Training and Development Handbook

Training and Development Handbook

A Guide to Human Resource Development

Third Edition

Sponsored by the American Society for Training and Development

Robert L. Craig   Editor in Chief

McGraw-Hill Book Company
New York St. Louis San Francisco Auckland Bogotá Hamburg
London Madrid Mexico Milan Montreal New Delhi Panama
Paris São Paulo Singapore Sydney Tokyo Toronto

Library of Congress Cataloging-in-Publication Data

Training and development handbook.

Includes index.
1. Employees, Training of. I. Craig, Robert L.
HF5549.5.T7T6648 1987   658.3'124   87-2629
ISBN 0-07-013353-0

34567890   DOCDOC   93210

ISBN 0-07-013353-0

The editors for this book were William A. Sabin and Jim Halston, the designer was Naomi Auerbach, and the production supervisor was Annette Mayeski. It was set in Meridien by Byrd Press.

Printed and bound by R. R. Donnelley and Sons

American Society for Training and Development

Handbook Advisory Board

Contents

Contents

Section 4 Training Applications

Foreword

The first edition of this handbook was published in 1967, a pioneering venture at a time we now see as a formative stage for the endeavor of training and development. This third edition comes upon a dramatically different human resource development scene, one that has changed not only in nature and extent but, more importantly, in the very role it plays. Employer-provided job training, when it was emerging in the 1950s and 1960s, was usually accepted as important but not critical to organizational purpose. Now, employee development, in its many forms, is seen as vital to the success of most enterprises and has, in fact, become the major form of continuing education and training in our whole society. And all indications are that ongoing development of the work force will necessarily increase and the employer share of that enterprise will grow even larger.

ASTD, as the professional organization of those with the dynamic charge of employee development, faces ever-increasing obligations to support practitioners in doing their jobs. This handbook, in its several versions, has been one of ASTD's responses over the years.

The principal purpose of this book is to provide a basic body of accepted knowledge of training and development—for use by those new to the field, but also intended as a reference source for more experienced trainers. In a field as broad and encompassing as HRD, even the mature professional has need for reliable referral sources as a refresher or to learn about not-too-familiar topics.

This new edition brings an updating of that body of knowledge to reflect what more has been learned, collectively, since the last edition, about how to do a better job of training employees.

The acceptance of the past editions of the handbook has been gratifying. The challenge for this edition, in the face of the greater expectations for employee training, is even larger. We hope it meets that challenge and serves its purpose well.

Curtis E. Plott
Executive Vice President
American Society for Training and Development
Alexandria, Virginia

Preface

Employee training and development (human resource development) has emerged as a major educational enterprise in the past three decades or so because of demand—demand in the workplace for employees, at all levels, to improve performance in their present jobs, to acquire skills and knowledge to do new jobs, and to continue their career progress in a changing world of work. Employer organizations depend directly on the competence and productivity of their work forces for survival in the fierce economic competition of the world marketplace. Technological change, economic change, demographic change, and other forces continually create new needs for learning by the work force.

Human resource development professionals play a primary role in managing and facilitating this learning of new occupational know-how—and the nature of their jobs changes, too. Hence, we have revised the *Training and Development Handbook* and produced a third edition to update the content of this reference work of what HRD people need to know and be able to do. (The first and second editions were published in 1967 and 1976, respectively.)

Because the field has changed so much, this third edition of the handbook is virtually a new work. Although many chapter titles remain the same, the substance has been changed and updated. We have added a number of new topics, too, so that our handbook users will have a reliable source of fundamental information about these advancing areas.

In keeping with the major trends in the field, the reader will find strong emphasis throughout this new edition on counting and measuring HRD and its accountability in general. HRD has become too important and too large and too central in the organizational scheme of things not to be subject to close management scrutiny. This emphasis on quantification throughout is intended to help those users who face this increased accountability.

Since line managers are so essential to successful employee development (and do the training in many instances), we have designed the handbook for them as well as for HRD professionals. Thus, it is intended as a comprehensive, convenient source of basic information for anyone who is serious about effective, professional development of their work force and improvement of organizational performance.

The handbook is a collection of the basic body of knowledge of employee training and development. Reference lists and bibliographies have been liberally included to provide extensive access to a broad range of literature and sources of aid in the field.

Developing and publishing a primary handbook such as this is a major undertaking and requires the dedicated efforts of a great many people. I must thank, profusely, the 61 authorities who contributed the 49 chapters. They are, of course, the source of the substance of this work. I am particularly pleased with the caliber of this edition's contributors and the work they have done.

My very special thanks must go to the ASTD Handbook Advisory Board who helped immensely. This group of distinguished ASTD members, all outstanding people in the field in their own right, have assisted me in both identifying the fine contributors and reviewing the manuscripts. Their constructive criticisms have added a great deal to the value of the book.

The Advisory Board members are: Vincent J. Byrne, President, Humanics Inc.; John W. Dreyer, Jr., Vice President, Wakefern Food Corporation; Eugene Fetteroll, Jr., Director of Human Resources, Associated Industries of Massachusetts; Dr. Ronald Galbraith, President, Management 21; Lawrence F. Lottier, Jr., Manager of Education, Dana Corporation; Francis A. McMullen, Executive Director, American Institute of Banking, New York chapter; Ed Schroer, Vice President, ASTD; Julie E. Walter, Manager of Training, Crouse-Hinds Company; and William N. Yeomans, Manager of Training and Development, J. C. Penny Co., Inc.

I hope this edition of the handbook serves you, the user, well.

ROBERT L. CRAIG
Editor in Chief
Fairfield, Connecticut

SECTION 1

The Training and Development Function

1
The History of Training *

Vincent A. Miller

Vincent A. Miller *has been, since 1983, a consultant specializing in technical training, management development, and cross-cultural training. He has been the U.S. Representative for the International Federation of Training and Development Organizations since 1982. For 28 years, he was Director of Consumer Affairs Education for Whirlpool Corporation. He is the recipient of two prestigious awards from ASTD: the Gordon M. Bliss Memorial Award for the most outstanding individual contribution to the training and development profession, and the International Trainer of the Year Award. Mr. Miller was President of ASTD in 1974, and served on its board of directors from 1971 through 1979. He was principal organizer and first director of the ASTD international division. He was one of the organizers, and first secretary/treasurer, of the International Federation of Training Organizations. He was a member of the board of directors of the Council on the Continuing Education Unit, from its inception in 1978 until 1984. Mr. Miller has been actively involved in training and development since 1947.*

It is generally thought that human beings began amassing knowledge at the beginning of the stone age. As they invented tools, weapons, clothing, shelter, and

* This history of training is a substantial revision of the chapter in the second edition of the handbook by Cloyd S. Steinmetz, now deceased. Mr. Miller has used some material directly from the Steinmetz work, revised other parts, and added major sections. The author of this chapter and the editor of the handbook gratefully acknowledge Cloyd Steinmetz' fine work as a source for this version of the history of the field.

language, the need for training became an essential ingredient in the march of civilization.

History tells us that the fastest form of long-distance transportation in the year 6000 B.C. was the camel caravan, which traveled at an average speed of about 8 miles per hour. It was not until the chariot was invented about 1600 B.C. that the average speed of long-distance transportation was increased to about 20 miles per hour.

Whether our ancestors stumbled upon or invented these facets of civilization is of very little significance. What is more important is that human beings had the ability to pass on to others the knowledge and skill gained in mastering these circumstances. This was done, not by written words, but by deliberate example, by signs, and by words. Through these devices, the development process called training was administered; and when the message was received by another successfully, we say that learning took place and knowledge or skill was transferred.

Discovery, application, communication, improvement, and more discovery. That is the probable cycle of inventions in the early days of human history. As communication improved, discovery and invention took giant steps forward. Inventions, or improvements that might have taken 50,000 years to accomplish in the stone age, might be reduced to hours, or even seconds, with today's electronic communication.

Training's Beginnings

Most scholarly dissertations on the history of communication begin with a description of early cave wall drawings, which served as the documentary record and textbook of the time. Isn't it conceivable that the etchings and paintings were also effective instructional illustrations, orienting primeval youngsters to such skills as fishing, and hunting, and how to protect themselves from the large woolly mammoths that roamed the land.[1]

As archaeological excavations continue to unearth clay or brick tablets on which is inscribed information about the lives of people living 6000 or more years ago, the place of training in the skyrocketing development of knowledge and civilization has become dramatically more evident.

The Sumerian Palace of Kish in Mesopotamia, built in 3500 B.C., is an example of the ancient use of brick. The Bible tells us that the Tower of Babel was also built of brick. The astounding architectural and masonry accomplishments of the craftspeople, embodied in the pyramids and ancient temples, such as Solomon's First Temple, are memorials to the stonemasons, the brickmasons, the carpenters, the artists, and the scientists of ancient times. But let us keep in mind that thousands of people worked on some of these projects. The work could not have been accomplished without *training*: without the transfer of knowledge from one person to another, or from one person to many people.

It must be remembered that in these early civilizations, literacy reached neither the craftspeople nor the peasantry. The skills and knowledge of the crafts could be transmitted only by direct instruction, from the skilled craftspeople to the not so skilled.

Historical Apprenticeship Data

Thus was developed an apprenticeship system whereby an experienced person passed along knowledge and skills to the novice, who after a period of apprenticeship became a journeyman, or yeoman. Provisions for governing apprenticeship were instituted as early as 1800 B.C. when such rules were included in the code of Hammurabi, who placed a code of his laws in the temple of Shamash (God of Justice) in Babylon.

The apprenticeship system was not restricted to artisans. The ancient temples taught religion and frequently art. The armies took the responsibility for training soldiers. In all walks of life, knowledge was passed from one person to another. Apprenticeship was the vehicle of instruction in medicine, law, and many other professions where the education is now in the domain of the colleges and universities. As recently as the 1920s, it was possible in the United States for a person to "read law in the office of a local attorney." Following a period of study, the apprentice lawyer took a government sponsored examination. A passing grade on the examination qualified the apprentice to practice law.

The apprenticeship system never seemed to work properly in colonial America. It involved a commitment of years, and imposed obligations and burdens on both the employer and employee. It proved inadequate as an efficient source of labor, although it provided a temporary source of cheap labor. One reason it did not work well was that adult male labor was very scarce. Most able-bodied men who would otherwise be candidates for apprenticeship were primarily on farms, or involved in the shipping trade.[2]

Guilds

Another development in the middle ages was the formation of guilds, which were associations of people whose interests or pursuits were the same or similar. The first guilds known were in England, before the Norman Conquest (1066).

By the end of the twelfth century, guilds were spread throughout the cities of Europe. The basic purpose of guilds was mutual protection, assistance, and advantage. In essence, guilds created private franchise, and at the same time established quality standards of products through quality standards of workmanship.

There were three classes of membership in the guilds: the master workers, who owned the raw materials and the tools, and directed the work; the apprentices, who usually lived with the master and who received practically no pay, except maintenance and training; and finally, the journeymen, who had passed through the apprenticeship stage but were not yet qualified as masters. Journeymen worked under a master, and received fixed wages for their labor.

The journeyman generally remained in the master's house. However, it was possible for the journeyman to save money, buy his tools, and take an examination in his craft. Once the journeyman had passed the examination, and had become a master craftsman, he could set up his own shop. However, as the markets expanded, more machinery and tools were required and becoming a master craftsman required a great investment, reducing the opportunities of a journeyman to become a master craftsman. As a result, the journeymen banded together and formed yeomanry guilds. The yeomanry guilds were the forerunners of today's labor unions.

During the peak of the guild system, between the twelfth and fifteenth centuries, the privileges of the members were protected by strict regulation of hours, tools, prices, and wages. The system required that all have the same privileges and pursue the same methods. In the craft unions of today, we still find restrictions as to the number of apprentices, regulation as to the quantity and quality of work, and the establishment of a base system of financial reward.

Craft Training

The nineteenth century ushered in an era of social legislation, and with it sizable changes in the concept of the workers' organization. Through all these changes, however, one constantly developing emphasis has been upon quality training of workers, and this has culminated in the staunch support of the unions for any legislation that provides a wide range of vocational education.

Industrialization meant two changes in work preparation. Specific training was now required before specific tasks could be performed. In the traditional craft and agrarian order, people had "grown up" into stable, lifelong occupations. The other change required a different orientation. Work activity was now focused away from the individual, family, or small group and toward a large impersonal organization, within a large, impersonal urban community. The industrial revolution required education for specific tasks, and education to function within the emerging corporate organization.[3]

One of the interesting sidelights in the history of education for business is that several of the early schools of business administration were established as a result of evening programs in business. It is commonly thought that the evening courses became an added service of existing schools of business, but in many instances the reverse is true. The evening courses came first, and were followed later by full-time colleges.

The history of the growth of the training which accompanied the great industrial expansion is fascinating. As early as 1809, the Masonic Grand Lodge of New York, under the leadership of De Witt Clinton, established vocational training facilities. Manual training began in the United States about 1825. However, most of the manual training schools that sprang up after 1825 were more disciplinary than vocational schools. The so-called state industrial schools were really places of incarceration for "bad boys." Nevertheless, the basic concept was correct. The schools gave idle hands training in such a manner that, in accompaniment with a trained mind, they would be able to make a contribution to society, rather than constitute a liability to it.

The concept of the application of higher learning to practical affairs has flourished in the United States since the Rensselaer Polytechnic Institute broke the classical barrier in 1824 to become the first college of engineering. Instruction in agriculture, education, business administration, accounting, journalism, and a variety of other fields has followed, and gradually there has developed the general acceptance of the notion that there is a bona fide link between education and training.

We could wonder why the universities failed to embrace training in the 1800s. Way back in 1830, the trustees of Columbia University established a new scientific curriculum, which meant that no Latin or Greek was required, and voted to make the courses available to young men "employed in the business and mercantile establishments." Apparently, the employers were not of a mind to grant the necessary time off, and the program failed to materialize. That there were no takers does not detract from the foresight of the Columbia trustees.

Cooper Union in New York instituted evening vocational classes in 1884. By 1886, private manual training schools were established in Cincinnati, Cleveland, Toledo, and Chicago, and public institutions of a similar sort were established in Philadelphia, Baltimore, and Omaha.

One of the great steps forward in the effort to free workers from the limitations of their immediate craft requirements was the passing of the Land Grant Act in 1862. When Abraham Lincoln signed this act, he initiated a means of higher education for the average man's children, which previously could be enjoyed only by the wealthy.

The Industrial Era Emerges

The industrial revolution began in England about 1750, and spread first to France and Belgium, then to Germany and the United States. After the Revolutionary War, Americans eagerly turned their energy toward the pursuit of prosperity, through power-driven machinery, steam engines, and a factory system that put useful knowledge and new technology to work. This early American drive for industrialization was so successful that, for example, in 1807 there were 15 cotton mills in the country, and by 1815 mills utilizing 500,000 spindles were employing 76,000 workers. These men, women, and children were already being called "industrial workers."[4]

The change from an agrarian to an industrial economy in the United States was evidenced by the rapid increase in the number of patents issued by the U.S. Patent Office. An average of 77 per year were issued between 1790 and 1811, and an average of 192 per year between 1812 and 1817.

Industry became employer, guardian, and patron of body and soul.[5] Industry was willing to become involved in broad issues of education and quality of life. Manufacturers recruited farm maidens to work in their mills. They provided, not just for a job, but for an entire set of living circumstances designed to nurture and educate. The girls lived in rambling boardinghouses, supervised by a matron. Literary evenings, elevating lectures, and circulating libraries were provided for them. They were expected to attend church on Sunday, and if they did not abide by stringent rules of conduct they were dismissed from their job.

Male workers also labored under the strict eye of the mill owners, particularly regarding morals, health, and well-being. The new "working class" wanted the opportunities industry offered as much as industry wanted workers with a certain level of intelligence, skill, and resourcefulness. The new system of manufacture meant that the machines were skilled, not necessarily the operator of the machine. Craftsmanship belonged to the past, industrial education to the future.

There was no American system of public education to provide "useful knowledge" for potential young workers in these early days of the industrial era. Training had to be within a company or trade group, out of necessity. But the companies did turn to the educational system for help, as is shown elsewhere in this chapter. During the period between the Civil War and World War I, the education of persons preparing themselves for a job in industry came to be known as "vocational education."

Many trainers do not know that two training techniques that we know and use today came into being and popular use during the emerging industrial era. Gaming simulation such as chess began thousands of years ago, but the Prussians started to apply gaming situations to military training in the early 1800s. They used games consisting of highly detailed maps, and color-coded blocks to represent troops. Players determined troop movements and appropriate armaments. Following the game, the players' decisions were discussed and critiqued. The war games became very popular and were adopted for military training throughout the world.[6] The case method was developed by Christopher Langdell at the Harvard Law School in the 1880s. This nondirective training technique to help students think for themselves slowly won acceptance in law, medicine, business, etc.[7]

Another training technique that has been around longer than most people would be willing to believe is role playing. Psychodrama and role playing was originated about 1910 by Dr. J.L. Moreno in Vienna, Austria. The technique became more publicized in the early 1930s, after Dr. Moreno came to the United States. He developed concepts of group play, role theory, and the use of creativity and spontaneity in therapeutic and educational contexts.

Factory Schools

One of the first factory schools established was in 1872 at Hoe and Company, a manufacturer of printing presses in New York City. The company had such a volume of business that it was forced to increase production. There was no time to train machinists by the apprenticeship method, and it was necessary to establish a factory school.

Similar factory schools were established at Westinghouse in 1888, at General Electric Company and Baldwin Locomotive works in 1901, and at International Harvester Company in 1907. Such companies as Western Electric, Goodyear, Ford, and National Cash Register soon installed factory training schools. Other companies saw the advantages of having factory schools, and they soon became a common practice.

Training Support from Other Sources

The YMCA was a key influence in the development of training. In 1892 the Brooklyn YMCA offered a course in freehand drawing. The Springfield, Ohio, YMCA offered trade training in patternmaking, toolmaking, and cabinetry. In 1905, the West Side New York YMCA offered 63 courses, 36 percent of which were commercial, and 26 percent industrial and scientific.

An innovation in education took place during the first decade of this century, when Dean Schneider of the University of Cincinnati, College of Engineering, introduced cooperative education. The student would go to school for a time and work in a factory an equal amount of time. Then the student would repeat the process, going to school for additional training and going back to the factory for additional practical experience.

America first saw correspondence instruction when the Chautauqua Literary and Scientific Circle offered several courses in 1882. The University of Chicago sponsored the first college-level correspondence courses in 1890.

The modern American correspondence school had its beginning in 1891, when Thomas J. Foster founded the International Correspondence Schools. The oldest date of an apprentice plan in conjunction with a correspondence school is 1903. The plan was worked out between ICS and a southern railway.[8]

By 1850, American unions were actively concerned with the restriction of entry into the skilled trades. They also were fighting with the employers for control of apprenticeship training. By 1900, they were setting up training schools that were sometimes in opposition to those set up or assisted by management. Nowadays, the unions and trade associations are utilized as educational resources by many employers. The unions have large training funds for training, and retraining, the workers. Sometimes, funds for retraining are built into the union contract with management.

The Ohio Mechanics Institute was started in Cincinnati, Ohio, in 1828. Horace Mann did much to improve the system of free public schools when he was a member of Congress from 1848 to 1852. However, despite all the grand arguments and some genuine reforms, the need for educated industrial workers continued. In 1876, while visiting the Centennial Exhibition in Philadelphia, President John D. Runkle of the Massachusetts Institute of Technology met Victor Della Vos, director of the Moscow Imperial Technical School. Della Vos had organized his school with shops for instructing boys in a definite method for each trade skill. He analyzed trades according to their component skills and devised a pedagogical order combining drawings, models, and tools into a graduated series of supervised exercises by which students could become proficient in a trade. That same year, MIT established instruction shops for engineering students and a new school of mechanical arts to offer manual education for industrial careers along with the scientific education curriculum.[9]

Industry Association Support

By the early 1900s, vocational education was sufficiently extensive that there was a great need for mutual assistance in this field. The natural outgrowth was the realization that in unity of action there is strength. In 1906, a group of 250 key educators interested in industrial education met at Cooper Union in New York City, and formed the National Society for the Promotion of Industrial Education. This society later merged with others to become the American Vocational Association.

In 1913, a meeting was held at New York University, and the National Association of Corporation Schools was organized. It started with 60 members representing 34 corporations. The association held four annual conventions. The first convention was held in Dayton, Ohio, in 1914. By 1918, the main interest of the organization had become "personnel." The name was changed in 1920 to the National Association of Corporation Training. Shortly thereafter, it merged with the Industrial Relations Association of America to become the National Personnel Association. Less than 3 years later, in 1923, the name was changed to the American Management Association.

The National Society for the Promotion of Industrial Education, mentioned earlier, changed its name to the National Society for Vocational Education in 1918, and merged with the Vocational Association of the Middle West (founded 1914) to become the American Vocational Association in 1925. The AVA membership is composed of more than 55,000 teachers, supervisors, administrators, and others interested in the development and improvement of vocational, technical, and practical arts education.

The National Vocational Guidance Association, organized in Grand Rapids, Michigan, in 1913, also supported the concept of training. It is now a Division of the American Personnel and Guidance Association, which was founded in 1952.

The National Association of Foremen was founded in 1925. This organization of business and industrial managers, from supervisory level to middle managers and above, was very much involved on the training scene from the time they were organized in 1925 through World War II. In 1944, the association organized a conference of educational directors in industry. The conference was held at Columbus, Ohio. Nearly 500 people from 28 states attended. In 1956, the National Association of Foremen changed its name to the National Management Association.

Training 1910 to 1920

By 1910, when the Ford Motor Company moved into a new plant at Highland Park, they had established a production line concept. However, it was not until August 1913 that the first test car began its journey as a bare chassis on one end of the "moving assembly" line, and ended up on the other end of the line as a finished Model T. Thus began the need for special training of the production line worker for a specific job.

World War I prompted a tremendous stimulus for training. Training has always grown best where emergency is the dominant thought. On September 12, 1917, the Emergency Fleet Corporation of the United States Shipping Board set up an educational and training section. There were 61 shipyards with 50,000 workers, and there was an urgent need for ten times as many workers, but not many more were available. The only answer to the problem was training of new workers. Charles R. Allen, as head of the program, ordered that all the training be done at the shipyards, and that the instructors should be the supervisors of these organizations.

Allen adopted the four-step method of "show, tell, do, and check" as his standard method of job instruction training to solve this World War I problem. Many lessons were learned during the war. The following statement was made at the time of the 1920 census: "The public is again reminded, through the census, of the lessons which the war should have taught regarding the tremendous loss in the ability of the public schools to reach out to all alike, and give them the educational and training equipment necessary for a life career."

Training in the 1920s

After World War I, a series of factors combined to compel companies to provide a stable source of competent future management. Many colleges and universities responded to the industrial need for managerial level personnel with business education programs.

The loss of men in World War I, and the inability of the economy of the late 1920s and early 1930s to support the surplus personnel required by the apprenticeship method of providing managerial talent caused that method (managerial apprenticeship) to die out.

The prosperity of the 1920s tended to discourage the application of training to industrial situations. However, by this time, correspondence schools had gained recognition and acceptance, and were serving the needs of the American wage earner. It was said that probably more men in American industry had gained the technical phases of their trades from correspondence schools than by any other means.

Sales training seemed to receive some stimulus during the postwar boom period of the roaring twenties. These were the years when the so-called modern appliances began to be heavily merchandised. The ownership of an electric refrigerator, or an electric range, or an electric washer was indeed a status symbol. Many salespeople were trained in door-to-door selling for these big ticket items.

Training in the 1930s—The Depression Years

As the economy plunged into the greatest depression in American history, more and more top-management people decided that training was not needed. The great number of workers whose jobs were terminated when businesses failed or reduced their working force provided an adequate supply of skilled and experienced workers.

The depression years of the thirties wrecked many internal training programs. Apprenticeship in the skilled trades was terminated in many industries. There were plenty of skilled workers waiting to be hired into any available job, and they voiced the cry: "Why train others, when we are here to do the job."

On the other hand, a great influence to the furtherance of training was stimulated by this same set of depression-laden circumstances. Unemployed people had time on their hands, and nothing to do with those hands. This problem became acute. A major effort to meet it was instigated by local, state, and federal governments. Perhaps the most widespread program was that involving the appropriation of federal funds for training in handicrafts. Hundreds of thousands of unemployed men and women occupied their spare time by learning leatherwork, weaving, art and painting, jewelry making, chair caning, etc. These people soon discovered that they could profitably occupy their time making useful things, and in some cases could provide some income by selling the articles which they made. People became training-conscious, and likewise became conscious of their own learning potential.

The training tools of the 1930s generally consisted of chalkboards, writing easels or chart pads, "magic lantern" slides, and in the later years of the decade some commercially prepared 16-mm sound motion picture films.[10] It was the development of the 16-mm sound movie projector that first brought the audiovisual technology into practical prominence in the classroom. Of course, there were some enterprising trainers at this time who were using "talking machines," both cylinder and disk, to give them some audio capabilities.

In the late 1930s, after Hitler sent his troops into Austria in March 1938, Britain and France began to increase their defensive armaments. Likewise, the United States began to bolster its defensive armaments. These "war" orders were eagerly accepted by American manufacturers and had much to do with improving the U.S. economy and reducing the size of the unemployment lines. The need for retraining was recognized, as people who had been unemployed or underemployed for years were again needed on skilled jobs.

The 1940s, and World War II Training

The National Society of Sales Training Executives became the first national training directors society when it was founded in 1940.

There was registration for the draft in the United States late in 1940, and many people who had never worked in a plant eagerly answered the call to replace those men who were drafted into the armed forces. These new people in industry needed to be trained as welders, as machinists, as riveters, etc. The United States entered the war in December 1941.

But who would do this training? By now, many of the vocational school instructors had taken higher-paying jobs in industry, and in some cases those who were left were not familiar with the needs of the employers. At last, business came face to face with the reality that they had too long ignored. Suddenly, the training function of the supervisor became paramount. In fact, management found that without training skills, supervisors were unable to produce adequately for the war effort. With it, new records were being established by industrially inexperienced, aged, handicapped, and women workers.

The training director became a necessity, and soon this was a common title in the management hierarchy. The wartime trainers suddenly needed to move vast numbers of people through orientation, attitude building, and technical instruction. To achieve their goal, they turned increasingly to training films and filmstrips, simulators, flip charts, flannel boards, and models which would help them get their message across. Role playing began to receive a lot of attention at this time.

The actual training of supervisors to become job instructors was developed to classic simplicity by the Training Within Industry Service (TWI), which was established in August 1940 by the National Defense Advisory Commission. On April 8, 1942, by presidential order, TWI became a part of the War Manpower Commission, and operated under the Bureau of Training. By the time TWI ceased operations in 1945, it had been instrumental in training 23,000 persons as instructors, and had awarded nearly two million certificates to supervisors who had gone through TWI programs in more than 16,000 plants, services, and unions.

JIT, or job instruction training, was developed to train supervisors in defense plants in the skill of instructing their workers as rapidly as possible. Train the Trainer Institutes were held all over the United States. Initially, the institutes were 3 days long. Fifteen to thirty persons attended. Later, the institutes grew to a 45-hour program.

JIT was all-inclusive. It not only taught how to instruct but also put emphasis on the related problem of human relations between the supervisor and the worker, and the equally important matter of determining the best job methods. It was quite natural then that other J programs followed; so we had

JRT—Job Relations Training

JMT—Job Methods Training

JST—Job Safety Training

Each program was a specialized facet of the fundamentals inherent in the JIT card. Added to the J programs listed above was a program development course (PDT), which was developed for executives who were unfamiliar with training techniques. More information on the J programs is included in Chap. 20, "Job Training," of this handbook.

The wire recorder was first used by the armed forces during the war years. It received extensive use as a training tool after the war, until the tape recorder was introduced in the early fifties. Another very popular training tool in use today, the computer, was used by the armed forces for other purposes during the war but was not used for training until many years later.

The training laboratory has become a highly respected and widely used learning method since its inception in Bethel, Maine, in 1947. Led by Leland Bradford, Ronald Lippitt, and Kenneth D. Benne, the National Training Laboratory conducted its first summer session. Since then, large numbers of training organizations have participated in NTL workshops, and this method of human relations training has spread around the world.[11]

We cannot leave the 1940s without mentioning that the American Society for Training and Development (ASTD) was formed, with its original name being The American Society of Training Directors. It was the emergence of the training director during the war years that set the stage, and a need to communicate with fellow trainers that was not fulfilled by any other national society that led to the organization efforts. A brief history of ASTD ends this chapter.

Training in the 1950s

Business gaming was not popular until the mid-1950s. One of the first business games to be widely used was the Top Management Decision Simulation, developed by the American Management Association. This game consisted of five teams of five players, each team representing the officers of a different firm manufacturing a similar product. Each of the firms competed for sales within a common market. After the appearance of this game, hundreds of other games were developed that covered all aspects of business practice.[12]

The wire recorder was mentioned as being used for training purposes after World War II. Trainers continued to use the wire recorder into the 1950s. With all its problems, it was the best thing available for recording audio, until after 1952 when 3M Corporation discovered the process for coating acetate and polyester tapes with metallic oxides. Now, magnetic recording, which was invented in 1899 by Poulsen, could be used by trainers. Most training departments began using the new reel-to-reel tape recorders.

It was not until about 1955 that videotape began to be used successfully in recording color and black-and-white television, although TV was used as a teaching medium starting about 1952, and its use grew steadily.

In 1957, the ASTD New Jersey chapter participated in a novel experiment, using closed-circuit TV to teach 2000 temporary postal employees the jobs that they were hired to do for the Christmas season.[13] The navy was using video for training about the same time. By 1958, there were 32 educational television stations in operation. They were teaching courses in typing, shorthand, sales training, and almost any phase of technical and professional skills that one can think of. Already, at the 1958 ASTD conference, there was a session on teaching by television. Both civilian and military utilization of TV were described, and there was a review of the key studies that had proved TV to be effective. Also, at the 1958 conference, there was a session titled "Human Factors in Automation." The session leader discussed what to do to overcome problems that follow progressive replacement of human labor by automation.

Trainers started to pay more attention to the evaluation of training in the 1950s. Up to this time, only a few trainers bothered to evaluate the results of their training. Many top companies and schools began using business games in their training of managers. "In-basket" exercises and other decision-making simulation games were very popular. Role playing was used extensively for training salespeople and industrial managers.

Training in the 1960s

In 1960, only one American business organization was using assessment centers, and even in the mid-1960s only a handful of companies were running them, but by 1970 about 100 companies were using assessment centers.[14]

The popularity of the training laboratory and other forms of sensitivity training increased tremendously during the 1960s. Trainers began to talk and write about their experiences with sensitivity training and behavioral change. Articles relating to these subjects, which appeared in the *Training and Development Journal*, increased from one in 1960 and 1961 to eleven in 1968.

By far the most popular technique used in training during the 1960s was programmed instruction. On July 28, 1961, the president of ASTD, Dr. Vernon Sheblak, appointed a committee on teaching machine technology. It worked with other committees from education and government agencies to exchange information, report on new developments, and prepare a set of recommendations. The recommendations of the joint committee appeared in the January 1966 *Training and Development Journal*. The National Society for Programmed Instruction, now known as the National Society for Performance and Instruction, was organized in 1962 with many of its charter members holding membership in NSPI and in ASTD.

In the early and mid sixties great promises were being made about programmed instruction. Its popularity carried through the sixties, then seemed to die out. However, the development process and the learning and teaching fundamentals, which were so much a part of PI, can be used in other training programs too.

By 1968 there were 10,000 video tape recorders in use. They were smaller now, and more economical, but the cost was still around $3000 to $7000 for a reel-to-reel, black-and-white recorder. Although acceptance was growing and the need great, many training departments did not purchase them because there was no compatibility between the different brands.

In addition to the teaching machines which were developed for use with programmed instruction, there was a great interest in the use of computers for training. Many reports were written about the potentials of computer-assisted instruction (CAI). Although the computer had not yet been miniaturized, trainers were looking toward the future, when they would be using computers.

Throughout the 1960s there was a growing awareness of how necessary it is for a trainer to be well grounded in the principles, and to use needs assessment and evaluation techniques. Another form of evaluation, performance appraisal, also came into popular use in the 1960s.

The need for management training was recognized more than ever before. Management training was almost as popular a subject as programmed instruction. Trainers started to hear about the systems approach and organization development near the end of this decade. More attention was paid to motivation. Also, the training director's job was being analyzed and was being given more recognition.

A nationwide Job Development Program was announced by President Lyndon Johnson on February 1, 1965. This was the beginning of a series of government-sponsored programs aimed at helping the unemployed, the poor, the disadvantaged, the minorities, and the hard-core unemployable. The Manpower Development and Training Act (MDTA) was extended. The Job Corps, designed to train young men for jobs in industry, was operating in otherwise unused army camps. Special training centers were set up in metropolitan areas to train the hard-core unemployed. Special attention was paid to the rights of all minorities.

The *Training and Development Handbook*, sponsored by ASTD and published by McGraw-Hill, was first introduced in 1967. It was the most complete training reference ever assembled up to that time.

Training in the 1970s

By 1970, 59 of the Job Corps centers had closed down, and smaller in-city centers had been established to handle local trainees. In the meantime, much attention was being given to the training of the disadvantaged and hard-core unemployed. More trainers were involved in this type of training from 1970 to 1972 than at any other time in history.

Gradually, starting about 1970, the training concerns shifted to a concern for minorities as a total grouping. Under government pressure, most organizations began serious efforts to fulfill established quotas for hiring and/or involving women and racial minorities in responsible management positions. Much of the training in the first half of this decade was aimed at upgrading them to supervisory positions.

Trainers became more professional during this decade. ASTD produced a *Professional Development Manual for Trainers*. Those who read the trade journals were bombarded with information about how to determine training needs, evaluation, management development, motivation, the training function, and training methods. Trainer involvement in national training societies increased by about 17,000 members, and additional trainer involvement in local training chapters was about the same.

Organization development (OD), which gained acceptance during the 1960s, became the most popular and the most talked about training technique or practice of the 1970s. OD was a combining of many interlocking components, including manager selection, personnel development, organization structure, management methods, interpersonal relations, and group dynamics. The trainers who became involved in OD were now concerned with much more than "people development," for which the name human resource development (HRD) had now been coined. Whereas the personnel and training departments were concerned with people, the OD consultant was concerned with the well-being of the entire organization. Many senior trainers became internal or external OD consultants in the 1970s.

The work that had been done in the area of needs assessment, task analysis, and evaluation laid the groundwork for the introduction of competency based learning, which came into popular use in the last half of this decade. Competency based learning is concerned with having the trainees develop certain specified competencies, after carefully studying their present competencies and the performance requirements of their job. It is a professional approach to instructional design, development, implementation, and evaluation.

There was a considerable amount of international training activity in the 1970s. ASTD received a $35,000 contract from the Agency for International Development (AID) for 1970–1971. Under the contract, ASTD was to prepare a report on the interest and extent to which companies located in developing countries would cooperate in developing organizations for professional training personnel. Among other things, under terms of the contract, ASTD was committed to establish at least one local and one national organization in Venezuela, and to prepare a plan for training participants in the methods and techniques needed to form such organizations. This was the beginning of a number of contracts that ASTD had with AID. Contract extensions provided funds for ASTD to sponsor the first International Training and Development Conference in Geneva, Switzerland, in 1972, and provided additional funds to support the establishment of a world federation of training organizations.

The International Federation of Training and Development Organizations was first proposed at the first international conference in 1972. Additional organizational efforts took place at the second international conference in Bath, England, in 1973. The formal signing of the IFTDO charter took place at the third international conference in Oslo, Norway, in 1974.

Another milestone for trainers was the opening of an ASTD Washington office in 1975 to foster closer relationships with federal agencies on behalf of member interests. This first Washington office was a branch office. The main office location remained in Madison, Wisconsin. However, the ASTD board of directors approved the move of all offices to Washington, D.C., in 1980, and the actual move to Washington offices was made in 1981.

Many advances in training technology in the 1970s came as a result of improvements in the training hardware. A few items which should not be forgotten are the variable speech control tape recorders, standardized video cassettes, availability of satellites for training use, and tremendous improvements in computers and availability of computer programs for training.

The 1980s and Beyond

One training movement that became very popular in the early 1980s was the Quality Circles movement. Actually, the Quality Circles movement came into the United States from Japan in the early 1970s. Quality Circles had been operating successfully there since 1962. Although the popularity has diminished, trainers will probably be involved with Quality Circles for many years to come. One reason for this projection is that the International Association for Quality Circles was founded in 1977, and their membership has grown beyond 5000 members.

Trainers became more conscious of their expenditures in the 1980s. Perhaps this was the result of the recession, but the fact remains that many training directors were studying methods of reporting their return on investment. Many articles have been written about ROI, but no one has yet developed a system that will apply to all, or even most, training operations. This is a challenge that can probably be accomplished with a computer program in the future.

The popularity of personal computers increased because of a reduction in computer prices, compatibility between various makes, and availability of many software programs at reasonable prices. Most primary and secondary schools had computers available for each classroom by the mid-1980s. Colleges and universities had overflow registration for their computer classes. Even so, the full potential of computers in training will not be realized for many years. The computer, in combination with other training hardware such as video equipment, will remain an indispensable training tool for many years.

Behavior modeling, which had been used since the early 1970s, became more popular in the early 1980s. Its greatest use was for management skills training, although it could be used for training in any skill. Actually, behavior modeling has been used since human beings were capable of communicating. In that sense (one person duplicating the behavior of another) it will be with us forever. However, the process is most likely to be integrated into training programs without mention that behavior modeling is taking place.

There was renewed emphasis on career development in the first half of the 1980s. Perhaps this was a direct result of the chartering of a Career Development Division within ASTD in 1979. According to leading career development theorists, we must give continuing attention to career development because of the ever-changing makeup of the work force, and changing social patterns and job structures. As we look beyond the 1980s we can only imagine what the future may be. We know from past experience that our training lives have been affected by wars, depressions, advances in technology, presidential elections, and our own eagerness to exchange ideas and improve on what has been taught to us.

Whether the past is prologue to the future is entirely dependent on each individual trainer. It is difficult to look at the present or the recent past in the perspective of history. It is much easier to look back 10 or 20 years and recall the rise and fall in the popularity and use of various training techniques and practices, because that is documented. Our responsibilities for the future of training are great. Our opportunities are unlimited.

The Early History of ASTD

A number of national organizations gave some support to training directors before ASTD was founded, but none of the organizations could embrace the entire body of trainers. The National Association of Foremen sponsored conferences for training directors in 1944, 1946, and 1947, but the emphasis was on industrial training. The National Society of Sales Training Executives was concerned with the welfare and training of sales trainers. The American Petroleum Institute had a committee on training, but naturally its concern was for training directors in the oil industry.

Perhaps the most factual report of the founding of ASTD was written by Thomas Keaty, the first president of ASTD. Some of the information used here is an edited account of a 1956 report which Mr. Keaty wrote, describing those early days of ASTD.

The idea of having a national training society that would cut across all industries was suggested on April 2, 1942, at a meeting of the American Petroleum Institute committee on training, which was held at the Roosevelt Hotel in New Orleans. Tom Keaty was delegated to develop a constitution, and to secure charter members. Copies of a proposed constitution were mailed out to 25 prominent training directors in the midcontinent area on June 15, 1942, with a request for comments, and an expression of interest. In the next 6 months a total of 12 charter members from eight states was secured. The constitution was approved by the charter members.

On January 12, 1943, fifteen members of the American Society of Training Directors met in Baton Rouge, Louisiana, for the first formal meeting under the constitution. Thomas S. Keaty was elected president. Dr. Andrew Triche was elected vice president, and J.W. Bowling was elected secretary and treasurer. By February 1944, the membership had grown to more than 100 members from 16 states. By late 1945, the membership had grown to almost 200 members from 28 states.

Coincident with the growth of ASTD, and in some cases preceding it, had been the formation of regional training directors associations such as Indiana Training Directors Association, Chicago Training Council, National Association of Training Directors in New York, Training Directors Association of St. Louis, and the Michigan Training Council in Detroit.

The first national convention of ASTD was held in Chicago, Illinois, on September 27 and 28, 1946. There was a program of speakers, but the main purpose of the meeting was to reconcile the viewpoint of ASTD and the regional training associations, and to agree upon a constitution and officers for a truly national association. A constitutional review committee was named. Thomas Keaty was again elected president. The cost of individual membership was set at $4 per year.

The first printed issue of *Industrial Training News* was published by ASTD in June 1945. All previous news bulletins had been mimeographed. The name of the ASTD publication was changed to the *Journal of Industrial Training* in June 1947, when it became a bimonthly journal. The name was changed again to the *Training Directors Journal* in 1958, when it became a monthly publication. It became the *Training and Development Journal* in 1966 and reached its present size of approximately 8 ½ by 11 inches in 1969.

It is a point of interest to note that the first issue of the *Journal of Industrial Training*, in June 1947, listed the requirements for full membership in ASTD as being a college or university degree and 2 years of experience in training and its related fields, or 5 years of experience in training and its related fields. Requirements for an associate member were that the person was to be engaged in training, or to be over 18 years of age, and attend a university.

The first permanent office for ASTD was opened in Madison, Wisconsin, about 1952, because the secretary-treasurer, Russell Moberly, who kept all the records lived there. By this time there were 32 ASTD chapters and over 1600 members. The national office remained in Madison, Wisconsin, until August 1981 when the entire national staff moved into new offices in Washington, D.C. ASTD had maintained a Washington office since 1975, but most board members thought that the more than 20,000 members and 119 local chapters would have better representation in government and association affairs if the entire staff moved there. The national offices were moved one last time in March 1985, when the national staff was moved into ASTD's own building at 1630 Duke Street in Alexandria, Virginia.

ASTD is still growing. The 1985 count is about 23,000 national members and 142 chapters, which also provide for the needs of about 23,000 local members. The tremendous growth in the society prompted a change in its governance structure.

Starting in 1984, a board of governors, made up of distinguished senior level leaders—HRD practitioners, academicians, government executives, and chief executive officers—establishes priorities and strategic direction for the society, while a smaller board of directors will receive input from the board of governors and serve as the decision-making body, in much the same manner as previous boards of directors have done before them.

References

1. O'Sullivan, Kevin, in Robert L. Craig, *Training and Development Handbook*, 2d ed., McGraw-Hill, New York, 1976, p. 43-2.

2. Eurich, Nell P., *Corporate Classrooms*, The Carnegie Foundation for the Advancement of Teaching, Princeton, NJ, 1985, p. 26.

3. Ibid.

4. Ibid.

5. Ibid., p. 29.

6. Coppard, Larry, in Robert L. Craig, *Training and Development Handbook*, 2d ed., McGraw-Hill, New York, 1976.

7. Pigors, Paul, in Robert L. Craig, *Training and Development Handbook*, 2d ed., McGraw-Hill, New York, 1976, p. 35-1.

8. "Industrial Training a La Carte," *Journal of Industrial Training*, November–December 1952, p. 24.

9. Eurich, Nell P., op. cit., p. 32.

10. O'Sullivan, Kevin, op, cit.

11. Dupre, Vladimir A., in Robert L. Craig, *Training and Development Handbook*, 2d ed., McGraw-Hill, New York, 1976, p. 37-2.

12. Coppard, Larry, in Robert L. Craig, *Training and Development Handbook*, 2d ed., McGraw-Hill, New York, 1976, p. 40-2.

13. Mark, Alexander, "TV in Christmas Season Post Office Training," *Journal of the American Society of Training Directors*, October 1958, p. 14.

14. Bray, Douglas W., in Robert L. Craig, *Training and Development Handbook*, 2d ed., McGraw-Hill, New York, 1976, p. 10-1.

2
Organization and Management of the Training Function

Jerry L. Pittam

Jerry L. Pittam is the Director of Management Education for Kraft, Inc., Glenview, Illinois. While the primary responsibility of his department is the full spectrum of management training and education, he and his staff are also concerned with the training needs of the total Kraft employee population. In his 15 years in the profession, he has seen— and fostered—the movement of continual education into the strategic operation of the business. He began his career in training as a means to merge his love of learning and teaching with a decided bent for practicality that he didn't always find in the "publish or perish" environs of academia. He received his B.A. degree (cum laude) from Florida State University and his M.A. from the University of California, Riverside.

Numerous adages suggest that people are the key to any successful business operation. Despite frequent lip service, there is nonetheless a fundamental truth to these clichés: no human enterprise can succeed without properly skilled and knowledgeable human resources. Hence ongoing employee development is critical to the short- and long-term success of every business (profit or nonprofit). All organizations, either formally or informally, must continually address the training and development of their people. To do otherwise is one means to assure obsolescence and eventual failure.

This chapter deals with the full spectrum of considerations in organizing training efforts, from the one-person shop to the multimember department. While actual organizational structure is considered, the primary focus is on the proper positioning of the training function, within the context of the objectives and needs of the overall enterprise. The principles involved are exactly the same regardless of ultimate staff size; however, as the complexity increases, so does the need for increased depth and breadth in the analysis for determining the scope and resulting responsibilities of a training function. Not surprisingly, the principles involved in effectively organizing and managing a training operation are exactly the same as those needed for any other functional area of a business, or for the business as a whole. Thus it follows that the better organized the entire business is, the easier it is to develop a complementary organization of the training required to assure the effective development of its human resources. Conversely, when the mission and overriding objectives of the business itself are unclear, it is more difficult to organize an effective training operation.

The major considerations include:

1. Collect relevant data.
2. Determine purpose.
3. Consider alternative strategies.
4. Determine most reasonable approach.
5. Determine what results to measure.
6. Sell approach.
7. Establish appropriate policies and procedures.
8. Track results and modify accordingly.

Collect Relevant Data

Collecting and interpreting a variety of data that impact the training function is the most critical step in the entire process. A thorough analysis is important from two perspectives:

1. Objective data are the *only* means to identify the mission and overriding objective of the training function and shift the focus from a reactive approach ("Let's give them only what they ask for") to a proactive one ("Let's demonstrate exactly where training can have a significant impact on the business").
2. The act of collecting and interpreting the data—when they involve numerous line and staff managers from throughout the business—is one of the most powerful marketing tools available to sell the resulting approach developed from those data.

If the collection and analysis of relevant data are done well, the appropriate organizational structure of the training function will be an obvious—almost secondary—outcome of identifying what the training function can contribute to the business.

The data collection usually takes two forms: face-to-face interviews and written documentation. It has one primary purpose: to develop the mission and overriding objective of the training function, which will ultimately lead to an appropriate organizational structure.

Establish Linkage to Business

When conducting informal discussions with line and staff management (one-on-one, through focus groups, etc.) and analyzing available documentation, keep two perspectives in mind:

1. What is the current scope of training operations? Why? What should it be? (Never assume that what is, is what ought to be.)
2. What is the overriding philosophy of the business, its mission, strategic plans, and operating plans?

Keep this dual perspective broad at this point, but begin to link the two together in order to determine how training can support the achievement of specific short- and long-term business goals. Both the big picture and the individual tiles that make up the entire mosaic are important. Assuring this linkage between business' operations and training can be one of the most interesting, exciting, and important aspects of organizing relevant training efforts. Yet it is frequently minimized or totally ignored, even by seasoned professionals in the field. While there may be any number of reasons (an already prescribed—usually limited—charter, inappropriate positioning of the training function within the organization, a personal reluctance to pursue the data, etc.), the potential payoffs of assuring this linkage for both the business and the function are extremely significant and can mean the difference between a proactive approach to addressing critical business needs and opportunities and a reactive stance of providing only what is requested.

Identify Customer Segments

As with many businesses, every training function has both "customers" (clients) and "consumers" (those who actually participate in education programs).
The "customers" for training include all critical members of the client base within the organization. These customers form the core group to whom the training function provides its services. It is this group's business goals that are most directly impacted by the efforts of the training function. Typically, the customer group is restricted to the highest members of management who are impacted by the scope of the training responsibilities. For example, a sales trainer within a particular operating unit might identify the regional sales vice president as the key customer, while also including members of the vice president's staff. This sales trainer might also identify the national sales training director as a key customer if there is a direct or dotted line relationship between the two.
Once the customers and their business objectives are identified, their specific needs—short- and long-term—must be delineated. Segment these needs into relevant classifications, such as functional and technical expertise (i.e., improved selling skills or product knowledge), cross-functional interrelationships (i.e., improved understanding of the R&D function by marketing experts), and common business practices (i.e., philosophy and culture, policies and procedures, planning skills, coaching, discipline, etc.). Obviously, one of the most effective means to gather this information is through face-to-face interviews with key customers and members of their staffs.

Identify Consumer Segments

Since the customers of training services are the ultimate clients within the organization, the consumers are the actual recipients of these services, whether they attend formal courses, participate in on-job training, or take self-study programs. In short, the consumers of training are the key populations that require continued education and development in order to achieve business objectives. Just as the needs of customers relate to their overall business objectives, so do the needs of consumers. Thus specific consumer groups and their particular needs must also be identified (i.e., major employee groups—within management, within support staff, etc.; breakdown of employees by job levels in the organization, highest degrees achieved, age, length of service, previously attended internal and external courses, etc.). Frequently, the richest source of data here is found in written documentation which is supplemented by selected face-to-face interviews, focus group discussions, etc. Once the information is collected, sift, sort, juggle, and scrutinize it for significance. For example, when length of service is compared with job levels, is the distribution equal across all levels or does length of service vary by level? More important, why? Where are degrees most prevalent? Why? What types of degrees? What does this signify in relation to this employee group?

Identify Staff Relationships

In addition to the identifying of specific customer and consumer segments, the relationship with other staff functions must also be carefully delineated. Particular attention should be focused on various appropriate aspects of human resource functions, such as succession planning, affirmative action, benefits, compensation, labor relations, employee relations, recruiting, and employment practices. Equal attention should be given to other staff functions such as legal, tax, public relations, accounting, and information systems. These interrelationships need to be explored from several perspectives: What services does each provide to the training function? (For example, how will accounting help to track direct costs related to training?) What services does training provide to each related staff function (as customer or consumer)? And what joint services are provided by the training function and other staff functions? (For example, will training design the orientation materials to be used by the employment specialists? Are there labor contract agreements that impact employee training?) Finally, the relationship with any other training functions in the organization must be explored and defined (i.e., relationships between corporate and business unit training operations or between sales training and management training if the two are in separate departments).

Determine Purpose

In determining the overall purpose of the training function, the answers to two overriding questions should emerge:

- What training and education exists now? Why?
- What should exist? Short-term? Long-term?

The answers to these questions are not a detailed needs analysis in relation to any particular problem or opportunity. Instead, the perspective is much broader and seeks to define the specific mission, objective, customers, consumers, and staff relationships of the training function. From this base, the various alternatives for organizing the function can be explored.

Establish a Mission Statement

The first step is to develop a mission statement for training and education within the specific organization, based upon the data gleaned earlier. A training mission statement identifies the principal reason for the existence of the training function and relates this reason to the overall mission of the business. It must take a long-term perspective (minimum of 10 years) on *why* the function exists and *what* it will contribute to the business. Does the scope of responsibilities include *all employees*? Or is it focused more specifically by particular *employee group(s)* (hourly, clerical, professional, management, etc.), by *functional area(s)* of the business (marketing, sales, production, distribution, research, etc.), by *geography* (southwest, east, north, etc.), by *business unit(s)* within the total company (consumer products, industrial products, etc.), or by some combination of these? Whatever the appropriate scope, the resulting mission statement must link directly to the overall philosophy of the business and its mission, strategic plans, and operating plans. Thus access to this information—whether formally established or informally understood—is critical to the definition of a viable mission statement for employee development.

Define an Overriding Objective

While the mission statement is intentionally broad and serves to prescribe a fundamental scope, the overriding objective—while still broad—narrows this perspective into specific, measurable, achievable, understandable terms. (Refer to any of a number of reliable sources for writing precise, usable objective statements. Charles E. Watson's work, *Results-Oriented Managing, The Key to Effective Performance*,[1] is an excellent starting point.)

Figure 2-1 provides a sample of the mission and key objective for the management education department of a diversified consumer products company.

Consider Alternative Strategies

With the mission, objective, customers, consumers, etc., at hand, the next step is to develop and evaluate several distinct approaches—overall strategies—that can achieve this mission and objective in relation to the needs of both customers and consumers. If the analysis has been thorough enough and the resulting mission and objective specifically targeted, the strategies will be relatively obvious.

Each strategy should include consideration of all available resources that will be required to assure achievement of the mission and overriding objective. For example, the full spectrum of resources might involve

People
  Training staff
    Line and staff managers as course leaders
    Line and staff managers as subject matter experts
    Support staff and departments (such as audiovisual and print production)
    Outside suppliers (writers and developers of custom materials, subject matter experts, etc.)
    Outside vendors (related hardware, prepackaged courses and programs)
  Budget
    What is in training budget (and what impact each item has on the control of cost, quality, commitment, etc.)
    Staff salaries and benefits
    Research
    Production

Figure 2-1. Mission and key objective statement.

MANAGEMENT EDUCATION DEPARTMENT

Mission

To help XYZ, Inc. achieve its position as the worldwide leader in its industry through the development of its management resources.

Key Objective

Provide staff assistance, built on a standard of excellence, for developing and improving managerial performance corporatewide. (See standards below.)

Customers

President and staff. Headquarters and business unit heads and staffs.

Consumers

All levels of management. (Definition: A manager is any line or staff professional who sets goals to meet his or her responsibilities.)

Product

Management development programs that address specific deficiencies in management skills, knowledge, and/or experience needed to attain company objectives. Scope of products includes individual, groupwide, and/or companywide.

Standards: 1. Needs identification
  (a) Establish course committee
  (b) Establish timetable for needs identification
  (c) Identify specific deficiency(ies).
  (d) Identify level(s) and number of managers involved
  (e) Identify number of sessions to be conducted
  (f) Identify potential resources (external and internal)
  (g) Complete cost-benefit analysis

  2. Objective
  (a) Identify terminal behaviors
  (b) Identify enabling behaviors
  (c) Establish timetable for design, development, pilot, and implementation

  3. Design
  (a) Identify content areas
  (b) Identify appropriate training methods, facilitation techniques, and media
  (c) Develop key point outline including time and events schedule and agenda

  4. Program development (all materials are targeted to audience level; concise, clear, and understandable by end users)
  (a) Administrative materials
  (b) Course leaders' guide
  (c) Participant materials
  (d) Supporting materials
  (e) Evaluation methodology and materials

  5. Delivery
  (a) Pilot
      (1) Evaluate course at 3.0 or higher on a 5-point scale (1 = low, 5 = high) immediately following the sessions
      (2) Course committee agrees that "80 percent" of course "on-target" meets objectives
      (3) Evaluate course instructor(s) at 3.5 or higher

(b) Train-the-trainer
  (1) Evaluate train-the-trainer course 3.5 or higher
  (2) Self-evaluation on confidence level to conduct program at 3.0 or higher
(c) Ongoing
  (1) Evaluate course at 3.5 or higher immediately following the session
  (2) Evaluate course instructor(s) at 3.0 or higher
  (3) Long-term evaluation and standards determined as appropriate
  (4) 90 percent identify at least one specific on-job application
  (5) 80 percent report at least one specific on-job application 6 months following course

6. Administration
  (a) Annual scheduling of course sessions meets at least 90 percent of requests
  (b) Sufficient course leaders trained when appropriate to address need
  (c) Informal feedback from course leaders and their supervisors indicates developmental value of being a course leader
  (d) Evaluate facility at 2.6 or higher
  (e) Adequate annual inventory in place for ongoing programs
  (f) Course implemented according to schedule
  (g) Not more than two complaints per course session

Consultants

Participant expenses (salaries and benefits, travel, meals, lodging, consultant fees, etc.)

Delivery methodologies (lecture and discussion, self-study, tutorial, structured on-job experience, role play, simulation, etc.)

Delivery technologies (paper and pencil, video, audio, print, 16-mm film, 35-mm slides, overheads, workbook, etc.)

It is important to consider the issues of people, budget, methodologies, and technologies as elements of strategy, because decisions at this point will prescribe the scope and limitations within which specific training needs are addressed. For example, whether the strategy includes or excludes nationwide video network capabilities will have a direct bearing on how specific training courses are designed, developed, and implemented.

Typically, significant variables in the training mission and key objective will lead to similar differences in strategies. For example, returning to the operating unit sales trainer mentioned earlier, the key customers include the region sales vice president, members of her staff, and the national sales training director. Key consumers identified might then include sales representatives, sales supervisors, sales managers, and area sales managers. The strategy to address the needs of this diverse group might focus on:

1. Use of national, internally developed courses whenever possible.

2. Reliance on self-study workbooks and slides or tapes for product knowledge.

3. Reliance on classroom sessions (lecture and discussion and behavior modeling) for sales skills.

4. Use of field sales managers as classroom instructors for sales skills courses.

5. Use of sales trainer for needs identification, design, development, and evaluation.

6. *No* use of outside suppliers or developers.

7. Use of area sales managers as subject matter experts.

8. Training budget for training staff compensation, research, and materials production only. All other expenses rebilled or paid directly by users.

Conversely, the data might indicate a substantially different strategy:

1. Use of selected mandatory national courses only.

2. Reliance on on-job training for product knowledge.

3. Reliance on on-job coaching for selling skills.

4. Reliance on classroom sessions to develop coaching skills of field sales managers.

5. Use of sales trainers for needs identification, design, development implementation, and evaluation.

6. Use of selected outside suppliers and developers.

7. Use of outside experts for course content.

8. Training budget for training staff compensation, research, materials production, consultants, and related course administration expenses (travel, lodging, meals, etc.).

As the scope of the training function broadens, the strategies (and resulting organizational issues) will become more complex in order to incorporate consideration of all customers, consumers, staff relationships, short- and long-range needs, etc.

Develop Alternative Organizational Structures

Each major strategy will suggest its own appropriate organizational structure that identifies specific positions (types and number), along with their responsibilities and reporting relationships, and the relationship of the training function to other functions in the business.

Advantages to Organizing

While effective organization of efforts requires considerable research and analysis, it is the key to making the data collection and analysis pay off, because it provides the systematic means to coordinate related resources so that specific objectives—whether for the entire function or for one particular project—can be reached efficiently and effectively. In short, organizing determines who will do what, with what resources, and within what reporting structure. It brings together all related activities and resources (people, money, equipment, etc.), establishes appropriate linkages by specifying the authority and responsibilities of positions within the hierarchy, and helps assure that everyone works together toward specific goals.

"Business Basics: What Managers Want Trainers to Know"[2] explores a variety of organizational structures (line, staff, committee, functional, and matrix), along with the advantages and disadvantages of each. As such, it can provide a benchmark for developing an appropriate structure for each major strategy.

Validate Organizational Structure

Once the most appropriate overall structure is identified and developed, it must be validated, or fine-tuned, in order to make sure it is, in fact, the most effective and efficient approach. Examine the selected organizational structure according to the basic principles described below.

Specialization of Work

Greater efficiency is achieved when work in the training function is divided so that individuals or groups perform a limited number of specific, related activities. Specialization increases productivity by improving each person's or group's level of performance. In general, a person's performance is determined by two factors:

- The individual's *ability* to do the work
- The individual's *willingness* to apply that ability on the job

When work is divided so that individuals can specialize their performance within a limited range of activities, each person's ability can increase. Rather than being a mediocre combination of carpenter, mason, electrician, general contractor, and landscaper, an individual usually functions better by specializing in one of these particular jobs. At the same time, each person's willingness to do a particular job may also be increased—because the responsibilities are within achievable limits. Rather than attempting to be a jack of all trades, the individual has the opportunity to be the master of one.

However, specialization works best when not carried to extremes. Overspecialization may decrease rather than increase an individual's level of performance. When work activities are divided into extremely small, repetitive units so that people have difficulty relating their performance to meaningful achievement, the ability required to do the job is so low that it can cause a significant drop in a person's willingness to do the job. The solution is to find a balance of specialization that considers how both ability and willingness can affect productivity.

As implied above, one approach to specialization within the training function can be based upon the major groupings identified in the initial analysis. That is, individual positions within the function can focus upon specific technical areas of the business (sales, production, etc.) or specific geographic areas (east, southwest, northeast, etc.). Conversely, specific positions can also be formed around all or parts of the overall training process itself (needs analysis, design, development, production, implementation, evaluation, administration, overall management of the function, etc.).

Span of Control

Within each level of the training function, each manager can supervise only a limited number of subordinates. To determine the span of control for a specific position, various factors must be considered. A manager's span of control can be *increased* if:

1. The level of *supervisory ability* is high.
2. The *subordinates' ability and willingness* are high.

3. The *activities of subordinates* are simple or quite similar.
4. The *interrelationship between subordinate activities* is low, so that one's activities *do not* affect another's activities.
5. The *subordinates' standards of performance* are specific and understood.
6. The *formal authority delegated to subordinates* is high.
7. The *availability of staff assistance* is high.

All these factors, when considered together, determine how many positions each manager at each level can supervise effectively. There is no set number that can be applied to all cases, but in practice top levels of an organization usually supervise from 3 to 11 subordinates, while spans from 6 to 30 are not unusual at lower levels. Determination of the "best" span should consider all the factors of a specific situation.

Consider Impact of Technology on Required Resources

Examine the selected organizational structure from the perspective of available technology that can either reduce the need for human resources or improve overall efficiency and effectiveness. For example, what is the potential impact of word processing, telecommunications, personal and mainframe computers, audiovisual equipment, etc.? How can the training function not only improve its own efficiency but also possibly serve as a model to the rest of the business in its application of technology?

Necessary Authority and Responsibility to Perform Identified Activities

Formal authority, informal authority, and responsibility are the threads that weave together related groups of activities within an organization. Thus a consideration of authority and responsibility must include not only the training function itself but also all other areas of the business that interact with the training function. For example, what position should have final approval of course content? Of overall training plans? Of hiring and promotion? Of budgets for course development? Of participant expenses for travel and lodging? Of training methodologies?

Formal Authority.   Formal authority is the rights delegated to a specific position in an organizational structure. Such rights are a part of the position itself and are not personal rights of the individual(s) who hold(s) that position. Formal authority includes the rights to (1) make decisions within the scope of delegated authority, (2) assign tasks to subordinate positions, and (3) require satisfactory performance from subordinates.

The delegation of formal authority from the top down through an entire organization results in three types of authority relationships: line authority, staff authority, and functional authority. Any single position may be based upon one primary type of authority, but most positions usually contain elements of all three types.

Line Authority.   Line authority is based upon the decision-making relationship between a superior and a subordinate position. Specifically, each superior position has line authority over those decisions that affect the specific objective it is accountable for. Line authority says "The buck stops here." For accomplishing any other objectives in the organization, that same position *may* have staff or functional authority.

Staff Authority. Staff authority is the right of one position to advise, assist, or offer service to another position in the organization. It is not decision-making authority; it is the authority to influence the decision made by someone in another position—one's boss, one's peers, or other positions in the organization. While line authority flows downward from the top of an organization to create supervisor-subordinate relationships, staff authority can flow in any direction to create advisory relationships.

Functional Authority. Functional authority is decision-making authority that is limited to a specific activity, or part of an activity—no matter where it occurs in the organization. Since functional authority is limited, it creates secondary (rather than primary) supervisor-subordinate relationships. Thus one position may have more than one boss—one line, the others functional. Typically, functional authority is more common at higher levels of complex organizations.

Any specific position may have one, two, or three types of formal authority. For example, a production manager's position has line authority for the operations assigned to that position, and staff authority to advise and assist related peer positions (marketing, distribution, finance, etc.) in meeting their objectives. The position of a business-unit safety manager has line authority for the positions reporting directly to it, staff authority in relation to other departments and positions, and perhaps functional authority for *some* activities (such as those directly related to safety standards) of a plant safety supervisor.

Informal Authority. If formal authority is the building block of organizational structure, informal authority is the mortar that holds the blocks together. To accomplish results day by day, most managers rely as heavily on informal authority as on formal authority. Informal authority develops over time; it is earned by individuals through their interactions with others in the organization. It usually increases as an individual's knowledge, experience, or skills are recognized and respected by others. Rather than a right dictated by one's position, it depends upon one's influence over others—subordinates, peers, higher management, or anyone else in the organization. Although it cannot be delegated formally, without it most individuals and organizations would not be nearly as effective. Conscious use and development of informal authority typically begets greater formal authority. In contrast, managers who rely solely on formal authority can rarely be as effective as those who also develop informal authority. In evaluating the selected organizational structure for the training function, it is critical to define formal authority explicitly and to consider how much the effectiveness of the operation depends upon informal authority. Since training is typically a staff function, the impact of informal authority can be critical, particularly in the start-up phase of any new approach. Figure 2-2 provides brief examples of formal (line, staff, and functional) and informal authority.

Unity of Command

Coordinating activities is easier when each position has only one superior. While specialization makes it possible to accomplish larger-scale tasks, it also requires

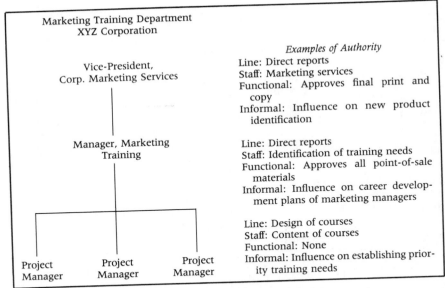

Figure 2-2. Examples of authority within a simple organizational structure.

careful coordination so that related activities are controlled by a central point. The activities of any group of subordinates are easier to coordinate if that group has only one boss. Although few would argue with the practicality of this principle, it is extremely difficult to apply in large, complex organizations. Specialization frequently divides knowledge and authority for some things among several positions which do not all relate directly to each other or to one superior position in the organization. For example, consider a training specialist who is designing a product knowledge course for sales representatives. This position reports directly to a sales training manager, who expects certain training design standards to be met. For this project, this position also "reports" to the director of new products, who has strong opinions on what the course content should cover and—equally important—how it should be covered. The training specialist also relies upon the services of the company's audiovisual production department, which has certain standards in relation to the production of the slides and audiotapes which are part of this particular training package. In short, the clear delineation of who has knowledge and authority over what requires careful attention. In practical terms, the result is that some people have more than one boss. In such cases, each position should have only one primary boss, with the authority of secondary bosses clearly spelled out and understood by all.

Centralization versus Decentralization

In general terms, the training function should be patterned after the overall approach of the organization which it serves. If that organization is centralized, the training function should also be centralized, and vice versa. While exceptions are possible, there should be ample evidence—based upon the preceding analysis—to justify such an approach. For example, balancing cost consideration against the necessity for a standard message concerning company culture and management practices, management courses might be centralized. In contrast, production technology courses (even with a cultural concern for "quality") could be effectively and economically decentralized. A "finance for nonfinancial managers" course could take any one of a number of approaches:

Cross-functional exposure is critical	Centralized course, with participants from variety of functions
Unity within function is critical	Centralized course, participants all from same function
Local teamwork is critical	Local course, local participants
Cost efficiency and speed of delivery are critical	Self-study, prepackaged course

Final Check Considerations

As a final confirmation that the selected organizational structure is the most appropriate for achieving the mission and objective of the training function, it should be evaluated in relation to the questions below:

1. Is the structure appropriate to the size and type(s) of business(es)?
   - Can the structure address all the identified business needs of key customers?
   - Is there a relationship between the size of the business (i.e., total dollar sales, capital intensity, employee count—or other appropriate measures of size) and the size of the training function in terms of total resources allocated (i.e., the simpler or more complex the business, the simpler or more complex the training structure)?

2. Does the structure address the needs of appropriate employee populations (sizes and types of consumer segmentations)?

3. Does the structure avail itself of quality "outside" resources?
   - Those outside the function, but within the business (example: use of internal resources as content experts, instructors, course designers, producers)?
   - Those outside the business (examples: consultants, prepackaged courses, universities)?

4. Does the structure eliminate weaknesses of any existing structure of the training function?

5. Does the structure incorporate the future direction of the business? (Is it designed to address both current and future needs?)

6. Is the structure compatible with relevant company policies and procedures?

7. Does the structure reinforce, or supplement, existing training programs? Should it?

8. Does the structure provide the means to achieve the training mission and key objective?

Once the selected organizational structure has been fine-tuned and validated as the best approach, the next step is to make sure the appropriate tracking measures are in place.

Determine Appropriate Results

The initial data regarding training's customers and consumers relate their objectives to specific needs that can be addressed, partially or fully, through some form of training. Thus, the data will also state or imply expected results when those needs are met. Once targeted results are known, appropriate tracking measures can be defined. Other chapters of this handbook deal with evaluation techniques that will be useful in prescribing appropriate overall tracking measures.

Sell the Resulting Approach

In reality, the marketing of the resulting approach begins with the initial collection of data that leads to the identification of the mission, key objective, and strategy of the training function, since—when done properly—this preliminary analysis indicates early that the intent of the exercise is to address the business objectives and related training needs of both customers and consumers. In the process, key decision makers are clearly identified, along with their primary concerns and expectations. These data form the basis of an effective marketing program to sell the resulting mission, objective, strategy, and organizational structure of the training function.

Several questions may still require additional amplification:

- How much do key decision makers already know about the potential impact of training on the effectiveness and efficiency of the business?
- How much do they need to know regarding the resulting approach?
  - Mission
  - Key objective
  - Strategy
  - Relationship of all three to business mission and objectives
  - Organizational structure
  - Key data from research
    - Customers
    - Consumers
    - Internal resources
    - External resources
  - End results to be expected and how these will be measured

Probably the easiest means to assure concurrence with the resulting organizational structure is to involve as many key people—customers and consumers alike—deeply in the process as early as possible. The resulting joint analysis and conclusions will then sell themselves.

Develop Policies and Procedures

Once the appropriate approvals have been achieved (or before, depending upon the typical process within a business), the resulting approach needs to be confirmed and reiterated through formal policies and procedures that define the process of implementation on a day-to-day basis. Even if the business itself does not require

EDUCATION AND DEVELOPMENT

POLICY:

While personal development is the primary responsibility of the individual, it is the company's policy to provide adequate, practical, job-related education and development, on a compensated basis, to all employees in order to help assure that they perform their responsibilities in the most competent and efficient manner possible.

SCOPE:

Education and development opportunities are available to all regular full-time, regular part-time, and seasonal employees without regard to race, sex, age, color, religion, national origin, or handicap.

Since education and development results in increased employee productivity, it is necessary that a structured education and development program be established companywide and in each business unit.

The following procedure describes corporate and business units' responsibilities regarding education and development.

DEFINITIONS:

Education and development is any interaction, formal or informal, which ultimately results in the enhancement of an individual's ability to perform a job and/or prepares an individual for additional responsibility and/or advancement.

RESPONSIBILITY:

The development of this policy and procedure is the responsibility of the management education department. Implementation of this policy and procedure is the responsibility of line management and each employee.

PROCEDURE:

Responsibility	*Action*
Corporate Management Education Department	1. Consults with business unit management on education and development needs.
	2. Develops and administers education and development programs and materials to be used on a companywide basis.
	3. Provides consultation on and development of programs and materials specific to particular business units.
Business Unit Human Resources Directors	4. Coordinate the programs and materials developed by the corporate management education department.
Line Manager and Subordinate	5. Determine, through a mutual process, what education and development is needed and seek help (where appropriate, and usually from the human resources representative) in deciding when, where, how, and by whom the education can be most effectively done.
	Note: This personal development step occurs naturally for exempt employees during the performance review, since its primary goal is personal performance improvement plans.
Line Manager	6. Provides necessary education and development to those individuals whose work he or she directs.
Subordinate	7. Assumes primary responsibility for own development.

Figure 2-3. Training policy and procedure.

such policies and procedures, if the training function has any degree of complexity, it is best to put specific policies and procedures in writing in order to assure smooth implementation. If the business does not already have its own standards for developing policies and procedures, *The New Playscript Procedure: Management Tool for Action*[3] is an excellent resource.

Figure 2-3 is the overall policy and procedure for a complex training function in a consumer products business. This policy is implemented through a number of specific procedures that address corporatewide needs analysis, identification, and scheduling of participants, evaluation of specific courses, etc.

Maintain Long-Term Perspective

After the data analysis has been completed, the mission and objective established, the organizational structure developed and evaluated, tracking measures put in place, and the entire approach approved and implemented, the work has only begun. Organizing and managing the training function is an ongoing process. It requires continued reevaluation and modification as the objectives and needs of the business change. Ultimately, it should lead to a strategic plan for the training function that is linked to and changes with the strategic plan of the business it serves. At a minimum, organization of the training function must be revisited and updated frequently enough to ensure that it continues to address its key customers and consumers through a mission and overriding objective that is concurrent with the objectives and needs of those customers and consumers. As with other staff functions, training is a service business within the business itself. Its viability, vitality, and effectiveness depend solely upon the continual assurance that it meets the needs it is intended to serve.

References

1. Watson, Charles E., *Results-Oriented Managing, The Key to Effective Performance*, Addison-Wesley Publishing Co., Reading, MA, 1981.

2. Callahan, Madelyn R., Managing Editor, "Business Basics: What Managers Want Trainers to Know," *Info-Line*, ASTD, Alexandria, VA, 1985.

3. Matthies, Leslie H., *The New Playscript Procedure: Management Tool for Action*, 2d ed., Office Publications, Inc., 1977.

3

Professional Development

Richard C. McCullough

Richard C. McCullough is the Executive Director of the Instructional Systems Association with a membership of over 75 firms producing generic and custom-designed training programs. Prior to this, he was the Vice President for Professional Development at ASTD. During that time he served as Staff Project Director for the ASTD Competency Study. For nearly 30 years, Mr. McCullough was engaged in training with the federal government holding such positions as Assistant Director for Training, U.S. Office of Personnel Administration; Deputy Director, Bureau of Training, U.S. Civil Service Commission; and Director of Training, Internal Revenue Service. He has written articles which appeared in the Training and Development Journal and Training magazine, presented at numerous national HRD conferences, and taught at the college level. He received his Master of Arts degree in Education from George Washington University with a specialty in Employee Training.

Why Professional Development?

You might ask why the need for a chapter on professional development in a handbook written for those who specialize in the training and development of others. The reason is that we sometimes overlook the obvious and are so busy helping others we forget the need closer at home. The truth is that training and development practitioners are in as much, if not greater, need for professional development as are their clients or customers.

First of all the field is relatively new and its core of knowledge is still being formulated. Few of us have had the opportunity of getting the type of formal education that professionals usually get before entering their field. We do not have the advantage that graduates of medical, law, or engineering schools have when first entering their profession. Therefore, much of what we will need will have to come from lifelong continued education or professional development.

Second, the training and development field is a changing and dynamic one. Not only are we constantly faced with new and better ways to provide learning opportunities (interactive videodiscs, computer-based instruction, and accelerated learning techniques to mention a few), but we are also faced with tremendous changes in the workplace. Changes in technology, market demand, and labor force demography demand that the training and development practitioner keep up-to-date through whatever means are available.

And finally, we training and development professionals need to serve as models for others. Surely you do not expect others to buy your services if you are not a partaker of them yourself. We should never get into the position of "do as I say, not as I do."

Educational Preparation

This is not to say individuals in training and development work are not well educated. Actually, just the opposite is true. A membership survey conducted by ASTD[1] found that 98 percent of its members had some college education, 89 percent had at least a bachelor's degree, 41 percent a master's degree, and 13 percent had their doctorate. *TRAINING* magazine's "Industry Report" for 1985[2] reported that trainers got their bachelor's degrees primarily in education (17.6 percent), followed by business and management (16 percent), social sciences (14.7 percent), and psychology (10.8 percent). Those receiving their bachelor's degree with a specialty in human resource development or training and development were less than 2 percent; however, this percentage increases to 6.1 percent for postgraduate degrees. The top four specialty areas for postgraduate degrees were the same as for the bachelors (education 31.6 percent, business/management 18.6 percent, psychology 10.4 percent, and social sciences 6.7 percent).

Occupational Preparation

But even with this strong evidence of academic preparation, those intending to make training and development their field of endeavor need professional development, not only for the four reasons stated above but also because the field does not seem to "grow its own."

The industry report mentioned earlier showed that 27.2 percent of trainers had held supervisory or managerial positions immediately prior to entering their training job; 21.7 percent had held other technical or professional positions; 17.3 percent had been teachers; 11.7 percent had been personnel specialists; and 7.2 percent had come from sales. The ASTD membership survey generally had reported similar findings, except that 24 percent of its respondents listed teacher or educator as their occupation prior to entering training and development. This seems to indicate that very few in training and development chose the field as their original occupation but rather that they came into the field after trying something else. This is another reason why professional development is particularly needed.

Emphasis of This Chapter

This chapter will stress the importance of planning your professional development efforts based on a careful analysis of your particular needs. It will describe in detail one way you can look at yourself, your job, and your future to plan where you want to spend your energy to achieve professional growth. It will suggest a variety of resources, formal and informal, that can be used when carrying out your plan. Emphasis will be on individual trainers and their struggle to maintain their competence and to advance in the training and development field. Only brief reference will be made to the supervisor's responsibilities for employee development, but much of what is covered can be easily applied.

The time frame used in this chapter is a short one, maximum of about 3 years; and therefore, the larger topic of career development is not explored in depth, but only in passing. But much that is said about professional development can easily be translated into career development.[3]

Definition of Professional Development

Professional development is defined here as the process by which individuals increase their understanding and knowledge, and/or improve their skills and abilities, to perform better in their current positions or to prepare themselves for a position to which they can realistically aspire in the near future. Professional development is very practical and results-oriented. You should be able to measure progress and its individual components should have recognizable beginning and ending points.

Often when professional development efforts fail, it is because they are too long-range, not job-related, not specific in their intended outcomes, have no time limits, or do not include a means for measuring success.

Doing the Analysis

Planning and carrying out professional development is much like taking a trip. It is not only important to know where you are going, it is essential to know where you are starting from. This requires you to take a careful look at the requirements of your present job and how well you are meeting them—and, if you are aspiring to another position, to look at its requirements and measure your ability to meet them. Where a gap exists between your identified level of competence to perform and the requirements of the job, current or future, a professional development need exists.

One method of analysis would be to compare your job description, or the job description of the position to which you aspire, with how well you are performing, or think you could perform. If your present job description is current and accurately describes what you do and its importance, this is a good place to start, particularly if it can be done in consultation with your supervisor.

However, another way to do this analysis is to analyze your training job in light of the work done over the past few years by those attempting to define the roles and competencies needed by training and development practitioners.

That approach is followed in this chapter.

Early Efforts

Over the years there have been numerous efforts to define the roles and competencies needed to do the training and development job. A few of the more significant ones are described.

In a 1967 article,[4] Leonard Nadler and Gordon Lippitt made one of the earliest attempts to describe the "emerging roles of the training director." They saw the job encompassing three roles:

A *learning specialist* who designed and presented training courses

An *administrator* who managed the function

A *consultant* who assisted line management with their efforts at problem solving, implementing change, and developing organization

While expanded by later studies, this article was a breakthrough in defining the training person's responsibilities in a manner understood by all. Dr. Nadler has continued to use this three-role breakdown in his teaching, consulting, and writing.[5]

A study done by the U.S. Civil Service Commission in 1976[6] identified five roles played by the federal employee development specialists:

A *career counselor* who facilitated the selection of training and development alternatives primarily for career development purposes

A *consultant* who was concerned with research and development and with providing advice and assistance on a variety of organizational problems

A *learning specialist* who designed, developed, conducted, and evaluated training

A *program manager* who set policy, managed the function, and interacted with top management

A *training administrator* who arranged, coordinated, and maintained the support services for the training function

The study also listed the tasks and competencies peculiar to each role and suggested resources for professional development. The results were used as guidance for federal training activities.

About this same time, the Ontario Society for Training and Development was studying the work of training professionals in Canada. The result of their work was a comprehensive guide[7] which lists four roles or categories of training and development personnel:

Instructor

Designer

Manager

Consultant

It also identified 11 areas of core competencies:

Administration

Communication

Course design

Evaluation

Group dynamics process

Learning theory

Manpower planning

Person-organization interface

Teaching practice

Training equipment and materials

Training needs analysis

A major contribution of this study was the matrix approach it used where core competency areas were matched with each role and specific examples of needed knowledge, understanding, and skill were given. It showed clearly that while the same core competency might be required by different roles, how that competency is expressed in behavior can vary greatly.[8]

As part of its accreditation (i.e., certification) activity, the American Society for Personnel Administration (ASPA) tested for four training and development roles:

Practitioner

Consultant

Educator

Researcher

On successful completion of the requirements and examinations, one can gain ASPA certification as a training and development specialist. ASPA provides a guide[9] covering these four roles for those wishing to study for the examination.

In 1978, ASTD's Professional Development Committee commissioned a study[10] of its then 14,000 members. The emphasis of the study, popularly known as the "Pinto-Walker study" after its authors, was on what the members actually did on the jobs. The final result was a list of 104 tasks, behaviors, knowledges, and abilities that were categorized into the following 11 activity areas:

Analyzing needs and evaluating results

Designing and developing training programs and materials

Delivering training and development programs and services

Advising and counseling

Managing training activities

Maintaining organization relationships

Doing research to advance the training field

Developing professional skills and expertise

Developing basic skills and knowledge

This study proved extremely useful to ASTD and its members. For several years it provided direction for the professional development activities and materials of the association. It also gave guidance to some universities and colleges in developing new training and development specialty curricula.[11]

Models of Excellence

While these early works have all been worthwhile and added greatly to the body of knowledge, the most recent and most useful work was done by ASTD from 1981 to 1983 and was made available in the publication *Models for Excellence: The Conclusions and Recommendations of the ASTD Training and Development Competency Study*.[12] It is this work that will be used as a basis for helping you analyze your needs and design your own professional development plan.

Some *background information* about the study should be helpful. The ASTD Professional Development Committee undertook the study with the following charge from the ASTD board of directors: "to produce a detailed and updatable definition of excellence in the training and development field in a form that will be useful to and used as a standard of professional performance by ASTD, organizations, educational institutions, training and development departments, and individuals practicing or expected to practice in the training and development field." Since publication, the study has been seen as fully meeting this charge in an exemplary manner. The products of this work are many and varied. This chapter will touch only on those directly related to professional development planning and execution. Others are using the results of the study for organizational decision making, selection of personnel, performance evaluation, counseling, and curriculum and course design.[13]

The identification of the *key roles* in the training and development field was a major contribution of the study. Based on a careful review of previous works, far beyond the ones mentioned in this chapter, and after several rounds of questionnaires with a panel of noted practitioners, 15 roles were found of key importance to the training and development field.

It is very important to make a clear distinction between "role" and "job" or "position." A role is a functional area with unique output requirements. Usually several roles are combined to make a job or position. On rare occasions, the role and the job may be identical. In different organizations, the same job titles could have wide differences in the roles encompassed under them. It is essential in professional development planning to get behind the job title and discover the actual roles being performed. Figure 3-1 lists the 15 roles identified in the ASTD study. Figure 3-2 provides the critical outputs for each of the roles.

With the roles identified, the next step was to determine the *critical competencies* needed to perform each of the roles. For this, the study directors called on 15 groups of "role experts" (a total of nearly 400 individuals) who, through a series of questionnaires, developed the list of 31 critical competencies found in Figure 3-3. When you combine this list of key roles with the list of critical competencies, you come up with a matrix like the one found in Figure 3-4.

To make the results as real as possible, the study provided a unique set of *behavioral examples* of what a competency would "look like" when it was being performed at various levels of expertise. To produce this product, the role experts were used again. Each was asked to submit examples of behavior which would exemplify expert performance in a particular competency for their role. These were then used to produce the intermediate and basic examples. The resulting descriptions were tested with groups of training practitioners for reliability and validity.

Figure 3-5 provides samples for the group process skills competency, the objectives preparation skills competency, and the training and development techniques understanding competency. These samples are presented to give you an idea of how descriptions of behaviors can be written and categorized by level of expertise. The reason each of the columns in Fig. 3-5 ends with "etc." is that it was the belief of the study directors that the best descriptions would be written by the individual reader. Companies and organizations have their own ways of determining what is "basic," "intermediate," and "advanced" in terms of their own situation. You, working with your supervisor and your peers, need to provide the appropriate behavioral examples, when working on your professional development needs analysis.

Six Steps in Analysis

As was said before, it is important to know where you are right now before you start off on any journey or professional development effort. Or, stated another way, by establishing where you are today professionally and comparing that with where

This study proposes that the T&D field consists of people who perform a different mix of roles. Some also perform roles which are outside the T&D area as we have defined it in this study. The fifteen roles below are those which emerged from literature reviews and after several rounds of review and questionnaires to experts in and around the T&D field. Some of the roles may be important in other human resource areas. We may assume that the competencies required to perform a T&D role will transfer to other areas where that role is important. The extent of transferability is the extent an individual can easily move between and among human resource areas—and to jobs outside human resources which require facility in the roles.

The roles below describe the major T&D functions which emerged in this study. They do *not* describe jobs. Individual jobs usually consist of several or many roles:

— EVALUATOR . . . The role of identifying the extent of a program, service, or product's impact.
— GROUP FACILITATOR . . . The role of managing group discussions and group process so that individuals learn and group members feel the experience is positive.
— INDIVIDUAL DEVELOPMENT COUNSELOR . . . The role of helping an individual assess personal competencies, values, and goals and identify and plan development and career actions.
— INSTRUCTIONAL WRITER . . . The role of preparing written learning and instructional materials.
— INSTRUCTOR . . . The role of presenting information and directing structured learning experiences so that individuals learn.
— MANAGER OF TRAINING AND DEVELOPMENT . . . The role of planning, organizing, staffing, and controlling training and development operations or training and development projects and of linking training and development operations with other organization units.
— MARKETER . . . The role of selling training and development viewpoints, learning packages, programs, and services to target audiences outside one's work unit.
— MEDIA SPECIALIST . . . The role of producing software for and using audio, visual, computer, and other hardware-based technologies for training and development.
— NEEDS ANALYST . . . The role of defining gaps between ideal and actual performance and specifying the cause of the gaps.
— PROGRAM ADMINISTRATOR . . . The role of ensuring that the facilities, equipment, materials, participants, and other components of a learning event are present and that program logistics run smoothly.
— PROGRAM DESIGNER . . . The role of preparing objectives, defining content, and selecting and sequencing activities for a specific program.
— STRATEGIST . . . The role of developing long-range plans for what the training and development structure, organization, direction, policies, programs, services, and practices will be in order to accomplish the training and development mission.
— TASK ANALYST . . . Identifying activities, tasks, subtasks, and human resource and support requirements necessary to accomplish specific results in a job or organization.
— THEORETICIAN . . . The role of developing and testing theories of learning, training, and development.
— TRANSFER AGENT . . . The role of helping individuals apply learning after the learning experience.

Figure 3-1. The 15 key training and development roles. (© *1983 by The American Society for Training and Development, Alexandria, Va. Reprinted by permission of ASTD.*)

Figure 3-2. The critical outputs for the training and development field. (© *1983 by The American Society for Training and Development, Alexandria, Va. Reprinted by permission of ASTD.*)

The following are the outputs which study respondents said are critical now and/or in five years. Some outputs are produced for internal use by the training and development functions. Others describe end products which go to the user (learners or client organizations).

Evaluator:
1. Instruments to assess individual change in knowledge, skill, attitude, behavior, results.
2. Instruments to assess program and instructional quality.
3. Reports (written and oral) of program impact on individuals.
4. Reports (written and oral) of program impact on an organization.
5. Evaluation and validation designs and plans (written and oral).
6. Written instruments to collect and interpret data.

Group Facilitator:
7. Group discussions in which issues and needs are constructively assessed.
8. Group decisions where individuals all feel committed to action.
9. Cohesive teams.
10. Enhanced awareness of group process, self and others.

Individual Development Counselor:
11. Individual career development plans.
12. Enhanced skills on the part of an individual to identify and carry out his or her own department needs and goals.
13. Referrals to professional counseling.
14. Increased knowledge by the individual about where to get development support.
15. Tools, resources needed in career development.
16. Tools for managers to facilitate employees' career development.
17. An individual who initiates feedback, monitors and manages career plans.

Instructional Writer:
18. Exercises, workbooks, worksheets.
19. Teaching guides.
20. Scripts (for video, film, audio).
21. Manuals and job aids.
22. Computer software.
23. Tests and evaluation forms.
24. Written role plays, simulations, games.
25. Written case studies.

Instructor:
26. Video tapes, films, audio tapes, computer-aided instruction, and other audiovisual materials facilitated.
27. Case studies, role plays, games, tests, and other structured learning events directed.
28. Lectures, presentations, stories delivered.
29. Examinations administered and feedback given.
30. Students' needs addressed.
31. An individual with new knowledge, skills, attitudes, or behavior in his or her repertoire.

Manager of Training and Development:
32. T&D department or project operating objectives.
33. T&D budgets developed and monitored.
34. Positive work climate in the T&D function or project group.
35. Department or project staffed.
36. T&D standards, policies, and procedures.
37. Outside suppliers and consultants selected.
38. Solutions to department or project problems.
39. T&D actions congruent with other HR and organization actions.
40. Relevant information exchanged with clients or departments (internal and external).
41. Staff evaluated.
42. Staff developed.

Marketer:
43. Promotional materials for T&D programs and curricula.
44. Sales presentations.
45. Program overviews.
46. Leads.
47. Contracts with T&D clients (internal and external) negotiated.
48. Marketing plan (developed and implemented).
49. T&D programs and services visible to target markets.

Media Specialist:
50. T&D computer software.
51. Lists (written and oral) of recommended instructional hardware.
52. Graphics.
53. Video-based material.
54. Audio tapes.
55. Computer hardware in working order.
56. Audiovisual equipment in working order.
57. Media users advised and counseled.
58. Production plans.
59. Purchasing specifications and recommendations for instructional and training software.
60. Purchasing specifications and recommendations for instructional and training hardware.

Needs Analyst:
61. Performance problems and discrepancies identified and reported (written or oral).
62. Knowledge, skill, attitude problems, and discrepancies identified and reported (written or oral).
63. Tools to assess the knowledge, skill, attitude, and performance level of individuals and organizations.
64. Needs analysis strategies.
65. Causes of discrepancies inferred.

Program Administrator:
66. Facilities and equipment selected and scheduled.
67. Participant attendance secured, recorded.
68. Hotel or conference center staff managed.
69. Faculty scheduled.
70. Course material distributed (on-site, precourse, postcourse).
71. Contingency plans for backups, emergencies.
72. Physical environment maintained.
73. Program follow-up accomplished.

Program Designer:
74. Lists of learning objectives.
75. Written program plans or designs.
76. Specifications and priorities of training content, activities, materials, and methods.
77. Sequencing plans for training content, activities, materials, and methods.
78. Instructional contingency plans and implementation strategies.

Strategist:
79. T&D long-range plans included in the broad human resource strategy of the client organization.
80. Identification (written or oral) of long-range T&D strengths, weaknesses, opportunities, threats.
81. Descriptions of the T&D function and its outputs in the future.
82. Identification of forces and trends (technical, social, economic, etc.) impacting T&D.
83. Guidelines and plans for implementing long-range goals.
84. Alternative directions for T&D.
85. Cost-benefit analyses of the impact of T&D on the organization.

Task Analyst:
86. Lists of key job or unit outputs.
87. Lists of key job or unit tasks.
88. Lists of knowledge, skill, and attitude requirements of a job or unit.
89. Descriptions of the performance levels required in a job or unit.
90. Job design, enlargement, enrichment implications or alternatives identified.
91. Subtasks, tasks, and jobs clustered.
92. Conditions described under which jobs or tasks are performed.

(Continued)

Theoretician:
93. New concepts and theories of learning and behavior change.
94. Articles on T&D issues and theories for scientific journals and trade publications.
95. Research designs.
96. Research reports.
97. Training models and applications of theory.
98. Existing learning or training theories and concepts evaluated.

Transfer Agent:
99. Individual action plans for on-the-job real-world application.
100. Plans (written or oral) for the support of transfer of learning in and around the application environment.
101. Job aids to support performance and learning.
102. On-the-job environment modified to support learning.

Figure 3-3. Thirty-one training and development competencies. (© *1983 by The American Society for Training and Development, Alexandria, Va. Reprinted by permission of ASTD.*)

The following model describes the knowledge and skill areas which the ASTD Competency Study has identified as important for excellent performance in the training and development field.
There are 31 competencies in this model:

1. *Adult Learning Understanding* . . . Knowing how adults acquire and use knowledge, skills, attitudes. Understanding individual differences in learning.
2. *Audiovisual Skill* . . . Selecting and using audiovisual hardware and software.
3. *Career Development Knowledge* . . . Understanding the personal and organizational issues and practices relevant to individual careers.
4. *Competency Identification Skill* . . . Identifying the knowledge and skill requirements of jobs, tasks, roles.
5. *Computer Competence* . . . Understanding and being able to use computers.
6. *Cost-Benefit Analysis Skill* . . . Assessing alternatives in terms of their financial, psychological, and strategic advantages and disadvantages.
7. *Counseling Skill* . . . Helping individuals recognize and understand personal needs, values, problems, alternatives, and goals.
8. *Data Reduction Skill* . . . Scanning, synthesizing, and drawing conclusions from data.
9. *Delegation Skill* . . . Assigning task responsibility and authority to others.
10. *Facilities Skill* . . . Planning and coordinating logistics in an efficient and cost-effective manner.
11. *Feedback Skill* . . . Communicating opinions, observations, and conclusions such that they are understood.
12. *Futuring Skill* . . . Projecting trends and visualizing possible and probable futures and their implications.
13. *Group Process Skill* . . . Influencing groups to both accomplish tasks and fulfill the needs of their members.
14. *Industry Understanding* . . . Knowing the key concepts and variables that define an industry or sector (e.g., critical issues, economic vulnerabilities, measurements, distribution channels, inputs, outputs, information sources).
15. *Intellectual Versatility* . . . Recognizing, exploring, and using a broad range of ideas and practices. Thinking logically and creatively without undue influence from personal biases.
16. *Library Skills* . . . Gathering information from printed and other recorded sources. Identifying and using information specialists and reference services and aids.
17. *Model Building Skill* . . . Developing theoretical and practical frameworks which describe complex ideas in understandable, usable ways.
18. *Negotiation Skill* . . . Securing win-win agreements while successfully representing a special interest in a decision situation.

19. *Objectives Preparation Skill* . . . Preparing clear statements which describe desired outputs.

20. *Organization Behavior Understanding* . . . Seeing organizations as dynamic, political, economic, and social systems which have multiple goals; using this larger perspective as a framework for understanding and influencing events and change.

21. *Organization Understanding* . . . Knowing the strategy, structure, power networks, financial position, systems of a SPECIFIC organization.

22. *Performance Observation Skill* . . . Tracking and describing behaviors and their effects.

23. *Personnel and HR Field Understanding* . . . Understanding issues and practices in other HR areas (organization development, organization job design, human resource planning, selection and staffing, personnel research and information systems, compensation and benefits, employee assistance, union labor relations).

24. *Presentation Skills* . . . Verbally presenting information such that the intended purpose is achieved.

25. *Questioning Skill* . . . Gathering information from and stimulating insight in individuals and groups through the use of interviews, questionnaires, and other probing methods.

26. *Records Management Skill* . . . Storing data in easily retrievable form.

27. *Relationship Versatility* . . . Adjusting behavior in order to establish relationships across a broad range of people and groups.

28. *Research Skills* . . . Selecting, developing, and using methodologies and statistical and data-collection techniques for a formal inquiry.

29. *Training and Development Field Understanding* . . . Knowing the technological, social, economic, professional, and regulatory issues in the field; understanding the role T&D plays in helping individuals learn for current and future jobs.

30. *Training and Development Techniques Understanding* . . . Knowing the techniques and methods used in training; understanding their appropriate uses.

31. *Writing Skills* . . . Preparing written material which follows generally accepted rules of style and form, is appropriate for the audience, creative, and accomplishes its intended purposes.

you would like to be represents your professional development need. It is not an easy task but will pay off in great dividends.

Step 1. Read carefully through the 15 key training and development roles in Fig. 3-1. Determine which of these are an important part of your current job. If you have trouble clearly understanding the role, refer to the critical outputs for the role listed in Fig. 3-2. Once you have identified all the roles that make up your current job, put them in priority order from most to least important in accomplishing what is expected of your position.

Step 2. Using a form like the one shown in Fig. 3-6, list the roles in priority order from left to right across the top of the page. In most cases, working on your top four roles should be sufficient to get you started.

Step 3. Using the roles and competencies matrix in Fig. 3-4, list down the left side of the form the key competencies needed in each of the roles you have identified as making up your job. You will notice that different roles require different competencies. For those competencies that do not apply to a particular role, simply draw an X through that box. If you have difficulty understanding a particular competency, refer to the definitions provided in Fig. 3-3.

Step 4. Continue your analysis by now evaluating your level of expertise in each competency for each role. To do this, rate yourself on a scale from 1 (little or no

This chart illustrates the level of expertise required in each competency area. Competencies and roles are both listed from most to least frequently occurring.

● = Advanced requirement.
○ = Intermediate requirement.

Requirements are listed only for competencies which 60 percent or more role respondents said are critical now and/or in five years for the role.

	Manager	Marketer	Instructional Writer	Media Specialist	Needs Analyst	Group Facilitator	Strategist	Evaluator	Individual Development Counselor	Instructor	Program Designer	Task Analyst	Theoretician	Transfer Agent	Program Administrator	
15. Intellectual Vers.	●	○	●	●	●	●	●		○	○	●	○	●*			12
11. Feedback Skill	●	○	●	●	●	●*			●	○	●	○		●		10
1. Adult Lrng. Und.	○		●	●	●	●			○	●	●	●	●*	○		9
25. Questioning Skill			●	○	●	●		●*	●	○	●	●				9
5. Computer Comp.	○	○	○	●*	○			○		○	○					8
8. Data Reduction Skill	●		●		●		●	●*				●	●			7
20. Org. Behavior Und.	●*	○			●	●	●		○		○	○	●	○		7
31. Writing Skills	●	●*	●	●	●						●	○	●			7
4. Competency ID.		○	○		●		○	○	○		○	●*	●	○		6
19. Object. Prep.	●		●	●							●*	○				6
24. Presentation Skill	●*		●	●					●	●	●*			●		6
27. Relationship Vers.	●					●*	●		●	○				○		6
30. T&D Techniques Und.			●			○				●	●*			○		6

Figure 3-4. The roles and competencies matrix. (© *1983 by The American Society for Training and Development, Alexandria, Va. Reprinted by permission of ASTD.*)

46

	18	16	14	10	10	10	14	8	9	9	9	7	7	3	
14. Industry Und.	●*	●	○					●	●				○		5
21. Organization Und.	●	●		○		●	●*	●			○				5
6. Cost-Benefit Analysis	●*	○	○			●	●								4
12. Futuring Skill	●	●				●*	●			○					4
13. Group Process Skill	●	●		●*		●					○				4
17. Model Building Skill		●			●	●				●					4
22. Perf. Observ. Skill				●	○		●		●		●*				4
18. Negotiation Skill	●	●*						●*	●			●*			3
28. Research Skills				○		●				●					4
2. Audiovisual Skill			●*					●	●*					○	2
3. Career Dvlp. Know.	○						●*	●*							2
7. Counseling Skill		○					●*								2
10. Facilities Skill			○												2
16. Library Skills		●*	○											●*	2
23. Pers. and HR Field Und.	○					●*									2
26. Records Mgmt. Skill									○						2
29. T&D Field Und.	●					●*								○*	2
9. Delegation Skill	●*														1
Totals	18	16	14	10	10	10	14	8	9	9	9	7	7	3	

* Indicates the highest expertise level for the competency.

47

EXAMPLE BEHAVIORS ILLUSTRATING LEVELS OF EXPERTISE

The COMPETENCY:	Basic:	Intermediate:	Advanced:
13. *Group Process Skills. . .* Influencing groups to both accomplish tasks and fulfill the needs of their members.	— A training group is hard at work in its second session when a new member arrives. The instructor stops the task work briefly; provides for the introduction of the member to the group, and vice versa; sets up a late informal get-together process; and quickly orients the new member to the ongoing task. — In a large group meeting of people who have successfully worked together before, the facilitator conducts a series of group involvement exercises and negotiates a "group contract" for the direction and goals of the meeting. — In a session where some different points of view are beginning to develop some negative feelings among group participants, the facilitator encourages the quiet participants to talk about their right to have a point of view. The discussion then returns to an open, highly participative one. — Etc.	— A line manager asks the T&D specialist to work with her in planning and conducting better staff meetings. The T&D specialist observes one meeting, interviews a few staff members, and recommends *various means for increasing group participation which will fit the needs and styles of the group members and the typical nature of the tasks.* — At the end of a training program, the T&D specialist senses a reluctance of the group to end the strong relationships built up. She talks about this with the group and allows members to talk about what the group and individuals in it have meant to them and how they feel about leaving it. — In a continually disruptive classroom situation, the T&D specialist *allows the disruptive group to air their issues and then is honest about her expectations and their alternatives should they choose not to cooperate. As a result, the general tension level in the group is reduced.* — Etc	— When asked to help a new task force learn the skills they will need in order to work together effectively, the T&D specialist *reviews and models several approaches for exploring ideas, reaching consensus, and managing conflict in a group.* — Having completed the "get-acquainted" phase with a new group, the facilitator finds that work on the task is being frustrated by a battle for control by three group members who are accustomed to being group leaders. *Understanding what is happening, the facilitator stops the task work, helps the group identify what is going on, leads them to a resolution of the problem, and gets them back to the task with all parties feeling they have been heard and are committed to proceeding.* — Etc.

Figure 3-5. The competency model for the T&D field. (© *1983 by The American Society for Training and Development, Alexandria, Va. Reprinted by permission of ASTD.*)

19. *Objectives Preparation Skill. . .*

Preparing clear statements which describe desired outputs.

— Asked by the personnel office to "find a film and conduct a 90-minute meeting for heads of offices on working with unmotivated workers," the T&D specialist draws on her past experience with the topic and drafts a letter which includes a *list of what people will learn in this session.*

— A T&D specialist receives a detailed task analysis and knowledge skill list for one segment of a toy assembler's job. He rewrites the task statements using *the language of behavioral objectives prescribed in established guidelines.*

— Etc.

— Asked by the personnel office to "find a film and conduct a 90-minute meeting for heads of offices on working with unmotivated workers," the T&D specialist draws on her past experience with the topic and drafts a letter which includes a *list of what people will learn in this session.*

— A T&D specialist is asked to help develop guidelines for independent learning projects which will occur as follow-ups to a formal management development course. She develops designs which include *lists of learning objectives for each module. These objectives include indicators that managers can use on their own to assess their progress.*

— A T&D specialist who has designed supervisory training programs before is asked to prepare a program to train new technical supervisors. He works with a task force of technical managers to identify special issues in technical supervision and *develops objectives for supervisory skills in the highly technical environment.*

— When given a list of clearly defined tasks, their skill requirements, and a description of the typical audience for a new program to train new technicians, the T&D specialist *writes objectives with observable behaviors, measurable performance criteria, and a description of conditions under which performance will occur on the job.*

— Etc.

— A T&D specialist with little experience in the technical area is asked to prepare a training plan based on a 200-page needs analysis report of the training needs for a high technology group. *She develops detailed training objectives to pass the review of a technical advisory board.*

— As part of a development strategy for auditors in a public accounting firm, the T&D specialist must develop objectives to guide the developer of course modules. Realizing that many outputs of successful auditing work are subjective, she develops *objectives which list a variety of indicators which can be used to measure each objective.*

— A T&D specialist is asked to design a strategy for upgrading the skills of a decentralized staff in a rapidly changing, highly technical job. Working with subject matter experts and with people who know the company's strategy, the T&D specialist identifies the critical skills which must be developed and prepares *objectives for use in on-the-job training.*

— Etc.

(*Continued*)

EXAMPLE BEHAVIORS ILLUSTRATING LEVELS OF EXPERTISE

The COMPETENCY:	Basic:	Intermediate:	Advanced:
30. *Training and Development Techniques Understanding*. . . Knowing the techniques and methods used in training; understanding their appropriate uses.	— In a presentation of a self-study supervisory development program, the T&D specialist *describes advantages and disadvantages of programmed instruction for this situation.* — In a presentation for new trainers, the T&D specialist *develops a list of commonly used training and development techniques and the advantages and disadvantages of each.* — Etc.	— As a result of a hiring freeze, the T&D specialist *reviews the training techniques used* throughout all divisions and subsidiaries in the corporation. After studying course records and research findings, he develops a set of recommendations which indicate: (1) which courses must have a *live instructor using group interaction techniques;* (2) which courses *could easily be converted to a materials-based, self-instructional format;* (3) which should remain as they are. — A lecture-based course has only been partially successful, although the content is accurate and complete for participant needs. The T&D specialist reviews the attitude and interest problems and proposes *six other ways the material could be more successfully presented.* — Because an off-the-shelf training package includes case studies which do not quite fit the company's situation, the T&D specialist recommends *several alternatives to the case modules,* including role plays, demonstrations, participant development cases, guided imagery, and other methods.	— A T&D specialist must develop a nine-module self-study program on drugs and effects for physicians. She sees her task as clearly presenting—in depth—a great deal of information, but also keeping the audience interested. She develops and uses a *format that incorporates graphics, space, summaries, case examples, diagrams, and short but clearly written essays.* Retention rates are 90 percent after the pilot. — A T&D specialist who is preparing a guidebook for use as an aid in designing training and development programs writes a *description of one hundred techniques used to help adults learn.* — In producing a multicourse program to train nuclear power plant technicians, the T&D specialist designs a program which incorporates *assessment, computer-aided instruction, workshops, mentoring projects, simulations, interactive video, field trips, case studies, and role plays.* Each technique is selected because of its leverage in helping achieve program objectives. — Etc.

Figure 3-5. Continued

NAME _____ *John Doe* _____ JOB TITLE _____ *Training Officer*

COMPETENCIES	ROLES			
	Instructor	Program Designer	Task Analyst	Transfer Agent
1. Adult Learning Understanding	4 4 0	4 4 0	X	4 4 0
4. Competency Identification Skill	X	4 2 +2	4 4 0	X
5. Computer Competence	1 4 −3	1 5 −4	X	X
8. Data Reduction Skill	X	X	4 4 0	X
11. Feedback Skill	4 4 0	X	4 3 +1	4 4 0
13. Group Process	5 4 +1	X	X	X
15. Intellectual Versatility	3 3 0	3 5 −2	3 4 −1	X
17. Model Building Skills	X	1 3 −2	X	X
19. Objectives Preparation Skill	X	5 5 0	X	X
20. Organization Behavior Understanding	X	1 3 −2	X	1 5 −4
21. Organization Understanding	X	X	X	2 5 −3
22. Performance Observation Skills	X	X	3 3 0	X
24. Presentation Skills	5 5 0	X	X	X
25. Questioning Skills	4 4 0	X	4 5 −1	X

Etc.

Note: From the above, it seems the six areas (#5, 15, 17, 20, 21, and 25) need to be included in John Doe's development plan.

Figure 3-6. Professional development worksheet. (© *1983 by The American Society for Training and Development, Alexandria, Va. Reprinted by permission of ASTD.*)

expertise) to 5 (advanced or high level of expertise). This is not always easy to do. It might help to review the behavioral examples given in Fig. 3-5 and think through what behaviors would be considered basic, intermediate, or advanced in your particular organization. Ask yourself if you exhibit those behaviors on a regular basis. Write the ratings you have given yourself for each competency in the appropriate boxes.

Step 5. Now you need to start over again and rate each competency for how important it is to your organization. This will differ among organizations. For example, "computer competence" appears as a key competency in 8 of the 15 roles. However, it may be that in your particular case neither your training organization nor your company as a whole uses computers to any great extent. In that case, it would be rated as having little importance. The same is true of all the competencies. While seen as "key" by the panels of experts who did the study, they may not be critical in your organization. On a scale from 1 (unimportant) to 5 (critical) rate the importance of each competency under each role in light of your own situation. When you finish, you should have two numbers in each open box on your form.

Step 6. Subtract the number you have given for "level of importance" from the number you have given for "level of expertise" to determine your professional development needs. A zero or plus number would indicate you have that competency well within the expertise level needed. A minus number would indicate that the importance of the competency to your current job exceeds your level of expertise. The higher the negative number the greater the professional development need. While it is a rather simplistic approach, taking the time to analyze your job by looking at its component roles and their concomitant competencies and then measuring your expertise and the importance of the competency in your situation can be a very productive exercise.

Role of the Supervisor

This analysis process will even be more effective if it can be done as a joint effort between you and your supervisor. In this case, together you would determine the roles that make up your job, prioritize them, agree on the level of expertise you possess for each competency, and set the level of importance in your organization of those competencies.

If done in an open discussion, with the sole aim being professional development, the results can be a far greater understanding and appreciation on both your parts. It could turn out to be one of the most productive discussions you two have had. In addition, working together to uncover areas needing professional development efforts can provide the start of a joint commitment as to how and when these efforts can best take place. Having a supervisor who understands what it is you want to accomplish in your own professional development can be a tremendous help.

There is a caution in this, however. Many personnel experts counsel that such professional development discussions between supervisors and employees should not be held as part of the performance appraisal or salary determination processes. It works out much better if the professional development discussions are disassociated from talk of "rewards and punishments."

Future Jobs

The procedure just described for looking at your present job can also be used to identify professional development need areas for a job you aspire to in the future

In that case the analysis would have to be done on that prospective job. Again, if possible, the involvement of your supervisor is usually helpful (particularly if the prospective job is under his or her supervision). But if not, it may be necessary, and even preferable, to consult with others who have firsthand knowledge of the roles that make up the position you hope to occupy in the future. They can tell you their opinions of the importance of the expertise needed but will be of less help in evaluating your current level of competence. This you will have to do. They can, however, be very helpful in pointing out the resources they have used in their own professional development.

Another 1983 ASTD Competency Study product can help in considering future positions. All 15 roles were compared with each other to determine which had common requirements. Correlations were completed based on the criticality of the competencies to the various roles. Those roles with intercorrelations of >0.5 were clustered together as shown in Fig. 3-7a and b. It should be noted that the roles of media specialist, individual counselor, and program coordinator did not correlate sufficiently with any other roles to warrant inclusion in a cluster.

In considering future positions, these data can be helpful in identifying other roles which require competencies similar to the ones you are already playing. This should assist you in uncovering areas where the transfer of your knowledge and skills can most easily be accomplished.

Writing the Individual Professional Development Plan

Once you have done the necessary analysis and determined the areas requiring professional development, your next important step is to write your individual professional development plan.

Guidelines

One of the most useful by-products of the ASTD Competency Study of 1978 was a self-development instrument.[14] It provided a worksheet similar to the one found in Fig. 3-6 and some very practical guidelines to consider when developing a professional development plan:

Limit your objectives. Don't try to improve more than two or three skills at once. Concentrate your efforts for quicker results.

Have at least one easy objective. Build your plan for a quick success to motivate further effort for the tougher objectives.

Include some actions you can take now. Getting started soon is essential . . . even if it is simply reading a book.

Select actions under your control. Some actions you have authority to implement. Others, such as attending a training program or working on a task force, may require your supervisor's approval. Mostly your plan should involve actions not requiring approval.

Look for on-job learning opportunities. Generally, more learning can happen on the job than in a classroom. Look for new projects and new responsibilities you can get involved in.

Get feedback. Let others know what skills you're trying to improve and ask for feedback on your progress. Feedback is rarely given unless asked for.

Define improvement. Define how you will know you've improved sufficiently.

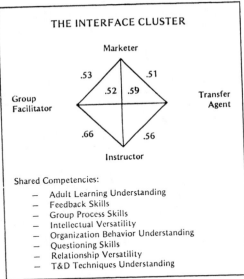

THE INTERFACE CLUSTER

Marketer

.53 .51

.52 .59

Group Facilitator

Transfer Agent

.66 .56

Instructor

Shared Competencies:
- Adult Learning Understanding
- Feedback Skills
- Group Process Skills
- Intellectual Versatility
- Organization Behavior Understanding
- Questioning Skills
- Relationship Versatility
- T&D Techniques Understanding

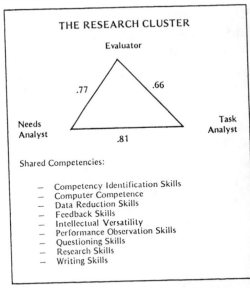

THE RESEARCH CLUSTER

Evaluator

.77 .66

Needs Analyst

.81

Task Analyst

Shared Competencies:

- Competency Identification Skills
- Computer Competence
- Data Reduction Skills
- Feedback Skills
- Intellectual Versatility
- Performance Observation Skills
- Questioning Skills
- Research Skills
- Writing Skills

Figure 3-7. Role clusters. (© 1983 by The American Society for Training and Development, Alexandria, Va. Reprinted by permission of ASTD.)

To these six guidelines, you should add two more, one at the beginning and the other at the end:

Put it in writing. Committing your plan to writing makes it clearer, more specific, and more binding, particularly if you share copies with others.

Celebrate your successes. As you complete a planned action, do something good for yourself. Celebrate. Take pleasure in what you have accomplished.

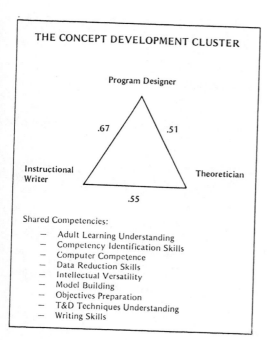

THE CONCEPT DEVELOPMENT CLUSTER

Program Designer

.67   .51

Instructional Writer   Theoretician

.55

Shared Competencies:

- Adult Learning Understanding
- Competency Identification Skills
- Computer Competence
- Data Reduction Skills
- Intellectual Versatility
- Model Building
- Objectives Preparation
- T&D Techniques Understanding
- Writing Skills

Unclustered:

- Media Specialist
- Individual Development Counselor
- Program Administrator

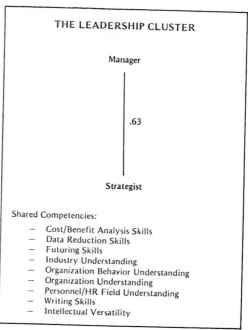

THE LEADERSHIP CLUSTER

Manager

.63

Strategist

Shared Competencies:

- Cost/Benefit Analysis Skills
- Data Reduction Skills
- Futuring Skills
- Industry Understanding
- Organization Behavior Understanding
- Organization Understanding
- Personnel/HR Field Understanding
- Writing Skills
- Intellectual Versatility

Figure 3-7. Continued

Suggested Format

There are many ways you can get your individual professional development plan into writing. Figure 3-8 provides one of those ways.

Column 1. Assessed need and learning objective. List the specific competency you want to improve and your objective in working on that competency.

Column 2. Resources, alternatives, and strategies. List the specific ways you will go about meeting the learning objectives described in column 1. List the resources you plan to use. Be flexible and have alternatives for meeting your needs.

Column 3. Starting and ending dates. Write down when you expect to begin your activity and when it should be completed. Again, be as specific as possible.

Column 4. Evaluation criteria. For each learning objective, write down how you will know when you have successfully completed an action regarding it. Make the criteria clear so that you can tell when you have had a success.

Column 5. Celebration. Be sure to give yourself the reward you deserve. Specify what it is you will do for yourself once you have had a success. Then note the date of your celebration activity after it is enjoyed.

While your plan is individual and personal, as suggested in the guidelines, it is often useful to share your plan with others. They can provide you with suggestions and encouragement.

Professional Development Resources

Such a wide variety of resources, methods, techniques, and approaches can be used in meeting professional development needs, no one should have any excuse for not using several in carrying out their professional development plan.

What Is Being Used

In an article[15] reporting on how trainers get trained, the most valued forms of professional development were ranked in the following order:

Seminars and workshops	46%
Training conferences	22%
Other conferences	8%
Periodicals	8%
Books	7%
Degree programs	4%
Self-study	4%
Films	1%

These percentages represent the response of the total population surveyed. It is interesting to note that these opinions on the most valued form of professional

NAME: John Doe   JOB TITLE: _____   Training Officer

ASSESSED NEED AND LEARNING OBJECTIVE	RESOURCES, ALTERNATIVES, AND STRATEGIES	STARTING AND ENDING DATES	EVALUATION CRITERIA	CELEBRATION
#5 Computer Competence				
— overcome my reluctance to use computers	— join the chapter computer special interest group	— next meeting and continuing	— attend at least 3 meetings	— treat myself to a special dessert
— learn how to use a pc	— buy myself an inexpensive pc	— Christmas and continuing	— learn to operate from manual	— buy myself a fun computer game
#15 Intellectual Versatility				
— broaden the way I look at problems	— attend a session on creative thinking at community college	— during spring semester	— take course and apply learnings to one course at work	— take a fishing weekend
#17 Model Building				
— learn more about the subject	— research journals for articles to read	— next month and two weeks later	— found, read, and understood at least five articles	— attend a movie I have wanted to see
#20 and #21 Organization Behavior and Understanding				
	— have lunch with my boss to find out more about company	— next week		
— be able to distinguish between the two and gain more knowledge about my company	— make this a discussion topic at a future "brown bag" meeting	— next meeting and as soon as possible	— when I can make the distinction and explain it to others	— buy my own copy of an organizational dynamics book
#25 Questioning Skills				
— improve my skills when talking to "clients"	— ask for feedback on next consultation	— next opportunity	— received direct, useful information	— take client out for a cup of coffee

Figure 3-8. Individual professional development plan.   (© 1983 by The American Society for Training and Development, Alexandria, Va. Reprinted by permission of ASTD.)

Years in field	Seminars and workshops	Training conferences
Less than 1	57%	6%
1–3	69%	27%
4–10	48%	27%
10–20	38%	24%
More than 20	47%	13%

development were different depending on how long one was in the field. It appears that seminars and workshops are seen as valuable regardless of how long an individual has been in the field, while training conferences seem of far less value to the very new and the very senior.

The *TRAINING* magazine "Industry Report" mentioned at the beginning of this chapter adds some additional information on the preferences training practitioners have for various modes of development. When asked what had contributed the most to their own development, the responses, given in rank order, were:

On-the-job experiences

Formal education (college, technical school)

Formal on-the-job training

Mentors

Networking

This leads us back to the opening statement in this section concerning the vast variety of resources available that we can draw upon to meet our professional development needs. We all do not have to do it the same way.

On-the-Job Opportunities

We often overlook those resources closest at hand, even though they may provide the best development opportunity possible. Right in your present job there are several ways you can carry out your individual professional development plan.

Job enlargement and special assignments are particularly valuable if you have involved your supervisor in the development of your plan. Taking on a new responsibility is an ideal way to increase your level of competence if done under the guidance of a knowledgeable and interested supervisor. There is no reason we cannot make work a learning and growing experience. The results of a survey already mentioned in this chapter indicate that people find on-the-job experiences extremely important in their development. Keep your eyes open for jobs to be done alone or with others on task forces.

Mentoring is another approach that works well if you are fortunate enough to be in a situation where there are expert performers in the competencies on which you are working. While mentoring has its supporters and detractors,[16] it is a resource that should not be overlooked.

The simplest approach is to directly contact the person who possesses the expertise in the competency you are working on and tell him or her that you would like to establish a mentoring relationship. You will be surprised that the "expert" you approach will more often than not be flattered and willing to share a great deal with you, as long as you are careful not to overstay your welcome. Be conscious of the amount of time you are using and sensitive to the one who is helping you.

Some of the earliest forms of training, going back to the middle ages, used a type of mentoring. Apprentices attached themselves to master craftsmen to learn a trade or profession. It still works today. While listed under "on-the-job opportunities," it can take place off-the-job as well through professional associations, academic institutions, or anywhere you can make professional contacts.

Company training programs are another resource for professional development. Be alert to offerings that are available, particularly on subjects which might meet your need for industry or business understanding. In addition, many companies often support lunchtime and after hours skill building courses on such topics as writing improvement or public speaking.

Professional Associations

As in all fields, training and development has its professional groups which are a rich resource for professional development opportunities. Most often these are thought of in terms of the services and products they have to offer, but not to be overlooked is the opportunity they provide you to grow and develop through participation.

Services and products differ from association to association; however, among the most common are:

A journal and other periodicals

National and local conferences

Seminars, workshops, institutes

Books, tapes, films (often at a reduced price)

Access to reference materials and experts through a centralized resource library or bank

Once you have joined an association, make use of the services and products available. You have a right, since you help pay for them with your dues.

Participation can provide a wealth of professional development opportunities. It gives you a place to acquire and test out competencies away from your regular job. Here are some suggestions:

Volunteer to serve on a committee.

Submit an article for publication.

Run for elective office.

Attend regular and special meetings.

Submit a proposal to make a presentation.

You will only get a small portion of the benefit that can come from belonging to a professional association if you do not get actively involved. As a start, it is often best to join a professional group at your local level where there are more opportunities for participation. However, if you plan to make the training and development field your career, membership in a national organization is a must. Here are three you should consider:

American Society for Personnel Administration (ASPA), 606 N. Washington Street, Alexandria, VA 22314, (703) 548-3440

American Society for Training and Development (ASTD), 1630 Duke Street, P.O. Box 1443, Alexandria, VA 22313, (703) 683-8100

National Society for Performance and Instruction (NSPI), 1126 16th Street, N.W., Suite 214, Washington, D.C. 20036, (202) 861-0777

All three have local chapters throughout the United States, publish journals and other materials, hold national conferences, and conduct educational programs for their members.

A more complete list of 100 associations related to the human resources field is published each year in the *Marketplace Directory*.[17] The list also includes the names of various trade associations which can be a valuable source of information on programs, seminars, and materials in their sphere of interest.

Conferences and Seminars

As pointed out earlier in this chapter, seminars, conferences, and workshops are rated by far the most preferred mode of professional development by trainers. If all of us were precise in our use of language, it would be easy to distinguish among these different types of educational offerings. But that is not the case. You should study the event announcements very carefully before deciding if they are likely to meet your professional development need. They can range from a 2-hour demonstration and discussion for 20 participants by a vendor on "how to operate a projector" to a week-long national conference for 5000 with as many as 500 separate sessions to choose from.

Attending a course or conference should be approached in a way that will be most productive for you. Planning should be thorough[18] and should include what you should do before attending, during the event, and as follow-up after you return home.[19]

When you join a national professional group, you are assured of a constant flow of information on conferences and seminars, because your name is placed on mailing lists which are sold to those who conduct them. The professional journals are another good source of information.

Academic Programs

A few years ago you could count on your fingers the universities and colleges offering degree programs related to training and development. That is no longer true. Responding to the tremendous growth of the field, many institutions of higher learning have developed or adapted curricula to meet the demand. ASTD published a directory that lists over 250 distinct programs in human resource development and training and development.[20] These programs are located throughout the United States in both state and private institutions. The programs can be found in various academic departments; however, a recent study[21] showed most were located in departments of education:

Education (including adult and vocational)	42%
Instructional media	28%
Business	13%
Communications	6%
Behavioral sciences	6%
Counseling	2%

The study also had some interesting data on the types of degrees that have been awarded through these programs:

Doctorate	44%
Masters	82%
Undergraduate	25%
Certificate	18%

This shows that the great majority of the degrees granted in the field are of the postgraduate variety. Other data from this study indicate that the awarding of postgraduate degrees has been going on in these institutions for an average of 10 years, while undergraduate degrees have been around only an average of 5.

While formal academic programs may not seem too appropriate to meet your immediate professional development needs, they should not be dismissed without some thought. By careful investigation, you may well find an academic program that will fit your short-term professional development needs at the same time it fulfills your longer-range career goals. Remember the data cited earlier which indicated that formal education was ranked second only to on-the-job experience as having been the experience of most value to trainers in their development.

Networking

A much overused and abused word in the past few years, networking is simply establishing and maintaining contacts with others for mutual benefit. Basically there are two types:

Formal groups have networking arrangements already available for you to tap into. Most professional societies have such subgroups with the main purpose of putting individuals in touch with others around some common interest. In ASTD, for example, there are six professional practice areas (sales and marketing, organization development, technical and skills training, international, media, and career development), 15 networks (including computer-based learning, consulting, minority, occupational safety, and women), and 36 industry groups (including agriculture, banking, forest products, hospitals and health, insurance, textiles, transportation, and utilities). Groups like these can provide specialized information and educational opportunities as well as serving as a communication channel between those with like interests and needs. They certainly facilitate networking.

Informal groups which you can join may already exist, but if not, there is no reason you could not be the catalyst for starting one. This type of less formal group is often called a "support group."

One author suggests[22] establishing "learning community groups" within your place of business where you and your peers can discuss books and articles you have read, work on a project or problem submitted by a member, make presentations to each other on subjects of interest, or even arrange a field trip to learn firsthand about some subject.

Regardless of the type of support group you find yourself in, the experience will not be rewarding or long-lasting unless careful attention is given to the "care and feeding" of the group. Over the years successful support groups have learned this,[23] while others have not and soon faded from sight. When informal groups work, they can be a powerful resource to use in your professional development effort.

Books, Magazines, Journals

Of all the ways to gather information on a particular competency need, reading is still one of the best. In this day of high emphasis on technology on the one hand and personal interaction on the other, this fact is sometimes forgotten.

Many reading lists already exist on a variety of subjects, but a good way to develop your own list is to make note of the references used by authors you particularly like. For instance, if you had completed your individual professional development plan prior to reading this handbook, you would have found several of the chapters especially relevant. In those you would note the references used by the author and then you would search these out to gather more information. You need not do original research on a topic when much of the work has been done for you already. And again, belonging to a national professional society will put you on the mailing lists of some of the major publishers of training and development books, such as McGraw-Hill, Addison-Wesley, Josey-Bass, John Wiley, and University Associates.

In addition, the societies' periodicals and others in the field not only have excellent articles that provide current material, but they also give reviews of the most recent books published in the field. The following four periodicals can be very valuable to you as you work on your professional development plan:

Performance and Instruction, National Society for Performance and Instruction, 1126 16th Street, N.W., Suite 214, Washington, D.C. 20036

Training and Development Journal, American Society for Training and Development, 1630 Duke Street, P.O. Box 1443, Alexandria, VA 22313

TRAINING: The Magazine of Human Resources Development, Lakewood Publications, Inc., 50 South Ninth Street, Minneapolis, MN 55402

Training News: A Monthly Newspaper for the Training Professional, Weingarten Publications, Inc., 38 Chauncy Street, Boston, MA 02111

In addition to these periodicals related to the training and development field, it is essential for your professional development to keep abreast of the latest in your organization's sphere of interest. Whether it be automotive, insurance, medical, public administration, or other, your ability to perform will be enhanced by your knowledge of the enterprise for which you are working. In a like manner, since in many ways "HRD Means Business" (the motto for the 1985 ASTD National Conference), it is incumbent upon you to know the trends in the general world of business also. The best way to do this is to regularly read the periodicals your top management is likely to be reading (e.g., *Wall Street Journal, Forbes, Business Week, Fortune*). Insularity and parochialism is a criticism often leveled at the training profession. We must consider this when are planning our professional development.

Cost of Professional Development

The earlier mentioned report of a study on how trainers got trained had some interesting data on how much trainers spent on their own development each year in terms of money and time. When you consider that the average cost of a public seminar is over $150 a day, and that the registration fee for a national conference is around $800, with neither figure including travel and expenses, these figures are not unexpected.

However, professional development does not have to involve a great expenditure of money. It can be done on a "shoestring."[24] Many of the resources listed in this chapter are not dependent on a lot of money. They are dependent on another element, time. There is no way your professional development plan can be carried out without a considerable expenditure of time on your part. Growth and development do not come easy. They do not happen overnight. They do require time and effort on your part. This is the cost.

Time, days	% of trainers	Money	% of trainers
0	4	0	5
1–2	11	$10–$150	7
3–5	33	$151–$300	11
6–10	27	$301–$750	21
10+	25	$750–$1200	23
		$1200+	33

Summary

This chapter has stressed:

The importance of professional development

The need for careful analysis

The essentiality of a written plan

The availability of a variety of resources

In so doing, it has provided specific guidance on how you can do your own analysis and how you can write your individual professional development plan based on current information regarding critical competencies needed in the training and development field.

This chapter has dealt with your future growth and development. That is an important topic. Chalofsky and Lincoln put it this way in the concluding paragraphs of their book:[25] "Above all we need to grow. We need to be open to new theories, new approaches, new techniques. . . . To grow and to strive for excellence is to be professional. What we, the authors of this book, believe is: your future in HRD is in your hands."

In similar fashion, Dugan Laird ends his very popular text[26] on the same note while speaking of the challenges facing the training and development department: "The impact of that challenge is more apparent when we stop to think that every behavior by a T&D specialist or a T&D officer impacts geometrically upon the organization. A successful class changes the performance of everyone who attends; a wise decision about how to solve a performance problem produces changed working conditions for entire populations . . . for incumbents and for employees yet to be hired. All the more reason for the careful selection and relentless energy in the continued growth of people on the T&D staff!" To those two statements, this author can only add—I agree.

References

1. Day, Richard, *Membership Survey of the American Society for Training and Development*, ASTD, Washington, D.C., 1981, p. 7.

2. Lee, Chris, "Trainers' Careers," *Training*, November 1985, pp. 75–76.

3. Stump, Robert W., *Your Career in Human Resource Development: A Guide to Information and Decision Making*, ASTD, Alexandria, VA, 1985.

4. Lippitt, Gordon L., and Leonard Nadler, "Emerging Roles of the Training Director," *Training and Development Journal*, June 1979, pp. 26–30 (reprinted from August 1967 edition).

5. Nadler, Leonard, *Developing Human Resources*, 2d ed., Learning Concepts, Austin, TX, 1979.

6. *The Employee Development Specialist Curriculum Plan: An Outline of Learning Experiences for the Employee Development Specialist*, U.S. Civil Service Commission, Washington, D.C., 1976.

7. *Core Competencies for Training and Development*, Ontario Society for Training and Development, Toronto, Canada, 1976.

8. Kenny, John B., "Competency Analysis for Trainers: A Model for Professionalization," *Training and Development Journal*, May 1982, pp. 142–148.

9. *Study Guide in Human Resource Management*, ASPA, Alexandria, VA, 1978.

10. Pinto, Patrick R., and James W. Walker, *A Study of Professional Training & Development Roles & Competencies*, ASTD, Madison, WI, 1978.

11. Olson, Elizabeth, and Ellis J. Berne, "Academic Preparation of HRD Practitioners," *Training and Development Journal*, May 1980, pp. 76–83.

12. McLagan, Patricia A., and Richard C. McCullough, *Models for Excellence: The Conclusions and Recommendations of the ASTD Training and Development Competency Study*, ASTD, Washington, D.C., 1983.

13. McCullough, Richard C., and Patricia A. McLagan, "Keeping the Competency Study Alive: Applications for the Training and Development Profession," *Training and Development Journal*, June 1983, pp. 24–28.

14. *A Self-Development Process for Training and Development Professionals*, ASTD, Madison, WI, 1979.

15. "How Do Trainers Get Trained," *Training News*, October 1985, pp. 8–10.

16. Clawson, James G., "Is Mentoring Necessary" and Kram, Kathy E., "Improving the Mentoring Process," *Training and Development Journal*, April 1985, pp. 36–43.

17. *Marketplace Directory, Training*, Minneapolis, MN, 1985.

18. Reynolds, Angus S., "How to Attend a Professional Conference Like a Professional," *Training and Development Journal*, April 1984, pp. 86–90.

19. McLagan, Patricia A., *Getting Results from Courses and Conferences*, McLagan & Associates, St. Paul, MN, 1982.

20. *ASTD Directory of Academic Programs in Training and Development/Human Resource Development*, 2d ed., ASTD, Washington, D.C., 1983. (Converted to the database in 1986.)

21. Pace, R. Wayne, and Brent D. Peterson, *A Booklet for Analyzing Human Resource Training and Development Academic Programs*, Brigham Young University, 1984.

22. Nadler, Leonard, "Learning Community Groups within an Organization," *Training and Development Journal*, July 1981, pp. 20–25.

23. McCullough, Richard C., "The Care and Feeding of a Professional Support Group," *Training*, May 1985, pp. 88–97.

24. O'Mara, Julia, Ruth Gentilman, and Jack H. Epstein, "Professional Development on a 'Shoestring'," *Training and Development Journal*, July 1981, pp. 26–30.

25. Chalofsky, Neal, and Carnie Ives Lincoln, *Up the HRD Ladder*, Addison-Wesley, Reading, MA, 1983, p. 147.

26. Laird, Dugan, *Approaches to Training and Development*, Addison-Wesley, Reading, MA, 1978, p. 287.

4

Recruiting and Selecting The Human Resource Development Staff

David W. Brinkerhoff

David W. Brinkerhoff is President of Abbott Smith Associates, Inc., a nationwide executive search firm based in Millbrook, New York. He consults with major corporations in determining their needs for staffing the human resource function. Prior to joining ASA 16 years ago, he was assistant dean at Purdue University and was responsible for the Continuing Education/Corporate Consulting program where he consulted with area industries on personnel and training problems. He designed many programs for International Harvester, Magnavox, and General Electric. He has written several articles and spoken to many professional groups. Brinkerhoff has been active in ASTD and was Region 1 Vice President and President of the New York Metro and Fort Wayne chapters. He is active in the O.D. Network, Human Resources Planning Society, and the Academy of Management. He received his B.A. and M.S. degrees from Purdue and has done additional studies toward his Ph.D. in Human Resources Management at Purdue and New York Universities. He was appointed to the executive board of the United States Statue of Liberty Foundation by the President, is President of New Horizons for the Retarded, vice president of the Millbrook Business Association, and past president of the Millbrook Rotary Club.

Recruiting the human resource development (HRD) staff has evolved over the years in a fashion similar to the growth of the HRD field in general. No longer is it appropriate to look through the corporate roster to find someone with a teaching background and make him or her a trainer. The old adage, "If you can't be a good engineer, you can always teach" no longer applies. This chapter will give the HRD manager a systematic method to recruit and select competent staff.

Is There Really a Position to Be Filled?

The budget process is in full swing, it has been a good year for the company, and your boss asks you (the HRD manager) if you need and can justify more staff. After you recover from your initial shock (about 10 seconds), you say "of course" and then proceed to quickly justify why you can use not only this person but also several more. All too frequently this is a true scenario. Or, one of your staff members is promoted to the line organization, and the vacant position is filled immediately with no questions asked.

Before any HRD position is filled, it should be examined closely to see if it is really needed. A good way to do this is to examine ASTD's "models for excellence" and determine the exact outputs of this function. Once these are determined, the critical competencies needed to perform these outputs can be identified. If either of these can't be done, perhaps the validity of the position should be questioned. However, assuming that everything is in order and there is a valid position, the HRD manager can then proceed to the next step in the recruiting process. The recruiting process itself is not a complicated one and can be shown as follows:

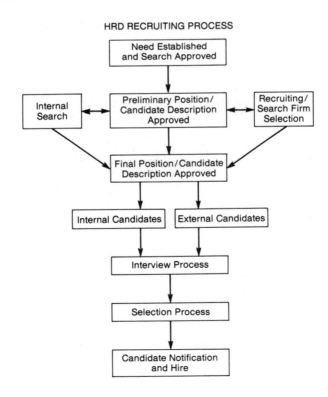

HRD RECRUITING PROCESS

Recruiting for HRD Positions . . . A Unique Experience

One of the difficulties in recruiting for HRD positions is definition. For instance, the title of "manager, management development" sounds obvious but in this field it is not. Many people with the title of "manager" manage no people and no budgets but do manage programs. So, if one is recruiting for a manager of the HRD function who has to manage people and develop budgets, this should be made very clear at the outset and the job descriptions should be written accordingly.

A second difficulty encountered in recruiting HRD professionals is where do they come from? Until recently very few colleges had a degree or even a series of courses exclusively devoted to HRD. Now there are several, but in most cases it is difficult to judge the quality of the graduate.

A third peculiarity of the HRD field is the diversity of the backgrounds of potential candidates. A 1982 survey of ASTD members showed that 30 percent had education or psychology degrees, and the remaining 70 percent had various degrees ranging from forestry to the culinary arts. This makes the recruiting process especially difficult when trying to compare one candidate with another.

The temporary nature of many training positions is another peculiarity in the HRD field. Many training positions are looked at as a steppingstone in the development of managers, especially in the sales area. When recruiting these people it is difficult to tell if they are true professionals or just in the position for a short time until they get promoted.

Another reason that recruiting for HRD professionals is unique is the difficulty in evaluating the work that a prospective employee is supposed to have done. A lot of HRD work is done by teams of program designers or presenters or needs assessors. Consequently, it is difficult at times to really know if a program was designed *entirely* by a prospective job candidate. Did they do just the needs analysis, or design only a chapter of an entire program? Or, what part did the candidate *really* play in the production of a videotape? These questions are hard to answer while respecting the confidential nature of the candidate's search for a new job.

For example, were the increased productivity results in a company directly attributable to the supervisory development program allegedly developed by the candidate, or were there other contributing factors such as new production machinery? In other fields it is very easy to find out if stated results were attained. An engineer who developed a new wheel bearing can bring it with him along with the patent for it. Unfortunately, most training programs and videotapes are not patented by anybody!

Finally, HRD people are usually very difficult to assess in an interview. Because of the nature of their jobs, they have to be "good on their feet" in front of groups. They know how to communicate well, and have probably had a few courses in "dress for success" and body language. Additional steps, as discussed later, should be taken to really be able to accurately assess the true capabilities of these people.

The Position Description

The most vital element of a job search is the position description, which must be developed before an internal or external search is initiated. Inputs for the description should be obtained from all parties concerned including (but not limited to) the person to whom the person reports, potential internal clients, subordinates, peers, and if possible the person who is leaving the position.

Many corporations have a standardized format for position descriptions, but in determining an HRD position description close attention should be given to the previously mentioned competency study. Once the competencies and outputs have been determined the position description can be developed. Anyone within the corporation who will be involved in making the hiring decision should be asked for inputs and should review the final document. If a search consultant is used, they will develop the position description in concert with the internal staff.

The components of the position description include three basic elements:

1. Brief description of the company and location of the job.

2. A description of the current HRD function and its reporting relationship within the corporation. Also, the reporting relationship of this position.

3. A description of the desired outcomes wanted in this position and the needed competencies.

An example of an actual position description is shown below:

1. Organizational perspective and background
   a. The Corporation. This $2.1 billion New York City–based division of a major international consumer products corporation is in a total transition phase. The corporate philosophy of "enduring renaissance" versus exploitation of short-term opportunities has given impetus to major change in the division. The first cycle of a comprehensive strategic planning process was completed in 1984. A second cycle, begun in 1985, will invest heavily in increased training and development to improve profitability. Employment in this division consists of 6000 managerial personnel and 18,000 salaried employees. The division, which enjoys a considerable degree of operational autonomy, has a very open, friendly, and aggressive environment. The new strategically oriented top management of the corporation reinforces a continued philosophy and backs this by approving large training budgets.
   b. The division human resources development function. The HRD function is in a state of transition in accordance with the new corporate strategic planning. In order to implement this change, the position of director, human resource development, has been established to be responsible for the development of top divisional management and sales management people in with the new human resource strategic plan. A training staff is now in place, but the new director will have the latitude to change and/or augment the current structure. The new director must develop good operating relationships with all internal clients and be able to manage the ongoing efforts of one of the nation's foremost external consulting firms. In addition, the new director must be able to determine management skills gaps and recommend programs to remediate these gaps.

2. The position and the challenge. This position, which reports to the vice president, human resources, is a demanding and challenging one. A training charter, which is congruent with the new strategic human resources plan, should be established as soon as possible. Current programs will have to be assessed for content, clarity, and currency. In essence, the major duties of this position include planning and development, administration, and program management and implementation, all within the context of the new corporate strategic plan.

   The focus of the position is with senior management and sales management staff which are undergoing significant cultural changes. The director must be a leader who can improve the level of professionalism of the department and the training in the corporation.

The Person Description

Once the position has been described, attention can be given to the kind of person needed to fill the position. As in the position description, the people involved in the hiring decision should be involved in the development of this document. Also, the external search person, if used, should be involved especially for comparative data.

The Individual

Potential candidates for this position must be unique. A required prerequisite is someone who has enjoyed success in a role similar to, if not the same as, the one defined. Experience as a "number one" or at least a "number two" person in an HRD function is necessary. The person selected must have skills, and a proven track record in strategic planning, business processes, organization design, and human resource planning. All this must be accompanied by solid experience in management and administration. The ideal candidate should have line-management experience in addition to an extensive HRD background. The person selected must be able to work with bright, creative managers, who are working in a changing environment and who are sensitive to a changing culture. In addition the person selected must have a high tolerance for ambiguity. Above all, the person selected must have a proven understanding of education and training in a corporate setting.

With the position description and the person description completed there should be a "common front" from the corporate (and search consultant, if used) standpoint. In other words, everyone involved in the recruiting effort should be looking for the same kind of a person. This will then carry over into the interviewing and hiring process. In addition, once the person is "on board," all of those involved will have the same expectation of the person hired.

How Is the Needed Person Identified?

Once the position-person description has been completed, the search can begin. The first place to start in most corporations is internally. If an internal job posting system exists, it should be fully utilized. Also, if the organization maintains a human resource information system, this should be accessed for viable candidates. In most cases, once the internal search has been completed (usually no more than 3 weeks), the external search can begin; however, to save time both searches can be conducted simultaneously. An external search strategy should be devised, so that it is a coordinated, cost-effective process.

If an external search firm is to be used, the following questions should be asked of that firm:

1. Has the search firm done specialized recruiting in the HRD area? If you, the client, have to spend a lot of time educating the firm on what HRD means, a lot of time and money will be wasted.

2. How long has the firm been in business? The longer the firm has been in business, hopefully in the HRD area, the better perspective they will have on the field in general.

3. How many offices does the firm have? If the firm can give nationwide service, the chances of identifying the "ideal" candidate are markedly increased.

4. What similar HRD positions has your firm recently filled? If the firm can point to a recent good track record, with references, the chances are pretty good.

5. How many searches are currently being conducted in the HRD area? Perhaps the firm is doing too many, or your firm will just get the spin-off from other searches.

6. To what professional societies do you belong? It is hard to conceive that someone who does not belong to ASTD, NSPI, ODN, etc., could do an effective job of recruiting in the HRD area.

7. How long will it take to fill the position? Find out exactly how long and why.

8. How do you bill? Industry average is 30 percent of the starting salary. Find out if there are any extras for which you must pay (candidate and search consultant travel are standard).

9. What is your code of ethics? Is the search firm going to keep its hands off your people for a year, 6 months, etc.? Will they replace a candidate who doesn't make it?

Whatever external firm is selected, it takes a tremendous amount of time and communication to find the right person. If college recruiting is the vehicle to be used, the corporate college recruiters should be enlisted. However, for HRD positions, most college recruiting will be at the entry level.

If advertising is going to be used, the entire cost should be determined. This will include not only the cost of the ad but also the cost of secretarial and administrative time.

One frequently overlooked resource is professional societies, which can provide an excellent, cost-effective source of candidates. Some, such as ASTD, have local chapters which provide a position referral service. Some of the HRD related professional societies that can be utilized are the following:

1. American Society for Training and Development (ASTD)

2. American Society for Personnel Administration (ASPA)

3. National Society for Performance Improvement (NSPI)

4. Organization Development Network (ODN)

5. Human Resource Planning Society (HRPS)

In addition, each of the above listed organizations has an annual conference at which recruiting activities are formalized, and usually at a minimal charge.

The Interview Process

Once candidates have been identified, the selection process is begun with an interview. In many cases, it is most advantageous and cost-effective to first conduct a telephone interview to ascertain a person's interest in the position and the company. If an outside search consultant is being used, it is their responsibility to determine the level of interest prior to an interview. After the initial interest has been established, it is time for the face-to-face interview. The candidate should be completely briefed beforehand by the company recruiting officer or by the search consultant on the company itself, the organization of the company and the HRD department, and most importantly, whom the interviewee will be seeing. More- over, all company people involved in the interview should be familiar with the elements of the job and what is expected of the potential employee. It is not infrequent that a candidate makes the comment, "I talked to three people at XYZ Company, and I could swear that they were each talking about a different job."

To prevent repetition and to provide a standard basis for an HRD position, the following is a suggested list of questions to be asked by the employer:

1. Tell me about yourself.
2. Why do you want to work for this company? In this industry?
3. How did you hear of this position?
4. What do you know about this company and industry?
5. What interests you about this position?
6. What type of supervisor do you work the best with?
7. What kinds of companies have you been interviewing with?
8. Why did you leave your past job?
9. What impact did you have on your past job?
10. What did you like best about your past job?
11. What are your greatest strengths and weaknesses (be brief)?
12. How are you doing in your present job search?
13. Where do you expect to be 5 years from now in your career? or What are your specific career goals?
14. How did you select this particular field?
15. In your last position how did you go about (developing a marketing training program, etc.)? How did you implement and monitor this program?
16. Which theorists influenced your thinking the most in this field?
17. How would you go about doing a needs analysis for this department?
18. Did you ever have a problem selling your training and development ideas to management?
19. Do you see any problems working in manufacturing as most of your background is in banking (or, from a nonprofit to a profit-making organization)?
20. How have you found your experiences in industry as compared with nonprofit, industry, teaching, social work, or hospital administration? (This question is usually asked of someone who has already made a career change into industry and is seeking a second industrial position.)
21. Are you free to travel? What percentage?
22. When would you be available to start working?
23. How long have you been looking for a new position?
24. What salary are you looking for?

Since most HRD people are very familiar with the interviewing process, their questions will sometimes be blunt and to the point. Some of the questions most frequently asked by candidates are as follows:

1. What is the career path for this position?
2. Where does this job fit in the organizational structure?

3. Is this a new position? If not, why did the last person leave?
4. What are the backgrounds of the others in the HRD department, and how does my job fit with theirs?
5. What is the mission of the HRD department, and is it supported by top management?
6. Is there a corporate strategic human resource development plan?
7. What opportunities exist for my own professional development (i.e., conference or seminar attendance)?
8. How much travel is involved in this position?
9. What do you expect me to have accomplished at the end of 1 month, 6 months, etc.?
10. What do you like most about this organization? What do you like least?

Interview Format

Many companies have a standard interview format; however, many have a haphazard approach which leads to confusion on the part of the candidate, and in some cases the loss of a good prospective employee. Jack Zigon, former director of human resources development at Yellow Freight, developed the following format which was given to all internal people involved in the interview process as well as to the candidate.

1. Candidates send résumés.
2. Yellow Freight System screens résumés and sends application packet.*
3. Candidate completes and returns application and questionnaire to Yellow Freight System.
4. Yellow Freight System reviews application and questionnaire. Yellow Freight System conducts phone interview to amplify questionnaire data. Candidate asks questions to amplify position description.
5. Yellow Freight System checks references.
6. Yellow Freight System has candidate visit corporate headquarters to:
   a. Deliver a short training presentation.
   b. Demonstrate consulting/counseling skills on a typical Yellow Freight System performance problem.
   c. Interview with manager of Human Resource Development and other key Yellow Freight personnel.
7. Yellow Freight System makes job offer.
8. Candidate accepts offer and okays routine background check and employment physical examination.
9. Candidate begins work.

Prior to the interview the candidate should be made aware of whom he or she will be interviewing. The length of interviews and the duration of stay should also be discussed. As an additional convenience to the candidate, the company should make travel and lodging arrangements and have them billed to the company. If a second or third interview is necessary, the candidate should be told immediately so

*Note that at any point between steps 2 and 8, either the candidate or Yellow Freight System can choose to end the process.

appropriate plans can be made before they depart the company location. Some HRD interviews require special scheduling. Such an example would be the person interviewing for a manager of instructional systems development position. Candidates should be told in advance to bring various samples of writing that they have done. If the company wants to keep some of the samples (which is not advisable), the candidate should get appropriate clearance, etc. Likewise, a candidate for a position that involves heavy stand-up instructing should be prepared to deliver a short sample program to the members of the HRD staff and a selected number of their clients.

The Selection Process

Once an acceptable number of candidates, usually three, have been through the interview process and are qualified for the position, several selection issues remain. After all acceptable candidates from outside the corporation are seen, how do the internal candidates measure up? How do the final three fit the culture of the organization? Is there a "chemical" fit with your organization? Several companies have a rating system based on a scale of 10, and the candidate with the highest score is the "winner" and gets the job offer. Whatever the process, the person to whom the candidate will report should have the final say. It is the most difficult area to discuss, because in reality most decisions made are subjective and made with a "gut feeling."

Psychological testing can be used at this stage of the process if the company is so inclined. Once a final candidate has been identified, the company can proceed to the next step, but the other backup candidates should not be immediately rejected. If references don't check, or if the number one candidate should reject the job offer, there will still be alternate candidates.

Reference Checking, the Job Offer, and Starting Days

Once a final candidate has been identified, reference checking can begin. The candidate should sign a release that gives the company or the search firm permission to check references. It is recommended that the person to whom the candidate will report do some of the actual checking. This gives firsthand information and a "feel" for the candidate. If a search consultant is used, it should be clear exactly what kind of reference is wanted by the company. Once all references have been checked and proven positive, it is time to move to the next stage. The job offer can be made on the phone or in person but should always be put in writing. The search consultant, if one is used, can be of great help in the offer stage by sounding out the candidate on expected salary, bonus, perks, etc. If the candidate declines the initial offer, the search consultant can act as a mediator. If the candidate ultimately does decline the offer, or if the offer is declined by the company, be sure that it is in writing.

On the other hand, once the candidate has accepted the position, the necessary moving assistance and other items necessary for a smooth transition should begin. The first days on the job are most important, especially in an HRD position. The new person should be introduced to all potential clients and be made part of the family as soon as possible. Again problems that arise can be negotiated by the search consultant, whose job should not end once the placement is made.

Recruiting within the Company for Short-Term Assignments (Two Years and Less)

In many companies HRD assignments are of short duration and used as a steppingstone to bigger managerial positions. However, staffing these short-term assignments (from 2 months to 2 years) can be most difficult. In most cases it involves a selling job on the part of the HRD manager. If a move is involved it is an even more difficult task.

A good manpower development program will alert both management and potential candidates to who is available. One major company informs people 4 years in advance, so that both can plan accordingly. A good internal referral system also helps develop appropriate candidates. Also, if the short-term position is viewed as a promotion, it is easier to get candidates.

Recruiting for Foreign Assignments

Recruiting for foreign assignments can be most difficult in today's political climate. There are, however, many people who like to work in foreign countries. Again, if there is internal recruitment, a human resource planning system will be a necessity.

If an external international HRD person is sought, all of the tools necessary for a "normal" placement must be utilized. Advertising in English-speaking foreign papers can help. The International Division of ASTD is an excellent resource, as well as the International Federation of Training and Development Organizations. Ex-military, ex-Peace Corps, and ex-government employees can be easily sourced through their respective organizations.

Conclusion

Recruiting for the HRD staff is not an easy task; however, if some of the methods described are used it can be made easier. One of the difficulties in recruiting in this area is that there are so few college "feeder" programs. This problem is being solved with the addition of academic programs in HRD at the bachelor's and master's levels. The George Washington University is one of the leaders. In addition to recruiting for current needs, attention should be given to the future needs of the HRD department. With advanced human resource and manpower planning techniques, and development within the "development" department, the necessity of going outside the organization should be minimized.

5

Records and Information Systems

Ralph T. Dosher, Jr.

Ralph T. Dosher, Jr., is *Corporate Education Manager at Texas Instruments, Incorporated. His 35 years at TI have been in four separate endeavors. Most recently, he established the corporate training and education function, developed a corporatewide orientation program for new hires, and initiated a technical education activity. Another quarter of his career was in general management. He was responsible for several TI businesses including TI's first automation products, the appliance, air conditioning, and automotive products, and TI's first factory systems products. It was at this time he invented the Decision Package concept of planning. His initial period at TI was devoted to engineering design and management when he was also responsible for the design of TI's first industrial instruments. Dosher holds a B.S. in Mechanical Engineering and M.S. in Electrical Engineering. He is a member of the Board of Regents of the Texas State Technical Institute, ASTD National Issues Committee, Design Committee of the ASTD National Conference on Technical and Skills Training, past chairman of the Metroplex Alliance for Engineering Education in Texas, founding member of the Technical Education Consortium, and served on the National Research Council panel on Continuing Engineering Education.*

Historically, the quality of training and education records has been determined by the stability of the organization and the administrative skills of the training department management. Training records are gradually yielding to computerization to increase quality and productivity. Therefore, this chapter will provide guidance on how to implement the records and information systems function to minimize the unfavorable aspects of organization and management change and maximize organizational acceptance of a computerized system.

Training Systems Needs		
Volume	Records	Cost Reduction
— Courses — Enrollments — Sites	— Budget and Planning — Product Planning — Job Performance — Career Pathing	— Negative Impact — Justification — Productivity — Product Cost
Legal and Organizational Requirements		

Figure 5-1. Areas of training systems needs.

System Requirements

Determining Needs

Before any project is started, the justification or need for the project must be rationalized. If a training records system is to have an extended life (as either a manual or a computerized system), the need must be carefully, very carefully, determined. Indeed, determining needs is the single most important task in the design and implementation of a records system. Because of the large expense for a computerized system, inaccurate system requirements can minimize or even eliminate the return on the computer investment. The need for a record system can exist in three areas—volume, records, and cost reduction; and the purposes must be defined to adequately develop system specifications. Figure 5-1 illlustrates the needs of a training system.

Training Volume Needs Training volume of courses, enrollments, and delivery sites must be defined but not in a static sense. These needs will vary in both time and mix. For example, when a specific program is established, it may be necessary to train all the existing employees, requiring that type of training, and then to train the new hires as needed. If the new hire enrollment volume is relatively small, the record system may be quite different from that required for a larger initial volume. If the number of classes is large, the enrollment volume per class will be small. The record system again could be different. In addition, if the courses are to be delivered at multiple or selected sites (vs. a single site), the needs peculiar to each site could be different. The projection of site mix, course, and enrollment needs over time is too often neglected in the rush to satisfy a current need. But the time spent to evaluate future demand can prevent designing a new record system every few years; or at least it will minimize the cost of updating the system as needs change with time.

Training Records Needs Training records that reflect the volume of training activity must also be rationalized. These records may be necessary for budgetary reasons only. However, more sophisticated needs have been evolving over the years. As the relationship between training and job and product performance becomes defined, the need for training records takes on more importance.

Budget and planning needs seem obvious, but often the training budget is just a number based on the prior year. With accurate data (both past and projected) the budget can be based on cost per enrollment or cost per course. Course cost should be separated into course delivery and course development. Course development cost may vary depending on subject matter, students, etc., as well as the type of delivery. Nevertheless, cost records are essential for budget and planning purposes.

Product planning for complex products and systems requires data on training requirements. It is easy to understand why training requirements must be included in a NASA "product plan," but training must also be included in planning autos, computers, retail stores, banks, etc. The need for data for such training is similar to the need for design and cost data in preparing a successful product plan.

Job performance is usually the result of appropriate training and education. More and more training is specified before job assignments are made. In a sense, future job performance may be projected by the training records. This has traditionally been practiced by requiring education records (a high school or college transcript) for entry-level jobs.

Career pathing needs training records for similar reasons. The employee or the employer may define the training required to prepare for a particular career path.

Cost Reduction Needs   Overhead cost reduction is the most common organizational need for training records, but it can have a negative impact on the training department. Training is often seen as an unnecessary expense when cost reductions are needed. Yet this may be the very time when training is needed most. If appropriate and adequate records exist, realistic cost reduction can be planned. Without such records the training department may be the victim of arbitrary cuts when budget reductions are necessary. However, the use of training records to escape organizational cost reductions should not be emphasized. The need for records should be expressed in a positive way.

Training justification can be expressed positively. Training (and the necessary training records) is the single greatest contributor to cost reduction. Its sole purpose is to increase the effectiveness of people and assets. But as noted in the Training Volume Needs section, there are various levels of need, and appropriate justification may mean a real reduction in the training budget.

Regardless of the budget level, training can increase productivity and thus achieve cost reduction. If training can be shown to improve the effectiveness of people and assets by reducing (or eliminating increases in) the people required by a certain percentage, a comparable amount could be justified as training expense. Trained people can do more than more untrained people. In other words, if training could reduce the payroll by, say 6 percent, then a training budget of 3 or 4 percent of payroll would be justified. That would be a productivity gain of 2 or 3 percent.

Product cost reduction may also represent a need. Customer or user training is often a significant cost of a product. As such, there is often a temptation to cut the training cost. Like the temptation to cut training to reduce overhead, the training need must be clearly rationalized. Again, accurate and appropriate records is where rationalization begins.

Legal and Organizational Requirements   There may be needs for a records and information system that cannot be rationalized or justified by internal needs. Government requirements for reports and taxes related to training are growing. The necessary data can only be provided by a viable records system. This need has existed for some time in many other countries; and the need in the United States is increasing. At times, it has appeared tuition reimbursement for employer-paid education would be taxed. The Tax Reform Act of 1986 only required tax on payments in excess of $5250 or on courses in sports, games, or hobbies. Nonetheless, for companies with many participants receiving tuition reimbursement, the need for a high-quality record system became quickly apparent. The need still exists. There have also been initiatives to provide employer tax incentives for training.

It may be that in the future training and education records will be required for government contracts, or government employment reports will require employee training records. For these and similar reasons, training records and information systems to fulfill government requirements are a real need that must be dealt with.

There may be organizational reasons for training records. For example, some companies stipulate that a certain dollar level of training and education be expended in each organizational unit. The money cannot be spent for other items and if not spent will be lost. The purpose is to encourage managers to invest in training. If the money is spent, a record system is necessary to measure the training activity.

System Selection

After the need for a training records and information system has been accepted, the specific system must be defined and selected. The need defines why a system is needed, but how those needs will be implemented designates a specific records system. That system will be defined by the selected hardware and software dictated by the specific applications.

Applications Applications cannot be defined by a single dimension. For example, if the application is to provide attendance records, the system may be a simple attendance book, or it may be a sophisticated computer system. It depends on the number of classes, the number of students, the number of people and organizations involved, how fast they want a report, and how many class sites are used. The format of the attendance records will also vary, even if the other variables are the same, among employee training, customer training, college classes, and other activities.

Employee training is usually people-oriented, i.e., providing employee job skills. If the organization is small, the training activity probably is not very complex and can be served with a manual system. On the other hand, if the organization is large, the training activity can be complex (e.g., many sites, training centers, and business areas) and will require a large computerized system. Most employee training systems, whether small or large, require more capability than customer training or formal education. Therefore, a computerized system can usually be more easily justified for a small employee training activity than for other applications.

Customer training is usually product- (vs. people-) oriented with an emphasis on conveying knowledge about a single product. As such, customer systems are usually less complex than employee systems. There are usually fewer students, fewer courses and classes, and less need for archiving. With fewer transactions, a manual and small computer system is likely to be appropriate.

Formal education (colleges or industry tuition reimbursement programs) applications have the characteristics of both employee and customer systems. They are people-oriented and also product-oriented. That is, the degree (the product) requirements are highly structured and predictable. However, they are sufficiently flexible to fit into either employee or customer training applications. High-volume applications should have a separate system to reflect the particular needs and improve effectiveness.

Geographical coverage or site structure present application requirements that also impact system selection. Applications involving several sites or organization obviously require a different system than a single-site or single-organization application. Multisite systems can be complex, but they are extremely cost-effective when all sites use common databases.

Hardware and Software Selection Hardware can be divided into four categories: (1) manual, (2) personal or microcomputer, (3) minicomputer, and (4) mainframe computer. The selection of a particular system can be based on the number of transactions per period required of the system. For example, if the record system is small with only a few hundred transactions per month, a manual system is perfectly adequate. But if the transactions are in the hundreds of thousands per month, a large central computer is indicated. Transactions are entries into a system for further action or for recording. Enrolling a single student is a transaction. So if the requirements are for enrollment and attendance only, there may be three or four transactions per student (enter name, mark attendance, record completion, and maybe tuition payment). If there are five one-day classes in a month and each class has 10 students, there will be about 200 or so (allowing for corrections and cancellations, which are transactions also) transactions per month. This small number could be handled by a microcomputer, but it wouldn't be necessary. A manual system would be suitable.

In addition to transaction type and volume requirements, site structure influences the selection of hardware and software. A single organization on a single site can define its system needs (transaction types or system functions) almost by fiat. But a multinational company with multiple sites and organizations will usually require a large mainframe computer system with sophisticated communications. To justify such a system, transaction volume must be in thousands per month.

Figure 5-2 relates the system functions, site structure, and transaction volume to hardware selection. The particular selection of hardware is a function of timing. Rapid advances in technology keep equipment designs changing on a continuing basis. Although specific equipment may meet the functional and site requirements, it may vary considerably from other commercial equipment in features, available software, peripherals, and price. Regardless, a selection can be made of one of the categories indicated, and then specific performance can be compared among available systems that meet the general functional and site requirements.

Manual and inexpensive personal computers can satisfy all but very large requirements. Minicomputers and minicomputer networks (local-area networks or

Site Structure	Transactions per month (100s)			
	0.1–1	1–10	10–100	>100
Single-site/Single-organization	M	PC	MC	RMF
Single-site/Multiorganization	M	PC	MCN	RMF
Multisite/Single-organization	PC	PC	MCN	RMF
Multisite/Multiorganization	PC	PC	MCN	RMF
System Functions				
Attendance Records	M	PC	PC	MC
+ Course and Class Schedules	M	PC	MC	MC
+ Enrollment	M	PC	MC	MF
+ Financial Records	PC	PC	MC	MF
+ Record Archiving	PC	PC	MF	MF

M = manual, PC = personal computer, M = minicomputer, MF = mainframe, MCN = minicomputer network, RMF = remote input mainframe.

Figure 5-2. Hardware selection.

telephone networks) will meet most large-volume requirements. Very large volume requirements will require a mainframe system with remote terminals and a high-capacity communication network.

Software selection is (apart from satisfying the application needs) a function of hardware selection. Although there is interchangeability of software among most personal computers, interchangeability among micro, mini, and mainframe computers is rare. Selection of a specific computer can be challenging, however, because of the wide variety of programs available. The best rule to follow is to carefully define the requirements so an appropriate design can be specified (see a later section on system design). Once an acceptable design is specified, selection criteria can focus on cost, features, and quality of the organization providing the software. Particular attention should be placed on the quality of the software provider. Unless that organization has the stability to provide continuous support, favorable cost and feature advantages can be lost.

Because software advances are more prevalent than hardware advances, planning for future needs is not as critical. Even so, future software requirements should be considered. The degree of influence of future requirements is a function of the growth rate of the record and information system. If the system requirements are projected to move from a personal computer (PC) to a mini or mainframe system in only a couple of years or so, software selection for the PC should not be influenced by future PC software developments. Rather, it should be influenced by the compatibility of the PC software format design with the larger system format design for increased transaction volume.

System Benefits

The most important consideration in defining the requirements for a system is determining the system benefits. As with any investment decision, there must be sufficient benefits to the user organization. These benefits will normally be direct training and education data processing benefits. (Even a manual system has data processing benefits.) But there will also be indirect benefits to activities outside the training and education operation. In preparation of the system requirements, both type of benefits should be defined.

Data Processing   Data processing benefits result from the organization of data so that they are easy to input into the system, easy to process, and easy to store. Easier data processing, manual or automatic, produces three tangible results that are important to any organization—cost reduction, cycle time reduction, and quality improvement.

Cost reduction normally results when a program is organized because it eliminates duplication, speeds learning, and simplifies storage and retrieval. Usually, training records and information systems are first perceived as needed because there are many ad hoc systems for various courses or organizations or sites. This duplication of effort can be costly, particularly when it is so easy to set up a small system on a personal computer. Even a small organization can benefit, and big savings can be made by eliminating duplication. Although it is difficult because each teacher or training manager does not want to be subject to standardization, cost reduction can be realized by installing a common system.

Labor cost savings over an extended period will usually result when a manual system is replaced by an automatic system. In a training system these savings can be substantial because most record systems are labor-intensive. There can be savings in both manual and computer systems simply from an organized approach to the records.

Data storage requirements increase as training records volume increases. With more data storage, retrieval can become complex and costly. A system approach, particularly a computerized system, will always simplify data retrieval. In relatively large training operations, installing a records system can produce significant cost reduction, and the longer the data must be stored, the more the savings multiply. Because more and more training data are required, storage costs will get increasing attention, and a share of cost reduction will be expected.

Cycle time reduction is a subtle but nevertheless, real benefit. Is enrollment weeks before a class starts, because of processing time, desirable? Is billing or issuing credit for a course weeks after completion desirable? Is generating reports when needed important? Depending on the size of the activity, a system approach to training records can materially improve cycle time on these issues and provide a significant benefit.

Quality improvement is a benefit for any product or service, and training records are no exception. Quality results from ease of data entry, consistent representation and interpretation of data, elimination of human errors (in automatic systems), and ease of consolidating data from various sources. Standardized formats encourage uniform and correct data input. Of course, quality data reduce cycle time and cost; but the benefit to system users, operators, and managers is more important.

Other Systems Support   The benefits of a records and information system to the training organization are important, but there are also benefits to other organizations. The training records provide data for other data systems, planning, customers, and tax and government reporting.

Employee files exist in most companies, regardless of size. Training records can provide important data for the files for many users (e.g., career planning, job qualification). When the training system is computerized, the data can be fed to the personnel system directly to keep it current. This is important when companies are fast-growing or declining. But even in relatively stable companies, easy access to training records is a benefit to the personnel department.

Operations planning must have data on all parts of the organization. Too often training costs are lumped in with some other organization. When training costs are available, the operating data are more refined and allow more precise planning. If the training records system is standardized and computerized throughout the company, consolidated data can be made available for operations plans.

Product introduction and delivery schedules can benefit from training records. When assembly workers, sales personnel, service technicians, etc., must be trained on a new product, the schedule to introduce the product can be affected—even severely—by the training schedule. Also, customer training may have to precede product delivery during an introduction cycle. Knowing the status of the required training (from the records and information system) can benefit the company and customer alike.

Financial systems benefit from training records systems cost data. Financial managers must have financial data for analysis, management decisions, and tax and government reports for all functions. Since training costs are becoming more and more important, training data can be a real benefit to the financial and tax departments.

System Design

System Configuration

System Elements Regardless of the size and type of system, certain elements are required. These elements are usually additive, and the larger the system, the more elements. For example, a small manual system may require only an attendance record; a larger system may require an attendance record, a class schedule, a completion report, and a financial report. A still larger system may require all of the above plus an enrollment system and a course catalog. The number of elements required determines the number of transactions, the hardware selected, and the software required. However, the number of elements does not determine the relationship of the elements to each other. There are certain elements that form the input to the system and certain elements that are outputs of the system. Also, the number of elements does not determine the primary user of the element data (i.e., the student always enrolls, the administrator always sets class schedules). The design relationships of the elements to each other and to the primary users are defined by a system diagram.

System Diagram A system diagram is the start of defining the system configuration. Figure 5-3 shows a sample system diagram of the various elements. These elements represent input data from external databases and on-line terminals. Output data elements feed external databases and on-line terminals and printers. System elements are controlled by

1. The training center that provides course and cost data into the system and can obtain data on course and class maintenance needs, class rosters, and enrollment status by class

2. The student who can search for available classes by subject matter, obtain data on specific classes and enrollment status, review history of completed courses, and input data for enrolling into a specific class

3. Databases that provide student data from personnel files and receive financial and student enrollment data

Hardware and software design are influenced by these elements, and they must be specified in a configuration that will meet the needs defined for the system.

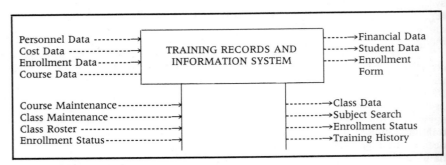

Figure 5-3. System diagram.

Hardware and Support Systems

Except for large mainframe systems, most training records and information systems can be designed locally. Even though many commercial systems are available, user-defined software can be acquired in word processor, spread sheet, database, etc., form. However, whether using such software or buying a commercial system, it is wise to go through a design process to assure the system meets the requirements. The hardware will vary depending on transaction volume (see Hardware and Software Selection section), but certain functions are common to all systems.

Manual System Design In the Determining Needs section it was shown that the specific application defined the makeup of the system. In this section are simple design rules for a manual system that have been valid many years.

Design Rules for Manual Systems

1. Minimize elements of the system. The simpler a system, the more likely it will be used.

2. Standardize forms and procedures. The operation of any "system" requires uniform inputs and outputs.

3. Make forms and procedures simple. Users should be concerned with content rather than form.

4. Provide system input locations at point of use. The user is the customer. Make the product available on the customer's terms.

5. Design as though the system will be implemented on a computer, for it probably will in the not too distant future.

The specific format of a manual system is not critical as long as it meets the needs. From a system point of view, there should be a course number, a class number, a schedule, an enrollment, and a completion. All these elements could be handled with a single piece of paper, particularly if there are few courses. However, it is usually best to use separate forms so as to have a structure ready to computerize. Financial format should conform to the standards of the accounting department or the customer. Since there is essentially no hardware involved in manual systems, the design is only constrained by the design rules.

Local Computer System The most common training records and information system now and probably for many years in the future is the local computer system. It provides opportunity for more system elements, data volume, and sophistication, and is more cost-effective. But most importantly, it provides a discipline difficult to maintain in a manual system.

Computer requirements for the local system are usually met with a personal computer. However, there is no reason why a single minicomputer could not be used if the transaction volume were sufficient. The primary requirement for the computer is that it be compatible with other hardware and software used in the organization. Also, it should be compatible with the most available and most applicable software and/or commerical administrative systems. The size of the training organization should be considered. A small operation not growing rapidly need not have a computer with power to waste. Likewise, a large operation will have more demands simply because of size and therefore should have a computer with power to spare. Finally, the computer should be compatible with the manual system it replaces (see the last design rule for manual systems). Users will appreciate needing a minimum effort to learn the new system. Also, it is likely there will be a period when both a manual and computerized system are used.

Input/output (I/O) capacity of the computer is important if there are plans to expand the system. I/O provides the means to add printers, communication to other computers, extra memory, and other peripheral devices. There should be at least three or four I/O ports to provide for system expansion and additional power.

More power means more speed and more capacity. Although more power can be obtained by a different processor, it is added to an existing system by adding more memory. More internal memory means processing larger programs and more data. Using a software shell (spread sheet, databases, etc.) or a commercial system, it is necessary to determine the required memory size to run the program. External memory can also be added with a floppy disk, but a hard disk (Winchester disk) is usually preferable as much more capacity can be obtained.

Design Rules for Local Computer Systems

1. Follow the manual systems design rules.
2. Use shell software compatible with most available hardware.
3. Set priority and schedule for system element implementation.
4. Regardless of element priority, hardware priority should be
   a. A computer with memory capacity to meet only initial processing needs.
   b. Printer.
   c. More memory.
   d. Additional local computers at different locations.
5. Purchase hardware required to meet system needs (based on element schedule and transaction volume) for no longer than 2 years. Requirements and available hardware changes are too great beyond 2 years.

Mainframe Centralized System   Only very large operations require a mainframe system. When capacity and communication requirements are not too demanding, a minicomputer can be perfectly adequate. In fact, many minicomputers are more cost-effective when system complexity is not a factor. Mainframe centralized systems differ from local computer systems not only in transaction volume but in complexity. They always involve communications to remote terminals or computers for input and/or output. They supply and receive data from several databases. This communication and data transfer task can be complex, and the design of mainframe centralized systems should be assigned to professional system designers. These designers can be the in-house information systems department, a consultant, or the supplier of the hardware. In some cases, they are a combination of all three.

Design Rules for a Mainframe Centralized System

1. Use professional system designers.
2. Implement an information management system (IMS), an electronic mail, or communication network before starting on the design of a training record system. A commercial system might be suitable and should be considered.
3. Identify the various databases that might supply or receive data from the training system and determine if there are any interface problems that would prevent their use.

4. Identify the various sites or locations where remote terminals will be required and determine if there are any communications problems to be resolved.

5. Determine if existing terminals or personal computers are compatible with the new mainframe systems and if terminal simulators are needed.

Software Design The operating system software (for micro, mini, or mainframe) will determine the flexibility and speed of the data processing. In mainframe and large minicomputer systems there is usually only limited choice of an operating system. However, a variety of operating systems are available for microcomputers. If commercial software is used for the local computer training system, the required operating system will probably be specified. If a software shell is used or the system is designed using a programming language, there is usually a choice of operating system. Choose the operating system applicable to the greatest number of software shells or currently in use on the local computer (depending on future requirements of the training system vs. other applications of the local computer). If a local area network or multitasking (running several programs at the same time) is planned for use with a microcomputer, specific operating systems may be required and thus requires careful planning.

The database structure design depends on the size of the training system. If the organization is large enough to require more than one local computer or has more than one training organization, the means of partitioning the database must be considered. There are various ways of partitioning, but partitioning by organization and site is most common.

Partitioning is not an issue for manual systems. For local computer sytems, the structure can be only one database or one for each site or each organization. But it is best to minimize the number of databases to maximize the benefits of a computerized system. Even in mainframe centralized systems the number of training centers should be minimized. When separate databases are desired, it is best to partition by organization in preference to site. The opportunity to hold classes and to enroll students at different sites is a real advantage of a computerized system.

Record Systems

Course and Class Records The structure of course records will determine not only the storage requirements but also the ease of use. Ease of use is very important in obtaining initial acceptance of the system. It is also important if multiple organizations and/or sites must be trained in its use.

Since course records do not involve student data, their structure can be independent of organization and site structure. This allows more flexibility in the design and data content. However, class records do require student data input and therefore are constrained by the student database. Class structure can be based on schedules, locations, cost, etc., but the easiest to maintain is one based on courses. If class structure is based on courses, the course structure must be designed first. So the hierarchy of the structure is the training center, the course (or curriculum, then course), and the class. At each level, the size of the database increases. For example, there would be one training center, maybe two or three curricula, five to ten courses per curriculum, and several classes per course.

Data requirements for course and class records can be as great or as limited as desired. Memory capacity requirements and cost, however, increase as data increase. The core data for a course are usually name, abstract (or description), and cost. Prerequisite courses and other requirements, course outline, textbook, course

```
┌─────────────────────────────────────────────────────────────────┐
│  ┌───────────────────────────────────────────────────────────┐  │
│  │                    Course Input Data                      │  │
│  │  User ID_____Password_____Training Center Name___  │
│  │  Course Number_____Course Name_____   │
│  │  Prerequisite Courses_____Text_____   │
│  │  Total Class Hours_____Course Cost_____Credit_____   │
│  │  Abstract:_____   │
│  │  _____   │
│  └───────────────────────────────────────────────────────────┘  │
└─────────────────────────────────────────────────────────────────┘
```

Figure 5-4. Sample course input form.

number, credit, and class hours may be added (see Fig. 5-4). To reduce cost, only core data could be in the computer database and the other data in a catalog (printed or in a separate database).

Core data for classes are name, schedule, and location. Other data that can be added are class number, instructor, maximum and minimum class size, and enrollment status (see Fig. 5-5). Since there may be more than one class per course, the class structure must be integral to the course structure. This is no problem for mainframe systems, but it will require careful planning when used on a local microcomputer system. For relatively small systems, course and class records can be installed into one database to minimize the integration problems.

For both course and class records, the input should be password protected. This means only the training organization may input data. Of course, output data from both are to be available without a password so anyone may obtain information on the courses and classes (see section on Records Security).

Student Records Volume requirements for student records can be large. If a record of every course taken by every student is retained, the file space or computer memory can be quite large. The key is to minimize the data stored relating to the courses completed. This can be done by utilizing several databases. For example, none of the student data retained in the personnel file need be duplicated in the training records system. Data on course description or class schedule need not be duplicated in the student records file if retained in the course and class files. The design of the student records system should call as much data from other files as available.

Legal requirements can influence the design of the student records system. For

```
┌─────────────────────────────────────────────────────────────────┐
│  ┌───────────────────────────────────────────────────────────┐  │
│  │                    Class Input Data                       │  │
│  │  User ID_____Password_____Training Center Name___  │
│  │  Course Number_____Class Number_____Course Name_____   │
│  │  Meeting Site_____Building_____Room_____   │
│  │  Start Date_____End Date_____Meeting Time_____   │
│  │  Max. Class Size_____Min. Class Size_____Instructor___  │
│  └───────────────────────────────────────────────────────────┘  │
└─────────────────────────────────────────────────────────────────┘
```

Figure 5-5. Sample class input form.

tax and government reporting, it may be necessary to include data on students not normally required. For example, job assignment, pay level, and education level could be required. Because these requirements add more volume to the records system, such data should be obtained from existing databases or a new database established. They should not be part of the student training records database.

Records retention may or may not be required. Of course, one reason for a training records and information system is to retain the records. As noted in prior sections, there are benefits to retaining the records. But how long and in what form has to be considered. If the student's training history is to be a system element, the retention design must allow on-line inquiry. If it is not required, the history can be obtained by an off-line report. The length of retention time must also be considered. The cost of retention for a large record volume for a long period can be too great for its worth. Regardless, records retention must be considered in the initial system.

Database sources that already exist should be used to the maximum extent. The personnel database will be the most valuable for student data. The financial databases (several might be required) can be used to pay tuition cost and to input training department costs. There might be existing databases for outside training, job descriptions (that specify certain training), and electronic bulletin boards. The more existing databases that can be used, the lower the development costs.

Enrollment Processing

Input Requirements Volume requirements for student data determine the format detail of the input. If the volume is small, students can use a paper form and the training staff can handle the input. If the volume is large, input should be via terminal or computer inquiry screens. The design of these screens should be very user-friendly and menu-driven to the extent possible. This will minimize errors and require less help from the training staff (less staff labor is one reason for the computer in the first place). Normally, the only data for the student to input would be the employee name, the employee number, the training center, the course number, the class number, and register or cancel. All other data (like the cost center, the mailing address, the phone number) should be obtained from the personnel database. These data can then be used to provide reports on classes, charges for attendance, notice of enrollment confirmation, etc. Figure 5-6 is a sample of an initial input screen (may be used on a local computer or a mainframe) to select a course and class. If the student does not know the course and class number, it can be determined via a search routine by entering the subject. If the course data are known, they can be entered directly. Figure 5-7 is a sample student data input screen. Here the student enters identifying data so additional data may be obtained from the personnel database. Data from the personnel database are

---

Course Selection

I would like to see a list of classes on the subject of

"_____"

I would like to enroll in the following class:

Training Center: _____
Course Number: _____
Class Number: _____

Press "enter"

Press "enter"

Figure 5-6. Sample course selection screen.

```
┌─────────────────────────────────────────────────────────────────┐
│                          Student Data                             │
│    My employee number is:                 My last name is:        │
│                                                                   │
│    ─────────                          ──────────────────────      │
│  `                                                                │
│         Press "enter"            •             Press "enter"      │
└─────────────────────────────────────────────────────────────────┘
```

Figure 5-7. Sample student data screen.

then automatically entered on the enrollment screen (Fig. 5-8) along with course data that were entered on the course selection screen. The student can confirm the data by entering an "x" in the register field (or in the cancel field) and pressing "enter." These screens can be varied to suit the particular system or need.

Registration and Confirmation   After all the enrollment data have been entered, hard copy can be printed out containing data for the desired approval cycle. When the signed off copy is returned to the training center, the registration can be made into an approved enrollment (which may be viewed on the computer by the student). This process is very effective on a computer system, but the same process can also be performed manually.

Before class starts it is desirable to send a reminder to the student (particularly if enrollment is opened several weeks before the start of class). This reminder can be generated automatically by the computer or sent as a manual memo. It can confirm the approval has been received (or has not yet been received) and give details on class time and place.

For systems with communication links to all plant locations, the automatic enrollment system allows students to enroll any time any place. This is cost-effective in administering industrial training where there are no regular semesters like those in universities. In fact the key to design is the flexibility to handle records and information in a nonrepetitive, nonroutine, and irregular fashion. This is different from many systems that have regularity.

Report Generation

On-Line Reports

On-line reports are available without delays caused by the transfer of data to different software. On-line means the software is always available to produce the

```
┌─────────────────────────────────────────────────────────────────┐
│                        Enrollment Data                            │
│                                                                   │
│  Employee Number  xxxxxxxxxxxxx Employee Name  xxxxxxxxxxxxx xxxxxxxxxxxxx │
│  Training Center xxxxxxxxxxxxxxxxxxx Course No.  xxxxxxxxxxxxxxxxx Class No. xxx │
│  Mail Address  xxxxxxxxxxxxx Phone  xxxxxxxxxxxxx Cost Center No.  xxxxxxxxxxxx │
│  Action: (  ) To register for class enter an "x"                  │
│          (  ) To cancel prior registration enter an "x"           │
│          Press "enter"                                            │
└─────────────────────────────────────────────────────────────────┘
```

Figure 5-8. Sample enrollment screen.

report. To always be available the software must be part of the main program. In mainframe systems this can be expensive. In minicomputer systems with communication networks, it can also be expensive. In local microcomputers, it is not expensive as the special software can be available quickly by simply inserting another disk.

Cost Trade-offs Because on-line reports can be expensive, it is important that the decision to make a report always available be carefully considered. Since computer capacity is determined by the amount of processing required per unit of time, the best usage is to spread out the processing over the 24 hours of the day. Any report that can be produced off-line during nonpeak periods (as in the middle of the night) will reduce the capacity demand and the cost. The degree of the cost reduction is a function of the degree of unbalance in the computer loading. The cost trade-off is proportional to the frequency of the report. If the report is required each time data are entered and processed, it obviously should be on-line. If it is required only once a month, off-line will be more cost-effective. The best rule to follow is to make all reports off-line unless waiting 24 hours will affect operations unfavorably.

Class Rosters Class rosters are regularly required and probably could be planned to be generated off-line. However, because they are somewhat volatile (there may be changes right up to the start of class), it is best to provide them on-line. Also, in large systems they are required at different times and different places where off-line rosters might be difficult to generate in a standard format. Rosters provide more data than just attendance. The report provides an opportunity for the data to be confirmed firsthand. Computer roster reports provide the opportunity for more data than the usual manual roster. For example, in addition to name and employee number, it is no problem for the computer to also print out the phone number (in case a last-minute call is necessary), address, and status of enrollment, i.e., registered only or registered and approved, or canceled.

Class Schedules Class schedules, particularly where there are several classes for one course, should be on-line. They will always be up-to-date, show what classes are full and/or still open, indicate location, and can provide special messages. Although class schedules should always be on-line, they can be printed out in catalog form if schedules are reasonably stable.

Enrollment Summary In large training organizations a summary of enrollment in all scheduled classes is important to training management. To be current, a report of enrollment status must be on-line at all times. The report can show enrollment count to date, the maximum and minimum count planned for the class, and the status of the enrollment count (similar to that provided on the roster).

Student Training History One advantage of a computerized system is the opportunity to draw on stored data to produce particular data. Student training history (or transcript) is a good example. Although common in the university setting, it has not been common in industry. Because training is having more impact on career planning and job placement, training history is taking on more importance. For this reason training history should be available to both the manager and employee; and it should be on-line because it may not be easy for employees to get off-line reports. The report should show the course and class, the time and place it was taken, and the grade (or completion). Other data, such as attendance, may be added.

Off-Line Reports

Cost Trade-offs   Off-line reports, unlike on-line reports, are almost always printed. While printing may have cost associated with it, the savings due to producing the report at low demand periods and being able to review it away from a terminal are significantly greater. Therefore, off-line reports are less expensive except when the waiting time is more costly than the storage for the on-line program.

Commercial Report Generators   Whether for manual, local, or mainframe computer, there are commercial report generators for producing off-line reports. The issue is not if report generators are available or if there are programs that meet requirements; the issue is what are the requirements? Software is changing so rapidly that requirements must be defined for at least 2 years. Even then, picking a commercial report generator can be risky. The first step is to decide on a general-purpose or special-purpose generator.

A special-purpose generator is already formatted in a way attractive for the intended use. An attendance report, a transcript or grade report, and a financial report are examples of special reports. Special-purpose report generators also perform certain calculations as part of the process. For example, often statistical reports are needed to analyze the training function. Report generators will perform the statistical calculations and print out the reports in one operation. Similarly, there are report generators that perform other special functions. While these special report generators simplify the process, a general-purpose generator might be preferable when the demand for the special-purpose design is limited.

General-purpose report generators allow selection of data for the report along with formatting design. When the database is large (as in most mainframe systems), it can be difficult to get to the data quickly. The report generators are actually a kind of programming language that will retrieve the desired data and present them in the desired format with almost the same flexibility as if programming in a regular programming language. Although the programming is special, some report generators can be used on both personal computers and mainframes. Still these reports require some programming to produce the report, but it is wiser to go with such generators than to produce a uniquely designed report.

Unique Reports   Considerable effort and cost are required in designing and programming unique reports. However, it is the only way to get exactly what is desired. To produce the report requires professional programming. But, because of the investment and the "design ownership," there is reluctance to change to other systems or to replace them. Also, it is usually difficult to maintain software support for the programs (unless a systems support group is available). This is particularly true if the program is to be moved to a different system. For example, it is no problem to transfer a manual report to a computer—you have to program it under any circumstances. However, if a program is written on a personal computer, it will be difficult to transfer it to a mini or mainframe computer. It may even be difficult to transfer it to another personal computer. A compromise alternative allows unique design and is usually transferable but requires minimum programming.

Spread Sheet Reports   Spread sheet and database software provides the opportunity to quickly design a report to meet a wide variety of needs. The format can be stored as a separate file for reuse any time. In fact, for local personal computer operations, the file can be so quickly recalled and used, it can almost be considered on-line. Similarly, if a manual database system is used, the desired reports can be produced on a personal computer (of your own or contracted). The primary advantage, however, is that spread sheet programs and databases are available for any size system and thus are readily produced.

Records Security

Data Protection Many records contain private data that should not be publicly accessible. Grades, career development data, course completions, class schedule maintenance, etc., can be protected by appropriate security software. However, a quality security system should be designed so that the ease of accessing the data (secured and nonsecured) is not compromised. The "user-friendly" performance of a records system is a primary benefit and to a large extent determines how much the system is used. But security is necessary and can be creatively designed just like other parts of the system.

Security for manual systems is controlled simply the way other files are secured. For computerized systems the approach can be more automatic. The usual approach is to require a password when requesting certain data. More security can be obtained by requiring identification (usually the employee number) when entering the password. Still more security can be achieved by changing the password frequently and/or requiring multilevel passwords. For example, one password can be required to enter the system, another password to obtain the desired data, and yet another password to obtain a different report. The rule is to let the security be appropriate to the privacy required.

Student Access The required privacy of student data is significant. Students obviously should have access to data relating to their training history, but it should be password protected (the password known only to the particular student). They all should have access to all data relating to class content and schedules without password protection. But there is no need for students to access financial data, class and course maintenance, or summary data. These data require passwords not known to the students.

Management Access All data should be accessible to the training organization management. To access the data the various passwords must be known to the appropriate managers. It is usually best to have a different password for each file, and it should be changed periodically.

Records Retention

Records retention of training data is just as important or unimportant as retaining other data. The retention period is determined by the cost of retention and the cost of reproducing the data (if, in fact, they can be reproduced). The issue, whether manual or automatic, is determining the importance of the data before retrieval is required.

Automatic Systems Retrieval in automatic systems is usually simpler than in manual systems, and storage is also simpler. For these reasons there is a tendency to retain more data than necessary. Detail class schedules need not be retained for more than a year. Student's course completion should be retained for more than a year. In either case the amount of computer storage is small; but when records for the whole company are considered, the computer can become full of data never retrieved. As a rule, inactive class and course data need not be retained more than a year. Student data should be retained as long as the student is employed. If this rule is followed consistently, the system must be designed so student data can be separated from class data for storage.

Storage and Archiving Legal requirements can be the primary reason for records retention. In many countries there are tax advantages to providing employee training. In the United States both the employee and the employer may receive tax advantages for certain types of training and tuition reimbursement. Although most tax benefits occur during the tax year, training records must sometimes be available beyond 1 year. Most company tax issues are resolved in less than 7 years. Storage of records for legal reasons can be off-line.

Employee history records are normally retained indefinitely even after the employee has left the company. Training records do not need to be a part of this storage. However, current employee history is very important to retain on-line for both employee reference and career tracking by management.

System Cost

Hardware Cost

Manual Systems Manual hardware cost is usually the cost of a calculator—$25 or so. Manual keysort systems are available, but they cost not much less than a personal computer, and the computer is preferable because it can do so much more.

Automatic Systems Computer hardware costs vary not only as a function of transaction volume but also as a function of the degree of automation. Elaborate software to produce a high degree of automation requires elaborate hardware. However, since most systems are designed for maximum cost-effectiveness, their costs are usually proportional to transaction volume. In the section on System Selection, the type of hardware for different transaction volume was indicated. Costs of computer hardware have been declining since they first came on the scene, and will probably continue to do so. But a cost range can be defined (Fig. 5-9).

Whether a $2000 personal computer or a $10 million mainframe computer, the cost can rarely be justified solely on the needs of the training records and information system. Transaction volume requires certain facilities and capabilities that by their nature provide considerably more transaction capacity. So in justifying the need for a records system when the hardware does not exist, consider other applications and include them in the plan.

Software Development Cost

Manual Systems Manual system cost is more a function of the particular organization than it is of the functional requirements. The same manual system

| Transactions per month (1000s) | 0.1–1 | 1–10 | 10–100 | > 100 |
| Hardware cost ($1000) | 0.1 | 1–10 | 100–1000 | > 1000 |

Figure 5-9. Hardware cost.

Transactions per month (1000s)	0.1–1	1–10	10–100	>100
Development time in months		1	1	1–6	12–15
Estimated cost ($1000)		1–3	2–6	10–50	50–200

Figure 5-10. System development cost.

data can be collected and processed in many ways when there is no discipline on how it is performed (as there is in a computerized system). The reason is that design and use occur at the same time—the system is designed on demand. For example, a simple roster may not be designed prior to a class. A blank piece of paper is passed around for the students to sign their name. The next time it may be name and employee number. Another class may require name, employee number, and phone number. Class schedules, report generation, and other records have the same problem.

However, if there is a repeat requirement for certain records, it is best to design a record that can be used over and over, i.e., planned design. The cost is primarily in printing the forms and not in the design (unless there is considerable drafting or artwork) or layout. Printing costs vary based on volume and quality of printing.

Automatic Systems Computerized systems vary as much as manual systems. A simple financial record system may require only a couple of hours using commercial spread sheet software. A companywide financial reporting system uniquely designed on a mainframe system may cost $30,000 and take 3 months. The same is true for other system elements. However, transaction volume generally requires and defines certain kinds of record systems for which the cost can be estimated (Fig. 5-10).

Operating Cost

Processing Cost Processing cost is a function of the systems elements provided and the number of transactions processed per cost period. It does not include storage cost. The cost of manual processing is primarily labor cost, and labor cost is a function of the skill of the labor. Because most manual systems are constrained to the available labor, processing per se is not a factor in the budget.

In computerized systems where the complexity of the element processing varies, the cost may vary up to 10 to 1. For example, entering names into a personal computer from a roster with complete data requires very little processing. But entering names without complete data may require the computer to obtain the necessary data from other databases, thus increasing processing and cost. Every time the "enter" button on a computer is pressed, a transaction takes place. Every time a transaction takes place, some type of processing is required. So total cost is determined by the type of processing and the number of times processing is required. A system processing 20,000 transactions per month may cost about $2000 per month in processing charges. Fewer transactions will increase the cost per transaction and more transactions, if required by complex processing, will increase the total cost.

Like manual systems, personal computer systems are labor constrained; i.e., only one person can work on the system at a time. With local area networks, data and program storage can be shared but processing is a one-person operation. So the processing cost for systems that use personal computers is the labor cost.

Transactions per month (1000s)	0.1–1	1–10	10–100	>100
Monthly processing costs ($1000)	0.2	1–3	2–5	>15

Figure 5-11. Monthly processing cost.

In large mainframe systems where many users are on-line at the same time, the cost is determined by the total volume. If the training system is the primary user, the cost will be much greater than when it is only a small user. At any rate, the reason for an automatic system is to reduce total labor cost. So a measure of the probable cost is how much the computerized system reduces administrative costs. Acceptable savings is usually around 40 to 50 percent. Processing costs can then be estimated based on administrative labor. For example, if the administrative labor is $10,000 per month (no overhead), a computer processing cost of something less than $5000 might be acceptable. The administrative labor with the computer would then be less than $5000. Figure 5-11 reflects probable costs based on estimated labor for different size systems.

Storage Cost   In addition to processing cost there is the cost of storing the training records. For manual systems, it is the cost of file cabinets. For personal computers, it is the cost of the disks on which the records are stored. For large mainframe systems, the records are stored on hard disks or tapes and there are costs related to operating the equipment and providing retrieval. This cost is usually based on the quantity of records stored. For attendance, class schedules, and other similar training records, the cost is 10 to 20 cents per month per record. But as noted in the Records Retention section, storage should be managed to minimize the volume.

System Upgrading and Maintenance

System Changes

Organization Turnover   Organization growth and new technology are the most common reasons to upgrade a system. Organization turnover can also be caused by internal and external mergers. Planning for external mergers can hardly be reflected in the system design, but planning for internal organization changes can. It is really only necessary in minicomputer and mainframe systems, as manual and personal computer systems are usually single organization systems. To allow for organization changes it is only necessary to design the databases so there is a separate database for each organization. This may cost a little more initially but will pay off in the long run. All organizations change in time.

Technology Turnover   Planning for technology is more difficult than planning for organization turnover but just as inevitable. In manual and personal computer systems it is necessary to buy new or upgraded versions of equipment and software. Technology changes come along about every 2 years for personal computers. The upgrades usually cost about 20 percent more. New equipment is usually about the same cost as the original but has increased capacity and features. Mainframe changes (new or upgrade) are usually determined by other applications, and the training records system gets the advantages.

Change Timing   When to make an upgrade or change from manual to automatic, regardless of the reason, must be carefully considered. Too often, a training organization wants to computerize because "everything else is being computerized." The System Selection and System Cost sections described the factors to consider in justifying an automatic system. Even though a new system has been adequately rationalized, the timing of the change can affect the success of the new system. The users must be ready for the system. If the users—the training organization and the students—are not ready, the very reason for the system can be lost.

When is the time to change systems? Not before the organization has accepted it. If the system is the first computer system, there may be fear of computers. If the system was designed outside the training organization, there may be a "not invented here" reluctance. If the users are forced to use it before they are adequately trained, they may ignore it. The best policy is to have the training organization deeply involved in the design of the system. Let them proceed at their own pace. If this means delays in realizing the benefits, so be it. It is better to be late than ignored.

Records Conversion   When a new system is installed, there is the question of what to do with the records from the old system. If a good records retention policy has been practiced, the old records will be minimal but important. If converting from a manual system to a computerized system, the manual data can simply be entered as though they were new data. If converting from a personal computer to a minicomputer or mainframe system, the data may be too voluminous to enter manually. In such cases, a special software program usually can be written to transfer the data. Otherwise, it is best to start a new record system with the new computer.

System Maintenance

Hardware Maintenance   Like any piece of equipment, computer hardware periodically requires maintenance. In a records and information system a failure can cause serious consequences. Although this is true for any computerized system, training organizations are not usually sensitive to this issue. Training organizations in large companies normally have a maintenance operation to provide the necessary service. However, in small and medium-sized companies, such a resource may not be provided and must be found elsewhere. In such cases the service can be provided by either the computer manufacturer or a local service company. Regardless of who provides the service, it is essential that a service plan be established before a computerized system is installed. This, of course, means service costs must be in the training organization budget. That cost, on an annual basis, runs between 10 and 20 percent of the original equipment cost.

Software Support   In the System Changes section the short life of software was noted and the opportunities for upgrading were noted. However, even in a short life, software needs maintenance as does hardware. In fact, system problems are caused by software failures far more often than by hardware failures. Also, consulting help to explain the subtle uses of the software is necessary. Therefore, provision must be made for support of the software. Commercial software will have fewer problems and is better documented than unique locally designed software. To facilitate their services, commercial suppliers usually have an 800 number. If the software is uniquely designed for the training organization, it is essential that complete documentation and diagnostic procedures be provided before the system is put into operation. When an automatic system is planned, the software support cost, like hardware maintenance, must be included in the budget. The amount varies with the size of the system, i.e., the number of software programs and the size of each program. A well-designed program will require annually about 10 percent of the original software cost for support. A not-so-well-designed program will require much more.

System Training

Training both the training personnel and the students in the use of the system is vital in the maintenance and upgrading of the system. System training is not a one-time activity at the original installation. It is an ongoing need and must be part of the overall program as is hardware maintenance and software support. Training department personnel and students are continually changing. Training can be a part of the local training department or it can be a part of the maintenance and software support organization. It could be contracted by an external vendor, but this is usually not best. It is best to have it in the local training organization. After all, they are trainers. The amount of training required and the cost will vary as a function of the type of system installed. If commercial spread sheet and database programs are used, the cost may be small. If a large unique program runs the system, training will be extensive. It should be planned just as any other training program is planned. Hopefully, training on the training system will be the most impressive training in the organization.

6

Training and the Law

Richard H. Mansfield III

Richard H. Mansfield III is a partner in the Washington, D.C., law firm of Mansfield & Ponticelli. He has been counsel to ASTD for a number of years, and has been involved in all areas of the law as it applies in the training environment. Prior to studying law, he interrupted his graduate studies in economics to serve as an officer in the United States Marine Corps in Vietnam and Washington.

Training is but one part of the seamless web of business enterprise. The legal complexity of the business world, and the large extent of government regulation, on both the local and the federal level, require a general knowledge of business law on the part of every manager.

The purpose of this chapter is to give those involved in employee training an overview of the laws which apply, either directly or tangentially, to their profession. But society and the laws are never static, and the limitations of information presented within the fixed covers of a book, as opposed to a computer-stored database, is such that new issues and new laws are covered only to the extent that they were such prior to the publication of the book. Unfortunately, as the adage goes, "Ignorance of the law is no excuse." Thus, each person, when faced with a real-life legal problem or decision, must consult with an expert. In this chapter I have attempted to summarize some areas of the law which most often and directly impact upon training, and to point out what appears to be, from today's perspective, those areas which will impact upon training in the near term.

A Primer on Contracts

It is probably a cliché to say that the business world has changed dramatically in the past few years. But it is true. Commerce has become far more formalized, far more regulated, and far more complicated. No longer can anyone close deals with a

97

handshake, as did our fathers. Now, almost everyone must regularly deal with multiple-page contracts, sales orders, and the like. Fine print often covers more square inches of the modern contract than does the subject of the agreement. This complexity requires a basic comprehension of the general law of contracts by all managers, whatever their operational area may be. By reviewing the basic principles, managers can become sensitized to critical issues and pitfalls, and will be able to consult with their legal advisors in advance so as to head off potential trouble, or to capitalize on potential benefits.

What this leads to is the absolute necessity for each trainer to be aware of the law which governs the formation and effect of the contracts they sign on behalf of their company. This section will deal with the basic law of contracts. The reader must remember, however, that states differ in interpretation of the law, and that because of this, specific legal questions must be reviewed by an attorney familiar with the law of the jurisdiction in which the question arises. But unlike the advice one so often hears, the variation of state laws is *not* a reason to forgo learning the basic rules of contract law. Many of the disputes which arise out of contracts could have been avoided or mitigated had the parties been aware of these general rules.

With this in mind, let us review the basics.

Definitions

First, a definition. A contract is defined as a promise for the breach of which the law gives a remedy, or for the performance of which the law recognizes a duty. This has been a part of our Anglo-American system of law for many centuries, and has accumulated a large body of applicable court precedents which further refine its elements.

Several actions must be present in order for a contract to come into existence: there must be mutual agreement of two or more persons or entities founded on sufficient "consideration" (money or similar remuneration) agreeing to do some act which is not contrary to law or public policy, and which is not obviously impossible. I will discuss these requirements in some depth below.

However, it is instructive to begin by reviewing some related terminology. Contracts can be expressed, implied, or constructive. Contracts are "express" when parties to the contract state the terms of the contract directly, either in writing or verbally. This is the most common form of contract. It appears in many forms: the formal written agreement, sales orders, purchase orders, and letter agreements, to name a few.

Contracts are "implied" when they are not express but are inferred from the conduct of the parties. These may seem unusual at first, but reflection will reveal that many contracts have at least some implied elements. For example, telephone orders may result in the transfer of goods without a verbal agreement as to price or discount, because both parties know the policy of the other.

Contracts are constructive when they are imposed upon parties by a court. In these rare cases, the court may impose an obligation based not on an agreement between two persons but upon ethical considerations or upon public policy. Since this type of contract is court-imposed, it is not of direct concern to most business and training situations.

Where the sale of goods (as opposed to services or real estate) is concerned, all states except Louisiana have adopted the Uniform Commercial Code (UCC) which governs many aspects of such sales, making the law the same from state to state. Other contracts are governed by the general contract law of the states.

Elements of a Contract

With this background, let us turn to an examination of the basic elements of a contract. These common denominators apply to UCC contracts as well as non-UCC contracts.

Meeting of the Minds It is a prerequisite of a contract that there must be mutual agreement ("meeting of the minds") of the parties to a contract on *all essential elements and terms.* There can be no contract unless all the parties intended to enter into one. However, the outward manifestation of a party's intention in the form of actions and words, and not the inward or subjective intention, determines legal intent. Different meaning attached by the contracting parties to ambiguous language may preclude the meeting of the minds and render the contract void. For example, where one party makes an offer which contains ambiguous language, and where the person accepting the offer reasonably understands that the offeror meant another thing, there is no contract. This is true even when both parties were acting in good faith.

Definiteness and Certainty A contact must be definite as to its terms and requirements. Absolute certainty is not required; only "reasonable" certainty is necessary. Subsequent conduct or words of the parties may eliminate any doubt as to the meaning of a contract, even where it may on its face be ambiguous.

Indefinite "contracts" are encountered more and more frequently in this age of printed forms. A reservation on the part of either party of an unlimited right to determine the nature and extent of its performance makes its obligation too indefinite for legal enforcement, and thus renders the contract void or voidable.

Formal Requirements A contract may be oral or written, or a combination. However, some contracts are required to be written by common law doctrine, the "statute of frauds," which has been incorporated in various forms in the statutes of most states. Generally, this statute requires the following to be in writing: (1) contracts which are not to be fully performed within one year of the date of signing, (2) promises to pay for the debt or default of another person or entity (novations), (3) contracts involving sale or lease of real estate, and (4) contracts involving the sale of goods in excess of a certain value (usually $500) where not covered by the UCC.

Except for contracts such as insurance policies which are regulated by statute, the physical form of a contract is immaterial. A valid contract may, and often does, consist of a series of letters or conversations between the parties.

If a contract is in writing, any alteration of the document made by one party without the permission of the other party is, of course, void. But note that parties may be bound by the terms of a contract even though they do not sign it if their subsequent action shows agreement to its terms.

Mistake, Fraud, or Duress A contract is void (if either of the parties so desires) on the ground of mistake of fact where the mistake is common to both parties and where it relates to a fact which is material and of essence of the agreement, such as the subject matter, the price, or the terms of the contract. Such a mistake is often referred to as a "mutual mistake."

A mistake on the part of one of the parties to a contract does not ordinarily void the contract. Contracting parties are bound by the meaning of the words used in a contract, even though one of the parties believed the words meant something different. This only applies, however, if the words in question are not ambiguous, and if the other party was not aware that there was a misunderstanding.

A person who enters into a written contract is presumed to know the contents and to agree to them, in the absence of fraud or misrepresentation by the other party. Because of this rule, failure to read the contents of a contract before signing it is no excuse, and all the provisions of the signed contract, whether read or not, are in force.

Special Rules for the Sale of "Goods"   For the remainder of this chapter, let us turn our attention to "sales," that is, to the sale and transfer of title to "personal" property, which, in legal terms, consists of things which are not attached to real estate. Services, such as consultant studies and legal advice, are not personal property. But the sale of training-related products falls squarely within this definition.

Definitions   Sales are covered by the Uniform Commercial Code, which has been adopted in all states except Louisiana. A sale is the transfer of ownership of property by contract. No special form is required for a valid sales contract, and the general rules of contract law must be followed. Often goods are delivered before payment is received. Who owns the goods until payment is received? This depends on the contract language and, in some cases where the contract is silent on this point, on the custom of the industry. Often a security interest is reserved in the goods until payment is made. In most states, security interests must be "perfected" by being filed with the state corporation commission or the clerk of the county in which the goods are delivered.

Warranties   A key issue in a sale is warranty. A warranty is a promise, either expressed directly by the seller or implied by law, concerning the goods. It is important to remember that a warranty may arise even if the word "warranty" is not used. All that is necessary is a statement or promise about the goods.

Under the UCC, any sale automatically makes a warranty on the part of the seller that it has good title, and that there are no liens on the goods. This is the basic statutory warranty.

"Express" warranties are those promises made directly by the seller. For example, the seller may "warrant this product for a period of one year."

In addition, the UCC specifies circumstances where an express warranty will arise, even without the words "warranty" or "guarantee"—or even without the intention of the seller to make a warranty. These warranties arise under the following conditions:

(a) Any affirmation of fact or promise made by the seller to the buyer which relates to the goods and becomes part of the basis of the bargain creates an express warranty that the goods shall conform to the affirmation or promise.

(b) Any description of the goods which is made part of the basis of the bargain creates an express warranty that the goods shall conform to the description.

(c) Any sample or model which is made part of the basis of the bargain creates an express warranty that the whole of the goods shall conform to the sample or model.

In addition to express warranties, other "implied" warranties are written into sales agreement by the UCC. The first of such warranties is that of merchantability. This means that the goods must pass without objection in the trade, and that they must conform to the description on their labels.

Another implied warranty which may arise is that of "fitness for a particular purpose." This warranty arises when "the seller at the time of contracting has reason to know any particular purpose for which the goods are required and that the buyer is relying on the seller's skill or judgment to select or furnish suitable goods."

A contract of sale may exclude warranties. To exclude the warranty of merchantability, the contract language must mention merchantability and it must be conspicuous: to exclude or modify any implied warranty of fitness, language such as "there are no warranties which extend beyond the description on the face hereof" may be used. And, unless circumstances indicate otherwise, all implied warranties are excluded by conspicuous language such as "AS IS," "WITH ALL FAULTS," or similar expressions.

In addition to the UCC, there is federal legislation, specifically the Magnuson-Moss Warranty–Federal Trade Commission Improvement Act, enacted in 1975, which applies to warranties and broadens the consumer's right in warranty disputes. However, this act applies only to the sale of consumer products used for personal, family, or household purposes. It does not cover the bulk of business-related purchases. The same applies to legislation presently in force in 11 states which precludes disclaimers and modifications of warranty.

Federal Taxation of Training

Business Expense or Fringe Benefit

The issue of federal taxation of training activities is one that has provoked much controversy and change over the last 20 years because training is incorrectly thought by some tax analysts to be a fringe benefit. Of course, most employers and employees believe the contrary, that training is a necessary working condition, and find it difficult to think of employee training as a fringe benefit. Rather, they argue, training is an essential business expense on the part of the employer, and though it has secondary benefits for employees, nevertheless, when provided by the employer training is primarily a direct business benefit to the employer. In addition, the social benefits derived from employer-provided training far outweigh the individual gain to the employee and thus should not subject the employee to federal income taxation upon the training received.

Federal Tax on Employee-Supplied Training

From the point of view of the employee, the rules have been stable for a number of years, and probably will continue to be so. The law is as follows for employee-supplied training, i.e., training paid for by the employee without reimbursement from the employer: Expenditures made by an employee to maintain or improve skills required in his or her employment or other trade or business, or to meet job requirements are deductible. That is, if the employee pays them out of his or her pocket, these expenses for training or education may be itemized and deducted on the employee's federal income tax return. However, these educational expenses are considered miscellaneous deductions, which, under the 1986 Tax Reform Act, are deductible only to the extent that all miscellaneous deductions exceed 2% of adjusted gross income.

The expenses for such training and education are also allowed even where the employee takes a temporary leave of absence from the job, so long as this is a temporary cessation of employment in order to maintain or improve skills for the job to which the employee is going to return. However, the deduction is not available merely because the employee vaguely intends to resume the employment at some future date.

The most troublesome and difficult aspect revolves around the issue of "maintaining or improving skills" versus "qualifying for a new job or profession." The former expenses are deductible, while the latter are not. This issue often arises where an employee receives education or training in a complementary yet different job area, for example, engineers who receive education or training in management-related subjects. It is clear in a case such as this that the engineer is training for a different position, albeit within the same organization. Yet it may be argued that the engineer, though trained in management, is merely improving skills for an engineering-type job, although with management-related aspects. The IRS treats every case upon its own facts, and often the taxpayer wins. This is a frequently contested area and there is much specific precedent available for review when such a case arises.

There is one series of exceptions to the general rule with respect to deductibility: educational expenses incurred to retain present status or to maintain or improve skills are nevertheless not deductible if that training or education (1) is undertaken for personal purposes or in order to satisfy general educational aspirations or (2) is required in order to meet minimum educational requirements for qualification in his employment or (3) is a part of a program of study which will lead the employee to a new trade, business, or position.

The Internal Revenue Regulations ("Regulations") allow deduction for travel, including meals and lodging, and transportation costs incurred to obtain training or education at a distant location so long as the education or training qualifies under the rules discussed above. One must be aware, however, that the rules of deductibility of travel and transportation costs are relatively complicated and should be consulted in each individual case.

Employer-Provided Training   Since the greatest number of individuals receiving training are beneficiaries of training provided by their employer, the rules governing their deductibility from the point of view of both the employer and the employee are of great importance to the training community.

Let us examine this issue from two sides. First, the easy part. The employer may pay the tuition costs directly or reimburse an employee for tuition costs which are job-related and which do not qualify the employee for a new business, or which are not designed to help the employee meet the minimum educational employment requirements of his or her present job. Since these expenses would have been deductible by the employee as discussed above, they are not wages subject to withholding or employment taxes, so long as the expenses are identified by a separate payment or by specifically indicating the separate amounts when both wage and expense allowances are combined in a single check or payment. This holds true for direct tuition payments made by the employer, for employer-provided group seminars, as well as for all other forms of employer-supplied training.

Now the more difficult part. These are the only types of employer-provided training which are clearly not subject to taxation and withholding, with the exception of payments made or benefits furnished prior to 1986 under a Qualified Educational Benefit Program [QEBP as defined in Section 127(b) of the Internal Revenue Code] so long as it was reasonable to believe at the time of the provision of benefit or payment that it would be excludable from the employee under the general rules. Because the provision of training of employees for *new* jobs has been considered by a few analysts as a fringe benefit, prior to 1986 the tax law provided a mechanism for an employer to set up a specific type of plan (QEBP or sometimes called an Educational Assistance Program, or generically, Employee Education Assistance, EEA) for its employees to provide a limited amount of training regardless of whether the training qualified the beneficiary for a new job level with the employer.

The IRS regulations on "qualified" QEBPs required a great amount of reporting and paperwork but did make it clear that *all* employer-provided training, except for instruction in sports, games, and hobbies, was exempt from taxation to the employee and was deductible by the employer, so long as the plan was nondiscriminatory. However, this exclusion of taxes for employees has twice expired since its first passage in 1978, and at this writing has been extended until the end of 1987 by the Tax Reform Act of 1986.

The law with respect to federal taxation of other types of training is presently in flux, and there are some tax analysts who argue that nonexempt training benefits are fringe benefits supplied by the employer to the employee, which may therefore be taxable to the employee under the fringe benefit rules.

Congressional action may be forthcoming with regard to both fringe benefits and employer-supplied training. Thus, the reader should consult with competent advisors regarding the latest laws and regulations in this area.

Copyright Law

This section will discuss the basic issues of copyright law and how these apply to training. Although most of the present impact of this law on trainers concerns the distribution of copyrighted material and the rights and obligations attached to it, the real significance of copyright law will be felt in the near future with respect to the distribution and ownership of computer-generated materials, either programs or data supplied on computers or computer media.

General Principles

The basis of copyright law is found in Article 1, Section 8 of the United States Constitution which empowers Congress to "promote the Progress of Science and useful Arts, by securing for limited times to Authors and Investors the exclusive right to their respective Writings and Discoveries; . . ." Congress has provided this protection through the Copyright Act of 1976, which is the latest in a series of copyright acts. This act preempts state law.

One of the most difficult concepts in understanding copyright protection is the distinction between idea and expression. The copyright law protects only the tangible expression of an idea. Ideas, procedures, processes, systems, methods of operation, concepts, principles, or discoveries, regardless of their form, are not protected by the law. Thus, for example, while the exact words used in a book are protected, the ideas in the book are not.

Three major common-law principles are used to distinguish idea from expression. The first is the "blank form principle," which states that blank forms such as blank columnar sheets are ineligible for protection since they do not express anything.

The second, known as the "scène à faire principle," limits copyright protection of expression essential to the treatment of an idea. For example, one cannot copyright the use of historical facts. Another example can be seen in board games such as Monopoly. Although the distinctive aspects of a board in a game are eligible for copyright, the general use of squares on a board game is not.

The third principle holds that a copyright will not be available for expressions of ideas which can only be expressed in a limited number of ways. For example, a contest instruction which instructed an entrant to place name, address, and social security number on a piece of paper and mail it to a stated address cannot be copyrighted because to protect this expression would be to protect the idea itself. Any implementation of the idea would require a similar expression.

Copyright Infringement

Generally, all that must be shown to prove copyright infringement is notice of copyright within the work, registration of the copyright, and copying of the work itself.

The question then arises as to how much copying is "copying." Here courts impose three different standards. The first standard is that of "substantial similarity," which was best described by a court as occurring when "the ordinary observer, unless he set out to detect the disparities, would be disposed to overlook them, and regard their aesthetic appeal as the same." The second standard, "outright copying," requires the two expressions to be virtually identical. Finally, the third standard would permit the deliberate adoption of a copyrighted expression; in essence, this standard operates as a complete bar and allows copying at will. In general, these standards of proof correspond to the common-law principles discussed in the previous subsection. In most cases, an allegedly infringing work must be at least "substantially similar" to the copyrighted work in order to establish infringement.

Rights of Copyright Holders

Once a work is copyrighted, the law gives five fundamental exclusive rights to the copyright owners: the rights of reproduction, adaption, distribution, performance, and display. The copyright owner has the sole right to exercise any of these rights, and to exclude others from exercising them, but these rights are qualified by various limitations in the copyright law, including that of "fair use."

Fair Use and Other Reproduction Rights

The Copyright Act of 1976 gave recognition to the "fair use doctrine" by allowing such use where it is for such purposes as criticism, comment, news reporting, teaching (including multiple copies for classroom use), scholarship, or research. There are no fixed definitions of what constitutes fair use because the concept is based on equitable principles, with each case raising the question needing to be decided on its own facts.

However, based upon the Copyright Act as well as its legislative history, some guidelines can be derived with respect to the reproduction of multiple copies of a copyrighted work for classroom use. Although phrased in terms of traditional classroom type instruction, it is clear that they apply to most, if not all, training. These guidelines were agreed upon by representatives of educational, author, and publisher organizations. They provide, with respect to books and periodicals, that a trainer may make a *single copy* of a chapter from a book, an article from a periodical or newspaper, a short story, short essay or short poem, a chart, graph, diagram, drawing, cartoon, or picture from a book for the purpose of scholarly research, use in teaching, or for preparation to teach a class.

Multiple copies for classroom use, not exceeding one copy per pupil in a course are permissible so long as each copy bears the copyright notice and the copying meets three tests: brevity, spontaneity, and cumulative effect. Brevity requires that excerpts from works be limited, in any event a maximum of 5000 words, and may include illustrations such as one chart, drawing, or picture. The spontaneity test requires that the copying be at the spontaneous need of an individual teacher. The cumulative effect test requires that the copying must be for only one course in a school and no more than nine instances of multiple copying can take place during one class term.

Copying of computer programs for use by students is not a "fair use" because of the need to copy the entire program. In addition, the copying of such programs may be a violation of the license agreement for the use of the programs.

In addition to the fair use doctrine, there are limitations upon the reproduction rights of a copyright holder. The first of such limitations is the statutory right of a library or archive which is open to the public or available to persons doing research in a specialized field. In such cases, reproduction may be made without infringing upon the copyright where there is no direct or indirect commercial advantage gained by the library or archive.

Under the Computer Software Act of 1980, a part of the copyright law, it is not an infringement for the owner of a copy of a computer program to make a copy or adaption of the program, provided (1) that the new copy is created as an essential step in the utilization of the computer program with the machine, or (2) that the new copy is for archival purposes only and that all archival copies are destroyed in the event the continued possession of the computer program ceases to be authorized. Copies made pursuant to this provision can be made by an owner but cannot be made accessible to any other person or entity.

Notice and Registration of Copyrights

A copyrighted work when published must contain a notice of copyright on each publicly distributed copy. Copyright notice is also required to protect sound recordings.

The proper form of notice consists of three items, the proper symbol (the word "copyright" or the abbreviation "copr." or the symbol ©), the name of the copyright holder, and the date of creation or copyright. In the case of sound recordings, the symbol ℗ is required instead. This copyright notice must be affixed to copies in a location to give reasonable notice to the claim, and there are regulations giving examples of methods of positioning the notice on various types of works (37 CFR Section 201.30). Although the copyright comes into existence upon the creation of the work, the owner, in a published or unpublished work, may register the copyright claim during the existence of the copyright by delivering to the Copyright Office the proper registration form and fees. These forms may be obtained from the Copyright Office.

Training and Equal Opportunity Statutes

Equal opportunity statutes have had a direct impact on training, and indeed on all employment practices. Although civil rights actions have been brought under numerous statutes and constitutional provisions, the laws which most directly affect training professionals are the Civil Rights Act of 1964, specifically Title VII, and the Age Discrimination Act of 1975.

Civil Rights Act of 1964

The Civil Rights Act of 1964 provides that it is unlawful for an employer to fail or to refuse to hire or discharge a person, or otherwise discriminate against that person, with respect to compensation or privileges of employment, because of the individual's race or color or national origin; or to limit or classify employees in any way which would deprive individuals of employment opportunities or adversely affect his or her status as an employee because of such race, color or national origin. The provisions of this act are administered by the Equal Employment Opportunity Commission (EEOC).

In addition to the federal civil rights statutes, virtually every state has its own civil rights statutes, often known as fair employment practices statutes, most of which require an individual who is discriminated against to file a complaint with an administrative agency.

Testing Procedures and the Civil Rights Act Since training does not normally encompass hiring or promotion, many of the provisions of the Civil Rights Act do not apply directly to it. However, training personnel are often involved in devising or administering testing procedures which may affect the promotion or hiring of employees. This area falls squarely within the act. The EEOC has written guidelines on employee selection procedures (29 CFR Section 1607.1 et seq.) which sets forth its position with respect to the fair administration, creation, and analysis of tests.

Of course, it is not illegal to use nondiscriminatory tests as a valid method of employee screening and promotion. However, the test must be just that: It must not be designed, intended, or used to discriminate because of race, color, religion, sex, or national origin.

Further, if a test or measuring procedure has a racially disproportional impact, it may not be used unless its use can be demonstrated to be a reasonable measure of job performance and that it has been validated as a predicter of job performance. Because of this, such a test should be used only where there is a compelling business purpose for its use. The burden of proving these criteria is squarely upon the employer or the organization administering the test.

As a final requirement, the EEOC guidelines provide that even if a test meets these requirements, it cannot be used unless the employer acting upon the test results can demonstrate that alternative suitable hiring transfer or promotional procedures are not available.

Apprentice and Similar Programs Title 7 of the Civil Rights Act makes it an unlawful employment practice to limit or segregate employees or applicants for employment in any way which will deprive them of employment or training opportunities because of their sex or race, except for such classifications as constitute bona fide occupational qualifications. The statute and case law make it clear that this includes discrimination with regard to the admission or employment in any program established to provide apprenticeship or any other type of training.

The Department of Labor has published regulations prohibiting sex discrimination in apprenticeship and training programs, and these generally require the recruitment, selection, employment, and training of apprentices during their apprenticeship without discrimination because of sex; the uniform application of rules concerning apprentices, including wages, promotions, job assignments, and the like; and the taking of affirmative action by the employer to provide equal opportunity in apprenticeship and training (29 CFR Section 30.1 et seq.). An example of the application of this rule is found in a 1978 EEOC decision which held that an employer's assertion that management trainees were required to work in dangerous neighborhoods did not justify the exclusion of women from such positions, where the employer could not prove that a woman applicant was not capable of performing the tasks required of the job.

Age Discrimination Act

In addition to the antidiscrimination rules mandated under the Civil Rights Act, most employers are also covered by the provisions of the Age Discrimination in Employment Act of 1967, and the amendment which makes its provisions applicable to activities receiving federal financial assistance. The act's purpose is to promote employment of older persons based upon their ability rather than their age, to prohibit arbitrary age discrimination in employment, and to help employers and workers find ways of meeting problems arising from the impact of age in employment. The protection of the act extends only to those individuals who are at least 40 years of age but less than 65 years of age. The Department of Labor has ruled that the act also prohibits discrimination within the 40 to 65 age group, as well as prohibiting discrimination as between those within and without the group.

Although there have been no cases to date on the applicability of the Age Discrimination in Employment Act to training, it would appear that it would prohibit discrimination in training matters based solely upon age without the bona fide occupational reason for the discrimination. However, on the face of the statute, it applies only against employer discrimination in hiring, discharge, compensation, or terms of employment against older employees.

The act specifically applies to labor unions, as well as employers.

Fair Labor Standards Act

Hours of pay and pay practices are regulated under the Fair Labor Standards Act, and under the Walsh-Healey Act. An understanding of the Fair Labor Standards Act is of critical importance to the training manager in the establishment of a training program. To those employees who are employed under federal government contracts, the Walsh-Healey Act is also significant, although the same principles are generally applicable under both. The substantive distinction is that the Fair Labor Standards Act requires payment of overtime after 40 hours of work in a work week, while the Walsh-Healey Act requires overtime after 8 hours of work in the work day.

The major area of concern in the field of training is whether time spent by employees in training activities must be considered compensable work time. This problem is particularly important with respect to training programs which are conducted at the end of the work day; if so, the employee will probably have to be compensated at the overtime rate.

It is important to note that both the Fair Labor Standards Act and the Walsh-Healey Act apply only to certain categories of employees, and there are numerous exceptions for executive, administrative, and professional employees.

Since neither act specifically deals with training activities, the administrators of the Wage and Hour Act and Public Contracts Divisions of the Department of Labor have published specific regulations concerning training (29 CFR 785). Under these regulations, attendance at lectures and training programs need not be counted as working time if four criteria are met: (1) attendance is outside the employee's regular working hours; (2) attendance is in fact voluntary; (3) the course, lecture, or meeting is not directly related to the employee's job; and (4) the employee does not perform any productive work during such attendance. Attendance is considered involuntary if it is required by the employer or if the employee is led to believe that his or her present job or the continuance of his or her employment would be adversely affected by nonattendance. Training is considered directly related to the employee's job if it is designed to make the employee handle the job more effectively, as distinguished from training for another job or a new or additional skill. However, even though a course indirectly improves an employee's skill concerning his or her regular work, the training is not considered directly related to the job if the course is instituted for the purpose of preparing the employee for advancement and not to make him or her more efficient in a regular job. Finally, an employee's regular attendance outside working hours at a training or educational program offered by independent institutions of learning is not considered as hours worked even if the program is established and paid for by the employer and is directly related to the employee's job.

Hours spent in an organized apprenticeship program may be excluded from working time if (1) the apprentice is employed under a written apprenticeship agreement or program which substantially meets the fundamental standards of the U.S. Department of Labor's Bureau of Apprenticeship and Training and which does not specifically provide that it is hours worked, and (2) the time does not involve productive work or performance of the apprentice's regular duties.

Many types of apprentices and individuals in training for a job are not covered by the Fair Labor Standards Act. This is a complicated issue, where professional advice is necessary, and which may require a ruling from the Department of Labor.

Eight Rules for a Successful Computer Contract

Purchasing even an expensive computer system need not be a difficult process. In this section, I will discuss eight elements of a good computer purchase contract, and the considerations which underlie each.

1. The contract is merely a written summary of the previously identified important details concerning the expected performance of the product and vendor, which have been discussed and agreed upon by both. It is the tangible result of a process, and is not an end in itself.

   Robert Frost, in one of his poems, noted that "good fences make good neighbors." This is equally true of computer contracts. Just as fences define the expectations of property owners about their property lines, so do computer contracts define the expectations of the parties to a computer purchase agreement. If there is an unmarked boundary, the expectations of the parties are likely to differ, causing at least the potential for conflict in a relationship which need not be contentious.

2. The computer purchase process must include at least the following components:
   a. Expert analysis of the operations of the company and realistic projections of its growth in the near term.
   b. Analysis of various proposals by vendors responding either to a "request for proposal" (RFP) or a detailed requirements report. In either case, the proposal must thoroughly show the hardware and software solutions

proposed by the vendor to the specific needs of the company. These specifications are incorporated into the contract and form its core.

c. Actual review by the company staff of a similarly configured system in operation. Ideally, this would be a "hands-on" session free from the presence of the vendor's marketing people.

d. Analysis of the company's organization and the requirements for organizational changes necessitated by the computerization.

e. Analysis of the service and quality reputation of the vendor.

f. Analysis of the scheduling necessary to have the system installed and working in the environment.

g. Consideration of the possible damages to the company should a failure of delivery or performance occur.

h. Discussion and resolution of all of the above with the vendor.

For the remainder of this chapter, I am going to assume that the process described by Rule 2 has been completed. At that point the contract is ready to be drafted.

In most instances, the staff itself will not have the expertise to perform the preliminary analysis and will have hired a consultant to aid in this process. It is important that the attorney also be brought in as early as possible, preferably during the initial stages of the preliminary analysis, so that he or she is aware of the details of the proposals. It is impossible for anyone to write a clear contract unless they are aware of and understand all aspects of the underlying agreement. It is equally important that the attorney have the technical and legal expertise in computer transactions necessary to help uncover and understand the possible areas of difficulties and pitfalls of the design, implementation, and installation procedure.

3. Get the total price in writing from the vendor. Then review all of the associated costs. If there are any ambiguities, set a ceiling.

The discovery of hidden costs is a common cause of computer contract disputes. Costs for special power requirements, construction and cooling of computer rooms, cabling costs, taxes, and the like should be required as part of the vendor's proposal.

Another hidden cost which can be significant is the cost of training. Even the best computers are complicated to use. Employees using them must be thoroughly trained in a "hands on" environment. Simply reading the (often unintelligible) manuals is not enough. The best contracts require training to accomplish the task, rather than specifying a fixed amount.

Most often, the hardware and software are purchased through different vendors. It is important that both proposals clearly set forth all the costs involved with the total package.

4. If there are two vendors, one supplying hardware and the other software, tie the two contracts together, so that a failure of one cancels the other.

Often hardware vendors recommend software suppliers and vice versa. In this case, the company is contracting with two companies. When this occurs, it is important that the contracts are specifically dependent upon each other. Otherwise, a company could end up with a computer without the software to run on it, or software with no computer to run it on.

Coordination of warranties and responsibility for damages between two vendors, specially when one of them is a major hardware company, is extremely difficult nd often impossible to do in a manner to adequately protect the purchasing ompany. Fortunately, more installations are now being done on a "turnkey" basis where a single vendor agrees to provide a total system—hardware, software, modifications, and training. So as long as the vendor has a "VAR" (value added reseller) or an "OEM" (confusingly a original equipment manufacturer) with the major hardware manufacturer, the contract can prudently require the vendor to make additional warranties which the major hardware vendors will never make. (In fact, most major hardware vendors generally will allow no changes to their own printed contracts.) Whenever possible, it is very advantageous for the purchaser to structure a purchase as a turnkey acquisition.

5. Demand warranties of performance of the hardware and software, but understand that both hardware and software companies will not agree to cover unlimited "consequential damages."

Every hardware manufacturer and most software houses have "standard" contracts which are written, not surprisingly, to protect their interests exclusively. Many of the provisions of these "standard" contracts are open to negotiation, and attorneys who have dealt with a company over a period of time realize where the maneuvering room is. However, there are many areas in which the manufacturer will not budge, and where it will forgo the sale if the customer insists. The major area in which this occurs concerns warranties.

Most hardware manufacturers give a warranty that the computer will perform according to its published specifications, or they will fix it within the specified warranty period. All other warranties are specifically denied. This is not enough. The purchaser should demand more protection, because, like automobiles, there are computer "lemons." Where possible, the contract should require the computer to be replaced where it breaks down or fails to perform more than once or twice during the warranty period. (Do not accept a computer without some initial warranty period from the manufacturer or vendor.) This warranty period is different from the service contract. A service contract is not a substitute for the initial warranty.

Carefully examine service agreements and warranties. Many of the latter require what is known as "depot maintenance." What this means is that the manufacturer will fix the product, *but only when it is delivered to its repair facility, often in another state*. It is for this reason that a service agreement is often required as of the date of installation of the product, as opposed to the date of the expiration of the warranty. A related problem is specifying the date of the commencement of the warranty. The contract should be clear on this point, especially if the central processing unit (CPU) is delivered before all its peripheral devices are delivered and installed. Make sure that the initial tests are performed satisfactorily, and preferably initiated by your consultant.

Software vendors must also warrant their product. If the software is specifically written for the company (not the usual case), it must be warranted to do everything in the specifications (RFP) which must be incorporated into the contract in all cases. In this case, the specifications are absolutely critical and should be carefully scrutinized by a technical consultant (if there are no in-house experts) and counsel. Agreement must be reached in advance as to what happens if the software does not work properly. Who fixes it? At what cost? What are the tests?

Where prewritten, or "canned," software is purchased, warranties must still be made. Agreement must be spelled out in the contract as to who will fix the software if it fails to perform, and the measures for determining whether it is, in fact, failing to perform.

In the usual case, software is a mixture of "canned" and custom programs, so that an amalgam of the two approaches must be used.

In all warranties, however, the contract must clearly specify the standards to which the hardware and software must be held, what constitutes a breach, and what events or penalties occur when a breach occurs.

In negotiating and specifying warranties, it is most often fruitless to demand that vendors expose themselves to unspecified "consequential damages," i.e., damages payable to the buyer for lost profits, or additional costs generated when the hardware or software breaches a warranty. One can always ask, but no reputable company would put its assets on the line in the average sale. It is much more fruitful to negotiate a "fix" in case there is a breach of warranty. This way, both parties know what steps must be taken in case of a breach, and litigation is often avoided.

6. Sign-off warranties or progress tasks must not be done until all aspects of the task have been tested.

For progress payments, as well as for acknowledgment of proper installation of hardware and software (the date which starts the warranty period), the contract should provide for proper prior testing and the standards to be used. It is important that the company not be forced to sign off on items until all aspects have been tested. Thus, for example, sign-off on a yearly accounting report should not be required until that report has been run successfully. Or, a company should not sign off on a totally integrated software package until all modules of the package are installed and running, and until it is demonstrated (in accordance with the specified tests) that the modules are, in fact, integrated.

7. Use progress payments and hold-backs as the primary means of assuring performance of vendors.

A good contract will set out specific agreed-upon dates for the installation and testing of the hardware and software. These dates are often critical for the effective implementation of the administrative changes necessary to computerize a company or division. However, in the press of business, vendors are sometimes slow in meeting deadlines.

The remedy to this situation is a careful setting forth of the time requirements in the agreement, coupled with provision of progress payments and significant hold-backs to ensure compliance.

8. Have the hardware vendor sign off on the computer's environment.

In the case of most minicomputers and some micros, there are specified climatic and electrical requirements for the operating environment. Be certain to have the vendor sign a statement certifying that the intended environment is in accordance with the specifications.

Following these eight rules will not guarantee a smooth and satisfactory computer purchase, but the result will be far better than if they were not followed.

Conclusion

This chapter has covered, in overview, the law of contracts, taxation, equal employment opportunity, wage and hour requirements, copyright, and computer contracting. Not all persons employed in employee training need be intimately familiar with all these legal areas. But as business and society grow inexorably more complicated, the odds are that the knowledge of these areas of law will become more and more important in the training world.

It has not been the purpose of this chapter to prepare the reader to become an expert in the law. Rather, it was written to acquaint or reacquaint the training manager with the broad overview of areas of law which will affect his or her activities, and to be able to know when to consult expert advice before problems arise.

7
Facilities

Charles J. Sener

Charles J. Sener *founded and directed the Bell Communications Technical Education Center (until the reorganization of the Bell System, the center was known as the Bell Systems Center for Technical Education) from its inception in 1965 until February 1985. He is a 15-year member of the American Society for Engineering Education (ASEE). He has served on the executive board of the Continuing Professional Development Division of the Society and as chairman of that division. A senior member of the Institute of Electrical and Electronic Engineers (IEEE), he has authored articles for IEEE and ASEE. He presented papers on the management of continuing engineering education at three world conferences. Sener is a past director of the Council for the Continuing Education Unit. He is a member of the National Nuclear Accrediting Board of the Institute of Nuclear Power Operations. Until recently, he was a member of the Engineering Education Committee of the United States Telephone Association. After 44 years in the industry, he left as Assistant Vice President, Bell Communications Research, Inc., to establish his consulting organization. He has a B.S. in Industrial Engineering from the Illinois Institute of Technology in Chicago.*

In this chapter, the size, characteristics, timing, and location of training facilities are discussed. The chapter has four major objectives:

- To give a conceptual framework for training facilities planning
- To provide a guide for analyzing existing facilities
- To provide a checklist for planning training facilities
- To suggest procedures for developing training facility strategies

Many individuals engaged in planning activities are doing so for the first time. Furthermore, many of these individuals have no planning experience of any kind

The four objectives of this chapter are designed to meet the needs of this group. However, even experienced training facility planners will benefit, too.

What Is an Overall Strategy?

An overall training facility strategy is a description of what training facilities will be needed during a long-range period (say 5 years), their location, size, and timing. This type of training facility strategy should be developed by the organization unit responsible for carrying out the training mission.

The objectives of an overall training facility strategy are to:

- Provide overall direction for training facility planning
- Resolve the strategic issues associated with the training facility
- Derive facility plans from plans for training development and delivery
- Provide a context and scope for facility planning

Overall training facility planning is an integral part of strategic planning for training and should not be carried out as an isolated exercise because of important interactions between the facility plans and other aspects of training planning.

Training delivery strategies are intimately linked with facility strategies. The affected strategy issues in delivery planning are:

- The modes of delivery (group-paced, self-paced, computer-based)
- Forecasted delivery volumes

The resolution of these issues is interdependent with resolution of training facility strategy issues.

Training development strategy is also linked to facility strategy. In the short term, trainers must develop courses that can be delivered in the available facilities and make efficient use of those facilities. In the long term, a shifting mix of types of courses (class size, instructional mode, etc.) can be planned concurrent with the planning for the facilities to house them.

Strategic Planning Tasks

A number of basic tasks must be performed in developing an overall training facility strategy. These tasks are:

- Define the scope of the overall training facility strategy.
- Develop or refine a training facility philosophy.
- Identify policy parameters, guidelines, and objectives.
- Determine the adequacy of existing training facilities.
- Develop a forecast of training requirements.
- Convert forecasted training requirements into facility requirements.
- Develop a training facilities plan to meet forecasted facility requirements.

The paragraphs that follow give a brief statement on each of these tasks.

Define the Scope

The scope statement defines the boundaries of the training facility strategy. Organizational, geographic, and time boundaries may be involved.

Develop a Philosophy

The training facilities philosophy statement sets out principles, beliefs, and assumptions governing training facilities planning.

Parameters, Guidelines, Objectives

Policy parameters, sizing guidelines, and utilization objectives will affect both the forecast of facility requirements and the selection and comparison of alternative training facility strategies.

Developing the lists of policies, guidelines, and utilization objectives requires a blend of objective data analysis and judgment. It is helpful to involve the managers of existing facilities in making the necessary judgments. The development of these policies, guidelines, and objectives is an important step since they will control many planning decisions.

Determine the Adequacy of Existing Facilities

Planning cannot be done without knowing what is already in place. The existing facilities are the starting point. These facilities must be analyzed as to their strengths, weaknesses, current operations, and existing plans.

Develop a Forecast

The forecast of training facility requirements is a prediction of the amount, type, and location of training facilities needed during the planning period. It should be expressed in capacity needed to support training activities subdivided by:

- Year (e.g., 1988, 1989)

- Location

- Intended use
    Instruction (trainee capacity, instructor offices)
    Development (developer offices)
    Administrative offices
    Number of bedrooms (if live-in facilities are to be provided)
    Support activities (number of square feet for support space)

This forecasting step is interactive with one of the following steps in the planning process, developing a training facility strategy. More than one forecast may be prepared considering different strategies.

Convert Forecasted Trainee and Staff Requirements into Facility Requirements

The mathematics of converting delivery, development, and staff forecasts to facility requirements forecasts are really quite simple. The main thing to remember is that no facility ever operates at 100 percent average fill, 365 days per year, 3 shifts. Fill factors must be accounted for. The average fill to be expected will vary depending on the strategy. The fill factors for the various strategies may be estimated from data obtained from existing facilities.

Develop a Training Facility Strategy

Developing a training facility strategy to meet forecasted requirements should result in a long-range, overall plan for training facilities coordinated with the company's long-range building plans. It should spell out the sizes, types, and general location of new facilities or additions to existing facilities to be built during each year of the plan. It should identify lease terminations, facilities to be abandoned, and major renovations to existing facilities.

Suggestions

Developing alternative strategies is creative work. There is no one best strategy, and each planner will arrive at a slightly different set of strategies. It is worth spending a reasonable amount of time generating a number of alternative strategies. A common mistake made by beginning planners is to develop a single strategy or only a few choices which appear to meet the forecasted requirements. A little extra work in developing more choices might uncover a plan which has substantial benefits over the first one or two choices. Getting other people involved in generating alternatives will help increase the range of choices available for analysis.

In comparing choices, the obvious losers should be weeded out without formal analysis; otherwise in comparative analysis there will be too many choices. Only the best three or four choices should be used for formal analysis.

Many strategic plans have failed for the lack of an implementation plan. The most important responsibility to identify is the individual or position responsible for controlling the overall implementation. The implementation plan spells out the steps to be taken in implementing the overall strategy, the timing of these steps, and the responsibility for their completion.

Defining Function and Space Requirements

The activities required to successfully implement the training curricula must be converted to building specifications. The object here is to identify and discuss the factors which must be considered when developing functional specifications for structural and hardware items incorporated into a training facility. The functional specifications communicate the trainer's need to the building engineer and/or architect.

Planning Inside Out

The types of training to be conducted within a facility and the mode of delivery affect the building layout. Group-paced and self-paced training represent the two basic modes of delivery. Each affects a training facility differently. Besides the two extremes, there are several other types of training.

If all training in a facility is to be group-paced, certain features should be designed into the facility to accommodate the characteristics of group-paced training. One of the first characteristics that must be considered is the movement of groups of people at specific times of the day. During the day, the groups will be moving from the classrooms to break areas, dining areas, or case rooms—sometimes referred to as break-out rooms. This group movement must be considered in planning the size of the corridors, the traffic patterns, and the acoustical treatment of the corridors.

In group-paced training the larger the group, the more noise generated by the movement of the people within the group. This affects the ability of the instructor to be heard above the din of the group noise. In this situation, acoustical treatment of the room must absorb the noise and at the same time enhance the instructor's lecture. Also, while lecturing, instructors generally use charts or projected media. The larger the class, the greater the difficulty of having the media visible to all members of the group. Proper room layout and room shape can increase the number of people who can comfortably see the presentation.

In contrast to group-paced training, a totally self-paced training environment would be made up of individuals working on their own, at their own speed. Consequently, large groups of people do not move in the halls at the same time. This reduced coincidence of people in the corridors means that the acoustical treatment of the corridor, while still important, may be accomplished for less expense.

Besides group-paced and self-paced training, several other types of training have significant impact on the structure and features of a training facility. Training requiring hands-on work with equipment or computer terminals or training conducted in small groups generates totally different space sizing and conditioning requirements than either of the two general types of training. The noise levels associated with hands-on equipment training are normally very high. The equipment usually requires a relatively large space with higher than normal ceilings. The heat loads generated by the equipment are usually relatively high, and the equipment often requires special electrical considerations.

In terminal rooms, the electrical loads are high and the noise generated by the printers is usually excessive. If individual practice is required on the terminals, many units may be needed. This will increase the electrical distribution and load requirements. As with most electronic equipment, terminals generate heat. The heating, ventilating, and air conditioning (HVAC) system must be capable of dealing with this additional load. Finally, most terminals use cathode ray tubes (CRTs). Normal fluorescent lighting produces glare on the screen and on the keys of the terminal. Eliminating this glare requires lighting treatment different from that for classrooms or carrel areas.

Small-group or case-oriented training increases the need for isolated spaces, either rooms or areas, where groups of individuals can discuss and work on common tasks. For normal class work, a classroom of 900 square feet might accommodate 20 students. However, if these 20 students are divided into five groups of four to work on a case, at least four additional areas of 140 square feet must be available for the case work. Small rooms affect traffic patterns, lighting, and HVAC distribution and control. If the case activities involve terminal work, the case rooms need to be equipped with computer terminals. This not only increases the electrical distribution and load but also may increase the distribution and load of the telecommunications system.

It is natural that training requirements will change, and with these changes comes the need to change the space where the training takes place. The need for unique space conditioning must be balanced with the need for flexibility.

Flexibility

The key to a successful training facility design is *adaptability*. Three change factors are present in today's training environment. First is the high rate of technological change in industry. The second factor is change in the manner of delivering training. The third factor is the significant growth in training both in total number of people and in new curricula. All three of these factors must be taken into consideration when planning for flexibility to accommodate changing conditions. These three factors affect the structural characteristics of the training facility. The question that must be answered by training managers is, "How flexible must this training facility be?"

Can too much flexibility be built into a training center? Increasing the flexibility of a building while at the same time maintaining performance standards raises the cost of construction. While wall construction to attain a given acoustical loss may be expensive, maintaining that same loss in temporary walls or folding partitions is considerably more expensive. A balance must be reached between flexibility and cost.

In design of a training facility, total flexibility is not needed. By analysis of the basic characteristics of the training to be conducted in the facility, a list of relatively standard training activities can be developed. These standard activities must be accommodated within the facility space, and the space must be conditioned appropriately.

Activity and Space Considerations

At this point in the planning process, the activities to be performed at the training facility have been identified along with the approximate amount of gross space required for each. The spaces required include classrooms, carrel arcades, dining rooms, a learning resource center, faculty space, and various types of administrative support space and storage space among others.

Space allocation in a training facility depends generally on three considerations: relationship of one activity to another, circulation patterns, and accessibility. The first consideration is the relationship that the activities of one space have with those of another space. Do the activities of one space depend upon the activities performed in another space? As examples, students move during the day from classrooms to case rooms to do case problems or from learning carrels to hands-on areas. The second factor to be considered is circulation. Who has to move between which areas, how often, and at what times during the day? Will the people performing activities in one space also be performing activities in another space? The final consideration related to circulation is access or nonaccess to specific areas. While students should have easy access to resource areas or individual study areas, they should not have to walk through administrative support areas to get to them. Access restriction is also needed for security. At the same time, various areas require different degrees of security.

DESIGNING TRAINING SPACES

At this point in the process of creating a training facility, much of the basic information is known. The size, shape, and content are to some extent fixed. However, because of the unique features inherent in a good training facility care should be taken to familiarize the building or architectural designer with these special features.

The eventual design will be expected to meet certain criteria beyond that specified in the planning statement. First of all, the newly designed facility will be expected to fulfill the functions intended, with a degree of flexibility. Performance of the various integrated systems such as lighting and HVAC clearly measures the design quality of any facility. Then too, from an operational point of view, reliability of the new design and its maintainability are interrelated. It is the design engineer's responsibility to provide reliable systems which can be readily maintained by the operations forces.

Architectural Considerations

The circulation pattern for students and staff within the facility will help define the image of the training facility. Corridors should be wide enough to permit groups of students to move between classes and to allow equipment to be moved from one location to another. Classrooms, dining rooms, and break areas should be arranged to minimize the student's travel during the training day. The circulation pattern also should prevent interference with the developmental staff and other administrative personnel. Since breaks are important for regenerating students' learning skills, break areas should be planned to facilitate break schedules. To minimize time lost in travel, it is reasonable to locate lounges with break services near classrooms, but not so near as to interfere with nearby classes in session.

Acoustics

Noise can be very detrimental to the learning process. It can have such a high energy level that prolonged exposure to it can be physiologically and psychologically harmful. It can also be irritating or distracting. It can interrupt students' train of thought, causing them to miss a point in a class presentation or to waste time rethinking a problem in a self-paced module. Guidelines for the control of sound within a training facility will be presented in this section.

Walls   One of the most critical features of a training facility is the way in which sound is controlled in the classroom area. As a standard, an ideal classroom wall will have a sound transmission class (STC) of 52. At this level, distracting sounds from outside the room are almost completely eliminated.

If construction methods are used which have lower STC ratings, some objectionable noise will penetrate the walls into the classroom. The net effect of this will be reduced effectiveness of the training activities and the learning process for some of the students.

Compromises must be made from time to time in the design of a training facility. Designs which allow flexibility in wall placement such as hollow metal partitions tend to reduce both sound absorption and sound transmission losses. Even a steel stud and dry wall partition with a sound attenuation blanket between the studs, constructed to the height of the dropped ceiling, will not provide an adequate sound barrier. Sound will spill from room to room through the ceiling void. However, as long as there is continuity in the sound barrier in the form of a sound attenuation blanket hung above the wall in the ceiling void, attenuation will occur.

Floors   The sound transmission properties of floors are usually adequate because of the mass and density of the floor materials which act as a sound absorber. However, from a sound reflectance point of view, floors can be a problem. The hard flat surface, even with vinyl tile applied, acts as a sounding board for noise generated within the room. Here carpeting is the best solution, increasing the sound absorption of the floor surface as well as eliminating the noise generated by furniture movement or pedestrian traffic.

Ceilings   Ceilings commonly used in office spaces, such as 2 by 4 lay-in metal pan or fissured mineral tile, all have excellent sound absorption qualities and can be used in the classroom with good results.

Doors   Doors located in carefully designed acoustical walls will reduce the effectiveness of the wall unless certain steps are taken to enhance the sound attenuation characteristics of the door opening. The STC ratings for doors are significantly less that those for a well-designed wall. If the doors are located in a vestibule off the corridor, these ratings can be improved somewhat.

Acoustical Problems and Solutions   The phenomenon of sound transmission between rooms is common when walls are hollow metal partition or when walls between rooms do not extend to the ceiling and floor slabs. Sound from an adjacent hallway or noisy equipment is likely to penetrate this type of wall construction.

The following are some ideas that can be utilized to treat the unwanted noise between rooms:

- The most effective way to minimize unwanted sound coming from another room is to treat it at the source or as close to the source as possible.

- If the source is noisy equipment, it may be possible to substitute quieter equipment.

- If the sound comes from an audiovisual presentation, the number of speakers in the room can be increased so that the volume of each speaker can be reduced.

- If the writing on a chalkboard in the adjacent room is disturbing, try mounting the chalkboard 6 inches from the wall instead of directly on the wall.

- Ventilating ducts transmit noise from one room to another. Generally, this can be controlled by placing absorbing linings within the ducts. In general, a layer of porous material, such as fiberglass or mineral wool impregnated with a light vinyl coating, lining a ventilation duct will attenuate a sound wave.

Electrical Systems

The most difficult system to design with adequate flexibility in the training facility is the electrical system. Lighting, varying electrical loads, and distribution all present unique problems for the designer.

Lighting Systems

Fluorescent Lighting   Probably the most commonly used lighting in the office and training environment is fluorescent lighting. Because of the high efficiency (lumens per watt) and the long life of the tubes, fluorescent fixtures are a natural selection for most, if not all, of the lighting needs in the training facility.

Two potential disadvantages of fluorescent lighting are the stark glare from the fixture and the occasional 60-Hz buzzing noise from the fixture's ballast. The ballast vibration can be controlled by making sure the fixtures are tightly assembled and gasketed according to manufacturer's recommendations. Glare can be controlled by the proper use and placement of lighting fixtures.

The 35-watt fluorescent tube has proven to be a real energy-efficient device. The lighting levels are only slightly sacrificed and the tube's performance and longevity have proven to be equal to the 40-watt tubes. However, the 35-watt energy saver tubes do not work well with fluorescent dimming systems and are not recommended for this application.

Incandescent Lighting   Incandescent lighting is usually not considered for commercial use except for special applications. This is true mainly because of the low light output of the regular incandescent bulb, the heat generated, and its low efficiency when compared with a fluorescent light source.

Task Lighting   Task lighting can be defined as that illumination which is located at the work station close to the task to be performed. No lighting beyond the immediate area of the task is achieved. For this reason, task lighting must be combined with other low-level ambient lighting for general viewing in the space.

Task lighting offers the potential advantages of lower power consumption with higher illumination levels at the task where it is needed. It has its best application in hands-on areas, carrel arcades, and to some extent in general office space.

Indirect Lighting   The indirect lighting method of illuminating space relies on reflected light off ceilings and walls to provide the proper level of ambient light in the space. One advantage of this lighting method is that the bright spot or glare from the source is not visible to the occupants in the space. The reflected light can be distributed uniformly about the space, minimizing or eliminating bright spot reflections in CRT screens and projected media screens.

Lighting Control   The level of lighting in classrooms should be adjustable to enhance projected media. To do this, three methods are commonly used: dimming, multiple circuiting, and a combination of the two. Dimming controls usually provide the most flexible control of a lighting system. Historically, fluorescent dimming has been not only expensive but marginal in performance, with flickering and flashing at low lighting levels. Today, advances in the control circuitry have corrected these problems as well as reduced the cost of the equipment. Incandescent dimming, commonly used in the past, is inexpensive and without the performance problems of the older fluorescent dimmers; however, it tends to introduce color distortion.

A combination of the two lighting systems, fluorescent for general classroom lighting and incandescent for dimmed lighting, provides a flexible lighting system, but unfortunately it is more costly to install and operate, introduces color distortion, and thus is not recommended.

Multiple circuiting of fluorescent tube elements within a fixture provides control of the lighting level in larger increments. For example, where the three tube fixtures are used, lighting levels of 0, 1/3, 2/3, and 3/3 can be achieved, controlled by two switches.

Low-voltage lighting control should be considered for use throughout the facility. These controls are usually made up of a single relay which may be controlled by any number of momentary contact switches. Low-voltage controls offer many advantages over standard switches:

- Lighting can be controlled from any number of locations.
- Low-voltage wiring may be used; e.g., bell wire, conduit, or other protected wiring is not needed for the switching controls.
- The system is easily adaptable to computer control or time clock control for energy conservation.

Electrical Power Loads

Planning the training facility includes careful estimation of the power requirements. These requirements will include the power supply to:

- Normal building requirements (such as lights, outlets, and air conditioning)
- Equipment for hands-on training
- Carrel rooms
- Audiovisual equipment
- Computer terminals, etc.

Normal requirements will be determined by the design engineer from the building specifications. The special power requirements of equipment for hands-on training can be determined only by a careful analysis of all courses to be taught in the facility and the associated equipment required.

Special consideration is required for carrel rooms because audiovisual devices and other hardware are used extensively in learning carrels. It is conceivable that a carrel could be equipped with an 8-mm cartridge film projector, two high-intensity lamps, a videotape monitor, and a videotape player. All items will not be used simultaneously in the same carrel; so plan for an average load rather than a total nameplate load.

Experience has shown that adding 25 percent to the total initial requirement is a reasonable provision for flexibility and growth. What should be remembered about future needs, however, is that the use of computer terminals in the training environment will, in all likelihood, continue to grow at a rapid rate as new operations and design systems come on-line. Planning for future use of terminals in classroom, carrel areas, case rooms, and perhaps some hands-on areas is recommended.

Distribution

To be sure that training facilities will meet current and future needs, wiring and cabling requirements must be identified. This is true not only when designing new facilities but also when making additions to existing buildings, upgrading or renovating available space, and preparing specifications for leased space.

Specific types of training facility services must be considered:

- Electrical services must be available for lighting and convenience outlets, and to support other services.
- Communication services such as telephones, security systems, and closed-circuit TV require their own wiring and cabling.
- Control systems for many training facility services have wiring and cabling requirements, including remote controls for projectors and other audiovisual equipment.
- Other wiring and cabling requirements exist when access to individualized audiovisual equipment is needed.
- Computer signaling cables and data links between certain hybrid training terminals, and equipment and host computers require special cabling.

Once the nature and scope of services requiring wiring and cabling have been determined, the procedures or system to provide them must be selected. It must be emphasized that at this point the most practical move is to consult with a qualified electrical engineer before moving ahead with your plans.

Heating, Ventilation, and Air Conditioning

Ventilation is the introduction of fresh air into occupied spaces of the building, and the removal of smoke and other unwanted gases from those spaces. Proper amounts of ventilation are essential to appropriately control the environment within a training facility.

The amounts of fresh air introduced to the building should be kept to a minimum consistent with good space conditions, since the treatment of fresh air generally increases the cooling and heating loads on mechanical equipment. Once the various uses of training facilities are defined, the building engineer can determine which areas require special ventilation and how best to accomplish their design objectives.

With current attention to individual rights, the mechanical designer must take into account the problem of smoking and the potential annoyance to nonsmokers. Air distribution to the classroom providing a room air change four to six times per hour should control all but the most severe smoke and odor problems.

Generally, the treatment of the training environment is a mechanical engineering consideration. Properly designed heating, ventilating, and air-conditioning systems will step from a properly planned training facility where the building design people are involved in the initial planning phases. The engineer's interest in this phase will be the special heat loads generated by equipment and location of this equipment within the building. Additionally the engineer will need to know the number of people anticipated in the various rooms so that their contribution to the heat loads can be determined. Finally he or she will want to know if there is to be equipment such as computers which have special environmental specifications. From this and other information gathered as the building design begins to stabilize, the basic mechanical design will take shape.

Even though environmental control is considered to be an important functional part of the training facility design, it is often neglected in the early stages of a project. This neglect results in a classroom environment that is either too hot or cold, too drafty or stuffy, too humid or dry. Any of these hamper trainee performance even with the best instruction and course material. The proper treatment of the training environment does not in itself create better training performance. However, the converse is certainly true. Poor environmental control can cause poorer training performance.

Each classroom should have its own temperature controls because of the potential for varying heat loads in each classroom space. This is true for conference rooms and carrel arcades as well. Because of the cost involved in providing individual controls, small rooms such as case rooms can be multipled on a single control with some risk of discomfort.

The success of a good heating, ventilating, and air-conditioning system largely depends upon its air distribution. To achieve the desired temperature and relative humidity levels, it is necessary to calculate the amount to be supplied to each room. To do this, the heating and cooling loads have to be evaluated for each space, based upon its physical characteristics, orientation, and occupancy.

Air velocities 3 to 5 feet above the floor should average between 25 and 50 feet per minute. Usually, there are complaints about stagnant air when the average air motion is less than 15 feet per minute; and drafts are objectionable when the average air velocity approaches 100 feet per minute.

When determining air velocities, the effect of the air on the occupants of the space during periods of extreme conditions of either heating or cooling must be considered. When the space temperature is at a minimum in the heating season, too high an air velocity will produce discomfort. Too low an air velocity at the high setting during the cooling season will also cause discomfort.

Renovating Existing Buildings for Training Facilities

At times it is economically justified to purchase, lease, or reuse an existing building for use as a training facility. Certain considerations regarding the appropriateness of the structure and its mechanical and electrical systems must be addressed. A thorough inspection by qualified engineering consultants will quickly determine any deficiencies in design and condition of the candidate structure.

Certain building features will have a significant impact on the usefulness of the building as a training facility. Column spacing, for example, must be great enough to permit desired classroom size. Column spacing of less than 20 feet may result either in the columns being exposed within the room, blocking vision and interfering with the room layout, or in classroom shapes inappropriate for using projected media effectively. If hands-on equipment is to be installed, floor loadings must be investigated. The HVAC system should be analyzed to determine its capacity for both heating and cooling, the serviceability and operational safety of the equipment and controls, and the flexibility of the design. The electrical system primary should be expected to meet all code requirements and be sized to handle the expected power demands of the training facility.

Comments

One final comment on the design of training space, the question of windows or no windows. Although the thought of a windowless space conjures up images of undesirable bland space, there are good reasons to support the windowless concept in a training facility. First, windows are a source of unwanted light which is difficult to control to the degree necessary in the classroom. Second, windows are a poor acoustical part of a wall and permit the transmission of unwanted sound from outside the building. Third, windows also permit the transfer of energy more readily than the walls around them. In cold weather, drafts and heat loss caused by windows will be obvious. Finally, windows are a source of distraction to the students.

To provide the student some contact with the outside world, windows can be provided in break areas or lounges. Some existing training facilities have used windows effectively in hallways outside of the classrooms, but in the training space, windows have only negative effects and should be avoided.

Where windows are used, Thermopane or other insulated glass can reduce the heat loss by up to 50 percent. Tinted glass or venetian blinds can be used to reduce the warming effect of the sun during the critical hours of the day. Then too, a heavy drape will accomplish a dual purpose by blocking out the unwanted light and reducing reflected noise from the hard surface of the window. All in all, windows are difficult to deal with, and if they are provided the problems should be well thought out in advance.

Providing Furnishings and Equipment

Much of the success of the training facility is determined by the training hardware used in the classroom. This hardware consists of visual training aids, hands-on equipment, mock-ups, projection equipment, terminals (communication gear), and furniture. The following paragraphs are intended to guide the training facility planner through the maze of options and accessories that must be faced to properly outfit the facility to meet the training objectives. Work station furniture including chairs, tables, and desks will be covered first, carrels second, modular furniture third, and finally training equipment. Audiovisual equipment will not be addressed, as it is covered in another chapter.

Work Station Furnishings

Chairs As stated earlier, student comfort cannot improve the learning rate of the student, but discomfort can certainly slow the learning rate. For this reason, some attention should be paid to providing student seating that will permit comfort for the largest range of body sizes. Tests have proven that the average person is capable of sitting in a chair for relatively short periods of time before anxiety caused by discomfort and fatigue begins to interfere with the learning process.

Seven primary factors in chair design will increase seating comfort and therefore forestall fatigue:

- Ergonomically designed seat and back
- Height adjustment capability
- Woven fabric upholstering
- Reclining ability with tension support
- Armrests
- Swivel ability
- Castered base

The features listed above can be divided into two categories: those which affec body support and those which enhance mobility. All major chair manufacturer make chairs which offer these features in several price ranges and choices of colors and styles.

An ergonomically designed chair is one which takes into account the physical structure of the seated body and provides support to the body in the proper places to permit good posture. Back, seat, and leg support should be provided without pressure points which inhibit blood circulation causing legs and feet to tingle or cramp.

Seat height should be adjustable from 16 to 21 inches from the floor. The seat and back of the chair should be fabric covered where it contacts the sitter. The woven fabric allows air movement and moisture evaporation from the surfaces in contact with the chair. Plastic upholstery inhibits this air flow and tends to cause moisture to collect, making the sitter feel damp and uncomfortable.

The armrest should be broad enough to provide a flat surface to rest an elbow or forearm and long enough to provide support even with changes in position. Upholstered chair arms provide the most comfort; however, they also show wear quickly. A plastic or wooden armrest is more practical. The armrest should be low enough to fit under the table without interference.

Reclining or tipping chairs greatly increase the length of time the students can stay seated by allowing the body weight to be transferred from the seat and legs to the back and shoulders. Classrooms with chairs lacking this feature will have students tipping the chairs onto back legs to find a comfortable position change, thus creating a potential safety hazard.

The pivot feature of the chair provides students with the ability to improve their viewing of displays or people located in various places around the room. The caster-equipped chair gives the student the ability to move quickly to consult with neighboring students or make room for another student to pass. In the carrel work station the castered chair gives the student the ability to move from the work table to the computer terminal to the book shelf and back again. Casters also make the chairs more mobile from an operational point of view. Chairs can be rolled from space to space rather than carried.

Tables and Desks For classroom use, tables are recommended rather than desks. They are less expensive and far more flexible. For additional flexibility, the tables can be provided with folding legs so they may be stored easily.

The work surface of the tables should have a light coloring to reduce the contrast with the papers and books that the student will be using. The reflectance level should be low, no more than 35 to 50 percent. A slight wood grain pattern enhances the surface aesthetically. Harsh or strong wood patterns should be avoided. The surface should have a matte finish to avoid any glare from overhead lighting. The top edging material should not be aluminum or chrome or other distracting or contrasting materials.

The surface area of the table should be large enough to hold all the materials the trainee needs simultaneously. The actual size of the table surface will depend upon management's decision as to how many students will be seated at a table. If the students are expected to have few reference volumes, a table width of 24 inches is sufficient. Where the student will be dealing with multiple references the table width should be increased to 30 inches.

The height of the work surface should allow the elbows to slide onto the surface. Standard height should be 29 inches from the floor to the top of the work surface. Other dimensions to be considered include:

- Knee room height—minimum of 25 inches
- Knee room width—minimum of 24 inches
- Knee room depth—minimum of 18 inches

Carrel and Work Station Furnishings The basic furnishings of a carrel, the chair and the work surface, should have the same characteristics as those recommended for classroom use. However, carrels do have additional consider-ations. These include the wall partitions, shelving arrangements, storage arrange-ments, and electrical requirements for possible audiovisual equipment.

Carrel Wall Materials Basic criteria for carrel walls are that they are of adequate size, attractive, provide adequate acoustic insulation, and are easy to clean. If the carrels are designed as part of a system, they can be easily rearranged and fitted with standard furnishings. Finally, they should be easily stored.

A movable wall system is desirable. Wall panels come in a variety of widths and heights. Each panel has a self-contained hinge mechanism so that panels can be connected easily. There is also a provision for running wires through the base of the walls. Each wall panel is made of a sound-absorbing inner substance and is covered on the inside and outside with removable fabric panels. The cloth panels are easy to clean and easy to replace. Manufacturers also make a wide variety of furnishings designed to fit, mount on, or replace the wall panels. Such things as horizontal work surfaces, shelving, and storage cabinets mount on the wall.

A movable wall system meets all the design requirements related to the construction of the carrel. In particular, it is so flexible that a set of panels and related hardware could be placed into one configuration and then modified to another in comparatively little time. Included is the capability of changing from a work surface appropriate to a seated height to one for standing height. Most of the movable wall systems meet the requirement of an attractive appearance. In general, any one manufacturer's product is truly a system and is coordinated in the design of its components. Product lines from companies such as All Steel, Steelcase, InterRoyal, Herman Miller, Westinghouse, and General Fireproofing, which are listed in *Sweet's Catalog* or in the *Office Product Master Catalog and Buying Guide*, should be investigated.

Recommended Design Features The following are design recommendations for learning carrels:

- Shelf units serve three basic functions: to hold audiovisual projection units, to hold instructional reference materials, and to serve as a base for attaching task lighting.
- Task lighting is needed because it is so difficult to provide overhead lighting which would be adequate for all of the many configurations of carrels that could be arranged in a given arcade. Furthermore, if carrels are being built in existing space, it is considerably less expensive to provide adequate task lighting than to modify the overhead lighting system.
- A work surface that is hung from the wall panel or from its structural components permits a wide range of height adjustments. After analyzing the training requirements, set the work surface at the appropriate height for the activity involved.
- In facilities without close-spaced ceiling ventilators, use panels 5½ feet high. Avoiding higher panels in these cases will provide better ventilation.

Modular Furniture and the Open Office Plan

Where office space is to be provided in the training facility for instructors, developers, and support personnel, keep in mind that it must be flexible and capable of change. Modular furniture and the open office concept provide the best options for planners and designers concerned with immediate space use and future requirements. An ideal office layout is one which creates a flexible, cost-effective environment which accommodates change, accepts growth, and allows people to use their work space effectively.

The following is a tally of desirable features in a modular or open office plan system:

- Variety in colors, finishes and materials, wood, laminates, metal, fabrics, nonglare surfaces

- Adequate physical design—hazard-free design, fire-retardant materials, and good sound-absorbing qualities

- Good maintenance characteristics

- Wiring capabilities for telephone, computer terminals, and power

The use of open plan modular systems in many cases displaces some of the permanent building costs, moving some of the costs into hardware rather than building investment. Modular systems utilize vertical space more efficiently than traditional office space. Costs incurred from reorganization and changes are greatly reduced. Standard grid arrangements for lighting and HVAC can be established to treat the general area, reducing these costs. Changes to HVAC and lighting systems can be minimized because office changes are made independent of building systems.

Defining Administrative and Operational Support Requirements

The following paragraphs provide an inventory of administrative, operational, and media support systems required for training facility operation. Some training facilities may have more systems, some less. Some functions may be grouped under a single heading, and others divided into even more specific functions. The intent of the inventory is to provide a menu of support, administrative, and media systems requiring planning, design, and space considerations prior to the construction of a new facility or remodeling of an existing facility.

Definition of Inventory and Support Systems

Systems which comprise a training facility can be divided into two main categories: Operational systems are those ongoing functions which result in or directly contribute to the end product of the organization's objectives. The end products of a typical training facility are (1) trained students and/or (2) developed and maintained courses.

Administrative systems are those which enable management to plan, organize, control, operate, and evaluate the business. This includes the records management and status tracking systems of the organization.

Some support systems have been categorized into a separate media classification. This is because media production groups and systems support both the administrative and the operational groups of a training facility. Media systems are those systems that produce, affect, and/or transmit informational or training messages to the staff or students in magnetic or audiovisual packages (i.e., video or audio tape, photographs, or drawings).

Inventory of Support Systems

Administrative

- Student registration
- Student relations
- Course, class, and case room scheduling
- Computer services
- Personnel
- Personnel and facility utilization tracking
- Accounting
- Financial
- Budget preparation and tracking
- Purchasing
- Inventory
- Storage
- Building and grounds maintenance
- Security
- Telecommunications
- Publications
- Transportation, receiving and shipping

Operational

- Technical and lab support
- Audiovisual support
- Centralized communications services
- Learning resources center
- Word processing
- Printing and reproduction

Media

- Television services
- Audio services

- Photography services
- Graphic arts

The following is a sample analysis format for the planning of administrative, operational, and media support systems.

System. The support function described.

Type of System. Whether the group function is operational, administrative, or media-related.

Functions Performed. What work functions, actions, or duties are performed in the area or room identified.

Personnel Considerations. The range of people who may work in the area, including the supervisor.

- The maximum number of people who work in this room or area at the same time
- Any special human-oriented considerations

Work Flow Interface. The primary groups, people, or areas with whom this group deals. Any groups, people, or areas that prepare, complete, or administrate work performed in this area.

Description of Space and Requirements. Description of current and suggested requirements for:

- Dedicated space (square feet)
- Lighting
- Floor covering
- Wall covering
- Acoustic treatments and conditions
- Air conditioning, ventilation, humidity, or filtration requirements

Furniture Requirements. Current and suggested requirements for:

- Seating
- Shelving
- Storage
- Decor
- Partitions

Communications Systems. List current and suggested communication facilities such as:

- What kinds of telephones, how many lines
- Kinds and types of communication terminals
- Intercom systems
- Other

Equipment Interface. The office and/or production equipment in the area and other devices and/or groups with which they interface.

Notes. Special considerations building planners, designers, or administrators should consider when planning for these office and production areas.

Television in the Training Facility

Television has become and will continue to be more prevalent in training because of the broad range of its application and its cost-effectiveness. Travel costs and other considerations will make electronic communication, including live and taped television, more attractive and more necessary.

Is teleproduction capability needed for a training organization? The answer to this question is probably "yes, of some sort." Is a television studio needed? The answer to that question is "it depends."

A teleproduction facility can range in size and scope from a black-and-white camera and one recorder in a workroom to a full studio with editing facilities. Following are some guidelines and considerations for determining individual needs.

First, the nature and size of the training organization will affect teleproduction needs. Small (less than 200 student capacity, non-live-in, leased or rented space) facilities can probably make-do with a couple of sets of cameras and recorders. If more complex taping is required, it is advisable to make arrangements with an outside production house.

For medium (200 to 400 student capacity) and large training facilities, in-house facility with editing equipment is recommended. A training facility of this size is usually heavily involved in course development. This is an ideal environment for cost-effective, in-house teleproduction.

Basic Videotape Recording Kit   A basic videotape recording kit includes black or low-grade color portable camera, portable recorder, microphone(s), and tripod. Approximate cost is $2500 to $5000 (format 1/2 inch VHS or 3/4 inch U-MATIC). With this basic equipment the following applications become possible:

- Instruction lectures can be recorded in the classroom for instructor appraisal and review purposes, and peer critiquing.
- Demonstrations involving equipment close-ups, off-premise facilities, etc., can be recorded.
- Meetings can be recorded for later or remote playback.

The above applications are appropriate primarily for in-house, staff, instructor, and administrative use. Tapes made with this kind of equipment are suitable for role-play situations, such as instructor performance reviews or role-play rooms. They are not suitable (under most circumstances) for playback to students. This is because the image quality, and usually the sound quality, too, will be low.

Only the master tape, the tape you record on, will have sufficient minimum quality for distortion-free playback. Copies made from this tape will gain noise and distortion from regeneration loss. The editing of such tapes involves rerecording that produces generation loss and further deteriorates the picture and sound quality.

This basic equipment is really in the audiovisual category, but it should not be stored, distributed, or used in the same way as audiovisual equipment. It should be maintained, administered, and operated by trained personnel who can operate it or instruct the potential user in its operation. If you plan to go beyond this level of equipment and operation, it is recommended that you seek qualified, professional assistance as early in the planning stage as possible.

Closed-Circuit Television Systems   There are three types of cable applications for closed-circuit television systems:

- Single-cable, single-channel separate audio, base band
- One-way, RF (single or multichannel)
- Two-way, RF (radio frequency)

Base Band   Base band is usually used in point-to-point dedicated transmission, such as from microwave dish reception to TV studio, or CCTV head end facility. A base band signal requires RF modulation to translate to ordinary television receivers. Base band can go directly into TV monitors. Base band systems are also suitable for:

- Classrooms or meeting rooms where temporary high-quality video is required for projection, live broadcast or cable-cast, or teleconferencing
- Special applications where two-way video is required

One-Way RF   The one-way (single-cable, multichannel) RF system is the most prevalent. It allows the transmission of up to the 108-channel capacity of current television receivers. For training facility use, 35 to 40 channels can be considered a high-end feasibility limit. RF cable can be connected directly to any television receiver.

Two-Way RF   Two-way RF uses the same coaxial cable as the above systems but requires special amplifiers, filters, and other equipment which can add at least 10 percent to the cabling cost.

Some typical applications of CCTV in a training facility are to provide cable to:

- Classrooms for presenting in-class taped materials
- Classrooms for live camera feeds of guest speakers or off-premise and remote premise demonstrations

Cabling Considerations   The first step in planning and designing a CCTV system is to determine the number of channels required. Cost-effective installations demand determining the total number of channels needed at the outset. Retrofitting an existing system for greater capacity can cost up to 50 percent of the initial installation costs.

The second determination to be made is what areas have access to which channels. Surveillance camera output, for instance, may be restricted to security personnel.

Once these determinations are made, it is again recommended that you seek the help of a professional CCTV consultant to design your system. This layout is of utmost importance to the quality of the service provided. Professional consultants can provide high-quality pictures for a reasonable cost. Although there is a temptation to do this design work in-house, experience has shown that for larger installations it usually becomes a costly, time-consuming trial-and-error procedure. Some considerations:

- Be sure to provide vertical access conduit in multifloor buildings for possible later cable installation.
- Systems over 52 channels are usually not feasible for training facility cost-effectiveness.
- Be sure that any "entertainment" channels provided will not violate copyright laws.
- Most current television receivers have lock-out features which can assist with channel access control.

Conclusion

The design and construction of a training center is not just the building of another school. Time should be taken to study the needs and requirements of students, instructors, and support staff before design work commences. Do not hesitate to make changes in plans while still in the design phase. At this stage you are dealing with lines on a piece of paper. But once your design has been released for construction proposals, changes will generally elevate your costs beyond their worth. Time to plan is never wasted.

Section 2

Program Design and Development

8

The Behavioral Sciences

Harold M. F. Rush

Harold M. F. Rush is a New York-based consultant in human resources management. His background includes research, teaching, consulting, and line management of human resources in public and private organizations and in academia. He was with Exxon Corporation for more than 10 years, responsible for manpower and organizational development at world headquarters, in Europe and Africa, and the Asia and Pacific regions. He was manager of personnel resources, development and planning, Exxon Minerals Company. Other experience includes Thiokol, where he served in human resources management and development positions. He worked on loan to the White House during the Kennedy and Johnson administrations, managing the first joint industry-government-community programs to hire, train, and upgrade minorities. He was associate director, Mayor's Office of Operations, New York City. He was Raoul de Vitry D'Avoucourt visiting professor of international human resource management, European School of Business (INSEAD), Fontainebleau, France, and visiting lecturer at other universities and schools. For nine years, Rush was a senior member of The Conference Board's professional staff heading the behavioral sciences and organization development function.

anager: a leader who enables people to work most effectively together by rforming primarily the work of planning, organizing, leading, and controlling.[1] Of the four basic managerial functions, none is more crucial to the success of the ganization than leading, for it is in performing this function that the manager's ility to manage is put to the acid test. It is in leading, more than in any other iction, that the manager must deal directly with the human resources of the ganization, and as any experienced manager knows, this is often a complex and difficult job, requiring knowledge and skill beyond that which the average person naturally possesses. People are variable; their behaviors are sometimes predictable, and sometimes not; people both think and feel; what worked well for management in the past often seems less effective when dealing with a more mobile, better-educated, more aggressive, and more affluent work force.

For these reasons, the managerial profession has looked outside the traditional business disciplines for insights and guidance in formulating strategies to manage the "people" part of the enterprise. Increasingly, the assistance is sought from a loosely bound collection of academic disciplines referred to as the *behavioral sciences* which may include sociology, anthropology, socioeconomics, the various subspe-cialities within psychology (clinical, social, experimental, etc.), and a host of other disciplines concerned with human behavior in social settings—in this case, the world of work and the work environment.[2]

An understanding of the contributions of the behavioral sciences and the implications of their theories and research findings is essential to the contemporary manager, who is, more than ever before, concerned about employee motivation and an accompanying increase in productivity. To sharpen his or her ability to manage people effectively and thereby help the organization to realize its objec-tives, it is incumbent upon the manager to know something about the inner workings of people and the resultant behaviors they exhibit in relation to the work they perform and the relationships that develop on the job between superiors, subordinates, and peers. One of the prime movers of the current generation of behavioral scientists, Douglas McGregor, pointed out that a substantial body of knowledge, based on research and scientific observation, now exists to enable the manager to manage people on a logical, professional basis, and not according to outdated myths and old wives' tales about what truly motivates people. In fact, he made an impassioned plea for enterprises to "exploit" the behavioral sciences and tap their contributions toward making management a science, as well as an art.[3]

While the coming together of management and the behavioral sciences has been a gradual process that continues to evolve even today, the heightened interest on both sides of the fence can be traced back only about three decades. However, there are some significant series of events which can be identified as precursors of the contemporary behavioral science-business interface. Principal among them are the so-called Hawthorne studies, the emergence of group dynamics research, and the group theory of organization.

The Hawthorne Studies

Beginning in 1927 and continuing for five years, the Hawthorne studies were conducted at Western Electric's Hawthorne plant near Chicago. A group of social scientists from Harvard was brought into the plant to study "the relation between conditions of work and the incidence of fatigue and monotony among employees." To do so, they set out to assess the influence of physical and environmental influences such as temperature, light, and humidity at the workplace and the relationship of rest periods to subsequent efficiency on the job. They selected experimental groups of employees, manipulated work conditions, and recorded the results. While they were able, in some instances, to determine cause-and-effect relationships between work conditions and efficiency, they also found that, almost regardless of what changes they made in the work environment, efficiency increased among their experimental groups of workers. This gave rise to what is called the *Hawthorne effect*; that is, the theory that employees perform more efficiently simply because they are given special attention.

More significant than the findings based on the original premise that physical conditions at the workplace affect efficiency were the unexpected findings that were gleaned from the Hawthorne studies. Because the researchers were, in effect, set back each time they tried to relate the various physical conditions to worker efficiency, the project, which was designed to last only one year, extended to five years. The reason: There were influences affecting efficiency and productivity much more strongly than working conditions—namely, group social structures, group norms, and group pressures. The researchers found, for example, that employees were more productive when working in groups than when working in isolation and that wage incentives alone did not determine product output, even on a piecework basis. Workers would sacrifice greater output for group acceptance.[4] Modern managers will find this no surprise, since they know and understand what happens to "rate-busters," but in the late 1920s—when most of industry was influenced heavily by "efficiency experts," time and motion studies, and incentive plans that were based on purely economic considerations—the social-group influences and interpersonal factors that were operating came as a surprise both to management and to the social scientists.

As a result, the research evolved to measure the human and social factors at play, and the investigation began to be concentrated on attitudes and motives of workers as individuals and on the social organization of work groups. With these findings documented, further research on the special roles of supervision and its relationship to the work groups began to be incorporated into the Hawthorne research, which served as the impetus for other groundbreaking behavioral research.

Group Dynamics Research

Although the principles of gestalt psychology had been applied to other areas of behavioral research, it was not until Kurt Lewin, the German-born American psychologist, and his colleagues began their experiments on interacting, face-to-face groups that the gestalt was adapted to social units or groups. The *gestalt* principle, most simply stated, is that the whole is greater than the sum of its parts. With this orientation as an underlying theoretical framework, Lewin and his colleagues made studies of groups as phenomena that were quite different from studies of individuals who compose groups. The research findings suggest that groups do, indeed, take on a distinct personality that supersedes the aggregate personality of its members, and for the first time in the history of social psychology, such terms as "group feeling," "group atmosphere," and "group goals" had an established scientific basis.

Moreover, it was found that the behavior of individuals acting in group situations is determined partially by the group's interaction and behavior, while influencing the norms and behavior of the group. In other words, there is a dynamic interaction, a give-and-take which occurs whenever groups function, that gives rise to what is referred to as *group dynamics*. Lewin and his associates studied group dynamics in the context of the "field" or "life space" in which the behaviors take place, and they posited that behavior can be understood only in the context of this field, thereby creating an analogy, however tenuous, to field theory in the physical sciences. Field theory in social psychology has been variously expressed in mathematical formulas, but the equation $B = f(PE)$, or behavior as a function of personality plus environment, underscores the situational nature of group dynamics and field theory. The personality of individuals may have many determinants, including heredity, early maturational experiences, beliefs, needs, etc., but any given behavior is a function of that personality *plus* the environment or field in which the individual interacts with others—therefore, behavior is changing and dynamic.[5]

Group Theory of Organization

Group dynamics research, which later produced the learning techniques of laboratory training (discussed later), clearly reinforced and gave explanation to the social-group phenomena that the Hawthorne research uncovered in factory work groups. It also formed the basis for large-scale research by Likert, Pelz, et al. on the roles of leadership and work groups, commonly referred to as the *group theory of organization.*

Prior to the Hawthorne studies, supervisors generally dealt with employees as individuals, using a corresponding managerial style designed to supervise on a one-to-one basis. With the research which demonstrated that organizations are actually composed of distinct and identifiable social groups, both formal and informal, and the complementary research on group dynamics and group behaviors, behavioral scientists—mainly from the University of Michigan—undertook extensive action research to identify where these groups exist in organizations, the patterns of group interaction in work situations, and the factors that encourage or impede group cohesion and effectiveness, the relationship of particular groups to other groups, and the individual's role in the several groups and subgroups to which he or she belongs.

Consistently it was demonstrated that the key to successful leadership lies in managers' recognition that they are not managing a collection of individuals—that they must couch their managerial strategies in terms of their relationships to the various groups to which they belong and particularly to the groups they supervise. This may involve an understanding of the function of informal groups in the organization, whose influence may be greater than is indicated by the work grouping that appears on the formal and official organization charts.[6]

Since an organization is more than a large collection of individuals, it is actually a series of overlapping groups—groups with the characteristics of individuals (norms, beliefs, values, feelings, inputs, outputs, etc.) but reinforced and modified by group interaction in any given situation. Crucial to the effective manager's role in relationship to these groups is the matter of *perception*—the way the manager perceives his or her role with the groups and the way the groups perceive the manager.

Behavioral Theories and Theorists Influencing Contemporary Management

With the backdrop of the foregoing breakthrough research findings, the behavioral sciences have produced a wealth of subsequent research and theory that have special relevance to the management of modern organizations. Some of these were produced quite independently from business organizations and were adapted by business enterprises because the problems they address are common in business organizations; others were carried out as developmental or action research in and for business organizations. It is impossible in this space to discuss in detail even the most significant findings, let alone others that may have made contributions to the growing body of behavioral research. However, some of the theories and research which seem to have most influenced the managerial process can be treated briefly in overview here.[7]

Since the work of some pioneers in the behavioral sciences first began to capture the interest of leaders, there have been noticeable, and sometimes dramatic, changes in the way organizations are viewed and managed. The influence of the behavioral sciences has been a steady one, and the business school graduates of today have been exposed to the field as a regular and routine part of their education for management. Some of the theories and research described here are no longer startlingly new to leaders and managers, but the contribution of the behavioral sciences to the overall body of knowledge and practice known as "management" is inescapable and undeniable.

Certainly, too, the research and contributions of behavioral scientists have expanded and evolved over the years, including those intervening years since the previous edition of this handbook was published. Limitations of space require some decisions and selectivity. We have chosen to deal with some of the fundamental theories, rather than with later refinements because it is important to know the seminal influences on what today has become a widely accepted "new" discipline known as organizational behavior.

This chapter also includes new material on stratified systems theory and the Myers-Briggs type indicator, both contributions that, in the opinion of the author, are powerful and practical tools and constructs whose time has come.

Kurt Lewin

As mentioned above, the group dynamics research which was headed by Kurt Lewin has had a weighty impact on subsequent behavioral science applications in contemporary organizations. The most widely applied facet of this research is one that has special interest to executives concerned with training and development: *laboratory training.*[8]

Laboratory training is the generic name for a variety of educational experiences designed (1) to increase individuals' sensitivity to their own motives and behavior, (2) to increase their sensitivity to the behavior of others, (3) to give them an understanding of how others perceive their behavior and are affected by it, and (4) to determine what factors facilitate or impede group effectiveness. The most common method of laboratory training used by business organizations, especially since the early 1960s, has been *sensitivity training* labs, the heart of which is the *T group* ("T" for training).[9]

While there are many variations on the basic T group, the traditional or "classic" one involves about 12 participants, usually strangers to one another, who meet for two weeks in an isolated spot without agenda and without hierarchical status to interact in face-to-face groups. Although designed to be an educational experience, the sessions are intended to encourage emotional or visceral learning, as contrasted with intellectual or "head-level" learning, which characterizes more traditional education. Further, there is no appointed leader or teacher, though an experienced "trainer" may act in the role of process observer and interpret the behavioral interactions of participants. The group's behavior is both the content and the process of the learning experience—totally experiential in nature. Participants learn to give and receive feedback on a completely candid and instantaneous basis, and the behaviors of individuals and the larger group are reacted to in terms of the "here and now," thereby underscoring Lewin's emphasis on understanding behavior in the "field" in which it occurs.[10]

Laboratory training is still widely used as a developmental technique, though in recent years organizations have tended to replace laboratory training or to supplement it with exercises designed to bridge the gap between the "pure" lab experience and on-the-job problems and situations. These exercises, however, owe much of their methodology to laboratory training. Among these are the Managerial Grid (discussed later in connection with Blake and Mouton), team building, intergroup building, and other methods associated with organization development.[11]

Rensis Likert

The name of Rensis Likert looms large in social psychology. Likert is widely known as the developer of one of the most popular opinion and attitude measurement scales, which has been in use for more than four decades. His more recent contributions, however, are directed more toward organizational behavior and the managerial process. A proponent of the group theory of organization, Likert has been actively involved in some of the most significant action research to be conducted in the world of work. His name is most often associated with the linking-pin concept and its companion, the interaction-influence principle; the four systems of organization; and human resource accounting.

The *linking-pin concept* concerns the manager's role in relation to the groups he or she supervises and the group's perception of their manager. The manager serves as a vital link between subordinates and his or her peers and superiors. Thus the manager is the channel of communication between organizational levels; the interpreter of objectives, policies, directives, etc., for subordinates; and the representative and advocate of the members of the work group for his or her peers and superiors. There is nothing new here, so far, since this is a primary function of *any* manager. The difference—and a crucial one—is that the linking pin is a *member* of at least two groups, and thus his or her behavior reflects the values, norms, and objectives of both groups. Usually the manager is the subordinate in one group (e.g., top management) and the superior in the other (e.g., middle management). Further, in order to be an effective linking pin, the manager must be perceived by both groups as a real member of the group, with corresponding identification with each group's activities, problems, accomplishments, etc.[12]

Interaction-Influence Principle. Even if the behaviors and perceptions of both groups are favorable in relation to the so-called linking pin, the *interaction-influence principle* must also be operative for the manager to be effective in an organization composed of overlapping and interfacing groups. Research on leadership styles and managerial effectiveness supports the necessity of a positive operation of the interaction-influence principle, with two essential variables at work.

First, the amount of influence a manager (linking pin) exerts upward in an organization directly determines the amount of influence he or she exerts downward. Stated simply, the more a manager is respected and listened to and can influence peers and superiors, the more effective he or she will be in managing subordinates. Managers who carry little weight with higher levels of the organizational hierarchy are apt to have little influence on the work groups that report to them.

Second, the more that managers allow themselves to be influenced by their subordinates, the more influence they, in turn, exert on subordinates. For example, in making decisions that will affect subordinates, the manager is more apt to get commitment and involvement from the work group in carrying out the decision if the work group has had some voice in determining the course of the decision. (See

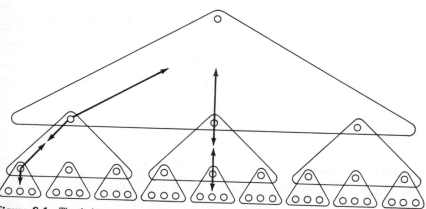

Figure 8-1. The linking-pin function. (*Source: Rensis Likert, New Patterns of Management,* McGraw-Hill Book Company, New York, 1961. Used with permission of McGraw-Hill Book Company.)

Fig. 8-1 for a graphic presentation of the linking pin and the directions of interaction and influence.)

The Four Systems. The interaction-influence principle clearly has strong implications for the development of a managerial style that is participative and involves the work group. And this is the style that Likert champions in his exposition of the *four systems of organization,* which is a comparative analysis of organizational and performance characteristics of four distinct types of organization. The systems are arranged on a continuum as follows:

System 1: Exploitive-authoritative

System 2: Benevolent-authoritative

System 3: Consultative

System 4: Participative-group

Several organizational variables are analyzed in terms of their existence in organizations typified by the respective systems and their corresponding organizational climates and management styles, including such variables as leadership processes used, character of motivational forces, communication processes, decision-making processes, and control processes. The four-system construct can be used to identify and describe organizations that are characteristic of the various points on the continuum, as well as to provide a model for normative organizational change.[13]

Throughout his work, Likert advocates a management that is based on the application of scientific research to human behavior in the social setting of the workplace. He sees the climate and managerial style inherent in his System 4 as the ones best founded on behavioral research and most conducive to effective achievement of organizational objectives, since System 4 relies most heavily on work-group participation and fuller utilization of human resources. Likert carries his emphasis on treating the "people" side of the organization as a resource to a logical extreme by developing a model for a method of accounting for the human resources.

Human Resource Accounting. Likert proposed formulas for assigning monetary values, often very specific ones, to the recruitment, hiring, training, and utilization of human beings, much as an organization would account for acquisition and usage of capital equipment. In human resource accounting, the human resources are accounted for in terms of gain or loss, appreciation or depreciation, and asset or liability, much as the material resources of the organization are accounted for, and they appear on the balance sheets as such.[14] While it remains to be seen whether human resource accounting is a viable or practicable technology for most organizations, a few firms have undertaken the practice on an experimental basis.

Douglas McGregor

Although Douglas McGregor made contributions to the body of behavioral research and had an active career as professor of management, management consultant, writer, and college president, his name is most often associated with his formulation of philosophical views of mankind, which he called *Theory X* and *Theory Y*.[15]

Theory X, basically a negativistic set of beliefs, includes the following assumptions (paraphrased):

1. People have an inherent dislike for work and will avoid it whenever possible.

2. Because they dislike work, people must be coerced, controlled, directed, or threatened with punishment in order to get them to exert sufficient effort toward organizational objectives.

3. People prefer to be directed, want to avoid responsibility, have little ambition, and seek mainly security.

Theory Y, in contrast, is an optimistic view of human nature:

1. Physical and mental work are as natural as play and rest.

2. People will exercise self-direction and self-control in achieving objectives if they are committed to the objectives.

3. Commitment to objectives is a function of the rewards associated with their achievement.

4. Under proper conditions, people learn not only to accept but also to seek responsibility.

5. Creativity, ingenuity, and imagination are *widely* distributed among the population; most people are capable of directing these abilities toward solving organizational problems.

6. Under conditions in most existing organizations, the average person's intellectual potentialities are being utilized only partially.

McGregor called these sets of assumptions *managerial cosmologies*, and he recognized that they represent only two of many possible "cosmologies"—a term related to *weltanschauung*, which is used in psychology and philosophy to denote a comprehensive conception of the world. They are therefore fundamental orientations or perceptions about the basic nature of human beings, particularly in relation to work and organizational life. While managerial styles and strategies logically are based on these theories, McGregor insisted that he was not proposing a "cook book" for managing. He adds, however, that Theory X most nearly sums up the view traditional management has taken toward the work force, while Theory Y represents an enlightened view of how most people are constituted, based on a considerable storehouse of research on human behavior.

"Consensus" Management?   Any management style starts with one's beliefs about the nature of people, and in most cases the sets of beliefs or assumptions held by managers become self-fulfilling prophecies when it comes to actual managing. If one's beliefs about people are consonant with those of Theory X, there is only one way to manage: by exerting external control on subordinates. On the other hand, if one views people in a way characteristic of the Theory Y assumptions, there is the possibility of allowing people to exercise self-control. This is what McGregor stated in his compilation of Theory Y, not a "soft" or "consensus" management, though critics often have leveled this charge.

There are qualifiers in Theory Y, and they are important to an understanding of what McGregor intended. For example, he specifies that people will exercise self-control and self-direction *if* they are committed to the objectives; people will accept and seek responsibility *under proper conditions*. McGregor realized that not all people are psychologically mature and that work is, in fact, a burden to some people, and he also realized that some people are passive and dependent and need to have external control. He adds, however, that people are not like this by nature; instead, their experiences in organizations have made them this way. While McGregor's own style and purpose reflected a Theory Y view of human nature and a management style consistent with Theory Y, he realized that if the manager cannot create the condtions that will lead people to use their creativity or if he cannot gain commitment and involvement, authority and imposed control must be exercised. The key to understanding the differences between the two theories is rigidity versus flexibility. Theory X allows for no flexibility in managerial style, while Theory Y suggests a wide range of styles, depending upon the work force and the situation.

McGregor argued that managing requires a special kind of skill and expertise because the manager's success is dependent upon effective utilization of the talents, minds, abilities, and efforts of other people. He therefore advocated a professional management founded upon scientifically obtained knowledge of human motivations and behaviors.[16]

Abraham H. Maslow

Maslow, a leader of the humanistic psychology movement, was concerned primarily with the fullest development of human potential; thus his burning interest was the study of superior people. He did not set out to develop a model of employee job motivation, though his theory of human personality has become probably the most influential conceptual basis for employee motivation to be found in modern industry. It is based on Maslow's theorizing and research into how the personality develops and grows and on the cardinal relationship of growth to motivation.

Starting with the assumption that human beings are wanting animals and are forever striving for goals of various kinds, Maslow posited that people want because they *need* these goals. Furthermore, while the finite expression of these needs may vary from individual to individual and from culture to culture, there are certain fundamental stages of need and growth common to all human beings—or at least the potential is present in everyone. Whether a person reaches the upper plateaus of these potential stages of growth depends upon the degree to which lower-level needs are adequately fulfilled. In fact, Maslow categorized these needs into a

Figure 8-2. Maslow's hierarchy of needs.

conceptual hierarchy, called, logically enough, the *hierarchy of needs*.[17] The five levels of the hierarchy, here represented in their ascending pattern of emergence, are

- self-actualization needs
- esteem needs
- love and belongingness needs
- safety needs
- physiological needs

Physiological Needs.   These are the needs for food, warmth, sleep, sex, and other primarily bodily satisfactions.

Safety Needs.   These include the need to be free from actual danger, as well as the need for psychological assurance of security.

Love and Belongingness Needs.   These are the basic needs for other people, social acceptance, and group membership, as well as the need to give and to receive love and affection.

Esteem Needs.   These include the need to have the respect and esteem of others, as well as the need for self-esteem.

Self-Actualization Needs.   These are the needs to realize one's potential fully, to become what one is capable of becoming, and to actualize the real "self," which is more than the basic organism.

The hierarchy implies that needs occur in the order in which they are presented, with physiological needs appearing first, then safety needs, etc. (see Fig. 8-2). This theory of personality and maturation states that until one level of need is fairly well satisfied, the next higher need does not even emerge. Moreover, once a particular set of needs is fulfilled, it no longer motivates. One is not driven to find safety if one is already safe, although if safety is taken away or threatened, it once again becomes the person's driving force or motivation, just as a fish is not motivated to seek water unless it is taken out of water. Stated simply, people are not motivated to achieve goals that they have already reached.

While Maslow posits these five sets of needs as inherently possible for all people, there are impediments of various kinds that can cause a person to reach a certain level of the hierarchy and cease to grow further. Even in relatively mature people, the lower-level needs remain and must be constantly maintained in order for motivation to be directed at the upper-level social and egotistic levels. In fact, the necessity of keeping the lower, more basic and primitive needs satisfied is a key factor in the Maslow model of personality and motivation. Because the lower-level needs are more immediate and urgent, if they are not constantly satisfied, they again come into play as the source and direction of a person's motivation. For example, a person who has climbed up the emotional ladder of the hierarchy of needs to the level of "esteem" will fall back to satisfy the safety needs if his or her safety is threatened.

While Maslow posits a serial nature of needs, it is important to keep in mind that an individual's motivation is not static, fixed, or "set in concrete." Whatever need is operative at a given time becomes the focus of an individual's striving to achieve satisfaction. Despite the tendency to fall back to a lower level if a lower-level need is insufficiently met, this lasts only until the need is satisfied. Then the individual's motivation is once again directed at the appropriate higher-level need. Maslow states explicitly that a person can be identified as being primarily at a given level— the level of prime motivation—at any given point in life. Emotionally healthy and mature persons are found striving to satisfy upper-level needs.

Self-Actualization Is Rare. However, while everyone may have a self-actualizing potential, Maslow's study of superior people indicates that few reach the level at which self-actualization is their prime motivation. Truly self-actualizing people are rare specimens. They are realistically oriented and are accepting of themselves, other people, and the natural world for what they are; they are greatly spontaneous; they are problem-centered, rather than self-centered; they have an air of detachment and a need for privacy; they are autonomous and independent; they have a fresh, rather than stereotyped, appreciation of people and things; they have had profound mystical or spiritual experiences, though not necessarily religious ones; they identify with all human beings rather than a subgroup; they have intimate relationships with a few specially loved people, and these relationships tend to be profound rather than superficial; they possess democratic values and attitudes; they do not confuse means with ends; they have a philosophical, rather than hostile, sense of humor; they have a great fund of creativeness and resist conforming to the culture; and they transcend the environment, rather than merely coping with it.[18]

The Maslow studies and the hierarchy of needs contain a wealth of personality theory and insights into human motivation, but the hierarchy alone has minimal relevance for average managers, except to broaden their understanding of human nature, unless it is related to the environment in general and the facts of organizational life in particular. This may be done by looking at the hierarchy in terms of the motivations of employees who compose the work forces in Western industry today.

Translation of Factors. Physiological needs—for food, shelter, clothing, etc.—require a job and a salary as a means to satisfy them. Safety needs are fulfilled through physical safety on the job, job security, and many fringe benefits. Belongingness needs may be satisfied by off-the-job relationships, by membership in work groups in modern industrial society, to a certain extent by work-connected social activities, and by unions and professional societies.

The pungent part of this anaology is what may *not* be satisfied: the need for esteem and the need for self-actualization. The key to real motivation lies in providing people the opportunity to satisfy their upper-level needs, rather than the lower-level ones, which most employees have already satisfied. It is important to remember that "a satisfied need no longer motivates."

Frederick Herzberg

Many managers, though intrigued and fascinated by Maslow's theory of personality and motivation, find it difficult to translate into concrete on-the-job application. However, the research and subsequent job redesign prescriptions of Frederick Herzberg and his colleagues are seen by large numbers of managers as a practical and workable means of increasing employee motivation. Yet the work of Herzberg can be understood only in terms of its extrapolation from Maslow's work, although on some fine points the connection is tenuous or represents an interpretation somewhat different from that of Maslow.

Herzberg's research, which has captured the imagination and loyalty of a host of followers (and has infuriated and alienated many others), began not as an inquiry into job redesign as such, but as an investigation of job factors and their relation to employee mental health. Herzberg and his colleagues were attempting to identify which kinds of on-the-job sequences contribute to job satisfaction and which ones cause dissatisfaction.

The research design is a simple one. Employees (originally accountants and engineers) were asked in semistructured interviews to recall specific events in the course of their work which made them feel particularly satisfied in their jobs; they were then asked to recall specific events that caused them to feel dissatisfied in their jobs. The interviews netted a large number of different kinds of events or circumstances, which Herzberg and his associates synthesized into several categories that describe in substance the multiple responses.

They found that rarely were the same sorts of events listed as sources of both satisfaction and dissatisfaction. In fact, allowing for some overlap, the things that caused satisfaction had a distinctly different character from that of the things reported as causing dissatisfaction.

Two-Factor Theory. Herzberg hypothesized, then, that the opposite of dissatisfaction is not satisfaction, but simply no dissatisfaction, and that the absence of satisfaction is not dissatisfaction, but no satisfaction. His postulating these sets of factors as different in character, separate, and discrete caused the theory to be called the *Herzberg two-factor theory of job satisfaction*. A listing of the basic factors—which he called *satisfiers* and *dissatisfiers*—may illustrate the substantive differences in their character, though not necessarily in order of importance within each set of factors

Satisfiers
Achievement
Recognition
Responsibility
Work itself
Growth
Advancement

Dissatisfiers
  Working conditions
  Policies and administrative practices
  Supervision
  Interpersonal relations
  Salary (all forms of financial compensation)
  Status
  Job security
  Personal life

Further analysis of the responses suggests that the satisfiers are all integral to the performance of the job, and therefore are referred to as job-*content* factors, while the dissatisfiers have to do with the environment surrounding the job itself, and thus are referred to as job-*context* factors. Herzberg called the satisfiers *motivators*, and the dissatisfiers *hygiene factors*, since they serve merely to support the climate for the job-content or motivating factors; therefore, the theory is often called the *motivation-hygiene* theory of job satisfaction.[19] He referred to the dissatisfiers as *replenishment needs* (they always go back to zero), since they must always be provided for, but their importance is realized only when they are inadequate or absent. The motivators are called *growth needs*, since they are the work elements that provide real motivation in this theory of job satisfaction. Generally speaking, the dissatisfiers, or hygiene factors, represent the lower-level needs on Maslow's hierarchy, and the satisfiers, or motivators, are *roughly* analogous to the upper levels of the hierarchy—esteem and self-actualization.

Job Enrichment versus Job Enlargement. Building on this model, Herzberg and his colleagues coined the term "job enrichment" to describe the process of redesigning work in order to build in or emphasize the motivators. They prefer the term "job enrichment" over the older term "job enlargement" because, in their view, enriching the job is quite a different thing from increasing the number of tasks. In fact, they refer to job enlargement as *horizontal job loading*, meaning that the job is redesigned to include additional tasks or operations of about the same difficulty as the core job. They insist that little, if any, real motivation will result from this kind of job redesign, since none of the motivators are accounted for, and that adding additional boring jobs to what is already a boring job may even decrease motivation. In contrast, job enrichment, or *vertical job loading*, involves building into the job the motivators by delegating some of the planning and controlling aspects, as well as the "doing" of the job.[20]

There has been widespread criticism of the theory from within the professional ranks of psychology as well as from practitioners in business and industry. Critics charge that the research design is simplistic and that people tend to tell an interviewer what they think the interviewer wants to hear. Perhaps a more telling criticism is based on people's innate ego-defensiveness, which may make them attribute satisfaction or success to themselves and dissatisfaction or failure to the environment or to other people. Nevertheless, Herzberg and others using his basic research design have replicated the original research on at least 16 different work populations, in addition to the accountants and engineers who composed the first sample, with similar results.[21] And cross-cultural studies, including ones made in the Soviet Union, Finland, and Israel, produce data similar to those gleaned from American work groups.

Robert R. Blake and Jane S. Mouton

Blake and Mouton are known among business people and organization development professionals principally for their development of a unique approach to
management and organization development called the *Managerial Grid.*®*

In the late 1950s, when laboratory training came into usage in business
organizations, the Grid was developed to meet the need for a means to bridge the
gap between pure laboratory training and the real problems and behaviors in the
"back-home" culture of the organization. It also served as a vehicle for experiential
learning—of the sort that laboratory training provided—without outside trainers,
thereby facilitating wide-scale exposure to the basic laboratory experience on an
in-house basis by using trainers from the sponsoring company.[22]

The Managerial Grid's underlying thesis is that two fundamental concerns most
often determine managerial styles: people and production. Too often these concerns are polarized in the manager's mind and resultant managerial style. Blake
and Mouton hypothesized that the dichotomy of people and production concerns
is both unnecessary and dysfunctional. In contrast, the two concerns are actually
complementary and mutually reinforcing, since a manager achieves results by and
through the efforts of others and since managing human resources effectively to
meet organizational objectives is the manager's primary obligation. However, most
managers adopt a managerial style that reflects an unbalanced concern for either
production or people, with consequent neglect of the other. The Managerial Grid is
a systematic program of management and organization development that is
designed to increase both the human and the economic or material concerns.[23]

The Grid is actually a graphic representation of the prevalent managerial styles,
with concern for people on the nine-point vertical axis and concern for production
on the nine-point horizontal axis (see Fig. 8-3). While theoretically there are 81
positions on the Grid, five points, representing five distinct managerial styles, are
those used for analysis of the manager's relative concerns and his or her typical
mode of managing. Ideally, the 9,9 position is the optimization of both the people
and production concerns.

The Six Phases.   The Grid is used by managers as an aid in assessing their own
managerial styles, as well as in assessing the styles of their fellow participants in a
laboratory training session called *phase 1*. While many of the pedagogical techniques in this basic laboratory are akin to those in more traditional laboratory
training, the focus is on analysis of managerial behaviors in relation to the job, as
contrasted with behavioral patterns in general.

Phase 1, the first of six overlapping and complementary phases, is called
management development, since it is designed to increase the *individual* participant's
awareness of his or her own managerial behavior and since it does not provide for
the larger organization's development.

Phase 2, a logical extension of the basic lab, is called *work-team development* or,
commonly, *team building*; in this phase managers begin to apply what they have
learned in phase 1 to their back-home work situations with their colleagues.
Individual and team standards of excellence are set, and personal and team barriers
to their achievement are analyzed in group or team sessions.

Phase 3 is the first phase called *organization development* because it has impact
upon the larger organization. It uses techniques similar to those of phase 2, but it
is concerned with work units and teams at their interface, whether line and staff or
different functional groups (e.g., manufacturing and sales). This phase is referred to

* Registered trademark of Scientific Methods, Inc.

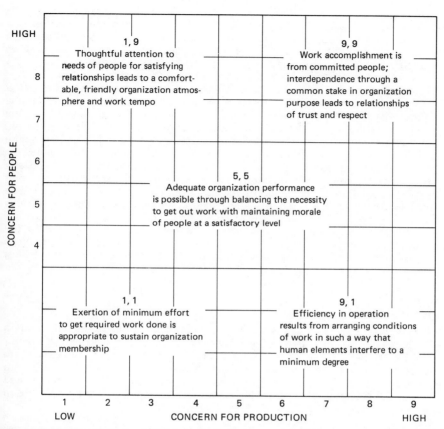

Figure 8-3. The Managerial Grid.® (© R. R. Blake and J. S. Mouton and Gulf Publishing Company, Houston.)

as *intergroup development*, and its principal aim is identification and resolution of barriers to intergroup cooperation.

Phase 4, *organizational goal setting*, involves top management in setting long-range organizational improvement goals and the development of strategies to reach them. The phase 4 plans deal with every aspect of the organization's operation, and the plans often detail specific objectives, e.g., 10 percent increase in profit or 10 percent reduction in employee turnover.

Phase 5 is *implementation* of the phase 4 plans, and—depending upon the nature of the various developmental goals, their time span, etc.—phase 5 may extend over several years. In this phase, task forces made up of members of the organization from different functional levels and multiple hierarchical levels are charged with the responsibility for monitoring and implementing the respective plans.

Phase 6, the *stabilization* phase, is primarily a measurement and evaluation phase to examine the organization's success in reaching its organizational goals. It involves critique and analysis of failures and shortcomings, as well as remedial action. It further involves recycling of the OD process at any or all of the preceding phases, whenever indicated.[24]

Grid organization development, while set up in six conceptual and implementation phases, is cleary a *systematic* method of organizational improvement that involves both the human and material aspects of the organization's operation. Just as in the phase 1 lab, in which production and people concerns are seen as complementary, the larger Grid program of OD is established to account for both concerns in its long-range effort to revitalize and renew organizations.

Not only is Grid OD designed to be followed in a set of logical sequences, but it also provides for a kind of "operation bootstrap" approach to organizational improvement. Even from phase 1, which often uses line managers as trainers, the OD process calls for participation and leadership from members of the organization, rather than reliance on outside trainers and resources. The people affected by the process are those most intimately involved in its implementation; therefore, the Grid is one form of *organic* organization development. Throughout the six phases, managers concerned with Grid OD use printed guidelines and forms to aid them in their efforts and to ensure that all relevant factors are considered and taken into account. These forms and guidelines are referred to as *instruments*, and the Grid is called *instrumented organization development*.[25]

While the Managerial Grid is intended as a basic format for any organization, the underlying concepts and techniques have been modified into several "spin-offs," with exercises and case materials adapted to the needs of various specialties, notably sales.[26]

Chris Argyris

A recurring theme in research and writing is the effects of organizational life upon the human personality. Because people are social animals, they construct organizations, formal and informal, to meet their need for social contact and to accomplish objectives that individuals cannot accomplish. Since the industrial revolution, there has been an ever-increasing tendency to institutionalize and formalize the aspects of organizations that capitalize on the economy of scale in order to increase output of goods and services.

One outcome, according to Argyris, is the alienation of the persons who make up the organization—a result of the fact that the view of "economic man" underlies and determines the operation of organizations. Ironically, the social and egoistic needs of the people in the organization are largely ignored, when taking them into account could result in the tapping of vast resources of creativity and in the obtaining of employee commitment to organizational objectives. Argyris states that modern organizations are often the source and *cause* of human alienation, apathy, and antagonism because such things as formalized structures, rigid channels of communication, prescriptive job designs, and pyramidal or hierarchical levels of authority are imposed on people in most organizations. People possess psychological energy which could be channeled toward making organizations more effective if these organizations allowed room for individuals to realize their needs. Instead, the psychological energy is often directed at fighting the system, or it is dissipated by individuals' frustrating attempts to realize their own needs within the context of organizational life.

Individual or Organizational Needs?   Argyris sees a fundamental dichotomy between individual and organizational needs, and because individuals by nature tend to place their own needs before those of the organization, neither their needs nor those of the organization are optimally fulfilled. Argyris argues that this will always be the case if individuals perceive that the organization's needs are given precedence over their own, and he contends that this is the case almost universally in contemporary organizations. He proposes as a solution a radical revamping of organizational practices to allow individuals the opportunity for self-realization in order for their psychological energy to be directed more toward organizational objectives.[27]

Argyris's complex prescription for improved organizational health includes an "open" organization, in which there are challenging goals for its members, work that permits some self-actualization, a highly developed sense of trust and supportiveness, interpersonal competence, a democratizing of decision making, and a decentralization of influence and authority, plus an awareness throughout the organization of the interdependence of its parts. He stresses, too, the dynamic nature of organizations, as opposed to a static view. Furthermore, for increased individual and organizational effectiveness, the dynamic nature of both must always be maintained by keeping the organization flexible enough to change, grow, modify, and adapt its internal structure, roles, processes, practices, and objectives to cope with pervasive change in its members and the environment in which it exists.

David C. McClelland

"Achievement" and "motivation" are ubiquitous concepts in the literature of the behavioral sciences that address themselves to the world of work. While some theories posit a connection between the two concepts, e.g., Herzberg's categorization of achievement as a motivating factor, there is a group of behavioral scientists whose central subject is the motivation to achieve. The best known of these researchers and theorists is David C. McClelland, noted for his studies of the degree of *need for achievement* in persons with varying personalities and social histories.[28]

McClelland and his colleagues have over the years studied individuals to determine how strong their need for achievement is. The research is based not so much on empirical observation of the subjects as on their response to several projective tests commonly used by psychologists in assessment of personality traits and in clinical diagnosis, notable H. A. Murray's Thematic Apperception Test (TAT). From among the 20 cards composing the TAT, which are untitled pictures, McClelland selected those with implicit "achievement imagery." The subject taking the TAT is given each card in succession and is asked to study each card and to imagine who the people in the picture are, what their relationships are, what the scene depicts, what led up to this scene, and what will happen afterward. Essentially the subject projects himself or herself into the picture and becomes one of the "actors" in the scene. The interviewer is alert to the various themes that emerge from the subject's narrative. An important theme, of course, is the need to achieve, a weighty personality and behavior variable.

Relevance of Need Achievement. In McClelland's model, persons are characterized as having either high or low need for achievement (nAch), which may be determined by the overall culture in which he or she was raised, familial relationships and experiences, interpersonal relationships, life experiences, etc. The nature of the nAch, as interpreted by McClelland and others who study achievement motivation, is a strong determinant in occupational choice and in the way people respond to the challenges or tasks that arise out of the job. For example, entrepreneurs predictably test out with high nAch, and among nonentrepreneurial types salespeople tend to demonstrate a high degree of need achievement.

People with high nAch typically are found to:

1. Prefer situations in which they can take personal responsibility for finding solutions to problems

2. Tend to set moderate and realistic achievement goals and to take "calculated" risks

3. Want concrete feedback on how well they are doing

There is a tendency for these people to make decisions themselves, not only to have better control over the outcome but to gain personal satisfaction from achieving. They usually are not given to sharing responsibility or to gambling on chance.

In setting moderate—or what they perceive as realistic—goals, people with high nAch are again selecting situations in which their need for achievement can be satisfied. If the goal is too easy to reach, they gain little sense of achievement; if it is too difficult, they are likely to fail and thus derive no sense of achievement.

The desire for concrete feedback on how they are doing is merely another example of such persons' need to do and achieve. Without the feedback, they do not know whether they are successful.

People with high nAch more frequently resume interrupted tasks after interpolated failure than after interpolated success. Once their need for achievement is satisfied—in this case, returning to a task repeatedly until they have completed or mastered it—they tend to go on to other challenges. On the other hand, people with low nAch tend to resume or to repeat tasks after success rather than after failure.

Cultural Determinants of nAch. The achievement motive, as already noted, can be determined by a complex interaction of experiences. The research indicates that the degree of emphasis placed upon achievement per se may vary from culture to culture; e.g., some American Indians test out with higher nAch than others, and the test results underscore the relative emphasis that the respective tribal nations place on achievement. But within a given culture or subculture there are discernible differences between individuals in terms of need for achievement, e.g., how much or how little the parents stressed achievement, what opportunities the individual encounters for psychological success, and how he or she copes with these opportunities. Regardless of the degree of nAch, two significant findings stand out in the diagnostic research on the achievement motive and the empirical research that correlates with the clinical assessments: (1) Rather than being an innate characteristic, the need for achievement is *learned* through a series of reinforcing learning experiences, and (2) it can be taught under the right circumstances.[29]

These two points are the most pungent parts of the achievement-motive research and theory. By first determining the degree of nAch in the individual and then ascertaining the maturational and other learning experiences that were responsible for it, new influences, experiences, and emotional climates can be created to raise the need for achievement. Whereas persons with high nAch require freedom to take risks, pursue challenging goals, and receive their gratification from successful completion of tasks, people with low nAch tend to be more concerned with acceptance by their peers, superiors, and subordinates; with affiliation; and with material rewards for relatively unchallenging tasks. People with high nAch more often seek the *intrinsic* rewards, represented by higher-level needs (à la Maslow), while people with low nAch tend to be motivated by the *extrinsic* rewards that are represented by lower-level needs.

B. F. Skinner

Sporadically throughout the history of psychology as a recognized discipline, the behaviorist school of thought has enjoyed a vogue, only to fall into disfavor with the majority of psychologists after a period of popularity. Virtually every introductory course in psychology includes a review of the early psychological experiments of Pavlov, the Russian physiologist, and his work with dogs. Other names associated with the behaviorist approach, Watson and Thorndike notably, are probably familiar to the layperson too.

Behaviorist psychology, also known as *stimulus-response* (or *stimulus-organism-response*) psychology, is actually a branch of experimental psychology (as contrasted with other branches, such as social and clinical) which is concerned with the kinds of stimuli that will produce a given response or responses and under what conditions. Members of this school tend to be interested in behavior per se and are not very concerned with the more abstract aspects of psychological theory—unconscious motivation, genetic predisposition, etc. Rather, they study the effects of the various stimuli and their ability to induce or modify certain behaviors by accompanying the stimuli with some kind of reward. Once a desired behavior or behavioral pattern is achieved through response to stimuli and rewards, the organism (or subject of the experiment) tends to maintain the behavior, even after the reward is taken away. All that is required, once the behavior is "locked in," is the stimulus associated with the reward, which produces a *conditioned response.*

For example, in the famous Pavlov research, there is the oft-cited experiment in which a bell was sounded simultaneously with the presentation of meat to the dog in his laboratory. After the dog had come to associate the repeated stimulus (bell) with the repeated reward (meat), Pavlov discovered that he could cease providing the meat, and the dog's response (salivation) would still occur each time the bell sounded.

Roots in Stimulus-Response Psychology. The work of B. F. Skinner follows generically the stimulus-response approach, though with some considerable modifications. Like his fellow behaviorists, he is concerned only with overt behavior that can be observed, predicted, and changed. He does not deny the existence of unconscious processes and motives or of genetic and cultural determinants of personality or behavior. He simply does not attempt to study them or take them into account in his highly scientifically controlled research. He states that modification of such things as genetically produced motivations is an extremely difficult and long-term task—because they are fundamentally resistant to change—while modification of overt behavior is relatively much more simple. He feels, therefore, that the minds, energies, and talents of psychologists ought to be directed toward changing behaviors, rather than delving into complex or metaphysical origins of behavior. Moreover, even when it can be shown that some aspect of behavior is due to season of birth, gross body type, or genetic constitution, the fact is of limited use. It may help in predicting behavior, but it is of little value in an experimental analysis or in practical control because such a condition cannot be manipulated.

Focus on Modifying Behavior. Skinner's chief interest is thus the manipulation and control of behavior. He proceeds on the assumption that all behavior is orderly and lawful and that the greater the understanding of cause and effect, the greater the potential for behavioral change, or, to use his term, *behavioral modification.* So far his position is not unlike that of other stimulus-response psychologists. The principal difference, however, is Skinner's emphasis on the *operant,* which he defines as "a response that operates on the environment and changes it." Operants are factors not necessarily directly associated with an applied stimulus—for example, a direct response to a stimulus, after the response has been sufficiently conditioned, such as the reflex of dropping a hot coal. Operants, while also logical and stimulated by something in the environment, cannot always be traced to an observable stimulus—for example, crossing from one side of the street to the other.[30]

The crux of Skinner's method of behavioral modification is *reinforcement*. Whenever a desired behavior occurs, whether in direct response to an applied stimulus or to an operant, it is rewarded, in order to increase the probability of its recurrence. This is positive reinforcement. Conversely, whenever an undesired behavior occurs, it is punished, in order to decrease the probability of recurrence. Frequent reinforcement of the operants will cause the behavior to become conditioned; therefore, the theory is often referred to as *operant conditioning* or *operant reinforcement*. The behavior becomes "locked in" if the reward (or punishment) follows the behavior immediately, because the subject more readily associates the reinforcing factor with the behavior. While this is an important factor in operant reinforcement, an almost equally important consideration is the schedule of reinforcement. Once the subject has associated the reward with the behavior, rewards are withheld and given irregularly. For instance, rather than administer the reward after each demonstration of behavior (which could lessen the subject's association of the operant and its reinforcement), one gives intermittent rewards, which are apt to increase the rate of response: the subject keeps performing the behavior until he or she is rewarded. Variable or intermittent rewards further tend to make the learned response more resistant to extinction.

While most of Skinner's research has been in laboratories using animals, mainly rats and pigeons, he and his disciples show no trepidation in extrapolating and generalizing the applicability of their findings to human behavior. In fact, the Skinnerian model has been adopted in a wide range of applications, including missile control, aspects of space technology, educational technology, treatment of the mentally ill, behavioral assay of psychoactive drugs, and the development of experimental cultures and societies.

Programmed Learning. The training and development professional is likely to be familiar with at least one educational technology that can be traced to Skinner, not only for its rationale and methodology, but also for its actual development as well. One of the first examples of "programmed learning" was developed by Skinner and his associate, J. G. Holland.[31] The Skinnerian principles are readily discernible in programmed learning systems, in which the learner gets immediate feedback on the solution to a problem or the answer to a question. The learner is usually told when an answer is correct (desired response) and instructed to continue (reward), but if the answer is incorrect or insufficient, the instruction is to try again or revert to previous material (punishment). Moreover, until the desired response is given, the learner may not proceed, and no further material will be supplied.

Recently there has been an upsurge of interest in operant reinforcement and behavior modification in business organizations, quite apart from interest in programmed learning. Increasingly, companies are applying Skinnerian techniques to improve on-the-job performance in a systematic way. Employees get instantaneous feedback on, and evaluation of, their performance of daily tasks. If a job is done well, the employee is rewarded for it, possibly by direct recognition from a superior, or possibly by the posting of his or her accomplishments for peers to see. The "reward" may also take the form of giving the employee a preferred work assignment.[32] And in some instances companies are trying to effect that often-heralded ideal of tying financial rewards and promotion to *actual* performance and, further, of associating performance with reward in employees' minds.[33]

Since the focus and aim of operant reinforcement are manipulation and control of behavior, many critics reject the approach as unethical and demeaning of human beings because of the "Big Brother" implications if behavior modification is carried to its logical extreme. Skinner acknowledges this possibility, but he argues that operant reinforcement *ought* to be used to improve broad social conditions and to resolve societal problems.[34]

Stratified Systems Theory

Stratified systems theory (SST) developed from the work of Elliott Jaques, whose early interest was in studying the nature of tasks and their complexity with a view toward establishing equitable rates of pay in industrial organizations.[35] It has evolved to a somewhat complex theory of organization and organization behavior with special implications for organization planning and structure, job design, and career pathing and development.

SST is basically a systematic theory of work in social organizations. Based on extensive study of organizations with a wide variety of purposes, it appears that there are fixed and observable hierarchical levels in most organizations, regardless of the nature or purpose of the organization and regardless of the environment or culture in which it exists. These levels or strata develop because the character of the work at successively higher levels is fundamentally different and more complex than at lower levels. For a given level to function properly, it must bring to bear a degree of thinking, perspective, and scope that not only builds upon the work of lower levels but integrates it into a larger and more complex framework. As one climbs the hierarchy one finds a greater number and a more complicated set of variables to deal with, and each successively higher level must have the capacity to integrate the work of the levels immediately below it. As a systems theory, SST posits not only that these levels are a natural outgrowth of social organization but that there is a mutual dependency among all strata or levels in order for the organization to do its work well and fulfill its mission or purpose.

Validation of the stratified systems theory has, to date, taken place in almost 30 countries with populations in excess of 250,000 individuals in manufacturing, service, religious, educational, and military organizations, among others.

Time-Span and Time-Frame. Although it is impossible in this space to discuss even simplistically all the concepts embodied in SST, it is essential to look at some related principles which are used to determine the nature of work at the respective organizational strata and for assessing the capability of people to perform well at each strata. Among the key concepts of SST are *time-span* and *time-frame*. Time is the common variable in both because, among the many ways of describing work and its structuring, the time factor is easily understood and readily measured.

Time-span refers to the task with the longest duration at respective hierarchical levels. Within the lower strata these tasks are of relatively short duration and are therefore completed within a brief time-span. At the highest levels, by contrast, the time-span encompasses strategic decisions and action, which by necessity have very long time-spans. At lower strata even the longest task may have relatively short duration, and its consequences will be seen immediately. At higher strata the duration and the impact are truly long-range.

Whereas time-span describes the tasks to be done in performing work and meeting job objectives, the related term *time-frame* is used to denote the complexity of the longest task people are capable of handling. *Time-frame* is a measure of the level or strata of work that people do. All work has certain prescribed limits or requirements which specify what a person must or must not do to accomplish the work. The qualifier in this construct is "discretion" in performing the work. The more complex the task, and therefore appropriate at higher organizational levels, the more discretion a person has in how to do the work and the more ambiguity he or she must deal with in exercising discretion in its performance.

In other words, most jobs involve a variety of tasks, but the *time-span* is based on which task takes the longest to complete. However, the longest tasks may not be the majority of the tasks to complete, but they are the most crucial measure of the work. *Time-frame* is a measure of the ability of an individual to perform at various hierarchical levels with increasing complexity. Another way of looking at *time-frame* is to assess how long a person can be left unsupervised to perform a task without veering off-course or causing problems for the organization.[36]

Stratified systems theory research suggest that time-frames of individuals develop at appreciably different rates throughout their lifetimes, but these rates of development and the inherent capacity of individuals to assume higher levels of responsibility and authority are broadly predictable. Using the time-frame construct, the large body of research data has been adapted to form a sophisticated system of *career path appreciation* and *career path mapping*. These career development methodologies cover such factors as intelligence, personality, social skills, aptitude, and specialized competencies—things usually covered by assessment centers—but also go beyond other methodologies to develop a highly personalized profile and career path.

Implications for Management. SST has enjoyed a vogue at several times in the past two to three decades, but it has failed to attract the large interest and following that some other organizational theories have experienced. This may be due partly to the special language employed by its theorists, language that sometimes seems unclear to a casual reader. It may also be due to people's not looking beyond the *prima facie* theory of hierarchical organization structures. There is some evidence, too, that the behavioral sciences have had sufficient influence on management and that there is a trend to push decisions down to the point of their impact rather than have data travel upward through organizational levels for decision making or "blessing," then travel downward to the locus of the problem or opportunity. If one considers the management implication of stratified systems theory, it not only appears consistent with decentralization and decision making at lower organizational levels but mandates an enriching of managerial jobs at lower strata.[37]

Figure 8-4 illustrates the various strata or levels of work, with time-spans ranging from 3 months to 50 years. This chart shows the seven levels that exist in most business organizations, with roughly analogous levels in military organizations. The description of the work appropriately done at corporate or strategic levels differs in its fundamental character from the work at "operations" and "comprehensive" managerial levels. In SST the highest level of "direct command" appears to be at Stratum V, and, while there are *official* reporting levels at Strata VI and VII, the actual relationships are most often that of colleagues who may possess complementary skills and who are properly concerned with long-range issues. From Stratum V and downward, clear boss-subordinate relationships, in the traditional hierarchical sense, obtain. A manager at Stratum IV may disagree with a superior at Stratum V, but it is usually accepted that Stratum V has the right to overrule decisions made by the Stratum IV manager.

Dysfunctional Organizations. Even in the most patently hierarchical organizations it is not uncommon to observe managers at the "strategic" level becoming involved in day-to-day operating matters, sometimes resulting in a truncating of the lower managers' authority (and motivation) and at the same time taking

Stratum or Level of Work	Time-span	Description	Civilian Organization	Military Organization
	50 years			
VII		Strategic design; development; deployment of complex systems	Corporation	Joint Chiefs of Staff
	20 years	_Strategic_		
VI		Direct deployment of complex systems	Group	Corps
	10 years			
V		Complex system; encompassing operating systems and modifying context	Subsidiary	Division
	5 years	_Comprehensive_		
IV		Alternative operating systems— general management	General Management	Brigade
	2 years			
III		Direct-operating systems— management of a mutual recognition unit	Unit	Battalion
	1 year			
II		Direct operating methods— supervision of a mutual knowledge system	Section	Company
	3 months	_Operational_		
I		Direct operating tasks	Shop Floor	Squad

Figure 8-4. Levels of work in civilian and military organizations.

higher-level managers themselves away from their jobs of charting and managing major change.

SST posits that the hierarchical levels—usually seven though theoretically eight in very large organizations—exist because they evolve naturally to advance the organization's purpose. They are not arbitrary levels or strata. If a higher level does not have the capability of and the responsibility for processing and integrating the work of lower levels, it serves no useful purpose. SST research has shown repeatedly that, regardless of the content of the work, a manager at a given stratum cannot effectively assess or integrate the works of others at the same stratum, let alone those with higher-level time-spans and time-frames. Yet many organizations are dysfunctional because they try to organize themselves and function with disregard for these principles.

For example, in some regionalized and decentralized organizations one finds research scientists, whose time-frame may be quite advanced and whose work has a time-span of 10 or more years, reporting to a unit manager whose time-span may be only 2 or 3 years. One result may be scientists who feel (and often are) misunderstood and unappreciated, and who nevertheless must defer to the management decisions of the unit manager (at Stratum III).

Another example of inefficiency and ineffectiveness may be found when one examines the various planning systems of many organizations. Typically, corporate-level management (Strata VI and VII) has responsibility for so-called long-range planning, whether or not there is a corporate staff department charged with this responsibility. Corporate strata may undertake to plan for the next 10 years or beyond, while "general" management (Strata IV and V) may do 3 year plans, and divisional management (Stratum III) may develop 18-month or 2-year plans. All these plans get reexamined, restated, and revised annually. SST research, using sophisticated trend extrapolation procedures and complex forecasting models, suggests that planning is most effective when it is tied to the median time-frame for each stratum. Further, there is a mathematical deterioration in the probability of accuracy with most planning tools and methods beyond 7 years. Moreover, the planning that usually occupies the corporate strata is not only inaccurate but unhelpful and dysfunctional, because the thinking, planning, and decision making that go on at corporate strata are extrapolative and linear. SST theory states that the "planning" at the top strata ought to go beyond linear forecasting. Instead, the corporate strategy ought to be concerned with environmental scanning, anticipating major events and trends, and creating the future that is wanted or needed. Then linear planning is left to lower strata, where its impact is felt and managed.

Redundant Levels and Positions. Despite some indications of new and experimental forms of organization, most organizations still hold on tenaciously to some traditional principles of span-of-control. SST proponents claim that if "true" strata are built into organizational design, span-of-control can be expanded appreciably. Not only does SST prescribe the basic seven managerial levels but it states that more levels or strata are unnecessary, even in *very* large organizations. (In the military whole, intact, fighting armies are managed by brigadier generals, Stratum IV managers.)

One obvious implication is the elimination of "assistant managers" or "assistants to," which usually connote one-on-one reporting relationships and a proliferation of redundant organizational and managerial levels. These "assistant" positions often signify an unwillingness to delegate and broaden span-of-control, and they may impede the flow of information in an organization, as well as retard decision making and the quick response organizations may need to manage change.

Myers-Briggs Type Indicator

The groundbreaking research of Carl Gustav Jung (1875–1961), the Swiss psychologist and psychiatrist, on the origins and development of personality must be described as monumental. Yet for a very long time, the contributions of Jung were eclipsed by those of his contemporary, sometime colleague, sometime adversary, Sigmund Freud. Each, along with Alfred Adler, was the founder of a school of psychology that stressed the importance of unconscious influences on feelings and behavior, as contrasted with the behavioral schools that stress observable behavior to the virtual exclusion of nonconscious motivations. Jung's position as a scientist has been derogated as unscientific by some persons who otherwise acknowledge his unique contributions to the study of humankind, possibly because of his interest in and use of the occult. Ironically, it can be argued that Jungian theories lend themselves more readily to verification, to controlled research, and to validation than those of many of his colleagues, notably his theories, and supporting research, into "racial memory" or the "collective unconscious." Similar beliefs, practices, and behaviors occur in disparate cultures, widely dispersed and having no common history or contact with each other.

Like Freud with the terms "id, ego, and superego," and Adler with his "inferiority and superiority complexes," some of the basic language of Jung's collection of work and theory, called "analytic psychology," have entered the common vocabulary without the average person's being aware of the origin of the terms. Two words that readily come to mind are *introversion* and *extraversion*, denoting fundamental differences in personality and behavior.[38]

The concepts of extraversion and introversion also happen to be key elements in one of the most dynamic and influential forces in the contemporary behavioral sciences, called the *Myers-Briggs type indicator* (MBTI). In a relatively short time MBTI has captured the interest of psychologists, psychotherapists, educators, clergy, and others in the "people professions." Not least among those attracted to MBTI and its multiple applications are businesspeople, especially those concerned with individual and organizational behavior, including training and organization development specialists. The MBTI is a psychometric instrument that, at the same time, depends completely upon Jung's work, while elaborating the basic concepts and adding related theoretical constructs that help to translate Jungian thought into a practical and useful tool.

The Two Attitudes. Carl Jung observed that all people are *constitutionally* disposed to view life differently, in either of two modes, *extraversion* or *introversion*, called *attitudes*. Because these terms have been adopted in popular language, it is useful to clarify what Jung actually intended them to mean. To the average person, an extravert is someone who is outgoing, easily accessible, open, and epitomized by the old-time salesman. And the introvert is commonly thought of as someone who is quiet, maybe somewhat shy or withdrawn, closed, and epitomized by the scholar or "bookworm." Directionally at least, these stereotypes are not without basis, but they are only stereotypes and often not descriptive of either the personality or behavior of persons characterized by either attitude.

The crucial element in understanding what is meant by introversion and extraversion is the flow of *energy*. Extraverts derive most of their energy from phenomena outside themselves, from events, things, environment, and other people. In the introvert energy comes from within themselves, and the energy is more often subjective than objective. Extraverts interact with the environment and *need* externals, including people. Introverts draw more on inner strengths and function quite well alone. Extraverts deal in empirical, concrete things. Introverts are charged by ideas and concepts.

All humans have the capacity for extraversion and introversion, but people typically develop a basic attitude or predisposition to *prefer* either an extraverted or introverted mode of existence. Well-developed extraverts deal very effectively with perceptions and ideas, and well-developed introverts deal ably with the external world when necessary, but introverts are usually more comfortable with reflection and what is inside them. *Preference* is the key to understanding these differences. These preferences develop *very* early in life, determined possibly by genetic or social factors—or both. The average person has two hands, and both are used constantly, but most people are decidedly right-handed or left-handed, a function of a fundamental predispositional makeup. A given reality or event may be experienced by two people, but the extravert tends to deal with the immediacy of the event and its impact, while the introvert may be more interested in the implications of the event than in its observable consequences.

Behavior is often situational, and the empirical behavior of a person does not *necessarily* indicate his or her basic attitude, whether it be extraversion or introversion. For example, extraverts may deal with concepts very effectively; and introverts may excel in certain professions that involve constant and close contact with other people. Some of the popular confusion about the terms may be due to Jung's choosing introversion to describe an attitude that connotes inward orientation, and people sometimes use it as a synonym for introspection, implying an inability to look beyond oneself.

It is important to note that, because all people possess the capacity for both extraversion and introversion, Jung acknowledged that rarely, if ever, does one find a "pure" introvert or extravert, certainly not in mentally healthy people. Further, the extent to which a person uses extraversion or introversion may change to accommodate circumstances, but the fundamental predisposition or preference does not change.

The Functions. While a grasp of the concepts of extraversion and introversion is absolutely essential to any understanding of Jung's work or to the Myers-Briggs type indicator, the two attitudes cannot stand alone. They must be complemented by what Jung referred to as "conscious psychological functions," which are, in a sense, subdivisions or subclassifications of the two basic attitudes. The functions are kinds of psychic activity that theoretically remain the same in varying circumstances.

Jung identified four psychological functions or modes of action:

1. *Thinking*: rational processes that elicit purpose or *meaning* from the object we observe, thereby forming a concept of it.

2. *Feeling*: informs us of the *value*, or use, of the object or occurrence.

3. *Sensing*: informs through the *senses* of sight, touch, smell, hearing, etc.

4. *Intuition*: the time dimension that points to *possibilities* that lie ahead.

In each of the above functions the key word in the definition is in italics. Additional clarification might include: *thinking* refers to conscious, objective, thought processes; *feeling* is highly subjective and highly individual; *sensing* is immediate and empirical; *intuition* refers both to vision of the future as well as to the often vague, sometimes undefined, "knowledge" on something of an instinctive level.

Just as humans possess introverted and extraverted attitudes, they also possess simultaneously all four functions, according to Jung. And, typically, people perceive life and its experiences predominately through one of the four functions, supported usually by a secondary function. In other words, we typically develop one function (and to a lesser degree another one) while neglecting the others in most instances. All are present in all of us, but we typically *prefer* one of the functions as our mode of dealing with events and ideas. Moreover, he saw the functions as two pairs of opposites, that is, sensing *or* intuiting, feeling *or* thinking.

Jung's typology describes a personality first in terms of introversion or extraversion, then in terms of the four functions. The result is eight basic types, e.g., extraverted thinker or introverted thinker; extraverted feeler or introverted feeler, and so on.

Origins of MBTI. Jung admitted that *possibly* there are more than four functions, but in his direct experience and from his extensive research into psychological types in many cultures, he could discover only four basic functions.

At first independent of Jung's work, but later influenced by it and revising her work to incorporate it, Katherine Briggs began in the first quarter of this century to develop her own psychological typology, mainly from biography. When Jung's typological theories were published in English (in 1923), her interest in psychological type intensified. Katherine Myers introduced typology into her family and profoundly influenced her daughter Isabel, who later married and kept her surname as well as that of her husband.

Isabel Myers-Briggs over a long lifespan collected data on psychological type, at first on an anecdotal basis and later with large research populations. Having received encouragement and some concrete support from principals in a major consulting firm and a developer of psychometrics, she eventually was able to test students in a public school system, using the early forms of what later was refined into the current MBTI instrument. Subsequently she had access to a medical school and tested the psychometric instrument on 10,000 nurses and 5000 medical students.

Her data bank grew and the instrument was modified several times to reflect subsequent findings. But Isabel Myers-Briggs found little interest and support among psychologists. This was due to several factors, among them a lack of general acceptance of the feasibility of measuring basic personality through psychometric instruments (more often the instruments used are projective techniques), the unpopularity of typological theories of personality per se, and surely the credibility of Myers-Briggs. Despite her diligent research, she was not a psychologist. She was basically self-taught in statistics and psychometrics. She persisted and gradually gained support from a handful of supporters. In 1962, Educational Testing Service published her test for research purposes but did little to promote it. Support and acceptance in the professional and academic communities continued to come slowly, but some support was forthcoming from a few respected academics. In 1975 publication of the MBTI and administration manuals was transferred to Consulting Psychologist Press. The Center for Applications of Psychological Type was established to carry out further research and to provide service to users of the MBTI.

The MBTI has been validated on a variety of populations, including students, teachers, nurses, physicians, marketers, administrators, and managers, among others.

Going beyond Jung. A significant departure from Jung, or possibly a further refinement of Jungian theory, is Myers-Briggs' addition of two extra dimensions to the total picture of a given psychological type. The MBTI incorporates these two dimensions as an integral part of the personality type. They are *perceiving* and *judging*.[39]

Perceiving is defined as a process of becoming aware of things, people, occurrences, and ideas, of gathering data. *Judging* includes the process of coming to conclusions about things that are perceived.

These two dimensions are viewed by Myers-Briggs as not only complementary to the Jungian personality theory but essential to a fuller understanding of the theory itself and to a more complete understanding of human personality. She posits that the methods of *perceiving* actually explain and make operational the *sensing* or the *intuiting*. In other words, intuiting and sensing are two different ways of perceiving. In a similar vein, Myers-Briggs sees *feeling* and *thinking* as two different ways of reaching conclusions about reality or *judging*.

People with a marked preference for perceiving are more comfortable with open-ended situations, to gathering more data. Those with a judging preference more readily make interpretations of data, reach conclusions, seek closure.

In summary, the Myers-Briggs typology comprises 16 basic types of personality, determined by one's basic predispositions toward:

- Extraversion (E) *or* introversion (I)
- Intuiting (N) *or* sensing (S)
- Thinking (T) *or* feeling (F)
- Judging (J) *or* perceiving (P)

The parentheses after each preference show the initials used in shorthand descriptions of each preference. With the exception of N for intuiting (to avoid confusion with the I for introversion) they are the first letter of each preference. The 16 types are described by the four letters that describe, respectively, each type; e.g., ISFP is an introverted, sensing, feeling, perceiver. The exact opposite on each dimension is an ENTJ, an extraverted, intuiting, thinking, judger. The 16 types can, and do, include various combinations of descriptive letters, each one of which describes a major modification in preference and type. There are ESFJs, ISFJs, INTPs, ENTPs, INTPs, ESTJs, etc.

The Four Temperaments.   While each of the 16 basic types contains significant differences on each dimension of choice or preference, there is a further grouping of type components called *temperaments*. While they may have considerable differences, their common preferences and behaviors are said to outweigh the differences. For example, an ESFP may be quite different from an ISTP, but they share the SP preferences and are likely to be more akin than different, the extraversion-introversion scale and their other differences notwithstanding, because they are sensing perceivers. The grouping of type components into the temperaments and the accompanying labels from Greek mythology is primarily the work of David Keirsey and Marilyn Bates. Many users of the MBTI agree with this categorization, but the temperaments construct and its assertion that the groupings are logical is not universally accepted as integral to MBTI thought or application.

The four temperaments have been variously described, but they are popularly described and labeled with the names of one of the Greek gods of mythology, with whom they share preferences and behaviors.[40]

1. *Dionysian (SP)*.   Seek freedom, value spontaneity, and resist being constrained or obligated. Does things because the *process* of doing them is pleasing, regardless of the goal or outcome. Action-driven, here-and-now, thrives on crisis situations requiring immediate action or response. Often optimists. Not easily controlled.

2. *Epithean (SJ)*.   Strong affiliation needs, sense of duty and obligation, keepers of traditions, gets satisfaction from serving and giving, strong work ethic. Want, but often cannot request, recognition and appreciation for what they perceive as merited. Often pessimists. Group acceptance serves as control and elicits conformity to group norms.

3. *Promethian (NT)*.   *Must* understand, predict, explain, and harness phenomena. Value competence above all else, in themselves and others. Thrive on challenge

ST	SF	NF	NT
I(S)TJ	I(S)FJ	I(N)FJ	I(N)TJ
IS(T)P	IS(F)P	IN(F)P	IN(T)P
E(S)TP	E(S)FP	E(N)FP	E(N)TP
ES(T)J	ES(F)J	EN(F)J	EN(T)J

Figure 8-5. Dominant Processes in MBTI (dominant process for each type circled).

and strive to control a variety of situations. Most self-critical of all, and constantly sets higher and higher goals of perfection; therefore, aware of own shortcomings and never satisfied with accomplishment. Embarrassed by praise.

4. *Apollonian (NF)*. Sets extraordinary goals, even transcendent ones, that are hard even for NFs to explain. Strive for "real" or "truest" self, and are always in process of "becoming." Work, relationships, efforts must be imbued with "meaning." Hard workers, if cause is deemed worthwhile, and tireless in pursuit of a cause. Can be a gadfly in pursuing one goal after another.

Dominant and Auxiliary Processes. In MBTI theory, everyone can be described by one of the 16 types, written as four-letter profiles. Just as people possess all of the type components but typically learn and prefer to use some processes more than others, they also have dominant and auxiliary processes within their own type. For example, ESFP describes someone who is an extraverted, sensing, feeling, perceiver. However, not all four letters play an equal part in determining the type and its resultant modes of behaving. In the ESFP person, the dominant mode is S for sensing, with the auxiliary F for feeling. By contrast, the ESTJ is characterized as having a dominant T for thinking, with the S for sensing as auxiliary.

There are several ways to find the dominant and auxiliary processes for each of the 16 basic types, some of them fairly complicated. True to form, the extravert's dominant process is more evident than the introvert's, because introverts do not show their dominant type in outward behavior. For quick reference a chart showing the 16 types appears as Figure 8–5. The dominant process for each type is circled.

Testing for Type. To ascertain a person's type, the psychometric instrument is a series of questions with multiple-choice answers, complemented by a group of word pairs. Persons being tested are told to choose their answers without second thoughts, on the assumption that initial reactions or choices are apt to be more spontaneous and therefore more indicative of the person's true preferences. There are no right or wrong choices, since the instrument is not normative. Rather it is intended to get a reading of the person's basic type, without any judgments or prescriptive biases.

Results of the test will type a person into one of the 16 basic types. It is important to note, however, that there are scales for each dimension; e.g., one person's S may be more pronounced than that of another person who also comes out an S.

The instrument has gone through several revisions and modifications, as validation data have been amassed and analyzed over the years. The test instrument comprises written questions and is self-administered. The form of the test in widest current usage consists of 126 items or questions. The test is scored by a trained professional, and feedback is given to the respondent. There is also an abbreviated version with 50 items that can be self-scored.

Although the Myers-Briggs type indicator (MBTI) is intended for "normal" or healthy populations and does not attempt to diagnose or otherwise deal with psychopathology, it is a controlled test, and the publishers try to restrict administration to those specially trained and approved for access to the test.

Language and Culture.   Jung maintained an abiding interest in the study of many cultures, including Oriental and African as well as European and Western civilizations. Indeed, he posited that his basic theories of personality transcend cultural barriers. However, the MBTI was developed on and for an English-speaking, fundamentally North American, population. Validation studies are ongoing, but to date there appear to be insufficient reliable data on other populations and cultures. Currently the MBTI is available in French and Spanish translations, with special attention devoted to removal of some slang and colloquialisms that appear in the English-language version.

Applications and Uses of MBTI.   In a relatively short time the MBTI has been adopted by a variety of professions. It is, arguably, the most widely used psychometric test for nonclinical, nonpsychiatric populations, although it was virtually unheard of a little more than a decade ago.

Although it is a relatively uncomplicated instrument that yields quick and easily understood data, aside from statistically controlled reliability and validity studies, users and proponents rate the MBTI as an unusually accurate descriptor of personality and behavior. While acknowledging that individuals are unique and that even among those whose type is described by the same four letters there are marked differences, the MBTI is nevertheless amazingly predictive of behavioral traits and predispositions. Given a particular event or phenomenon, observed or experienced by a variety of people, those with the same MBTI type have a high probability of interpreting and acting on the stimulus in a recognizably similar manner, because they share a constellation of personality components.

The MBTI has found widespread usage in formal education, from early school through higher education; individual, couples, family, and group counseling; career guidance; and communications, to name but a few.

Organizations, including business organizations, have found the MBTI especially useful in training and development and organization development, because of its relevance and applicability to a host of concerns, including selective placement, career pathing, management style and leadership, team and intergroup development, management of individual differences, conflict resolution, and adult learning methodologies.

Summary

Any review of the behavioral science research and writings reveals that there are many aspects to the complex subject of human behavior. There are differing points of view concerning the facets of personality that are the most relevant to human motivation, a point that usually comes through strongly, even in a cursory overview of a few of the leading theories, such as the one presented here. However, it becomes equally clear, despite the variety of approaches, that all are concerned with gaining greater understanding of the causes and forms of human behavior, especially in the context of organizations.

In some instances the contributions of the behavioral sciences offer specific guidelines or "how-to" action steps for improving the motivational climate. In other instances the contributions are in the forms of insights into the inner workings of personality and behavior, which are translations of research findings but which remain in the realm of theory. Even these theoretical or "philosophical" contributions can be useful, insofar as they provide a conceptual framework for understanding people and the behaviors they exhibit.

This is no small consideration for the manager, who, by definition, accomplishes objectives through and with the efforts of other people. In fact, the manager's skill is greatly dependent upon his or her ability to look beyond the overt behaviors of people into the sources and causes of those behaviors. Most managers who are successful in their jobs exhibit an understanding of the human as well as the material side of enterprise. To do this one need not be an "armchair psychologist" or an "office sociologist," although in managing today's work force the inputs of the behavioral sciences are in many ways as relevant as the physical or material concerns facing the manager.

Despite the tremendous advances of modern technology, successful management of the enterprise is greatly dependent upon effective utilization of the most important asset of any organization—the human resources.

While the process of motivation is always complex and often elusive, it is incumbent upon the manager, *at the very least*, to work toward removing the demotivating factors in the organization's culture and in his or her own interpersonal style in dealing with peers, superiors, and subordinates. This is not an easy task, regardless of the degree of sensitivity and insight the manager possesses, but at the heart of the matter is a recognition that motivation is inextricably linked with individual growth and development.

Development of subordinates is properly a line responsibility. But the training and development professional has a special role to fulfill in the process, which consists in keeping abreast of the developments within the field of human behavior and in serving as a valuable resource for the manager who is trying to create a climate in which motivation flourishes.

References

1. Allen, Louis A.: *Professional Management: New Concepts and Proven Practices*, McGraw-Hill Book Company (UK) Limited, London, 1973.

2. Rush, Harold M. F.: "What is Behavioral Science?" *The Conference Board Record*, January 1965.

3. McGregor, Douglas: *Leadership and Motivation* (edited by W. G. Bennis, E. H. Schein, and C. McGregor), The M.I.T. Press, Cambridge, Mass., 1966.

4. Roethlisberger, F., and W. J. Dickson: *Management and the Worker*, Harvard University Press, Cambridge, Mass., 1939. Roethlisberger, F., and W. J. Dickson: *Counseling in an Organization: A Sequel to the Hawthorne Research*, Harvard University Graduate School of Business, Boston, 1966.

5. Lewin, Kurt: *Resolving Social Conflicts: Selected Papers on Group Dynamics* (edited by Gertrude W. Lewin), Harper & Row, Publishers, Incorporated, New York, 1948. Cartwright, Dorian, and Alvin Zander (eds.): *Group Dynamics: Research and Theory*, 2d ed., Harper & Row, Publishers, Incorporated, New York, 1960.

6. For a discussion of what constitutes a true group, see Rush, Harold M. F.: "Work Units, Teams. . . or Groups," *The Conference Board Record*, January 1967.

7. Rush, Harold M. F.: *Behavioral Science: Concepts and Management Application*, National Industrial Conference Board, Inc., New York, 1969. (This book deals in greater depth with the nature and contributions of the various behavioral sciences, the work and writings of most of the theorists discussed in this handbook, and three approaches to behaviorally oriented training. It includes 10 case studies of business applications of behavioral science technology.)

8. Schein, Edgar H., and Warren G. Bennis: *Personal and Organizational Change through Group Methods*, John Wiley & Sons, Inc., New York, 1965.

9. For a discussion of typical sequences of events in T groups for business people, see Rush, Harold M. F.: *Behavioral Science: Concepts and Management Application*, chap. 3.

10. Marrow, Alfred J.: *Behind the Executive Mask*, American Management Association, New York, 1964. (Marrow discusses the rationale for laboratory training for managers and gives an excellent narrative account of behavioral interaction in a "classic" T group.)

11. For a discussion of organization development, see chap. 31 of this handbook. See also Kuriloff, Arthur H.: *Organizational Development for Survival*, American Management Association, New York, 1972. Rush, Harold M. F.: *Organization Development: A Reconnaissance*, The Conference Board, New York, 1973.

12. Likert, Rensis: *New Patterns of Management*, McGraw-Hill Book Company, New York, 1961.

13. Likert, Rensis: *The Human Organization: Its Management and Value*, McGraw-Hill Book Company, New York, 1967.

14. Ibid.

15. McGregor, Douglas: *The Human Side of Enterprise*, McGraw-Hill Book Company, New York, 1960. (Although McGregor wrote many articles for business and professional journals, *The Human Side of Enterprise* is his only book-length work published before his death. Its influence on the behavioral science movement within the business community is inestimable.)

16. McGregor, Douglas: *The Professional Manager* (edited by Caroline McGregor and Warren G. Bennis), McGraw-Hill Book Company, New York, 1967.

17. Maslow, Abraham H.: *Motivation and Personality*, 2d ed., Harper & Row Publishers, Incorporated, New York, 1970.

18. Maslow, Abraham H.: *Toward Psychology of Being*, 2d ed., Van Nostrand Reinhold Incorporated, New York, 1968. Maslow, Abraham H.: *Eupsychian Management: A Journal*, Dorsey Press, Inc., Division of Richard D. Irwin, Inc., Homewood, Ill., 1965.

19. Herzberg, Frederick: *Work and the Nature of Man*, The World Publishing Company, Cleveland, 1966.

20. Rush, Harold M. F.: *Job Design for Motivation: Experiments in Job Enlargement and Job Enrichment*, The Conference Board, New York, 1971.

21. Ford, Robert N.: *Motivation through the Work Itself*, American Management Association, New York, 1969. Myers, M. Scott: *Every Employee a Manager: More Meaningful Work through Job Enrichment*, McGraw-Hill Book Company, New York, 1970. *Work in America*, report of a special task force to the Secretary of Health, Education, and Welfare, The M.I.T. Press, Cambridge, Mass., 1973.

22. Blake, Mouton, Barnes, and Greiner: "Breakthrough in Organization Development," *Harvard Business Review*, November–December 1964. Rush, Harold M. F.: *Organization Development: A Reconnaissance*. (The article by Blake et al. reports the development of the Managerial Grid and initial validation research with Humble Oil Company (now Exxon Company, U.S.A.), using a pseudonym for the company. The book by Rush includes a capsule discussion of this development research in a case study which also deals with Humble's experience with several approaches to organizational improvement.)

23. Blake, Robert R., and Jane S. Mouton: *The Managerial Grid*, Gulf Publishing Company, Houston, 1964.

24. Blake, Robert R., and Jane S. Mouton: *Corporate Excellence Diagnosis*, Scientific Methods, Inc., Austin, 1968.

25. For a comparison of instrumented OD with other forms, see Rush: *Organization Development: A Reconnaissance*. This work also compares practices in "OD" and "non-OD" companies.

26. Blake, Robert R., and Jane S. Mouton: *The Grid for Sales Excellence: Benchmarks for Effective Salesmanship*, McGraw-Hill Book Company, New York, 1969.

27. Argyris, Chris: *Integrating the Individual and the Organization*, John Wiley & Sons, Inc., New York, 1964. Argyris, Chris: *Interpersonal Competence and Organizational Effectiveness*, Dorsey Press, Inc., Division of Richard D. Irwin, Inc., Homewood, Ill., 1962.

28. McClelland, David C., et al.: *The Achievement Motive*, Appleton-Century-Crofts, New York, 1953.

29. McClelland, David C., and David J. Winter: *Motivating Economic Achievement*, The Free Press, New York, 1969.

30. Skinner, B. F.: *Science and Human Behavior*, The Macmillan Company, New York, 1953.

31. Holland, J. G., and B. F. Skinner: *The Analysis of Behavior: A Program for Self-Instruction*, McGraw-Hill Book Company, New York, 1961.

32. Laird, Dugan: "Why Everything Is All Loused Up, Really (and What to Do about It)," *Training in Business and Industry*, March 1971. (Laird's article reports on widespread *conscious* application of behavior-modification techniques within Emery Air Freight, a company that pioneered adaptation of Skinnerian principles to day-to-day operations.)

33. "Where Skinner's Theories Work," *Business Week*, Dec. 2, 1972.

34. Skinner, B. F.: *Beyond Freedom and Dignity*, Alfred A. Knopf, Inc., New York, 1972. (This best-seller is a defense of Skinner's position on the use of operant reinforcement as a means of control over people to accomplish broad social goals of societies and cultures. It is also an excellent exposition of operant reinforcement theory and method, couched in lay terms.)

5. Jaques, Elliott: *Equitable Payment*, John Wiley & Sons, Inc., New York, 1961.

6. Jaques, Elliott: "Taking Time Seriously in Evaluating Jobs," *Harvard Business Review*, September–October, 1979, pp. 124–132.

7. Jaques, Elliott: *Free Enterprise, Fair Employment*, Crane Russak, New York, 1976.

8. Jung, C. G.: *Psychological Types*, Bollingen Series XX, The Collected Works of C. G. Jung, vol. 6, Princeton University Press, Princeton, 1971.

9. Myers-Briggs, Isabel (with Peter B. Myers): *Gifts Differing*, Consulting Psychologists Press, Inc., Palo Alto, Calif., 1980.

0. Keirsey, David, and Marilyn Bates: *Please Understand Me; Character & Temperament Types*, Prometheus Nemesis, Del Mar, Calif., 1978.

9
Adult Learning

Malcolm S. Knowles

Malcolm S. Knowles *is Professor Emeritus of Adult and Community College Education at North Carolina State University. Previously, he was Professor of Education at Boston University, Executive Director of Adult Education Association of the U.S.A., and Director of Adult Education for the YMCAs of Boston, Detroit, and Chicago. He received his A.B. at Harvard College in 1934 and his M.A. and Ph.D. from the University of Chicago in 1949 and 1960, respectively. Since his retirement in 1979, he has been actively engaged in consulting and conducting workshops with business and industry, government agencies, educational institutions, religious institutions, voluntary agencies, and ASTD chapters and conferences in North America, Europe, South America, Australia, Japan, Singapore, Thailand, and Korea. He is the author of 17 books, the most recent being* The Adult Learner: A Neglected Species, *Gulf Publishing, rev. ed. 1984, and* Andragogy in Action, *Jossey-Bass, 1984, and over 170 articles.*

Wherefore Pedagogy?

All formal educational institutions in modern society were initially established exclusively for the education of children and youth. At the time they were established there was only one model of assumptions about learners and learning—the pedagogical model (derived from the Greek words *paid*, meaning "child," and *agogus*, meaning "leader"; so "pedagogy" means literally "the art and science of teaching children").

This model assigned full responsibility for making all decisions about what should be learned, how it should be learned, when it should be learned, and if it had been learned, to the teacher. Students were given the role of being submissive recipients of the directions and transmitted content of the teacher. It assumed that they were dependent personalities, that they had little experience that could serve as a resource for learning, that they became ready to learn what they were told they had to learn (to get promoted to the next level), that they were subject-centered in their orientation to learning, and that they were motivated by extrinsic pressures or rewards. The backbone methodology of pedagogy is transmission techniques.

As educational psychologists started researching educational phenomena around the turn of the century they were governed largely by these assumptions, too. But they were not really looking at learning; they were investigating reactions to teaching. And the more they found out about how teachers could control learners' reactions, the more controlling teaching became. Pedagogy was king.

When adult education began to be organized systematically in the first quarter of this century, pedagogy was the only model teachers of adults had to go on, with the result that until recently adults were taught as if they were children. I believe that this fact accounts for many of the troubles adult educators encountered, such as a high drop-out rate (where attendance was voluntary), low motivation, and poor performance. When training began emerging as a specialty within the general adult education movement almost half a century later, this was the only model available to trainers, as well.

Then Came Andragogy

The first inkling that the pedagogical model may not be appropriate for adults appeared in a book by Eduard C. Lindeman, *The Meaning of Adult Education*, in 1926.[1] Based on his experience as both an adult learner and a teacher of adults, Lindeman proposed that adults were not just grown-up children, that they learned best when they were actively involved in determining what, how, and when they learned. But it was not until the 1950s, when we began getting empirical research on adults as learners, that the notion that there are differences between youth and adults as learners began being taken seriously.

A seminal study by Houle[2] spawned a crescendo of studies (Tough,[3, 4] Peters,[5] Penland,[6] and others) of how adults learn naturally (e.g., when they are not being taught). These studies document the fact that adults do indeed engage in more intentional learning outside of formal instruction than in organized programs and that they are in fact highly self-directed learners. Meantime, knowledge about adult learners was coming from other disciplines. Clinical psychologists were providing information on the conditions and strategies that promoted behavioral change (which is what education should be about, too). Developmental psychologists were illuminating the development stages that adults experience throughout the life span, which are a main stimulus of readiness to learn. Sociologists were exposing the effects that many institutional policies and practices have in inhibiting or facilitating learning (especially the inhibiting effects of rules and regulations, requirements, registration procedures, time schedules, and the like). Social psychologists were revealing the influences of forces in the larger environment, such as social attitudes and customs, reward systems, and socioeconomic and ethnic stratification.

Early in the 1960s European adult educators were feeling a need for a label for his growing body of knowledge about adult learners that would enable them to talk about it in parallel with the pedagogical model, and they coined the term (or actually rediscovered the term that had been coined by a German adult educator in 833) *andragogy*. It is derived from the Greek word *aner*, meaning "adult" literally, "man, not boy"). It was initially used to mean "the art and science of elping adults learn," but, as will be shown later, the term has taken on a broader teaning. It is a term that is now widely used around the world as an alternative to edagogy.

What Do We Know about Adults as Learners?

The research cited above leads to the following assumptions about adults as learners, on which the andragogical model is based:

1. *Adults have a need to know why they should learn something.* Tough[4] found that adults would expend considerable time and energy exploring what the benefits would be of their learning something and what the costs would be of their not learning it before they would be willing to invest time and energy in learning it. We therefore now have a dictum in adult education that one of the first tasks of the adult educator is to develop a "need to know" in the learners—to make a case for the value *in their life performance* of their learning what we have to offer. At the minimum, this case should be made through testimony from the experience of the trainer or a successful practitioner; at the maximum, by providing real or simulated experiences through which the learners experience the benefits of knowing and the costs of not knowing. It is seldom convincing for them to be told by someone (like the boss) that it would be good for them.

   To practice what I preach, let me try to make a case for your learning about "Treating Adult Learners as Adults." Let me quote from an article I wrote for the *Training and Development Journal* of September 1976, "Separating the Amateurs from the Pros in Training":

> When I first got into training in 1935 the assumption was made that one didn't need to have qualifications much different from any other administrative role to do a good job as a training director. The role was defined essentially as that of managing the logistics of organizing and operating activities for various groupings of individuals. If one had any experience in planning schedules, building budgets, getting out promotional materials, hiring people, and filling out reports, he [there were no she's at that time] was qualified. We were all amateurs. . .But no longer. During the intervening years there has been a body of knowledge about how adults learn and a body of technology for facilitating that learning that is changing the role of trainer and requiring that he or she know things few teachers know and probably none of his or her associates knows. The trainer must know *andragogy* —the art and science of helping adults learn—and how it differs from *pedagogy* —the art and science of teaching youth. . .This is the mark of the pro.

I am assuming that all who are reading this chapter want to be pros.

2. *Adults have a deep need to be self-directing.* In fact, the psychological definition of "adult" is one who has achieved a self-concept of being in charge of his or her own life, of being responsible for making his or her own decisions and living with the consequences. At the point at which we arrive at this self-concept we develop a deep psychological need to be seen and treated by others as being capable of taking responsibility for ourselves. This fact creates a special problem for us in adult education and training in that although adults may be completely self-directing in most aspects of their lives (as full-time workers, spouses, parents, and voting citizens), when they enter a program labeled "education" or "training," they hark back to their conditioning in school and college and put on their hats of dependency, fold their arms, sit back, and say, "Teach me." The problem arises if we assume that this is really where they are coming from and start teaching them as if they were children. We then put them into an inner conflict between this intellectual map—learner equals dependent—and their deeper psychological need to be self-directing. And the way most people deal with psychological conflict is to seek to withdraw from the situation causing it. To resolve this problem adult educators have been developing strategies for helping adults to make a quick transition from seeing themselves as being dependent learners to becoming

self-directed learners. My little paperback book, *Self-Directed Learning: A Guide for Learners and Teachers*[7] describes some of these strategies.

3. *Adults have a greater volume and different quality of experience than youth.* Except in certain pathological circumstances, the longer we live the more experience and more varied experience we accumulate. The greater reservoir of experience affects learning in several ways:

- Adults bring into a learning situation a background of experience that is itself a rich resource for many kinds of learning for themselves and for others. Hence, in adult education, the greater emphasis on the use of experiential learning—techniques, such as discussion methods and problem-solving exercises, that tap into the accumulated knowledge and skills of the learners, or techniques, such as simulation exercises and field experiences, that provide learners with experiences from which they can learn by analyzing them.

- Adults have a broader base of experience to which to attach new ideas and skills and give them richer meaning. The more explicit these relationships (between the old and the new) are made—through discussion and reflection—the deeper and more permanent the learning will be (see Boud et al., 1985).

- It is predictable that a group of adults, especially if there is an age mix, will have a wider range of differences in background, interests, ability, and learning styles than is true of any group of youth. Adult groups are heterogeneous groups. Accordingly, increasing emphasis is being placed in adult education on individualized learning and instruction, through contract learning, self-paced multimedia modules, learning resource centers, and other means.

- But there is a potentially negative consequence of this fact of greater experience—it tends to cause people to develop habits of thought and biases, to make presuppositions, to be less open to new ideas. (How often have you heard somebody react to a new proposal, "It won't work. We tried it five years ago and it didn't work"?) Some techniques have been developed to try to counter this tendency—sensitivity training, open-mindedness scales, creativity exercises, and others.

But the difference in quality of experience adults bring with them is also significant. Few youth have had the experience of being full-time workers, spouses, parents, voting citizens, organizational leaders, and of performing other adult roles. Most adults have. Accordingly, adults have a different perspective on experience: it is their chief source of self-identity. To youth, experience is something that happens to them. But adults define themselves in terms of their unique experiences. An adult's experience is who he or she is. So if adults' experience is not respected and valued, is not made use of as a resource for learning, they experience this omission not as a rejection of their experience but as a rejection of them as persons. Evidence indicates that this phenomenon is especially characteristic of undereducated adults.

4. *Adults become ready to learn when they experience in their life situation a need to know or be able to do in order to perform more effectively and satisfyingly.* The pedagogical model makes the opposite assumption—that people become ready to learn what they are told by some authority figure (teacher, trainer, boss), that they have to learn because it's good for them or the authority figure demands it. Adults experience "being told" as infringing on their adultness—their need to be self-directing—and tend to react with resentment, defensiveness, and resistance. Adults learn best when they choose voluntarily to make a commitment to learn.

This principle is often difficult to apply in business and industry, since, rightly or wrongly, employer-provided training tends to be perceived as employer-required training. Indeed, often attendance is compulsory. When I sense that there are people in one of my activities who have been "sent," I do two things to try to reduce the resistance it induces. First, I make it public that I realize that there may be some people in the room who aren't there because they want to be, and that I am sorry about this because it tends to get in the way of learning. But, I explain, there is nothing I or you can do to change this at this time, so let's accept it as a given and see if we can't have a pleasant and profitable time together anyway. More importantly, I try to involve them in discovering for themselves—through participating in simulation exercises, self-diagnosing their learning needs through competency-based rating scales, or observing role models of superior performance—the value for their own lives of learning what the program has to offer.

One of the richest sources of readiness to learn is the transitions people make in moving from one developmental stage to another. As Havighurst[8] points out, as we confront having to perform the development tasks of the next stage of development, we become ready to learn those tasks; and the peak of our desire to learn them he calls the "teachable moment." A typical sequence of developmental tasks in work life would be (1) to begin a process of career planning, (2) to acquire the competencies required for a first job, (3) to get a first job, (4) to become oriented to the first job, (5) to master the competencies required to perform excellently in the first job, (6) to plan and prepare for a next-step-up job, and so through a cycle of career development. The final developmental task would be to prepare for retirement from a career. A main implication of this concept is the importance of timing our educational offerings to coincide with the worker's developmental tasks. Indeed, some of the great goofs of training have occurred as a result of forcing people into training activities before they are ready for them—as, for example, pushing people into supervisory training programs before they feel they have mastered the work they are to be supervising.

5. *Adults enter into a learning experience with a task-centered (or problem-centered or life-centered) orientation to learning.* Children and youth have been conditioned by their school experience to have a subject-centered orientation to learning; they see learning as a process of acquiring the subject matter necessary to pass tests. Once that is done, their mission is accomplished. This difference in orientation calls for different ways of organizing the content to be learned. In traditional education the content is organized into subject-matter courses—such as Composition I, in which the rules of grammar are memorized, Composition II, in which sentence and paragraph structures are memorized, and Composition III, in which rules of outlining, syntax, and the like are memorized. In adult education the content is organized around life tasks: Composition I becomes "Writing Better Business Letters," Composition II becomes "Writing for Pleasure and Profit," and Composition III becomes "Improving Your Professional Communications."

I have found that this principle is commonly violated in orientation programs, in which the sequence of topics might be (1) The History and Philosophy of XYZ Co., (2) The Market and Products of XYZ Co., (3) The Personnel Policies of XYZ Co., and so on, instead of starting with a census of problems and concerns, along with problems and concerns of the organization and trainer. But I strongly urge trainers to review their entire programs and restructure the units around tasks, problems, or life situations. The participants will see the program as much more relevant to their lives and they will learn the content with the intention of *using* it.

6. *Adults are motivated to learn by both extrinsic and intrinsic motivators.* One of the most significant findings of the research into adult learning is that adults are motivated to learn. Allen Tough,[4] the researcher who has to date accumulated the largest volume of information about how adults learn in normal life, has yet to find a subject in his research who had not engaged in at least one major learning project (a mininum of 7 hours of intentional learning) in the preceding year, and the average number of learning projects was over seven. The problem (and our

challenge) is that they may not be motivated to learn what we want to teach them; hence the importance of following through on the first assumption above—developing a need to know.

The pedagogical model makes the assumption that children and youth are motivated primarily, if not exclusively, by extrinsic motivators—pressures from parents and teachers, competition for grades, diplomas, and the like. Adult learners respond to extrinsic motivators—wage raises, promotion, better working conditions, and the like—up to the point that they are reasonably well satisfied. But the more potent and persistent motivators are such intrinsic motivators as the need for self-esteem, broadened responsibilities, power, achievement, and the like Wlodkowski[9]). The message here, as I read it, is to appeal to both the desire for job advancement and life enrichment in promoting your programs.

Implications for Practice

The assumptions of pedagogy and andragogy have a number of implications for what we do as human resource developers. One basic implication is the importance of making a clear distinction between a *content plan* and a *process design*.

When planning an educational activity, the pedagog thinks in terms of drafting content plan, and he has to answer only four questions to come up with a plan: 1) What content needs to be covered (the assumption being that they will only learn what he transmits, and therefore he has to cover it *all* in the classroom)? So he draws up a long laundry list of content terms. (2) How can this content be organized into manageable units (1-hour, 3-hour, etc., units)? So he clusters the content items into manageable units. (3) How can these content units be transmitted in a logical sequence (rather than the sequence in which the learners are ready to learn it)? So he arranges the units in a sequence according to chronology (history, literature, political science) or from simple to complex science, math). (4) What would be the most effective methods for transmitting this content? If unit 1 is heavily loaded with information, the method of choice will probably be lecture and assigned reading; if unit 2 involves skill performance, the method of choice will probably be demonstration by him and drill, drill, drill by them. By answering these four questions, he ends up with a content-transmission plan.

The andragog, on the other hand, when she (get the gender change?) undertakes to plan an educational activity, sees her task as being twofold: first, and primarily, to design and manage a process for facilitating the acquisition of content by the learners; and only secondarily to serve as a content resource (she perceives that there are many content resources in addition to her own—peers, supervisors, specialists, and a variety of materials in the learner's environment, and that an important part of her responsibility is to keep up to date as to what these resources are and to link learners with them). So the andragog has to answer a very different set of questions to come up with a process design. (Notice that it is not a matter of the pedagog's being concerned with content and the andragog's not being concerned with it; rather, the pedagog is concerned with transmitting the content and the andragog is concerned with facilitating the acquisition of the content by the learners.)

The questions raised by the andragog have to do with implementing the following elements of an andragogical process design:

1. *Climate setting.* A prerequisite for effective learning to take place is the establishment of a climate that is conducive to learning. Two broad aspects of climate must be considered: institutional climate and the climate of training situation.

Among the questions that might be raised regarding institutional climate are: Do the policy statements of the institution convey a deep commitment to the value of human resources development in the accomplishment of the mission of the institution? Does the budget of the institution provide adequate resources for the support of significant human resources development (HRD) efforts? Is the HRD staff involved in the decision-making process as regards personnel policies and programs? Are adequate physical facilities for HRD activities provided? Does the reward system of the institution give credit for the achievement of personal growth on the part of individuals and their supervisors?

As regards setting a climate in a training situation, these are the conditions that I think characterize a climate that is conducive to learning, and the questions that might be asked in creating a process design to achieve those conditions:

- A climate of mutual respect. I believe that people are more open to learning if they feel respected. If they feel that they are being talked down to, embarrassed, or otherwise denigrated, their energy is diverted from learning to dealing with these feelings. I do several things to try to bring such a climate into being: First, I provide name tents—5 by 8 cards with their names printed on them with bold felt pens—so that I (and they) can start calling on them by name. Then I put them into small groups of five or six persons (preferably sitting around tables) and ask them to share their "whats" (their work roles); their "whos" (one thing about themselves that will enable others to see them as unique human beings); any special knowledge, skill, or other resources they would be willing to share with others; and any questions, problems, or concerns they are hoping will be dealt with in this program. I ask one person in each group to volunteer to give a high-point summary of this information about each group. I feel that this hour is the most important hour in the whole training event, since it starts the process of creating a climate that is conducive to learning.

- A climate of collaborativeness rather than competitiveness. The above sharing exercise causes the participants to start seeing themselves as mutual helpers rather than rivals. For many kinds of learning, the richest resources are within their peers, hence the importance of making these resources available.

- A climate of supportiveness rather than judgmentalness. I think I largely set this climate by being supportive in my own behavior, but the opening exercise also tends to establish peer-support relationships.

- A climate of mutual trust. In order to reduce the instinctive mistrust with which people typically react to authority figures, in presenting myself I emphasize who I am as a human being rather than as an expert, and I urge them to call me by my first name.

- A climate of fun. Learning should be one of the most joyful things we do, and so I do everything I can to make the experience enjoyable. I make a lot of use of spontaneous (not canned) humor.

- A human climate. Learning is a human activity; training is for dogs and horses. So I try to establish a climate in which people feel that they are being treated as human beings, not objects. I try to care for their human needs—comfortable chairs, frequent breaks, adequate ventilation and lighting, availability of coffee or cold drinks, and the like.

The first question an andragog asks in constructing a process design, therefore, is "What procedures should I use with this particular group to bring these climate conditions into being?"

2. *Creating a mechanism for mutual planning.*   A basic law of human nature is at work here: people tend to feel committed to a decision or activity to the extent that

they have participated in making the decision or planning the activity. The reverse is even more true: people tend to feel uncommitted to the extent they feel that the decision or activity is being imposed on them without their having a chance to influence it.

In planning a total program—all the courses, workshops, seminars—of an institution, the usual mechanism is a planning committee, council, or task force. To be effective, it is critical that it be representative of all the constituencies the program is designed to serve. (See Houle[10] for helpful guidelines.)

For a particular program, such as a course or workshop, I prefer to use teams of participants, with each team having responsibility for planning one unit of the program.

The fullest participation in planning is achieved, however, through the use of learning contracts, in which case the learners develop their own learning plans (see Knowles[7, 11, 12]).

The second question the andragog answers in developing a process model, therefore, is "What procedures will I use to involve the learners in planning?"

3. *Diagnosing the participant's learning needs.* The HRD literature is rich in techniques trainers can use for assessing training needs as perceived by individuals, organizations, and communities (Boone,[13] Brown and Wedel,[14] Davis and McCallon,[15] Knowles,[16] McKenzie and McKinley,[17] Mager and Pipe[18]). These needs are the appropriate source of goals for a total program (Knowles,[16] pp. 120–126). But in a particular training event involving particular individuals, a learning need is not a need unless so perceived by the learner. One of the highest arts in training is creating the conditions and providing the tools that will enable learners to become aware of their training needs and therefore translate them into learning needs. A new body of technology is being developed for facilitating this process, with emphasis on such self-diagnostic procedures as simulation exercises, assessment centers, competency-based rating scales, and videotape feedback (Knowles,[16] Wlodkowski[9]).

So the third set of questions the andragog asks in constructing a process design is "What procedures will I use in helping the participants diagnose their own learning needs?"

4. *Translating learning needs into objectives.* Having diagnosed their learning needs, participants now face the task of translating them into learning objectives—positive statements of directions of growth. Some kinds of learning (such as machine operation) lend themselves to objectives stated as terminal behaviors that can be observed and measured (Mager[19]). Others (such as decision-making ability) are so complex that they are better stated in terms of direction of improvement (Knowles,[11] pp. 128–130).

So the fourth question the andragog asks is "What procedures can I use for helping participants translate their learning needs into learning objectives?" (For suggested procedures, see Knowles,[7] pp. 25–28.)

5. *Designing and managing a pattern of learning experiences.* Having formulated the learning objectives, the next task of the trainer and the participants is to design a plan for achieving them. This plan will include identifying the resources most relevant to each objective and the most effective strategies for utilizing these resources. Such a plan is likely to include a mix of total group experiences (including input by the trainer), subgroup (learning-teaching team) experiences, and individual learning projects. A key criterion for assessing the excellence of such a design is, how deeply involved are the participants in the mutual process of designing and managing a pattern of learning experiences?

So the fifth question the andragog asks is "What procedures can I use for involving the learners with me in designing and managing a pattern of learning experiences? (For suggested procedures, see Knowles,[16] pp. 235–247.)

6. Evaluating the extent to which the objectives have been achieved. In many situations institutional policies require some sort of "objective" (quantitative) measure of learning outcomes (Kirkpatrick,[20] Scriven,[21] Stufflebeam[22]).But the recent trend in evaluation research has been to place increasing emphasis on "subjective" (qualitative) evaluation—finding out what is really happening inside the participants and how differently they are performing in life (Cronbach,[23] Guba and Lincoln,[24] Patton[25, 26, 27, 28]). In any case, the andragogical model requires that the learners be actively involved in the process of evaluating their learning outcomes (Knowles[12]).

The sixth question, therefore, that the andragog asks is "What procedures can I use to involve the learners responsibly in evaluating the accomplishment of their learning objectives?"

By answering these six sets of questions, the learning facilitator emerges with a *process design* —a set of procedures for facilitating the acquisition of content by the learners.

But Not Andragogy *versus* Pedagogy

When I first began conceptualizing the andragogical model I perceived it as being antithetical to the pedagogical model. In fact, in the book in which I first presented the andragogical model in detail, *The Modern Practice of Adult Education,*[16] I used the subtitle "Andragogy versus Pedagogy." During the next few years I began getting reports from elementary and secondary school teachers saying that they had been experimenting with applying the andragogical model in their practice and finding that children and youth also learn better in many situations when they are involved in sharing responsibility. And I got reports from teachers of adults that they had found situations in which they had to use the pedagogical model. So when I revised the book in 1980 I used the subtitle, "From Pedagogy to Andragogy."

As I see it now, whereas for 13 centuries we had only one model of assumptions and strategies regarding education—the pedagogical model, now we have two models. So we have the responsibility now of checking out which set of assumptions is realistic in which situation, and using the strategies of whichever model is appropriate for that situation. In general, the pedagogical assumptions are likely to be realistic in those situations in which the content is totally strange to the learners and in which precise psychomotor skills are involved, as in machine operation. But even in these situations, elements of the andragogical model, such as climate setting, might enhance the learning. And I use elements of the pedagogical model, such as reinforcement, in my andragogical practice. So my stance now is not either-or, but both—as appropriate to the situation.

Preparing for the Future

In the third quarter of this century we accumulated more research-based knowledge about adults as learners than was known in all of previous history. In the past decade that body of knowledge has at least doubled. I am confident that the present body of knowledge will at least double in the next decade. My colleagues in the biological sciences assure me that their disciplines will contribute some of the major breakthroughs, especially as regards the physiological, chemical, and neurological (such as right-brain, left-brain) processes involved in learning. The technology of making resources for learning available is already in a state of revolution, especially with the development of computers and communications satellites. My own conviction is that by the end of this century most educational services will be being delivered electronically to learners at their convenience in terms of time, place, and pace.

What a challenge we in human resources development face if we are to avoid the obsolescence of our work force. I can foresee this challenge requiring that we reconceptualize a corporation (or any social system) as a system of learning resources as well as production and service-delivering system and redefine the role of HRD away from that of managing the logistics of conducting training activities to that of managing a system of learning resources. We would then ask a very different set of questions from those we have traditionally asked in training and development. The first question would be, "What are all of the resources available in this system for the growth and development of people?" Then we would have to ask, "How well are these resources being utilized now, and how might they be more effectively utilized?" We might come up with a chart that looks something like this:

Managing a System of Learning Resources

Resources	Strategies for Enhancing Their Utilization
Scheduled training activities (courses, workshops, seminars)	Revise time schedule so as to make them more accessible to employees
	Revise programs so as to make them more congruent with adult learning principles
	Train presenters in adult education methods
Line supervisors and managers (the most ubiquitous resources for day-in-and-day-out employee development)	Build responsibility for people development into their job descriptions
	Build into supervisory and management training programs sessions on principles of adult learning and skills in facilitating learning
	Give credit in personnel appraisals for performance as people developers
Libraries, media centers (printed materials, audiovisual and multimedia programs)	Arrange to be open during hours accessible to all employees
	Make information about resources available to all employees
	Provide help in using them
Individual employees, specialists, and technicians (many people in organizations have knowledge and skills others would like to learn)	Store this information in a data bank and make it available to employees through an educational brokering center
Community resources (courses, workshops, specialists, etc., in colleges and universities, community organizations, professional associations, commercial providers, etc.)	Include in the above data bank

If nothing more is done than what has been described so far, the quality of human resource development in a corporation would probably be improved. But learning would still be episodic, fragmented, and disconnected. It can be made more systematic, incremental, and continuous through the use of learning contracts or development plans (Knowles[12]).

A contract simply specifies what an individual's objectives are for a given learning project, what resources will be used in fulfilling the objectives, what evidence will be collected to demonstrate that the objectives have been fulfilled, and how that evidence will be validated. In one corporation the contract is negotiated between the individual and the HRD staff; in another, it is between the individual and his or her supervisor; in another, it is between the individual and a team consisting of the supervisor, a representative of the HRD department, and a peer. Progress toward fulfilling the contract is monitored, and the evidence is validated by these same parties. Several corporations with a management-by-objectives program have incorporated the contracting process into the MBO process.

Several things happen when a systems approach is adopted. A heavier responsibility is placed on the line supervisors and managers for the development of their personnel than traditionally has been the case. This integrates the HRD function more closely with the operating function, and line supervisors and managers derive added self-esteem and job satisfaction from their developmental role once they have become adept at it.

Employees find that their personal and professional development are more integrated with their work life. A much wider ranger of resources for learning are available to them, and employees are more directly involved in planning and achieving their own development—adding to their self-esteem and satisfaction.

For HRD professionals, the systems approach represents a major shift in role. They are less concerned with planning, scheduling, and conducting instructional activities, and are more concerned with managing a system. One of their major responsibilities is to serve as consultants to the line—a closer and more functional relationship, and one more central to the operation of the business.

How much more fulfilling a role!

References

1. Lindeman, Eduard C., *The Meaning of Adult Education*, New Republic, New York, 1926.

2. Houle, Cyril O., *The Inquiring Mind*, University of Wisconsin Press, Madison, WI, 1961.

3. Tough, Allen, *Learning without a Teacher*, Ontario Institute for Education, Toronto, 1967

4. Tough, Allen, *The Adult's Learning Projects*, 2d ed., Ontario Institute for Education, Toronto, 1979.

5. Peters, John M., and S. G. Gordon, *Adult Learning Projects: A Study of Adult Learning in Urban and Rural Tennessee*, University of Tennessee, Knoxville, 1974.

6. Penland, Patrick R., *Individual Self-Planned Learning in America*, Final Report of Project 475AH60058 under grant No. G007603327, U.S. Office of Education, Office of Libraries and Learning Resources. Unpublished manuscript, Graduate School of Library and Information Sciences, University of Pittsburgh, 1977. Available as ERIC document. Also available from the University of Pittsburgh bookstore under the title *Self-Planned Learning in America*.

7. Knowles, Malcolm S., *Self-Directed Learning: A Guide for Learners and Teachers*, Cambridge Book Co., New York, 1975.

8. Havighurst, Robert, *Developmental Tasks and Education*, 2d ed., David McKay, New York, 1970.

9. Wlodkowski, Raymond J., *Enhancing Adult Motivation to Learn*, Jossey-Bass, San Francisco, 1985.

10. Houle, Cyril O., *The Effective Board*, Association Press, New York, 1960.

11. Knowles, Malcolm S., *The Adult Learner: A Neglected Species*, 3d ed., Gulf Publishing Co., 1984.

12. Knowles, Malcom S., *Andragogy in Action*, Jossey-Bass, San Francisco, 1984.

13. Boone, Edgar J., ed., *Serving Personal and Community Needs through Adult Education*, Jossey-Bass, San Francisco, 1980.

14. Brown, F. Gerald, and Kenneth R. Wedel, *Assessing Training Needs*, National Training and Development Service Press, Washington, DC, 1974.

15. Davis, Larry N., and Earl McCallon, *Planning, Conducting, Evaluating Workshops*, Learning Concepts, Austin, TX, 1974.

16. Knowles, Malcolm S., *The Modern Practice of Adult Education*, 2d ed., Cambridge Book Co., New York, 1980.

17. McKenzie, Leon, and John McKinley, ed., "Adult Education: The Diagnostic Procedure," *Bulletin of the School of Education*, Vol. 49, No. 5, Indiana University, Bloomington, 1973.

18. Mager, Robert, and Peter Pipe, *Analyzing Performance Problems*, Fearon Publishers, Belmont, CA, 1970.

19. Mager, Robert, *Preparing Instructional Objectives*, Fearon Publishers, Belmont, CA, 1962.

20. Kirkpatrick, Donald L., *Evaluating Training Programs*, ASTD, Washington, DC, 1975.

21. Scriven, N., ed., *Evaluation in Education*, McCutchan Publishing Corp., Berkeley, CA, 1974.

22. Stufflebeam, Daniel, et al., *Educational Evaluation and Decision Making*, Peacock Publishers, Itasca, IL, 1971.

23. Cronbach, Lee J., et al., *Toward Reform of Program Evaluation: Aims, Methods and Institutional Arrangements*, Jossey-Bass, San Francisco, 1980.

24. Guba, Egon G., and Yvonne S. Lincoln, *Effective Evaluation: Improving the Usefulness of Evaluation Results through Responsive and Naturalistic Approaches*, Jossey-Bass, San Francisco, 1981.

25. Patton, Michael Q., *Utilization-Focused Evaluation*, Sage Publications, Beverly Hills, CA, 1978.

26. Patton, Michael Q., *Qualitative Evaluation Methods*, Sage Publications, Beverly Hills, CA, 1980.

27. Patton, Michael Q., *Creative Evaluation*, Sage Publications, Beverly Hills, CA, 1981.

28. Patton, Michael Q., *Practical Evaluation*, Sage Publications, Beverly Hills, CA, 1982.

Additional Reading

Boud, David, Rosemary Keogh, and David Walker, eds., *Reflection: Turning Experience into Learning*, Nichols Publishing Co., New York, 1985.

Cross, K. Patricia, *Adults as Learners*, Jossey-Bass, San Francisco, 1981.

Knox, Alan B., *Adult Development and Learning*, Jossey-Bass, San Francisco, 1977.

10

Group Norms: Their Influence on Training

Robert F. Allen

Robert F. Allen is the president of Human Resources Institute of Morristown, New Jersey. He is also a professor of psychology and policy sciences in the graduate division of Kean College of New Jersey. He is the author of more than 200 books, articles, and films on personal, organizational, and community change. His three most recent books are Lifegain: A Culture-Based Approach to Positive Health (Appleton-Century-Crofts, 1981), Beat the System: A Way to Create More Human Environments (McGraw-Hill, 1980), and The Organizational Unconscious (Prentice-Hall, 1982). Dr. Allen is a fellow of the American Psychological Association and the Menninger Foundation. He is the president of Healthy America, a national coalition for health promotion. He is also a marathon runner and an award-winning poet and film maker. His film "Toward a Caring Community" received an award from the New York Film Festival. Dr. Allen has pioneered in the development of the normative systems culture-based approach to change. He and his staff at the Human Resources Institute have been responsible for over 600 broad-scale organizational and community change programs over the last two decades. His programs are being used in hospitals, businesses, union organizations, colleges and universities, and communities throughout the United States and in western Europe.

Norms of group behavior, or the expected behaviors of the individuals within an established group setting, are major factors in determining how that group performs. The effect of group norms needs to be taken into account in the design and implementation of training efforts intended to improve organizational performance. These norms, often elusive and unrecognized, have tremendous power

They can aid and abet, or drastically undermine, the work of the professional trainer.

This potent behavioral force is the product of the organizational culture itself. The culture might be a store, an office, a factory, a school—or, more correctly, the groups of human beings who work there. A basic understanding of the teaching role of this organizational structure is an important and frequently overlooked ingredient in the development of training strategies. Many, many programs have been rendered ineffectual because they have come into contact with the *real* training being carried out by the day-to-day culture in the organization. What the culture supports and what it fails to support, and often actually attacks, provide the real curriculum for learning, regardless of what is "taught" in the seminar, class, or training session.

Astute trainers will be aware of the potent teaching force of the culture and will use it to make their programs work. They will be aware that they cannot hope to be successful if they are working at cross-purposes with the "shadow" training being carried out by the powerful yet elusive norms of the group.

How Does the Culture Teach?

A clear understanding of how the culture goes about its business quietly, imposing its insidious power over us, is of prime importance to the professional trainer. It behooves those of us concerned with organizational norms, effectiveness, and change to understand thoroughly what norms are, how they operate in a culture, and how they can be changed. Our experience has been that when norms are considered, understood, and dealt with creatively and systematically, training programs can and will prove successful.

What Are Norms?

What the culture supports is passed on by examples set in people's behavior. The expected or anticipated ways of behaving within a group are called *norms*. A norm is an idea that exists in the minds of members of the group regarding the behavior that will be *expected*. The norms form a code of behavior established for the group, and support ways of behaving that determine so much of what we do.

Whether a norm is a matter of fashion (hairstyle) or a tradition (giving Christmas presents) or an expression of value ("do your own thing"), it must have group support to exist. Support may be in the form of encouragement from group members to adhere to the norm or in the form of rewards to members who do. The group has power to enforce its norms by applying pressure on members to conform. Sometimes it is only through a raised eyebrow ("I wonder where he got such a crazy idea?"), while at other times it is much more explicit, "I don't think he would be happy working in this company."

This power is evident when a new behavior is taught and then comes into conflict with an old, established behavior. Experience shows that the old norm nearly always wins out.

Norms in Conflict

Let us look at two conflicting behaviors in an organization. One has been taught in a training session; the other had been taught by the culture.

A young lady—Sally Jenkins—accepts employment as a cashier in the XYZ Supermarket Company. This company prides itself on the quality of its cashier training program, particularly in the area of customer courtesy. The program itself is well designed, is 4 days in length, costs a good deal of money, is led by skillful trainers, and uses the best equipment and best procedures possible. Sally Jenkins has enjoyed her training experience and feels that she has learned a great deal about customer service. Her first day on the job, however, leads her to question what she has learned. It is 10:30 a.m. that first day, and things have been going rather well. Two customers are lined up at Sally's checkout counter, and Jane, an experienced checker from the next register, calls over: "Sally! It's time for coffee. Let's go."

Sally looks at the two customers, turns to Jane, and says, "Jane, you go ahead. I'll finish up with these customers and be with you in a jiffy." But Jane's reply puzzles her because it contradicts what she has learned in the training program.

"Look, Sally, around here when it's coffee break time, it's coffee break time. They can find another line."

Sally is caught in a dilemma. If she follows Jane's suggestion, she will be ignoring what she has been taught, she will disappoint two customers, and possibly she will also violate her own value system. If she does not go along, however, she may not receive a very friendly reception from her fellow checkers when she does take her break. She may not be invited to go to lunch or to join the bowling league. Sally may even appear on the turnover statistics in a few days, stating: "Somehow, this just isn't my kind of place."

The setting may change, but the problem of conflicting norms is the same. The expected behaviors of the culture form the training curriculum for the employee within the company, whether he or she is the newest recruit or the president of the corporation. Training programs are valuable and successful only to the extent that they are skillfully used to seed new norms or to reinforce existing norms within the organization. In some cases training programs actually ask people to behave in ways that would be harmful to them if they were to follow instructions. Consider the young man who has been told in a sensitivity training session to be open, direct, and honest in providing feedback to his boss when this is contrary to the norms of his boss and his department. Perhaps it is fortunate that people don't always follow the instructions that we give them in training sessions.

What Influences Norm Development?

The development of norms in organizations is affected by a number of key influences. They must be considered by the trainer if the training program is to be effective.

It is important for trainers to see how norms get established, for therein lies the answer to changing them. Most norms are established in a subtle fashion. They come into being over a period of time without anything actually being said, so that members of the group are hardly aware that the norms exist. They just become "the way things are done around here."

Following are some of the more important influences on norm development.

Leadership Commitment

One of the major factors shaping norms in an organization is the level of leadership commitment. This needs to be more than commitment to the training program; it must be commitment to the *desired behavior*. Unfortunately, too often a behavior like "teamwork" that is taught in a training program has little or no real commitment from the organizational leadership. In such a situation the teamwork norm may be verbally espoused, but go no further. However, when leadership commitment to a behavior is visible and active and is backed up by realistic supports, the desired behavior is more likely to be reinforced and maintained.

The supervisor is a key to an effective norm change program. What he or she supports is likely to be reinforced in an organization, while what he or she downplays or opposes has little chance for continuing growth. One of the most important responsibilities of a trainer is to see that the supervisor is fully "on board" before the training is begun.

Modeling Behavior

Leaders in groups often serve as models, and others readily copy their behavior. In this way, norms are established or reinforced. Take, for example, the ease with which a "coming in late" norm can be established. If one person comes in late habitually, other employees will begin to think, "If he can get away with it, I can too." When the person modeling the behavior has any special status—say it is the boss—the behavior will quickly be accepted as bearing the stamp of approval, and a norm will be well on the way to being established. If leaders wish to institute positive norms or to reduce the impact of negative behaviors, the tremendous influence of modeling behavior cannot be overlooked.

Information Feedback

Norms tend to be most readily reinforced in an organization where information feedback is provided. Where there is little information flow, norms tend to be rapidly forgotten. If productivity and cost-effectiveness are regularly and widely communicated within a positive environment, norms relating to them are likely to be developed and maintained. Where employees and their managers are kept apprised of their success or lack of success in a given area, norms within that area are likely to be reinforced.

Trainers should also see that current information systems are examined to determine the normative impact of information being transmitted. Sometimes comparative ratings on individual and department sales foster competition—in conflict with the teamwork between departments that the organization is trying to encourage. When these reports are modified, cooperation between departments will be facilitated, and norms involving joint problem-solving efforts are more likely to be developed.

Individuals need to have the necessary information to support change efforts. Adequate information flow about important decisions is a requirement for successful change.

After a training program is underway, it is essential to have feedback on the progress being made in the change effort. Those involved should be told how they are doing, for knowledge of improvement is a powerful reinforcement. The trainer can help this flow of information by setting up instruments of evaluation concerning member behavior as it affects desired norms.

Recognition and Reward

Behavior that is rewarded will tend to be repeated. If the reward gives satisfaction, or is continued, the behavior will come to be performed regularly and thus become a norm for the group in question.

The "payoff" for a desired behavior can take the form of supervisory acknowledgment and praise or of administrative decisions affecting pay, promotion, and other benefits.

We need to answer these questions: What do we reward? What are the rewards? Are positive behaviors being given positive reinforcement? Do we punish people for behaving the way we want them to? Are people being inadvertently punished for doing the right thing?

Knowledge and Skill Development

Nothing will wipe out a norm more rapidly than lack of knowledge and skills necessary to develop it. Witness the supervisor who has not been helped to develop the skills of leadership. As a result, the tendency is to downplay the importance of these skills within the organization. Too often we set up a situation where people are encouraged to develop a commitment to new norms but are not provided with an opportunity to learn the skills necessary for their implementation. The development of improved job performance norms will be of little value if the people concerned with these norms are not given the opportunity to acquire the necessary job performance skills.

Orientation

The time when a person joins a company or accepts a new position is one of their most teachable moments. However, what passes for orientation at this time is often nothing more than a review of company benefits, a routine rundown of the rules, and a halfhearted pep talk. The orientation program can, however, be utilized to introduce the positive norms existing in the organization as well as the organization's norm goals.

Work Group Support

In carrying out norm change programs, attention should be paid to influential team members and informal leaders, for they will be crucial to the group's acceptance of the norm, via their modeling behavior.

Through work groups, a seeding process can enhance norm development and change. For their initial placement, employees may be seeded into work groups that have strong positive norms. Often what happens is that the new employee is taken aside by an old hand and told "how things are really done around here."

In addition, positive employees can be "seeded" into work groups with poor norms. This is most effective when the group has undertaken a norm change effort. Otherwise, the "positive" employee, because he or she is not given support, may be influenced by the "negative" majority.

Norm Influences as Primary Trainers

These influences are the primary "trainers" in an organization, and good use of the knowledge of norm development and maintenance will be invaluable to the trainer.

None of what we have said here denigrates the value of a well-planned, well-executed training program. It points instead to the need for such training programs to be supported in the day-to-day experience of people on the job. A good training program can help seed new norms and refine old ones.

The Normative Systems Approach

This focus on building a supportive environment has caused us to use the term *normative systems* to describe our particular approach to training and organizational development. This approach stresses the key influence of norms on personal and organizational effectiveness. It seeks to increase people's understanding of the influence of culture upon their lives and helps them to devise ways of making certain that the cultures they are part of reflect their highest goals and aspirations. Over the past 20 years the normative systems approach to training has been applied to over 600 different change settings ranging from corporate offices to industrial plants and from colleges and universities to police departments and hospitals.

Possible Applications

There are five major areas of application:

Introducing New Organizational Programs. "How can we get this new program off the ground?"

"How can I successfully introduce this new training concept?"

When an organizational program is being introduced, it is important to realize that its success depends almost entirely upon its ability to develop new norms or ways of behaving within the organization. A management by objectives program that remains "only a program" tends to use up large amounts of organizational time and energy, while contributing little to behavioral change. When a new program seems to be hard to get going, chances are that old norms are getting in the way and need to be addressed.

Strengthening Existing Programs. "How can we get the men to wear the proper safety equipment?"

"How can our orientation for new employees be made to stick?"

Sometimes programs that already exist within an organization are really not doing very well. Usually the failure can be traced to their inability to modify existing norms. We saw this in our example of the new checker in the supermarket. Here we can see the importance of modeling behavior. If influential members of the work group are practicing the desired norm, it will be picked up by new people coming in.

Many organizations have long-standing programs that look well on paper but never have really been practiced by the people. With a good understanding of the dynamics of norm change, the trainer can strengthen and make otherwise "unworkable" programs workable.

Solving Perplexing Human Factor Problems. "How can we reduce absenteeism?"

"Why won't our employees work harder?"

Many times our most perplexing human factor problems are deeply embedded in norms. In a warehouse setting, low productivity may be supported by the culture.

The person who breaks this norm and strives for greater productivity may be in serious difficulty with fellow workers. Examining the norms and norm influences will help us deal with this problem.

Launching New Work Groups or Work Teams.   "How can we make this new factory, store, or department even better than those we've had in the past?"

A golden opportunity exists for seeding positive new norms at the time a new work group or work team is being established. Positive employees can be seeded into the new work groups. Training directed at on-the-job teams can help work groups get off to a strong start, with desired norms a part of the initial process.

It is important to remember that a short time after the new unit begins operation, it will have its own set of norms. To a considerable extent, the initial developmental process will determine whether the new norms will be positive or negative. It has been our experience that under these conditions new employees will choose positive norms if they have an opportunity to consider the alternatives.

A Total System of Organizational Intervention and Change.   "How can we increase the effectiveness of our total organization?"

By viewing the organization as a total culture, it is often possible for the training specialist to assist the organization's members in bringing about comprehensive and sustained change at a number of different organizational levels and at a number of key organizational pressure points. Such broad-scale organizational development effects usually begin at the top of the organization and continue downward through each of the organizational levels and departments. In such a process, the purpose is to help people modify the cultures of which they are a part so that these cultures can more accurately reflect individual and organizational needs and aspirations.

Normative Change: A Four-Phase Process

The normative change process, whether concerned with a single training intervention or a comprehensive organizational change program, makes use of the same four-phase process that is shown in Fig. 10-1.

This four-phase change process begins with an analysis and objective setting phase followed immediately by a systems introduction phase and a systems implementation phase, and finally, by carefully integrated evaluation and renewal activities which allow for the ongoing recycling of the project on a continuing basis.

These four phases are in turn undergirded by certain key implementation

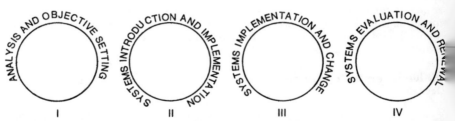

Figure 10-1. A simplified version of the basic normative systems model.

principles. Although their emphasis may vary from program to program, there are nine important principles that are usually involved. When effectively implemented, these become a way of life within the organization and serve as ongoing criteria that can be used to determine the appropriateness of various actions being considered.

General Principles of Cultural Change

- Involving people in the problems and programs affecting them
- Creating a sense of community and teamwork
- Using win-win, positive non-blame-placing approaches
- Focusing on results, both short- and long-range
- Working from a sound information base
- Being systematic and using multilevel change strategies
- Integrating concern for people and achievement
- Emphasizing sustained culture change

This is accomplished with the help of the people who are actually participating in the establishing and reinforcing of the norms. They have an opportunity, usually in a high-involvement workshop, to try out the kind of culture they desire and begin to create an environment in which change can take place.

This intensive and systematic study of the norms which define the organization and significantly influence individual and organizational efficiency and goal attainment is rapid, and feedback on the findings can be provided quickly.

Information Gathering. The technique here includes selected interviews with top management, on-site observations, and the administering of certain survey instruments. A leadership norm indicator (Fig. 10-2) pinpoints who the leaders are and what type of leadership is operating, and an associate opinion survey samples opinions of personnel, including lower-echelon employees. The information report includes identification of weak norm areas and recommendations for change.

A "norm pack" is developed which provides a description of those norms that make a crucial contribution to the success or failure of the organization or the program in question. Actual examples of both positive and negative norms in each of the critical norm areas are included. These samples are usually written in such a way as to reflect verbatim employees' statements and concerns. A normative profile is drawn as a graphic indication of the strength of the various norm areas in the organization. It shows both normative strengths as they actually exist and the strengths desirable or necessary for the organization to operate at peak effectiveness. The "norm gap" highlights the differences between the existing normative profile in an organization and the profile desirable for peak effectiveness.

Making use of the data gathered from various parts of the organization, a norm profile (Fig. 10-3) is developed. This profile shows the disparity between what the organization wishes and what actually takes place. Periodic evaluation of this norm gap provides an ongoing method of measuring the progress of the program.

Experience has indicated that an organization will have approximately 10 to 12 critical norm areas that contribute to success or failure. Common to many organizations are the following:

Organizational and personal pride. This is a feeling that "This is our organization."

IF AN EMPLOYEE IN YOUR COMPANY WERE
TO:

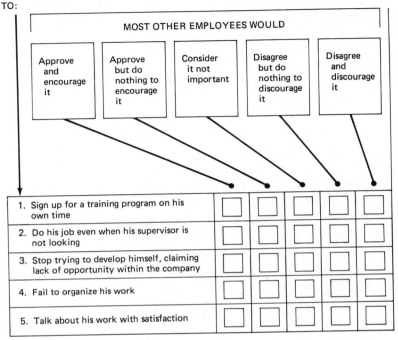

Figure 10-2. Extract from norm indicator.

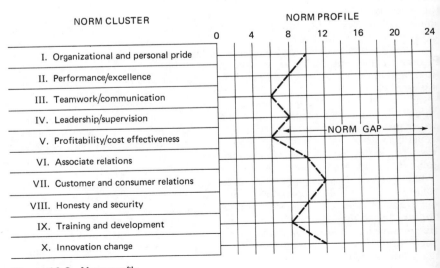

Figure 10-3. Norm profile.

Performance and reward systems. Support desired behavior or interfere with their development.

Information and communication. The type of information and the way it is communicated have a powerful impact on behavior.

Leadership and supervision performance. Supervision is viewed as a constructive relationship and sharing of problems, and leaders are given tools to accomplish them.

Profitability and cost-effectiveness. Emphasis on assuring profitability and reducing unnecessary costs.

Associate relations. Concern for good relationships between employees and management.

Customer and consumer relations. Focus on high quality of customer service.

Honesty and security. A high value placed on personal integrity and a concern for the organization.

Training and orientation. Importance placed on training and development activities.

Innovation and change. Actively seeking out positive continued improvements.

Modeling behavior. Behavior throughout the organization is affected by what leaders are *perceived* as doing.

Work teams. Every worker is part of a work team. Subcultures are often formed at informal meetings of the work team.

Organizational policies and procedures. These convey clearly the organization's cultural priorities.

Once the norms, positive and negative, have been identified and the distance between these norms and the goals has been determined, it is time to establish priorities and move into change strategies. In this way each program is tailored to the particular needs and concerns of the particular organization where it is being applied.

Phase I. Analysis and Objective Setting

The first step in applying the culture change process is that of determining the nature of the existing culture and of identifying the key norms and norm influences that are affecting it. This is accomplished through the use of interviews, field observations, and the use of normative survey instruments such as the leadership norm indicator depicted in Fig. 10-2. Such instruments help to pinpoint norms and norm influences that can affect the program's success and the success and failure of the organization.

Phase II. Systems Introduction and Involvement

It is here that the members of the culture have an opportunity to come together to consider the possibilities of change. Making use of high-involvement workshops, each individual and each department group within the culture has an opportunity to try out the new norms of the culture that they wish to create and begin to build the type of supportive environments in which change can take place and be sustained.

The workshop is organized into three parts: understanding, identifying, and changing. In it, people have an opportunity to come to understand the importance of the areas that have been selected for emphasis and the importance of the cultural norms that influence these areas. They also have an opportunity to identify for themselves the norm influences that are affecting their own performance and the performance of the organization as they affect those areas. Most importantly, they have an opportunity to plan and to begin to organize a strategy for change and to begin to build the teamwork and positive interrelationships that will be necessary to successfully implement the changes that they have decided upon.

Phase III. Systems Implementation

This is the phase during which the various elements of the organizational culture are systematically modified so that they can more effectively contribute to the achievement of objectives. During this stage, four key elements are emphasized: individual development; work team or peer group development; leadership development; and the development of the policies, programs and procedures of the culture. Specific change programs are usually required in each of these four elements, with each program being directed toward modifying the norm influences that have previously been identified. All three levels of goals—performance, programmatic, and cultural—are emphasized, with the cultural level particularly stressed so that not only are problems solved, but new ways of handling problems are built into the culture. Norm changes are put into practice within the day-to-day activities of the group and are reinforced by rewards and support systems.

In order to bring about change, it is necessary that people within the organization examine and modify each of the various norm influences that we have described. If a given change is not supported by these norm influences, it is not likely to last very long. If it is contradicted by the norm influences, it may never be practiced at all outside the training session. Norm influences such as management commitment, modeling behavior, and information and reward systems are a necessary prerequisite to any organizational change.

Working on a single norm influence is not likely to bring about change. It is necessary to work on many, if not all, of the influences simultaneously if significant change is to be developed and maintained. Too often we work on a single influence—by providing a pay raise or instituting a new training program, for example—and are then disappointed that the actions we have taken do not bring about the desired results.

Phase IV. Evaluation and Renewal

The fourth phase provides ongoing feedback about the effectiveness of the change program. It includes reevaluation and renewal meetings, which continue as long as the change program is in effect. These meetings provide a periodic opportunity for members of the organization to review the positive norms, either to strengthen them or to modify them according to the changing times, and to lend further support to the internalization of skills dealing with both human and technical problems. Results on all three goal levels are evaluated. Extension to other areas of the organization or to other concerns is now possible and serves to strengthen achievement of the original project goals.

These four phases make up the basic process of any normative systems program.

Whether the training objective is to increase productivity on an assembly line, to achieve a more harmonious work force in an office, or to humanize a small committee or a whole community, the basic model is the same. Each step is important and cannot be omitted if change is to be successful and continuing.

Organizational Change Begins at the Top

It is important that organizational change not be sought at the lower levels until it has been achieved at the level immediately above. Effective norm programs begin at the top of the organization and continue downward through all levels of the organizational structure. It is difficult, if not impossible, for planned change to be developed at the lower levels without the commitment, support, and visible modeling behavior of supervisory and management level personnel.

Not Blame Placing, but Problem Solving

Rather than trying to find out who's to blame for the problems, the emphasis needs to be on finding solutions by which everyone will benefit. In a well conceived norm change program, problem solving without blame placing is a constructive asset.

When all parties are encouraged to deal with problem behavior as it is related to norms, there is minimal risk of arousing personal defenses. It is easier to take the criticism, "The norm around here is to arrive fifteen minutes late. Can we change it?" than it is to take, "You guys are always holding up the meeting."

In other words, it is less threatening and less accusative to focus on norms than to blame people for things for which the overall organization may well have been responsible.

Focus on Results, Not Mere Promises

Rather than focusing on promises or on mere activities, the norm needs to be that people search for solutions and are oriented to achieving results. Without this focus on results, we get caught up in abstractions and unfulfilled promises. If we focus on results—on what we actually do—the excitement of achievement begins to feed on itself.

Continuing emphasis on results not only replaces empty promises, it also replaces the negative norm of blaming. Finger-pointing behavior is bypassed when the orientation is toward accomplishment and concrete results. The negative norm of helplessness is also undermined, for the realization that something is being accomplished spurs people on. Attention can be paid to excellence and to solving the next part of the problem, and there is a feeling of being in control. Many people at first think that change is not really possible, but they can be convinced that things can happen when they actually see some results.

Successful change programs set specific, measurable short- and long-range goals that everyone agrees will constitute satisfactory cultural change. The short-range goals need to be ones that can be achieved in a reasonable period of time and that lead to early, visible results.

The long-range goals must also be clearly defined, for mere "activities" that aren't framed in the larger context are, in the long run, as disappointing as meaningless promises.

Sustained Cultural Change

Instead of treating symptoms, the group needs to deal with the root causes of problems and try to develop norms of support that will be long-lasting. It we really want to change, we must be willing to commit ourselves to an effort that will extend over a long period of time, for negative norms are often deep-rooted, and building support for positive ones is crucial. Often it would be better not to start a program at all than to start it when we are not prepared to continue with it.

In an organization or community, this recognition of a sustained effort is particularly important, for there are many levels to reach and many people to involve. The necessity for a long-term effort need not be discouraging, however, if coupled with simultaneous work on achieving immediate results in some areas.

The Trainer as a Change Agent

In summary, what we are suggesting here is that trainers see themselves as *change agents*. Since the primary influences within organizations are those cultural differences which shape behavior, our role is to be certain that these influences work to the mutual benefit of the individual and the organization of which he or she is a part.

When each individual training program is being considered, it is important that certain questions be carefully considered. A beginning list of these questions would include the following:

1. Have we defined our training objectives in terms of the desired normative outcomes?
2. Do we have a workable approach to involving the people most directly affected?
3. Is there visible commitment by management to the behavior change being sought? If not, what do we need to do to build it?
4. Have we assured that management personnel and other key reference groups are prepared to model the desired behavior visibly?
5. Has a system been set up to keep people informed about how well they are doing in achieving the desired goals?
6. Have we checked to see that people will be rewarded or at least not penalized for the desired behavior?
7. Have we made certain that people will have an opportunity to develop the knowledge and skills that may be required?
8. Can the formal orientation program and procedures be used to recommend the desired behavior?
9. Are we prepared to make use of the informal leadership of the work group to strengthen the desired norms?
10. Have we developed the support of supervisory personnel for what we are trying to achieve?

11. Have we developed a systematic way of working on a number of influences simultaneously and in coordination with one another?

12. Has the program been designed in such a way as to assure that no level within the organization is asked to make changes until the level above has developed a full commitment to the change being sought?

13. Is the program designed in such a way as to avoid blame placing and constitute instead a constructive problem solving approach?

14. Is the program results-oriented? Do we have a clear focus on what we are trying to achieve?

Conclusion

It is important that the information gained as a result of this work with group behavioral norms not be seen as a method of merely securing greater conformity to managerial directives. Rather, it is a method of helping people from all levels of the organization—from top management to the lowest and newest employee—to become involved in creating their own environments instead of being merely the victims of whatever currently exists. Because they are involved from the start, they are not conforming to outside pressures but are taking an active part in the systematic norm change process.

The basic question we have been attempting to answer here is one raised in executive suites across the country; it is a crucial question for all who are interested in developing effective training programs: "With all the dollars we've invested in training," the managers ask, "where is the payoff? Why don't training programs work better?"

One of the major troubles with the most traditional methods of training is that they have been dealing only with symptoms, without touching that underlying culprit that we mentioned at the start—the "shadow trainer." Negative organizational norms too often do their silent work, undermining hardworking trainers. But if this shadow trainer is understood and dealt with, the culture can be a positive force, adding strength to the professional trainer's efforts. Training *can* be successful and significant, even indispensable, if it is treated in the context of the organizational culture and its powerful norms.

Bibliography

Allen, Robert F., and Charlotte Kraft, *Beat the System: A Way to Create More Human Environments*, McGraw-Hill, New York, 1980.

Allen, Robert F., and S. Silverzweig, "Changing the Corporate Culture," *Sloan Management Review*, a Journal of the Alfred P. Sloan School of Management, Massachusetts Institute of Technology, Cambridge, MA, spring 1976.

Allen, Robert F., and S. Pilnick, "Confronting the Shadow Organization: How to Detect and Defeat Negative Norms," *Organizational Dynamics*, Journal of the American Management Association, spring 1973.

Allen, Robert F., and Richard Murphy, "Getting Started: The Development of a New Company," *Business*, Vol. 29, No. 4, July–August 1979.

Allen, Robert F., and Charlotte Kraft, *The Handbook for Cultural Analysis and Change*, HRI Press, Morristown, NJ, 1980.

Allen, Robert F., "The Ik in the Office," *Organizational Dynamics*, winter 1980.

Allen, Robert F., and Shirley Linde, *Lifegain: A Culture-Based Approach to Positive Health*, HRI Press, Morristown, NJ, 1980.

Allen, Robert F., S. Pilnick, and S. Silverzweig, "Norms in the Supermarket Industry: A Self-Instructional Program," SRI Press, Morristown, NJ, 1970.

Allen, Robert F., and M. Higgins, "Ousting the Absenteeism Culture," *Personnel*, January 1979.

Allen, Robert F., and Sara Harris, *The Quiet Revolution*, Rawson Associates and Signet, New York, 1978.

Allen, Robert F., S. Pilnick, and Colin Park, "The Accounting Executive's Shadow Organization," *Management Accounting*, Journal of the National Association of Accountants, Vol. IV., No. 7, January 1974.

Allen, Robert F., and Frank J. Dyer, " A Tool for Tapping The Organizational Unconscious," *Personnel Journal*, March 1980.

Allen, Robert F., and Stanley Silverzweig, "Changing Community and Organizational Cultures," *Training and Development Journal*, Madison, WI, July 1977.

Allen, Robert F., "When Are Results Not Results," A Selected Paper of the Organization Development Division, ASTD, March 1979.

11
Instructional Design*

George L. Gropper

and Paul A. Ross

George L. Gropper *received his Ph.D. in psychology from the University of Pittsburgh, his M.A. in psychology from the University of California at Berkeley, and his A.B. in social relations from Harvard College. He has been with the American Institutes for Research, Florida State University, and University of Pennsylvania. He is currently with the Digital Equipment Corporation. He has been a contributor to "Instructional Design" from its inception in the late 1960s. His publications include, among other titles,* Instructional Strategies, Diagnosis and Revision in the Development of Instructional Materials, *and* Criteria for the Selection and Use of Visuals, *all published by Educational Technology Publications. His latest work, from Lawrence Erlbaum Associates, is "A Behavioral Approach to Instructional Prescription" in* Instructional Design Theories and Models.

Paul A. Ross *is a personnel manager at Digital Equipment Corporation, responsible for quality of work life, satisfaction, and productivity of two major work forces—field service and software services. He manages compensation, benefits, recruitment and staffing, organization development, training and development, employee relations, Affirmative Action and Equal Employment Opportunity, and personnel information systems. Previously, he was responsible for education, training, and development in the Educational Services Development and Publishing Group at Digital. Ross has broad experience in academe, business, and government. He has lectured at the Harvard Graduate School of Education and Lesley College and at major training conferences. Ross has a Doctorate in Organizational Development and Management Theory from the University of Massachusetts, Amherst. In 1983, he was elected to the ASTD board of directors and currently serves on the executive committee as secretary of the society.*

* The views expressed here do not necessarily reflect those of the Digital Equipment Corporation. The authors are grateful to William Bylund for reviewing a draft of this chapter.

Criteria for a Training Development Process

The design of consumer goods provides an appropriate, if surprising, model for the design of training. Like an automobile, a typewriter, or a television set, a *training program* is something to be planned, engineered, developed, tried out, sent back to the drawing board, tried out again, and delivered in final form. If developed in this disciplined fashion, like other products, the training program will do the job it was designed to do.

Overview of Desirable Development Characteristics

Consistently effective training outcomes are attainable only if training professionals have at their disposal a training development *process* that is systematic, generalizable, and valid. To meet these criteria, the process must possess the following characteristics:

For systematic development	For generalizable development	For valid development
• Standardization • Comprehensiveness • Internal consistency • Reliability	• Applicability to varied jobs • Applicability to varied audiences • Applicability to varied needs	• Job-relatedness • Relevance • Effectiveness

Systematic Development

To be *systematic*, a training development process has to be standardized, comprehensive, internally consistent, and reliable. If a training development process has these qualities, what is it like?

Standardization. A standardized development process requires highly formal rules. There must be prescribed rules for the gamut of development decisions that need to be made: what to do, when to do it, how to do it, when to do it in an alternative way, what should be produced, what standards to apply, and what to do next. Rules governing all such decisions are key to standardization.

If, in contrast, the development process relies on the artistic or unique skills of individual developers, however professional, there can be great variability in both process and outcomes. Implicit rules make poor guarantees. Explicit rules, on the other hand, make possible a training development process that is standardized and repeatable. They are critical for a dependable and accountable training operation.

Comprehensiveness. Many tasks are involved in the training development process. Since there are intimate dependencies among them, the success of any one of them depends on the success of the remaining tasks. A letdown or omission for any one of them can create a weak link in the overall process. Therefore, in the interest of the integrity of the entire process, all training development issues must

)e comprehensively addressed. The process, and its governing rules, must cover all
critical development tasks.

nternal Consistency. Since most development tasks build on the results of
prior tasks, it is as important to have formal rules for making connections between
asks as it is to have them for individual tasks. Each task can then properly build on
he results of specific, prior tasks. All the tasks can then be performed in an
appropriate sequence. Formal rules for connections between tasks, in effect, allow
he overall process to take place in an internally consistent way.

Reliability. It is not enough simply to have development rules in place. For a
raining development process to produce its expected effects developers must *adhere*
o the rules. All developers must follow the rules and implement them in the same
way. The same developer must follow the rules and implement them in the same
way on different occasions. A training development process can be effective only if
he rules are actually implemented and only if they are implemented in a
consistent, reliable way.

The hallmarks of *systematic* development are standardization, comprehensiveness, internal consistency, and reliability. From a technical point of view, these
properties are prerequisites for implementing a training development process
effectively. From a management point of view, they are prerequisites for monitor-
ng the training development process and holding those who implement it
accountable.

Generalizable Development

To be *generalizable*, a training and development process must be able to encompass
raining development for *any* type of job, *any* type of audience, and *any* type of
raining need. If a training development process has these capacities, what is it like?

Applicability to Jobs. A training development process is useful if it applies to
broad range of jobs. It has to be applicable to jobs calling for motor skills as well
s intellectual skills, recall of facts as well as solving problems, following fixed rules
s well as inventing them, working with paper and pencil as well as dealing with
people, or working on equipment as well as doing things in one's head, etc. The
process has to identify and then accommodate any of these job requirements.

Applicability to People. A training development process is useful if it applies
o any trainee audience: audiences with or without verbal skills, with or without
isual skills, with or without special aptitudes, with or without interest in learning,
with or without prior experience, etc. The process has to identify and then
accommodate requirements of any of these audience characteristics.

Applicability to Training Needs. To be of use to the broadest range of
evelopers a training development process has to be adaptable to varied applica-
ons. It has to apply to any type of training: initial, follow-up, refresher, or
remedial. It has to apply to a diversity of delivery mechanisms: lecture, audiotape,
paper-and-pencil, film or TV, computer, etc. It has to apply to varied training
formats: self-paced, fixed pace, job aids, case studies, etc. The process has to identify
and then accommodate any of these requirements.

Valid Development

To be *valid*, a training development process has to be job-related, relevant, and effective. If it has these qualities, what is it like?

Job Relatedness. Training programs need to address skills and knowledge that are critical for job performance. Therefore, a training development process has to be able to distinguish between what is job-related and what is not. As a basis for making this distinction, it has to have a methodology for gathering information about job requirements. Decisions about course coverage can then be dependably based on what people actually do on the job.

Relevance. Even if developers successfully and reliably follow training development rules, questions still remain. Does this make a difference? Are the parameters they use in analyzing learning requirements helpful? Will the treatments they prescribe for meeting those requirements lead to satisfactory trainee learning? Or would some other way of analyzing training requirements or some other set of prescriptions be more productive? To produce effective training outcomes, the issues a training development process addresses and the way it addresses them have to be relevant.

Effectiveness. The effectiveness of a training development process or of the training programs it produces can be evaluated only in an empirical way. Inspection alone cannot be depended upon to provide reliable or conclusive evidence. Both training development process and training programs have to be formally tried and their effectiveness actually assessed.

Training program results are needed to answer questions about how well the programs work. Results are needed to diagnose what is wrong with programs that do not work. And results are needed to decide on the repairs that will ensure that they ultimately work. Program tryout and revision is essential in assuring program effectiveness.

From a technical point of view, "job-relatedness" and a "relevant" process are prerequisites for effective training development. Without these qualities a training development process cannot have a positive impact on job performance. With respect to "effectiveness," the technical and management points of view coincide. One needs to know so that, when necessary, changes can be made in training programs or even in the development process itself. The other needs to justify its investment in training.

A Highly Disciplined Approach

Adhering to all three criteria—systematic, generalizable, and valid—makes for a highly disciplined approach to training development. There may be training requirements for which shortcuts may be acceptable. But there are many training situations in which anything less formal, less disciplined, or less complete may lead to common and, in many situations, unacceptable training failures. Personnel may not get up to speed at all or quickly enough. They may fail to gain confidence in their ability to perform effectively. They may commit serious or dangerous errors on the job. They may have a negative impact on the performance of others. They may require remedial training. These are costly, unnecessary, and avoidable consequences and need to be *weighed* against the cost of a training development process that can avoid them.

Overview of "Instructional Design"

Having made its appearance as late as the 1960s, instructional design is relatively young. Its first proponents intended that it be systematic, generalizable, and valid.

Major Tasks

Trainers skilled in "instructional design" typically perform the following development functions:

- Identify a need for training.
- Identify all the tasks performed on the job.
- Determine the learning requirements for those tasks.
- Appraise the intended audience's capacity to learn those tasks.
- Formulate a training approach that matches both learning requirements and audience capacities.
- Develop a training program that implements the approach.
- Try out the program with a sample of the intended audience.
- Make revisions based on test results.
- Try out and revise the program again (if time and money permit).
- Install the final version of the program.
- Monitor job holder performance in order to appraise continuing program effectiveness.

Multiple Instructional Design Models

There is widespread agreement among instructional design theorists and practitioners as to the role of major instructional design tasks. There is no such agreement as to the detailed mechanics for carrying them out. The fact is, there is no single, universally accepted instructional design model.

There are behavioral models, cognitive models, and hybrids. Some are more systematic and more detailed and comprehensive than others. Some are more generalizable. And, given the varied analytic and prescriptive approaches they employ, some are likely to be more valid than others (there is no evidence to compare them). How did all this come about?

Some History

Active Practice and Feedback

Elements of "instructional design" owe their origin to some early research and training efforts. During World War II military trainers, influenced by behavioral psychology, built "active practice" into training films. They replaced passive watching with active practice. They created occasions during a film for trainees to practice making the responses they would have to make on the job. And, as also required by behavioral psychology, they provided feedback about the correctness of the responses.

In the decades that followed the war, active practice and feedback also became a part of instructional television both inside and outside of the military. At about the same time, programmed instruction assigned active practice an even more central role. Today active practice is part of most instructional design approaches— no matter what their theoretical orientations.

Programmed Instruction

Programmed instruction, also a product of behavioral psychology, broke subject matter up into small chunks. Each chunk, generally a presentation frame, contained a practice problem and the information needed to help a learner solve it. A lesson consisted of a deliberate succession of such practice frames. By practicing appropriate responses, learners went from mastery of partial skills to mastery of more complex and complete skills.

In addition to this graduated approach, programmed instruction allowed learners to progress from frame to frame, from practice problem to practice problem, from mastery of one set of skills to mastery of another, at their own pace—one ingredient thought necessary to accommodate individual differences among learners.

With entire lessons built around active practice and graduated problem tasks, development of lessons had to be based on highly analytic considerations. Decisions had to be made about which responses to practice, the sequence in which they were to be practiced, the frequency with which any given response would be practiced, the type and variety of contexts in which responses would be practiced, the type and amount of help to provide for each practice problem, how gradually to withdraw help, etc. This analytic, systematic design of a learning experience marks programmed instruction as a forerunner of instructional design.

Today, programmed instruction, still used, can be thought of as a specialized subvariety of instructional design. Both are prepared in highly systematic, formal ways. A key difference lies in their presentation formats. Programmed instruction is still more apt to rely on a frame-by-frame presentation. While instructional design might on occasion also do that, it allows for greater latitude and variety.

Piloting

There was some "piloting" or tryout in early film and TV training. Some involved reviews of a lesson by *experts*. Some involved *learners* actually taking lessons. However, only with the maturing of programmed instruction did piloting become a routine, thoroughgoing feature of the training development process.

Programs were tried with a sample of the target audience. Learner failure on individual practice problems and on tests that followed revealed when something was wrong. It also became the basis for diagnosing what was wrong and what needed to be done about it.

Early Instructional Design

Just as programmed instruction, in its adoption of analytic and systematic techniques, represented an advance over earlier training efforts, early instructiona design took this approach one step farther. Conceptual schemes evolved for analyzing job tasks or subject matter knowledge and for making prescriptions based on the results. These very first approaches owed a debt to learning principles derived from behavioral psychology.

Skills emphasized in behavioral psychology (e.g., discriminations, generalizations, associations, and chains) were used to analyze the subject matter to be taught. Training approaches, also derived from behavioral psychology (e.g., shaping, fading), were selected to accommodate these skills. This was an early, explicit, and systematic matching of "conditions" and "treatments."

Subsequent instructional design approaches, to this day, have formulated different analytic approaches (some behavioral, many cognitive, and some eclectic mixtures of the two). They have also formulated different, prescriptive training approaches to accommodate the new analytic categories. But they all equate analyzed learning requirements with "conditions." And they all equate training approaches with "treatments." All current instructional design models consist of formal rules for *matching* these conditions and treatments.

Instructional design now consists of (1) "front-end" tasks that seek to identify "conditions" that will have to be accommodated, (2) middle tasks that prescribe and implement "treatments" capable of accommodating those conditions, and (3) concluding tasks that try out and revise training programs produced by this matching process.

Instructional Design Tasks

The major tasks listed in Table 11-1 describe a training development process currently accepted by many instructional design theorists and practitioners. They may not perform these tasks in exactly this order. And they may allow for detours and loopbacks. But, at their most systematic, they perform them all.

Because there are formal interconnections among the tasks, in virtually all instructional design models each task uniformly builds on the results of prior tasks. This striving for internal consistency, this comprehensive, rule-driven approach to individual tasks and to their interconnections distinguishes instructional design from other less systematic approaches to training development.

By studying actual job requirements, instructional design ensures that training will concentrate on job-related skills. Further, trying out training programs and, when necessary, revising them, ensures that training for those requirements will be effective. The aim in both cases is a valid development process.

Each task in instructional design, from needs analysis to formative evaluation, has its distinctive *purpose*. Each employs distinctive *methods*. And each produces distinctive *results*. A discussion of these issues for each task can, by way of introduction to instructional design, convey something of its systematic flavor.

Needs Analysis

Improved performance is a main motive for approving training outlays. To justify them, a training development process requires a mechanism for determining whether there is a genuine need to improve performance and, if there is, for identifying its nature and extent. In instructional design that mechanism is *needs analysis*.

Purpose. Developers seek demonstrable evidence of inadequate performance. They collect data to determine whether there is a gap between current performance

Table 11-1.   Instructional Design Tasks

Tasks	Purposes	Methods
Needs analysis	Identify gaps between current and expected skill levels	Ratings of performance and estimates of deviations from expected levels
Task description	Gather detailed data regarding required job tasks for new or existing jobs	Direct observation of experts doing job tasks Reports from interviews or questionnaires about what experts do on a job
Task analysis	Identify learning requirements for job tasks Forecast potential learning difficulties	Classification or analysis of types of learning involved
Sequencing	Arrange order in which tasks or topics are to be learned	Identification of relationships among tasks or topics—making sequences necessary or facilitating
Stating objectives	Provide descriptions of expected performance that can serve as a specification	Review of task description information and formulation of condensed, clear statements of job tasks or knowledge skills
Developing tests	Create testing instruments for evaluating training program	Development of tests to capture or simulate the same performance described in objectives
Formulating instructional strategies	Select an approach that can accommodate the learning requirements imposed by job skills and audience characteristics	Review of task analysis results to identify the "conditions" that must be accommodated and prescribing "treatments"
Developing materials	Translate strategies to create an appropriate learning experience	Creating practice items, presentation materials, and instructions for taking program
Formative evaluation	Try out program with sample of audience to find out what works and what does not—as a basis for revision	Administration of program Diagnosis and revision of training program

and expected performance. Which job areas show evidence of a gap? Which job holders, other than new hires, are responsible for the gap? Evidence of a gap between current and expected performance can determine whether training will be needed, the performance areas needing it, how much training each may need, and which job holders make appropriate candidates for training.

Results. A useful datum that assessing employee performance may provide is the percentage of employees falling below, at, or above expected performance levels. In the following table, the percentages of employees falling short of an expected level for each job area are readily apparent. Data of this type identify job areas for which there are gaps between current and expected performance. They also identify the extent of those gaps. Priority ratings may be assigned to each job area to indicate importance.

Percentage of Personnel Rated at Each of Five Performance Levels

	Low 1	Expected			High 5
		2	3	4	
Installation		20	65	15	
Maintenance	5	10	70	10	
Diagnosis	10	30	60		5
Repair			75	15	10
Interpersonal		20	75	05	

Method. Approaches to needs analysis range from reliance on armchair judgments about training needs to quantitative ratings of current performance. For jobs whose performance requirements have yet to be defined, experts may be asked for their judgments about the kinds of training needed. For jobs whose requirements are known, supervisors may be asked to rate actual subordinate performance. In either approach, priorities are based on judgments about which job areas are most critical for overall job performance or most merit a training effort. At its most dependable, needs analysis is based on empirical data. Collected and analyzed as objectively as possible, *data* are relied on to establish whether there is a genuine need.

Task Description

To make decisions about what to cover in a training program and what to leave out, a training development process has to have a mechanism for identifying what is relevant to train for and what is not. In instructional design that mechanism is *task description*.

Purpose. The results of a task description, sometimes called "job description," become the basis for defining job requirements and identifying what is relevant. Developers collect data about job activities. The questions they ask, the respondents they choose, the instruments they use, the analysis they make, the entire methodology they use for collecting information, are all geared to an objective, comprehensive, and reliable definition of job activities. As important, by basing the definition on empirical data about those activities, the definition is expected to be valid as well.

Results. The end product of a task description is a catalog of job activities. The catalog may be presented in outline—with major activities subdivided into tasks and tasks subdivided into steps—and so on down to some desired level. Or the end product may display job activities as a job flow.

The description of job activities may typically include the following kinds of information:

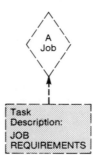

- Input situations job holders face
- Decisions they have to make
- Actions they have to take
- Tools or job aids they use
- Outcomes of each action
- Standards for each action or for each outcome

In effect, a task description provides a comprehensive description of how experts perform their jobs.

Method.   Approaches to task description can range from direct observation of experts actually performing a job to the collection of questionnaire or interview descriptions of what experts do on the job. Some, if not most, approaches concentrate on the overt behaviors experts exhibit. Others concentrate on the mental processes that go on in experts' heads as they perform job tasks. Task description is at its most dependable when it uses empirical data to determine what is relevant to train for and what is not, and when it collects those data as objectively and comprehensively as possible.

Task Analysis

Since performance requirements vary from job to job, learning requirements can be expected to vary as well. Some jobs may require learning facts, some problem solving, some following procedures. Therefore, *learning* to perform one job can be expected to impose demands on trainees that are different from those imposed by another.

To prescribe an appropriate training approach for a job, the training development process has to have a mechanism for analyzing specific learning requirements. In instructional design that mechanism is *task analysis*.

Purpose.   An analysis of job tasks addresses interrelated issues bearing on how easy or difficult learning those tasks will be. All will be involved in later decisions about the type of practice and the type of presentation that will be required.

What kinds of skills are involved in the performance of job tasks: motor or intellectual, creative or reproductive, verbal or quantitative, dependent on short- or long-term memory, etc.? Under what conditions will the skills be exhibited performance from memory or with job aids available; new, varying situations to be

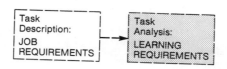

dealt with or constant repetition of old, uniform situations; recalling facts or applying them; etc.? Are there characteristics of the skills that can make learning them easy or difficult: easy or difficult decisions to make; a small or large number of facts to recall; a small or large number of steps to execute; etc.?

Are there audience characteristics that can help or hinder in learning required skills: high or low learning abilities; high or low verbal or visual skills; high or low levels of related or of prerequisite skills; etc.? Answers to questions of this sort define specific *conditions* for which specific *treatments* will have to be prescribed.

Results. A task analysis may produce a categorization of the tasks to be performed. Tasks may be categorized based on such *learning* requirements as recalling facts, applying facts, giving definitions, following procedural rules, solving problems, or giving explanations. How the tasks are taught will ultimately depend on how they have been *categorized*.

Alternatively, a task analysis may produce a highly detailed analysis of the component skills that make up each task. These might include the "behavioral" skills: discriminations, generalizations, associations, and chains. Or they might include "cognitive" requirements for long- and short-term memory or other information processing requirements. In this approach, any given task is analyzed for such components. How the tasks are taught will ultimately depend on how they have been *analyzed*.

Characteristics of the target audience may also be given closer scrutiny at this time. Efforts may be made to determine how audience characteristics will affect learning ease or difficulty or how these characteristics might interact with the learning demands imposed by the skills to be learned.

Method. Some approaches to task analysis address the overt behaviors that job holders perform and either categorize them or analyze them for their component skills. Others address the processes that go on in job holders' heads and, similarly, adopt one or the other of these two contrasting analytic approaches.

In either approach developers may do "top of the head" analyses or laborious, minute analyses. Theoretical preferences or practical considerations of time and money often determine which point on this continuum developers select.

Task analysis is likely to be most effective when it identifies the conditions likely to affect learning ease or difficulty as exhaustively as possible.

Sequencing

Learning order can make a difference. Learning one task may be impossible or, at best, difficult until another is learned. Learning one task before another, even though not required, may facilitate learning a second. Learning two tasks together may be feasible and, under some circumstances, desirable. How to make decisions about a learning order that is right for all job tasks?

To prescribe a sequence that will facilitate learning, the training development process requires a mechanism for analyzing relationships among tasks. In instructional design that mechanism is *sequencing*.

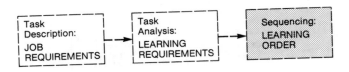

Purpose. Some tasks may *have to be* scheduled in a particular order. Others may prove *helpful* if scheduled in a particular order. Still others may be scheduled in any order without consequence to themselves or to remaining tasks. In the training development process sequencing seeks to discover which contingency applies to which tasks.

Sequencing decisions attempt to identify and capitalize on the relationships (if any) among job tasks. It is the type of relationship between any two tasks that has a bearing on the order in which the two should be learned.

Results. Sequencing decisions identify the order in which all activities, tasks, steps, substeps, etc., will be learned. They also identify the order in which facts, rules, and principles that support job tasks will be learned.

Method. Generally, sequencing involves an inspection of task description results for evidence of the nature of relationships among job tasks. The results may reveal evidence of hierarchical relationships, sequential relationships, or nonrelatedness— whichever types of relationships a given approach to sequencing considers critical.

Some tasks may be subordinate to others. Some tasks may be superordinate to several others. Some may be neither but simply follow one another in performance. And some may be unrelated to others in any of these ways. Sequencing decisions are made based on the presence or absence of such relationships.

In some approaches, subordinate tasks or tasks lower on a hierarchy are scheduled first because they are treated as prerequisites. In other approaches superordinate tasks (e.g., use of higher-order rules) are scheduled first because that sequence is thought to facilitate the learning of one or more lower-order tasks (e.g., use of lower-order rules).

In some approaches, tasks *performed* early are scheduled to be *learned* early. In other approaches it is the tasks *performed* late that are schedule to be *learned* early. Thus performance sequence and learning sequence may differ. Sequencing is more likely to be effective the more successful it is at accurately identifying prerequisite and facilitating relationships among job tasks.

Stating Objectives

An objective functions as a specification for either an end-of-training or an on-the-job outcome. An objective must therefore clearly and explicitly identify the outcomes a training program is expected to produce.

To craft a training program that can produce specified outcomes, the training development process has to have a mechanism for formalizing a specification for those outcomes. In instructional design that mechanism is *stating objectives*.

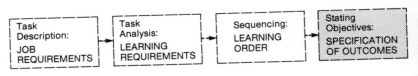

Purpose. Stating objectives translates and compresses information gathered earlier. It creates a tool that facilitates the conduct of remaining tasks in the training development process.

Previous "front-end" tasks may produce vast amounts of information about job requirements. The information may be very detailed, stated at varying levels of generality (tasks, subtasks, steps, etc.), appearing in varied formats (lists, flows, etc.), addressing varied issues (decisions, standards, actions, supporting knowledge, etc.), and covering job tasks varying in scope.

A developer needs to digest all this information and translate it into a form that can be easily used in subsequent development tasks. Objectives perform that function by (1) compressing collected information, (2) highlighting key performance elements a developer needs to concentrate on, (3) weeding out unnecessary information, (4) creating units of performance of roughly comparable scope, and (5) standardizing how performance requirements are depicted. What results are objectives that are brief summary statements of performance requirements.

Results. Substantively, an objective may describe several or all of the following performance ingredients:

- The types of situations a job holder encounters
- (If applicable) reference materials or job aids used
- The actions needed to respond to each type of situation
- (If applicable) tools that are used in performing an action
- Outcomes or products that are produced
- Standards for actions taken or for products produced

The more of these ingredients included in a statement of objectives, the more informative and helpful an objective will be. Other desirable substantive characteristics include a performance orientation and job-relatedness.

Formally, the choice of language used to state an objective can make the difference between an objective that is informative and helpful and one that is not. Like any specification, an objective cannot be ambiguous. Language that is understandable and explicit is preferable to language that is subject to varied interpretations. A large literature concentrates on standard statements of objectives.

Method. Developers base objectives on task description results. Inspecting those results for the types of information needed for an objective and for units of performance of roughly comparable scope, they translate the results into an objective. The more accurately and unambiguously the objective specifies a training outcome, the more helpful it will be to developers in subsequent development tasks.

Developing Tests

A training development process will ultimately need to evaluate the effectiveness of the training. For this purpose it must provide for reliable and valid testing instruments. They must accurately reveal how much trainee improvement occurs following administration of the program.

To generate useful evaluative information about a training program, a training development process has to have a mechanism for producing testing instruments tailored to the targeted outcomes of the program. In instructional design that mechanism is *developing tests*.

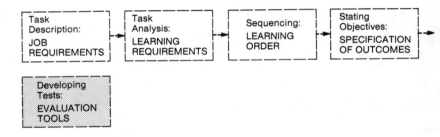

Purpose. Administered before and after training, tests provide evidence about the adequacy of a training program. They are key to "evaluation" both during the development of training programs and later in their routine administration.

Test results are used for different purposes at these different stages of the training development process. During development they provide *developers* with evidence about the adequacy of a program. Revisions to the program made during trial runs are based on such evidence. Later, during the routine administration of a certified and installed training program, tests provide *management* with feedback about trainee progress as well as about the continuing effectiveness of the program.

Results. The closer tests approximate the performance requirements of a job, the more representative of actual job performance and the more predictive the results will be. Directly or in simulated form tests must capture the skill requirements of a job. They can be delivered by the same medium that delivers the training or by different media including paper and pencil, computer, TV or film, equipment in the laboratory, etc. They can require multiple-choice, matching, or production responding. They can be self-scoring or externally scored. The only "instructional" criterion they must meet is that they make the same demands of the trainee (or as nearly the same) as specified in objectives. Beyond that, administrative and cost considerations may affect a choice from among these varied options.

Method. "Tests and measurement" is a highly developed subdiscipline within psychology. Accordingly, the principles and guidelines for test construction, about which there is also a large literature, are well established and widely known. They apply to developing test instruments in training settings.

"Objectives" define the types of tasks that need to be incorporated into test items. Developers create items that, at their best, impose the same performance requirements.

Formulating Instructional Strategies

Developers decide on a training approach suitable to the conditions uncovered in prior analyses. They now prescribe treatments to match these conditions. To attain the outcomes specified in objectives, a training development process must have a mechanism for identifying what are suitable matches between conditions and treatments. In instructional design that mechanism is *formulating instructional strategies*.

Purpose. An instructional strategy prescribes a type of learning experience needed to promote mastery of job tasks. The strategy is more apt to succeed the

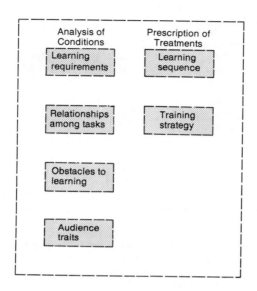

more responsive it is to the types of learning required for mastery of specific job tasks.

If, for example, an objective calls for *applying* facts, rather than simply recalling them, a strategy is selected to meet that learning requirement. One element in an appropriate strategy might be to provide examples of situations for which the facts do and do not apply. If, on the other hand, only recall of facts was required, a lesser strategy would be in order.

A strategy must also accommodate other parameters that characterize conditions: obstacles to learning particular job tasks, audience capacities to learn them, the setting on the job in which job tasks must be performed, etc.

Results. A strategy characterizes learning experiences trainees will undergo. It identifies the type of practice trainees will engage in, the type of presentation that will be used to prepare them for it, and the medium or media that will deliver both practice and presentation.

Generally, practice consists of the same types of tasks described in objectives. The closer practice requirements approximate job requirements, the more beneficial their effect is likely to be. However, in many training situations trainees may require

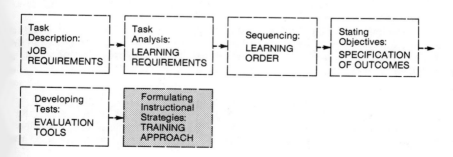

preparatory practice. Being easier than joblike practice, this form of graduated practice prepares trainees for the more demanding joblike tasks that will follow it.

Training presentations are designed to accommodate anticipated difficulties and to facilitate both joblike and prior, easier practice tasks. The ingredients of presentations that prepare trainees for practice generally include:

- Telling trainees what to do and how to do it

- Examples of:
  Situations to which actions apply
  Actions being taken
  Outcomes

- Rules governing the performance

For "concept learning," trainees might be told how to define a concept, given examples of it, and then allowed to practice stating the definition and producing instances of the concept or simply recognizing instances of the concept. For "procedural learning," trainees might be told how to carry out procedures, given examples of situations to which they apply, possibly be given some guiding rules or principles, and then be allowed to practice the procedures.

A medium is usually selected on the basis of its capacity to "carry" the type of presentation to be offered and the type of practice that will follow. Cost and administrative feasibility also guide such decisions. Where the latter considerations override instructional issues, simulation and less expensive media are readily available options.

Method. Developers review the results of prior tasks to identify the conditions that need to be accommodated. Results of task description, stating objectives, and developing tests identify the types of tasks that must be performed on the job. Results of task analysis identify the types of learning that must take place in order to master those tasks. Results of an audience analysis identify characteristics that might affect trainee ability to learn those tasks. Results of sequencing decisions identify what is judged to be an optimum order for learning all job tasks.

An instructional strategy is formulated that identifies treatments that can accommodate these conditions. At its best, a strategy makes as nearly close a match as possible between treatments and conditions—for all objectives.

Developing Training Materials

A developer must now find the words, pictures, or symbols that will create the practice opportunities and supporting presentation specified in an instructional strategy. The developer has to translate that strategy into training materials and procedures.

To develop a training program capable of producing specified outcomes, a training development process has to have a mechanism for translating a strategy into an end product. In instructional design that mechanism is developing training materials.

Purpose. A program has to implement the specifications spelled out in an instructional strategy. Developers have to create instances of all the ingredients that go into a training program: practice items, definitions, examples, illustrations, etc. They have to fashion all the ingredients needed to produce an entire learning

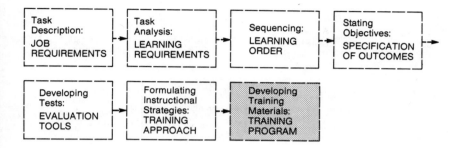

experience—from first practice task to the last, from supporting presentation to supporting presentation.

An instructional strategy constitutes only a most general blueprint for the character of a prescribed learning experience. The training development process, therefore, has to have more specific rules for developing all needed program ingredients. What should the ingredients consist of? How many of them should there be? How should they change from one instance to the next? In what order should they occur? Thus, developers need detailed guidance for translating highly general prescriptions into specific lesson ingredients.

Results.   A training program is meant to deliver a complete, prescribed learning experience. Whether on paper, on film, or on computer tape, the program must contain all the ingredients needed to create an appropriate learning experience. There must be specific instances of telling trainees what to do and how to do it; examples of situations, actions, and outcomes; rules or principles governing a performance; and practice problems.

There must be sufficient numbers and variety of instances. The instances must be there in a prescribed order and with adequate transitions among them. All told they must create a cumulative learning experience that constitutes an appropriate treatment for the conditions identified in front-end analyses. Properly crafted they represent a concrete implementation of the instructional strategy that prescribed that treatment.

Method.   One approach to program development starts with the preparation of practice items. Only then are supporting presentations prepared. With a practice task clearly in mind, it becomes easier to conceive of the kind of presentation support it will take to prepare the learner. A major advantage to this approach is the possibility it allows of only presenting what is needed to prepare learners for practice items. Training programs have a chance to remain lean, less time-consuming, and less costly. The more accurately and completely developing training materials implements and spells out the details of an instructional strategy, the more likely the resulting training program is to achieve targeted outcomes.

Formative Evaluation

Like a consumer product, a training program is the end result of much planning, engineering, and implementation. For all the sophisticated design that may go into its preparation, there remains uncertainty, as in the case of the consumer product, as to the program's actual capacity to do the job it was designed to do.

To assure delivery of a product that works, a training development process

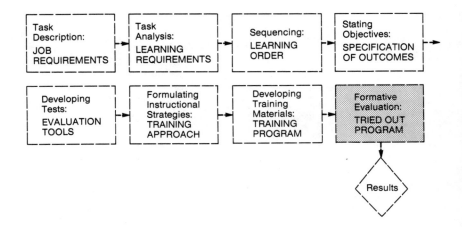

requires a mechanism for trying out the product, determining whether it can do its job, and if it cannot, identifying what needs to be changed, and making those changes. In instructional design that mechanism is *formative evaluation*.

Purpose. Developers evaluate the effectiveness of a training program by administering it to a sample of the target audience. Using tests specifically developed for that program, they assess how well trainees in the sample learn what they are supposed to learn. Then, using the results of the tryout, they diagnose shortcomings in the program and make revisions.

If time and money permit, multiple cycles of tryout and revision provide still greater assurance that a training program will be effective. The more cycles there are, the greater that assurance.

Results. The end product of formative evaluation is a training program that has been revised in the light of tryout results. It might contain any of the following kinds of changes: coverage of topics not previously included, a rearrangement of the sequence of topics, additional materials such as graphics or tables or more examples or practice items, revision of existing materials, etc. The changes chosen are made in response to explicit problems that have been diagnosed during the tryout.

Method. A training program is administered to a sample of a target audience. With all conditions as nearly representative of an ultimate, intended training setting as possible, data are collected about program adequacy.

Varied instruments and methods are possible. Results on tests and on practice problems are prime candidates. Interviews or questionnaires can be used to gather trainee reactions to how easy or difficult the program was. Trainees can identify whether they had difficulty and, if so, with which topics or with which presentation element or with which practice problem. Trainees can also indicate how interesting or satisfying they found the program.

All this information is pooled and analyzed for evidence of shortcomings in the program. Is information missing? Is some information there, but in insufficient detail? Is some information provided flat out wrong? Is some information simply misleading or confusing? Based on the diagnosis reached, developers make necessary revisions. Additional tryouts may be held to verify whether the revisions improve the original product.

Formative evaluation has its best chance of performing its intended function if time and money permit it to continue until specified outcomes are reached.

Summary

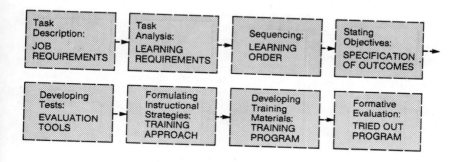

Conclusion

A sizable literature provides theoretical support, methodological underpinnings, and procedural guidelines for all these instructional design tasks. It can help newcomers to the discipline to sort out the various available instructional design models and to select one or more they might wish to try.

Trial of an instructional design model in a training development effort can provide evidence about its value: How easy is it to learn? How easy is it to implement? Can it be implemented in comparable ways by different developers? Can it accommodate varied applications? Does it produce programs that require little revision when tried out? Does it produce training programs that are effective?

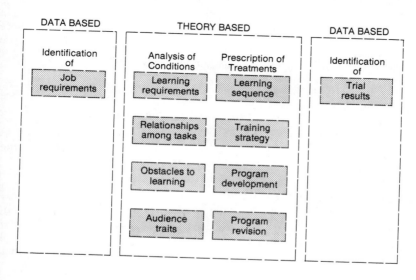

How much time and money does its use entail? What cost-benefit results does its use produce?

An instructional design model that requires training programs to undergo formative evaluation should itself be subject to the same requirements. A training operation might itself profitably modify or adapt instructional design models that tryouts reveal to be flawed in one way or another. Or, it might select another.

There are many models to choose from. Most are highly sophisticated. Most share many ideas. The next handbook that is published may be able to focus on a more universally agreed-on model. In the meantime different theories animate the different models that are currently available. But caveat emptor is *not* a necessary warning for any model that, at a minimum, carries out two especially critical instructional design tasks: (1) performs a task description to identify what is relevant to train for and (2) subjects a training program to formative evaluation to ensure that it is effective. Both, more or less unencumbered by theory, reach out to the real world for dependable, concrete data and thereby contribute to the validity of the development process. These two tasks represent useful and reassuring safety valves for a training operation. One ensures relevant coverage in a training program, the other program effectiveness.

Bibliography

Systematic Design of Instruction

General
Braden, R.A., *One Hundred Book Titles: A Twelve-Foot Shelf of Basic References for Instructional Design and Development*, Educational Technology Publications, Englewood Cliffs, NJ, 1981.
Gordon, I.J., ed., *Criteria for Theories of Instruction*, Association for Supervision and Curriculum Development, Washington, DC, 1968.
Langdon, D.G., ed., *The Instructional Design Library Series*, Educational Technology Publications, Englewood Cliffs, NJ, 1980.
Merrill, M.D., ed., *Instructional Design Readings*, Prentice-Hall, Englewood Cliffs, NJ, 1971.
O'Neill, H. F. Jr., ed., *Procedures for Instructional Systems Development*, Academic Press, New York, 1979.

Active Practice
Allen, W. H., "Research on Film Use: A Student Participation," *Audio/Visual Communication Review*, Vol. 5, pp. 423–450.

Programmed Instruction
Lumsdaine, A., and R. Glaser, eds., *Teaching Machines and Programmed Learning*, Department of Audiovisual Instruction, National Education Association, Washington, DC, 1960.
Markle, S. M., *Good Frames and Bad*, 2d ed., Wiley, New York, 1969.
Skinner, B. F., "The Science of Learning and the Art of Teaching," *Harvard Educational Review*, 24 (232), 1954, pp. 86–97.

Early Instructional Design
Gagne, R. M., *The Conditions of Learning*, 3d ed., Holt, Rinehart and Winston, New York, 1977.
Gilbert, T. F. "Mathetics: The Technology of Education," *Journal of Mathetics*, 7–73, 1962.
Mechner, F., "Behavioral Analysis and Instructional Sequencing," in P. Lange, ed., *Programmed Instruction: 66th Yearbook of the National Society for the Study of Education, Part II*, University of Chicago Press, Chicago, 1967.

Snelbecker, G. E., *Learning Theory, Instructional Theory, and Psychoeducational Design*, McGraw-Hill, New York, 1974.

Models

Andrews, D. H., and L. A. Goodson, "A Comparative Analysis of Models of Instructional Design," *Journal of Instructional Design*, summer 1980, vol. 3, No. 4, pp. 2–16.

Reigeluth, C., ed., *Instructional Design Theories and Models: An Overview of Their Current Status*, Lawrence Erlbaum Associates, Hillsdale, NJ, 1983.

Instructional Design Tasks

Needs Analysis

Birnbrauer, H., and L. A. Tyson, "How to Analyze Needs," *Training and Development Journal*, August 1985, vol. 39 (8), pp. 52–55.

Georgenson, D., and E. Gaizo, "Maximize the Return on Your Training Investment through Needs Analysis," *Training and Development Journal*, August 1984, vol. 38 (8), pp. 42–47.

Mager, R. F., and P. Pipe, *Analyzing Performance Problems*, Lear Siegler, Inc./Fearon Publishers, Belmont, CA, 1970.

Steadham, S. V., "Learning to Select a Needs Assessment Strategy," *Training and Development Journal*, January 1980, vol. 34 (1), pp. 56–61.

Zemke, R., "Needs Assessment: A Brief Overview," in Birnbrauer, ed., *Technical Skills Training Programs*, ASTD, Washington, DC, 1985.

Task Description

Gael, S., *Job Analysis: A Guide to Assessing Work Activities*, Jossey-Bass, San Francisco, CA, 1983.

Gardner, J. E., *Training Interventions in Job Skill Development*, Addison-Wesley, Reading, MA, 1981.

Miller, R. B., "Task Description and Analysis," in Robert M. Gagne, *Psychological Principles in System Development*, Holt, Rinehart and Winston, New York, 1962.

Rossett, A., "Relevance Revisited Systematically," *Journal of Instructional Development*, summer 1981, vol. 4, pp. 9–13.

Task Analysis

Bloom, B. B., ed., *Taxonomy of Educational Objectives: Handbook One, Cognitive Domain*, David McKay, New York, 1956.

Gilbert, T. F., *Human Competence: Engineering Worthy Performance*, McGraw-Hill, New York, 1978.

Merrill, P. F., "Task Analysis: An Information Processing Approach," *NSPI Journal*, 1976, vol. 15 (2), pp. 7–11.

Zemke, R. J., and Thomas Kramlinger, *Figuring Things Out: A Trainer's Guide to Needs and Task Analysis*, Addison-Wesley, Reading, MA, 1982.

Sequencing

Gagne, R. M., "Analysis of Objectives," in Leslie J. Briggs, ed., *Instructional Design: Principles and Applications*, Educational Technology Publications, Englewood Cliffs, NJ, 1977, pp. 114–115.

Gilbert, T. F., "Mathetics: The Technology of Education," *Journal of Mathetics*, 1962, 7–73.

Nadler, L., *Designing Training Programs: The Critical Events Model*, Addison-Wesley, Reading, MA, 1982.

Popham, W. J., and E. L. Baker, *Planning an Instructional Sequence*, Prentice-Hall, Englewood Cliffs, NJ, 1970.

Stating Objectives

Bloom. B. S., et al., *A Taxonomy of Educational Objectives*, Longman, New York, 1977.

Davies, I. K., *Objectives in Curriculum Design*, McGraw-Hill, New York, 1976.
Kapfer, M. B., *Behavioral Objectives in Curriculum Development, Selected Readings and Bibliography*, Educational Technology Publications, Englewood Cliffs, NJ, 1971.
Mager, R. F., *Preparing Instructional Objectives*, Pitman Learning, Belmont, CA, 1875.

Developing Tests

Berk, R. A., ed., *Criterion-Referenced Measurement: The State of the Art*, The Johns Hopkins University Press, Baltimore, 1980.
Copperud, C., *The Test Design Handbook*, Educational Technology Publications, Englewood Cliffs, NJ, 1979.
Hively, W., ed., *Domain Referenced Testing*, Educational Technology Publications, Englewood Cliffs, NJ, 1974.
Thorndike, R. L., ed., *Educational Measurement*, American Council on Education, Washington, DC, 1971.

Formulating Instructional Strategies

Bell, C. R., "Criteria for Selecting Instructional Strategies," *Training and Development Journal*, October 1977, vol. 31. no. 10, pp. 3–7.
Davies, I., *Instructional Technique*, McGraw-Hill, New York, 1980.
Dwyer, F. M., *Strategies for Improving Visual Learning: A Handbook for the Effective Selection, Design, and Use of Visualized Materials*, Learning Service, State College, PA, 1978.
Gropper, G. L., *Instructional Strategies*, Educational Technology Publications, Englewood Cliffs, NJ, 1974.
Markle, S., *Designs for Instructional Designers*, Stipes Publications, Champaign, IL, 1978.
O'Neill, M. F., Jr., ed., *Learning Strategies*, Academic Press, New York, 1978.

Developing Instructional Materials

Dick, W., and L. Carey, *The Systematic Design of Instruction*, 2d ed., Scott Foresman, Glenview, IL, 1895.
Gagne, R. M., and Briggs, L. J., *Principles of Instructional Design*, Holt, Rinehart and Winston, New York, 1974.

Formative Evaluation

Baker, E. L., and M. C. Alkin, "Formative Evaluation of Instructional Development," *Audio Visual Communication Review*, vol. 21, no. 4, 1973, pp. 389–418.
Cronbach, L. J. "Course Improvement through Evaluation," reprinted in D. A. Payne and R. F. McMorris, eds., *Educational Psychological Measurement*, General Learning Press, Morristown, NJ, 1975, pp. 243–256.
Gropper, L. J., *Diagnosis and Revision of Instructional Materials*, Educational Technology Publications, Englewood Cliffs, NJ, 1975.
Lawson, T. E., *Formative Instructional Product Evaluation: Instruments and Strategies*, Educational Technology Publications, Englewood Cliffs, NJ, 1974.

12
Determining Needs

Geary A. Rummler

Geary A. Rummler is president of the Rummler Group, a research and consulting group specializing in the design and development of organization performance systems for business and government. Prior to founding the Rummler Group, he was president of the Kepner-Tregoe Strategy Group, specialists in strategic decision making; cofounded and was president of Praxis Corporation, an innovator in analysis and improvement of human performance; and cofounded and was director of the University of Michigan's Center for Programmed Learning for Business. Rummler was a pioneer in the application of instructional and performance technologies. His clients have included the aircraft, automobile, steel, food, rubber, office equipment, pharmaceutical, chemical and petroleum, retail, banking, and airline industries. He has worked with such federal agencies as IRS, SSA, HUD, GAO, and DOT. His work has taken him to Europe, Japan, Mexico, and the United Kingdom. He received his M.B.A. and Ph.D. from the University of Michigan. He is a member of the Training Research Forum, was president of the National Society for Performance and Instruction, member of ASTD Research and Strategic Planning Committees, and editorial board of Training magazine.

The new training director of Property Casualty, Inc., has just received the following message from the vice president of claims: "Welcome aboard. We are long overdue for some training for our claim representatives and their bosses, the claim supervisors. I would appreciate your recommendations on what training we should provide."

The task the training director faces is determining training needs. It is the starting point of all training. There is no more critical task in the training process. How well this step is done impacts

- The trainees—is the training relevant to their jobs?
- The organization—will this training improve performance?

- The quality of the training program—can we measure the effectiveness of the training course?
- The effectiveness of the training function—does training make a difference? Have an impact on the organization?

"Determining training needs" is not just a training process issue. It is also a training management issue, reflecting the mission, philosophy, and strategy of the training function.

This chapter will examine why we train, present a framework for linking training and performance and evaluating approaches to determining training needs, and discuss four basic approaches to determining training needs. The emphasis in this chapter is not as much how to as *when* to use each approach and *why*.

Basic Premise

A basic, beginning premise for this chapter and the discussion of determining training needs is the following:

The primary objective of training is to improve individual *and* organization performance.

Training is used—or misused—to do a variety of things from informing, motivating, rewarding to changing behavior and improving performance. However, the goal of the training professional (as shown below) is to have the training *input* impact the performance *output* of the trainee.

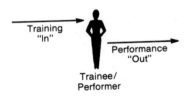

With this objective for training in mind, the training director of Property Casualty, Inc., should interpret the request of the vice president of claims as follows: "What training is required to improve the *performance* of our claim representatives and the claim supervisors, and consequently, the performance of the claim function and the bottom line of Property Casualty, Inc.?"

There are a number of ways we can go about answering the vice president's question—of determining what training is required. Before we can determine which way is appropriate, it will be helpful to have a framework for looking at training and performance.

A System View of Training and Performance

If the goal of training is to improve performance, it is important that we have a framework for looking at and understanding the relationship of training and performance. A very useful framework is a *system* view. This will provide us with a framework for looking at how training can impact performance, what the roles of the training function can be, the significance of accurately determining training needs, and the alternative approaches to determining training needs.

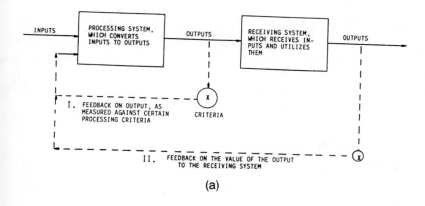

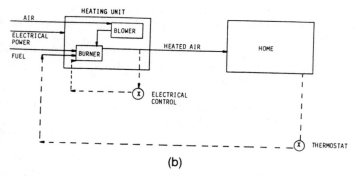

Figure 12-1. (a) General systems model; (b) a home heating system.

A Basic System Model

Our look at training is based on general systems theory, which suggests that we can view many aspects of our world as processing and receiving systems, as illustrated in Fig. 12-1a. Specifically,

1. The processing system converts inputs, through various process systems, into outputs. A home furnace is a processing system (Fig. 12-1b) taking in air, fuel, and electrical power, and converting them into hot air.

2. For every processing system, there is a receiving system. And therefore, every output of a processing system is an input to another system, a receiving system. The rooms in a home are the receiving system for the home furnace. The hot air output of the furnace is the heat—the input—that the rooms require.

3. Systems are driven by the feedback they receive. There are two *primary* levels of feedback. Loop I is the measurement that the processing system makes of its output against internal criteria. In the furnace, this feedback regulates the level of fuel, air, and electrical power used to produce the hot air. Feedback loop II originates from the receiving system, measured against the receiving system

criteria. If the processing system and receiving system are in fact operating as a total system, the processing system will respond to both feedback loops and will alter its output accordingly. In a house, the receiving system criteria are represented by the thermostat. When the temperature falls below a certain level, the thermostat mechanism sends a signal to the furnace for more hot air.

A fundamental system truth is that processing systems respond to the receiving system requirements. If they fail to do so, they fall into disuse or are replaced.

A System Look at Organizations

One aspect of the world that can be profitably viewed as a system is an organization—any organization. In fact, understanding that organizations function as systems is key to analyzing individual and organization performance and determining training needs.

Figure 12-2 shows a macroview of an organization as a system, wherein we can see:

1. Organizations function as processing systems, converting inputs (orders, materials, labor, capital, technology, etc.) through various subsystems (functions, departments) to produce valued outputs (products or services) for a marketplace or constituency (receiving system).

2. The processing system and organization responds to various levels of feedback: (I) self-evaluation against internal criteria for product quality, cost, etc., and (II) evaluation by the marketplace or constituency. Ultimately, all organizations respond or adapt to their receiving system. They respond or they disappear.

3. All the subsystems (i.e., functions, departments) support the basic organizational process of converting inputs into outputs. The subsystems have basic processing systems—receiving system relationships with each other (e.g., R&D and manufacturing, manufacturing and sales) and likewise respond to the two primary sources of feedback. As the total organization adapts to the changing

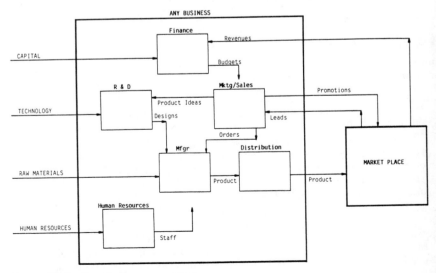

Figure 12-2. Organizations as a system.

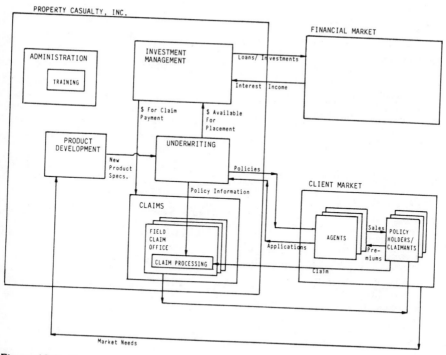

Figure 12-3. Property Casualty, Inc., as a system.

requirements of its marketplace or constituency, the subsystems must adapt to the changing requirements of the organization.

As we said earlier, this concept or view of organizations as systems is key to determining training needs. For example, if the training director of Property Casualty, Inc., understands the concept, then he or she will know that:

1. Property Casualty, Inc., is a processing system that must ultimately respond to its receiving systems of policyholders and investors (see Fig. 12-3).

2. The vice president of claims manages a key subsystem of the company which must produce outputs critical to the performance of the total company.

3. The claims function is made up of a number of key sub-subsystems or processes, one of which is the claim handling function in the field that requires specific performance from claim representatives and claim supervisors.

If the training director believes the objective of training is to improve the performance of individuals and organizations, then understanding that Property Casualty, Inc., has the basic system relationship listed above provides a framework or road map for determining how claim representatives' and claim supervisors' performance impacts the performance of the claim function and the total company.

There is a second system view of organizations that is important to our training director of Property Casualty, Inc., and relevant to determining training needs in general. This is a look at the training function as a system.

A System Look at Training

As you might expect, the training function of any organization can be viewed as a key subsystem of that organization, as shown in Fig. 12-4. This system view suggests that:

1. The training function is a processing system, converting training needs data, training technology, training expertise, budget, and untrained personnel into trained personnel for the various operating functions or units (receiving systems). (Training organizations may perform other functions such as brokering outside training resources, which are not shown in this model for reasons of simplicity.)

2. The primary inputs of training needs and untrained personnel are converted into the output of trained personnel through subsystems such as analysis, design, development, delivery, and evaluation (to identify a few).

3. The training processing system is subject to the same "system laws" regarding responding to receiving systems that apply to organizations and the general systems model. Like the other processing systems we have discussed, there are two primary sources of feedback:
   Self-evaluation against internal criteria. This might involve cost of training, course evaluation, etc.
   Evaluation by the receiving systems against their criteria. This may include response time to requests for training and the subsequent performance of the trainee.

As with other processing systems, the training subsystem must be responsive to its receiving systems or it will perish and/or be replaced. This means that:

1. The internal criteria must be in "synch" with the criteria used by the receiving systems and/or clients. If the client is expecting increased performer and organization performance (sales increase, reduction in manufacturing costs of new products) and the training function is evaluating the quality of the training output by a "smiles test" or "happiness index," the training subsystem may be producing an unacceptable output as far as the client is concerned.

2. The training output is going to be only as good as the training needs data input that the training subsystem is processing.

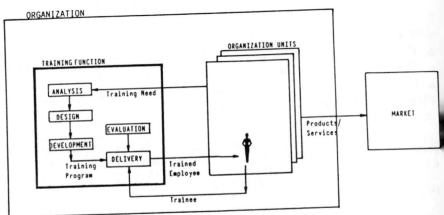

Figure 12-4. The training function as a key organization subsystem.

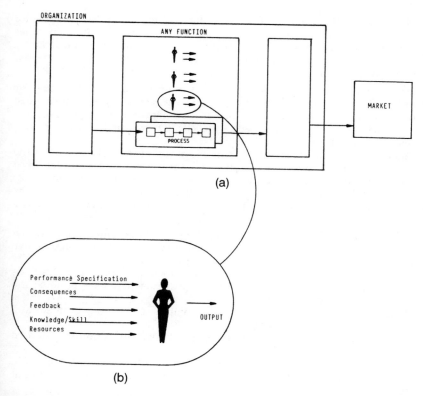

Figure 12-5. A systems look at the trainee performer: (a) Performance Context; (b) Peformance Factors—Inputs required to produce an output.

This system view of training has implications for the design and management of the training function, as well as for determining training needs. For our training director of Property Casualty, Inc., it makes the point that he or she manages a key subsystem and if the output is "training that improves performance," then a most critical input to the function is the right kind of data on training needs.

The quality of the training output is only as good as the training needs data input. If the training needs have not been properly identified, then both the training course *and* the training function are in jeopardy.

A System Look at the Trainee-Performer

Now let's take our system view of the world one more, final step and look at a trainee-performer in a system context. This allows us to understand what circumstances training can impact performance and what are possible approaches to determining training needs.

To do this, we will take a more microscopic look at the organization as a processing system. Referring to Fig. 12-5, we see:

1. Any subsystem, such as the claim function of Property Casualty, Inc., is linked to the organization system through key inputs and outputs (see Fig. 12-5.)

2. Each subsystem is composed of processes for getting work accomplished—for converting inputs into outputs. The Property Casualty, Inc., claim function has a claim handling process that converts policyholder claims into settled claims. (Processes may not be well defined or articulated—or even agreed upon—but they always do exist.)

3. There is a hierarchy of performers who exist to operate and support the basic process. Their outputs "drive" the process. The claim representative must produce various outputs for each step in the claim handling process. (For process step one—"claim assigned"—the claim representative must review caseloads, develop a work schedule, etc.)

   Likewise, the claim supervisor must produce various outputs to support the claim representative and the process. And the claim office manager must produce outputs to support *all* the key processes in the claim function, to see that all the necessary subsystem outputs are being produced. As we move up the hierarchy, the responsibilities of performers become broader, but there always is the focus of making the processes and the total function work effectively.

4. The output of any performer is a function of several performance factors, which we can show as critical inputs (see Fig. 12-5). That is, the claim representative (or any performer) is going to produce the desired output *only* if:
   a. They know what performance is expected of them (*performance specification*).
   b. They do not encounter negative consequences when they produce the desired output (*consequences*).
   c. They receive adequate feedback on the output so they can evaluate and correct it if required (*feedback*).
   d. They have the necessary tools, time, and budget to perform as desired (*resources*).
   e. They *know* when and how to produce the desired output (*knowledge and skill*).
   f. They have the physical and emotional capacity to produce the output (*individual capacity*).

This final system look at performance reveals some significant implications for training and how we determine training needs. Based on the system view of the trainee-performer, we realize:

1. Every trainee is *always* a performer, operating in some performance context of expectations (possible unclear or conflicting), consequences (possibly more negative than positive), varying levels of resources, and varying degrees of feedback. Given this, training (i.e., knowledge and skill input) is but one factor in producing job performance. The training analyst must know what performance can be impacted by training and what performance can't, and what performance factors must *also* be altered if the recommended training input is to result in meaningful performance output.

2. Every trainee-performer does (or should) impact organization performance in a fairly direct way. A training analyst needs to learn *how* the performer impacts the organization for the training to have any impact. They must uncover that linkage between performer and organization, as obscure as it may be.

As a way of reviewing the whole system look at training and performance, let's summarize the implications for the training director of Property Casualty, Inc. That is, if our training director fully subscribed to this view, he or she would:

1. Understand that the training function is a subsystem of Property Casualty, Inc., and that its major output is "training that improves individual and organization performance." The training function would be evaluated on how well its

training outputs affected individual and organization performance. The training director would also realize that the quality of the training output will be only as good as the quality of information they receive (input) on the training needs.

2. Interpret the request for the vice president of claims for recommendations on training needs for claim representatives and claim supervisors as, "What training is required to improve the *performance* of our claim representative and the claim supervisors and, consequently, the performance of the claim function and the bottom line of Property Casualty, Inc.?"

3. Realize that the claim representatives and claim supervisors exist in a very real performance context. If training of claim representatives and claim supervisors is to make any difference—to impact individual and organization performance—then the approach to determining training needs must involve learning that performance context. That means that the approach to determining the training needs of claim representatives and claim supervisors requires determining:

   a. The performance goals of Property Casualty, Inc., and how the claim function impacts them, thereby determining the critical performance areas of the claim function.

   b. How the claim handling process impacts those critical claim function performance areas.

   c. How each step in the claim process impacts the total process output, and how each step might fail.

   d. How the claim representative and claim supervisor affect each step in the claim handling process and how that performance by them can vary and why.

   e. What knowledge and skill is required to have the claim representative and claim supervisor produce the outputs necessary for the claim handling process to operate effectively.

   f. What other performance factors must be altered (e.g., measures and feedback on performance) if the claim representative, claim supervisor, and claim process are to be effective.

The result would be a training course and strategy that would improve the performance of claim representatives, claim supervisors, the claim function, and Property Casualty, Inc., and a training function and/or subsystem that was responsive to the business demands of its receiving system.

Now that we have the broad framework for understanding the relationship between training and performance, let's look at several approaches to determining training needs.

Basic Approaches to Determining Training Needs

In the preceding section we described a scenario for how the training director of Property Casualty, Inc., might respond to the request of the vice president. It is, in fact, an ideal scenario. In reality a number of factors might interfere with carrying out the approach described above, including:

- Not enough time (the vice president wants an answer within 2 weeks).

- Not enough training resources to do the desired level of analysis.

- Management (the vice president of claims) doesn't share the notion that training should improve performance. They want training activity, not training results.

- Management isn't sure it wants some outside staff folks poking around very deep in their operations. They would prefer a superficial look at alleged training needs.

These are all organization realities. Therefore, the goal of a training analyst is twofold: to be responsive to the vice president's request and still do the best job he or she can of recommending training that will make a difference. Our first project with the vice president may produce a relatively superficial analysis, but if we meet the manager's perceived need, we will no doubt have a second project where we might have a better chance to link to performance, and a third with an even better chance, etc. This being the case—being reality—we need several approaches to determining training needs.

There are many approaches to determining training needs, but we want to focus on four popular approaches. To put these four approaches in perspective, let's review the basic linkage between training input and performance output, as shown in Fig. 12-6 and illustrated with the example of a claim supervisor at Property Casualty, Inc. There are five major links, starting with the input:

1. *The knowledge and skill input to the performer.*

2. *The knowledge and skill base or repertoire of the performer that results from the knowledge and skill input.* This performer repertoire or capability is popularly known these days as "competences." The competency of "claim analysis skill" for the claim supervisor is a result of knowledge and skills such as "interpreting policies" and "estimating extent of loss."

3. *The tasks which the performer actually performs.* Something gets done, gets produced. This is the first level of output. The knowledge and skill input can (and should) be linked directly to the task output, as is illustrated with the claim supervisor's task of "$ expense estimated."

4. *The job outputs.* What is actually accomplished by the performer—the results of all the tasks being done correctly. The tasks shown for the claim supervisor all contribute to the successful job output or accomplishment of "claim assigned."

5. *The process or function outputs.* What the organization requires of the process or function in question. The job outputs are necessary to produce the desired process or function outputs. The process in question for our example is the claim handling process and the output is a "claim processed."

Summarizing the linkage from output to input (right to left) in order for the claim handling process to consistently produce the desired output of "claims processed," the claim supervisor must produce specific job outputs which require that certain tasks be done, and these tasks require specific knowledge and skills.

These five links between training and performance correspond to four popular approaches to determining training needs. Each of those approaches "taps" into this linkage at a different point, usually with different results.

First we will quickly overview the four approaches and then each will be discussed in some detail. The four approaches are (see Fig. 12-7):

1. *Performance analysis*, which starts with links 5 and 4. Using this approach the training director of Property Casualty, Inc., would *begin* the needs analysis by determining the desired process and job output, and then determining the tasks required for each job output and ultimately what knowledge and skill was required to perform the various tasks. This approach will also identify the other performance factors such as consequences and feedback—in addition to training—that are required if the job and process outputs are to occur.

2. *Task analysis*, which enters the linkage at point 3. If applying a task analysis approach to determining the training needs of claim supervisors, the training director of Property Casualty, Inc., would begin by determining the *tasks*

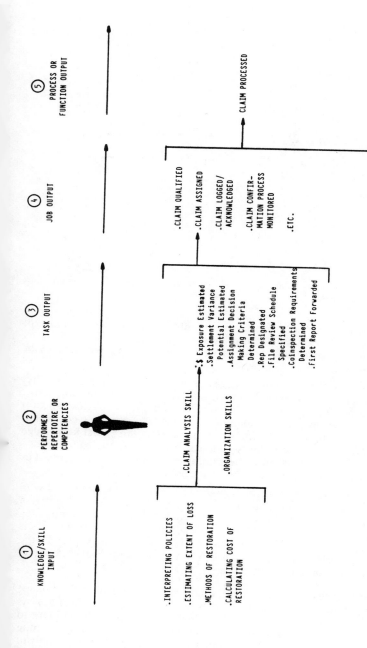

Figure 12-6. A view of the linkage between training input and performance output (an example for a claim supervisor).

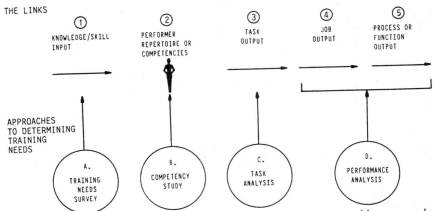

Figure 12-7. The linkage between training input and performance output and four approaches to determining training needs.

performed by the supervisor and then ascertaining what knowledge and skill was required to successfully perform those tasks. This approach to needs analysis is output focused but does not tie directly into job performance or address the other performance factors.

3. *Competency study*, which enters the linkage at point 2, the performer repertoire. If this were the approach used by the training director of Property Casualty, Inc., he or she would begin by determining what experts in the claims function thought the competences or capabilities of a claim supervisor were (claim analysis skills, organization skills, etc.) and then ascertaining what knowledge and skill was required to have the capabilities or to display the competences. This approach does not directly link the training input to performance output or address the performance context of the performer.

4. *Training needs survey*, which enters at point 1. This is a very straightforward process where the training director of Property Casualty, Inc., would survey a range of informed sources within the claim function and ask what training they thought was required by or would be beneficial for claim supervisors. This is basically an informed opinion survey and begins and ends at point 1 in the linkage. This approach to needs analysis is relatively quick but makes no direct link to performance output at any level.

These four approaches to determining training needs, to entering the linkage between training input and performance output, are summarized in Fig. 12–8. As you can see, the four approaches vary in how tightly they link training input to performance output and therefore in the quality of the information on training needs. But the quality of information must be balanced against the constraints of time, resources, and client sophistication.

In reality, where the training analyst starts the needs analysis process (which of the four approaches) depends on circumstances. Specifically it will depend on:

- The size and type of trainee-performer population.

- The complexity of the jobs in question.

- The opportunity to "make a difference."
  Is this a population or area important to organization performance?

TRAINING-PERFORMANCE LINKAGE / ALTERNATIVE TRAINING NEEDS ANALYSIS	KNOWLEDGE/ SKILL REQUIRED	COMPETENCIES/ REPERTOIRE	TASKS OUTPUT	JOB OUTPUT
TRAINING NEEDS SURVEY	① What training do you think you/they need?	?	?	?
COMPETENCY STUDY	② What knowledge/ skill is required to be competent in these areas?	① What competency do you think you/they need?		
TASK ANALYSIS	② What knowledge/ skill is required to perform these tasks?		① What tasks are required/do you do on this job?	?
PERFORMANCE ANALYSIS	③ What knowledge/ skill is required to perform these *critical* tasks?		② What tasks are required to produce the *critical* accomplishments?	① How does this job impact the performance of the organization? What are (or should be) the *critical* job accomplishments and how is each critical?

Figure 12-8. Summary of four approaches to determining training needs.

Is this a "quick fix" or will it be a multiyear training plan?
- The time available.
- Client commitment.
  Do they want improved performance or some training "flash"?
  Will they make changes in other performance factors to support the recommended training?
- The resources available.
  The manpower to do the analysis.
  The budget for the training product. (If there is only $1500 for the training product, you won't get much training; so a precise, comprehensive analysis is not worthwhile.)

In short, is this a training opportunity where you *want* to make a difference? Where you *can* make a difference?

Keeping in mind that when you use which approach depends on the circumstances, we will discuss each approach and how they might be used by the training director of Property Casualty, Inc., to respond to the request of the vice president.

As shown in Fig. 12-9, each approach has advantages and disadvantages and is

	TRAINING NEEDS SURVEY	COMPETENCY STUDY	TASK ANALYSIS	PERFORMANCE ANALYSIS
STARTING POINT	What knowledge and skill is required?	What competences are required?	What tasks are required?	What job performance is required?
GENERAL APPROACH	1. Ask key people what knowledge and skills they think or feel the trainee-performers require to do their job (or "X" portion of their job). 2. Prioritize the knowledge and skills recommended and summarize as a topical list, a training agenda, curriculum, etc.	1. Ask key people what competencies they think or feel the trainee-performer requires to do the job (or "X" portion of the job). 2. Determine the knowledge and skills required to attain the stated competences. 3. Prioritize the knowledge and skills recommended and summarize as a training agenda or curriculum.	1. Determine what tasks are required of the trainee-performer in order for the job to be performed correctly and successfully. 2. Determine the knowledge and skills required to correctly perform the tasks identified. 3. Prioritize the tasks, and thereby the knowledge and skills, and summarize as a training design document, training agenda, or curriculum.	1. Determine what performance is required. 2. Determine the critical job outputs or "accomplishments." 3. Determine what tasks are required of the trainee-performer to produce the job outputs or "accomplishments." 4. Determine the knowledge and skills required to correctly perform the tasks identified. 5. Determine what other factors (in addition to knowledge and skills) influence job performance (such as job design, resources, consequences, and feedback). 6. Prioritize the knowledge and skills required based on impact on job performance and summarize as a training design document, training agenda, or curriculum. 7. Summarize recommendations to

ADVANTAGES OF THIS APPROACH	• Fast, inexpensive • Broad involvement • Low risk • Low visibility	• Relatively fast, inexpensive • Broad involvement • Consensus • In addition to training needs, articulation and agreement on a success "profile" for the performer • Identify generic training needs covering a broad population (e.g., first-time supervisors, first-time managers)	• Precise identification of tasks and required knowledge and skills • Is a form of output and can be measured • Broad involvement • Objective, validated by observation	modify negative influences on performance, as identified in 4, above. • Links knowledge and skills requirements to job performance. • Can validate, evaluate. • Addresses other factors affecting performance. • Impact of job outputs is established and therefore can prioritize knowledge and skills input.
DISADVANTAGES OF THIS APPROACH	• Not precise or specific • Based on opinion, albeit "expert" • Difficult to validate • Difficult to set priorities • Difficult to relate to output, to evaluate importance of training • Once you ask people what training they feel is important, there is an implicit expectation that you will deliver it	• Difficult to relate to output, to evaluate training • Difficult to assess relative importance of competences and therefore difficult to set priorities for knowledge and skills input. • Consensus will not necessarily identify the critical difference between exemplary and average performance. • Does not address other factors influencing performance • Can be highly visible	• Takes time and skill • Visible • Difficult to assess relative importance of tasks and therefore difficult to set priorities for knowledge and skills input • Does not address other factors affecting performance	• Takes time and skill • Visible

Figure 12-9. Comparison of four approaches to determining training needs.

more appropriate under different circumstances. However, a professional trainer is likely to profitably employ all the approaches at some point in his or her career.

Approach A—Training
Needs Survey

This is the most frequently used approach to determining training needs. It is quick, but the results are based on opinion. The key to effectively using this approach is the quality of the opinions received.

A General Scenario

The task confronting the training director of Property Casualty, Inc., is to answer the question "What training do the claim representatives (and/or claim supervisors) require?" The basic approach is to seek the opinion of (i.e., survey) knowledgeable people regarding the performance of claim representatives and claim supervisors. The following is a typical sequence.

1. Identify the data sources—whose opinion will be sought. In the case of PC, Inc., that might include claim representatives, claim supervisors, claim office managers, and region managers. (See the organization chart in Fig. 12-10.)

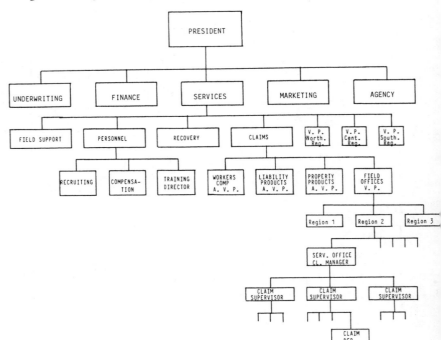

Figure 12-10. Organization chart for Property Casualty, Inc.

2. Develop a questionnaire that solicits the opinions.
3. Interview the following sources, using the questionnaire as a guide.
   One region manager—what knowledge and skill is required by the claim representative and claim supervisor?
   Three or four claim office managers—what knowledge and skill is required by claim representatives and claim supervisors?
   Five or six claim supervisors—what knowledge and skill is required to do your job? What knowledge and skill is required by claim representatives?
   Five or six claim representatives—what knowledge and skill is required to do your job?
   Refine the questionnaire during the interview process.
4. Mail the questionnaire to the following:
   All claim office managers not yet surveyed.
   Two claim supervisors and four claim representatives from every claim office. The issue is not statistical sample size, but assurance that you have heard from a wide spectrum. (An alternative to steps 3 or 4 is to assemble small focus groups of four to six participants for a discussion of the knowledge and skill requirements. These discussions could be "free-form" or be guided by the questionnaire. A group of claim office managers would discuss the knowledge and skill requirements of the claim representatives and claim supervisors. A group of claim supervisors would focus on their knowledge and skill requirements and those of the claim representatives. And the claim representatives would address the knowledge and skill they felt they required.)
5. Organize the responses to the survey into categories. In this case, the knowledge and skill requirement for the claim representative might be organized "by basic technical knowledge and skills," "advanced technical knowledge and skills," and "interpersonal skills." The categories for claim supervisor might be "technical knowledge and skills" and "management skills."
6. Prioritize the training needs. This is difficult to do with this approach to determining training needs because there are no data on the relationship of the knowledge and skill to critical job performance. However, prioritization might be accomplished in this case by:
   a. Considering the frequency with which various knowledge and skill subjects were mentioned by the participants (the design of the questionnaire can facilitate this).
   b. Discerning some pattern or logic in the categories that suggests that, for example, claim representatives should be trained first in basic technical knowledge and skills, then interpersonal skills, and finally advanced technical skills.
7. Present the findings in some form of proposed training plan. This could be as straightforward as a list of training that should be provided claim representatives during the next year or as comprehensive as a proposed multiyear curriculum for the career claim representative. (The latter might be risky since there is no link between the proposed training input and performance output.)
8. Distribute an abbreviated summary of the survey findings to the parties who participated in the survey, along with an indication of what action will be taken as a result.

The following section will discuss some of the specific issues that arise in data gathering and data analysis when following a scenario such as that just described.

Data Gathering

A training needs survey is seeking opinions on "what knowledge and skill is required" for a particular job or class of performer. Whose opinion should be sought and how?

Data Sources

Potential sources of data (opinion) on knowledge and skill needs include:

1. Supervisors and managers of the job in question, who may identify what knowledge and skill components explain the difference between good and poor performers.
2. Past incumbents (which may or may not include the above source).
3. Incumbents.
   Senior successful performers, who may identify what knowledge and skill has contributed to their success.
   Juniors or beginners, who may be able to articulate what knowledge and skill would make them better prepared for the job that looms ahead of them.
4. Representatives of functions in and out of the organization that interface with the job in question. They may identify what knowledge and skill makes job incumbents effective in working with their function.

Sometimes there are secondary sources of information which may provide a general perspective about a job rather than specific information about knowledge and skills. These sources include:

- Senior management
- Subordinates of the performer in question
- Customers

Seeking the opinion of these sources is relatively easy, and it is thereby possible to solicit a broad base of input. However, there are two reasons to restrict your data gathering to those sources who will give you the best data.

1. The more people you include in your data gathering, the more people you must keep informed as you progress. (If you ask an opinion, you have an implicit responsibility to follow through on it—either to respond to it or explain why you have not.)
2. The more people included, the more data to be processed, analyzed, prioritized etc. It is easy to become overwhelmed with the data.

In determining training needs, more is not necessarily better.

Data Collection

Data can be collected from the various sources via:

1. A questionnaire, which is mailed to the source.
2. A one-on-one interview, which might be guided by a questionnaire.
3. A small group meeting, which is unstructured or guided by a questionnaire.

A combination of these processes might be used in any given training needs analysis effort.

There are also degrees of structure that can be employed when seeking the opinion of the various sources. The structure will impact the quality of the opinion. The following represent a range of "structure," from little to considerable:

1. Basic—simply ask (questionnaire or interview): "What knowledge and skill (training) do you think the X's need in their job?"

2. Performance context—ask (questionnaire or interview):
   "Given the current business challenges we face, what knowledge and skill is required of the X's?" or
   "What are the business challenges you think we face in the next three years? What are the knowledge and skills required of the X's to meet each of these challenges?"

3. A critical incident—ask (questionnaire or interview): "Think of a critical incident during the past 6 weeks involving an X handling an employee grievance. What knowledge and skill would have helped the X handle the situation?" (The critical incident process is a specific technique widely used over the past 40 years. For more information see the references at the end of this chapter.)

Data Analysis

The data analysis requirements are not great nor are the procedures sophisticated. The data must be categorized in some fashion (e.g., technical knowledge and skills, interpersonal knowledge and skills) and the needs prioritized. This approach does not establish any link with performance output; so the major form of prioritization is by frequency of mention in the survey.

The results can be summarized in a list of training needs or a proposed training agenda for the next X period of time, or as a proposed curriculum for X job.

Advantages

The advantages of this approach include:

1. Being fast and inexpensive.

2. The potential to have broad involvement. A wide spectrum of people can participate relatively inexpensively.

3. Having low visibility, if desired. A representative number of people can be surveyed quickly with little expense and a small investment of time on their part.

4. Involving little risk.

Disadvantages

The potential disadvantages of this approach include:

1. The results are imprecise. For example, the level of response will most likely include such things as "communications," "finance," and "statistics." Unless the data are gathered in an interview format that allows for follow-up questions,

such as "What do you mean by 'finance'?" and a response like "Well, budgets— preparing budgets and reading the operating statements," it is difficult to identify specific knowledge and skill requirements.

2. The data are opinion (hopefully expert), and not necessarily supported by objective performance data. Therefore, it is difficult to relate the recommended training to a specific performance output, and thereby almost assuring that you can't objectively evaluate the impact of training.

3. Difficulty setting priorities. Since the knowledge and skill is not tied to performance output, there is no basis for setting priorities other than frequency of mention or some logic such as "we teach technical skills before interpersonal skills (or the reverse)."

4. An implicit commitment to train. Once you ask people's opinion on what training is required, they are left with an expectation that you will act on their recommendation. As a result, you must be responsive to their recommendations or explain why you are not. Seeing or hearing no response to their input will seriously jeopardize any future cooperation regarding training need survey.

When and Where Not to Use

Recognizing the limits on the quality of data obtained, this approach can be used for most all levels and type of jobs. It is most appropriate when there is low client commitment, a short response time, and little opportunity to seriously impact organization performance.

Approach B— Competency Study

This is an increasingly popular approach to determining training needs. It is relatively quick and can result in a broad consensus on training needs. However, it still starts the needs analysis process on the "input" side of the formula.

A General Scenario

The task of the training director of Property Casualty, Inc., is to answer the question, "What training do the claim representatives (and/or claim supervisors) require?" The project might proceed as follows:

1. Select a group of "experts" to identify the general competences of a good claim supervisor and claim representative. The goal is to articulate a model or profile of a claim supervisor and claim representative. There might be several group meetings including:
   a. Regional and claim office managers with experience as claim supervisors and claim representatives, and in managing them.
   b. Experienced claim supervisors and claim representatives.

2. Distribute the preliminary model to a larger circle of experts, conceivably to all claim office managers, regional managers, and claim supervisors. These managers will add to or delete from this preliminary list.

3. Assemble the input from the broader survey and review with the initial expert groups (step 1). Finalize the list of competencies.

4. Have the original expert groups identify and prioritize the knowledge and skills they believe are required to have the desired competencies. A larger number of managers could participate through a survey similar to step 3 if broader involvement was desirable.

5. Organize the knowledge and skill requirements into a training plan. The requirements might be classified as "basic" and "advanced" for claim supervisors and "technical" and "interpersonal" for claim representatives. The training plan could be a list of recommended training or a more comprehensive multiyear curriculum for claim representatives and claim supervisors.

Following are more of the specific issues that arise in data gathering and data analysis when using this approach.

Data Gathering

As with a training needs survey, we are relying on the opinions of "experts" as to the desired competencies of the performer in question.

Data Sources

The sources should be people who have performed the job, managed the job, and possibly been recipients of the job's outputs. It helps if they are articulate and have credibility with the performance population in question and the organization as a whole.

Data Collection

The primary forms of data collection are the group meeting with experts and the survey questionnaire. The guidelines discussed under data collection for a training needs survey are applicable for a competency study.

Data Analysis

The data analysis requirements include determining what knowledge and skill supports what competencies, determining some system of prioritization for the training, and possibly structuring a multiyear curriculum. The results of the analysis might be displayed as follows:

COMPETENCY—KNOWLEDGE/SKILL LINK

COMPETENCIES	KNOWLEDGE/SKILL AREA			
	A	B	C	D
I. _____	X	X	X	
II. _____		X	X	
III. _____	X		X	

CURRICULUM			
COMPETENCIES	Year 1	Year 2	Year 3
I. _____			
II. _____			
III. _____			

Advantages

The advantages of this approach include:

1. It is relatively fast and inexpensive.
2. It involves broad participation and results in consensus.
3. In addition to determining training needs, it requires the organization to articulate and reach agreement on a success profile for the performer role in question.
4. It identifies generic training needs for broad performer population, such as "first-time supervisors," "first-time managers," and "trainees."

Disadvantages

The potential disadvantages of this approach include:

1. It is difficult to relate competencies and the resulting knowledge and skill requirements to job output and organization performance. Therefore, validation and evaluation are difficult.
2. It is difficult to assess relative importance of competencies and therefore difficult to set priorities for the knowledge and skills input.
3. The consensus of experts will not necessarily identify the critical difference between exemplary and average performance, which is key to identifying training input that will impact job output.
4. The findings tend to be general, identifying topics such as "financial planning" versus "skill in preparing requests for capital appropriations."
5. It does not address other factors influencing the performance of the job in question. The individual may be "competent" as defined by the knowledge and skill input, but we will not necessarily see the desired job output because performance factors such as feedback and consequences.

When and Where Not to Use

Understanding the limitations on the forthcoming data (not tied to performance output), this approach is more appropriate for managerial and professional jobs with broad, difficult-to-define job responsibilies than for jobs with specific, well-defined outputs. In the case of Property Casualty, Inc., a competency study would be more useful in examining the jobs of "staff manager" or "underwriter" than a claim representative.

In general, this approach would be appropriate for determining training needs when there is a relatively short lead time, resources are limited, and/or the client would benefit from a consensus profile of the job in question.

Approach C—Task Analysis

"Task analysis" is an effective and widely used process to determine training needs. It requires time and effort, but the results are based on objective, "hard" data. This approach makes it possible to link the resultant training input to measurable performance output.

A General Scenario

The task is to answer the question,"What training do the claim representatives (and/or claim supervisors) require?" Since this approach is more appropriate for analyzing the claim representative job than for the claim supervisor job (the reason will be discussed later), this scenario is for the claim representative job only. The following is a sequence the training director of Property Casualty, Inc., might follow:

1. Identify claim representatives who are considered to do their job well. Ideally claims management has hard performance data to assist in this identification. If there are different types of claim representatives (big claims vs. little claims, property vs. casualty), you will be identifying several task lists and therefore need good performers in all relevant categories.

2. Gather data on what tasks are involved in processing a claim. The data gathering effort might include some or all of the following:
   a. Observe and interview claim representatives as they perform the job.
   b. Interview claim supervisors to determine what they feel are the critical tasks.
   c. Assemble small separate focus groups of claim representatives and claim supervisors to generate a list of tasks. (These are in descending order of effectiveness.)

3. Develop a list of tasks and subtasks (and perhaps sub-subtasks) describing what a claim representative *should* do to correctly process a claim. As we said in step 1, there may be several such lists representing different types of claims or claim representative jobs.

4. Refine the list by:
   a. Presenting it to small separate groups of claim representatives and claim supervisors for their review. They are asked to delete and expand on the task list. They also might comment on which tasks are most critical.
   b. Distributing the initial list to a number of claim representatives and claim supervisors for their additions, deletions, etc.

5. Finalize the list of tasks and assess their relative criticality.

6. Determine what knowledge and skill is required to perform the critical tasks and subtasks. The knowledge and skill can be determined by:
   a. The training analysts using themselves as a reference point. Based on their understanding of the task (based on their firsthand observations and interviews), what would they require to successfully perform the task.
   b. Assembling small separate groups of claim representatives and claim supervisors to review the task and discuss the knowledge and skill required to perform properly.
   The knowledge and skill requirements can be listed by major tasks or they can be summarized by categories such as "claim process knowledge," "product knowledge," "negotiating skills," "interpersonal skills," etc.

7. Present the findings in some form of proposed training plan. The plan should reflect some priorities for the training. Since the training director started the project by identifying the task output, the priority can be established several ways, including:
   a. Referring back to those tasks designated as critical and making the related knowledge and skills top priority.
   b. Reviewing which tasks are currently not done well and making the related knowledge and skills top priority.

Following is a discussion of some specific issues in conducting a task analysis.

Data Gathering

The initial thrust of this analysis is to determine what tasks are required of the performer in question. It is important that these data be valid—based on the analyst's *observation* of the desired tasks. If we ask various people what tasks they *think* the claim representative performs or should perform, we have another opinion survey which has little more validity than what we might have learned with approach A.

In effect, we want to be able to say, "These are the tasks that successful, effective claim representatives perform when handling claims. And less effective representatives don't perform all the tasks and don't perform them well. If a claim representative performs these tasks they should also be effective" (barring performance environment factors).

Data Sources

The primary data source for a task analysis is the performer—first "good" performers and then a few not-so-good performers to help highlight the critical tasks and subtasks. (It is important that you identify the major types of performers—small claims, big claims—and that you first observe the *best* of each type.) Secondary (but important) sources include immediate supervisors and former "master" performers.

Data Collection

The primary form of data collection should be observation and interviews of performers. The data might be collected by flowcharting the steps followed by the performer or by listing tasks and subtasks.

Once you have a basic task outline of the job based on your observation, you should go to secondary sources such as supervisors and have them confirm, expand, and modify your task list.

Data Analysis

Once the task data are gathered they can be organized in various formats for analysis and communication. For example:

1. Showing the difference between type of jobs.

MASTER TASK LIST	TASK BY TYPE OF CLAIM REP		
	BIG CLAIMS	SMALL CLAIMS	SPECIAL CLAIMS
A. _____	X	X	X
B. _____		X	
C. _____	X		
D. _____	X	X	X

2. Linking task to knowledge and skills requirements.

TASKS	SUBTASKS	Job: BIG CLAIMS KNOWLEDGE/SKILL REQUIREMENTS
A.___	1.___	
	2.___	
	3.___	
B.___	1.___	
	2.___	

The results can be summarized in some training plan format varying from a list of knowledge and skill types to a curriculum for new claim representatives.

Advantages

The advantages of this approach include:

1. Clear identification of required tasks and the required knowledge and skills.
2. The tasks can be validated—good performers perform these tasks this way.
3. The task is a form of output, which can be measured. We can link the training input to the task output.
4. The training recommendations are based on fact and there is little room for debate. There are data to support the training recommendations.

Disadvantages

The potential disadvantages of this approach include:

1. It takes time (60 to 90 days) and skill (you should have some training in this before trying it).
2. The project will be visible—which is a potential positive and negative. A large number of people will have to be aware of the analysis effort. Observing and interviewing will also be mildly disruptive to certain operations in the short run.
3. It is possible to set priorities by surveying what people feel to be the critical tasks. However, the link is not necessarily made between tasks and total performance ("Of these 50 tasks, which 12 are most critical to job performance?")
4. The approach does not address other factors in the performance environment which affect how well a task is ultimately performed.

When and Where Not to Use

This approach is particularly useful for jobs such as claim representatives, telephone installers, and office machine service representatives—where a large number of people perform similar tasks, work on similar equipment, follow similar processes, and perform very specific tasks.

This approach is a less useful starting point for supervisory and management jobs. A better starting place for determining the needs of a management job is the job output—determining first how the job impacts overall process and organization performance.

Approach D—
Performance Analysis

"Performance analysis" is a relatively new (20 years) but proven process for determining training needs and improving individual and organization performance. This method requires time, skill, and management commitment but can directly and significantly impact organization performance as well as produce relevant training programs. The essence of this approach is the determination of the performance context of the trainee, and therefore the training input is directly linked to individual and organization performance.

A General Scenario

The primary task of the training director of Property Casualty, Inc., is to answer the question, "What training do the claim representatives (and/or claim supervisors) require?" This approach does two additional things:

1. It will identify the training necessary to impact *job performance.*

2. It will identify the other factors affecting job performance that must be present. These other factors must be dealt with if the training is to impact performance.

The following is a likely scenario:

1. Determine *how* claim representatives and claim supervisors affect the performance of the organization—Property Casualty, Inc. The link between the claims representative and the claims supervisor and the organization performance is the *claim process.* This is the key process that the claim representative and the claim supervisor affect or make work.

2. Analyze the claim handling process. This requires:
   a. Describing how each step in the claim handling process *should* be performed.
   b. Describing how each step in the claim process is usually or currently performed.
   c. Identifying the gap between desired and actual performance of each step in the process.
   d. Identifying the impact of the gap in performance of each step of the process on the overall effectiveness of the process and on the organization (claim function and corporation).
   e. Identifying the cause of the gap between desired and actual performance of each step.
   This step will result in a summary such as that shown in (*a*) on p. 243.

3. Determine how the claim representative and claim supervisor impact the performance of the claim process—i.e., each step in the process. We want to make this linkage [see (*b*) on p. 243].

4. Determine what knowledge and skill is required of the claim representative and claim supervisor in order to produce the desired job outputs [see (*c*) on p. 243].

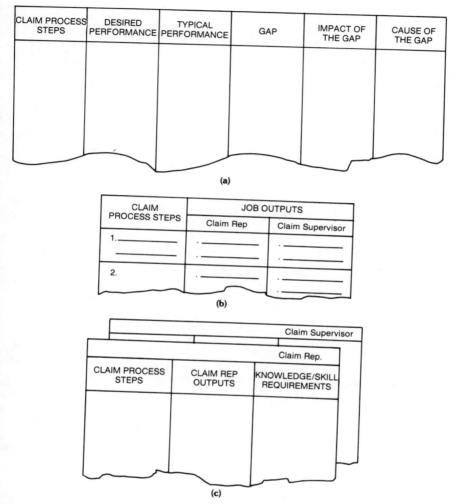

CLAIM PROCESS STEPS	DESIRED PERFORMANCE	TYPICAL PERFORMANCE	GAP	IMPACT OF THE GAP	CAUSE OF THE GAP

(a)

CLAIM PROCESS STEPS	JOB OUTPUTS	
	Claim Rep	Claim Supervisor
1. _____	. _____	. _____
_____	. _____	. _____
2.	. _____	. _____
		. _____

(b)

Claim Supervisor

Claim Rep.

CLAIM PROCESS STEPS	CLAIM REP OUTPUTS	KNOWLEDGE/SKILL REQUIREMENTS

(c)

5. Determine what other elements of performance support are required if the job and process are to be performed properly.

   The data gathering and analysis process to accomplish the preceding steps might be as follows:

   a. Select a well-performing claim office to begin the data gathering.
   b. Interview the claim office manager for a review of the claim handling process and how it can impact the performance of the office and the total organization. Have the manager identify the high-performing supervisors and claim representatives.
   c. Observe and interview two well-performing claim representatives. (Literally ride with them while they call on claimants.)
   d. Observe and interview two well-performing claim supervisors.
   e. Observe and interview a poor-performing claim representative and a new (less than 6 months on the job) claim representative.
   f. Summarize the findings (first draft) in the format shown in steps 2 and 3.
   g. Repeat steps b through f in at least two other claim offices. During these

CLAIM PROCESS STEP	CLAIM REP OUTPUTS	KNOWLEDGE/SKILL REQUIREMENTS	OTHER PERFORMANCE SUPPORT REQUIREMENTS

Claim Supervisor

Claim Rep.

interviews the analyst should begin to discern the cause of the gaps in performance and what knowledge and skill is critical to good performance.

h. Summarize these findings in the formats shown in steps 2 to 5.

i. The knowledge and skill necessary can be determined as was done with task analysis. How many more claim representatives and supervisors should be interviewed depends on the diversity of types of claims.

6. Present the findings. You are presenting a training plan, as in the other approaches. However, in this case you have some additional horsepower; you can:

a. Link training to job performance.

b. Prioritize training in the terms of relative impact.

c. Articulate other organization issues that (1) must be addressed if the training is to have any real lasting impact on the organization and (2) may have greater impact on individual and job performance than training.

The presentation may consist of a list of recommended training or a multiyear curriculum. In each case you can support your recommendations and priorities with a sound link to job performance. In addition, you can also recommend what must be done to support the training.

Following is a discussion of some specific issues in conducting a performance analysis project.

Data Gathering

The essence of this approach to needs analysis is to determine:

1. What job *performance* is desired?

2. What is the actual, typical performance?

3. What is the gap between desired and typical or actual performance?

4. What is the impact of the gap on function and organization performance?

5. What is the cause of the gap in performance? There are several things to consider when gathering and analyzing data to make these determinations.

Data Sources

The two primary sources of data for these determinations are *documents* containing relevant performance data and *people*.

When possible, the definition of performance—at the organization function and job level—should be substantiated with performance data such as sales figures, labor dollars, and scrap.

When identifying people to observe and interview, you need to be able to distinguish among very good or "master" performers, average performers, and poor performers. Master performers are the source for determining how the process and job *should* be done, and generally, they should be observed or interviewed first. The average and poor performers will provide insight into the critical difference between good and not-so-good performance and the impact of the discrepancy on the process.

Data Collection

The primary form of data collection is observation and interviews. In the case of Property Casualty, Inc., the approach might be:

Claim office manager. 1½-hour interview and discussion on how a claim office is measured and how the claim handling function impacts these measures, plus observations on the difference between master and average claim representatives and claim supervisors.

Claim representatives and supervisors. Literally travel in the car with them for a day or two, observing what they do and questioning them on the why and how.

An important aspect of this approach to analysis is *observing* the difference between performers.

An issue can be how much data to collect. Performance analysis does not require large samples of performers. It does not require talking to dozens of performers to determine what performance is desired. The training analyst can build the model of what the claim process should be and what claim representatives should do by observing and interviewing five to eight master performers. (In fact, at some point you will not learn anything new from spending time with a performer and you will know that you have enough data on what is desired.) Likewise, you don't have to talk to many average and poor performers to understand what performance is typical and what are the causes. A common error of new performance analysts is to gather too much data before trying to analyze it in the formats described earlier.

In some circumstances it is important to involve more people in the data gathering to assure acceptance of the findings across the organization. When this is the case, you should build your basic models as described above in one unit of the organization and then review these models with other units. This makes the "data gathering" task with these secondary units one of reviewing and elaborating on the models versus the extensive work of building models.

Data Analysis

The essence of this approach—of performance analysis—is to build a model or profile of what is desired and what is typical and then to explore the difference between the two—the impact and cause of the difference. Recommended formats for doing the analysis were illustrated earlier.

There are two additional points to note while doing the data analysis.

First, it is beneficial to describe the desired performance of functions, processes, and jobs in what Gilbert has called "accomplishments." Following are some accomplishments for the claim representative job:

- Claim qualified
- Work schedule developed
- Claim confirmed
- Loss scoped
- Reserve determined
- Settlement obtained
- File closed

Note that they are not behavior or tasks, but the results of behavior are tasks—the results or conditions we want to exist. There are a number of advantages to using accomplishments, but the major one in this context is their clarity and the ability to evaluate if they have been obtained.

Second, the training analyst will have to *interpret* the data that have been gathered, arrive at conclusions, and make recommendations. You will have to say "based on what I have seen, *this* should be the desired output." There will be more responsibility and judgment involved than listing those items people told you during interviews. In the case of Property Casualty, Inc., there will be several different ways claim representatives handle claims. But the training director will have to make a recommendation as to what is the best process to follow in terms of benefits to the company.

Advantages

The advantages of this approach include:

1. It clearly links knowledge and skill requirements to job performance.
2. Because of advantage 1, it is possible to set priorities for training. If the major job performance opportunity is in the "qualifying claims" step in the process, that suggests that training in that area receive number one priority.
3. Also because of advantage 1, it is possible to evaluate the impact of training on job performance.
4. It addresses the other factors affecting performance.

Disadvantages

The potential disadvantages of the approach include:

1. It takes times and skill. (As in task analysis, you should have some training in this approach before attempting it.)
2. It usually requires a management commitment in terms of making people available and in responding to the results. If management only wants a training needs "wish list," they will not be prepared for the comprehensive results of this approach.
3. It will be quite visible, raising expectations (and perhaps some anxiety).

When and Where Not to Use

This approach is useful when:

1. Job performance is critical—the organization really needs increased productivity and quality, reduced costs, etc.
2. You have a specific job such as claim representatives and claim supervisors. This

is in contrast to determining the training needs of "first-level supervisors" or "first-time managers" for a multidivision organization.

3. You have enough lead time. A project like this takes time to do correctly. A half-baked job will be disastrous (e.g., in Property Casualty, Inc., if you went to just one claim office). A project such as we described for Property Casualty, Inc., will no doubt take 60 to 90 calendar days to complete.

It is not useful when:

1. Management wants a quick, general response to the question, "What training. . . ."

2. There is no budget or commitment for training development.

3. Management is not prepared to consider changes in the performance environment to support the training.

Summary

The basic premise underlying this chapter is that the objective of training is to improve individual and organization performance. With that as a given, we have looked at the task of determining training needs.

The general systems model was used to show the critical linkage between training input and performance output. Determining training needs is basically the process of establishing this critical linkage between performance needs and knowledge and skill requirements.

We reviewed four approaches to determining training needs, in descending order of likelihood to link training input to performance output:

- Performance analysis
- Task analysis
- Competency studies
- Training need survey

Which approach is used is a balance between the quality of the needs data (the degree of linkage to performance output) and project constraints such as lead time, resources, and client commitment.

Determining training needs is the starting point of all training efforts. The quality of these data—the linkage to performance output—will determine the effectiveness of the training course and, ultimately, of the training function.

Bibliography

Bolt, James F., and Geary A. Rummler, "How to Close the Gap in Human Performance," *Management Review*, January 1982.

Boyatzis, Richard, *The Competent Manager*, John Wiley, New York, 1982.

Front-End Analysis Workshop, Harless Performance Guild, Newnan, GA.

Gilbert, Thomas F., *Human Competence (Engineering Worthy Performance)*, McGraw-Hill, New York, 1978.

Mager, Robert F., and Peter Pipe, *Analyzing Performance Problems*, Fearon, Belmost, CA, 1970.

McLagan, Patricia A., "Competency Models," *Training and Development Journal*, December 1980.

Performance Design Workshop, The Rummler Group, Summit, NJ.

Training Studies and Task Analysis Workshop, The Jacklich Corporation, Lisle, IL.

Zemke, Ron, and Thomas Kramlinger, *Figuring Things Out* (A Trainer's Guide to Needs and Task Analysis), Addison-Wesley, Reading, MA, 1982.

13

Assessment Centers

Joseph L. Moses

Joseph L. (Joel) Moses has been actively involved in assessment center research, applications, and practice for almost 20 years and has been responsible for many of AT&T's pioneering activities in this area. He developed and has managed AT&T's Advanced Management Potential Assessment program and its Assessment and Development Program for Middle Managers. Moses was one of the early leaders in the assessment center movement and has conducted extensive research on this topic. He directed AT&T's research on management women and designed an assessment center program to facilitate the movement of women in management. His current research interests center on ambiguity and change, particularly as it affects both individuals and organizations. Moses received his Ph.D. in Industrial Psychology from Baylor University. He heads the Management Continuity Research and Programs Unit at AT&T and is a founding partner of the Applied Research Group, a management consulting firm. Active in many professional organizations, he is a Fellow of the American Psychological Association and holds a Diplomate in Industrial and Organizational Psychology. He is a former national board member of ASTD, is Research Professor of Psychology at New York University, and is a Visiting Professor at Columbia University's Teachers College.

You probably have formed an opinion about assessment centers by the time you read this chapter. Some people think that it is a wonderful technique, others think that it is a mismanaged tool. Some view it as providing unique insights concerning managerial behavior; others feel that it is an artificial process. Some feel that assessment centers are accurate predictors of future potential; others think that they ignore inputs about present job performance. Some believe that assessment results are remarkably accurate; others question whether a few days of assessment outweighs a long and rich performance record.

This chapter will attempt to put these views into perspective. It will define assessment centers, trace their history and uses, provide examples of a typical program, suggest ways of getting started or modifying an existing program, and provide the interested reader with some reference sources for further reading.

One major theme will be stressed throughout this chapter. Assessment programs are major organizational interventions. Assessment centers can have a significant impact concerning how organizations go about staffing their key human resources. In this context, assessment centers are more than a technique—they represent strategies to estimate management needs for today and for the future.

Background

Since its early beginnings, the assessment center method has helped to create an understanding of the complex world in which a manager functions. Initially developed to select foremen, it is now used to select, develop, or place individuals in a variety of assignments in management, sales, and technical positions. Assessment centers are used in industry, in governments, in education in virtually every industrialized country in the world.

During its 30-year applied history, the primary use of assessment centers has been to select those with the potential to advance to more challenging job assignments. Considerable research has demonstrated that the judgments made at an assessment center predict potential with a high degree of accuracy.

Assessment center data have been used for other staffing decisions as well, including estimates of development needs, placement recommendations, and career planning. An emerging use of assessment centers allows researchers to study complex organizational behaviors such as career motivation, approaches to stress, and an understanding of how managers confront ambiguity.

An assessment center is both a place and a process. It is a physical center where individuals are evaluated for potential or for development or placement outcomes. While attending the center individuals can indicate abilities needed in more complex assignments by demonstrating behaviors which are not easily seen or are difficult to measure in current assignments. The assessment center process relies on measurement procedures which are designed to ensure that the judgments are made in a fair, objective, and job-related way.

Assessment Centers Defined

While there are many forms of assessment procedures, the term *assessment center* has a specific meaning. As defined by the Task Force on Assessment Center Standards,[1] an assessment center must meet the following criteria:

1. It must contain an explicit definition of the determinants of managerial effectiveness. Often these are called dimensions or assessment variables. These are identified using a variety of job analytic techniques to ensure that the behaviors measured are relevant.

2. Multiple measurement techniques, including simulations, are used. Simulations are exercises which provide the participant with behavioral stimuli representing important aspects of job behavior.

3. Performance of behavior is observed and evaluated by a selected, trained team of managers who are knowledgeable about the target position.

4. Integration of information occurs after all the measurement techniques are completed, at an assessment evaluation session. Here, ratings made on specific

dimensions are pooled and discussed, and overall predictions of potential, placement strategies, or development needs are made.

A number of outcomes, in addition to measuring or identifying further potential, occur as a result of participating in an assessment center. From the participant's point of view, the assessment exercises provide many opportunities to demonstrate a wide array of abilities. Well-designed simulations allow the opportunity for an extensive sampling of behavior in diverse settings. Analyzing one's performance in simulations designed to tap different aspects of a manager's job can be very useful when making diagnostic inferences concerning situations of optimal performance or situations where one might need additional support. This kind of input can provide valuable insights when considering future placement and development assignments.

Extensive feedback is typically provided to both participants and their management on the strengths and weaknesses identified. This kind of feedback can contain a wealth of diagnostic information including insights concerning situational effectiveness which can be used for development, placement, and self-insight purposes.

For the assessors themselves, participating as a member of an assessment team also provides unique developmental experiences. One of the most powerful management development experiences is serving as a member of an assessment center team. Recent research[2] suggests that assessor training and experience enhances a number of key management skills, particularly those related to performance feedback and evaluation.

Assessment centers can also have a significant impact on organizational behavior. Well-designed programs often are major organizational interventions which raise critical issues such as the interrelationship of the assessment data to existing training and development programs, which managers will have access to the assessment results and how the results will be used, should participants be able to nominate themselves, and what other data will override assessment ratings. Articulating answers to these kinds of questions often forces an organization and its managers to take a critical view of existing staffing and development programs.

Rich insights about organizational behavior can be obtained when the assessment center data are aggregated on a group rather than a case-by-case basis. This requires the assessment of a large enough sample of managers in order to be able to make some inferences about the organization itself. Aggregated assessment data can provide an excellent organizational diagnosis of the strengths and weaknesses of existing managers, their style and approaches to contemporary business problems. This kind of information can be extremely valuable when developing recruiting, selection, training, or staffing strategies for both current and future needs. For example, it may be that a desired behavior is absent in many of the managers assessed. This might suggest the design of a development program, or alternate recruiting and/or selection standards, or the need to "seed" the organization quickly with experienced managers who have demonstrated that they possess the behaviors that are desired. Assessment data used in this way can serve as a valuable early warning system for the organization.

Assessment Center History

Much of the early history of assessment centers can be traced to Dr. Henry Murray and his pioneering efforts at the Harvard Psychological clinic in the 1930s. Murray, trained in medicine, used the clinical concept of "grand rounds" (where a team of specialists would diagnose and recommend treatment) as a method for integrating information about a person. Murray was interested in studying personality and developed a method, the Diagnostic Council, which enabled the pooling of independent sources of information. This became the forerunner of the evaluation session used by all assessment centers.

Murray was asked, with the advent of World War II, to adapt his methods to help select spies for the Office of Strategic Services. This led to the first assessment center program. Using ideas taken from German military studies during World War I, Murray and his staff developed a series of ingenious simulations designed to assess one's capabilities of being a spy. This early research was published in a classic book,[3] and a popular version of this appeared in *Fortune Magazine* in 1946.

AT&T was the first business to use assessment centers. In a series of pioneering research studies,[4] assessment centers were used to predict progress in management. Data collected at assessment, at reassessment 8 years later, and at a subsequent reassessment 20 years later showed that the assessment center predictions were significantly related to actual progress in management.

Operational assessment centers, for selecting foremen, were first installed at AT&T in 1958. Assessment centers were gradually introduced in a number of large companies such as Sohio, Sears, and IBM. A conference on this topic sponsored in 1968 drew considerable interest. A group of researchers formed the Assessment Center Research Group that year, and in 1972 the International Congress on the Assessment Center Method was formed. One of its early products was the development and dissemination of standards for assessment centers.[1]

Two other events were occurring coincident with the emergence of assessment centers during the late 1960s. First, assessment concepts were adapted in education. An assessment center was integrated into the educational curricula at Alverno College, a pioneer in demonstrating linkages between assessment and education. Similarly, the National Association of Secondary School Principals established a nationwide assessment program for school administrators in 1976.

A second seminal event during this period was the passage of the Civil Rights Act of 1964, the formation of the Equal Employment Opportunity Commission, and the demonstration that assessment centers were useful and fair techniques for the identification of potential among women and minorities. Even the EEOC itself established and used an assessment center for its own staffing needs. The result was a proliferation of assessment center applications to many state, federal, and local governmental agencies.

At present it is estimated that over 5000 organizations use assessment centers. While it is hard to estimate the number of people assessed, the numbers run into the hundreds of thousands. AT&T and the Bell Telephone Companies alone have assessed over 300,000 men and women during the last 25 years.

There are several major reasons why assessment centers have survived and flourished. First, assessment centers rest on a strong research base. Well over 100 published studies indicate that assessment center judgments are valid. A number of these are cited at the end of this chapter. Much of the research was conducted prior to widespread implementation, and the technique continues to be studied by researchers and practitioners. Interest in assessment centers continues, and the International Congress of the Assessment Center Method draws participants from all of the world and soon will be celebrating its fifteenth consecutive annual meeting. Second, the focus of assessment has been on behavior, rather than abstract traits or characteristics. Feedback is provided that stresses what was done, rather than what was intended. Finally, both job analytic techniques and assessment center instrumentation have been made available through commercial vendors to any organization interested in exploring this technique.

Assessment Center Components

There are four distinct components to a successful assessment center program: a set of dimensions or characteristics which are to be measured; a series of exercises or simulations which stress behaviors related to the dimensions identified; a trained assessment staff which can observe, report, evaluate, and feed back these behaviors; and most importantly, a management system which intelligently uses the results of this program.

Well-run assessment center programs emphasize all four components. A carefully executed job analysis is often a key step. While there are several types of job analysis, the process helps to identify critical dimensions of managerial performance. It also provides useful insights for designing simulations to reflect the organizational context in which a manager operates. Once dimensions and techniques are developed and schedules established, a staff needs to be trained. In well-run programs considerable attention is given to staff selection and training, with assessors chosen from the very best of the management team. Finally, considerable care and attention is given to how the results will be used and, as importantly, how the results will not be used. Frequently, important policy-capturing meetings are established with key users to develop policies concerning assessment center use well before the program gets under way. Procedures for monitoring the program, the use of results, and evaluating program predictions are usually established at this time as well.

Poorly designed, hastily constructed assessment center programs (unfortunately, they do exist) typically imitate rather than initiate. They tend to rely on superficial job analysis (if one is conducted at all), take givens as truth, and are more concerned with the speed with which they can install the latest fad, in this case assessment centers. Consequently they borrow techniques, taking whatever is available; use definitions of dimensions which make sense in other organizations but may make little sense in the host organization; rely on a meager "content" analysis as the "scientific" basis for the center; and provide sketchy training of assessors, or use assessors from a companion agency or other organization who may have little understanding of the relevance of the behaviors observed to behavior in the host organization. Policy issues often are developed after the fact, and the assessment center implementors may have little power or credibility in the organization. No attempts at evaluation or follow-up are made, and the organization relies on the good faith efforts of other organizations and their research results to justify the existence of their program.

Often these programs are short-lived, or result in litigation. A recent article[5] provided an excellent review of assessment center litigation. The overall history of assessment centers as a valid and defensible technique results from many programs that have been designed and managed in accordance with the Ethical Standards for Assessment Centers.[1] In centers which result in adverse litigation efforts, a pattern emerges. Issues concerning lack of standardization, inappropriate use of results, or lack of training and/or management of the assessment center process are raised suggesting that those responsible for implementing the program have little awareness of this technique. One other trend has recently been noted, when contrasting assessment programs which have flourished to those with short lives. Assessment programs which are exclusively designed for development tend to be less rigorous and few last for more than a short time. The message is clear. Assessment centers that are well received meet organizational needs. They are installed with care and effort. They are evaluated. They work.

The Typical Center

Describing a typical assessment center is analogous to trying to describe a typical family. There are literally hundreds of variations around a theme. Take assessors, for example. Most assessors are drawn from the host organization. Many organizations use line managers; others use staff drawn from human resources or training organizations; others use some combination of line and staff people. Some centers are staffed exclusively by psychologists, others (the majority) do not have any psychologists on the assessment staff, while other organizations combine psychologists with lay assessors. Assessor training also widely varies, ranging from a few hours (probably not an effective strategy) to three weeks or more. Assessment centers are conducted for diverse populations as well, ranging from high school students to candidates for general manager and other senior-level management or sales-marketing assignments, but centers have been conducted to select blue collar workers as well as CEOs.

The length of assessment also varies, ranging from a few hours to three days or more. Centers are conducted in schools, in hotel facilities, on company locations, and in dedicated assessment quarters. The number of people assessed at one time also varies and can range from as few as 1 to as many as 15. Similarly, the number of assessors used in any given session may range from 3 or 4 to 11 or 12. The length of the assessment program also varies from a half day to programs lasting almost a week. The length of the assessor tour also varies. In some centers managers serve as full-time assessors for 6 months or more at a time. Other programs use assessors just once.

With this in mind, the "typical" assessment center evaluates 12 participants during a 2-day period. The participants, all of whom have been oriented to the nature and purpose of the program, arrive at the assessment center on a Monday morning. After a brief orientation which reviews the program schedule and introduces the six management assessors who are on the staff, the program begins.

The assessment phase consists of a number of group exercises, a series of simulated role plays, one or more in-baskets, individual analysis, and presentation exercises, all of which have been tailored to reflect behaviors related to organizational success. During their two days at the center, participants will make presentations, solve problems, serve as organizational consultants, respond to marketing and sales issues, work as a team of task force members, supervise or manage peers and subordinates in a variety of organizational settings designed to elicit behaviors relevant to effectiveness in the target position. On Tuesday evening they will leave the center, usually somewhat exhausted, after receiving a final briefing which reviews the process and describes feedback procedures and any follow-up activities that are planned.

During Monday and Tuesday each assessor will observe many of the assessees as they participate in the various simulations. Assessment reports are prepared immediately after each exercise, with some extra report preparation time provided on Wednesday morning. Each assessor has been assigned to approximately 8 or 9 participants, and typically prepares only one report on each of these individuals. No participant is exclusively seen or evaluated by a single assessor. On Wednesday afternoon the assessors convene and divide into two teams. Each team is responsible for evaluating 6 of the 12 participants. Each individual is evaluated separately, and the evaluation process for a single individual takes several hours to complete.

First, individual assessment reports are read. For example, the assessor who observed the participant during the group exercise reads his or her report. Next, a different assessor who conducted the in-basket interview reviews this material. This continues until all the assessor reports are read. While listening to the reports, the assessors take notes and then make ratings on the dimensions or characteristics measured in the program. Ratings are discussed, differences are resolved, and then an overall prediction of further potential is made. Then recommendations for development, next job assignments, or placement strategies are reviewed. This process continues on Thursday until all six participants are completed by each team. Friday is used to provide feedback to previous participants and to prepare reports going to both the individual and his or her management.

This overview is very general. Some centers have very different evaluation procedures, ranging from an attempt to rate dimensions after each exercise, to weighting of ratings based on some preestablished format. In some programs no attempt is made to make an overall rating; in others the participants are rank ordered based on the group seen that week; in others the ranking is never done or is compared with a larger population. Feedback procedures vary also. Some programs provide immediate feedback after each exercise; others do not provide any feedback (other than a pass-fail) at all. Some programs restrict the assessment data to a very few; others encourage widespread use of assessment centers results.

The most common form of feedback is provided to the participant by a member of the assessment center staff. This usually occurs shortly after the assessment week. Most feedback sessions are conducted either at the center itself or near the work location. Feedback interviews last several hours and performance in the program is reviewed. Developmental suggestions and follow-up topics are covered. Assessment feedback often is markedly different from other forms of performance feedback. The person providing the feedback data is emotionally removed from the participant. The data are objective and are based on performance in the program and on observations made by many assessors. Feedback is concrete, immediate, and descriptive. And most importantly, the staff person providing feedback, whether an assessor or a member of the assessment staff, has been trained to conduct the feedback interview.

In addition to face-to-face feedback, most centers prepare a report for management. Who sees this report is a function of the program. Most typically, a written report is prepared and is shared with those levels of management responsible for long-term career and staffing decisions. The written report is usually not as detailed as the oral report given to the participant. Rather, it is designed to highlight areas of strengths and weakness and to suggest developmental, training, and placement assignments. Many centers provide a copy of this report to the participant as well.

The gist of all this suggests that assessment center programs take on the value and needs of the organization. The richness of assessment is its ability to be adapted to a variety of organizational settings and needs. Assessment center outcomes vary from selection to further identification of potential, to career planning, to development, to programs where these activities are combined or treated as independent events.

Assessment Center Outcomes

Most assessment programs are geared to a specific outcome such as selecting a candidate for further advancement or using data collected to help place an individual in a future assignment or prescribing development or training needs.

Assessment center outcomes are often best reflected in the composite or overall rating provided. Centers that are geared to assist with selection or advancement activities rely on an overall rating. Centers which do not provide an overall rating but emphasize individual dimensional ratings such as leadership and decision making tend to be used for placement and/or development purposes. Often, however, these distinctions are blurred or confused.

If an overall rating is provided, it makes a big difference if this rating is a composite arrived at by averaging or weighting dimensions according to some predetermined format. These result in *descriptive* judgments. Most centers for entry-level sales or management jobs are of this nature. Assessors are trained to observe behaviors and determine whether or not they occurred. The evaluation process focuses on whether behaviors did or did not occur. Exercise reports and evaluation discussions are driven to describe what did occur. For example, in-basket exercises can be scored based on the relationship of a response to an item and its assumed importance to an external criterion.

A second kind of assessment overall rating is the result of inferences and judgment. These result in *predictive* outcomes. Assessors in this type of setting are trained to integrate information in order to make a prediction concerning the overall likelihood of success in the target job. These kinds of judgments are more common in assessment centers for higher-level management jobs. The emphasis of the evaluation process shifts from a discussion of whether or not a behavior has occurred to the impact of observed behavior when predicting subsequent performance. This kind of discussion also requires agreement on whether or not the behavior did occur but goes beyond a descriptive dialog to indicate whether or not the behavior appears to be typical (and therefore highly predictive) or less typical. Assessors are trained to integrate data from many simulations rather than "scoring" each simulation in a discrete fashion.

There are major differences in overall ratings arrived at by description or prediction approaches. As noted, description-oriented assessment programs tend to rely on a composite assessment score. Assessors are trained to either weigh specific dimensions to reflect job analysis findings or to add up and average individual ratings in order to determine a composite score. Assessors may use formal or informal approaches depending on how they were trained or the folklore of the center. In any event, the goal of these centers is to ensure consistency in ratings. Discussions are designed to resolve differences in assessor ratings and to arrive at a consensus decision on individual dimensions. Most of the evaluation session is aimed at making sure that the individual dimension ratings are as accurate and as descriptive as possible. When an overall rating is made, there is usually little disagreement since it represents an averaging of composite dimension ratings.

Prediction-driven assessment ratings tend to look for patterns of performance rather than a composite. Compensatory judgments often appear. These are judgments which reflect the fact that an individual may perform differently in different situations. For example, an individual's leadership style may vary in different simulations. Let's suppose that a participant was very effective in one situation and demonstrated a great deal of leadership talent. In another group exercise, however, this person did little to lead others but was a helpful, supportive group member. Rather than averaging leadership ratings, i.e., very effective as a leader in one situation and less effective as a leader in another situation equals an "average" leadership rating, prediction-oriented centers tend to look at the context in which the behavior occurred. For example, this individual may be most effective when leading others in structured tasks and has more difficulty taking the lead when the task is unstructured; or this person is best when leading others in competitive situations but is less effective when faced with cooperative tasks. The overall assessment rating reflects more than a composite rating. it is a prediction of overall effectiveness; i.e., an outstanding rating means that this individual will have little difficulty in almost any aspect of more complex management jobs simulated at the center, and a poor rating suggests that this individual will have difficulty making a transition to more complex job demands.

As seen from this discussion, description-oriented programs emphasize dimensions while prediction-oriented programs focus on simulations. Prediction-oriented approaches allow greater flexibility for placement, development, and selection outcomes, while description-oriented programs work best when they focus exclusively on selection issues.

Unfortunately these distinctions are often blurred. Description-oriented assessment programs require a less sophisticated staff. Assessors can come from almost anywhere and may not need to know much about the host organization. The training of assessors is usually shorter and less detailed than in prediction-oriented programs. The typical training consists of teaching assessors to indicate whether or not a behavior occurred and assessors are encouraged to use check lists, behavior observing report forms, predetermined report forms, or other techniques to ensure consistency. Description-oriented programs tend to use commercially available assessment exercises, forms, and rating instruments. If a job analysis has been performed, its purpose was to verify that existing commercially prepared exercises do reflect aspects of performance in the host organization. As noted, these kinds of programs are very popular for assessing entry-level sales and management jobs.

Prediction-oriented assessment programs tend to require a more sophisticated assessment staff. While some description-oriented programs have exceptionally talented assessors, many operate with assessors who are available rather than requested. Assessors in a prediction-oriented program must have extensive knowledge about the target jobs and must be able to differentiate among important aspects in these jobs. For example, assessors should be able to differentiate which positions require considerable work as an individual contributor versus which jobs require team effort; which jobs demand little supervision of the incumbent versus which jobs are characterized by close supervision; which positions are fundamentally unstructured versus jobs that follow standard procedures; which positions require an incumbent to think on his or her feet versus which positions allow the individual to have a great deal of time before giving a response. In contrast to description-oriented programs, prediction-oriented assessment programs tend to develop rather than purchase simulations and are most frequently used for middle and upper management positions.

Starting a Center

In hundreds of organizations that wish to start assessment centers, the most frequently asked questions concern the availability of assessment materials. For example, commonly asked questions include where one can purchase exercises dimensions, schedules, training materials, etc. While these are important questions they are of secondary importance in starting a center. Considerable assessmen software exists, but it may be of little value if key policy issues are either addresse superficially or ignored.

Our preceding discussion of assessment outcomes is a good case in point. Mos new users, when asked about optimal outcomes, will probably indicate bot selection and development. As we have seen, however, there are wide difference in staffing and training strategies which can be used, depending on the purpose c the center.

Throughout this chapter we have stressed the idea that assessment centers ar major organizational interventions. Assessment centers can have a major impact o staffing decisions, placement strategies, succession planning efforts, feedback pol cies, and training and development activities. Or assessment programs can b conducted in a vacuum, with little or no interface between the program and oth human resource activities. We can think of a continuum of human resour interventions. At one end are programs that are integrated and feed one anothe

These activities often are described as key elements in a human resource development system. At the other end of this continuum are many discrete programmatic activities. The key distinction which places an activity toward either end of this continuum is whether it is integrated into a larger system or whether it is a programmatic activity which is essentially independent of other human resources events.

Assessment programs can fall at either end of this continuum. Depending on where it is positioned, however, there are large differences in both acceptance of the center and its longevity. Assessment centers which are essentially independent, nonintegrated programs are frequently viewed with suspicion, skepticism, and fear by participants and users. They may be installed as a response to a specific need, i.e., not enough minorities in management, or because "everyone else is doing it." Response times between idea and action are short, and programs are purchased with few attempts to modify preexisting dimensions, exercises, staffing requirements, staff tours, training, or schedules. These programs are often short-lived, and if an analysis is done concerning why the program failed (rarely is this done) blame is placed on the assessment center as a concept rather than the lack of fit or lack of support of the program. Often these kinds of issues could have been addressed had more thought been given to these issues earlier.

Assessment center programs which are integrated into a human resource system tend to be well accepted, are established as helpful activities in the development of a manager, modify techniques and outcomes as an organization goes through different life cycles, and tend to use the data for understanding complex human behaviors. Frequently considerable research data are available as well. Often the key determinant of the success, impact, and longevity of an assessment center program is the early decisions made in establishing a center. Each organization needs to view its assessment center somewhat differently, and must adapt techniques and procedures to fit its own uniqueness. Programs which are sold as "generic" or applicable to all interested parties have little likelihood of long-term survival or positive impact. Let us then review some of the key steps in getting started.

1. *Establish an oversight committee.* This committee should consist of key senior-level management policy makers, many of whom may be ultimate users of the assessment center results. This committee should have oversight of the program. The committee needs to determine clear policy objectives for the center. For example, what is the purpose of the center? Who will attend? Can individuals nominate themselves? Who will have access to the assessment results? Can a person be reassessed? Who will provide feedback? Who will receive it? In what form? These and a myriad of other issues are the foundation of the program. It is at this point that a determination can be made whether the assessment center will be a stand-alone program or integrated into other aspects of a human resource system. Well-designed programs have most of these policy issues established prior to actual implementation of the program. The discussion of many of these issues may result in a clearer understanding of what assessment centers can (and cannot) do for an organization. Often, it is just this initial discussion which sets the stage for assessment centers as a key input as an organizational intervention. Setting policy is not difficult. Setting good policy is. A consultant who is experienced with many forms of assessment center approaches may be a very helpful resource at this stage.

2. *Determine where the program will reside.* This step does not mean the actual location of the center (although this could be decided at this time as well) but reflects organizational responsibility. There are no obvious choices, but this decision often sets the tone for the assessment program. It obviously should be placed with an organizational unit that has a great deal of credibility, respect, and

confidence with the management team. Depending on organizational culture, it could be placed in a central headquarters unit or could be decentralized. Experience indicates that there are several advantages to positioning assessment center activities in a centralized setting. Development, training, and administrative costs can be shared, with substantial cost savings. Assessors can be drawn from multiple organizational units. This has many advantages. It markedly decreases the impact of lost management time on a single unit; it markedly increases the objectivity of the program by introducing managers who have little or no prior work history with the assessees; it affords valuable opportunities for managers from different organizations to work with one another and learn more about the global nature of the business; it sets the stage for other organizational interventions; and it positions the program to help understand organizational differences and successes, including viewing high-potential managers as corporate resources, developing research, and other intervention activities as needed.

While there are examples of quite successful decentralized assessment programs, this is the exception rather than the rule. Decentralized programs have the advantage of potentially being very responsive to local management's needs. At the same time, there is a tendency for decentralized efforts to cut costs or look for shortcuts, particularly when assessor training and assessor participation conflict with operational needs. Since assessors are the most important element in the assessment judgment process, anything which results in a lowered performance quality impacts on the success of the program.

A final issue concerning program responsibility reflects the extent to which assessment operations are seen as unique. This can be a key decision which may need a fair amount of thought. For example, different organizational staff units have different perspectives. Positioning assessment responsibility within a college employment group may be quite different from positioning the program in a training group or a strategic planning group or a succession planning group or a personnel research group or an industrial relations group. These groups often have different networks both in and outside the organization and may be viewed differently by key organizational users. The choice for program responsibility should rest with the strongest unit, not simply the unit who initiated exploring this concept.

3. *Determine if a consultant is needed.* This may also be one of the major decisions which affects the success of this program. The decision is a simple one based on the subject matter expertise of existing staff. As we have seen, assessment center programs require a considerable amount of professional knowledge; simply having worked as an assessor does not provide sufficient qualifications to design or implement a program. Since policy formulation is often a key aspect in developing a program, the subject matter expert must have the confidence of policy makers and must be able to confront and advise decision makers as appropriate. For this reason, an outsider may be useful.

If an external consultant is desired, considerable care should be given to selection. Assessment center judgments may have considerable impact on the lives of program participants, and the consultant must be able to demonstrate familiarity with the rich literature on assessment centers including contemporary problems and issues, assessment center concepts, measurement and statistical issues, job analysis, research design, ethical issues, and the management of training, development, and implementation procedures.

The consultant should be very familiar with the Ethical Standards for Assessment Center Operations. If assessment center decisions may have an effect on promotional or career opportunities, care should be given to choosing a consultant who has sufficient credentials to appear as an expert witness in litigation or arbitration hearings. If the consultant is a psychologist, he or she should be licensed or certified, or a diplomate in industrial and organizational psychology. (If in doubt, check with the local state licensing agency.) Finally, the best test of an assessment center consultant is to consult with some of the major contributors to the field. As a rule these individuals have made a lasting professional contribution through research, scholarship, and writing. They may have much at stake in seeing that assessment centers are properly implemented and can be very helpful sources. As with any business decision, multiple opinions may be very fruitful. There are many self-proclaimed assessment center "experts." Frequently they are salespeople who are minimally trained and are taught to push a prepackaged program. A good early-warning signal is to ask how long it will take to install a program. If you are told that it can be installed in only a few weeks, watch out. I have found that well-designed, lasting programs take time to implement. Six months from the initial contact to actual program implementation is quite common.

4. *Conduct a job analysis.* Job analysis procedures vary, and it is beyond the scope of this chapter to review this technique. Several good sources[6,7] are provided in the references at the end of this chapter. Well-done job analyses take time but are well worth the effort. A thorough job analysis not only will identify key management dimensions but will be able to differentiate skills needed at different management levels. A detailed job analysis forms the basis for determining what types of activities are critical aspects of a target job and how they should be simulated. This information also is extremely useful in designing simulations. Job analysis data are necessary to document the job relatedness of the assessment techniques and form the basis for any validation strategy that will be employed. A well-designed job analysis can provide useful insights concerning development, particularly which on- and off-the-job developmental experiences are critical for management success. Finally, a sophisticated job analysis strategy can provide useful insights into emerging management behaviors which may be essential in the future.

The job analysis is the second most important aspect in starting a center. (Establishing an oversight function is the first.) Yet, this is the step which may often be ignored, overlooked, or minimized. It is easy to see why, because job analysis takes time, requires research, and may not provide immediate tangible payoffs. It may also be beyond the technical expertise of many self-styled assessment "consultants," who will minimize this step with statements such as "research has shown that most management jobs have the following dimensions," and then attempt to sell a prepackaged assessment center program. Job analysis procedures provide a snapshot of the skills and knowledge required for effective performance. Such snapshots can be time-bound, reflecting the current state of the business. A well-designed job analysis strategy provides opportunities to update information as an organization, its jobs, and its people change. This can have a major impact on the types of simulations used, dimensions chosen, etc. Such a job analysis also can be used as a benchmark to help understand how an organization changes as well.

5. *Determine characteristics to be assessed.* These decisions are heavily influenced by the job analysis findings. They are not based simply by reviewing what other programs have found to be useful. Often, a number of dimensions can be added to reflect program outcomes. For example, if participants are expected to enroll in development or educational programs, one can determine the extent to which an individual will benefit from these interventions by assessing a person's development potential. If placement outcomes are critical, one can assess a person's adaptability for change, etc. This is often a good time to check the job analysis results with existing potential appraisal forms. Often these can be modified to incorporate new information provided by the job analysis.

Once dimensions are identified, they need to be carefully defined. These should be reviewed with the oversight committee. A number of criteria should be met in defining assessment characteristics. The dimensions should be stable; i.e., they should be aspects of behavior that are unlikely to easily change as a result of the measuring process; the dimensions should be observable as a result of the assessment process; the dimensions should be simple rather than complex; the dimensions should be independent of one another, and they should be definable in terms which are free of jargon, emotion, or racial or sexual overtones.

6. *Develop or purchase simulations.* The decision to develop or purchase existing simulations reflects the extent to which the assessment program mirrors a preconceived view of it. While many excellent commercially developed simulations are available, this author has found that simulations developed for a specific program have many advantages. First, they reflect the organization, its problems and procedures. In this respect they often provide the participant with a "realistic job preview" of responsibilities in more complex management jobs. Next, they are very useful to contrast different organizational requirements such as working in stable versus unpredictable environments. Such simulations are valuable as placement indicators.

Specially developed simulations can be used to indicate specific performance needs. If the simulations are integrated, they may actually reflect an entire organization. Such integrated simulations have the advantage of increasing the familiarity with each new assessment simulation as the names and functions of simulated people and organizations are constant; they also, if not well designed, have the disadvantage of introducing measurement error if early performance determines later performance in the simulation.

7. *Develop assessment schedules.* These include schedules for participants, assessors, and program administrators. They also include training schedules, schedules for practice candidates used in training, and testing and/or research instrument schedules. These schedules take into account the pacing of the program, optimal use of participant and assessor time, and degree of difficulty of exercises. This is not an aspect of the program which should be taken lightly. How participants and assessors are treated can often be indicated by the care given to scheduling activities.

8. *Develop informational materials.* Assessment programs, particularly if they are new to the organization, can be well received if participants, assessors, and management users are well informed concerning the purpose of the center and its relationship to other human resource activities. Brochures, newsletter items, management briefings, informational sessions with prospective participants, etc., all can be extremely useful in positioning the program. A well-designed marketing campaign including videotapes, slide presentations, and meetings with key assessment center staffers may make a major contribution to the overall acceptance of the program. Its importance cannot be minimized.

9. *Recruit, select, and train assessors.* This is one of the major determinants of the success and acceptance of the program. Assessors should be managers who are widely respected throughout the organization, who are those individuals who can least be spared, and who are individuals of considerable potential themselves. Often, assessors benefit from the assignment and are chosen as a part of their development as high-potential managers. Developing a staffing strategy to make such key people available should be the responsibility of the oversight committee. If it is delegated to a personnel or training organization, staffing becomes more difficult, depending on the "clout" of the personnel department. With little power, assessors will be chosen because of availability rather than impact; or as often is the case, the program will be staffed from external sources. While such a staff might be

competent, they are rarely perceived so by either participants or management users. As is so often the case, "you get what you pay for" applies. If assessors are drawn from the best of the organization, there is a strong message that this program is important. The staffing of the initial center sets the tone for the future. Often, assessors are the program's best salespeople. Well-respected assessors are difficult to get because everyone else wants their time. Yet, since assessment is a judgmental process, the perceived respect of the judges is one of the major determinants of the center's success.

The training of assessors is also a key factor. Assessors should be able to understand how to measure, report, and evaluate behavior. If they also provide feedback, training needs to be provided for this aspect of the program as well. Often assessor training is a source for shaping organizational behaviors, particularly if the trainer is able to provide meaningful feedback. Most managers think they can judge behavior; surprisingly few know how to do so. Assessor training can provide a rich framework for acquiring these kinds of skills.

The role of the trainer is critical here. Most assessors will be unfamiliar with the process. Most managers, when placed in unfamiliar situations, tend to learn by imitation. This is particularly true of assessors. Different tones can easily be established. It is here where description- and prediction-oriented centers differ greatly. Description-oriented centers focus on accuracy and consistency. Prediction-oriented programs focus on determining which elements are most predictive of long-term success.

The length of training varies. Most well-designed programs view assessor training as an investment rather than an expense, and assessor training is determined by the demands of the program. It generally takes about one week to train an assessment staff.

Most well-designed programs assess the assessors. Some have certification requirements which must be met in order to participate as assessors in the program. In general, such certification requirements are well received as they provide behavioral criteria related to assessor activities such as acquiring, interpreting, and evaluating information. Frequently such training simulates the assessor's job, providing both a realistic preview of the assessor's role as well as feedback concerning performance expectations.

10. *Develop evaluation and monitoring strategies.* This is a major activity which often determines the long-term effectiveness of the program. Such monitoring and evaluation can take many forms. For example, valuable insights can be obtained from both participants and assessors. Many of these kinds of inputs relate to program design issues ranging from participant selection and preparation to the pacing, difficulty, and usefulness of the assessment experience itself. A second kind of evaluation input should be collected from the assessment center users. Was the feedback timely and useful? What data were most helpful? A whole host of user-oriented information can be collected ranging from the impact of the assessment data on promotional or staffing decisions to the impact on stimulating development strategies. This kind of data could be included along with other survey data collected by the organization or could be independently collected. A useful source of items for such an analysis is provided in reference 8.

Another form of evaluation, known as validation, is also required. This is a complex topic, often having legal overtones. Basically, validation activities document that the judgments made in assessment process are demonstrably related to job outcomes. If the outcomes of assessment are selection or promotional decisions, the documentation must show that these decisions are made in a job-related way. If the assessment outcomes are development, similar logic applies. Determining validation documentation is a complex topic, well beyond the scope of this chapter. In general, however, either statistical or evaluative documentation must be offered in accordance with professionally accepted standards.[9] A well-designed and well-documented job analysis is necessary in any validation effort. Whether such a job analysis is sufficient depends on the validation strategy employed.

The above "10 commandments" of assessment implementation should be helpful when starting a center for the first time, as well as for reviewing an ongoing program.

Further Readings

There is a rich body of literature on this topic. For those interested in the history and development of assessment centers, the pioneering work of Murray[3] is valuable. The pioneering AT&T research[4] should also be reviewed. A number of texts[10, 11] summarize both research and appplication issues facing the assessment center practitioner. For those who wish an update of major assessment center research and issues, the *Annual Review of Psychology* provides such a perspective, beginning with the 1972 chapter on Personnel Selection and continuing every other year with similarly titled chapters. Finally, both *Personnel Psychology* and the *Journal of Applied Pyschology* provide many contemporary studies of assessment centers.

References

1. Task Force on Assessment Center Standards, J. Moses, Chair, "Standards and Ethical Considerations for Assessment Center Operations," *The Personnel Administrator*, 1980, 25, 35–38.

2. Lorenzo, R. V., "Effects of Assessorship on Manager's Proficiency in Acquiring, Evaluating and Communicating Information about People, *Personnel Psychology*, 1984, 37, 617–634.

3. Office of Strategic Services Assessment Staff, *Assessment of Men*, Rinehart, New York, 1948.

4. Bray, D. W., R. J. Campbell, and D. L. Grant, *Formative Years in Business*, Wiley, New York, 1974.

5. Byham, W. C., "Review of Legal Cases and Opinions Dealing with Assessment Centers and Content Validity," Monograph IV, Development Dimensions International, Pittsburgh, 1979.

6. Jeswald, T. J., "Issues in Establishing an Assessment Center," in J. L. Moses and W. C. Byham, *Applying the Assessment Center Method*, Pergamon Press, New York, 1977.

7. Gael, S., ed., *Job Analysis Handbook*, Wiley, New York, 1986.

8. Dodd, W. E., "Attitudes Towards Assessment Center Programs," in J. L. Moses and W. C. Byham, *Applying the Assessment Center Method*, Pergamon Press, New York, 1977.

9. Division of Industrial and Organizational Psychology (Division 14), American Psychological Association, *Principles for the Validation and Use of Personnel Selection Procedures*, 2d ed., Dayton, OH, *Industrial/Organizational Psychology*, 1980.

10. Moses, J. L., and W. C. Byham, *Applying the Assessment Center Method*, Pergamon Press, New York, 1977.

11. Thornton, G. C., and W. C. Byham, *Assessment Centers and Managerial Performance*, Academic Press, New York, 1982.

14
Writing Training Materials[*]

Kenneth H. Silber

Michael B. Stelnicki

Kenneth H. Silber is currently manager of Quality Control and Instructional Design, Interactive Products Group, Advanced Systems, Inc., Arlington Heights, Illinois. Prior to coming to ASI, he was a supervisor, instructional technology, for AT&T Communications. Silber has been professor, Instructional and Training Technology, at Governors State University. As a training consultant, Dr. Silber has done instructional design and training for several Fortune 100 companies. He has published a book and over 50 articles in the training field and has conducted numerous workshops on instructional design and performance analysis—including the workshop on which this chapter is based. Silber is currently active in the National Society for Performance & Instruction, serving as reviewing editor for its journal, Performance & Instruction, and as president-elect of the Chicago chapter; he has also been active in the Association for Educational Communications and Technology, serving on its board of directors, and as president of its Division for Instructional Development.

Michael B. Stelnicki is currently university professor, Instructional and Training Technology, at Governors State University, University Park, Illinois. He conducts courses in instructional design and development, training videotape production, training research, training techniques, and managing and evaluating HRD systems. Prior to coming to GSU, Stelnicki worked as an associate editor at a Chicago-based publishing firm, and produced and directed instructional television programs in Wisconsin. He has consulted with major business and

*This article is based on the copyrighted materials used in workshops of the same name given by the authors, Stelnicki and Silber (1985).

educational organizations on the writing of training materials. Stelnicki conducts workshops (as well as university classes) on applications of message design principles to writing training text materials and to producing training videotapes. He has presented these to a variety of groups, including ITVA and NSPI chapters, and at the annual NSPI conference. He has been a member of ASTD, the Illinois Training and Development Association, and AECT. Currently his memberships include NSPI, and the Chicago chapters of NSPI and the National Academy of Television Arts and Sciences.

Introduction

Why Use These Principles. Have you ever tried to learn from training materials that were poorly written? Did you feel you had wasted your valuable time? Were you annoyed with the person who wrote the materials? Did you feel your company had wasted its money having you go through the training? When you write training materials, you can avoid all of above. How? By applying the 14 simple principles explained in this chapter as you write lessons. Why? Why go through the effort of reading this chapter, learning its principles, and applying them as you write training? What's in it for *you*?

First, applying these principles will make your job *easier*:

- Writing training lessons will be simpler.

- Writer's block will be almost eliminated.

- The time it takes to write training materials will *not* increase (and, in most cases, will decrease).

- The principles are easy to apply.

- The principles become automatic after you use them a few times.

Second, applying these principles will make the training you develop *better*: Specific advantages will be explained throughout the chapter.

Third, applying these principles will get you *recognized as a superior trainer:*

- Most competent and successful trainers use these principles.

- You will produce more cost-effective training that will translate into bottom-line savings for your company.

Who Says So. The principles in this chapter come from the practical experience and research of both gurus and everyday practitioners in the training field. They come from journals you are familiar with: *Training and Development, Training, Performance & Instruction.* They come from books and articles by authors whose names are probably familiar to you (see the bibliography at the end of the chapter). The principles include some tried and true ones that have been around for years, and some of the newest thinking on how people learn—and how to help them do it.

What You'll Learn. By the end of the chapter, you will be able to use the job aid table in the chapter to write the introduction, explanation, and summary sections of a training lesson incorporating the 14 principles explained in this chapter.

Table 14-1. Sections of a Training Lession

Section	What the section does
Introduction	Gets the trainees ready to learn, and previews what is to be learned
Explanation	Presents the information to be learned, including examples and practice
Summary	Reviews the information taught, and helps trainees remember and apply it

Where They Fit In. Applying these principles when writing training materials relates to several other chapters in this handbook:

- It is a description of how to do the developing training materials phase of the instructional design chapter.
- It assumes you have already determined the training need (see Chapter 12).
- It assumes you have already selected your media, as explained in Chapter 29, Audiovisual Methods, and other chapters.

Organization. To relate these principles to something concrete, and to present them in small groups that will not overwhelm the reader, this chapter will divide a training lesson into three sections, as defined in Table 14-1. The principles that apply to each section will be explained separately, in the context of how they would be used in that section. The chapter will then summarize all principles in a job aid table that will include, for each principle, a checklist of questions to ask as you write your materials.

To make each principle as easy to understand as possible, the explanation will include the following parts:

- What it means—a simple description of why and how the principle helps trainees learn.
- Using it—a translation of the principle into what must be done in training.
- Example—a reference to some portion of this chapter, and how it is written, that shows one correct use of the principle.*

Principles To Be Used in the Introduction Section

Introduction

Why Use Them. In addition to making your job easier, following these principles in writing the introduction section of your training lessons makes the trainee's job of learning easier because:

---

* Ideally, this chapter should include a separate example showing the use of the principle, as well as a "poor" example, showing the principle's misapplication. It should also include, to model the principles it is teaching, more headings, some practice exercises and feedback, and another example in the summary. Unfortunately, these elements must be omitted because of space limitations.

- Trainees learn if:
  - They see how the information will help them on their jobs.
  - They see the "payoff" for the extra effort they will have to spend to learn something new.
  - They believe the materials training them know more than they do.
- It is easier for trainees to learn if:
  - They know what they are to learn.
  - They see or understand how the information being taught is organized.
  - The information is explained in terms of something they already understand.

Where You Have Seen Introductions Before.   You are already familiar with the principles of introductions—even though you may not have recognized them as such.

- When you have watched "coming attractions" or "teasers" of a movie or TV show, you were watching introduction sections that piqued your interest.
- When you have heard someone recite a long list of a speaker's past achievements, you were listening to an introduction that established the speaker's credibility.
- When you have been asked, at the beginning of training sessions, to list your concerns about the topic, you were part of an introduction that established what was important to you.
- When you have read the agenda of a training session, you were reading an introduction that organized the content for you.

How This Section Is Organized.   The principles to be followed in writing a good introduction section are:

- Attention/motivation
- Influence/credibility
- Objectives
- Context/familiarity
- Mental set

Principle 1: Attention/Motivation

What Attention/Motivation Means.   Trainees learn only when they pay attention to training. If their minds are on something other than the training, they won't learn—no matter how well the training is written. Motivation helps maintain that attention. The motivation stems from some benefit or value in the training. Without motivation, trainees will almost certainly forget whatever they learn the minute they put down the training materials.

Using Attention/Motivation.   Write something that will grab the trainees' attention and create a desire to learn subsequent information. This *cannot* be accomplished by merely saying "OK, pay attention" or "learn this because the boss says so." This can be accomplished by showing and telling the trainees *how* this training will help them. This is called giving them a WIIFM, that is, what's in it for me.

The introduction section should contain the following information to make up a good WIIFM. Explain to the trainees, in the context of their job:

- *How* the content relates to the "real world"
- *How* the content is important to
  - The trainees
  - The job
  - The organization
- *How* the content will make the trainees' job
  - Easier
  - Better
  - More pleasant
  - More interesting
  - More important
- *How* learning the content will make trainees
  - Happier
  - More productive
  - More intelligent
  - Better qualified
  - Rewarded by others

Example.   The section in the introduction to this chapter entitled "Why Use These Principles" is an example of a WIIFM, addressing each of these issues, that hopefully got your attention and motivated you to read the rest of the chapter.

Principle 2: Influence/Credibility

Introduction.   Trainees only believe, listen to, and learn from people and materials that they consider to be "influential" or "credible." Materials are influential/credible if they:

- Have expertise
- Are attractive to trainees

What Expertise Means.   Trainees do not learn from training materials if they believe they know more than the materials. No matter what they have already read or heard about the subject, they must believe the training materials contain the definitive, authoritative word on what they are learning.

Using Expertise.   Write materials that convey the impression that the materials:

- Are based on the most current information available.
- Are based on information sources that trainees regard as true (research, experts in the field, documentation, professional practice, etc.).
- Include information they have heard or read.

Some ways of showing the expertise of training in the introduction section are:

- Stating the credentials of the author.
- Citing research, books, documents, experts, or accepted professional practice on which the training content is based.
- Making reference to the most current ideas about the topic of the training.
- Making reference to ideas trainees have heard or read elsewhere.

What Attractiveness Means. Trainees tend to believe things and people they find attractive to them. While this applies more to video and people than to print, print materials must also be visually appealing enough to entice trainees to read them.

Using Attractiveness. Prepare training materials to make them look like something trainees want to read. Some ways to make the materials attractive are:

- Using "slick" binders
- Using neat typesetting and page layout
- Having error-free typesetting and figures
- Liberally using appropriate diagrams and pictures

Example. The section "Who Says So" in the introduction to this chapter is an example of using the principle of expertise—citing training field "gurus" who have articulated these principles.

Principle 3: Objectives

What Objectives Mean. Trainees learn best when they know, at the outset, exactly what they will be learning and what they will be able to do after they finish the training. Knowing the objectives enables trainees to focus on the essential information and eliminate extraneous or distracting information. Objectives also provide a goal against which they can measure their own progress.

Using Objectives. Tell the trainees, in the introduction section, the objectives of the training lesson. The objectives are most useful to the trainee when stated:

- In terms of skills the trainee will gain
- In words that are:
  - Specific
  - Concrete
  - Behavioral
  - Real world

Example. This chapter incorporated this principle when it stated, in the section called "What You'll Learn" in the introduction, what the reader would be able to do after reading the chapter.

Principle 4: Context/Familiarity

Introduction. Trainees learn most easily when the information being taught is put in the context of something they already know, and is taught using familiar concepts and terminology.

What Context Means. Trainees learn new information by linking or relating that new information to something they already know or understand. When presented with new information, they search their minds for something the new information "is like." Then they "hook" the new information onto the already known.

If the new information trainees are trying to learn is explained using these "links" and "hooks," they learn it more easily because they know exactly what to hook the new information onto. If the new information is *not* explained in terms of existing "links" or "hooks," then learning is more difficult and takes longer, because trainees first have to figure out what the "hooks" are.

Using Context. Apply context to written training materials by:

- Linking or relating the information being taught to something that the trainees already know
- Making it clear to trainees which existing "links" or hooks to use

Some ways to do this are:

- Use analogies ("this is like XYZ because. . ." or "this is not like XYZ because . . .").
- Use situations familiar to the trainees.
- Generalize from examples to the principles.
- Add details to already known information.

What Familiarity Means. Trainees learn new information by building on blocks of information (facts, ideas, procedures) they already know. They take the new information and add it to these "building blocks" to create new knowledge.

If the new information is explained using these building blocks, the trainees learn it more easily because they know which blocks to add onto. If the new information is *not* explained in terms of existing building blocks, then learning is more difficult and takes longer, because trainees have to start from the "ground up," learning the basic building blocks before they can learn the more complicated information.

Using Familiarity. Write training materials that:

- Let the trainees know exactly which building blocks the new information should be added to.
- Explain the new information using the building blocks—the facts, ideas, and procedures—the trainees already know.

Some techniques for making training materials familiar to trainees are:

- "Recalling," or bring back to mind, what they already know
- Explaining how the information builds on what they already know
- Using vocabulary or concepts they already know to explain the new information

Example. In the sections "What It's Like" and "Where You Have Seen Introductions Before," this chapter has tried to provide both context and familiarity through situations most readers would recognize. In addition, the explanation of the principle provided above used familiar, understandable concepts ("hooks" and "building blocks") rather than complex psychological definitions.

Principle 5: Mental Set

What Mental Set Means. Trainees learn best when, in addition to having "hooks" for the new information, they have a "mental set," or picture of the "whole forest," before they go into detail about each of the trees. Trainees receive a mental set when provided with an overall structure of the new information at the beginning of training. This is done by explaining the information to be learned in a brief and succinct, yet accurate, form.

The mental set helps trainees in several ways:

- It focuses their minds on the information they will be learning and helps block out extraneous or irrelevant ideas.

- It provides them with an overall structure (like the border of a jigsaw puzzle) in which to fit the small pieces of information which will be coming.

- It shows them the organization of the training lesson, letting them know "where they are" in the body of information being learned.

Using Mental Set. Apply mental set by:

- Presenting the information to be learned in a brief and succinct, yet accurate, form

- Explaining how the training lesson is organized by:

  - Sequence of content

  - Sections of the lesson and format in which it is written

Some ways to present the information in a brief and succinct, yet accurate, form are:

- Tell the trainees "In this lesson, you will learn . . ." or "The X parts of a Y are . . .".

- Write a paragraph of no more than seven sentences which summarizes the major concepts, principles, or procedures to be taught—one per sentence.

- Write a topic outline listing the major concepts, principles, or procedures to be taught—limit = 7.

Some ways to explain how the content is sequenced in the training lesson are:

- A numbered topic outline

- A table, with numbers in the left column and topics in the right column

- A flowchart showing the flow of topics

- A "lesson map" which puts each topic in a box, and shows sequence by the arrows connecting the boxes

Some ways to explain the sections of the lesson, and the format in which it is written, are:

- List, by name, the sections of the lesson.
- Briefly describe what will be in each section.
- Describe the format in which the lesson is written, highlighting:
  - Any unique features of the writing style or page layout (bullets, marginal headings, different type styles indicating different types of information).
  - Any unique activities trainees must do (e.g., respond).

Example. This chapter has provided the reader with a "mental set" in several ways: the outline at the beginning of the chapter, and the several sections on "organization" throughout it, provide both a brief, succinct summary of the content and a description of the way the chapter is organized.

Review

This section of the chapter has discussed the five principles to be followed in writing a good introduction section to training materials:

- Attention/motivation
- Influence/credibility
- Objectives
- Context/familiarity
- Mental set

A more detailed review of each principle, summarizing how it is applied in training, is found in the Job Aid at the end of this chapter.

Principles to Be Used in the Explanation Section

Introduction

Why Use These Principles. In addition to making your job easier, following these principles in writing the explanation section of your training materials makes the trainees' job of learning easier because:

- It is easier for trainees to learn if:
  - They are given something along the way to help them organize the information being presented.
  - The text material is arranged so that it is easy to follow and so that key points are highlighted.
  - They are presented with an amount of information that is within their visual or auditory ability to absorb it.

- Everything is presented to them using both words and appropriate illustrations.
- They have the opportunity to practice what they've learned.
- They are given examples illustrating what they've learned.

Where You Have Seen Explanations Before. While the introduction section discussed above contains the "Why to Learn It," the explanation section contains the actual information or content to be learned. You are already quite familiar with other versions of explanations:

- The middle part of a novel, film, or TV show usually "explains" the plot or the subject matter.
- The portion of the speech in which a speaker "develops" the ideas is the explanation part.
- When, during a training session, the instructor demonstrates how to perform a skill, the instructor is conducting the explanation part of the lesson.
- The main section of any text or handbook where the actual "content" is presented is the explanation portion of the book.

How This Section Is Organized. The principles to be followed in writing a good explanation section are:

- Chunking
- Illustrations
- Intra-organizers
- Relevant examples
- Text layout
- Frequent relevant practice
- Feedback

Principle 6: Chunking

What Chunking Means. Trainees can perceive only limited amounts of information at one time. Research shows this capacity to be seven meaningful pieces of information, plus or minus two pieces (7 ± 2). If the amount of information presented to trainees at once exceeds this limit, they may have difficulty in initially processing and ultimately absorbing it.

Trainees can perceive and remember larger amounts of information if the information is grouped, or "chunked," so that each chunk contains:

- A label naming the chunk
- No more than seven items in the chunk itself

Trainees then perceive and remember:

- All the label names as a separate group
- The items under each name as separate groups

Therefore, a list of 15 steps in a procedure could be grouped into 3 major "chunks" of 5 steps each. Trainees remember the names of the 3 groupings as 1 chunk (with

3 items in it), the 5 steps in the first grouping as another chunk (with 5 items in it), etc.

Using Chunking. Break down and group, or "chunk," larger pieces of information (complex facts, procedures, rules, etc.) into smaller, easier-to-process groupings. A procedure for doing this is:

- Decide if there are more than 7 points, ideas, steps, concepts, etc., in the lesson; if yes. . . .
- Divide them into logical groups of seven or fewer items.
- Make up a name for each grouping.
- Present, first, the list of "grouping" names.
- Next, take the first grouping name and list the steps, points, concepts, etc., under it.
- Next, do the same for the second grouping.
- Repeat until all groupings have been covered.

Example. This chapter has chunked the 14 principles being explained in the following way. First, a training lesson was divided into 3 parts, named Introduction, Explanation, and Summary (chunk 1). The first 5 principles were then grouped under Introduction (chunk 2), the next 7 principles were grouped under Explanation (chunk 3), and the final 2 principles were grouped under Summary (chunk 4).

Principle 7: Illustrations

What Illustrations Mean. Trainees learn better from training materials that combine text and illustrations. This follows from the old "one picture is worth a thousand words" adage. Often the word message can be enhanced or made more understandable by a relevant, properly prepared, illustration. Conversely, an illustration can be made more understandable when accompanied by appropriate labels and/or word messages.

Specifically, when they are used with words, illustrations can help trainees visualize:

- Representatives of ideas, concept, things
- Relative sizes of objects
- Steps in a process
- Specific details of objects
- Parts of objects
- Generalized shapes
- Relative distances

Using Illustrations. Use illustrations alone, or illustration and word combinations, to:

influence,
direct,

- control,
- organize, or
- simplify

trainees' perceptions of instructional messages. Some techniques for using text and illustrations effectively are to:

- Make illustrations attractive to the trainee.
- Use captions, questions, or explanations, with illustrations, to:
  - Help the trainee classify the illustration.
  - Tell the trainee what to look for in the illustration.
  - Help the trainee remember the illustration.
- Initially use less detailed graphics to convey an overview of the concept or object.
- Later, use more detailed graphics to show specific examples or portions of a concept or object.
- Use line drawings, rather than pictures, to show or highlight the details of the object.
- Use lines, arrows, color, and highlighting in illustrations to:
  - Emphasize items.
  - Separate items.
  - Indicate movement.
  - Show hierarchical relationships.
- Follow the "chunking" principle in deciding on the complexity of illustrations— show a maximum of seven points per diagram, and chunk if there are more.
- Make each chunk a clearly discrete step of the process or part of the object.
- In sequencing illustrations, go from the "big view" illustration to the discrete parts illustrations and back again to the big view illustration—and do so frequently to keep trainees oriented.

Principle 8: Intra-organizers

What Intra-organizers Mean.   Intra-organizers perform the same function as the "mental set" principle discussed earlier; they help to guide trainees through the materials and to ready them for the upcoming topics. Intra-organizers differ from mental set in two ways:

- They appear throughout the explanation and summary sections of the lessons instead of just in the introduction.
- They help remind the trainees where the current topic fits in relation to all the other topics in the lesson.

They are extremely important in long or complex lessons, in which the trainee can get lost among the trees and forget what the whole forest was about.

Using Intra-organizers.   Place intra-organizers where natural breaks occur within the training sequence, i.e., where one topic, subtopic, unit, lesson ends and a related one begins. Intra-organizers can take the form of:

- Subheadings
- Short phrases previewing the material about to be taught
- One- or two-column tables listing all the topics to be covered in the lesson but highlighting the topic to be taught next
- A flowchart, or map, of the whole course, highlighting the topic to be taught next

Example. The "How This Section Is Organized" segments at the beginning of each section of the chapter are examples of intra-organizers.

Principle 9: Relevant Examples

What Examples Mean. Trainees learn ideas better when—and often only learn them if—they are presented with examples of those ideas. Examples are "typical instances" of the ideas or concepts being taught that:

- Illustrate the ideas or concepts with real world objects, situations, or descriptions.
- Contain all the important characteristics of the idea or concept that make it unique.
- May contain varying degrees of other characteristics that are not unique to the idea or concept.
- Vary in amount of difficulty trainees will have in recognizing them as examples— from a very easy (a "bull's eye") example to a very difficult (a "borderline") example.

Descriptions and examples are not enough, however. Trainees also need "nonexamples" to contrast with the examples. Nonexamples:

- Contain only some, or none, of the unique characteristics of the idea or concept.
- Vary in amount of difficulty trainees will have in recognizing them as nonexamples—from a very easy (a "far out") nonexample to a very difficult (a "borderline") nonexample.

These examples and nonexamples help trainees:

- Recognize the boundaries of the idea—what it includes and what it does not.
- Discriminate one idea from another that may seem identical but is not.
- Generalize from the "ideal" description of the concept presented in the training setting to the many different forms the concept might take in the "real world job" situations.

Using Examples. Write training materials that include both examples and nonexamples for each idea, concept, principle, procedure, etc., taught:

- Use examples that are relevant to the audience.
- Use many examples and nonexamples (at least two of each) to show the variety of instances falling under that idea, concept, principle, etc.
- Start with the easy "bull's-eye" examples and "far out" nonexamples, and move, at the end, to the difficult "borderline" examples and nonexamples.

Example. While limited in the number of examples presented (because of space limitations), this chapter has shown how some sections of its serve as examples of the principles explained.

Principle 10: Text Layout

What Text Layout Means. It is easier for trainees to learn when the training materials format helps, rather than gets in the way of, understanding and organizing the information. Use of good text layout principles can aid the learning process by:

- Making the text easier to read
- Relating the words and illustrations in the text clearly
- Giving an obvious organizational pattern to the content
- Emphasizing what is important
- Directing attention to key points
- Separating blocks of information
- Facilitating rapid scanning and retrieval of information
- Providing note-taking space

Good text layout involves:

- The placement of space and text on the pages of the training materials
- The use of words or phrases to headline, highlight, or distinguish blocks of text
- The use of underlining, boldface, italics, boxes, and lines to highlight key ideas
- The use of tables, graphs, matrices, flowcharts, and diagrams to simplify and highlight concepts and procedures
- The placement of words and illustrations in proper relation to one another so they work together

Using Text Layout. Use the following guidelines to format the pages of the training materials:

- Leave lots of white space on a page to break up the density of the text.
- Use short topic or subtopic words or phrases on the left side of the page with corresponding explanations on the right side.
- Put boxes around text portions of special interest or importance.
- Use boldface and/or italics or underlining for points to be emphasized.
- Place illustrations and related word explanations next to each other.
- Use "bullets" instead of numbers for lists—except when the list is a procedure with steps that must be performed in a certain order.
- Use short lists separated by headings.
- Leave lots of blank space for note taking.
- Write short sentences.
- Organize sentences into short paragraphs.

- Use various type faces and sizes to differentiate chapter, topic, subtopic, and small units of information.
- Use matrices, tables, and flowcharts to:
  - Highlight the attributes of one concept.
  - Compare the attributes of two related, but different, concepts.
  - Show sequential steps in a procedure.
  - Emphasize decision points and appropriate actions to take in each situation.

Example. This chapter has been formatted following the text layout principles identified above.

Principle 11: Frequent Relevant Practice

What Practice Means. If trainees are to learn, it is not sufficient for the materials to merely explain the information well. In addition, trainees must have the opportunity to respond to the information, or practice the skills, being taught. Training materials provide this opportunity by asking questions about the information or by providing exercises which require trainees to apply the skills. This responding serves at least two functions:

- It increases learning:
  - The more trainees practice a skill (within some limitations and conditions), the better they learn it.
- It gives trainees confidence in their learning:
  - By trying out their new skills, and finding out if they are learning them correctly, the trainees feel more confident that they have indeed learned.

What Relevant Means. Practice alone, however, is not enough. The type of practice trainees have is crucial to whether the practice helps them learn. The questions asked about the information and the exercises requiring skill practice must match the way the knowledge and skills will be applied in the real world. Thus, reciting from memory the list of steps in a procedure usually does not help learning, since this is usually *not* the skill that is required on the job. On the other hand, actually performing the procedure on a real (or at least simulated) problem like one found on the job *will* have the desired effects.

What Frequent Means. The practice must also be frequent. A single test at the end of training is *not* sufficient. Trainees should have the opportunity to practice each part of a new skill or apply each new piece of knowledge *when* they learn it. When learning a six-step procedure, for example, trainees should have the opportunity to practice each step as they learn it, before going on to learn the next step. In addition, trainees should have the chance to practice each part of the skill *several times* throughout the training. When they learn the third step of the six-step procedure, for example, they should have a chance to practice not only the new step but the first two steps of the procedure again.

Using Frequent Relevant Practice. Build opportunities for frequent relevant practice into training materials by:

- Inserting opportunities for practice at least at the end of every "chunk" of knowledge and skill taught
- Providing many exercises or questions that call for the trainees to practice a skill—not just one or two
- Spreading the opportunities to practice a skill throughout the entire lesson—not just bunching them all in one place
- Writing the exercises and questions trainees must answer so that they:
  - Match the objectives of the training
  - Match the application of the skill and knowledge on the job
  - Require thinking and processing of information, rather than mere memory
- Encouraging trainees to practice on their own as they read the training materials—even before the materials provide formal practice exercises

Principle 12: Feedback

What Feedback Means. Once trainees have practiced a skill, they need information about how correct their responses were. If trainees' responses were correct, they need information that confirms that correctness. If trainees' responses were incorrect, they need information that:

- Tells them that the responses were incorrect
- Tells them why the responses were incorrect
- Tells them what the correct responses were and why they were correct

Providing feedback to trainees in training materials serves several functions:

- It allows trainees to check on the quality of their learning.
- It builds into the training a way to correct trainees' incorrect learning.
- It "reinforces" some trainees for their learning efforts and correct responses—thus motivating them to continue learning.

Using Feedback. Include feedback in the training materials *immediately follow-ing* each "practice":

- The layout of the materials should ensure that trainees cannot see the feedback before they make their own response.
- The feedback should come immediately after the response—no extra time or other text pages should separate them.

The feedback should contain:

- An explanation of how to use the feedback to judge the correctness of the responses
- The correct response to the practice
- An explanation of why the response is correct—using words different from those used to explain the concept or procedure in the first place
- Statements of praise or other information designed to encourage trainees
- If possible, a description of some likely incorrect responses, and an explanation of why they are incorrect

- Suggestions about what trainees whose responses were incorrect should do.

Feedback sequences should:

- Be simple and to the point
- Not belabor the obvious, especially for simple, low-level responses

Review

This section of the chapter has discussed the seven principles to be followed in writing a good explanation section in training materials:

- Chunking
- Illustrations
- Intra-organizers
- Relevant examples
- Text layout
- Frequent relevant practice
- Feedback

A more detailed review of each principle, summarizing how it is applied in training, is found in the Job Aid at the end of this chapter.

Principles to Be Used in the Summary Section

Introduction

Why Use Them.   Following these principles in writing the summary section of your training lesson facilitates your work and makes the trainees' job of learning easier because:

- Trainees learn better if all the information they've learned is:
  - Tied together for them at the end.
  - Said in yet another way at the end.
  - Generalized to yet another example.
  - Presented in a form that makes the key points stand out.
- Trainees can only apply what they've learned if:
  - They remember what they learned.
  - They remember when to apply it.
  - They have reference materials to help them apply it.

Where You Have Seen Summaries Before.   You are already quite familiar with things and people that use these principles in their summaries—even though you may not have recognized them as such:

- When you consult your automobile owner's manual for the steps to change your oil, or your cookbook for the proportions of ingredients to use in making veal marsala, you are using a reference guide.
- When you learned "ROY G BIV" as a way to help remember the colors of the rainbow, you were using a mnemonic.
- When you hear a speaker "tell you what you've been told," the speaker is reviewing the information presented in speech.
- When you read the summary section of a chapter in a textbook, you are reviewing the information in the chapter, stated in different words.

How This Section Is Organized. The principles to be followed in writing a good summary section are:

- Review
- Memory/reference

Principle 13: Review

What Review Means. Trainees learn best when, after being presented with a large amount of information, they are given a summary of the information that repeats and ties together all the pieces for them. Repeating the information in the same words is not enough, however. To help trainees better understand and apply what they've learned, the summary must explain it in a slightly different way.

Since the trainees are dealing with a large amount of information, it helps them to have the information summarized in a way that highlights the key points. To help trainees generalize what they have learned to new situations, they need a final example that shows all the pieces of information being applied together.

Using Review. Include a review at the end of each lesson that:

- Contains all the essential information tied together
- States the information in a different way
- Highlights the key points
- Gives an example that extends the information to new situations

Some ways to write a review at the end of a lesson that includes all the elements are:

- Use a format that ties together, states in different ways, and highlights the information:
  - Outline
  - Table
  - Checklist
  - Flow or stage diagram or schematic
- Limit the information reviewed to the essential "large chunks."
- If all information is reviewed, keep it in a "chunked" format.
- Restate the information in the form of key words or questions.
- Repeat the "mental set" and "intra-organizers."

- Present another example that:
  - Applies *all* (vs. pieces of) the information in one complete smooth flow.
  - Uses a situation that is different from any used previously in the training.

Principle 14: Memory/Reference

What Memory/Reference Means. Trainees cannot be expected to remember all the information they've learned during the training lesson. Therefore, they need three things to help them remember and use the information on the job.

First, they need some simple memory jogger (key words, analogies, mnemonics) to help them call the information to mind and recall all the details.

Second, they need a final practice (sometimes called a test) which asks them to recall or apply all they have learned.

Third, they need some reference, called a job aid, that:

- Summarizes the information in an easy-to-read format.
- Can be used by trainees back on the job.

Using Memory/Reference. Include three memory/reference aids in the summary of the lesson:

- A memory jogger
- A final practice or test
- A job aid

Some ways to include these three elements in a summary are to provide:

- Memory joggers:
  - Key words
  - Mnemonics
  - Analogies
  - Symbols
  - Figures
  - Familiar situations or stories
- Practice
  - A synthesizing end-of-lesson test that:
    Is at the application, *not* memory, level
  - Applies *all* (vs. pieces) of the information in one complete smooth flow
  - Uses a situation that is different from any used previously in the training
- Job aids in the form of a:
  - Checklist
  - Table
  - Reference document
  - Blank form

Table 14-2. Job Aid for Writing Training Materials That Work

Principle	Key questions to ask about training materials
	The Introduction Section

1: Attention/motivation	• Does the "What's in It for Me?" explain how the lesson content:
	  • Is important to the trainees, job, and organization?
	  • Will make the trainees' job easier and more interesting?
	  • Will make the trainee more productive and rewarded by others?

2: Influence/credibility	• Are the credentials of the author stated? • Is the research or professional practice on which the training is based cited? • Is reference made to new ideas or ideas trainees may have heard elsewhere? • Is the packaging and printing visually appealing to the trainees?
3: Objectives	• Are the objectives stated overtly? • Are they stated in terms of skills the trainees will gain? • Are they stated in behavioral terms?
4: Context/familiarity	• Is the information being taught linked or related to what trainees already know? • Are the trainees told which existing links or "hooks" to use? • Is previously learned, related content "recalled?" • Do explanations use already known concepts and vocabulary as "building blocks?"
5: Mental set	• Is the information to be learned presented in a brief and succinct, yet accurate, form? • Are the organization, sequence, format, and unique features of the lesson explained?
6: Chunking	• Are large amounts of information broken down into "chunks" of seven pieces per chunk? • Does each "chunk" have a label naming it? • Are the names of all the chunks presented first, followed by a breakdown of each chunk in sequence?
7: Illustrations	• Are illustrations combined with captions or explanations to aid understanding? • Are illustrations sequenced from the less detailed, overview type, to more detailed, specific point type? • Are line drawings, not pictures, used to show details of objects? • Are color, highlighting, arrows used to emphasize or separate key items? • Are a maximum of seven elements shown in each illustration?

8: Intra-organizers	• Are the logical subsections of the lesson identified and highlighted by:
	  • Subheadings?
	  • Course maps?
	  • Short phrases?
	  • Tables?

9: Relevant examples	• Are at least two examples of each concept or idea used to show the variety of forms the concept can take?

Table 14-2. Job Aid for Writing Training Materials That Work

	• Do the examples contain all the important characteristics that make the idea unique?
	• Are at least two nonexamples of each idea paired with the examples to show the limits of the idea or concept?
	• Are the examples and nonexamples relevant to the trainees?
	• Are the examples and nonexamples sequenced from easiest to most difficult?
10: Text layout	• Is there lots of white space on the page?
	• Are matrices, tables, and flowcharts used to organize procedures or contrast concepts?
	• Are different typefaces and type styles used to highlight key points?
	• Are words or key phrases used as marginal notes or subheadings to facilitate rapid scanning, reading, and retrieval?
	• Are lists of items (except for sequential procedures) "bulleted?"
11: Frequent relevant practice	• Are there exercises or questions at the end of each chunk of content presented?
	• Does the practice match both the training objective and on-the-job skill application?
	• Are there at least two practices for a skill?
	• Are the practices for each skill spread out through the lesson, not bunched in one place?
12: Feedback	• Does the feedback come immediately after the response?
	• Is the correct answer given, and why it is correct explained?
	• Are statements designed to praise and encourage the trainee used?
	• (if possible) Are likely incorrect answers given, with an explanation of why they are incorrect?
	• Are the trainees prevented from seeing the feedback before they respond on their own?
13: Review	• Is all the essential information included and tied together?
	• Is the information stated differently?
	• Are the key points highlighted?
	• Is there an example that extends the application of the information?
14: Memory/reference	• Are there memory joggers:
	• Key words?
	• Analogies?
	• Mnemonics?
	• Figures?
	• Is there a synthesizing practice and test that:
	• Applies all that has been learned?
	• Uses a new problem situation?
	• Is there a job aid, in the form of:
	• Checklist?
	• Blank form?
	• Flowchart?
	• Glossary?
	• Table?
	• Reference document?
	• Diagram?
	• Example?

- Flowchart
- Diagram
- Glossary
- Example
- Chapter index

Review

This section of the chapter has discussd two principles to be followed in writing a good summary section to training materials:

- Review
- Memory/reference

Summary Reference Aid Table

Review.   This chapter has discussed why principles should be followed in writing training materials. It has explained 14 principles to be used in the introduction, explanation, and summary sections of a lesson, including what they mean and why they work. It has also described how to use each of the 14 principles to write effective training materials. Finally, it has pointed out how this chapter is written to model, or provide an example of, most of the principles.

Applying the Principles.   It is not expected that you will remember all these principles; doing so is *not* necessary for you to successfully apply them on your job. To help you use them to meet the objective of this chapter—writing training materials using all 14 principles—the chapter concludes with Table 14-2, a job aid which includes:

- The name of each principle
- A summary of questions to ask about training materials based on the principle

Using the Job Aid.   You can use this job aid as reference when you are going to:

- Write a training lesson yourself
- Evaluate a training lesson someone else has written

Training materials that work should provide a "yes" answer to every question in the job aid. If any questions are answered "no," some revisions in, or additions to the training materials are indicated.

Bibliography

Davies, Ivor, *Instructional Technique*, McGraw-Hill, New York, 1981.
Fleming, M., and H. Levie, *Instructional Message Design*, Educational Technology Publication, Englewood Cliffs, NJ, 1978.

Gagne, Robert M., *The Conditions of Learning*, 3d ed. Holt, Rinehart and Winston, New York, 1977.

Hartley, James, *Designing Instructional Text*, Nichols Publishing Company, New York, 1978.

Horn, Robert, *How to Write Information Mapping*, Information Resources, Inc., Lexington, MA, 1976.

Knowles, Malcolm S., *The Modern Practice of Adult Education*, Association Press, Chicago, 1980.

Laird, Dugan, *Approaches to Training and Development*, Addison-Wesley, Reading, MA, 1982.

Mager, Robert F., *Troubleshooting the Troubleshooting Course*, Pitman Learning, Inc., Belmont, CA, 1982.

Mager, Robert F., *Preparing Instructional Objectives*, 2d ed., Pitman Learning, Inc., Belmont, CA, 1984.

Mager, Robert F., *Measuring Instructional Results*, 2d ed., Pitman Learning, Inc., Belmont, CA, 1984.

Stelnicki, M. B., and K. H. Silber, *Writing Training Materials That Work: Workshop Materials*, Governors State University, Park Forest South, IL, 1985.

Tiemann, P. W., and S. M. Markle, *Analyzing Instructional Content*, Stipes Publishing Co., Champaign, IL, 1983.

Wlodkowski, Raymond, *Enhancing Adult Motivation to Learn*, Jossey-Bass Publishers, San Francisco, 1985.

Zemke, R., and S. Zemke, "30 Things We Know for Sure about Adult Learning," *Training/HRD*, June 1981, pp. 45–46, 48, 52.

15
Testing

Mary L. Tenopyr

Mary L. Tenopyr is *Division Manager—Employment and Staffing Systems at AT&T. She also holds an appointment as a member of the Army Science Board. Previously she held psychological research management positions with the U.S. Civil Service Commission and Rockwell International. She was also previously on the faculty of the Graduate School of Education at the University of California at Los Angeles. She has taught at other universities, including the University of Southern California and New York University. She was awarded a Ph.D. from the University of Southern California, where she specialized in psychological measurement. She has held numerous offices in professional and scientific organizations and is currently president of the ASPA Foundation. In 1984, she was given the Society for Industrial and Organizational Psychology's award for outstanding professional practice.*

This chapter is designed to define testing, explain the various roles testing has in relation to training, describe and relate information about the testing's most important characteristics, describe developments in selection testing, relate information about the status of achievement testing, and provide a summary of the topics covered.

Definition of Testing

Testing is a process whereby one obtains a quantifiable estimate of some aspect of performance at a given point in time. Although the term "quantifiable" implies numerical measurement, it also applies to categories such as "excellent" or "good," to letter grades such as "A" or "B," and to gross categories, such as "pass" or "fail." All these categories can be translated into numbers. The term "performance" in the definition of testing is not meant to imply that actual hands-on work is required to define a test. Most tests consist of constructed tasks upon which performance is measured. For example, both the task of answering questions about job knowledge and the handling of simulated in-basket materials are constructed tasks.

Although the distinction is not always clear, tests may be divided into two general categories. First there are tests of maximum performance, in which the examinee is instructed to do his or her best. The typical training test is in this category. The other type of test is a habitual performance test in which the examinee reports in terms of what he or she believes or feels, or how the person would habitually act in a given situation. Most of the instruments used to measure personality, character, interests, or attitudes fall in this category. In terms of training, these habitual performance instruments are of limited interest; they are probably most useful in evaluating training designed to change beliefs and attitudes.

Various Roles of Testing

Testing, essentially, has five roles in training. These are (1) selection of trainees, (2) diagnosis of training needs, (3) evaluation of training adequacy, (4) evaluation of trainee achievement, and (5) use as criterion for selection test results. A purpose of this chapter is to relate clearly the interdependence of testing and the training development and delivery processes. Testing cannot be considered in isolation from the total training system, and testing in one of its roles cannot be considered apart from the way it functions in its other roles. This chapter also gives an overview of current knowledge relative to each of the roles of testing and indicates the relationships among roles and the implications of the law for each of these roles.

Appropriate testing in training cannot be accomplished unless one considers the whole system in which training is embedded. Despite the fact that test development and application are important, basically a test can be no better than the training upon which it was based. Of course, the training can be no better than the needs analysis upon which the training was designed. In turn, the needs analysis depends upon adequate definition of the job for which training is to be developed, followed by appropriate measurement of job performance or other job behaviors, so that training needs can be adequately delineated. Here, diagnostic testing may take place and influence later selection and evaluation testing. Finally, the definition of the job depends upon the allocation of the tasks which the organization decides need to be done to achieve its goals.

Thus, the situation in its simplest form is a chain: organizational goals, task definition to achieve these goals, task allocations to jobs, job definition, performance measurement, needs analysis (possible diagnostic testing), training development, training delivery, and testing.

Any inadequacies along this chain will render the final process less than perfect. For example, if the job is poorly defined or performance on it is not measured adequately, any training needs analysis will suffer; the training will be poorly developed, and any measurement of trainee success may have little relevance with respect to performance of the job and, in turn, achievement of the goals of the organization.

Also, one can conceptualize the simple chain configuration relative to training as complicated by various feedback loops which are characteristic of a system. For example, training can result in a situation in which the job is redefined, because of different skills of job incumbents.

Furthermore, training and related testing are intricately involved with other personnel practices of the organization. For example, changes in wage rate may affect the general skill level of job applicants and dictate the need for different training. Conversely, the fact that an organization offers the opportunity for training may affect the wages the employer has to offer to attract job applicants.

Examples could be given of many other interactions with the equipment procurement system or with a production control system. What has been presented here, of course, does not represent the totality of the many interactions training and its associated testing can have in the systems and subsystems within an organization or those impinging on an organization, but it should be sufficient to indicate that training testing does not exist in a vacuum. Training testing is highly dependent upon many factors within and outside the organization and cannot be developed or evaluated without consideration of its whole role in the total organization.

The ensuing discussion of the roles of testing in training will have a more narrow focus than the preceding material; however, the reader is cautioned to keep in mind that testing is usually a reflection of the steps that preceded test development and the interactions of those steps with many processes within and outside the organization.

Testing Characteristics

Validity

The most important concept relative to test use is validity, which refers to the accuracy of inferences made from test scores.[1] Test validation is a process of investigation, relative to determining such accuracy. Various types of investigation may be involved, depending upon the exact situation, but in all cases, the type of investigation is dependent upon the use to which the test is to be put. It is inappropriate to speak of "validating" a test; one investigates the validity of a test for a particular use. It is equally inappropriate to speak of a "valid test"; rather one should speak of "valid test use." A test which is used validly for one purpose may not be validly used for another purpose. Although there are various strategies for investigating validity, it is important to recognize that validity is essentially a unitary concept related, of course, to the specific use. Since 1954,[2] there has been a tendency to categorize validity into categories. This unfortunately has led to a situation in which various types of validity have been discussed separately by numerous writers and the underlying unity of validity has been, for the most part, ignored.

It is common now to speak of three strategies for investigating validity; however, the use of different strategies for validation does not define different types of validity. The three strategies are criterion-related, content, and construct. Depending upon the use to which a test is to be put, one may wish to emphasize one of those strategies more than others; however, this action does not constitute using one "type" of validity.

Criterion-Related Validity.   The criterion-related strategy is used when one specifically wants to relate test use to some outcome called a criterion. The criterion may be singular, such as grades in training, or it may be a composite of several outcomes, such as training time, job performance, and tenure. In any event, the criterion is the primary variable of interest and it is the relationship of the test with the criterion one wishes to investigate. For example, one may establish training time as a criterion and wish to know how well aptitude tests given at time of hire relate to later training time. The relationship is usually expressed numerically through a statistic called a "coefficient of correlation" or some variation thereof. In the validation situation, these coefficients are often referred to as validity coefficients. A typical validity coefficient is a unit-free index number, not to be confused with a proportion, and it can take on values from +1.00 to −1.00. A coefficient of +1.00 indicates a perfect positive correlation; that is, the person who scored highest on the test scored highest on the criterion. The person who scored second highest on one scored highest on the other. With a coefficient of correlation of +1.00, the same relationship exists point-for-point throughout the two sets of data. In work with testing, this degree of relationship rarely if ever occurs. A coefficient of correlation of zero indicates a pure random relationship between the test and the criterion. In this situation, the best prediction of criterion performance one can make from the test score is to say that regardless of test score, every examinee will be average in criterion performance. This is, in practical terms, equivalent to no prediction at all. A coefficient of correlation of −1.00 means the same as one of +1.00; only the relationship is reversed. The person who scores highest on the test does poorest on the criterion. In testing, a negative coefficient of correlation is most likely to occur when the "good" ends of the test and the criterion scales are in different directions. For example, aptitude tests often correlate negatively with training time, because high test scores are "good" and high training time is "bad." When scales are in the same direction, correlations between aptitude tests and training success criteria are usually positive. They are also usually of moderate size, roughly in the range from .15 to .60. Coefficients of correlation of this magnitude, whether they be positive or negative, show that test scores are useful in making predictions of criterion performance.

Earlier writings[3] differentiated between types of criterion-related validity depending upon the type of design used in the validation study. The most common differentiation was between "predictive" and "concurrent" validity. The term "predictive" was used to describe studies in which job applicants are hired regardless of test score (predictor) and criterion data (e.g., course grades) are collected later. The term "concurrent" was reserved for use in situations in which the predictor and criterion data are gathered at approximately the same point in time. In organizations, the latter type of design usually involves testing of present employees and gathering criterion data, e.g., supervisors' ratings, at the same time.

Later writings[4,5] have indicated that the distinction between the two types of design is not always clear and that many design variations are possible. Also Schmitt, Gooding, Noe, and Kirsch[6] have indicated that there are relatively small differences in the validity estimates for three classes of design.

Content Validity.   A second type of validation strategy is the content-oriented strategy. It consists mainly of investigating a domain of content such as a collection of job tasks, sampling from that domain, and building a test on the basis of that sample. This strategy relies heavily on systematic use of expert judgments, although some numerical techniques may be used in developing a content-oriented test. The content-oriented strategy is the one most meaningful for training achievement tests. It is the method most used for diagnosing training needs and evaluating training and trainees. It is also important in selecting trainees when the objective is to select those who already have some knowledge or ability in the area in which training is to be done. Another use is to develop criteria for validation studies involving selection tests.

The first step in content-oriented test construction is to define a content domain. In training, defining the domain theoretically consists of all the steps in the chain preceding testing, as presented earlier; however, in practice, one usually starts with the training as it has been developed and delivered. In other words, the domain is what has been taught.

This raises an interesting philosophical question. What if the training itself is not valid? Questioning the validity of the training process could lead to an almost infinite regress. One could question the needs analysis, the performance measurement on the job, the delineation of job tasks and requirements, etc. Failures in any of these could serve to make the final training test, based on training content, not valid for making inferences about job performance or other job-relevant behavior.

The training organization should not assume that training tests are valid for inferences about later job behavior unless the total training system is well developed and every link in the chain of events leading to the training test is properly performed. The best test construction cannot compensate for poorly developed or delivered training. The moral of the story is to avoid the question of whether the training itself is valid by following professional techniques in training development and delivery and by influencing those in charge of job design and other facets of the organization relevant to the training situation to perform their functions properly.

Defining an appropriate job domain upon which to base training developments almost always requires careful job study. Many methods have been advanced for job analysis. Some are more useful than others in training development. Some of the recent writings on this subject are contained in Bemis, Belenky, and Soder,[7] Gael,[8] Levine,[9] and McCormick.[10]

After the job domain is defined and appropriately narrowed by a needs assessment, the objectives of training set, the training developed and delivered, one is ready to speak of a training domain. This is the total content of the training as actually delivered. It is this training domain, the content domain, which should be the basis for developing training tests for diagnosis, trainee evaluation, and use as a criterion for selection tests.

The second step, after defining the content domain, is the sampling from that domain to obtain the tasks, knowledges, skills, or abilities which are to be the basis for actual test questions or other tasks. Many methods can be used for sampling, but the basic guide to sampling should be the course objectives.

In some cases, it is critical that trainees know some material taught extremely well whereas other parts of the material need not be known so well. Developing a test which reflects differences in criticality of content is usually best achieved by sampling extremely heavily from the more critical areas and less heavily from those areas of lesser importance. The instructor may wish to engage the services of independent subject matter experts to determine criticality at this point; however, the judgment as to what is critical should have been done during training development and the steps which preceded it.

For some jobs, such as airline pilot, the notion of sampling has little meaning. When everything the trainee does is critical, every aspect of the training domain should be subject to testing.

Content sampling should result in a sample sufficient in size to provide later a test which will yield stable measurement. This is basically a question of test reliability, which is the degree to which test scores are free from errors of measurement.[11] Reliability will be discussed in more detail later; however, in general, longer tests provide more freedom from one type of error of measurement; this does not mean that inappropriate lengthening of a test is advisable. The inclusion of irrelevant material in the content sample just for the sake of lengthening the test is not a justifiable procedure.

Content sampling also should be cast, if possible, in terms of what the examinee has to do later on the job. Samples should be described in terms of "action" verbs, e.g., "Records the trouble call number to line 5 of Form 220."

If one follows the standard prescriptions for writing training objectives,[12] the sampling should follow directly from the objectives. Writing the description of the members of the sample in this way will also help preclude the development of a test which is based upon rote memorization of facts.

Content sampling should not be heavily based on the ease with which test items can be written for a particular subject. Often the most critical parts of training require the most creative test writing. Especially to be avoided is oversampling in areas in which it is easy to write questions with simple numerical answers which are subject to rote memorization.

The content sampling is best summarized in a document variously known as a "test outline" or a "test budget." Various procedures for developing this document have been proposed, but there is no evidence that any format other than the traditional outline format as taught in elementary school is necessary. However, for organizational training purposes there are several criteria this document should meet: (1) it should be closely allied with the course objectives, i.e., it should accurately reflect what was taught; (2) it should deal in actions at every step in the outline; (3) it should be broken down into fine enough units so that the number of test tasks to be developed for the finest outline unit is small (some recommend that the units should be so fine that no more than five test questions are assigned to any given unit); and (4) it should provide a training-relevant test as long as is reasonable and feasible.

When a training test is used in a way that will have any effect on a trainee's future in the organization, it might be wise to have the test budget reviewed by one or more independent subject matter experts and their judgments recorded. This not only will serve as a quality control measure but will also aid in possible later legal defense, if the test is challenged.

Construct Validity. The third major strategy is construct validation. This strategy focuses primarily on the test score as a measure of a psychological characteristic of interest. The term "construct" is used because one is trying to measure something intangible that has essentially been constructed. In the mental ability area, one can speak of characteristics such as verbal comprehension, spatial visualization, and numerical facility as constructs. Constructs in the personality area are harder to define, but such characteristics as friendliness and sociability are often used as if they were constructs.

Early conceptions of construct validation, such as that of Cronbach and Meehl,[13] implied that every construct had to be embedded within a complex and continually developing theory. This idea was developed through the years and refined.[14] The use of the term "construct," however, came to be applied without all the theoretical support that early writers had contemplated. Possibly in recognition that ideals would never be fulfilled, later writers have looked upon constructs as requiring less rigorous definition. However, few writers would disagree that a construct has to be embedded in a conceptual framework and have a body of empirical evidence supporting its definition. Terms implying constructs are in use in everyday language. Conversations are sprinkled with terms like "drive," "enthusiasm," or "introversion." Yet many of these terms do not have the research-based empirical support to justify their use in testing or in precisely describing individuals. One should be cautious in applying such labels and also examine carefully any claims that a test "measures" such abstract constructs.

A language of constructs has not been agreed upon by psychologists. Throughout psychology one can find a proliferation of terms used to describe people. However, definitions of the same term often vary from researcher to researcher, and there seem to be no clear paths to truth. The situation is complicated by the fact that even very narrow personal characteristics, such as the ability to type, can be considered constructs.[15] Thus, one can conceive of an almost infinite number of constructs.

Unless one attends to construct validation, one has little evidence about the meaning of test scores beyond the specifics of the exact training situation. One may know that scores on a certain test requiring reading correlate with success in a course designed to train retail clerks; however, one cannot explain the reasons for this relationship without invoking constructs. It is highly likely that certain constructs affect both performance on the test and performance in training, but without further evidence, we do not know what those constructs are and hence cannot fully discern the meaning of the relationship.

Construct validation takes on particular importance in training when one engages in efforts designed to change attitudes, leadership abilities, or other such characteristics which are hard to define. For evaluation of trainees and training, there is often a tendency to select commercial tests on the basis of the label applied to the test or unsupported claims in the test manual. Often labels are misleading; test names may suggest some relationship to the objectives of the training course, but the same test name can be used for a number of tests which are not highly related, and the test user has no guarantee that the test chosen has any relationship to the objectives of a given training course.

In situations where the trainer is dealing with constructs, he or she is well advised either to choose commercial tests carefully or to avoid their use. An alternative is to base training measurement on the content of the training course. The distinction between content and construct validity is not always an easy one to make. Content-oriented test construction strategies can form strong evidence of construct validity.[15,16] The training developer, however, may have considerable research to ensure that the content of the course is relevant to the constructs he or she wants to develop in trainees.

Reliability

Classical Reliability Theory. Reliability refers to the freedom of test scores from errors of measurement or, in more general terms, consistency of measurement. As it is inappropriate to speak of the validity of a test, it is equally inappropriate to speak of the reliability of a test. Reliability is essentially a generic term, and different reliability coefficients are appropriate depending upon purpose. The commonest ways of estimating reliability are (1) to administer the same test to the same people a second time and obtain the coefficient of correlation between test and retest results, (2) to administer an alternate form of the test to the same people and obtain the coefficient of correlation between forms, and (3) to determine the coefficients of correlation among items or other parts of a test administered only once and estimate the reliability on the basis of these coefficients. The latter method yields what is commonly known as an estimate of internal consistency.

Each of these methods or variations thereof is useful for different purposes. For example, the stability of test scores over time is best estimated by test-retest with a suitable time interval between test administrations.

Possibly the most common ways of estimating reliability for training tests are the various internal consistency methods.[17] Because they depend upon only one administration of the test and do not require the development of an alternate form of the test, they are the least expensive to use. All these methods, such as the split half and the various Kuder-Richardson methods, depend on the degree of homogeneity of response to the content of the test. The source of unreliability indicated by internal consistency methods is differences in response to different parts of the test. This source of unreliability may often be traced to different content in different parts of the test.

The internal consistency methods do not indicate other possible sources of unreliability, such as examinee's changing their responses to items on a retest or differences in content between two forms of a test. The internal consistency methods, because of their convenience and cost, tend to be used at times when other reliability estimation methods may be more appropriate. For highly speeded tests, the use of internal consistency methods may lead to a falsely high estimate of reliability. When the content within a test varies widely, as might be the case for a beginning building maintenance test which might involve several subjects such as electricity, carpentry, and plumbing, an internal consistency method might yield a lower estimate of reliability than other methods.

One of the newest developments relative to reliability is generalizability theory, which has been developed by Cronbach, Gleser, Nanda, and Rajaratian.[18] This theory's use is becoming more common and accepted.

Reliability in testing is most important for its support for validity. Generally, a test which is not reasonably reliable cannot be very valid. Reliability is never a substitute for validity. The fact that a test gives consistent results does not mean that it is measuring the right thing.

Special Reliability Considerations in Achievement Testing. When tests are developed to be criterion-referenced,[19] i.e., developed to communicate the examinees' performance relative to what he or she can do, as opposed to norm-referenced, designed to communicate the person's standing relative to some group, classical reliability theory is often not applicable. Although many organizational training tests can provide both norm-referenced and criterion-referenced interpretations, when a training test is designed to be interpreted only in terms of specified performance standards, e.g., "can (or cannot) assemble a widget correctly in 90 seconds," special reliability formulas may apply. These have been summarized by Berk.[20,21] A review of methods for estimating the reliability of mastery-nonmastery classifications in criterion-referenced testing has been prepared by Subkoviak.[22]

The literature relative to the reliability of criterion-referenced tests continues to develop. The reader is advised to monitor the educational research literature continually.

Selection for Training

Basics of Selection

In selecting persons for training, there are two approaches. When, in general, training is to start at a low level of mastery, and relatively untrained people are to be selected, the use of aptitude tests supported by the results of criterion-related validation is appropriate. When training is to start at a higher level of mastery, and trainees are to be selected on the basis of current level of learning, an achievement test may be appropriate. The distinction between aptitude tests and achievement tests is not clear. The difference is usually cast in terms of the way the test is used. When the test is used to predict, it is usually referred to as an aptitude test. When a test is used to reflect past events, such as amount previously learned, it is called an achievement test.

The distinction between aptitude and achievement is not in test content.

Obviously, answering simple arithmetic questions on a test which is called a "numerical aptitude test" requires some past learning, but if the test is used to predict later learning success, the test is properly referred to as an aptitude test. Also, when tests indicating specific training content mastery are used to predict later performance, such as degree of achievement in a higher-level training source, they are essentially being used as aptitude tests. However, despite being somewhat inappropriate, in the ensuing discussion the term "achievement" will denote tests which are direct reflections of degree of mastery of training content, and the term "aptitude" will be reserved for tests of the more general abilities usually used to predict later training or job success.

In selecting for training, it is often difficult to establish clear-cut roles for aptitude and past achievement. The question of what action to take with regard to a person who has had some previous training but cannot pass validly used aptitude tests often arises. No test is a perfect predictor; consequently this situation can occur in the case of some individuals. The only solution to the dilemma imposed is thorough criterion-related investigation involving both the aptitude tests and a measure of training achievement.

Relative to aptitude tests used for trainee selection, evidence of criterion-related validity is usually necessary. This need is supported not only by principles of good professional practice[3,11] in psychology but also by federal government guidelines on testing,[23] numerous state and local regulations on testing, and a developing body of case law.

It should be emphasized that conducting criterion-related validation studies requires a great deal of rigor and knowledge. Earlier writings, however, suggested that any little study would be sufficient. Those wishing to conduct such studies are advised to seek the assistance of an industrial psychologist or a psychometrician.

Recent Developments

There have been a number of recent developments in selection testing; Some render older ideas meaningless. For example, it has been shown[24] that to detect validity one needs much larger samples of persons to study than was previously believed. The typical test validation study as historically done, i.e., one involving 30 to 100 people, will often not give validity results which even approximate the "true" validity. Rather than do small studies which may be meaningless, one is advised to seek expert advice and seek approaches other than criterion-related validation in the exact situation.

One such approach which has recently emerged is based upon the validity generalization literature.[6,25,26,27,28] The authors of this research assert that all aptitude tests are validly used for predicting success in all jobs. This does not mean, however, that all tests are equally valid for any job or any purpose. It means only that in all likelihood any aptitude test will offer at least a minimum level of prediction for the usual job and training success criteria. In other words, this does not mean that any test for selecting trainees is valid enough to be useful for any course. Validity, as mentioned previously, is not an all-or-none phenomenon, and the closer the value of the validity coefficient to +1.00, the more accurate is the prediction and the more useful the test is, in general. The trainer should seek expert advice to achieve the highest validity he or she can in selecting trainees.

The fact that certain tests are generally highly valid for selecting clerical employees has been demonstrated; the literature does not seem so conclusive relative to blue collar jobs. Also managerial selection on the basis of aptitude tests needs further study to determine the degree of generalizability of selection tests.

The question of possible discrimination against various groups in the population has been a subject of much heated debate and research over the past two decades. The definition of discrimination in selection has essentially been agreed upon by professionals.[11] Discrimination is not a matter of differences in passing rates on selection tests; it is rather a question of whether differences in scores on selection tests are reflected in differences in job or training performance. In other words, do people who score low on the test also do poorly in training, and vice versa?

Using this kind of definition, the research literature indicates that racial discrimination on selection tests is, in general, not a scientific problem[29,30] in employment or education settings. The research literature with respect to sex differences is not conclusive. However, sex differences on most selection tests are often not of any practical significance.

Another area which has received considerable attention during the last decade is the utility of tests. Utility generally is interpreted in terms of the cost benefits of using a test. Determination of savings from the use of tests or any other personnel practice has always been difficult; however, for selection tests, new methods of estimating utility have been developed and are being widely used.[31,32]

A final area in which research results have become fairly conclusive is choosing among various selection procedures.[6,28] It is clear that aptitude tests, along with work samples and peer ratings, are the best-known predictors of measures of job success, including training success. Traditional selection procedures like interviews and education and experience evaluations are relatively poor predictors of job or training performance. Also the typical validity found for aptitude tests, based on all the published literature and much of the unpublished literature, is high enough to afford good prediction of job success. Furthermore, aptitude tests predict training achievement even better than they do job performance. Consequently, for most situations in which there is to be selection for training, it is advisable to use aptitude tests rather than some other selection method.

Measuring Training Achievement

Types of Achievement Testing

Training achievement tests can be used in any of the five roles of testing: (1) selecting trainees, (2) diagnosing training needs, (3) evaluating training needs, (4) evaluating trainee achievement, and (5) serving as criteria for validating selection tests.

How one develops and evaluates achievement tests depends upon the philosophy of training in the organization and the specific policies and goals affecting the training organization. The selection of training test development procedures may at times depend also upon the nature of a specific course's overall objectives.

It is in the organizational training area that classical test theory and the newer test theories are most likely to be at least philosophically different. Classical test theory involves norm-referenced testing in which an individual's test performance is related to one's standing in some reference group. Criterion-referenced testing, on the other hand, is purposely constructed to provide measurements relative to specific performance standards. Although not necessary to do so, most criterion-referenced tests are usually interpreted in terms of mastery or nonmastery, and the standards for mastery are usually specified in the course objectives.

Regardless of what type of achievement test, norm-referenced or criterion-referenced, the instructor sets out to develop, a wide number of test development guides are available, e.g., Green;[33] Gorth, O'Reilly, and Pinsky;[34] Gronlund;[35] Hopkins and Antes;[36] Martuza;[37] Popham;[38] Rahmlow and Woodley;[39] Smith;[40] Swezey;[41] Thyne;[42] and Tuckman.[43] More advanced treatments of criterion-referenced testing may be found in Berk;[44] Berk;[45] Popham;[46] and Hambleton, Swaminathan, Algina, and Coulson.[47] These are only a small sample of the hundreds of publications on the subject. There is little doubt that criterion-referenced measurement has become and will continue to be a major force in American education. The methods of test construction have become well developed, and the psychometric questions are being answered, although there is still some debate.

Test Standards

The question of setting standards for criterion-referenced testing was well covered in a 1978 special issue of *Journal of Educational Measurement*, which was edited by Lorrie A. Shepard. Livingston and Zieky[48] have provided a useful manual for setting standards.

A special problem in standards setting is the situation in which everyone masters training and training time is the only variation among trainees. Here, although subject matter experts may be asked for judgments, it is often useful to do a criterion-related study to determine the relationship between training time and an appropriate measure of later job behavior. The same technique may be used for a combination of degree of mastery and training time.

Validity of Achievement Tests

The questions of validity of criterion-referenced test score use are essentially the same as those for norm-referenced. The test score use must be validated with reference to the inferences to be made from it.[16,49] In organizational training, however, there are many practical problems in achieving ideal validation. If training was developed on the basis of careful needs assessment and job study, and the tests were developed on the basis of course objectives, one may make a claim for content validity when one's goal is to measure training achievement. It is recognized, however, that ideal development of training achievement tests on such a systematic basis is not always possible. Also when a published test is used as a measure of training achievement, content-oriented methods often will not suffice; furthermore any claim that a particular test is relevant to some construct must be strongly supported. Certainly, test names and unsupported claims in promotional literature in test manuals are not evidence of construct validity.

Many inferences made from training achievement tests, such as those about future job performance, are often best supported by criterion-related evidence. When a training test is used for selection or otherwise affects a trainee's career, the question of whether the test predicts later behavior on the job becomes paramount. In this situation, the trainer is often faced with a dilemma. As mentioned previously, a study on a small number of trainees may fail to detect validity. Also, adequate measures of job performance or other job behavior are often not available, and one is sometimes faced with judging a good test on the basis of its relationship to a bad criterion. In many cases, a small sample study involving a hastily developed supervisor's rating criterion or an unreliable production measure may be worse than no study at all. If one is to do criterion-related studies or training achievement, they must be done in the same careful manner as those for trainee selection tests.

A further complicating factor is that when training and associated training tests are used for selection, they fall under the purview of government guidelines on testing.[23] According to the guidelines, if the use of such tests results in different passing rates for different race, ethnic, or sex groups, the user of the tests should be prepared to submit evidence of validity.

There is no question that many training achievement tests indicate different levels of achievement for different groups. An obvious solution is to devote extra attention in training to those who have difficulty in mastering the training material, so that most members of the affected groups master the course. Another course of action is to implement a valid trainee selection program, so that those who cannot master training are likely to be screened out before training. This solution, it should be noted, merely shifts the burden of validation to the employment organization instead of the training organization.

However, satisfying legal requirements does not relieve the training organization of the responsibility for valid measurement of achievement. Valid measurement is necessary for all uses of training achievement tests. Possibly the best course of action for a training organization to achieve valid measurement of training achievement is to concentrate on test development and ensure content validity. When it is feasible to conduct appropriate criterion-related studies, one should probably do so.

Certainly, however, it is necessary to mount an integrated effort to achieve effective training measurement. Content appropriateness, quality of the measuring instruments, and appropriateness of the tests relative to the various inferences which may be made from test results must all be considered.

Summary

It has been emphasized that training and the steps preceding it are intertwined with testing. Good training is a necessary but not sufficient condition for having a good test. However careful the test construction, testing will probably not serve its intended purposes unless the training upon which the testing was based is appropriate. This applies in all of the five roles of testing in training.

Selection research has progressed in the past two decades. It was once believed that validity associated with aptitude tests was specific to the situation. Summaries of the research now indicate that there is much more generality to validity than previously believed. On the basis of the literature, it is possible to choose tests for selecting clerical trainees; however, relative to blue collar workers and managers, the literature is less conclusive. It has been found that employee selection tests, in general, do not technically discriminate on the basis of race. Results with respect to sex are less conclusive. There were more problems than heretofore believed in doing validation studies on small samples, and cost benefits of testing can be more easily estimated than previously thought.

Also it has been found that among traditional selection procedures, tests are among the most validly used for predicting training achievement, and education, interviews, and experience are relatively poor predictors. In measuring training achievement, criterion-referenced testing is nearing maturity. Many techniques for developing tests and analyzing test data are available in such form that a practitioner can use them. Various aspects of criterion-reference testing are still a subject of debate.

The field of testing should not be considered to be without further need for research and reasoned contemplation. Despite the notable developments in the last two decades in selection research and achievement testing, there are still many questions, and the reader is advised to keep current on further developments.

References

1. Cronbach, Lee J., "Test Validation," in Robert L. Thorndike, ed., *Educational Measurement*, 2d ed., American Council on Education, Washington, DC, 1971, pp. 443–507.

2. American Psychological Association, American Educational Research Association, and National Council on Measurement in Education, "Technical Recommendations for Psychological Tests and Diagnostic Techniques," *Psychological Bulletin*, vol. 51, 1954 (supplement).

3. American Psychological Association Division of Industrial/Organizational Psychology, *Principles for the Validation and Use of Personnel Selection Procedures*, Berkeley, CA, 1980.

4. Barrett, Gerald, James S. Phillips, and Ralph A. Alexander, "Concurrent and Predictive Validity Designs: A Critical Reanalysis," *Journal of Applied Psychology*, vol. 66, 1981, pp. 1–6.

5. Guion, Robert M., and Charles J. Cranny, "A Note on Concurrent and Predictive Validity Designs: A Critical Reanalysis," *Journal of Applied Psychology*, vol. 67, 1982, pp. 239–244.

6. Schmitt, Neal, Richard Z. Gooding, Raymond A. Noe, and Michael Kirsch, "Meta Analyses of Validity Studies Published between 1964 and 1982 and the Investigation of Study Characteristics," *Personnel Psychology*, vol. 37, 1984, pp. 407–422.

7. Bemis, Stephen, Annholt Belenky, and Dee Ann Soder, *Job Analysis: An Effective Management Tool*, Bureau of National Affairs, Washington, DC, 1983.

8. Gael, Sidney, *Job Analysis: A Guide to Assessing Work Activities*, Jossey-Bass, San Francisco, 1983.

9. Levine, Edward L., *Everything You Always Wanted to Know about Job Analyses*, Mariner Publishing Co., Tampa, FL, 1983.

10. McCormick, Ernest J., *Job Analysis: Methods and Applications*, AMACOM, New York, 1979.

11. American Educational Research Association, American Psychological Association, and National Council on Measurement in Education, *Standards for Educational and Psychological Testing*, American Psychological Association, Washington, DC, 1985.

12. Mager, Robert F., *Preparing Instructional Objectives*, Palo Alto, CA, Fearon Publishers, 1962.

13. Cronbach, Lee J., and Paul E. Meehl, "Construct Validity in Psychological Tests," *Psychological Bulletin*, vol. 52, 1955, pp. 281–302.

14. Ghiselli, Edwin E., John P. Campbell, and Sheldon Zedeck, *Measurement Theory for the Behavioral Sciences*, W. H. Freeman, San Francisco, 1981.

15. Tenopyr, Mary L., "Content-Construct Confusion," *Personnel Psychology*, vol. 30, 1977, pp. 47–54.

16. Messick, Samuel A., "The Standard Problem: Meaning and Values in Measurement and Evaluation," *American Psychologist*, vol. 30, pp. 955–966, 1975.

17. Guilford, Joy P., and Benjamin Fruchter, *Fundamental Statistics in Psychology and Education*, 6th ed., McGraw-Hill, New York, 1978.

18. Cronbach, Lee J., Golda C. Gleser, Harinda Nanda, and Nageswari Rajaratan, *The Dependability of Behavioral Measurements: Theory of Generalizability for Scores and Profiles*, Wiley, New York, 1972.

19. Glaser, Robert, and David J. Klaus, "Proficiency Measurement: Assessing Human Performance," in Robert M. Gagne, ed., *Psychological Principles in Systems Development*, Holt, Rinehart and Winston, New York, 1962, pp. 419–474.

20. Berk, Ronald A., "A Consumer's Guide to Criterion-Referenced Test Reliability," *Journal of Educational Measurement*, vol. 17, 1980, pp. 323–349. Erratum, vol. 18, 1981, p. 131.

21. Berk, Ronald A., "Selecting the Index of Reliability," in Ronald A. Berk, ed., *A Guide to Criterion-Referenced Test Construction*, Johns Hopkins University Press, Baltimore, 1984, pp. 231–266.

22. Subkoviak, Michael J., "Estimating the Reliability of Mastery-Nonmastery Classifications," in Ronald A. Berk, ed., *A Guide to Criterion-Referenced Test Construction*, Johns Hopkins University Press, Baltimore, 1984, pp. 267–291.

23. Equal Employment Opportunity Commission, Civil Service Commission, Department of Labor, Department of Justice, "Adoption by Four Agencies of Uniform Guidelines on Employee Selection Procedures," *Federal Register*, vol. 43, pp. 38290–38315, 1978.

24. Schmidt, Frank L., John E. Hunter, and Vern W. Urry, "Statistical Power in Criterion-Related Validation Studies," *Journal of Applied Psychology*, vol. 61, 1976, pp. 473–485.

25. Schmidt, Frank L., and John E. Hunter, "Development of a General Solution to the Problem of Validity Generalization," *Journal of Applied Psychology*, vol. 62, 1977, pp. 529–540.

26. Callender, John C., and H. G. Osborn, "Development and Test of a New Model for Validity Generalization," *Journal of Applied Psychology*, vol. 65, 1980, pp. 543–558.

27. Raju, Nambury S., and Michael J. Burke, "Two New Procedures for Studying Validity Generalization," *Journal of Applied Psychology*, vol. 68, 1983, pp. 382–395.

28. Hunter, John E., and Ronda F. Hunter, "Validity and Utility of Alternative Predictors of Job Performance," *Journal of Applied Psychology*, vol. 96, 1984, pp. 72–98.

29. Linn, Robert L., "Single Group Validity, Differential Validity, and Differential Prediction," *Journal of Applied Psychology*, vol. 63, 1978, pp. 507–512.

30. Schmidt, Frank L., and John E. Hunter, "Employment Testing Old Theories and New Research Findings," *American Psychologist*, vol. 36, 1981, pp. 1128–1137.

31. Schmidt, Frank L., and John E. Hunter, "Individual Differences in Productivity, An Empirical Test of Estimates Derived from Studies of Selection Procedures Utility," *Journal of Applied Psychology*, vol. 68, 1983, pp. 407–414.

32. Boudreau, John W., "Effects of Employee Flows on Utility Analysis of Human Resource Productivity Improvement Programs," *Journal of Applied Psychology*, vol. 68, 1983, pp. 396–406.

33. Green, John A., *Teacher-Made Tests*, Harper & Row, New York, 1963.

34. Gorth, William P., Robert P. O'Reilly, and Paul D. Pinsky, *Comprehensive Achievement Monitoring, A Criterion-Referenced Evaluation System*, Educational Technology Publications, Englewood Cliffs, NJ, 1975.

35. Gronlund, Norman E., *Constructing Achievement Tests*, 2d ed., Prentice-Hall, Englewood Cliffs, NJ, 1977.

36. Hopkins, Charles D., and Richard L. Antes, *Classroom Measurement and Evaluation*, F. E. Peacock, Itasca, IL, 1978.

37. Martuza, V. R., *Applying Norm-Referenced and Criterion-Referenced Measurement in Education*, Allyn & Bacon, Boston, 1977.

38. Popham, W. James, ed., *Criterion-Referenced Measurement, An Introduction*, Educational Technology Publications, Englewood Cliffs, NJ, 1971.

39. Rahmlow, Harold F., and Katheryn K. Woodley, *Objectives-Based Testing, A Guide to Effective Test Development*, Educational Technology Publications, Englewood Cliffs, NJ, 1974.

40. Smith, Fred M., *Constructing and Using Achievement Tests in the Classroom. A Competency Based Text*, Peter Lang, New York, 1984.

41. Swezey, Robert W., *Individual Performance Assessment: An Approach to Criterion-Referenced Test Development*, Reston Publishing, Reston, VA, 1981.

42. Thyne, James M., *Principles of Examining*, Wiley, New York, 1974.

43. Tuchman, Bruce W., *Measuring Educational Outcomes. Fundamentals of Testing*, Harcourt Brace Jovanovich, New York, 1975.

44. Berk, Ronald A., *Criterion-Referenced Measurement: The State of the Art*, Johns Hopkins University Press, Baltimore, 1980.

45. Berk, Ronald A., ed., *A Guide to Criterion-Referenced Test Construction*, Johns Hopkins University Press, Baltimore, 1984.

46. Popham, W. J., *Criterion-Referenced Measurement*, Prentice-Hall, Englewood Cliffs, NJ, 1978.

47. Hambleton, R. K., H. Swaminathan, S. Algina, and D. B. Coulson, "Criterion-Referenced Testing and Measurement: A Review of Technical Issues and Developments, *Review of Educational Research*, vol. 48, 1978, pp. 1–47.

48. Livingston, Samuel A., and Michael Zieky, *Passing Scores: A Manual for Setting Standards of Performance on Educational and Occupational Tests*, Educational Testing Service, Princeton, NJ, 1982.

49. Linn, Robert L., "Issues of Validity in Measurement for Competency-Based Measurement," in Mary A. Bunda and R. Sanders, eds., *Practices and Problems in Competency-Based Measurement*, National Council on Measurements in Education, Washington, DC, 1979, pp. 108–123.

16
Evaluation

Donald L. Kirkpatrick

Donald L. Kirkpatrick is Professor of Management at the University of Wisconsin Management Institute in Milwaukee. His business experience includes positions as personnel manager of Bendix Products Aerospace Division and training supervisor with International Minerals and Chemical Corp. He served on the National Board of Directors of the American Society for Personnel Administration and was national president of ASTD. He has written six management books including Supervisory Training and Development, How to Improve Performance through Appraisal and Coaching, No-Nonsense Communication, and How to Manage Change Effectively. He has frequently appeared as a seminar leader for numerous organizations in the United States, and on programs in Mexico, Hong Kong, Taiwan, Australia, Thailand, and India. He has regularly appeared as a speaker on the national conferences of ASTD and on programs sponsored by the American Society for Personnel Administration and other professional societies. He has developed supervisory and management inventories on communication, human relations, safety, time management, managing change, and modern management. He received B.B.A., M.B.A., and Ph.D. degrees from the University of Wisconsin, Madison. His dissertation was entitled "How to Evaluate a Human Relations Training Program." Kirkpatrick is an elder in his church and a member of Gideon's International.

Effective training directors will make an effort to evaluate all their training activities. The success of these efforts depends to a large extent on a clear understanding of just what "evaluation" means. This chapter will attempt to accomplish two objectives: (1) to clarify the meaning of evaluation and (2) to suggest techniques for conducting the evaluation.

These objectives will be related to "in-house" classroom programs, one of the most common forms of training. Many of the principles and procedures can be applied to all kinds of training activities such as performance review, participation in outside programs, programmed instruction, and the reading of selected books.

The following quotation from Daniel M. Goodacre III is most appropriate as an introduction:

> Managers, needless to say, expect their manufacturing and sales departments to yield a good return and will go to great lengths to find out whether they have done so. When it comes to training, however, they may expect the return—but rarely do they make a like effort to measure the actual results. Fortunately, for those in charge of training programs, this philanthropic attitude has come to be taken for granted. There is certainly no guarantee, however, that it will continue, and training directors might be well-advised to take the initiative and evaluate their programs before the day of reckoning arrives.[1]

Evaluation Clarified

Nearly everyone would agree that a definition of evaluation would be "the determination of the effectiveness of a training program." But this has little meaning until we answer the question: In terms of what? We know that evaluation is needed in order to improve future programs and to eliminate those programs which are ineffective. The problem is how to begin.

Evaluation changes from a complicated, elusive generality into clear and achievable goals if we break it down into logical steps. these steps can be defined as follows:

Step 1: *Reaction*. How well did the conferees like the program?

Step 2: *Learning*. What principles, facts, and techniques were learned? What attitudes were changed?

Step 3: *Behavior*. What changes in job behavior resulted from the program?

Step 4: *Results*. What were the tangible results of the program in terms of reduced cost, improved quality, improved quantity, etc.?

With this clarification of the meaning of evaluation, training directors can now begin to pinpoint their efforts at evaluation. They better realize what they are doing, and they recognize the limited interpretations and conclusions that can be drawn from their findings. As they become more experienced and sophisticated in evaluation design and procedures, they slowly begin to obtain more meaningful results on which future training can be based.

These four steps will now be defined in detail with examples and suggested guidelines. it is important to stress that the described *procedures* and *techniques* can be used in almost any organization. It is also important to stress that the *results* from one organization cannot be used in another organization. Obviously, there are many factors that would influence the results. These variables include the group, the conference leader, and the approach to the subject.

Step 1: Reaction

Reaction may best be defined as how well the trainees liked a particular training program. Evaluating in terms of reaction is the same as measuring the feelings of the conferees. In fact, it is measuring "customer satisfaction." It is important to emphasize that it does not include a measurement of any learning that takes place

Guidelines for Evaluating Reaction

1. Determine what you want to find out.
2. Use a written comment sheet covering those items determined in step 1.
3. Design the form so that the reactions can be tabulated and quantified.
4. Obtain honest reactions by making the forms anonymous.
5. Encourage the conferees to write in additional comments not covered by the questions that were designed to be tabulated and quantified.

The comment sheet shown in Fig. 16-1 was used to measure reaction at an ASTD summer institute that was planned and coordinated by the staff of the Management Institute, University of Wisconsin.

ASTD INSTITUTE

Leader _____ Subject _____

Date _____

1. Was the subject pertinent to your needs and interests?

   ☐ No   ☐ To some extent   ☐ Very much so

2. How was the ratio of lecture to discussion:

   ☐ Too much lecture   ☐ O.K.   ☐ Too much discussion

3. Rate the leader on the following:

	Excellent	Very good	Good	Fair	Poor
A. Clarifying objectives					
B. Keeping the session alive and interesting					
C. Using audiovisual aids					
D. Maintaining a friendly and helpful manner					
E. Illustrating and clarifying points					
F. Summarizing					

What is your overall rating of the leader?

☐ Excellent   ☐ Very good   ☐ Good   ☐ Fair   ☐ Poor

4. What would have made the session more effective?

_____

_____

_____

_____

                                   Signature (optional)

Figure 16-1. Reaction form.

Those who planned this ASTD program were interested in reactions to subject, technique (lecture versus discussion), and the performance of the conference leader. Therefore, the form was designed accordingly. The conferees were asked to place a check in the appropriate spaces so that the reactions could be readily tabulated and quantified.

In question 3, concerning the leader, it was felt that a more meaningful rating would be given the leader if the conferees considered items A through F before checking the overall rating. This question was designed to prevent a conference leader's personality from dominating group reactions.

Question 4 encouraged the conferees to suggest any improvements that came to mind. The optional signature was used so that follow-up discussions with conferees could be done. In this ASTD summer institute, about half of the conferees signed their names. With this type of group, the optional signature did not affect the honesty of their answers, in all probability. It is strongly suggested that unsigned sheets be used in most in-house meetings, however.

In most cases, a simpler comment sheet is sufficient. Figure 16-2 shows a form that obtained significant information on reaction and requires minimum time from participants. This form can be used for each leader. Of particular importance is the separation of "subject" from "leader."

To evaluate a total program that includes a number of sessions, a final comment sheet (Fig. 16-3) can provide additional valuable information for improving future programs. So that "standards of performance" can be established for the quality of instruction, the reactions can conveniently be converted to numerical ratings. For example, on the forms shown in Figs. 16-2 and 16-3 the following ratings can be used: excellent = 5, very good = 4, good = 3, fair = 2, and poor = 1. An example of reactions from 27 participants might be:

10 Excellent	$10 \times 5 = 50$
10 Very good	$10 \times 4 = 40$
5 Good	$5 \times 3 = 15$
1 Fair	$1 \times 2 = 2$
1 Poor	$1 \times 1 = 1$
27 Total participants	108 Total points

Dividing 108 (total points) by 27 (total participants), we get a rating of 4. Experience in a particular organization can provide data for the establishment of a standard of performance for all instructors.

I firmly believe in getting a comment sheet on each subject and each leader. In the case where the same leader is conducting a series of meetings with the same group, it may not be necessary to get reactions after each session. In a nine-session program, for example, it may be sufficient to obtain reactions after the third, sixth, and ninth sessions. A final comment sheet should also be used to get an evaluation of the entire program.

It has been emphasized that the form should be designed so that tabulations can be readily made. In my opinion, too many comment sheets are still being used in which the conferees are asked to write in their answers to questions. A form of this kind makes it very difficult to summarize comments and to determine patterns of reaction.

How to Supplement the Evaluation of the Conferees

At the Management Institute of the University of Wisconsin, sessions are always evaluated in terms of the reactions of the conferees. Occasionally the coordinator of

REACTION SHEET

Please give us your frank reactions and comments. They will help us evaluate this program for possible improvement in future programs.

Leader _____ Subject _____ Date _____

1. How do you rate the subject content?

☐ Excellent   COMMENTS:
☐ Very Good
☐ Good
☐ Fair
☐ Poor

2. How do you rate the conference leader?

☐ Excellent   COMMENTS:
☐ Very Good
☐ Good
☐ Fair
☐ Poor

3. What benefits do you feel you got from this session?

☐ New knowledge that is pertinent.
☐ Specific approaches, skills or techniques that I can apply on the job.
☐ Change of attitude that will help me in my job.

OTHER:

4. What would have made this session better? (Use other side if necessary.)

Figure 16-2. Reaction form.

the program felt that the group reaction was not a fair evaluation of the effectiveness of the program. Sometimes the conference leader's personality made such an impression on the group that this person received a very high rating. In other sessions, the conference leader received a low rating because he or she did not have a dynamic personality. Therefore, some members of the Management Institute adopted a procedure by which the conference leader was rated by the coordinator as well as by the group. The form shown in Fig. 16-4 was used.

This procedure in which the coordinator of the program also evaluates each conference leader was also used in an ASTD summer institute. It was found that a coordinator's rating was usually close to the group's rating, but in some instances it varied considerably.

It is suggested that the training director in each company consider this approach. A trained observer such as the training director or another qualified person would

---

FINAL REACTION SHEET

NAME OF PROGRAM _____ DATE _____

1. How would you rate the overall program?

    ☐ Excellent   COMMENTS:
    ☐ Very Good
    ☐ Good
    ☐ Fair
    ☐ Poor

2. To what extent will it help you do a better job for your organization?

    ☐ To a large extent
    ☐ To some extent   COMMENTS:
    ☐ Very little

3. What were the major benefits you received? (Check as many as you wish.)

    ☐ Helped confirm some of my ideas.
    ☐ Presented new ideas and approaches.
    ☐ Acquainted me with problems and solutions from other companies.
    ☐ Gave me a good chance to look objectively at myself and my job.

    Other benefits:

4. How were the meeting facilities, luncheon arrangements, etc?

    ☐ Excellent   COMMENTS:
    ☐ Very Good
    ☐ Good
    ☐ Fair
    ☐ Poor

                  (OVER)

Figure 16-3. Final reaction sheet.

fill out an evaluation form independent of the group's reactions. An analysis of the two would give the best indication of the effectiveness of the program.

Conclusions about Reaction

The first step in the evaluation process is to measure the reactions to training programs. It is important to determine how people feel about the programs they attend. Decisions by top management are frequently based on one or two comments made by people who have attended. A supervisory training program

5. What would have improved this program?

6. Would you like to attend future programs of a similar nature?

    ☐ Yes
    ☐ No
    ☐ Not sure

7. Other comments and suggestions for future programs:

Signature (optional) _____

Figure 16-3. Final reaction sheet (*continued*).

may be canceled because one superintendent told the plant manager that "this program is for the birds."

Also, conferees who enjoy a training program are more likely to obtain maximum benefit from it. According to Spencer, "for maximum learning you must have interest and enthusiasm." In a talk given by Cloyd Steinmetz, of Reynolds Metals and a past president of ASTD, he stressed: "It is not enough to say, 'here is the information, take it?' We must make it interesting and motivate them to want to take it."

To evaluate effectively, training directors should begin by doing a good job of measuring the reactions and feelings of people who participate. It is important to do this in an organized fashion, using written comment sheets which have been

COORDINATOR'S RATING OF LEADER

Name of leader_____Subject_____

Date _____

	Very much so	To some extent	No
A. PREPARATION 1. How well prepared?			
2. Preparation geared to group?			
B. CONDUCTING 1. Held interest of group?			
2. Was enthusiastic?			
3. Used audiovisual aids?			
4. Presented material clearly?			
5. Helped the group apply the material?			
6. Adequately covered subject?			
7. Involved the group?			
8. Summarized during and at end?			

C. CONSTRUCTIVE COMMENTS
What would you suggest to improve future sessions?_____

_____

_____

D. ADDITIONAL COMMENTS

_____

_____

_____

Figure 16-4. Leader rating sheet.

designed to obtain the desired reactions. It is also strongly suggested that the form
be so designed that the comments can be tabulated and quantified. In the
experience of the staff of the Management Institute, it is also desirable to have the
coordinator, training director, or another trained observer make his or her own
appraisal of the session in order to supplement the reactions of enrollees. The
combination of these two evaluations is more meaningful than either one by itself.

An instructor who has effectively measured the *reactions* of conferees and finds
them to be very favorable can feel extremely proud. However, the instructor should
also feel humble because the evaluation measurement has only begun. Even
though he or she has done a good job of measuring the reaction of the group, there

is still no assurance that any learning has taken place. Neither is there any indication that the behavior of the participants will change because of the training program. And still further away is any realistic way of judging any results that can be attributed to the training program.

Step 2: Learning

It is important to recognize that a favorable reaction to a program *does not assure* learning. All of us have attended meetings in which the conference leader or speaker used enthusiasm, showmanship, visual aids, and illustrations to make a presentation well accepted by the group. A careful analysis of the subject content would reveal that the speaker said practically nothing of value—but said it very well. It is also important to recognize that an unfavorable reaction probably assures no learning. It takes effort to learn, and "turned-off" participants won't try.

Learning Defined

For the purpose of evaluation, learning is defined as follows: attitudes that were changed, and knowledge and skills that were learned. It does not include the on-the-job use of the attitudes, knowledge, and skills. This application will be discussed later in this chapter in the section on behavior.

Guidelines for Evaluating in Terms of Learning

Several guidelines should be used in measuring the amount of learning that takes place:

1. The learning of *each conferee* should be measured so that quantitative results can be determined.

2. A before-and-after approach should be used so that any learning can be related to the program.

3. Where practical, a control group (not receiving the training) should be compared with the experimental group which receives the training.

4. Where practical, the evaluation results should be analyzed statistically so that learning can be proved in terms of correlation or level of confidence.

These guidelines indicate that evaluation in terms of learning is much more difficult than evaluation in terms of reaction, as described earlier. A knowledge of statistics, for example, is desirable. In many cases, the training department will have to call on the assistance of a statistician to help plan the evaluation procedures, analyze the data, and interpret the results.

Suggested Methods

Classroom Performance. It is relatively easy to measure the learning that takes place in training programs that are teaching skills. The following programs fall under this category: job instruction training, work simplification, interviewing skills, reading improvement, effective speaking, and effective writing. Classroom activities such as demonstrations, individual performance of the skill being taught, and discussions following a role-playing situation can be used as evaluation techniques. The training director can organize these in such a way that he or she will obtain a fairly objective evaluation of the learning that is taking place.

For example, in a course that is teaching job instruction training (JIT) to supervisors, every supervisor will demonstrate in front of the class the skills of JIT. From their performance, the training director can tell whether the supervisors have learned the principles of JIT and can use them, at least in a classroom situation. In a work simplification program, the conferees can be required to fill out a "flow process chart," and the training director can determine whether they know how to do it. In a reading improvement program, the reading speed and comprehension of the participants can be readily determined by their classroom performance. In an effective speaking program, each conferee is normally required to give a number of talks, and an alert training director can evaluate the amount of learning that is taking place by observing the individual's successive performances.

Thus in situations like these, an evaluation of the learning can be built into the program. If it is organized and implemented properly, the training director can obtain a fairly objective measure of the amount of learning that has taken place. He or she can set up before-and-after situations in which the conferees demonstrate whether they know the principles and techniques being taught. In every program, therefore, where skills of some kind are being taught, the training director should plan systematic classroom evaluation to measure the learning.

Paper-and-Pencil Tests. Where principles and facts are taught rather than skills, paper-and-pencil tests can be used. In some cases, standardized tests can be purchased to measure learning. In other cases, training directors must construct their own.

To measure the learning in human relations programs, for example, the *Supervisory Inventory on Human Relations* might be used. Sample test items are listed in Fig. 16-5 (answered by circling A for "agree" or DA for "disagree").

SUPERVISORY INVENTORY ON HUMAN RELATIONS

1. Anyone is able to do almost any job if he or she tries hard enough.   A   DA
2. Intelligence consists of what we've learned since we were born.   A   DA
3. If a supervisor knows all about the work to be done, he or she is therefore qualified to teach others how to do it.   A   DA
4. A well-trained working force is a result of maintaining a large training department.   A   DA
5. In making a decision, a good supervisor is concerned with his employees' feeling about the decision.   A   DA
6. The supervisor is closer to his or her employees than to management.   A   DA
7. The best way to train a new employee is to have him or her watch a good employee at the job.
8. Before deciding on the solution to a problem, a list of possible solutions should be made and compared.   A   DA
9. A supervisor should be willing to listen to almost anything the employees want to say.   A   DA

Copyright © 1983 by D. L. Kirkpatrick. Published by Dr. D. L. Kirkpatrick, 1920 Hawthorne Drive, Elm Grove, WI 53122.

Figure 16-5. Test to measure learning.

Standardized tests are also available in such areas as communications, time management, managing change, modern management, and safety. In following the guidelines that were suggested in the beginning of this chapter, this kind of standardized test should be used in the following manner.

1. The test should be given to all conferees prior to the program.

2. If practical, it should also be given to a control group which is comparable with the experimental group.

3. These pretests should be analyzed in terms of two approaches. In the first place, the total score of each person should be tabulated. Second, the responses to each item of the inventory should be tabulated in terms of right and wrong answers. This second tabulation not only enables a training director to evaluate the program but also provides some tips on the knowledge and understanding of the group prior to the program. This means that in the classroom, the training director can stress those items most frequently misunderstood.

4. After the program is over, the same test or its equivalent should be given to the conferees and also to the control group. A comparison of pretest and posttest scores and responses to individual items can then be made. A statistical analysis of these data will reveal the effectiveness of the program in terms of learning.

One important word of caution is necessary: Unless the test or inventory accurately covers the material presented, it will not be a valid measure of the effectiveness of the learning. Frequently a standardized test will cover only part of the material presented in the course. Therefore, only that part of the course covered in the inventory is being evaluated. Likewise, if certain items on the inventory are not being covered, no change in these items can be expected.

Many training directors and others responsible for programs have developed their own paper-and-pencil tests to measure learning in their programs. For example, the American Telephone and Telegraph Company incorporated into its Personal Factors in Management program a short test measuring trainee sensitivity and empathy. First, each individual was asked to rank, in order of importance, 10 items dealing with human relations. The participants were then assigned to groups which worked 15 minutes at the task of arriving at a group ranking of the 10 statements. Following this 15-minute "heated discussion," each individual was asked to complete a short inventory, which included the following questions:

1. *a.* Were you satisfied with the performance of the group? Yes ____No ____
   b. How many will say that they were satisfied with the performance of the group?
2. *a.* Do you feel that the discussion was dominated by two or three members? Yes ____No ____
   b. How many will say that they thought the discussion was dominated by two or three members?
3. *a.* Did you have any feelings about the items being ranked that, for some reason, you felt it wise not to express during the discussion? Yes ____No ____
   b. How many will say that they had such feelings?
4. *a.* Did you talk as often as you wished to in the discussion? Yes ____No ____
   b. How many will say that they spoke as often as they wished?

The successive class sessions then attempted to teach each conferee to be more sensitive to the feelings and ideas of other people. Later in the course, another "empathy" test was given to see whether there was an increase in sensitivity.

In Morris A. Savitt's article entitled "Is Management Training Worthwhile?"[2] he described a program that he evaluated. He devised a questionnaire which was given at the beginning of the program "to determine how much knowledge of management principles and practices the conferees had at the beginning." At the end of the 10-week program, the same questionnaire was administered to test the progress made during the course. This is an example of a questionnaire tailored to a specific program.

Paper-and-pencil tests can be used effectively in measuring the learning that takes place in a training program. It should be emphasized again that the approach to this kind of evaluation should be systematic and statistically oriented. A comparison of before-and-after scores and responses can then be made to prove how much learning has taken place.

Conclusions about Learning

It is easy to see that it is much more difficult to measure *learning* than it is to measure *reaction* to a program. A great deal of work is required in planning the evaluation procedure, in analyzing the data that are obtained, and in interpreting the results. Wherever practical, it is suggested that training directors devise their own methods and techniques. As has been pointed out in this section, it is relatively easy to plan classroom demonstrations and presentations to measure learning where the program is aimed at the teaching of skills. Where attitudes, knowledge, and skills are the objectives of the training program, it is advisable to use a paper-and-pencil test. Where suitable standardized tests can be found, it is easier to use them. In many programs, however, it is not possible to find a standardized test, and training directors must use their skill and ingenuity in devising their own measuring instruments.

If training directors can prove that their programs have been effective in terms of learning as well as in terms of reaction, they have objective data to use in selling future programs and in increasing their status and position in the company.

Step 3: Behavior

A personal experience may be the best way of introducing this section. When I joined the Management Institute of the University of Wisconsin, one of my first assignments was to sit through a one-week course called "Human Relations for Foremen and Supervisors." During the week I was particularly impressed by a foreman named Herman from a Milwaukee company. Whenever a conference leader asked a question requiring a good understanding of human relations principles and techniques, Herman was the first one who raised his hand. He had all the answers in terms of good human relations approaches. I was very much impressed, and I said to myself, "If I were in industry, I would like to work for a man like Herman."

It so happened that I had a first cousin who was working for that company. And oddly enough Herman was his boss. At my first opportunity, I talked with my cousin Jim and asked him about Herman. Jim told me that Herman might know all the principles and techniques of human relations, but he certainly did not practice them on the job. He performed like the typical "bull of the woods" and had little consideration for the feelings and ideas of his subordinates. At this time I began to realize there may be a big difference between knowing principles and techniques and using them on the job.

Five requirements must be met for change in behavior to occur:

1. Desire to change

2. Know-how of what to do and how to do it

3. The right job climate

4. Help in applying the classroom learning

5. Rewards for changing behavior

The third requirement refers primarily to the boss of the person being trained. If he or she established a preventive or discouraging climate, no change in behavior is likely to occur even if the trainee is anxious to change and has acquired the necessary knowledge and skill. If the climate is neutral or encouraging, the change in behavior is apt to take place.

Several guidelines are to be followed in evaluating training programs in terms of behavioral changes:

1. A *systematic* appraisal should be made of on-the-job performance on a *before-and-after* basis.
2. The appraisal of performance should be made by one or more of the following groups (the more the better):
   a. The person receiving the training
   b. The person's superior or superiors
   c. The person's subordinates
   d. The person's peers or other people thoroughly familiar with his or her performance.
3. A statistical analysis should be made to compare performance before and after and to relate changes to the training program.
4. The posttraining appraisal should be made 3 months or more after the training so that the trainees have an opportunity to put into practice what they have learned. Subsequent appraisals may add to the validity of the study.
5. A control group (not receiving the training) should be used.

A "Supervisory Skills" Institute[3]

At the Management Institute, University of Wisconsin, a 3-day institute called "Supervisory Skills" was evaluated. The institute covered six topics: order giving, training employees, appraising employee performance, preventing and handling grievances, decision making, and initiating change. A questionnaire was completed by each supervisor who attended the institute to obtain information on the participant, the company, and the participant's relationship with his or her immediate boss. Specific information was obtained on:

1. The participant: job, experience, education, age, reasons for attending the program, and what he or she hopes to learn

2. The company: size, type, and climate for change

3. The participant's boss: years spent as boss, the climate he or she sets for change, and involvement in sending the person to the institute

Interviews were conducted with each participant within 2 to 3 months following the institute. The interviews were conducted in the participant's company to obtain information regarding changes in behavior that had taken place on the job. In addition, interviews were conducted with the participant's immediate supervisor as another measure of changes in the participant's behavior.

Examples of specific questions are shown in Fig. 16-6. In addition to measuring changes in behavior, an attempt was made to determine what results were achieved. Questions asked of both the participant and his or her boss are shown in

Training employees	Yes		No		Not sure	
a. *Since* the supervisor attended the program, are his or her new or transferred employees better trained?						

Training method	Participant always	Participant usually	Participant sometimes	Participant never
b. *Before* the program, who trained the workers?				
c. *Since* the program, who trained the workers?				

Progress in training effectivess	Does not apply	Much more	Some-what more	No change	Some-what less	Much less	Don't know
d. *Since* the program, if someone else trains the employees, has the supervisor become more observant and taken a more active interest in the training process?							
e. *Since* the program, if the supervisor trains the employees, is he or she making more of an effort in seeing that the employees are well trained?							
f. *Since* the program, is the supervisor more inclined to be patient while training?							
g. *Since* the program, while teaching an operation, is the supervisor asking for more questions to ensure understanding?							
h. *Since* the program, is the supervisor better prepared to teach?							
i *Since* the program, is the supervisor doing more follow-up to check the trainees' progress?							

Figure 16-6. Examples of supervisor interview questions in Kirkpatrick study.

Fig. 16-7. Although the design of the evaluation was relatively simple, it provided data to indicate that significant changes in both behavior and results were achieved.

Conclusions about Behavior

The future of training directors and their programs depends to a large extent on their effectiveness. To determine effectiveness, attempts should be made to measure in objective terms. Measuring changes in behavior resulting from training programs involves a very complicated procedure. But it is worthwhile if training programs are going to increase in effectiveness and their benefits are to be made clear to top management.

It is obvious that very few training directors have the background, skill, and time to engage in extensive evaluations. It is therefore frequently necessary to call on industrial psychologists, research people, and consultants for advice and help.

Step 4: Results

The objectives of most training programs can be stated in terms of results such as reduced turnover, reduced costs, improved efficiency, reduction in grievances, increase in quality and quantity of production, or improved morale. From an evaluation standpoint, it would be best to evaluate training programs directly in terms of results desired. There are, however, so many complicating factors that it is extremely difficult, if not impossible, to evaluate certain kinds of programs in terms of results. Therefore, it is recommended that training directors evaluate in terms of reaction, learning, and behavior first and then consider results.

Certain kinds of training programs, though, are relatively easy to evaluate in terms of results. For example, in teaching clerical personnel to do a more effective typing job, you can measure the number of words per minute on a before-and-after basis. If you are trying to reduce grievances in your plant, you can measure the number of grievances before and after the training program. If you are attempting to reduce accidents, a before-and-after measure can be made. But a word of caution: A difficulty in the evaluation of training is evident at the outset, technically called "the separation of variables"; that is, how much of the improvement is due to training as compared to other factors? This is the problem that makes it very difficult to measure results that can be attributed directly to a specific training program.

"Cost-Reduction" Institute

A number of years ago, two graduate students at the University of Wisconsin attempted to measure the results of a cost-reduction institute conducted by the Management Institute. Two techniques were used. The first was to conduct depth interviews with some of the supervisors who had attended the course and with their immediate superiors. The other technique was to mail questionnaires to the remaining enrollees and their supervisors. Following is a brief summary of that study:

Depth Interviews

Interview with Trainees

1. Have you been able to reduce costs in the few weeks that you have been back on the job?

1. To what extent has the program improved the supervisor's working relationship with his boss?

         ☐   To a large extent
         ☐   To some extent
         ☐   No change
         ☐   Made it worse

2. Since the program, how much two-way communication has taken place between the participant and his subordinates?

         ☐   Much more
         ☐   Somewhat more
         ☐   No change
         ☐   Somewhat less
         ☐   Much less
         ☐   Don't know

3. Since the program, is the participant taking a more active interest in employees?

         ☐   Much more
         ☐   Somewhat more
         ☐   No change
         ☐   Somewhat less
         ☐   Much less
         ☐   Don't know

Figure 16-7. Interview questions for supervisor and boss in Kirkpatrick study.

Replies: 13 — Yes
            3 — No
            2 — Noncommittal or evasive
            1 — Failed to answer

2. How? What were the estimated savings? Different types of replies indicated that the 13 people who said they had made cost reductions had done so in different areas. But their ideas stemmed directly from the program, according to these trainees.

Interview with Superiors.   Eight of the cost-reduction actions described by the trainees were confirmed by the immediate superior, and these superiors estimate total savings to be from $15,000 to $21,000 per year. The specific ideas that were used were described by superiors as well as by the trainees.

4. On an overall basis, to what extent has the supervisor's job behavior changed *since* the program?

Supervisory Areas	Much Better	Somewhat Better	No Change	Somewhat Worse	Much Worse	Don't Know
a. Order Giving						
b. Training						
c. Decision Making						
d. Initiating Change						
e. Appraising Employee Performance						
f. Preventing and Handling Grievances						
g. Attitude toward Job						
h. Attitude toward Subordinates						
i. Attitude toward Management						

5. In regard to the following results, what changes have been noticed *since* the participant's attendance in the program?

Performance Bench Marks	Much Better	Somewhat Better	No Change	Somewhat Worse	Much Worse	Don't Know
a. Quantity of Production						
b. Quality of Production						
c. Safety						
d. Housekeeping						
e. Employee Attitudes and Morale						
f. Employee Attendance						
g. Employee Promptness						
h. Employee Turnover						

Figure 16-7. Interview questions for supervisor and boss in Kirkpatrick study (*continued*).

Mailed Questionnaires. Questionnaires were mailed to those trainees who were not contacted personally. The results on the questionnaire were not nearly as specific and useful as the ones obtained by personal interview. The study concluded that it is probably better to use the personal interview rather than a questionnaire to measure results from this type of program.

Conclusions about Results

The evaluation of training programs in terms of "results" is progressing at a very slow rate. Where the objectives of training programs are as specific as the reduction of accidents, the reduction of grievances, and the reduction of costs, we find that a number of attempts have been made. In a few of them, the researchers have attempted to segregate factors other than training which might have had an effect. In most cases, the measure on a before-and-after basis has been directly attributed to the training even though other factors might have been influential. An article called "Evaluating Training Programs: Evidence vs. Proof"[4] describes a philosophy and approach that are appropriate for most programs.

Summary

One purpose of this chapter is to stimulate training people to take a penetrating look at evaluation. Their own future and the future of their programs depends to a large extent on their ability to evaluate and use evaluation results.

Another objective has been to clarify the meaning of evaluation. By breaking it down into reaction, learning, behavior, and results, the training professional can begin to do something about it and can gradually progress from a simple subjective reaction sheet to a research design that measures tangible results.

Articles on evaluation will continue to appear in the *Training and Development Journal* and other magazines. Some of these articles are well worth studying because they describe effective principles, procedures, and methods of evaluation.

This chapter has not provided the answers to the training director's problem of evaluation. It has attempted to provide an understanding of principles and methods. Better understanding will come from continued study of new principles and methods that are described in articles written in professional journals. Needless to say, skill in using proper evaluation methods can come only with practice.

References

1. Goodacre, Daniel M., III, "The Experimental Evaluation of Management Training: Principles and Practices," *Personnel*, May 1957.

2. Savitt, Morris, "Is Management Training Worthwhile?" *Personnel*, September–October 1957.

3. Kirkpatrick, Donald L., "Evaluating a Training Program for Supervisors and Foremen," *The Personnel Administrator*, September–October 1969.

4. Kirkpatrick, Donald L., "Evaluating Training Programs: Evidence vs. Proof," *Training and Development Journal*, November 1977.

Special References

The following helpful booklets are available. They contain evaluation articles from the *Training and Development Journal* and *Training* magazine.

Kirkpatrick, Donald L., ed., "Evaluating Training Programs," ASTD, 1630 Duke Street, Alexandria, VA 22313, 1975.

Zemke, Ron, Linda Standke, and Philip Jones, eds., "Designing and Delivering Cost-Effective Training and Measuring the Results," *Training*, 731 Hennepin Avenue, Minneapolis, MN 55403, 1981, Section 7.

Bibliography

Kirkpatrick, Donald, *Supervisory Training and Development*, 2d ed., Addison-Wesley Publishing Co., Reading, MA, 1983, Chapter 9.

Laird, Dugan, *Approaches to Training and Development*, Addison-Wesley Publishing Co., Reading, MA, 1978, Chapters 15–16.

Odiorne, George, *Training by Objectives*, The Macmillan Company, New York, 1970, Chapter 10.

Suessmuth, Patrick, *Ideas for Training Managers and Supervisors*, University Associates, La Jolla, CA, 1978, Chapters 30–33.

Tracey, William R., ed., *Human Resources Management and Development Handbook*, AMACOM, New York, 1985, Chapters 106–108.

17

Measuring Results

Martin E. Smith

Martin E. Smith *manages New England Telephone's "Management Development System," which enables managers and executives to analyze and address their educational and developmental needs. He has worked for NET since 1973 where he has managed the design, delivery, and evaluation of generic management, instructional technology, and technical curricula. He established an evaluation group that evaluated literally hundreds of courses over a 10-year period and experimented with a wide variety of evaluation techniques. He and his staff coauthored (with colleagues from Illinois Bell) the most widely used training evaluation manual in the Bell System. He wrote another manual on evaluating training staffs and has published over 30 journal articles on evaluation. Prior to NET, Smith worked 7 years at the Bell Telephone Laboratories where he did research on instructional media and evaluation methods. He conducted several large studies that helped establish instructional technology and programmed instruction in the Bell System. In 1967, he received his Ph.D. in Industrial Psychology from Purdue University. He is a member of the American Psychological Association, American Educational Research Association, and National Society for Performance and Instruction.*

The intent of this chapter is to provide the reader with suggestions for evaluating the impact of training upon job performance. The immediate objective is to quantify, often in monetary terms, the benefits of a particular program. While the focus is on a specific program, the underlying objective may be to demonstrate the contribution of the training department to the corporation.

As Scherman[1] noted, "Managers faced with constricted budgets, higher costs and fewer people to do the job, are demanding a higher return on their training investment." Line management is not hesitant to blame poor performance on ineffective training. As training budgets grow, top management is scrutinizing the training department's budget and staff size as closely as it reviews line organizations. Top management is demanding more evidence of training's contribution to the "bottom line."

Training managers recognize that attendance data (e.g., "we achieved a 25 percent increase in student days . . .") and trainee reactions (e.g., "students rate the XYZ program a 4.5 out of a possible 5.0 on the dimension of . . .) mean little to executives. Trainers would do well to relate their programs to the "numbers" by which line managers measure their own success: productivity indexes, quality measures, sales figures, customer complaints, etc.

At one level, this challenge is a technical or methodological problem: How do you design an evaluation to produce the necessary data? This chapter will deal with that question. The more subtle issue embedded in the methodological question is how to get executives to believe the data and to influence their support and use of training resources. This question is a strategic and a political issue. After 20 years as a researcher and practitioner, I still struggle with the issue, and the latter part of this chapter will present my current opinions.

Operational Measures of Job Performance

There are countless ways of measuring job and organizational performance. At the risk of oversimplification, we will use three broad categories: productivity, quality, and work force measures. These categories will be defined, and examples will be cited. Criteria for selecting appropriate measures will be discussed. The extrapolation of evaluation findings to monetary consequences will be illustrated. Finally, several "do's and don'ts" will be offered to increase the likelihood of success.

Examples

Table 17-1 summarizes 28 reports of operational measures used to evaluate training and other performance improvement programs. Specific measures are listed under the headings of "Productivity," "Quality," and "Work Force." The programs are described under the heading of "Intervention." The jobs to which the measures and interventions apply are also identified. The purpose of Table 17-1 is to show the range of measures that can be used to evaluate the impact of training.

This chapter is divided into four sections. The first describes ways of measuring job performance. The second outlines several research designs for collecting performance data. The third discusses the evaluation of the training department as distinguished from the evaluation of specific programs. Finally, suggestions are offered for gaining client support. It is not an exhaustive summary of published examples.

Productivity. This term includes the quantity of output per unit of time. Productivity may be calculated per individual worker, per work group, or for a larger organizational entity, such as a work shift or a plant. This heading also includes efficiency measures where actual productivity is compared with an objective or an expected level of output, e.g., percent of productivity quota. Productivity measures are generally associated with manufacturing, but Table 17-1 lists examples for clerical jobs, service jobs, sales work, and even professional jobs.

Quality. These measures represent discrepancies between the actual product or service and the expected product or service. Discrepancies may be identified

Table 17-1. Examples of Operational Measures

Reference	Job	Type Of Intervention	Productivity Measure	Work Quality Measure	Work Force Measure
Baum [2]	Automotive production and maintenance jobs	Attendance control policy			Casual absences (short duration at employee's discretion)
Chaney & Teel [3]	Machine parts inspectors	Training and job aids		% of true defects found	
Cullen, Sawzin, Sisson & Swanson [4]	Plastics extruders	Formal training vs. on-the-job training	Training hours to reach minimum job standards	Production wastes (pounds of raw material)	
Dolton & Todor [5]	Non-technical, service jobs in public utility	Flextime program			Grievance rate
Gommersall & Myers [6]	Assemblers, welders and inspectors (electronics)	Orientation	Unspecified		Unspecified
Gustafson [7]	Telephone Operators	Initial job training handled per hour	Mean no. of calls		
Gustafson [7]	Telephone frame workers (wire central office equipment so customers can be connected to network)	None	Efficiency defined as actual time to complete daily work load divided into standard time expected for that work load		
Hahne [8]	Sales Representatives who sell tires, oil etc., to stations for a large oil co.	Sales training	% of sales people showing increased sales, summarized by product		
Holoviak [9]	Coal Mining managers	Company support for manager training	Output per man-day in terms of tons of coal, completed by company		

Table 17-1. Examples of Operational Measures (Continued)

Reference	Job	Type Of Intervention	Productivity Measure	Work Quality Measure	Work Force Measure
Horrigan [10]	Programmers analysts, technicians managers & support people	Training and development programs (collection of courses)			Turnover
Jones & Moxham [11]	Garment makers (machine operators)	Job training based on task analysis	Average output per person in terms of "minute value" of work done in one hour		% of workers leaving in first year of employment
Kelley, Orgel & Baer [12]	Production line supervisors	Supervisory skills training	Products produced per week		
Kelley, Orgel & Baer [13]	Sales persons, Sales managers	Sales training, Sales Manager Training	Gross sales revenue		
Kim & Campagna [14]	Employees in a county welfare	Flextime Program	Cases approved per hour; routine actions per hour; cases		Individual absence categorized by short vs. long-term (2 hours or more), paid vs. unpaid
Latham & Kline [15]	Pulpwood Logging operators	Training in goalsetting	Measure used but not described		Injuries, turnover, absenteeism
Lawler & Hackma [16]	Janitors	Participate decision-making plan			% scheduled hours actually worked (measure of absenteeism)
Lefkowitz [17]	Sewing Machine Operators	Vestibule Training, on-the-job training	Average daily output for 35 days after training		% operators quitting within 40 days
Luthans & Maris [18]	Bank Employees	Attendance program using social rewards and feedback from supervisors			% attendance calculated

Table 17-1. Examples of Operational Measures (*Continued*)

Reference	Job	Type Of Intervention	Productivity Measure	Work Quality Measure	Work Force Measure
Macy & Mirvis [19]	Assembly workers	Union Management "quality of work life" program	Output per employee (productivity data available by unit only)	Production under standard, product rejects, machine downtime, variance between actual and budgeted supply use	Total absences for plant completed for 5 time phases of project; voluntary turnover; involuntary turnover; accidents (4 types); grievances
Meyer & Raich [20]	Retail Sales (appliances, radios, tvs)	Behavior modeling training	Per-hour commissions		
Mikesell, Wilson, & Lawther [21]	State tax auditors	Training	Dollar tax payer error found per audit; dollar taxpayer errors found per hour; change in new liabilities less new refunds per auditor		
Mirvis & Lawler [22]	Bank Tellers	None		Number of teller shortages or overpayments to customers	"Unauthorized" absences of less than 3 days; voluntary turnover
Murphy & Beauchemin [23]	Telephone Operators	Listening Training	Average length of customer contact	Courtesy & accuracy as rated by supervisors (each operator is observed in a specified no. of contacts each month)	
Reber & Wallin [24]	Employees in farm machinery manu-facturing firm	Training, goal setting, knowledge of results			On-the-job injuries reported according to OSHA

Table 17-1. Examples of Operational Measures (*Continued*)

Reference	Job	Type Of Intervention	Productivity Measure	Work Quality Measure	Work Force Measure
Robinson [25]	Customer service reps (wholesaler of automotive parts)	Training		Complaints per month escalated to manager level	
Rosentreter [26]	Dept. managers (manufacturing)	Educational program on goal setting with subordinates			Turnover (6 mos. before vs. 6 mos. after); incidents of tardiness; "level 2" grievances
Smith [27]	Telephone supervisors	Training in attendance control		Accuracy and completeness of employee attendance records	Group attendance rates
Smith [28]	Telephone installers	Basic Training	Work units per hour; work delays; service orders per day; number of items sold	Trouble reports per 100 service orders; quality inspections by supervisor	

internally, as by quality control inspectors, or externally by customers or government inspectors. Quality defects may range from aesthetic to structural properties. Quality measures include scrap, customer complaints, machine downtime, accuracy, and courtesy.

Work Force.   This category includes statistics which describe the stability and competence of a group of employees. Measures include turnover, absenteeism, accident rate, grievances, and promotions. These measures are often used to evaluate supervisory training and organizational development (OD) interventions, such as quality circles and participative management.

Selection

The determination of which measures to use begins with an analysis of the jobs and organizations targeted for performance improvement. The intermediate objective is a list of potential measures. This list may include ways in which performance is measured now and ways in which it could or should be measured. Each measure on your list is then compared with the following criteria. These criteria will help you select the most feasible measures for your evaluation.

Does the Measure Reflect Program Objectives?   Is it logical that the measurements will vary as a direct consequence of the intervention? If you train supervisors on how to control attendance, is it probably not reasonable to expect work quality to improve?

Is the Measure Valued by Top Management?   The importance of a measure is usually indicated by its use. Measures may be used, for example, to appraise the job performance of supervisors, to set corporate or departmental objectives, or to justify disciplinary action. If a measure is not widely used, it may be valued if you can explain its relationship to other measures, especially financial indicators. For example, you may select as your evaluation measure the number of hours for a new employee to reach a productivity standard. While the organization may not use that particular statistic, it is reasonable that overall productivity will improve the faster employees reach the standard.

Can the Measure Be Computed for Specific Employees?   Measurements are generally aggregated by work group, location, production line, etc. The benefits of a training program are usually realized on an individual basis. Lumping the trainee's performance data in with the group average virtually precludes any hope of demonstrating the effects of training. Often, however, production or quality data are collected by individual and then summarized for the work group. If the evaluator can gain access to the individual data, the measure becomes practical to use for evaluation.

Is the Measure Available on a Timely Basis?   Evaluation studies generally have an explicit or implicit deadline if they are to influence business decisions. If the measurements cannot be collected and summarized in time for the decision, there is little justification for the evaluation design. I once took 18 months to evaluate a course with the consequence that the decision makers, including the line manager who commissioned the study and the training managers who "owned" the course, were all transferred to other jobs by the time the study was completed.[29]

Can Enough Data Be Collected for Reliable Measurement?   Reliability means consistency or stability. The more reliable the measure, the more confidence you can have in drawing conclusions from the data. There are different techniques for checking reliability (see Guilford and Fruchter[30] or Guilford[31] for a discussion), but they all depend upon the amount of data. Statisticians offer a variety of formulas and suggestions for determining how much data to collect (see Smith[32] for a summary), but the minimum sample (e.g., number of trainees) seems to be at least 30 people. Smith[33] describes a study in which reliability problems limited the interpretation of results.

Is the Measure Free from Known Biases?   A bias is an extraneous factor that distorts the measure and makes it difficult to determine the effects of the intervention. Biases are often situational differences between the trainees and the employees to whom the trainees are compared. Biases may include seasonal variations, weather, quality of raw materials, or customer characteristics. For example,

- Sales trainees are given less desirable territories than the comparison group.
- Production trainees are assigned to older equipment more prone to break down.
- Repair trainees are given the easy jobs or are assigned as helpers to more experienced repair technicians and thus are not given the chance to practice their new skills.
- Trainees are directed not to use the "school" method by their supervisors who, instead, want the work done by local methods.

Extrapolation

To put training results in perspective, it may be useful to extrapolate productivity or quality gains into monetary terms. There are many ways to do the extrapolation, and Table 17-2 (Brandenburg and Smith[34]) presents 10 examples of the extrapolation process. These examples represent a range of jobs as well as the three categories of operational measures.

The following example (Smith[45]) explains the process in more detail. The example involves a clerical job called station assigner. Assigners maintain records of the equipment serving each telephone customer. In this example, the presumed benefit is the reduction of errors. The measurement plan involves analyzing posttraining work samples for two groups of station assigners. One group attended a newly developed course. The others graduated from the old course being replaced by the new course.

The first column of Table 17-3 lists five types of errors. The second column shows the frequency of errors for graduates of the old course. Error rates are expressed as the number of errors per 100 pairs assigned. (The term "pair" refers to the two wires that run from the central office to a terminal near the customer's location.) The next column shows the errors for graduates of the new course. The last column shows the difference between the error rates for the two groups. These differences are taken as the estimated benefits due to the new training.

The next step is to price the benefits. In Table 17-4, the price is considered to be the cost of correcting each error. Correcting an assignment error may require work by three types of employees: assigners, installers, and framemen. To correct a wiring error (top row) requires an average of 10 minutes of an assigner's time. Ten minutes is one-sixth of an hour. One-sixth of the loaded hourly wage is $2. The last column presents the average dollar cost of correcting each type of error.

The next figure shows how the cost data and the observed error rates are used to

Table 17-2. Translating Performance Gains into Monetary Terms

REFERENCE	JOB	PROGRAM	BENEFITS	MEASUREMENT	FORMULA
Allen, Amacher and Yaney [35]	Machine Operators	Re-structure of work group	Reduced turnover and, hence, reduced cost of replacing skilled employees.	Factory turnover was monitored before and after creation of "unit work teams."	(Turnover before change – turnover after change) X employees X average replacement cost.
Fauley [36]	Supervisors	Speed reading course	Improved reading speed which makes time available for other activities.	Pre– and post– course reading speeds are compared.	Supervisors X hours saved per day X days X hourly wage.
Jones and Moxham [37]	Sewing Machine Operators	Initial job training	Productivity gain due to less time to reach standard reduced turnover, and increased efficiency.	Productivity and turnover of trainees compared to employees hired (a) before program was implemented and (b) after it was halted.	$(P_2R_2 - P_1R_1)V - (W_2R_2 - W_1R_1)$ Where: P = productivity R = retention time with company V = unit value of output W = wages Subscripts 1 and 2 represent "before" and "after" the program, respectively.
Mikesell, Wilson and Lawther [38]	Tax Auditors	Tax audit workshop	Identification of tax payers' errors which led to more tax revenue for state.	Trainees were compared to their audit division before and after the work-shop.	(Post minus pre-workshop revenue for trainees)–(Post minus pre-workshop revenue for audit division).
MacFarland and Keeler [39]	Construction Job	Initial job training	Reduced time to reach standard and reduced supervisory time.	Foreman rating of recent graduate vs. crew in terms of productivity and time spent coaching.	Productivity gain = trainees X work hours X hourly wage X .5; time = foremen X hours saved X hourly wage.
Smith [40]	Foremen	Attendance administration course	Reduced absence rates.	Work groups' absence rates tracked for foremen who were trained vs. foremen who were not trained.	(Predicted absences – actual absences) X daily wage.
Rosentreter [41]	Production Managers	Management training program	Reduced employee turnover (3 others not significant).	Turnover measured before and after for treatment and control groups.	Turnover expected–Turnover observed X employees X replacement cost.
Cullen, Sawzin, Sisson and Swanson [42]	Semi-skilled Machine Operators	Structured vs. unstructured (OJT) training	(1) decreased time to achieve job competency (2) decreased scrap (waste) (3) increase in solving problems	(1) mean to achievement in hours (2) scrap in lbs. per worker (3) simulation of problems	(1) none (2) scrap for group S – scrap for group U X employees X cost of material per lb. (3) none
Zigon [43]	Truck Terminal Managers	Management training	(1) decreased cost per bill (2) increased bill/hr., lbs./hr., labor cost/hr. (3) reduced overtime	(1) bill count and cost (2) bill, lbs., labor (3) amount of overtime	(1) compare vs. previous (2) compare to previous (3) compare over 5 months
Reber and Wallin [44]	Skilled & Semi-skilled Manufacturing Employees	Safety training	Increased safety performance.	Questionnaire observation of performance.	Compare over four time periods; overall injuries decreased from 84.8/100 to 55.1/100.

Table 17-3. Error Rates for New vs. Old Training

ASSIGNMENT ERRORS	ERRORS PER 100 PRS. ASSIGNED		
	OLD TRAINING	NEW TRAINING	DIFFERENCE
WIRING LIMITS	1.14	0.25	0.89
CLERICAL ERRORS	2.22	0.89	1.33
RECORD ERRORS	1.28	0.60	0.68
WORKING PAIR ASSIGNED	1.34	0.32	1.02
WORKING EQUIPMENT	1.70	0.58	1.12

Table 17-4. Estimated Costs of Errors

ASSIGNMENT ERRORS	LOADED COST OF LOST TIME PER ERROR			
	ASSIGNER $12/HOUR	INSTALLER $18/HOUR	FRAMEMAN $12/HOUR	TOTAL COST
WIRING LIMITS	$2.00	$6.00	$0.75	$ 8.75
CLERICAL ERRORS	$0.50**	$0.75**	$1.00*	$ 2.25
RECORD ERRORS	$1.00	$1.50	$0.00	$ 2.50
WORKING PAIR ASSIGNED	$2.00	$6.00	$3.00	$11.00
WORKING EQUIPMENT	$2.00	$0.00	$3.00	$ 5.00

* LOST TIME ESTIMATED TO OCCUR FOR 50% OF THE ERRORS.
** LOST TIME ESTIMATED TO OCCUR FOR 25% OF THE ERRORS.

Table 17-5. Savings by Error Category

ASSIGNMENT ERRORS	DIFFER- ENCE	TOTAL COST	COST SAVED
WIRING LIMITS	0.89	$8.75	$7.79
CLERICAL ERRORS	1.33	$2.25	$2.99
RECORD ERRORS	0.68	$2.50	$1.70
WORKING PAIR ASSIGNED	1.02	$11.00	$11.22
WORKING EQUIPMENT	1.12	$5.00	$5.60
		GRAND TOTAL	$29.30

estimate the savings achieved by reducing errors. For each error category, the difference in errors between graduates of the old and new courses is multiplied by the cost of correcting that type of error. Savings are summed for the five categories.

The cost savings per 100 pairs assigned is multiplied by the average annual work volume. The cost of training is subtracted. The result represents the value of sending an assigner to the new course, based on one year of work. The calculations look like this:

(Unit saving × work volume) − cost of training = value per trainee

($29.30 to correct errors per 100 pairs × 10,000 pairs assigned in a year) − $600 to train one assigner = $2330.00

Comment

Even though most of the examples relate to training, the advice given here applies equally to other performance improvement interventions, such as incentive and compensation systems, changes in management style, and feedback processes. Second, our examples usually emphasize one measure. In reality, most situations permit multiple measures which increase your chances of demonstrating tangible benefits of your program.

It must be acknowledged that most efforts to relate training effects to dollars fail. Before you can expect to demonstrate the economic impact of training, certain conditions must be met. I'd like to propose six prerequisite conditions.

First, there must be a performance criterion that can be improved, e.g., productivity, sales, scrap, overtime. In general, there has to be a problem.

Second, this problem must in part be due to some knowledge or skill deficiency.

Third, the training program must be designed to correct specific deficiencies.

Fourth, other factors which contributed to the problem, i.e., factors beyond the employee's control, must be corrected, or else they will negate the effects of training. These factors include such things as poorly documented work methods, obsolete equipment, and no supervisory support.

Next, a chain of events must occur. Employees must be trained. They must apply the new skills, i.e., must change their job behavior. The change in employee behavior must produce an improvement in the performance criterion.

Finally, employees must continue the new behavior patterns; they must be rewarded and not punished. Reward can come from the boss's encouragement or from knowledge of improved operating results. Punishment can come from increasing productivity quotas and from no feedback.

Research Designs

A research design is a plan. This plan specifies the types of measures to be collected, the procedures for collecting the measurements—including data sources—and the procedures for analyzing the data. This plan enables you to estimate the impact of training in terms of operational measure(s). At a minimum, the plan must include (1) a sample of data based upon the posttraining job performance of course graduates and (2) a sample of job performance data unaffected by training.

This section describes five research designs that are commonly used to evaluate training results. Four are called "quasi-experimental" designs because the assignment of people or groups to treatments is not random. True experiments present less equivocal data but are often impractical in field settings because of the difficulty in randomly assigning people or withholding treatments from groups. Furthermore, true experiments sometimes break down and have to be analyzed as quasi-experiments.

Equivalent Comparison Group Design

In this design, the researcher randomly assigns participants to either a treatment or a comparison group. The treatment (or experimental) group receives the program, while the comparison (or control) group does not. The performance of both groups is measured following the program and possibly before the program. If the treatment is effective, the treatment group should outperform the control group and/or show greater pretest-posttest gains. Other treatments, alone or in combination, may be added to the experimental design.

This design was used by Chaney and Teel[46] to evaluate, singly and in combination, the effectiveness of a training program and job aids upon the performance of machine-parts inspectors. Performance was measured before and after training. The group who received training reduced defects by 32 percent. Those using the job aids improved by 42 percent. Inspectors who had both the training and the job aids achieved a 71 percent increase in accuracy. The control group showed no change in performance.

This experimental design is discussed by Campbell and Stanley,[47] Fuqua,[48] McGehee and Thayer,[49] and Parker.[50] Other studies which exemplify this design are Lefkowitz[51] and Rosentreter.[52]

Nonequivalent Comparison Group Design

If participants cannot be assigned randomly to groups, the research design is then called the nonequivalent group design. The training evaluation of an attendance administration course I described in an article[53] was originally conceived as an equivalent group design. However, the random assignment of supervisors to training and the control group was disrupted by vacations, transfers, and overriding work commitments. Nevertheless, it was found that employee attendance improved only when the second-level manager was trained. Training the first-level supervisor had no impact on employee attendance.

This design is useful and quite common, even though threats to validity are less well controlled than in a true experiment. Cook and Campbell[54] discuss this design in detail.

Reversal Design or ABA Technique

This strategy uses one group. This group is administered the program, and then the treatment is removed. The group's performance is measured before the treatment, when the treatment is in force, and later after the treatment is removed. If the treatment is effective, performance should improve during the treatment and then deteriorate when the treatment is removed. Extensions of this design include administering the treatment a second time or administering two different treatments separated by the absence of any treatment.

Luthans and Maris[55] used the reversal technique to evaluate the impact of a behavior modification program upon absenteeism. A baseline attendance rate was established from 1 year's worth of data (i.e., the A condition in the ABA design). Then an attendance program was administered for 2 months (the B condition). Supervisors were trained to administer social rewards (attention and recognition) and feedback for employee attendance and to extinguish absence behavior by removing reinforcers. After 2 months, the program was withdrawn (repeat of the A condition). The supervisors were instructed to revert to the traditional means of enforcing the attendance policy. Two months later, the program was reinstituted (repeat of the B condition). Dramatic fluctuations in attendance were produced by applying and removing the behavior modification program.

The reversal design is also discussed by Cook and Campbell,[56] who call it "removed treatments with pretest and posttest," Clark and Snow,[57] Brethower and Rummler,[58] and Kazdin.[59] Other ABA studies are described by Jones and Moxham[60] and Dolton and Todor.[61]

Multiple Baseline Design

This design is appropriate when a program is introduced to different organizational units at different times All groups are measured throughout the phased introduction of the program. If the program is effective, each unit's performance should improve shortly after they receive the program. Groups receiving the program later can serve as control groups for evaluating the program's impact on groups receiving the program earlier.

Brethower and Rummler[62] provide a hypothetical example of this research strategy:

> A training program is begun January 1st in Region A, and yields a 17% performance improvement. The same program is started February 1st in Region B and yields a similar performance improvement. This pattern is repeated March 1st in Region C, and April 1st

in Region D. By starting the programs at different times, rather than all at once, factors such as changes in the market place, workload, quarterly business cycle, and personnel intake are spread. If, in each of the four regions, the introduction of the training program leads to improved job performance, then one can attribute the change in performance to the training program with more certainty than if only one region had shown such improvement.

Discussions of this design may be found in Brown[63] and in Brethower and Rummler[64] and Campbell and Stanley,[65] who call it the recurrent institutional design; Clark and Snow,[66] who call it the staged innovation design; and Cook and Campbell,[67] who call it the interrupted time series with switched replication. Other examples are described by Kelley, Orgel, and Baer,[68] and Reber and Wallin.[69]

Interrupted Time Series

This design involves repeated (continuous) measurement, such as productivity or sales records, before and after a program is implemented. If the program is effective, there should be an abrupt change in the measurement trend.

One example (cited by Cook and Campbell[70]) is a study by Lawler and Hackman.[71] Weekly attendance records were used to calculate the impact of participative decision making upon absenteeism among janitors. Attendance was tracked for 12 months prior and 16 months after program implementation. The "before" and "after" attendance rates did not significantly differ, but, as Cook and Campbell[72] point out, the last week before the new program had an unusually high level of absenteeism and would have led to a wrong conclusion if a short pretest-posttest measurement period had been used.

The time series design is discussed by Cook and Campbell,[73] Campbell and Stanley,[74] and Clark and Snow,[75] who call it the "intensive time-series design."

Additional References

Several writers have discussed the process of planning an evaluation. Phillips[76] describes an 18-step process for evaluating HRD programs. He offers additional guidance in instrument design, sampling, analysis, and reporting of results. Chabotar and Lad[77] offer a manual for evaluating training programs. Elsbree and Howe[78] present an extensive account of an evaluation project, with the first two articles concentrating on planning. Cook and Campbell[79] offer an extensive discussion of field research and evaluation.

Evaluation of the Training Department

The term "training results" can refer to the consequences of a particular program or to the training department's contributions to the corporation or sponsoring agency. The first two sections dealt with the first meaning; this section and the next consider the departmental perspective.

Training managers need ways of demonstrating contribution to corporate goals and, second, efficient management practices. I propose four approaches to measuring training organization, its services, and its internal operations. The four techniques are: (1) client satisfaction surveys, (2) focus groups, (3) training statistics, and (4) organizational audits. All four focus on the organization, not on individual programs. Techniques 1 and 2 look at the training organization from the clients' perspective. The third approach deals mostly with the internal functioning or efficiency of the training organization. The last is a combination of internal and external measures for a broad analysis of the training organization.

Client Satisfaction Surveys

This technique involves a brief questionnaire administered by mail or telephone to managers who send people to training. Questions deal with how the client managers perceive the training organization, usually focusing on satisfaction with particular services or functions. Questions tend to be brief, and "closed-ended" questions predominate.

Table 17-6 is an excerpt from a survey developed for use in a large company. It consists of 49 Likert-style questions that cover seven factors: perceived value of training, feedback from trainers to field managers about trainee performance, timeliness of training, satisfaction with vendor training, instructors' competence, client managers' knowledge of training services, and satisfaction with training facilities. This survey is used separately for each curriculum rather than for the entire training organization.

The value of this technique is that it provides a lot of data quickly about potential problems. The emphasis is on problem detection or identification rather than analysis. Consequently, another data collection effort is required to determine the causes of any problem detected by the survey.

Focus Groups

A focus group is an ad hoc group convened to discuss an issue. Focus groups have been used for "brainstorming" a problem and for market research in determining

Table 17-6. Excerpt from Client Satisfaction Survey

Remember: Please read each statement carefully and circle the number which most accurately reflects your opinion.

To guide you:
"1" means the statement is true to an extremely small extent, never or not at all.
"4" means it is true to an average extent, or about normal in degree or frequency.
"7" means it is true to an extremely high extent, always or without fail.

Of course, you may use the other numbers:
"3" and "2" represent varying degrees between average and extremely low.
"5" and "6" represent varying degrees between average and extremely high.

	extremely small extent, never, not at all			above average, normal			extremely great extent, always
1. Course schedules are well publicized so you know when a course you need is coming up	1	2	3	4	5	6	7
2. Training enables my people to be self-sufficient more quickly	1	2	3	4	5	6	7
3. Courses are available when needed	1	2	3	4	5	6	7
4. Instructors put in a full day's work	1	2	3	4	5	6	7
5. Requests for training are usually met with good and timely responses	1	2	3	4	5	6	7
6. My training budget is a very worthwhile expenditure	1	2	3	4	5	6	7

a product's image. This technique can be adapted for examining the training organization and its relationship to its clients. Focus groups can be organized for one occasion or they may meet periodically. Our discussion of "client's commitment" included an example of this technique.

In leading focus group meetings, it is crucial to probe for the reasons or critical events that have shaped people's impressions. Conversely, the facilitator must take care not to bias opinions by inadvertently encouraging or discouraging certain types of comments.

Training Statistics

A training statistic describes some characteristic of an organization's internal operations or external services. It is time-bound, meaning that it portrays the organization for a specific period of time, e.g., monthly, quarterly. Statistics may deal with such functions as program development, delivery, and scheduling. Statistics may represent such dimensions as volume (frequency, amount), cost, efficiency, timeliness, or quality. Examples include: average cost to train one employee for one day, "seats" scheduled as a percentage of "seats" requested, and percent of students successfully completing training. Training statistics serve as problem indicators. They are a "warning system" which should trigger further data collection to determine the causes of negative trends.

Table 17-7 shows a 1984 survey of the training measurements used by five former Bell System companies. Many of these statistics were experimental and are no longer used. This list is presented to illustrate the variety of possibilities.

There are two common problems with using statistics to evaluate groups within a training department. The first problem is the unfair comparison of training groups. Training statistics are affected by such variables as differences in client demands, e.g., seasonal fluctuations, or high-volume courses versus low-demand courses; differences in delivery strategies, e.g., self-paced versus group-based training, or field site versus training center; differences in program development, e.g., purchase of "off-the-shelf" courses versus contracting for customized courses versus "in-house" designed courses; differences in staffing strategies, e.g., part-time versus full-time trainers, use of contractors, use of instructors borrowed from other departments. Training statistics should be used to understand critical variables that shape the training department's activities. Appropriate standards come from historical trends developed for a particular training group rather than intergroup differences.

The second problem is the use of self-reported measures which are easily distorted. We are familiar with one training department that relied upon project managers to report project completion dates versus project target dates. Over a 4-year period, no project was ever completed behind schedule. The most reliable measurements are often derived from data gathered for other purposes by nontrainers. For example, the "cost per trainee hour" can be compiled from the course scheduling process (trainee hours) and the accounting process (cost data).

Organizational Audits

An audit is an intensive study of an organization for the purpose of finding ways to improve how the organization operates. Individual programs are evaluated but only as samples of the organization's work. Audits may employ a variety of data collection techniques and usually require a substantial investment of time and people. Audits are usually staffed by people from outside the audited organization.

Table 17-8 comes from one company's audit plan.[80] The columns represent

Table 17-7. Partial Listing of Training Measurements Tried by Five Companies

MEASUREMENT	Co. "A"	Co. "B"	Co. "C"	Co. "D"	Co. "E"
Relevance (rated by graduates)	X	X			
Effectiveness (rated by supervisors)	X	X			
Delivery cost per trainee (on hour)	X	X	X		
Demand vs. capacity in terms of student days	X		X	X	
% seats cancelled (management and non-management)	X		X	X	
% courses developed @ Training Development Standards	X	X			
% projects completed on time	X	X			
% seats provided to requested seats		X		X	
% Training Manager observations completed		X			
Average time in initial training		X			
Student days per instructor day	X	X	X	X	
Student/instructor ratio	X	X			
% follow up evaluation completed/committed		X			
Developer hours/instructional hour	X	X		X	
Development cost/instructional hour	X	X			
% developer days spent on developing		X			
Trainee cost/trainee hour by training center			X		
Instructor utilization (% time in class)	X				
No. trainers per 1000 employees					X
Delivery hours per 1000 employees					X
Delivery hours/1000 customer contacts					X
Delivery hours/number of new hires, transfers, promotions					X
Delivery hours/$1000 capital investment					X
Delivery hours/$1000 revenue					X

methods for collecting data. The rows represent variables which can be measured in an audit. Other audit plans have been presented by Tracey,[81] Lien,[82] Gaskell and Svenson,[83] Chellino, Rice, and Dinneen,[84] and Olivas.[85]

Audits generate much information but at great cost. It is important to involve the audited management team in defining study objectives and, second, in interpreting data. The goal is to develop the commitment of training managers to act upon the audit findings.

Client Support for Training

Measuring the results of training is a tactic often used to gain corporate support for the training department. No matter how sophisticated the evaluation, it may not

Table 17-8. Training Evaluation Exercises and Variables

Exercises (columns):
1. Trainee Questionnaire
2. Trng. Delivery Mgr. Interview
3. Analysis of Seat Cancellations
4. Analysis of Classroom Use
5. Analysis of Instructor Use
6. Instructor Interview
7. Analysis of Test Procedures
8. Analysis of Test Data
9. Observation of Instructors
10. Graduate Questionnaire
11. Methods Mgr. Interview
12. Review of Course Content
13. Anal. of Dvlpmt. Project Statistics
14. Compliance with Development Stds.
15. Trng. Development Mgr. Interview
16. Graduate's Supervisor Questionnaire
17. Observations of Graduates
18. Field Manager Interview
19. Anal. of Delivery Expenses
20. Anal. of Instructional Design
21. Compliance with Adaptation GL

Variables	1	2	3	4	5	6	7	8	9	10	11	12	13	14	15	16	17	18	19	20	21
Scheduling Process		X																X			
Timeliness of Training	X	X																			
Prerequisites (Compliance)	X	X				X															
Pre-training Briefing of Trainees	X	X				X															
Training Requests vs. Scheduled Training		X																X			
Seat Cancellations		X	X																		
Curriculum Planning		X																			
Classroom Utilization				X																	
Instructor Utilization					X																
Instructor Performance (Evaluation)							X	X	X												
Procedures for Evaluating Instructors		X					X														
Testing and Grading							X	X	X												
Delivery Expenses																			X		
Learning Problems of Trainees							X		X												
Post-Training Work Assignments		X										X				X					
Post-Training Job Proficiency												X				X	X				
Training vs. Field		X														X		X			
Feedback from Field to Trainers		X																X			
Instructors vs. Developers		X												X							
Development Priorities		X												X							
Timeliness of Development		X												X		X					
Course Implementation Problems		X				X										X					
Instructor's Change of Course						X										X					
Productivity of Development Group														X		X					
Efficiency of Development														X							
Efficiency of Adaptation														X							
Cost of Development, Adaptation														X							
Compliance with Training Dev. Stds.													X								
Compliance with Adaptation GL																					X
Quality of Materials & Design		X				X	X			X				X						X	
Relevance of Course Content						X				X		X				X					
Evaluation of Development Projects															X	X					
Methods Staff vs. Instructors		X									X					X					
Methods Staff vs. Developers																X					
Conversion Training		X											X			X					
Special expertise required?	No	No	No	No	No	No	Y-	No	Y-	No	No	Y-	No	Y-	No	No	Y-	No	No	Y-	Y-
Preparation Time (in days)	1	½	¼	¼	¼	1	½	½	1½	5	½	½	½	½	½	5	1½	1½	½	1	½
Administration Time (in days)	3	½	0	0	0	1½	0	0	3	15	½	3	0	0	½	15	8	1½	0	6	0
Analysis Time (in days)	1	½	¼	¼	¼	1½	1½	1½	3	1½	3	3	3	3	½	3	3	1½	1	3	1½
Sample Size (*per course)	10	1	NA	NA	NA	1*	NA	NA	1*	15*	NA	NA	NA	NA	1	15	5*	3	NA	NA	3

compel any more support from the client departments. The issue can be approached from two perspectives: the immediate program at hand or the longer-term relationship with the client or decision maker.

Specific Programs

Let us assume that you have created a program for a client organization, and you want to evaluate that program to show the clients how the program has benefited them. You are faced with such questions as: How to get the client to act upon the findings and recommendations? How to get the client to articulate the issues proposed for investigation? Who can speak for the client organization?

We advocate face-to-face discussion with the department head to determine if he or she sees the need for an evaluation study, what decisions the evaluation should support (e.g., whether or not to send employees to the program), what data would be considered "valid" or acceptable for enabling that decision, what the constraints are—especially time, who should participate in the planning process, and who approves the evaluation plan. Many times you must deal with a representative of the department head. That is fine, as long as the department head has, in fact, empowered the representative to act on his or her behalf. The objective is to develop a sense of "ownership" in the study by the decision maker.

A recent personal case illustrates this process. The request was to evaluate a management training curriculum designed for one department. I proposed looking at productivity measures, comparing performance before and after managers attended training. The client did not arrange for the training to improve productivity (which, incidentally, was not a problem). Rather, the client department was experiencing high turnover in lower management levels. The client simply wanted to know if first- and second-level managers perceived any change in the management style within the department and, second, what needed to happen for the style to improve. Through discussion about the department's objectives, we decided on a simple strategy.

Several groups of lower-level managers were selected. Every 4 months, half-day discussions were held with each group about how they saw the department and higher levels of management, how useful they considered the training, what problems they were experiencing, and what advice they had for reinforcing the desired changes. The groups' membership remained intact throughout a year's study. In essence, the evaluation was conceived as an ongoing "consumer research" study rather than a "one-shot" experimental study as originally proposed.

The evaluation enhanced not only the client's sense of ownership of the curriculum but also the organization's confidence in training services generally. Training statistics showed that this particular client group went from an annual average of 2 hours of management training per management employee to a yearly average of over 3 days per manager.

Long-Term Support

The long-term objective should be to build a consulting relationship with the client organization. Evaluation should be viewed as one of the services made available to the client. One vehicle for promoting the desired relationship is a steering committee that oversees the training (or "human resources development") services provided to that client organization. The committee may commission needs analyses, direct the design of training programs (and other performance improvement efforts), and oversee the implementation of these programs. Evaluation becomes a means for the committee to gather data about the effects of its decisions. Thus, the client management assumes responsibility for identifying and correcting its problems, and the training or HRD organization serves as the instrument of the client.

Steering committees are typically populated with midlevel managers delegated by the senior management. The training or HRD organization is represented by someone at the same management level as the client representatives. There may be as many committees as major client departments.

Beyond the committee process, the evaluator would do well to learn as much about the client organization as possible if there is to be an enduring relationship. Some things to know include: What are the pressing issues facing the department?

Who are the key decision makers and how do they make decisions? Who are the opinion leaders in mid and lower management? How does that organization measure its success? There is no magic to discovering this information. It simply requires talking to your client managers, usually in a very informal fashion.

Some Last Thoughts

Any permanent training organization needs a quality control function to support a variety of decisions, e.g., purchase of new programs, course maintenance, assurance of on-the-job support, or instructor certification. Quality control requires a variety of evaluation techniques, including the capability to measure training results. In general, it is expensive and time-consuming to measure the results of specific programs. Therefore, I would like to offer advice to get the most "mileage" from this type of evaluation:

1. Get client input to the evaluation plan, as outlined in the section on client support.
2. Make sure that the project can meet the prerequisites outlined at the end of the section on operational measures.
3. Assign the project to someone with the professional background to handle the experimental design.
4. Be alert to research opportunities. Research seeks to formulate rules and principles to guide future decisions, while evaluation is concerned with the "here and now" of judging a specific program, product, activity, etc. Research and evaluation involve similar activities. With modest effort, research requirements can be incorporated into an evaluation. (I discuss how to recognize these research opportunities in a recent article.[86])

References

1. Scherman, I.A., "Training, Directions for the 80s," *Training and Development Journal*, 1980, 34(1), pp. 50–55.
2. Baum, J.F., "Effectiveness of an Attendance Control Policy in Reducing Chronic Absenteeism," *Personnel Psychology*, 1978, 31(1), pp. 71–81.
3. Chaney, F.B., and K.S. Teel, "Improving Inspector Performance through Training and Visual Aids," *Journal of Applied Psychology*, 1967, 51(4), pp. 311–315.
4. Cullen, J.G., S. Sawzin, G.R. Sisson, and R.A. Swanson, "Training, What's It Worth?," *Training and Development Journal*, 1976, 30(8), pp. 12–20.
5. Dolton, D.R., and W.D. Todor, "Unanticipated Consequences of Union-Management Cooperation: An Interrupted Time Series Analysis," *Applied Behavioral Science*, 1984, 20(3), pp. 253–264.
6. Gommersall, E.R., and M.S. Myers, "Breakthrough in On-the-Job Training," *Harvard Business Review*, 1966, 44(4), pp. 62–72.
7. Gustafson, H.W., "Job Performance Evaluation as a Tool to Evaluate Training," *Improving Human Performance Quarterly*, 1976, 5(3–4), pp. 133–152.
8. Hahne, C.E., "How to Measure Results of Sales Training," *Training and Development Journal*, 1977, 31(11), pp. 3–7.
9. Holoviak, S.J., "The Impact of Training on Company Productivity Levels," *NSPI Journal* (now called *Performance and Instruction*), 1982, 21(5), pp. 6–8.

10. Horrigan, J.T., "The Effects of Training on Turnover: A Cost Justification Model," *Training and Development Journal*, 1979, 33(7), pp. 3–7.

11. Jones, A., and J. Moxham, "Costing the Benefits of Training," *Personnel Management*, 1969, 1(4), pp. 22–28.

12. Kelley, A.I., R.F. Orgel, and D.M. Baer, "Evaluation: The Bottom Line Is Closer than You Think," *Training and Development Journal*, 1984, 38(8), pp. 32–37.

13. Ibid.

14. Kim, J.S., and A.F. Compagna, "Effects of Flexitime on Employee Attendance and Performance: A Field Experiment," *Academy of Management Journal*, 1981, 24(4), pp. 729–741.

15. Latham, G.P., and S.B. Kline, "Improving Job Performance through Training in Goal Setting," *Journal of Applied Psychology*, 1974, 59(2), pp. 187–191.

16. Lawler, E.E. III, and J.R. Hackman, "Impact of Employee Participation in the Development of Pay Incentive Plans: A Field Experiment," *Journal of Applied Psychology*, 1969, 53, pp. 467–471.

17. Lefkowitz, J., "Effect of Training on the Productivity and Tenure of Serving Machine Operators," *Journal of Applied Psychology*, 1970, 54(1), pp. 81–86.

18. Luthans, F., and T.L. Maris, "Evaluating Personnel Programs through the Reversal Technique," *Personnel Journal*, 1979, 58(10), pp. 692–697.

19. Macy, B.A., and P.H. Mirvis, "Organizational Change Efforts: Methodologies for Assessing Organizational Effectiveness and Program Costs versus Benefits," *Evaluation Review*, 1982, 6(3), pp. 301–372.

20. Meyer, H.H., and M.S. Raich, "An Objective Evaluation of a Behavior Modeling Training Program," *Personnel Psychology*, 1983, 36(4), pp. 755–761.

21. Mikesell, J.L., J.A. Wilson, and W. Lawther, "Training Program and Evaluation Model," *Public Personnel Management*, 1975, 4(6), pp. 405–411.

22. Mirvis, P.H., and E.E. Lawler III, "Measuring the Financial Impact of Employee Attitudes," *Journal of Applied Psychology*, 1977, 62(1), pp. 1–8.

23. Murphy, J., and A. Beauchemin, "Results of the Effective Listening Special Study: DAS-1 System," Human Performance Division, New England Telephone, December 1982.

24. Reber, R.A., and J.A. Wallin, "The Effects of Training, Goal Setting, and Knowledge of Results of Safe Behavior: A Component Analysis," *Academy of Management Journal*, 1984, 27(3), pp. 554–560.

25. Robinson, D.G., "Training for Impact (How to Stop Spinning Your Wheels and Get into the Race)," *Training*, 1984, 2, pp. 42–47.

26. Rosentreter, G., "Evaluating Training by Four Economic Indices," *Adult Education*, 1979, 24(4), pp. 234–241.

27. Smith, M.E., "An Illustration of Evaluating Processes, Design Features, and Problems," *Improving Human Performance Quarterly*, 1978, 7(4), pp. 337–350.

28. Smith, M.E., "An Illustration of Evaluating Post-training Job Performance," *Improving Human Performance Quarterly*, 1979, 8(3), pp. 181–201.

29. Smith, ref. 27.

30. Guilford, J.P., and B. Fruchter, *Fundamental Statistics in Psychology and Evaluation*, 5th ed., McGraw-Hill, New York, 1973, chapter 17.

31. Guilford, J.P., *Psychometric Methods*, McGraw-Hill, New York, 1954, chapter 14.

32. Smith, M.E., "How Big a Sample Do I Need for My Evaluation?" *Performance and Instruction*, 1980, 19(10), pp. 3–7ff.

33. Smith, ref. 28.

34. Brandenburg, D.C., and M.E. Smith, *Evaluation of Corporate Training and Programs*, TMR

Report 91, ERIC Clearinghouse for Measurement and Testing, Educational Testing Service, Princeton, NJ, May 1986.

35. Allen, D.C., H.R. Amacher, and J.P. Yaney, "The Economics of Management Change: Cost Estimating," Paper presented at the annual meeting of the National Society for Performance and Instruction, Atlanta, April 2, 1976.

36. Fauley, F.E., "Cost Models: A Study in Persuasion," *Training and Development Journal,* 1975, 29(6), pp. 3–8.

37. Jones and Moxham, ref. 11.

38. Mikesell, Wilson, and Lawther, ref. 21.

39. MacFarland, R., and K. Keeler, "Assessing the Value of a Training Course," Paper presented at the annual meeting of the National Society for Performance and Instruction, Washington, DC, April 1975.

40. Smith, ref. 27.

41. Rosentreter, ref. 26.

42. Cullen et al., ref. 4.

43. Zigon, J., "Increasing Bottom Line Results of Training," *Performance and Instruction,* 1984, 23(2), pp. 18–20.

44. Reber and Wallin, ref. 24.

45. Smith, M.E., "Performance Indices for Managing a Training Development Organization: Two Years of Experience," *Improving Human Performance Quarterly,* 1978, 7(3), pp. 303–318.

46. Chaney and Teel, ref. 3.

47. Campbell, D.T., and J. Stanley, "Experimental and Quasi-experimental Designs for Research on Teaching," in N.L. Gage, ed., *Handbook of Research on Teaching,* Rand McNally, Chicago, 1963. Also published as *Experimental and Quasi-experimental Designs for Research,* Rand McNally, Chicago, 1966.

48. Fuqua, D.R., "Measurement Issues and Design Alternatives: Selection Criteria for the OD Consultant," *Improving Human Performance Quarterly,* 1979, 8(4), pp. 277–290.

49. McGehee, W., and P.W. Thayer, *Training in Business and Industry,* Wiley, New York, 1961.

50. Parker, T.C., "Statistical Methods for Measuring Training Results," in R.L. Craig, ed., *Training and Development Handbook,* McGraw-Hill, New York, 1976, chapter 19.

51. Lefkowitz, ref. 17.

52. Rosentreter, ref. 26.

53. Smith, ref. 27.

54. Cook, T.D., and D.T. Campbell, "The Design and Conduct of Quasi-experiments and True Experiments in Field Settings," in M.D. Dunnette, ed., *Handbook of Industrial and Organizational Psychology,* Rand McNally, Chicago, 1976, pp. 249–256.

55. Luthans and Maris, ref. 18.

56. Cook and Campbell, ref. 54.

57. Clark, R.E., and R.E. Snow, "Alternative Designs for Instructional Technology Research," *Audio-visual Communications Review,* 1975, 23(4), pp. 373–394.

58. Brethower, K.S., and G.A. Rummler, "Evaluating Training," *Improving Human Performance Quarterly,* 1976, 5(3–4), pp. 103–120. Reprinted in *Training and Development Journal,* 1979, 33(5), pp. 14–22.

59. Kazdin, A.E., "Methodological and Assessment Considerations in Evaluating Reinforcement Programs in Applied Settings," *Journal of Applied Behavior Analysis,* 1973, 6(3), pp. 517–531.

60. Jones and Moxham, ref. 11.

61. Dolton and Todor, ref. 5.

62. Brethower and Rummler, ref. 58.

63. Brown, M.G., "Evaluating Training via Multiple Baseline Designs," *Training and Development Journal*, 1980, 34(10), pp. 11–16.

64. Brethower and Rummler, ref. 58.

65. Campbell and Stanley, ref. 47.

66. Clark and Snow, ref. 57.

67. Cook and Campbell, ref. 54.

68. Kelley et al., ref. 12.

69. Reber and Wallin, ref. 24.

70. Cook and Campbell, ref. 54.

71. Lawler and Hackman, ref. 16.

72. Cook and Campbell, ref. 54.

73. Ibid.

74. Campbell and Stanley, ref. 47.

75. Clark and Snow, ref. 57.

76. Phillips, J.J., *Handbook of Training Evaluation and Measurement Methods*, Gulf Publishing Co., Houston, 1983.

77. Chabotar, K.J., and L.J. Lad, *Evaluation Guidelines for Training Programs*, Midwestern Intergovernmental Training Committee, Lansing, MI, 1974.

78. Elsbree, A.R., and C. Howe, "An Evaluation of Training in Three Acts," *Training and Development Journal*, 1977, 31(7), pp. 10–14; 31(8), pp. 12–19; 31(9), pp. 30–35.

79. Cook and Campbell, ref. 54.

80. Smith, M.E., "Exchanging Ideas on Evaluation: 15. New England Telephone's Training Management Operational Review Plan," *NSPI Journal* (now called *Performance and Instruction*), 1979, 18(6), pp. 44–47.

81. Tracey, W.R., *Evaluating Training and Development Systems*, American Management Association, New York, 1968.

82. Lien, L., "Reviewing Your Training and Development Activities," *Personnel Journal*, 1979, 58(11), pp. 791–794ff.

83. Gaskell, R., and R. Svenson, "Exchanging Ideas on Evaluation: Training Operational Reviews—A Multipurpose Tool," *NSPI Journal* (now called Performance and Instruction), 1978, 17(2), pp. 20–21.

84. Chellino, S.N., R.L. Rice, and M. Dinneen, "A Corporate Training Audit," Paper presented at meeting of the National Society for Performance and Instruction, San Francisco, March 1978.

85. Olivas, L., "Auditing Your Training and Development Function," *Training and Development Journal*, 1980, 34(3), pp. 60–64.

86. Smith, M.E., "Recognizing Research Opportunities," *Performance and Instruction*, 1985, 23(1), pp. 9–12.

18

Return on Investment

Henry L. Dahl, Jr.

Henry L. Dahl, Jr., is Director, Corporate Employee Development and Planning, at The Upjohn Company, Kalamazoo, Michigan. He is responsible for human resource planning, management and executive development, organization development, and employee training. He is a member of the Corporate Planning Steering Committee, which administers the company's Five-Year Plan. He has been at Upjohn since 1957, serving in many corporate and divisional human resource positions. Prior to his present position he was Manager, Manpower Planning and Manager, Employment. In 1983–1984 he participated in a White House Conference on Productivity. He has lectured widely on the subject "Measuring and Improving the Return on Human Resource Investments." He was coproducer of two award-winning management development motion pictures, "Me! & You" and "Me! and We." He is an Accredited Personnel Diplomat of the American Society for Personnel Administration, a director of the Mid-West Human Resource Planning Association, as well as a long-standing member of ASTD. Dahl is a 1955 graduate of the University of Minnesota with a B.B.A. in Industrial Relations.

The Competitive Edge

Every enterprise, private or public, must have a competitive edge to survive and grow. Perhaps it is a unique product or market. Perhaps it is a special competence or natural resource. Perhaps it is a special method of production, sale, or distribution. Perhaps it is a government charter or a public service. Whatever it is, it will cease to exist and grow without a competitive edge.

Analysis by many scholars reveals that very fundamental elements are at work in developing these "edges." Successful people have stated many times that they can quickly obtain all the resources they need—markets, products, methods of sales, production capabilities, and distribution systems—except one, *the human organization*, the knowledge, skills, and motivation of people. The human resource is the most critical limiting factor in developing the *competitive edge*. Not only can the

343

human resource be the limiting factor in building an edge, it has tremendous untapped and unused potential for greatly enhancing a competitive edge.

Consider also that all decisions, all functions, all effort in an organization's life are the result of people. People determine everything in an organization's success.

Human Resource Economics

Some economic facts further emphasize the importance of human resources in organization success. Most organizations spend more money for human resources than for any other resource. Yet the primary financial tools managers use—the profit and loss statement, the balance sheet, and the cash flow statement—contain no information on the cost of people.

Further, in the United States and around the world, the cost of human resources has been, is, and will be increasing significantly because of inflation, increasing cost of employee benefits, increasing proportion of knowledge workers, and collective bargaining. In capital-intensive organizations, the value and importance attached to facilities and equipment is increasing dramatically. The need for competent people to use those assets efficiently will increase at least proportionately.

More and more organizations are becoming labor-intensive as the service components of the U.S. economy become more prevalent. In labor-intensive organizations the key to the competitive advantage is the ability of the management team to optimally manage the human resource of the organization.

Unfortunately, data published by the Chamber of Commerce of the United States show that the return on human resources in the United States is declining as the cost of people has increased faster than profits. A study published by The Upjohn Company in 1983 reports that each new position or employee added to the organization represents, in effect, an eventual investment of 160 times the initial annual salary. A $20,000 a year employee becomes a $3.2 million investment. A $40,000 a year employee is $6.4 million, a $60,000 is $9.6 million, etc. The implications of these investments are enormous. Their analysis and justification in most organizations gets much less attention than equivalent or lesser investments in facilities or equipment.

Consider the amount of money spent by organizations to house, maintain, and improve the output of a $1 million production machine. Are equivalent sums spent to house, maintain, and improve the output of every employee? Probably not.

In most organizations the expenditure for human resources each year is greater than the total value of the plant, property, and equipment they own. Of course, this will vary according to the nature of the organization and its capital intensity.

Quite a bit of evidence shows that the return on human resource investments has been and is declining. How much of the drop in U.S. productivity is due to lower return on the investment in the human part of the organization? National and industry data suggest the ROI on human resources has been declining for several years. No wonder the United States is losing much of its production capability to other nations.

The ability of an organization to develop a competitive edge depends on its human resources. People make the decisions about utilization of other resources, and because the people costs are so large, these decisions are especially significant.

Developing a Competitive Edge

Seven key actions are required for developing human resources into a competitive edge: (1) the organization must be strategically positioned; (2) it must have the optimum organization structure to achieve its goals; (3) jobs must be effectively designed; (4) each job must be staffed by a person who has the potential to perform the job at least satisfactorily; (5) the person on each job must have the knowledge and skills to successfully perform the job; (6) the climate or culture must activate, energize, and motivate people to use their knowledge and skills effectively; and (7) there must be an effective method to measure the resulting performance.

Training and Development Role

Consider the airline company which appeared to provide outstanding programs in developing its human resources into a significant competitive edge. This organization has developed exceptionally fine market segments; knows the nature and direction of its efforts for the next 10 years; has fine equipment, unique services, a strong financial base, and the ultimate in job and organization design; has state-of-the-art performance evaluation programs; and has each of its jobs filled by individuals who are dedicated, have high potential, and want to do a good job.

Consider further, you just completed an excellent flight with this airline. The plane arrives at the gate for deplaning, the passengers stand to leave the aircraft and wait for 15 minutes . . . an apologetic crew member announces the delay has been caused by a new employee learning to position the ramp at the aircraft doorway.

All the excellent programs and the excellent flight were useless because one employee did not have the knowledge and skills to do the job well. The competitive edge was lost. Will the passengers remember the good flight? Probably not; they will remember the "snafu."

Training and development must help the organization equip each employee with the knowledge and skill needed to perform his or her job effectively now and in the future. *The entire human resource management system fails if employees do not have the knowledge and skills to do the job.*

Well-trained people can be somewhat effective without well-prepared strategic plans, organization structure, culture and climate, and motivation programs. But, without knowledge and skills, everything collapses. Planes can't fly because pilots are not certified, planes can't fly because of maintenance, and passengers are turned away because of poor service at the reservation check-in counter, by flight attendants, and by baggage handlers. Each person must have the knowledge and skill required by the job in order to generate a competitive advantage.

Good relations cannot do it alone. A truly competitive edge comes from people who know why they are there, what their job is, and how their job fits into the large picture. They are attracted to the organization and want to stay and are properly placed in jobs that use their strengths. They feel good about the climate and rewards, *they have the knowledge and skills they need*, and they know how well they are doing.

Role of Management

The responsibility for developing human resources into a competitive advantage lies squarely with the management team. Profitability, success, growth, productivity, and employee relations are all directly related to the competency of the management team.

Therefore, developing of the management team's knowledge and skills is a number one priority for human resource development. Each supervisor, manager, director, officer, general manager, and CEO must have the knowledge and skills required for success at their level. The knowledge and skills needed to manage all resources of the organization are important, but managing the human resource is doubly important because all other resources of the organization are managed by people.

Measuring ROI

Some work has been done to measure the return on investment in human resources, but more needs to be done. We need to develop effective and meaningful ROI measures of the total human resource before we can do the pieces (staffing, training and development, environment, performance evaluation, etc.).

The Upjohn Company has a model which links the seven management actions (see previous list) to its "human resource return on investment" model. Training and development is one of the "management actions" in the model. Since so little is known about the relationship between training and development and profitability, or organization success, the Upjohn model contains an estimate of what it is. It also estimates the relationship between training and staffing, placement, motivation, and performance. Much more work is needed to establish the real relationship between these key areas of human resource management.

ROI Role

The implications of this discussion for the human resource development function become increasingly clear and important.

- Human resource development must become "partners" in assisting the organization to survive and grow.
- Human resource development must place a high priority on helping management develop and maintain a competent management team.
- Human resource development must assist management in identifying the knowledge and skills required for success in the jobs of the organization.
- Human resource development must assist management in finding, identifying, or developing cost-effective methods for employees to learn needed knowledge and skills.
- Human resource development must assist management in evaluating employee learning experiences and continuously evolve more effective learning technology.
- Human resource development must develop and promote valid and useful ways to measure the return on investment in human resources and especially human resource development.

Economic Measures

Human resource development people must know something about the economics of the human resource in the organization. Some beginning actions are outlined below.

Calculate the Cost per Person in Your Organization. Find out from your financial people the total dollars spent for payroll, benefits, and employee-related taxes for your organization. Divide the total figure by the number of regular employees in your organization. This will tell you *employee costs per person*. Plot this for the past 5 to 10 years. Project it 5 years into the future based on the best estimates you can get or develop. If the information is available for various parts of your organization, plot these separately. These resulting graphs will help you answer the questions:

- What is the average cost per person in your organization?
- What has been the trend?
- What will it be in 5 years?
- Which parts of our organization have the highest costs per person? Why?
- What is happening to the various components of employee costs? Are any of the components becoming a larger portion of employee costs? Why? Does this seem reasonable?

Calculate the Earnings* of Your Organization per Person. Using your annual report, write down the profit (preferably pretax) for each of the past 10 years. Divide the profit figure for each year by the total number of regular employees to show dollars of pretax earnings per employee. Graph this for the past 10 years. If information is available, calculate and graph this ratio 5 years into the future and by parts of your organization if you have separate profit centers. These graphs will help you answer questions like:

- What is the trend in dollars of earnings per employee? Why?
- What will happen in the next 5 years if we carry out our present plans? Is it what we want? If not, what should we do about it?
- How does our ratio of earnings per employee compare with our competition? Is it what we want? What should we do about it?

Calculate the Dollars of Assets per Employee. Ask your financial people for an asset amount that represents facilities and equipment. Divide this by the number of employees in your organization. Graph these numbers as you did before. This information can help you answer questions like:

- What is the value of the facilities and equipment our average employee is responsible to use, maintain, and operate? Is the trend up or down and why?

Which parts of our organization require more employee competencies to optimally use its facilities and equipment?

Organizations which have a low ratio of dollars, facilities, and equipment per employee are very labor-intensive. This is important for human resource development people to know, because in these organizations the key to success is the effective management of people and we know people managers require very complex and important skills and knowledge to be successful.

For more advanced quantitative measures important to human resource development people, refer to Chapter 14 in the book *White Collar Productivity* edited by N. Lehrer and published by McGraw-Hill in 1983.

*Assuming you are a profit-making organization.

Calculate the Dollars Spent for Training and Development in Your Organization

- What is the average amount spent for each employee for training and development? What should it be?
- How much is spent per person in different job categories—supervisor, manager, sales, professional, technician, plant, office? What should it be?
- What are the trends? Is the money spent in areas of greatest potential payoff?
- Is the training and development money being spent to support important business needs?
- What is the relationship between training and development investments and productivity? Profitability? Turnover? Lost time? Safety statistics? Employee morale? Use of equipment and facilities? Return on investment in human resources?

Summary

In summary, this chapter says:

- The human resource is, in the final analysis, the most significant competitive advantage of an organization.
- Seven actions determine the effectiveness of the human organization.
- The knowledge and skills of the people is a critical element of these actions because without it the entire system fails.
- The knowledge and skills of the organization's management team are a number one priority.
- More work is needed to measure ROI on human resources and more specifically on the training and development component.

Bibliography

The Consultant, Vol. 3, No. 1, The Office & Information Systems Groups, Digital Equipment Corporation, 1986.

Dahl, Henry, "Measuring the Human ROI," *Management Review*, January 1979.

Drucker, Peter F., "The Danger of Excessive Labor Income," *The Wall Street Journal*, January 6, 1981.

Flamholtz, Dr. Eric G., "Human Resource Accounting," Jossey-Bass, San Francisco, CA 1985.

Lehrer, Robert, *White Collar Productivity*, McGraw-Hill, New York, 1983.

White House Conference on Productivity Report, A Report to the President of the United States, April 1984, National Technical Information Service, Department of Commerce, 5285 Port Royal Rd., Springfield, VA 22161.

19

Brain Dominance Technology

Ned Herrmann

Ned Herrmann is chairman of the board of The Whole Brain Corporation. He is recognized as the father of brain dominance technology and is known internationally as an expert in this new field. Herrmann's interest in the brain is a culmination of a lifelong awareness of his own duality, which in turn resulted in his pursuit of the nature and source of creativity. As a young man, he excelled in mathematics and science while pursuing a career in music and performing arts. His education in physics prepared him for his brain research work over the past 8 years. His interest in the arts and experience in performing led him to a second career as a painter and sculptor. In the last 10 years of his long career at General Electric he integrated these interests with his interest in teaching, culminating in his corporate position, Manager of Management Education. His ability to function with ease in the class-room, office, art studio, laboratory, and boardroom has been key to his creation, development, and application of the Herrmann Brain Dominance Instrument and the Applied Creative Thinking workshops that have come from the brain model he developed.

Much has been said and written about the brain in recent years that has potentially significant implications for people involved in education and training. Why should this subject be of interest to human resource development professionals? Simply stated, the brain is involved in all aspects of the learning process. It is the single body organ that is the central processor of all learning activities.

Contemporary understanding of human brain functions establishes that each brain is unique and that brains in general are specialized. While experts argue about the degree of specialization, there is general agreement on the fact of specialization. There is also agreement on the concept of dominance: eye dominance, hand dominance, foot dominance, ear dominance, and brain dominance. While the body is symmetrical in terms of organ duality, that is, humans have two eyes, two ears, two hands, two feet, and two hemispheres, experts agree that in the use of these dual organs there exists a general asymmetry. In other words, we use one to a greater degree than the other. When combined, the concepts of specialization and asymmetry or dominance produce within each human being a distribution of specialized preferences that affect general behavior. Specifically included is the unique individual's learning style.

An immediate implication for the education and training profession is that the assumptions about the learner must now be completely reconsidered. Intelligence is no longer one-dimensional but rather includes the notion of multiple intelligences. Each individual is now being thought of as a unique learner with learning preferences and avoidances different from those of other learners. This means that learning designs must somehow factor in the uniqueness of the individual learner so that the subject matter is understood by all the participants in the learning experience, not only equally in terms of comprehension but also consistently in terms of intended meaning.

Each one of us, as an HRD professional, is also a unique human being with a unique learning style. If we consider our own experience throughout our personal learning history, the face validity of these concepts would likely be strongly substantiated. We did much better in some subjects than in others. We responded much more to some teaching methods than to others. We retained some material more accurately and for a longer time than other material delivered in a different way. We remember the three or four outstanding teachers and we have forgotten many others who for us were not effective. The reason for that, and this is probably true for you and for most others, is your personal uniqueness and individual learning style that differentiates you from others in terms of content, delivery, learning environment, and teaching techniques.

The concept of whole brain teaching and learning provides the basis for bridging the gap between the unique individual learner and the design and delivery of the learning. The reason that HRD professionals who have made use of whole brain teaching and learning concepts are so enthusiastic about this approach is that it works effectively for a much larger population of learners in a much wider variety of subject areas.

The concept works because:

- The brain is specialized.

- Individual brains are unique.

- The brain is situational.

- Learning is mental.

- Unique individuals have different learning styles.

- Learning designs can accommodate individual differences.

- Delivery of learning can respond to personal uniqueness.

- Unique people can be made an integral part of the learning design.

- Learners can be grouped to make the learning more effective.

- Learning through affirmation and discovery can be more effective, fulfilling, and enjoyable and can last longer.

- Learning programs that are based on the specialized brains of unique participants work to the advantage of everyone—including the trainer.

The brain provides a wide array of specialized functions. Many of these specialized modes are allocated to specific locations in the two hemispheres. Even though in some instances the degree of lateralization between the left and right hemisphere is relatively small, the effect of dominance causes the differentiation to be very large. Therefore, from a practical point of view none of these specialized modes can be ignored when it comes to the unique person in a learning situation. It is far better to assume that specialization exists than to rationalize that it is too small to matter. Experience with thousands of learners in workshops where such differences are made visible has clearly shown that to pay attention to these differences is highly beneficial to the individual learner and also to the entire learning group.

The Thinking Processes

The concept of whole brain teaching and learning is based upon a distribution of specialized modes throughout the brain system. The model that has been developed divides the brain into four separate quadrants, each one different and equal in importance (see Fig. 19-1). Two of these quadrants represent the more cognitive, intellectual modes, associated with the two cerebral hemispheres. The other two quadrants represent the more visceral, emotional modes associated with the limbic system. Two of the four quadrants are specialized in left-mode thinking processes. These are the more logical, analytic, quantitative, and fact-based modes contained in the cerebral left quadrant, and the more planned, organized, detailed, and sequential mode processed in the limbic left quadrant. In contrast, the other two quadrants make up right-mode specialization. These include the more synthesizing, integrating, holistic, and intuitive modes, associated with the cerebral right

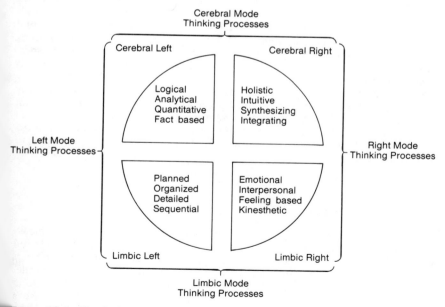

Figure 19-1. The thinking process.

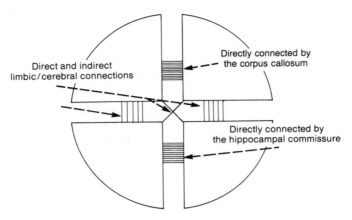

Figure 19-2. The interconnected brain system.

quadrant, and the interpersonal, emotional, kinesthetic, and feeling modes associated with the right limbic quadrant.

The brain is physiologically composed of two separate hemispheres, which are known as the left and right hemispheres. There are two sets of major structures which are connected together between the two hemispheres. These include the two cerebral hemispheres connected by the corpus callosum, and the two halves of the limbic system, connected together by the hippocampal commissure (see Fig. 19-2). These represent massive connections that allow for direct interaction between the two halves of the cerebral system and the two halves of the limbic system.

We know a lot more about the function of the two cerebral hemispheres than we do about the function of the limbic system; however, more and more understanding emerges each day about both of these specialized areas. While the cerebral hemispheres are thought of as the more cognitive, intellectual parts of the process, the limbic system is becoming known as the more organized and emotional aspect of learning. A key function of the limbic system is to transform information as it is entered into the brain system, so as to position it for appropriate processing. By reason of this role, the limbic system has a major effect on memory. There are many who believed that memory is essential to learning, and that indeed without memory, learning is not possible. Therefore, because of the organized and structured aspect of limbic processing, plus its role as the emotional processor, these two quadrants of the teaching and learning model represent a significant aspect of the learning process.

Brain Dominance

With the sponsorship and funding of General Electric Company, I was able to develop and validate an instrument to aid in measuring an individual's preferred mode of thinking. This tool is called the "Herrmann brain dominance instrument." It is a paper-and-pencil questionnaire that provides the basis of a personal profile. This profile (see Fig. 19-3) represents a metaphor of an individual's thinking preferences across the total spectrum of mental options that comprise the four parts of the brain described in the whole brain teaching and learning model. As of

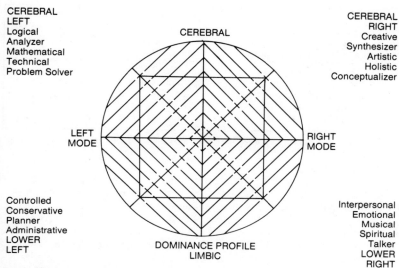

Figure 19-3. The brain dominance profile.

January 1986, close to 200,000 have completed this instrument. A study of 15,000 participants in a variety of workshops shows an even distribution of preferences in all four quadrants. Therefore, considering the world at large, the assumption must be that people are equally distributed throughout the teaching and learning model in terms of their mental preferences.

Figure 19-4 shows the differences in the learning styles represented by the specialized modes of each of the four quadrants. Experience has shown that different design and delivery approaches facilitate learning in each of these four specialized quadrants. Figure 19-5 shows these four different design and delivery approaches.

Brain dominance data indicate that individuals in similar occupations tend to have the same general profile; therefore, accountants in one division of the company have profiles similar to accountants in another division of the same

Cerebral left	Cerebral right
LEARNS BY:	LEARNS BY:
—Thinking through ideas	—Self-discovery
—Values logical thinking	—Constructs concepts
—Needs facts	—Values initiative
—Forms theories	—Is concerned with hidden
Builds cases	possibilities
Limbic left	Limbic right
LEARNS BY:	LEARNS BY:
—Testing theories	—Listening and sharing ideas
—Values structure and process	—Values intuitive thinking
—Oriented to skill attainment	—Works for harmony
through practice	—Integrates experience with self

Figure 19-4. Learning styles represented by the specialized modes of the four quadrants.

Cerebral left Formalized lecture, data-based, case discussions, textbook, program learning, and behavior modification	Cerebral right Nonstructured, experiential, experimental, visual, aesthetic, individual, and involved
Limbic left Structured, sequential, lecture, text- book, organizational case discussions, program learning, and behavior modification	Limbic right Experiential, sensory movement oriented, musical, people-oriented case discussions, and group-interactive

Figure 19-5. Design and delivery approaches for the specialized modes of the four quadrants.

company. The same is true comparing accountants in one company with accountants in another company. It is also true when comparing accountants in a company in India with accountants in companies in Stockholm, New York City, Johannesburg, and Singapore. It is clearly evident that work is a common denominator, not only between companies but also between cultures.

Figure 19-6 shows a sample distribution of brain dominance profiles of selected occupations. Note that some occupations are primarily focused in one quadrant, while others represent multiple dominances in two, three, or even four quadrants. These distributions of preferences by occupation represent a significant issue for training and development professionals as they design and deliver learning programs to people in these occupational groups.

Experience has shown conclusively a strong correlation between a person's personal profile, occupational profile, and learning profile. The array of learning profiles, when correlated with the four-quadrant brain dominance concept, provides the bases for the creation of a whole brain teaching and learning model (see

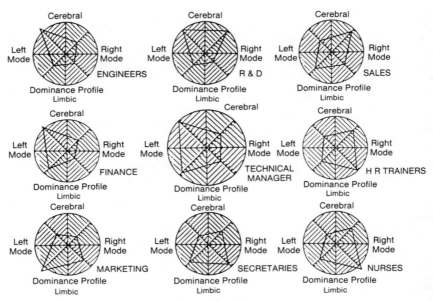

Figure 19-6. Brain dominance profiles in selected occupations.

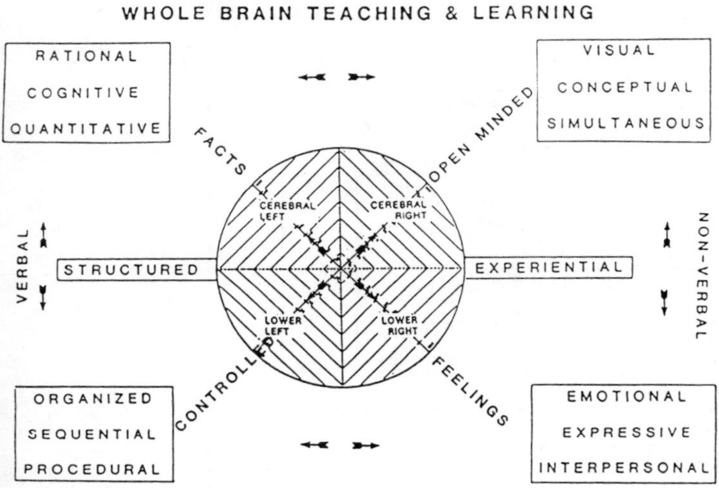

WHOLE BRAIN TEACHING & LEARNING

Figure 19-7. Teaching and learning design model.

Fig. 19-7). Incorporated into the metaphoric model are key descriptors that differentiate each quadrant from the others in terms of major teaching and learning modes, procedures, and processes. The arrows indicate the iterative nature of the process as it correlates with the physiology of the interconnected brain.

It is essential to consider the uniqueness of the learning group when designing educational programs for that group. Using the model as a diagnostic tool it is possible to gain critical understanding of the preferences of a particular occupational group or organization so as to better design the learning program to meet that unique requirement.

Whole Brain Learning

Direct experience with several specific workshops involving the participation of several thousand people clearly indicates that the most successful approach to learning, design, and delivery is to create a "whole brain" experience for a "composite whole brain" learning group. This is done by designing the learning experience to dynamically move back and forth in its delivery of each key learning point to equally distribute the learning across all four quadrants of the model.

Moving back and forth helps ensure that participants with different interests are able to learn effectively and consistently. The nature and extent of these different interests are summarized in Fig. 19-8. Shown are key descriptors of each quadrant of the whole brain model, typical professions that have strong preferences in those quadrants, typical types of individuals that choose those professions, and examples of specialized areas of interest of those individuals.

Learning Design and Delivery

When the unique learning styles associated with each quadrant are added to these profound differences, it becomes clear that traditional approaches to design and

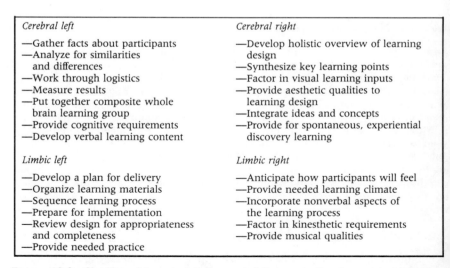

Figure 19-8. Learner interest factors.

delivery fall short of desired results when dealing with a composite group. Using the model as a guide, it is possible to design a learning module, a workshop, or an entire course.

Figure 19-9 is a four-quadrant checklist that shows the distribution of key design and delivery elements that need to be factored into the kind of whole brain approach required for a composite learning group. Given that there is a learning

Cerebral left	Cerebral right
—Gather facts about participants —Analyze for similarities and differences —Work through logistics —Measure results —Put together composite whole brain learning group —Provide cognitive requirements —Develop verbal learning content	—Develop holistic overview of learning design —Synthesize key learning points —Factor in visual learning inputs —Provide aesthetic qualities to learning design —Integrate ideas and concepts —Provide for spontaneous, experiential discovery learning
Limbic left	Limbic right
—Develop a plan for delivery —Organize learning materials —Sequence learning process —Prepare for implementation —Review design for appropriateness and completeness —Provide needed practice	—Anticipate how participants will feel —Provide needed learning climate —Incorporate nonverbal aspects of the learning process —Factor in kinesthetic requirements —Provide musical qualities

Figure 19-9. Checklist of important design and delivery aspects of a successful training program.

need, the best way to take advantage of this whole brain approach is to create a composite whole brain learning group by selecting the learners to represent all the learning styles contained in the whole brain model. This is done by choosing people with brain dominances that range across the complete brain dominance spectrum. Putting together multifunctional groups composed of both males and females is a good way of getting started. This is of course not the way that most organizations deal with their training and development activities. However, when the advantages of this process are understood, many organizations have been willing to change the culture so that learning groups can be formed this way.

Benefits

The results are spectacular in a number of different ways.

1. The participants find this heterogeneous learning group much more interesting than the typical homogeneous learning group.
2. The learning group, by reason of the differences contained in it, can now become part of the learning resource. This allows for discovery learning to take place through interaction of the learners.
3. The composite whole brain learning group forces the design of the learning experience to also be whole brain. This means that each key learning point must be considered from the perspective of each discrete quadrant.
4. The whole brain learning group and the whole brain design require a very different delivery than traditional approaches. The workshop leaders or trainers involved must now factor the uniqueness of learners and the specialized delivery of the material into their teaching.

Design and Delivery Diagnosis

Using the models and exhibits already shown, it is possible to diagnose an existing workshop or module of a workshop to determine the degree to which its design and delivery is appropriate to the subject matter and the learning group involved. Experience has shown that most learning designs are greatly suboptimized in this respect. Through diagnosis, it is possible to identify the principal elements of design and delivery that fall short of a balanced design, and by reason of identification provide direction for taking correcting action.

When diagnosing an existing program or designing a new learning experience, it is important to review both the thinking style preferences of the participants as well as thinking style demands posed by the learning design. Figure 19-10 shows the distribution of thinking styles and modes in the whole brain model. First, consider the learning group and check off the thinking styles you assume they prefer. Second, review the learning design and circle the thinking style that the program requires. By comparing the checks with the circles, you can get a rough profile of each. Analysis of the similarities and differences will give important clues. When starting from scratch to design a learning experience, either an individual module or an entire workshop, it is possible to accelerate the process by using the checklist worksheet in Fig. 19-9.

Conclusion

After working with these concepts for the past 10 years, I have concluded that there is a great deal to gain and almost nothing to lose through their application to

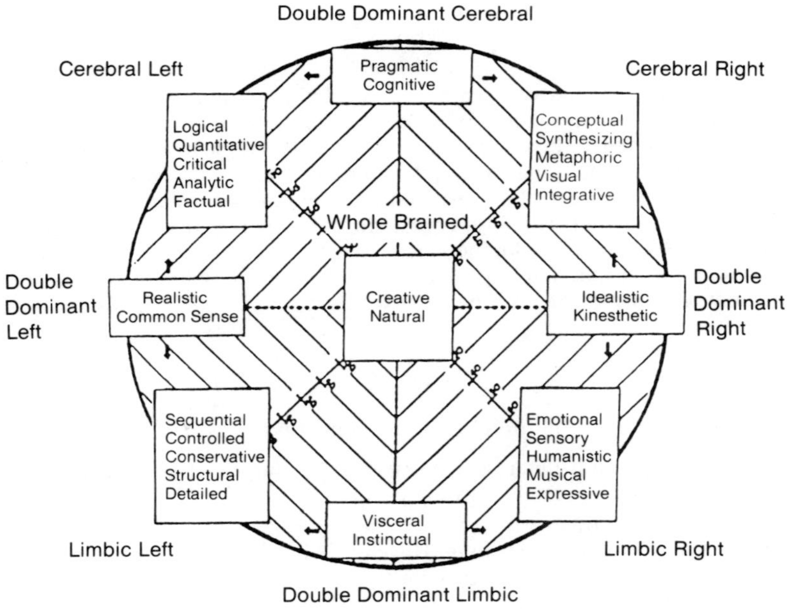

Figure 19-10. Thinking styles.

—Provides design and delivery appropriate to all learning styles.
—Improves correlation of learning outcomes with course objectives.
—More fun for participants and trainers.
—More impactful and longer-lasting.
—Learning groups more interesting.
—Provides a greater opportunity for experiential and discovery learning.
—Stimulates and exercises multiple intelligences.
—Provides the basis of greater self-understanding.
—Enhances participants' communications skills.
—Reduces learning fatigue.
—Provides the basis for greater understanding of participants' similarities and differences.
—Makes learning more exciting.
—Provides development opportunities for the trainers and facilitators.
—Provides the basis for assembling a more diversified, balanced learning group.
—Positively enhances male and female differences.
—Minimizes or eliminates age as a consideration.
—Opens up new developmental opportunities.
—Provides the basis for training in "untrainable" areas, i.e., creativity.
—Enhances previous learnings and job experiences through its organizing principles.
—Increases likelihood of consistent learning outcomes.
—Reveals the roots of personal boredom, confusion, and procrastination.
—Stimulates significant personal action after the training experience.

Figure 19-11. A summary of ways that brain dominance technology can contribute to training effectiveness.

HRD-related work. The assumptions, the concepts, and the methodologies all enhance the design and delivery of learning to unique individuals. Extensive experiences in many companies, with many occupations, in many subject areas, under highly differing circumstances have all resulted in positive outcomes. Of special significance to all of us in the HRD profession is that not a single person who has designed and led programs based on these concepts wants to return to the traditional modes. These concepts work to the advantage not only of the learner but also of the trainer.

Section 3

Media and Methods

20
Job Training

Alice Bird McCord

Alice Bird McCord is Senior Vice President, Planning and Research, for the National Retail Merchants Association in New York. Her prior experiences include positions as personnel director and director of executive recruitment and development in two divisions of the May Department Stores Company. Prior to this she was director of training and development with a major New York City retailer. In addition to positions in the retailing personnel field she has experience in consulting, serving as manager, personnel and organizational consulting, with a major international consulting firm. She is a member of a number of professional organizations including ASTD, is an associate of the American Psychological Association, and was a contributor to the second edition of the Training and Development Handbook. She has a B.S. degree from New York University and an M.A. from Columbia University.

More persons have gone through job training programs than through any other training program. Job training is concerned with performance rather than with subject matter; persons learn to perform the tasks required on the job in the actual job setting under the guidance of a supervisor. Techniques of job training are useful in teaching skills in numerous organizational and educational settings: at the work station, in the shop, at the desk, or in the laboratory. Regardless of the level of the learner, job training offers an equal opportunity and an equal chance to learn for all learners, since it is concerned only with what an individual does on the job. Techniques of job training reduce frustration by giving the individual an opportunity to perform actual tasks as quickly as possible and help reduce alienation of new employees by training in the actual work environment, using supervisors and peers in the instructional process.

On the job, learning takes place continuously, regardless of whether or not there is a planned training program or a supervisor who assumes responsibility for training. Learning occurs as the result of interaction between coworkers, dealing with superiors and subordinates, and through feedback, whether positive or negative.

Few, if any, companies admit that they do not use on-the-job training. Yet, in many companies job training means that there is no formalized program and employees are left to learn their jobs in whatever way they can: working along with a helpful fellow employee, applying what they have learned elsewhere to the new job situation, or modifying or improving their performance through negative feedback. This is true in large organizations as well as in small ones.

In this chapter, a distinction is made between informal, unorganized job training, usually known as "on-the-job" training (OJT) and formal, organized job training that occurs in the work setting. In OJT, the learning is predominantly opportunistic, with the skills or knowledge coming from a supervisor, from an experienced worker, or by discovery. Job training, or formal, organized, and directed training in the work setting, is the primary concern of this chapter and the training professional. It received major impetus during World War II from the wide use of job instruction training (JIT) and related methods as part of the "Training within Industry" (TWI) program instituted to train wartime production workers, as will be discussed later.

Regardless of whether or not a formal training program exists, behaviors that are reinforced in the work environment are more important in the individual's performance than are those acquired in formal training programs. The work group, the supervisor's expectations, and the feedback and "reward system" all interact to influence the way in which an individual performs.

Job training, when carefully planned, is an organized method of training, designed to help an employee, through supervised instruction, learn skills while actually working in an assigned job. Job training may be designed to bring a beginning student or employee from entry level to mastery, to overcome skill deficiencies, to strengthen a formal training program, and to upgrade an employee's skill for job enlargement or advancement. It can be used with semiskilled and skilled workers, as well as with persons in technical, staff, and management positions.

OJT and JIT

Two commonly used methods of job training are OJT (on-the-job training) and JIT (job instruction training). Although similar in intent, the focus is different. In OJT, employees are expected to learn while doing the job under the watchful eye of a supervisor or an experienced worker. JIT was originally developed for use with World War II production workers and is based on a mechanical step procedure requiring the instructor or teacher to present the material in an orderly, disciplined manner. It is most frequently used in teaching a motor skill.

Benefits of Job Training

The new employee learns through doing the job, experiencing the same problems that will be faced daily in the job. Learners are permitted to work at their own speed, thereby gaining confidence and a sense of productiveness. If they learn in the actual work environment, an understanding of the job and the opportunity to correct errors before they become established is assured. By receiving reinforcement from the supervisor, the superior-subordinate relationship is strengthened.

When job training is related to the specific needs of an individual or group, it should:

- Help the new employee to be assimilated more quickly into the organization
- Give the employee a sense of satisfaction in performing the new job
- Indicate that the company has a stake in the new employee's career

The responsibility for job training gives the supervisor understanding of the work done by subordinates, provides the opportunity to identify problems or discrepancies in job methods and procedures, and encourages the development of leadership skills. Rather than decreasing the role of the training department, job training is a means through which the training staff can maintain centralized coordination of all training. In addition, the development of job descriptions, standard procedures, and manualized job instruction is a part of the job training system.

Background of Job Training

Vocational training began in the earliest civilization when parents gave job instruction to their children. Apprenticeship training can be traced to ancient times. It was brought to the American colonies from western Europe. Later, when the growth of the factory system gave rise to tyrannical bosses, it became evident that better methods of industrial training were needed. Gradually, as a result of the influence of Frederick Taylor in the early 1900s, developments in education and psychology, and what had been learned during World War I, direction shifted from driving workers to produce to viewing the supervisor's role as one of obtaining production through people.

Influence of Frederick W. Taylor.   The major thrust of Taylor's work was to increase production. By talking with managers and workers, he discovered that managers often did not know what they wanted from workers and that workers, in turn, did not know what managers wanted. Taylor studied methods and equipment and analyzed the steps important in doing a job. He divided the work into simple, elementary movements and discarded the ones he considered useless. Then, by observing the fastest and most skilled worker and by using a stopwatch, he recorded each motion. Thus, through mathematical calculations, he could determine the proper length of time required to do almost any job. This process enabled him to establish standards for both quality and quantity.

Taylor has been criticized as preoccupied with equipment because he considered workers only in terms of skill and production. However, Taylor placed emphasis on standardization and development of superior methods, and he believed that it was possible, scientifically, to select and train workers. He developed what was probably the first training aid, an instruction (or method) card which gave a worker each specific part of the job to be performed together with the time required for each step or operation.

Influence of Educators and Psychologists.   Johann Friedrich Herbart, a nineteenth century German psychologist, sought to prove that education is a science. In teaching that the student's learning is the result of the teacher's instruction, he influenced educational methods in the United States. Herbart believed that the mind receives and assimilates new ideas in a certain pattern. Therefore, any subject might be presented to the student according to a standard format. He outlined four steps of instruction in the learning process:[1]

Clearness	Analysis and synthesis
Association	The ability to build on what is already known

| System | Organizing new information with what is already known |
| Method | Practice |

A number of American educators also influenced the development of industrial training methods. Among these were Horace Mann, who taught that useful knowledge was more important than philosophic wisdom, and John Dewey, who saw learning as an orderly process and placed emphasis on practical experience.

Edward Thorndike, experimenting with animals, developed two fundamental laws of learning: (1) the law of habit formation, which states that the right movements can be put in the proper sequence and practiced until they become routine, and (2) the law of effect, which states that a response is strengthened when a task is performed correctly, while annoying or less satisfying responses are weakened.[2]

These persons and others contributed to the development of training methods which use procedural steps to condition the learner by presenting one step at a time, demonstrating and explaining it until it is done correctly.

Training in World War I. The Emergency Fleet Corporation of the U.S. Shipping Board at the beginning of World War I needed 450,000 additional workers. A former vocational instructor of the Massachusetts State Board of Education, Charles R. (Skipper) Allen, aided by his group in the Emergency Fleet Corporation, developed a method to train shipbuilders. It was based on Herbart's four steps of instruction. Allen named these:

Preparation	Show
Presentation	Tell
Application	Do
Inspection	Check

From Allen's findings, and those of the Army during World War I, the following principles were developed as the basis for industrial training:

- Training should be done within industry.
- Training should be done by supervisors. (The ability to instruct is an important part of the supervisor's job.)
- Supervisors should be trained in how to instruct.
- The best group size for training is 9 to 11 people.
- The preparation of a job breakdown is an important step before training.
- Break-in time is reduced when training is done on the job.
- When given personal attention in training, the worker develops a feeling of loyalty.

New meaning was given to training and its role in helping management solve its production problems. Advances in training were achieved as programs that solved production problems for both supervisors and workers were developed. Learning by doing resulted in significant savings of training time. Ways of measuring and evaluating training resulted.

Although Allen received recognition for his work and books on how to instruct appeared during the twenties and thirties, not until the need for defense production became serious in 1940 were steps taken to develop a method of instruction.

Development of Job Training

In 1940, the need for trained defense workers caught American industry off guard. The World War II emergency called for shortcuts in assimilating new recruits into the nation's work force.

Establishment of Training within Industry

Training within Industry (TWI), an advisory service formed by the National Defense Advisory Commission, was given the responsibility for finding ways to help contractors achieve maximum utilization of manpower resources. As a result, TWI developed three training programs designed to solve production problems. All were developed because of demands for assistance with real needs, all were tried out in numerous situations and settings, and all were a merging of ideas among numerous people.

The first bulletin issued by TWI, on September 24, 1940, announced: "The underlying purpose of this activity is to assist defense industries to meet their manpower needs by training within industry each worker to make the fullest use of his best skill up to the maximum of his individual ability." The programs that TWI developed tended to serve two purposes: they solved new or recurring production problems, and they gave a sense of satisfaction to supervisors who participated. In all, three job programs were developed, based on the same fundamentals. Each was:

1. Subjected to extensive tryouts and revisions to make it simple and practical, using shop rather than theoretical terms.

2. Developed to help supervisors solve their own problems.

3. Standardized so that large numbers of persons could be reached—a task which otherwise might have been impossible. (Standardized materials were developed in the form of manuals which frequently directed the instructor to illustrate major points on a blackboard. Other audiovisual devices had been considered and discarded because in 1940 they were not readily available in most organizations.)

4. Based on learning by doing, using actual case problems. Each case involved instruction, action, drill, improvement, training, and checking. (Of these, drill became the most important. "What to do" is not enough. Only when people are drilled in "how to do it" does action result.)[3]

5. Founded on "multiplier principles": training persons who, in turn, could train others.

6. Dependent upon creating the proper atmosphere by setting a tone of informality. (Terms such as "class," "teacher," and "student" were avoided. Instead, "meeting," "instructor," and "learner" or "worker" were used.)

7. Planned for 10 persons in five 2-hour sessions, scheduled witin a 2-week period—on company time and at company expense.

The TWI Policy. The three fundamental principles of TWI were that it (1) convinced management that training is an everyday operating tool, (2) helped industry to instruct its supervisors, and (3) served as a clearinghouse of information on ways industry could meet production problems through training.

During the first year of operation, TWI acted primarily as an advisory service to defense contractors. By its second year of operation, it had shifted its emphasis, influencing industry to do its own instruction through supervisory training and improvement.

Much of the credit for the industrial job training during World War II was rightfully given to the work done by Training within Industry. But TWI did far more than enable American industry to meet its wartime production needs. New ideas and new ways of viewing the human side of an organization resulted. Management, preoccupied with production needs, suddenly became aware of the relationship between the development of products and the development of the people who did the work.

One of the most critical manpower shortages was for skilled lens grinders and polishers. Fulfilling its role as an advisory service, TWI held a conference with representatives from major lens-grinding and precision instruments plants. Twenty separate jobs were involved in grinding, and it was considered necessary for each operator to learn all of these, requiring approximately 5 full years.

The outcome of the conference was a recommendation to upgrade the present workers in precision optical work to the most highly skilled jobs and to break in new workers on one simple job. This required that a number of jobs and operations be broken down, job specifications written, and a training program developed.

In breaking down each part of the job, a few critical points were identified. Since these areas were the keys to good work, they were called "key points." They later became the basis for the job breakdown. In developing a lens-grinding program, the instruction steps developed by C. R. Allen during World War I were expanded to a seven-step method of instruction:

1. Show workers how to do it.

2. Explain key points.

3. Let them watch you do it again.

4. Let them do the simple parts of the job.

5. Help them do the whole job.

6. Let them do the whole job—but watch them.

7. Put them on their own.

Because of the influence of Allen and Taylor, as well as the fact that most wartime jobs required primarily motor skills, the focus in job training was concerned with breaking down each step of the job into separate steps, and with repetitive practice and drill.

Major Points of JIT

Job Breakdown.   The TWI manual required that before instructors developed the job breakdown in the first JIT session, they explain, verbally, how to tie a fire underwriter's knot. Since tying this knot is somewhat complicated and since few, if any, of the participants knew how to do it, the point was apparent: simply telling someone how to do a job is not enough. This was an appropriate lead-in to having the group prepare a job breakdown (see Fig. 20-1) considered essential to JIT. (The underwriter's knot is so named because of its specification in insurance policies. It is used in most electrical fixtures and appliances, and it helps relieve the strain on wire connections.) In adapting the program to peacetime use, other tasks, not widely known to participants, such as how to make a sign writer's cup, were often used.

SESSION OUTLINE

Timetable 5. Break down the fire underwriters' knot.   References

    a. Here's a quick simple way to make a breakdown.

    b. Explain that here is what you did to get fire underwriters' knot
        clear in your mind before instructing.

        NOTE: Pass out blank Breakdown Sheets and explain headings,
        important steps, and key points.

    c. Take wire and go to board.

        +Write down headings PART and OPERATION. FILL in.

        +Do the first important step, then write it on the board.

        +Do the second important step, write it down, and so on through.

        +Then tie the knot again, step by step, bringing out each key point.

        +Ask yourself aloud the three questions for each step and answer
        them yourself.

    d. Establish the breakdown on the board in numbered steps as follows:

Part: Twisted Lamp Cord	Operation: Tie Fire Underwriters' Knot
Important Steps	Key Points
(1) Untwist and straighten	6 inches
(2) Make r.h. loop	in front of main strand
(3) Make l.h. loop	pull toward you
	under stub
	behind main strand
(4) Put end through loop	
(5) Pull taut	end even,
	knot snug

WORK FROM THIS OUTLINE–DON'T TRUST TO MEMORY

Figure 20-1. Session outline.

    The instructor or supervisor prepared a job breakdown on the job while watching an experienced worker perform each step of the job. The preparation of the breakdown ensured that supervisors covered all the steps in the job, helped them organize their thinking so that they introduced each step of the operation in the right sequence, and required that they become familiar with all aspects of the job, particularly the mechanical operations, with which they may have had little or no previous experience. As they observed each step, they recorded it on a breakdown, sometimes called a blueprint (see Fig. 20-2). (A well-written job breakdown should be detailed enough to serve as a step-by-step procedure so that an individual, unfamiliar with the job, can perform each step satisfactorily.) The operation was recorded in a single, brief statement, for example, "Adjust the tension."

JOB BREAKDOWN SHEET FOR TRAINING PURPOSES

DEPARTMENT _Lens Grinding_ JOB _Centering_
BREAKDOWN MADE BY _Joseph Nelson_ DATE _Sept. 2, 1941_

IMPORTANT STEPS (WHAT TO DO) A logical segment of the operation, when something happens to advance the work	KEY POINTS (HOW TO DO IT) Anything that may: Make or break the job Injure the worker Make the work easier to do
1. Place piece on plate against regulating wheel	Knack - don't catch on wheel
2. Lower level wheel	Hold at end of stroke (count 1, 2, 3, 4) Slow feed. Watch - no oval grinding
3. Raise lever - release	
4. Gauge pieces periodically	More often as approach toleranœ
5. Readjust regulating wheel as required	Watch - no backlash
6. Repeat above until finished	

Figure 20-2. Job breakdown sheet for training purposes.

Next, the key point was recorded. This was the part of a step that was the "key" to doing it correctly—to making it easier to perform. Instructors were taught to ask three questions in determining the key points: Is there anything in the step that will make or break the job? Hurt the worker? Make the work easier to do? Key points did not include every possible thing that might be done. The purpose of the list was to make certain that the supervisor did not overlook the key points which were crucial in training a new worker. Knowing what the key points were and being able

HOW TO GET READY TO INSTRUCT

Have a Time Table—
how much skill you expect him to have, and how soon.

Break Down the Job—
list principal steps.
pick out the key points.

Have Everything Ready—
the right equipment, materials, and supplies.

Have the Work Place Properly Arranged—
just as the worker will be expected to keep it.

Job Instructor Training

WAR MANPOWER COMMISSION
BUREAU OF TRAINING
TRAINING WITHIN INDUSTRY

KEEP THIS CARD HANDY
16—26793-4   GPO

HOW TO INSTRUCT

Step 1—Prepare the Worker
Put him at ease.
Find out what he already knows about the job.
Get him interested in learning job.
Place in correct position.

Step 2—Present the Operation
Tell, Show, Illustrate, and Question carefully and patiently.
Stress key points.
Instruct clearly and completely, taking up one point at a time—but no more than he can master.

Step 3—Try Out Performance
Test him by having him perform job.
Have him *tell* and *show* you; have him explain key points.
Ask questions and correct errors.
Continue until you know *HE* knows.

Step 4—Follow Up
Put him on his own.   Designate to whom he goes for help.
Check frequently.   Encourage questions.   Get him to look for key points as he progresses.
Taper off extra coaching and close follow-up.
16—26793-3

If Worker Hasn't Learned, the Instructor Hasn't Taught

Figure 20-3. Job instruction card.

to identify them quickly constituted one of the most important aspects of the job instruction process. For example, when using a knife, a key point is "Cut away from you."

The Four Basic Steps.   The four steps in a job instruction pocket card format were first used by C.R. Allen during the 1920s. The four steps of "How to Instruct," introduced during session I, appeared on one side of the card, and the four-step method on "How to Get Ready to Instruct," introduced during session II, appeared on the reverse side of the card (see Fig. 20-3).

On-the-Job Training (OJT)

On-the-job training is the most common method of training. Like JIT it permits the employee to learn new skills and behaviors through observation and guided practice while working "on-the-job."

The major difference between OJT and JIT is that in OJT the learner generally works under the guidance of someone actually performing the job. Where JIT is best used in teaching motor skills, OJT is best suited to jobs requiring mastery of several behaviors and skills such as in sales, customer contact, office and clerical jobs, and supervisory positions. OJT may merely consist of having an employee learn a job by observing an experienced employee at work. It may also be used to give an experienced employee an opportunity to gain a broad, overall picture of the operation by becoming familiar with other jobs as well as to ensure that an adequate number of persons are trained who are able to perform various jobs.

The danger in OJT occurs when the program is completely unstructured and the responsibility for training is not assigned to someone knowledgeable in instructing and coaching. In this case, it is unlikely that OJT will be successful, and the

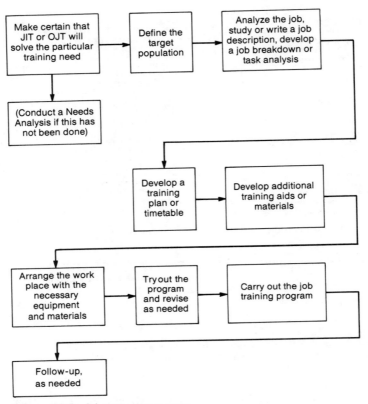

Figure 20-4. Job instruction process.

likelihood is increased that the learner will acquire incorrect or undesirable behavior or skills. The key to successful OJT is in the selection of the person who can establish a warm, friendly feeling with new employees.

Developing the JIT Program

The primary reason for using job training is to enable new workers to become fully productive as quickly as possible. Preliminary planning and analysis is considered the most important part of the job instruction process (see Fig. 20-4).

Conduct the Needs Analysis

A needs analysis is generally used to diagnose performance deficiencies of employees presently on the job. Before conducting any training, it is important to consider the level of competency of the learners. It is relatively easy to determine the competency of current employees since their present job performance can be measured. This is done through conducting a needs analysis. However, in training new hires assumptions need to be made about their learning needs by considering the transfer of previous experience and education. This is often referred to as defining the target population.

A number of short, easy diagnostic methods can be used to assess training needs and indicate whether or not job instruction is the best training method. Since job training is performance based, most of the diagnostic methods suggested identify where standards of performance are being met. These are best suited in determining training needs for skilled and semiskilled workers since output is often more difficult to measure in office, service, and supervisory positions. In conducting a needs analysis, select the method(s) which is (are) most closely related to the position. For example, in a highly standardized job where there are measurable units of output, use methods which measure productivity. In positions where output is difficult to measure and standards of performance may not exist, observational measures are probably more useful.

Productivity and Performance Measures. Operational audits are generally used when it is beneficial to measure costs and indicate where improvement in performance would have the greatest payoff. An audit of any of the following will measure present output and identify where performance can be improved:

- Labor costs
- Output per employee
- Quality of units produced
- Waste and scrap
- Piecework earnings
- Ratio of salary to sales, or units of sales per salesperson
- Commission earnings

Reviewing personnel records will often give an indication of training needs. Among these are:

- Performance appraisal system
- Grievances
- Absenteeism and tardiness
- Disciplinary actions
- Accidents
- Employee turnover by position or department

Observational Measures. Personal observations by supervisors or persons skilled in observational techniques can be an effective way to determine training needs.

- Personal observations (i.e., observing the way employees perform their jobs); where a large number of employees are involved, a sample may be used. Observation may be continuous over a period of time or at various times of day for a specified work period.
- Personnel inventory, forced choice, or ranking of individuals by supervisors.
- A checklist of job behaviors observed by the supervisor.

Surveying Employees. One of the easiest, yet a seldom used method, is to ask employees what they believe their training needs are. Employees who have completed their training period yet are relatively new to the job are often articulate in expressing their needs.

- Questionnaires or other survey methods particularly designed for the purpose of assessing training needs may be among the least expensive techniques. (When attitude surveys are used and have not been specifically designed for this purposed, skilled analysis is required to determine training needs.)
- Training needs checklists (employees are asked to check off from a list their own individual training needs).
- Formal interviews.
- Group interviews (ask employees as a group to list the problems they are currently faced with).
- Critical incident (what situations make for significant differences in the ways jobs are; these can be gathered by talking with supervisors to determine the outstanding and ineffective behaviors in job performance).

Diagnostic and Situational Measures. These are primarily used for supervisory and managerial personnel and are best when used in connection with human resource planning.

- Position descriptions
- Skills inventory
- Replacement charts (where there is a lack of promotable individuals at any job level, the reason is often lack of training to prepare people for the next job level)
- Annual personnel inventory
- Periodically administered achievement tests (these must be relevant and reliable and must meet validity requirements)

Concerns of Management. When used in connection with other information, needs expressed by management can be an effective aid in determining needs and can help involve management in the training process. However, where an expressed concern of management is hurriedly responded to without thorough and careful analysis, it is unlikely that there will be any lasting result.

Define the Target Population

It is often assumed that all individuals entering a job training program are at the same level of competency or, if newly hired, are all inexperienced. Since it is unlikely that either of these is the case, it is important to define the population in order to determine the level of knowledge or skills of learners in relation to the standards of performance required in the job.

Standards required in the job

Job training should make up this gap

Entry level (where the learners or employees are prior to entering the program)

By defining the target population, questions such as: Who are the learners? What are their characteristics? What experiences do they bring with them? can be

1. Job requirements (state in terms of skill, previous job experience, education, or training)_____

_____

_____

2. What are the trainees expected to know or be able to do at the time they enter training?

_____

_____

3. Age (what is the age range of persons who will be going through the program? How will life experience affect learning?)_____

_____

_____

4. What is the level of motivation (what's in it for them; . . . acquire the basic skills to perform the job; advance to a higher skill level?) _____

_____

_____

_____

Figure 20-5. Form for determining the target population.

answered. This information can be obtained in large part through examining the personnel records. A form such as that shown in Fig. 20-5 can be used.

Analyze the Job

The third and most important step is that of analyzing the job. First, study the job description, or write one if it does not exist. Although the job description does not serve as the basis for the program content—or even show how to perform the job—it serves an important function since it lists the major tasks performed in a job, the conditions under which they are performed, and any special training or education required. It also helps get agreement on the responsibilities of the job and the standards of performance. A job description may simply be a paragraph describing the activities of the job (see Fig. 20-6).

Job descriptions for skilled jobs used for wage classification purposes may contain more detail. However, job descriptions are never detailed enough to enable

POSITION: Senior Statistical Clerk
REPORTS TO: Statistical Department Manager

Under general supervision, performs routine statistical clerical work involving collection, compilation, and verification of statistical data. Prepares and presents data in such forms as tables and diagrams. The individual should possess knowledge of the subject matter and with the methods so that minimal supervision is necessary. The position does not require knowledge of advanced statistics, ability to interpret data, or the use of judgment in meeting new problems.

Figure 20-6. Simple job description.

an employee to perform a job or to use for training purposes, since they do not break down each task and subtask.

Prepare the Job Breakdown

For simple tasks requiring no more than five or six different operations, the job breakdown (or blueprint) developed for the TWI programs may be used. It is generally prepared by the supervisor or training instructor while watching an experienced worker perform each step. It includes two columns, Important Steps and Key Points. A step is a significant action which advances the task or operation toward completion.

The key point indicates the "key" to the right way of doing a step. Key points are:

- Hazards or cautions about safety
- Factors which make or break the action
- Pointers which make the job easier to do—knacks, tricks, additional bits of information, special timing

Examples

Hazard.   When using a knife, a key point is to "cut away from you."

Tolerance Fermentation.   In preparing bread dough, there is, among others, a key point—fermentation tolerance. The gassing power of the yeast has ripened the dough structure to the optimum.

Feel.   When putting a micrometer on a piece of stock, the key point is "how tight"—a matter of feel.

Knack.   When riveting, it is important to know when to remove the pneumatic riveter. The key point is to listen. The sound will change when the pieces are solidly together.

Prepare the Task Analysis

In jobs requiring more complex skills, a task analysis should be developed which contains more detail than the job breakdown. It describes what the individual does in performing each action of each task and subtask. (A task is a group of related actions or activities performed in close sequence and required for the completion of a work objective.) For example, in learning to operate a drill press, there are a number of tasks which must be completed before the machine can be operated. The learning objective might be: to make the necessary adjustments before operating the drill press. The tasks are:

- Secure the work firmly.
- Fasten the cutting tools in the spindle.
- Change the spindle speed for the particular job.
- Center the work in position under the drill.
- Adjust the stop for the depth of the hole to be drilled.

The task analysis may also state the standards or criteria of each task and the conditions under which it is performed and may indicate time or performance standards. There is no rigid format that must be followed, and with a little experience, the supervisor or instructor can probably develop a format best suited to the particular job.

One way of developing the task analysis is to simply list all the tasks which occur in a particular job. A person doing the task analysis who is familiar with the job can probably list most of these. Next, these tasks are ranked as nearly as possibly in the order in which they are performed. Some tasks are far more important to successful job performance than are others and therefore should receive greater attention. For example, being able to bring a sale to a satisfactory close is the most critical task in a sales job. If the salesperson can perform every other task but is unable to close the sale, he or she will not be a successful salesperson.

It is also helpful to estimate just how difficult each of the tasks and subtasks is for the learner. It is quite probable that the learner will already be able to perform some or many of the tasks required. It is helpful to estimate the learner's ability to ensure that adequate attention will be given to new material and that known procedures are not overly emphasized.

Even if the person preparing the analysis is totally familiar with the job several workers should be observed and any differences in the way they carry out each task or operation identified. This ensures that no important step is overlooked and gives the supervisor or instructor the opportunity to ask why tasks are done in a certain way. Some firms videotape employees as they are working and then develop the task analysis from what is recorded on tape.

In preparing the task analysis, record each activity or step in the left-hand column under Main Step (see Fig. 20-7). Each Key Point, important in completing the step, is recorded in the next column. Next, indicate any necessary materials, equipment, or tools. It is helpful to include the reason for the task and standards of performance for the job on the task analysis sheet. Standards may be stated in terms of some measurable unit of output.

The task analysis is checked by actually performing the job, following only the instructions given. If a step or point has been omitted or is not entirely clear, it is apparent since the task cannot be completed. A well-designed task analysis should enable someone to perform each step of the process with little—if any—additional instruction.

Develop the Training Timetable or Schedule

In addition to developing the task analysis or job breakdown an additional step is preparing the training timetable specified in the TWI program. Just as the task analysis is the master plan for the content of the training program, the timetable specifies what major topics will be covered with the trainee, indicates what amount of time will be devoted to each major topic, and assigns responsibility for each aspect of training. Formats may be developed to meet the needs of a specific situation. The timetable shown (see Fig. 20-8) is designed to serve as a control that specific training has been covered with each employee.

Job training is based on thorough, adequate planning and preparation. If each of the steps in these phases has been followed, the supervisor or instructor will be ready to begin the process of instruction.

Recent Developments in Job Training

Integrated Training

The mix of skills in any particular job is dependent on the particular job and its level. JIT may be used effectively in unskilled and semiskilled jobs requiring the

TASK ANALYSIS

JOB_____ Baker's Helper _____
TASK_____ Baking Bread _____

Main Step	Key Point	Procedure (Material Equipment, Tools)	Reason	Standards of Performance
Knead dough	Put light coating of flour on hands Flatten dough by curving fingers over dough and pushing down with heel of palm Turn dough one-quarter, fold and push down, repeat process for 8–10 minutes	Mixed dough Flour Flat surface	To keep hands from sticking to dough. Flour added later will coarsen texture	Prepare dough and bake evenly formed loaves of bread
Place dough in lightly greased mixing vats to rise	Turn dough once on greased surface Cover with a cloth Place in warm area 82° until double in size, tolerance fermentation	Cloth	Prevents crust from forming	
Form into shape for baking	Divide dough into 6-inch balls Cover and let rest, 10 minutes Flatten into 10 by 14-inch rectangles Form loaves by rolling dough toward you Break bubbles in surface Seal ends by pushing with side of hand; fold top of dough around sides Cover and let double in bulk, 1 hour		Leaves a smooth crust after baking	
Preheat oven 375°				
Bake for 50 minutes	Crust should be lightly browned			

Figure 20-7. Sample task analysis.

development of simple motor skills and OJT for routine jobs requiring mastery of several skills. Many jobs today require more complex skills, with the acquisition of these skills over an extended period of time. In addition, many jobs require a mix of skills, which may be most easily taught by using integrated training methods. This is particularly true in positions requiring human relations and administrative skills, such as in service, sales, supervisory, and managerial positions. The training

TRAINING TIMETABLE

Employee's Name_____ Department_____

Job Title _____ Date Hired_____

Tasks	Instruction Time	Place of Instruction	Day and Hour of Instruction — Day Hour	Trainee Signs Here	Instructor Signs Here

NOTE: Instructions to Trainee
—Report to place of instruction on time.
—Return your copy of the Training Timetable to your supervisor.
Instructions to Instructor
—Sign this form at the end of each instruction period.

Figure 20-8. Training timetable form.

method selected should parallel as closely as possible the skill requirements of the job. For example, JIT may be a good training method for teaching a simple manual skill, but it would not be very useful in training in human relations skills where visual demonstration, such as role playing, would be a more effective technique. Where higher skill levels and a longer training time is required than JIT or OJT permits, classroom training is often integrated with JIT and OJT as in apprenticeship training.

In selecting methods for job training, the following factors might be considered:

What is the skill mix in the job?

How many persons will be trained for the particular job?

Is a trainer available to develop the program?

What are the differences in experience levels among trainees? Must individual differences be accounted for?

What principles of learning would most likely apply to the trainees?

Vestibule Training. Sometimes it is more feasible to conduct job training away from the actual work situation. Vestibule training is similar to JIT but has the advantage of having employees learn in a specially designed area adjacent to the work setting. This may be more conducive to learning when the work situation is hazardous, where a new employee might disrupt the work of other employees, or when it might be beneficial for the employee to learn certain segments of the job before starting in the work situation.

Programmed On-the-Job Training. A type of programmed training can be used for job training which offers the flexibility of using—or integrating—several methods of training. Programmed OJT is generally used where training is best spaced over an extended period of time, where multiple skills are involved, and where learners should have the opportunity to transfer and apply skills and knowledge to the job before progressing to the next stage. A combination of classroom and OJT can be used to solve a number of job training needs.

Programmed OJT is frequently used with employees in supervisory, managerial, and sales positions, since each of these jobs requires competency in a number of areas. Programmed OJT offers practice on the firing line when the individual is dealing with real problems of increasing complexity while working under supervision. The advantage of this type of OJT is that although highly structured to ensure transfer of classroom training, it is flexible and can be designed to solve a number of training needs.

Advantages of Job Training

JIT and OJT are personalized methods based on person-to-person instruction giving employees a sense of responsibility while learning a job. Job instruction offers a number of advantages to companies not large enough to have a training staff or where the number of persons to be trained does not warrant a formal training program. The advantages offered by JIT over OJT are in the development of motor skills and where massed practice is required in mastering a complex skill.

Shortcomings of Job Instruction

Job instruction tends to focus on the way a job is presently being performed by an experienced employee. Because of this, there may be a tendency to include advanced skills not needed by the beginning worker. It might be better to analyze what the new employee needs to know to perform the job, rather than the way an experienced worker performs it.

The four-step method of instruction assumes that the sequence of steps used in the production process are the same as those which are the best for training. However, the order in which a task is performed may not always be the best order in which to learn it. An additional weakness of the four-step method is its failing to give the reasons why a task is done in a certain way. This deficiency can be adjusted through the choice of training materials and the coaching process.

The greatest weakness of OJT is that it lulls the supervisor—and management—into assuming that, when a worker is left alone to learn a job, this is job instruction. Job training efforts, in which the objective is to improve employee performance, are not successful when:

- Supervisors are not held directly responsible for training and performance
- The content of the program is not related to the requirements or standards of the job and will be reinforced on the job

It is questionable whether or not job training should be used unless it:

- Reduces the learning time to perform a job
- Reduces early turnover among new employees
- Improves the quality of production

- Increases productivity
- Reduces costs
- Produces a material or skill that will be used as a regular part of the job

Use and Application Today

"Why should an organization still use methods of instruction that were developed decades ago?" If automation, product diversification, and decentralization mean that it is difficult or impossible to find large numbers of workers with the required skills, the answer lies in training and in the upgrading of skill levels. Until quite recently, most jobs were fairly static, the training or education needed were obtained early in one's career, and there was no need for acquiring additional skills. Since both the educational or training process and the job remained static, training was an end in iself. Today, factors such as the need for improved productivity, better quality, more skilled workers, increasing obsolescence, and need for new skills have made training and education more important throughout an individual's career.

There is an increased interest in job training, both by companies not having formal training and by larger ones whose experience with centralized and highly structured training may no longer be successful because of decentralization. Job training has also become increasingly important in teaching basic skills to workers in developing countries.

Although job training may take a back seat to more recent sophisticated methods, it remains a vital method when used properly. To be successful, it must be carefully planned, organized, supervised, and controlled. Its objectives should be clear, job-relevant, and stated in behavioral or performance terms. Job standards must be established which are descriptive of the job and competent persons selected and trained to conduct the program.

Although the original work by TWI during World War II contributed greatly to the field of training, perhaps its single top accomplishment was making industry aware of the contributions gained when new employees are trained to perform the skills to make them productive employees.

References

1. *Training within Industry Report, 1940–1945*, War Manpower Commission, Bureau of Training, Washington, DC, September 1945, pp. 185–186.

2. Garrett, Henry E., *Great Experiments in Psychology*, Century Company, New York, 1930, p. 120.

3. *Training within Industry Report 1940–1945*, War Manpower Commission, Bureau of Training, Washington, DC, September 1945, p. xi.

Bibliography

AMA Encyclopedia of Supervisory Training, American Management Association, New York, 1961, pp. 156–174.

Gold, L., "Job Instruction: Four Steps to Success," *Training and Development Journal*, Vol. 35, September 1981, pp. 28–32.

Hess, L., and L. Sperry, "Psychology of the Trainee as Learner," *Personnel Journal*, Vol. 52, September 1973, pp. 781–785.

Kainen, T.L., et al., "On the Job Training and Work Unit Performance," *Training and Development Journal*, Vol. 37, April 1983, pp. 84–87.

Levinson, Harry, *Organizational Diagnosis*, Harvard University Press, Cambridge, 1972.

McGehee, William, and Paul W. Thayer, *Training in Business and Industry*, Wiley, New York, 1961.

Morrison, James H., "Determining Training Needs," *Training and Development Handbook*, ed. by Robert L. Craig, McGraw-Hill, New York, 1976, pp. 9-1–9-17.

Phifer, S.H., "Need for On-the-Job Training," *Training and Development Journal*, Vol. 40, December 1978, pp. 30–34.

Pulich, M.A., "The Basis of On-the-Job Training and Development," *Training and Development Journal*, Vol. 29, January 1984, pp. 7–11.

Tosi, H.L., and R.J. House, "Continuing Management Development beyond the Classroom," *Business Horizons*, Vol. 9, Summer 1966, pp. 91–101.

21
Classroom Instruction

Martin M. Broadwell

Martin M. Broadwell *is President and General Manager of the Center for Management Services, Inc., an Atlanta-based firm specializing in customized, in-house training programs. His activities in the field of consulting have taken him to some 45 countries, as well as most states in this country. He spent nearly 20 years with the Bell System as an engineering manager, serving as both personnel and training director. For 15 years he was a corporate partner of Resources for Education & Management, Inc., where he worked on audiovisual training programs as well as doing in-house training. He is the author of 13 books and over 200 articles in the field of training and supervision and has appeared in two video-based, comprehensive training packages. He has been a guest lecturer at the University of Michigan's Executive Training Center for 25 years. He holds degrees in Physics, Mathematics, and Management.*

Informal studies show that perhaps 95 percent of adult training is done in the classroom, and in many organizations the figure is 100 percent—and all this in the face of such advances as computer-assisted instruction, closed-circuit television, teaching machines, self-instructional devices, and the newer learner-controlled instruction. Why, then, is so much still going on in the classroom? There are many reasons; neither time nor purpose permits listing all of them here, but a few are important. There is an ease and convention about the classroom that does not exist with the other techniques mentioned. It is easy to do classroom instruction, for all one has to do is find a room, assemble an instructor and students, and have all the ingredients for carrying on instruction—not necessarily the *best* instruction, but nevertheless.

This ease of operation is perhaps the main reason for the popularity of the classroom. After all, a "room" can be a storage room, a motel room, a banquet room, a conference room, or a training room. There are other reasons why the classroom is popular. Everybody is exposed to the same message at the same time in the classroom setup. Everyone gets to start and stop at the same time and see the same film at the same time, and they are all there to interact with the same people at the same time. All this can be done with just one instructor, and once a course gets under way, it is possible to continue without revision. (Remember, we are talking about what can be done, not necessarily what *should* be done or what produces the best results.)

A typical classroom has the advantage, too, of being flexible. There is an opportunity for small-group activity, individual work, and total-group work. There can be screens, chalkboards, and easels at the front of the room, as well as models and demonstration gear. Tables can be provided and rearranged, allowing the trainees to work around them or on one side of them, or the tables can be removed and an auditorium arrangement set up. Also, facility costs can be kept to a minimum, with the classroom arrangement, as opposed to many other styles of instruction or techniques. As long as the rooms are occupied to their fullest, the cost per trainee is minimal. When the room is not being used for training, it can be used for other purposes, and this keeps the training costs down.

Disadvantages.   There are disadvantages, however, and we should mention them early in the chapter. While the classroom method of instructing is the most popular with training people, it is also perhaps the most *ill used* of all the possible techniques. Anything that can be put together as easily as we talked about earlier is bound to have drawbacks. The drawback is simple: It is just as easy to have *bad* training in a classroom as it is to have *good* training. It may even be easier. A room, a group of trainees, and an instructor guarantee only a classroom situation, not success. In fact, the ingredients mentioned lend themselves to poor instruction. When there is a teacher who knows the subject and learners who do not, the most natural thing for the instructor to do is to start to tell them what he or she knows. When this happens, and it often does, we have one of the oldest and poorest forms of teaching there is. We can expect very little learning to come from this kind of situation, at least not for long, anyway. There is another drawback which will be covered in more detail later. That is the matter of the difficulty of getting feedback from *all* the learners. When there are 10 to 20 trainees in the room and the instructor has much to cover, before long many of the learners will be at different points, but the instructor may not know it. Unless there is frequent feedback, the instructor will be unable to tell where the learners are. It is difficult to get this feedback when all learners have equal time to listen and respond if they want to. Worse, *there may be no requirement to respond at all.*

We should also know the limitations of the classroom. There are things the classroom can do quite adequately and other things it cannot do. It can provide a situation for getting people together who need to be together to learn. It can provide an atmosphere for learning using the stimulation of an effective instructor and of the students themselves. It can bring together people with like problems and let them share their solutions. It can bring together cross sections with different problems. It can create and encourage furtherance of interactions between people who would never get this type of interaction in other teaching-learning situations. But there are some things the classroom is limited in doing well or at all. It cannot guarantee that 95 percent of the people entering will make 95 percent on a given test, as programmed instruction might be able to do. It does not promise to allow each student to progress at his or her own pace, as self-instruction does. It cannot let each learner follow his or her own learning paths, as computer-assisted instruction can do. It cannot let each student negotiate for specific learning goals, as the open classroom allows. So there are limitations. All we have to do is admit them, work around them, and determine those things the classroom can do best. We also need to avoid trying to make the classroom do things *it does not do very well.*

Elements of the Classroom

Let us look now at the elements that make up any classroom. It is easier to talk about the components of the classroom than about the classroom situation as a whole. The first element is the *instructor*. Not that the instructor is the most important factor, but it is his or her presence that makes the classroom different from most other forms of training. We shall have more to say later about the selection and training of instructors, but in this section we want to see the influence this element has on the learning process.

The instructor brings to the classroom a certain amount of knowledge and experience—usually more than learners possess. If the instructor has not had more actual years of experience, probably he or she has had more *meaningful* experience—experience that is organized and prepared for sharing with others. The students may or may not respect this experience or knowledge, but it is there nevertheless and influences the outcome of the teaching-learning activity. Usually, the instructor is not one of the gang, nor should this be the case. This is not to say that there should be an aloofness, but rather a degree of commitment. There is generally nothing wrong with an instructor's sharing pleasantries with the group, but to overdo this just to get in "good" with the class will usually lessen his or her effectiveness.

Most people like to think of the instructor as being the great leader and producer of learning. We would like to soften that considerably by suggesting that the best way to think of the instructor is as a *facilitator of learning*. It should be the aim of every instructor to provide opportunities for learning, whatever it takes. If it means getting little or no credit for the outcome, then that should not be a consideration. Those instructors who find the classroom a place for an ego trip are *misusing* the students, not helping them.

The Trainees

The next ingredient is the group itself, those trainees who make up the class to be trained. It is this ingredient that makes the training necessary. Without them, there would be no need for either the instructor or the classroom. The best instructors remind themselves of this fact frequently! No two trainees are alike. Each has a different ability to learn, a different desire to learn, a different background to build upon, and a different environment to go to after the training is over. No one technique will work equally well with all the trainees. What motivates one may turn another off. What is exciting to one may bore the other. A learner may try to find excuses for not performing well, such as a dull teacher, a hot room, or hard chairs, and indeed these will hurt learning. Another may ignore these things or even try to defend them. The point is that the learner is an individual, and in a classroom situation it is difficult to be treated as one; it can be done, however, as we shall see later.

The Material

Another ingredient is the material to be taught. The purpose of training is to overcome a deficiency, to produce behavior change. The ideal situation is one in which both the trainer and the trainees know exactly what the deficiencies are and what the specific behavior change is going to be. In other chapters this is spoken of as setting *behavioral objectives*. For our purposes, let us just say that it is best when the learner knows where he or she is going, since this can be of some help in getting

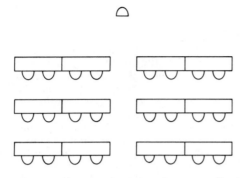

Figure 21-1. Traditional classroom arrangement.

there. Without a set of directions, training is like driving a car blindfolded, waiting for someone else to say when to start, stop, turn, and so on. Many classrooms give this impression, as the learners grope for meaning in the instructor's discussion.

There has been quite a shift in thinking about preparing material over the years. Most training people now recognize that the material is just a means to an end. They no longer talk about "covering material." Rather, they talk about reaching objectives and overcoming deficiencies. But the material to be taught is an integral part of the teaching-learning situation. Material should be selected on the basis of its contribution to the behavior change required, rather than its presence in other, similar courses. The "We've *always* taught this material to this group" syndrome is to be avoided.

The Environment

The last ingredient we need to mention is the *environment*. This includes the tables and chairs and room temperature and ventilation, of course, but much more than these things. It includes also the *climate for learning*, which is difficult to measure but is a very significant part of the learning situation. Do the students feel free to ask a question? Do they feel free to experiment with an answer? Is it punishing to question the teacher? Are there leaders in the group who keep others from participating? These are all part of the environment and need to be taken into consideration when deciding how well the training is going. Poor results may be due not to poor teaching and poor learners or to the selection of the wrong subject matter but rather to the fact that the environment for learning was poor. We shall discuss some things that produce and change the environment later on in this chapter. Let us not forget, however, that the physical things mentioned do affect the learning and have to be considered. Even with the best instructor, it is difficult to concentrate if the room is smoky, hot, or noisy or if the chairs are too hard or too soft.

Classroom Arrangements

Having mentioned the physical aspects of the classroom, let us look now at the various designs for setting up a classroom and see what effect classroom arrangement has on learning. In the *traditional* arrangement (Fig. 21-1), the trainees sit in rows facing the front of the room. They may be at tables which are lined up across the room, or they may be seated theater style without tables. Much training is done in this fashion, and it has some advantages and some disadvantages. For example, it is a very efficient arrangement as far as use of space is concerned. It requires only space for an aisle up the middle. The tables or chairs can come right up to the front of the room within a foot or two of the instructor's equipment and can extend to the back wall. An aisle in the middle allows for projection equipment; an overhead projector can be used without blocking much of the view, and so all the space is accounted for. All the trainees are in full view of the screens and easels and can see the instructor equally well, except for the heads in front of them, of course.

The disadvantages of this arrangement are not as obvious as the advantages. The traditional arrangement is essentially teacher-oriented, with the teacher completely in control. The likelihood that the learners will voluntarily respond is small, and the possibility that they will talk and exchange ideas with one another is even smaller. When interactions do occur, they are likely to be between the teacher and an individual student. When there is a series of exchanges, they usually go from teacher to student to another student to teacher to still another student, and so on, with the instructor being the focal point all the time. The instructor also can determine the direction of the discussion by choosing to respond to a certain question or statement or to let it drop. New instructors tend to like this approach because it gives them some security and makes up for a lack of confidence.

Another arrangement may be called the *chevron* design (Fig. 21-2). This is a variation on the traditional arrangement in which the tables are moved back slightly down the middle at an angle so that the students can see one another as well as the instructor. This arrangement is to be preferred over the traditional one because it produces much more voluntary responding from the trainees. There is still the advantage of being able to see the front visuals and the instructor, there is still the aisle for projection equipment, and there is still a strong element of control available to the instructor, though perhaps this is less obvious than in the traditional arrangement. Informal studies indicate that the flow of conversation is across the aisle and that the learners tend to talk to the people they can see, rather than the ones behind them.

This matter of visibility is important in the classroom because whatever arrangement the instructor chooses will result in the learners' either being able to see the front of the room well, and fellow students not so well, or being able to see one another well, but not the front of the room. In the *circle* arrangement (Fig. 21-3) nearly half of the group cannot see the front of the room without moving their

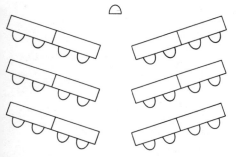

Figure 21-2. Chevron classroom arrangement.

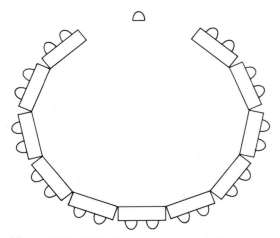

Figure 21-3. Circle classroom arrangement.

chairs and/or tables. A good compromise is the *U-shaped* arrangement (Fig. 21-4), which allows the learners to see one another fairly well and at least the center of the front very well. This limits the use of the front of the room to the center because the sides are obscured by students. Another problem with this arrangement is that the students along each edge of the U cannot see the others in that row, and so they tend to talk across the opening. The trainees at the back tend to interact more with the instructor than with the other trainees. A *V-shaped* arrangement (Fig. 21-5) makes more of the front of the room available, but the students see less of one another. In this arrangement, there are fewer people across the back and more down each side, which conserves space across the room. Obviously, the circle and the U- and V-shaped arrangements are the least efficient in terms of use of space, since the entire center is generally unused.

Psychology of Design

Several things are obvious in a discussion of classroom arrangement. First, there is no perfect system for all training needs. Next, how they are seated makes a

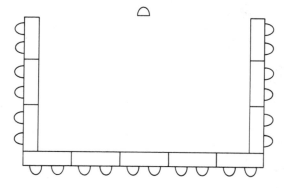

Figure 21-4. U-shaped classroom arrangement.

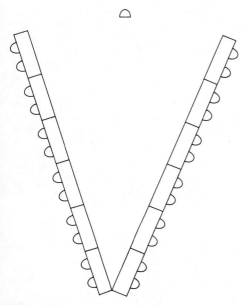

Figure 21-5. V-shaped classroom arrangement.

difference *to the learners* in terms of whom they talk to, how they feel about the instructor's role, and how well they can see the visuals. It should also be obvious that the availability of space will determine the arrangement to a certain extent. Another consideration that needs to be expanded, however, is that we can divide the types of arrangements roughly into two categories: teacher-centered and learner-centered. Those arrangements which tend to limit participation (by their design) are essentially teacher-centered. This means that the teacher controls the activities. The teacher directs the flow of the conversation and the learning patterns. The teacher is very visible in the sense that the learners have a greater dependency on the instructor and must get their instructions constantly from him or her.

Learner-Centered Arrangements

The arrangements that allow for the learners to participate and to interact easily with the others in the group are considered learner-centered. The visibility of the instructor is reduced considerably as far as controlling the step-by-step processes toward learning is concerned. The flow from one activity to another is more natural, and the learners are generally less aware of the change. The instructor has not lost real control—just some of the visibility in exercising control. For example, when the arrangement is in a U shape, the instructor can regain attention simply by moving slightly into the U and taking over. The learners will immediately be quiet since they will not want to talk around the instructor. Again, this arrangement makes use of the instructor's visibility as a means of keeping control, especially where the learners are very dependent on the instructor. What we have done is to convert the U shape from a learner-centered arrangement to an instructor-centered one.

When the learners are gathered around tables in small groups, there is an even more learner-centered situation. The teacher will find it harder to get back into the center of things, especially when the students are busily engaged in a discussion that is meaningful and relevant to them. One way for the instructor to regain control is to have each group report on something. When the groups have finished talking, it is easy for the instructor to take up where he or she left off in the planned program. The instructor can also regain control by beginning some instruction—perhaps merely calling the students' attention to a common problem that the instructor has observed while listening to the groups. He or she can use the chalkboard, an overhead, or an easel to point up the problem, and that action in itself will bring the control back to the instructor. This same process may be used with the circle arrangement. This is a very hard student-centered situation to break at times, since the learners have gotten themselves into a very comfortable process of sharing equally with one another and with the instructor. Turning control over to one person—the instructor—may not please them very much. Often, though, the instructor can regain control by simply standing up or going to the board, as just mentioned with respect to the U-shaped configuration.

Teacher-Centered Arrangements

Teacher-centered arrangements do not suffer from the problem of getting the learners to relinquish any control, since they rarely have any under these arrangements anyway. The traditional "all-seats-facing-the-front" arrangement is the best example of this. The instructor is more highly visible than in any other teaching design, standing in the front of the room with all the students looking in his or her direction. Even the chevron design loses very little of the teacher-centered aspect, although the learners do get to see one another and to talk more in this design. The instructor can simply begin to do something at the front of the room, and all the learners will direct their attention there.

Classroom Techniques and Systems

Involvement

Let us look now at some basic requirements for successful classroom instructing. There are three characteristics to look for in a successful situation. First, there is the matter of *involvement*. Since none of us ever learn much without being involved in the learning situation, it is most important that the learners be involved as much as possible. They must not be just killing time or participating without having set a specific learning goal. Their involvement must be meaningful and well directed. The learners, as much as possible, should see where their involvement is taking them and why they are doing the particular thing they are doing that has gotten them involved.

The involvement can be of several kinds. A small group of students may work together on a common problem; individual learners may work on problems separately; or the instructor may mention a problem and ask the students to think about it. There does not have to be physical involvement in order to get mental involvement, but many a good instructor has been fooled by thinking that what he or she is saying is so provocative that all the learners are mentally engrossed in every word—hence involved—when in reality they are bored, confused, or thinking about something else altogether. It is an assumption at best to think that learners are involved mentally when there is no concrete evidence of this. Only when they have *said* something or are *doing* something can the instructor be sure of the extent of their involvement.

Accountability

The second ingredient to look for in a successful classroom teaching-learning situation is student *accountability* for the learning activity. Since learning is a *self*-activity, the students need to know that they are responsible for learning. When there is a specific objective, they need to think of it as an objective *they* must reach, not one the instructor must *make* them reach. In the case of a small-group activity, homework, or outside reading, the learners must feel that they have the responsibility for reaching the particular learning goal in the assignment. The instructor should plan activities that will let the learners take on some of the responsibility for the learning—hence the term "accountability." If the learners know the objectives ahead of time and see that a certain assignment will allow them to reach that goal, they will more readily accept the accountability for performing the activity. This places a burden of responsibility on the instructor to see that the learners really do take the responsibility for the learning, however. Often, instructors tend to overprotect the learners by accepting the accountability for the learning themselves. They say things like "You'd better listen to this because it's important." An instructor may reach all the conclusions for the learners, rather than risk letting them do it. The successful instructor will present just enough information to allow the conclusion to be reached and then will let the students reach that conclusion themselves. This approach makes the learners, rather than the teacher, accountable for the thought processes required to reach the conclusion. If the instructor presents all the facts and then reaches the conclusion, the learners really have little or nothing to do during the teaching-learning process.

Feedback

A final characteristic of a good classroom situation is a high amount of *feedback* from the learners. Feedback is that ingredient which allows the instructor to know just where the learner is at any given time during the instruction. There is an obvious truism here: The more feedback there is, the more the instructor will know about the success of the instruction. Feedback can be obtained in many ways. Unfortunately, many instructors tend to depend upon watching the *faces* of the learners for a large amount of their feedback. If the students look fairly pleasant or satisfied, if they seem interested, or if they smile and nod their heads positively, the instructor reads this as feedback that says, "Things are going great." Experienced instructors have usually learned not to be surprised when they finally ask for some verbal feedback from a group such as this and hear a student say, "Uh, I don't know . . . I haven't been able to follow you very well."

Successful instructors have learned to depend only upon that which they *hear* for sure, or *see* for sure, to tell them what they *know* for sure about the class. Feedback in a class can be compared with instruments or dials on a machine that tell us how a particular operation is going. The more accurate the feedback, the better the control. The lights and meters on the dashboard of a car are there to tell the driver how well the car is functioning. Without them the driver would worry about the oil pressure, the fuel level, and overheating. The same is true in the classroom: without feedback, the instructor worries constantly about how well the students' minds are functioning. As we look at the various systems for teaching, it will be obvious how large a part feedback plays in determining what we *call* the "system."

When we talk about techniques, it is easier to think in terms of the three characteristics just discussed than to classify the techniques. For example, it is meaningless to speak of the "discussion method" unless we know what is going on during the discussion. The method is one in which the students and the instructor engage in discussions of some sort about some subject. Neither the amount of talking done by the students nor the number of students doing the talking is defined, but we know we need that information if we are to judge the effectiveness of the teaching. Are the students being asked to reach conclusions as they "discuss" the topic? Is the instructor getting feedback from the students in such a way as to test the success of past teaching or set the direction for future instructing? Are all the students offering feedback, or just one or two? We can say the same for the "question and answer" technique. What are the questions doing for the instructor? Is there usable feedback? What is the learner getting out of the question and the answer? How much responsibility—accountability—does the individual learner have for the answers? How involved are the students as a whole? Is the questioning and answering just between the instructor and one or two students, or are there small subgroup sessions in which the individuals give their inputs; a consensus opinion or answer is arrived at, which is in turn presented to the whole group; and a final conclusion is reached that represents all the thinking of all the learners? Any instructor can evaluate the processes being used by applying these three criteria to the situation: involvement, accountability, and feedback. It is better to use these as a measure of a particular method, rather than whether the instructor "feels comfortable" with it or even whether the students like it. Rather than list different methods and comment on them, let us look at different systems of instruction and see how it is possible to introduce methods into these systems.

Teaching-Learning Systems

We can best understand what is happening in the classroom if we divide the possibilities into three different systems or formats. These systems are not absolute. Not everything that happens in the classroom can be said to be a part of one of these systems, nor can a teacher stay only in one of these systems all the time. The important thing is to begin to think about what is happening in the classroom in terms of what the student is doing and what the instructor is doing.

Direct Teacher Input Systems

The first system is the *direct teacher input system*. As the term implies, the inputs to the class come directly from the instructor or from some source other than the learner. This system has the lowest possible amount of involvement. There is no feedback, and the accountability must consist in something other than the learner's responses or their work on a project. The simplest form of this system is the lecture, but this is not the only form. Anytime there is a complete input of new information from an external source (other than the learner), we have this system. Showing a movie, a filmstrip, or a series of overhead transparencies or slides is an example of this system *if nothing else happens during the time of the showing*. If there is just the presentation of the material, with no accountability during the presentation, then all the input is directly from a teaching source. Building in the subtlety of having the students look for points of disagreement, requiring role playing at the completion of the showing, or listing the key points on the board as the students call them out from their notes results in a different system.

The important thing about this system is that it requires nothing of the viewers or listeners, other than their presence. Any conclusions that are reached, any new information that is brought out, and any discoveries that are made are all due to the instructor, not the students. The students may like this, by the way. There is something that we may call the "podium syndrome" that makes some students feel very comfortable when the instructor is talking. For some, it is a kind of "security blanket" in the classroom—they like to feel that things are well organized and that the instructor will cover all points clearly and precisely, with the students staying out of it to prevent confusion. This is not to say that all students are like this, but perhaps too many are. Such students do not take too well to doing work on their own or to reaching their own conclusions. Unfortunately, they do not retain nearly as much as they need to of what they *hear* the instructor say during these comfortable moments, and so they do not make very good learners from this point of view. Even when the instructor gets them involved and they come up with their own conclusions and thus are in a position to learn more and remember more, they may still end up saying, "Why didn't the instructor just tell us that without going through all that effort to get us involved?" This does not remove the instructor's responsibility to do the best possible job of instructing, even though the students may not recognize the instructing as being the best.

Teacher Modification System

The next system, which moves up a level in student involvement, we call the *teacher modification system*. In this system the teacher provides the original inputs of new information or conclusions, but does some questioning of the learners to see whether they interpreted the information correctly. If they did not, the teacher "modifies" their words or ideas to make sure they hear the correct information again. This is a superior system to the first one because the learners are likely to take more home with them—since they got involved—than they would under the direct teacher input system. When the instructor gets the learners involved in a discussion of the material presented, whether presented on film or in a lecture, and when they review what has already been said without drawing new conclusions, the teacher is operating in the teacher modification system or mode.

We must remember, though, that if the learner comes up with any *new* conclusions, the instructor is no longer operating in this system. Only when the instructor puts in all the new material, ideas, and conclusions, either in lecture form or by some other means, and then gets the learners to feed this information back through some form of questioning or discussion can we describe the process as teacher modification. We use the term "modification" because if the feedback shows that the learner does not have all the information or has the wrong idea on some things, the teacher "modifies" the learner's perceptions and presents the correct idea or concept. The process is simply one of the teacher giving out new information, having the learner feed that information back, and then making a correction if necessary. The instructor has all the control and all the responsibility for what gets corrected and what does not. The instructor—and usually *only* the instructor—knows the specific learning objective. Only the instructor can "pass" on the success of the learning experience. While this system helps the learners retain some of the information better, especially information with which they became involved, it still lacks the degree of accountability that ensures the greatest amount of learning.

Learner Discovery System

A still more effective system is called the *learner discovery system,* in which the learner begins to draw conclusions and supply some of the learning activity under teacher *guidance* rather than *control.* The idea is for the teacher to supply only those facts which the learners cannot find themselves and for the learners to come up with their own discoveries as much as possible. Instead of feeding "old" information back to the teacher—as in the teacher modification system—the learners furnish new conclusions or concepts and even new factual information they have found on their own. Here we have a much better situation for retention to take place, since the learners are accountable for the learning and must know where they are going in order to see whether they have gotten there. This is a more effective type of involvement, and the instructor gets very good feedback.

One thing to notice here, however, is that the teacher still determines whether there is just modification or actually discovery. A case study, for example, is an excellent way to get a group involved in coming up with some good conclusions that they might have missed if the teacher had just told them about a management principle or described an abstract situation. Some instructors, however, are so afraid that the students will miss the point that they provide the conclusions themselves instead of waiting for the learners to come up with them. In this case—even though the learners may have been involved in role playing during the learning experience—the teacher is still operating in a teacher modification system or maybe even direct teacher input system. If all the new conclusions come from the teacher, who ends up by saying something like, "Now, are there any questions?" little more than a glorified lecture has taken place.

The same is true if a videotape is made of the salesperson's performance in a simulated sales effort. If the instructor ends up telling the salesperson all the things he or she did wrong and right and why, then the instructor just took a long time to get around to the lecture. The learner was not allowed to learn anything alone. The feedback went to the learner in the form of seeing the videotape replay, but the conclusions that could have been reached by the salesperson were reached instead by the instructor, and so the instructor got no particular feedback on how the learner saw the situation. We could make the same illustrations with in-baskets and management games.

Just having the learners go through some involvement does not automatically get the teaching process into the highest order of teaching, no matter how sophisticated the equipment used or the method employed.

Learner-Controlled Instruction

Another system is the open-classroom system, or learner-controlled instruction. This is quite different from the systems talked about here, in that it takes an altogether different approach to the learning process. It is concerned less with technique or methodology than with obtaining the desired performance through a "contracting" process that gets the instructor and the learner agreeing on several things before the training begins. They agree on the goals—objectives in behavioral terms—and they agree on the measuring devices for seeing whether these goals are actually met. Since the learner and the instructor agree on the goals, the learner is obligated to do the tasks assigned; the instructor is obligated to see that the assignments will guarantee that the learner gets to the goals if the assignment is completed. From a mental standpoint, there is total accountability and involvement. Since there is constant measuring, feedback is always individual and accurate. Above all, the majority of the instruction (and learning) is self-paced.

Supervisory or Management Training

Specialized arrangements are needed for doing supervisory or management training. The difference lies in the fact that this is the place that realism is perhaps most needed and the most difficult to get. While it's easy to simulate a computer problem by having a computer in the room, it is impossible to have an entire work force on hand for the supervisors to "practice" on. We substitute simulation activities for the work force. We use case studies and role playing and in-baskets and action mazes and management games and other types of activities that are taken directly from the real world. But this often requires a little different kind of room arrangement and certainly different kinds of instructing.

First, there is frequently the need for "break-out" rooms, places where small subgroups can go and work on a common problem, decide on a decision, and prepare for presenting this solution to the entire group. This means that the rooms should be large enough to accommodate as many people as might be in the maximum-sized subgroup. Further, the rooms should be equipped with easels, transparencies and markers, and any other things that will facilitate preparing a presentation. There should be enough rooms to keep the subgroups to no more than five or six, less if possible.

Next, the training rooms themselves should be such as to allow for flexibility in arrangements. There will be times when everyone needs to face the front, in a traditional mode. Usually this is to get instruction, to see films or video, and to see things develop on the board. This would also allow for the instructor to get into a group role play. Next, the rooms should allow for easy movement of chairs so the participants can turn around, have multiple role plays, or meet in small groups without leaving the room. Since there will be times when the students will need to move across the room, place things on the walls, exchange ideas with other individuals and groups, and perhaps have discussions or even debates, the chairs and tables should allow for all of this to happen.

As we've mentioned, there is often a need for video or movies; so the room should have easy access to the screen or monitor viewing by the participants. If the visuals aren't immediately viewable, the chairs and room arrangements should be such that it is easy for the students to roll or move their chairs quickly and quietly for this viewing.

Technical Training

Much training is now technical in nature and requires special considerations. First, there is the need often for equipment, such as computer terminals or models of field equipment. This is enhanced by furniture and room sizes that allow for a number of people to gather around one piece of equipment or for each person to have his or her own individual equipment. When equipment is taken into traditional rooms with traditional tables and traditional arrangements, there is seldom a very good result. The instructor should have freedom to move about, have access to the individuals working on the equipment, and be able to get the entire class's attention and be seen by them.

Frequently, manuals are needed and/or specification sheets and other reference material. This requires at least a 30-inch table, and plenty of room for the instructor to visit each learning site. Also, there should be room enough for each student to have materials available all the time, without worrying about interfering with other students.

One of the problems with teaching technical materials is that it is so easy for the instructor to simply lecture on the materials in the manuals. The students soon get bored, wonder why they had to come to the class to have someone read to them, and usually take little home with them that's usable. An alternative to this approach is to have the instructor design problems that are solved by the students using the manuals to find the answers. This can easily be done by starting all the class off with a simple problem, one that can be found reasonably quickly in the manual or reference materials. As soon as each finishes, he or she is given another problem, slightly harder—or taking slightly longer to answer—and soon each will be working on different parts of the problem. The instructor talks only to those students who are having problems, and all are working at their own pace. To keep one or two from getting too far ahead, there can be some additional, alternate problems with more depth than is required usually on the job, but challenging and interesting enough that the faster students can enjoy the diversion. They shouldn't feel punished for being ahead, and if the exercises are done properly, they may not even know (at the time) that they are ahead of the rest of the group. The advantage of this method is that they are solving problems from the same source they should be using to solve them at home on the job: from the manuals. They are also building confidence in the reference material by seeing that they really can get solutions from the material, and not becoming dependent on the instructors. If the instructors will spend their time talking only to the students who are lost or cannot find the information in the reference books, and then only give them some clues for finding the solutions, not the actual answers, the teachers are doing what they should be doing best: overcoming deficiencies, not boring students who already know the answers. Admittedly, this isn't as exciting to some instructors as standing up in front of a class and expounding on a technical subject, showing what great prowess and command of the subject the instructor has . . . but it will produce better learning and longer retention. And that's the whole idea of teaching in the first place!

Evaluation

Evaluation of instruction is complicated by the fact that we often evaluate the wrong things. For example, we tend to evaluate the instructor when we are talking about classroom teaching. But if we have failed to choose the correct material to teach, we are looking at the wrong thing when we look at (evaluate) the teacher. The best instructor available cannot produce employees who can perform correctly if the subject matter does not deal with their deficiency on the job. By the same token, we cannot expect the best instructor in the world to help improve the organization if the wrong students are selected. So part of our evaluation has to do with the organization's skill in selecting subject matter, setting specific objectives, and getting the proper employees to the training location. Even then, we may evaluate the wrong thing. We may watch an instructor in action and decide that he or she is doing a good job because there is a lot of action, movement, and variety. The instructor is a good performer: he or she does not lean on the podium, does not talk while facing the board, and gets a lot of eye contact. We have to remember that what we are looking for is not a good public speaker, but a good *facilitator of learning*. So far we have pointed out the characteristics of a good learning situation: accountability, feedback, and involvement. We can best judge the worth of an instructor by the extent to which these things are present in the classroom. The amount of accountability, feedback, and involvement in the learning situation tells us whether the instructor is doing the job required. It may be that these things are present to the point where the learners are not even aware of the instructor's position at the speaker's stand or of the amount of eye contact. The students are too involved in the learning process to observe the teacher's actions on the platform. When this happens, we can say that the instructor has developed a good classroom technique.

22
Meetings, Conferences, Workshops, and Seminars

Jack L. Reith

Jack Reith is Manager of Personnel Development and Public Relations at Santa Barbara Research Center, Santa Barbara, California (a Hughes Aircraft Company subsidiary). Prior to this he was a management consultant based in Lake Arrowhead, California. He has had experience in the fields of banking, retailing, military and consumer electronics, metal processing, law firms, public utilities, government agencies, real estate, aerospace, management communications, conglomerates, and small business.

Reith graduated from Yale University with a degree in Industrial Administration and Engineering. For his graduate studies in organization behavior, he attended UCLA and the Claremont Colleges, and received special training from the NTL Institute for Applied Behavioral Science. Reith has published many articles in various professional journals and was also a contributing author to the first and second editions of the Training and Development Handbook. His wide experience, coupled with his understanding of organizational behavior, have given him an unusual ability to identify management problems which constrain productivity and organizational growth.

While working as a program manager in the complex field of airborne inertial navigation systems, Reith developed a special interest in the conduct of meetings. While operating in this difficult matrix management environment, he wrote his first article on meetings in 1970.

This chapter first describes how to conduct a meeting, including planning, caucusing, the agenda, the meeting room, conducting the meeting, techniques for keeping on schedule, summarizing, action items, minutes, and follow-up. This is followed by a short discussion of meeting dynamics—the understanding of which is the key to successful meetings.

Next, 16 types of meetings are defined. Finally, a complete checklist is provided for setting up conferences, meetings, workshops, seminars, and conventions. The checklist covers accommodations, meetings, facilities, equipment, registration, speakers, and many other checklist reminders.

Planning and Conducting a Meeting

Planning the Meeting

The success of almost any meeting depends, in large part, upon the planning and preparation which preceded it. The first step is to define the objective or objectives for the meeting.[1] Objectives may take whatever form most readily fits the needs of the participants, the subject matter, and the circumstances of the meeting. The objectives can be simply a statement of what you hope to accomplish by having the meeting.

Much has been written about defining objectives for organizational management,[2,3] as well as objectives for learning experiences.[4] Equally important is defining objectives for meetings.

The following list may help in defining objectives for business meetings of various types. Meetings are often held to:

1. Inform

2. Instruct

3. Define and plan

4. Clarify

5. Create

6. Resolve and decide

It is interesting to note that as you proceed from the top of this list to the bottom, the number of attendees for an efficient meeting will tend to decrease. For example, large numbers of people may attend a meeting where the primary objective is to inform. On the other hand, only a handful of people may be efficiently and effectively involved in a meeting called to resolve a difficult problem. A meeting, of course, may be designed to accomplish a number of objectives.

After an objective has been defined, it should be examined to see whether a meeting is the best way to accomplish it. A meeting may not be needed at all![1]

Prior Contact with Participants

A very effective way to start the planning is to contact participants before objectives for the meeting have been completed. Contact with participants will help clarify meeting objectives, begin to prepare the participants to participate in the meeting, and possibly identify needs of the participants. Additional agenda items can then be added.

Caucusing

Some very effective meeting leaders consistently have prior meetings or caucuses with those attendees whose opinions or recommendations will significantly affect the results of the meeting. I have found this approach to be particularly effective when new ideas, proposals, or plans are being submitted for approval at a meeting. Usually among the meeting participants will be formal or informal leaders whose understanding and approval of the proposal will greatly influence its acceptance by the group. Prior understanding of the proposal may put these people in a position to render positive opinions regarding the proposal.

Of special importance is a premeeting with speakers and presenters to discuss the material they will be presenting, to plan the sequence of events, and to correlate their material with the total meeting agenda. This can be done most effectively in person, but the telephone can be used if person-to-person contact is impossible.

Soliciting Agenda Material

As mentioned earlier, participants will feel more a part of the meeting and will be more likely to participate and support the meeting's conclusions if they are asked to review the planned agenda and to make recommendations for changes or additions. Again, this is most effectively done in person, but of course the telephone can often save a great deal of time.

Developing the Agenda

In any event, the mailing of an agenda in advance will greatly help all participants know the objectives and sequence of items for a planned meeting. One exception is when it is decided to build the agenda at the beginning of the meeting. This technique will be described later.

A meeting agenda should include a statement of objectives, time (beginning and end), location, participants' names and identifications (e.g., title, organization), and a list of subject matter or problems to be discussed or presentations to be made. Also, an agenda may include a definition of expected actions to be taken by participants following the meeting.

Timing of Agenda Items

Effective meeting leaders have developed different ideas about the sequence of items on a formal agenda. Some feel that the most important items should be first. Others feel that the first items on the agenda should be warm-up items to get the group started toward active participation.

Certainly attention should be given to the location of complex items so that the group will be fully alert and capable of understanding the problems discussed; otherwise, Mr. Parkinson's prediction may become a reality: The same amount of time may be spent on a $10 million decision as on one involving only $10.[5]

The Meeting Room

Selection of the room is very important in planning a meeting. The meeting room should be convenient to the participants, quiet, and selected to minimize (even discourage) interruptions by those not scheduled to attend the meeting. Preparing a meeting room is also important. A comprehensive checklist for large meetings, conferences, and conventions is included later.

Beginning the Meeting

I have been conducting meetings of various sorts and sizes and types for nearly 30 years. If there is one error I make most frequently, it is that of assuming that everyone at a meeting knows the other people there. I urge that at the beginning of any meeting, the meeting leader be certain that all those present know one another or have been introduced. The meeting leader can accomplish this simply by introducing people he or she is sure have not met. Often it is a good warm-up to ask the participants to introduce themselves. Name tags that attach to the participants' clothing are helpful, and "table tents" in front of each participant will aid not only participants but also the speakers or conference leaders as they talk with the meeting participants.

Next, at the beginning of the meeting the agenda should be reviewed, particularly the objectives of the meeting. If an agenda has not been prepared, the objectives of the meeting should be stated at this time, and an agenda may be "built" at the meeting.

Building an Agenda at the Meeting

As mentioned earlier, some meeting leaders like to use an agenda-building technique to get early involvement of participants. Agenda building consists of getting the recommendations from meeting participants as to what the agenda items should be. The meeting leader can, of course, include his or her own. This can be done on a blackboard or newsprint chart by first listing all the recommendations made by the group and the meeting leader and then obtaining group agreement as to the sequence in which the agenda items will be covered.

If desired, to assure coverage of the entire agenda, the meeting leader can obtain concurrence from the group as to the amount of time to be spent on each item. Although this may seem time-consuming, those who use it believe that, overall, it creates a more effective meeting and reduces the total meeting time.

Techniques for Keeping on Schedule

As mentioned in the previous paragraph, obtaining concurrence of the participants as to the amount of time to spend on each item is one way of keeping on schedule. As a minimum, the meeting leader can place on his or her copy of the agenda a time objective for the conclusion of each agenda item.

Keep the meeting focused on the agenda items. Stimulate discussion, but watch your time schedule. Call a coffee break if a hot argument goes on too long.

A technique I have seen used effectively for long meetings with large numbers of speakers is to provide more than adequate time for coffee breaks. This effectively provides a "pad," which is often needed.

Above all, the leader should never lose control of a meeting.

Recognizing or Restraining the Individual

The most skillful meeting leaders seem to have an uncanny talent for leading a group in such a way that the people who really should participate in the meeting do participate, while those who tend to "overparticipate" are restrained from doing so. Part of this talent consists in being sensitive to where individuals are at every moment, and to where the group is at every moment, during the meeting. This sensitivity can be developed and improved through training, particularly training in meeting dynamics, as discussed later.

Quiet individuals must be invited to participate by the meeting leader, often repeatedly. Those individuals at the meeting who tend to talk at every opportunity must be restrained. Often, if the right atmosphere is created by the meeting leader, others at the meeting will tactfully "turn off" the overcontributors. If it does not turn out this way, the meeting leader must interrupt, perhaps saying something like, "Bill, let's hear what John and Mary have to say on this subject before we go on to the next item."

Meeting Control

Although some meetings seem to function effectively with little leadership, all meetings require a leader, and that the leader has considerable responsibility. People who attend meetings are, in effect, delegating to the meeting leader a part of their valuable time to be used effectively, during the meeting, in order to accomplish the objectives of the meeting. This delegation charges the meeting leader with responsibility for efficient utilization of their time.[1]

An awareness of meeting dynamics and an understanding of group process will certainly help a leader become more effective. Often, however, a meeting leader must simply confront time itself and direct the meeting toward a conclusion.

Summarizing

Summarizing is a key responsibility of meeting leaders; it helps them effectively control a meeting and facilitate the accomplishment of meeting objectives. The summary may cover where the meeting is with reference to the agenda, where the leader thinks the group is in reference to a decision on an agenda item or the solution of a problem, or the position taken by one of the participants. In any event, mastery of this technique can help a meeting leader be more effective in managing the meeting.

Action Items

What I call the "assignment" and "commitment" aspect of a meeting is one that has not been adequately covered in many discussions of meetings. Both the assignment of responsibility for the solution of a problem and the commitment by the individual or individuals responsible are extremely important. Too often a great deal of the value of a meeting is lost because it is not clear who will take responsibility for significant actions which the group has agreed upon and which will make the time spent at the meeting worthwhile. It is the meeting leader's responsibility to assure that the assignment is clear and that the commitment is made.[1]

Minutes of Meetings

Minutes seem very formal and time-consuming to some people, but they are the assurance to all concerned that the objectives of a meeting were achieved and therefore that the meeting time was well spent. Furthermore, when more than one person is involved in any communications process, there is not only the chance for error in understanding but also the probability of it. Therefore, minutes of meetings are an essential part of the follow-through to see that meeting objectives are achieved.

Some minutes include simple statements of the following:

1. Conclusions reached
2. Action items and assignment of responsibility
3. Matters unresolved
4. Next meeting date and time

More complete minutes will include a statement of:

1. Date, time, and location of the meeting
2. Objectives
3. List of participants
4. Matters discussed, item by item, including the expressed opinions of the people who attended
5. If the meeting involved voting, the names of those making motions and seconding the motions, as well as the result of the vote
6. Action items assigned, with expected results and dates
7. Matters not covered, or postponed, with an explanation
8. Next meeting: date, time, place, agenda

Follow-Up

Some of the most effective leaders it has been my pleasure to work with over the years are those who personally follow up on action items and decisions made at meetings they have held. Not only do most of us appreciate a reminder, but the contact made by the meeting leader helps overall communications and prepares the meeting leader to build the agenda for the next meeting.

Meeting Dynamics: The Key to Successful Meetings

What really happens *between people* during a meeting is critical to the outcome of the meeting. Unfortunately, this "dimension" is often overlooked.

It is important to remember that *everyone* who comes to a meeting comes with attitudes, needs, and, in effect, "agenda." The effective meeting leader will be aware that the interaction between the participants' "agendas" and the meeting "agenda" will significantly affect the conduct and results of the meeting.

Task versus Process

Any time two or more people are called together by one of them (leader), there is a meeting. For meetings there are *always* two dimensions:

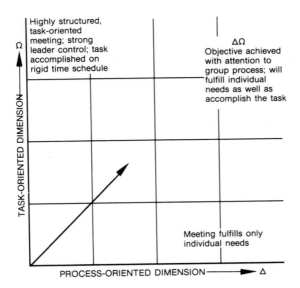

Fig. 22-1. Meeting matrix.

1. The task or goal

2. The process—what is happening between people within the group

The task or goal may be all that the leader recognizes, and he or she may try to achieve this goal without interest in, attention to, or recognition of the process. As leaders become experienced, they can learn to understand the dynamics which occur in any group and to use the dynamics to help attain the task goals. A matrix may be developed to represent the two dimensions as shown in Fig. 22-1.

The omega (Ω) dimension is the task-accomplishment dimension and is exemplified by a highly structured meeting with strong leader control, which may result in the achievement of task goals on a perfect time schedule.

The delta (Δ) dimension is the process-oriented dimension, in which the meeting fulfills the needs of the individuals without necessarily accomplishing all the tasks or achieving all the leader's objectives.

If the tasks can be accomplished and the objectives achieved with effective individual participation (the $\Delta\Omega$ of the matrix), the meeting will often be completed more rapidly, and the commitments made will later be supported more enthusiastically by the participants.

For more information on meeting dynamics, refer to references 6, 7, and 8 at the end of this chapter.

Types of Meetings, Conferences, Seminars, and Workshops

There are many different kinds of meetings. The person responsible for planning a meeting or a learning experience or a problem-solving session must arrange the principals and participants, and the physical resources, so as to best accomplish the objectives defined for the meeting.

Here, 16 kinds of meetings will be defined.[9,10,11] The definitions come primarily from the work accomplished at the Bureau of Studies in Adult Education at Indiana University and from books written by the members of that organization.

Speech-Lecture. A speech or lecture is a carefully prepared oral presentation of a subject by a qualified individual. It is generally characterized by formality. It is an easy type of program to organize. However, it provides no opportunity for audience participation, and hence it provides for communication in one direction only.

Speech-Forum. The speech-forum is a learning method which consists of an organized speech given by a qualified person and a period of open discussion immediately following. The speech-forum provides for minimal two-way communications. In addition to the speaker, there is usually a chairperson to act as moderator during the discussion.

Panel. A panel is a group of three to six persons who carry on a purposeful conversation on an assigned topic. The panel members are selected on the basis of previously demonstrated interest and competence in the subject as well as their ability to verbalize before an audience. The panel members are usually seated at a table in front of the audience. Conversation among panel members is started by a moderator, who usually prepares questions in advance which he or she uses to start and sustain the discussion. In the strictest definition, there is no audience participation in the panel.

Panel-Forum. A panel-forum is a panel which is immediately followed by an audience-participation period involving free and open discussion by the panel members on questions submitted by the audience. A moderator usually acts as a go-between for panel members and the audience. Questions can be presented directly from the floor by members of the audience, or they can be written on cards collected and read by the moderator. Sometimes questions are collected from the audience in advance by the moderator.

Symposium (Ancient Concept). A symposium (ancient concept) is a group of 5 to 20 persons who meet in a private dining room to enjoy good food and fellowship and who desire to discuss, informally, a topic of mutual interest. During dinner, the previously selected topic is introduced by the moderator (symposiarch). Group members are then free to talk informally about the topic if they wish. When everyone has finished eating and the table is cleared, the group carries on a more systematic (but still informal) discussion of the topic under the guidance of the moderator. As a rule, this technique is used for leisurely exploration of a topic, rather than for problem solving or discussion of highly controversial issues.

Symposium (Modern Concept). A symposium (modern concept) is a series of related speeches by two to five persons qualified to speak on different aspects of the same topic or on closely related topics. The speeches vary in length from 3 to 20 minutes, depending upon the number of speeches, the amount of time available, and the topics. The speakers do not converse with one another. They make presentations to the audience. A chairperson is usually in charge.

Symposium-Forum (Modern Concept). A symposium-forum (modern concept) is a symposium followed immediately by an audience-participation period of free and open discussion. A moderator acts as a go-between for the speakers and the audience. He or she is skilled in handling an audience and stimulating group participation. Like the panel-forum, the symposium-forum provides for a limited degree of two-way communication.

Colloquy.   A colloquy is a modification of the panel, using six to eight people. Three or four of the people are resource persons or experts, as in a panel. However, in addition to the experts, three or four people representing the audience also sit on the stage. These people ask questions, express opinions, and raise issues to be treated by the experts. A moderator usually directs the proceedings. The moderator may sit at a small table in the center of the stage, with the three or four experts behind a table on the left side of the stage facing the audience, and the three or four audience representatives behind a table facing the audience on the right side of the stage. Usually the members of the audience just listen, but occasionally they participate under the guidance of the moderator. A particular advantage of the colloquy is the opportunity it provides to reduce the natural barriers that usually stand between a large audience and the experts on the stage, thereby helping to establish rapport between the audience and those on the platform.

Group Discussion.   As defined by Bergevin, Morris, and Smith,[10] group discussion is purposeful conversation and deliberation about a topic of mutual interest among 6 to 20 participants under the guidance of a trained participant called a leader. Maximum opportunity is provided for the individual participant to share his or her ideas and experiences with others. The discussion method is often used as a part of education and training programs and courses of all sorts. The leader is particularly important in group discussions; special training for leaders is desirable wherever possible.

Conference.   A conference is a group composed usually of 2 to 50 persons who represent different organizations, departments, or points of view but who have some common interest or background. They gather information and discuss mutual problems, with a reasonable solution as the desired end. Problem identification and solution is often the objective of a conference. However, the conference is also used to interchange information and to improve cooperation.

Convention.   A convention is an assembly of representatives or delegates from local units of a parent organization who have a common interest, or an assembly of representatives or delegates from different organizations or professions who have a common interest. These persons meet to explore and act on problems of common interest. A convention is a medium which often uses a combination of other group activities, such as speeches, panels, forums, and group discussions. Planning is essential to successful conventions. Careful attention must be given to the selection of a chairperson, appointment of a planning committee, and selection of speakers and group discussion leaders. Often a large convention will involve many committees covering all pertinent responsibilities, from finance to hospitality.

Committee.   A committee is a small group of individuals appointed or elected to perform a task that cannot be done efficiently by the entire group. A committee is usually appointed and authorized by, and responsible to, the parent group; there is a presiding officer, who is usually designated, but sometimes elected by the group. The powers and duties of a committee are often fixed by the parent organization or by the constitution and bylaws of the parent organization. Committees are usually established to study a particular problem (including carrying out research essential to solving the problem), to reach a conclusion on the basis of study of the problem, and to act if action is indicated and authorized. A report is usually prepared as the final act of a committee. The report is submitted to the parent group which established the committee.

Institute.   An institute is a series of meetings arranged for a group of persons who come together to receive instruction in, and information about, a specific field of work. The series may be held on one day or may continue for weeks, months, or years, in a planned and organized manner. Authoritative instruction is emphasized. An organized body of knowledge is presented to the learners, or issues are raised for their consideration. Often various group activities are utilized: speech, symposium, panel, group discussion, etc. The participants learn in groups, but individual study is also involved.

Institutes have been established by the practitioners in many special disciplines. These institutes run from a few weeks to years, and the longer ones often qualify the participants to carry on work within the discipline. Usually a certificate is awarded at the end of an institute.

Seminar.   A seminar is a group of persons gathered together for the purpose of studying a subject under the leadership of an expert or learned person. Often the procedure followed is to identify the problem, explore the problem, discuss or lay out necessary research involved in the solution of the problem, conduct the research, share the findings with others in the group, and reach a conclusion on the basis of the research.

Workshop.   A workshop is a group of persons with a common interest or problem, often professional or vocational, who meet for an extended period of time to improve their individual proficiency, ability, or understanding by means of study, research, and discussion. The workshop allows considerable flexibility, and the emphasis is on improving individual proficiency and understanding. Theory and practice are often treated concurrently. The learner is encouraged to work out a program of personal study and receives help with this program from the other participants and resource people. The learning situations tend to be based on interests and needs identified by the participants themselves, rather than by experts.

Clinic.   A clinic is a meeting of a group of people with common interests; it is established for the purpose of diagnosing, analyzing, and seeking solutions to specific problems. The group usually confronts real-life situations to establish a manner and method to meet them more successfully. Often case studies, demonstrations, role plays, speeches, field trips, and shared real-life experiences form the basis for the diagnosis and solution of problems.

Meeting, Conference, and Convention Checklist[12]

Accommodations

Agreement with Hotel or Facility before Meeting

1. Approximate number of guest rooms needed, with breakdown on singles, doubles, and suites

2. Room rates

3. Reservations confirmation

4. Copies of reservations to those concerned

5. Date that majority of group is arriving

6. Date that majority of group is departing

7. Date that uncommitted guest rooms are to be released

8. Understanding regarding rooms to be assigned to VIPs, special guests, etc.— those to be paid by company and those complimentary by hotel

9. Hospitality suites needed

10. Checkrooms, gratuities, bars, snacks, service time, and date

Meetings

Check with Hotel before Meeting

1. Floor plans furnished

2. Correct date and time for each session

3. Room assigned for each session; rental

4. Headquarters room

5. Seating number, seating plan for each session, and speakers' tables

6. Meetings scheduled, staggered for best traffic flow, including elevator service

7. Staging required—size

8. Equipment for each session (check against equipment and facilities list)

9. Other special requirements (check immediately before meeting)

10. Checkroom open and staffed

11. Seating style as ordered

12. Enough seats for all conferees

13. Cooling or heating system operating

14. PA system operating; mikes as ordered

15. Recording equipment operating

16. Microphones—number and type as ordered

17. Lectern in place, light operating, gavel, block

18. Water pitcher, water at lectern

19. Water pitcher, water, and glasses for conferees

20. Guard service at entrance door

21. No smoking signs or ashtrays, stands, matches

22. Overhead projector, screen, and extension cord

23. Teleprompter operating

24. Pencils, note pads, paper

25. Chart stands, easels, blackboards, related equipment

26. Piano, organ, signs, flags, banners
27. Lighting as ordered
28. Special flowers and plants as ordered
29. Any other special equipment
30. Directional signs if meeting room is difficult to locate
31. If meeting room is changed, notice posted conspicuously
32. Stenographer present
33. Photographer present
34. Assignment of someone to remove organizational property after the meeting
35. Check for forgotten property

Equipment and Facilities

1. Special notes to be placed in guest boxes
2. Equipment availability lists and prices furnished
3. Signs for registration desk, hospitality rooms, members only, tours, welcome, no smoking
4. Lighting—spots, floods, operators
5. Staging—size
6. Overhead projector, 16-mm projector and reel, slide projector and trays, stands of correct height
7. Blackboards, flannel boards, magnetic boards
8. Chart stands and easels
9. Lighted lectern, teleprompter
10. Gavel, block
11. PA system—microphones, types, number
12. Recording equipment, operator
13. Video players and stands
14. Special flowers and plants
15. Piano (tuned), organ
16. Phonograph and records
17. Printed services
18. Dressing rooms for entertainers
19. Parking, garage facilities
20. Decorations (check fire regulations)
21. Special equipment
22. Agreement on total cost of extra services
23. Telephones
24. Photographer
25. Stenographer

26. Flags, banners—whether hotel furnishes United States, Canadian, and state flags, etc.
27. Radio and TV broadcasting
28. Live and engineering charges
29. Closed-circuit TV
30. Computers for registration, etc.
31. Telephone access for computer hookup

Registration

1. Time and days required
2. Registration cards—content, number
3. Tables—number, size
4. Tables for filling out forms—number, size
5. Chairs
6. Ashtrays, no smoking signs
7. Typewriters—number, type
8. Personnel—own or hotel's
9. Water pitchers, glasses
10. Lighting
11. Bulletin boards—number, size
12. Signs
13. Notepaper, pens, pencils, sundries
14. Telephones (check immediately before opening)
15. Personnel—their knowledge of procedure
16. Information desired on registration cards
17. Information on badges
18. Handling of guests, dignitaries
19. Program and other material in place
20. Emergency housing
21. Hospitality desk
22. Wastebaskets
23. Copies of registration lists
24. Training of registrars in registration system and computers

Speakers

Check before Convention

1. Have speakers been invited early?

2. Have speakers been informed of length of time available to them?

3. Have speakers been informed of type of talk desired?

4. Are financial arrangements understood? Fee or expenses only? Fee or fee plus expenses? When is payment to be made?

5. Are biographical material and photos available for publicity and introduction?

6. Is speaker's spouse or guest coming?

7. Has hotel reservation been made?

8. Will speaker require special equipment?

9. Has speaker been furnished with program or tentative program as early as possible?

10. When is majority of group arriving?

11. Are any local people closely related (personally or businesswise) to speaker, and should they be invited to hear him or her speak?

12. Has someone been designated to meet speaker upon arrival in city?

Check Immediately before Meeting

1. Has speaker been personally introduced to officers and head table? Have special needs been met?

2. Is blackboard or easel in place?

3. Are pointers and chalk in place?

4. Will help be needed in turning charts?

5. Are projector or TV monitors properly placed?

6. Is projector stand available?

7. Is projectionist or TV operator on hand?

8. Is material to be passed out? By whom?

9. Will speaker need assistance?

Other Important Points

1. Is emergency speaker available in case of a "no-show"?

Miscellaneous

Decorations

. Have decorations and storage space for decorations prior to use been arranged for?

. In case of elaborate decorations, have fire regulations and hotel policy been checked?

Entertainment

Has an interesting entertainment program been planned for men, women, and children?

Guests

1. Have local dignitaries been invited and acceptance received?
2. Have they been provided with tickets?
3. If expected to speak even briefly, have they been forewarned?
4. Have arrangements been made to welcome them upon arrival?

Publicity

1. Has an effective publicity committee been set up?
2. Have city editors and radio and TV program directors been personally called on?
3. Has an integrated attendance-building publicity program been prepared?
4. Have newsworthy releases been prepared?
5. Have arrangements for photographs for organization and publicity been made?

Recording

1. Have arrangements been made to take minutes of the meeting, to type resolutions, to copy proceedings?
2. Has permission been obtained from the speakers to make audio- or videotapes of their presentations?

Registration List

1. Have arrangements been made to copy registration lists?

Sign Checklist

1. Registration desk, hospitality room, tickets, information, members only, special events, hospitality committee, special tours, spouses' committee, no smoking, welcome, advance registration

Signs

1. Have adequate signs been prepared to assure smooth operation, and is masking tape available for mounting?

References

1. Reith, Jack, "Meetings Cost Money—Make Them Pay Off!" *Training and Developmen Journal*, October 1970.
2. Odiorne, George S., *Management by Objectives*, Pitman Publishing Corporation, New York 1965.
3. Morrisey, George L., *Management by Objectives and Results*, Addison-Wesley Publishing Company, Inc., Reading, MA, 1970.
4. Mager, Robert F., *Preparing Instructional Objectives*, Fearon Publishers, Inc., Belmont, CA 1962.
5. Parkinson, C. Northcote, *Parkinson's Law*, Houghton Mifflin Company, Boston, 1957.

6. Benne, Kenneth D. and Paul Sheats, "Functional Roles of Group Members," *Journal of Social Issues*, vol. 4, no. 2, pp. 42–46, 1948.

7. Brilhart, John K., *Effective Group Discussion*, Wm. C. Brown Company Publishers, Dubuque, IA, 1967.

8. Miles, Matthew B., *Learning to Work in Groups*, Teachers College Press, Teachers College, Columbia University, New York, 1959.

9. Bergevin, Paul, and Dwight Morris, *Group Processes for Adult Education*, Community Services in Adult Education, Bloomington, IN, 1951.

10. Bergevin, Paul, Dwight Morris, and Robert M. Smith, *Adult Education Procedures*, Seabury Press, Inc., New York, 1963.

11. McKinley, John, and Robert M. Smith, *Guide to Program Planning*, Seabury Press, Inc., New York, 1965.

12. Reprinted by permission of AMACOM, a division of the American Management Associations, Licensee, from B. Y. Auger, *How to Run Better Business Meetings*, © 1972 by Minnesota Mining and Manufacturing Company, pp. 156–161.

23
Case Method

Paul Pigors

Faith Pigors

During 62 years of marriage, Paul and Faith Pigors have integrated their ways of thinking and doing things to make the most of their human resources. This experience is reflected in the Pigors Incident Process.

Paul Pigors, *Harvard University, 1920–1924; B.S. cum laude; Ph.D. Harvard University, 1927. He taught at Harvard, the University of Rochester, and Tufts College. In 1941 he joined the MIT faculty, retiring in 1965 as Professor Emeritus, Industrial Relations. During and after his teaching years, he published books, articles, and pamphlets. His best-known book (with Professor Charles A. Myers) is* Personnel Administration: A Point of View and a Method. *The ninth edition appeared in 1981. Until 1978, the senior author also served as impartial arbitrator of labor disputes and as conference leader at Georgia Tech, Cal Tech, Washington University, the American Management Association, and in all three branches of the Armed Services.*

Faith Pigors, *2 years at the Ecole Normale de Musique, Paris, and attendance at Radcliffe College. She was for many years Consultant in Management Development for the Bureau of National Affairs, Washington, D.C. She also coauthored several books and three sets of cases published by BNA for the Incident Process. She worked with Paul, as participant observer-reporter, in courses at many U.S. business organizations as well as at summer sessions in England, Mexico, Hawaii, and Japan.*

Perhaps the greatest challenge in education—and the most puzzling one—is to discover what it is that keeps alive in some people the natural spark of curiosity, eagerness, hunger for life and experience, and how we may rekindle that spark when it flickers out. If we ever solve that problem, we will be at the threshold of a new era, not only in education but also in human experience.[1]

Constituent Elements of Case Method

One basic ingredient is the *case report*. In thinking about such a report (even by one's self), a second ingredient comes into play: *case analysis*. Talking about a case report with other people brings in the third ingredient: *case discussion*. Every form of case method necessarily uses all three ingredients.

Outstanding Applications of Case Method

The Harvard Method

This way of reporting actual situations and analyzing case reports is the oldest and most generally respected form. To many people, it is *the* case method. Originated in the 1880s by Christopher Langdell at the Harvard Law School, this nondirective way of helping students to think for themselves slowly won acceptance in law, medicine, business administration, and social work.

A major aim of the Harvard method has always been showing students how to learn by independent thinking—discerning in the "ever-tangled skein of human affairs"[2] principles and ideas which have lasting validity and general applicability.

In the Harvard method, teachers function as catalysts: they assign cases for study and provide a permissive environment for group discussion. They do not attempt to cover a topic by "telling 'em" (the lecture method). Instead, they help students to discover for themselves the facts and ideas—displayed in case reports—which are most meaningful to them.

The role of a Harvard teacher, in such a course, has been described operationally by Glover and Hower:

> "Let me summarize what I think I heard you say, to see if I caught what you were driving at." . . . "Would you mind elaborating that? I'm not sure it is clear to most of us." . . . "Is this what you mean?" . . . "I think I see your point, but I am having difficulty relating it to your previous interpretations (or to what Mr.——has just said, or to the situation as developed in the discussion so far)."[3]

Another hallmark of the Harvard method is the completeness of their published case reports.* For case writing, few institutions can equal the research division of the Harvard Business School. Members of its staff spend years in the field before writing case reports which faithfully describe actual situations.

However, to some students the Harvard reports have seemed overly detailed and time-consuming to read as preparation for case discussion.

---

* For examples, see John D. Glover and Ralph Hower, *The Administrator: Cases on Human Relations in Business*, 5th ed., Richard D. Irwin, Inc., Homewood, IL, 1973. Particularly useful to a course director are the excellent bibliographies compiled by Grace V. Lindfors: *Intercollegiate Bibliography: Cases in Business Administration*, Intercollegiate Clearing House, Soldiers Field, Boston. See also *Case Bibliography and Index: Management of Organizations— Europe*, Jean Burleson, ed., 1973.

The Wharton School "Live" Case Method: Then and Now

The "live" case approach was originated by Walter B. Murphy and instituted, in the early 1950s, at the Wharton School of Finance and Commerce. In its original form, each case was presented to students by an executive from an organization where the case situation had developed and where the difficulty recently had been, or currently was being, tackled. The immediacy of that approach was a convincing way to give what is nowadays referred to as "credibility" to the facts reported and immediacy to the issues which students were invited to analyze and discuss.

The procedure for study was as follows: (1) a brief written statement of an actual difficulty was given to students the day before the first classroom session at which (2) an executive presented the case orally, allowing most of the hour for questions. (3) Next, students met informally, in small groups, and each student wrote a brief analysis of the problem, adding his or her own solution and summarizing the report in a one-page letter to the executive. (4) At the second meeting of the whole class a student led the discussion. An instructor then selected 10 reports which he considered as the best and forwarded them to the executive. (5) The executive studied those reports, added comments, and returned the material to the instructor before meeting again with the whole class. (6) At this final meeting, the executive told the students about the historical solution to the problem, and commented on the student papers that had been sent to him. The meeting ended with a general discussion of solutions by management and by students.

Over the years that approach has been considerably modified. And as currently used at Wharton, the original name of the method has been dropped. But the authenticity of cases studied has been retained and the vitality of the approach has, in at least one course, been enhanced. These statements about current procedure were documented in a letter from Leonard Rico (Associate Professor, Department of Management, The Wharton School of the University of Pennsylvania). Here are the salient points:

> We emphasized exposure to "real world" problems, doing this in several ways. Guest lecturers, (line/staff) from area firms, provide students with up-to-date information from their own companies. And students do research in organizations. Numerous variations of what was formerly called the "live" case method are applied by instructors in the various Wharton disciplines.
>
> In my own courses I use the Incident Process and the Harvard case method to bring reality into the classroom. I also use project teams to evaluate problems of human resources in area firms. Teams act as consultants on problems defined by executives. They then make oral reports to the class and to company representatives, who evaluate these oral reports. Some firms also have teams report to representatives of upper management. Comments and suggestions on oral reports are incorporated into final, written reports which students submit at the end of the semester.

Centre Europeen D'Education Permanente

The following paragraphs are taken, with permission, from a 1985 description dictated by Professor Salvatore Teresi, general manager of CEDEP:

> This center for Permanent Education, founded in 1971, is located in Fontainebleau, adjacent to the European Institute of Business Administration (INSEAD). It constitutes a major development in the training of European executives. The principal teaching methods are participative—for example, the Harvard case method, various forms of group dynamics and micro-computer assisted learning.

The most innovative feature of this international Center is its associative and cooperative character. Originally founded by six major European industrial concerns, it now has a membership of 20 different companies from industry and service who actually manage the Center in collaboration with a staff of professional teachers, mostly from INSEAD.

The major educational program of CEDEP is the General Management course: a 12-week program divided into six training periods of two weeks each (at CEDEP) with an interval of three months (between each residential period) during which participating managers return to work in their respective companies. During the 3-month recesses, managers keep in touch with one another and with CEDEP staff members. INSEAD provides backup services, such as library and duplicating facilities.

The major objective of CEDEP is rapidly to create a "critical mass" of executives who have followed the same type of management development program. Within each member company, this will stimulate the development of a coherent "business culture" which will permeate the organization with managerial values, principles, and styles that have been approved by member companies.

Additional programs at CEDEP include: a 3-week course, for junior managers, on Efficient Management of Resources and Opportunities; a 5-day seminar, for senior managers, on competitive environmental changes and company responses; and a series of tailor-made programs designed to meet the training requirements of a given member company.

This venture of working with, and in, current situations is well designed to foster continuing self-education by executives.

These three outstanding examples of differing applications show a few ways in which case material can be presented, analyzed, and discussed. Below are a few other ways.

Other Varieties of Case Reports and Ways of Presenting Them

An easy way to cope with the recurrent problem of student resistance to assigned homework for case analysis is to invent a short case illustration.

The Fictitious and Abbreviated Case

A short case can be put together by using fragments from firsthand experience or from collateral reading, doctored to fit a specific purpose of some course director. However, no one truly interested in the development of human resources can afford to overlook the costly disadvantages of concocted case material. As discussants set to work on a fabricated case, some of them are sure to ask for more information. But discussion leaders who try to invent "facts," however adroit they may be as ad-libbers, are likely to become entangled in the web they weave. As they fumble for words, and perhaps contradict themselves, students tend to lose confidence in the leader's ability and integrity. Worse still, their interest in the case—now evidently fictitious—is likely to evaporate.

Labor Arbitration Reports

A far more useful form of abbreviated case material is provided by the American Arbitration Association. Their education department publishes monthly summaries of awards and opinions that were rendered under the rules of the association. These can be developed by anyone who has the time and ability to utilize the full-length report which can be purchased from the Arbitration Association.* (Of course, when that has been done, the case is no longer an abbreviated report.)

The Single Problem Case

This kind of case report offers factual data, but the material is *unrealistic*, because it is oversimplified. Students who have been "trained" by studying only this type of case report may think they have learned something useful. But they may be in for subsequent disappointments. No real life situation presents neatly packaged problems, labeled "Here I am. Solve me and you're all set." A case report that misrepresents reality to that extent offers no learning material for anything except academic problem solving. This undesirable consequence was (accidentally) emphasized by a student who, having graduated from a school of business administration, failed miserably in his first job. He put his dilemma in a nutshell with the comment: "If only someone would give me a problem, I know I could solve it. But all I can see here is a mess." He had made no progress in acquiring practical managerial skills, such as: (1) ferreting out relevant facts (for example, to clarify conflicting statements by two parties to a dispute); (2) disentangling different kinds of interactive difficulties (organizational, technical, and in human relations); (3) setting up a timetable (to determine which difficulty needs to be tackled "right now"); and (4) clarifying immediate issues (for decision and short-term action) in a way that avoids oversimplifying a complex situation or running contrary to long-term organization-wide policies and goals.

A convenient way to present a real life situation is with audiovisual presentations. This approach has important advantages for both teachers and students. Teachers don't need to do the research and writing required to prepare a full-length report. And a film that contains dialogue, as well as body language, stimulates students to develop feelings of identification with the characters portrayed.

The Pigors Incident Process (PIP)

Busy managers and graduate students, alike, have appreciated the fact that in this variation of orthodox case method there is *no required homework*. Instead, the case report is put together orally, during a class session. Current procedure is as follows:

Steps in a Cycle of Case Analysis

Step 1: Starting with an Incident.† Students begin work on a case by reading a page or less that depicts some point of climax in a case. Appended to this incident is the suggestion that conferees imagine that the incident has just occurred

* For an example, see Paul Pigors and Charles A. Myers, *Personnel Administrator: A Point of View and a Method*, 9th ed., McGraw-Hill Book Company, New York, 1981, case 17, pp. 550–555: "What Price the Corporate Image?"

† For a sample incident and a detailed description of techniques used, and results obtained, during a PIP course, see Vol. 29 of *The Instructional Design Library*, Educational Technology Publications, Englewood Cliffs, NJ, pp. 23–49, 1980.

and that (collectively) they adopt the role of a management representative responsible for coping with it promptly and effectively. Quick and casual readers can run their eyes over this brief sketch in a minute or two. But serious and perceptive students—able to read between the lines—search for possible clues to the total situation in which the incident developed.

Step 2: Getting and Organizing Factual Information on the Case as a Whole. Using the incident as a launching pad, students now question the discussion leader ("the man with the facts"). Alert and attentive questioners can usually bring out all the information needed to make a short-term decision about the incident in 20 to 30 minutes. But, at that point, they have on their hand a welter of facts. This "mess" needs to be sorted out, and reduced to manageable proportions, in a concise but complete summary. When working on their first case, it may be that no one feels willing to do this job off the cuff. If no one volunteers to sum up the facts of the first case, a written summary may be distributed— preferably for this session only.

Step 3: Visualizing Key Facts as Interrelated Factors and Formulating an Action Issue. At this stage, key elements in the case are highlighted, by diagraming issues. This diagram can also show interrelationships between these factors, and indicate their relative importance. When the elements for decision are thus displayed, students are well prepared (as management representatives responsible for coping effectively with this incident): what do we need to decide and do "right now"—while keeping in mind corporate policy and long-term organizational goals? Members of a study group always differ on this point. Therefore, the group at large divides into subcommittees of like-minded members.

Step 4: Making, Presenting, and Testing Reasoned Opinions. Members who agree on a decision for action usually disagree in their reasoning. But because each subcommittee is preparing to compete with the others, in "proving" that their decision is the best one, members are predisposed to listen to one another attentively. And usually defense mechanisms, which so often impede clear thinking, are put aside.

Next comes presentation of subcommittee opinions to the reconstituted group at large. This is done—either by elected spokespersons (who emphasisze reasoning) or by role players (who demonstrate what they would do, leaving the audience to infer the reasoning).

After the full range of opinions has been presented to the group at large, two ways of appraising these decisions follow. First, student decisions are compared and appraised during group discussion. Then the test of history is applied. What actually was decided and done in the case situation, when the incident was a current event?

Now comes what has proved, for some course directors, a flaw in the situation of the study group. Having decided and appraised various decisions for coping with an incident, conferees tend to feel that they have finished with the case. What remains to be done?

Step 5: Reflecting on the Case as a Whole. For purposes of managerial development in making the most of human resources what remains to be done is vital. In *re*-viewing an actual situation, case students can learn from opportunities that are often overlooked, or have to be skimped, by busy managers. In everyday life it may seem impractical, or even impossible, to spend time *looking back* over a sequence of events to see how a given difficulty built up, or *looking ahead*—to consider how the recurrence of a similar difficulty might be prevented. But case students have time to reflect.

To make the most of this culminating phase of case analysis, students may now be invited to promote themselves (collectively) to the organizational role of a senior executive—unless, of course, students in this particular course already *are* executives. At that organizational level, a major responsibility is to engage in long-term, high-level thinking. And that is what remains to be done now, in regard to the case-for-the-day.

To rekindle the interest of students who may be suffering from a sense of letdown, a tested technique is inviting them to consider—in small groups—one or more of the following questions: (1) What *favorable features* of the case (viz., organizational relationships, previous managerial actions, personalities, and company practices) were—or might have been—used as resources for productive interaction? (2) What *shortcomings in behavior, or other situational flaws*, seem to have been accountable (rather than who was to blame) for difficulties that showed up in the incident? (3) What needs and opportunities can be identified in the case with regard to corporate goals?

When students have selected the question(s) they wish to think about, small group work can begin. Elected spokespersons report the views of their constituents, while the discussion leader lists them, in three columns, where everyone can see them. (And the observer-for-the-day takes notes that will later be part of a report on that meeting.)

Another graphic way to record this stage of analysis is to diagram the major issues that have been discussed. They represent what may be called the heart of the case. If time runs out before this is done in class, the observer can incorporate the major-issues diagram in the report that will be rendered to the group. When such a diagram is made toward the end of a course, it will surely show that most of these same issues have emerged during discussion of several cases.

Conferees who make the most of opportunities offered during this five-step cycle of case analysis can develop their managerial and executive skills. However, two other features of the program can greatly increase the possibilities of learning from experience—both directly and vicariously.

Other Features of PIP

One such characteristic is shared leadership (in teamwork and by rotation among students as deputy leaders). The other is a course structure that takes account of the facts that: (1) when group members continue to meet together, each session is somewhat different from the previous one; and (2) each meeting is an integral part of an ongoing case situation.

Sharing Leadership Responsibilities. From the very beginning, shared leadership has been characteristic of PIP. At early meetings in MIT courses, natural leaders volunteered as summarizers or were elected to serve as spokespersons or role players. After group members had got the hang of the five-step cycle, deputy leaders prepared cases and led discussions (each for one meeting).

During the 1960s, shared leadership was instituted at a higher level, when the author delegated to his wife the duties of participant-observer-reporter. That staff role supplements the work of course directors who have their hands full preparing cases, answering fact-finding questions (in step 2), and diagraming issues. Meeting those responsibilities leaves little time for observing conferees who remain silent. Moreover, in appraising performance after each meeting, a teammate can be useful, especially one who has taken careful notes and has tried to understand why some students seem uninterested in what other participants are doing. In talking things over after a meeting, teammates may be able to think up a suggestion that will energize someone who has been virtually a nonparticipant. But sometimes the transition from inactivity to active participation comes about spontaneously, as a shy person responds to recognition by fellow members of a small group. Other changes in behavior come about during a series of meetings.

A Progressive Series of Meetings. Successive meetings may be called "progressive" when each one, after the first, builds on the previous session(s)—especially when periodic stocktaking and observer's reports enable case students to appraise past performance with course objectives and to set new targets.

To facilitate this kind of self-education, the current structure of a PIP course is as follows: mutual introductions, orientation, and induction. The nature of the first meeting takes account of the fact that the first need is for fellow students to become acquainted. Even in an in-house course, many conferees do not know one another by sight. And a printed name card cannot communicate nearly as much as is conveyed by the voice and manner of the person who sits behind the card.

After *mutual introductions* comes *orientation* to goals of the course, which students are invited to share. This objective can be met in various ways.* Toward the end of the first meeting time should be allowed for *induction* into the technical method that students will start using at the next meeting. This can be done by distributing copies of the five-step analytical cycle, allowing time for questions and explanations.

Demonstration and Practice Sessions. Having three of these meetings allows conferees to get the hang of the technical method. At the first one, minimum standards are set, and, especially if group members study a written report (prepared by the observer on the "first team"), these standards can rapidly be raised.

During these sessions a course director inevitably demonstrates a managerial style. (For PIP purposes, participative management has obvious advantages.) And, when course leadership is by a team, its members also communicate, by their behavior, what they believe about teamwork and about productive ways to function in a line and staff relationship. Toward the end of the last demonstration session, a course director may ask which conferees would like to volunteer as deputy discussion leaders and observer reporters.

Interim Stocktaking and Planning Session. Attention is now focused on "this case," as students—starting their work in subcommittees—consider the same three questions that they have been asking (in step 5) about "those cases out there." When subcommittees are small, each conferee has ample opportunity to participate.

As spokespersons report to the group at large, course directors should be prepared for some negative criticisms. If no "flaws" are reported, it is a sign that the atmosphere is not as free and informal as it needs to be. Often, however, negative comments turn out to be based on misunderstandings. If so, a course director is alerted to the possibility that more, or better, explanations during early meetings may be advisable in the future.

A written report by the "first team" observer can summarize subcommittee opinions as presented by spokespersons, and subsequent discussion and decisions can be made by the group as a whole. Toward the end of this meeting, or immediately afterward, several volunteers may be expected to sign up for leading roles.

---

* For two such ways, see Vol. 29, *The Instructional Design Library*, op. cit., pp. 57–59.

A Working Session. At the start of this meeting, conferees team up as deputy leaders. (During a 12-session course, each of five volunteer teams will be responsible for one meeting.) Preliminary work by those teams can be done at this session—thereby reducing the time needed for work outside the classroom. Another advantage of preparatory work done now is the opportunity to consult with members of the "first team" if deputy leaders have any questions.

Sometimes the size of a team (or of several) is now increased by including a "free observer." (Conferees who serve in that role are *free from* preparing a written report, and *free to* spend a whole meeting taking notes of what other participants are doing.) At best, dates are now set for all meetings which will be conducted by deputy leaders.

Meetings Led by Conferees. As leaders-for-the-day come "up front," the first team can appropriately step down—taking the seats vacated by deputy leaders. Naturally, however, the course director *retains accountability* for what gets done by deputy leaders. And the participant-observer-reporter doesn't stop taking notes of what seems to be happening in the group as a whole, as well as *in* some participants when their expressive behavior is picked up as a clue.

Final Stocktaking and Planning Meeting. This session can best start with subcommittee work. One committee can be composed of deputy discussion leaders. Another may consist of observer-reporters. Each of these subgroups is invited to consider questions such as: What have we learned by taking these leading roles? What might we have done better? Might any changes in our job descriptions, or in course procedure, have been helpful? Members who have worked in neither leading role can constitute a committee for overall evaluation. Items on their agenda typically include: objectives and structure of the course, techniques and procedures used, leadership abilities needed and demonstrated for such work, and perceived progress since the course began. Changes in procedure suggested by conferees at such meetings have benefited members of future courses, as PIP gradually evolved.

People who know about PIP only by reading about it might well ask: "When so much work is done in subcommittees, and nearly half the meetings are conducted by deputies, is there much left for a course director to do?" Anyone who has actually conducted such a course knows that course directors have their hands full. Here is an outline of the overall assignment.

A Multiple Role for Course Directors. Before and during a series of meetings, interlinking responsibilities include functioning as:

Planner. For each course as a whole, for cases to be used in demonstration sessions, and for the special meetings which focus on "this case."

Representative of Group Purpose. Demonstrating by everything they do (and refrain from doing) an appropriate role for a case student who is also a responsible leader.

Communicator. Largely by "who" they are. Personality is inevitably communicated in a course director's willingness and ability to listen attentively and empathically, to speak and write clearly, to encourage participation, and to welcome criticism.

Manager. Of people working together for effective results.

Host and Supervisor. Beginning at the first meeting, when major responsibilities include mutual introductions, orientation to goals that case students are invited to share, and induction into procedures and techniques that will be used.

Provider of Factual Information. About PIP as a technical method and, in step 2, during demonstration sessions.

Technical Consultant. On tap to offer advice to deputies—when requested.

Pinch Hitter. If some leader-for-the-day has been unable to finish preparatory work or if a deputy observer is unavoidably absent or was never signed up. Pinch hitting as an observer-for-the-day can be instructive for someone whose usual responsibilities allow little time for watching what happens during a meeting.

Perennial Student. Evincing willingness to accept suggestions for changes in current practice, and even—if comments at stocktaking meetings suggest that it would be advisable—to make changes in their own behavior.

The above outline of a course director's role shows one aspect of PIP. Another view can be given by considering criteria for the constituent elements of case method.

Criteria for Constituent Elements of Case Method

Case method can't do all it might do unless all its constituent elements meet high standards. For example, when the goal of case study is to acquire proficiency in techniques and arts of developing human resources, starting with a fictitious *case report* may be a total waste of time or worse. A fabricated case can block realistic learning. Worse still, it may induce boredom and distrust. Similarly, when *case analysis* is hurried, superficial, and done by one person alone, the result may be biased to the extent that it does more harm than good. Even *case discussion* can be fully productive only when a range of views is clearly presented by participants who feel free to say what they think, and whose comments are attentively listened to. Such talking and listening can lead to a useful integration of the best elements in all expressed.

For best results, the three constituent elements of case method must—in our opinion—meet the following standards.

The Case Report

Such a word picture should:

Show facts, not give the writer's opinions. Conferees are then free to make up their own minds as to the relative importance of reported data and the immediate issues.

Be objectively stated, not seriously warped by bias. However, *facts-as-perceived* cannot be identical with *facts-as-they-are.* Therefore, all reporting is to some extent selective and interpretive.

Give a multiple, inside view. This can be done when case writers interview participants (especially those whose views of issues and even, perhaps, of certain facts differ considerably). By interviewing insiders, it is also possible to show that facts of feeling can be more powerful in shaping events than are objectively verifiable facts.

Indicate interpersonal relationships—both formal and informal.

Portray process. How did the situation change during the time span of the case report?

Case Analysis

Analyzing a case situation (or case report) should meet some of the same criteria already listed for case reporting. It should:

Be comprehensive and many-sided. These standards are much easier to meet in group work, and when there is time to do a more thorough job, than when a person does it alone and in a hurry.

Be relatively objective. This criterion, also, is more nearly attainable in group work than when attempted by a single individual. Members of a group can be expected to express different views, especially about issues. Unwarranted assumptions and biases are likely to be challenged.

Be flexible. Searching a case report for meaning should not be limited by a checklist of questions automatically applied to every case. Each situation is to some extent unique.

Offer practice in problem solving and decision making. Case analysis in a group presents opportunities to experiment with a variety of techniques that can contribute to realistic solutions for many kinds of problems, and for decisions that will stand up (because they are based on verified facts and supported by sound reasoning).

Focus periodically on "this case." Thus students can see the practical uses of academic techniques when applied in a current situation.

Culminate in reflection on the case as a whole. Unless reflection is part of a cycle used—in regard to both "those cases" and "this case"—conferees are unlikely to carry with them the kinds of general ideas that are applicable in a variety of situations that they live through.

Case Discussion

To offer a full measure of learning, discussion of a case should:

Achieve coverage. This criterion entails talking about all aspects of a case at the level of facts, considering issues (both short- and long-term), and bringing out the full range of conferee opinions (on issues and decisions).

Be focused at each stage. Talk that swings back and forth between facts, issues, and opinions sinks to the level of a bull session.

Keep moving. At any given time, group attention should be centered on only one aspect of the case, and in one stage of case analysis. But it should not become stalled by unprofitable argument—as happens when two or more speakers go round and round in arguing some difference of opinion. How fast should talk move? Managerial skill is required to set a pace that is approximately right for the group as a whole—not too slow to hold the attention of quick-thinking members or so fast that slower thinkers cannot keep track of what is being said.

Be free and informal. Freedoms that can and should be made available include trying out ideas for size, citing firsthand experience (relevantly and briefly), and speaking one's mind—in considered opinions—without regard to the status of those who differ.

Students who have practiced a form of case method whose elements meet the above standards have had a variety of opportunities to work productively both as independent problem solvers and decision makers, and as cooperative group members.

Factors That Favor Progress by Case Students

As in any other situation where people work together for results—on a baseball field, as crew members in a space shuttle, or as players in a string quartet—forces that affect what a current situation can become may be grouped under the following headings.

Technical Factors

In a case study group, these include: *selection of cases* for study (Well adapted to capacities of students? Presented in a way that brings the case report to life? CEDEP and Wharton are outstanding examples of what can be done.); *method of case analysis* (as in PIP, for example); use of *group dynamics*; and practice offered in a *range of skills* (for example, as at Harvard, Wharton, and in PIP).

There is no hard-and-fast line between technical and human and social factors. The degree of success achieved by using any technique depends, in large measure, on the individuals who use it and on social factors which affect individual feelings and behavior. Nevertheless, there are significant differences between these situational features.

Human and Social Factors

These include professional qualifications and experience of official leaders, as well as their attitudes and behavior; student qualifications (overlapping with, and reinforcing, those of official leaders) such as concern for and interest in work associates; intelligence, vitality, alertness, and curiosity; willingness to work (occasionally on overtime, as volunteers); courage (to speak up in ways that promote group process, as when someone says: "Sorry. But I don't understand what you're talking about."); size and mix of the study group (large enough to provide some range of difference, yet small enough to permit active participation by every group member and, for an in-house course, with a mix of professional interest, in people from several organizational levels); age and length of experience represented by case students (preferably not so young that they think they know all the answers, but with enough experience as organizational subordinates and supervisors so that they already know how much they need to learn).

A third situational factor affects all the others.

Space and Time Dimensions

For a case study group, significant aspects of space and time include location, arrangement, and size of the conference room. (Reasonably accessible to all conferees? Relatively remote from noisy operations outside, and protected—by previous agreement—from outside interruptions by telephone calls? Arranged with chairs around a table—thus permitting easy communication among all conferees? Large enough so that subcommittees can confer, periodically, around smaller tables, with some degree of privacy?) Significant aspects of the time factor include *timing* and *length* of formal sessions. Especially in an in-house course, it is advantageous to schedule classes for an early morning hour—preferably before conferees have embarked on their regular (organizational) work assignments. On that schedule they are likely to feel more free to concentrate on the academic case-for-the-day, instead of being preoccupied by current difficulties in their full-time work situation—perhaps a problem whose solution could permanently affect their career. Two hours are needed for thoroughgoing case analysis. A weekly interval between meetings allows time for students to assimilate new ideas, and possible to try out a few of them. (The CEDEP schedule is exceptionally favorable in this respect.) *Length* of the course is another key factor (and here again CEDEP is outstanding). Ten to twelve sessions is a minimum time within which to expect learning at the level where students consider making attitudinal and behavioral changes. A semester-long course is greatly preferable.

A fourth situational factor also affects progress in a study group.

Climate

Significant features of the psychological climate are both external and internal. For an in-house course, the attitudes of top executives and the behavior by immediate organizational superiors are crucial. (Does top management regard this kind of educational opportunity by their subordinates as a worthwhile organizational investment? Does the daily behavior of immediate organizational superiors reinforce new ideas?) Within the study group itself, a favorable climate can—to a considerable extent—mitigate chilling blasts from skeptical or authoritarian superiors. (Inside the study group, do official leaders set the tone for an atmosphere that is friendly and informal? Do natural leaders within the group help to generate the degree of warmth in which new ideas can grow and proliferate, while differences can melt away?)

When most of the above-mentioned features are favorable, steady progress toward a long-term goal of the case method can confidently be expected. However, the pace of progress and the stage reached naturally differs among individual participants. Some people enter the course at a point ahead of that where others finish. But all educable persons who want to develop their managerial skills—in making the most of human resources—can make headway from wherever they start.

Milestones toward a Long-Term Goal

Proficiency in Academic Techniques

Skills emphasized, and kinds of practice offered, differ according to different methods used. A number of these techniques and practices have been described in earlier pages and need not be repeated.

Effective Teamwork

To us, the term teamwork denotes two things: (1) team spirit, plus sufficient practice to ensure quick and smooth coordination of action, and (2) communication so effective that it can often take place without spoken words.

Farther along the road, and reached by relatively few case students, is the milestone marked case-mindedness.

Case-Mindedness

This term denotes ability to view a current situation—in which one is personally and emotionally involved—with something of the objectivity that befits a case student. Emotional detachment enables a person to think clearly and dispassionately about facts and issues, to take into account the feeling-facts that motivate other participants, and to make decisions for short-term action that incorporate thinking about long-term goals of paramount importance. Case-mindedness includes incident-awareness—recognition that even superficially trivial incidents may, if ignored, grow into big problems.

Reaching the milestone of case-mindedness marks a double gain because it also indicates that case students have made headway in learning how to learn vicariously, as well as by firsthand experience. From then on, questions they ask in reviewing one of "those cases" habitually include: What seems to have been accountable for what went wrong? Might available resources (technical, human, or organizational) have been used more effectively? And in trying to prevent the recurrence of difficulties that showed up in that case, how might similar resources be put to good use in future?

Changes in Attitude and Behavior

Not far beyond case-mindedness, the next milestone carries a sign saying: "Change attitudes here." These changes, to be expected toward the end of a semester-long course, were well described by a highly qualified psychologist. From close observation of case students at Harvard, the late Professor Irving J. Lee derived the following generalizations:

> [At first they tend to see themselves as critics.] They begin what is easier, judging, approving, condemning . . . [But gradually their] easy praising and blaming gives way to asking, searching, listening . . . [Thus a conference room] can become a testing-ground on which each member can measure the reach of his own arts and habits of communication.[4]

Our own experience suggests that those statements are somewhat overgeneralized. In how many study groups do *all members* make such changes?

A Triple Blend of Understanding: A Long-Term Goal

A milestone still farther from where most of us start, and closer to an unattainable ideal, is nevertheless useful as an aim to work toward. This goal is a blend of understanding which combines a high degree of the following ingredients:

1. *Intellectual capacity.* Ability to think clearly, at all levels of abstraction; rapidly to assimilate and organize a mass of information; skill in identifying, formulating, and integrating issues for short- and long-term action; aptitude for deriving from current events guidelines for future action; awareness of one's own strengths and weaknesses; the art of gaining insight from information and of using both insight and hindsight to develop foresight; agility in going "up and down the ladder of abstraction," ascending from facts to the level of general ideas and coming down again, to take action at the level of facts—practicing the art of generalizing from experience in a manner at once realistic and flexible. To that end, it is useful to employ working hypotheses—generalizations with a broad base of observation, but not set in concrete. A working hypothesis earns its pay by keeping the mind of

a person who employs it open to fresh perceptions. A working hypothesis is subject to performance appraisal and—if it hasn't worked well—to replacement.

2. *Sensitivity, empathy, and interpersonal skills.* These elements of understanding add up to social literacy. *Sensitivity* enables a person to become aware of inner meanings in other people, deeper than those that can be discerned by intelligence alone. *Empathy* contributes to appreciation even of feelings that one does not share. Such appreciation can power the hypothesis that beneath any apparently unreasonable act there is always some kind of reason. And *interpersonal skills* often make it possible to *work with* a person who has been driven into what seems (to outsiders) like utterly unreasonable behavior.

3. *Common sense.* This relatively rare ingredient of understanding is partly intuitive. But experience in any given field of activity—supplemented by case analysis—can improve a person's practical judgment of what will work and what won't partly because a given decision will or will not prove acceptable to those upon whom one must depend to make it work. Common sense can include organization sense. For a subordinate, this entails knowing when to speak up, how, and to whom—if organizational practice permits any such activity from managerial representatives at lower organizational levels.

Although perfection is unattainable, case study can offer guidelines, practice, and motivation for anyone in search of this blend of understanding. And one reason why case study is useful is that it stimulates the habit of questioning. It has been well said that "to live is to ask questions of life." Is that why so many people find case study so enlivening?

In our opinion, case method can be far more educational than the lecture method in developing human resources. How much mental stimulation and learning can be gained during the relatively passive state in which many people attend an average lecture? Observation suggests that often a state of somnolence grips many "listeners," rendering them unfit to ask even one question when the lecturer hopefully concludes his remarks with the invitation: "Are there any questions?" Case method, on the other hand, offers little opportunity for dozing and many opportunities for doing. Thus case students tend to become interested and invigorated to the point where they not only want to learn but actually do learn— with associates and by themselves—continuing this process as a means of lifelong self-education. When the aim is managerial development, can more be asked of any method for developing human resources?

References

1. Gardner, John W., *No Easy Victories*, Harper & Row, New York, 1968, p. 105.

2. Redlich, Josef, *The Common Law and the Case Method in American University Law Schools*, a report to the Carnegie Foundation for the Advancement of Teaching, Bulletin No. 8, New York, 1914, p. 12.

3. Glover, John D., and Ralph M. Hower, "Some Comments on Teaching by the Case Method," in Kenneth B. Andrews, ed., *The Case Method of Teaching Human Relations and Administration: An Interim Statement*, Harvard University Press, Cambridge, MA, 1953, p. 20.

4. Lee, Irving J., *Customs and Crises in Communication: Cases for the Study of Some Barriers and Breakdowns*, Harper & Brothers, New York, 1954, preface, p. xii.

Bibliography

Beaumont, P.B., "The Diffusion of Human Resource Management Innovations," *Relations Industrielles*, 1985, Vol. 40, No. 2, pp. 243–256.

Boeker, Warren, Rebecca Blair, M. Frances Van Loo, and Karlene Roberts, "Are the Expectations of Women Managers Being Met?" *California Management Review*, vol. XXVII, No. 3, Spring 1985, pp. 148–157.

Gardner, John W., *No Easy Victories*, Harper & Row, New York, 1968.

Glover, John D., and Ralph Hower, *The Administrator: Cases on Human Relations in Business*, 5th ed., Richard D. Irwin, Inc. Homewood, IL, 1973.

Lee, Irving, J., *Customs and Crises in Communication: Case for the Study of Some Barriers and Breakdowns*, Harper & Brothers, New York, 1954.

Muczyk, Jan P., Eleanor Brantly Schwartz, and Ephraim Smith, *Principles of Supervision: First- and Second-Level Management*, Bell & Howell Co., Columbus, OH, 1984, Case Two: "Will More Money Be a Motivator?" pp. 360–366.

The Pigors Incident Process: Case Studies for Management Development, Series I. "Practical Supervisory Problems (Blue Collar Cases)," Series II. "Government Cases—Federal, State and Local," Series III. "Office Supervision and Middle Management (White Collar Cases)," published by The Bureau of National Affairs in packaged sets for use in group work.

Pigors, Paul, and Faith Pigors, *Case Method in Human Relations: The Incident Process*, McGraw-Hill, New York, 1961, Case VI. "Inside a Study Group," pp. 301–327; Case IX. "A Critic Criticized," pp. 349–368.

Pigors, Paul, and Charles A. Myers, *Personnel Administration: A Point of View and a Method*, McGraw-Hill, 9th ed., New York, 1981, Case 17, "What Price the Corporate Image?" pp. 550–555.

Pigors, Paul, and Faith Pigors, "The Incident Process—A Method of Inquiry," *Nursing Outlook*, October 1966, Vol. 14, No. 10.

Pigors, Paul, Faith Pigors, and Marita Tribou, *Professional Nursing Practice: Cases and Issues*, McGraw-Hill, New York, 1967.

Pigors, Paul, L.C. McKenny, and T.O. Armstrong, *Social Problems in Labor Relations: A Case Book*, McGraw-Hill, New York, 1939.

Redlich, Josef, *The Common Law and the Case Method in American University Law Schools*, a report to Carnegie Foundation for the Advancement of Teaching, Bulletin 8, New York, 1914, p. 12.

Sutton, Charlotte Decker, and Kris K. Moore, "Executive Women—20 Years Later," *Harvard Business Review*, September-October 1985, Vol. 63, No. 5, pp. 42–66.

24
Role Playing*

Phyliss Cooke

Phyliss Cooke is director of professional services; dean of the Master of Human Resource Development Degree Program; dean of the HRD Intern Program; and senior consultant for University Associates, Inc., San Diego, California. Cooke conducts workshops in organizational development, small-group training theory and practice, experiential learning technologies, program design and delivery, communications skills, conflict management, and facilitating organizational change. She conducts customized training and consults with public and private organizations and the military. Cooke trains others in training technologies such as role plays, structured experiences, and instrumentation. She coaches managers in developing work groups, planning and conducting meetings, team building, and communication. Recent consulting has taken her to the Far East, Australia, and Canada. Cooke is a certified Situational Leadership trainer. She received a Ph.D. in counselor education from Kent State University. She was administrative director of the Cleveland Institute for Rational Living, psychologist for the Cleveland Board of Education, and a therapist in private practice.

Role playing is the most effective training technology available to the group facilitator for the dual purpose of helping individuals (1) to develop and enhance behavioral skills and (2) to explore attitudes that affect their behavior. Furthermore, because many of the principles for using role playing also apply to the implementation of other highly experiential technologies, mastering the role-play technology can enhance a facilitator's general effectiveness.

To be able to make role plays as useful as possible for training purposes, the facilitator should have at least a general understanding of the relationship between

* The content of this chapter has in part been extracted and adapted from Pfeiffer;[1] from Jones and Pfeiffer;[2] and from Shaw, Corsini, Blake, and Mouton.[3] All material has been used with the permission of the publisher.

430

attitudes and behavior as well as an appreciation of the complex psychological processes through which new behavioral patterns are formed. Although most facilitators do not have advanced degrees in these areas of cognitive processing, most *do* have enough background in the behavioral sciences to allow them to develop the skills needed to employ this technology sensitively in their training and educational events.

The following section is a review of various experiential training technologies and is intended to provide a conceptual framework for discussing the general principles for using role plays in training and educational endeavors.

Major Training Technologies

Figure 24-1 depicts a number of major training interventions along a continuum from didactic to experiential (based in part on Hall[4] and on Tannenbaum and Schmidt[5]). It also shows the relationship between visible learner involvement and the source of meaning of the material being learned. With experiential approaches—those that primarily stress active participant involvement in contrast to passive receptivity—the learning is presumably internalized and is therefore more effective.

Across the bottom of Figure 24-1, there is a classification of human relations training approaches and techniques, ordered according to the extent to which each incorporates visible learner involvement. The least involving intervention is reading, in which the learner is in a *reactive* mode, passively receiving and vicariously experiencing. The most involving intervention is the intensive growth group, in which the learner is encouraged to be *proactive*, to take responsibility for his or her own learning. In between these two extremes are activities that range from lectures to structured experiences.

The experiential lecture is more involving than the traditional lecture approach because it incorporates activities on the part of the "audience." These interruptions are designed to personalize the points of the lecture and/or to generate readiness for the next topic.

Discussion is a time-honored teaching intervention that has been extended and refined in participation training, particularly by adult educators at Indiana Univer-

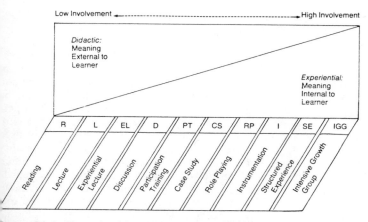

Figure 24-1. The technology of human relations training.

sity. The case-study method, developed and popularized in business education by professors at Harvard Business School, is closely related to role playing, in which a "case" is acted out in a semistructured format.

The use of paper-and-pencil instruments involves learners in self-assessment. The didactic component comes from the theory underlying the items of the particular scale that is used in the instrument. Structured experiences stress high participation and "processing" of data generated during interactive activities.

Intensive growth groups exist in many forms, such as counseling, T-groups, encounter, and therapy. They are characterized by high learner involvement and interaction. The data for learning come from the life experiences and here-and-now reactions of the group members. Participants are expected to integrate their learning into new self-concepts on their own terms.

The involvement dimension in Fig. 24-1 could be replaced with any of several other dimensions that would vary similarly. For example, at the highly didactic end of the scale (reading) would go low *risk*, low *self-disclosure*, and low *interaction with others*. The other end, highly experiential (intensive growth group) is associated with high values on these same dimensions (risk, self-disclosure, and interaction). Each of the training approaches and techniques is, of course, useful for certain purposes, and there are various training situations that are most appropriate for one or another.

Facilitators are continually faced with the task of planning activities to meet the learning needs of participants. The choice of an effective intervention is made after the participants' learning needs have been assessed and a statement of training objectives has been formulated.

Three factors determine which approach is used: the maturity of the group, the skill and experience of the facilitator, and the environment in which the training takes place. The key to success in using role plays lies in accurately assessing these three factors. Because the participants' learning needs represent a *critical* design consideration, it is imperative that the participants understand and accept the facilitator's decision to incorporate role playing into the training design as well as the relevance of the data to be generated during the role-play activity. If the facilitator is successful in promoting understanding and acceptance, resistance to role playing is minimal and the participants' interest in the activity carries the design.

The Objectives of Role Playing

Another critical design consideration is clarity of objectives. A number of objectives in human relations training can be realized through role playing. The approach can be used to demonstrate various skills and concepts in interpersonal relations and communications. Problems being experienced by a participant group can be "staged" to achieve a different perspective. Role playing can be applied to personnel selection, as in assessment centers. It can provide a powerful means of experiencing different behaviors in order to evaluate their effects. It can also be used to create a database for interpersonal feedback within a human relations laboratory learning situation. Inasmuch as many experiential learning concepts are often difficult for participants to apply to their everyday work, role playing offers a vehicle for delivering theory input in an engrossing and stimulating way that is relevant to real-world problem situations. Theoretical concepts can be incorporated into role descriptions and into the role-play problem. Role playing also has the additional potential of generating affective content for purposes of exploring relationships between feelings and behavior in human interactions. Role plays can be selected or devised to study the probable effects of different behaviors on the participants in a problem situation, thereby providing a potential learning opportunity for individuals to develop an increased sensitivity both to their own and to others' feelings. Shaw, Corsini, Blake, and Mouton[3] suggest that role plays are conducted for one or more of the following purposes:

1. *Diagnosing.* Establishing a better understanding of the role players by seeing and hearing them in action

2. *Informing.* Giving observers (those participants who are watching and listening but not actively engaged in the role play itself) an opportunity for vicarious learning

3. *Training.* Providing the role players with insights as well as an opportunity to practice behavioral skills (by experiencing a nearly "real" situation and then receiving feedback that might help them to understand themselves and to improve their behavior)

4. *Evaluating.* Providing a sample of behavior for purposes of analyzing and evaluating performance or responses

Given the various purposes that can be served, it is easy to see why role players must clearly understand the specific training purpose(s) of a particular role play if that role play is to succeed. In fact, the *primary* reason that role plays often evoke negative feelings in participants and are considered to be the hardest technology to implement is that the facilitator is not clear about or has not clearly communicated the purpose(s) to be served. For example, the facilitator may be intending to provide an opportunity to *practice* effective communication skills, but the participants may feel that they are being "evaluated" and may be unwilling to take advantage of the opportunity to make mistakes while learning these complicated skills. In other instances, past experiences in which the participants felt criticized may inhibit their ability to profit from direct practice with corrective feedback. It is up to the facilitator to set and maintain a tone that is conducive to learning and psychological safety in exploring current attitudes and/or behaviors.

Advantages and Disadvantages

Although role playing has a number of obviously desirable applications, it also presents some potential disadvantages. The facilitator needs to be aware of both the advantages and the disadvantages in order to be able to optimize the benefits and minimize the potentially negative aspects.

Potential Advantages

Participants typically experience role playing as an engaging activity. Because almost everyone know how to play someone else's role, participants tend to enjoy role plays, and it is unnecessary for them to learn new skills in order to benefit from the process. Also, role playing is often fun, although overplaying a part can detract from the learning. When role playing is conducted skillfully, the situations have a high credibility for participants, thereby reducing resistance to learning relevant skills and theory.

The technique is highly flexible. The facilitator can change the role play as it is being conducted, and the materials can be edited to fit particular situations. Role playing can be engaged in for brief or long periods. The technique often minimizes the threat of interpersonal interaction in human relations training: it is sometimes easier to explore oneself by projecting oneself into a role than to expose oneself directly. Participants are allowed to carry out decisions without the danger of embarrassing or incriminating themselves in "real" situations. Role playing can increase participants' awareness about the effects of feelings on social behavior.

Perhaps the most decided advantage of role playing in a training or educational context is that it uses the experiences of participants in ways that increase their ownership of learning. Because it provides a vehicle for focused feedback to individual participants, it can assist in developing the expressing of feelings. Through the medium of role playing, various problems in systems can be studied in a way that brings the "human factor" of organizational situations into sharper focus. Because it has the potential to develop skills in self-expression, listening, communicating points of view, and interpersonal interaction, role playing can raise participants' consciousness about the need for skills in human relations training. It can also permit the simulation of problem issues that arise infrequently in personal or work situations but are very important when they do arise. Thus, role playing offers participants the opportunity for hard-to-obtain experience in dealing with such situations.

Potential Disadvantages

Several potential disadvantages are inherent in the role-play technique. One obvious one is that the artificiality, superficiality, or apparent oversimplification of the situations depicted in role-play situations can allow participants to discount the value of their learning. A second problem is that sometimes participants lose themselves in roles and engage in inadvertent self-disclosure, exposure, and ventilation. It is important that the facilitator point out this possibility to participants. The facilitator should be particularly aware of this disadvantage in order to avoid the ethical breach of allowing people unknowingly to make themselves vulnerable. Role playing can be a threatening experience for a significant minority of participants, and the facilitator needs to be sensitive to the pressures faced by those participants.

A third disadvantage is that roles sometimes reinforce stereotypes and caricature people's behavior. This unfortunate side effect can be avoided if the facilitator ensures that role descriptions are credible and nonstereotypical and that role players are instructed not to portray their roles as caricatures. Fourth, role playing can deteriorate into play, and the serious learning potential inherent in the process can thereby be jeopardized. A fifth problem arises when role plays are staged in front of an audience: the passivity of the audience can lessen the impact of the learning. In such a case, it is important that members of the audience have active roles as observers or coaches.

Sixth, role plays can overpersonalize problem situations; for example, in role plays conducted in connection with team-building efforts, problems facing organizational work units are sometimes aggravated by the participants' tendency to perceive feedback personally and to see issues in terms of individuals. Role playing can, through such overinvolvement, generate excess affect, and the facilitator should be aware of the need to keep the learning focus sharply delineated.

Designing Role Plays

In designing role plays, the facilitator can avoid the potential disadvantages of the technique through certain design considerations, choice of role-play problems, dimensions of role-play structure, careful development of materials, and detailed preparation.

Design Considerations

Several design considerations are useful in creating role-play situations. Within the situation itself and the descriptions of the roles and individual players, it is often important that there be a broad range of human problems. Unless the role play is intended to demonstrate ineffective behavior, participants should be given an opportunity to behave effectively. This is particularly true if the major objective of the role play is to develop skills, in which case the emphasis should be on acknowledging and reinforcing the desired results.

In the role-playing situation it is ideal to have conflict and variety. Generally it is desirable to avoid getting too close to actual, current organizational situations. Using actual problem situations as the content of role-play activities can have a number of negative consequences, including the following:

1. Defensive behavior on the part of participants may be evoked.

2. Participants may concentrate on solutions rather than focus on aspects of the problem.

3. Basic disagreement on issues may be generated, leading to polarization within the participant group.

4. The organizational situations commonly addressed in organization development have many causes, and the human dimensions within them are obscured. Role playing may oversimplify such situations and lead to misleading generalizations.

In setting up role-play situations it is therefore best to use simulated problems before attempting to use real organizational problems. If, however, real problems are being used, it is better to focus on existing problems rather than ones that have been "solved," in order to minimize blaming.

Choice of Role-Play Problems

Many types of problems can be suggested for creating role-play situations. It is possible to focus on personal problem behaviors such as being unable to say "no" or being shy. Problems inherent in leadership situations can easily be set up for role playing: boss-subordinate interactions lend themselves well to exploration; and performance appraisal, a special type of boss-subordinate behavior, can be studied effectively. It is easy to establish role-play situations that simulate various aspects of staff meetings, such as the influence of hidden agendas on the conduct of the meeting. Integration problems, such as a "we-they" attitude, can be studied effectively. Peer relationships between colleagues can be role-played also. It is perhaps more ambitious but entirely possible to design role plays that explore any aspect of a functioning organization.

Some Dimensions of Role-Play Structure

At least four common dimensions of role-play structure can be identified.

Extent of Active Involvement. A role play may be acted out by several groups at once or by only one group. Obviously the total number of participants will affect the facilitator's decision; one could not have four role-play groups of five people each if the total number of participants were ten. However, the facilitator typically does have a choice regarding the extent of active involvement.

The *multiple role play*, in which several groups act out the same role play at once, often in the same room, is probably most common, and it does have certain advantages; it gives maximum opportunity for everyone to participate; it enables comparisons to be made of the several outcomes to the same situation produced by different groups; and it often helps shy or reticent participants to overcome these feelings and become involved.

The *single-group role play*, however, in which one group carries out the role play "on stage," in front of an audience, also has several advantages: it aids in diagnosing others' feelings through observation of their behavior; it is highly appropriate for small groups (fewer than ten people); it is particularly useful for advanced or intensive training; it permits audience members to develop observational skills and to serve as external consultants to the role players; and it makes it possible to stop the action at critical points and start again, giving the facilitator much more control over the role-play process and allowing him or her to capitalize on what happens in the role play without losing sight of the learning goals. Because only one set of behaviors occurs, the details that have been observed by everyone can be discussed, and individual role players can receive highly focused feedback on their behavior.

Degree of Situational Structure. The second dimension centers on the degree to which the role-play situation is structured. At one extreme a written skit calls for role players to act out their roles from a line-by-line script. This has the advantage of producing a highly focused demonstration, but the impact of the participants' spontaneous involvement in their roles is minimal. Skit completion begins with a highly structured reading of lines, but at some point the script ends and participants continue spontaneously. Perhaps the most common degree of structure is represented by the dramatized case, which is read silently and individually by each role player. The case may be in the form of a script but is more often simply a page or so of background material. Role players pick up on the action in a spontaneous way, at the point at which the written case concludes. The higher the degree of structure, the more certain it is that specifically defined learning points will be made, but the lower the participants' personal experiential involvement will be.

Degree of Role Multiplicity. The third dimension is the degree of role multiplicity. That is, it is often desirable to have one or more persons act as backups or "alter egos" to a particular role player. At one extreme, an audience can be divided up so that each segment identifies with one of the role players in a single-group, on-stage role play. A kind of minimum condition, at the other extreme, would be assigning observers to be limited alter egos, for a multiple role play. The alter ego can coach the role player to help him or her analyze a situation more objectively, can help keep him or her "in role," can provide support for the role player in difficult situations, and can step in and change places with the role player if desirable. Using one or more alter egos actively involves more participants in the role play and is advantageous from that standpoint.

Degree of Nonverbal Emphasis. Finally, an often-neglected dimension concerns the degree of nonverbal emphasis in the role-play situation. Role plays can be used to focus exclusively on nonverbal behavior (through the use of pantomime for all communication, for example). Although this approach generates awareness of nonverbal factors in interpersonal behavior, a more realistic approach might involve explicit role instructions that include directions about nonverbal behavior. Observers' instructions, too, can be designed to focus on this dimension.

The four dimensions described here are independent, and they can be combined in almost any imaginable way. For example, a multiple role play can be designed with an incomplete (open-ended) script, using two alter egos and concerning scripted nonverbal behaviors. Equally possible is a single-group, on-stage design using a dramatized case with everyone but the role players being observers and with nonverbal behavior left unexamined. Specific designs depend on the learning goals, the specific content issues, the nature of the population, and the facilitator's preferences, along with other factors. Awareness of these dimensions and the range of choices they imply should help the facilitator in the design process.

Development of Materials

It is important to develop clear, concise, and highly focused materials for use in a role play: they should be readable and not too lengthy or too complicated for a participant to remember. Ordinarily a role play requires some case-background data to set the scene for participants. Occasionally, further information ("bulletins," "telegrams," "letters," "notes," and so forth) is used to affect the role play as it progresses. The role descriptions should be written in uncomplicated language for the individual players and should include some hints on how to play the role. Observer background-data sheets need to be provided for people in the "audience." It is highly desirable for observers to have paper-and-pencil instruments to focus their reactions. Otherwise there may be a tendency to overpersonalize the observation and to fail to focus on the specific learning intended.

Instead of using prepared, written role materials provided by the facilitator, participants can create their own roles. This approach minimizes the need for printed materials, but it is often more difficult for the facilitator to handle in that the outcome is less predictable and may not be consistent with the expressed learning goals.

Preparations for Role Playing

It is important for the facilitator to prepare for the role play by establishing a proper set, continually keeping the objectives clear, and ensuring that the entire experience has an obvious logic to it.

The importance of establishing a proper set early cannot be overemphasized. Since the term "role playing" can connote "fun and games" for some people, it is up to the facilitator to establish that the activity is intended to promote learning. The objectives should be specified beforehand, except in a situation intended to explore covert interpersonal processes (for example, the use and impact of hidden agendas). Even in such a case, however, the facilitator needs to be constantly aware of the objectives.

In setting up the situation the facilitator should provide an overview to establish who is going to be involved and how. Participants can be selected to play roles by one of four basic methods: using volunteers, type-casting participants on the basis of their personalities, making assignments on the basis of some other knowledge of participants, and utilizing role reversals. The fourth method, for example, might involve having someone with high organizational status play a low-status position and vice versa. In briefing role players, the facilitator should not make the mistake of assuming that people know how to get into their roles; a bit of coaching on role taking may be necessary. One way of briefing role players is to designate support groups that can function as coaches during caucusing sessions. These groups can be established either randomly or through volunteering, and they can provide each role player with a support base for getting into and staying in role. A variation on the support group is the reference group, consisting of participants with similar jobs. For example, secretaries in a workshop could be the reference group for an individual who is going to role-play a secretary.

In briefing observers it is important to clarify their task: are they simply observers or are they permitted to talk with one another? Are they expected to make a report? Are they going to meet with individuals? Any forms that they are to use in recording their observations should be examined. If the observers are to be permitted to intervene in the role play with process observations, this procedure should be made explicit. If the observers are to function as alter egos, this role should probably be demonstrated by the facilitator.

In staging a role play, several arrangements suggest themselves. The "group-on-group" role play, conducted in the center of the room with observers circled around it, increases the sense of involvement. Alternatively, the role play can be staged with the observers in a semicircular arrangement so that the role players can be seen from the front. In multiple-group role plays each group should be arranged in such a way that it can interact with minimal interruption from the other groups. If there are several groups, or if the role play is likely to be fairly noisy, the role plays can be conducted in separate rooms.

Conducting Role Plays

In order to use role playing effectively, the facilitator should be aware of some special considerations in conducting the activity. Perhaps the most important is to keep the objectives of the role play and the facilitator's role clear throughout the entire process. The facilitator needs to be confident that the objectives are being met and that the activity can be focused adequately within a narrow range of learning goals.

Maier's[6] seven directions, outlined as follows, are useful in instructing participants on how to role-play.

1. Accept and adopt the facts of the role.

2. *Be* the role.

3. If it is appropriate to do so, change your attitude(s) during the action.

4. Let yourself become emotionally aroused.

5. Make up data, if necessary, but do not alter the spirit of the case.

6. Avoid consulting your role notes during the role play.

7. Do not overact; it may detract from the learning goals.

These instructions can also be included on any role-description sheets that are handed out to role players prior to the activity.

While the role play is being conducted, the facilitator must be able to modulate the intensity of the event. This can be done in a number of ways. Humor can be used to lighten a heavy interaction; the role play can be put "on hold"; participants can be assigned different roles during the role play; the interaction can be stimulated through intervention on the part of the facilitator; role players can be instructed to remain in their roles. The facilitator can tell participants to reread their role descriptions and coach one another on roles; then there can be interim caucuses between observers and support or reference groups and/or the role players. The role play should be ended before it either becomes boring or loses its focus on the learning goals.

After the role play has been concluded, the facilitator needs to be thorough in helping participants to share and process what they have experienced and to generalize and apply what they have learned. Forms and guided procedures can be extremely useful mechanisms in helping participants to share experiential data, but the facilitator must assist participants in using the forms and in explaining and tracking the procedures.

Ensuring that participants do not dwell on the content of the roles is crucial for effective processing. One method of "de-roling" the role players is to encourage them to "ventilate" or to explore in an expressive way the feelings that they experienced during the activity. They can also be invited to finish unfinished business by making statements such as "If I had been the boss . . . . " Another way of helping role players to separate themselves from their roles is to instruct them to write analyses of the role-play situation. Still another way is to have individual consultants work with role players in order to "finish" the experience.

Role players often can give one another interpersonal feedback in a role as a means of ending the activity and progressing beyond it in order to explore its generalizable learning. To encourage participants—both role players and observers—to focus their learning, the facilitator can instruct them to concentrate on comparing feelings with observable behavior and to develop generalizations about the worlds that they ordinarily live and work in, while avoiding any discussion about personalities within the role-play situation. The facilitator should also reiterate the objectives of the activity. Often it is useful if the objectives are prominently posted on newsprint. The facilitator needs to be particularly conscientious about encouraging the generalization and application of what has been learned; if these steps are omitted, practical, transferable learning is left to chance.

Use of Video in Role Plays

In recent years it has become increasingly popular to incorporate videotapes into a role-play design. For example, some facilitators play prerecorded videotape vignettes showing people interacting in various situations, and others tape the participants' role plays during the session for future processing. The use of videotapes offers both advantages and disadvantages. A videotaped "record" provides irrefutable proof of what has occurred, and this record can be reviewed numerous times for continual learning. In this way a videotape can add tremendously to the participants' ability to maximize insights and to relate to their behavior as seen by others. However, these advantages can become disadvantages when the participant is unable to accept the "evidence." Seeing oneself on a screen is a type of "out-of-body" experience; care must be taken to ensure that the participants feel safe in the presence of others who are viewing these tapes and that they feel mentally prepared to observe themselves objectively so that they can "own" their recorded behavior and learn from viewing it. The sensitive facilitator can use any of several simple techniques to provide the necessary security.

1. Have participants be in charge of taping one another (rather than assuming this responsibility himself or herself).

2. Have participants decide prior to the taping which behaviors are to be concentrated on.

3. Have participants be in charge of playing back the tapes (that is, using the remote-control device so that they can stop the tape or advance it past sections that make them feel uncomfortable).

4. Have participants work in pairs to review the tapes and coach each other, with the facilitator adding supplementary comments.

The general idea is to provide strategies that will increase the participants' comfort in learning about themselves through the use of this medium.

Behavior Modeling

Many firms now specialize in developing video-based training programs that help people to acquire the verbal and nonverbal behaviors associated with skillful performance in a variety of interpersonal situations (such as disciplining an employee or responding to an angry customer). In the videotaped portions of these programs, role players typically demonstrate both appropriate and inappropriate behaviors. These behavioral models are then used as standards that can guide participants as they work to shape their own behaviors.

Although these videotaped role plays can enhance certain kinds of training designs, they typically do not provide the type of high-impact, highly experiential learning opportunity that is available through personalized tapes.

Summary

Role playing is one of the most exciting techniques available to the group facilitator in training and development activities. Because role playing is active learning, it requires detailed planning for both content and logistics; because it is not a "show," it necessitates care in processing, or talking through, the experience before crystallizing its learning. Finally, role playing creates practical, transferable learning that participants own and are likely to apply in their everyday lives. Utilizing the technology of role play in training and education demands and deserves careful planning on the part of the facilitator. Implemented with sensitivity, it is a highly useful and versatile training vehicle.

References

1. Pfeiffer, J. W., *Reference Guide to Handbooks and Annuals*, 1985 ed., University Associates, San Diego, CA, 1975, pp. 1–3.

2. Jones, J. E., and J. W. Pfeiffer, "Role Playing," in J. E. Jones and J. W. Pfeiffer, eds., *The 1979 Annual Handbook for Group Facilitators*, University Associates, San Diego, CA, 1979, pp. 182–193.

3. Shaw, M. E., R. J. Corsini, R. R. Blake, and J. S. Mouton, *Role Playing: A Practical Manual for Group Facilitators*, University Associates, San Diego, CA, 1980.

4. Hall, J., *The Awareness Model: A Rationale of Learning and Its Application to Individual and Organizational Practices*, Teleometrics, Conroe, TX, 1971.

5. Tannenbaum, R., and W. H. Schmidt, "How to Choose a Leadership Pattern," *Harvard Business Review*, May–June 1973, pp. 162–164, 166–168.

6. Maier, N. R. F., A. R. Solem, and A. A. Maier, *The Role Play Technique: A Handbook for Management and Leadership Practice*, University Associates, San Diego, CA, 1975.

Bibliography*

Bavelas, A., "Role Playing and Management Training," *Sociatry*, 1947, 1, pp. 183–191.

Bradford, L. P., and R. Lippitt, "Role Playing in Supervisory Training," *Personnel*, 1946, 27, pp. 358–369.

Calhoun, R. P., "Role Playing as a Technique for Business," *Michigan Business Review*, 1950, 2(6), pp. 29–32.

Fantel, E., "Psychodrama in the Counseling of Industrial Personnel," *Sociatry*, 1948, 2, pp. 384–398.

Kellogg, E. E., "A Role Playing Case: How to Get the Most Out of It," *Personnel Journal*, 1954, 33, pp. 179–183.

Lippit, R., "The Psychodrama in Leadership Training," *Sociatry*, 1943, 6, pp. 286–292.

Liveright, A. A., "Role Playing in Leadership Training, *Personnel Journal*, 1951, 29, pp. 412–416.

Maier, N. R. F., A. R. Solem, and A. A. Maier, *The Role Playing Technique: A Handbook for Management and Leadership Practice*, University Associates, San Diego, CA, 1975.

* Excerpted from M. E. Shaw, R. J. Corsini, R. R. Blake, and J. S. Mouton, *Role Playing: A Practical Manual for Group Facilitators*, University Associates, San Diego, CA, 1980. Used with permission of the publisher.

25
Team Building

Joseph C. Christen

Joseph C. Christen is the Manager of Human Resource Development at The Andersons in Maumee, Ohio, where he is responsible for the development and implementation of programs to meet the needs of individuals and groups for professional growth and development. He has conducted programs in team building, performance appraisal, MBO, interpersonal communications, problem solving, constructive discipline, principles of management, stress management, and sales. Christen has a master's degree in Organizational Development from Bowling Green University and is working on a doctorate in Counseling and Human Services at The University of Toledo. He has conducted workshops for community agencies and business organizations such as General Motors, American Feed Manufacturers Association, Sylvania Savings Bank, Southern Iowa Farm Services Bank, Bowling Green State University, The University of Toledo, American Management Associations, ASTD, Deibold Corporation, and General Motors de Mexico. A member of the Greater Toledo chapter of ASTD, he received the ASTD Torch Award for Community Service in 1982.

Team building is a process which has been in existence since the beginning of time. The notion of people working together for a common cause dates back to the beginning of civilization, when physical survival of individuals and groups often depended on their ability to get along with one another. The difference between this historical perspective of team building and the process that exists today is the deliberate effort to create and maintain a group of people who can work well together toward the accomplishment of common goals and objectives, and enjoy doing so. Team building is a set of activities which accelerate the normal socialization process of a work group and does not rely on evolutionary development of working relationships.

Team building is not just another of the current fads in organization and management. It has matured and found its appropriate place as a management tool (Dyer).[1] Team building remains a viable process in management and an important aspect of a company's environment. Donald E. Peterson, Ford Motor Company's chairman and chief executive officer, was quoted in the December 3, 1985, issue of the *The Wall Street Journal* as stating that "being part of a team is a much more productive environment" (Guiles and Ingrassia).[2]

The team building process helps managers share a vision, align with the strategic direction of a company, and develop the interpersonal competence necessary to achieve excellence in group performance. Team building is a natural extension of the "human relations laboratory training" presented by Vladimir A. Dupre.[3]

Team Building History

Sports teams, work teams, service teams, special teams, and family teams are all examples of the importance being placed on teams today. Reilly and Jones[4] characterized a description of earth's civilization as given by a creature from another planet, "they play in groups, live in groups, and work in groups."

Where did this all begin? The first notable studies of people working together are the Hawthorne studies. They were conducted at the Western Electric plant in Hawthorne, Illinois, in the late 1920s and early 1930s. A group of Harvard professors were interested in studying the relationship of area lighting to work output (productivity). They also studied the effects of rest periods, incentives, and other independent variables relative to productivity. The results indicated that work output, or productivity, was a function of something other than the lighting, rest periods, and incentives, and other independent task variables. The development of a "team" spirit was considered to be the most significant independent variable which influenced productivity.

One of the researchers, Elton Mayo,[5] summarized the critical factors which he observed as being present in the experimental group. The factors he identified in 1928 include:

The boss:

Had a personal interest in each person's achievement

Took pride in the record of the group

Helped the group work together to get its own conditions of work

Faithfully posted the feedback on performance

The group:

Took pride in its own achievements

Had the satisfaction of outsiders showing interest in what they did

Did not feel they were being pressured to change

Was consulted before changes were made

Developed a sense of confidence and candor

These factors were identified in 1928 and are still important considerations for managers today. Since the Hawthorne studies there have been virtually thousands of studies of group behavior and team effectiveness. Researchers and managers were influenced by the results of the Hawthorne studies and subsequent studies of group behavior and productivity and believed that it may be worthwhile to formulate the concept of teamwork.

Both Kurt Lewin's[6] work with group dynamics and the laboratory methodology developed in Bethel, Maine, in 1947 seemed appropriate methodologies to train individual managers in the value of effective group functioning. The focus was on the individual manager to develop a sense of self-awareness and personal impact in a group context. The early efforts in management development included human relations laboratory training, otherwise known as T-groups, sensitivity training groups, or encounter groups. The T-group experiences provided individuals with personal growth and learnings; however, there seemed to be limited transferability of these learnings to the team since the other team members did not share in this learning experience. The T-group and laboratory training methods were, and continue to be, valuable for individuals to experience personal growth and understand group dynamics. However, it was not considered an effective developmental process because of the limited impact on the team. The main criticism of these techniques for team development was the absence of the other team members.

The T-group or laboratory process was then used within the work groups to develop stronger working relationships. Beer[7] would describe this as the interpersonal model of group development. The T-group approach to group development or team building is relatively unstructured and is focused principally on the relationships between team members. T-groups and laboratory training became viewed as too heavily relationship-oriented and not enough task-oriented for the more pragmatic manager.

A different approach to team building emerged during the late 1960s and early 1970s. The goal setting model (Beer[8]) was generally more structured and seemed to address the concerns of the critics of team building as simply a touchy-feely feels-good exercise, with little practicality for improving team effectiveness. This emerging model emphasized agreement on the strategic direction of the organization as well as specific goals such as sales, return on investment, and profit. Strategic planning meetings are useful in gaining commitment, resolving conflict surrounding goals, and motivating people toward goal accomplishment.

Recent Trends

T-groups continue to serve a valuable purpose in the management development process for individual human relations training. Strategic planning is present in one form or another in practically every organization. Recent trends in group development include matrix organizations, quality circles, gain sharing groups, employee participation groups, and quality-of-work-life programs. It is becoming very apparent to managers of large and small organizations that "people" and "people working together" are the deciding factors between successful and unsuccessful organizations. Team building has become a blend of the T-group methodology and the strategic planning approach to management. The proverbial task-relationship combination surfaces. However, this time it is at a group level rather than an individual leadership level.

Team building is a process which provides an individual the opportunity to align with the strategic direction of the organization and develop the necessary relationships to realize a synergistic contribution to the goals of the team. Individual alignment with the strategic direction of the team is essential for maximum success of the team efforts. Figure 25-1 depicts the concept of individual and organization alignment.

The more overlap between the individual's values, goals, style, perception, semantics, or personal agenda and that of the organization, the more closely

Figure 25-1. Individual and organizational alignment.

aligned will be the strategic, tactical, and operational activities. Team building helps examine the degree of alignment and appropriate adjustments or changes necessary to the task or relationships to achieve excellence in performance. Byrd[9] has identified this approach as the "heart of team building." "When differences affect the productivity of the team, and when the manager can't discuss the differences in a way to bring about a constructive exploration and resolution, they need team building."

Focus and Definition

Team building activities may relate to task issues, the way things are done, the needed skills to accomplish tasks, the resource allocations necessary for task accomplishments; or they may relate to the nature and quality of the relationships between the team members or between the team members and the leader; or they may relate to any combination of these task and relationship issues. It is a process of deliberately creating an energetic group of people who are committed to achieving common objectives, who work well together and enjoy doing so, and who produce high-quality results (Francis and Young).[10]

The focus of these activities is on the impact that the task and relationship issues have on the group's ability to implement the strategic plan of the organization. It is through the day-to-day operational and administrative processes that the tactical (short-term) plans of any organization are realized and contribute to the strategic (long-term) plans of an organization. The group's examination of how they function on both levels and the determination of how to improve any dysfunctional behavior or situation is considered a significant part of the team building process.

Instruments such as Schutz's fundamental interpersonal relations orientation—behavior (FIRO-B) scales,[11] the Myers-Briggs type indicator,[12] and Geier's personal profile system[13] are useful in the examination of individual and group behavior. The use of instruments is another means of adding structure to the process yet focusing on relationships.

Identifying the Need for Team Building

Dyer[1] has identified 12 key symptoms or conditions that frequently serve as a stimulus for a manager to consider team building. These are:

1. Loss of production or unit output

2. Increase of grievances or complaints within the staff

3. Evidence of conflicts or hostility among staff members

4. Confusion about assignments, missed signals, and unclear relationships

5. Decisions misunderstood or not carried through properly

6. Apathy and general lack of interest or involvement of staff members

7. Lack of initiation, imagination, and innovation, resulting in routine actions being taken

8. Ineffective staff meetings, low participation, minimally effective decisions

9. Start-up of a new group that needs to develop quickly into a working team

10. High dependency on or negative reactions to the manager

11. Complaints from users or customers about the quality of services

12. Continued unaccounted-for increases in costs

The manager or any member of the team may recognize one or more of these symptoms which indicate a need for team building. There is no specific number of indicators that need to be present for team building to be appropriate, but rather it is the number and the intensity with which these are present that suggest team building as an appropriate intervention.

Once the manager recognizes the presence of these factors within the work group the manager may approach a facilitator or third party consultant to discuss the possibility of team building. With the help of a trained facilitator the manager will determine if team building is the appropriate organization development intervention to address the issues that have been identified. After it is agreed that team building is an intervention that will effectively bring about improvement in group functioning, it is necessary to identify the team.

Who Is the Team?

Defining the membership of the team is not always easy. The complexity of today's organization requires flexibility in the membership of work groups. Therefore, what is represented on the formal organization chart may not in fact be an accurate representation of the team. Francis and Young[10] identify three levels of membership:

1. *Core team members.* Their contribution is necessary over an extended period, and significant reorganization would be necessary should they withdraw. These individuals are likely to appear on the formal organization chart within the normal reporting relationships to the manager.

2. *Supportive team members.* Their contribution aids the team to do its work effectively. They do not greatly assist tasks to be performed or spark creative effort. Rather, their contribution is to ease, support, and provide assistance, raw materials, or information. Individuals within this group often do not appear on the formal

organization chart; however, they work on a regular basis in assisting the core team in meeting its objectives. Members in this level are often in staff positions.

3. *Temporary team members.* Their contribution is specific and time-bound. It may be that a particular assignment requires skills absent from the team. An outside person can then become a temporary team member while his or her special contribution is required. The person then withdraws and ceases to be a team member. While it may seem inappropriate to include temporary team members as part of the team building process, one must keep in mind that team building has both near-term and long-term implications. Temporary team members may be disruptive to the normal operation of an organization or unit which could be disruptive to the day-to-day operations and ultimately impact productivity or contribution to the strategic plan.

Once the manager and facilitator clearly understand the perceived need for team building and know the members who will be participating in the team building process, it is necessary for the facilitator, manager, and team to meet and collectively decide on the group's readiness for team building. It is important that managers and members of the team understand that team building is an ongoing process, one which needs to integrate into broader organizational development activities that contribute to the strategic direction of the organization.

The Facilitator's Role

Reilly and Jones[4] identify the facilitator's role in team building as a "process" consultant rather than an "expert" consultant. The facilitator's role in team building should help the group solve its own problems by making it aware of its own group process and the way the process affects the quality of the team's work. The facilitator's allegiance is to the entire group, not to the manager or to a particular clique within the team. It is very important that the manager and the group members understand the facilitator's role in the team building process.

A Model for Team Building

Several approaches can be used in the team building process. The approach used will depend on the facilitator's personal style, the nature of the issues which prompted the exploration of team building, the culture of the organization, the manager, and the group. The following model or approach is one which integrates the interpersonal model with the goal-setting model and examines the impact of the relationships within the team on the strategic direction and performance of the group (see Fig. 25-2).

Entry, Initial Diagnosis, and Contracting

The team building process begins with a meeting between the facilitator and the manager, or in some instances a team member and the facilitator, in which the two discuss the issues that have surfaced and prompted the investigation into team building. This is the facilitator's entry into the group. After this initial diagnosis, the facilitator, manager, and team members meet to discuss the issues influencing the team functioning, the group's readiness to engage in team building, and the

Entry	• Manager or team member discusses team functioning with facilitator (third party consultant)
Initial Diagnosis	• Facilitator clarifies the presenting issues in relation to the need for team building
Contracting	• Facilitator meets with manager and team members to discuss initial diagnosis and appropriateness of team building • The facilitator and team contract to proceed with team building after a clear understanding of process, roles, objectives, and risks
Data Collection and Analysis	• Interviews • FIRO-B • Team Review Questionnaire
Team Skills Training	• Exercise conducted during off-site meeting to encourage communication, build trust, increase openness, feedback, and cooperation • Personal Profile System or the Myers-Briggs Type Indicator present a means of understanding one's own behavior as well as the behavior of others
Data Confrontation	• The information from the interviews is shared and discussed between team members
FIRO-B	• The results of the FIRO-B scales are discussed as they relate to team member interaction and the impact on team effectiveness
Team Review Questionnaire	• The results from the Team Review Questionnaire are reviewed and discussed with recommendations for needed changes with ways to improve team performance
Individual Action Planning	• Individuals discuss the specific actions that they intend to take in an effort to improve their contribution to the overall goals of the team. Information provided through the Personal Profile System, FIRO-B scales, interview data, and group discussion will be beneficial in helping each team member develop a specific action plan
Group Action Plans	• The entire team discusses the specific actions that they intend to take as a group, which will enhance the team effectiveness and overall performance. Information gained through the group discussion of the interview data on group description and issues, as well as the information provided through the team review questionnaire, provides a basis for group-level action planning. Included in the group action plan will be the targeted date for the team building follow-up session
Critique	• A critique of the session as well as the process will be beneficial for the individuals on the team as well as the facilitator. Identification of the most valuable aspects of the team building process as well as recommendations for changes in the future become part of the critique. The critique session also provides a sense of closure for that particular team building session

Figure 25-2. A team building model.

establishment of a contract or agreement between the facilitator and team to proceed with the team building intervention. The contract or agreement clarifies the process, roles, objectives, and risks associated with team building so the ground rules are clear to everyone. Facilitators must clearly explain their role as well as the expectations and demands that will be placed on the manager and the team members as they proceed through the various steps of team building. A general explanation of the activities that will be engaged in by the manager and group members is necessary for their understanding of how it fits into the overall organization development plan for the unit. The data collection, analysis, data feedback, and action planning phases will be described along with the expectation of each individual's and the group's participation within each phase. It is extremely important that the facilitator emphasize the confidential nature of the team building process as well as the ground rules surrounding the interpersonal communications and feedback. The team must understand that the facilitator's role is to maintain a psychologically safe environment during the exchange of feedback and personal risk taking.

The group's readiness to engage in team building is determined by their willingness to accept the issues discussed as valid and in need of change, to commit the necessary time and resources to the team building process, to take personal risks in examining their own as well as the group's performance, and to be willing to change in the areas that require improvement.

It is often helpful for the facilitator to solicit the group expectations and concerns regarding any aspect of the team building process as outlined. Beer[7] points out that a manager's decision to enter into team building strongly influences the group norms and the direction of open self-examination. A willingness to engage in this process ultimately becomes a requirement for group membership, a requirement that may not match each member's needs and expectations, but which does ensure a more efficient, effective, and healthy group in the long run. With the decision to proceed with team building, the facilitator begins the data collection process.

Data Collection and Analysis

The data collection process can take many forms such as questionnaires, interviews, or sensing. The model being presented here begins with individual interviews between the facilitator and members of the team including the manager. The facilitator points out that the information shared during the interview will be given to the group during the team building session which will follow. While the information given is not confidential, it is anonymous since it will be shared with the other members of the team during the team building session. However, no individual will be identified with the feedback. Personal identification and ownership of the feedback will occur during the team building session with the group.

Each member of the team is asked to reflect on his or her perception of every other member of the team and to share this perception with the facilitator. Specifically, the team members are asked to identify the particular strengths that the other members bring to the team, as well as areas that may be developed for improved contribution to the team's objectives. Often these developmental areas are considered to be "weaknesses"; however, it is important to recognize that development may be the extension of a strength rather than the overcoming of a weakness. After individual team members have described the strengths and developmental areas of another team member, they are asked to give a self-description based on what they believe is the other person's perception of them. This information is helpful in that it gives the facilitator an idea of the level of

THREE HUMAN NEEDS THAT AFFECT GROUPS

NEEDS	ACTIONS	
	EXPRESSED	WANTED
INCLUSION Prominence, or who is "in"	I make efforts to include other people in my activities and to get them to include me in theirs. I try to belong, to join social groups, to be with people as much as possible. Always ◁———▷ Never	I want other people to include me in their activities and to invite me to belong, even if I do not make an effort to be included. Always ◁———▷ Never
CONTROL Dominance, or who "pecks" whom	I try to exert control and influence over things. I take charge of things and tell other people what to do. Always ◁———▷ Never	I want others to control and influence me. I want other people to tell me what to do. Always ◁———▷ Never
AFFECTION Closeness, or who likes whom	I make efforts to become close to people. I express friendly and affectionate feelings and try to be personal and intimate. Always ◁———▷ Never	I want others to express friendly and affectionate feelings toward me and to try to become close to me. Always ◁———▷ Never

Figure 25-3. FIRO-B scales.

communication or feedback being exchanged between individual members, as well as the team.

Strengths which may be identified for individuals could include task-oriented as well as relationship-oriented behaviors. For instance, a manager may be described as a strong leader, decision maker, delegator, communicator, as well as friendly, personable, understanding, or considerate. Developmental areas could include such things as organization, decisiveness, technical knowledge, attention to detail, follow-through, or listening, diplomacy, or discipline. During the interview, individuals are also asked to identify the major issues which are facing the group. These issues could include group functioning, profitability, or any group issue considered significant by the individual. The group level issues will be useful for comparison and specific clarification of the results of the team review questionnaire.

Following the discussion of the other team members, each person is given a set of prework instruments to be completed and returned to the facilitator prior to the team building session. The first instrument is Schutz's[11] FIRO-B scale. The FIRO-B measures six human needs: expressed inclusion, wanted inclusion, expressed control, wanted control, expressed affection, and wanted affection (see Fig. 25-3). This scale was specifically designed to measure interpersonal relationships and provides valuable data for understanding the interaction between members within the group.

The second instrument is the Team Review Questionnaire, developed by Francis and Young.[10] The Team Review Questionnaire consists of 108 statements regarding effective team functioning. Members are asked to indicate which of these statements are true and which are false. These statements are then factored into 12 dimensions of effective team functioning. When successful teams are examined, we find that they have achieved definite progress in the following distinct areas:

1. *Appropriate leadership.* The team manager has the skills and intention to develop a team approach and allocates time to team building activities. Management in the team is seen as a shared function. Individuals other than the manager are given the opportunity to exercise leadership when their skills are appropriate to the needs of the team.

2. *Suitable membership.* Team members are individually qualified and capable of contributing the "mix" of skills and characteristics that provide an appropriate balance.

3. *Commitment to the team.* Team members feel a sense of individual commitment to the aims and purposes of the team. They are willing to devote personal energy to building the team and supporting other team members. When working outside the team boundaries, the members feel a sense of belonging and representing the team.

4. *Constructive climate.* The team has developed a climate in which people feel relaxed, able to be direct and open, and prepared to take risk.

5. *Concern to achieve.* The team is clear about its objectives, which are felt to be worthwhile. It sets targets of performance that are felt to be stretching but achievable. Energy is mainly devoted to the achievement of results, and team performance is reviewed frequently to see where improvements can be made.

6. *Clear corporate role.* The team has contributed to corporate planning and has a distinct and productive role within the overall organization.

7. *Effective work methods.* The team has developed lively, systematic, and effective ways to solve problems together.

8. *Well-organized team procedures.* Role are clearly defined, communication patterns are well-developed, and administrative procedures support a team approach.

9. *Critique without rancor.* Team and individual errors and weaknesses are examined, without personal attack, to enable the group to learn from its experience.

10. *Well-developed individuals.* Team members are deliberately developed and the team can cope with strong individual contributions.

11. *Creative strength.* The team has the capacity to create new ideas through the interactions of its members. Some innovative risk taking is rewarded and the team will support new ideas from individual members or from outside. Good ideas are followed through on into action.

12. *Positive intergroup relations.* Relationships with other teams have been systematically developed to provide open personal contact and identify where joint working may give maximum payoff. There is regular contact and review of joint or collective priorities with other teams. Individuals are encouraged to contact and work with members of other teams.

Energizing individuals to change relationships with other team members is one of the prime objectives of team building (Varney and Hunady).[14] Generally, the entry and contracting phases of the team building session followed by the individual interviews and distribution of questionnaires energizes individuals and the group prior to the offsite meeting. Some benefit is derived out of the anticipation of the team building session. Once the data have been collected through interviews and the instruments returned and analyzed, the facilitator meets with the group away from the workplace (offsite) in order to avoid day-to-day interruptions and pressures. Depending on the size of the group, the offsite session may take 2 to 3 days.

Team Skills Training

The offsite team building session may also include a team skills training activity (Christen and Nykodym).[15] With the inclusion of team skills training, the agenda for the offsite meeting would include:

1. Expectations and concerns from group members regarding the session
2. Review of tentative agenda
3. Team skills training (Personal Profile or Myers-Briggs Type Indicator)
4. Interview feedback
5. FIRO-B results
6. Team Review Questionnaire results
7. Individual action plans
8. Group action plans
9. Critique

This variation of the team building approach includes team skills training. Team skills training is referred to here as an exercise which helps team members gain an understanding of their personal behavioral styles in a general sense, and how their styles are compatible or incompatible with other styles. Specifically, the Personal Profile System developed by Geier[13] is used to help team members discuss the individual behavior patterns of dominance, influence, steadiness, and compliance and gain an understanding of other team members. The Myers-Briggs Type Indicator[12] may also be used to help team members understand themselves and others. The exercise creates an atmosphere which encourages commitment, openness, feedback, and risk taking. Self-understanding and the understanding of others and their behavioral styles as it relates to group functioning is a typical outcome of the team skills training activity. This step provides for more meaningful exchange of feedback and clarification for understanding when the interview data are discussed between group members.

Data Confrontation

Following the team skills training exercise, the data collected during the interviews are given back to team members. Each person is given the collective input from every other member of the team as well as their self-perception as identified by them during their own interview. Individuals receive their personal feedback and the group issues and description, but not the personal descriptions of other team members. The discussion of the interview data is very similar to the process developed in the team skills training session. Individuals can solicit additional feedback or ask for clarification of anything included in the interview data.

Sufficient time needs to be given to allow individuals the opportunity to exchange feedback regarding specific behaviors as they relate to group functioning and task accomplishment. Additional information is provided through the results of the FIRO-B and the effects of the individual interpersonal needs as they relate to group interaction. The individual results of the FIRO-B scales and discussion of group interaction as identified with these results enhance and "energize" individuals to consider behavioral changes which will enhance their contribution to the team. The Team Review Questionnaire results identify the key areas that need attention at a group level. A discussion of these areas facilitates the group-level action planning for improved group performance along specific dimensions.

Action Planning

Once the data have been confronted on an individual and group level, the facilitator helps the group develop specific action plans to improve performance and contribution to the organization's strategic plan. Group action plans will include specific actions to be taken, the person responsible for initiating and carrying out those actions, the time frame within which they will be carried out, as well as the expected result (measurement) of the action. The group action planning process provides the team members with the opportunity to commit to the changes required to improve group effectiveness.

The information provided through the Personal Profile System, the interview data feedback, the FIRO-B, and the discussion that takes place during the team building session provides a very good basis for individual action planning to improve each team member's contribution to the team. Following the individual and group action planning activities the facilitator and team need to establish a date and time for a team building follow-up session. The facilitator will emphasize that team building is not a program with a beginning and an end, but rather a process that becomes a way of life which influences the climate conducive to risk taking, openness, and effective problem solving. During the first session, the group will make progress toward this end; however, it is generally necessary for team building follow-up sessions for the group to begin to learn to facilitate itself without the help of the outside facilitator.

Critique and Follow-up

The length of time between the initial team building session and the follow-up session will vary by group and the issues that are being addressed. The action plans established for individuals in the group should provide sufficient time for individuals and the group to undertake the activities outlined and can also be a gauge for the timing of the follow-up session. Once a time has been established for the follow-up session, the facilitator may lead a brief critique of the session, bringing closure to that particular meeting. The critique session also gives the team members an opportunity to offer feedback to the facilitator regarding the various aspects of the process to this point in time.

When Not to Use
Team Building

Team building, and a decision to pursue it in an organization, rests on a number of critical, implicit assumptions. Team building should not be considered a general activity that all work units should experience. Before any team building process is started, the following conditions should be assessed:

1. Is the work unit one where collaborative action is essential for good achievement?
2. Is the manager familiar with and committed to the idea of team improvement and the related amounts of time and resources required to affect this effort?
3. Is there a feeling of "hurt" or a need to see improvement by the manager and the team?
4. Are people in the work unit willing to look at their own unit and engage in problem-solving actions?
5. Is there enough time and availability of personnel to start such a program?
6. Are the manager and others in the work unit willing to look at their own performance and the work of the unit, willing to give and receive feedback, and honestly interested in making change? Have people already made up their minds what the problems are and what must be done?

If these questions cannot be answered in the positive, team building is not the appropriate intervention to improve overall team effectiveness (Dyer).[16]

Benefits of Team Building

Team building is time-consuming and can be expensive. It is important to identify how this approach can benefit the organization. Francis and Young[10] identified five benefits of the team building process to the organization. These are particularly important to today's rapidly changing world.

1. Team building provides for the effective management of complexity. With advancing technologies in every field of endeavor it is becoming increasingly more important for managers and members of work units to be able to effectively manage the complexities of organizations in both the public and private sector.
2. Rapid response to ever-changing environments and work demands is another outcome of the team building process. Teams who work well together are able to anticipate the needs of other team members and the organization, and respond to those in ways which prevent problems rather than react in ways which require the correction of problems.
3. Team building results in a high level of motivation for the individuals within the team and the entire work unit. Increased levels of task accomplishment, improved levels of job satisfaction, and camaraderie result in higher levels of motivation.
4. Higher quality of decisions results from mature teams who are capable of making better decisions than even the most brilliant individual. In addition to the quality of the decisions being improved, the commitment to carrying out the decisions by individuals on the team is much higher.
5. There is a collective strength or synergism that occurs when a group participates in an effective team building intervention. Organizations who support team building efforts for their work units realize these benefits and believe that they offset the time and expense associated with engaging in the team building process.

The benefits outlined affect individuals, groups, and entire organizations. The process is not restricted to work groups within large organizations. Team building can benefit individuals, management teams, project teams, representative teams, and even committees who are working together toward the accomplishment of goals that are common to each individual and the group.

Conclusions

Team building or team development has matured as a viable management tool useful for improving team effectiveness. The methodologies and the approaches have changed and will continue to change as new developments and refinements are made in the management processes relative to group behavior and strategic planning. Team building is effective because of its multidimensional focus on the individual, the intergroup, and the group behaviors as they relate to the accomplishment of task and contribution to the organization.

References

1. Dyer, William G., *Team Building: Issues and Alternatives*, Addison-Wesley, Reading, MA, 1977.

2. Guiles, Melinda G., and Paul Ingrassia, "A Better Idea? Ford's Leaders Push Radical Shift in Culture as Competition Grows," *The Wall Street Journal*, December 3, 1985, pp. 1, 26.

3. Dupre, Vladimir A., "Human Relations Laboratory Training," in Robert L. Craig, ed., *Training and Development Handbook—A Guide to Human Resource Development*, McGraw-Hill, New York, 1976.

4. Reilly, Anthony J., and John E. Jones, "Team-Building," *The 1974 Annual Handbook for Group Facilitators*, University Associates, Inc., San Diego, 1974.

5. Mayo, Elton, *The Human Problems of an Industrial Civilization*, Division of Research, Graduate School of Business Administration, Harvard University, Boston, 1933.

6. Lewin, Kurt, *Field Theory in Social Science*, Harper & Brothers, New York, 1951.

7. Beer, Michael, *Organization Change and Development—A Systems View*, Goodyear Publishing Company, Inc., Santa Monica, CA, 1980.

8. Beer, ref. 7, p. 143.

9. Byrd, Richard E., "The Heart of Team Building," in Roger Ritvo and Alice Sargent, eds., *The NTL Manager's Handbook*, NTL Institute, Arlington, VA, 1983.

10. Francis, Dave, and Don Young, *Improving Work Groups: A Practical Manual for Team Building*, University Associates, Inc., San Diego, 1979.

11. Schutz, W.C., *The FIRO Scales*, Consulting Psychologists Press, Palo Alto, CA, 1967.

12. Briggs, Katherine C., and Isabel Briggs Myers, *Myers-Briggs Type Indicator*, Consulting Psychologists Press, Palo Alto, CA, 1977.

13. Geier, John G., *Personal Profile System*, Performax Systems International, Minneapolis, MN, 1979.

14. Varney, Glenn H., and Ronald J. Hunady, "Energizing Commitment to Change in a Team-Building Intervention: A FIRO-B Approach," *Group & Organization Studies*, University Associates, Inc., San Diego, December 1978, 3(4), 435–446.

15. Christen, Joseph C., and Nick Nykodym, *Process Consultation: A Tool for Organization Renewal and Change*, ASTD, Madison, WI, 1980.

16. Dyer, ref. 1, pp. 133–134.

26

Games and Simulations

Thomas C. Keiser

John H. Seeler

Thomas C. Keiser is senior vice president, Management Division, Forum Corporation, Boston, Massachusetts, where he is responsible for management, executive, and supervisory training conducted by the Forum. During his 14 years at Forum, he has been a principal architect of several standard programs and many customized programs. Formerly, he was MidAmerica regional vice president based in Philadelphia and held other field positions. Prior to his field experience, he was Forum's market manager in Sales and Marketing. He was also senior consultant in Forum's Management Consulting Group and new product manager for the Forum Research and Development Division. He has worked extensively on the design, development, and implementation of specialized programs for Forum clients including Citicorp, Chemical Bank, Continental Illinois Corporation, CBS, U.S. Department of Commerce, E.I. du Pont de Nemours, General Electric, Hercules, Mellon Bank, Morgan Guaranty, Prudential Insurance, Sun Oil, Trans World Airlines, U.S. Department of State, and U.S. Steel. He graduated cum laude from the University of Pennsylvania with a double major in Honors Sociology and History. He received a master's degree in Sociology at the same time as his bachelor's degree.

John H. Seeler is director of training for TAD Technical Services Corporation of Cambridge, Massachusetts. His responsibilities include the planning, design, implementation, and assessment of entry-level and intermediate training and development programs for sales and recruiting staff, as well as programs for other nontechnical personnel. Previous to this, he was a teacher, writer, editor, and instructional designer. He graduated magna cum laude with a degree in history from Bowdoin College in Brunswick, Maine, and is doing graduate work in *adult education, instructional design, and human resources at the Boston University School of Education. He is a member of the Massachusetts chapter of the ASTD.*

Games and simulations have become increasingly popular with learners and trainers alike. Learners find them intriguing and fun, while many trainers feel they are unparalleled in motivating the learner and making learning compelling.

Games and simulations are applied to a wide range of training situations. They can be used as introductory lessons for novices and advanced ones for experts; they may be high-tech or low-tech, 20-minute or 3-day exercises. And, although business games and simulations have been used for decades, the field has been expanding and changing rapidly.

History of Business Games and Simulations

In a sense, games and simulations are an old, even ancient, technique. Today's business games and simulations can trace their roots back to the war games of centuries ago—a millennium, if one includes chess, a stylized depiction of ancient warfare. The modern war game was first played by the Prussian army in the early 1800s; opposing teams battled each other by maneuvering soldiers representing military units on large, chessboard-like maps. Over the course of the nineteenth century all the elements of simulation games were added: elaborate simulations of activities, consideration of the influences of extraneous environmental factors, and the effect of time. The war game achieved the essentials of its current form by World War I. During this century, it has been used to train players in tactics and strategy, test war plans, and evaluate scenarios.

Two twentieth century innovations would also contribute to the development of business gaming and simulation: game theory and computers. Game theory, invented by mathematician John von Neumann, quantitatively describes decision-making behavior under conditions of competition and uncertainty. Von Neumann's *The Theory of Games and Economic Behavior*, published in 1944,[1] by explaining the logic and strategy of game playing, made the principles he described available for game design and provided a vocabulary for describing the characteristics of competition. The development of the computer provided greatly improved logistics. The computer simplified the mathematical component of game theory. It eliminated the drudgery of calculations and greatly increased the speed and quantity of data analysis. By providing a "black box," the computer made it unnecessary for the game administrator to master an elaborate quantitative model in all its detail. And it provided greater authenticity and the impression of impartiality to computerized games and simulations.

The first business game was inspired by the war game simulations played during the 1950s. Frank Ricciardi of the American Management Association applied the gaming and simulation principles he had observed as a visitor at the Naval War College to the development of a business game. A year's work resulted in the debut of the American Management Association's Top Management Decision Simulation in 1957. A computerized general management game, it was designed for competitive, interactive team play pertaining directly to the skills used in business. Participants were assigned to the management of make-believe companies and competed with rivals for a share of the market. Each team's decisions were made on the basis of its knowledge about its own company's situation, and more limited information about the market and industry. Each round of play represented a quarter; decisions submitted for each quarter were analyzed by a computer which generated financial statements for use in the next quarter. The game concluded with a session to compare performances and review the decisions and strategies of the participants.

The American Management Association game and a manual game designed by G. R. Andlinger shortly afterward received a lot of attention and were influential in the development of other business games and simulations. Soon after their advent a number of companies and universities had employed the games or had designed their own, both general management games and games which addressed functional areas of management, such as marketing strategy or finance. Their number and use expanded rapidly; by 1962 two-thirds of the nation's major business schools were using business games.

Games and simulations are now employed in many fields, not just in business training but in planning, research, and education as well. Games and simulations developed for one purpose may be adapted for another, crossing over from research to training, or from military to corporate applications.

Current Trends

Though games and simulations have been used for training for decades, their current popularity can be attributed to significant changes in technology, to new management needs, and to the greater availability of games and simulations.

The computer has been a part of many business simulations and games since the first one was played in 1957. The recent advent of the personal computer has significantly affected the field.

Although the computers used in the first games offered vast advantages over the manual alternative, the difference between them and the technology available today is not one of degree but of kind. In the traditional business simulation game, the computer would operate in cyclical batches, it would be physically separate from participants who would not interact with it, and it would be tended by specialists. And, of course, participants had to have a computer available—a rare and expensive thing in decades past; an hour's time on a mainframe computer of 20 years ago could cost as much as an entire personal computer today.

Today, with the wide availability of powerful, inexpensive personal computers, computer simulations and games are no longer restricted to mainframes; they are developed for or adapted to the personal computer. Because they are less expensive and more accessible, many more companies are using personal computer-driven games and simulations and making them available to a wider range of their people—people who themselves tend more and more to be computer literate. With the personal computer has come the possibility of widely used interactive simulations. Instead of operating remotely using a batch mode, the computer can be employed to engage in a "dialogue" with the user and to play an interactive role in the actual process of the simulation. Supplying realistic data and results in a complex, interactive mode has the effect of greater realism and authenticity.

As computer technology has become more sophisticated, it has become more reliable and simpler to use. Game and simulation design can make better use of the technology rather than be governed by it. Expert systems—software programs which can act as a consultant to the learner—have the potential of playing a major role in the future.

Another significant change to affect training has been the recognition of the importance of the middle manager to the long-term success of the organization. While in the past only the top had to know how the different elements of the organization fit together, now many more people need to have a bird's-eye view of the organization and how it functions. Greater emphasis is being placed on the individual manager, his or her contribution, and his or her potential. This changing emphasis is a response to the clearly perceived need for change when comparing American companies' performance to the Japanese, or to America's best as described in *In Search of Excellence*.[2] Especially emphasized is individual creativity and motivation, effectively exercised within the organization. As an expression of this, games and simulations are being employed as team building exercises to more effectively integrate and utilize the individual manager. This development has a parallel in a debate within war gaming circles during the nineteenth century, in which one side argued against employing lieutenants in the roles of generals, feeling that it would "ruin them as subalterns." The opposition prevailed, its response being that the army must benefit by developing all its officers' comprehension of the army as a whole, its mission, and their role within it. Games and simulations provide the opportunity for participants to "see the forest" despite the trees, to better understand their own performance, and to evaluate their strengths and weaknesses in working with others. At the same time, games and simulations provide the opportunity to observe and evaluate the individual.

In addition to changes in technology and attitudes about management, a third factor has contributed to the popularity of games and simulations. This is the introduction of sophisticated new games and simulations which are more "ambitious" and elaborate than most of their predecessors. Among these are the Center for Creative Leadership's *Looking Glass*, the Strategic Management Group's *Strategic Management Game*, Executive Perspectives Inc.'s *Executive Perspectives Simulation*, and the Sony Management Systems Company's *International Management Game*.[3]

These games and simulations contrast with the ones which preceded them, many of which are quick and simple and emphasize a specific lesson. The newer, more complex games and simulations are not quick. Including playing and debriefing time, an exercise may be measured in days. They also are not simple, in some cases having taken years to develop, and requiring an exhaustively prepared team of trainers to run. In keeping with the organization-building trend in management, their objectives are not limited to teaching a particular skill, but instead they immerse the participant in a wide range of management issues. While all involve business tactics and strategy, many emphasize the role of individual behavior and group dynamics in the organization. And all of them provide the individual with a broader perspective than that of the isolated specialist, and allow him or her to experience the workings of the organization as a whole.

It is the combined influence of the personal computer, of the new emphasis on the individual manager, and of the availability of a new class of sophisticated games and simulations which has caused the expansion of their use. More credible with top management, they have become a more popular training option.

Games and
Simulations Defined

A variety of terms are used by practitioners of games and simulations to describe the field; different practitioners may use terms differently or interchangeably. For the purposes of this chapter, we shall use the following definitions:

A *game* is a structured activity in which two or more participants compete within constraints of rules to achieve an objective.

A *simulation* is an operational model, using selected components, of a real or hypothetical process, mechanism, or system.

A *simulation game* combines the characteristics of games and simulations in a game based on a simulation.

Games

To fulfill most definitions of a game, an exercise will have the following characteristics:

- It will involve competition. The competition may be directly between players, either between individuals, as in chess, or between teams, as in bridge. Or the competition may be between players and the game itself, as in solitaire, golf, or a solo video game.

- It will have rules, a set of arbitrary constraints on the players' behavior. Rules govern play and consequences. They may be minimal, as in pick-up basketball, or very elaborate, as in a business simulation game depicting the operations of the marketing division of a consumer products company; such a game may be governed by a volume of rules. Rules are by nature contrived and inefficient; they give artificial value to a goal or objective, and then restrict the manner in which a player can pursue it.

- It will have closure. Games come to an end after a certain amount of time, number of rounds or points, etc. Nonsimulation games usually have a simpler way of determining winners than simulation games.

A "pure" game does not simulate anything. Such nonsimulation games include poker, Scrabble, and checkers. (Games such as chess and Monopoly may be viewed as not strictly "pure," because they can be seen as stylized simulations, respectively, of medieval warfare and the real estate business.)

A prominent type of nonsimulation game used in training is the resource-allocation game, in which players must decide how to allocate an insufficiently available resource in the most effective way to meet a goal. As a "pure" game, the resources may simply and literally be chips; as it shades into a simulation game, the resource may represent spaces on a lifeboat or personnel during a hiring freeze. Two nonsimulation resource-allocation games are *Wff 'n Proof*, in which players use logic to build systems, and *Equations*,[4] a mathematical game. The rationale for using nonsimulation games for training purposes is the notion of "transfer": that the learning achieved from playing the game can and will be applied in practical settings. Nonsimulation games are appropriate for teaching facts and concepts in a specific area of subject matter.

Simulations

A simulation is a model of a mechanism, process, or system. A model is a representation of a view of reality; it is restricted to including those components considered necessary to its purpose. A simulation differs from other models in that it is an operating model; it represents the model not only as it appears at one particular time but also as it changes. A simulation represents the resources, restrictions, and consequences of the reality it models. A participant in a simulation can by his or her decisions and actions effect changes in it, and be affected by it.

There are three kinds of simulations: all-machine, people-machine, and all-people.

- All-machine simulations are completely computerized. The computer alone makes decisions and responds to their consequences; there is no interaction with —or interference by—humans. Such simulations are used not for training, but for research and planning.

- In people-machine simulations, people participate with the computer in making decisions which affect the simulation. In a batch-mode system, the computer may perform high-speed calculations and issue intermittent updates or status reports. In an interactive system, human participants interact with a computer which contains the simulation model and responds to the participants' actions.

- All-people simulations involve no model-containing machines. The model is described by rules by which the participants abide, and which define their roles, environment, resources, and constraints. Actions are initiated and consequences are calculated by people in accordance with the model.

An example of "pure" simulation—a simulation with no game component—is the use of computer-based simulators to replace training on actual equipment. One of the most familiar examples of this people-machine simulation is the use of flight simulators to train pilots. Both civilian airlines and the military use simulators extensively, and can train pilots at a fraction of the cost in fuel, equipment, and labor required in using actual aircraft. Flight simulators reduce training time, and—because they do not actually crash—they eliminate the risks faced by first-time pilots. Simulators can also provide authentic, hands-on practice when the real thing is not practical or not available to use for training purposes, as in training soldiers to fire missiles or technicians to operate nuclear power plants. Because simulators and trainers are expressly designed for training, a well-designed simulation can provide more efficient and effective training than the use of the actual equipment.

Simulators and trainers involve no game component because the actual mechanisms and processes which they model do not. Because they are models, they include only selected components considered important for the task of training; a flight simulator needs an instrument panel, but not wings.

Two examples of "pure" business simulations are the Center for Creative Leadership's *Looking Glass*[3] and New York University's School of Business's *Financial Services Industry*[5] simulation. No overt competition is designed into either exercise, so they are simulations, not simulation games; the exercises involve problem solving but do not deliberately pit participants against each other.

Simulation Games

A simulation game combines the elements of a game—competition for an objective, rules, and closure—and those of a simulation. Because it is a simulation, elements of the game correspond to reality through the selected components which comprise the model. Thousands of simulation games are in use today, and appear in many forms. However, they share certain common characteristics. Three elements of which all simulation games are composed are the roles assumed by participants, the simulation's scenario, and an accounting system.

Roles define the parts played by the participants in the simulation. They may correspond more or less precisely with the real or hypothetical situation which the simulation represents, depending on whether its intent is verisimilitude or flexibility. A role may represent an individual or a group of individuals.

The scenario describes the subject which the simulation represents, and can range from very simple to very elaborate. It can be provided to participants in a variety of materials—the *Looking Glass* scenario is described in part by the company's annual report—or be presented by the trainers. The scenario includes the rules prescribing the players' actions and their objectives. The accounting system monitors play and provides feedback on the simulation's progress. In an all-people simulation game, the accounting system involves a referee; in a people-machine simulation game, a computer calculates the effects of actions and decisions.

Most simulation games fall into one or more of the following categories:

Gamut-running games employ the familiar format of board games. Players move along a path, overcoming obstacles, until they reach a goal.

Allocation games were described earlier in the example of the resource-allocation game. Other types of allocation games include budget allocation, in which the scarce resource is money; and power- and influence-allocation games.

Group interaction games use the contrived circumstances of a game not so much to simulate a real or hypothetical system or situation as to present a human relations problem in which the participants are invested. Their purpose is to expose participants to new points of view by experiencing them.

General systems games are complex simulations which model the total system of an organization—a company, industry, city, etc. Usually, these are very structured people-machine simulations.

An example of a popular people-machine simulation game is *Zork*.[6] *Zork* is an interactive computer-based simulation game. It presents the player with a simulated world; although a fantasy world, it is a "real" simulation, because a simulation can model the hypothetical as well as the actual. In *Zork*, the player competes against the game itself, gaining points by working through an unseen world, overcoming obstacles, and amassing treasure. The game can continue until the player masters it, or it can abruptly end if the player "dies." Played on a personal computer, *Zork* demands both thought and imagination on the player's part—the play appears as text, not images, on the screen, and the player's imagination must supply the visuals. Because it is an interactive computer simulation, the player and the game respond to each other's decisions. Although businesspeople play it—and through transfer it could conceivably provide skills to apply to business—*Zork* is a nonbusiness simulation game played for fun.

An example of a business simulation game is the *Executive Perspectives Simulation*. Both a game and a simulation, it involves interteam competition in a simulated business setting. Like a number of games and simulations, the *Executive Perspectives Simulation* has evolved in stages. First developed 20 years ago as a business school simulation game, it was purchased and made commercially available 5 years ago. Created before the personal computer existed, the simulation has been "retrofitted" as a personal-computer-based exercise, and periodically undergoes both technological and content updates. Although some games and simulations contain designed-in lessons, the *Executive Perspectives Simulation* does not. Like other sophisticated simulations, it is designed to represent the real world as authentically as possible, so that principles which apply to the simulation may also apply to the real world.

The *Executive Perspectives Simulation*'s basic model can be used off-the-shelf, but it is usually modified to represent different industries under different conditions depending on the user's purpose. It is employed to teach three different kinds of skills, either singly or in combination: strategy and planning skills; functional skills, such as marketing or financial operations; and human behavior skills, such as leadership or communication. It is employed both as part of existing programs and as a stand-alone exercise.

Typically, the *Executive Perspectives Simulation* is a 2-day exercise requiring 1/2 day of introduction, 1 day of simulation, and 1/2 day of debriefing. Participants assume roles and receive assignments in a make-believe but authentic business setting. Because the purpose of a simulation game is often to provide the participant with a different or broader point of view, roles are usually assigned; a manager may be assigned an executive position; financial and marketing executives may exchange roles; or a seller may take the part of a customer. Participants often become absorbed by an authentic simulation without realizing it, and become committed to their roles. The progress of the simulation game is carefully observed by trainers.

The debriefing session with which the program concludes is an integral and critical part of any training game or simulation. The debriefing gives the participants the opportunity to examine how the whole operation worked and to reflect on their own performance and how they interacted with others.

The *International Management Game*, the *Strategic Management Game*, and the *Executive Perspectives Simulation* display some of the differences and similarities between sophisticated business simulation games.

The *International Management Game* is a table game which employs cards, plastic pieces, and a game board. The *Strategic Management Game* and the *Executive Perspectives Simulation* are personal computer-based simulations operated by participants. The *International Management Game*, developed by Sony, teaches the "Japanese-style" management philosophy adhered to by that company, which is reflected by the choices designed into the game. The *Strategic Management Game* and the *Executive Perspectives Simulation* emphasize certain strategies or skills but allow the player the latitude of more than one "right" choice. And the three simulation games differ in the degree of realism afforded their participants; some practitioners feel that the degree of realism directly relates to the transferability, or later application, of a simulation's experiential learning.

The *International Management Game*, the *Strategic Management Game*, and the *Executive Perspectives Simulation* all include interteam competition. All usually employ a seminar format, and engage participants in a breadth of management planning and strategy issues. And all take not minutes or hours, but days, to play.

Applications

Games and simulations are used by trainers as learning exercises, and also as problem-solving and evaluation tools. Here are five of their applications:

1. Games and simulations are particularly suited to teaching problem-solving and decision-making skills. Such skills are best learned not in a linear, abstract, passive context, but in a complex, realistic, active environment. Well-designed games and simulations provide a realistic environment with concrete referents while effectively emphasizing the essentials for learning in a structured and coherent way.

2. Simulations provide an effective vehicle for affective learning. Because participants adopt roles, they frequently also adopt feelings. Often they find new understanding—not on an abstract but on an affective level—of issues which involve emotions, values, and attitudes. This is a function of a simulation's potential to involve the learner. A persuasive model of reality can become as compelling as the real-life situation, and participants can find their emotional involvement with a simulation's characters and situations to be convincingly "real" as well. Other points of view can be perceived, and perceptions of systems, problems, and roles better understood.

3. Games and simulations are often used to develop the specialist's awareness and comprehension of the elements and systems which make up the whole. This is the "not just the trees, but the forest" feature which has appealed to recent

management development trends. Within their fields, specialists are responsible for a great amount of information, while as part of the organization as a whole, the specialist must understand the organization and be able to communicate with its other members to contribute optimally. Especially useful in exploring the relationships between parts of a system and their interaction with each other, games and simulation are employed as an integrative learning method.

4. Because a simulation models reality, it can be not only educationally useful, it also can be used to explore and solve real problems for an organization in the process of teaching. Through taking part in simulations which emphasize problem solving and decision making based on real-life models, participants can reach both an understanding of and new solutions to real problems.

5. In addition to teaching, games and simulations are used as an evaluation tool to identify and assess the individual's strengths and weaknesses. A familiar application of this appears in the assessment center method. A business game is a part of the typical assessment center program, along with other activities such as group discussions, in-basket exercises, written tests, and interviews. Although a business game, because its purpose is not to test experience, the game requires very little business knowledge; play is expressly designed so that the inexperienced participant will not be at a disadvantage. Usually the game's object is to trade simple or abstract items—the first assessment center game used Tinker Toys—at a profit. The game's purpose is to provide a medium in which the assessors can observe the participants' characteristics which are relevant to performance as a manager, including decisiveness, organization, leadership, reaction to stress, and relationships with others. A well-designed game is involving and challenging and elicits the kind of interpersonal behavior which the assessors might not have the opportunity to observe during other components of the program. Assessment results are used in a variety of applications, including hiring, placement, advancement, and development.

In addition to assessing individual personality traits and potential, simulations are employed to assess individual or group learning. In such an evaluation a simulation is designed to represent an actual job situation as realistically as possible. Performance in the simulation is evaluated and the learner is provided feedback. This technique is useful before planning later training, as well as to provide the trainer with a measure of the effectiveness of prior training. With feedback to the participant, games and simulations provide the opportunity for self-assessment as well.

Advantages

Practitioners feel that games and simulations offer the following characteristics to their advantage as training tools:

1. As a learning experience, a simulation is an efficient substitute for reality. Because it is a model, a simulation contains only those components considered important; a teaching simulation selects and concentrates on only those aspects of reality which are important to its learning objectives. A simulation compresses time, and provides the opportunity for a greatly accelerated "learning by doing" experience. The learner gains insights through nondirect experience in a quicker alternative to real-life learning experiences. This is especially valuable when time constraints are a factor.

2. Because neither the activity nor its consequences are real, games and

simulations offer a nonthreatening opportunity to explore, experiment, take risks, communicate, and reflect. Participants in games and simulations have permission and encouragement to learn, without having to worry about self-defense. This is particularly salutary for cooperative, problem-solving, or communication exercises. In the case of communication, games and simulations can provide a setting to broach controversial issues and provide participants with the opportunity to express—and listen to—points of view not normally discussed.

3. Games and simulations motivate the learner. Learning which is seen as just a means to an end—such as a grade or the fulfillment of a requirement—lacks the compelling element of learning in which the learner is involved. Games and simulations contain their own goals and motivations for the learner, through either competition or immediate feedback. People learn best when motivated. Motivation created in a simulation may extend beyond the learning exercise to the reality which it represents.

4. Because different people learn in different ways, it is wise to employ different teaching methods. Some learners may have trouble absorbing training content when its vehicle is passive. And those who do learn by reading and listening to lectures can benefit from the active medium of games and simulations as well.

5. Games and simulations can be intriguing, compelling, and fun. They are popular with learners as an engaging way of learning, and with trainers as an alternative to conventional "spray and pray" teaching methods. Games and simulations provide an ingredient to add in the training "mix" to keep it lively and interesting.

6. Simulations employ models of the context in which learning will be applied. In theory, this encourages the transfer of learning from the simulated setting to the real one. Success in a simulated activity builds confidence. This confidence may be "transferred" from the simulation to the reality which it models.

Limitations and Disadvantages

Practitioners also recognize limitations and disadvantages which apply to the use of games and simulations:

1. Although a simulation models reality, no simulation is truly realistic. Because the model consists of selected components, the variables included and their relative importance reflect the designer's model of reality—a simplified, "filtered" reality. A compelling simulation can appear to be genuine even when it is not—as the effect of Orson Welles' *War of the Worlds* broadcast illustrated. A simulation which is persuasive but inaccurate can effectively teach misinformation or biases. Because the simulation and its consequences are not real, the actions of its participants will reflect this. This has a positive aspect, as noted earlier; the participant is freed from constraints which may inhibit learning. At the same time, participants, by being more or less cautious, more or less serious than in real life, will not be behaving completely realistically, and therefore not drawing completely realistic lessons from the experience.

2. The competitive experience of a game can dominate the learning experience. Competition is key to making a game a game; an advantage of employing a game as a learning exercise is that the fun of competition motivates and involves the learner. Competition becomes counterproductive when participants become totally involved in the "win/lose" process, at the cost of exploration and reflection. This

depends on the design and administration of the game, and the learning—and competitive—styles of the players.

3. A game or simulation can be costly in time and money. This is true whether developed by the user or purchased commercially. The more elaborate and sophisticated, the more costly; and when a computer or special equipment is involved, the cost of programming, equipment time, and operating personnel must be included. Alternative training methods are usually less expensive.

4. There is no conclusive evidence about the effectiveness of games and simulations, no clear set of theories to predict and describe their effects and the reasons for them. Three main areas of game simulation effectiveness must be evaluated: their acceptability to students; their power to motivate; and the quality and quantity of learning they provide, that is, how well learning from games and simulations transfers to real life. Claims made about games and simulations' effectiveness still rest only on anecdotal evidence. It is widely felt that games and simulations work, but no one really knows exactly why, nor can they prove it.

Selection and Design

Should the user design a game or simulation or acquire one? That depends on the user's resources, expertise, and the desired outcome. With their increase in popularity, a wide variety of games and simulations are now commercially available, representing a full range of characteristics: simple or complex, brief or lengthy, all-man or man-machine, directed or open-ended, abstract or highly realistic, dating from three decades ago (*The Executive Simulation*,[7] a computer-based game developed at UCLA in 1958, is available in a personal computer version) to newly released, from personal computer diskette to a 3-day session guided by specialized trainers at the designer's headquarters.

The user must be a selective consumer. Not only is there the wide variety from which to choose, training objectives must be matched with the different, and sometimes multiple, objectives of available games and simulations. Many games and simulations are modified versions of each other. If no game or simulation is available which meets the trainer's needs closely enough, it may be practical to modify an existing one to meet different training requirements. If this is not feasible, and a game or simulation is the best training approach to meet the instructional need, a new one must be designed.

The developer must have expertise both in instructional design and in the subject of the game or simulation. Game and simulation development varies greatly in both expense and time required, depending on the ambition of the project; the most sophisticated run into a number of man-years and several hundred thousand dollars. Next to actually having designed games or simulations, the best experience for a designer is to have administered and participated in different kinds, and be familiar enough with them to be able to adopt appropriate principles and components from them.

The design of a game is the systematic construction of ideas into an operating model. Here is a brief, general guideline outlining the four main steps of game and simulation design. Some of its elements apply to games, some to simulations, and all to simulation games.

1. *Determine the training objectives of the exercise and its intended users.* Both the objectives and the uses may be defined precisely or broadly, depending on the game or simulation's purpose. Also at this step, the designer should determine whether to proceed further by asking: Is a simulation or game the most effective method of

meeting the stated training objectives with the intended users? And if so, does an appropriate game or simulation already exist? Assuming the answers to the questions are "yes" and "no," respectively, the designer should proceed with the next step.

2. *Develop the basic specifications of the exercise.* At this point the simulation model should be built, and the expectations and parameters of the exercise established. In clear terms, the exercise's content—the messages it will convey—should be described; and its format—the vehicle it will use—determined. Content may be cognitive, affective, or a combination, depending on training objectives. The format chosen should be appropriate to achieve intended instructional objectives, by providing an effective medium for content while remaining within the designer's production constraints.

3. *Develop the components of the exercise.* These include the scenario, rules, roles, and an accounting system. The scenario should be sufficient—neither too simple nor too complicated—and appropriate both for the intended users and to meet training objectives. Similarly, the number of roles should be sufficient to represent characters important to the situation, without including so many as to make the exercise unnecessarily complex.

4. *Construct and test a prototype of the exercise.* Because testing is useful in the design process itself, a prototype should be built early and tested often. Final stages of this step involve field testing by users, and finally actual field use.

Conducting Games and Simulations

A crucial factor in a game or simulation is how it is conducted. All games and simulations share four major phases of administration: preparation, introduction, operation, and debriefing.

The preparation for a game or simulation requires particular thoroughness. Because of their intensity and the often paramount need for realism, interruptions during the course of a game or simulation can seriously disrupt the exercise and its effectiveness. The trainer must be thoroughly familiar with the exercise to be adequately organized and prepared. This requires an understanding of how the game or simulation matches the participants' instructional needs, and how it integrates within the overall instructional context. The trainer must account for all practical contingencies, and prepare schedules, space, materials, personnel, and responsibilities.

The introduction sets the tone for the game or simulation itself. It is here that the trainer must resist the impulse of the exhaustive explanation. Because games and simulations are experiential exercises, participants must be given the opportunity to learn as much for themselves as possible. Trainers facilitate the learning. It is the trainer's responsibility to provide enough information so that participants may proceed on their own; to explain the exercise's purposes; and to be supportive, understanding, and enthusiastic.

The operation of the game or simulation also requires the trainer to stifle the teacher's impulse and suspend the usual role of leader for the period of the exercise, allowing the participants to think, decide, act, and learn for themselves. The trainer's main responsibility is to observe and evaluate as the exercise proceeds.

The conclusion and debriefing phase is one of the most important parts of a game or simulation learning exercise. It is during this period that participants can capture what occurred by discussing actions and impressions. The trainer acts as discussion leader. The debriefing usually is divided into three phases. During the first phase, participants express their views of the experience. This is important, not only for relief but also so that everyone involved can understand each other's feelings. The trainer's role is to keep the discussion enlightening and not allow it to become confrontational. The second phase is an analysis by participants of their own and others' roles. The third phase involves an examination of the game or simulation's "lessons," and how they apply to the world to which the participants will return.

Summary

Games and simulations' unique ability to engage the learner has made them an attractive and increasingly popular training option. But although engaging the learner is an important element in effective learning, it is by no means all that is required; games and simulations are useful only if they teach, not just compel. Games and simulations are learning tools which, to be effective, must be designed and used purposefully and appropriately. Therein lies the challenge of games and simulations for the designer, trainer, and learner alike.

References

1. Von Neumann, John, *The Theory of Games and Economic Behavior*, Princeton University Press, Princeton, NJ, 1944.

2. Peters, Thomas J., and Robert H. Waterman, *In Search of Excellence: Lessons from America's Best-Run Companies*, Harper & Row, New York, 1982.

3. *Looking Glass, Inc.*, Center for Creative Leadership, 5000 Laurinda Dr., P.O. Box P-1, Greensboro, NC 27402. *The Executive Perspectives Simulation*, Executive Perspectives, Inc., 92 Main St., Charlestown, MA 02129. *The Strategic Management Game*, The Strategic Management Group, 3624 Market St., Philadelphia, PA 19104. *The International Management Game*, Sony Management Systems Co., 9 W. 57 St., New York, NY 10019.

4. *Wff'n Proof* and *Equations*, Wff'n Proof Learning Games Associates, 1490 South Blvd., Ann Arbor, MI 48104.

5. *The Financial Services Simulation*, Associate Professor Stephen A. Stumpf, The Financial Management Simulations Projects Group, New York University Schools of Business, 40 W. 4 St., New York, NY 10012.

6. *Zork*, Infocom, Inc., 125 Cambridge Park Dr., Cambridge, MA 02140.

7. *The Executive Simulation*, University of California, Los Angeles, 405 Hilgard Ave., Graduate School of Management, Los Angeles, CA 90024.

Resources

Thousands of games and simulations, and books and articles about them, are available. This bibliography lists selected books and journals about games and simulations.

Books

Abt, Clark, C., *Serious Games*, The Viking Press, New York, 1970.
Adair, Charles H., and John T. Foster, Jr., *A Guide for Simulation Design*, Instructional Simulation Design, Inc., Tallahassee, FL, 1972.

Adams, Dennis, *Simulation Games: An Approach to Learning*, Charles H. Jones Co., Columbus, OH, 1973.

Barton, Richard A., *A Primer on Simulation and Gaming*, Prentice-Hall, Inc., Englewood Cliffs, NJ, 1972.

Boocook, Sarane S., and E. O. Schild, *Simulation Games in Learning*, Sage Publications, Beverly Hills, CA 1968.

Coombs, Don H., *Simulation and Gaming: The Best of ERIC*, Stanford University, 1976.

DeKoven, Bernard, *The Well Played Game*, Doubleday, Garden City, NY, 1978.

Duke, Richard D., *Gaming: The Future's Language*, Malsted, New York, 1974.

Dukes, Richard L., and C. Seidner, eds. *Learning with Simulations and Games*, Sage Publications, Beverly Hills, CA, 1978.

Gibb, G. I., *Handbook of Games and Simulation Exercises*, Sage Publications, Beverly Hills, CA, 1974.

Gibb, G. I., *Dictionary of Gaming, Modeling and Simulation*, Sage Publications, Beverly Hills, CA, 1978.

Greenblatt, Cathy S., *Gaming—Simulation Rationale, Design, and Applications*, Malsted, New York, 1975.

Greenblatt, Cathy S., and Richard D. Duke, *Principles and Practices of Gaming—Simulation*, Sage Publications, Beverly Hills, CA, 1981.

Horn, R., and H. Cleaves, *The Guide to Simulation Games for Education and Training*, 4th ed., Sage Publications, Beverly Hills, CA, 1980.

Maidment, R., and R. M. Bronstein, *Simulation Games: Design and Implementation*, Charles E. Merrill Publishing Co., Columbus, OH, 1973.

Suits, Bernard, *The Grasshopper: Games, Life, and Utopia*, University of Toronto Press, Toronto, Ont., 1978.

Thiagarajan, Sivasailam, and Harold D. Stolovitch, *Instructional Simulation Games*, Vol. 12, *The Instructional Design Library*, Educational Technology Publications, Englewood Cliffs, NJ, 1978.

Zuckerman, D., and R. E. Horn, *The Guide to Simulations/Games for Education and Training*, Information Resources, Inc., Lexington, MA, 1973.

Periodicals

Simulation/Games for Learning, Society for Academic Gaming and Simulation in Education and Training (SAGSET), Centre for Extension Studies, University of Technology, Loughborough, Leics. LEII 3TU, England.

Simages, North American Simulation and Gaming Association (NASAGA), University of North Carolina, Asheville, Asheville, NC.

Simulation and Games: An International Journal of Theory, Design, and Research, Sage Publications, Beverly Hills, CA.

27

Computer-Based Training

Frank A. Hart

Frank A. Hart is manager, educational services, General Electric Information Services Company, Rockville, Maryland. Prior to joining General Electric, he managed the Advanced Technology Training Program at the Xerox Training Center, Leesburg, Virginia. In the 10 years before joining Xerox, Hart held key training positions in the Army in which he was responsible for testing and implementing new training technologies. He was commander of the U.S. Army Research Institute for the Behavioral and Social Sciences, director of the Army's Training Development Institute, and president, Combat Arms Training Board. He is a member of the Association for the Development of Computer-Based Instructional Systems, National Society for Performance and Instruction, and ASTD. He is chair of the Society for Applied Learning Technology Special Interest Group on Microcomputers. He holds a B.S. degree from the U.S. Military Academy and an M.A. from Stanford.

The training community is in the midst of turmoil concerning the application of the computer to support the profession. Technology has been a lure for trainers throughout the twentieth century. The successive introduction of motion pictures, television, video recorders, video conferencing, and videodiscs suggested to trainers that the use of such technologies would bring considerable benefits. Conference proceedings of the past 20 years, particularly, are replete with predictions about the ability of computers to decrease the cost and increase the effectiveness of training. *Time* magazine's selection of the computer as the "Man of the Year" in 1984 symbolized the strong, almost overwhelming, presence of computer technology in the business and government world. Training managers confront the phenomenon regularly at training association meetings where they encounter a growing number of panels, presentations, and exhibits which are devoted to computer-based training (CBT), and they are greeted by a plethora of catalogs, mailers, and announcements descending upon their desk daily.

Bells and whistles have always been used as a substitute for effective training by the many "song-and-dance" artists of our profession. The careful craftsman has wisely subordinated technology to its role as supporter or enhancer of skill development. Does the smart training manager join this movement to CBT or ignore it? Have the predictions about the role of computer-based training come to pass? What are the possibilities for the application of computer technology to the training requirements of your organization?

The purpose of this chapter is to aid the trainer, training developer, or training manager who is not an expert in technology-based training but wants to evaluate its potential for application to his or her training requirements. The chapter discusses the critical questions and issues and provides an approach for resolving them. It is not a detailed "how to" treatment. Some "how to" examples are found in the bibliography. The chapter treats the subject of computer-based training from a business perspective, providing questions and a general approach to evaluate the potential use of computer-based training for your organization.

Why Should Organizations Want to Use CBT?

Let us begin the examination of computer-based training by considering its benefits. What results can training managers obtain that would justify a CBT investment to the management of their organization?

The decision to use computer-based training should occur only because it provides specific benefits which are important to your organization. You should concert a strategy that will obtain those benefits. If you are not focused on the benefits, your organization could waste resources as it acquires CBT to "just try it out."

Computer-based training has the potential to provide two major benefits. It can reduce the cost of training and/or increase the effectiveness of training. Reducing the cost of training enables you to provide more training for the same cost. CBT has become particularly attractive to larger companies with dispersed work forces.

Reduced Costs

- *Reduced student travel and living costs.* Students do not have to travel to class sites. In many cases the computer hardware can be placed in dispersed locations so that the student takes the training at or near his or her work site. For large companies with a geographically dispersed work force this can become a very large saving.

- *Reduced length of training.* There is considerable evidence to support the industry's claim that students in CBT programs complete the training in about 30 percent less time than if they had been trained in the same program in a classroom. This reduction in training time is primarily a function of the ability of each person to proceed at his or her own speed and not to be constrained to the pace of the slowest person in the class.

- *More timely training.* A CBT training program can be provided to a student as soon as he or she requires it. New hires do not have to wait for sufficient people to organize a class. They may begin a CBT orientation program as soon as they join the organization. Timeliness also means that individuals may take CBT programs at odd times during the day or night rather than during prescribed class hours. Timeliness makes employees productive faster.

- *Increased student to instructor ratio.* Whether the reference is to an instructor or facilitator who manages students on terminals in a classroom or to the instructor who is at the end of the phone to answer questions from students scattered across the country, the result is the same. The instructor or facilitator of a CBT program can manage or support considerably more students, perhaps severalfold more, than can the instructor in a more conventional form of training. The result is a reduction in the instructor/facilitator staff for the same student load.

- *Reduced amount of operational hardware.* When a training program includes operational hardware which students are learning to operate or maintain, the amount of hardware required to support training can be decreased significantly by the use of computer simulations. For instance, the copier company which teaches copier maintenance on a personal computer simulation generates considerable hardware savings. A classroom with six $5000 enhanced personal computers and one $40,000 copier can produce the same training result as a classroom with six $40,000 copiers.

- *Reduced equipment damage.* When the student is learning equipment operations or maintenance, his or her mistakes are less costly on a computer simulation than when performed on an expensive piece of equipment. The ultimate example is the airplane flight simulator on which pilots develop their skills rather than training on the more expensive airplane. The same principle applies, in a less dramatic fashion, when a technician learns to apply equipment troubleshooting diagnosis and repair on a computer simulation rather than on the copier, the aircraft engine, or the radio. If a student makes a mistake on the actual hardware, it could be costly. If he or she makes the same mistake on a simulation, only student pride may be damaged and he or she can learn from the error.

Increased Effectiveness of Training

In addition to making training more efficient, CBT can make the training more effective. The impact on effectiveness is seen in the following ways:

- *Standardized delivery.* Unlike the human instructor, the computer delivers the instruction the same way every time. It doesn't have good days or bad days. Every day is the same. It is important to note that the standardized delivery is only as good as the design and development behind it. Standardized delivery could be standardized poor delivery if the program was ineffectively developed.

- *Standardized feedback.* Each time a student responds to a situation, the computer can provide standardized feedback.

- *Individualized student program.* CBT can individualize student programs in three different ways. It can tailor an entire program to the capabilities of a student as determined by testing before the course begins. At predetermined places within a course, it can tailor the remainder of a course to a student based upon performance to that point in the course. Finally, it can tailor the work within a module or segment of a course based upon the student performance in the beginning of the module. Individualization can be expensive because of the increased computer programming required. Both the computer memory required to handle individualization and the programming costs have been the principal constraints to its being used more than it is.

■ *Increased performance practice.* One of CBT's major contributions to effectiveness is seldom recognized. The computer can offer each student sufficient opportunity to practice a skill until proficient. It is often difficult within instructor-delivered programs to provide each student the opportunity to practice until proficient while delivering accurate, consistent feedback for each student attempt. CBT can, and while doing so, guarantees a performance result. Once again, that performance result reflects underlying training expertise required.

These benefits are impressive. For companies with large work forces, and particularly where the work force is geographically dispersed, the cost savings can be considerable and the training more effective. However, a computer-based training solution for a program of any size provides risks as well as rewards. The key to success is the ability to perform a cost-benefit analysis. Effective cost-benefit analysis is dependent upon a knowledge of CBT benefits and their derivation.

Computer-Based Training Use

The cliché about "no free lunch" certainly applies to CBT. Computer-based training is usually a "high risk—high reward" venture whose risk side is seldom appreciated. All the commotion about CBT may lead you to believe that everyone, or at least a large number of companies, are using computer-based training and that its use represents a significant proportion of training budgets. This is hardly the case. Surveys of *Fortune* 500 companies over the past 4 years indicate that 40 to 50 percent of the companies employ computer-based training in one form or another. Larger surveys, such as the one *Training* Magazine conducts annually, indicate that 20 to 25 percent of the surveyed companies use CBT. The larger companies are more likely to try CBT because they can afford to experiment with new forms of training or because their training requirements are sufficiently diverse that they can match some of their needs against commercial CBT capabilities. However, surveys which addressed quantity or budget questions indicate that among those companies which employ CBT, the budget devoted to that technology, or the amount of the company's training requirement addressed by it, varies from less than 1 to 10 percent. Hence the proliferation of CBT is still very limited.

The important question for any organization considering CBT is why its use is not more widespread. The short answer is there are enough failures and disappointments to prevent CBT's growing by leaps and bounds.

The failures and disappointments with CBT are similar in scope to those experienced when other technologies have been uncritically applied to the training process. Infatuation with the technology saw CBT applied to situations in which it was not appropriate much less a workable training solution.

The learning curve involved in developing successful CBT is steep. CBT requires the integration of training's instructional systems development process with the computer industry's software engineering process. Neither is easy. Too many CBT programs have ended up showcasing the skills of the computerist rather than those of the trainer.

Another reason for CBT's present limited use is the small amount of generic CBT available for off-the-shelf purchase. Only one community—data processing—can choose from among a significant amount of CBT training materials. While the number of CBT commercial niches is increasing, the number is small on a relative basis; and each niche supports only a fraction of the training requirements in the area in which it operates. An interesting example is sales training, which is a large item in the training budget of any company with a sales force. Over the past 2 years commercial CBT companies have developed a large number of disk-based training programs to support sales training. However, these programs address prerequisite skills or knowledge that the salesperson should have before beginning more traditional sales training programs or in other ways support the traditional programs.

If you can't buy CBT off the shelf, you have to build it or contract to have it built. CBT is expensive to develop. Where good training organizations may spend 20 to 40 development hours for each delivery hour of conventional instruction, good development teams require from 50 to 500 hours to develop each hour of CBT. The ratio swing depends on the training requirement, the form of CBT, and the development approach chosen. This means that CBT can cost from $2800 to $28,000 per hour to develop. How many organizations can afford this cost?

The corollary to the excessive initial cost of CBT is the longer time required to develop it than to develop conventional training. A CBT program may take several times longer to develop than would the same program developed for conventional delivery.

The history of training in the seventies and the early eighties includes a large number of CBT prototype efforts which did not last through the early trials. Organizations who want to develop their own CBT will quickly discover the risks described above. Despite these risks there are sound reasons for organizations to consider CBT and to employ it. The benefits described earlier are real. The training community has considerable experience dealing with CBT and understands its selection and development much better than it did a few years ago. In the remainder of this chapter we will examine a decision process to help organizations determine whether CBT is appropriate for them, examine the trends in the technology, and conclude with reasons why the training community should feel optimistic about this technology.

CBT Decision Process

The initial need for any organization considering CBT is to have a systematic process that will take into account the major variables and issues necessary to good decision making. Shown in Fig. 27-1 is such a decision process to help you decide whether or not CBT is appropriate for your organization. It will address the roles of computer-based training, the development process, and the issues concerning implementation. This process provides a systematic approach to your assessing the viability of computer-based training for your organization.

Determine Requirements

Step one in the process is to determine the training requirement. In other words, you must determine that you have a performance problem that training can correct and be able to define the training requirement in behavioral terms. Instructional technologists use a variety of terms to describe this process. "Needs analysis" appears to be the term most frequently used to convey the process envisaged. It is quite useful to conceptualize three processes occurring. One ought to begin with a performance analysis of the type described by Robert Mager. It will determine the performance problem or issue and lead to a conclusion concerning the role of training. Second, a job analysis of the specific job or function being addressed determines the array of job tasks to be addressed. Finally, a task analysis is used to define behaviorally each job task. The result of this first step is a set of behaviorally defined job tasks which describes the performance results the proposed training

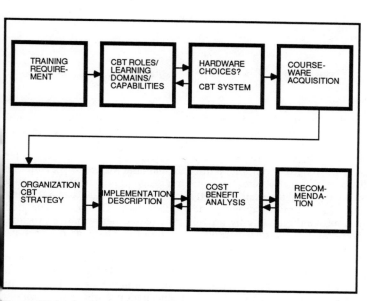

Figure 27-1. Computer-based training decision process.

program should achieve. There is no incremental difference in time or cost in the process required to determine the training requirement for CBT from the process always required to generate behaviorally based systems training.

Match Needs with CBT Capabilities

Step two consists of three parts:

List appropriate CBT roles.

Determine the learning domains inherent in the training requirement.

Determine the CBT capabilities required by the learning domains.

You emerge from step two with a statement of CBT capabilities required to train effectively in the learning domains of the training objectives. You learn how much graphics capability will be required.

The beginning of step two is to determine what CBT roles are appropriate for the training requirement described in step one. The computer can perform three roles. It can manage the training process, deliver training, or provide administrative support. The management of training is called "computer-managed instruction," or CMI. Although CMI is less glamorous than the delivery role, it can provide major benefits. CMI keeps records of student activity and performance, generates instructional prescriptions, and tests students. Organizations have used CMI to manage students in classroom settings where self-paced materials were being employed. Hence, CMI can be used in conjunction with non-CBT training delivery.

Computer delivery of training is usually labeled computer-assisted instruction, or CAI. Listed below are examples of the way in which the computer can deliver instruction:

Drill and practice

Tutorial

Simulation

Games

Inquiry mode

Based upon the training requirement and the benefits you would like to obtain, make a list of those CBT roles which would be appropriate. You are not making decisions at this stage, but rather constructing alternatives. If your primary interests are to reduce the cost of training, you will want to deliver training via the computer in order to reduce the length of training, reduce the demand for instructors, and be able to provide training at the job site. If you are interested in improving the quality of training, you have several alternatives. CMI can improve the quality of a training program through its ability to provide individualization. Computer-delivered instruction can improve the quality by providing increased performance practice, consistent delivery, and standardized feedback. None of the benefits or roles are mutually exclusive.

If you determine that computer-delivered instruction is necessary, you have to determine what capabilities must be provided by your CBT system. The link between computer roles, training objectives, and the computer capabilities is not well developed within the CBT community. All objectives are not taught equally well by the computer. It facilitates the learning of certain objectives better than others. Moreover, the different forms of computer capability such as graphics are more critical to the learning of certain forms of objectives than to others. The general rule is that the more precisely you can define a training objective, the better the computer can support the learning of that objective through computer-assisted instruction. The computer does not support vaguely defined objectives very well.

To determine the CBT capabilities that may be necessary, it is important to determine the learning domains inherent in the training objectives. Do the key objectives center about the cognitive, affective, or psychomotor domains? Figure 27-2 arrays five types of training often found in the business sector, lists the skills contained therein, and suggests the types of CBT required.

The importance of Fig. 27-2 is that it provides insights into the characteristics of

Functional area to be trained	Data processing	Technical training	Sales skills management training communications skills
Learning domains	Cognitive skills concepts	Cognitive skills Psychomotor skills	Cognitive skills Psychomotor skills
Types of CBT required	Any form of CBT	Graphics supported CBT for simulations to support psychomotor skills Any form for cognitive skills	Graphics supported CBT for psychomotor skills video supported CBT fulfills this best Any form of CBT for cognitive skills—which are usually the enabling tasks for this requirement

Figure 27-2. CBT capabilities and learning objectives.

	Main frame CAI nongraphic	Main frame CAI with graphics	Mini-computer CAI with graphics	PC developed CAI limited graphics	PC developed CAI simulation rich
Development ratio (hours of development per hour of delivery)	40-1 to 100-1	100-1 to 300-1	50-1 to 200-1	30-1 to 50-1	100-1 to 500-1
Development cost per hour of delivery	$2300 to 5600	$5600 to 17,000	$2800 to 11,200	$1700 to 2800	$5600 to 28,00
Supports	Cognitive domain ————————————————————————————————→				
		Psycho-motor	Psycho-motor	Psycho-motor	
	Affective domain ————————	increasingly easier	————————————————————→		

Figure 27-3. CBT development costs.

the particular CBT system required to support learning objectives of a specific type. This match of functional training area to domain to CBT capabilities reflects an early understanding within the profession of these relationships. It needs to be taken farther and matched with the comparative CBT development effectiveness of the various CBT systems.

Figure 27-2 suggests that any form of CBT can support data processing training effectively. The implication of this suggestion is that cheaper, nongraphics CBT systems are quite sufficient for data processing. More expensive graphic systems may contribute not much beyond increased cost. The procedure based skills which underlie both data processing training and technical training can be taught effectively by CBT because of the precision of the performance objectives that can be developed.

Moving to the concepts and interpersonal skills inherent in sales training, management training, and communications training, one faces a very different situation. Training objectives in these areas lack the hard precision one finds in technical or data processing training. More important, the terminal performances inherent to sales skills and management skills require interpersonal practice. On the other hand, an examination of the enabling skills and knowledge of sales and management terminal performances would quickly show that many, if not most, of such subordinate skills could be taught and practiced by computer-based training. This observation means that the total program to provide any of the major terminal performances in sales or management training would require some instructor-delivered training in addition to CBT.

Figure 27-3 adds to the information contained in Fig. 27-2 by indicating which learning domains are supported by the major CBT hardware types and providing representative cost ratios.

Now that you have listed appropriate CBT roles and determined the learning domains inherent in the training requirement, you need to complete step two by constructing alternatives concerning the CBT roles that you envisage and the implications for CBT capabilities. If you are going to deliver technical training, you need graphics supported CBT to develop the necessary simulations. Any form of

CBT can support the cognitive skills found in sales and management training. However, providing the interpersonal situations critical to sales or management training requires video-supported training. Computer-driven videodisc systems meet this requirement.

When you complete step two, you should ensure that you have determined alternatives that will meet the training requirements in step one and provide the benefits considered important to your organization.

Step three has two components: hardware choices and CBT system. First, specify viable hardware choices. Hardware choice is dictated by the training requirement, the features and functions it requires, the location of the training population, the hardware available, and the CBT system necessary to support the requirement. Current hardware choices include mainframes, minicomputers, microcomputers, and networked systems. The changing nature of computer technology is blurring the distinctions among micro, mini, and mainframe systems and creating new options. However, the following information will enable you to deal with the terminology and hardware categories being used.

Mainframe.   A centralized mainframe system used in a timesharing manner was the early operational mode for CBT systems and is still used extensively. The mainframe provides a large amount of storage capacity for both management functions and courseware. Further, additional terminals can be added at small incremental costs. Mainframe systems have their drawbacks. When too many terminals are using the system at the same time, the system's response is degraded. Reliability is another concern. Any time the central processor ceases operation, all the terminals stop functioning also. An important issue when considering mainframes is whether graphics will be required. Some mainframe systems, including the popular IBM instructional system (IS), do not provide graphics for instructional purposes. Other systems, including Control Data's PLATO system, do provide graphics. This is an example of the interrelationship of different mainframe capabilities and specific CBT systems. CBT systems will be addressed later.

Minicomputers.   Minicomputers driving terminals in a timesharing situation are similar to timesharing mainframe systems. While minis may lack the capacity of the large mainframe host, a minicomputer may be the correct business solution any time capacity requirement will not overload mini capabilities.

Microcomputers.   Microcomputers or personal computers serving as stand-alone systems are increasing in popularity because of their flexibility, low cost, and transportability. On the other hand, they lack the ability, management, and resource sharing capability of the mainframe system.

Networked Systems.   One of the more popular hardware solutions is the networked system in which geographically distributed personal computers are linked to a mainframe. Instructional software can be transmitted to the micros and course results uploaded to a management system. Further, course revision can take place on the mainframe and then be downloaded electronically.

The evolving nature of computer hardware means that this is an area that will require close scrutiny. While costs are falling, power and capacity are increasing almost geometrically. The distinctions among different forms of computers described above may be meaningful only for a few more years. However, some conclusions about hardware are still in order. If the students are geographically dispersed, you need either stand-alone personal computers or distributed personal computers networked to a mainframe or mini. The networked solution usually is more cost-effective than stand-alone systems. A second critical issue concerns whether or not the training requirement will need graphics. Some mainframes and mainframe-based CBT systems provide graphical support and some do not. You have to research this issue when you consider CBT.

As a minimum, you should conclude your examination of hardware with tentative conclusions about whether you need a networked system, stand-alone micros, or timesharing mainframes or minis and whether graphic support is critical to the instructional success of your requirement.

Select CBT System(s)

The next step is to select one or more CBT systems that would be appropriate to your requirements. In early 1986 over fifty different CBT systems are available on the commercial market. Each system is built around an authoring system or authoring language which constitutes the system software for the instructional system. Authoring languages and authoring systems enable courseware developers and development teams to create the training material. Each language and system has its own strengths and weaknesses and set of features. Many are linked directly to specific hardware configurations. You have no choice but to research market availability and system capabilities. Significant new systems are being added almost every month.

Selection of a CBT system begins by returning to the statement of the training requirement and determining exactly what capabilities are required of your CBT delivery system. Does it require graphic support? Will skills or knowledge or both be taught? How will student performance be evaluated? Can the program be delivered in a linear manner or will branching be required? Several of the sources listed at the end of the chapter provide excellent checklists to help you.

The key in examining each CBT system is recognizing the embedded instructional system contained therein. The developer of an authoring language or system begins by formulating an instructional approach. The developer next builds a software package to ease the development of training materials that use that instructional approach. Further, the authoring language or system is enhanced with additional features to make the developer's job easier. An example of an additional feature is "screen capture" which permits the entire screen of an application software package to be captured and inserted directly into a CBT package with only one or two keystrokes rather than having to copy the entire screen. The embedded instructional system dictates the way in which the instructional program will be delivered. Some developers use high-level programming languages such as PASCAL to have more flexibility in their instructional delivery. At least two prices are paid to use high-level programming languages rather than authoring languages or systems. The high-level authoring languages take longer for developers to master and may require several times more development time for a specific training program. On the other hand, certain graphics-rich simulation may be possible only in high-level programming languages. Enough advances have been made in more flexible authoring languages and systems over the past 2 or 3 years to make this an interesting area to explore as you consider your CBT decision.

Acquire Courseware

Step four is to determine how you will acquire courseware. Courseware is the term used to describe the CBT instructional software. It is the learning material. You can buy courseware off-the-shelf, contract for its development, or form an in-house development group. Each approach is the appropriate answer to certain situations. The major variables are cost, time, maintenance of courseware, and requirements for continuing expertise. If you can find off-the-shelf courses which meet your precise objectives and which will run on your hardware and operating systems, buy them. The critical question is how closely the objectives of the off-the-shelf courseware match your learning objectives. More to the point, you probably will have great difficulty finding off-the-shelf courseware whose objectives are sufficiently close to yours. Except for certain specialized areas, the number of lessons available will be small. In such areas as data processing training, a sizable CBT commercial industry has emerged. The commercial activity is strong because of the degree of standardization present among data processing operations in terms of hardware, software, and training objectives. Similarly, an increasing number of CBT lessons are becoming available to support personal computers and their standard software packages. Another recent growth area is CBT training to support important enabling knowledges and skills and productivity tools in sales training and management training. You need to investigate the CBT vendors to determine what can be provided you.

Contracting for courseware development is an appropriate solution when the organization lacks in-house capability, wishes to avoid the CBT development learning curve, and has a time-sensitive requirement. Contracting may also be the solution for a specific project which can be described well or for the first project of a company which is exploring CBT. Usually, a contracted effort will cost less than an effort provided by an in-house group in its early days. Finally, experienced CBT development groups may contract to expand their capability during peak periods.

If an organization intends to make a long-term commitment toward a CBT program, it may want to consider forming its own group. While it will have to pay for the learning curve of its fledgling in-house group, the organization will reap several benefits. All the experience gained goes directly into the skills of the in-house group. The in-house group will be in a position to update its own courseware. Finally, the in-house group will be able to bring its acquired experience to bear on new CBT challenges and provide new CBT solutions.

It is not unusual to see organizations use all three approaches to acquire courseware, not only when they are beginning their CBT program but even during the mature stage. Do not arbitrarily rule out any of the three approaches. Each has its place.

Determine Business Strategy

Step five is to determine a company CBT business strategy. The CBT planner must determine whether the initial CBT project will be a stand-alone effort in which experimentation is permitted or whether it will be the first project in a larger system and hence must be compatible with the design of the eventual larger system. Experimental projects offer considerable advantages. They enable an organization to leap quickly into its first CBT effort since they do not put constraints upon the selection of hardware, software, authoring systems, and operating systems. In the experimental project, the organization can experiment with the forms of computer-delivered instruction, the kinds of hardware, and the methods of developing the courseware.

In those instances in which the organization can define with confidence its eventual system and possesses sufficient in-house CBT expertise to understand what it is about, it makes sense to make the pilot effort compatible with the final system. The point is that organizations should not back into a decision concerning their choice of system and system design. They should make conscious decisions as to whether they are experimenting and for what purposes, and as to when they intend to develop a system design for their program.

Plan Implementation

The next step is to describe the implementation which will occur. What training courses will be provided? Who is the target audience? Where are they located and where will they be trained? Who will be the instructors or facilitators for the CBT program? What will be their responsibilities? What will be the relationship between the CBT development group and the course instructors? What is the hardware upon which the training will take place? You will probably describe two or more different implementations to reflect the alternatives you are considering.

As an example, you may be considering centralized training of software consultants in the COBOL language and you would like to establish a computer-managed instructional system to manage their individual progress through a self-paced course. You are interested in eliminating the travel costs of the students; so you consider converting the self-paced course to computer-delivered instruction which is delivered at the job site. The CAI program is computer managed as well. Establishing detailed descriptions of the implementation of each alternative enables you to complete the cost-benefit analysis which is the next step.

Cost-Benefit Analysis

Once a company strategy has been outlined and the alternative implementations described, it is time to complete step seven, the cost-benefit analysis. Cost-benefit analyses are neither mysterious nor exotic. Rather, they should be viewed as a commonsense examination to determine whether development and implementation of a specific CBT system makes business sense in a particular situation. The starting point of the cost-benefit analysis is the formula in Fig. 27-4. Use of this formula and development of a cost-benefit analysis is well explained in the various works by Glen Head which are listed in the bibliography. Key to easy use of this formula is recognition that the primary benefits will be reduced student costs

```
TRAINING
SYSTEM      =
COSTS


STUDENT COSTS
    +
    INSTRUCTOR COSTS
        +
        FACILITY COSTS
            +
            EQUIPMENT COSTS
                +
                ADMINISTRATIVE COSTS
                    +
                    COURSEWARE ACQUISITION COSTS
```

Figure 27-4. Cost-benefit analysis.

through shorter learning time and reduced travel costs and instructor costs through higher student to instructor ratios and shorter courses. In turn, these benefits must be weighed against the primary cost increases, which will be courseware and hardware acquisition, each of which should be amortized over a realistic period. Although hardware may appear to be the largest new expense, experience indicates that the courseware is the major new cost factor.

When the planner completes the cost-benefit analysis, he or she must engage in an interactive process of examining the effect of various assumptions on the alternatives examined. They should also consider qualitative issues in the context of the cost-benefit analysis. It may be impossible for a high-tech company to compute the value of providing computer-based training to its clients or being the first in the industry to do so, but the benefit may be sufficient to tip the scales when alternatives of similar value are being considered.

Now the planner is in a position to make a recommendation to the organization.

Development

Because the development of CBT is a cross-disciplinary effort, it is important to highlight several aspects of the development project. Several sources listed in the bibliography provide detailed discussions concerning how to proceed with development.

First, it must be recognized that computer-based training development is the merger of two complementary but different processes: the systems approach to training and the software engineering process. The systems approach to training is a structured way to manage the training process from requirement to implementation and evaluation. Figure 27-5 shows a generic model usually referred to as the "instructional systems development" or ISD process.

Several features of the ISD model are critical and epitomize its purpose and use.

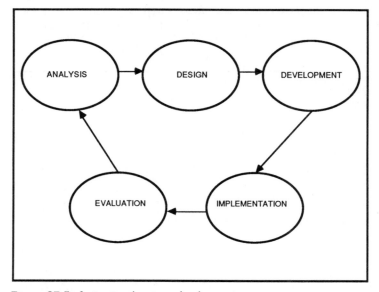

Figure 27-5. Instructional systems development process.

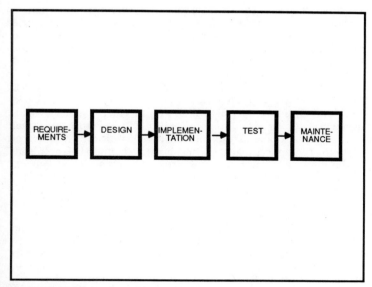

Figure 27-6. Systems engineering process.

The model stresses the importance of an analysis phase that is based upon examining members of the target population in order to determine exactly the target requirement and then conducting a behavioral analysis so that the requirement can be expressed in behavioral terms as performance objectives with tasks, conditions, and standards. The design and development follows a standardized process, but the key is the systematic testing, or validation, of increasingly larger components of the training on typical members of the target population to ensure that the training works. The ultimate test of the training itself occurs in an evaluation phase to test the students to ensure that they have acquired the skills and knowledge that are the purpose of the training. Finally, evaluation occurs on an ongoing basis with the results fed into each phase of the model to revise the program.

Different forms of the system approach to training appear, but they are all quite similar to the generic model pictured above and share the characteristics described above.

A second process is the systems engineering process, which is the approach necessary to develop any computer software program. The process is outlined in Fig. 27-6. The critical point of any system engineering process is the requirements phase. Many unsuccessful software programs owe their downfall to the absence of a good requirement descriptions document reflective of sufficient work in the requirements phases. One particular point to note is the extra time required in the testing phase to ensure that the program runs on the computer exactly as it is supposed to run.

Another major issue in development is the form of the development organization. The computer-based training effort, during its early period in any organization, requires a management approach that will treat the effort in a holistic fashion. The management choices are functional management, project management, and matrix management. A case can be made for each in certain situations depending upon the decision criteria emphasized. However, our concern, for the most part, is not with the upgrade of existing CBT systems or the development of single experimental prototypes. These are both simple projects that probably can be handled by functional management approaches. The larger challenge is the organization which makes a conscious decision to establish a computer-based training system and to begin the development of courseware. The expenses involved, the sophisticated nature of the technology, the time length of the project, and the probable size and cost are all factors that may combine to defeat a functional organization. "Business as usual" will destroy an emerging CBT system.

Project management with its clear lines of control but its cross-functional capabilities may have the best potential to cope effectively with the challenge of building a CBT system. The project manager must build a carefully balanced staff that includes all the disciplines covered by the project. Planning, development, implementation, and evaluation of a CBT project is a truly interdisciplinary effort.

Another key aspect of the management challenge is to ensure that the expectations of the different parties agree. Most military CBT efforts of the 1970s failed because the research and development expectations of the developers differed substantially from the operational expectations of the users upon whom the products were imposed. Early phases of any large CBT effort will by their nature include more development and evaluation aspects than may be included later in the project. The potential users must not only understand this; they must share in the development and evaluation. Finally the project manager must adhere to a serial development of critical components during the early phases of the program. Hardware and software environments must be stabilized before courseware is developed. Unfortunately, parallel development is often used because of time constraints. It leads to situations in which hardware and software shortcomings create courseware errors and ultimately slow and make more expensive the courseware development.

Another development issue concerns the choice of programming environment. Authoring languages and systems and high-level programming languages were discussed earlier.

Implementation

A great deal has been written about implementing CBT systems. Several of the items cited in the bibliography contain excellent detailed discussions of CBT system implementation. Planning must address both beginning the implementation and maintaining it. Key areas include management of the instructors, maintenance of the courseware, administration and reports, budgeting, program reviews, and relationship with contractors.

However, the most important implementation issue addresses people relationships. The principal challenge in implementing a new CBT system is one of transferring computer-based training technology from a group of developers, steeped in the technology and comfortable in its characteristics, to a group of users who wonder what strange apparition is about to be imposed upon them and upset the order and stability of their world. Instructors, trainers, and administrators must be won over. They must be continuously involved so that they feel they "own" the program. This means that the principal user groups, especially the instructors and facilitators, must be included in the initial planning groups as the organization first considers CBT. If they own the CBT system, the instructors and facilitators will sell it to the students and will be in the forefront of continuously refining and updating it to improve it.

New Capabilities

Videodisc-Based Training. This technology combines the capability of the videodisc to random access 54,000 still frames of information or 30 minutes of motion sequences with a personal computer's text and graphics and its capability to control the interaction between the information on the videodisc and that on the personal computer. The capability to display actual photographs and video sequences provides the training developer new opportunities.

Videodiscs were first used in training in the late 1970s. Early applications were primarily in Defense Department technical training programs and in nuclear industry operator training. The last 3 years have seen considerable growth in the number of videodisc-based training programs in both the Defense Department and the private sector. The major areas of use at present seem to be in those training requirements which can employ machine simulations and in interpersonal skill training. Commercial programs have been developed for both sales and management training. They use video sequences of interpersonal activities to enable the student to draw conclusions about certain activities, to practice categorizing behaviors, or to see the consequences of his or her selection of a course of action.

Student reaction to videodisc-based training programs is usually so much more favorable than it is to more conventional CBT that we should see increasing use of this technology as a component of training programs. Videodisc-based training is more expensive than CBT and takes considerably longer to produce. These shortcomings will remain for some time.

CD/OD ROM. Compact disc read-only memory (CD-ROM) and optical disc read-only memory (OD-ROM) are new technologies that can provide an incredible increase in storage capacity to computer systems. CD/ROM is a small, laser-read disc, about the size of a personal computer floppy disc drive, that can provide a storage capacity that is the rough equivalent of 250,000 pages of text. Currently, this technology is being used in electronic publishing, but it should soon be used in training to provide quantum increases in personal computer storage capability.

Expert Systems/Artificial Intelligence. This technology combines advances in the cognitive sciences with the large increases in computer computational power to create tools to help workers in job situations. The expert system makes original judgments about a situation based upon the general facts and rules programmed in its database and the responses of the user to a series of questions. Expert systems can be used to create an investment portfolio, to solve an electronic troubleshooting problem, to receive medical symptoms and generate a diagnosis, or to perform an intelligence analysis. Although some rule generating programs are being marketed for personal computer use, the general understanding of expert systems is that the term applies to complex endeavors that will require very large databases to program the knowledge and rules that define a particular context. The expert systems assistance in helping the worker to solve a problem is not the result of a program but rather of a series of inferences by the system. This requires far more computer capacity than is found in today's personal computers. Eventually, expert systems should be found in support of the more difficult technical training requirements as well as being part of the job package in sophisticated, procedurally oriented jobs.

Trends

Several trends are having a significant impact on the future of CBT. Probably the first trend that should be noted is the increased realism concerning the use of technology-based training that can be seen in the professional training community. Trainers and developers increasingly see CBT as another useful and important tool in their bag of capabilities rather than as a panacea. They ask tough questions of the CBT vendors and display a business-oriented approach to CBT purchases.

Second, the pervasiveness of the personal computer in both the office and home has a major impact. A larger portion of the business world is becoming computer literate, which means they should be more receptive to using computers in training and more capable of using them. The increased presence of personal computers in business has spawned a strong CBT market niche. Hundreds of floppy-disc–based CBT programs have been created to train people to use personal computer applications like word processing and spread sheet programs. While many of these programs are unsophisticated pageturners, many exhibit sound instructional design. The CBT tutorials marketed with major new PC application programs have become increasingly effective and sophisticated. In the process they both acclimate more users to CBT and generate certain expectations concerning its effectiveness. These CBT tutorials may begin to serve as a benchmark for measuring training effectiveness in other areas by computer literate management.

Authoring Systems.   The increasing number of authoring systems being sold and the features and sophistication displayed in the recent entries in this field should raise the quality of the CBT that is being built. There is no reason not to expect this trend in improved authoring systems to continue.

Networking.   Commercial data communications networks have become an important part of the information services industry. It is becoming increasingly easier for companies to consider networked solutions to their CBT training system and to have several commercial choices.

Mixed Programs.   Increasingly, we should see CBT as a component of a training program rather than as the entire training program. For example, prerequisite work for classroom training should be provided via CBT. Student completion of prerequisites should be computer tested. Interpersonal skill programs, especially in sales and management, can mix CBT programs with instructor-intensive components. Technical training programs can employ videodisc-based simulations to cause the technician to master a troubleshooting procedure before he or she performs it once on a real piece of hardware to validate the performance on CBT. The options are endless once the trainer and developer perceive CBT as another important tool and not the solution.

Bibliography

Buck, John A., and Lori Gillespie, *Computer-Based Training (CBT) Starter Kit*, Longman Crown, Inc., Reston, VA, 1985.

Data Training, special CBT issues: March 1984, March 1985, March 1986.

Gery, Gloria, "I Want It All: Trade-offs in System Selection," *Data Training*, March 1985.

Gery, Gloria, Evaluating the Emerging Market: A Resource Guide to Computer-Aided-Instruction, *Data Training*, Warren-Weingarten, Inc., Boston, MA, 1982.

Gordon, Jack, "Computers in Training," *Training*, October 1985.

Ham, Michael, "Playing by the Rules. State of the Art: Artificial Intelligence," *PC World*, January 1984.

Harmon, Paul, and David King, "The Engineers Behind Expert Systems," *Computerworld*, March 18, 1985.

Harmon, Paul, "Expert Systems, Job Aids and the Future of Instructional Technology," *Performance and Instruction*, Vol. 25, No. 2, March 1986.

Harney, Heather, and Paul Pangaro, "Conversational Technology: Beyond Computer-Based Training," *Data Training*, May 1985.

Head, Glenn E., *Training Cost Analysis, A Practical Guide*, Marlin Press, Washington, DC, 1985.

Journal of Computer-Based Instruction, Association for the Development of Computer-Based Instructional Systems, summer 1984. Special issue on authoring tools.

Kearsley, Greg, *Computer-Based Training, A Guide to Selection and Implementation*, Addison-Wesley, Reading, MA, 1983.

Kearsley, Greg, *Costs, Benefits, and Productivity in Training Systems*, Addison-Wesley, Reading, MA, 1982.

Kearsley, Greg, "Helps, Simulations, and Intelligent Tutors," *Data Training*, May 1985.

Kemske, Floyd, ed., *Data Training 1984 Computer-Based Training Guide*, Warren-Weingarten, Inc., Boston, MA, 1984.

Kemske, Floyd, "Guide to Authoring Systems," *Data Training*, April 1984.

Mager, Robert F., and Peter Pipe, *Analyzing Performance Problems*, Fearon Publishers, CA, 1974.

Montague, William E., and Wallace H. Wulfeck II, "Computer-Based Instruction: Will It Improve Instructional Quality," *Training Technology Journal*, winter quarter 1984.

O'Neil, H. F., Jr., ed., *Computer-Based Instruction: A State of the Art Assessment*, Academic Press, New York, 1981.

O'Neil, H. F., Jr., ed., *Procedures for Instructional Systems Design*, Academic Press, New York, 1979.

Reynolds, Angus, "Computer-Based Learning: Deciphering the Alphabet Soup," *Training/HRD*, January 1983.

Training, September 1985, special edition on computers and training.

28
Self-Instruction

Marjorie L. Budd

Marjorie L. Budd is Chief, Advanced Instructional Systems, with the Internal Revenue Service. Budd has over 15 years of experience in the field of training and development, serving in both instructional design and managerial positions at the University of Carolina School of Medicine, the U.S. Army Engineer School, and the IRS. She has been responsible for the development of several hundred self-instructional courses, and has received the U.S. Army Commander's Award for Outstanding Civilian Achievement and the IRS Assistant Commissioner's Award for her work in self-instruction and computer-based training. She received a bachelor's degree in English from the University of Florida and a master's degree in educational technology and Ph.D. degree in adult education from the University of North Carolina at Chapel Hill. Her special areas of interest include program evaluation and quality assurance systems. She has given numerous presentations and workshops in the United States and Africa and has published articles in professional journals. She is a member of the American Educational Research Association, Association for Educational Communications and Technology, and past president of the Federal Educational Technology Association.

Training professionals now view self-instruction as a powerful and legitimate method for teaching, based on the accumulation of over 30 years of experience and research in its use. However, many organizational managers remain unconvinced of the merits of self-instruction. The stereotypes of "reading in a closet" and "wasting time" still survive, with attitudes that question how information could possibly be conveyed without live experts lecturing at the podium, or how trainees could possibly apply themselves without instructors standing over them.

Thus, training professionals still have much educating to do to win acceptance for the method, in addition to the challenge of creating successful self-instructional programs, if given the opportunity. To those ends, this chapter provides information on the various forms, versatility, and effectiveness of self-instruction, the advantages and disadvantages associated with the method, the ways it can go wrong, and the critical steps that must be taken to make sure it does not go wrong.

Self-Instruction Defined

Self-instruction is an all-inclusive term used to describe any teaching situation where students take responsibility for their own learning. A wide range of decisions can be allocated to the trainee, including the topic of study, objectives, resources, schedule, type and sequence of activities, environment, media, learning strategy, etc. Generally in organizational training, independent decision-making areas are limited to those within an established framework of a course. This is understandable: training is for a job, and most jobs have well-defined duties and responsibilities. Job requirements and organizational goals will dictate many of the decisions before trainees are ever involved. However, trainees usually work without direct supervision, set their own pace, and are often given the opportunity to select activities, resources, and learning environments in self-instructional training programs.

Approaches to Self-Instruction

Several different approaches to self-instruction have been popularized over the years. The terms used to identify the approaches have often been used interchangeably in the literature, providing evidence that differences have blurred as the inevitable shake-out of the best characteristics has occurred.

Approaches that have received the greatest amount of attention in the world of adult education include programmed instruction, individualized instruction, the personalized system of instruction, learner-controlled instruction, correspondence study, and self-study.

Programmed Instruction (PI)

Built upon B. F. Skinner's principles of operant conditioning, programmed instruction was the first major effort toward designing materials for individual study.[1] The approach generated much excitement in the 1960s, but as with all educational innovations, PI could not live up to its disciples' promise as a panacea. Waning interest in subsequent years was attributed in part to an initially rigid and redundant (and boring) design of materials, instructors' fears and lack of knowledge about the use of programmed instruction, and relatively high costs of materials.[2]

Today there are fewer classic programmed instructional materials on the shelves of training departments, but the legacy of PI has been one of tremendous impact. There are those who hold that the field of educational technology originated with PI.[3] Consider the basic features of PI:

- Specification of behavioral objectives and level of acceptable performance
- Systematic structuring of content
- Presentation of content in small steps
- Requirement of learner responses

- Immediate knowledge of results
- Self-pacing
- Empirical development of materials

Who among us has not seen the use of objectives in classrooms, seminar workshops, and text as well as in materials prepared for self-instruction? Who ha not used the systems approach or has not considered one or more of learnin theories in the structuring of content? Who would ever bypass the critical step developmentally testing self-instructional materials before actual implementatio of the program? Clearly, the effect of PI on the field of training and developmen has been pervasive. And it continues with increased impetus as trainers seek in features the most effective ways to design computer-assisted instruction.

Individualized Instruction (II)

Individualized instruction refers to an instructional strategy which allows traine to work at their own rates, through carefully structured course materials designe to accommodate individual needs. This is a very general definition of the ter which is frequently used to describe any type of self-paced program. However, more complete definition distinguishes II from other approaches. Truly individu alized instruction, in addition to being self-paced and carefully structured, will ha diagnostic testing, which is used to select individually tailored paths based c trainees' entry-level knowledge, and alternate forms of instruction.[4] These el ments put emphasis on the "individualized" aspect of the strategy. Most progra will also employ the use of behavioral objectives and mastery learning.

Personalized System of Instruction (PSI)

The personalized system of instruction has had a great impact on college teachir and its use is beginning to extend into government and business training progran In the academic sphere, it is being used in thousands of college courses coveri almost every discipline, and it has been the subject of hundreds of research report Developed and first employed by Fred Keller in 1964, the method is often referr to as the Keller method, or Keller's personalized system of instruction. The ba features of PSI are:

- Self-pacing
- Mastery learning, with frequent testing and repeated testing, if necessary, order to advance
- Study guides which direct students through units of course content
- A few scheduled lectures for stimulation and motivation
- The use of student proctors for quiz evaluation and immediate feedback performance

Unlike PI, the emphasis is more on the system of directing students through entire individual study experience, and less on the precise design of the instr tional materials. In fact, PSI content units may use programmed instructio materials, or texts, or any other source of information available to satisfy instr tional requirements.

Learner-Controlled Instruction (LCI)

Headlined as a method that incorporates the principles of adult learning, learner-controlled instruction delegates considerable control of instructional decisons to the learner.[6] Trainees are initially provided with a set of parameters and options: a statement of objectives, a variety of content informational sources, and the requirements for demonstrating mastery of skills. Trainees are given the power to control the sequence and pacing of their learning as well as the selection of methods and media according to their needs and preferences. In some instances, trainees also participate in the development of their own objectives and mastery criteria. A major aim of LCI is to incorporate training into the "real-work" job environment as much as possible.

Correspondence Study

The term correspondence study indicates that self-instructional materials are being used in a situation where the instructor or administrator is physically separated from the trainee.[7] Interaction takes place with the exchange of materials, responses, and feedback, usually by mail. There are potential economic benefits that are unique to correspondence study, in that if appropriate home study courses can be identified from among the thousands offered from outside institutions, the employee's organization saves not only the development time but also course administration and instructor time.

Self-Study

When used generically, as it frequently is, self-study refers to any program of study using a self-instructional approach. Basic requirements are that trainees are mastering the content on their own without direct supervision, and usually working at their own pace.[8] Occasionally the term self-study will be used to describe specific types of situations, such as the study of oneself, e.g., an organizational self-study or managerial self-study, or the study of materials from an outside institution without any requirement for exchange of responses and feedback.[7]

Research Findings and Recommendations

Over the years, all forms of self-instruction have been shown to be as effective or more so than conventional classroom instruction.[9] The results for PSI are quite extraordinary, showing consistently higher levels of achievement and less variation in achievement.[9] PI has exhibited increasingly higher levels of effectiveness, suggesting that the design and implementation of PI materials are improving with experience.[10]

The most dramatic and consistent finding for self-instruction is a significant reduction in training time over conventional instruction.[11] This time savings, along with reduced resource requirements and a decreasing need for travel and per diem expenditures, has made self-instruction a far more efficient method than conventional instruction. The Navy has reported savings due to course length reductions and staff reductions of over $1.5 million for only one of their schools during a

3-year period.[11] AT&T has estimated savings at $40 million dollars after converting classroom training to self-paced training.[12]

Generally, trainee attitudes have been favorable toward all forms of self-instruction.[13] Ratings have often indicated preference for the method over conventional classroom methods. When negative attitudes exist, they have been attributed primarily to a lack of understanding about self-instruction, lack of organizational commitment and support for the method, and inadequate orientation to the changing roles and structure required.[14]

With so much research and experience in self-instruction now documented, a pattern of key components for success begins to emerge. Drawing upon the findings and recommendations for each of the approaches, a list of the most important factors can be developed:

- Good orientation program to the method
- Strong administrative support system
- Specification of objectives
- Frequent quizzes and practice
- Immediate feedback
- Mastery requirements to reach a specified performance standard
- Job-related performance requirements
- Procedures for review after original learning
- Self-pacing, or self-pacing within prescribed limits
- Systematic approach to content structure
- Empirical evaluation of materials

By referring to this list, training professionals can design their own self-instructional programs using one of the established approaches or their own adaptations, and ensure that they have accounted for each of the important factors in their design.

Versatility of Self-Instruction

Frequently, organizations which have not had extensive experience with self-instruction have a decidedly narrow view of what it is and how it can be used. There are many options for designing and structuring self-instruction: the training professional's responsibility is to be aware of all of them and to educate the organization. Options exist in a number of areas:

- Since self-instruction is a method, it can be communicated through various media—print, audiovisual media, or computer-based training (CBT). (Indeed, many of the attributes now being acclaimed for CBT can be traced back to the method of self-instruction being delivered through that medium.)

- Instructors can be present, on call, or nonexistent, depending on the needs of the program. Monitors or aides can be used for administrative purposes, or computers can manage course data requirements.

- Implementation can take place in learning centers, the work area, classrooms, libraries, at home, or any other place where the resources and suitable study environment are available. (A note of caution about the work area: too often managers, or even employees, who may not take self-instructional training as seriously as classroom training, are tempted to allow ongoing work requirements to interfere with the time allocated for employee study when employees are at their desks.)

- Self-instruction can be used for preclassroom instruction (thereby ensuring that all trainees have the same prerequisite skills and knowledges), continuing professional education, as a full course, or as part of a course. It can be inserted into formal classroom courses as required, optional, remedial, or enhancement material. It can be used in combination with different methods, such as small group discussions, role plays, simulations, or field projects. It can even be used to select employees for jobs or promotions, through the miniature job training evaluation process.

An example of an IRS course designed by the author demonstrates how self-instruction can be mixed with other methods to best satisfy varying instructional needs and the availability of resources. The first 4 weeks of recruit internal revenue agent training were converted from classroom training to self-paced training. The course was designed to be conducted at the trainees' post-of-duty, at a learning center equipped with enough computer terminals to achieve the ratio of one terminal for every three trainees. A full-time instructor was needed for these new recruits, for purposes of counseling, tutoring, monitoring trainees' progress, scheduling and managing the instruction, and diagnosing and solving learning problems.

Twenty-five self-instructional modules were developed, covering introductory material, tax law, and IRS policy and procedures. The tax law modules were developed in a print format (since tax law required extensive reading and practice with abstract concepts), and each module was followed by computer-delivered drill and practice and testing. Some of the introductory modules were delivered via videotape, such as the preview of the revenue agent profession, to bring reality into the training environment.

The introductory and tax law modules were designed to be taken in strict sequence, since the information was cumulative in nature. However, modules covering topics that could be taken at any time (such as rules of conduct, travel procedures, disclosure regulations) were designated as randomly scheduled modules. These modules provided flexibility for the trainees in determining their own schedules, and prevented queuing problems at the computer terminals since the modules did not require the use of computers.

Three instructor-led small group sessions were interspersed throughout the course, to allow trainees to apply their knowledge to case studies and discuss with their instructor and peers all the "what if" questions that accumulate during the learning of tax law. Three field activities working with "live" revenue agents were also scheduled at certain times during the training, in order to enhance the trainees' understanding of job requirements at an early stage.

(Results for this program were similar to other research findings: a 25 percent time savings as compared with classroom instruction, with learning and performance equally as effective, and a projected annual cost savings of $6 million for nationwide implementation of the program.)

In this example, a variety of methods and media were employed, not for entertainment value, but for sound instructional reasons. Trainees learned tax law by reading printed self-instructional lessons. They practiced and tested their knowledge of tax law with self-instructional CBT, receiving immediate feedback. They discussed issues, participated in role plays, and practiced interviewing taxpayers in small group sessions. Finally, they worked with "live" revenue agents on actual casework to familiarize themselves with the job.

It was not difficult to mix methods. When trainees were at a certain point in their learning (some were even beyond that point since lessons were self-paced), instructors scheduled a group session. Field activities were scheduled individually, again based on where trainees were in their learning.

The versatility of self-instruction provides a tremendous potential for the training professional to find creative solutions to learning problems.

Advantages and Disadvantages

The advantages of self-instruction are numerous for employee training and should merit serious consideration by any organization with training requirements. Advantages include:

1. *Flexibility.* Self-instructional courses can be structured to be run at any time, thereby ensuring that trainees receive the instruction they need when they are ready for it. Moreover, trainees can complete their learning at their own pace in order to demonstrate mastery of the objectives.

2. *Consistency.* Presentation of information to several audiences remains consistent in the self-instructional format, because it is not instructor-dependent. Trainees will acquire the same skills and information regardless of differing environments.

3. *Mobility.* Self-instruction can often take place where classroom facilities are not available. And it can accommodate a variety of work and travel schedules that are realities for employees within an organization.

4. *Effectiveness.* As previously stated, self-instruction works, and has been shown to be as good as or better than other teaching methods.

5. *Cost savings.* When employees learn independently, they inevitably cover the same instruction in less time as compared with group-paced classes. Cost savings are realized, then, when trainees get back to work sooner, and when centralized training programs (with travel, per diem, facilities, and resource costs) are no longer needed.

6. *Compatibility with adult learning principles.* Within the field of andragogy, it is now recognized that adults prefer to direct their own learning,[15] that they have vast experience which they can utilize in their learning, and that they should share in the responsibility for their learning.[16] Self-instruction is one mechanism for providing a good climate for adult learning.

7. *Focus on the learner.* When instructors no longer stand on the platform, and the need for preparation of lectures has disappeared, and 30 or more trainees do not have to be moved from one topic to the next in lockstep fashion, attention can be directed away from the classroom presentation and toward the individual learner. Learning difficulties can be diagnosed through regular checks on time and achievement, and tutoring, counseling, and remediation can be provided as individual needs arise.

The disadvantages to self-instruction are few, but important to recognize. Sometimes there are ways to overcome them, but sometimes they cannot be overcome. Disadvantages are:

1. *High development time for materials.* There is no getting around it: self-instruction takes longer to develop than classroom instruction.[17] Materials must be

carefully structured so trainees can follow them without guidance from an instructor, extensive practice exercises are required, and materials must be tested and revised until they work. Some organizations will try to deny this ("just do something quick and dirty") and some will be defeated by it ("we've got to have it by next week, so just make a workshop"). But the time for development is a necessary requirement and can only be overcome if one is fortunate enough to locate already-prepared or commercial materials that are appropriate for, or can be adapted to, instructional needs of the moment.

2. *More difficult to update or revise.* The degree of difficulty in revision really depends on the medium through which self-instruction is delivered, the approach being used, and the level of distribution of materials. For example, if self-instruction is delivered through CBT, revision can be easily and almost instantaneously accomplished. If an approach like PSI or LCI is used, it may be possible to quickly change the guidelines for using materials rather than the materials themselves. But if materials are self-contained, with all the structure, course content, and guidelines within themselves, and if they are in a print format, and if they are widely distributed to individual trainees, then revisions present a major undertaking. One might long for the "good old days" of classroom training when a short addendum to the instructor guide would suffice.

3. *Lack of interaction with peers and instructors.* There are two aspects to consider here. First, if training objectives require interaction, e.g., interviewing taxpayers, negotiating contracts, then self-instruction is not an appropriate method to consider. On the other hand, if the objectives are suitable for individual study, and self-instruction is the method of choice, the training professional must be sensitive to the "learning in isolation" factor. Valuable learning experiences can be missed and motivation can suffer when trainees are deprived of interaction with peers and instructors for long periods of time. This is not so much a concern with short courses as it is for courses which run for several days or longer. It would be wise to consider a mix of methods for more lengthy courses, and to build in regular discussions between the trainee and instructor or administrator.

4. *Extensive planning requirements.* If self-instruction is to succeed, there must be a rigorous approach to planning. Self-instruction must be built solid from the beginning. It is like a product that must survive the wear and tear of many different types of customers, and must develop a reputation of reliability to generate and maintain its market. It should be a "stand-alone" system, planned so well that there is no need for an authority (instructor, manager, etc.) to "save" it, give it credibility, organization, or meaning.

Problems and How to Avoid Them

Those who have been in the training field for any length of time have probably heard one or more war stories about the problems with self-instruction. But most of the problems, in retrospect, never had to happen and could have been avoided altogether with careful and informed planning. Sources of major problems have been traced back to the following:

Wrong subject matter chosen for self-instruction

Resources and/or facilities inadequate

New trainee and/or instructor roles not clearly defined or trained

- Guidelines for implementation not complete or precise
- Design of materials flawed (writing unclear, ambiguous directions, topics a practice not job-related, etc.)
- Organization not committed to the method (didn't take individual learni seriously, or perceived that the program would "take care of itself")
- Intent of self-instruction lost (became pageturner in CBT, or intensive reading a lockstep classroom)

Steps should be taken to eliminate these problem sources during the planni and development stage for two very important reasons: (1) problems are extrem difficult to solve after they have surfaced, with frustrated and discouraged traine instructors, and managers, and (2) there is a tendency to blame the method for problems. Most members of the organization, who lack the training profession understanding of the complexities of the situation, will simply dismiss se instruction as "no good." It could be years before the subject is ever conside seriously again.

If the author were asked what were the most important lessons learned avoiding problems after many, many years of developing self-instructional p grams, here would be the top 10:

1. *Select appropriate content for self-instruction.* If the objectives require hun interaction, if the tasks or procedures are not well defined, if there are no right wrong answers but many "gray" areas that require discussion, if the conten subject to frequent changes, or if there is a need to inspire and motivate train with dynamic human presentations, then the content is probably not appropri for self-instruction. Self-instruction works best for teaching factual informati well-defined procedures and relationships, and even complex concepts that requ extensive explanation and interaction.

2. *Consider all options in designing a course.* For a lengthy course, develo course map which provides alternate paths, flexible entry and exit (so that train can begin and end the training based on individual needs and progress), allocat of resources (if they are limited), and an appropriate mix of methods. Approac creatively, and then structure it carefully and precisely.

3. *Provide adequate orientation to the organization.* Inform managers and e ployees alike of the philosophy, basic principles, procedures, and requirement self-instruction. Let them know that trainees might be moving about indep dently, and taking their own breaks and lunch hours at different times, and that doesn't mean that work isn't being accomplished. Let them also know that t required to complete training should not be a basis for assessing train performance. As long as trainees are pacing themselves within a range of accepta limits, their mastery of the objectives is the primary concern.

4. *Attend to the instructor role (if any).* If this valuable resource is to be use the program, make certain that significant responsibilities are built into the r Having an expert come in to do nothing but menial, monotonous tasks is sure-fire way to destroy a program. Bored and unmotivated instructors will set tone for all the trainees. Consider having instructors on call, or on a part-time ba if their full-time presence can't be justified. Monitors or aides can take care of routine tasks that must be performed. Instructors are critical for counsel tutoring, diagnosing and solving learning problems, leading group activi scheduling, and managing individual paths through the course.

5. *Ensure that trainees and instructors know their roles.* The responsibility learning now rests with the trainee, and this calls for a certain amount of initia

that may not have been needed in past training experiences. Additionally, instructors now focus on the individual, rather than on the classroom lecture and the performance of the group. These simple shifts have many ramifications on how trainees and instructors ought to conduct themselves in a self-instructional course. All expectations should be spelled out in printed guides and in opening sessions of the program. Specialized training for instructors of self-instructional courses may even be necessary.

6. *Take special care in the development of materials.* Make sure they work before the program is implemented. After preparing first drafts of the materials, try them out with a few people who are representative of the target audience, and take copious notes on every problem and comment they have. This process is called developmental testing, and it's a good idea to prepare "lean" materials at this initial stage. Provide only the important information and practice needed to achieve the objectives. The try-out people will point out the gaps, and revisions can be made accordingly. It is much easier to identify undertraining than overtraining, and thus arrive at a point where the materials are both efficient and effective. After the materials have been tried out and revised, they should be validated. A validation criterion should be established that indicates the success rate desirable for the instruction, such as 80/80 (80 percent of the trainees pass 80 percent of the objectives), 80/90, or 90/100, and a group of trainees should complete the materials to see if this criterion can be met. In order to statistically project the results for the entire population, a group of 25 to 30 trainees should be used. When materials are validated, there is statistical proof that they teach an acceptable number of trainees to an acceptable level of mastery. If the decision is to purchase materials rather than develop them in-house, look for evidence of validation. Likewise if materials are to be tailor-made by an outside contractor, use validation as a final step for acceptability of the product. If for any reason it is not feasible to conduct a validation, at a very minimum try out materials in final form with a few trainees. There are enough concerns in implementing a new self-instructional program without having the concern of whether or not the materials are any good.

7. *Insist on proper facilities.* Trainees need a place where they can relax and concentrate. If the learning center is that part of the library that is the main thoroughfare to other parts of the building, that won't do. If the resources (computer terminals, video monitors, print materials) are separated two floors up from the study area, that won't do. If the work area is a hub of human activity, that won't do. Facilities do not have to be elaborate, but they do need to be quiet, comfortable, and in close proximity to all required resources.

8. *Be aware of the target audience—adult learners—when developing the style of the materials and the design of the system.* For example, never patronize the learners. Don't "talk down" to them, don't belittle them (even in jest), and don't try to be unnecessarily cute or flip in the materials. Such a style will offend some adults, will soon become tiresome to many more, and will distract all of them from the seriousness of the learning. The proper tone of the materials should imply respect for learners, and a consideration of them as equals in the learning process. Along similar lines, try to give adults real freedom to make decisions within the established limits of the program. Nothing kills enthusiasm more quickly than to be told one is responsible for one's own learning and then to be given no way to demonstrate that responsibility.

9. *Answer all the "what if" questions about administration beforehand.* What will be done with early finishers, late finishers? What incentives can be provided to prevent procrastination? What can be done if a trainee is found to have a problem with procrastination? What alternatives can be provided if equipment (such as a

computer terminal or videotape monitor) breaks down, or activities need to be rescheduled, or instructors are unavailable for a period of time? Anticipating all possible problems and at least a set of first steps to cope with them will give everyone connected with the program a greater sense of confidence as implementation draws near.

10. *Continue to evaluate the program during and after implementation.* Collect data for each of the four steps—reaction, learning, behavior, and results—described by Kirkpatrick in Chapter 16 in this handbook. Evaluation studies will provide valuable information on how to improve the training, as well as evidence to justify the training.

Summary

This chapter has provided information on what self-instruction is, how it has been approached, the findings of research, the versatility, advantages, and disadvantages of the method, and key ways to avoid problems. Ample evidence exists to indicate that self-instruction can efficiently and effectively satisfy certain training needs of an organization. The method ought to be among those seriously considered whenever performance problems occur that can be solved through training. For further information on the techniques for designing self-instruction, consult books on the systematic approach to design and development of instruction. Similar steps and principles constitute the building blocks for all types of instructional materials. Several recommended texts are listed in the bibliography.

References

1. Henderson, E. S., and M. B. Nathenson, eds., *Independent Learning in Higher Education,* Educational Technology Publications, Englewood Cliffs, NJ, 1984.

2. Hanna, M. S., and J. W. Gibson, "Programmed Instruction in Communication Education: An Idea Behind Its Time," *Communication Education,* vol. 32, pp. 1–7, January 1983.

3. Morgan, Robert M., "Education Technology—Adolescence to Adulthood," *Educational Communication and Technology Journal,* vol. 26, no. 2, pp. 142–152, summer 1978.

4. Micheli, G. S., and L. H. Ford, *Survey of the Extent of Individualized Instruction in Navy "A" and "C" School Courses* (TAEG Report No. 83-7), U. S. Navy Training and Evaluation Group, Orlando, FL, September 1983. Bangert, R. L., J. A. Kulik, and C. C. Kulik, "Individualized Systems of Instruction in Secondary Schools," *Review of Educational Research,* vol. 53, no. 2, pp. 143–158, summer 1983.

5. Kulik J. A., P. Jaksa, and C. C. Kulik, "Research on Component Features of Keller's Personalized System of Instruction," *Journal of Personalized Instruction,* vol. 3, no. 1. pp. 2–15, spring 1978.

6. Wydra, Frank T., "Learner Controlled Instruction," *National Society for Performance and Instruction Journal,* vol. 17, pp. 4–10, December 1978.

7. Salinger, Ruth D., "Correspondence Study," in R. L. Craig, ed., *Training and Development Handbook,* 2d ed., McGraw-Hill, New York, 1976.

8. Bynum, M. M., and N. Rosenblatt, "Self-Study: Boon or Bust?" *Training Journal,* vol. 21, no. 11, pp. 61–64, November 1984.

9. Cox, J. H., "A New Look at Learner-Controlled Instruction," *Training and Development Journal,* vol. 36, no. 3, pp. 90–94, March 1982. Ford, John E., "Application of a Personalized System of Instruction to a Large, Personnel Training Program," *Journal of Organizational Behavior Management,* vol. 5, nos. 3/4, fall/winter 1983. Hanna and Gibson

ref. 2. Hall, E. R., and J. S. Freda, *A Comparison of Individualized and Conventional Instruction in Navy Technical Training*, (TAEG Report No. 117), U.S. Navy Training and Evaluation Group, Orlando, FL, March 1982. Kulik, C. C., B. J. Shwalb, and J. A. Kulik, "Programmed Instruction in Secondary Education," *Journal of Educational Research*, vol. 75. pp. 133–138, 1982. Kulik, J. A., C. C. Kulik, and P. A. Cohen, "A Meta-Analysis of Outcome Studies of Keller's Personalized System of Instruction," *American Psychologist*, vol. 34, no. 4, pp. 307–318, April 1979.

10. Kulik, J. A., "How Can Chemists Use Educational Technology Effectively?" *Journal of Chemical Education*, vol. 60, no. 11, pp. 957–959, November 1983.

11. Goldstein, I. L., "Training in Work Organizations," *Annual Review of Psychology*, vol. 31, pp. 229–273, 1980. Cox, ref. 9. Ford, ref. 9. Skinner, B. F., "The Shame of American Education," *American Psychologist*, vol. 34, no. 9, pp. 947–954, September 1984. Zajkowski, M. M., E. A. Heidt, J. M. Corey, D. V. Mew, and G. S. Micheli, *An Assessment of Individualized Instruction in Navy Technical Training* (TAEG Report No. 78), U.S. Navy Training and Evaluation Group, Orlando, FL, November 1979.

12. Shoemaker, H., "The Evolution of Management Systems for Producing Cost-effective Training: A Bell System Experience," *National Society for Performance and Instruction*, vol. 18, pp. 3–15, October 1979.

13. Bangert et al., ref. 4. Hanna and Gibson, ref. 2. Kulik et al., "A Meta-Analysis of Outcome Studies of Keller's Personalized System of Instruction," ref. 9. Hinton, J. R., "Individualized Instruction: What the Research Tells Us," Paper presented at the annual meeting of the Association for Educational Communications and Technology, Kansas City, MO, April 19, 1978. Kulik, ref. 10.

14. Zajkowski et al., ref. 11.

15. Zemke, R., and S. Zemke, "30 Things We Know for Sure about Adult Learning," *Training Journal*, vol. 18, no. 6, pp. 45–52, June 1981.

16. Knowles, Malcolm, *The Adult Learner: A Neglected Species*, Gulf Publishing Co., Houston, TX, 1973.

17. Smith, Martin E., "Self-Paced or Leader-Led Instruction," *National Society for Performance and Instruction*, vol. 34, no. 2, pp. 14–18, February 1980.

Further Reading

Branson, R. K., G. I. Raynor, J. L. Cox, J. P. Furman, F. J. King, and W. H. Hannum, *Interservice Procedures for Instructional Systems Development*, 5 vols. (TRADOC PAM 350-30 and HAVEDTRA 106A) U.S. Army Training and Doctrine Command, Ft. Monroe, VA, 1975.

Diamond, R. M., P. E. Eickman, E. F. Kelly, R. E. Holloway, T. R. Vickery, and E. T. Pascarella, *Instruction Development for Individualized Learner in Higher Education*, Educational Technology Publications, Englewood Cliffs, NJ, 1975.

Dick, Walter, and Lou Carey, *Systematic Design of Instruction*, 2d ed., Scott, Foresman and Co., Glenview, IL, 1985.

Fleming, Malcolm, and W. Howard Levie, *Instructional Message Design*, Educational Technology Publications, Englewood Cliffs, NJ, 1978.

Gagne, Robert M., *The Conditions of Learning*, Holt, Rinehart and Winston, New York, 1977.

Henderson, E. S., and M. B. Nathenson, eds., *Independent Learning in Higher Education*, Educational Technology Publications, Englewood Cliffs, NJ, 1984.

Kemp, Jerrold E., *The Instructional Design Process*, Harper and Row, New York, 1985.

Knowles, Malcolm, *The Adult Learner: A Neglected Species*, Gulf Publishing Co., Houston, TX, 1973.

Langdon, Danny G., *Interactive Instructional Designs for Individual Learning*. Educational Technology Publications, Englewood Cliffs, NJ, 1973.

Posner, George J., and Alan N. Rudnitsky, *Course Design*, 3d ed., Longman, Inc., New York, 1986.

29
Audiovisual Methods

Clint Wallington

Clint Wallington is director of three related but distinct programs—
*audiovisual communications, instructional technology, and career and
human resource development—at the Rochester Institute of Technology, Rochester, New York. He has been active in ASTD—a member of
the Professional Development Committee, involved in the ASTD
competency study, Models for Excellence, and other national and local
activities. His department does instructional development for RIT and
other clients. He was on the board of directors of the Association for
Multi-Image and has written and produced award-winning multi-image
presentations. He writes the multi-image column for AV Video and is a
featured presenter in AV Video's "All-Pro" seminars. Before RIT, he
was with the Association for Educational Communications and Technology. Prior to AECT, he did graduate work at the University of
California, where he received a Ph.D. in instructional technology with a
minor from the USC cinema school. His bachelor's degree is from the
University of Missouri at Kansas City. He is a member of ASTD,
National Society for Performance and Instruction, Association for
Multi-Image, Instructional Television Association, and the National
Education Association (life member).*

Training and the role of *audiovisual communications in training* have changed
significantly since the last edition of this handbook. Sophisticated training techniques have brought about equally sophisticated audiovisual materials. The audiovisual spectrum ranges from flipcharts to interactive video, enough information to
easily fill several books, let alone a single chapter. Of necessity, the chapter will be
selective, yet it will still provide the basics of selecting and using the more common
training media. The chapter has a threefold purpose:

- To acquaint you with key factors involved in selecting an audiovisual medium

- To quickly review the characteristics of the more common media

- To offer guidelines and specific recommendations for using media in a training presentation

The chapter's three major sections reflect these three purposes. It may seem complex, but then so is today's world of training and audiovisual.

Media Then, Media Now

It hasn't been long since audiovisual was considered an "add on"—an extra—to training. In those early days, decisions about audiovisual were more easily made. The lesson or speech was written and key points were extracted and placed on flipcharts, transparencies, or slides. Or the training film was shot for classroom use knowing an instructor would introduce it and do a follow-up. While these practices are still much in use—and validly so—audiovisual has changed.

Much of the credit for change goes to the highly visible hardware side of audiovisual—items like portable videocassette players, multiprojector slide shows, quick access videodiscs. In reality, a concurrent but less visible revolution in training has been taking place—a major change called "instructional development" or "instructional design." Briefly stated, instructional design is a systematic approach to training that breaks the training into small steps and then applies specialized knowledge to each step. (Instructional development and its related processes are covered in more depth in other chapters of the handbook.) The net result of the changes in the media themselves and the design of training is a different look at audiovisual methods in training.

Making Audiovisual Decisions

Today's trainer is faced with a number of directly interrelated questions which shape the design, development, and subsequent use of any audiovisual materials in training—yet the questions themselves do not seem, at first glance, to be media-related. For example,

- How many times will the training take place?
- Do I have an adequate number of trainers to conduct the training session?
- Where will the training take place?
- What sort of trainee performance—cognitive, affective, psychomotor—do I want at the end of the training?
- How will the training session be followed up in the workplace to be sure that the trainee is performing as desired *on the job*?
- Is formal training really needed or are there other solutions to the performance problems?

The above may not seem to be audiovisual questions, but they are. For example, if the training is relatively simple skill training that must be conducted at a number of geographically scattered job sites, an audiovisual training package is a reasonable solution. Or, if an organization does not have an adequate supply of *good* platform (classroom) trainers, it is far easier to design audiovisual materials that do most of the training and then use the trainers (or subject matter experts) as coaches or course managers. Or, if the performance problem can be solved by a job aid—one form of audiovisual material—rather than by a formal training session, why spend the time and resources developing and conducting classroom training?

This new, analytical approach to audiovisual communications in training means more *results-effective* and more *cost-effective* training. However, even though many of the basic psychological principles that support audiovisual remain the same, the factors that affect the *use* of audiovisual communications are far more complex. Good use of a range of audiovisual communications methods will require more forethought and planning than ever before—but then the probability of successful training is concomitantly increased.

Part One: Audiovisual Selection and Planning

Key Factors

At least six key factors affect media selection—and even more in many situations. Choosing the right audiovisual is usually a series of trade-offs, balancing one factor against the others. While there is no guaranteed selection procedure, ASTD's publication, *Selecting and Developing Media for Instruction* (Anderson), offers a detailed process for matching the medium to the training. The following factors are food for thought rather than inflexible rules.

1. Media Use—Speaker Aid, Shared Time, or Stand Alone.   One of the early design decisions affecting media is the way in which the training will actually be presented or "delivered." There are three basic ways to use audiovisual materials in training and presentations—audiovisual as a *speaker aid,* as *shared time,* and as *stand alone* media. The difference among the three lies in the amount of human control in the presentation process.

In using audiovisual as a *speaker aid,* the "live" trainer totally controls the direction and pace of the lesson. It is he or she who determines at what point each audiovisual item will be used and how. There may be a plan or outline to be followed, but the final presentation remains under the direct control of the presenter. Traditionally, media like flipcharts and overhead transparencies are considered speaker aids.

At the opposite end of the spectrum, the lesson or training module is without any human intervention. The lesson is in a totally audiovisual or "mediated" format. This is the *stand alone* presentation. It may be designed to be highly interactive with the trainee and have any number of branches or paths but the overall pattern is fixed and cannot be changed without human intervention. Computer-assisted instruction—and before that, programmed instruction—are classic examples of the *stand alone* format.

Between these two opposites, speaker aid and stand alone, lies a middle ground where the two blend—the *shared time* presentation. In *shared time* use, a live presenter "shares" the burden of training with media segments. In this case, the audiovisual segments are essentially *stand alone* units that can be utilized in different ways with different sorts of introduction and follow-up by the human presenter. The classic example of a shared time medium is the training film that has a live introduction and summary or review.

The decision of *how* the audiovisual materials will be used—*speaker aid, shared time,* or *stand alone*—is critical because the kind of use determines the media selection and development of the audiovisual segments. Stand alone lessons or units generally need more care and field testing in their development simply because there is no one present to answer the trainee's questions. Speaker aid materials have more flexibility in their use simply because the presenter can vary the elements of the presentation—level of language, trainee involvement—to fit different audiences.

2. Audience Characteristics. Of equal importance is the audience. While a majority of adult trainees learn equally well from most nonprint media, subtle differences do exist in the relationship between trainee and presentation. And the presenter (or instructional designer) should take special pains to tailor the language level to the trainee's level of understanding.

3. Training Objectives. A third factor is the type of training objective. In situations where the objective deals primarily with facts or information and the training method is exposition and explanation, any simple, straightforward audiovisual presentation—from speaker aid to stand alone—works reasonably well. Where it becomes necessary to bring audiovisual examples or simulations into the training, the audiovisual requirements become more complex.

4. Training Environment. A fourth factor, closely related to "how" the materials will be used, is "where" they will be used—the learning environment. The platform trainer using simple speaker aid media can be adapted to a wide variety of situations and audience sizes. Stand alone media that rely on special equipment are less easily adapted to different circumstances. Simple elements of the physical environment—like control of the light or height of the ceiling and shape of the room—may dictate the type of media that can be used.

5. Production Considerations. Next, when deciding on the audiovisual materials to be used in the training, some of the logistics of production may play a deciding role. How many copies will be needed? How many times will each be used? Will changes or updates be needed? Are the personnel and the production capabilities readily available? How long will it take to develop and produce? Even though there may be a clear-cut need for a particular audiovisual material, the logistics of producing not only the original but copies may militate against its development.

6. Cost, Effectiveness, and Efficiency. Finally, pervasive in all decisions is cost. Generally speaking, the more complex the audiovisual segment and the more the audiovisual is developed for the *stand alone* mode, the more costly it will be. Two key factors in justifying training costs are the number of uses of the training materials and the critical nature of the training. An example of critical training is preparing flight crews to deal with inflight emergencies. Using paper-and-pencil training is hardly a good measure of the skill needs. Yet, creating actual (not simulated) aircraft emergencies could easily have serious consequences. The solution: complex flight simulators that react much as a real aircraft would. The cost of the simulator is readily justified in terms of lives saved and actual dollar loss from an accident. In less critical (at least in terms of lost lives and property) skill training, the expense of a complex computer-assisted training is hardly justified for a few people. But when literally thousands of geographically scattered employees must be trained in corporate procedures, the costs of developing and producing audiovisual materials for training greatly reduce the per unit cost as well as add consistency and reliability to the training.

As mentioned earlier, the foregoing questions must be answered in the initial planning stages. Waiting until after the lesson is completely designed can either limit the possible audiovisual options or lead to costly major revisions.

Part Two: Media Attributes

With so many choices and elements, where does instructional design leave off and audiovisual start? When the audiovisual materials carry the total load of formal training—including trainee motivation, lesson presentation, testing and feedback, and choosing the next instructional segment—the audiovisual delivery system is tightly constrained by the instructional design.

Presentation Media

However, this use of the audiovisual, while steadily increasing, still represents only a fraction of the total use of audiovisual in training. Far more common is the use of media only to present information and, in some cases, to motivate. These are the "presentation media." In the previous section, audiovisual was divided into three categories of use—speaker aid, shared time, and stand alone. The most common uses of audiovisual in presentations are by far the speaker aid and shared time uses. These uses allow the human presenter to modify a lesson to meet different objectives and audiences—maximum flexibility.

The most common speaker aid audiovisual formats are flipcharts (including chalkboards and display boards), overhead transparencies, and speaker support slides. The common shared-time media are motion picture, video, slide+tape, and sound filmstrips. Almost all shared-time media use projected visual materials with an accompanying sound track. All are more complex to produce than speaker aid materials.

Knowing how the media will be used will help in planning presentations, but each medium—regardless of how it is used—still has its own special features and constraints. Let's look at those next—medium by medium.

Flipcharts, Chalkboards, Display Boards

The ubiquitous chalkboard and flipchart are probably the simplest and most common of the trainer's audiovisual tools. Chalkboards, once black, are now generally green and are being replaced in upscale locations by white display boards where the presenter writes with a special erasable marker. While the flipchart can be used as a chalkboard or display board, it has the added advantage that the material written on the sheet can be saved. In addition, flipchart materials can be prepared ahead of time and, if done on heavy enough paper, can be reused in other presentations. Other flipchart characteristics include:

- Simple to prepare
- Low-cost materials (although custom artwork can be expensive)
- No special equipment needed other than the flipchart, an easel, and markers (or chalkboard and chalk)
- Easy to use but requires skill in writing in large, bold, legible letters
- Can be time-consuming if the presenter must write all the information as the presentation develops
- Fixed maximum size and viewing distance and hence limited audience size

One variation of the display board is covered with material to which Velcro will adhere. You cannot write on the board but you can hang objects (even heavy ones) on the board. Some display boards are made of metal, and magnetized objects will adhere to them.

Overhead Projection

The overhead projector, like the flipchart, is a widely used training tool. The overhead projector—known in some circles as the Vu-Graph—came into prominence in military training almost 50 years ago. It can be used like a chalkboard except that the writing is projected, thus allowing a large audience to view the materials. In addition, already prepared graphic materials can be used. The overhead projector will also accept 8- by 10-inch color reversal transparencies, although the cost is somewhat prohibitive and projection quality worse than with a slide projector. Other characteristics include:

- Can be used with normal room lights on.
- Speaker faces toward the audience while using or writing on a transparency.
- Needs electricity (110 volts) and most models have a cooling fan which can be noisy in a small room.
- Requires a screen and some projection distance.
- Lens is a fixed focal length, which results in the size of the projected image being controlled by the lens-to-screen distance.
- Transparencies are easily manipulated by the speaker.
- Transparencies are generally words or graphics (including illustrations).
- Transparencies can range from inexpensive, simply made transparencies to multicolored transparencies with several parts or "overlays."
- Some already prepared transparencies are available. Besides handmade transparencies, transparencies can be made inexpensively with thermal and electrostatic copiers.

Speaker Support Slides

Slides—technically, transparencies in a 2- by 2-inch mount—are another of the more common trainer's speaker aid tools. They can vary from simple pictures or word slides to elaborate graphics slides. As with any speaker aid medium, the slides can be edited and rearranged for different audiences. In addition to carrying the same kind of information as overhead transparencies, slides can also use "real" images (photographs). Slides are a little less flexible *during* the presentation because the speaker cannot spontaneously rearrange them or write on them—as is possible with overhead transparencies. Other characteristics include:

- Slides provide compact, portable presentations, are easily stored and easily edited and sequenced (prior to presentation) for different audiences.
- Pictures allow the presenter to show things not easily visible or brought into the training room.
- It is easy to mix charts, graphs, and text with actual pictures.
- Needs electricity (110 volts ac), and most slide projectors have a cooling fan which can be a bit noisy.

- The projector is usually at the back of the room, away from the speaker, although the speaker can easily operate it with a remote control.
- Most projectors have zoom lenses which allow the image size to be varied from a fixed projection distance.
- Slides require a screen, generally a more reflective screen than required by an overhead projector.
- In most cases, the room must be darkened for acceptable viewing, especially for pictures.
- Slide projectors are somewhat expensive (slightly more than the overhead projector), but they are readily available within most large organizations.
- Slides are almost always made by a photographic process which generally adds to the cost of production but which allows for the use of original materials of varying sizes.
- Elaborate "special effects slides" can be produced, but they are relatively expensive.

Slides can also be shown on a rear projection screen that allows the projector to be behind the screen on which the image appears. Many presenters now use a dissolve unit that controls two slide projectors and allows one image to dissolve into another rather than have a second of darkness between images. Some corporate and sales slide presentations use multiple projectors, a dissolve unit, and a program stored in computer memory to produce animation effects in the presentation. Slides can easily be the most impressive of the speaker aid media.

Slide+Tape

Slide+tape is a slide presentation synchronized to a sound track. Slide+tape is a rapidly growing medium. It offers a relatively inexpensive way to produce presentations. New control units, especially microprocessor controlled dissolve units, have greatly increased program reliability. Computer-generated synchronization tracks minimize the problem of the slides being out of synchronization with the sound track even when the tape recorder is stopped or the slide projector fails. This reliability and a desire for more sophisticated presentations has led to an increase in the number of multiprojector shows, especially two- and three-projector shows. Multiple projectors allow a far smoother flow of images which along with animated special effects better holds the audience's attention. Because the production uses individual slides, single images are readily updated or changed. Other characteristics of slide+tape include:

- Like slides, slide+tape requires electricity (110 volts), a screen, a darkened room, and sound reproduction equipment.
- While the majority of slide+tape presentations have some synchronized data channel on the tape, some presentations still use an audible tone or a script from which an operator advances the slides.
- Multiprojector slide+tape presentations may require specialized dissolve units; however, there is no standardization in synchronizing cues—thus, what will run on one brand of dissolve unit will not run on a different brand.
- Equipment is more expensive than slides because of the audio system and synchronizer needed.
- Production is far less expensive than comparable motion picture or video productions.

The slide+tape medium is probably one of the most popular media for shared time and stand alone productions. In the past years, the slide medium (slide+tape and speaker support slides) has shown the greatest growth increase of all media.

Filmstrips

Filmstrips are similar to slide+tape presentations, but the images are on a consecutive strip of film instead of each individual film chip being in a separate slide mount. A slide show may be converted into a filmstrip by a production company with the proper equipment. Filmstrips are generally available from commercial production companies and cover a topic in a general manner, relying on the trainer to adjust the audience to the filmstrip . . . or vice versa. Other characteristics of filmstrips include:

- Like slides, filmstrips require electricity, a screen, and a darkened room.

- Like slides, the content of images may range from text and graphics to real pictures.

- Unlike slides, filmstrips may *not* be resequenced.

- Filmstrip projectors are generally less expensive than comparable slide projectors, although various attachments can easily raise the cost.

Filmstrips are becoming less common, although they are far from disappearing. Because they become cost-effective (as compared with slides) only in large quantities and because the image sequence cannot readily be changed, they are rarely produced for custom training applications unless an organization has a widespread training need. Hence filmstrips are found more commonly in generic skills training or education than in specialized training applications.

Audio (Only)

Audio as an accompaniment to other media is an integral part of shared time and stand alone presentations. Audio is rarely used alone in group presentations. Audio (only) is more commonly used in cassettes for individual listening. Other characteristics of audio include:

- Audio requires minimal equipment for playback, especially for individual use.

- The portability of the equipment means that audio can be used easily in almost any situation, as in an automobile or at home.

- Audio is relatively easy to record, but good-quality audio is more difficult to produce than is commonly assumed.

- Music and sound effects can be used to evoke vivid mental images and moods.

- Audio cannot be easily revised or resequenced.

Audio (only) has been used quite successfully in information and motivational audiocassettes, but the use is somewhat specialized. Audio is also used to capture an event, like a conference session. This use is reasonable but falls far short of achieving the potential of good audio presentations.

Motion Pictures

The 16-mm sound motion picture is another familiar audiovisual training tool. Although being supplanted somewhat by videotape, motion pictures are still visually superior in situations requiring large screen images. Also, for large screen use, motion picture projectors are still more commonly available in most organizations than are video projectors. Other characteristics of motion picture are:

- Like slides, motion pictures require electricity (110 volts ac), a screen, and a darkened room.
- Motion pictures have full lip synchronization in sound tracks.
- Motion picture projectors are readily available in most large organizations or through rental agencies.
- In-house production is relatively expensive, as are duplicate prints.
- Films covering an enormous range of training topics are readily available for purchase or rental.

Motion pictures and video are quite similiar in style and message structure. For small group situations, in-house video production is supplanting motion picture production.

Videotape

Videotape has many of the advantages of motion pictures except for use with large audiences. The style and structure of video is quite similar to motion pictures. Other characteristics include:

- Relative ease of use and availability of equipment, although there are different *and incompatible* videocassette formats.
- Especially appropriate with small groups.
- Can be used with large groups by using video projection but the quality of large images is less than comparable motion picture or slide images.
- Simple presentations are easier to produce and less expensive than comparable motion picture productions.
- Duplicate copies are less expensive than slide+tape or motion picture and can be erased and reused (with some possible loss of tape quality).
- Like motion pictures, a wide range of training tapes is available for purchase or rental.

The videocassette is becoming more and more common in training, especially for individuals or small groups. Simple presentations and demonstrations are relatively easy to produce although there are technical complexities (and concomitant cost increases) when special effects are introduced. The use of videocassettes will probably continue to increase, especially where training programs are to be widely distributed.

Interactive Media

Interaction between trainee and presenter or between trainee and lesson is independent of the delivery medium. The Socratic dialogue exemplified interactive learning some 2500 years ago. It still works. Structured interaction between lesson and trainee with appropriate feedback reaches back to the earlier part of this century: A little over two decades ago, programmed instruction was built on this sort of interaction. Programmed instruction was followed by computer-assisted instruction (CAI), also with full interaction, but because of storage capacity, computer-assisted instruction is generally limited to text and graphic display. To add video materials, an interface between computer and a videotape player was developed. The interface allowed the CAI program to select the next video segment to be viewed (usually based on the trainee's responses) and then rewound or fast-forwarded the videotape to the appropriate starting point. The tape movement, however, generally resulted in a slight delay between instructional segments—delays that could break a trainee's concentration. The optical videodisc is a proposed solution to both the storage and the delay problems. But trainers should be wary of claims based only on hardware and information storage systems. No audiovisual delivery system can guarantee interaction or quality instruction. Good training is good training—with or without media. Audiovisual delivery systems—media—can significantly improve training, but the ultimate responsibility always remains in the hands of the instructional developer and the trainer.

Part Three: Guidelines for Media in Training Presentations

Overview

It takes more than good presentation skills to use media well. Behind any successful audiovisual presentation is a great deal of thought—about the presentation environment, about the equipment, about the techniques. Part three of this chapter offers some guidelines for using the three most common presentation media—flipcharts, overhead transparencies, and slides—with a few suggestions about motion pictures and video.

The Environment

Like any training technique, audiovisual is highly dependent on its environment. Any training room or presentation area should be reasonably comfortable and free from distractions. Desk or table space should be provided if the trainees will be writing or doing workbook exercises. Seating should be comfortable yet offer firm support—especially if trainees will be seated for extended periods of time. If the room is to be used for a number of different training functions, the furniture should be movable.

Lighting and Light Control

Illumination should be even and free of harsh pools of light and glare. The overall level of illumination should be adequate for trainees to read and to take notes. With display media (as opposed to projected media) like the flipchart or chalkboard, all room lights can be left on. In fact, the display material should be well illuminated so the trainees can see it easily. Most projected media have limits to the amount of permissible room light. When using the overhead projector, the room lights can be left on *if* no light is shining directly on the screen. Slides, motion pictures, and projected video require the room to be darkened, especially any light source that falls on the screen surface. Because the room must be dark around the screen yet still have enough illumination for trainees to take notes, separate light banks (and switches) for different room areas are desirable. Even better is a system of separate light banks, each with a control for variable illumination levels. This allows the room light to be adjusted to suit individual audiovisual needs.

Screens

All screens are not alike. Besides size differences, screens differ in other ways. First, a screen may be either front or rear projection. Rear projection screens are translucent (rather than opaque) and the images are projected from behind the screen. This keeps the equipment out of sight, and if the screen is properly shielded, room lights can be kept on. Rear projection is usually used only for slides, motion pictures, and video where—unlike overhead projection—the presenter needs to be near the projector to manipulate the transparency.

In front projection—except for overhead projectors—the projector is usually at the back of the meeting room behind the audience. From there, it projects on the front (audience side) surface of the screen. In front projection, the kind of screen material used strongly affects the brightness of the image and the angle of acceptable viewing. In general, the more highly reflective the screen surface, the narrower the acceptable viewing angle. In actuality, the acceptable viewing angle depends not only on the actual screen used but also on the ambient light falling on the screen *and* the visual information being projected. The three commonly available front projection screens and the *approximate* viewing angle of each are:

Matte—not especially reflective, 70 to 80 degrees

Beaded—a surface with small reflective beads embedded in the surface, 45 to 55 degrees

Lenticular—an embossed surface, 40 to 55 degrees, although not as dim as beaded outside of the main viewing angle

Screen Size and Placement.   The general guideline for screen placement is to place the screen flat against a wall and to center the screen in relation to the audience (Fig. 29-1). However, in a situation where this placement would cause a speaker to be in the way or where ambient light would fall on the screen and wash out the images, the screen can be moved to a corner of the room . . . if the audience

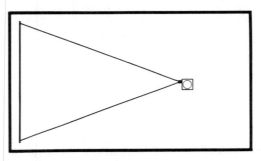

Figure 29-1. Screen and projector placement in a room with normal darkening and no ambient light from outside.

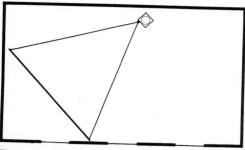

Figure 29-2. Screen and projector placement in a room with ambient light from windows.

remains within the viewing angle and can still see the screen clearly. Every effort should be made to darken the windows or other sources of ambient light that might fall on the screen (Fig. 29-2).

The screen should be high enough so the last row of viewers can see the bottom over the heads of those in front of them (Fig 29-3). For a small group, this usually places the *bottom* of the screen at a *minimum* of 4 feet above the floor. For larger groups, this minimum height may be as great as 7 or 8 feet—or more for very large groups.

The need to raise the screen above the viewers' heads often causes problems in a meeting room with a low ceiling. In such a room, a horizontal—rather than vertical—slide format is recommended (Fig. 29-4). The horizontal format maximizes the restricted viewing area.

The projector(s) should be placed so the lens is in the center of the screen at a right angle to the screen. If the screen is elevated, the projector(s) should also be elevated. While this placement is readily done with slide and motion picture projectors, it cannot be done for overhead projectors because while slide and motion picture projectors are located toward the rear of the room, the overhead projector is placed at the front of the room at a height where the speaker can easily use it. Off-center placement of the projector leads to a condition called "keystoning" (Fig. 29-5).

On those occasions when the projector cannot be moved, the screen should, if possible, be tilted or angled to minimize the keystone effect (Fig. 29-6).

Screen and Audience Size.   How big should a screen be? How far away can a viewer be? How close? The actual maximum viewing distance depends on any number of factors—how reflective the screen is and the viewing angle, the ambient light in the room, and the kind of images and information projected. One common guideline is that the maximum viewing distance should not be more than 6 screen

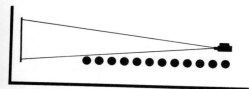

Figure 29-3. Screen raised above audience to allow clear view; projector raised to project at right angles to screen and thus avoid "keystoning."

Figure 29-4. Examples of screens with vertical and horizontal image format where screen cannot be raised: left, vertical image with less image area; right, horizontal image with greater image area.

widths. For example, for a viewer 30 feet away, the minimum screen width would be 5 feet. Conversely, with a 7-foot-wide screen, maximum viewing distance is 42 feet. This guideline assumes that the image fills the full width of the screen.

Some organizations recommend using screen height—rather than width—as the maximum distance measure. This is especially useful in wide-screen presentations. The guideline for screen height is a maximum viewing distance 8 times the screen height. With this guideline, the maximum viewing distance for a 5-foot-high screen would be 40 feet. This assumes that the image fills the full height of the screen.

Whether using the screen width or screen height guideline, the *closest* viewer should not usually be closer than 2 screen units—height or width—unless the presentation is wide-screen (3:1 ratio or wider). For most presentations with a 5-foot-high or -wide screen, 10 feet is the minimum viewing distance. Part of the guideline is derived from how wide the front row of the audience can be and still see the projected images clearly. You can violate the minimum viewing distance guideline more readily than the maximum viewing guideline because the minimum viewing distance deals more with off-center viewing and viewer comfort while the maximum viewing distance affects the size of the information on the screen and how easily it can be recognized. Remember, too, that the closer the audience is to the screen the higher the bottom of the screen must be to avoid the front row's blocking the projected image (Fig. 29-7; refer to Fig. 29-3 also).

Lenses and Image Sizes. All the guidelines about viewing distances assume that the projected images *do* fill the screen width. The overhead projector has a fixed-focus, noninterchangeable lens. That means that the image size is determined by the distance between the lens and screen. The closer the lens is to the screen, the smaller the projected image.

A range of lenses, including variable focal length lenses (called zoom lenses), is readily available. The shorter the focal length of the lens, the larger the image on the screen will be. Zoom lenses are particularly handy because of the variable focal lengths. For example, a 4- to 6-inch zoom lens has a full range of focal lengths from

Figure 29-5. Examples of the shape of a "keystoned" image: left, projector is lower than the center of the screen; right, projector is to the right of the center of the screen.

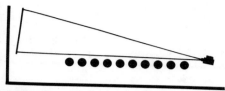

Figure 29-6. Screen tilted at right angles to projector to avoid image "keystoning."

4 to 6 inches. Table 29-1 shows the image size projected by the more common focal length lens at the distances generally found in the majority of training situations. For special situations, shorter and longer focal length lenses are available. For very short lens-to-screen distances, some companies make short focal length lenses with a mechanism to compensate for keystoning.

Legibility. Legibility of text on the screen is a complex issue, but here are four guidelines that cover the majority of situations involving legibility.

First, use a medium or bold typeface. Avoid light or thin letters. Use a simple, clean typeface without frills or serifs. Keep titles short, using only keywords. A simple rule of thumb for horizontal (3:2 ratio) slides is to have no more than 4 lines of 15 characters each. The actual number of characters will depend on the actual typeface used. The less the audience knows about the information—and, hence, the less recognizable the information is—the more important legibility becomes. Trainees can fill in gaps in known information more readily than in new information.

Second, as mentioned earlier, lighter letters, especially in a contrasting color, on a darker background are easier to read than dark letters on a light background. Avoid clear, white, or very light backgrounds. In a room with high ambient light, deep saturated colors will be hard to see. Use a dark background and bold, pastel letters.

Third, assuming the maximum viewing distances mentioned above (8 times screen height or 6 times screen width), the *absolute minimum* letter height for an overhead transparency is 1/8 inch. This is bigger than even the largest (pica) typeface on a typewriter—ordinary typing will not work. A more realistic minimum height for lettering on an overhead transparency is 3/16 inch. Major captions or headings should be even bigger. If the artwork for text on a slide is 8 1/2 by 11

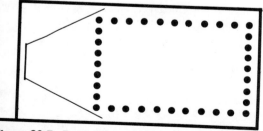

Figure 29-7. Example of audience at approximate acceptable viewing distances. Note that if the screen reflected the image more widely, another row might be added at the front row of the audience.

Table 29-1. Common Focal Lengths, Projection Distances, and Image Sizes

The lens-to-screen distances are based on a 3:2 image ratio, full frame slide with the wide part of the image (about 1½ inch wide) placed horizontally in the projector.

Screen width	Focal length of lens, inches						
	2	3	4	5	6	7	8
	Lens to screen distance ("throw" distance)						
36"	4'10"	7'2"	9'7"	11'10"	14'5"	16'9"	19'2"
40"	5'4"	7'11"	10'7"	13'	15'11"	18'6"	21'2"
50"	6'6"	9'10"	13'1"	16'1"	19'7"	22'10"	26'1"
60"	7'9"	11'8"	15'6"	19'1"	23'4"	27'2"	31'1"
70"	9'	13'6"	18'	22'2"	27'	31'6"	36'
7'	10'9"	16'1"	21'5"	26'5"	32'3"	37'7"	42'11"
8'	12'3"	18'4"	24'5"	30'1"	36'8"	42'9"	48'11"
10'	15'2"	22'9"	30'4"	37'5"	45'7"	53'2"	60'9"
12'	18'2"	27'3"	36'4"	44'8"	54'6"	63'7"	72'8"

Courtesty of D.O. Industries, Rochester, NY, makers of Navitar projection lenses. Excerpted from a larger lens chart available from D.O. Industries.

inches, 3/16 inch is the minimum height for lettering. The rule of thumb for text legibility on a completed slide is to hold the slide at a comfortable arm's length (about 15 inches) and try to read the text. If it is readily legible, it can probably be read at the maximum viewing distance.

Fourth, and most important, legibility guidelines are just that—guidelines. There is no substitute for projecting or displaying the information under the actual circumstances—the same room, the same equipment, the same lighting conditions—in which it will be viewed. Ask a colleague unfamiliar with the information to read the information from the farthest viewing distance. If he or she can read it, it is acceptable for use in the presentation.

The Last Step—Rehearsal

Preparing a presentation without rehearsing is akin to a football team drawing up a game plan and not practicing. The guidelines are only a starting point. There is no substitute for experience, for practice—rehearsing the presentation. If there is no opportunity to completely rehearse the presentation on site, the rehearsal should be conducted under circumstances as similar to the actual presentation as possible. Good presenters take nothing for granted. They make arrangements well in advance, check and recheck them, and then arrive for the presentation early enough to double check all details and do at least a quick run-through.

Summary

Using audiovisual techniques and materials definitely requires a substantial amount of work. Is it really worth the effort? The answer is generally "Yes." For five reasons.

First, even though audiovisual is not an automatic guarantee to save bad training, *most* training situations are definitely improved by the use of audiovisual materials and techniques. This is especially true in skills training, in training where visual and auditory cues are part of the skill to be developed, in situations where the trainee's attention must be held. When used well in carefully planned training, audiovisual *does* enhance learning.

Moreover, audiovisual materials can bring to the training session sights and sounds and simulations that might not otherwise be possible or feasible. From dangerous, yet critical, situations to distant locations or past events, audiovisual is a communications vehicle that can take the trainee's mind to times, places, and occurrences outside the immediate training area.

Second, audiovisual materials and techniques integrated into the training provide a base or "floor" for instruction. The materials help to structure the lesson. Instead of being entirely dependent on an instructor's interpretation each time it is delivered, the lesson's audiovisual materials provide a consistency and reliability from lesson to lesson.

Third, this capacity for consistency and learning reliability has led to a new look at the cost-effectiveness of audiovisual training, especially using "stand-alone" media. With media-based instruction handling the bulk of simple training, good trainers can be spared the boring redundancy of offering the same presentation week after week. They can concentrate instead on developing new courses and lessons. And the more times a lesson is successfully used by trainees—especially when it leads to reduced trainer time—the greater the cost-effectiveness of that lesson.

Fourth, while research has shown differences in individual's learning styles, most training is designed as though all trainees were alike. Incorporating audiovisual materials into the training is at least a start in accommodating different learning styles.

Fifth, the use of audiovisual materials—more sophisticated materials than the simple flipchart—has come to be the hallmark of the professional trainer. With the growth and acceptance of instructional design, training has become more than group facilitation or platform training. Training and development has entered a new era, and audiovisual communications is part and parcel of today's—and tomorrow's—training.

Selected Bibliography and Comments

Anderson, Ronald H., *Selecting and Developing Media for Instruction*, 2d ed., Van Nostrand Reinhold, New York, 1983. A very practical and useful "how-to" guide to choosing media for training. Also has advantages and disadvantages of each medium as well as a checklist to follow in selecting and developing training in each medium. Perhaps a bit simplistic for the experienced media user or producer but quite down-to-earth and useful.

Audio-Visual Equipment Directory, Fairfax, VA, International Communications Industries Association (formerly National Audiovisual Association), new editions annually. A directory covering a wide variety of audiovisual equipment, furniture, and accessories. Includes handy tables (like projection tables) and lists of manufacturers and distributors. Good reference tool for *hardware*.

AV Video magazine, Montage Publishing Company, Suite 314, 25550 Hawthorne Blvd., Torrance, CA 90505. A controlled circulation trade publication aimed at producers of various media. Has monthly columns on various media formats as well as articles about new media developments and audiovisual applications. Aimed toward the "nonspecialist" working in audiovisual communications in an organization.

Heinich, Robert, Michael Molenda, and James D. Russell, *Instructional Media and the New Technologies of Instruction*, John Wiley & Sons, New York, 1982. More oriented toward teachers than trainers but still contains both utilization *and* production techniques. Also has information on lesson planning and development and operation of basic audiovisual equipment.

Laird, Dugan, *A User's Look at the Audiovisual World*, 2d ed., Fairfax, VA, International Communications Industries Association (formerly National Audiovisual Association), 1974 (new edition under preparation). A fairly detailed guide to the selection, planning, production, use, and storage of various audiovisual materials. Oriented more toward training manager and audiovisual generalist and includes more hardware use than Anderson (above).

Section 4

Training Applications

30

Leadership Development[*]

Charles A. Reiner

Harvey Morris

Charles Reiner is a founder and principal at Vector Management Systems, Inc., a New York–based consulting firm. As a program designer and trainer he works extensively in the areas of management simulations, negotiations, motivation, and conflict management. His consulting work is primarily in the area of cultural modifications and strategic planning. Reiner is also president of Vector Selection Systems, an executive search firm. Since 1978 he has had an affiliation with the Center for Creative Leadership and has been closely involved in the Looking Glass simulation from both a design and delivery standpoint. His current active contracts include GTE, Sun Oil, Celanese, Sandoz, Eli Lilly, Uniroyal, Armco Steel Co., and Citibank. Reiner, who was formerly on the faculty of Cornell Medical School, received his Ph.D. in psychology in 1973.

Harvey Morris is the president of Vector Management Systems, Inc. He has worked extensively with organizations in such diverse industries as chemical and petroleum processing, heavy manufacturing, electronics and defense, pharmaceuticals, communications, and utilities. He received a Ph.D. in Psychology from the University of Nebraska in 1970, where his research focused on the dynamics of small work groups. Throughout his professional career, Dr. Morris has been involved in the design and implementation of management development activities, and in conjunction with the Center for Creative Leadership (where he is an adjunct staff member) he has been actively involved in the Looking Glass simulation.

* The authors wish to acknowledge the assistance of Martin J. Cohen, a New York–based training consultant, in the preparation of material for this chapter.

What Is Leadership?

A Plethora of Research: A Paucity of Results

Anyone who has reviewed the leadership literature of the last two decades cannot help but be struck by a sameness in the typical opening remarks—in effect, decrying the state of knowledge in a field as well researched as any in the behavioral sciences. Here is a typical comment:

> Four decades of research on leadership have produced a bewildering mass of findings. . . . It is difficult to know what, if anything, has been convincingly demonstrated by replicated research. The endless accumulation of empirical data has not produced an integrated understanding of leadership.[1]

Nevertheless, the recent proliferation of books, articles, and programs on leadership attests to the fact that interest in the subject remains lively, that definitive answers remain elusive, and that the field is still "wide open."

The reasons for the disarray are real and abundant. The search for a unified leadership theory has been hampered by a series of obstacles including a general lack of agreement about terminology and methods of study, the tendency to pursue a single, limited aspect of the topic, and the lack of an overall framework to integrate the diverse findings that have been reported.

Some writers[2] have been so discouraged by the apparent chaos in the field as to suggest that the concept of leadership be discarded entirely, while others[3] strongly defend its usefulness. Certain writers[4] express doubt that leaders exert any significant influence at all in organizations with so many confounding factors operating, while still others[5] consider leadership the critical element in attaining organizational goals. Current approaches to leadership effectiveness have, to differing degrees, all failed to overcome flaws in theory or research methodology and thereby demonstrate their ultimate value. While the majority of research to date has led to contradictory or inconclusive results, there is still reason to conclude that progress is being made.

Recently, a new understanding and perspective appears to be emerging which offers hope for an eventual integrated theory of leadership. There is increasing recognition that no single approach to date has supplied all the answers, and that while fundamental disagreements remain, enough is now known to provide a foundation for significant future advances.

Rather than focus on the already well-documented areas of contention, this chapter, after a brief review of the field, will aim to add evidence to support or refute existing concepts using a new vantage point—observations from full-scale management simulations—as the data source. This overlay brings its own unique set of advantages and limitations but when matched to past research findings will hopefully offer some useful insights into the state of the leadership art.

Definitions

The focus of this chapter is on managerial leadership—the kind that takes place in formal organizations like businesses, schools, and government. Although a great deal has been written on the subject, there is still no generally accepted definition of leadership. This is both a symptom and a cause of the problem. Researchers have tended to define the term according to the particular viewpoint and dimensions they favor. And the variations are not just semantic, leading to basic differences in the choice of phenomena to be studied and in the interpretation of the findings. The dilemma, then, is to pick the leadership definition that seems to make the most sense and risk losing important insights from other, incompatible approaches, or commit to none of them—keeping an open mind—and risk being unable to reach any conclusions for lack of a meaningful frame of reference. There is, of course, another option—the compromise position—to use the broadest, least restricting definition, which for purposes of this chapter will offer the greatest advantages.

Perhaps the most common elements mentioned in leadership definitions are that it involves a group context and an influence process of leaders over followers. Just to underline the ambiguity on the subject, even this oversimplified conception of leadership is not free of controversy. Some writers have questioned the validity of the "leader-group" focus, noting that leaders frequently spend as much, or more, time dealing with peers, superiors, and outsiders as with subordinates.[6]

According to one authority, the presence of effective leadership in an organization is felt through a sense of energy and "empowerment" that characterizes the work force. This empowerment is manifested in several ways:[7]

- Employees have a sense that they are important to the organization.

- Employees are enthusiastic about the work.

- Employees feel part of a team.

- Employees care about learning and improving themselves.

- Employees care about excellence in performance.

Such a description of leadership seems to place it in a category beyond typical conceptions of management. Are they the same, or different? If different, how?

Leadership vs. Management

While many writers use the terms leader and manager interchangeably, important distinctions must be made. To start with, clearly not all leaders are managers, and it can be easily argued that not all managers are leaders. "Manager" is a job title that is earned or conferred, while "leader" is a term with a more subjective, even emotional connotation.

Many organizations are said to be well managed but poorly led. For those who make this distinction, the focus of management is clearly on its administrative aspects, such as the development of organization charts, plans, objectives, and control systems. Traditional conceptions of management work include four or five major functions, with "leading" being one of them, making it merely one of several roles managers must play. Other writers, however, contend that leadership transcends the normal sphere of managerial functions, placing it in a different dimension. Leadership for them involves concepts like motivation, inspiration, and direction setting, and is often seen as an amorphous process requiring special talents.

For the present, there does not seem to be any entirely satisfactory answer beyond acknowledging that both sets of skills or qualities are necessary for a well-rounded executive. All leadership and no management would be just as incomplete as the reverse.

The basic underlying question that historically has driven leadership research is "what makes leaders effective?" Although approaches differ widely here too, the most common definition of effectiveness is "the extent to which the leader's group or organization performs its task successfully and attains its goals."[8] Other measures of leader effectiveness include the attitudes of followers, and the leader's contribution to the quality of the group process. The selection of criteria has depended on the objectives and values of those making the effectiveness judgments.

Scope and Influence of Leadership

Whether leadership is defined narrowly as a piece of the manager's job, or set aside on its own small pedestal, important questions remain about the nature and context of the phenomenon. What are the characteristics of the environment in which leaders operate? How much influence can leaders have on group and organizational outcomes? What are the realistic limitations on what they can accomplish?

Studies of what leaders and managers actually do on the job reveal a work environment that contrasts dramatically with the static and orderly depictions of most textbooks.[9] Careful field observations[10] have revealed that managerial work is characterized by:

- A large number of activities
- A majority of activities that are of short duration
- Frequent interpersonal contacts, many outside the immediate work group
- Communication primarily through verbal interaction
- Change as a constant fact of life

The implications of these findings for improving leadership are significant. For example, programs such as those teaching complex problem-analysis and decision-making techniques, a common subject in managerial skills training, may be seen as having more limited applicability given what is now known about the frantic pace of an executive's usual day.

Overall, the research evidence concerning the amount of influence of leaders over followers, and the impact on results is equivocal. Some things that have been established with a fair degree of confidence[6,11] are that:

1. Cooperative relationships between leaders and followers tend to improve group effectiveness.
2. Follower motivation and commitment may be heightened by their participation in making certain types of decisions.
3. Leader technical expertise is necessary to gain and maintain influence with followers.
4. Upward and lateral influence enables the leader to represent the group and keep it viable through the appropriation of needed resources.
5. An important element of leadership is that the reciprocal nature of influence, that is, leader behavior, may be as much a result of follower behavior as a cause of it.
6. A high level of personal motivation is a prerequisite for leadership, probably to overcome the extreme complexities, pressures, and responsibilities of the job.

One of the benefits of scientific research is that without knowing absolutely what something is, valuable insights are possible by understanding what has clearly been ruled out. For instance, it is reasonably certain that leadership is not simply an ability a person has or does not have—a mysterious gift bestowed on a special few at birth. There are numerous interactive factors operating at any given time that determine not only a leader's effectiveness, but even whether an individual may be considered a leader at all. Most theories assume that leaders have more control over the work environment than is actually the case. For example, studies which have looked at the impact of environmental factors such as union strikes, natural disasters, accidents, and shortages of raw materials indicate that they can effectively nullify a leader's influence and power. Nor is leadership, as popularly conceived, an ability required only at the top of the organizational pyramid. Leadership must exist at all levels for true organizational effectiveness. It is not only the visionary president, but the inspirational managers and creative supervisors working in concert, that bring about successful outcomes. Internal company structures and systems, as well as external forces, can limit both the leader's and the group's prerogatives. So the way that leaders maneuver within, around, and through these constraints is a gauge of leadership effectiveness.

The Schools

A Brief History of the Major Approaches

Given the communal nature of human beings, it is an apparent truism to say that leadership has always existed. The wiser or richer or stronger of the species have always been able to gather followers around them; the process has been a source of unending fascination and awe to all those who do not lead but wish they could.

The earliest writings on the subject speculated about the qualities of famous political, military, and religious leaders, and it was not until the 1920s that any sort of systematic investigation of leadership began. From the start, leadership research and theory has been characterized by a wide diversity of approaches with few attempts to integrate or build on earlier work. Behavioral scientists have studied traits, power and influence, behaviors, and situational factors in their search for an understanding of how leaders gain and maintain power, influence followers, and achieve group goals.

Trait Approach

Not surprisingly, much of the early work on leadership attempted to discover those personal traits, skills, and characteristics that distinguish leaders from nonleaders, or effective leaders from ineffective leaders. Early notions of leadership ascribed success to the possession of extraordinary abilities such as powerful insight, penetrating intuition, excellent timing, and unusual persuasiveness. Hundreds of correlational studies scrutinized every imaginable trait but were, in the final analysis, inconclusive. The initial intention of researchers to develop a list of traits by which to single out leaders from the crowd has not succeeded.

The conception of leadership as a simple function of personality traits seems, at best, oversimplified. While leaders were found to be slightly higher on certain personality factors, it is still unclear whether these factors represent a cause or effect of being in a leadership position, or both. Furthermore, the personal characteristics that have been shown to relate to leadership do so only in the context of specific situations, and it has not yet been demonstrated which traits are most effective in which situations.

Although trait theory as originally developed has failed to deliver the promised formula, certain useful findings have come out of the research that may be integrated at some point with data from other approaches. Research into traits and skills has shown that effective leaders tend to:

- Be more concerned with achieving results than with sticking to policies and procedures, more practical than philosophical or idealistic

- Rate higher than followers on dimensions such as self-confidence, maturity, persistence, energy, and tolerance for frustration and stress

- Be highly motivated, with strong needs for achievement and power, and to a lesser extent, for affiliation

- Be more willing to absorb interpersonal stress, and to confront people constructively on work-related issues, than to avoid potential conflict

- Have higher levels of managerial competence in conceptual, technical, and human relations skills

- Be more interested in the work itself than in matters such as benefits and working conditions

- Exceed their average follower in intelligence (only slightly), knowledge, achievement, socioeconomic status, and sense of humor

- Communicate with others openly and honestly, rather than being secretive and political

- Be more likely to encourage participation of followers in planning, problem solving, and decision making than to operate autocratically

- Incorporate a task orientation with a people orientation without having to trade one off against the other

- Have a positive attitude toward authority, and identify more with superiors and the organization than with subordinates

More recent trait research, as reported in Stogdill's book,[1] has improved its methodology and has consequently been seen as more promising. These later studies have identified more relevant traits, use more accurate trait measures, and look at trait patterns rather than just individual correlations. Most significantly, greater attention is being paid to how the situation affects the relevant importance of various traits.

Power and Influence Approach

Another major line of research has examined leader effectiveness in terms of the source and amount of power, and the way in which leaders exercise their power over followers. Whatever their focus or level of complexity, most definitions of leadership include some reference to it as a process of "influencing the activities of others." So the concept of influence is generally seen as somehow fundamental to the exercise of leadership.

Broadly speaking, power is a person's potential to influence others, and in an organizational context may be said to take two forms: "position power" and "personal power." Position power is the potential influence of a leader deriving from the authority vested in the job position. The potential influence stemming from characteristics of the person in the position is called "personal power." The most effective forms of personal power are the leader's expertise based on demonstrated competence, attractiveness based on personal qualities, and loyalty based on cooperative relationships developed over time.

Although the terms and relationships have been defined in many ways, one classic description[12] outlines five sources of power through which leaders may attempt to influence others:

1. *Reward power.* Influence through distribution of rewards (e.g., promotions, bonus)

2. *Coercive power.* Influence through threat of punishment (e.g., demotion, dismissal)

3. *Legitimate power.* Influence through "rights" conferred by position in an organization (e.g., authority)

4. *Expert power.* Influence through ability to persuade with facts and knowledge (e.g., technical expertise)

5. *Referent power.* Influence through followers' admiration for or personal identification with the leader (e.g., charisma)

To fully understand the influence process between leaders and followers, it must be recognized as reciprocal. Followers depend on leaders for direction, inspiration, guidance, and support in their work. Leaders must rely on followers to perform well, to maintain cooperative relationships, and in some cases, to keep them in power. This counterbalance of influence serves to curb the leader's exercise of "position power" and keep it constructive.

While a great deal of conceptual confusion surrounds influence processes, their apparent centrality to any notions about leadership has led to considerable research, and a number of key findings have emerged:

- Leader-follower influence processes are reciprocal, with both parties sending and receiving attempts to shape their behavior.

- Effective leaders tend to rely more on personal power than on position power, although both are necessary.

- Leaders require sufficient authority in their position to make necessary changes and distribute rewards, or they cannot be effective.

- The manner in which power is used is critical to the result, that is, whether the influence attempt is welcomed, rejected, or simply tolerated.

- Effective leaders tend to exercise their power more subtly, remaining sensitive to status differences and possible threat to others' self-esteem.

- When power is used to inspire and encourage followers, it is more productive for the organization and the individual than when it is used to dominate and control them.

- Charismatic leaders tend to use a blend of both the positive and negative styles in their use of power.

Behavior Approach

Since early trait research yielded consistently disappointing results, investigators started looking in a new direction for answers, specifically toward a behavior-centered approach to understanding leadership. The focus shifted from what effective leaders should *be* to what they should *do*. In effect, there was less interest in how to choose the "right" people, and more in how to train the ones you have in the necessary leadership behaviors.

Some of the more influential studies of leadership behavior were conducted at Ohio State University in the early 1950s. The most significant finding from this body of research was the isolation of two key factors said to differentiate effective from ineffective leaders. The factors—"initiating structure" (i.e., task orientation) and "consideration" (i.e., people orientation)—were later investigated in hundreds of studies seeking to clarify the relationships between these behaviors and leader effectiveness. The results, once again, left troubling unresolved issues, which were attributed to conceptual and methodological shortcomings.

Another notable series of leadership studies, carried out at the University of Michigan during the same period, concluded that effective managers paid considerable attention to administrative tasks but at the same time remained considerate, supportive, and trusting in dealing with subordinates. In terms of specific behaviors, the most commonly found categories were planning and coordinating, supervising subordinates, carrying out position responsibilities, and maintaining good relations with coworkers.

While research continues on leadership behavior categories and activity patterns, the most significant findings to date show that:

- Leadership involves complex patterns of behavior carried out in a complex environment.
- It is likely that several different patterns of behavior may be equally effective in a given situation, and that one type of behavior may be effective across a variety of situations, depending on the mix of factors involved.
- There is no generally accepted list of leadership behaviors at present, but behaviors directed at accomplishing the work of the group, supporting and maintaining the group, and representing the group are known to be important.
- Broader behavior categories apply to more leadership situations but tell correspondingly less about leader effectiveness; it is a trade-off between specificity and applicability.
- Effective leaders are able to increase follower commitment by involving them in appropriate decisions and projects.
- Effective leaders are more inclined to establish clear performance expectations for followers, and to treat them in a respectful, supportive way.
- Effective leaders are more likely to attempt to influence and motivate followers by using praise and recognition as well as monetary incentives.
- Effective leaders use both consideration and initiating structure to improve work group performance and satisfaction.
- Effective leaders tend to defend the weak and timid, and encourage their involvement.
- To be effective, leaders must have a flexible outlook and style, and be able to function in ambiguous situations. This ability, sometimes called "conceptual complexity," is important to both creativity and information processing, and involves processes such as analyzing situations, going beyond the "givens," ignoring distractions, and experimenting with variations of behavior.
- Abilities that characterize both effective leaders and creative people include risk taking, complexity, and dealing with opposites and contradictions.

To date, behavior research has also been inconclusive. There are two likely reasons for this. First, the lack of agreement among researchers on levels, terminology, and types of behavior variables to study has inhibited comparisons. Second, in many cases, situational variables were not taken into account.

Situational Approach

The finding that different traits and behaviors lead to effective leadership under certain conditions and not under others has led to a situational approach to leadership research. Situational theorists maintain that neither traits nor behavior are as important as the specific factors operating in any given situation. Based on a contingency model, this approach emphasizes the importance of situational variables such as the nature of the task, the leader's authority, and the role expectations of superiors, subordinates, and peers.

A summary of the most significant findings from situational and contingency approaches includes:

- The nature of the managerial job is essentially reactive, so there cannot be one "best" leadership style or strategy as some have proposed. The choice of a style will depend on who or what is being managed, and under what circumstances.

- In recognizing the importance of "situationality," managers are reminded of the need to treat different subordinates differently, and to treat the same subordinates differentially in different situations.

- Effective leaders are those who can either obtain a position that makes best use of their ability or can adapt the situation to achieve a better match.

- Effective leaders have the capacity to structure social interactions in a way appropriate to the situation.

- Task-oriented leaders are most effective when the situation is characterized by either high or low control, while relationship-oriented leaders excel when the level of control is somewhere between the two extremes.

- An understanding of leadership dynamics must take account of the leader's characteristics, the followers' needs and goals, and the demands of the situation.

- Because of the enormous complexities, it is unlikely that people will ever be able to be fully "programmed" for leadership roles—nor would people be likely to accept being "robotized" to that degree.

In general, situational theories have tended to be complex, conceptually weak, and difficult to test. In fact, none have yet been verified, once again leaving inconclusive results. The situational approaches have, however, been useful in identifying important variables, such as task structure, task independence, and environmental uncertainty, that need to be taken into account in developing an understanding of leader effectiveness.

Aside from the conceptual and methodological problems, some behavioral scientists have questioned even the potential value of complex situational leadership theories for improving leadership effectiveness. They point out that situational concepts are useful only if the leader has sufficient time to analyze a situation and choose an appropriate response style, which is rarely the case. They are simply too busy to use a complicated model.

A Continuum

In summarizing the history of leadership research, what has appeared to be several distinct lines of inquiry, each with its own following, can be seen through a

Table 30-1

Approach	Assumptions	Questions
Trait	Great leaders possess personal characteristics that ordinary people do not have	What traits or skills make someone a leader?
Power and influence	It's not what you *are*, but what you *have* and how you *use* it that matters	What are the sources of power, and the means of influence used by leaders?
Behavior	It's not what you *are*, but what you *should* do that matters	What are the behaviors and activities that effective leaders engage in?
Situation	It's not what you *are* or what you *do*, but the *circumstances* that are important	What are the conditions under which certain skills, styles, or behaviors are most effective?

different lens as a fairly orderly progression. The logic of this evolution in leadership theory can be understood by viewing the pattern of this research in terms of the basic assumptions and questions posed by each succeeding group of theorists (Table 30-1). As each series of studies yielded some answers but raised additional questions, fresh assumptions evolved to stimulate and guide the next wave of research. Further research continues on each of the approaches, but the emphasis tends to be more on reconciling previous contradictions than on maintaining a "purist" position.

Observing Leaders in Action

Recent Research

Increasingly, in the last decade, writers[13,14,15,16] have been pointing out how different the actual work environment of the manager is from the textbook descriptions of calm, logical, orderly behaviors. These investigators report that the reality of managerial work, in sharp contrast to the "armchair assumptions" of theoreticians, is characterized by numerous, brief interpersonal encounters, frequent interruptions, and a hectic atmosphere of continual change. Against this backdrop, it is no wonder that these researchers find it difficult to imagine the methodical performance of prescribed behaviors such as planning, organizing, controlling, and directing, ever taking place on the job.

The complexity of the work environment is the main issue here, and it carries important implications for all leadership approaches. For example, far from sitting quietly at their desks strategizing, most managers spend the bulk of their time interacting with others and working energetically to develop and maintain a network of crucial work relationships. If this description is valid, as many believe, rather than teaching content, such as planning and control systems, and rational decision processes, leadership training might be more relevant if it is based on actual leadership situations, that is, the "context" of the leader's job, and on the use of focused feedback to assist participants in evaluating their performance and its impact. One type of intervention that meets these qualifications is a management simulation.

Simulations are highly realistic recreations of work situations, with physical trappings, procedure, and problems all devised to make participants feel, and hopefully act, as they would on the job. Recently, large-scale management simulations have been used with increasing frequency and apparent success, essentially for self-diagnostic and self-developmental purposes. Simulation represents a promising development for leadership research because it combines the advantages of field observation studies (realism) with those of laboratory studies (partly controlled situation). In effect, they make the richness and complexity of an ongoing organization available for systematic study.

A Unique Opportunity to Observe

The authors of this chapter have been conducting the oldest and most popular of these simulations for several years, specifically Looking Glass Inc. (LGI), developed by the Center for Creative Leadership in 1978. Having worked with and observed thousands of managers in action, the authors found themselves in a unique position to make systematic observations on leader effectiveness.

The management simulation offers not only a new vantage point but also an opportunity to integrate some of the findings from earlier research while overcoming some of its major limitations. Performance feedback, for example, considered by many to be vital to employee development, tends to be poor or nonexistent on the job; and there is certainly little time for reflection or self-examination. Simulations remedy both these concerns, as well as facilitate the transfer of learning to the job because of their high level of realism.

Accumulating Evidence

In this section, we will first outline what we feel are the clearest and most significant things we have learned about leadership from observing and debriefing large numbers of managers participating in the LGI simulation. Then, we will attempt to relate these observations to the research literature to see where they support or contradict what has been reported. These are our observations and comments:

1. *Calling up the reserves.* An important aspect of leadership is being able to call upon behaviors that are in the manager's repertoire, but below the awareness threshold, and apply them appropriately as the situation requires. Although the simulation provides participants with numerous opportunities to experiment with behaviors, we have often found that the potential for leadership is not exercised. This willingness or unwillingness to risk taking action in unfamiliar circumstances seems to be a key discriminator of leadership ability. The simulation eventually enables the risk takers to see the linkages between their behaviors and simulation outcomes, and perhaps to generalize them to their real work situations. A lot of current leadership training fails because these linkages are not apparent and not understood. So leadership is, first, having an insight or "vision" and then risking to act on and implement that insight. Leadership is being proactive—willing to take action.

2. *Reaching beyond.* Effective leaders appear to have the ability to "break set," that is, to go beyond the obvious parameters of a problem in search of a solution. This ability to "extrapolate" from the givens has much in common with accepted

definitions of creativity and the creative process. This ability may be facilitated by a penchant for routinely questioning assumptions and asking penetrating questions.

3. *A delicate balance.* Effective leaders are often able to achieve a delicate balance between seemingly contradictory (polar) dimensions operating in a given situation. For example, they appear to be able to experience the environment in two distinct ways simultaneously. They can balance the subjective and objective aspects of an issue; they can effectively trade off between intellect and intuition, and rely on both. This "style flexibility" permits them to flip back and forth, and to use different behaviors at different times as necessary to achieve resolution of the problem. An example of this flexibility is the effective and selective use of humor to motivate a group that may be "too up" or "too down." This balance allows them to operate tactically while maintaining a strategic framework (a rare talent!).

4. *Seeing the forest.* Effective leaders often demonstrate an uncanny ability to select key issues from among many, and stay focused despite numerous potential distractions (unless something truly more important comes up) until the issue is resolved. Effective leaders are able to "manage the context" while delegating the content. They can discern the big picture and avoid getting caught up in handling draining details—they *can* see the forest for the trees.

5. *What's in a question?* This talent for sifting and sorting through the endless stream of problems, and setting appropriate priorities is related to the ability of effective leaders to maintain good communications with subordinates, to accept feedback, and to ask discerning questions. They are not afraid to admit what they do not know, and know how to seek assistance. They are also very sensitive to "process." They ask questions like, "How did this happen?" and "What worked well?" so they can trust their "intuition" because it is based, in fact, on a series of ongoing analyses.

6. *Steady as she goes.* Effective leaders have the courage to make unpopular decisions, knowing perhaps that they will not be "liked" but will (at least in the long run) be respected for their stand or action. This ability entails being able to maintain a global perspective while dealing with specific aspects of the situation. They must keep an underlying belief in what they are doing, and that it will be seen as helpful.

7. *Now hear this.* Effective leaders are able to delegate effectively, showing trust and respect for subordinates. They are also able to establish structure around group action (e.g., in leading a group meeting, put up an agenda with time frames and stick to it).

8. *Know thine own self.* Effective leaders tend to be more "accurately introspective." They tend to give thoughtful consideration to their actions, and have a good sense of their limitations as well as their strengths.

Some Things That Get in the Way

Effective leadership may be derailed by personality factors or by factors operating in the work environment. Some of these factors include:

- *Company values.* Short-range thinking, such as the demand for maximizing profits on a quarterly basis, often thwarts a leader's strategic initiatives.

- *Intragroup conflict.* The assertive actions that leaders must sometimes take may result in competition and conflict, often leading to avoidance behavior and failure to reach productive outcomes. When, for example, "turf issues" arise, it may be difficult for leaders to enlist the cooperation needed for effective action.

- *Overconfidence.* Leaders have been known to suffer from what may be called "the surgeon complex"—the need to believe unwaveringly in what they are doing (or they could not "cut"). This absence of self-doubt is a necessity, but is a double-edged sword in that it limits their willingness to consider alternatives.

- *Inflated ego.* There is always the danger of leaders' losing perspective and sacrificing substance for style. Once a leader's image has been established, a compulsion may develop to maintain the status quo, leading to more conservatism toward risk taking and a likely reduction in effectiveness.

- *Yea sayers.* A classic, and classically fatal, error for a leader is to become surrounded by "yes men and women." When a defensive environment develops and the openness ceases, the risks of failure multiply quickly.

Awareness of these risk factors should help the astute leader in sidestepping them.

Common Themes

As was noted earlier, leadership research has been characterized by highly segmented and narrowly focused studies, with little attempt at pulling together what has been learned. While each school has tended to go essentially in its own direction in search of the "one best way," more recent writers have seen merit in each of the positions, finding more overlap than was formerly recognized. Table 30-2 is an attempt to highlight the areas where findings from the various approaches, including our own experiences with LGI participants, converge into common themes. Table 30-2 shows that the importance of task-related knowledge and skills has emerged as either a predictive or an explanatory factor in the leadership research of each of the major schools, as well as in our own observations. Similarly, maintaining good relations with followers, letting followers have a say in certain decisions, having influence with peers and superiors, and having high personal motivation have all been found—to one degree or another—to enhance leader effectiveness.

Table 30-2 is not a comprehensive attempt to summarize all that is presently known about leadership. Rather, it highlights five areas where research from divergent theoretical positions can be seen to lend some support to each other. Although many of the connections are still tenuous and incomplete, they are nevertheless there, and suggest a way that an integration of findings may be approached. By taking what has been established and noting the points of interdependence, we can begin to form a model which uses the "cross-validated" findings to set the direction for continuing research. This model can also indicate the most productive approaches to leadership development while we wait for more definitive answers.

Improving Leadership

The old controversy about whether or not leaders are endowed at birth with some sort of "leadership genes" appears to have finally been settled. The early assumptions that some people are "born leaders" or that certain personal traits are universally necessary for effective leadership have never been demonstrated in several decades of research. Now, it is recognized that certain traits increase the likelihood but do not assure that leaders will be effective in certain situations.

Table 30-2

Common themes	Approaches				
	Trait	Power and influence	Behavior	Situational	Simulation (context)
Task-related expertise	Technical and conceptual skills essential for most kinds of leaders	Basis for expert power, and necessary for influence such as persuasion	Technical and conceptual skills and knowledge essential for many effective leadership behaviors and for external representation	Trait and behavior research findings often presented as situationally dependent	Effective leaders are able to recognize, select and focus
Cooperative and respectful leader-follower relations	Human relations skills (e.g., tact, listening) and skills facilitating charisma (e.g., speaking, acting) are necessary for fostering good relationships	Referent power is an important source of influence over subordinates and followers	Consideration by leader important determinant of follower satisfaction; providing recognition, decision participation, etc., contributes to better leader-follower relations	Variables such as subordinate's competence, maturity, performance, and level in organization, etc., important for leader-follower relations	"Style flexibility," and the ability to achieve a delicate balance between seemingly contradictory dimensions (e.g., tactical and strategic frames of reference) enhance leader's stature and effectiveness with followers
Decision participation	Certain leader traits predispose greater use of decision participation by followers; conference lead-	Participation increases the amount of reciprocal influence vs. leaders who make decisions autocrati-	Leader effectiveness increased in problem-solving group meetings if leader uses appropriate proce-	Decision acceptance and decision quality are key variables in determining decision participation; level in	Effective leaders are able to encourage open communications, and to delegate effectively, trust and

	ership requires conceptual skills	cally	dures to overcome problems in group process	organization important—lower level managers less likely to use participation	respect for followers
Upward and lateral influence	Upward influence enhanced by critical knowledge and expertise; technical and human relations skills important for upward and lateral influence	Significant upward influence to acquire necessary resources, improves leader's influence and status with followers	Leaders spend a lot of time interacting with superiors and peers, especially in representational role; also coordinate and facilitate vertical communication in the organization	Relative to degree of lateral interdependence (i.e., extent to which leader's group must rely on other groups to work effectively)	Effective leaders tend to be more "accurately introspective" (i.e., know own strengths and limitations well), which enhances their ability to deal realistically with peers and superiors
Managerial motivation	High degree of managerial motivation and other traits (e.g., self-esteem, stress tolerance) necessary to handle hectic pace and administrative functions	Leaders are likely to have a strong need for power and positions of influence	Leader's high degree of ambition, initiative, persistence, and energy more likely to be channeled into necessary leadership behaviors (e.g., planning, organizing)	Function of the organization, size of group, and degree of administrative responsibility relevant (e.g., more stress and responsibility presumably requires higher levels of motivation)	Effective leaders seem especially able to call upon appropriate behaviors in crises, showing a willingness to act; overcome inertia and the tendency to let others take the risks. Also, demonstrate self-confidence and courage in making unpopular decisions, believing in their ultimate recognition as helpful

Adapted from Gary A. Yukl, 1981.

Choosing the Most Appropriate Approach

The extent to which the trait approach is valid is the extent to which selection methods hold the key to improved leadership. Traits and skills that can accurately be identified as critical for effectiveness in a given leadership position may be used as screening criteria for potential applicants. If the behavior approach is in fact more valid, then training and development techniques are more appropriate. Rather than having to choose the right people, effective leaders could be "grown." On the other hand, if it truly "all depends on the situation," then situation shaping or job design holds the answer to improving leadership. Of course, if all the approaches contain some truth, as the prevailing view holds, a multifaceted approach would yield the best results.

Implications of Simulation Findings for Developing Leaders

Our experience as simulation facilitators has left us with some very clear notions about how to nurture leadership potential. Whether embedded in formal training activities or ingrained in daily work interactions, these are the things we feel matter most in developing leaders.

1. Ensure that the basic tools are in place. A foundation of supervisory and management skills such as appraisal, delegation, interpersonal communication, and conflict management is necessary before moving to the higher plane of leadership. Since these skills are often lacking, a program covering this "remedial work" is recommended first.

2. Establish an environment that encourages experimentation with behavior. Let managers know that it is all right to fail and that reasonable risks are viewed as worth taking. Ways should be sought to get managers to go beyond their immediate, familiar responses to challenges—to dig deeper into their repertories for uncommon responses.

3. Provide opportunities for managers to learn how to analyze complex situations. This may be accomplished through a training program to teach a problem-solving, decision-making technique, or on the front lines with a challenging assignment. These are the shaping experiences that build self-confidence and "vision."

4. Reinforce the importance of balance and flexibility in confronting problems. Encourage managers to be simultaneously subjective and objective, tactical and strategic, analytical and synergistic—to be able to move back and forth comfortably as the situation demands.

5. Pace the manager's development with incremental steps keyed to the individual's capability. Keep the manager "on the edge" by easing into increasingly threatening situations but remaining just this side of failure, and where possible, with the safety net at hand.

This sharing of our thoughts has not been intended as an exhaustive or even a very scientific treatment of the subject. We see it as offering some potentially valuable guidelines, derived empirically from our extensive work with simulation participants, and offering corroboration of some of the findings in previous research.

Gaps Remain

Although the recent beginning attempts to pull things together seem promising, there are still many more questions than answers, and significant conceptual difficulties to be surmounted before success can be achieved. Perhaps the most obvious shortcoming is the well-established tradition in the field to pursue narrowly focused research on a single set of variables. Greater efforts at integration and building and less on "pushing one's pet theory" are needed to break the pattern. To enhance their potential contribution to a unified theory of leadership, each of the major schools has gaps to fill. The trait proponents must continue to improve the selection and measurement of traits, and clarify their relationships to situational variables. Considerably more must be learned about reciprocal influence processes and the consequences of exercising different forms of power.

The dynamics of political power acquisition and use is also inadequately understood. After innumerable studies, the specific behaviors that contribute to leader effectiveness have not been satisfactorily identified, nor is enough known about the timing, frequency, and content of these behaviors. As with traits, more must be learned about the implications of situational factors such as role expectations, nature of the work, and group cohesiveness on the effectiveness of leadership behavior. Leadership models which emphasize "style" have little explanatory value beyond the leader-subordinate relationship.[17,18] The situational, and other approaches, all need to deal with the fact that interaction with superiors, peers, and people outside the organization comprises a substantial part of the leadership role. It seems clear that the work needed to integrate the various approaches will require a framework broad enough to encompass leader traits, influence modes, behaviors, styles, roles, and situational variables. A difficult task, but not impossible.

References

1. Stogdill, R. M., *Handbook of Leadership: A Survey of Theory and Research*, Free Press, New York, 1974.

2. Miner, J. B., "The Uncertain Future of the Leadership Concept: An Overview," in J. G. Hunt and L. L. Larson, eds., *Leadership Frontiers*, Comparative Administration Research Institute, Kent State University, Kent, OH, 1975.

3. Hunt, J. G., and L. L. Larson, "We March to the Beat of a Different Drummer: An Overview," in J. G. Hunt and L. L. Larson, eds., *Leadership Frontiers*, Kent State University, Kent, OH, 1975.

4. Pfeffer, J., "The Ambiguity of Leadership," in M. W. McCall, Jr., and M. M. Lombardo, eds., *Leadership: Where Else Can We Go?*, Duke University Press, Durham, NC, 1978.

5. Katz, D., and R. L. Kahn, *The Social Psychology of Organizations*, 2d ed., Wiley, New York, 1978.

6. Lombardo, M. M., *"Looking at Leadership: Some Neglected Issues,"* Technical Report Number 6, Center for Creative Leadership, Greensboro, NC, 1978.

7. Bennis, W., "The Four Competencies of Leadership," *Training and Development Journal*, August 1984.

8. Yukl, G. A., *Leadership in Organizations*, Prentice-Hall, Englewood Cliffs, NJ, 1981.

9. McCall, M. W., Jr., *"Leaders and Leadership: Of Substance and Shadow,"* Technical Report Number 2, Center for Creative Leadership, Raleigh, NC, 1977.

10. Mintzberg, H., *The Nature of Managerial Work*, Harper & Row, New York, 1973.

11. Yukl, G. A., *Leadership in Organizations*, Prentice-Hall, Inc., Englewood Cliffs, NJ, 1981.

12. French, J. R. P., and B. Raven, "The Bases of Social Power," in D. Cartwright, ed., *Studies in Social Power*, Institute for Social Research, Ann Arbor, MI, 1959.

13. McCall, M. W., Jr., and M. M. Lombardo, eds., *Leadership: Where Else Can We Go?*, Duke University Press, Durham, NC, 1978.

14. Sayles, L. R., *Leadership: What Effective Managers Really Do and How They Do It*, McGraw-Hill, New York, 1979.

15. Burke, M. W., "Leaders: Their Behavior and Development," in D. A. Nadler, M. L. Tushman, and N. G. Harvany, eds., *Managing Organizations: Readings and Cases*, Little, Brown and Company, Boston, Toronto, 1982.

16. Kotter, J. P., *The General Managers*, The Free Press, New York, 1982.

17. Blake, R. R., and J. S. Mouton, *The Managerial Grid*, Gulf Publishing Company, Houston, 1964.

18. Hersey, P., and K. H. Blanchard, *Management of Organizational Behavior*, 3d ed., Prentice-Hall, Englewood Cliffs, NJ, 1977.

31

Organization Development

Glenn H. Varney

Glenn H. Varney is professor of Management and director of The Master in Organization Development program, Bowling Green State University, also, president of Management Advisory Associates, Inc., a consulting firm in Human Resource and Organization Development. He has three books published, with three more due to be published. These include Goal Driven Management, Teambuilding, and The Change Process. To his credit are over 50 articles in a variety of professional journals. Varney is past director of the OD division and vice president of ASTD. He holds several awards, including the ASTD Torch Award. He has a Ph.D. from Case Western Reserve University in Cleveland, Ohio.

At no time since the industrial revolution have society's attitudes, values, and beliefs about work and the work force and their relationship to organizations undergone such intensive scrutiny, debate, and change. Evidence of this change is all about us and has been recorded and discussed in a flood of articles, books, and reports. In the early seventies when the problem was beginning to be felt, it was described as follows:

> Because work is central to the lives of so many Americans, either the absence of work or employment in meaningless work is creating an increasingly intolerable situation. The human cost of this state of affairs is manifested in worker alienation. But the essential first step toward these goals is the commitment on the part of the policy maker in business, labor, and government to the improvement of the quality of work life in America.[1]

In general, American managers are faced with changing the cultural influences that relate to how people work in organizations. To the dismay of many managers, they find that their knowledge, skills, and techniques are not in tune with what has been described by Dr. Allan Filley as the second "great age of social experimentation."[2] They are faced with acquiring new managerial competencies and skills which involve learning to manage in a way which successfully influences a changing human work force seeking a quality work life. Thus in virtually every modern organization, those persons charged with responsibility for human resources management are seeking improved and new skills as well as a better understanding of the complex and changing relationships of human behavior in organizations.

One of the visible recent responses is the emergence of organization development (OD) as a framework for study within which professional managers, researchers, and academics alike can come to grips with the complexities involved in organizing and managing human resources. Four factors are involved in the evolving practice of OD:

1. It is a long-range effort to introduce planned change on a diagnosis which is shared by the members of an organization.

2. An OD program usually involves an entire organization or a coherent system or parts thereof.

3. Its goal is to increase organization effectiveness and enhance organizational choice in self-renewal.

4. The major strategy of OD is to intervene in the ongoing activities of the organization, facilitate learning, and make choices about alternative ways to proceed.[3]

Definition of OD

One of the most difficult things in compiling a manual on organization development is defining it exactly, so that the person unfamiliar with OD will have a sense of what it is and what it can do. There are at least four well-accepted definitions.*

1. OD is a planned change effort evolving the total system managed from the top to increased organizational effectiveness through planned interventions using behavioral science knowledge (Richard Bechart).

2. Using knowledge and techniques from the behavioral sciences, organization development attempts to integrate individual needs for growth and development with organizational goals and objectives in order to make more effective organizations (National Training Laboratories Institute).

3. OD is a process of planned organizational change which centers around a change agent who in collaboration with a client's systems attempts to apply valued knowledge from the behavioral sciences to client problems (Warren Bennis).

4. Achieving an idea of corporate excellence to strive toward and perfecting a sound system of management which can convert driving into action (Blake and Mouton).

The key words in these four definitions are:

Planned change

Total company

---

* See *Bibliography of Organizational Development Literature*, ASTD, Alexandria, VA, 1984.

Increased organizational effectiveness

Interventions

Behavioral science knowledge

Individual needs and company goals

Change agent

It seems clear from these definitions that the one main element is the word "change." To put it another way, it involves looking at the organization and helping the organization to change in the direction it desires to go.

In OD terminology, such a planned change for the total organization is called an "intervention." Basically, OD attempts to make use of the social and behavioral sciences. The "change agent," as referred to in the organization development field, is the person who serves as the catalyst or prime mover of the change strategy. The change agent may be an internal consultant, a manager, or an external change agent. For purposes of our discussion, think of the manager as a change agent. We believe every manager is responsible in some way for bringing about change in the organization, and therefore is the most likely person to be involved in OD.

One major corporation in the United States defines its OD approach as a "plan for applying appropriate resources to organization revitalization." It says, "It is a planned intervention in the ongoing management process with the explicit intent of applying new knowledge, new technology, new resources, and new individual organizational authenticity to the achievement of the organization's goals in a dynamic and uncertain environment." It furthermore states that the objective of the program is to "increase earnings now" and "to do so in such a way that the organization's capacity for continued growth and earnings is within its own control."

In addition, it states that the program is "a means of changing the management process from one of dependence on previous experiences to one of autonomy based on the utilization of total technical and human resources." This particular company does not think of OD as a programmatic effort. On the contrary, they see it as management in an organization renewal effort being conducted on a continuing basis.

Like other areas in the field of management practices, OD is based squarely on a variety of knowledge, skills, and experience. It is firmly rooted in such disciplines as psychology, organization behavior, and sociology.

The bulk of the literature applicable to OD is drawn from a variety of subject areas, such as:

History of organization behavior	Informal organization
Organization theory	Organization structure
Decision-making processes	Interpersonal dynamics
Organizational communication	Sociology
Nature and impact of technology	Organizations as systems
Behavioral analysis	Organizational effectiveness
Perceptual processes	Role theory
Learning process theory	Power and authority
Motivational theory	Leadership
Personality development	Small-group theory

In summary, the combined forces upon organizations from societal changes require managers in organizations to be more aware, more responsive, and more able to bring about change in accomplishing the organization's basic objectives and

540

tasks as well as in meeting the desire for human fulfillment now being expressed throughout American society.

History of OD

Dr. Wendell French (University of Washington) describes the early history of OD as follows:[4]

> Organization development programs emerged about 1957 and have at least three origins. One origin centers around the late Douglas McGregor's work with Union Carbide in an effort to apply some of the concepts and insights from laboratory training to a large system.
>
> The second origin centers around a headquarters human relations research group at the Esso Company. About the same year Douglas McGregor was beginning to work with Union Carbide, the Esso group began to view itself as an internal consulting group offering services to field managers—rather than as a research group writing reports for top management. In addition, with the help of Robert Blake and Herb Shepard, this group began to offer laboratory training in the refineries of Esso.
>
> Certainly a third origin of OD stems from the experience that researchers were gaining at the Survey Research Center at the University of Michigan in the use of attitude surveys and in feeding back survey results in an effort to change organizations. For example, Howard Baumgartel reported some research in 1959 which, in retrospect, was an article of very good insight on OD.* In his conclusions he stated,

> "The results of this experimental study lend support to the idea that intensive group discussion procedure for utilizing the results of an employee questionnaire survey can be an effective tool for introducing positive change in a business organization. It may be that the effectiveness of this method, in comparison to traditional training courses, is that it deals with the system of human relationships as a whole (superior and subordinate can change together) and it deals with each manager, supervisor, and employee in the context of his own job, and his own problems, and his own work relationships."

> At the present time, OD efforts are becoming visible in England, Norway, Sweden, Holland, Japan, Canada and perhaps other countries, as well as in the United States. They are appearing in a wide range of kinds of institutions, including business firms, schools, police departments, and hospitals.

Is OD Different from Other Employee Relations Activities?

A typical question asked by managers is, "How is organizational development different from other employee relations activities?" The easiest way to show the difference is to contrast other personnel activities such as manpower planning, recruiting and selection, and managerial and supervisory development. We look at the goals, the scope, the signs of how these particular programs fail, strategies for correcting systems failure, processes and activities that are used, typical problems encountered, the kind of time frames that the programs work under, organizational initiative (where does the impetus come from?), and the capability of specialists to perform the functions. We have summarized these differences in Fig. 31-1.

---

* Howard Baumgartel, "Using Employee Questionnaire Results for Improving Organizations: The Survey Feedback Experiment," *Kansas Business Review*, Vol. 12, pp. 2–6, December 1959.

Figure 31-1. Manpower resource management—functional interdependency (a description of how various manpower functions interrelate to support an effective program of manpower resource management).

Dimension	OMP Organization and Manpower Planning	OD Organization Development	RS Recruitment and Selection	MD Manager Development	MD Manpower Development
1. Goals	1. Relate and design organization to meet growth plans and changing environmental conditions to assure that organization will be able to accomplish its future objectives. 2. Assess present manpower strength and weaknesses in light of future manpower requirements with the objective of providing the needed talent to accomplish future objectives.	1. Improve organization effectiveness. 2. Utilize manpower resources more fully. 3. Facilitate change. 4. Manage conflict (internal and external). 5. Provide system for evaluating effectiveness of organization and its components.	1. Improve organization effectiveness. 2. Continuous supply of needed skills and talent (ability) required to man the organization today and in the future. 3. Provide internal inventory of manpower resources.	1. Improve organization effectiveness. 2. Identify high-potential manager. 3. Develop high-potential manager. 4. Provide adequate supply of managers.	1. Improve organization effectiveness. 2. Provide needed skills today and in the future. 3. Utilize and develop total manpower resources more fully.
2. Scope	Total organization and its components	Total organization and its components	Total organization and its components	Managers (as distinguished from supervisors; i.e., responsible for significant part of business—middle to top)	Total organization and its components

541

Figure 31-1. *Continued*

Dimension	OMP Organization and Manpower Planning	OD Organization Development	RS Recruitment and Selection	MD Manager Development	MD Manpower Development
3. Signs of system failure	1. Falling behind competition 2. Organizational conflict 3. Organization conflict (internal and external) 4. Profit decline 5. Lack of organization thrust (i.e., motivation)	1. Low acceptance ratios 2. High recruitment costs 3. Poor public image	1. Lack of manager replacement 2. High turnover of managers 3. Ineptness of managers (mistakes)	1. Inadequate skills 2. High turnover 3. Lack of identification with organization goals	
4. Strategy for correcting systems failure	1. Organization structure diagrams 2. Manpower audit and analysis	1. Organizational diagnosis 2. Organizational confrontation of problems	1. Design revision of strategy around OD diagnosis.	1. Design MD activities around OD diagnosis.	1. Design MD activities around OD diagnosis.
5. Processes and activities used	1. Reorganization—restructuring 2. Management systems change 3. Policy modification 4. Long-range planning	1. Confrontation meeting 2. Team building 3. Action research 4. Survey feedback 5. Intergroup problem solving	1. Confrontation meeting 2. External and internal environment research 3. Survey feedback, external and internal	1. Courses, conferences 2. Coaching 3. Job rotation 4. Manager assessment programs 5. Career paths	1. Courses, meetings 2. Communication media 3. Participative techniques

6. Typical problems encountered	1. Unpredictable organizational consequences 2. Shortages of manpower 3. Unsatisfactory manpower forecasting techniques lead to inaccurate forecasting.	1. Management failure to recognize need of OD approach to manpower resource management 2. High degree of suspicion of OD 3. Inadequate techniques and tools 4. High cost	1. Failure to provide resources to attract good people 2. Inability of management ro recognize cost of ineffective recruitment. 3. Lack of global approach to problems	1. Unwillingness to invest in MD 2. Failure to identify contributing managers 3. Inability to identify developmental needs 4. Manager resistance 5. Lack of useful techniques for MD	1. Unwillingness to invest in MD 2. Inability to identify developmental needs 3. Poorly designed, ill-conceived program
7. Time frame	Continuous	Continuous	Continuous	Continuous	Continuous
8. Organizational initiative	Top executives Personnel executive All managers Consultants	Top executives Personnel and OD executives All managers Consultants	Top executives Personnel executives All managers	Top executives Personnel and OD executives All managers Consultants	Personnel and OD executives All employees Consultants
9. Capabilities of specialists required.	Organization analysts Consultant Planner Statistician Operation research skills	OD diagnostician Consultant Catalyst	Systems analyst Decision maker Evaluator Salesperson	Diagnostician of MD needs Designer of programs	Diagnostician of needs Designer of programs Teacher

A Model for Systematic Change

OD relies on orderly change, change which has been carefully planned and thought through to assure that the end results have been reached without unforeseen or undesirable events. Those who practice OD use what is commonly called "action research." Action research means systematic analysis of an organization to understand the nature of the problems and forces within the organization. Furthermore, it means using the organization's own resources to solve problems and change the organization.

Models for systematic analysis abound in OD and serve a very important function. They provide a framework for studying organizations based on known theories of organization behavior. The practice of OD would indeed falter were it not for the models used by OD consultants.

Usefulness of a Model—A Framework for Analysis

Models are used in almost any endeavor or facet of our lives. For example, when an automobile is undergoing a new design, the architects always develop a model prior to the actual production process. Physicians doing diagnostic work-ups use a conceptual model of the illnesses using the symptoms as indicators. Models are used to design clothing. They are used to explain human activities; they're found in psychology to describe personalities. Models in general are very useful. They guide us in our search for information and understanding.

The values of a model for systematic change are many.

1. A model serves as a guide through a series of steps. In this way one is assured of not overlooking some aspect or failing to carefully analyze or study some particular part of the problem.

2. A model assures that attention is given to each step in proportion to its value to the total result. It is not uncommon for humans to emphasize one aspect of life or a particular problem and to deemphasize another. The model also serves to place proper emphasis at the most important and least important points.

3. Management, like any other field, has a strong need for systematic analysis. Systematic analysis is applied rigorously in the technical aspects of business where we apply computer technology, engineering technology, and so forth. It often does not show up in management practice. Therefore, a model assures managers of a more careful analysis, resulting in more accurate and correct decisions relative to the social and technical equation.

4. As in project management, models serve a manager by providing a tracking method for following the progress of change. For example, well-conceived models can be used in developing critical path plans for implementing change.

5. One of the least understood but most important values in a model is its utility in selling management on the need for change as well as the way in which the change is going to be managed. The advantage is the appearance of being organized and not "shooting from the hip." It gives the impression of doing your homework and having systematically examined the problem.

6. Explaining the need for change as well as exactly what is going to be done is more readily accomplished when a specific model of change is used.

Probably there are other reasons to justify the use of a systematic model for change; it suffices to say that any model used is better than no model at all.

Goals of Change—Improving Results and Outputs

Any time a change is made in an organization, it has the underlying purpose of improving the way the organization is functioning. In simpler terms, to increase productivity of a unit, group, or organization is the primary basis for change. Without the end result of improved productivity, there would be no need to change.

The following model emphasizes effectiveness of the organization, from the perspective of both efficient technology as well as efficient human performance, resulting in both high productivity and high satisfaction. It involves a smooth intermeshing of technical and human management of the organization.

The Change Process Model

The model which we propose is laid out in Fig. 31-2. The following is a brief description of each of the stages and associated steps.

Stage 1. In stage 1 we have identified separate segments of change associated with assessing the need for change and selling change goals within the organization. The steps involve conducting a *preliminary scan* of the organization to generate a problem statement or hypothesis statement which results in a series of questions to be answered for a particular problem or change objective to be accomplished.

Stage 2. Stage 2 attempts to understand the goal problem within the context of this organization's character so that we are assured that the correct targets have

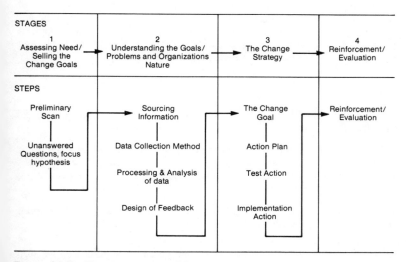

Figure 31-2. Change process model.

been identified and the problem clearly defined to avoid errors in the implementation of a strategy. This stage involves sourcing information within the organization, in other words, determining where the needed information is located. Second is development of methods and actual collection of the needed information. Third is processing and analyzing the data, and fourth is designing a feedback process for explaining what the data say and how they answer the specific questions outlined in stage 1.

Stage 3.   Stage 3 represents the actual change strategy for bringing about the desired adjustments within the organization. Four steps are involved:

1. The preparation of the change goal. Here we are attempting to clearly define what it is that we are trying to change in terms of behaviors, practices, and new assets.
2. Development of the action plan.
3. Testing the action plan. To make sure that it is the correct action and that it meets the change goals.
4. Implementing the action.

Stage 4.   Stage 4 involves reinforcement and evaluation of the change. In this stage the change agent is required to develop reinforcement processes and mechanisms and also to develop some form of evaluation. The purpose of the evaluation is to assess the degree to which the change strategy has actually brought about the desired change. In other words, to what degree has the problem been solved or the goal met?

The model at this point gives an overview of the change process. As we delve into each stage, we will cite the specific skills required for successful implementation of that stage.

We stress that a practicing manager or a student of management need not be fully qualified to use all the skills required at each stage. It is common practice in organizations to ask for assistance in particular areas as needed. For example, if statistical knowledge is required, you could call upon a statistical quality control analyst or a systems analyst to assist you. It is a commonly accepted belief, however, that managers must know enough about each of the skills to know when to seek assistance. All too often managers avoid a particular aspect of the change process because they do not have the needed skills and expertise.

How to Use a Model
for Change

The application of a model as a part of systematic and orderly change management has been emphasized several times. It cannot be emphasized enough. Change must be carefully conceived and systematically implemented. Several points need to be made regarding how to use this model.

1. A model can serve as a basis for laying out a project for change or it can become the framework for a proposal for change.
2. The model can be used as a road map for change. This guides the manager and members of the organization through the change process in a step-by-step systematic way.

3. The model can serve as a reminder of the need for a systematic discipline of change. Frequently managers and students of change do not apply adequate discipline to the change process, dismissing rigor as unnecessary and not accepted within the organization. Other excuses for not being systematic include "it is too costly," "it leads to incorrect decisions," and "we don't have time to think through what we need to do."

4. Whenever change starts to take place, you must recognize that you are entering into a *dynamic process*. This simply means that none of the variables, factors, or conditions will be constant—the entire system begins to change. It appears illusively clear to managers that there is a start and a finish to any change process. Because of the abstract nature of our thinking, this is probably necessary. However, it is almost impossible to point exactly to where change starts and where it finishes. As you work with the change process you must always keep in mind that when you initiate a particular aspect of change you are automatically affecting other aspects. In the process of using the model you need to recognize that factors are in a constant state of change and that the evaluation of each aspect or stage of the change process must be carefully reviewed. For instance, when you start to implement an action plan in stage 3, you begin immediately to change the definition of the problem identified in stage 1. The change agent must continuously reexamine the questions asked, the problem definition, and the resulting decisions.

Other Diagnostic Models

In the preceding section we introduced a change process model designed to assist change agents in systematic change analysis. OD abounds with diagnostic and explanatory models designed to guide practitioners in the process of change. Our purpose in this section is not to list all these models but to simply give you some other options.

Weisbord's Six-Box Model

Marvin M. Weisbord of Organizational Research & Development has designed a six-box diagnostic model.[5] The model is portrayed in Fig. 31-3.

The six boxes are purpose, structure, relationship, reward, helpful mechanisms, and leadership. These constitute the internal factors which the organization seeks to keep in balance. In general the organization as a whole, and each of its various subunits, must do something about each of these six factors. What it does and how it does it will depend to some extent on its environment. Basically the environment means forces difficult to control from inside that demand a response from the organization. Such forces include customers, government, unions, students, families, friends, and so forth. It is not always clear where the boundaries are between the external and internal environment. Basically the *purposes* of the organization include such things as goal clarity and agreement on goals by members of the organization. What is the organization attempting to do and where is it attempting to go? *Structure* has to do with the way in which the organization is put together. Common factors here include functions to be performed, products and services offered, and how they are to be combined into a cohesive organization which makes it possible to accomplish the goals stated under the heading of purpose.

Relationships are basically between people, such as peers, boss, and subordinate, between units within the organization, and between people and their technologies.

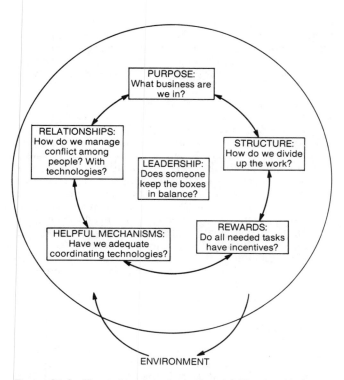

Figure 31-3. The six-box organizational model. Visualize this figure as a radar screen. Just as air controllers use radar to chart the course of aircraft—height, speed, distance apart, and weather—those seeking to improve an organization will observe relationships among the boxes and not focus on any particular blip.

Rewards have to do with satisfying the personal needs of people, including physiological safety, belongingness, esteem, and personal growth.

Helpful mechanisms simply mean do we have the technologies and systems in place within the organization to make it possible to accomplish things.

Leadership, as the word implies, means the ability the leaders have to direct the organization in a way which makes it cohesive, coherent, and able to perform its needed task to accomplish its goals.

Nadler Systems Model

David Nadler has designed a model which essentially covers most of the same factors that Weisbord covers but portrays them in a different way.[6] His model is shown in Fig. 31-4.

Nadler portrays the systems diagnostic model as a input-output model or a systems model, the input factors being the factors from within the environment, the kinds of resources that are needed to accomplish the tasks within the organization, and the history of the environment and the factors leading up to accomplishment of the particular task at hand. The transformation part of it has to do with the

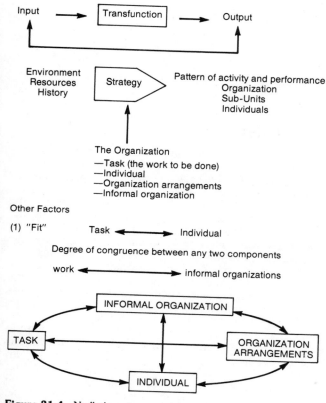

Figure 31-4. Nadler's systems model.

design of strategies which will use the environment resources history in a way which will accomplish the outputs. The factors which must be considered in organizing coherent strategy include the tasks that people must perform, the nature of the individuals performing those tasks, the way in which the organization is arranged or structured, and the informal structure or informal organization and how it operates.

The outputs are such things as patterns of activities and the way in which the organization performs, from an organizational point of view, from the point of view of subunits, and from the point of view of individuals. Nadler uses the process of organizational change and diagnosis as one of developing congruencies between the various components within the organization or, as he refers to it, "It is a fit between the tasks and the individuals trying to accomplish the tasks," or the degree of congruity between any two components within the organization. He portrays this concept in the following way: Combining the individuals who perform tasks, arranging the organization in a structure that will accomplish the goals, and recognizing the presence of this informal organization all interact together. Having these factors fit appropriately and with few or any discongruities would be the objective of an OD practitioner, for in Nadler's model the practitioner looks for misfits among the four systems.

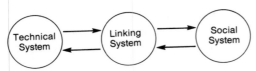

Figure 31-5. Basic organizational system.

A Social-Technical Model

Any organization is comprised of three basic components, the technical component, the linking component, and the social component. These three major systems must interface and function efficiently and coherently for the organization to accomplish its objectives. The model is shown in Fig. 31-5.

A technical system is comprised of factors such as the physical facility, the equipment, the materials, the manufacturing systems, the flow of materials, the layout of the plant, lighting, and the physical environment in general.

A social system is comprised of the individuals within the organization, the subgroups within the organization, the informal organization, interpersonal relationships, and the personal needs and wants of each individual.

The linking system is comprised of the leadership in the organization, the procedure and practices and policies, the organizational structure, and any factors needed to combine the technical system with the social system in order to achieve the objectives of the organization.

This approach to organizational analysis is a simple way of characterizing the factors which must be taken into consideration when analyzing how a particular organization functions. A misfit between any of the systems can create a problem or an incongruity. The diagnostician using a model such as this looks for misfits and incongruities. Also this model can be used for tracking or mapping to look for the cause and effect relationships of problems. The social-technical systems model provides a convenient way of going to the source of the problem. Or it can be used as an organizational planning model. When considering change, for example, of a physical layout of a plant, this model can be used to track the impact that the change will have on the social as well as the linking system.

The three models we have presented represent only a fraction of the models available. Others are Hornstein and Tichy's emergent pragmatic model, Lawrence and Lorsch's contingency models, and Levenson's clinical historical approach, to mention a few.

Organizational practitioners will find the systems analysis model to be very helpful in two ways: (1) as a means of assuring that systems diagnosis is done in an orderly way, (2) as a way to communicate clearly and concisely with the client organization.

OD Techniques and Interventions

In this section we will discuss various techniques and approaches used in OD. The approaches described are not the only ones available. Also, depending on the organization and the consultant using it, a given approach may be known by more than one name. The purpose is to give a general idea of the techniques and

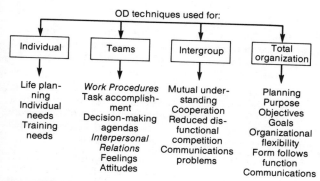

Figure 31-6. Use of OD techniques.

approaches. To assist in implementing changes, this section concludes by giving an example of how a strategy can be built using OD techniques.

Overview of OD Techniques

Figure 31-6 illustrates a variety of techniques. Different approaches are recommended at different levels within the organization. No attempt will be made to go into detail; however, the definitions and explanations which follow should help in understanding the techniques.

Description of OD Techniques

Seven OD techniques follow:

1. *Laboratory Training.* This ranges in length from 2 to 3 days to 2 weeks. It is aimed primarily at giving participants a better understanding of what makes them tick and what makes groups function as they do, as well as a greater understanding of interpersonal and intergroup communication. The focus can vary from great emphasis on organizational values and problems to great emphasis on inter- and intraindividual values and problems.

  a. *Strangers laboratory.* Participants are usually from different organizations and may include both men and women. Participants commonly have widely varying backgrounds, skills, professions, and trades.

  b. *Cousins laboratory.* Participants from the same business, educational, or governmental organization, but usually no bosses in the same group with subordinates and no two people from the same work subgroup.

  c. *Family laboratory.* Usually includes the manager and the people reporting directly to him or her. It sometimes includes other key people in the manager's organization.

2. *Team Building.* The focus is on early identification and solution of the work group's problems, particularly the interpersonal and organizational roadblocks

which stand in the way of the team's collaborative, cooperative, creative, competent functioning.

    a. Establishing new teams. The focus is upon the participants and the manager developing a common framework and common goals within which they can work, also on identifying problems which would prevent team members from working with each other, e.g., task forces, proposal teams.

    b. Strengthening existing teams. This activity looks back over the recent past to determine what the strengths and the problems have been in the way the organization has conducted its business, to develop action plans to solve the problems, and to capitalize on the unit's strengths.

    c. Re-forming teams. Much like 2(a) above, but here many of the participants have worked with or perhaps even for each other (e.g., because of mergers and acquisitions). The focus is on problems the participants anticipate will develop in working together.

3. *Diagnostic techniques.* The main thrust here is diagnostic, i.e., to find out what the problems are with little emphasis on solutions.

    a. Vertical sensing. This involves interviewing, usually in small groups, an entire vertical slice of an organization to find out the nature of the main problems and the degree to which these problems are felt or make waves at the different levels within the organization. As nearly as possible the interviewers all report to each other in a vertical slice and would be able to discuss the impact of problems as they were understood and felt in the various levels in the organization. This procedure can be carried below the exempt-salaried level through the entire organization to the least-skilled employee.

    b. Horizontal sensing. This is usually done in small groups on a random basis, but participants come from no more than three or four levels in the organization, as contrasted with 3(a) above. The focus is upon identifying problems most relevant for a general grouping of people—such as middle-level managers, engineers, and manufacturing specialists. Though people at several levels are polled, participants in any one meeting are usually from only one or two organizational levels.

    c. Division consulting teams. This team is usually comprised of a division's general manager, its personnel manager, and an outside consultant. The latter is someone skilled in organizational development technology, usually on a university faculty or with a private consulting firm. Sometimes the outside consultant is an expert from within the company, but not in that particular group or division. This team meets regularly, usually monthly, to discuss the current climate or health of the division, to review effectiveness of ongoing personnel programs, to spot new problems, and to plan future actions.

    d. Organizational mirroring. In this technique, people from a number of functional units within the organization are interviewed to gain a comprehensive picture of how one of those units appears in the eyes of the others. Example: A manufacturing organization wants to know more about how it is viewed by others—what its interface problems are. A sample of people in manufacturing are interviewed to determine how they see themselves and how they assess their relations with other units. Then people from the other organizations with whom manufacturing must work (sales, engineering, personnel, etc.) are interviewed to determine how they see manufacturing. When these results are combined, manufacturing can see from the data how they appear to the other organizations as well as how they see themselves.

4. *Intergroup meetings.* This is primarily a problem-solving mechanism. Such meetings are usually held when problems are known to exist and have become somewhat acute. The focus is on putting the cards on the table in such a way that the really difficult hang-ups are spotlighted and solutions, with time lines, are proposed.

    a. Subgroups of an organization. Example: The sales engineers in a sales unit are technically trained as engineers but have been making promises to the customers about engineering changes in the product without the knowledge of the people in the engineering unit. The focus of the meeting would be on what kind of damage is being done and how this damage can be minimized or avoided.

    b. Line and staff. Examples of difficulties here are frequent and need not be cited. Because of the nature of their work, line and staff people frequently (though most inadvertently) step on each other's toes. From time to time meetings are in order to help clear the air between them.

    c. Customers. Perhaps the most difficult intergroup meeting to design. Usually if the buyer is willing to talk, the customer is not—and vice versa. These meetings should be designed carefully, and a high level of skill is required. Potentially, however, its payoffs can be among the highest.

5. *Third party facilitation.* This involves the use of a knowledgeable, sensitive, and skilled third person to help diagnose, understand, and resolve the problems. Usually the helping mode is that of the consultant working intensively with the manager to help him or her work through some particularly difficult problems which he or she has encountered.

    a. Improving managerial effectiveness. Example: A manager who is unsure of his or her impact on others, or perhaps of how efficiently he or she uses time, invites a third person to be with him or her for half a day or a day. The manager's job is business as usual. The consultant's job is to observe and listen to the content and the process of everything the manager does during that time period. Then the consultant and the manager go back over the consultant's notes and the two discuss the manager's style and possible ways it could be improved.

    b. Debriefing staff meetings. A manager should regularly use the last 10 or 15 minutes of staff meetings to ask those present what they thought of the staff meeting and how it might be improved. From time to time, the manager might find it helpful to ask a third party to sit in. Preferably the third party would be someone who knows the group and has a level of acceptance in the group. This person's job is to observe how the staff meeting is conducted and how the members of the staff interact. The observer often provides feedback to the group and to the manager at the end of the meeting.

    c. Difficult one-to-one discussions. A third party is invited by two individuals to sit with them as they try to work out some particularly difficult situation. Often this is a manager and one of the employees working for him or her. The need frequently arises when one or both are somewhat shy or nonconfronting and find it difficult to discuss the problem. In this case the problem usually stems from their attitudes toward each other and not from the work itself. Sometimes it is because the manager is an overpowering person, and the subordinate needs some emotional support in talking about the issue with him or her. No matter the reason for the third party, it should be clearly understood that the third party is not a judge and does not have a final say in any element of the confrontation. He or she is there to help each say what must be said, to pick up hidden themes which may emerge, and to help them invent solutions.

6. *Consulting pairs.* Many times the manager can benefit from a close and continuing relationship with someone outside of his or her own organization (an external consultant). This should be someone the manager trusts, who has a good understanding of managerial skills, who is willing to learn about the manager's organization and its problems, who can help the manager spot problems early, and who can help develop solutions for these problems. One advantage of this kind of pairing rests in the fact that the consultant, not being in the organization all the time, can often see trends and roadblocks more objectively than the manager. Often a member of the personnel department can function as a consultant to a manager.

7. *Consultant network.* In an effective organizational development effort, those who participate in the program may come to see themselves as consultants to each other. In fact, an OD effort cannot be truly successful unless a great majority of the participants are willing to help each other when asked to do so. It becomes a group norm. Once such a norm is established, with little extra organizational effort an internal "consultant" network can be formed. From this network (which is also an OD skills bank) a manager or supervisor can draw the kind of help needed to solve particularly tough or knotty problems.

It is almost a certainty there will be situations for which none of these procedures seems appropriate. The best bet in that case, or indeed in any case, is to get together with your own "external consultant" or OD resource and design a program or strategy as appropriate as possible for your situation.

In this section we have sketched out some basic techniques and approaches used in organizational development. Sources of information relative to other approaches are available as indicated in the resources list at the end of this chapter. Figure 31-7 is an inventory of the OD techniques which will be helpful.

Role Description

The following example includes most typical activities performed by an organization development function.[7]

Organization Planning and Systems Development

Charter. To help develop a fully functioning organization whose goals and objectives are achieved through optimal use of its human and material resources.

Organization planning and systems development are primarily the responsibility of operating management. The role of the organization and systems group is to provide technical assistance to management for achieving its goals and objectives. This group serves as an internal consultant to line management on a variety of issues regarding (1) organization structuring, (2) management system design, (3) performance evaluation, and (4) problems that often involve interfacing groups.

Approaches, Techniques	Application			
	Individual	Team	Intergroup	Total Organization
Strangers laboratory	_____	_____	_____	_____
Cousins laboratory	_____	_____	_____	_____
Family laboratory	_____	_____	_____	_____
Team building				
New teams	_____	_____	_____	_____
Strengthening existing teams	_____	_____	_____	_____
Reforming teams	_____	_____	_____	_____
Diagnostic				
Vertical sensing	_____	_____	_____	_____
Horizontal sensing	_____	_____	_____	_____
Consulting teams	_____	_____	_____	_____
Organizational mirroring	_____	_____	_____	_____
Intergroup confrontations				
Subgroups	_____	_____	_____	_____
Line and staff	_____	_____	_____	_____
Customers	_____	_____	_____	_____
Third-party facilitation				
Improve managerial effectiveness	_____	_____	_____	_____
Debriefing staff meetings	_____	_____	_____	_____
Difficult one-to-one discussions	_____	_____	_____	_____
Consulting pairs	_____	_____	_____	_____
Consulting network	_____	_____	_____	_____
Life planning	_____	_____	_____	_____
Job enrichment	_____	_____	_____	_____
Individual consultation	_____	_____	_____	_____
Group observation	_____	_____	_____	_____
Peer coaching and counseling	_____	_____	_____	_____
Start-up meetings	_____	_____	_____	_____
Group development for training	_____	_____	_____	_____
Boss-secretary meetings	_____	_____	_____	_____
Husband-wife teams	_____	_____	_____	_____
Unit staff program	_____	_____	_____	_____
Use outside professional assistance	_____	_____	_____	_____
Consistency in compensation	_____	_____	_____	_____
Goal setting (MBO)	_____	_____	_____	_____
Developing data	_____	_____	_____	_____
Training for change	_____	_____	_____	_____
Integration of manpower	_____	_____	_____	_____
Interdisciplinary task teams	_____	_____	_____	_____
Job movement	_____	_____	_____	_____
Self-development	_____	_____	_____	_____
Role playing	_____	_____	_____	_____
Getting acquainted	_____	_____	_____	_____
Nonverbal encounters	_____	_____	_____	_____
Other _____	_____	_____	_____	_____

Figure 31-7. Checklist of OD approaches and techniques.

Goals

1. To develop a fully functioning organization that optimizes its human and material resources in accomplishing its specific goals and objectives
2. To develop a work climate built on openness, trust, and respect for individual members
3. To develop a proactive organization that anticipates problems (where possible) before they occur and plans for them as soon as it is realistically possible
4. To affix appropriate authorities and responsibilities for organization members and facilitate the development of a work climate that encourages individual initiative and personal fulfillment
5. To create, develop, and maintain effective management systems that are designed to facilitate optimal organization performance

Responsibilities and Authorities

1. Assist management in diagnosing organization or system problems and implementing plans to overcome them
2. Conduct studies to ascertain optimal organization structure or management system design
3. Develop and implement plans for initiating and maintaining organization or management system changes
4. At management's direction, assess the effectiveness of designated corporatewide or divisional programs with respect to their stated goals and objectives
5. Identify and develop plans for increasing management effectiveness and improving work relationships
6. Participate in the design or redesign of organizations or management systems
7. Coordinate the implementation of newly established functions

Approach

To provide an internal consulting resource to management

1. To identify barriers to effective organization performance
2. To analyze conditions which impact the organization and affect its performance
3. To propose action plans which can resolve organizational problems through effective problemsolving and decisionmaking
4. To assist management in designing and implementing plans to resolve problems

To assist client organizations in

1. Identifying and clarifying goals and objectives
2. Identifying barriers to achieving goals and objectives
3. Analyzing possible causes of continuing organizational problems
4. Developing effective problem-solving mechanisms
5. Designing and implementing plans to overcome problems identified

Typical Activities

Organization

- Analyzing functions (who does what)
- Organization structuring
- Identifying authorities and responsibilities
- Job design and redesign

Systems

- Mapping out the present system
- Identifying dysfunctions caused by duplication, omissions, inefficiencies
- Planning for attaining system improvement

Planning

- Identifying short- and long-term goals and objectives
- Anticipating problems
- Developing plans to maximize organizational effectiveness
- Improving communication, feedback
- Enhancing problem-solving capabilities at lowest possible level

Applied research

- Analyzing policies, procedures, and practices of the client organization
- Assessing organization effectiveness as it relates to its external environment, interfacing organizations, members' perceptions
- Identifying or clarifying goals and objectives
- Developing standards of performance
- Examining management practices
  - Hiring
  - Promotion
  - Grievance handling
  - etc.
- Evaluating ongoing programs
- Operating plans
- Manpower plans
- Succession planning
- Minority programs
- High-potential programs
- Professional development

Procedures

1. Ascertain the objectives of the project to be undertaken with the client
2. Gather data that clarify the extent of the problems that relate to the project objectives
3. Present preliminary findings to the client for further clarification and/or direction
4. Propose a specific plan of action that will

- Clearly identify the problem
- Identify a feasible problem-solving model
- Implement proposed solutions
- Evaluate outcomes

5. Conclude the project when satisfactory results have been achieved

Specific Competencies

1. Problem identification

- Intrapersonal
- Interpersonal
- Interorganizational

2. Data gathering

- From surveys
- From interviews
- From existing historical data
- etc.

3. Data feedback

- Clarification of felt problems
- Climate analysis
- Management systems performance

4. Designing problem-solving models

- Appropriate to the situation
- Collaborative
- Participative (as appropriate)

5. Developing action plans

- Specific to the task
- Supported by the client
- Within target dates

6. Evaluating outcomes

- Consultant's actions

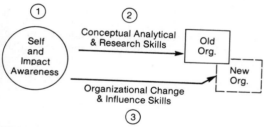

Figure 31-8. OD professional development.

- Effectiveness of the project's design
- Establish criteria for evaluating effectiveness of action plans

OD Skills

The skills needed in professional development for OD are shown in Fig. 31-8.[8] This design attempts to describe the three areas in relationship to the individual practitioner and the client organization involved.

Self- and Impact Awareness

This developmental area emphasizes the knowledge that an individual has of his or her own personal needs, values, and abilities including such factors as the need for control and power, need to achieve, and need for affiliation. Before an individual can work effectively with others he or she must have thorough awareness of self. OD practitioners who try to explain the importance of values in an organization while not aware of their own value structure and the role their values play in influencing approaches to an organization's problems will defeat themselves.

Although self-awareness has been given considerable attention, it has been from the point of view of personal growth, not from that of the client-consultant relationship. For instance, consultants need to be continuously aware of the role they are playing as an influence agent. Are they persuading and selling an organization to change toward their own goals and values, or are they trying to help the organization select, sift, and sort out its values and goals? Many OD practitioners, under the guise of helping their clients, teach them participative leadership, collaborative decision making, and open communications whether the client wants it or not.

A second part of self-awareness is a clear understanding of the impact that one has on another person or on an organization. In other words, how do practitioners use their personal traits or style to convey help or influence the client organization? A number of OD practitioners proudly and openly talk about learning to dramatize their points in order to persuade the client to action. Personally, I see nothing wrong with using personal skills to help an organization but not when individuals become so enamored with their personal style that it takes precedence over the client's needs.

There is a more subtle way in which the consultant's personal style can interfere with accurate OD actions. Any time that a consultant or third party enters a system, that entrance, even if just to collect data, will change the dynamics of the organization. The consultant has to have a sense of the degree to which the client (whether the client is an individual, group, or total system) has adapted to the consultant's presence. Clearly, any intervention is only as good as the accuracy of the diagnosis, and many interventions are based on hasty conclusions that ignore the impact of the consultant.

Conceptual, Analytical, and Research Skills

The second developmental area involves conceptual, analytical, and research skills. These skills are normally considered to be reserved for the social researcher. Many OD practitioners do not feel that these skills are needed or are of value in their work as organizational consultants. I take a contrary position and do not believe that OD professionals can serve their clients without a thorough development of these skills. The ability to develop hypotheses about the organization's behavior and prepare analytical formats for collecting information to prove or disprove the hypotheses is crucial if we are to move beyond the state of an intuitive art to an objectifiable science. These skills require an intimate knowledge of the conceptualization process, data collection processes, and statistical analytical procedures that are necessary to any carefully designed research.

Discussions with OD practitioners on this particular skill area will, of course, generate a wide range of viewpoints. The time has arrived for OD professionals to see themselves as social researchers as much as organizational "artists." OD practitioners can retain art skills while developing scientific skills. The combination of both, plus being sensitive to the organization and its constructs while at the same time being thorough, analytical, and careful, can only increase the ability to help the client organization.

Organizational Change and Influence Skills

The third skill area is closely allied with the first: both require personal development. The difference is that the third area is more task-specific. It requires the development of such specific skills as the ability to design interventions to meet particular situations and the ability to make conscious choices about the change strategies to be recommended. When a particular problem occurs, a well-trained OD professional should be able to develop a specific intervention to fit the unique learning needs of that organization. Unfortunately, too many consultants feel that the right exercise can always be found in the "OD manual." Second, the individual consultant needs to be able to design well-conceived plans and strategies for helping the organization move from point A to point B. This is not dissimilar to the types of planning that engineers use when laying out "critical data" for construction projects. The set of learnable skills associated with systems planning are just as appropriate to OD as to engineering.

References

1. *Work in America, Report of Special Task Force to the Secretary of Health, Education and Welfare,* MIT, Cambridge, MA, 1973.

2. From casual conversation with Dr. Allan Filley at the Academy of Management meeting, 1976.

3. Sherwood, John J., *An Introduction to Organization Development*, Experimental Publication System, American Psychological Association, Issue 11, 1971.

4. French, Wendell, "A Definition and History of Organization Development: Some Comments," *Proceedings of the 31st Annual Meeting of the Academy of Management*, Atlanta, GA, Aug. 15–18, 1971. Used by permission.

5. Weisbord, Marvin M., *Diagnosing Your Organization*, Organization Research & Development, Division of Petrella Assoc., 1976.

6. Presented during the 1981 Annual Conference, Human Resource Planning Society, Tampa, FL.

7. Partin, Jennings J., *Current Perspectives in Organization Development*, Addison-Wesley, Reading, MA, 1973.

8. Varney, Glenn H., "Training Organization Development Practitioners: A Need for Clarity and Direction," *Organization Behavior Journal*, Vols. III, IV.

Resources

Various universities and colleges throughout the United States have programs designed to train OD practitioners. They are:

The American University
Institute for Human Resources
Development
215 Ward Circle
Washington, DC 20016
(202) 686-7910
Degree: AU/NTL Master's Degree
in Human Resource Development

Boston University
School of Management
685 Commonwealth Ave.
Boston, MA 02215
(617) 353-2680
Degree: DBA in OB or OD
Ph.D. in Social Psychology with
OD concentration

Bowling Green State University
College of Business
Dept. of Management
Bowling Green, OH 43403
(419) 372-2946
Degree: Masters in Organization
Development

Brigham Young University
Dept. of Organization Behavior
790 TNRB
Provo, UT 84602
(891) 378-2664

Degree: Masters in Organization
Behavior

Case Western Reserve University
Dept. of Organizational Behavior
Sears Library Building
Cleveland, OH 44106
(216) 368-3055 or 368-2000
Degree: MS in OD and Analysis
(open only to people who live
and work full-time in NE Ohio)

Clark University
Dept. of Management
950 Main St.
Worcester, MA 01610
(617) 793-7400
Degree: MBA—Concentration in OD

Columbia University
Teachers College Box 6
525 W. 120th St.
New York, NY 10027
(212) 678-3249 or 678-3000
Degree: MA in Organization
Psychology (Doctoral
Program Planned)

Eastern Michigan University
Department of Management
504 Pray-Harrold
Ypsilanti, MI 48197

(313) 487-3240
Degree: MSOD: Masters of
   Science in Organization
   Behavior and Development

The Fielding Institute
226 East de La Gucara
Santa Barbara, CA 93101
(805) 963-6601
Degree: MA in OD (Ph.D. in OD
   planned)

George Washington University
School of Government and
   Business Administration
Washington, DC 20052
(202) 676-6205
Degree: DBA, MBA

Loyola University
Program in Community & OD
820 North Michigan Ave.
Chicago, IL 60611
(312) 274-3000
Degree: MA in Community and OD

Massachusetts Institute of
   Technology (MIT)
Sloan School of Management
50 Memorial Dr.
Cambridge, MA 02139
Degree: Ph.D. in OB, MS in
   Management (Organization
   Studies)

New York State University
Graduate School of Business
   Administration
90 Trinity Place
New York, NY 10006

(212) 285-6060
Degree: MBA in OD

Pepperdine University
School of Business and
   Management
3415 Sepulveda Blvd.
Los Angeles, CA 90034
(213) 306-5598, (408) 354-4041
Degree: MS in OD

Purdue University
School of Management
Krannert Building
W. Lafayette, IN 47907
(317) 494-4525
Degree: Ph.D. in Organization
   Behavior

University Associates
8517 Production Ave.
San Diego, CA 92121
(619) 578-5900
Degree: Masters Human Resource
   Development

University of New Hampshire
Whittemore School of Business
McConnell Hall
Durham, NH 03824
(603) 862-2771, 862-1234
Degree: MBA (OD concentration
   second year)

University of West Florida
School of Business
Pensacola, FL 32514
(904) 474-2308
Degree: Masters in OD

Associations and groups specifically involved in organization development are
listed below.

Academy of Management
OD Division
c/o Boston University
School of Management
621 Commonwealth
Boston, MA 02215

American Society for Training
and Development
Curtis E. Plott, Exec. Dir.
1630 Duke St. Box 1443
Alexandria, VA 22313

(703) 683-8100
*Training and Development
Journal* (monthly)

R. Wayne Boss, Editor
AM-OD Div. Newsletter
c/o University of Colorado
Campus Box 473
Boulder, CO 80309
(303) 492-8488

Center for the Study of OD
Ethical Dilemmas

Mark S. Frankel, Ph.D., Dir.
Center for the Study of Ethics
in the Profession
Illinois Institute of Technology
Chicago, IL 60616
(312) 567-3017

Certified Consultants Intern. CCI
(Formerly IAASS)
Dr. Stanley Hinkley
Box 573
Brentwood, TN 37027
(615) 377-1306

International Registry of OD
Professionals
Dr. Donald W. Cole, RODC, Editor
6501 Wilson Mills Rd., Suite K
Cleveland, OH 44143
Organizations and Change
(monthly), *The OD Journal*
(quart.), *International Registry
of OD Professionals* (annually)

NTL Institute
Joseph Potts, Exec. Dir.
P.O. Box 9155, Rosslyn Station
501 Wilson Blvd.
Arlington, VA 2209
(703) 527-1500

The OD Interorganization Group
(worldwide)

Dr. Donald W. Cole, RODC, Cont.
11234 Walnut Ridge Rd.
Chesterland, OH 44026
(216) 461-4333

The Organization Development
Institute
Dr. Donald W. Cole, RODC
11234 Walnut Ridge Rd.
Chesterland, OH 44026
(216) 461-4333
Organizations and Change
(monthly), *The OD Journal* (quart.),
*International Registry of OD
Professionals* (annually)

Organization Development
Network
Tony Petrella, Exec. Dir.
c/o Block/Petrella Assoc.
1011 Park Ave.
Plainfield, NJ 07060
(201) 561-8677
The OD Practitioner

University Associates, Inc.
8517 Production Ave.
San Diego, CA 92121
(619) 578-5900
800-854-2143 except
California, Arkansas, and
Hawaii

In this chapter we have attempted to provide the reader with a concise overview of organization development. The field is expanding rapidly, requiring a continuous updating of knowledge and skills. To keep abreast of these changes is part of responsible professionalism.

32

Executive Development

Walter R. Mahler

Walter R. Mahler is chairman of Mahler Associates, Inc., of Midland Park, New Jersey. He is best known for two books: Executive Continuity, written with Bill Wrightnour, and Succession Planning in Leading Companies, written with Frank Gaines. He has contributed to the design of executive development programs for many of the Fortune 500. Over four hundred executives have graduated from the Advanced Management Skills Program for General Managers designed by Mahler. The 8-week program, scheduled 1 week a quarter, incorporates many novel features. In addition to the above books, Mahler has authored The Succession Planning Handbook for the Chief Executive, How Effective Executives Interview, Structure, Power and Results, and Diagnostic Studies (for Human Resources). Mahler graduated with a B.A. from Northern Colorado University and with an M.A. and Ph.D. from Columbia University. He is a member of ASTD, The Psychological Association, and the American Association for the Advancement of Science.

Executive Development: What Is It?

Day after day, human resource development practitioners are admonished about their responsibilities. The list of responsibilities keeps getting longer and longer. Dire predictions are made to increase the sense of urgency. Before adding to the list of critical responsibilities, let me first discuss what executive development is about. There may be five key positions in a small organization or five hundred in a mammoth company. Periodically, the key positions become open. They must be filled. Your organization has an effective executive development effort if:

- You can fill key positions without delay.
- You can fill the positions without going outside.

- You can fill the positions with confidence.
- Your choices prove to be quite successful.
- Talented personnel don't quit very often.

This definition permits us to say that executive development is one of the primary responsibilities of the human resource practitioner. Executive development is critical to the continued success of every organization.

A Systems Approach Is Necessary

I firmly believe that the critical challenge of executive development can be successfully accomplished. It can be accomplished, but it takes a comprehensive approach.

Major Requirements for a Systems Approach

Any attempt to identify the major requirements in a comprehensive executive development system cannot avoid a certain arbitrariness. I suggest that there are 10 major requirements. It might be asked if there are other major ones. Possibly, but the 10 recommended ones have proven themselves in a variety of organizations. Some skeptic may well question if all 10 are necessary. No they are not. Considerable progress toward the executive development purposes can be made with sustained action on three or four of the requirements. However, experience with numerous companies suggests that the organization which implements more of the requirements increases its likelihood of achieving successful results. The 10 major requirements have to do with:

1. The purpose of executive development
2. Top-management action
3. Professional staff contribution
4. Human resources review
5. A helpful data system
6. Corporatewide selection
7. Development of future high-level managers
8. Getting results from an investment in manager education
9. Getting a developmental contribution from an objectives program
10. Integration of the executive development effort with other management programs

First Requirement: Establishing Purposes

Why do we put purpose as the number one requirement? In the last decade, most large organizations have become much more deliberate about their executive development. Systems and procedures are in place. But this is the crux of the problem. Procedures, policies, and programs came into being because they were the popular thing to do. Several bellwether companies had established executive development programs. Scores of companies began the visitation routine to copy the bellwethers. The bellwether companies' procedures, techniques, and methods became widely disseminated. No one started by establishing purposes. Company after company rushed into program mechanics. Time went by and disillusionment set in. The programs didn't live up to their promises. So what happened? One of three things. A new staff executive was hired, a new program was introduced, or the forms were changed. The cycle of hope and disappointment was again repeated. Watching this sequence of events occur, over and over, finally leads to the conclusion that the "Achilles heel" of executive development is the lack of well-thought-out purposes and philosophy. Some years ago, a participant in our semiannual executive development workshop bought our suggestion about purposes being a first step. A new chief executive wanted to revitalize an established program. The human resources executive worked out the following purposes with the top executive. The purposes were:

1. For every key position, management will have at least one "ready-now" backup.

2. Ninety percent of key management position openings will be filled from within.

3. Critical turnover will not exceed 4 percent. (Critical turnover was defined as a key manager who resigned or retired early that the company did not want to have leave.)

4. Managers appointed to key management positions will have been previously identified as backups at least 90 percent of the time.

5. An individual will not stay in a key management position for longer than 7 years.

6. Selection successes will be 95 percent or better for internal selections and 75 percent for external selections.

I can report that the executive development program has been revitalized, as shown by the achievement of their purposes. All levels of management now understand why new or revised methods have been introduced. Let us now consider some suggestions on what you might do about purposes and philosophy pertaining to executive development.

Suggestions for Those Who Are Getting Underway with a New Executive Development Program

1. *Start with one specific purpose.* You probably have a major concern right now. Fine, let's convert that into a specific purpose. Pick a very basic purpose, one that has a significant impact upon the future of the organization. Yes, we do have a favorite purpose. Do give it serious consideration. It is: The company will have at least two well-qualified, internal candidates for each key position to be filled.

2. *Avoid borrowing methods from another company.* There is a natural tendency to get started by "borrowing" from another company. With a few exceptions, companies with a well-established executive development program have complex ones. They do five or six things. They do them simultaneously. It is quite likely that you should do only one thing to start with and do it well.

3. *Do a self-analysis about your purpose.* Earlier I suggested concentrating upon one specific purpose. Before rushing into a program it is wise to do a bit of self-analysis. Let's assume that you established the purpose we mentioned above: The company will have at least two well-qualified, internal candidates for each key position we have to fill. Ask yourself two questions:

- What things are helping you currently?
- What things are currently hindering you?

Remember, getting the desired results requires that you get executives to change some habits. Techniques and processes do help, but it takes dedication and discipline to get a change in habits.

Suggestions for Those with an Established Executive Development Program:

1. *Establish three or four very specific purposes.* The purposes should reflect the concerns of top management. Identify where they would like to have a competitive advantage.

2. *Request that all current executive development processes be backed up by purposes.* Have you ever been asked to describe your executive development effort? In responding, most of us begin by mentioning a series of processes. Mention will likely be made of:

- The recruiting effort
- The initial training effort
- The performance appraisal process
- The annual human resources review
- The in-company management courses

Prepare a list of major processes in the executive development effort. Then prepare one or more purposes for each process. This task is more thought-provoking than you might at first expect.

Second Requirement: Top-Management Action

We have already stressed that purpose is the first and most important requirement for an effective executive development program. Close behind is the requirement for decisive top-management action. Top management must dictate the purpose or purposes. Top management must clarify the philosophy guiding the executive development process. In addition, top management must act.

Top-Management Types

Experience with many large companies leads me to conclude that the way top executives view their responsibilities for executive development can be categorized into four types. They are:

- The "I could care less" type—they see no need for executive development.
- The "omnipotent" type—they rely entirely on themselves.
- The "we must do something" type—they see a need to get started.
- The "fully dedicated" type—they are actively involved.

Trends at the Top

One basic trend is a steady increase in the number of fully dedicated types. There is also a steady decrease in the "I could care less" types. The latter type of executive rarely changes. They just seem to die out. The second trend is a most interesting one. Both direct and indirect reports we get reveal that very few top executives are satisfied with their current executive development efforts. The third trend has to do with expectations. Our experience tells us that top executives are beginning to place much higher demands on their human resources function. I noted earlier that a strong dissatisfaction existed with current executive development programs. This dissatisfaction has led executives to ask for modifications and improvements in major aspects of their ongoing programs. Intense board involvement is a most obvious trend, and it is becoming widespread. Ten years ago the word "rubber stamp" was quite frequently used to describe the role of the board with regard to executive development and selections. Not any more. In well-managed companies board involvement in executive development is taken for granted.

Suggestions for Those Who Want to Revitalize an Established Program:

1. *Find out just what results you are now getting.* A good first step is to get data on just how well your purposes are currently being achieved. You may also find that future business plans call for new purposes. Remember, you are dealing with a pipeline problem. Results have to be gained at each step of the way if you are to get the needed results year after year.

2. *Concentrate on getting managerial commitment to the purposes.* We have a tendency to design a new process or modify an old one by changing procedures. The mechanics can often be improved. But the "Achilles heel" of many an executive development effort is a lack of commitment at successive levels of management.

3. *Resolve to get better evaluative data on key executives.* Have you ever looked at the file folder for a key executive? The evaluative information most companies have on their key executives can best be described as "pitiful." We will deal with this issue under the fifth requirement.

Third Requirement: A Professional Staff Contribution

Let's look at the above words in reverse. A contribution is required. Purposes won't be achieved unless you get a contribution from a "staff" individual or group. The term staff suggests a catalyst role. Managers are stimulated to give attention to a responsibility they might otherwise neglect. The word "professional" is chosen deliberately. You need individuals who really know their stuff. The challenge of executive development requires specialized knowledge and talents. It's no place for amateurs or beginners. In particular, it is not a place to put those who have failed.

Basic Responsibilities of the Human Resources Function

The basic responsibilities are:

- Overall systems design
- Staffing and directing the function
- Process development
- Process implementation
- Providing advice and counsel
- Program measurement and redesign

Let's consider an actual example. A chief executive recently hired a "pro" for the top human resources position. At the end of the first year, this chief executive reported that his human resources executive had:

- Kept the chief executive from hiring a "bum" from outside.
- Encouraged the chief executive to remove a nonperformer in a key position.
- Got the chief executive to stop "ranting and raving."
- Slowed down the frequency of changes being made in organizational structure.
- Got the company to move on a major redundancy problem that had been around for years. The purpose set was an interesting one: to get all the unemployed off the payroll.
- Increased the financial reward differentiation between the outstanding and the "just satisfactory" performers.
- Got the chief executive to give increased attention to top-level communications.
- Come up with a unique development move for a key executive.
- Discouraged making an acquisition because of evidence about questionable management talent.

This chief executive was getting his money's worth. The organization was more competitive.

Fourth Requirement: The Human Resources Review

The most important single program in an executive development program is, in our opinion, the human resources review. The review process usually takes place once a year. Managers, at each level, prepare for the review by completing prescribed forms having to do with various questions about human resources. Each manager then has a discussion with higher-level management. Out of these discussions come the plans for developing and moving personnel.

What Should an Organization Expect of the Review Process?

The organization should consider this the most important aspect of the entire executive development process. The organization should expect great things from the review process. Reviews should make a direct and observable contribution to the purposes discussed earlier. The review provides the organization with the best opportunity to become knowledgeable about the quality and depth of executive resources. The communication exchange during the review is, primarily, for the benefit of management. The review process should require that managers from the chief executive on down will do four things:

1. Think thoroughly about a specific set of human resources questions or issues.

2. Have an intensive discussion of their thinking with higher-level executives.

3. Decide upon precise action plans to reflect the thinking and the discussion.

4. Subsequently, implement the planned action.

Review Questions

Let us now discuss the basic questions to be included in the review. We suggest that there are eight basic types of questions.

1. *Business plan.* Does your most recent strategic business plan have any major impact upon management personnel within your organization?

2. *Organizational structure.* Do you contemplate making any organizational changes in the next 12 to 18 months? (Consider the two organizational levels below you.)

3. *Performance evaluation.* What is your evaluation of the current performance of those individuals who report directly to you?

4. *Promotability forecast.* Who do you predict will qualify for your position? Who do you predict will qualify for the positions one level removed from you?

5. *Forward plan.* What is the nature and timing of moves, if any, for individuals in the positions reporting to you? Look ahead 5 years.

6. *Individual development plan.* What is the nature and timing of specific developmental acts for direct reports? What is the nature and timing of specific developmental actions for other individuals who appear on promotability forecasts and forward plan?

7. *Special programs.* (A question can be raised about any special program deemed important. The following programs are illustrative only.)

▪ What is the status of your high-potential program?

▪ What is the status of your Equal Employment Opportunity (EEO) program?

▪ What is the status of your college recruiting program?

8. *Quarterly action schedule.* What specific action is to be taken each quarter of the year ahead pertaining to the prior set of questions?

I will not go into detail on these basic questions. They have been dealt with in great depth in the book, *Succession Planning in Leading Companies*, by Walter Mahler and Frank Gaines, published by Mahler Publishing Company, Midland Park, New Jersey, 1984.

Fifth Requirement: A Helpful Data System

If you want a shock, just arrange to get all the data your organization presently has on:

- A recent college recruit
- A 5-year employee
- A 10-year veteran
- A 20-year veteran

Unless your organization is most unusual, you will not only be shocked, you will be dismayed. We see a need for a significant contribution having to do with data.

1. *The human relations staff should concentrate on getting basic data in an accurate, timely, and readily usable form.* There are two types of data which deserve the term "basic." One is the basic demographic data we usually find on a "work history." You should expect to have a work history for every employee. It is likely that a comprehensive work history can readily be designed. Once designed, it can readily be put on the computer. However, many a data system overlooks the need to keep the work history up to date on a regular basis. It should also be possible for you and other managers to have the work history readily available. A second type of basic data has to do with compensation history. Here, the challenge is to have data which are accurate, timely, and maintained under strict security. Another type of basic data has to do with "career aspiration" information.

2. *The human resources staff should get more and better evaluative data from the human resources review process.* We suggest you experiment with a "tutored review" alternative. It is designed to secure greatly improved evaluative data. You not only get better data, the review discussions improve and the review plans of actions improve. The tutored review involves an experienced staff person talking through the above questions with an individual manager prior to the review discussion.

3. *The human resources staff should design a comprehensive, career-long data system.* Most data programs have evolved a piece at a time. They can hardly be called a system. Rarely is attention given to a career-long approach to getting data. It's an interesting challenge for the human resources staff to design a comprehensive career-long data system. This will require some pioneering, for you will be entering into unexplored territory.

4. *The human resources staff should contribute meaningful evaluative data of their own.* This suggestion is particularly appropriate for the large, diversified company. Higher-level management is entitled to two inputs when it comes to evaluative data. They should get an input from "line managers" in the human resources review. The higher-level managers are also entitled to get a very significant contribution from their human resources function.

Sixth Requirement: Selection on a Companywide Basis

To achieve the critical purposes of a well-designed executive development program, it is essential that there is an effective, companywide selection process. You must not only develop the talent, you must make proper use of the talent.

Executive Selection Process

The selection process is often as informal as the back of an envelope. In a few companies it has become an elaborate process. The executive selection process to be recommended will be in between these extremes. We recommend that each executive be required to use the executive selection process for all executive appointments. There are five steps in the process:

1. Identification of results expected

2. Listing of more important plans required to achieve the results

3. Preparation of specifications

4. Evaluation of several candidates against the specifications

5. Final decision

Seventh Requirement: Developing Future High-Level Managers

For the last decade, we have conducted a semiannual executive development workshop. Participants, more often than not, came from large companies with established high-potential processes. The participants prepare a thorough assessment of their executive development efforts. Without exception, the participants express disappointment with their current processes for development of future general managers. What are the consequences of the failure to develop the future general managers we need? You handicap yourself in the tough challenge of competing on a global scale. You endanger your ambitious growth plans.

A Philosophy for Developing Future High-Level Managers

The traditional approach to the development of general managers has been characterized by many activities. Most companies try one technique and then another. The entire process is quite haphazard. Belatedly, we have come to realize that a complex problem requires a systems approach. To be effective, a systems approach must combine numerous activities into an integrated whole. Doing this requires a well-conceived philosophy. We would like to share our philosophy of developing future high-level managers with you. It will help in talking about our philosophy if you keep the hierarchy in Fig. 32-1 in mind. We will present the philosophy in the form of a series of statements:

1. The outcome we desire is a steady flow of well-qualified individuals to fill general manager's positions in the future.

2. We need to divide the challenge into two parts. One part has to do with *improvement plans*, the other part with *development plans*.

3. Improvement plans are aimed at securing improvement in current performance. Referring to Fig. 32-1, each successive level of management works our improvement plans with the level below them.

4. Development plans are aimed at developing talent to perform effectively, in the future, in high-level positions. Again, referring to Fig. 32-1, individuals at level

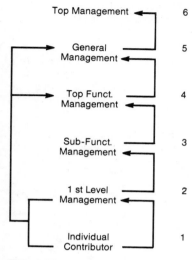

Figure 32-1. Management hierarchy.

1 or 2 are to be developed for positions at level 4, 5, or 6. At this time, we will concentrate on level 5, the general manager position.

5. The primary basis for development is a series of challenging work situations. The situations have to be genuine and one has to stay in them sufficiently long for real development to take place. Our present assumption is that 2 to 4 years is about the right length of time. Development benefits from a series of well-selected learning opportunities provided over a period of years.

6. It becomes a necessity that supervisory development opportunities begin relatively early. We suggest 27 to 32 years of age as about the right timing.

7. You aren't selecting future executives at an early age. You are identifying individuals who are deemed worthy of an opportunity for deliberate development. At one time, we used the term "accelerated development." Frankly, we don't want that. We want deliberate development.

8. You will need to establish observable characteristics to help in making the initial identification of youthful talent.

9. You will need to identify developmental opportunities relevant for the general manager position. A similar need exists for other high-level positions.

10. This entire process requires the personal interest and active support of an executive about three levels above where the moves are being made. A high-level "power figure" has to be actively "behind" the entire effort.

11. The number of individuals in this effort should be quite small, but newcomers need to be introduced regularly, year after year.

12. Participants must make effective use of each development opportunity in order to get another one.

13. A superior and subordinate can prepare an improvement plan on their own; however, developmental plans, as we define them, cannot be left to lower-level operating managers. *To be more precise, you should not expect immediate*

superiors to prepare development plans. Please reread this statement. Its implications are crucial. It is an extremely rare company that is in tune with this philosophy. Why this insight came to us so belatedly suggests an example of arrested development on our part.

14. Implementing the above philosophy requires a significant human resources staff input. This input has not been provided to date. Rigorous studies must be conducted. Once the operating managers have the benefit of these studies, the responsibility for implementing developmental planning can be turned over to high-level operating managers.

It becomes apparent that the described program is a major undertaking. There is a lot of new work to be done. The needed support work will require a significant staff contribution to design, install, and maintain the program.

Involvement is most critical. The entire program must be a "line manager" program. As mentioned earlier, a power figure, such as a general manager, must "implement" the program. Development of the methodology is best done with involvement of the concerned managers. The "developmental scenario" for each participant needs the contribution of both line managers and staff managers.

The entire program is analogous to a forester with a reforestation program. The program has to go on year after year, decade after decade. Top executives can come and go, but this program must go on and on. The program doesn't benefit from a short burst of enthusiasm. It requires dedication, persistence, and patience. Therefore, it must be institutionalized.

Eighth Requirement: Getting Results from an Investment in Manager Education

Manager education is the eighth requirement for your overall system approach. It doesn't deserve top priority. Neither does it deserve to be neglected entirely. In a well-designed system, you must invest in management education, and, even more importantly, you *must* get results from your investment.

Prevailing Patterns of Advanced Management Programs

Both business and nonbusiness organizations have made extensive use of formal educational programs. Practically every major university has an advanced management program. The American Management Associations have conducted a 4-week management course for more than 20 years. A few large companies have their own advanced management programs. Many other organizations rely on short courses. These may be conducted as an internal program or as part of an external program. Let us give attention to each of these basic alternatives.

University-Sponsored Programs

One can identify major changes in university programs by a sequential analysis of *Bricker's Directories.* Only one of the twelve leading universities can be credited with a major modification of their program in the last 10 years. An analysis of the summary derived from *Bricker's Directory* permits the following conclusions:

- The class size of 52 is large. Some participant discussion and interaction can occur but not very much for any one participant.
- The heterogeneity of participants is great. They vary greatly in age, in position level, in business affiliation, and in national background. Such vast differences require that instruction be dealt with in rather broad terms.
- The instruction calls for 4 to 13 consecutive weeks with a few exceptions. The potential value of spaced instruction has rarely been tested by university programs.
- The data on average salary and percent of participants who are in general management reveal the majority of the participants are middle-level managers and not profit-center-type executives.

In-Company Programs

Some large companies have had an established internal management education effort for years. In recent years, many other companies have initiated their own internal programs. Internal programs are similar in style. The more common characteristics are:

- One-week programs. A few companies offer 4-week programs. Rarely are programs longer than 4 weeks.
- Instruction is provided by professors or consultants. Occasionally, a company will have its own professional staff. Some actually put their line officers to work as instructors.
- Group size varies widely but is likely to range from 30 to 40 participants.
- An increasing number of companies have their own educational facilities, but the majority make use of temporary facilities.
- The selection of participants is somewhat haphazard. In some companies, the supervisor and the subordinate play an active role in the decision. In many cases, the decision is a centralized one.

There seems to be an interesting ebb and flow in the support of internal education. AT&T, General Electric, and International Business Machines have provided sustained support for decades. Not many other companies have. For 3 to 5 years, a big "educational" push is on, and then the support wanes. The main reason for the difference appears to be that of culture. In some companies, there is a deep-seated conviction that management education is important. In other companies, the authors feel, a CEO may be enthusiastic about education, but the next CEO may be negative on educational expenditures.

Pitfalls in Prevailing Patterns

The prevailing pattern of educational programs, whether done externally or internally, has failed to produce the needed results because of recurring pitfalls. The first pitfall to be found in advanced educational programs is that top management will assume that the educational programs will do the job of developing their future managers. A second pitfall occurred with the advent of advanced management education. Many years ago, universities found there was a new market—the executive. They designed an advanced program tailored after their undergraduate program. Heavy reliance was placed upon case studies. The basic pitfall was getting underway in the absence of a thorough need-determination process which governs the choice of subject matter, size of group, nature of group, educational method, and type of instructor. Unfortunately, the entire advanced management process is continuing today, using the same premises and the same methodology that were in vogue 25 years ago. A third pitfall has to do with the heterogeneous nature of participants. The instructor in the average university program is faced with 52 diverse students. Often the number is 80. The students come from organizations differing greatly in size, from different types of businesses, with different backgrounds and unique personal needs. Often, one-third of the students are from offshore. The instructor must strike a general pattern which appeals to most of the students, most of the time. Such a general course seldom meets specific needs. A fourth pitfall has to do with selecting the participant. In many organizations, the executive who can be made available for 6 weeks or longer is sent. This means that the "real-comers" often miss out on an educational experience. A fifth pitfall is that the educational process is not programmed as a continuous effort stretching over the entire career of a manager. Once in a manager's career, usually at some random interval, they are given an opportunity to take a 6-week educational program. Often this constitutes the first and last formal educational experience they receive. A sixth pitfall has to do with the need to improve managerial ability. Educational programs have the avowed purpose of broadening an executive's knowledge and awareness. Application of this knowledge calls for skills, and these skills are almost never included in an advanced management program.

Our Philosophy of Manager Education

Again, we come to the question of philosophy. And, for a basic reason! Education is a very complex process. The traditional overly simplified approach to a manager education has produced disappointing results. One of the reasons for the failure to get results is the lack of a well-thought-out philosophy about manager education. This is true not only of line executives but also of educational specialists. Let us share our philosophy of education with you. The philosophy will be presented in the form of a series of statements. The statements are not in order of importance.

1. Education can make a contribution to the development of executives. Getting this contribution becomes more important as the executive's life becomes, predictably, more complex. It doesn't help to be completely allergic to education; neither does it help to be overly enthusiastic about it.

2. An organization will benefit if its executives realize, from actual experience, that they are expected to keep on learning, year after year. It's possible the actual course content isn't that consequential.

3. You get more leverage if the human resources staff, the line manager, and the educators work together to establish specific educational outcomes and then work to achieve them.

4. We need much more investment in "front-end" work (determining needs, designing specific courses) to develop programs tailored to achieve very specific outcomes.

5. University programs have to be general and theoretical because of the heterogeneous student body and the lack of practical experience of the professors. This means you get one kind of a result from university programs. It's appropriate at certain stages of a manager's career. However, you cannot rely exclusively on university programs for all your educational needs.

Ninth Requirement: Getting a Developmental Contribution from an Objectives Program

The ninth requirement for an effective executive development effort has to do with objectives. We feel you can and should get a developmental contribution from an objectives program. It may seem strange to you for us to introduce objectives in a chapter about executive development. It may seem stranger yet to imply that you should get a developmental contribution from an objectives program. But that is exactly what we propose to do. We propose to do more than that. We hope you will discover that you and your organization no longer need to struggle with performance appraisals. Isn't that wonderful? But this switch from performance appraisals to objectives isn't an easy one. Getting an effective management-by-objectives program presents complexities of its own. We feel that an objectives program with stress on self-control can give a significant contribution to the development of individuals and the development of teams. To get this contribution we need to come up with a new philosophy about objectives.

Needed: A New Philosophy about Objectives

You can begin to clarify your own philosophy of managing by objectives by thinking about the purposes of the objectives effort. It will help if you separate primary purposes from secondary ones. Let us argue for two primary purposes and only two. They are:

- Self-management
- Teamwork

The primary purpose of the objectives effort is to provide managers with a tool by which to manage themselves. You will achieve this result when managers prepare an objectives document, review it regularly with others, and get a strong feeling of pride or of guilt. If the term "guilt" sounds too strong, substitute the word "anxiety." Pride and guilt are two strong motivators. Notice the superior does not complete an appraisal and inform the subordinate of it. There is no "report card." Rather, subordinates appraise their own progress and discuss both progress and variances with their superiors. This problem-solving type of discussion permits superiors to coach, to encourage self-insight, to suggest areas of improvement. This brings us to the second primary purpose—teamwork objectives provide a staff group with regular opportunities for problem-solving discussions. The interaction occurs in a timely manner. Discussion of successes comes easily for each of us. Discussion of "failure" is more difficult.

Needed: Appropriate Objective Documents

Because of our own somewhat delayed development, we did not discover, until recently, that you need two types of objectives documents to implement the philosophy just discussed. One document is needed to achieve the primary purpose of self-management. You also need another document for other purposes, such as improved team play, improved communications, increased motivations, and finally, granting of financial rewards. The first document we refer to as the RIO document. That stands for the three parts of the document:

- Responsibilities
- Indicators
- Objectives

Responsibilities are major areas of a position. The individual holding a position is responsible for achieving certain results in each area. The sum total of the responsibilities encompasses the entire position. Responsibilities are usually stated in terms of brief titles. Qualifying sentences can also be used.

Indicators are those things to be examined in determining when a responsibility is well done. Some executives like to use the term "measurements." It is quite appropriate. Indicators are not objectives. They are "bridges" to get from responsibilities to objectives. Notice that indicators don't tell how much. They don't reflect how high you commit yourself to jump. They just describe the nature of the results you commit yourself to achieve.

Objectives are statements of end results to be achieved within a given time period. Objectives define the level of performance. If you want subordinates to feel pride and guilt about their entire job, the objectives must be comprehensive. If you are an advocate of a small number of objectives, please don't expect the objectives effort to fulfill the two primary purposes stressed earlier. You had best admit you are giving a secondary purpose top priority. This may be a desirable step to take, but let's not kid ourselves. You might get decisions made on bonus awards, but that is likely to be all you get.

The second document we refer to as the pride document or pride chart.

Major Parameters of the Pride Document or Pride Chart

What are some of the major parameters of the pride document or pride chart? First, it is quite simple. It is a list of the 10 most important results to be achieved if you and your staff are to be proud of yourselves. "You" refers to the top manager and all those who work under the top manager. The most important results appear at the top of the list. However, there is no weighing. There are 10 statements reflecting the 10 results. Usually each statement consists of a single phrase or sentence.

The message is the important thing. Does everyone who reads the statement understand what it says? Remember, we aren't measuring, we aren't evaluating. We are communicating. We are motivating ourselves and others.

Each quarter you can reflect the extent of accomplishment. You will be amazed at the effort generated to get to where we can be proud. The critical requirement is for the pride chart to be visible, in your office, at all times. Imagine, everyone who walks in your office knows what your objectives are and what you are committed to achieve.

Tenth Requirement: Integration of Executive Development with Other Management Programs

Earlier we recommended that many new things should be undertaken to get executive development results. We have used the term "systems approach" quite frequently. The term implies we are dealing with a complex process. In using the "systems" term with respect to executive development we are calling attention to the challenge of getting a large number of busy executives to introduce several new processes and to sustain the processes, year after year. The challenge is to get a significant change in habits. But the expected executive development results are not forthcoming. Why? Because other important management programs are at odds with the executive development program. Let us concentrate attention on three very important management programs. They are:

- Business planning
- Organization planning
- Motivational planning

Quite often, there is a gap, a lack of relationship between the executive development program and the above management programs. In the case of business planning, the more frequent situation is one not of cross purposes but of lack of relationship. The business plan has critical human resources requirements. These requirements are identified in the business plan, but the executive development program doesn't produce the expected results. The interrelationship between organization planning and executive development programs is an interesting one. The prevailing pattern of organization planning for most large companies is that of changing the structure at the top three levels quite frequently. Rarely is much weight given to the abrupt change in number or type of executives needed. In the case of motivational programs, a company quite often has a financial reward system which works at cross purposes to the executive development program. It doesn't help when executives who do a great job with executive development are financially penalized. It is amazing how widespread the phenomenon is. Don't assume too quickly that it isn't operating, right now, in your company.

Summary

Executive development is a complex business. The human resources practitioner needs to read practically every chapter in this handbook. When you look at the entire people flow process you realize it starts at recruitment. It reaches a climax at the executive level. Action is still needed on retirements. The impact of a talented leader or a poor leader is, of course, greatest at executive levels. There is no question; the human resources practitioner has both a great challenge and a great opportunity, entitled "executive development."

33

Management Development

Richard A. Eastburn

Richard A. Eastburn is a principal in the consulting firm of Benoit Eastburn Cowin in Cleveland and greater New York City. This firm works in partnership with management to improve innovation and competitive advantage through use of capital, plant, people, and technology. The firm works in areas of manufacturing, high technology, human resources, government, service, and advertising. Eastburn's experience includes development of approaches to change an organization's status quo. He has managed an international human resources function and consulted on major organization issues. His experience has been gained at TRW, Inc., American Standard, Digital Equipment, and RCA's defense business. He has been a successful entrepreneur, developing a premier $44 million retirement community in Hudson, Ohio, and is currently engaged in a new business requiring product development and marketing. He holds a master's degree in Business from Columbia University and in Organization Behavior from Temple University. He resides in Chagrin Falls, Ohio, with his family.

Change is the hallmark of the modern business environment. A whole new range of products, sparked by space-age technologies, is altering the way we live and do business. Manufacturing is becoming ever more intellectually challenging and complex as methods change to meet new productivity demands. Product life cycles are shrinking while the time to design and develop new products grows longer. World markets are changing, requiring major adjustments in marketing strategies.

As we near the close of the twentieth century, the sheer velocity of change and fluctuating personal and business values seems to intensify. The ability to anticipate these changes is critical to the success of a business, as well as the management of people. Management development professionals play a major role in helping their companies develop effective managers and business systems for working within this fast-paced environment. To do this they must:

- Continually track changes in technology, business strategy, economic conditions, competition, and human values.

- Focus on the requirements of their particular industry and the needs of their own company.

- Acquire new skills in business and expand their skills in the social sciences and education.

- Develop their critical thinking and conceptual skills.

What Is Management Development?

Management development is the preparation and education of managers to effectively manage their people while at the same time achieving the strategies and goals of their company. This generally includes those individuals above the first two levels of supervision and below senior management.

A major change in this field has come about in the *way* the management development professional carries out his or her role. Figure 33-1 maps out the roles, functions, and changes that are driving the professional, giving some examples under each major heading. The roles are noted as policy development, education and training, development systems, and consulting and advising. The major functions are needs identification, design projects, marketing, and evaluation. The change drivers are the business environment, management expectations, organizational politics, competence of the professional, and the pace of change.

Being responsive to organizational goals and alert to changes in the business environment is an important function of the management development professional. It can lead to significant impact on the bottom line. For example, during the inflationary times of the mid-1970s, many companies, G.E. among them, found that they must place major emphasis on asset management to succeed or survive. G.E. management quickly placed top priority on its cash management objectives. The company's training professionals were alert enough to respond to this new need and set up a cash management training program for over 600 managers. As a result of the training program, and the support of management, the company was able to gain $600 million of additional cash during the 18-month period following the program. Such success speaks well for the professionals who can make it work.

Management development is skilled at helping people and organizations learn and change. Understanding how people learn and work together productively in organizations, choosing the most appropriate methods for achieving specific goals, and the cost effectiveness of different development and training methods determine the success of a program.

In fulfilling this element of management development responsibility, choosing the appropriate teaching technique is important. For example, the lecture format is not particularly successful in changing behavior. Lecture methods are effective, however, for communicating specific information and, used appropriately, can be highly beneficial. Similarly, video-aided instruction, computer-aided instruction, business simulations, etc., all have their appropriate function in effective learning and change.

Role of T&D	Needs Identification	Design Projects	Marketing Programs	Evaluation
Policy Development	Unique organizational needs Identify general approaches Impact of future System implications	Performance evaluation policy Internal search policy Succession policy	Determine critical decision maker target Develop multi-teaching approach Market test in needs and design phase	Track performance and compliance
Education and Training	Unique organizational needs Identify general subject matter Identify existing programs System implication	Plant managers seminar Leadership workshop Strategic management seminar	Same as Test above	Accomplishments of objectives
Development Systems	Unique organizational needs Identify general approaches Impact of future System implications	Performance evaluation procedures Internal search procedures Succession procedures	Same as above	Track compliance and performance
Consulting and Advising	Assist management to see real needs Identify methodologies to approach issue Organize and convey data collected at seminars	Develop alternate solution Implement	Very tailored Political impact	Referred new assignments Qualitative check of objectives accomplished

↑   ↑   ↑   ↑ CHANGE DRIVERS ↑   ↑   ↑   ↑

Business Environment   Politics of Organization   Management Expectations

Competence of Professionals (T & D)   Pace of Change

Figure 33-1. Roles and functions of management development.

Management Development: Change Agent

Management development helps prepare managers for growing responsibilities and more complex tasks. Management development also needs to provide a system for identifying people for future responsibilities to prepare them to assume new tasks. The appropriate developmental assignments—functional, geographic, and external—are critical for shaping the character, effectiveness, and style of a high-potential general manager. Having the right managers available to a company also helps it manage its future more effectively.

Development professionals operating in this complex set of systems must be change agents. As such, they must understand and help managers understand the dynamics of environmental and corporate systems (see Fig. 33-2). Understanding a business organization from the viewpoint of the strategy and systems at work frees the manager to make informed changes easily as external business conditions change. Seeing the organization as fluid, rather than as cast in concrete, makes it possible to anticipate change and train personnel before a crisis becomes unmanageable.

IBM, for all its size and 370,000 employees, has developed a relatively fluid

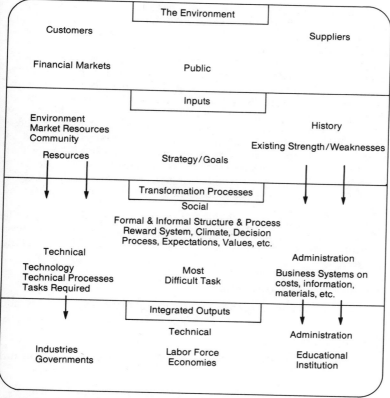

Figure 33-2. A model of organizational dynamics.

organization which allows shifts of power and influence in ways which expedite business. When a new product is coming on stream, for instance, the engineering department develops the product without undue constraints from marketing or sales. As the product goes into manufacturing, so does the primary influence and responsibility. This encourages superior performance and minimizes power struggles. When the product is ready to be launched, marketing takes over. The operating procedures of the company allow a timely and fitting response to needs as they arise during the various phases of the development process.

There is a time lag between change in the external environment and a business organization's response. The more doctrinaire, the more rigid the organization, the longer it will take to respond. Competition from Japan taught Detroit's automobile companies that they need a more fluid structure and a greater awareness of the necessity of changing the distribution of power, authority, and responsibility as the industry and the environment change.

A narrow, academic, behavioral science approach to training and development has meant that business and competitive issues have too frequently been ignored. This limits the effectiveness of development and hurts its image. After all, the managers being trained have to cope both with the behavior of their staff and with business problems. In the real world it is difficult to separate the two; however, many training and development programs do just that. This makes it difficult for managers to translate what has been taught into action on the job. Before long, training programs are perceived as meaningless academic exercises.

One training and development professional learned the importance of anticipating change and integrating behavioral and business programs the hard way. While working for a major defense contractor, he was asked to help solve the problem of an unacceptable delay between the receipt of new government contracts and the organization of a team to deal with them. A survey uncovered great mistrust among section heads, making cooperation virtually impossible. After 4 to 5 months of team building meetings, a new contract came in and, within a spectacular 4 hours, the team was organized to deal with it. Within a month the division in which this team worked was totally reorganized and its members scattered throughout a new corporate structure. While the experience was intellectually satisfying and a good team-building effort, months of time and effort were improperly focused. A discussion with the division vice president to discover his view of the competitive factors and the direction of the business would have fostered the development of a more effective team-building approach within the constraints of a possible division reorganization. The months spent in altering behavior should also have been used preparing for the reorganization.

In facing a future alive with change, it is imperative that professionals understand the issues facing their businesses. Only in this way can development programs be used to competitive advantage. Some critical issues facing most businesses over the next several years are:

- Cost competitiveness on a global scale

- Global management approaches to producing and marketing products and services

- Fluidity of organizational systems and structures

- Transfer of skills and capabilities from one business to another in spite of turf issues

- Balance between long-term qualitative strategy and short-term financial performance

- Effective utilization of human resources at all levels of the organization to capture the energy and imagination of people
- Shifting value systems in an atmosphere of competition, change, and instability

How development people respond to these issues will depend upon their ability to understand the business, to understand and help manage change, and to master educational and learning processes.

Role of Policy in Management Development

Corporate policy grows out of the needs of the organization and must be reviewed frequently and modified as conditions change. It supports the vitality of the organization, sets a cultural tone, guides management behavior, and provides equity of treatment among employees. Well-thought-out development policies can improve the strength and continuity of management. Finally, and perhaps most significantly, policy should support achievement of superior performance.

The development professional should be involved in creating and modifying policies through careful analysis of the organization's needs. Considerations for policy development include an overall development policy that prescribes how the organization views the development of managers and what kind of "permission" they have to participate in their own development. One approach to this particular policy is to allow managers a certain number of hours or days a year for development activity. Another is to give support to managers so they can pursue development activities noted on their performance evaluation.

Other policies of importance to development include performance evaluation, succession, internal search, management intern programs, and use of university executive programs. Some companies include external search among policies in development. They take the view that external search supplements internal development and should assure that all qualified employees are considered before an external search candidate gets a job.

Development Programs

Policies are usually supported by programs and procedures. For example, there may be a performance evaluation system and, frequently, a seminar to help managers gain the skill to conduct evaluations. An internal search policy is often supported by a job posting procedure to identify those interested in applying for openings and career counseling seminars for managers so they can support the process and have appropriate attitudes.

Each company's unique set of characteristics determines which development programs may be appropriate. The strategy of the company, its history, and its size will determine the type of development programs it establishes. The development professional needs to understand his company, its business, management, climate, and norms to recommend and develop the appropriate policies and programs.

Policy and Program Marketing

Both policies and programs need to be carefully implemented and publicized. Both need to be marketed and made attractive to managers so they can understand the benefits and applications of the policies and programs in their department.

Marketing must be a continuous process. Much of managers' lives is spent determining which message they will respond to, which cry for help they will answer, which priority they will address today. It is impossible to respond to all messages. Unless managers are reminded of the benefits, the development professional's memos will lose out to those receiving more "air time" and consequently more management attention. Essential to marketing management development activities is a budget to support a marketing plan.

Education and Training

The development professional designs, purchases, and conducts both educational and training programs. There is a difference between education and training. Education challenges the individual intellectually, uncovers latent talent and ability, and improves performance at doing and thinking. Concepts, values, ideas, and incidents discussed in the classroom force the student to *think*, improve problem-solving capability, and clarify values. Training teaches specific skills or procedures. It is more narrow and specific than education. Many learning programs use both educational and training elements to achieve their objectives.

In either case, it is *learning* that must be emphasized by the management development. Most concepts can be taught in a host of different ways. Therefore, it is important to discover the method that will assure learning takes place. To do this, the development professional's first question about a learning objective should be, "How will these particular managers learn this most effectively?" Only after this has been answered can the question be asked, "Given what I know about learning, how can this be taught most effectively?" These questions help to place the emphasis on the student. Selecting methods and techniques appropriate to a particular group or environment is the hallmark of effective training and education programs in business and industry. This track record for quality education, however, is no cause for complacency. It's time for a new look to see how to increase the power and effectiveness of corporate education and training.

Establishing Focus

Effective management education and training starts with determining an appropriate focus. To do this, a professional must decide what objectives are essential; are we trying to convey new information or new skills, alter attitudes or values, change management behavior, or change the behavior of a whole organization?

A single program may deal with several objectives in varying depth. A seminar, for instance, may convey information and at the same time bring about behavior change. In the right-hand column below are examples of the most useful techniques for achieving the objectives identified in the left-hand column. The list of techniques or methods is not exhaustive. Rather, it suggests types of activities that will most effectively achieve the desired objective.

Objective	Technique or method
Information	Lecture
Skills	Demonstration, practice
Attitude	Group discussion, peer pressure
Individual behavior	Dilemma, feedback, experience
Organization behavior	System compatibility, common language, management follow-through, team building

To the extent that a behavior change is an objective of a learning experience, classroom work is only part of the task. The behavior expected and taught needs to fit with the environment in which the behavior will occur. People seldom do what their environment does not support. The problem for the development professional is that many of our developmental activities contradict this fundamental principle. The skills or concepts taught in the classroom often have no support back in the workplace and so are laid aside, forgotten, and the learning experience wasted. Often, employees learn teamwork skills at a seminar only to return to an office run by an autocratic manager intolerant of team techniques.

Before a student returns to his workplace, he must have opportunities to practice the new behavior or capability in a risk-free environment. New behavior or capability can be tested in the classroom without fear of failure, damage to the person's career, or creation of a business problem.

This requirement cannot be met either by on-the-job experience or by conventional academic approaches. Given the rapid change in the business world, managers do not have the time to learn a concept, experiment with it for a few years, and finally decide whether it works or not. Stan Pace, when president of TRW, stated flatly, "We just don't have time to allow managers to learn by experience alone. There must be short cuts to learning how to be a better manager and that's what we expect the management development department to help us with."

Listed below are some differences between the approaches of the businessperson and the academic:

Business and commerce	*Education and academic*
• Do it	• Study it
• Rewards performance	• Rewards discovery of new knowledge
• Knowledge is for competitive advantage	• Knowledge is for sharing
• The present is urgent	• The present is not as important as past experiences and future questions
• Answers have a specific practical purpose	• Answers are theoretical
• Promotions result from achieving tangible results	• Promotions result from research and publishing
• Uncertainties tend to be avoided	• Uncertainty tends to be analyzed and explored
• Education is paid for by the company	• Education is paid for by the student

A general academic approach is, by nature, ill-equipped to deal precisely with the objectives unique to a given company. Each company will emphasize the objectives it believes most important. If the professional development person, therefore, tries to apply textbook approaches to in-house management education and training, the results will be far from satisfactory. Topical education and training, without a direct connection to the needs of the organization, waste the participants' time and the organization's money.

Another dimension of focus is the manager's role in the organization. The information, skills, attitudes, and behavior change as the manager moves from one role in the organization to another. Because of major differences in roles and concurrent responsibilities, a transferred or promoted manager takes anywhere from 6 months to 2½ years to thoroughly learn and adjust to a new position. Education and training can cut this time in half.

A plant manager's function in the organization differs from that of a general manager. Time horizons, strategic operational focus, and business issues vary from one role to another. As a result, teaching the same thing about manufacturing

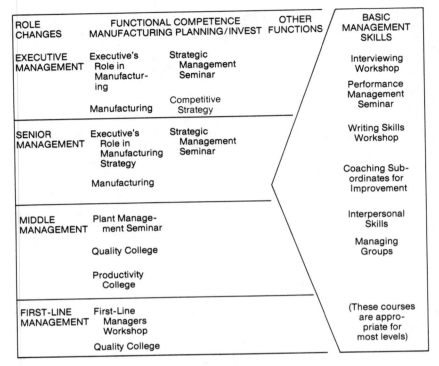

Figure 33-3. Conceptual model—management courses.

strategy to executive and plant managers causes virtually no substantial change in the organization's effectiveness because the focus is too general. Figure 33-3 describes elements of an integrated management and training system and differentiates the roles managers play in the organization.

Objectives and Capabilities

To establish focus one also has to understand the capabilities of the organization, which can be divided into three categories—individual, functional, and organizational. *Individual* capabilities of employees include their technical, administrative, and managerial abilities as well as the ability to think, resolve problems, and make decisions.

Functional capabilities are used by the organization to conduct business. They include manufacturing, engineering, finance, human relations, law, etc. Functional competence and its effective use and development is a significant issue in many organizations. Problems frequently result from the underutilization of staff people and the demotivation that results from not being challenged. The area of developing functional competence is frequently given little attention.

Organizational capabilities include an organization's ability to make decisions that result in a competitive advantage at the macro level. This could mean readjusting traditional expectations or organizational principles to enable a new division to be effective in the marketplace, as IBM did with its personal computer division; or appointing a marketing specialist to a top position, as Apple did to help it deal with IBM's entry into the personal computer market. Such decisions are strategic in nature and demand considerable skill for conceptual problem solving. This is generally done by senior management of a corporation or a major division.

Learning Objectives and Discriminating

Essential in determining the focus is identification of key issues in a learning opportunity. This requires the ability to collect and interpret data, understand the need, develop the materials, and identify the learning process. Data collection should clarify learning objectives and teaching approaches. It can also unearth information and insight into critical business problems, or the management of people, which should be relayed to management.

Several sources of data need to be explored to determine appropriate education and training activities for managers. They include:

- The business strategy

- Speeches and statements of senior officers

- Clarity on the work and tasks that need to be done through discussions with relevant managers

- Understanding of the capability and needs of the managers in the organization

- A discernment of the various roles and responsibilities within the organization now and how that may need to be shifted in the future

- An understanding of the business systems within the organization and how those business systems compel and restrain various kinds of behaviors

- Surveys of the relevant employee group

- An understanding of the norms, values, and politics of the organization and their impact on the material to be taught

The success of education and training is measured by this rule: can the student transfer a concept into practice? An effective "learning system" has a built-in compatibility between what managers are expected to learn and what they are expected to do in their work. This kind of learning expects, encourages, and supports change, and realizes that if change does not occur, the business is not going to reach its objectives.

It is particularly helpful to begin the needs identification process by looking at the organization as a system in order to sort out the sources of data that are most important to the assignment.

For example, when asked to design a program to help plant managers use manufacturing more competitively, one professional began by gathering information about the plants from superiors, subordinates, and the plant managers themselves. Business performance data were also used to compare the company's output with expected performances.

To facilitate the collection of information, two groups of 15 to 20 plant managers were organized. Each manager was asked to come to a meeting prepared to answer four to six questions that were carefully designed to elicit the necessary information. At the meeting, the plant managers, divided into groups of five or so, were asked to discuss the list of questions. Each group then made a presentation to the others, who were encouraged to ask questions and state opinions. The presentations clarified the thinking of the plant managers. The same process was repeated with the division vice presidents who supervised the plant managers. The questions were modified to fit their roles and to bring out their perception of the plant management job. The information gained through these sessions was invaluable in targeting the precise subjects, capabilities, and attitudes to be covered in the training program, including:

- The current level of capability and self-image in the group for which the seminar is designed

- The expectations of the management level above that group

- The impact of changes for the environment over the next 5 to 6 years

- The systems used by the targeted group and how those systems will impact on the learning objectives

- The norms and politics of the organization

- The factors that lead to success in the targeted population, as well as those that lead to failure

- The impact of the business strategy on this group

Determining an Approach

Once the needs are determined, the educational objectives can be set and a determination can be made whether to purchase an existing program or create a new one. It is also possible to customize by combining an existing program with new material. The critical issue here is a cost-benefit analysis. There must be a balance among what you are trying to achieve, the needs, resources, and costs. Though cost is a factor, the primary driver of the relationship between customization and cost should be the learning objectives.

Learning Objectives and the Business Strategy

The business strategy is important for the development professional in identifying education and training objectives. Often this is overlooked or considered too high-powered for the development function, whereas it is essential in creating effective learning programs.

The strategy of a business can be either written or behavioral. Even if it does not have a well-formulated and documented strategy, the actions a business takes in the marketplace to achieve and maintain a competitive advantage reveal its strategy. The development of a comprehensive business strategy demands that the people running the business understand their competition, industry, company's structure, customer base, relevant technology, suppliers, etc.

In Fig. 33-2 illustrating the dynamics of organizational systems, a number of items were listed in the environmental area. An understanding of each item is imperative in evolving a strategy. Anyone attempting to develop managers must understand the strategy of the organization and how management development can contribute to its success.

Fitting the Environment of the Organization

A third key concept important to development professionals is fit. Effective behavior for them in organizations needs not only the capability of the person but the support of the organizational environment to maximize education and training.

To design effective learning experiences, management must take into account the norms of the organization—how things really happen, its needs, and management's readiness to change. Where possible, it is also important to identify key "domino" issues that, when dealt with effectively, will help solve other problems within the organization.

It would be futile for an organization to attempt to change focus to a strategic one when all the reward systems support a short-term approach. People in organizations generally do what management rewards. The system within which we work structures a great deal of our behavior. But management often wants something taught yet fails to recognize that the system norms and organizational values must change for the learning to be applied.

Gathering information on the impact of the organization's systems is important in identifying needs. Understanding the roles and responsibilities of the people who are the focus of the training and the systems in which they work are two issues of equal importance. Also necessary is an understanding of the norms, values, management behavior, and organizational climate. If the norms support cautious "cover your tracks" behavior, risk taking and innovation will seldom occur, even if management says it wants managers to take risks and be innovative. If senior managers say, "We want everyone to obey all laws of doing business and to act in a thoroughly ethical way," and then put heavy pressure on their staff to "produce next quarter's profits no matter what," managers will bend the rules, and sometimes break them, to hold their jobs.

Issues of values, behavior, and systems are all intertwined with any effort that involves learning and change. The "fit" of the learning experience with any follow-up work and the organization's values and systems are critical to achieving results from the learning experience.

Learning Application

The most important concept is application. Unless managers are able to apply what they have learned, the whole learning experience will have been wasted. Often, training programs are put together to resolve a certain problem, teach a new skill, or help managers acquire a new behavior. At the end of the program, the managers talk about it; they just can't do it!

For example, market segmentation is a tool widely taught in business schools and executive programs. The ability of managers to segment a market correctly is apparently quite another thing. Many managers know the concept, can define it, and could pass a business school test on it. There are, however, many times when senior managers reviewing a business strategy still find the market segmentation done incorrectly and the strategy and supporting plans, therefore, off target.

Another notorious area where application doesn't match theoretical knowledge is in performance evaluation. How many courses have been run on this subject? Certainly enough to have developed the kind of behavior that we want. Yet survey after survey on the practices of managers reveals that, in most companies, the area where managers are least competent is performance evaluation.

Application of learning comes, first of all, from determining the learning objectives. What kind of objectives are we dealing with? What is the desired behavior? What information needs to be conveyed? What new skills are to be acquired? What values and attitudes need to be instilled?

Application results from selecting the best methods to achieve each of these objectives. It also comes from focusing the training on specific roles and functional areas and having only those people who fit that category attend the program. Providing a learning experience that is highly involving and participatory encourages application by the student.

Assisting Managers to Learn

Managers are busy, intense, practical people. Because they have a lot to read, they tend to read superficially, scan pages quickly, pick out key words and phrases. When put into a structured learning experience, they must change their reading habits to gain the most from assignments. Trainers can help by digesting readings into a *Reader's Digest* format for quick, easy reading.

Managers' learning styles tend to be determined by their experience on the job. David Kolb, formerly of MIT, has researched the learning styles of managers and developed an experiential learning model that is depicted in Fig. 33-4. Kolb's cycle consists of four stages. Immediate concrete experience is the first stage. This forms the basis for observing and reflecting on what one has experienced. These observations, reflections, and the meaning derived from them are used to create a concept, or "theory," from which new criteria for action can be developed. This model indicates that the manager learns first from a concrete experience. The manager then needs to learn from observing and reflecting. This in itself is a skill of no small consequence. Based on the observations and reflections, the manager can derive some meaning and some generalizations from the experience. The generalizations can then be tested to see if they hold up. If they do, the manager will lock onto the new concept, or "theory," and modify behavior accordingly. While all

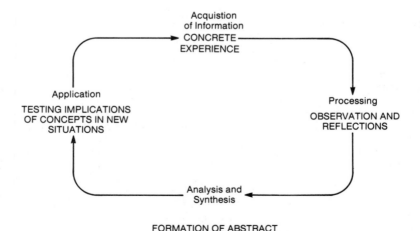

Figure 33-4. A model of the learning process.

four stages are steps in a continuous process, people usually have preferred styles. Therefore, they are better at one or two stages of the process than at others. Kolb's model can be used in the design and development of management learning. Since people prefer to learn in different ways and really need all four steps in the process, a seminar needs to provide all four steps for the most potent learning experience.

Education in business has become known for the use of participatory techniques; however, it must be recognized how important it is for managers to have an opportunity to observe and reflect and to develop abstract generalizations, based on their educational experiences. Frequently, these experiences will confound the manager because they are contrary to his or her current practices. This challenge to conventional thinking is one of the most useful aspects of any learning opportunity. An opportunity to test these generalizations must also be provided. The manager can then arrive at a new conclusion which will bring definite growth. At this point, it is time for the manager to go back to the job and apply the new generalizations and theories. It is also extremely helpful for managers to have opportunities to return to the classroom for periodic follow-up sessions to discuss their successes, failures, and questions with their peers and instructor.

Assisting Managers to Think

Management thinking demands at least three types of problem solving. Management development must prepare people to deal with all three levels as their jobs demand.

First there is the solving of discrete problems, such as an annoying breakdown in the office heating system. This problem is not connected to any other system in the office. The heating contractor is called and a repair is made.

A second level of thinking is systems-oriented. Systems problems may occur at the organizational level or sublevel. For example at *sublevel*, a business claims to give superb customer service. However, when customers call the plant no one can discover the status of their orders. Obviously the order processing system is not set up to accommodate customer inquiries regarding order status. The total system needs to be adjusted to rectify this weakness. The marketing department, the manufacturing department, and in some cases the engineering department may be involved in solving this problem.

Finally, there is a strategic level of thinking. An example is a plant that supplies all the dashboards to every car line and plant in a large, decentralized automotive company. Structuring the company this way was a strategic decision. However, it means this particular plant controls the schedule of every other plant in the company. If a wildcat strike occurs, no cars can be produced once their dashboard inventory is depleted. Tremendous pressure is put on the plant, and this generally causes labor problems, significant stress, high turnover, and absenteeism. All the workers and managers see the problems, but not in terms of business strategy. The plant manager, who has to deal with the problem and with the superiors who made the strategic decision, may have the clearest view of its impact. It will take managers and executives who are comfortable thinking strategically to analyze the problem correctly and solve it. Education and training can equip managers to identify and resolve each type of problem successfully. This means more than just training managers to think successfully in three ways. It also means training senior managers how to coach their subordinates and set up systems that support the development and use of these skills.

Assisting Managers to Learn about Self

A philosophy professor told the first class of the new semester that the smartest one wouldn't get the best grade. The students looked at him in disbelief. How could that be? Feeling puzzled was part of the course! The professor then went on to say that the person who got the best grade was the person who was most motivated to do the best thinking. There is a point here for managers. Being smart is not enough. Self-knowledge is essential. This includes values, emotions, energy level, physical capabilities, as well as intellect. A smart manager who is well motivated but who has a poor self-image and lacks the self-confidence to do the job will not perform well. Experiences in the business environment can be developed so that managers have the opportunity to learn about themselves. The development professional can build self-learning into each program.

This is also important because of the increased competitiveness of our times. Prior to the early 1970s, inflation and international competition was not as much of a threat as it is today. Currently, a manager whose values were formed in the fifties and sixties could have significant problems with regard to views toward work, competitiveness, and managing people. However, a manager who has an opportunity to look at his or her values, understand them, look at the work and strategy of the business, and the environment, has an opportunity to change and modify his or her values to keep up with the demands.

New Educational Technologies

Technology is changing management development. Video-aided instruction, computer-aided instruction, and the videodisc are finding applications in the field. A pitfall of new technology is the ease with which one is beguiled by all the glamorous electronic equipment. This can cause one to purchase more than needed or use the "gadget" as a substitute for sound learning approaches. Again, it is essential to be guided by the learning objectives in selecting techniques and materials. Computer-aided instruction may be intriguing to operate but totally inappropriate in terms of learning objectives.

Video-aided instruction is particularly useful in demonstrations of appropriate management behavior and skills involving motion, modeling, and specific operations. The greatest use for computer-aided instruction will be to provide information and build certain skills, primarily on an individual basis.

The world of business simulations is broad, diverse, and interesting. Simulations cover the gamut from simple management games using Lego blocks, tinker toys, and paper cutouts to computerized simulations of complex management or organization problems. Many of these techniques can be used to develop effective and useful "in-house" simulations. Companies like Strategic Management Group, Center for Creative Leadership, and Sterling Institute have developed computer simulations that can be purchased and used effectively in-house (see Chapter 26).

Videodiscs provide a more interesting version of programmed learning because they integrate the computer with television. The widest application is with large groups learning a skill that requires the visual medium of television and the speed of the computer to pick out specific pieces of information. It can be effective in demonstrating management behavior and helping managers learn specific skills, operations, or behaviors in a surprisingly short time, since its focus is on the essentials of any skill or operation. Development costs are very high, as in computer simulations.

Teleconferences via satellite and microwave transmission are in their infancy. Over the next 5 to 10 years, they are sure to be one of the training tools with wider use. The present format for most transmissions is the "talking head," and greater flexibility will be needed to meet the learning objectives relevant to management development. To be most effective, all parties at each location need to have a video monitor, video cameras to cover all participants as they speak, and telephone linkage. The cost, although relatively high, should be offset against the alternative travel time and cost.

External Management Development Resources

Training Materials

American industry spends millions of dollars every year on packaged management training programs. If the needs of the company have been correctly identified, the selection of these packages is relatively easy. However, too often selection of a package is based on something less than the critical objectives. One training house may help develop individualized applications of their package while others will not allow any deviation (see Chapter 22).

Outside consultants provide additional input for the development professional's programs. The needs of the company will dictate whether an academic or a consultant in private practice is required. Be sure to check out the experience of other companies with a consultant and find out if the style, approach, flexibility, and material are appropriate for your company. The training professional must be specific and clear with the consultant about what is needed. Since the consultant is working for the development professional, he or she needs to be managed in the same way a staff member is managed. The consultant will have a bias which should not contradict or interfere with the objectives of the learning program of the development officer (see Chapter 47).

The Role of Higher Education

Most business schools offer a variety of executive management development programs. Each has a particular bias and set of assumptions. One program may be appropriate for a certain type of manager but not for another. Just because the name of Harvard, Stanford, Columbia, or other prestigious school is associated with a program does not mean it will automatically meet a particular need. The development professional must help management evaluate the programs. An excellent reference is *Bricker's International Directory of University Executive Programs*, published annually by Samuel A. Pond, of Woodside, California. The directory presents a thorough assessment of each university's executive management programs. It is organized in a number of ways: general management programs by level of management, functional programs, and programs by subject. Each school is reviewed with detailed information about each program. Additional information can be obtained from individual schools. Because programs are expensive, it is worth the time to assess them carefully.

Executive MBA programs provide a general business education that helps managers perform at higher levels. Descriptions of these programs are available from each university. They differ, ranging from programs that require attendance on a specific day of the week for 2 years or that meet on Fridays and Saturdays for 1 year to 18 months, to others that bring managers in for 3 or 4 days at a time monthly. These class schedules often may determine whether or not a manager can receive further education and still remain on the job (see Chapter 46).

Government Programs

As government becomes more intrusive in business, many managers need greater understanding of government operations, particularly at the federal level. Two programs are worth consideration if this is an important objective for a company in its management development program. The President's Commission on Executive Exchange reports directly to the White House and focuses on the executive branch of government. Participants attend for a year and are on the government payroll while maintaining benefits in their home company. The participant usually reports to a high-level cabinet officer or a specific office, such as the Office of Budget and Management. The manager finds out firsthand how the executive branch works. Self-confidence is increased by being thrust into new, unknown, and challenging circumstances.

The Conference Board's Washington office coordinates a program called Congressional Assistant Program. The focus is on the legislative branch of government. Participants are assigned to a Senator or a Representative, and usually the manager will be given responsibility for one or more of the Congressman's committee assignments. Managers increase their understanding of the legislative branch, and again, self-confidence is gained. The government gains from these programs, too, through having contact with industry representatives as well as the assistance of the managers. Of critical importance to the success of these programs is returning participants to a job in the company where their new insights and confidence can be used. This requires much preplanning.

Conclusion

Development education and training is a vehicle for change and competitive advantage in an organization. Employee involvement, strategic management, and other programs are applications of development education and training which the professional can help design and implement.

Cost competitiveness, a key issue in business, can be the focus of programs and can be used to help managers understand ways to improve costs and enhance quality at the same time. In the past, American businesspeople have been able to isolate themselves from world competition in ways that European managers have not. A European manager has to deal with far more complexity, government regulation, union intervention, and cultural differences than is found in the United States. The pressure to internationalize our markets, however, is forcing managers to take a more appreciative look at the way overseas managers operate. Experience is proving that learning can be a two-way street with a corporation's international divisions. Management development can play a significant role in accelerating this change and helping managers understand how to manage a business than spans time zones, continents, and cultural differences.

Social values of the population and the workplace are changing. What was proper behavior yesterday may be improper or illegal today. During the early 1980s a number of senior executives found this out and lost their jobs in the process. These managers, in most cases, did nothing that had not been done before, and, in fact, they may have learned their behavior from their superiors. Managers need to learn how to keep their ear to the ground and assess the shifting values of a population and provide leadership that will keep the organization proactive and out of defensive legal and social issues. It is also important to understand the values of a population in order to manage and lead people effectively. Management development has an important role to play in this area—both identifying the shifts and helping managers deal successfully with them.

Training and development can bring a competitive advantage to any company. To maximize the opportunity to contribute to corporate success, the professional must understand company strategy and structure, industry structure, company products or services, department functions and operations, specific organizational processes, and the norms and politics of the organization. Second, the professional must understand the dynamics of the business from a general perspective which includes the implementation of strategy, the financial dynamics of the business, technology, and how people function in the organization.

The professional also needs a thorough grounding in behavioral sciences and their application to business. This involves not only an understanding of effective management of people in organizations but how people learn and how effective organizations change to master their future. All these things lead the professional to speak the language of business and to avoid becoming "behavioral monks"— who live in their own cloistered society. If Tom Peter's findings are correct about the corporation's need to be "close to the customer" (discussed in his books *In Search of Excellence* and *A Passion for Excellence*), they also apply to the development function. The customers of development professionals are the managers of the company. Being close to those managers and meeting their needs is essential not just to the career of the development professional but to the success of the business.

To achieve "closeness" to the customer, time must be spent with managers— joining their staff meetings, working to understand how they think and behave, going out in the field with the salesperson, working alongside people on the manufacturing floor, and working with people in the accounting department. Reading *The Wall Street Journal*, the *Harvard Business Review, Business Week, Fortune,* and other business publications on a regular basis builds an appreciation of the business. Some of these activities are the most relevant personal development activities a management development professional can do.

Bibliography

Digman, Lester A., "How Well-Managed Organizations Develop Their Executives," *Journal of Organization Dynamics,* autumn 1978, pp. 63–79.

Foulkes, Fred K., *Company Profiles: Management Development Survey—Nine Leading Companies,* a study done for AT&T Long Lines, 1980.

Incole, D. A., I. M. Rubin, and J. M. MacIntyre, *Organizational Psychology, A Book of Readings,* 2d ed., Prentice-Hall, Englewood Cliffs, NJ, 1974.

Kolb, David A., "On Management and the Learning Process," in Kolb, D. A., I. M. Rubin, and J. M. McIntyre, *Organizational Psychology—A Book of Readings,* 2d ed., Prentice-Hall, Englewood Cliffs, NJ, 1974.

Kolb, David A., I. M. Rubin, and J. M. McIntyre, *Organizational Psychology: An Experiential Approach,* 2d ed., Prentice-Hall, Englewood Cliffs, NJ, 1974.

Peters, Tom, and Nancy Austin, *Passion for Excellence,* Random House, New York, 1985.

Peters, Thomas J., and Robert H. Waterman, Jr., *In Search of Excellence*, Harper & Row, New York, 1982.

Pond, Samuel A., ed., *Bricker's International Directory*, 15th ed., Samuel A. Pond, Woodside, CA, 1984.

Rognetta, Vince, and Richard A. Eastburn, Unpublished study of 100 companies' management development practices, 1985.

Shaeffer, Ruth Gilbert, *Developing Strategic Leadership*, The Conference Board, New York, 1984.

34

Supervisor Development

Lester R. Bittel

Lester R. Bittel *is currently professor of management and director of the Center for Supervisory Research at the College of Business of James Madison University. An internationally recognized authority in the field of management and supervision, he is the coeditor of the Handbook for Professional Managers and author of the best-selling text, What Every Supervisor Should Know. Before accepting his academic post, Bittel was editor and publisher of Factory magazine and later director of information systems for the McGraw-Hill Publications Company. Prior to that, he was a field engineer for the Leeds & Northrup Company, an industrial engineer for Western Electric Company, Inc., and plant manager and training director for the Koppers Company. Bittel was a principal consultant and contributor to the massive Modular Programme for Supervisory Development published by the International Labour Office in 1981. He was also the designer of the Professional Development Certificate Program used as a standard by the Commonwealth of Virginia for training its public service supervisors. In 1981, Bittel, together with Jackson E. Ramsey, launched the first of an ongoing series of studies of supervisory attitudes and practices, widely reported in such journals as the* Harvard Business Review.

The supervisory management force, two million strong, holds the power to turn on—or turn off—the productivity of organizations. These are the men and women who provide the tenuous interface between the management hierarchy in every organization and the vast body of employees who put their hands on, or apply their minds to, the real work of enterprise, public as well as private. These unique hybrids are, in most instances, technically as well as legally, members of management. But their loyalties are strongly divided. Three out of four have risen from the ranks of labor—either blue-collar or white-collar. They rarely enjoy the privilege of establishing the goals of the organization they serve. Their upward mobility is severely limited. Yet their efforts ultimately ignite or defuse the productive spirit of the more than 70 million people who generate the nation's output of goods and services.

Historical Background

Supervisory development began, conceptually at least, during World War II, with the development of the Training within Industry Programs. These programs, fathered by Channing Dooley of the Standard Oil Company of New Jersey and Glen Gardiner of the Forstman Woolen Company, targeted three supervisory skills: job instruction training (JIT), job methods training (JMT), and job relations training (JRT). Only the JIT program remains today in anything like its original form. The other two programs have been largely forgotten. Nevertheless, it is possible that JMT was the predecessor of today's courses in job design, although its emphasis was upon the technical rather than the self-determinant aspects of an employee's work. It also seems certain that JRT was the forerunner of modern human relations skills training. In any event, it is safe to say that supervisory development is rooted deeply in contemporary organizational culture. Almost certainly, supervisory training is the foundation from which management development has emerged.

A Distinctive Segment of Management

Despite its linkage to management development, supervisory development remains in most instances clearly differentiated from it. The reason stems from the unique character of the supervisor's role in the organizational structure. Of all managers in the hierarchy, supervisors are the only ones who must function at a dual interface, relating on the one hand to rank-and-file operatives below them and on the other hand to the policy-oriented managers above them. Supervisors' employment origins are significantly different from other managers, too. In 1981 nearly three-quarters of all supervisors rose from the nether ranks rather than entering their managerial positions directly from college or from a high-level, professional, or specialized occupation. Both the unique nature of the supervisory job and the premanagement conditioning experienced by so many incumbents have acted to produce a supervisory segment of managers that is distinctive from other managers.[1]

Environmental Pressures

The supervisor's job has also been shaped by the changing and ever-intensifying pressures placed upon it by the environment. From what was once a simple emphasis upon the job and work requirements, factors external to the immediate job concerns have evolved to make the supervisor's job incredibly more complex and demanding.[2] The implications for supervisory training are extensive and are reflected in contemporary development programs.

The Role of Supervisors in Organizations

The design and conduct of supervisory development programs derive from an analysis of (1) the traditional concepts of the supervisor's role in the organization, (2) the competencies needed to fulfill that role, and (3) the knowledge, skills, and attitudes that supervisors bring to their assignments.

Traditional Role Concepts

In the early years of this century, supervisors became known as the "people in the middle," literally, in the hard place between genuine managers on the one hand and rank-and-file employees on the other. More recently, Keith Davis characterized supervision as "the keystone in the organizational arch," the supporting structural member between management and the work force.[3] In his book, *New Patterns of Management* (1961), Rensis Likert described supervisors more pragmatically as the "link-pins" between the upper and lower planes of an organizational structure.[4] Viewed in Likert's way, supervisors act as a series of flexible couplings, transmitting orders and instructions from above while absorbing shocks and disturbances from below. Likert's more realistic version still applies, although the Taft-Hartley Act of 1947 placed supervisors unequivocally in the ranks of management. The act specifically prohibits supervisors from joining unions of production or clerical workers, although they may form a union composed exclusively of supervisors. In the main, however, supervisors have not formed unions and have cast their lot, often with varying degrees of enthusiasm, with the management hierarchy, where they remain the bottommost figures on what is essentially a totem pole.

In the last two decades, the viewpoint of M. Scott Myers has become popular. Myers conceives of a supervisor's role as one of "facilitating," a person who makes resources and information available to subordinates while allowing them to plan and implement their own work. Such "goal-oriented" supervisors intervene to exercise control only when necessary.[5]

Supervisor's Role by Titular Definition

While there are many popularly accepted definitions of the widely used title of "supervisor," a simple one seems to serve best. It was developed by the International Labour Organization after considerable study of the literature:

> Supervisors are usually first-line managers whose major function is working with and through non-management employees to meet the objectives of the organization and needs of the employees.[6]

A modification of this definition is observed by the Opinion Research Corporation. It suggests that within the limits of this definition another distinction can be made: there are supervisors (*first-level supervisors*) who manage only nonmanagement employees, and there are also supervisors (*second-level supervisors*) who manage other supervisors in addition to nonmanagerial employees.[7]

Role by Self-Analysis

Granting the inherent flaws in self-appraisal, the National Survey of Supervisory Management Practices of more than 8500 supervisors found them drawing these conclusions[8] about their roles:

1. They see themselves as the boss, often operating independently on their own best instincts and judgment rather than according to policy. Their alignment with management is tentative at best. Only 40 percent say they "feel a part of company management"; 19 percent say they "feel closer to my employees than to company management." Another 17 percent "feel closer to other supervisors" and still another 18 percent say, "I feel that I am on my own as a manager most of the time." Some 6 percent say, "I feel that my boss and I are the company management."

2. Their thinking is in line with the traditional values of hard work and experience leading to achievement. The seniority principle, by which service is rewarded by promotion and security, appears to be "a good idea" to more than three-quarters of them. Performance appraisals as effective guides to motivation and discipline get the same degree of approval.

3. They are ambivalent about employee motivation. On the one hand, 93 percent of all supervisors say that "most employees want to do a good job," and 83 percent say that "most employees willingly accept responsibility for their own work." On the other hand, 66 percent say that "the main interest of most employees is to get enough money to do the things they want to do," while 61 percent say that "employees require close supervision," and 41 percent say that "most employees have to be pushed to produce."

4. All in all, however, supervisors are a vital, rather happy group. They are almost unanimous in saying (95 percent) that "what happens in my company or organization is really important to me." Only 24 percent say that "money is what's most important about my work." Eight out of ten (82 percent) say, "Generally speaking I am satisfied with my job."

Supervisory Segmentation for Training Analysis

Generalizations about supervisors—and the training they will need—become more meaningful when they are segmented according to certain basic classifications. As a consequence of the NSSMP survey mentioned earlier, it is very helpful to segregate supervisors according to the four-cell matrix illustrated in Fig. 34-1. There are significant demographic and attitudinal differences between each of the four groups: (1) blue-collar, first-level; (2) white-collar, first-level; (3) blue-collar, second-level; and (4) white-collar, second-level. These differences will impinge heavily in program design.[9]

Further analysis of survey data showed significant differences according to the operating area in which supervisors were employed. These include production, marketing, engineering, and purchasing.[10,11,12,13] It is not unlikely that there are also significant differences among supervisory roles and attitudes according to the industry in which they are employed.

Basic Supervisory Competencies

Supervisory training programs, of course, should spring from a clear knowledge of the competencies required by employers of their supervisors. Here again, general-

Educational Levels
8-12 years, 46%
13-15 years, 31%
16-20 years, 23%

- Production supervisor in manufacturing plant.
- Supervisor of greatest number of employees (union).
- Man rather than woman.
- Oldest; extensive supervisory experience.
- Relatively modest educational level.
- Satisfied with pay, although not highest paid.
- Feels greatest pressure by far to keep costs low.
- Less than positive in beliefs about employee motivation.
- Most tolerant of minorities.
- Moderate alignment with management.

BLUE-COLLAR, SECOND-LEVEL

Educational Levels
8-12 years, 19%
13-15 years, 21%
16-20 years, 60%

- Supervisor of clerical, accounting and staff employees.
- Supervisor of relatively few employees (non-union).
- Youngest; most experienced in supervision.
- Best educated.
- Highest paid.
- Greatest authority in hiring; greatest support in disciplinary matters.
- Least supportive of seniority principle.
- Least tolerant of minorities.
- Highest alignment with management.

WHITE-COLLAR, SECOND-LEVEL

Educational Levels
8-12 years, 55%
13-15 years, 27%
16-20 years, 18%

- Production supervisor in manufacturing plant.
- Supervisor of large number of employees (union).
- Promoted from shop floor.
- Least educated.
- Lowest paid.
- Least authority in hiring; least support in disciplinary matters.
- Most supportive of seniority principle.
- High degree of tolerance toward minorities.
- Low alignment with management; most likely to want to return to old job.

BLUE-COLLAR, FIRST-LEVEL

Educational Levels
8-12 years, 23%
13-15 years, 26%
16-20 years, 51%

- Supervisor of clerical, accounting and staff employees.
- Supervisor of fewest number of employees (non-union).
- Women rather than man.
- Feels that paperwork is heavy burden.
- Relatively high educational level.
- Most poor paid; lower end of pay scale.
- Low degree of tolerance toward minorities.
- Feels least pressure to keep costs low.
- Least aligned with management.

WHITE-COLLAR, FIRST-LEVEL

Figure 34-1. Segmentation of supervisors. (*Adapted from Lester R. Bittel and Jackson E. Ramsey, "New Dimensions for Supervisory Development," Training and Development Journal, March 1983, p. 15.*)

zations are not nearly so good as those gathered by each organization through observation and research. Nevertheless, many helpful hypotheses of necessary supervisory competencies have been gathered by authorities close to the scene.

Carroll and Anthony,[14] for example, asked the question, "What Do Supervisors Do?" and concluded that five responsibilities were involved:

1. *Supervisor's responsibility to higher management.* This includes items such as plan the work of the department, coordinate the department's work with other

departments, interpret and implement management policies, make production decisions, maintain both morale and discipline, keep control of costs, and send recommendations for change upward.

2. *Supervisor's responsibility to employees.* This includes items such as stand up for employee when being treated arbitrarily from above, handle employee problems promptly, be fair in all departmental matters, distribute all departmental amenities fairly, discuss proposed changes before change takes place, maintain a safe and clean work area, and plan work so that work loads are as stable and predictable as possible.

3. *Supervisor's responsibilities to coworkers.* This includes items such as coordinate whatever work flows or paper work needs to be exchanged among supervisors, communicate with other departments about mutual needs and problems, give them support as members of the same management team, and coordinate policy interpretations with other departments to assure consistency and uniformity.

4. *Supervisor's responsibilities to staff departments.* This includes items such as comply with reasonable requests for information from staff managers, utilize whatever standardized reporting forms are necessary, and listen to and consult the counsel of staff managers pertaining to matters which fall into their expertise.

5. *Supervisor's responsibility in labor matters.* If a union is present, this might include items such as become knowledgeable about the labor agreement, attempt to maintain a conciliatory atmosphere in the relationship with the union, respect the terms of the agreement, effectively administer the grievance machinery, treat employees fairly even though they are union members, and represent management, for that is where a supervisor's first loyalty lies.

Baker and Holmberg[15] analyzed data gathered by the American Management Association and found that the supervisory time spent on managerial functions can be ranked from most to least in this order; implementing, planning, organizing, delegating, evaluating, innovating, and staffing.

Cover,[16] however, takes issue with generalized managerial aspects of supervisory competencies and urges a "return to basics." These would emphasize production, quality control, sales support and customer relations, cost control, people, housekeeping, safety, administration, personal relationships, innovation, and attention to identification and establishment of performance improvement objectives.

In probably the most exhaustive research ever extended in the identification of competencies, AT&T isolated and ranked 14 principal duties of supervision as illustrated in Table 34-1. These are examined in detail as a guide for the development of supervisory training programs in Charles R. Macdonald's *Performance Based Supervisory Development.*[17] AT&T's analysis identified not only the 14 basic duties but also the major tasks, decision points, skills, and related knowledge areas associated with each.

Selection of Supervisors

Roughly one in five supervisors in the NSSMP survey volunteered that they would return to the ranks if they could do so without loss of face or reduction in pay.[18] This group of supervisors ranked significantly lower in every aspect of satisfaction and confidence than the others in the survey. It would appear, therefore, that prudent human resources management in this area should begin, not with supervisory development, but with a more careful and effective selection process Extensive studies reported by the University of Pennsylvania in 1978[19] conclude

Table 34-1. Dimensions of Supervisor Competencies

Principal duties	Major tasks	Decision points	Skills	Knowledge	Total items
1. Planning the work	15	6	12	32	65
2. Controlling the work	9	6	13	36	64
3. Problem solving	11	4	14	17	46
4. Performance feedback	24	4	28	60	116
5. Coaching subordinates	22	1	22	25	70
6. Motivative atmosphere	13	3	10	19	45
7. Managing time	9	2	17	44	72
8. Communication	6	1	1	16	24
9. Informal oral communication	19	5	21	20	65
10. Self-development	8	1	7	17	33
11. Written communication	11	3	21	23	58
12. Representing company	5	1	—	3	9
13. Career counseling	17	3	2	32	54
14. Meetings	18	2	28	39	87
Total	187	42	196	383	808

Adapted from Charles R. Macdonald, *Performance Based Supervisory Development: Adapted from a Major AT&T Study*, Human Resource Development Press, Amherst, MA, 1982, p. 24.

that employees with the greatest supervisory potential do not necessarily fill the key ranks. To begin with, selection systems are poorly planned and implemented. Preferences are traditionally given to friends and relatives. The seniority syndrome, too, carries over into supervisory selection. In effect, it says, give the longest-service employee a shot at the job first. But the selection system is only part of the problem. Many good workers will not move into supervision if it means shift work. Pay differentials between hourly employees and their supervisors are narrow. Hourly jobs are seen as more secure, supervisory work as full of frustrations. This view is supported by Benson,[20] who contends that "superworkers" continue to be rewarded by promotions to supervision, a position that is often inappropriate for their skills or without any promise of advancement. "We may be building failure into the selection process," warns Benson.

Good selection programs start with a study of the work to be performed. This is easier said than done. All too often it is the product of a facile job-description writer rather than a careful study of the work, especially its make-or-break aspects. Progressive organizations develop historical data that help them to associate personal characteristics (measurable ones preferred) of successful performers with each job requirement. Selection dimensions are derived from these studies. The selection process is then precisely prescribed and implemented. The better programs involve a combination of screening techniques—testing, multiple interviewing, in-basket exercises, and psychological evaluations.[21]

Training Needs Assessment

Ideally, the assessment of supervisory training needs should be the resultant of a comparison between (1) the required competencies of the position (AT&T calls these "mastery models") and (2) the measured knowledge, skills, and attitudes of the incumbent supervisors or supervisory candidates. In actual fact, a great many organizations begin with generalized lists of competencies. They then use a number of techniques to establish the training gaps, or needs, between this list and presumed capabilities of their supervisory participants.

Capability Assessments

To establish the levels of capabilities already possessed or attained by an organization's supervisory population, human resource analysts commonly use as sources (1) *performance reviews*, from which specific and cumulative identification of less than satisfactory performance against appraisal criteria is gathered; (2) *critical incidents*, gathered from formal records or through interviews with supervisors, their peers in staff departments, and their superiors; (3) *attitude (or climate) surveys*, from which general indicators of unsatisfactory employee relationships are identified. In a relatively few instances, diagnostic instruments are also used. These are available commercially from a number of psychological test development organizations.

Needs Inventories

The most common approach in designing most supervisory training programs, however, is to rely upon an assessment of needs (made judgmentally) by the managers to whom supervisors report, by HRD professionals, by the supervisors themselves, or by some combination of these three. Occasionally, employees will also be asked to contribute to this assessment. Such needs assessments, or inventories, may be made by direct interview, by written survey, or through nominal group techniques (NTG) in which training needs are itemized and ranked in group sessions conducted by HRD professionals. Alternative formats for conducting written needs-inventory surveys are shown in Figs. 34-2 and 34-3. Burack[22] cautions that inventories gathered from self-assessments are liable to contain biases and should be subjected to "reality checks" from peer's subordinates, peers, and superiors.

A traditional, simplified needs-inventory format and content is shown in Fig. 34-2. This form, developed by Training House,[23] asks that items be rated as 3, "extremely important"; 2, "fairly important"; and 1, "not too relevant." Other formats offer space for suggesting training needs not listed.

The trend in needs inventories is to expand definition of the items in order to more clearly specify the areas of deficiency, as shown in the excerpt in Fig. 34-3, developed by Langdon.[24]

Another source of needs-assessment data is for an organization to use a standardized inventory instrument and compare results with standards established for a national, industry, or functional database. The survey instrument used by the Center for Supervisory Research at James Madison University (Harrisonburg, Virginia 22807), for example, is especially appropriate not only for determining current training needs but also for monitoring trends in supervisory attitudes development.

Course Content

Typical course content for supervisory development can be inferred from an examination of established competencies and needs-analysis inventory lists. Beneath the surface of the subject matter, however, it is important for the training coordinator to establish beforehand exactly what the learning thrust of each course or topic will be. Specifically, almost any subject or course may be approached with an objective of conveying *knowledge*, imparting or improving *skills*, or reinforcing or shaping *attitudes*. Many subjects, of course, lend themselves readily to classifications as knowledge or skill, but the deeper aspect of content should not be overlooked,

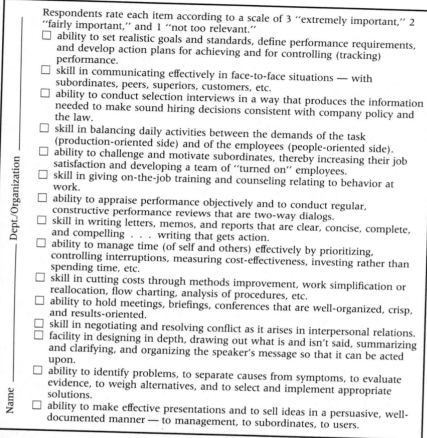

Respondents rate each item according to a scale of 3 "extremely important," 2 "fairly important," and 1 "not too relevant."

☐ ability to set realistic goals and standards, define performance requirements, and develop action plans for achieving and for controlling (tracking) performance.

☐ skill in communicating effectively in face-to-face situations — with subordinates, peers, superiors, customers, etc.

☐ ability to conduct selection interviews in a way that produces the information needed to make sound hiring decisions consistent with company policy and the law.

☐ skill in balancing daily activities between the demands of the task (production-oriented side) and of the employees (people-oriented side).

☐ ability to challenge and motivate subordinates, thereby increasing their job satisfaction and developing a team of "turned on" employees.

☐ skill in giving on-the-job training and counseling relating to behavior at work.

☐ ability to appraise performance objectively and to conduct regular, constructive performance reviews that are two-way dialogs.

☐ skill in writing letters, memos, and reports that are clear, concise, complete, and compelling . . . writing that gets action.

☐ ability to manage time (of self and others) effectively by prioritizing, controlling interruptions, measuring cost-effectiveness, investing rather than spending time, etc.

☐ skill in cutting costs through methods improvement, work simplification or reallocation, flow charting, analysis of procedures, etc.

☐ ability to hold meetings, briefings, conferences that are well-organized, crisp, and results-oriented.

☐ skill in negotiating and resolving conflict as it arises in interpersonal relations.

☐ facility in designing in depth, drawing out what is and isn't said, summarizing and clarifying, and organizing the speaker's message so that it can be acted upon.

☐ ability to identify problems, to separate causes from symptoms, to evaluate evidence, to weigh alternatives, and to select and implement appropriate solutions.

☐ ability to make effective presentations and to sell ideas in a persuasive, well-documented manner — to management, to subordinates, to users.

Dept./Organization

Name

Figure 34-2. Needs inventory format. *(Adapted from Scott B. Parry and Edward J. Robinson, "Management Development: Training or Education?", Training and Development Journal, July 1979, pp. 8–13.)*

since it will have a significant impact upon the effectiveness of course material and subsequent evaluation of the training by participants and their sponsors.

Course Levels

The most common classification of course material has been according to level of experience of the participants, rather than by course topic. Course content, emphasis, and technique may vary, but the great majority of supervisory topics might be taught at any level of experience. Many in-service programs and a great many institutional supervisory training programs are constructed, however, according to whether or not the participants are classified as (1) *presupervisory,* (2) *entering* or relatively inexperienced (1 to 5 years), or (3) *experienced* supervisors with more than 5 years of experience at that level. An integrated program was designed

—1. Analyzing problems and making decisions:
   - ☐ a. Identify the problem and describe it clearly.
   - ☐ b. Determine whether or not the problem is worth spending time on.
   - ☐ c. Use a systematic approach to collect information.
   - ☐ d. Identify the most important characteristics that a solution should have.
   - ☐ e. Generate a series of possible solutions and select the one which best meets the needs. Consider the characteristics of each possible solution.
   - ☐ f. Prepare an effective action plan for the solution you select.

—2. Conducting fact-finding discussions:
   - ☐ a. State the need or the information in such a way that the employee will be encouraged to provide what you need.
   - ☐ b. Indicate clearly the kind of information you want.
   - ☐ c. Probe for relevant information (both positive and negative) even though the employee may be reluctant to speak.
   - ☐ d. Uncover all the relevant data without creating hostility or distrust.
   - ☐ e. Record the facts you collect.
   - ☐ f. End the discussion so that the employee feels he or she has made a significant contribution.

—3. Motivating:
   - ☐ a. Identify situations that result from motivational problems rather than from lack of skill or organizational support.
   - ☐ b. Identify causes of motivational problems.
   - ☐ c. Indicate clearly the behaviors that you want to motivate.
   - ☐ d. Develop a plan for removing demotivating elements from the work environment.
   - ☐ e. Identify incentives in the work environment which can be used to motivate the employee.
   - ☐ f. Demonstrate how to give effective motivational feedback.

—4. Dealing with emotional situations:
   - ☐ a. Face up to, rather than avoid or be intimidated by, emotional situations.
   - ☐ b. Recognize and avoid using "emotional blackmail" as a way of controlling others.
   - ☐ c. Demonstrate respect for the feelings of others.
   - ☐ d. Handle emotional situations by calming.
   - ☐ e. "Defuse" the emotions of others so that the real cause of problems can be uncovered.
   - ☐ f. Avoid responses that escalate emotional behavior.

Figure 34-3. Detailed items for a needs inventory. (*Adapted from Danny G. Langdon, "The Individual Management Development Program,"* Training and Development Journal, *March 1982, pp. 78–82.*)

along these lines for the Commonwealth of Virginia for the offering of a Certificate in Professional Development to its public-service supervisors. Its designations are: Level 0, presupervisory to accommodate open enrollment and to prescribe preparatory requirements; Level I, for basic (or inexperienced) supervision; Level II, for advanced (or experienced) supervision; and Level III, for middle managers.

Basic Supervisory Course. One of the most comprehensive lists of course offerings for supervisors at all levels of experience was designed by the International Labour Office,[6] as shown in Table 34-2. Extensive, detailed course outlines for instructors and trainees are available from ILO.

Table 34-2. Comprehensive List of Basic Courses

A Basic Modular Program for Supervisory Training
I. Supervision
    M-I-01   The Organization and the Supervisor
    M-I-02   Principles of Supervision

II. Supervisory Techniques
    M-II-03   Planning and Scheduling
    M-II-04   Work Study and Organization
    M-II-05   Directing and Coordinating Work
    M-II-06   Controlling Work
    M-II-07   Quality Control
    M-II-08   Finance and Cost Control
    M-II-09   Decision Making and Problem Solving
    M-II-10   Role Analysis
    M-II-11   Introducing Changes
    M-II-12   Communications and Records

III. The Main Supervisory Areas
    M-III-13   Utilization of Equipment and Facilities
    M-III-14   Maintenance Supervision
    M-III-15   Material Handling
    M-III-16   Energy Utilities and Auxiliary Services
    M-III-18   Office Supervision
    M-III-19   Purchasing
    M-III-20   Marketing

IV. Supervising People
    M-IV-21   Leadership
    M-IV-22   Informal Organizations and Groups
    M-IV-23   Individual and Group Discussions
    M-IV-24   Staffing
    M-IV-25   Motivating Workers
    M-IV-26   Job Evaluation
    M-IV-27   Performance Appraisal
    M-IV-28   Salary Administration
    M-IV-29   Training and Development
    M-IV-30   Interpersonal Relations and Behavior in Supervision
    M-IV-31   Industrial Relations
    M-IV-32   Safety, Health, Security
    M-IV-33   Maintaining Discipline and Morale
    M-IV-34   Complaints and Grievances
    M-IV-35   Supervising Special Groups

Adapted from J. Prokopenko and Lester R. Bittel, "A Modular Course-Format for Supervisory Development," *Training and Development Journal,* February 1981, p. 15.

Advanced Supervisory Course. Many colleges, universities, and community colleges divide their for-credit supervisory curriculum into basic and advanced programs of a semester length. One such program, offered by the U.S. Department of Agriculture follows this format, and its course listings are shown in Table 34-3.

Focus Clusters. It is popular in the in-service field to offer short courses containing clusters of related topics focusing on a particular skill or knowledge area. Many such courses are designed around selected chapters in a particular text or reference book. For example, the following focus clusters are commonly used in conjunction with one popular book in the field.

Interpersonal Relations. Work group behavior, conflict and cooperation, appraisal of employee performance, the arts of leadership, effective oral and written

Table 34-3. Basic and Advanced Course Content, U.S. Department of Agriculture

Modern Management and Supervision: Part I (40 hours)
Motivation
Employee development
Self-confrontation
Team leadership
Problem solving
Decision making
Performance assessment
Analysis of efficiency
Consultation skills
Communications
Organization theory

Modern Management and Supervision: Part II (40 hours)
Supervision and management awareness
Behavior analysis
Interpersonal relations
Self-confrontation
Creativity
Employee development and performance appraisal
Performance standards
Incentives and recognition
Authority, strategies, and decision making
Managing time
Delegation
Equal employment
Labor-management relations
Adverse actions
Information sharing and communications
Conflict resolution
Planning an organization system
Synthesis of management concepts
Practical problem solving
Self-development

communications, giving orders and instructions, counseling troubled employees, handling complaints and grievances, how and when to discipline.

Management Process. The supervisor's management job, supervision and the management process, making plans and carrying out policy, exercising control over people and processes, problem solving and decision making, organizing an effective department, staffing with human relations.

Productivity and Quality Improvement. Supervision and the management process, training and development of employees, job design and enrichment, job assignments and work schedules, improving productivity and controlling costs, toward a higher quality of workmanship.

Personal Skills Building. Problem solving and decision making, taking charge of your career, managing time and handling stress, putting your best foot forward in the organization.

Special Interest Courses. There are always a number of topic areas that enjoy a brief popularity and a relevance to current problems. Other courses hold high value periodically for any organization. Among both kinds of special interest subject areas, these seem to retain perennial value: performance appraisal, equal employment opportunity, employee training, productivity improvement, time management, stress management, grievance handling, leadership, communications, transactional analysis, and problem solving.

Methods and Techniques

Supervisory development draws from the same array of locales, sources, methods, and techniques as do other training segments. Certain alternatives, of course, seem more appropriate and effective than do others, although documented evidence is scarce.

Locale and Source

Bula[25] in 1982 found that supervisory training budgets were apportioned according to Table 34-4. This survey does not shed light, however, on the more basic concern of the extent to which such training should be conducted off the job or on the job.

On-the-Job Training vs. Off-the-Job Training

In an earlier study by the Conference Board,[26] the implications were that 90 percent of all formal training for supervisors takes place off the job in a classroom, seminar, or workshop format. Only about 10 percent of all companies surveyed conducted formal supervisory training *on the job* that met a three-part criteria: (1) stated, written objectives for each participant, (2) one or more designated individuals (line managers or HRD professionals) to guide the experience of the trainee, and (3) a specific schedule setting forth the types of experience to be obtained and a timetable of intended progress. *Off-the-job classroom-type* training is obviously more convenient for the trainer and easier to control. The Conference Board survey showed a distribution of methods used in off-job classroom training for supervisors to greatly favor group discussion (95 percent) and formal presentation or lecture (90 percent), followed by case study (85 percent), role play (60 percent), required reading (55 percent), and business games (40 percent). These figures do not tell the whole story, since other comments regarding this survey indicated that case studies and role play were accorded less than 20 percent of the training time by those

Table 34-4. Primary Source and Locale of Training for Supervisors, Percent

Internal	57
Outside	36
Vocational technical on site	30
Vocational technical off site	26
University on site	19
University off site	27
Other organizations on site	9
Other organizations off site	14

Adapted from Ronald J. Bula, "Survey of Management Training Needs in Wisconsin," *Training and Development Journal*, January 1985, pp. 64–65.

organizations using them. In a related study of off-site meetings attended by supervisors, McKeon[27] provides some specific insights into the elements of classroom methods that can make them effective. Participants observed that presentations and discussions accounted for about 60 percent of their training time and yielded 43 percent of the perceived learning value of the activity; working on problems in small groups took about 25 percent of the training time and accounted for about 27 percent of the perceived value. Interestingly, required reading and related outside work accounted for about 15 percent of the time and 16 percent of the value. The balance of perceived value was derived from incidental exchanges during meals and coffee breaks. The conclusion is that small-group assignments and self-paced learning for supervisors appears to be more effective, hour for hour, than formal presentations.

The Conference Board survey also indicated that HRD professionals provided the faculty for 75 percent of in-house, off-the-job classroom training for supervisors. The balance of the faculty was provided by line managers and other functional specialists in the organization.

Methods Selection

As with other training, the methods used for supervisory training should be of a balanced variety to achieve the established objectives with the greatest simplicity and economy. The generally agreed-upon advice regarding choice of methods is this:

- To increase *knowledge*, consider especially assigned reading, lectures, guided discussions, observational tours, case studies, programmed learning, and self-tests.

- To increase *skill*, consider especially modeling, role playing, demonstrations, case studies, problem-solving conferences, job rotation, and supervised practice on or off the job.

- To influence *attitudes*, consider especially role playing, demonstrations, case studies, problem-centered conferences, job rotation, and films.

In general, supervisors tend to prefer and to learn more effectively from specific concrete examples, experience and reality-oriented practice, and interactive exercises than from abstract, conceptual presentations or from reading assignments.

Program Planning and Design

Once all the variables in competencies, selection, needs assessment, course content, and method selection have been reviewed and assembled, the trainer faces the major task of strategy determination and implementation. These two elements are encompassed by the planning and design phase of supervisory training.

Objectives

It is essential that the program objectives be clearly defined and put into writing. Agreement must be secured beforehand, *in fact* from the principal line managers, and *by inference* from the supervisors themselves. Objectives are typically expressed in terms of incremental improvements in knowledge, skills, and/or attitudes directly related to acknowledged competency requirements and an assessment of developmental needs. The more quantitatively these goals can be defined, the better, although the state of the art will leave many in purely qualitative terms. Some examples of program or course objectives are:

Basic Objectives of Supervisory Training

1. To give the participant the essential knowledge of his or her responsibilities so as to make decisions that are compatible with company goals and policies

2. To give the participant the knowledge essential to good management practices so that this knowledge may guide day-to-day management decisions

3. To give the participant the skills to direct the work of his or her department and people in a positive and productive manner

Objectives for Introduction to Supervision. To provide inexperienced supervisors with a basic understanding of management functions and of their specific responsibilities in applying them in their organization.

Objectives for Advanced Supervision. To provide experienced supervisors with a review of job-related fundamental management practices and to introduce them to a selected variety of important new concepts and techniques directly applicable to their work.

Objectives for Time Management. To instill in supervisors an awareness of the degree to which personal time may be controlled and to provide them with a number of specific tools and techniques for increasing the productive use of their time on the job.

Whenever possible, objectives should also include a statement of the way in which acquired learning will be evaluated. These evaluation measures can include a number of methods such as (1) before-and-after comprehension testing; (2) self-evaluation feedback from supervisors after returning to their jobs; (3) evaluation of critical incidents by superiors; (4) routine performance appraisal criteria; (5) measurement of performance-related data from a supervisor's department, such as absence and turnover rates, grievances lodged, productivity, and quality measures; and (6) identifiable achievements such as reports prepared, problems solved, and conflicts resolved.

Format Choices

In addition, decisions must be reached as to what extent programs should be conducted (1) on the job or off the job (the great proportion occurs off the job in classroom settings); (2) on site or off site (most full-scale programs are conducted on the premises); (3) during working hours or after (most are held during working hours, although this choice varies widely); (4) continuously or on intermittent schedules, such as 2 hours per day for 2 weeks or 1 day a week for 10 weeks (schedules vary widely, but intermittent schedules prevail); and (5) internal HRD faculty, line faculty, or outside organizations such as vocational-technical institutes, community colleges, university extensions, or independent consultants or professional societies.

Participant Selection

Another question to be resolved is whether or not for conference-type training to mix supervisors with those from other departments and with middle and upper managers. Most authorities agree that much is to be gained by placing line supervisors from different departments and divisions in the same classes as well as including equivalent-level staff supervisors. Interactions are likely to be democratic and vigorous with valuable exchanges of on-the-job as well as course-related information and perspectives. In general, however, there are risks involved in mixing widely separated echelons of management. The learning experience can be threatening to lower-level supervisors and their degree of participation in discussions inhibited. On the other hand, some courses may lend to exchanges of viewpoints for higher, as well as lower, levels.

Traditional vs. Modular Format

Because the number of subjects that might be judged as essential parts of supervisory development is so large, some authorities advocate a departure from this traditional approach to program design.[23] They believe that training is made more effective and less costly by targeting selected elements in modular fashion. Each module is thus integrated into a comprehensive, long-range program for supervisory development. There is considerable justification for this approach, as illustrated by the example in Table 34-5.

Planning Guidelines

Broadwell[28] cautions about a new generation of supervisors who are younger, better educated, and impatient with the ponderous, didactic methods used in traditional approaches to supervisory training. He also calls attention to the increasing number of white-collar, knowledge-oriented supervisors whose expectations and life styles differ from before the "baby boom." Fulmer[29] advises that the focus of supervisory training programs would not exclude the need to regularly familiarize supervisors with the internal workings of their own organizations. And Short[30] urges that program design allow for "unlearning" well-entrenched, ineffective habits on the part of supervisors. He observes that good design will entail discomfort or "disequilibrium" and its success will depend, in large measure, on the supervisor rather than exclusively upon the trainer.

Byham[31] also emphasizes how important it is that training actually *change* a supervisor's behavior—and performance. Accordingly, he offers these negative precepts to guide program design:

- Practice does not make perfect.
- Tenure does not make a good supervisor.
- Experience is a poor teacher.
- Learning by mistake is a waste of time.
- Systems can't change people.
- Self-study is not enough.
- Bosses are often poor models.

On the positive side of program design, Byham advises that:

1. Adequate diagnosis of training and developmental needs is vital.

	Traditional management development	Modular management development
Scheduling	Meetings are scheduled at the convenience of the instructor, usually same time each week (e.g., Tuesday mornings for 8 weeks). Or, if many participants are required to travel, course may be held at hotel or conference center and run continuously (e.g., over 1 week)	Meetings are held as often as demand requires, at the convenience of participants. Thus, if 67 people sign up for "Time Management," it will be run four times (16–17 persons each time); a topic with 34 enrollees will be run twice. Offerings can be scattered throughout year
Length of sessions	Each class meeting is same length as others. Some topics are "rushed" or "crammed" to cover all the content; others fit comfortably	Length of meeting is determined by content and intent. Half day, full day, 2 days with 2 weeks between, and so on
Participants	Same people go through course cycle together. They become a group and function as such after the first meeting	Different faces at each meeting. Composition of group is based on need to know and availability to attend
Enrollment	Selection is usually done by personnel or training departments. Participants are drafted, with the approval of their immediate supervisor. Such programs usually try not to mix too wide a spectrum of grade levels in any one group: senior managers attend first, then middle, then first level	Selection is done by department heads, who fill out a "selection matrix" at start of year. They then confer with their subordinate managers (the participants) and enroll. A boss and subordinate can attend the same offering without disrupting their work flow or the group composition
Content	Over time, all members of the organization's management team get the same common core of concepts, skills, procedures, and policy. It becomes part of the "puberty rites" of passing into management in the organization. Once a manager has attended, there is often no further training within the organization	Different managers take different selections, based on their needs (e.g., some supervise people, others manage projects; some do a lot of writing, or negotiating, or presenting, or running of meetings; others don't). Of course, some matrix offerings can be required of everyone (e.g., those dealing with policy and procedures, budgeting, etc.)
Instructor	The instructor carries the burden of responsibility for making the course a success. Usually the same person(s) will teach all subjects and should speak with authority on all topics	Different instructors can be used for different modules, so the most qualified person (from within or outside) can be made available for a given topic
Follow-up	End-of-course activities are done on a group basis (e.g., graduation, postcourse evaluation, joining of supervisory association, follow-up meeting to report on composite action plans). Usually there is little or no follow-up	Follow-up is the responsibility of participant and immediate boss. There is more time to implement action plans after each module attended, and more commitment to do so. Better communication is possible between instructor and participant-and-boss, who can function more as a team

© 1978 by Training House, Inc. / 100 Bear Brook Road / Princeton Jct. NJ 08550
Adapted from Scott B. Parry and Edward J. Robinson, "Management Development: Training or Education?" *Training and Development Journal*, July 1979, p. 9.

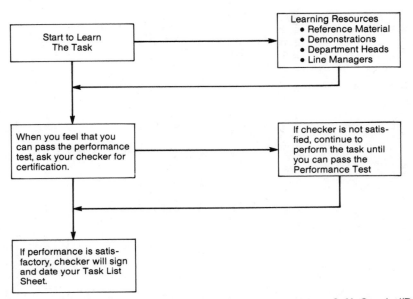

Figure 34-4. Performance-based planning model. *(Adapted from C. V. Crumb, "Performance-Based Line Supervisor Training," Training and Development Journal, September 1981, p. 44.)*

2. The supervisor's immediate superior is vital in bringing about behavioral change.

3. The individual's needs must be integrated into program design.

4. Development plans must be put into writing.

5. A follow-up procedure must be integral with the program.

Planning Models

In principle, planning for supervisory training follows, with only slight modifications, the same process as for any kind of sound training. A model that emphasized the performance-based approach[32] for supervisory program design is shown in Fig. 34-4. Still another model, linking supervisory training to career planning[33] is illustrated in Fig. 34-5.

Program Management

Management of supervisory development programs differs from others only to the degree that the supervisory population is more pliable (or manipulable) than the middle or executive levels of management and less manipulable than nonmanagerial trainees. Thus, in the main, the individual providing supervisory training can focus on program management mechanics rather than paying undue attention to the typical problems of attendance and out-of-class preparation.

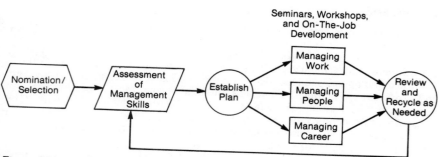

Figure 34-5. Integration of supervisory training with career development planning. (*Adapted from Marlys C. Hanson, "Training Employees and Managers for Their Roles in Career Development," in Career Management: Implications for Organizations and Individuals, Career Development Division, ASTD, Alexandria, VA, 1980, p. 10.*)

Maximizing Outcomes

In any case, prudent trainers will seek to manage the program in such a way that results will be maximized. Rosenthal and Mezoff[34] suggest that supervisory development practitioners first make certain that the supervisors' managers understand the benefits to be derived from the training and then follow a series of steps during the development process to assure that what happens during the training occurs in the most favorable organizational atmosphere. Rosenthal and Mezoff suggest that trainers inform the supervisors' sponsors of the "ceremonial effects" of the development program: (1) it acts as a motivator and a builder of confidence and self-esteem, (2) it serves to remove stress and helps newly appointed supervisors to make the crossover to management more effectively, and (3) it facilitates improved working relationships between participants and their coworkers and employees. These two authors also suggest the following 10-point program for assuring the optimum learning environment:

1. Inform participants about training well in advance of the training event.

2. Conduct a pretraining interview with participants.

3. Encourage sponsoring managers to discuss the program beforehand with their participating supervisors.

4. Design the training to address issues of the supervisor's organizational role.

5. Provide ample opportunities for participants to discuss work-related issues.

6. Structure the program to include free time for social interaction and individual reflection.

7. Conduct training off site or at a location that minimizes distractions and interruptions.

8. Structure the training to make it significantly different from the normal work routine.

9. Publicize the training in the organization's newspaper or newsletter.

10. Provide certificates of completion.

Certification

An attractive way to emphasize the importance of, and lasting value of, supervisory training is to integrate it with the certification opportunities provided by the Institute of Certified Professional Managers. This organization, jointly sponsored by the National Management Association and the International Management Council, is located and operates independently on the campus of James Madison University in Harrisonburg, Virginia. It conducts a full-scale, recognized certification program based upon education, experience, and three certification examinations. The substance of the certification examinations parallels the range of subjects offered in a comprehensive supervisory training program, and participant and trainer's manuals are available for preparation purposes.

Program Monitoring

It is essential that training sessions begin and end at the stated time and that their conduct follow principles of good management. The HRD professional becomes an important role model in this regard. Rigorous attendance records should be kept; absences should be followed up (in a sensitive manner, of course) to determine their cause and to let individuals know that their participation was missed. If the program calls for out-of-class assignments, these, too, should be logged in, to indicate their importance to the training experience and to the trainee's progress. If assignments are optional, make certain that this is clear to all participants, although it is better for assignments to be an integral and required part of the program if they are to be included at all. It is often a good idea, too, to maintain contact with participants' sponsors during the program in order to receive ongoing, current feedback and also to sustain motivation at that end.

Program Examples

Supervisory training programs vary widely in content, length, and format. Most comprehensive programs, however, contain subjects and topics described earlier in this chapter. It will probably be more helpful at this point to look at how different aspects of supervisory development have been treated and at a few programs with distinctive features but with broad application elsewhere.

Policies

At Morrison-Knudson,[24] a large diversified construction, design, and engineering firm with 35,000 employees and based in Boise, Idaho, the supervisory program is constructed on explicitly stated policies and criteria, especially when selecting vendor supplied components. The policies state that all content must:

- Be needs-assessment based.
- Employ performance-task objectives.
- Be how-to, or skill, oriented.
- Be highly interactive.
- Incorporate behavioral modeling.
- Utilize job aids, reminders that can be taken back to the job.

- Concentrate on team effort.
- Involve the supervisor's manager in the planning process.
- Fit into an ongoing employee-performance and career-development program.
- Be demonstratably cost-effective.

Selection

At Tri/Valley Growers Plant 7 in Modesto, California,[35] the success of its supervisory training program was founded on a complete redefinition of the supervisor's role in the organization and a more effective selection process. Key elements in these phases included (1) differentiation between roles that were heavily weighted toward administration and those requiring technical know-how, (2) documentation of each position as to content and required skills, (3) redefinition and clarification of relationships between supervisors and staff department, (4) screening of supervisory candidates through an assessment center conducted by an outside consultant, and (5) changes in supervisory responsibility, authority, and method of selection made clear to the union.

On-the-Job Retail Supervisor Training Program

Zale Corporation,[36] a major operator of jewelry stores with 1100 retail outlets, designed and utilizes a comprehensive, trainee-paced, modular supervisory training program that "must take place on the job and complement, rather than interrupt, regular duties." The CPD program (for Career Development Program) is divided into three phases: (1) learning experiences that are related directly to the company's products and processes, (2) management experiences that are oriented to aspiring or relatively inexperienced supervisors, and (3) management experiences for supervisory trainees and incumbent supervisors. Each of the latter two phases contains 12 management learning projects that direct the trainee through a series of step-by-step on-the-job experiences. The procedure for each project encompasses several steps and takes about 1 year:

- A supervisor or manager trainee is assigned to a limited area of the store as a surrogate manager of that area. The trainee is encouraged to experience, observe, and participate in as many management activities related to that area as possible.
- A list of skills and knowledge (learning objectives) required and reference resources for self-study are provided.
- The trainee performs management learning exercises which provide an information base for the follow-up analysis and develops basic proficiencies in the assigned area.
- A management analysis of the assigned area is made by the trainee who makes a creative listing of all areas with potential for improvement in that department. This is an indicator of the trainee's conceptual and creative depth.
- All the possible improvement activities listed in the above step are compared with store policies, budgets, inventory constraints, etc., and the listing is modified to allow for realistic implementation within the restrictions of the store's environment and management climate.
- The trainee prepares a plan of action which documents how improvement

activities can be compiled, prioritized, and applied in the store to increase productivity, sales, and profits.

- The trainee implements those activities which will enhance, rather than interfere with, normal store operations.

- The store manager and/or district manager evaluate the trainee's plan of action, activities attempted, sales and efficiency results, and management effectiveness.

- When the trainee has satisfactorily completed all requirements in a project, the store manager certifies the trainee's ability to effectively manage that particular area. The trainee can then proceed to the next project as dictated by his or her job assignment in the store.

- If the trainee's results are not judged by the store manager as the best possible, the trainee is asked to repeat the learning project and plan of action until he or she achieves acceptable results.

- Once an employee completes all three phases of the program and has gained some expertise in all areas of store management, he or she is given an opportunity to manage an entire store for up to 2 weeks, often while the manager is on vacation.

- Assuming the trainee has met an acceptable standard of achievement throughout the program, he or she attends a 6-day Management Candidate Seminar in Dallas for an intensive week of review and additional management training.

Orientation Programs

Ramsey[37] provides an example of a supervisory orientation (Table 34-6) illustrating a program that combines on-the-job exposure to a large variety of company functions and activities with counseling, self-study (using computer-aided instruction), and classroom training.

Supervisors and Organization Change and Development

The supervisor's role in the organization is increasingly difficult to generalize about. Each organization places supervisors in a slightly different context from other organizations. Generally, however, the supervisors' role has emerged from one that was clearly defined for one-on-one authority relationships with subordinates, as shown in Fig. 34-6, to one requiring some form of team or group relationship not wholly dependent upon a concept of institutionalized authority.[38]

As mentioned earlier, nearly 20 percent of supervisors feel that they are miscast and ineffective in their current roles. Part of this dissatisfaction arises from the ambiguity of their position and the lack of a strong organizational support system.[18] Wolfe[39] observes that for supervisors to be effective, their roles must be established by a realistic organization strategy. He faults the present concept of the supervisor's role for the following conditions:

- Supervisors are expected to act as the linkage between management and nonmanagement, which requires balancing two divergent viewpoints.

- Supervisors are expected to be action takers when change is required, even though their authority for introducing change is often nonexistent.

- Supervisors are frequently at a dead end in terms of promotability, even though

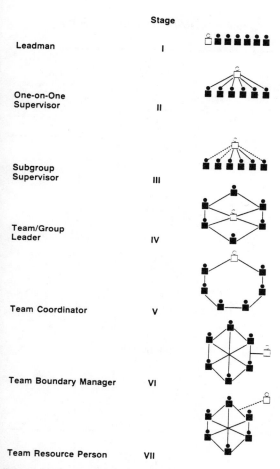

	Stage
Leadman	I
One-on-One Supervisor	II
Subgroup Supervisor	III
Team/Group Leader	IV
Team Coordinator	V
Team Boundary Manager	VI
Team Resource Person	VII

Figure 34-6. The changing role of the first-line supervisor. (*Adapted from Carl A. Bramlette,* "Free to Change," Training and Development Journal, *March 1984, p. 39.*)

they may be fully committed to the management team. Cummings[40] deplores this. He says, "To be promoted to a supervisory position early in one's career and never again be promoted can create a demotivating attitude. . . . Career development and human resources planning programs can appear incoherent and paradoxical to these supervisors."

Wolfe also observes that "The supervisor's job has little real authority and, in a practical sense, is not viewed as a real management job." That is a harsh conclusion to draw, but it is one that should get greater attention from organization development people. Wolfe goes on to say since supervisors have so little authority-related leverage, they must learn to exercise influence and to use available resources, especially through staff specialist groups. This influence, Wolfe says, should have two dimensions: (1) functional information which requires that the supervisor know not only their own jobs but their subordinate's jobs well

Table 34-6. Combined On-Job, Off-Job New-Supervisor Training Program

Assignment	Presented by (contact)	Where (location)	Schedule Minimum	Actual	Date assigned (exclude Sat. Sun. and holidays)
		Part 1			
Orientation:					
Orientation (introduction and local tour)			1 day		
Orientation (carton and mill tour)			1 day		
Orientation (filer mill)			1 day		
Staff services			1/2 day		
Personnel and industrial relations			1/2 day		
Accounting			1 day		
Sales function:					
ROI			1/2 day		
Sales office			1/2 day		
Sales visit			1 day		
Production planning and control					
Factor scheduling			10 days		
Other scheduling			5 days		
Waste control			1 day		
On-the-job training with press supervisor			18 wks (on trainee specialty)		
On-the-job training with finishing supervisor			7 wks (other departments)		
Parts room supervisor					
Concurrent Counseling and review:					
1. Policies and procedures			Continual		
2. Objectives, plans profit concepts			Continual		
3. Waste control			Continual		
4. Community relations			Continual		
5. Fundamental of supervision			Continual		
6. Cost reduction			Continual		
7. Safety			Continual		
8. Labor relations			Continual		
		Part 2			
Self-instruction:					
Supervisor's self-development course or similar formal program			Concurrent		
Cost reduction and control—prime I			Concurrent		
Safety and the supervisor—prime II			Concurrent		
Labor relations and the supervisor—prime III			Concurrent		

Table 34-6. Combined On-Job, Off-Job New-Supervisor Training Program (*Continued*)

Assignment	Presented by (contact)	Where (location)	Schedule Minimum	Schedule Actual	Date assigned (exclude Sat. Sun. and holidays)
Part 2					
Formal seminar:					
1. Basic economics			5 days		
2. Fundamentals of supervision					
a. Human relations					
b. Supervisor's roles as manager					
c. Discipline					
d. Selection, orientation, and placement of hourly employees					
3. Methods of instruction					
4. Communications					
5. Method of improvement and creative thinking					
6. Administering provisions of the union contract agreement					
7. Safety, housekeeping, and fire prevention					
8. Container division policies and objectives					
9. Company, profit, and marketing concepts					

Adapted from Jackson E. Ramsey, "Supervisory Development," in *Human Resources Management & Development Handbook,* William R. Tracey, ed., Amacom, New York, 1985, pp. 979–980.

enough to supervise them effectively and (2) all the managerial-process and interpersonal skills needed to build an effective work group. As a consequence, Wolfe suggests a more functional definition of the supervisor's role:

> The role of the supervisor is to use influence and management work to maintain and measurably improve the return on the use of organizational resources at the point where physical work takes place.

Such a definition would help to make supervisory training objectives more concrete. It would depend, however, upon (1) a specific articulation of how supervisors are to perform management work, (2) greater clarification of the kinds of relationships supervisors should have with management and nonmanagement personnel, and (3) improved reinforcement and support from middle and upper-level management.

Participatory Pressures

There is some indication that the popular trend toward emphasizing participatory management again places the supervisor in the middle. In fact, top management is increasingly likely to hold supervisors as scapegoats for obstructing the process.[41] In fairness to supervisors, it is they who must deal with the reality of employees' inclination to cooperate or not or to become involved or not in planning and decision making. And, as is always true, the extent to which lower-level managers will develop participative approaches will depend in large measure upon the participation opportunities extended to them by upper management.

Self-Development for Supervisors

Kur and Pedler[42] believe that the greatest improvement in supervisory performance will occur through self-development, using selected organization development techniques. They agree that self-development "is the most complex, difficult form of learning" but they emphasize that it "results in more mature, more competent individuals." They advise that such learning takes place at three levels: (1) participants first acquire the learning specified by the organization of which they are a part; (2) they then identify their own needs and the resources available and how to evaluate, monitor, and control their own learning processes; and (3) they learn to manage through egalitarian, people-centered means.

The OD approach that Kur and Pedler discuss includes several techniques such as action learning, field study and joint development activities, and body-mind approaches. The most appropriate OD techniques for supervisory development, however, would appear to be:

Structured experiences, which place the supervisor in a learning situation of accelerated experience, following a preprogrammed or structured set of activities requiring various levels of interaction. Emphasis is upon discovery of information and new ways of behavior leading to problem solving rather than upon expository learning. Structured experiences usually involve activity over relatively short intervals, seldom exceeding 3 hours.

Coaching, in which an informed helper assists the supervisor in problem solving or mastering new skills. In sales training, this is often called "curbstone coaching." One variant used in supervisory development has the trainer "shadowing" a supervisor for several days, after which the two "process" or discuss each event, assessing the supervisor's handling of each event and identifying alternative approaches that might be used in similar situations in the future.

Experiential groups, including T-groups, sensitivity training, and encounter groups. Learning takes place as individuals discuss with group members the events that unfold during the life of the group. Though such groups were once very popular, results are often contradictory and nonproductive unless the learning sessions are conducted by professionally trained leaders under widely accepted professional guidelines.

Evaluation

Program evaluation encompasses five basic elements:[43] (1) identification of the decision makers who seek information and/or validation of the effectiveness of a particular training program (these people influence the budgets that support the program, and it is essential that their expectations be determined in advance); (2) clarification of the goals and objectives of the program, along with a specifically defined statement of their content; (3) translation of these objectives into criteria or standards for postcompletion evaluation; (4) a method of obtaining the measurements; and (5) interpretation of the evaluation information provided by the measurements.

Table 34-7. Evaluation Criteria for Supervisory Training Programs Ranked According to Frequency of Usage

Subjective criteria:
156 Trainee's reactions, during or at close of program
90 Reactions of immediate superiors of trainees
42 Trainer's evaluation of the program
41 Trainee's reactions, 3 to 6 months after training
33 Reactions of higher management
30 "Informal observation"
392 Total mentions

Objective criteria:
41 "Department's records"
38 Review of performance appraisals of trainees following training
22 Records—of production, costs, quality, safety, or other factors
28 Records—of absences, turnover, tardiness, or grievances in trainee's unit after training
19 Testing at end of course
12 Testing, before and after course
10 Attitude surveys among employees being supervised by trainees, following training
9 Formal program evaluation studies, conducted by company or by outside organization
8 Accomplishment of specific objectives
187 Total mentions

Adapted from Walter S. Wikstrom, *Supervisory Training*, The Conference Board, New York, 1973, p. 39.

Evaluation Criteria

Evaluation criteria can be classified as either subjective or objective, qualitative or quantitative. The Conference Board[26] surveyed over 300 companies offering supervisory training and found that the use of subjective training criteria occurred two times more frequently than objective usage, although almost all companies used two or more of the criteria ranked in Table 34-7.

Evaluation Techniques

The more traditional evaluation methods are indicated in the list in Table 34-7. Swierczek and Carmichael,[44] however, enlarge upon these in a conceptual fashion. They suggest, for example, the following:

- *An open-ended questionnaire* distributed at the end of a program segment. Two questions are asked: "What skills did you learn at this seminar?" and "How will you apply these skills back at work?" No instructions are provided the respondent in order to reduce the bias inherent in conventional evaluation checklists.

- *Administration of standard "how-supervise" type of instruments* before and after the seminar. One that proved to be particularly effective uses a series of questions based upon Likert's systems 1 to 4 (confidence in subordinates, feel free to talk, subordinates' ideas used, responsibility for goals, communications by goals, levels at which decisions are made, etc.).

- *A follow-up survey checklist administered before the training as well as 6 months after.* Validated skill areas included: (1) identify and attempt to eliminate interruptions and time wasters, (2) assign tasks to subordinates, (3) provide subordinates with exact references to behavior in order to document performance problems, and (4) facilitate feedback from subordinates. This technique also uncovers supervisory resistance to, or failure to adopt, theoretically sound practices such as "setting priority tasks on a regular basis" and "keeping daily logs."

Environmental Influences

Almost all evaluations, other than those dependent exclusively upon performance documentation, are subject to uncontrollable influence in the supervisor's environment. Accordingly, Clement and Arand[45] remind trainers of three contingency variables that should be considered when interpreting evaluations: (1) influence from the organizational setting (objectives, policies, practices, supervisor's authority to administer rewards and punishment, work group expectations, etc.); (2) nature of the supervisor to be trained (education, experience, expectations, etc.); and (3) problems to be solved by the training program (ranging from simple, tangible, and immediate to complex, ambiguous, and long-term). The authors observe, for example, that supervisory training is more effective with young, relatively new supervisors, responsible for a small number of subordinates, and with a short period of total service.

Objectives Commitment

One particularly effective method that not only provides valid evaluations but also extends and reinforces supervisory training is reported by Morrisey and Wellstead.[46] They take the position that "a participant in one of our supervisory training programs has not completed the program at the end of the scheduled class sessions. All participants must commit themselves to specific objectives on how they will apply some of what was learned. Then, they must send in a progress report 60 days later in order to earn their certificate of completion." Follow-up procedures include these five additional steps:

1. Form letter sent to participants after 30 days reminding them they will be receiving a report form in about 3 weeks and encouraging them to keep working at their objectives.

2. Report form sent to each participant 1 week before due date asking the following questions: (1) What results, both positive and negative, have you had so far in implementing your objectives? (Include any appropriate documentation you may have.) (2) What other specific changes have you made in the way you do your job as a result of the training program? Please describe the results of these changes, both positive and negative. (3) Based on your on-the-job experience since the end of the program, what two aspects would you change to make the program more meaningful for people in positions like yours?

3. Instructor receives completed report, reviews and either approves it for a certificate or contacts the participant for additional action as needed.

4. Certificate sent with cover letter to participant's superior asking that it be awarded to him or her at an appropriate time.

5. Follow-up letter sent to all participants who have not returned their reports 1 week after deadline allowing them an extra week in which to report and opening the door for individual consultation if needed.

Summary

Supervisory development remains a unique form of improvement activity, distinctive from the broader areas of management and executive development. It requires from the HRD professional (1) a practical recognition of the innate qualifications, limitations, and aspirations of the supervisors participating in such development, (2) a genuine knowledge of the specific competencies required on these supervisors in their work assignments, and (3) a particular sensitivity to the roles and relationships imposed upon the supervisors by the organization structure and culture in which they perform.

References

1. Bittel, Lester R., and Jackson E. Ramsey, "The Limited, Traditional World of Supervisors," *Harvard Business Review*, July–August 1982, pp. 26–36, and Lester R. Bittel and Jackson E. Ramsey, *Report of the National Survey of Supervisory Management Practices*, Center for Supervisory Research, James Madison University, Harrisonburg, VA, April 1982.

2. Bittel, Lester R., *What Every Supervisor Should Know*, 5th ed., McGraw-Hill Book Company, New York, 1985, p. 13.

3. Davis, Keith, "The Supervisory Role," in M. Gene Newport (ed.), *Supervisory Management: Tools and Techniques*, West Publishing Company, St. Paul, MN, 1976, p. 5.

4. Likert, Rensis, *New Patterns of Management*, McGraw-Hill Book Company, New York, 1980.

5. Myers, M. Scott, *Every Employee a Manager*, McGraw-Hill Book Company, New York, 1970, p. 99.

6. Prokopenko, J., and Lester R. Bittel, "A Modular Course-Format for Supervisory Development," *Training and Development Journal*, February 1981, p. 1422.

7. *Foremen Thinking—A Survey for the Foremanship Foundation*, Opinion Research Corporation, Princeton, NJ, 1970.

8. Ramsey, Jackson E., and Lester R. Bittel, "Men and Women Who Turn the Key of American Productivity," *National Forum*, winter 1984, pp. 43–46.

9. Bittel, Lester R., and Jackson E. Ramsey, "New Dimensions for Supervisory Training and Development," *Training and Development Journal*, March 1983, pp. 12–20.

10. LaForge, R. Lawrence, and Lester R. Bittel, "A Survey of Production Management Supervisors," *Production and Inventory Management*, fourth quarter 1983, vol. 24, no. 4, pp. 99–112.

11. LaForge, R. Lawrence, Mary C. LaForge, and Lester R. Bittel, "A Survey of Supervisory-Level Marketing Managers," *Akron Business and Economics Review*, summer 1984, vol. 15, no. 2, pp. 47–52.

12. LaForge, R. Lawrence, Jackson E. Ramsey, and Lester R. Bittel, "A Survey Profile of the Problems, Practices, and Attitudes of Engineering Supervisors," paper No. 84-WA/Mgt-1, American Society of Mechanical Engineers, New York, December 1984.

13. Seguin, Vernon L., "Are Purchasing Supervisors Different?" *Journal of Purchasing and Materials Management*, fall 1984, vol. 20, no. 3, pp. 27–31.

14. Carroll, Archie B., and Ted F. Anthony, "An Overview of the Supervisor's Job," *Personnel Journal*, May 1976, pp. 228–249.

15. Baker, H. Kent, and Steven H. Holmberg, "Stepping Up to Supervision: Making the Transition," *Supervisory Management*, September 1981, vol. 26, no. 9, pp. 10–18.

16. Cover, William H., "Stepping Back to Basics," *Training and Development Journal*, November 1975, pp. 3–6.

17. Macdonald, Charles R., *Performance Based Supervisory Development*, Human Resources Development Press, Amherst, MA, 1982, p. 24.

18. Bittel, Lester R., and Jackson E. Ramsey, "Misfit Supervisors—Bad Apples in the Managerial Barrel," *Management Review*, February 1983, vol. 72, no. 2, pp. 8–13.

19. Northrup, H. W., R. M. Cowin, L. G. Vanden Plas, and W. E. Fulmer, *The Objective Selection of Supervisors: A Study of Informal Practices and Two Models of Supervisory Selection*, The Wharton School, University of Pennsylvania, PA, 1978.

20. Benson, Carl A., "New Supervisors: From the Top of the Heap to the Bottom of the Heap," *Personnel Journal*, April 1976, pp. 176–178.

21. Byham, William C., "Assessment Center Method," in L. R. Bittel and J. E. Ramsey, eds. *The Handbook of Professional Management*, McGraw-Hill Book Company, New York, 1985, pp. 40–43.

22. Burack, Elmer H., "Self-Assessment: A Strategy of Growing Importance," *Training and Development Journal*, April 1979, pp. 48–52.

23. Parry, Scott B., and Edward J. Robinson, "Management Development: Training or Education?" *Training and Development Journal*, July 1979, pp. 8–13.

24. Langdon, Danny G., "The Individual Management Development Program," *Training and Development Journal*, March 1982, pp. 78–82.

25. Bula, Ronald J., "Survey of Management Training Needs in Wisconsin," *Training and Development Journal*, January 1985, pp. 64–65.

26. Wikstrom, Walter S., *Supervisory Training*, The Conference Board, New York, 1973.

27. McKeon, William J., "How to Determine Off-Site Meeting Costs," *Training and Development Journal*, May 1981, pp. 116–122.

28. Broadwell, Martin M., "Supervisory Training in the 80s," *Training and Development Journal*, February 1980.

29. Fulmer, William E., "The Making of a Supervisor," *Personnel Journal*, March 1977, pp. 140–141.

30. Short, Ronald R., "Managing Unlearning," *Training and Development Journal*, July 1981, pp. 37–44.

31. Byham, William C., "Changing Supervisory and Managerial Behavior," *Training and Development Journal*, Part I, April 1977, pp. 3–8, Part II, May 1977, pp. 10–16.

32. Crumb, C. V., "Performance-Based Line Supervisor Training," *Training and Development Journal*, September 1981, pp. 44–47.

33. Hanson, Marlys C., "Training Employees and Managers for Their Roles in Career Development," in *Career Management: Implications for Organizations and Individuals*, ASTD, Alexandria, VA, 1980.

34. Rosenthal, Steven M., and Bob Mezoff, "Improving the Cost/Benefit of Management Training," *Training and Development Journal*, December 1980, pp. 102–106.

35. Doud, Ernest A., Jr., and Edward J. Miller, "First-Line Supervisors: Key to Improved Performance," *Management Review*, December 1980, pp. 18–24.

36. Kelley, Nancy, "Zale Corporation's Career Development Program," *Training and Development Journal*, June 1982, pp. 70–75.

37. Ramsey, Jackson E., "Supervisory Development," in *Human Resources Management & Development Handbook*, William R. Tracey, ed., Amacom, New York, 1985, pp. 979–980.

38. Bramlette, Carl A., Jr., "Free to Change," *Training and Development Journal*, March 1984, pp. 32–40.

39. Wolfe, Edward H., "Supervisory Development: The Need for an Integrated Strategy," *Training and Development Journal*, March 1983, pp. 28–31.

40. Cummings, Paul W., "Supervisory Expectations versus Organizational Reality," *Training and Development Journal*, September 1976, pp. 37–41.

41. Apcar, Leonard, "Middle Managers and Supervisors Resist Move to More Participatory Management," *Wall Street Journal*, Sept. 12, 1985, p. 31.

42. Kur, C. Edward, and Mike Pedler, "Innovative Twists in Management Development," *Training and Development Journal*, June 1982, pp. 88–96.

43. Bakken, David, and Alan L. Bernstein, "A Systematic Approach to Evaluation," *Training and Development Journal*, August 1982, pp. 44–51.

44. Swierczek, Fredric William, and Lynne Carmichael, "The Quantity and Quality of Evaluating Training," *Training and Development Journal*, January 1985, pp. 95–99.

45. Clement, Ronald W., and Eileen K. Arand, "Evaluating Management Training: A Contingency Approach," *Training and Development Journal*, August 1982, pp. 39–43.

46. Morrisey, George L., and William R. Wellstead, "Supervisory Training Can Be Measured," *Training and Development Journal*, June 1980, pp. 118–121.

35

Engineers and Scientists

Robert W. DeSio

Robert W. DeSio is Director of University Relations, IBM. For 9 years, he was director of IBM Corporate Technical Institutes, comprised of the Research, Manufacturing Technology, Software Engineering, and Quality Institutes. He joined the IBM Applied Science Division in 1953 and has held many IBM management positions including Director of Advanced Market Development, Director of Scientific Computing and High Performance Systems, and Director of Systems Engineering. He is a member of the American Society of Engineering Education; Board of Advisors, National Technological University; Board of Advisors, Institute of Systems Science, National University of Singapore; Board of Advisors, Management School of Worcester Polytechnic Institute; and Committee for Continuing Education, Institute of Electrical and Electronic Engineers. He is on the board of governors of ASTD and board of overseers for Regents College Degrees and Examinations, New York State Department of Education. DeSio is a graduate of Rensselaer Polytechnic Institute with a bachelor's and master's degree in Physics. He also attended the University of Minnesota and Harvard University prior to joining the 20th Air Force in the Asia Pacific Theater in World War II.

In a sense continuing education and training today is an implicit national strategy. In fact it is a strategic necessity if we are to realize true success in the world of international competition. The process of education and training of people in business, industry, and government is dependent on a true partnership between the academic world and the industrial, business, and government sectors. This partnership truly exists in the United States today and is being implemented in other parts of the world such as Southeast Asia. The partnership is in reality a mutual set of dependencies—each driving the other. The reasons, the way in which the partnership manifests itself in the training and education process will be described in what follows.

The engineering and scientific community is one of our most precious resources and assets. In a sense they are the creators of change and innovation which drives the world today. On the one hand they create and innovate and on the other they apply and implement their creations. The need for continuing education and training of this community is a top priority because of its relevancy to the goodness and success of the industrial and business sectors. The root factor is change, and that is what drives everything.

A World of Change

It has been said that the learning experienced during the past 45 years is equivalent to that occurring during the prior 450 years and this in turn is equivalent to the previous 4500 years. Using this scale, that would translate into learning during the next 4 to 5 years that is equivalent to the past 45 years.

This phenomenon is attributed primarily to the explosion of knowledge. It is interesting to note that technology itself has been a primary factor in accelerating the generation of new knowledge. Also, it is noted that there has been explosive growth not only in the generation of knowledge but also in the application of knowledge, and that is the basic mission of industry and business.

Today we speak about the "half-life phenomenon." In the world of science, half-life deals with radioactive decay. The half-life of engineers and scientists relates to the technical obsolescence of these professionals. Not too many years ago one was set for life when a degree from a university was acquired. In a sense there were at least three phases in life—learning, working, and hopefully, retirement. Of course that belief is as archaic as the buggy-whip.

In many technical disciplines such as electrical engineering and computer science, the half-life is in terms of 2 or 3 years. In contrast, 30 years ago engineers were set for 12 to 14 years in their chosen profession, but now the dynamics of change has caught up with the professions. One learned engineering psychologist states that an engineer in semiconductor technology today should read 40 to 50 professional articles each day just to keep up with the state of the art.

The change is a moving target and the half-life phenomenon is very real. The price of not addressing this phenomenon is obsolescence. That is why industry and business is concerned and in many instances preoccupied with the subject.

The Environment

The process of continuing education or, more important, continuing development of engineers and scientists must be looked at in the context of the environment. In addition to change there are other environmental factors of importance.

International competition is significant; one has but to reflect on the impact of this competition in the automotive and electronic sectors. International competitors have demonstrated the capability of being the low-cost producer of high-quality products. The consequences have been seen in a vivid manner in these two sectors. In certain areas the dichotomy among design, development, and manufacturing has been a real impediment. It is one thing to conceptualize and design a product, but this must be related to the pragmatics of building the product. Today we talk about design for manufacturability and that development and manufacturing must be a continuum. We had to learn this, and in reality it is an educational problem. It took international competition to awaken us.

Another key environmental factor is that the world is one of specialization and specialization is an imperative. At the same time the world is becoming more interdisciplinary, especially in engineering, science, and technology. This is a reality in business and industry as well as in the academic world. The vertical lines of specialization must be related and be compatible with the horizontal interdisciplinary lines. Reconciliation has been a very difficult challenge, and the organizational constraints in university departments or in the functions of business and industry have been inhibitors in so many areas. The implications of teaching and preparing professionals to be specialists but operating in an interdisciplinary world are of primary importance to industry and business.

There has been a steady decline in the number of engineers in critical disciplines going on to full-time graduate work once the first degree has been received. The attractive salaries and job opportunities offered by industry have siphoned off potential graduate students. An implicit condition of employment is to enable new young engineers and scientists to continue graduate work on a part-time basis once they have joined the ranks of the employed. Many corporations, partially because of the need as well as the competition for new graduates, are having to provide the opportunities for continuing education leading to an advanced degree.

The shortage of faculty in certain engineering and scientific disciplines is another dominant environmental factor. Many studies have been made which conclude that in computer science and electrical engineering there has been a constant shortage of faculty in the 20 percent area for the past few years. This is of concern not only to those in the academic world but also to those in industry who are hiring potential new faculty.

Because of these environmental factors, especially international competition, industry has had to take the initiative in innovation and the application of technology. There has been a tremendous investment in capital equipment in both development and manufacturing. In the area of material science and semiconductor manufacturing, industry has had to be on the leading edge. Invariably, the process used is in advance of an understanding of the base science and underpinnings. Unless concepts and theories are married to the application of the technology, the long-range consequences are obvious. The result is that in certain areas industrial laboratories are ahead of university laboratories. This dictates the necessity for a close liaison between the academic and industrial communities. This is one of the reasons why partnerships are so vital and important today between industry and academe.

The Partnership

A tremendous set of dependencies confronts us. As stated earlier, the university-industrial partnership is a reality. The fundamental mission of the university is education and research. The fundamental mission of industry and business is the application of knowledge. The partnership manifests itself in the new extended mission of the university. The extended mission is not only to provide education to the human resource that will be filling the ranks of industry and business, but also to provide the continuing education to this same resource in a lifelong sense. This continuing education is both degree- and non-degree-related. The National Technological University's (NTU) sole mission is providing education at the master's level in six disciplines to professionals in industry, business, and government. There are over 50 universities whose extended mission is providing both degree and nondegree education to working professionals using instructional television (ITV). In some cases there are no residency requirements.

Industrial Perspective

Continuing education and training has become an integral part of corporate strategies. No longer is the process relegated to the lowest functions of business and industry. More and more corporate education strategies are tied to the corporate goals and strategies of the enterprise. The scenario can be stated as follows:

- Continuing education and training is an integral part of the job. There is no longer a separation of the process of training from the work of the individual.

- Training and education should be delivered to the individual's workplace to the highest degree possible. The intent is to make it readily available and easy to acquire.

- In order to bring education and training to the individual's workplace, extensive usage of educational technologies will be required. These technologies include the use of microwave and satellite transmission in the delivery of courses.

- Both the academic community and industry play fundamental roles in continuing education and training.

- There must be a balance between training and education in preparing a person to do the job today while staging the employee in a career sense for the future.

The evidence that education and training is of the highest priority is demonstrated in many studies conducted in the past few years. Some experts project the annual educational expenditures of business and industry to exceed 60 billion dollars. If one includes corporate benefits and similar indirect costs, the annual expenditures are in excess of 100 billion dollars. This is more than the total annual expenditures of all the colleges and universities in the United States. Needless to say this is a big business, and top management is becoming more involved in making sure it is directed properly.

The terminology training and education has been used extensively. It is important that the distinction is made and understood.

Technical Education and Training

Basically, training deals with the job and education is related to the individual's career. In earlier days, the job of education was left to the university and training of employees was left to industry and business. The distinction is shown below.

Technical education	Technical training
• Conceptual and generic	• Application of knowledge
• Base knowledge in science and engineering	• Application of knowledge
• Short-range and tactical	• Long-range and strategic
• Job-related—specific skills, product knowledge	• Career-related

More and more attention and focus is being given to continuing education. This is in distinct contrast to former times when people were set for life once their academic education was completed. It is recognized that knowledge is expanding at an accelerating rate. The corporation that concentrates on training at the expense of education will find itself going down a path of short-range success and long-range failure.

In business and industry, training occurs in a natural way. Management, especially lower levels of management, will provide the training necessary to do the job today. That same local management may be more reluctant to provide education for the employee that has strategic relevancy for the future and career of the individual. Upper management in many cases is concentrating on educating and making sure that the opportunities are provided, both internal and external—reflecting the strategic needs of the business.

There is another distinct phenomenon. Even though the primary mission of the university is education, in technical areas industry and business are frequently providing the education from within. In fact one can find courses and total curricula being offered in corporate education centers that might be found in university catalogs. Why does this happen?

As mentioned above, there are those areas where industry is leading in the application of technology. In many cases these are interdisciplinary areas. Because of the pressures to stay ahead, industry has had to conduct the education using its own professionals as faculty to contend with the new technology. In a sense this is a short-term phenomenon that occurs out of desperation. When such discrepancies occur it is important that they are minimized, and that is why the partnership is essential. Many corporations have taken the initiative to encourage and work with the university community in changing their curricula and course offerings. This manifests itself in grants, donations, and similar programs from industry to the university community.

Going Rates

It is not uncommon for engineers and scientists to spend 15 to 20 days a year in continuing education and training. This is over and above informal programs such as self-study courses. Some corporations have minimum annual education objectives and goals for their technical professionals. These are monitored and followed by management to make sure that they are realized. Some corporations have extensive tracking systems and databases to pinpoint employee performance and educational completion.

It is more proper to talk about continuing self-development rather than continuing education. The real goal is learning, and that encompasses not only formalized classes but also rotational job assignments, active participation in professional societies, sabbatical assignments, and frequent use of literature and the library. Even though this chapter is concentrating on training and education these other activities are essential.

What should be the going rate? This is a very difficult question, and in reality there is no single answer. Education and training should be an integral part of the job. Some experts feel that 10 percent of the time should be dedicated to self-development. This translates to 4 to 5 hours a week. The important thing is for the corporation and the individual to have a sound partnership and program for continuing self-development. That development of the individual, both short- and long-range, is of the highest priority.

Delivery Mechanism

The emergence of a vast menu of new educational technologies is one of the significant occurrences during the past 5 years. Indeed, education is much more accessible today. The use of technologies such as telecommunications, personal computers, and academic work stations is a whole new world. These technologies employed in the learning environment offer new dimensions in the learning process. Technology is now a partner to the teacher in the process of education. Interactive training systems, self-study courses, and long-range transmission of courses via satellite are important factors in improving the quality of education. At the same time they can enhance education productivity, especially where there are faculty and instructor shortages.

Also it is significant that some of the most meaningful innovations in using new technologies in education and training are emanating from corporate education facilities. Today, there are corporate education centers that are truly on the leading edge in using new educational technologies to enhance learning. The full integration of voice, video, and data in industrial education centers is a reality. State-of-the-art mini-universities exist within industrial walls.

Instructional Television (ITV)

The use of educational technology such as ITV has been a significant vehicle for delivering education to industrial employees. ITV has been used by universities since the middle 1960s and today extensive usage of ITV is made by industry in providing continuing education. ITV comes in a number of flavors:

- Videotape courses

- Tutored videotaped instruction (TVI)

- Microwave transmission of courses

- Satellite transmission of courses

The videotaping of courses from candid (live) classrooms is the basic form of ITV. These videotapes are then made available to be used for educational purposes. The use of a local tutor with the tapes (TVI) has proven to be a most effective method of delivery, and excellent results have been achieved. Stanford University has been a pioneer in the use of TVI. This success dates back to a master's degree program for professionals at Hewlett Packard. The tutor stops the tape at frequent intervals and functions as a moderator to stimulate discussions in the classroom.

Courses delivered in real time from live classrooms to remote students were pioneered over short distances using microwave transmission. Again, the candid classrooms have cameras placed strategically; each is a source of transmission and technicians operate the cameras. There is one-way video transmission from the source classroom to the remote-receive classrooms. Two-way voice communications enable direct interaction to occur. In a sense the remote classrooms are an extension of the source classroom. In many cases there is daily courier service between the university faculty members and the remote students for handing in homework assignments. Such systems offer working professionals the opportunity to take both degree and nondegree courses from university campuses, without leaving their work locations. Many universities use such technology in providing education to industry as part of the new extended mission of the university. These universities are serving the needs of professionals in the regions in which they are located. Maryland, Minnesota, and Stanford are a few of the universities that have well-established programs.

The extension of microwave transmission is the use of satellites for sending courses over long distances. The use of satellite transmission enables industrial students to take courses emanating from classrooms hundreds of miles remote from the workplace. In a sense professionals can now pick and choose the best of education regardless of their distance from the source of the education. The physical world has not changed, but electronically we have linked university campuses with industrial classrooms so that these classrooms are an extension of the campus.

Living Examples of ITV

Many examples demonstrate the educational partnership that exists between the university community and industry (see "ITV Resources" at end of chapter for addresses).

AMCEE (Association for Media Based Continuing Education for Engineers) established in 1976 is a nonprofit consortium of over 50 universities providing a catalog of over 500 videotape courses produced on university campuses. In most cases these videotapes are produced in live-candid classrooms, are packaged and become a library of programs made available to industry for a fee. Linkage is made between students and faculty by electronic mail, regular mail, or courier service.

GENESYS was one of the initial two-way microwave regional programs hosted by the University of Florida providing graduate courses to NASA contractor professionals in the Orlando area. During the period 1965–1972 over 250 completed their master's degree work in this pioneering educational activity.

Stanford University, beginning in 1969, was a leader in the use of ITV, including microwave transmission of courses, videotape, and TVI. There are over 120 industrial classrooms and four video channels in the system linking the campus with remote industrial locations.

Colorado State University since 1967 has had the SURGE system serving professionals in the Colorado region. They have one of the most extensive videotape delivery systems for industrial usage. Over 45 locations are being served with 90 courses going to over 1000 professionals.

In the Dallas area the TAGER system, established in 1967 with Southern Methodist University as one of the universities involved, has used a wide variety of transmission facilities including ITFS, cable TV, and microwave as well as videotapes.

One of the most innovative examples involving a partnership among universities in pooling their efforts to provide education to industry, business, and government is the National Technological University (NTU). This new university, established in 1984, consists of a consortium of 21 universities. The total mission is dedicated to part-time advanced degree programs for working professionals. The vehicle for delivery is ITV, both videotape and satellite transmission. There are six master's degree programs in six different technical disciplines. Ultimately each of the 21 schools in the consortium will have an uplink satellite transmission facility for delivery of courses. The faculty for each of the six disciplines come from the 21 participating universities. The remote students must fulfill the admission requirements of NTU. Industrial students then pick courses in each of the six disciplines. These courses are subsets of graduate courses offered at each of the 21 universities. The courses are taken by the students in their industrial classrooms and the courses are delivered over the NTU satellite network. As the courses are completed fulfilling the credit requirements of each of the participating universities, they are accumulated by NTU and the degree is given by NTU. Also, over the same network AMCEE courses are made available for these professionals not pursuing advanced degree programs but who have a pressing need for advanced technical education. In May 1984, during the early stages of NTU, a 2-week special education program of elective technical courses was delivered to some 17,000 professionals at 70 industry locations. This program with one-way video and two-way audio totaling 45 hours on the air was one of the most extensive demonstrations of continuing education using satellite delivery—a precursor of what was to follow. The role that NTU can play for those professionals in remote locations with no local university presence is obvious.

Not only are universities playing a fundamental role in the education of scientists and engineers but also professional societies. IEEE has demonstrated leadership in continuing education not only through local chapters but nationwide using satellite transmission. During the past few years they have offered four 1-day courses annually in high-priority areas such as artificial intelligence. Thousands of professionals have participated in these interactive courses.

Industrial satellite networks used for educational purposes are becoming strategic vehicles for keeping working professionals current. Hewlett Packard has an extensive network tying together its employees for both educational and communication purposes. A special program was established between the California State University at Chico, California, and HP to deliver live courses from the campus to HP professionals throughout the United States. The courses were transmitted live from the university via microwave to a neighboring HP location and then uplinked via satellite and transmitted nationally to HP professionals participating in a computer science master's program.

Today some nine corporations employ their own satellite delivery systems for the education of employees. In addition to the ability to reach out and provide continuing education, there are the savings of travel and living costs. There can be significant savings and long-term return on investment using ITV.

Other Living Examples

There are many examples of model education programs being employed by industry. The role that universities are playing is very significant, especially in providing advanced technical education. Many corporations have set up their own extensive training and education staffs. The investment in "bricks and mortar" and the establishment of mini-campuses inside industrial walls is becoming more common. The use of scientists and engineers from the corporation as full-time or part-time faculty has become a significant part of the changing scene.

This is especially true where industry is in a leadership role out of necessity, as in advanced manufacturing systems engineering and materials science. There is a need to keep the engineering and scientific community on the leading edge. Because of the rapidity of change, frequently there is no other choice but to use in-house professionals to teach other professionals. There is one other advantage, and that is the ability to cross the line between theory and concepts to the pragmatics of applying theory in a real way. The teacher is master of both.

One of the pioneering mini-campuses for training and education was the Bell Communication Technical Education Center in Lisle, Illinois. It was a primary source for training technical professionals in the Bell operating companies. This 800,000 square foot facility is a mini-campus in every sense of the word with classrooms, laboratories, and 800 dormitory rooms for resident students. For technical education and training this center is a showcase for corporate technical education and was a model that others emulated.

Xerox, GE, Motorola, and Texas Instruments all have extensive education programs and in many instances have invested considerably in education facilities that are in reality mini-campuses. The dialogue occurring in education within the industrial and business sector is considerable, with an intent to learn from each other. This sharing of experience in providing education and training is very important because of the change in the education process. There are discussions of sharing generic, nonproprietory courses to the benefit of all.

"Smart" Facilities

Technology has provided new opportunities for state-of-the-art educational facilities. Today the thrust is to wire the building for the future, and this is especially important for educational facilities. Again, it is a moving target and intuition plays a key role. Academic work stations, PCs, and integration of voice, video, and data is the accent in planning new educational facilities. Technology is a primary factor in the improvement of the quality of education. In Hartford, Connecticut, Aetna Life & Casualty has a state-of-the-art education complex which is futuristic in every sense of the word—raised floors in the classrooms, PC work stations, and innovative classroom projection systems. With today's technology change a building or an educational complex can become obsolete in a matter of a few years. That is why universities and industry are spending so much time looking ahead in the planning and design of classrooms, laboratories, libraries, and dormitories. The objective is to electronically link together all parts in a unified way. That is the university or industrial campus of tomorrow.

IBM, like many other corporations, has a dependency or academe for continuing education. Over 3600 technical professionals in U.S. laboratories and plants are taking courses leading to a master's degree on a part-time basis. This education is provided by local universities and in many instances courses are delivered from more remote sources via microwave and satellite.

In Thornwood, New York, a new 285,000 square foot corporate technical education facility became operational in October 1985. The Corporate Technical Institute (CTI) is made up of four institutes—Systems Research, Manufacturing Technology, Software Engineering, and Quality. There are 60 full-time faculty, most of whom have come from the laboratory or the field. Adjunct faculty from universities play a key role in providing education at CTI. Technical professionals spend up to 10 weeks in residence and 70,000 student days are delivered to resident students annually. This mini-campus has 12 classrooms on raised floors to facilitate reconfiguring the classroom for work stations and PCs. Twelve break-out rooms are used by students on projects. Each of the 250 dormitory rooms is equipped with PCs as part of a local area network with a "gateway" to a large computer center.

Over 700 PCs are installed for faculty, student, and administrative usage. Voice, video, and data are integrated point to point throughout the complex. The library has over 10,000 volumes and 400 periodical titles. There is a full set of laboratories supporting the education, including robotics, instrumentation, process, and microcomputer labs. CTI is transmitting live courses via satellite initially to six IBM laboratories throughout the United States. By the end of 1987 there will be 23 locations on line. Courses are being delivered 5 hours a day via satellite from one candid classroom. By the end of 1986 there will be two candid classrooms delivering courses over two channels in this extensive satellite network.

Each of the 23 locations will have two receive classrooms. Electronic mail facilitates additional interaction between CTI faculty and remote students. Courses transmitted are videotaped at CTI as well as at the receive locations for future usage. These same videotaped (or live) courses can be viewed in the dormitory rooms by the students as "refresher" courses. By 1988 it is estimated more than 50 percent of the student days will be delivered remotely via satellite.

The Future

The future of training and education of scientists and engineers is difficult to predict. It is certain that education will become an even more integral part of corporate strategies. The partnerships will grow in strength and the education process will go through dramatic change as technology is introduced. Linkage between university and industrial satellite networks with lectures, seminars, and courses transmitted both ways will become a reality. As indicated above, the university and industry-business-government communities are dependent on each other. Within the law there will be even more dramatic cooperation between the sectors in professional education. There will be even greater accent on education in the career development of the technical community along with taking care of the job training needs of today.

In looking ahead, more effective ways of providing education and training to small firms and businesses must be found. The use of video and electronic networks certainly will facilitate continuing education for smaller firms. They will have the same opportunities as the larger corporations, and the education will be available in a cost-effective way. As costs come down, interactive training systems employing PC-videodisc technologies that are self-paced and driven will be of particular importance to engineers and other professionals in small companies.

The partnership can be facilitated even more, with industry-based education being made available to university faculty and students. Where industry is ahead, every possibility should be examined for the transfer of this experience to university campuses, perhaps in short courses, seminars, and lectures. The vehicles would certainly include the use of industrial adjunct teachers and sabbatical assignments. The use of industry satellite networks with courses, seminars, and lectures emanating from industrial classrooms to university campuses is being discussed actively today. All this will be important in developing and providing state-of-the-art continuing education for engineers and scientists in industry, government, and business.

Future success will be dependent on the excellence of training and education available from the academic community as well as industry operating in a true living partnership.

Bibliography

Eurich, Nell P., *Corporate Classrooms: The Learning Business,* The Carnegie Foundation for the Advancement of Teaching, Princeton, NJ, 1985.

"IBM and U.S. Universities, An Evolving Partnership," Dr. Lewis Branscomb, May 1985 *IEEE Proceedings.*

National Research Council Report, *Continuing Education of Engineers,* National Academy Press, Washington, DC, 1985.

National Research Council Report, *Engineering Graduate Education and Research,* National Academy Press, 1985.

National Research Council Report, *Engineering Technology Education*, National Academy Press, 1985.
National Research Council Report, *Support Organizations for the Engineering Community*, National Academy Press, 1985.

ITV Resources

AMCEE (Association for Media-Based
Continuing Education for Engineers)
225 North Avenue, NW
Atlanta, GA 30337-0210

GENESYS
102 Nuclear Sciences Building
University of Florida
Gainesville, FL 32611

IEEE (Institute of Electrical and Electronic
Engineers)
Computer Society
1730 Massachusetts Avenue, NW
Washington, DC 20036-1903

NTU (National Technological University)
P.O. Box 700
Fort Collins, CO 80522

SURGE
Colorado State University
Engineering Research Center
Fort Collins, CO 80523

TAGER
2601 North Floyd
P.O. Box 830688
Richardson, TX 75080

36

Technical Skills*

W. J. Mallory

W. J. Mallory *is with Management and Technical Training at Ford Motor Company. In the last 8 years, he has managed the instructional design and development activities associated with 16 performance-based, high-technology-oriented manufacturing technical skills training programs. He was the primary architect in the design and implementation of a technical skills training delivery capability which has provided approximately 155,000 hours of technical training to date. Mallory has also authored Ford Motor Company's Technical Training and Job Aid Specifications. He was recognized for his contribution to his employer, to his profession, and to ASTD in 1983 when ASTD named him its Technical Skills Trainer of the Year. Prior to his work at Ford, he managed the Technical Services Division of Applied Science Associates, Inc. There, he was responsible for providing job-performance aid and technical training products to a number of industrial and governmental clients.*

This chapter's focus is on the training concerns of the corporate or in-house technical trainer: the subject matter expert drafted into a training job, the liberal arts major with training responsibility in a personnel department, or the manager or supervisor with a new product or process facing deadlines and the need to improve human performance. In short, this chapter will try to identify and look at

*The author wishes to express his appreciation to the following individuals and organizations for time and information contributed to the preparation of this chapter: Ford Motor Co.: Ruth Gramlich, supervisor, salaried personnel and training, Ypsilanti plant, Electrical and Electronics Division; and Robert Kasper, supervisor, apprentice and launch training, North American Automotive Operations. Livonia, Michigan, public schools: Dennis Laurain, vocational education specialist. Michigan Governor's Office for Job Training: Larry Goode, associate director of marketing; and Jan Urban-Lurain, associate director. The views expressed are solely those of the author.

major technical training issues from a corporate point of view, rather than from the viewpoint of an educator or consultant.

In the last 30 years, an incredible amount of time and resource has been expended developing and testing the techniques and methods which comprise the instructional development process as we now know it. The process, when followed, is capable of producing stunning results. However, today's technical training programs, in an alarming proportion, are produced and conducted in a fashion similar to programs done 20 to 30 years ago. The only noticeable difference in many cases is the subject matter. Task analysis, performance-based, interactive, and self-instructional are a few of the current "buzz-words" used by technical trainers. However, the first thing one learns about a new instructional concept is how much more expensive it is than the old way. The second thing corporate trainers learn is how incredibly long the development process is when they are facing an immediate need. It's not hard to guess why improved instructional technology comes slowly to industry. In some cases, industry is laboring just to maintain the pace set many years ago.

Microcomputers, robots, remotely guided vehicles, lasers, electron discharge machining, flexible manufacturing—the list is seemingly endless; there is no doubt about it, the workplace is filled with a plethora of high-technology devices. The only thing more exciting than the length of the list of high-tech equipment is the speed at which new items are being added to the list. We would be naive to expect the rate of high-tech innovation to slacken; shrewd planners might expect the opposite. There are many technical training needs associated with the current barrage of high-tech products. One kind of need is produced when new technology is introduced in the workplace—the need to train the work force to perform a new job somewhat different from the old one, using a state-of-the-art laborsaving gadget. If a large work force is affected, there is a high volume of employees requiring this training. A mass shift to office automation in a large corporation is an example of this high-volume need. This first type of need is not so new or frightening because when the number of potential trainees is large, it's easy to see the need and it's easy to justify the training.

A second, more insidious, type of need is high volume with respect to the number of different programs required by a particular work force. This type of need becomes more of a problem as the size of the audience or work force shrinks and as more and more different jobs require training. In this case, it may be difficult to justify training as a viable alternative. Selection may be an answer, depending upon labor agreements.

A third type of need is associated with training today. This need does not deal directly with programs or trainees but rather with a need to demonstrate results. Corporate technical training must be accountable for results. Line management is preoccupied with cause-effect relationships; the ones which produce profitable results are obviously favored. Top management knows that technical training is necessary in some situations but tends to view it as something of a luxury when times are tough. This perception of training persists because training has failed to produce results, or even worse, training may have failed to measure and communicate results achieved. To be a full partner in the business environment, training must accept responsibility for improving human performance on the job; and training must demonstrate measurable results to management. Accountability for results is a terrific strategy for changing the perception of training from a luxury to a necessity.

There is a fourth category of training need which is descriptive of how technical training ought to conduct its business—a need for excellence in technical training. In industry, excellence is not achieved by spending a fortune on technical training. Excellence is achieved by producing the necessary results on time with the lowest possible investment. This means that a lot of people with varied interests and responsibilities must work together as a cohesive team. The corporate training activity, a service organization, must realize that its customers are both trainees and management. Without one or the other, there is no need for training.

The Environment

Technical skills training jobs may be broadly classified as either administrative or instructional. Instructional jobs are those such as instructor, instructional developer, and instructional designer. Administrative posts handle support functions like "program prospecting," coordination, and scheduling. In many organizations, skills training is restricted because the training structure is biased either instructionally or administratively. There are shortcomings of either structure which can be lessened by a blending of skills and job responsibilities.

Administrators tend to be reactive, responding to each new problem identified by management by looking for existing programs. Analytical developers will study the problem and attempt to create the "best" solution under the circumstances; while a subject-matter expert (SME) will pass if the problem is beyond the SME's expertise. A better approach would be to study the need and determine if training is an appropriate solution. If training is necessary, needs should be assessed, tasks analyzed, and objectives set before any existing programs are evaluated or any new program developments undertaken. The better approach requires both instructional and administrative skills.

The best solution is when training anticipates the problem, acquires the necessary instructional material, and implements the solution before management identifies a difficulty. This is the best solution because lost productivity, between the time the problem emerges and the time management labels it, is saved.

Resources

Apprenticeships

Established apprentice programs represent a resource which should not be overlooked since these programs produce employees with entry-level skills through a combination of education, task-specific training, and hands-on practice. The mechanism to utilize the potential of an apprentice program is through the fine tuning of program content. While the fundamentals may change slowly over time, tasks on the job tend to constantly evolve. This perpetual evolution should result in periodic updates to the program. At Ford Motor Co., the apprenticeship program content is monitored and reviewed by a Joint Apprenticeship Committee, a group composed of United Automobile Workers of America (UAW), representing skilled trades workers, and company management.

For information regarding the establishment of a registered apprenticeship program, one should contact the Bureau of Apprenticeship and Training, U.S. Department of Labor.

Government Aid Programs

A variety of state and federally funded aid programs may be valuable resources for corporate skills trainers. The opportunities available will vary somewhat because of programs designed to solve local problems. For example, the Michigan Skills Partnership program is an amalgamation of the following:

- Michigan Business and Industrial Training Program. If a firm is considering a move into or an expansion within Michigan, this program will help the employer obtain skilled workers. This program is administered by the state department of labor.

- Quik Start. The state department of education makes grants to educational institutions to train employees: for new business or industry, for expanding business or industry, and to operate new equipment. In Michigan, this program also provides funds for curriculum design, development, and materials.

- Project Opportunity. Corporate expansions or relocations to the state may receive grants for retraining of workers whose previous jobs have been eliminated. The Governor's Office for Job Training administers this program.

- Job Service. The state employment security commission offers a free source of job applicants to interview. This service includes defining skill needs and applicant screening prior to employment interviews.

- Private industry councils. Private councils throughout the state operate programs to train unemployed workers with low incomes for new jobs. This effort is administered by the state department of labor, while policy is set by the Job Training Coordinating Council.

- Community colleges. Vocational assistance to expanding and relocating businesses through community colleges is also coordinated at the state level.

- Special populations. The Governor's Office for Job Training also provides training assistance to employers willing to hire special segments of the work force including workers 55 and older with low income, veterans, handicapped individuals, and public assistance recipients.

The Michigan programs described above are either federally funded and administered by the state or funded and administered by the state. The best advice on obtaining information about governmentally funded programs is to contact your state government for pertinent program facts. While the names of agencies will vary from state to state, there is one organization which will be found in each state; in each of the 50 states there is a Job Training Coordinating Council to advise the governor on job training programs. To pursue local opportunities start with your governor's office.

Vocational Education

Vocational education is a different type of aid program in that federal and state government funds are matched with regional funds to support local career preparation at the high school and junior college level. Government funding to these institutions is most readily available to support education in "high-demand" fields like computerized accounting. The corporation has a community obligation to work hand in hand with local vocational schools to shape the design and content of courses supplying new candidates to the local job market. To this end, corporate SMEs should work with community advisory councils. The resource value is in preparation of the potential work force before employment.

Junior colleges represent additional resources because of access to vocational education specialists who may be retained as consultants or commissioned to prepare and present customized programs strictly of corporate interest.

Organized Labor

Corporations with labor agreements should consider the labor union(s) as a job-related technical skills training resource. For example, both Ford Motor Co. and General Motors Corp. have individually teamed with the UAW to address skills training in high-tech areas. Financial support for these programs has come primarily from training funds accrued in proportion to the number of hours worked by UAW represented workers. In addition, joint union-company administrative bodies have successfully petitioned for governmental funding assistance in vocational and retraining programs.

Off-the-Shelf Courses

Off-the-shelf training programs can represent a valuable, ready source of courses at a relatively modest cost. Off-the-shelf programs have the virtue of being readily available, eliminating the requirement for long-range planning to detect the need and the long months of extensive preparation and testing necessary to produce a program. Additionally, the cost of materials per trainee is likely to be less for an off-the-shelf program, unless the population targeted for training is quite large (i.e., several hundred or more).

Caveat emptor—let the buyer beware—off-the-shelf programs should be considered in favor of custom-developed programs only if existing courses truly meet the needs. This is one very large "if." Too many off-the-shelf programs are purchased on the basis of title, description, or subjective program evaluations. Off-the-shelf materials should receive an objective analysis and a thorough testing. The objective analysis should be based upon a task analysis which (at a minimum):

- Identifies job-related tasks
- Determines task frequency
- Determines task criticality
- Considers safety implications
- Identifies target audience
- Determines measurable indicators of task performance and defines acceptable performance
- Sets performance-based objectives

If the program of interest appears to contain sufficient information and hands-on practice of important job tasks, it merits a tryout. The tryout results should be based on before- and after-training comparisons of task performance by representative members of the target population. If satisfactory performance is achieved after training, the program is a bargain.

Associations

Professional associations are valuable resources. Through professional organizations, one can learn about skills training from fundamentals to fine points of instructional design including the latest research findings. Some associations with excellent national reputations are listed below.

American Society for Training and
Development (ASTD)
Box 1443
1630 Duke Street
Alexandria, VA 22313

Human Factors Society (HFS)
Box 1369
Santa Monica, CA 90406

National Society for Performance and
Instruction (NSPI)
1126 Sixteenth Street, NW, Suite 214
Washington, DC 20036

Society for Applied Learning Technology
(SALT)
50 Culpepper Street
Warrenton, VA 22186

Custom-Developed Programs

Having a skills program custom-developed by an equipment vendor, training consultant, or expert in the field is an alternative when there are no available programs to meet a specific need. There are no perfect solutions; with custom programs, generally longer lead times are involved, and the development cost is likely to be several times the cost of typical off-the-shelf programs. Since higher development cost is, for all intents and purposes, a factor in custom courses, one must ensure that the custom effort is maximally effective, thereby providing maximum value and return on investment. Again, as was observed above, the buyer has a strong obligation to perform a task analysis and preliminary program design. Without the information produced by these activities, the buyer has no basis for objective analyses of proposals and developmental materials.

Contract Instructors. Some consultants are available to teach courses in their field of expertise. These consultants may offer proprietary or made-to-order programs. When one employs the consultant as an instructor, in addition to reviewing task analysis and course content, course format should be checked. Since many consultants also tend to be lecturers, one should be sure that necessary job skills are practiced during training and that practice is evaluated with immediate feedback to the trainees. Finally, since you are employing an instructor, look into the individual's ability and past results in similar situations by checking references.

In-House Development. In-house development suffers from some of the same lead time and cost penalties associated with custom-developed programs. Advantages of in-house development include control of proprietary information, better understanding of local culture, and utilization of local SMEs.

Many major corporations rotate key technical personnel through skills training jobs to take advantage of technical expertise. While in the training function, these SMEs are given some exposure to training for trainers which usually concentrates on presentation skills. That's fine, but what about instructional technology? Most competent instructional technologists are college graduates with advanced degrees; we should not expect to impart a detailed understanding of training principles in a 1- or 2-week "Train the Trainer" course for nontraining professionals. The answer is to maintain a mixed-disciplinary staff. A few skilled instructional designers are necessary to create and maintain a coherent program while guiding, coaching, and counseling the SMEs' efforts.

Tools, Methods, and Suggestions

Product Specification

Regardless of program source: off-the-shelf, custom-developed, in-house-developed, or some combination of the above, the only reasonable course of action is to develop a functional description of the necessary training. As individuals, we would not select and purchase a new car while wearing a blindfold; we might get a dune buggy when we meant to buy a sports car. Why then, as members of management, would we blindly choose a training program?

Ford Motor Co. has developed a Technical Training and Job Performance Aid Specification to provide some base-line training process and product consistency. This specification is as valuable to training administrators as it is to training developers. While the Ford specification may not satisfy the training or operational needs of others, it illustrates a concern and commitment to improving the results of technical skills training.

The following discussions cover core topics for an industrial technical training development specification, given the perspective of the task as described here. The following topics pertain to both internally and externally developed programs.

Task Analysis.   Task analysis is many things to many people. For our purposes, a task is defined as "a group or collection of individual, single-purpose steps (e.g., Set switch A to ON) to accomplish a single purpose (e.g., Disassemble the Theta Axis Drive Motor)." Tasks have the following characteristics:

- A definite beginning and end
- Involving human interaction with equipment, media, and/or other people
- Producing meaningful, measurable results
- Encompassing a mixture of decisions, perceptions, and/or physical activities[1]

For nondevelopmental (administrative) trainers, task analysis is limited to some relatively straightforward steps. The elements of task analysis necessary for proper program specification and evaluation were suggested above in the discussion of objective analysis of off-the-shelf programs. The following is representative of these task analysis requirements.

A task analysis should be performed prior to program design or development. The task analysis should produce the following products:

- A task identification matrix
- A target audience description
- A list of tasks beyond current capability
- A task frequency, danger, difficulty, and criticality matrix
- A list of tasks to be covered
- Measurable indications of task performance
- Acceptable levels of performance
- Performance-based objectives

Task Identification Matrix (TIM).   A TIM should be produced which attempts to identify task relationships in the workplace. The matrix row headings should be comprised of physical objects and/or characteristics of the work environment which are interacted with by the task performer (e.g., control panel, word processor, wrench). The matrix column headings should be action verbs which describe interactions with the work environment (e.g., clean, operate, adjust, repair, troubleshoot). At each matrix row and column intersection a "T" should be entered if the verb-noun combination describes a real task performed by the target audience; if the combination does not produce a task, a "—" should be entered. Refer to the following table for an example:

	Align	Operate	Replace	Connect
Power switch	—	T	—	—
Volume control	—	T	—	—
Balance control	—	T	—	—
Line fuse	—	—	T	—
Power cord	—	—	—	T

Target Audience Description (TAD). A TAD should be prepared to describe general features of the target audience. Typically one should pursue the following areas when searching for common factors in the target audience:

- *Prerequisites.* What skills, knowledge, education, or work experiences are common to task performers through position requirements?

- *Perceptions.* What are the common perceptions about the job and/or the task? Attitudinal related advantages and disadvantages may be discerned by probing target audience perceptions.

- *Job.* The position's duties, responsibilities, and placement on the organization chart may hint at common audience features. For example, entry-level positions are generally filled with new employees. Programs for new employees should include orientation to the corporation as well as dealing with the task to be trained.

- *Experience.* Many positions require prerequisite experience in similar positions or in allied fields. If this bond of common similar experience exists, those qualifying experiences should be examined for target audience commonality.

- *Motivation.* What motivators will drive members of the target population while in training? The answer to the "What's in it for me?" question is a determiner of adult motivation. If a program is perceived as necessary or job-related, the target audience is likely to be positively motivated. However, if the audience is negatively motivated, they will probably fail to achieve the desired results regardless of program quality.

- *Physical characteristics.* One should check for relevant, job- or task-related common physical attributes. For example, it's common for the lens of the human eye to stiffen with the aging process causing eyestrain when attempting to focus on near objects such as words on a page; that's why people over 40 frequently require glasses for the first time, or why those who wear glasses go to bifocals. If the average age of the target population was 45 years, it would be reasonable to expect corrected vision or a substantial number of vision problems when close visual discrimination or large amounts of reading are required. The correct reaction to this information is to redesign the task and/or training to address target population characteristics. In the above example, an appropriate response would be to consider using a larger, sans serif character font for written materials.

A word of caution—it is against the law to discriminate on the basis of race, sex, or age. These characteristics should be considered only if they are relevant to task performance, as illustrated in the preceding example. One should draw conclusions carefully based on audience characteristics. For example, if a majority of the audience graduated from an apprentice program, we could conclude that the audience had that experience in common. We could not deduce or predict performance at a task. The safest policy is to test for task-related ability levels. If reading ability is critical to task performance, then reading-level tests can help to prescribe reading levels for course materials or perhaps remedial reading training. A further word of caution about testing: the operative phrase is "job-related." Most mental tasks can be performed in a variety of ways; judge the product, not the process.

Tasks Beyond Current Capability (TBCC).

The tasks identified on the TIM should be reviewed with the TAD and current similar tasks performed by the target audience. The objective should be to eliminate all tasks identified on the TIM which the target population is capable of performing without additional attention. The tasks remaining after this culling process are those tasks which are beyond the current capability of the audience. By definition, these TBCC tasks are those to be dealt with by training and performance aids.

Task Frequency, Danger, Difficulty, and Criticality Matrix (TFDDCM).

A matrix expressing the expected frequency, difficulty, danger, and criticality of task performance should be prepared. Matrix column headings are defined as follows:

- Frequency—high, at least once daily
- Difficulty—high, complicated decisions, fine discriminations, physically demanding
- Dangerous—high, improper task performance is life-threatening
- Criticality—high, the parent organization's mission is jeopardized

The matrix row headings should consist of a list of the TBCC. On a three-point scale, rate each matrix cell as follows:

- High = 5
- Med = 3
- Low = 1

Refer to the following table for an example.

	Freq	Diff	Dang	Crit	Total
Operate power switch	5	1	1	1	8
Operate volume control	5	1	1	1	8
Operate balance control	1	1	1	1	4
Replace line fuse	1	1	5	5	12
Connect power cord	1	1	5	5	12

The matrix row totals provide a basis for decisions regarding the importance of covering tasks with training and/or performance aids. The higher the score, the more likely a task is for inclusion in the training plan. However, the rule of reason must still be applied. Any task receiving a score of 5 in either the dangerous or critical category should also be considered for treatment.

List of Tasks to Be Covered.   The original TIM contained an exhaustive list of tasks associated with the activity considered for training. The purpose of identifying tasks which are within current capability or which are simple, noncritical, and harmless is to remove them from further analysis and consideration. The remaining new, difficult, dangerous, or critical tasks should be consolidated into a list of tasks to be covered by training and/or job-performance aids. Particular attention should be given to flagging low-frequency critical tasks for inclusion in job-performance aids.

Measurable Indications of Task Performance.   For each task to be covered, measurable indications of normal or acceptable performance should be provided. Indications of acceptable performance are critical since these specifications are statements of overt performance upon which the performance improvement materials will be judged. Measurable indications may include aspects such as performance accuracy and performance time.

Acceptable Levels of Performance.   Performance levels are quantitative criteria which specify benchmark measures of acceptable performance. For example, in the task "Align the Shaft Coupling," accuracy could be specified as "within $\pm$ 0.0001 inch"; while performance time could be stated "within 3 minutes." Thus the performance criteria cover accuracy ($\pm$0.0001 inch) and time (3 minutes or less).

Performance-Based Objectives.   Each task statement should be phrased as overt performance, criteria, and relevant environmental conditions. For example, analyze the following performance-based objective: "Bring water to a boil over a campfire in 10 minutes or less; given two matches, kindling, a driving rain in a 20 mph wind." The objective's components are as follows:

- *Overt performance.*   Bring water to a boil over a campfire.
- *Criterion performance.*   In 10 minutes or less.
- *Environmental conditions.*   Given two matches, kindling, a driving rain in a 20 mph wind.

   The environmental conditions tie task performance back to the reality of the workplace. Overt performances, performance criteria, and environmental conditions combine to form performance-based objectives.

General Requirements

Once the task analysis has been accomplished, there are several project management steps to accomplish before the desired program is ready, completed, and ready to use. These additional administrative steps include:

- Prepare a program specification.
- Develop a plan of instruction.
- Detail performance-aid coverage.
- Develop criterion-referenced tests.

- Develop materials.
- Conduct a validation.
- Prepare an evaluation.

The following requirements specify suggested products and activities for these administrative steps.

Program Specification. Before a development source (internal or external) is selected, a program specification should be prepared. The program specifications should address the following concerns:

- Audience information including TAD data, common educational and employment experiences, entry-level skill requirements, and results of any audience testing.

- Delivery media considerations such as company-required hardware configurations, particularly in the video, microcomputer, and interactive video equipment areas. Existing delivery systems and delivery format preferences should also be listed.

- Quotation validity desired should be specified. This is usually stated as the period of time, after proposal due date, for which the quoted price is frozen. The period length is usually set to cover the time necessary to obtain management approvals and to have the purchasing department place the order.

- Validation details should be specified including vendor responsibility, required support materials and services, validation acceptance criteria, and measurement technique. A typical acceptance criterion is that 90 percent of the trainees achieve 90 percent mastery of course materials.

- The specification should detail any requirements to make the instructional design process explicit. It is recommended that key design documents be required to present an opportunity for in-process reviews during the development phase. Suggested products for review include task analysis products as described earlier, plan of instruction, criterion-referenced tests, draft training and performance-aid products, and final copies.

- The specification should detail any house format or content requirements. Any proprietary requirements for publication formats, computer software standards, or interactive video format or content requirements should be specified.

- The specification should describe the working relationship including chain of command and relationship of the project team to the organization. The developer's interface with the organization should be made explicit.

- The specification should state the corporation's standard terms and conditions for externally developed programs. These terms and conditions cover areas such as title to work product, copyright license, and confidentiality. The purchasing department is the place to get the correct set of standard terms.

- The specification should contain, at a minimum, a complete set of performance objectives.

Plan of Instruction (POI). A POI should be prepared which addresses the following points:

- An accounting of which objectives should be satisfied by training, and a listing of objectives to be handled by performance aids. In situations where there is overlap in coverage between training and performance aids, the roles and responsibilities of each should be detailed.

- A definition of instructional modules. Objectives to be handled by training should be coalesced into related groups. Each group should represent a training module.

- An ordering of modules into reasonable instructional progressions. To accommodate branching, for each module, prerequisite and dependent modules should be indicated.

- Within each module, the objectives should be sequenced to develop the instructional progression from fundamental knowledge and skills to highly specific job skills. Typically, performance objectives are statements of desired results and therefore are "terminal" or criterion objectives for the module. To detail a complete instructional process, enabling objectives should be developed to present primary and intermediate skills and/or knowledge necessary to achieve the terminal objective.

- Instructional material, training equipment, the instructional approach, and estimated length of instruction to satisfy each terminal and enabling objective should be included. It is recommended that the instructional approach be formatted as a scenario which describes the roles and relationships among trainee, instructional media, and training equipment.

Performance-Aid Coverage Plan. A performance-aid coverage plan should be developed based on the list of objectives to be satisfied by the performance aid, which was developed as part of the POI. The coverage plan should address organization and format of the performance aid(s).

Criterion-Referenced Tests. Before the development of instructional materials, criterion-referenced tests (CRT) should be developed to demonstrate achievement or mastery of terminal and enabling objectives as set forth in the POI.

Material Development. Once the POI, coverage plan, and CRTs have been developed and approved, material development may begin. The function of the plans is to provide detailed content and format guidance for the performance-improvement products. The CRTs amount to detailed statements of what the training must accomplish. The CRTs are the tests which cover the material which training must teach.

Validate the Materials. The validation represents a dress rehearsal or tryout of the entire set of program materials using a limited number of trainees who are typical of the target audience. The program developer should prepare a validation plan which addresses areas such as:

- Checking validation participant's credentials

- The statistical method to be employed including data to be collected, scoring or treatment method, minimum number of participants required

- An administrative plan detailing the particulars of how the validation would be managed, including establishing roles and responsibilities of vendor and client

Evaluation. Program evaluation is distinctly different from validation. Validation is a process to measure the quality of program materials. Validation usually presents the opportunity to collect prescriptive repair information to improve deficient areas in the instruction. Evaluation, however, is a test of the corrected, validated program. Evaluation is a measure of how well the trained audience now performs the tasks or activities of concern. Performance tests which compare on-the-job performance before and after training are appropriate for evaluation purposes. Ideally, the measurable indications of task performance identified in the task analysis will be used as the performance test. In a properly developed course, after-training performance will equal or surpass the acceptable limits of performance determined in the task analysis.

Trainer's Responsibilities

The trainer's responsibilities, while following these product specifications, are either developmental, supervisory, or some combination of both. The specifications serve as a road map, charting the developmental process to be followed in achieving the desired results. The supervisory and administrative role of the trainer affects the management of the development effort (scheduling resources, etc.) and is responsible for the quality, content, format, and ultimate utility of the program. The following paragraphs contain some methodology to assist the trainer in the administrative-supervisory part of the developmental process.

Review Task Analysis. Each of the discrete task analysis products as described earlier should be reviewed as follows:

- *TIM.* Since the row and column entries on the TIM establish the limits of task analysis, the row heading entries should be carefully reviewed with the physical work environment to be sure that all elements of the environment which are interacted with are present. Similarly, review the action descriptors which convey the types of interactions the task performer has with the environment. Each matrix cell entry should be tested for validity by asking the question "Does the task performer do this?" not "Can we handle this now?" If a task is performed, the cell should contain a "T." It is recommended that separate reviews be conducted by trainers and SMEs, with the trainers responsible for coalescing the results and interacting with the developer.

- *TAD.* The TAD should be reviewed to ensure that audience-descriptive data are relevant to the task performed. TAD should be reviewed by training, SMEs, the legal department, and perhaps an industrial psychologist.

- *TBCC.* Initially the TBCC should be reviewed to confirm that all tasks identified on the TIM are included. The next step is to review the decisions reflecting which tasks are—and are not—beyond the current work force capability. These decisions should be reviewed by training and the SME. Any conflicts should be resolved by performance testing after measurable indications and acceptable limits of performance have been established.

- *TFDDCM.* The matrix row headings should be checked with the TBCC to be sure that all TBCC tasks are included. Second, the cell entries for frequency, difficulty, dangerous, and critical tasks should be double-checked. Reviewers of this product should include training, SMEs, safety, and operations. Disagreements over cell assignments, and therefore treatment, should be resolved in favor of the highest numerical value suggested by the review team.

- The list of tasks to be covered should be checked for correspondence with the review team results from the previous step.

- *Measurable indications of task performance.* Each task on the list of those to be covered should be addressed. The indications of performance should be tested to ensure that product or output characteristics are described rather than irrelevant process features. The review team at this step should consist of training, SMEs, and operations.

- *Acceptable levels of performance.*   For each measurable indication of performance from above, humanly possible levels of performance should be listed. Training's responsibility is to ensure that it is reasonable to expect human beings to achieve and sustain the indicated levels of performance. Operations must accept (buy in) the specified levels, since these levels describe a theoretical maximum limit on human performance. If operations does not buy in to program objectives, it's likely that the finished program will not satisfy their needs. If the result is that given the current task and task environment, it is not humanly possible to achieve operations' performance requirements, then the problem is not solvable with training; it's time for engineering and/or industrial engineering to examine the problem.

- *Performance-based objectives.*   There should be at least one performance-based objective for each identified task. Each objective should have one or more associated measurable indications and the related quantitative values described in the statements of acceptable performance. Since this is primarily an administrative check to be sure that nothing has been omitted or added, review responsibility falls to training.

Review Program Specification.   If the design work was accomplished by a consultant, it is strongly recommended that the analysis phase be completed and a separate procurement held to select a developer. There is a compelling reason for this suggestion; the estimated cost will be much more accurate after the design work is accomplished. A second consideration would be to disqualify the specification consultant from bidding on the development project, thereby removing the possibility of conflicting interests.

Program specifications should be reviewed prior to requesting vendor proposals. The specification contents should be as described earlier under General Requirements of the Product Specification. Once training is satisfied with the content, the draft specification should be submitted for the review of the legal and purchasing departments.

Review POI.   Generally the POI is the first instructional design document prepared by the training developer on a project. The POI is the developer's first detailed response to the format and content requirements of the specification. All aspects of the POI should be very carefully checked to be sure that the vendor's documented understanding of the program requirements matches the specified needs. It is usually true that some significant differences will be found. Vendors should be encouraged to identify suggested improvements separately from the general response to the specifications. It is not unusual to work through two or three submissions of the POI before agreeing on the complete approach. POI review cannot be emphasized too much, since it determines the exact treatment for the materials to be developed.

Of particular interest in the POI is "head-book trade-off"; this is the accounting of how course objectives will be handled. Objectives to be handled by training (head) should be generalizable kinds of skills or knowledge; information easy to remember and easy to recall should be earmarked for inclusion in training. Sequences of procedural steps, large numbers of exact values, and highly descriptive information should be relegated to performance aids. For example, an objective dealing with proficiency in arithmetic multiplication would teach memorization of the multiplication tables from zero through nine and the multiplication process for the conjunction of real numbers containing one or more digits. In another example, a performance aid would be superior to training in an objective which required rapid and frequent access to six-place logarithmic tables. A performance aid would also be the clear choice for a critical task which is not performed often enough to recall the correct sequence of steps.

Review Criterion-Referenced Tests. Criterion tests must provide the trainee with the opportunity to demonstrate the performance described in the terminal and enabling objectives. In the case of performance tests, the CRT should consist of the actual test administration form, instructions, scoring directions, etc. Performance tests should be reviewed for conformity with performance objective requirements.

For knowledge-based objectives, CRTs will be achievement exercises, and reviews should center on the quantity and appropriateness of the items submitted. A rule of thumb is that there should be between five and ten test items for each knowledge objective.

Review Draft Instructional and Performance-Aid Materials. The draft materials must be reviewed for conformance:

- *To the format specifications.* The editorial aspects of the draft materials should be checked including grammar, spelling, composition, cross references, illustration appropriateness, and format compliance.

- *To content requirements.* The content must be checked side by side with the associated CRT. At the very least, there should be some content dealing with each CRT item. It's difficult to argue whether coverage is adequate. Doubts of treatment adequacy may be voiced, but if the developer disagrees, the only positive test is validation. If the material validates, it was obviously adequate.

- *To the mediation decisions.* Check that coverage is provided in the appropriate media; training should contain all the "head" objectives, and the "book" objectives should be in the performance aid.

Conduct Validation. The validation should be managed and the data collected and analyzed according to the approved plan. In addition to these objective measures, it is recommended that a senior representative from training monitor the activities apart from the planned validation. The monitor should concentrate on debriefing the trainees module by module as the validation progresses. The trainee's assessment of length, difficulty, validity, etc., will be invaluable in designing course improvements.

A running item analysis is another excellent technique for identifying problem areas for additional improvement. In the running item analysis, trainees' responses to CRTs are pooled and the item is scored (e.g., 15 of 20 trainees incorrectly responded to item 12). In debriefing the trainees regarding item 12, one might discover inadequate coverage, an ambiguous item, a technical error, or many other possible problems. If the analysis is maintained in real time, then as soon as problems occur, research on the solution may be performed and alternative treatments proposed and perhaps tested. If relatively few problems are encountered, this may substitute for a later revalidation.

Review Final Materials. If the draft review was thorough and the validation was moderately successful, the review of final materials will consist of making only the improvements discovered to be necessary during validation. If the validation was less than successful, the materials should be redrafted and revalidated.

Program Evaluation. The final responsibility of the trainer is to evaluate the program in terms of its strategic mission—whether it produced desired performance on the job. The best evaluation is an on-the-job performance test under normal working conditions. If the actual performance is equal to or better than the specified criteria, then the program was a roaring success. If the validation was successful but the evaluation failed to demonstrate the desired capability, then there are either some nontraining factors impeding performance or the task analysis overlooked some key tasks or objectives. In this situation, look for other factors such as motivation or noise (confusion-task interference). If the problem is not related to any of these factors, review the task analysis findings with a master task performer.

The last step of the evaluation is to report back to management. Management should be kept informed throughout the development process, particularly when the work force possesses new capabilities to be utilized.

Train the Trainer

The previous discussions have not attempted to do more than suggest appropriate actions and responsibilities for industrial technical skills trainers. It would be impossible to attempt serious skill building here. However, it is possible to outline a skills program which parallels the previous discussions. For many current corporate technical trainers, we need to look at the job and ask if the position objectives are consistent with tasks described here.

Suggested Course. The following recommendations parallel the Ford Motor Co. course "Needs Assessment and Training Program Evaluation."

Audience. The intended audience of this program should be the current technical training staff including SMEs; trainers from the hourly ranks as well as those from salaried positions are true trainers and will greatly benefit from the instruction.

Media. While all forms of instructional media are available to us, it is suggested that an expert-led group session may contain the greatest advantage. One advantage is that the expert-led program can be implemented much faster and at a lower cost, given that in any given corporation the population of trainees is likely to be very small. The course format should emphasize hands-on case-study-type exercises. The case-study exercises should be worked in teams of four or five trainees. This grouping should follow the line of natural work groups if possible, to promote teamwork. Team grouping will also permit the facilitator to monitor the cooperative efforts and interact with groups requiring additional help.

Objectives. The following objectives are recommended for inclusion in a training program for corporate trainers. Close inspection of these objectives will reveal that indications of performance and acceptable levels of performance have been omitted. These parameters should be added at the local level to suit the audience, tasks, and responsibilities.

Introduction. The trainee shall demonstrate:

- A knowledge of the course's purpose.

- A knowledge of the course's content.

- A knowledge of the course's organization.

- A knowledge of the course's format, media, and media interactions including practice exercises.

- A knowledge of the course's objectives. This shall be accomplished on a unit-by-unit basis.

Task Analysis. The trainee shall demonstrate:

- A knowledge of performance-based training; a knowledge of what performance-based training is, how it works, and what it accomplishes.
- A desire to implement performance-based training because of its advantages to employees and to the company.
- The knowledge that a task is a group or collection of individual, single-purpose steps (e.g., set switch A to ON) to accomplish a single purpose (e.g., disassemble the Theta axis drive motor).
- The knowledge that a task has a definite beginning and end.
- The knowledge that a task involves human interaction with equipment, media, and/or other people.
- The knowledge that a task performed results in a meaningful product.
- The knowledge that a task includes a mixture of decisions, perceptions, and/or physical activities.
- The knowledge that an activity is a complex duty which is accomplished through performance of two or more tasks.
- The knowledge that a subtask is a sequential group of task steps less than a complete task but perhaps common to several different tasks.
- The ability to develop a task inventory.
- The ability to define a program's target population.
- The ability to determine task difficulty, frequency, criticality, and safety.
- The ability to determine and list frequently performed, difficult, critical, and dangerous tasks which are beyond the current capability of the audience.
- The ability to locate and interpret quantitative task-performance data.
- The ability to locate task information sources.
- The ability to establish observable and measurable dimensions of task performance.
- The ability to establish quantitative values for acceptable task performance.
- The ability to establish performance-based objectives.

Mediation. The trainee shall demonstrate:

- A knowledge of how adults learn.
- A knowledge of objectives, information, and performance-related subjects most and least likely to be satisfactorily accomplished by training.
- A knowledge of objectives, information, and performance-related subjects most and least likely to be satisfactorily accomplished using job-performance aids.
- The ability to correctly allocate objectives to the most effective format (training or performance aid) for accomplishment.
- A knowledge of job-performance aid: characteristics, formats, format strengths, and format weaknesses.

- A knowledge of common technical training: delivery media, media applications, delivery media strengths, and delivery media weaknesses.

Evaluation. The trainee shall demonstrate:

- The ability to evaluate existing programs by synthesizing program objectives, comparing program objectives and job-performance requirements, a review of the "head-book trade-off," reviewing program and performance-aid media selections, and on-the-job performance testing of program graduates.
- The ability to evaluate programs in development by in-process reviewing the POI and draft instructional materials, conducting a validation, performance testing program graduates.
- The ability to evaluate vendor proposals against program objectives.
- The ability to compare multiple vendor proposals for the same product.

Summary

Today in industry, we are facing some of the most compelling challenges ever—to become competitive. The engineering sciences are near the asymptote in their hardware-based productivity equations. The most significant improvements in quality and productivity will come to those corporations and individuals who effectively invest in human capital. Performance-based, task-oriented technical skills trainers should be franchised as partners, by management, to manage the development of the human resource. This chapter has presented some basic, proven-effective techniques which, if followed, can be of immense value in dealing with the challenges facing today's corporate skills trainers.

Reference

1. Schumacher, S., and Z. Glasgow, *Handbook for Designers of Instructional Systems*, Vols. 1–5, Air Force Human Resources Laboratory, Wright-Patterson Air Force Base, OH, March 1974, AFP 50-58.

37
Sales Training

C. E. Hahne

C. E. (Gene) Hahne is Manager of Training—Human Resources, Products Employee Relations, Shell Oil Company, Houston, Texas. His group is responsible for training the 20,000 employees in manufacturing, pipeline, technical operations, and sales, and operates four retail learning centers to train jobbers, dealers, and distributors. Hahne has received Shell Oil's Excelsior Award, ASTD's Distinguished Contribution to Employer Award, and ASTD's 1984 Torch Award. He served on both the old ASTD board and the board of directors under the new governance structure; as treasurer of the society; chair, budget and finance committee, and on many national committees and task forces. He was director of the ASTD Sales and Marketing Division and received the 1981 James R. Ball Award. His contributions to the community include work with Texas A&M University, University of Texas, Houston Baptist University, North Harris Community College, and the University of Houston. He helped design and implement a management development program for the state of Texas and has conducted workshops throughout the world. He has been named to Who's Who in the South & Southwest, Who's Who in Finance & Industry, Personalities in the South, Personalities in America, Men of Achievement in the World.

This chapter, a reference resource for sales trainers, is a block of practical information to help develop and maintain effective training programs. The principles of sales training, however, work just as well for *any* type of training.

Purpose of Sales Training

Productive sales training increases sales permanently by enhancing the knowledge, skills, work habits, attitudes, self-confidence, and on-the-job behavior of an organization's sales force. The end result is *learning*, which occurs only when a salesperson permanently changes behavior for the better.

The bottom-line sales training goal is the same as that of sales and marketing management: apply the organization's sales and marketing plan effectively to maximize both current sales and the long-term growth of the organization.

Selling is the process of human interaction to achieve the goal of persuading another person to make a decision that you support. In selling you identify needs and wants—and then communicate in a persuasive way to convince someone that you can satisfy those needs and fulfill those wants.

Every person, every day, is involved to some degree in selling, as an inevitable part of interacting with other people. Some sell suggestions . . . ideas . . . "what ifs" . . . recommendations. Others directly promote specific, tangible products and services. All selling, however, involves a learnable core of basic skills that apply to any sales position, no matter what industry or field of endeavor.

Sales training is changing behavior by exposing people to knowledge and skills that allow them to communicate with others in a persuasive way. It is, in fact, *the process of creating an environment in which individual sales personnel can feel motivated to develop effective sales skills and a productive attitude that can lead to achieving personal and business goals.*

Such training is an *ongoing process,* fed by a series of programs that expose the individual to key skills and knowledge. This in-depth exposure to personal communication skills is valuable to *all* personnel in any organization (in purchasing, finance, etc.) who need to enhance behavior in order to persuade others to accept recommendations for action.

Any complete sales training process should include exposure to these knowledge and skill areas:

- Organizational philosophy, policies and procedures, structures, and strategies
- Business knowledge and skills
- Time and territory management
- Legal considerations
- Sales and negotiation skills
- Planning and goal setting
- Self-awareness and personal development
- Communication skills

Obviously each individual salesperson has a specific set of needs; no two are exactly alike. Ongoing programs to change behavior, therefore, must be adaptable to the various degrees of training need among the sales force. The long-term goal, of course, is to bring all sales personnel up to the same productive level of sales behavior so they can all achieve maximum potential in reaching individual and company goals.

Benefits of Sales Training

Everyone wins with good training. *Mutual benefit* is the prime principle:
The *salesperson* receives

- Greater self-confidence
- Ability to communicate more persuasively
- Greater fulfillment in achievement

- Enhanced career opportunities
- Greater feeling of pride and loyalty in contributing to the well-being of the customer and the organization
- Increased income from greater sales

The *customer* receives

- A solution to immediate problems and needs
- End-user benefits of the product or service
- Overall better service
- A valuable resource for information and help (salesperson) who cares about customer needs
- A valuable resource for reliable products and services (the company)

The *company* receives

- Increased revenue from sales (short- and long-term)
- Increased profits (the return on training investment)
- Long-term stability of repeat business from satisfied customers
- Reduced employee turnover and cost
- Improved employee morale
- Growth potential in the marketplace

And the *sales training group* receives

- Greater credibility with management
- Greater use of developed programs
- Enhanced job stability and protection from recession
- Increased job satisfaction

How to Create and Maintain Sales Training Results

We accomplish result-getting training by following *ten steps to productive sales training:*

1. Get and maintain management support and credibility.
2. Analyze and clearly identify the actual needs of both the organization and the sales personnel.
3. Develop a training action plan and present it to management.
4. Find and/or design and develop criterion-referenced training material.
5. Design a comprehensive measurement and follow-up plan.
6. Select and train trainers.
7. Validate the program with a pilot group.
8. Collect data, analyze these, and adjust the program.

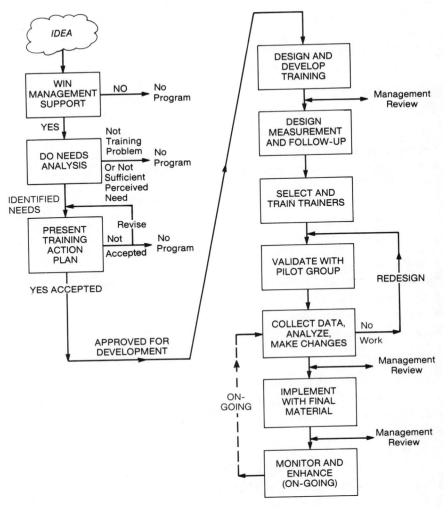

Figure 37-1. Sales training program development process.

9. Implement the training program.

10. Monitor and enhance the program over the long term.

Throughout this 10-part cycle you must communicate with management to keep key individuals informed of the progress and direction of the program. This communication is vital to maintaining your credibility as a valuable management resource for consultation and effective solutions.

Look at Fig. 37-1. This flowchart shows the process of the 10 steps in sequence. Notice the various times to communicate with management to protect the program and the credibility of your sales training group.

Also note the *options for no training program.* The first question to ask yourself is always, "Is it a training problem?" Only a lack of knowledge or skill requires training; any other reason requires management action of another sort. Options for no training could also be the result of a trainer's lack of credibility, an irreconcilable difference in opinion about what the real needs are, an unconvincing training action plan, and so forth.

The most critical phase of the whole process, however, is usually *assessing needs and communicating them to management*. The problem is often a conflict in how the needs are perceived.

Managers tend to identify good training as that which provides what they want, based on their goals and their distanced view of life on the front line. As sales trainer, you must make sure your programs maintain a sensitive balance between what management wants (perceives as needs) and what the sales people want (perceive as needs). You must understand your organization's objectives and goals, its abiding philosophy, its strategic marketing plan, in order to identify the most important needs to address. At the same time, you must also be able to satisfy management with your solutions.

Step 1: Win Management Support (Credibility)

Your *first* and most important job is to gain the support of management, and keep it.

Success in getting funds and support for training will be in direct proportion to your ability to develop and maintain credibility among management. The best training program ever made can gather dust on the shelf if management doesn't believe in the product and what you can do for the organization. Sales training succeeds best when you convince your management of the worth of each training program, as well as the value of your contribution as a sales training resource.

You must be the effective salesperson yourself in order to convince management to make the best use of your ability to create powerful learning experiences that result in increased performance of the sales force. This work includes thorough fact finding, netting out bottom-line impact of decisions, managing expectations, and delivering what you said you would, when you said.

The most persuasive position you can take is to be visible, involved, constantly communicating with all levels of the organization. *The successful sales trainer develops workable programs by being a persistant diplomat who regularly communicates the bottom-line benefits of sales training to all members of the organization.* This attitude provides the foundation for management support throughout the development process, gives you important positive communications, and enhances your position as training consultant and valuable management resource.

So use *regular communications* and *management credibility* as the driving force for your application of the 10 steps to productive sales training.

Step 2: Analyze Training Needs

You can't improve bottom-line sales results if you don't train your sales force in exactly the right skills. And you can't do that without knowing their specific needs in detail.

So the first job in training is to *analyze and identify the real-world needs* of the sales force. This work is best done by either your training staff or a qualified consultant, or some combination. It is an *objective* process that leaves little room for value judgments—an unemotional, unbiased snapshot in time of both personal and organizational needs.

Please note: *every* training program needs and deserves a needs analysis of some degree. The halls of corporatedom are littered with old programs, hanging around for years, that never met the real needs in the first place. *Every* program worth doing is worth doing right . . . and right doesn't have to mean expensive, just *thorough*. If you don't have much budget for a program, there are two clear choices:

1. Spend most of the budget identifying specific needs and presenting them in an in-depth training action plan.

2. Add the money to another program's budget so you can at least do one program right. (That is, why waste what little money you have—and everyone's time and energy—if you aren't going to give your training program a chance to achieve the results that it could?)

A *well-designed analysis instrument* is absolutely essential for an accurate, objective picture of the need. Your survey questions should probe these areas:

- Objective facts about common processes, job tasks, problems, challenges
- Feelings that might indicate attitude problems
- Weaknesses; areas in which the sales personnel feel a need to strengthen their skills (i.e., they would feel more confident with these skills)
- What the respondents would teach if they were trainers.

The needs analysis instrument (survey, questionnaire, etc.) should be exactly the same for all people interviewed and for all interviewers. Short questions are best. For getting objective information, ask short direct questions that can be answered with only a few words. To get feelings and open the interviewee up to discuss hidden concerns, use open-ended questions that start with "why," "how," "what would you do if . . .," and so on. Try to design it so that interview time is no more than an hour or so per person.

Another method of needs analysis is to *study the job description*, if a complete description exists. Use deductive reasoning to back off from the overall tasks to find subtasks, skills, and knowledge necessary to accomplish the job.

Other approaches include *studying performance appraisals* to highlight performance problems and weaknesses, *conducting group interviews, observing behavior on the job, attending sales team meetings* to discuss problems, *studying sales correspondence* for the previous sales period (such as the previous complete quarter), and *studying other records* such as turnover and performance reports.

On-the-job observation gives immediate feedback. You can tell if a salesperson preplans a call, whether he or she is taking that extra step to get involved in helping the customer solve problems and meet needs. Make sure you communicate that you're not there to judge or inhibit their work, but rather to understand their needs so you can help them have the opportunity to improve their career opportunities.

While observing on-the-job behavior, you can begin to *establish credibility* for your training programs and generate enthusiasm and a sense of expectation. In causing dialogue, you encourage their support and commitment to the program. Get them talking about training and themselves (which, according to Dale Carnegie, is everyone's favorite subject). When they're involved, you've created *ownership;* it's not just the company program, it's *theirs*. When you deliver what they had hoped for, you're a hero and they're inspired to make the most of the opportunity.

Be sure to *interview management.* . . . and follow up with reports of results. Senior management responds best in one-on-one interviews. For middle managers and line participants, try group interviews (much easier to conduct and less demanding on your communications skills). For large numbers, send questionnaires and surveys that are easy to compile. Such instruments give a large amount of data in a short time for relatively little expense. Include in your group those outside the sales organization, including customers.

In needs analysis, be careful not to blindly accept information on face value. Many will try to hide true feelings, especially their limitations. Others concentrate on complaining about matters of emotional interest, but which are unrelated to actual work performance. Make sure you create a comfortable, trusting environment when talking with salespeople during your needs analysis.

There is a strong case for using outside consultants for some of the one-on-one "bare-your-soul" sessions. Employees often feel safer with an outsider who assures them he or she will report the facts without using anyone's name. Sales trainers, after all, are usually perceived as serving management, rather than their employees. Analyzing consultants' qualifications is easy: just study their samples and call the companies that have used them to find out how well their training programs are meeting the needs. Their proof is in the pudding, and studying their record of accomplishments is essential.

Special Note about Foreign Countries. Consider foreign cultures, taboos, and manners when training salespeople who will do business outside the United States. This subject merits considerable needs analysis attention, and perhaps a separate questionnaire. You would do well to seek consultation from a knowledgeable local native for this task. One slip of the tongue or careless gesture can ruin years of building relations in a foreign culture—showing the bottom of your shoe in Saudi Arabia, or giving a white wedding gift in China (funeral color there), or using gestures that don't mean the same as in America.

The end result of a well-conceived and well-executed needs analysis will tell you exactly how to design your training program:

- Who needs training

- When training should occur

- What *exact* skills and knowledge need to be learned

- What methods to use in the training experience, for new or experienced employees

- Who should be the trainer—instructor—facilitator, and what methods that person should use

- What results management can expect in improved performance, and how to measure them

What can salespeople learn in a good training program? How a successful salesperson operates; product and service knowledge (yours plus competitors'); company policies and procedures; internal organization; corporate strategy; how to plan, organize, manage time, manage a territory and its paperwork, such as call reports, make a sales call, handle objections and close the order, follow up and build a long-lasting relationship with customers; the most productive attitudes; why other salespeople succeed; how to develop accurate forecasts; and the many personal skills involved in communicating one-on-one, persuasively and effectively. The list, of course, will come from your thorough needs analysis and will therefore be tailored to the specific needs of your sales force, individually and collectively.

Then be sure to *manage ongoing needs analysis* by

- Keeping your finger on the pulse of the organization and its day-to-day functioning

- Keeping ears and eyes open at training sessions

- Becoming a part of the management planning process
- Constantly communicating with people at all levels of the organization
- Encouraging feedback through a confidential open-door policy at all times

Your needs analysis can be the door through which the organization learns to communicate—thus reaping substantial long-term rewards far beyond simple skills training.

Step 3: Sell Training Action Plan to Management

One half of your job is building lasting value into your training programs. The other half is convincing management of your accomplishments.

One proven method (and step 3 in developing any training program) is to produce a *training action plan* and sell it to management. Notice in Fig. 37-1 that the rest of the training process depends on this vital step.

An effective action plan includes these parts:

1. *Description of audience.* Who exactly needs the training and who doesn't, highlighting the variety of needs in the group to be trained.

2. *Summary of results of needs analysis.* Prioritized specific needs and the net impact to the organization of meeting those needs. (Keep it brief; talk net impact, results, benefits, bottom line.)

3. *Descriptions of objectives of your program.* There are three types of objectives for you to identify and explain:

- *Business* objectives that impact management's financial and strategic goals. You must interface with management in strategic planning sessions in order to be aware of the proper business objectives for your programs. Business objectives are net tangible results in sales and profit, the company's return on its investment of money and resources for training.

- *Learning* objectives that describe what specific skills and behavioral change the participants can expect from the program. On the heels of learning objectives are *application* objectives, which are simply the application on the job of the skills and knowledge learned in the program.

- *Training* objectives that identify the trainer's set of goals for creating and managing the learning experience. These include factors of creating the most stimulating, yet protective, learning environment possible. For example, one vital part of your training job is to shelter trainees from having their performance in the program be exposed to management. You can't afford to allow intimidation to stifle participation, shut down candor, muffle honesty, or in any way inhibit the individual's opportunity to take risks and step beyond normal habits to new and improved behavior. Role-play video and audio tapes, for example, are private experiences that are for trainees and trainers only. Training isn't the time for management to observe and evaluate performance—it's time to experiment, make mistakes, learn by doing to *increase* the level of performance back on the job. You lose credibility with trainees (and therefore your pipeline of feedback and communication) if you appear to be management's ears and eyes. Your commitment to trainees must be total to meet your overall commitment to management.

All learning objectives must be

- *Specific* (exact yet simple)
- *Realistic* (challenging yet achievable)
- *Measurable* (quantifiable yet not limiting)

For example, it isn't useful to tell management that you're going to teach salespeople how to *probe* a customer for information. Tell management instead that you're going to teach each participant how to increase sales by ten percent—or improve the call closing percentage by 25 percent—or boost sales to existing accounts by 5 percent in the next quarter. These are *specific, realistic,* and *measurable* goals that management wants to hear. Remember, to increase sales you must establish and maintain credibility with management. Set doable goals, meet them with a finely tuned training program, and you will have successfully managed the expectations of a group of people very important to your future opportunities.

Most sales training will involve primarily cognitive (thinking) and affective (feeling) objectives; use high-level verbs within those categories whenever possible. Note that *understand* is not a specific measurable, doable skill and thus is too vague a word to properly identify an important objective. Keep in mind that you are building *criterion-referenced* training with specific, realistic, and measurable learning objectives. In other words, each objective becomes a criterion upon which you'll build training exercises such that no important objective is left unfulfilled and no activity or concept in your program is without direct relation to an objective. The danger of setting such specific objectives (especially business goals that relate to performance) is that others in the organization may want to share the glory and claim part of the credit for sales increases. You must therefore have a system of *measuring training results,* which means you need measurable objectives in the first place. Another danger is *not achieving the results* predicted. Here's where the successful trainer shines, because he or she is willing to be held *accountable* for results of training. That's not so hard, actually, when you have a sound needs analysis that tells you exactly what needs to be done to increase sales and achieve those measurable results. All you have to do is trust the natural inclination of humankind to want to achieve goals and do well in order to receive the pride of recognition in our society.

4. *Detailed tasks.* The fourth part of your training action plan should be a complete *task analysis.* This document lists tasks (job skills), by category, which are necessary for a salesperson to achieve the success expected and hoped for by management. A good task analysis often causes management to rethink job descriptions and update them to a more specific, measurable form—making them the vital criteria for performance upon which enlightened performance appraisals and career counseling are based. Use any form you wish, though here's an example of one of the most common formats (the content, of course, depends on your group's specific needs):

Learning task for salesperson:

1. Plan a sales call.
   1.1 Develop a practical sales call planning form.
       1.1.1 Find and study available forms.
       1.1.2 Interview successful salespeople to determine most useful aspects.
       1.1.3 Use the best ideas to customize a sales planning form that fits your specific style and territory.
   1.2 Practice the planning form effectively.

1.2.1 Plan a complete sales approach for an actual customer in your territory.
1.2.2 Makes the sales call along with your sales manager.
1.2.3 Evaluate the effectiveness of your techniques with your manager.
1.2.4 Adapt your planning form to include better ways to plan and make a sales call.
2. Cold-call a prospect by telephone.
  2.1 Plan your strategy.
    2.1.1 Identify your objective for the call.
      2.1.1.1 Establish a business goal.
      2.1.1.2 Identify action you want the prospect to take as a result of your call.

Whatever form you use, be specific with *command verbs* that specify *action* and identify doable tasks. Keep your tasks *in parallel;* that is, begin them all with command verbs.

5. *Summary of available resources.* Management will want you to identify options for achieving the identified goals. You can cause the desired *action* on your training report and recommendations if you specify exactly what it will take in

- Money
- Manpower
- Management support

to accomplish the goals. Be sure, as well, to point out the *return on investment* in specific terms, to put even the most adventurous company commitment in its proper light in terms of *net value to the organization's business goals.* Management will surely want to know the best training approach, challenging you to defend any one of a number of options:

- Use off-the-shelf program material as is (probably the most common solution to meet training needs).
- Customize such material (watch out for copyright laws).
- Update existing in-house material (if it's even close to addressing the basic needs you've uncovered).
- Develop an entirely new program (tailored *exactly* to fit the specific needs of the current sales force).
- Create some combination of the above (be careful your management committee doesn't turn your submitted horse into the proverbial camel).
- Hire consultant(s) to help do any of the above. Consultants are most valuable when (*a*) you have limited staff expertise in a specific area, (*b*) your training staff is too busy, or the deadline too quick to handle in-house, (*c*) the issues are so sensitive as to require a neutral third party, or (*d*) management feels that they and the training staff are too close to the tree to see the forest and need an objective, "disinterested" viewpoint on key issues and observations. The consultant you hire should
- Have a verifiable track record.
- Be absolutely trustworthy for confidentiality and meeting deadlines.
- Be a people person who can relate to others easily.
- Be able to contribute to the credibility of your training group.

And some valuable advice: Create a detailed, professional working contract with each consultant to outline specifically what each party's duties are, the consultant's availability, key deadlines, training approach to take, content of program, description of deliverable materials, approval cycles, what determines acceptable quality of deliverables, how to cancel the agreement, etc. (obviously carefully scrutinized by your legal department and purchasing, where applicable). You'll find that 99 percent of the time, this complete and careful agreement serves the sole purpose of managing expectations and making absolutely clear what's expected of each party; only rarely does it have to be enforced as a binding legal contract.

- Final option: *back off* and have no program at all—an option that management always has with any program proposal if there isn't sufficient *business and/or organizational value* identified.

Present your training action plan in a *formal stand-up presentation* to management.

- Net it out with bottom-line results and benefits.

- Use graphics, readable charts, computer slides, etc., to present a professional image.

- *Sell* your plan! Get management *commitment* to support the program with money, time, and verbal communication of support to people at all levels of the organization. Your goal is *management buy-in to your specific program plan recommendations.*

Be prepared to justify your findings and recommendations with facts at hand and detailed predictions of net impact. Then be prepared for approval and the opportunity to put your money where your mouth is!

Step 4: Develop Instructional Material

Once you have a specific, well-developed training action plan, developing instructional material should be just a matter of carefully filling in the blanks.
Instructional design for sales training typically involves these major components:

1. Completing the needs and task analyses
2. Choosing appropriate training media and methods
3. Identifying trainer's specific role
4. Developing the program material

The *choice of media* and methods is critical to your job of helping trainees change behavior. For example, *group discussion* is usually best for exploring decision making and behavior options that apply to the trainee's real world. *Role playing* is best for practicing concepts and techniques to create new behavior. *Slides* often work best when the content of the program changes often or when you need to show it often to large audiences. *Videotape* is especially good for giving a perspective to a problem, process, or procedure and leaving the viewer with a memorable mental image that makes subsequent exposure to details easier and more effective. Audiotape, especially combined with a mostly graphic (few words) manual to follow, helps people who are not especially print-oriented to step through a process in a way that simulates the actual experience.

Special Note. Consider *logistics* of your sales organization's equipment and training facilities before making final decisions on training methods and media. Videotape may be best for presenting certain tasks and objectives, but your sales locations may have slide projectors instead of video players. You then must weigh the cost of video players against the added value that videotape can provide over slides or audiotape. Be prepared to justify your recommendations in dollars to management. (You are probably aware that management usually frowns on recommendations for increasing capital expenditures and personnel, for financial reasons that relate to your company's balance sheet and P&L statement.)

There are several key concerns in *identifying the trainer's role* in the program. The question is whether you want the trainer to "impart knowledge" or "manage the learning experience." *Stand-up lecture*, by the way, has been proven to be one of the least effective means of causing learning—a tough fact for most lifelong instructors to accept! Just remember that training can't make a person learn—it can simply create an environment in which the individual's own will and desire can best function to allow the individual to learn important skills and concepts. Trainers make best use of their time by leaving the presentation of basic terms and concepts to the precise, consistent, and compact form of audiovisual materials—allowing trainers to concentrate on *application, discussion facilitation,* and *one-on-one tutoring*. Remember that "trainer" is actually a misnomer, since "learning" is a process that goes on in the learner's mind based on a voluntary acceptance of ideas. In fact, the same principles apply to effective "training" that work in effective "management."

For your *choice of methods* for sales training, consider these approaches:

- *Seminars* and *workshops* provide opportunities for participation that are necessary for learning and change in behavior. They encourage the facilitator role for trainers, rather than stand-up lecturing.

- *Role playing* is a powerful means of reinforcing terms and concepts by giving the trainee the chance to practice techniques in realistic settings. *Audiotape* role playing is excellent for learning telephone sales techniques, with special emphasis on the impact of words (which convey only 10 percent of the complete message) and tone of voice (which conveys another 38 percent of the message, leaving 52 percent to body language) on the sales process. *Videotape* role playing is excellent for the words and tone, as well as the body language so important to one-on-one relationships and sales effectiveness. *Trio group* role playing is a way to experience the sales situation from both sides; three participants in a group take turns acting out a situation as salesperson, customer, and observer.

- *Case studies* provide the real-world atmosphere within which to practice skills and techniques. The above role playing works best when, instead of using generic simulations, you provide an actual real-life situation with the opportunity to compare the trainees' solutions with what actually occurred on the job. Take plenty of care in writing case studies:

  - Keep them relatively simple with one major point or skill as a focus.

  - Use dialogue to simulate what went on before the trainee takes over the call.

  - Use real facts.

- *Exercises* are short activities designed to reinforce a single concept or technique through (1) definition, (2) example, (3) practice, and (4) reinforcement of proper technique. Keep exercises short and specific. Hand out the exercise instructions or forms only when it's actually time to do the exercise. Do one example with the whole class; then let individuals or small groups complete the actual exercise. Finish with a group discussion of key points learned.

- *Special guest speakers* can add interest and valuable job-related knowledge and ideas to your program. Consider inviting especially successful salespeople, sales managers, and even customers to share their particular approach to achieving personal and company goals. Welcome discussion afterward as a valuable means of personal involvement and motivation.

- *Nonclass activity.* Your program may well include such learning experiences as *self-paced study, one-on-one counseling and tutorial guidance,* and *self-directed practice* and development.

- *Self-analysis tools.* The first step in communicating with others is to know yourself. A salesperson must be sensitive to the impact of his or her personal style on others, to avoid offending a prospect and to be the most persuasive salesperson possible. Consider two types of self-analytical tools in your sales training:

  1. *Style analyses.* Numerous self-graded or computer-graded style analysis programs are available on the market. Each in some degree helps the individual see him or herself clearly as others do. The result is often an increased sensitivity to behavior, to the needs of others, and to the use of words, tone of voice, and body language in order to create a desired impression.

  2. *Feedback from others.* Commercial programs are available to provide questionnaires for a salesperson's coworkers, subordinates, managers, and customers to evaluate the individual's effectiveness as a communicator. The result is often an amazed new awareness of what others *really* think of the trainee, and more often than not an increased desire to listen to constructive ideas for improvement and to attempt to improve behavior.

- The beauty of a good needs and task analysis is that it practically spells out the right method for each task to be learned. Your trainees, in effect, designed the program.

Developing program material is much easier if you have a well-executed instructional design. Materials development involves several key steps:

1. *Write copy* for exercises, case studies, workbook text, audiovisual scripts, etc. You'll need someone who specializes in writing training material, and not simply an expert on the subject of your program. The expert knows content detail but is too close to the subject; the writer is more of a layperson who knows how to package and present the key details in the clearest and most learnable style. Training copy should be

- Clear and direct
- Conversational (rather than stiff and formal, which alienates the reader, using passive verbs and long multisyllable words, for example)
- Logically organized, with clear transitions connecting the different parts
- True to the program's objectives, tasks, and the instructional design
- Tied specifically to graphics and visuals
- Checked by subject-matter experts, management, sales personnel, and the legal department
- Final-edited by one single person who can apply consistent style, format standards, and editing principles throughout

The best-designed program in the world can't withstand a mediocre writer (nor can an excellent writer rescue a program improperly designed and lacking in substance). When in doubt on content, trust the subject-matter expert; on presentation, trust the writer. Take the time to test audio and video scripts by reading them aloud for flow and natural feeling, especially those that contain dialogue. Have others read the case studies and exercises to make sure they make sense and don't confuse the reader or viewer. If anything confuses even one reader, make it clearer.

2. *Develop graphics and printed material.* Simple line drawings in one or two colors is sufficient for almost all training programs. Effective doesn't have to mean expensive. Use such techniques as screens (shading) and variety of type boldness and size to create the impression of more visual interest. Use colored paper sometimes to add an extra color dimension. Keep graphics and printed material clean and simple. Typeset before printing whenever possible. Hire an artist to clean up any artwork. Include photos when possible; use artwork when photos aren't available or feasible. Use the most practical form of binding. *Note:* For the first version of the material, consider using a neatly typewritten version photocopied for the pilot group of trainees (more on this subject under step 7). Save most of your graphics budget for the final improved version of your program (see step 8).

3. *Produce audiovisual segments.* Training programs don't have to be (and shouldn't be) Hollywood productions that entertain and "wow" but rather should make it easy for trainees to learn and change behavior. Consider these important guidelines for audiovisuals in sales training:

Slides. For graphics use few words, try computer graphics (many labs now let you call in on personal computers to compose your own, at a nominal cost), and keep them colorful but simple. For photographs, take the time to create professional pictures that are in focus, are well lighted, and illustrate exactly what you're discussing. Use two projectors with a dissolve instead of one, for smooth uninterrupted visual transitions. Use multiple projectors (multi-image) sparingly in training, because that approach is usually overkill in your department.

Video. Use ½-inch video for economical productions. Hire a local production crew rather than a big agency. Keep production simple: Use computer-generated titles to identify key points (they would be headings and subheadings in a book). Hire a narrator who is conversational and easy to listen to, but not condescending in tone. Use your company personnel for posing, but hire local actors for acting. Avoid humor unless you're extremely good at it. Stick to real people rather than cartoons, which are old hat and generally don't work well with adult audiences in training. Stay absolutely true to the purpose and objectives of your program. Copies, by the way, should be ½-inch VHS format in most cases to match the majority of machines available today. Be sure to make special copies to conform to different machines and electric currents for foreign countries.

Film. Follow the same general guidelines for video.

4. *Prepare trainer's guide.* Develop a compact summary of what the trainer needs to know to conduct the training experience:

- Role of trainer and facilitator
- Objectives of program
- Overall program outline
- Section-by-section lesson plan, with time, location, and description of activity for each step of the program
- Exercises, case studies, and other class material to present to participants
- Answer keys, lists of questions, and other support material for trainer—facilitator

- Reference material to help in preparation for the program
- Copy for flipcharts, overheads, slides, etc., for use in the seminar or workshop

Well-prepared instructional material makes the rest of the training process much easier.

Step 5: Design Measurement and Follow-up Plan

Measuring training results can be the difference between having management look on your efforts as an expense (burden) or an investment (asset). When times get tough and money tight, you'll want to be considered a wise investment to keep around.

The operative word is *payoff*, and measurability is your primary means of proving the bottom-line worth of your training programs to the long-term organizational business goals. You measure training results to

- Establish credibility, power, and commitment for your training group
- Help sell future programs to management
- Determine if you need to change your program and/or trainers to be more effective
- Make sure the program satisfies the organization's and individuals' needs and achieves objectives
- Determine if and when a follow-up program is needed and, most importantly,
- Prove to management that there is real benefit in spending money for sales training

A "fail-safe" way to measure the results of training depends on having specific, realistic, and measurable objectives—learning, business, and training objectives—originally developed in your needs and task analyses. The specific form and nature of each objective and task determines the measurement method you can use.

The implication behind all measurement of training results is *accountability:* your willingness as a trainer to identify specific objectives and put your credibility on the line in measuring how well your program achieved those objectives. Remember, however, that your objectives originally were the result of a joint effort with your sales force, management, and others in the organization. If your training program is true to the original objectives and tasks, it has an excellent chance of achieving its goals.

What exactly do you measure?

1. *Trainee's mastery* of a body of information. Use a pretest before the program to check the trainee's initial knowledge of terms, concepts, and techniques in sales. Use the same test at program's end to determine improvement as a result of the program experience. Be sure the questions are exactly the same to have a valid comparison. Each question, by the way, should relate directly to a major learning objective, and the test as a whole should present all the major concepts in the program.

2. *Trainee's perception of value* from the training. Measure this factor by interview, questionnaire, or program critique which the trainee fills out. A positive attitude and willingness to apply the program techniques are both signs of perceived value. Proof of the pudding, however, lies in behavioral changes on the job.

3. *Manager's perception of value* from the training. Use a one-to-one interview or a questionnaire to determine the manager's perception, and compare it with that of the trainee. If there is a difference, it is probably attributable to the trainee's tendency to judge himself or herself based on *intentions,* vs. the manager's tendency to judge the trainee based on *actions.*

4. *Tangible changes and results* from the training. You can measure how well the trainee applies the new concepts and techniques by getting feedback from the field. Increased sales, greater number of new customers, higher closing rate, greater average sale amount—these are some of the quantifiable results of good sales training. *Performance ratings* are useful to track, if you first establish control groups of individuals who did and didn't go through the training, all other factors being equal. Then the increase in average performance rating for your trained group over the other can be a measurable, tangible indication of improved behavior and results on the job.

Again, the key to proving the value of your training programs—and enhancing your credibility with management—lies in setting up the criteria upon which your posttraining comparisons will be based. Specific, realistic, and measurable criteria (objectives and tasks) provide the foundation for provable return on the training investment.

When do you measure training results? Give a posttest at the end of the program. Then look down the road 2 or 3 months to get initial indications (through interviews or questionnaires) of changed behavior and preliminary results. Check again at 6 months and then 1 year from end of training program. Involve anyone who can give feedback on the value of the training: management, customers, peers, subordinates.

Measure knowledge immediately. Measure skills after a period of application on the job. Measure change in behavior after several months of proving that the change is permanent. Measure bottom-line results at the end of the sales accounting period during which the posttraining performance occurred.

Design your measurement program early and you'll have the tools for proving the value of your work.

Step 6: Select and Train Trainers

Once you've decided on the role of your program's trainer(s)—instructor or facilitator—you know the level of experience and preparation your trainer(s) will need.

Who does your training?

First consider whether you want (*a*) someone who has sales background but needs to be trained in instruction, or (*b*) an outside training professional who needs to learn your company's products, services, policies, and abiding principles. Look for these qualities in your potential trainers:

- Ability to sell themselves, their ideas, and their organization
- High level of energy and enthusiasm
- Upbeat, positive, can-do approach to work and life
- Insatiable appetite for learning and new experiences
- Vision of the job as stimulating and a source of personal growth
- Ability to deal with big egos
- Problem-solving focus, rather than tendency toward emotionalism

- Ability to facilitate group interaction
- Respect for the ideas and needs of others
- Platform skills, or the quick-study ability to learn them enough to seem natural

You want fast-track people who are going places and doing something constructive, who can add fresh ideas to the training experience. At the same time, by involving various personnel in training you're contributing to the enhancement of the overall performance across the board in your organization. Added benefit: You're filling the sales and marketing organization with people who appreciate sales training and the commitment it takes from everyone for the programs to have their maximum impact.

Here are some sources to draw from for trainers:

- *Training staff.* A good deal of regular training can be handled by your staff. But there are often other concerns besides simply conducting the program well.
- *Sales management.* You can get management involved in supporting the program, in its "ownership," by giving them the chance to interact and communicate with others in the organization.
- *Others in the organization.* Use as many people as possible to present sales training. Get many people involved and you have everyone talking about training.
- *Outside consultants.* Use outside expertise whenever you need fresh ideas, specific experience, and added training staff.

It is your responsibility as sales trainer to

- Train each of them in "train the trainer" workshops.
- Give each one clear learning objectives and guidelines for their roles.
- Provide assistance in structuring their presentations and refining them. When they look good, so do you and your training program.

The more you involve management (field sales, district, regional, etc.) in your program as coaches, cheerleaders, troubleshooters, experts, the more credibility your program will carry.

Step 7: Validate Program with Pilot Group

Your program can die with the test group if you don't choose one carefully. For your pilot program—the "litmus paper" test that management wants to see before committing major resources—you'll want to select participants who

- Have a high degree of motivation
- Feel positive about their jobs and the company
- Have pride in doing a good job
- Understand their role in helping refine and improve the program before it goes out to the rest of the field

You *don't* want troublemakers, skeptics, stubborn argumentative souls to destroy the credibility you've worked so hard to achieve. So pick a group that will help achieve your main goal of refining the program and getting it off the ground. You're not stacking the deck, because you want and will get honest feedback. What you're doing is making sure the participants will play the game and take this opportunity seriously.

The best system for a pilot program is to form groups or teams of five people, with a "one" (top performer) and a "two" (supportive performer) on each team. Use preliminary material (see step 4). Arrange the facility, equipment, etc., for maximum comfort.

Step 8: Collect Data, Analyze, Modify Program

Step 8 is your opportunity to get all the feedback you can and hone your program to its sharpest edge.

Collecting data is similar to *needs analysis.* Gather data on participant reactions through (1) questionnaires, (2) one-on-one interviews with participants immediately after the program, (3) one-on-one interviews with participants' managers, and (4) comparison of notes among facilitators.

One of the best ways to collect data is to observe the same participants in the field that you observed before the program. See whether they are better able to handle the challenges of sales situations.

Use *questionnaires* as a quick and inexpensive means of polling participants and their managers on the value of the training. Look through *company records* for signs of improvement after the trainees have been back at work in the field. Keep in mind that behavioral change is extremely slow and requires plenty of practice and positive feedback. One by-product of this communication process is letting the sales organization know that the training group cares about the impact of its efforts.

Once you've analyzed the data, put them into a formal report. Identify all recommendations for change. Then identify changes you've made as a result of this process. Make the alterations to audiovisual and printed material.

Next *present to management* the results of the validation and analysis. Find out what management expects the program to do at this point. *Sell* the benefits and results based on your collected data. Identify benefits to all managers present in the meeting. Close the sale! Your continued credibility depends on being able to say, "See, it's just as great as I said it would be!"

Step 9: Implement Training

Now you put the rest of your salespeople through the program. At this point you've done all the hard work and decision making. Now you simply

- Follow your proven plan exactly.
- Keep your program on schedule.
- Get a good mix of individuals in each group (identify potential problem participants and strategize on the best way to get them involved early in the program).
- Keep management posted of the program's progress.

You've tested the content, proven the process. Your trainers are trained. Management supports you. Terrific?

If you've opened the book to this page and want to learn how to implement your training programs, be assured that the proper way to do so lies in the preceding pages—not once the program is complete. We call this well-prepared approach being *proactive:* anticipating needs, planning, and organizing so you're always a step ahead of the game. As stated earlier, your success in training will parallel your ability to proactively manage two processes: (1) training development and (2) creation and maintenance of your credibility with management.

Step 10: Conduct Ongoing Monitor and Enhancement Process

Now that the program is over, it isn't over. The point is, you can't stand still. You must certainly work to keep your programs effective. Most trainers can start a program and run it well for awhile. How many are still perfecting and managing it a year later?

What makes this ongoing process vital is this one fact: *the world is constantly changing*. What worked last year may not be exactly the answer this year. Or maybe it is. Management commitment can gradually disappear.

Your sales force needs to stay up-to-date:

- There are new techniques sprouting constantly.

- They need follow-up reminders to good sales practices and techniques.

- You need to spot the return to bad habits and be ready with fresh solutions and support.

Your best ongoing tool is a good *calendar* for posting follow-up activity over time for each program. Your most productive follow-up work is communication with the field, including field trips with sales managers and salespeople. Consider sending out regular training bulletins, reminders via regular newsletter, audiocassettes on various subjects of sales training, and videocassettes for the same purpose. Have periodic meetings in the field with salespeople to discuss challenges and how to apply learned techniques more effectively.

See how other companies are handling sales training by being a part of organizations such as Sales and Marketing Executives (SME), Sales and Marketing Professional Practice Area of ASTD, and the National Society of Sales Training Executives (NSSTE). Encourage the sales force to participate in outside programs, to read books, to continually improve their personal skills.

Use *coaching* and *counseling* skills to help individuals continue their learning experience and hone their skills.

- *Coaching* is the process of encouraging the individual to improve both job skills and knowledge.

- *Counseling* centers on helping each salesperson handle attitude and motivation problems and maintain a winning attitude toward the job.

You can best help each individual by being a good listener, observing performance strengths and weaknesses, presenting ideas for improvement as positive alternatives rather than finger-point criticism, and then helping the individual develop an improved action plan that lists specific steps to take to improve personal skills and achieve greater goals.

After all, training is really self-development. Your counsel and encouragement after the fact can go a long way to ensure the most productive climate for individuals to feel confident and able to control their performance and contribute to long-term organizational goals.

Sales Training Checklist

How do you make sure you've followed the 10 steps to productive training programs?

Figure 37-2 is a suggested sales training checklist. Use it to check off each stage of a program as you complete it. Put the completion date so you can look back to analyze how well the development cycle went for each particular program. Such retrospection provides you with important feedback for improving your next

---

Course Title/Subject: ――――――――――――――――――――――
Intended Participants: ――――――――――――――――――――――
Department: ―――――――――――――――― Manager: ――――――――――――――
Training Deadline: ―――――――――――――― Budget: ――――――――――――

PREDEVELOPMENT QUESTIONS:
— Is this training necessary? Is a new program necessary? Would an existing program serve the same purpose?
— Bottom-line value to organization:

10 STEPS IN DEVELOPING PRODUCTIVE TRAINING: DATES
    1. Win Management Support of the project.
    2. Analyze Training Needs:
      — Design analysis instrument.
      — Conduct analysis, study, and observation.
    3. Sell Training Action Plan (TAP) to Management:
      — Summarize results of needs analysis.
      — Define program objectives.
      — Prepare detailed task analysis.
      — Identify available resources.
      — Present TAP to management.
    4. Develop Instructional Material:
      — Choose training media and methods.
      — Identify trainer's role.
      — Develop program material:
        ... Copy
        ... Graphics, printed material
        ... Audiovisual segments
      — Prepare trainer's guide.
    5. Design Measurement and Follow-Up Plan.
    6. Select and Train Trainers.
    7. Validate Program with Pilot Group.
    8. Collect Data, Analyze, Modify Program:
      — Send and gather questionnaires.
      — Study company records, etc.
      — Present results to management.
    9. Implement Training.
    10. Conduct Ongoing Monitor and Enhancement Process:
      — 3-month review
      — 6-month review
      — Ongoing long-term reviews
FINAL CHECKS:
Have I kept management informed at each step?
Has this program contributed to my group's credibility?
What would I do differently to improve performance next time?
What's my next step to monitor and improve this program?

Figure 37-2. Sales training checklist.

training program. The checklist also gives a ready visual confirmation of your progress in response to management requests for an update.

Sources and Resources for Sales Training

Here's a recap of important concepts in the chapter regarding support for your training objectives.

Training the Sales Manager.   Companies are usually quite willing to spend money to train salespeople, but not so eager to spend it for training sales managers. Research has proven that a good salesperson does not always make a good sales manager; a different set of skills is involved in the two positions. The promoted salesperson must learn how to

- Be more of a coach than a cheerleader or super salesperson
- Develop management skills of planning, organizing, leading, delegating, and controlling
- Create and maintain the proper climate for motivation
- Reinforce sales skills
- Manage the achievement of key business goals through the efforts of others in the sales force

Networking and Professional Development.   Sales trainers have someone else to develop: themselves. One powerful means of enhancing personal skills and potential is called *networking*. It's the process of interacting with other trainers and other organizations, such as

- Sales and Marketing Executives International
- National Society of Sales Training Executives
- ASTD Sales and Marketing Professional Practice Area

By interacting you learn what other companies are doing, how they do it, and what the results are. You learn what works and what doesn't, without having to experiment with your own sales force. So to further develop yourself,

- Constantly read and look at new programs.
- Participate in training programs yourself.
- Share ideas with other trainers.
- Participate in your local chapter of ASTD.
- Put together a network of trainers in your own city, people with common goals and objectives in your industry.

In short, do as good a job of managing your own behavioral growth and personal development as you do for your sales force. The more you enhance your skills, the more you become indispensable to your organization.

Understand your organization's needs. Develop specific training and business objectives. Make professional presentations to management. Monitor and evaluate the results of your programs. Keep them up-to-date and productive. Be in touch with professionals in your industry, and with management at all levels of your organization. Constantly communicate to let people know what you're doing and the impact of training on their objectives.

Be a risk taker. Be proactive. Make your job the most exciting way to work and grow. Use this handbook as a regular reference and apply the sales training checklist to every program. By doing so you'll build a broad base of support for training in your organization and for achieving your own long-term goals.

Bibliography

Harrison, Jared F., *The Management of Sales Training*, Addison-Wesley, Reading, MA, 1977.
Harrison, Jared F., *The Sales Manager as a Trainer*, Addison-Wesley, Reading, MA, 1977.
McLaughlin, Ian E., *Successful Sales Training: How to Build a Program That Works*, CBI Publishing, Boston, 1981.

38

Office and Clerical Skills

Robert S. Fenn

Ruthie Bush Mathews

Robert S. Fenn is National Director of Training for The Travelers, where he is responsible for both management and office automation training. He has recently completed overseeing the design and construction of a new state-of-the-art $20 million plus training center in Hartford, Connecticut, that will allow The Travelers to more effectively capitalize on various forms of automated training. Prior to joining The Travelers in 1982, he held positions as Consultant; Vice President, Citicorp; Vice President, NYC Off Track Betting; and International Personnel Director, Celanese Corp. He has an M.A. from Columbia University and a B.A. from the University of California. He also studied in Peking, China, and at Yale Graduate School.

Ruthie Bush Mathews is Assistant Director, Program Administration with Corporate Training and Development Division, The Travelers in Hartford, Connecticut. She is responsible for the administration and implementation of automated skills, supervisor and management training in the home office and field office locations. From 1980 to 1983 she directed The Travelers clerical skills training program—MOST/BEST. Prior to joining The Travelers in 1980, she directed both federal and state funded programs for the Urban League of Greater Hartford and the Greater Hartford YWCA. She is a member of ASTD and the Administrative Management Society, and a board member of Connecticut Literacy Volunteers.

Historically, people in the clerical support function have been women; and today, they make up 99 percent of the secretarial-clerical support work force.[1]

The position of secretarial-clerical support person was viewed by management, and even the incumbent, as having limited functions. This image, and the attitude that the support person is *capable* of handling only the traditional functions has caused problems for educational institutions as well as businesses. The primary problem stems from the fact that technology has changed not only the equipment used but the way in which the secretarial-clerical support position functions. Further, the institutions that educate secretarial-clerical personnel have failed to keep pace with the changes.

Office and Clerical Functions

The traditional task of a secretarial-clerical support position included:

- Typing
- Filing
- Mail processing
- Shorthand
- Microfilming
- Greeting and directing visitors
- Answering telephones
- Making travel arrangements
- Arranging meetings
- Ordering supplies

With the changes in technology these have expanded to include such tasks as:

- Maintaining budgets
- Designing and producing graphs
- Automated record keeping and retrieval
- Electronic mail
- Voice mail

Technology and its effect on office automation are major problems in both educational institutions and business today. Neither seems able to keep up with the developments. This results in educational institutions improperly equipped to train the secretarial and clerical support person needed by business, and business constantly changing their requirements for "qualified" personnel.

Issues of Training

Educational institutions have come to realize that the traditional secretarial training curriculum is obsolete. The fact that an estimated 80,000 secretarial and clerical positions go unfilled by business each year clearly emphasized that educational institutions lag behind in training for the skills that businesses need. This realization has even reached the high school level and they, too, are soliciting advice from the business community. There is continual communication between educational institutions and businesses to try to provide students with the skills needed to fill the automated secretarial positions in the future.

However, schools find that it is almost financially impossible to keep pace with the changing technology. To equip schools with state-of-the-art technology needed to train for automated job functions requires capital investments that many schools do not have. Complicating the situation is that businesses are not looking just for individuals who have had generic word processing training but for individuals who can function effectively on specific equipment.

Many schools also have a second concern. They have difficulty finding and keeping qualified staff who are willing to adapt to constantly changing technology and office automation.

A third concern is that staff in educational institutions are finding it difficult to determine what the secretarial-clerical curriculum should be. They are aware that training should include the more automated training course, i.e., word processing, spread sheet applications, and database management. But the question still remains, "Can the schools provide the job specific training required by businesses today?" Figure 38-1 provides a look at the kinds of job-specific training required by businesses.

Accountability

Webster's Encyclopedia Dictionary defines accountability as "the state of being accountable, answerable, liable or responsible." This definition does not give a clear understanding of instructor accountability in a business training situation. Perhaps a more appropriate definition of accountability for instructors of secretarial and clerical skills training might be:

the guarantee that the training provided will achieve the predetermined levels of learning and/or skills necessary for their present or future positions.

Instructor Accountability

As schools and businesses struggle to provide cost-effective secretarial and skills training, greater responsibility for the outcome of the training is being placed with the instructor.

In the past, the learner was viewed as the individual solely responsible for learning taking place. The idea was that it was the responsibility of the teacher to teach and the learner to learn. If the learning did not take place, it was assumed that the learner was responsible and not the teacher. Schools and businesses now realize that both the instructor and the learner must be held accountable for the communication of information and the acquisition of learning. Neither can be held totally accountable for an effective learning process.

Instructors are being preassessed for subject matter knowledge, instructional behaviors, and personal characteristics that are considered prerequisites. The preassessment may be accomplished in a number of ways; however, a mock training situation provides an excellent opportunity to assess instructors' "intrinsic behaviors." These behaviors can influence and motivate students and affect the way students react to information being presented. The instructor assessment form in Figure 38-2 provides a checklist of those behaviors or characteristics considered prerequisite behaviors. The form may be modified to fit particular needs.

In all fairness to the instructor, the students should also be preassessed. What are their skill levels? What are their objectives? What are their abilities? Will they have an opportunity to use the new skills? These are just a few of the questions that should be answered prior to training. It is extremely difficult to hold an instructor

PERSONNEL REQUISITION TheTravelers	POSITION TITLE Secretary			JOB POSTING NUMBER	
DEPARTMENT/DIVISION	EMPLOYMENT COUNSELOR'S NAME			EMPLOYMENT COUNSELOR'S TEL. EXT.	

POSITION CODE	JOB GROUP CODE	PAYROLL CODE	SALARY GRADE	SALARY RANGE MINIMUM MAXIMUM	SHIFT/HOURS	BUILDING LOCATION

Duties and Responsibilities:

1. Types letters, forms, memos, reports, statistical tables, etc., from handwritten drafted material, shorthand notes, or dictaphone.
2. Take and transcribe dictation, often confidential, through the use of shorthand skills or cassettes.
3. Perform calculations and keep records to prepare unit reports, for example, statistical, productivity, cost allocations, etc.
4. Sort and organize incoming mail. May route to others for answering. May date stamp or log in mail and prepare outgoing mail.
5. Organize appointment calendar, arrange meetings and make travel arrangements.
6. Greet callers, answer and route telephone calls, furnish information, record messages.
7. Maintain filing system, including correspondence files, personnel files, general files and pending files.
8. May assist in processing confidential or Personnel related work for the unit, i.e., absence reports, vacation schedules, paycheck, overtime, salary increases, etc.
9. May prepare miscellaneous forms, such as purchase orders, furniture and equipment requisitions, expense accounts, etc.
10. May assist secretaries of Department Management with telephone, mail, etc.; may substitute for them during absences.

Knowledge and Skills Requirements:

1. Must be an expert in secretarial skills, including typing, filing systems, grammar, spelling, telephone and interpersonal skills, and organization.
2. May be required to compose letters and must have basic knowledge of the line of business in which he/she works.
3. Reading skills to read correspondence and material for filing. Often this material includes contracts, technical field specific material, memos, manuals and other documents.
4. Writing skills to write simple correspondence or reports with little direction provided. Interpersonal skill to give and receive information tactfully. Often handles confidential material requiring significant discretion.
5. Basic number skills required.
6. Knowledge of Displaywriter, IBM-PC-Displaywriter III is required.

Physical Effort Demands and/or Working Conditions:

RESPONSIBILITY CODE	DATE OF REQUISITION	HAVE PRESENT EMPLOYEES BEEN CONSIDERED FOR THIS POSITION	YES ☐ NO ☐	REASON FOR REQUISITION ☐ ADVANCE REPLACEMENT
SIGNATURE (SUPERVISOR)	TEL. EXT.	SIGNATURE (DEPT. PERSONNEL REPRESENTATIVE) TEL. EXT.		☐ INCREASE IN STAFF ☐ REPLACEMENT

Figure 38-1. Secretarial job description.

accountable for learning if the student does not bring the need and capacity for learning to the training, and particularly so if the instructor is not aware of the student's abilities, knowledge, and job requirements.

The instructor is more likely to meet the standards set for training as well as feel more comfortable with the concept of accountability if the training has been developed to meet certain guidelines.

Developing Training

There is nothing magic about developing training for clerical skills. The same process and principles apply to developing training for a secretary that would apply

CORPORATE TRAINING AND DEVELOPMENT INSTRUCTOR SKILL ASSESSMENT

Instructor Name:_____Observer:_____

Module Presented:_____Date:_____

SUMMARY RATING

____1_____2_____3_____4_____5_____6_____7_____8_____

| little skill—
needs much
work | some skill—
needs
attention | skills are
good | very
professional |

BEHAVIORS/CHARACTERISTICS ASSESSED:

PRESENCE—(relaxed; confident; knowledge of subject matter; effective body positioning; good class management)

PRESENTATION—(clear, understandable, appropriate language, appropriate visual aids)
ORGANIZATION—(comfortable, natural flow of information; appropriate learning materials; good transitions)

FACILITATION—(promotes group interaction; good listening; lively discussion; enthusiasm; good eye contact; supportive)

HANDLING DIFFICULT SITUATIONS—(dealing with dissension, respecting participants' perceptions)

CREATIVITY—(innovation to promote learning)

Figure 38-2. Behavior, skills, and characteristics of an effective instructor.

to developing training for engineers. Other chapters in this book, *Training and Development Journal, Training* Magazine, or a good library can provide well-researched step-by-step processes for a training professional to follow when developing clerical training.

Because of this ready availability of process models, the focus here is on selected conditions or guidelines that, too often, are ignored in the development of training in general and particularly in developing clerical training.

Critical Guidelines

The responsibility of the developer of training is to create an optimal learning situation in which the learner can obtain the particular skills and knowledge identified as necessary for accomplishing the learner's present or future job. To create that optimal learning situation, the developer must be sure that the design included the following:

- Trainee awareness of the purpose of the training, its intended results, and their significance
- Recognition of the learners' current skills and attitudes that may assist or hinder achievement
- The time to learn at one's own pace
- Relevancy and reality of the task or knowledge to be learned

- Review and repetition
- Feedback, appraising

Each of these conditions is critical to effective learning, and an absence of any of them will tend to inhibit learning. The more complex or difficult the skill or knowledge to be learned, the more inhibiting the absence becomes.

Awareness of Purpose

Have you ever been asked to attend a class without being told why? Perhaps you thought it was a reward. Perhaps a punishment? Perhaps you wondered if you were about to be given a new job. Whatever your guesses, if you didn't *know why*, you could only speculate about what you were supposed to achieve in the class.

We are not creatures who respond to every stimulus or situation equally. We want to know where we are going and how we are going to get there before we can accept that the journey is worthwhile. The unknown raises fears and questions which, unanswered, can cause misdirected energy and attention.

The learner should be given, at the beginning of the program, the overall goals. As each module is started, its goals must also be stated. They should be stated carefully for an awareness of both what is to be learned and its significance to the learner. The learners must also be told how they will know they have mastered the knowledge or skills. Only in this context can they effectively focus their attention.

However, being aware of the desired direction does not always create a need to go that way. Learners will relate the goals of the program to their particular situations and decide whether they have a need to achieve the goals. For this reason, the significance of the goals to the individual learners is of utmost importance. Let's look at an example.

A new word processing system is about to be introduced in a unit. It will improve the efficiency of the unit, make corrections easier, reduce spelling errors, allow fast retrieval of data, simplify layout, and generally make work easier. The old system will be removed in 3 weeks.

The members of the unit must be taught the new word processing system through a learning program. The goals of that learning program will have different significance to each of the members of the unit depending upon their concerns. To some, the significance may be that work will be easier; to others, it may be that they will be able to spell correctly. To still others, it may be that the old system is being removed in 3 weeks and they must learn the new one whether they like it or not.

If no announcement of the introduction of the new system has been made before the start of the training, significance would be sharply changed—particularly for those who might be motivated by the removal of the old system in 3 weeks. They would not understand why it would be imperative they learn a new system. Awareness of the purpose of training and relating that purpose to the learners sets the stage for achievement. If not done effectively, it can sharply reduce learning.

Recognition of Current Skills and Attitudes

One of the breakthroughs in recent training design has been the creation of programs, particularly computer-based or interactive video, that have the capability of assessing a participant's knowledge, job skills, and attitudes and providing a path through the training that takes these into consideration. Though presenting interesting design and development challenges, such a process is a major step forward as it potentially provides a series of benefits:

- Avoids learners studying materials or skills in which they are already competent
- Allows programs to address individual attitudes or concerns person by person
- Provides job-related examples and practice that can vary by individual
- Increases creative options for the developers of the training

Such programs become almost custom-designed to the individual learner. Since most are learner-controlled, they also have the advantage of allowing learners to move at their own pace.

Historically, lack of recognition of current skills and attitudes of learners has been a common failing of both training and education programs. School systems and businesses have identified what was required to be known by the end of the program and then presented that to the learners. They have ignored the fact that learners bring to a program differing knowledge, skill levels, interests, learning aptitudes, experiences, and attitudes. It has been up to the learner to adapt to whatever methodology the program developer and instructor utilize. The result has been that individuals vary widely in what they learn from a common program. The bell-shaped grade curve is an interesting example of this.

Recognition of learners' current skills and attitudes is important to both the training developer and the learner. The developer must be aware of these so that the learning situation can be designed to either rapidly develop a common level of skills and attitudes among the learners or be prepared to deal with each individual at varying levels of entry skills and attitudes that exist upon entry. Obviously, this may differ sharply from one learner to another.

Three methods are commonly used to determine current skills and attitudes. First, as a part of the process for designing and developing a program, entry skills and attitudes can be determined through focus groups, interviews, or paper-and-pencil survey instruments. Second, diagnostic testing can be used either just prior to entry into a program or upon entry. Third, in group programs, a process can be built into the program by which the group identifies its own range of skills and attitudes at the beginning of the course or program. The method used may vary from program to program depending upon what is appropriate for the particular circumstances.

Time to Learn at One's Own Pace

Since no two learners bring to any program identical skills, attitudes, abilities, or learning aptitudes, it stands to reason that no two learners will progress at the same pace. Despite this, most training is developed around the idea that learners should be able to achieve a predetermined level in a specific number of hours or days. This seems to be primarily for the convenience of the developer and instructor. "Fast" learners (those who because of their entry skills, attitudes, or learning aptitudes respond well) may be somewhat frustrated at the lack of pace. "Slow" learners (those who don't respond as well) may never achieve mastery. And those in the middle, hopefully, achieve mastery. This means that the time of the "fast" learners has been wasted, the "slow" learners haven't met the program objectives, and those in the middle may have efficiently achieved what the developer and instructor intended.

We have discovered that almost every learner can master the given tasks or information if provided with the necessary tools and time. In truly efficient learning situations, mastery is defined and each learner takes the time that she or he needs to achieve it. The focus in such learning is upon individual mastery, not just presenting a certain amount of information or doing a specific set of exercises in a certain time. Clerical training is particularly adaptable to this approach since it tends to have easily definable levels of mastery that are, in most cases, readily measured. Such skills as word processing, filing, and telephone responsiveness are examples.

Designing training so that it addresses the needs of each individual rather than the overall needs of a group normally requires greater development efforts and costs. However, if the audience is large enough, overall costs will be reduced because of the efficiency of learning; and in many cases, delivery of self-developed computer-based instruction may cost only a fraction of the cost of conducting classroom courses where travel is involved.

Relevancy, Reality

Have you ever attended a course where it was obvious that the instructor or course developer was going to be sure that you were told everything there was to know about a subject whether or not you needed to know it? You probably soon became so frustrated that the relevant parts of what was being presented were lost to you.

Too often, particularly with teaching how to use a piece of equipment such as a typewriter or word processor, the course developer focuses on the capabilities of the equipment rather than on the needs of the learner. The result is a course that covers everything the equipment is capable of doing, a high percentage of which the learner may never use. This is typical of courses designed by equipment vendors who want to demonstrate the power of their products.

The alternative to looking at the capabilities of the equipment is to examine the learner's job and determine the extent or frequency of use of the various equipment capabilities. Training can then be focused on what is relevant for a particular job. For instance, if the only use a learner has for a word processor is the typing and issuance of letters, there is little purpose in teaching how to develop graphs. Not only will training time that could be spent on practicing producing letters be lost, but the graph development skills will soon be forgotten because of lack of usage and reinforcement on the job.

If it is not possible to examine the jobs of the learners closely before designing training, it is acceptable to design the training around the capabilities of the equipment or a wide variety of possible tasks that might be related to the job. If this is done, a method must be built into the training whereby the learners' needs are diagnosed and only those portions of the training directly related to the individual's job are taught. In this manner, a comprehensive, widely applicable course may be developed out of which learners will take what they need for their particular job.

Relevance is one key to efficient training. Reality is another. What is taught may be recognized as relevant, but if it represents reality to the learner, its relevance increases. As learners are successful in tasks that are identical, or at least very similar to those that are done on the job, they tend to become increasingly motivated to learn because they feel that learning is consequential to them. In other words, they see a payoff for themselves.

If the course developer analyzes clerical tasks from job to job, it becomes clear that training that is close to reality is not terribly difficult to create. For instance, by developing memos on several carefully selected topics for learners to practice typing, most of the learners in a class can select a memo that will be fairly typical of their job. In most businesses, a list of memos on such topics as personnel-related matters, customer services, sales, and a budget overrun will provide the majority of learners with a choice of memos that are real for their jobs.

As a general rule, the more relevant and real training is, the more meaningful it will be to the learner. The more meaningful it is, the more that motivation to learn is likely to increase.

Learning by Doing

There is no way of assuring mastery of a skill or body of knowledge other than having the learner demonstrate it. Similarly, the most effective way to prove to learners that they are capable of learning is to have them prove it to themselves by performing the skill or using the information being taught. If learners actually learn by doing, they tend to gain greater confidence in their own abilities and retain the learning longer.

Where tasks are complex or difficult, learning can be developed by steps, keeping the learning process simple and logical. Each step should be addressed separately and then related to and practiced with previous steps.

It is not difficult to build learning exercises into a program and make learning more interesting. However, such exercises should be designed to repeat and review critical knowledge or skills.

Review and Repetition

Learning is a building process. As learners progress, they keep adding to their ability or knowledge. Unless review and repetition are built into learning, what has been taught early can easily be forgotten. It is therefore critical that the process of learning be one of constant review of prior teachings and repetition of constantly expanding exercises.

A goal of most learning programs is to achieve fluency. This can be defined as the ability to utilize what has been learned automatically and accurately. Fluency is best obtained by repetition under varying conditions until responses require little thought. An example of the difference between someone who is fluent and someone who is not can easily be seen in the ability to use a keyboard. Familiar to most of us is the person who hunts and pecks—painfully spelling out words. The lack of fluency is obvious. In contrast is the individual who types 70 or more words per minute, never stopping to check the work or think about it. He or she is not only faster but more likely to be accurate.

Initially, review is also required. Once the basics are known, the review process becomes less frequent and the repetitions more frequent until fluency reaches the predetermined mastery level.

If learning is to remain with the learners, the principles of review and repetition are a basic requirement of effective program design.

Feedback, Appraising

Closely related to review and repetition are feedback and appraising. Although both terms mean providing information to the learner, there is a subtle difference between them. Feedback is the process of providing learners with the results of their efforts. Appraising carries with it the connotation of causing the learners to know and understand how and why their performance brought about the results it did. For our purposes, we will use the terms interchangeably, assuming that they mean providing learners with the necessary information about their performance for them to either correct it or realize that they are performing according to expectations.

Feedback is a key to successful learning. It should provide both reinforcement and correction. Properly designed, it will enlighten and motivate. Without feedback, learners may not be sure whether their interim or final objectives have been achieved. Like annual performance appraisals, they don't know until it is too late how they are doing or what they can do to improve.

Effective feedback has several characteristics. It must be timely, diagnostic, and prescriptive. Timely feedback occurs immediately after the learner has attempted to demonstrate or practice a skill or use specific knowledge. As such, feedback during learning should be frequent, occurring at planned checkpoints interspersed so that the learner can never fall so far behind that it becomes difficult to correct a learning problem.

Diagnostic feedback focuses on the individual and provides the answer to the questions "What did I do right?" and "What did I do wrong?" It provides correctional steps.

Prescriptive feedback tells the individual how to correct behavior or failure to learn. It prescribes additional review, practice exercises, or sources of information that will bring the learner back on course.

Feedback is one of the most crucial elements of good training and one of the most ignored. Mastery of a skill or body of knowledge occurs at different rates of speed and in different ways in a group of learners. Without feedback, neither the learner nor the instructor knows whether the individuals in the group are ready to proceed. Feedback can be designed in many ways including skill tests, games, group exercises, self-diagnostic devices, case problems, etc. It is a must for effective training design and should be timely, diagnostic, and prescriptive.

The purpose of most clerical training is to achieve mastery over a set of skills or a body of knowledge. Mastery will be consistently achieved by the learners only through effective design of the learning process. Such design is achieved through following a proven process and applying the logical guidelines just presented. The focus of the training must be the individual, not the group. The challenge is for each learner to achieve mastery. It is a reasonable and reachable goal.

Unique Aspects of Clerical Training

Much of what has been presented here is applicable to most kinds of training, clerical or otherwise. However, there are important aspects of today's clerical positions that call for somewhat unique training responses.

One of these is that despite the rapid automation of clerical functions, certain basic skills and knowledge seem to continue to be important. They are the basis for accomplishing common clerical functions whether done manually or electronically. In particular, keyboarding skills and filing theory seem to be important in many clerical positions. Too often trainees are taught these skills as a part of learning a specific software program. When this occurs they tend to associate the skills with the program and not see them as transferable. If they are addressed separately, they are instilled as basic skills which then facilitate the learning of any software program. In such a situation, they are likely to be better understood and learned more thoroughly since the skills are the primary focus.

A second somewhat unique aspect of today's clerical positions is that not only are the functions changing but the automated systems that cause changes are themselves constantly changing. An example of this is the software word processing package call "Displaywrite." It now has three versions, each issued at a different time. Software packages often are replaced or modified with a year or two of their issuance. This, of course, can help keep the training professional in business since it assures a constant need for training. However, it also presents the trainer with the potential nightmare of not having any ideas of what the shelf life of a training program will be and of being faced with the constant need to revise programs recently put in place. To respond to the situation, the trainer should be extremely careful when committing program funds to be sure that:

- The shelf life of the program and size of the audience will warrant the expenditures

- Programs that are likely to be revised have "windows" built into them at likely modification points that will allow for easy revision

With care and creative planning the potential nightmare can often be reduced to a bad dream.

A third aspect of today's clerical functions that bears attention by trainers is the rapid growth in decision-making responsibility. As more and more information becomes available at the clerical person's fingertips, increasingly their level and volume of decision making rises. Perhaps the best example of this is the field of medical claims processing. In the past the claim processor (a clerical person) was primarily responsible for recording claims, making a decision based on guidelines as to what or whether to pay, and issuing checks. Anything complex or over a specified dollar amount was referred to a supervisor. Today, in a fully automated claims department a claim can arrive by electronic transmission from a claims clearinghouse, be entered from a tape into the insurance company's claim system, and result in a check being issued for transmission to the hospital. The claims processor oversees the process and makes decisions only on the claims that are very complex present problems to the automated system or are so large that a human approval is required. In other words, the clerical person is now making the decisions that the supervisor used to make. This raises the value of the job but also raised the risk of error. It is up to trainers to recognize such changes and be sure that clerical personnel have the knowledge and skills needed to analyze problems and make effective decisions. Depending upon the nature of the decision making, the trainer can provide such training either in conjunction with teaching specific processes (such as claim processing) or as a separate skill to be applied to a variety of situations or processes. The need for decision-making skills is likely to increase rapidly in the foreseeable future. It should be anticipated and responded to as it occurs.

Clerical training will be one of the continuing challenges to the trainer because of both its importance and the problems it faces. Proper planning and creativity will be crucial elements in meeting demands. Another crucial element will be the ability to recognize and control training costs.

Costs and Benefits of Training

What are the costs and benefits of training? This question has caused debate for many years. It has seldom been satisfactorily answered.

Many trainers and managers believe that the training they do has a positive impact on morale, enhanced skills, and/or increased productivity. But a feeling or belief is no longer enough in today's competitive world. The demand today is proof.

Calculating Costs

An article written by Lyle M. Spencer, Jr., for *Training* Magazine in July 1984 addresses the costs and benefits of training. The article, "How to Calculate the Costs

CALCULATING THE FULL COST OF A TRAINER'S TIME

The full cost of a person making the current HRD specialist's average salary of $25,000 and paid on the basis of a 260-day (2080-hour) year is calculated as follows:

EXPENSE	CALCULATION FORMULA	AMOUNT
1. Salary	S	$25,000
2. Plus: fringe benefits @ 35% salary	.35 × S = .35S	8,750
3. Subtotal	1.35S	$33,750
4. Plus: overhead @ 125% of salary and fringe	1.25 × 1.35S = 1.69S	42,188
5. Total full cost/year	3.04S	$75,938
6. Total full cost/day	$75,938 (direct cost/ year) ÷ 260 (days worked/year)	$292.07
7. Total full cost/hour	(direct cost/day) ÷ 8 (hours worked/day)	$ 36.51

Figure 38-3. The cost of a human resource development person. S = salary.

and Benefits of an HRD Program" is concise and provides easy to follow examples on calculating the two major expenses:[2]

- Labor costs
- Direct costs

Labor costs are calculated by determining the personnel/trainer salaries, all overhead costs, and fringe benefits to produce a per-day or per-year labor cost. Figure 38-3 shows the worksheet for calculating the labor cost, that is, the complete cost of the human resource development person.

Calculating direct costs (Fig. 38-4) for training involves adding the nonlabor expenses of a specific project. These expenses include per diem expenses, material costs, computer time, etc.

Trainers have used a number of methods to demonstrate the benefits of training. However, for too many years, the most popular method has been program evaluation forms or "smile sheets" for gathering participant feedback. Such a system provides data that are of highly questionable validity. Telephone surveys have also been popular. Pretest and posttest are probably the most reliable in measuring gains made by students taking secretarial and clerical skills training. But how can you measure these gains in terms of increases or decreases in expenses or the dollar benefit to the company?

Measuring Benefits

Measuring benefits is more difficult than measuring costs. One school of thought on measuring benefits is that training should result in measurable on-the-job increase in productivity. This can be done in many production-related jobs (including a number of clerical positions) by determining pretest and posttraining production and quality rates and putting a dollar value on the difference.

If this method is used, the posttraining studies should be made several months after the trainee returns to the job. Waiting several months will minimize the so-called Hawthorne effect (increase in productivity due to the attention paid to the learner).

However, after several months, other job-related factors such as poor working conditions or oppressive supervision may have caused the trainee's productivity to drop to or below the pretraining level, negating the positive effects of training. This may then raise questions about the validity of the training because the cause of the poor performance may not be recognized and the effects of the training are really still unknown.

A second school of thought believes that the skills and knowledge that will result in improved productivity and quality should be studied and identified prior to the development of training. From such a study, mastery levels of skill or knowledge can be set as objectives.

Testing the trainee upon entering a training program can then determine the level of skill or knowledge brought to training, and testing at the end of training can determine exit skill levels and whether mastery has been achieved. The problem with this is that those exit skill levels and knowledge may never be transferred to the job because of the same kind of job-related factors that destroyed the validity of testing in the first school of thought.

The advantage of the second school of thought, however, is that there is assurance that the trainee has achieved "mastery" of the skills. Though it may not be possible to prove that this caused increases in productivity, it can at least be stated that the skills were higher than upon entry and that the skills taught were those identified as related to productivity.

We believe that the latter approach is applicable in almost any training situation. It makes the training function accountable for proper task analysis, course objectives, program design, selection of delivery media, and achievement of agreed-upon mastery levels.

A third method of determining benefits should be mentioned. This is to determine average cost for training new people *on the job* until they have achieved mastery level and then comparing that with the cost of reaching mastery through *formal training*. While applicable in some situations, the same job factors that interfere with measurement in the other methods cause the same kinds of problems with this approach.

If a cost-benefit analysis is made it should not be assumed that the analysis is an everlasting justification for a training program. Job functions and factors change. Training approaches change. Costs change. This means that training programs must constantly be audited to assure that they remain cost justified. Trainers and developers, as well as managers and supervisors, must be alert to such changes or the cost-effectiveness of a program can be destroyed and hours of training wasted.

Summary

Secretarial and clerical training is an exciting field today because it is in constant transition. As the challenges faced by trainers are solved, new ones appear. Obviously, automation is one of the major causes of the problems, but it is also one of the solutions, one with tremendous potential.

However, the key to the future does not lie in one or another method of delivering training. It is in our ability to focus on the individual. We must develop methods of assuring that the training each individual receives is appropriate for him or her. We must make sure that it helps the individual to achieve mastery of the needed skills and knowledge within a reasonable amount of time while being

Figure 38-4. Step-by-step worksheet to calculate full cost of human resource development. K = thousand; S = salary; T = time; M = full-cost multiplier. "A good estimate of the full cost of an instructor . . . is roughly three times his/her direct salary cost."

COSTING WORKSHEET

Analysis Step*	Labor Costs						Direct Costs or Step/Unit Totals				Totals
	Labor ("Who?")	(1) #	Full Cost/ Time	(2)	(3) Time	(4) Cost (1)×(2)×(3)	Expenses	(5) Cost/Unit	(6) × #Units	(7) Cost = (5)×(6)	(8) = (4)×(7)
1. Development of course	Smith (HRD Person)	1	S $\frac{\$30k \times M3}{T\,260}$ = $346/day		× 10 days =	$ 3,460	Materials	$260	× 1 =	$260	$ 3,720
Step 1 Total						$ 3,460				$260	$ 3,720
2. Trainer training	Smith (Trainer)	1	S $\frac{\$30k \times M3}{T\,260}$ = $346/day		× 5 days =	$ 1,730	Per diem	$ 20	× 5 days =	$100	$ 1,830
	Plant Supv.	8	S $\frac{\$25K \times M3}{T\,260}$ = $288/day		× 5 days =	$11,520	Materials	$50 Person	8 × people =	$400	$11,920
			S $\frac{\times M}{T}$ =	×	=		Travel to training site	$350 person	8 × people =	$2,800	$ 2,800
			S $\frac{\times M}{T}$ =	×	=		Per diem	$75/ person/ day	4 days × 8 people × = 40	$3,000	$ 3,000
			S $\frac{\times M}{T}$ =	×	=		Training room	$150/day	× 5 =	$ 750	$ 750
						$13,250				$7,050	$20,300

3. Delivery of training	Plant Supv. (Trainers)	8	$\dfrac{S\ \$25K\times M3}{T\ 260}$ = **\$288/day** × 3 days (16 hrs delivery, 8 hrs prep) = \$ 6,912			=	\$ 6,912
	Head Foreman	80	$\dfrac{S\ \$20K\times M3}{T\ 260}$ = **\$231/day** × 2 day = \$36,960	Materials	$\dfrac{\$50}{\text{person}}$ × $\dfrac{80}{\text{people}}$ = \$4,000		\$40,960
Step 3 Total			\$43,872		\$4,000		\$47,872
4. Evaluation	Smith (HR Person)	1	$\dfrac{S\ \$30K\times M3}{T\ 260}$ = **\$346/day** × 3 day = \$ 1,038	$\dfrac{100}{\text{time}}$ × 1	= \$ 100		\$ 1,138
Step 4 Total			\$ 1,038		\$ 100		\$ 1,138
			Total Labor Cost \$61,620	Total Direct Costs \$11,410			\$73,030 TOTAL

* Fill in number and name of step; draw heavy horizontal line to show where one step ends and next begins; put step, labor, and direct cost subtotals on this line. Continue this procedure, and use as many costing worksheets as you need.

cost-effective. If we do this, we will have proven our worth as trainers as well as having made a major contribution to our organizations, whether business or educational.

References

1. Kolbert, Elizabeth, "What's New in the Secretarial World," *The New York Times,* August 4, 1985.
2. Spencer, Lyle M., Jr., "How to Calculate the Cost and Benefits of Training," *Training,* July 1984, pp. 40–44, 48–51.

Bibliography

Alternative Learning Styles in Business Education, National Business Education Association, Reston, VA, 1979.

Erdle, Steven, "Personality, Classroom Behavior, and Student Ratings of College Teaching Effectiveness: A Path Analysis, *Journal of Educational Psychology,* vol. 77, No. 4, August 1985.

Spencer, Lyle M., Jr., "Calculating Costs and Benefits," *Human Resource Management and Development Handbook,* American Management Association, New York, 1985.

39

Computer Skills

Ann W. Armstrong

Alice McElhone

Ann W. Armstrong is cofounder of The Forhan & Wakefield Group, Inc., a Westport, Connecticut, computer education company specializing in high-technology software documentation, training, and product support. Armstrong is directly responsible for curriculum design and development and implementation of programs for the Computer Education Group, managing more than twenty-five professional trainers in the field. In this capacity, she is responsible for managing the firm's contract with IBM Corporation to provide customer education in IBM product centers on the east coast. Armstrong is author of two books: Using Lotus 1-2-3 for Electronic Spreadsheet Models and Using Lotus 1-2-3 for Database, Graphics and Macros. She has written software documentation for such clients as Western Union, Merrill Lynch, Kensington Microware, Manufacturers Hanover Trust, and IBM. She has served as seminar leader for the Computer Literacy Week sponsored by Training magazine and other professional organizations. Armstrong graduated from Randolph-Macon Women's College in 1970 with a Bachelor of Arts degree in Economics. She received her Master of Arts degree in Economics, specializing in Monetary Theory and Policy, from the University of Cincinnati in 1973. She attended the New York University Graduate School of Business Administration Advanced Professional Program in Computer Sciences and Information Systems in 1982. Armstrong is a member of ASTD, the Advanced Computer Machinery Society, Women in Management, and Omicron Delta Epsilon, the national honor society in Economics.

Alice McElhone is Vice President of Marketing Communications for The Forhan & Wakefield Group, Inc. She is responsible for managing the firm's marketing communications projects for major vendors and corporations including software documentation, market testing and

*evaluation, interface design, sales support materials, sales training
curricula, promotion, and advertising. Her group's clients include such
corporations as General Electric, Manufacturers Hanover Trust, Merrill
Lynch, Pitney Bowes; and vendors including IBM, Dun & Bradstreet,
Western Union, Kensington Microware, and Monroe Systems for
Business. McElhone came to Forhan & Wakefield from Exxon Office
Systems Corporation, where she was manager of Curriculum Design
and Publications, responsible for software and hardware documentation, training curriculum, and sales support materials for five extensive
product lines. McElhone has been a contributor to business publica-
tions, such as MIS Week, and is a member of the Society for Technical
Communication, Women in Communications International, and
Women in Management.*

Computers are no longer a fad. They have moved from the domain of the hackers
and data processing professionals into the offices of finance, marketing, human
resources, and training. To address this migration, training professionals need to
become knowledgeable about the kinds of skills and the type of information people
must acquire to use these tools effectively in their jobs.

Professional computer training must solve three specific problems inherent in
learning these new systems: fear of technology, resistance to change, and long
learning curves. In addition to learning to use the computer to improve job
performance and productivity, the new computer student must learn a completely
new language and totally unfamiliar concepts: magnetic media, memory, operating
system. The novice faced with a new machine and pounds of user documentation
can expend untold hours of unproductive effort getting started and making costly
mistakes. Even worse, it is not unusual for a novice to be overwhelmed and give up
altogether. A good trainer knows how to induce readiness to learn, knows where
to start, how to assuage fear, how to assess progress, and when training should end
and practice begin.

This chapter deals with computer education for adults. Adult learners are
unusual subjects, bringing to the learning climate their fully formed prejudices and
a great variety of experience, motivation, ability, and need. Computer education
designers should structure programs to capitalize on this wide range of learner
experience by creating curricula that allow each learner to be self-directed.
Designers should also understand that adults learn best when the learning
atmosphere is supportive.

What is the key to implementing a successful computer education project? The
most important ingredient in a company setting is management support. Management must be convinced the short-term cost of training in time and money will be
repaid many times over in long-term gains in productivity. For a successful
outcome, project leaders must be sure management understands the process and
accepts these concepts:

- Computer education requires concentration—an adequate schedule of uninterrupted training time.

- Training is the beginning; practice completes the process. Management must be
  made aware that new graduates of a training program will not be fully competent
  until they have had adequate practice.

- Successful outcomes are directly related to motivation, and motivation is directly
  related to the degree of management support perceived by the students.

Purpose and Benefits

One way project leaders can gain the support of management is to hold a management seminar prior to computer training. During this seminar the project leader should clearly outline the purpose of formal computer education:

- Increase productivity.

- Reduce duplication of effort: For example, staff trained to develop financial applications according to a company standard can share data.

- Minimize the impact of staff turnover by standardizing procedures, facilitating retraining.

- Maximize use of capital equipment. An idle machine is a drain on finances.

- Maintain a competitive position: A fully automated office with a trained staff works faster and smarter—sending, receiving, and analyzing vital information in a timely way.

During the management seminar, emphasis should be placed on the benefits of computer education which are important to management and trainees alike:

- Computer competency alleviates a good part of routine, tedious work, freeing the individual to plan, make better decisions, and perhaps contribute directly to the bottom line.

- Computer literacy increases the individual's usefulness, offers a career path, and promotes job satisfaction.

Ownership

In computer education, ownership is important in two ways: personal ownership of the individual training process and management ownership of the overall outcome.

Management Ownership

As part of the needs assessment, it is imperative that the training project leader determine where the true management ownership of the outcome lies, which may not be the same as the individual driving the project. As described below under Stage I: Needs Assessment, support from management is a key ingredient in delivering successful computer training programs.

Personal Ownership

As part of the training process, individual students must be given ownership of their own training. As little as we know about how adults learn, it has been established that adults must see a concrete benefit to themselves for assimilating new knowledge. Adults will learn what they perceive they need to know. The trainer's task is to make the benefits clear.

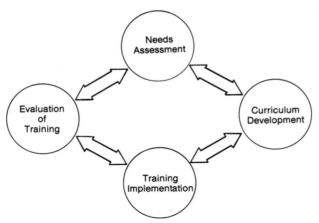

Figure 39-1. The four stages of implementation. (*Copyright 1985, The Forhan & Wakefield Group, Inc.*)

The Four Stages of Implementation

Once management has agreed to the need for computer education, the training project should be organized in four stages:

- Needs assessment
- Curriculum development
- Training implementation
- Evaluation

Each of these topics is treated in detail later in this chapter. Figure 39-1 details the four stages of implementation.

Stage 1: Needs Assessment

According to Malcolm S. Knowles' andragogical model, adults learn faster and more effectively when they are required to know something to perform better in some aspect of their lives. Because of this motivation to learn, adults will respond more receptively to a learning situation that is designed to be task-centered or problem-centered and that directly relates to their job situation.

The implications of this theory for computer training in business are twofold: first, to design effective training one must ensure that the learner perceives the training to be necessary; second, the critical functions or work products produced in the learner's job must be identified and integrated into the training curricula.

Top-Down Fact Finding

To implement effective computer education programs in business, the curriculum project manager needs to know what type of training is required, the attitude toward computers and training that prevails in the business, and the resources available within the organization. To facilitate this process, begin at the top level of management and conduct a series of fact-finding interviews. It is important that this process begin at the top because positive support at this level almost always ensures a successful training effort. Any negative attitude toward the training effort at this level will produce obstacles to training and should be addressed before the process moves any further.

The Executive Survey.   With the aid of the executive survey form (Fig. 39-2), the curriculum project manager can identify the attitude of senior management toward computerization and computer education and can uncover those functions and work products critical to the business goals of the organization.

The Work Product Data Sheet.   The work product data sheet shown in Fig. 39-3 is used to find the business applications that are appropriate for computer

Figure 39-2. The executive survey. (*Forhan & Wakefield.*)

EXECUTIVE SURVEY   Date _____
Training Implementation
Section 1: Project Owner Identification

Name: _____

Title: _____

Organizational Unit: _____

Telephone: _____

Section 2: Computerization goals
What is the goal of your organizational unit in terms of computerization?

Section 3: Organization
Identify those individuals in your organization requiring computer training. Indicate department names, managers, etc.

(Continued)

Figure 39-2.   (*Continued*)

EXECUTIVE SURVEY
Training Implementation
Section 4: Critical functions and work products
Identify those functions which need to be computerized to achieve your business goals.
Identify key contacts for more information.

Critical function or work product	Key Contact	Phone #

Section 5: Applications to be automated in order of priority

---

training. These applications can then be used to design training centered around the
tasks the learner is required to perform for the job. Collect actual samples of the
learner's work products to utilize this form effectively.

The End User Questionnaire.   Because adults enter any learning situation
with dramatically differing experiences, it is beneficial to know as much about these
experiences as possible when designing and implementing computer training. The
end user questionnaire (Fig. 39-4) can be used to gather this type of data. Once
these data are gathered they should be passed on to the trainer, who can use
individual strengths and specialized knowledge to enhance the learning experience
of the group.

Stage II: Curriculum
Development Process

Whether executed by in-house staff or by computer education companies, curriculum development requires careful step-by-step project management.

Project Scoping and Proposal

The needs assessment provides the inputs for project scoping. By clarifying the
training need, coming to agreement as to the target learner population, determining broad course objectives and dependencies, and identifying expert resources, the
curriculum project manager is able to develop a detailed proposal for carrying out
the training project. A project has a tendency to grow if not formalized, making it
difficult to budget and even more difficult to evaluate the end result.

EXECUTIVE SURVEY
Section 6: Microcomputer comfort level on all of the following

Type of Equipment/software	Very comfortable	Comfortable	Un-comfortable
Keyboard			
Data processing terminal			
Micro/personal computer			
Electronic mail			
Electronic spreadsheets			
Database management			
Word processing			
Problem solvers			
Graphics			
Operating systems			

Section 7: Indicate your desire to learn the following

Type of Equipment/software	High desire	Desire	No desire
Keyboard			
Micro/personal computer			
Electronic spreadsheets			
Basic computer literacy/terminology/ concepts			
Databases			
Word processing			
Problem solvers			
Graphics			
Operating systems			
Comments			

(Continued)

The proposal should address the components of the project, the delivery medium, staffing requirements, schedules, internal and external expert resources, the costs, and the *assumptions* on which the costs are based.

Establishing the Approval Cycle

The owner of the project is the final authority on the acceptability of a training program. Therefore, at the beginning of the project, a design plan and outline of the components should be submitted to that person for written approval. The limits of the project are thus clearly defined and responsibility for the training plan is shared between the project leader and the project owner.

The second approval required is for technical content of the program. The subject matter experts designated by the owner should be included in this review cycle. It

Figure 39-2. (*Continued*)

EXECUTIVE SURVEY
Section 8: Departmental equipment installed or to be installed

Type of Equipment/software	Vendor Name	Model	Date of Install
Personal computer			
Terminal			
Word processing software			
Database management software			
Electronic spreadsheet software			
Problem solvers			
Graphics			
Operating systems			
Programming languages			
Other			

Section 9: Indicate the time frames in which your people would be available for training

Month, Day, Number of Hours

is important to establish specific schedules and ground rules for review of any curriculum under development. For example, reviewing manuscript, software-based training, and existing outside training programs takes time. Build into the schedule sufficient time for the reviewers to give an informed assessment so the end result is not a disappointment. Insist on reviewers adhering to the schedule, and on confining their reviews to their own areas of expertise.

The last review should be of the final training program, and requires only the owner's signature.

Research and Analysis

If the subject of training is an established software program, it is probably cost-effective to select one of the existing training packages or hire a company that specializes in computer education, rather than attempt to develop new materials in-house. Ask for evaluation copies of the training materials you are interested in and/or attend a class taught by the training firm.

Courseware developers and curriculum project managers must study the subject matter in depth to be able to select or design effective training; they must become expert users before they can become expert trainers. A close look at the hardware or software product and any available reference material (end user manuals, help

WORK PRODUCT DATA SHEET
Training Implementation   Date _____
Section 1: Work Product Identification

Name: _____

Title: _____

Work Product Name: _____

Telephone: _____

Section 2: Describe in detail the method currently used to create the work product. List all steps. Attach a sample of the final work product.

Major Steps

Section 3: Application(s) to be automated
Describe the applications to be automated. If known, in which applications category do they fall: For example, electronic spreadsheet, word processing, database management, graphics, communications, etc.

Work Product	Type of Application

Figure 39-3. The work product data sheet. (*Forhan & Wakefield.*)

files, tutorials, existing courseware, and others) will enable developers and project managers to define measurable objectives for training and to determine the possible alternative methods of training.

On completion of this phase, a report of findings detailing measurable objectives, subject matter, and training alternatives should be presented to the project owner for approval.

Course Design

Meeting the needs of adult learners requires creative approaches to training. This is particularly true for computer education design where the learners' backgrounds can differ drastically on several different levels: conceptual relating to applications knowledge, conceptual relating to knowledge of the computer, and finally in terms of technical skill and manual dexterity. For these reasons, it is important that designers and selectors of computer education programs learn the importance of providing curricula that allow learners to move at a pace consistent with their learning ability and in directions appropriate for their experience.

THE END USER QUESTIONNAIRE

Name ————————————————— Course ———————————————

Department ———————————————————— Phone # ——————————

To assist us in offering the best possible computer training for you, please answer the following questions:

Do you have any experience with a keyboard? ———————————————————
If yes, explain. ————————————————————————————————————

Do you have any experience with a computer? ——————————————————
If yes, explain. ————————————————————————————————————

What is your reason for taking this course? ——————————————————

———

What do you hope to gain from this course? ——————————————————

———

What software, if any, do you currently use? —————————————————

———

For what applications? ————————————————————————————————

Do you feel you need additional training? ——————————————————

If yes, what type(s)? ————————————————————————————————

Thank you.

Figure 39-4. The end user questionnaire. (*Forhan & Wakefield.*)

This section deals with two types of computer education materials:

- Guided learning
- Self-paced training

Guided Learning. Guided learning requires that a trainer be present during the learning experience. The trainer can then provide the "high touch" human element needed by many computer novices, especially those who are afraid of the technology. Lecture format can be an effective way to transfer facts and concepts in a short training session if the objective is to achieve a general knowledge base. If the objective is to acquire a specific skill, however, a format of hands-on practice with the trainer serving as facilitator is more appropriate. Ideally, the training schedule allows a combination of lecture and practice. To guarantee transfer of skills, practice should include working with the student's own work products.

Longer training programs lend themselves to the learning contract (Fig. 39-5) between trainer and student, defining agreed-upon training objectives and criteria for measuring the outcome.

LEARNING CONTRACT—COMPUTER EDUCATION

Learner: _____

Trainer: _____

Learning Objective	Resources and/or Strategies	Evidence of Completion	Target Completion Date	Evaluation Method

Signed, Trainer _____   Date _____

Signed, Learner _____   Date _____

Figure 39-5. Learning contract.

Self-Paced Training.   Self-paced training works well in a classroom, in conjunction with guided learning. It is essential in situations where classroom training is not feasible. In the real world, many people will learn a new product in a work setting, in the noisy, busy mainstream. For this setting tutorial training, whether software-based, paper-based, or audiovisual, is best designed in discrete units to allow for start-stop sessions. Built-in reviews and progress checks will strengthen the assimilation of the material. Each new unit should begin with a review of the last unit, as considerable time may elapse between training sessions.

Once past the required basics, students can choose key topics that apply to their own work. A well-designed tutorial teaches just enough to get the student started. Practice and other learning aids, such as quick references and mnemonic devices, complete the job.

Medium Selection.   A rich variety of delivery systems is available to the computer trainer today, but choosing the right medium for the message is not an easy task. The selection of the medium depends on a variety of factors: learner preference, time availability, equipment availability, and cost. Here are a few rules of thumb:

1. Classroom seminars are ideal for learners who are afraid of the technology. In fact, this type of training is often necessary to help new users to get beyond the first step. Guided classroom learning provides the learner with the opportunity to interact with an expert, an environment that is very conducive to learning. It also allows the learner time away from day-to-day responsibilities, therefore allowing concentration to be placed on learning the computer. Classroom training is easier to customize than other forms of computer training.

When using classroom training consider the number of students per computer. In some training situations, it is best to use one computer per student. In others, it is best to have two students share a computer. One per student is more advantageous for practice and drill sessions. Two students sharing one computer can be better in problem-solving training sessions.

Flipcharts are ideal for small groups but are expensive to produce in quantity. Color transparencies are the next best choice for low-cost, easy-to-produce visuals. Projected computer output is an excellent choice for demonstrating procedures; to be effective, it requires two people for delivery: one leader and one computer operator. 35-mm slides are a poor choice for computer training as it is difficult to provide a learning environment where information can be presented and the learners can practice simultaneously.

2. Video works well to break up heavy material and to deliver concepts but is not especially handy in combination with hands-on practice. It does, however, afford the learners the opportunity of proceeding at their own pace and reusing the material as often as desired. A major disadvantage of this type of medium is that the learner must have a videotape recorder available. If used in conjunction with a computer, it can be difficult to get the two systems comfortably located near one another.

3. The print-based tutorial is a low-cost method for engaging the student directly with the computer. Whether used in conjunction with guided learning or as a self-paced learning tool for individuals learning on their own, tutorials should be designed with proper ergonomic considerations, attractive illustrations, and modular teaching units.

4. Computer-based training for self-paced instruction is relatively low-cost to deliver but is only as good as its response time. Some CBT programs are unacceptably slow in performance. The student must be involved in the process, with interaction about every three screens. Poor screen design and too much page turning without action is the mark of ineffective CBT. A good system is menu-driven, allowing the learner to select key topics, and offers built-in progress checks for self-testing. CBT is best for topics not subject to frequent updates. It is cost-effective: once purchased it can be used over and over to train many students.

5. Interactive laserdisk training is the top-of-the-line medium and can be designed to combine guided learning, CBT, and moving and still visuals. Unfortunately, it is expensive to revise, difficult to sample test, and requires additional delivery hardware as well as the computer system. Another major drawback to this type of training is lack of standards. Buyers of one kind of interactive videodisc system cannot run applications from other companies on their hardware. However, once these hurdles are overcome and the initial investment is made, the system can be used to train many students.

6. Audio-supported self-paced material is low in cost but in computer training is not advised for novices. A multimedia assault on the senses can impede the learning process.

Sample Module.   If you decide to design your own courseware rather than purchase existing material, make certain you create a sample module early in the

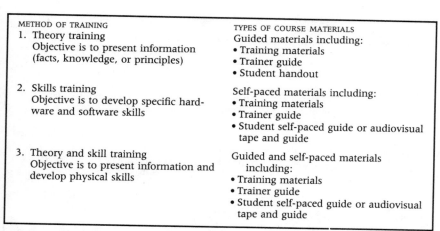

METHOD OF TRAINING	TYPES OF COURSE MATERIALS
1. Theory training Objective is to present information (facts, knowledge, or principles)	Guided materials including: • Training materials • Trainer guide • Student handout
2. Skills training Objective is to develop specific hardware and software skills	Self-paced materials including: • Training materials • Trainer guide • Student self-paced guide or audiovisual tape and guide
3. Theory and skill training Objective is to present information and develop physical skills	Guided and self-paced materials including: • Training materials • Trainer guide • Student self-paced guide or audiovisual tape and guide

Figure 39-6. Methods and materials for computer education.

design process. Select one topic of average difficulty and develop it to completion and then test it on typical users. Involve the project owner in the process of validation to find out if any design changes are needed before proceeding further. Figure 39-6 identifies types of course materials appropriate for different methods of computer training.

Material Development

If you have chosen to design rather than purchase, the next step is to write the material based on the approved sample module—the storyboards and script for electronic media, and manuscript for print-based educational materials. Trainers may review and critique the materials, both for their own preparation and to uncover any problems remaining. As part of the courseware, student critique forms are prepared, and last, validation guidelines and standardized forms are produced. All materials are submitted for technical and contextual editing.

Pilot Program

All trainers are given course materials and rehearsed for the pilot program in a setting emulating the actual training environment. The entire course is then tested on typical users. Neutral observers, following written guidelines and using standardized forms covering objective and subjective responses, monitor the pilot program. Students are asked to complete standard critique forms at the end of the course. This fine tuning of the courseware guarantees a fail-safe training program. Figure 39-7 summarizes the curriculum development process.

Stage III: Training Implementation

Preparation is an integral part of implementing successful computer education. Remember, many of the learners may be approaching the learning experience with

PHASE	PROCESS	OUTPUT
Project Scoping and Proposal	Meeting with key parties to: —Clarify topic(s) —Identify learner population —Identify broad course objectives —Detail any restrictions —Identify both internal and external resources	Proposal with recommended training project plan including developmental process, schedule, staffing and outside resource requirements, estimated costs, and approval cycle
Research and Analysis	Research, learn, and analyze software and/or hardware required for course design	A report of findings and recommendations including: —Measurable course objectives —Subject matter —Key topics —Alternative methods of training
Course Design	Develop creative approaches and alternatives for delivering the course objectives, subject matter, and key topics	A report including: —Course description —Course outline detailing subject matter and key topics —Agenda with timelines —Selection of training methodology and materials required
Material Development	Develop or select learning materials Test materials Prepare trainers	Training materials Trainer's guide Student materials
Pilot Program	Test program by conducting it with actual participants Revise topics and/or materials based on results of the pilot	Required course design revisions Revise training materials and/or student materials

Figure 39-7. Curriculum development process summary.

fear—fear of technology, fear of failure, fear of job obsolescence. Students approaching the training with apprehension will lose all confidence if the equipment fails at the beginning of the session. It is important that the stage be set to reduce these fears. Prior to training, certain steps can be taken by the trainer to ensure the comfort and confidence of the students. Before each training session, complete this checklist:

1. All computer equipment is properly installed and in good operating condition.

2. All software required for training is available and set up correctly.

3. All training materials and equipment are available and operational.

4. The training room is set up to ensure comfort and to stimulate learning.

Using the Training Project Schedule

A training project schedule form like the one in Fig. 39-8 can be helpful in assuring that all materials needed for the training are ready and available. This form should be customized for the type of training being delivered.

Client: _____
Course Date: _____
Instructor(s): _____

TRAINING PROJECT SCHEDULE

To Do	Date Needed	Who Responsible	Date Completed
Agendas			
Objectives			
Manuals			
_____			
_____			
_____			
Flipcharts			
_____			
_____			
_____			
Overheads			
_____			
_____			
_____			
Disks			
_____			
_____			
_____			
_____			
_____			
_____			
Handouts			
_____			
_____			
_____			
Templates			
_____			
_____			
_____			
Name Tags			
Equipment			
_____			
_____			
_____			
Evaluations			
_____			
_____			
_____			

Figure 39-8. Training project schedule.

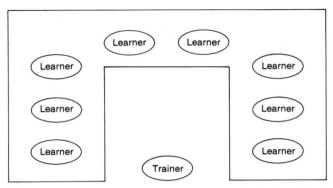

Figure 39-9. The horseshoe classroom. (*Copyright 1984, The Forhan & Wakefield Group, Inc.*)

Preparation for Class

Prior to training, the project leader should ensure that all materials detailed on the training project schedule form are delivered to the classroom. The classroom climate is an important element in the computer education design process. The typical classroom setup with desks and chairs placed in rows with the trainer standing at the front is the least conducive to computer learning. In this environment adult learners revert to childhood expectations of the learning process where knowledge is a one-way transmission from trainer to student. Self-directed learning, which is the key to the andragogical learning process, is stifled. Augmenting this problem, the trainer is placed in a situation where the learners' computer screens are not within view, making it impossible for the trainer to observe the progress of the students easily and unobtrusively.

The Horseshoe Classroom

Setting up the classroom so the learners are sitting in a horseshoe configuration with the trainer closing the horseshoe creates the correct physical and psychological climate for computer learning. Figure 39-9 shows how to set up the horseshoe.

Why a Horseshoe? From the physical environment perspective, the horseshoe allows the trainer to be in constant touch with the learner's progress without appearing to be looking over the learner's shoulder. The psychological climate is one of openness, mutual trust, respect, collaboration, and supportiveness: all essential ingredients in adult learning. And most important, this setup facilitates two-way transmission from trainer to learner, learner to trainer, and learner to learner.

Creating a Humane Learning Climate

Adult learning is fostered when the learning climate is set up to be humane—where human beings can be comfortable. This is particularly important when adults are being educated to use the computer, a machine notably lacking in humanity. The correct learning climate can be partially attained by tending to those elements that ensure human comfort, like comfortable chairs, work surfaces that are at the correct height and depth, adequate lighting, good ventilation, and freedom from noise distraction.

In *Megatrends*, John Naisbitt refers to the world of high tech, high touch, meaning that without the human element it is impossible to reap all the productivity benefits associated with computerization. Effective computer training provides the high touch element critical to effective implementation of high tech.

The trainer can foster a climate of high touch by providing an atmosphere of caring and cheerfulness in the classroom. Name tags for both the trainer and students should be mandatory in computer learning situations where the trainer and learners do not know one another. Care should be taken during the opening of the course to remove any concerns the learners have about the training, and the stage should be set for an atmosphere that is open and encourages questions and student participation.

Stage IV: Evaluation of Training

The final stage of implementation of computer training is the evaluation process. How can we most effectively evaluate the success of a computer training program? Three techniques of evaluation can be used during this stage.

The Course Critique

A course critique similar to the one in Figure 39-10 should be passed out at the end of the training session and filled in by all the course participants. The course critique measures student reaction to the training program, the trainer, and the course materials rather than learning or behavior changes resulting from the training.

Postclass Telephone Surveys

Like the course critique, the postclass telephone survey is used to measure student reaction to the training experience. If conducted by someone other than the trainer, it can often provide more objective feedback on the reaction of the learner to the training.

Applications Survey

Use the interview forms from the needs assessment stage of implementation to perform an applications survey to ascertain which work products or functions have been automated as a result of the training. Applications surveys should be conducted several months following computer training. Although time-consuming to conduct, the applications survey will provide information on the actual learning, behavioral modification, and business results derived from the computer training program. Use the results of this survey to determine the effectiveness of the training program and to reveal any additional computer training requirements for the business.

Name _____ Address _____

City _____ State _____ Zip _____

Company _____ Your Title _____

Industry _____ Phone _____

Company Training Coordinator _____

	Excellent	Above Avg.	Avg.	Fair	Poor
1. What was your overall impression of the class?	5	4	3	2	1
2. Was the course material clearly presented?	5	4	3	2	1
3. Instructors' knowledge of the material?	5	4	3	2	1
4. Instructors' presentation of the material?	5	4	3	2	1
5. How well did the class hold your interest?	5	4	3	2	1
6. How was the pace of the course?	5	4	3	2	1
7. How did the course rank in meeting defined objectives?	5	4	3	2	1

The duration of the course was: Too long _____ Too short _____ Correct _____

What did you like most about the course? _____

_____

What improvements do you suggest for future classes? _____

_____

How did you hear about this course? _____

What other courses would you be interested in taking? _____

_____

For Internal Use Only:

Instructor _____ Date _____

Course _____ Product Center _____

Figure 39-10. The course critique.

Resources for Computer Training

Computer Manufacturers. The manufacturers of the equipment your company uses may be a resource for hardware and software training, although more and more manufacturers are recommending third party training specialists, rather than assuming training support for their equipment.

Computer Education Companies. Companies like The Forhan & Wakefield Group in Connecticut and Applied Computer Consultants in California offer training, software documentation, and product support. Usually these firms will offer training on popular software products as well as provide custom education for specialized and nonstandard software, such as applications developed by your company.

Computer Retail Stores. Stores like the NYNEX Business Centers (formerly IBM product centers) offer training on popular software products for personal computers and minicomputers. Training through these sources can often be offered at the product center or at your location.

Custom-Designed Courseware. Publications such as *Data Training* regularly evaluate custom training firms. Another source for finding companies that can deliver custom-designed training is information industry trade shows.

In-House Training. Often it is more convenient to offer training at your location. In-house staff, computer education company trainers, and authorized trainers from the hardware and/or software manufacturers can be used to perform the training. Course materials can also be produced or purchased from outside sources.

"Off-the-Shelf" Training Programs. Certain computer skills can be learned from prepackaged audiovideo or software programs. Deltak, McGraw-Hill, and Wiley Systems are major providers of this type of training. Evaluate these programs carefully to see if they meet the needs of your target population.

On-the-Job Training. Although not the ideal training methodology for computer education, on-the-job training cannot be overlooked by the small company with limited resources. A word of caution—when using this type of training ensure that the learner has some quiet time available for practice.

Private Institutions. A growing number of private trade and business schools offer courses in word processing, data processing, computer languages, and some software applications. Classes are given at the school, which may not be convenient. Check the credentials of these schools carefully. Ensure that the curriculum is designed for adult businesspeople.

Professional Associations. Some of the latest developments in computer education are discussed, demonstrated, and published by professional organizations like SALT (Society for Advanced Learning Technology), the Society for Technical Communication, and the American Management Associations. Computer associations also give seminars that might prove helpful.

Public Schools. Community colleges are a major resource for computer-related learning. For small groups or individuals who must be trained in specific skills, such as computer operations, the community college provides a solution.

Software Development Companies. Some well-established software companies offer training classes for purchasers of their software. Some computer education companies are authorized training vendors and centers for software companies.

User Groups. Many communities and businesses have user groups that provide computer training to their members. Often, groups will specialize in a particular brand of hardware, software, or business application. Many computer retail stores can provide you with a listing of these groups in your community. In large corporations, a listing of corporate user groups can be obtained from the data processing department.

Bibliography

Birren, F., *Light, Color, and Environment*, Van Nostrand Reinhold, New York, 1969.

Knowles, Malcolm S., and Associates, *Andragogy in Action*, Jossey-Bass Publishers, San Francisco, CA, 1984.

Knowles, Malcolm, *The Adult Learner: A Neglected Species*, 3d ed., Gulf Publishing Company Book Division, Houston, TX, 1984.

Naisbitt, John, *Megatrends*, Warner Books, Inc., New York, 1982.

Rogers, Carl R., *Freedom to Learn*, Charles E. Merrill Publishing Company, Columbus, OH, 1969.

Rogers, Carl R., *A Way of Being*, Houghton Mifflin, Boston, MA, 1980.

Smith, Barry J., and Brian L. Delahaye, *How to Be an Effective Trainer*, John Wiley & Sons, New York, 1983.

40
International Training

Michael J. Copeland

Michael J. Copeland *is a personnel manager in the Procter & Gamble International Division. He is currently working in the relocation and compensation areas and maintains an active participation in the development of group training projects in the United States. He has been the primary contact for the development of the integrated cross-cultural and language training model used within the company for organizational training and development in Japan and Saudi Arabia.*

Organizations which have interests and responsibilities abroad face unusual difficulties in keeping subsidiaries current in the latest developments in both management techniques and technology. Top managers often identify needs within organizations which can be satisfied with international training but they are usually unaware of the problems inhibiting the rapid transfer of both general and technical solutions.

To enable managers to execute desired international training, several unique aspects need consideration. Training time and costs will normally be increased because of language and cultural differences between the home location of the employees being trained and the host country. Depending on the scope of the differences, costs are often between one and a half and two times the cost of training home country employees.

Overall costs normally associated with the training need to be carefully analyzed to ensure that the surcharges for the international aspects of the training and the variation in the time required for satisfactory completion of training are estimated properly. Variables include the location of training, time needed, interim travel home, incremental expense per employee or family, medical insurance, and incidental expenses reimbursed by the organization.

The selection of employees to be trained is more difficult owing to the extended time required for training and language and cross-cultural barriers identified prior to the training program start-up. In some cultures, dual-career couples complicate long-term training, or secondary school–aged children result in the deselection of key employees for training.

The unfamiliarity of the sending and receiving line management with the desires of each other's organization is a further complication of international training. Line managers are often hesitant to communicate internationally because of perceived language barriers or assumptions about the overseas organization. This results in poor initial training and additional costs once deficiencies are recognized and corrected.

Until these issues are addressed and resolved, international training will not be satisfactorily accomplished.

Costs of International Training

The cost of relocating employees and families can be double their usual salary plus benefits. Once in the new location, these costs can continue to be double those of a locally employed person. Depending on the sending and receiving locations and tax laws of both countries, these costs can become the most difficult aspect of the training initially. In many instances, line managers responsible for the decision to obtain training have no frame of reference for these costs and often resist this information as unrealistic or unacceptable. The trainer is left with the onus of including these transfer and ongoing support expenses as part of the total cost of the training and is put in an unfavorable position at the outset unless this aspect of the process is understood prior to the decision to move people for training.

Information about the costs of the transfer is best obtained from the internal resources responsible for international moves. If these are not available, companies who habitually transfer employees internationally can explain their process and costs if asked. Very little information is considered proprietary and those doing the work are usually willing to share their system. Large organizations like the National Foreign Trade Council, National Association of Manufacturers, or American Council on International Personnel can act as referral agencies if your company is a member of one or more of these organizations.

Defining the Training Objective

This is a hurdle which requires a great deal of attention prior to any training. It is often overlooked and leads to unproductive time and frustration on the part of all involved.

Strategic decisions about transfers are made at an organizational level removed from the execution of training. The first difficulty to be overcome is the communication of the major decisions which will result in training to the rest of the organization. The larger the organization, the more levels the information must filter through before the trainees obtain access to the decision. The training objectives which flow from the strategic decisions are left to the middle managers involved in most cases. It is up to the trainer to get the middle management to define what the training is to accomplish. Once these decisions are communicated, direction to develop training generally follows.

General objectives are usually available. For example, "Transfer the technology for the production of this product from the U.S. to the new facility being built for the joint venture in Indonesia" is seen as adequate as far as the operations vice president and manager of manufacturing are concerned. However, the trainers need specific objectives for each functional area of the production process and for each individual to be trained. A close relationship between the operating and training organizations has to be developed in this phase of the project.

If training is to be done by employees rather than vendors or consultants, much of the training objective setting is accomplished implicitly since organizational expectations and standards are commonly understood by both trainers and line managers. In this instance, objectives can be more general to start with and become fine-tuned as the training progresses.

If training is to be done by subcontracting, the organization desiring the training must be specific about objectives and expectations. It is not an overstatement to say that the lack of specific objectives is the root cause of unsuccessful training when outside resources are responsible for the execution of the training task.

In any case, both the sending and receiving parties must agree on the objectives in advance. Once agreed, the objectives need to be shared with the employees to be trained prior to the training. At the same time an estimate of the time expected for the accomplishment of the objectives needs to be communicated. The employees to be trained should understand that once the objectives are met, they can expect to return to the home location to put newly acquired skills to use.

Determining Training Location

If the training objectives can be met by having the trainer(s) go to the trainee's location, significant savings can often be realized. This is best done when the training is specific and can be accomplished in less than a month or two. In these cases, the trainer has to be self-sufficient in the subject to be taught and the training materials to be used. Linguistic and cultural barriers must be addressed and removed in advance.

If the individuals to be trained go to the trainer's location, the trainer has access to far more resources than outside the home location and the trainees have the opportunity to participate in ongoing activities not available in their home location. These peripheral opportunities can be readily worked into the core training to enrich the experience abroad for the trainees.

Group training usually requires the group to go to the trainer's location if the subject is too complex to be dealt with using portable training aids. Technology transfers are an example of complex subjects which for successful training require that a group relocate to the location where the technology is in operation. This enables the group to observe and to operate the process in a functioning environment.

Time References for Training Assignments

Training assignments are normally designed around one of three time frames.
Short-term training is generally less than 6 months long. This decision is tax-related in cases of reciprocal tax treaties. If a tax treaty exists between the home and host countries, the customary stipulation is that individuals traveling between

the two countries are subject only to their home country tax system if the travel is less than 183 days in a taxable year. In assignments of this nature, it is not usually cost-effective to move families and personal effects. Instead, interim trips are used to stay in touch with home country responsibilities.

Medium-term training is generally more than 6 months and less than 2 years. The majority of personal development training for high-potential employees falls into this category. Normally, the employees and immediate family relocate. Many dual-career families can participate in this kind of training. Leaves of absence are generally available for 1 to 2 years for the spouse not employed by the company transferring the employee for training. The preponderance of individual training is normally completed in the medium-term range.

Long-term training is in excess of 2 years. This time period involves as much development, in the sense of growth and individual skills enhancement, as training. Except in unusual and complex circumstances, the employee is normally a productive member of the organization rather than simply a trainee.

Short-term training tends to be the most task-oriented for all involved. Culture shock and adaptation problems are minimized since there is little or no need to integrate into the community or to learn cross-cultural skills or a new language.

Medium- and long-term assignments involve the complexities of adjustment to life abroad, specific language and cultural issues, and the reintegration to the home location after the assignment. Unless these assignments are thoroughly planned and analyzed, employees will predictably suffer a drop in productivity and motivation, at least initially. These issues need careful attention during the planning for international training.

The Selection of International Trainees

Before the development of a training program is considered, the selection of participants must be addressed. Language skill, adaptability, commitment to the training objectives and organization, openness to the new location's norms and values, and other similar characteristics need to be included in the selection process.

Many international transferees are selected almost exclusively on the basis of technical expertise, availability, and willingness to accept the assignment. These factors are legitimate criteria but do not represent a complete list of items to be considered.

Selection can be done by consultants without the inherent biases of the organization's selection process. The organization needs only to nominate equally qualified candidates and let professional evaluators predict success abroad. Final designation is retained by the organization after recommendations have been made by these consultants.

Once the selection process is determined, other issues need to be addressed. For example, in group training, it is desirable to have both an experience and hierarchy mix. This mix will provide stability, maturity, and a sense of purpose without the need for leaders to identify themselves from within the group, establish their position, and spend time and energy informally influencing the rest of the group.

Less experienced employees will find readily available role models from more experienced employees. At the same time, the less experienced are more willing to try new ideas and stimulate the more experienced to try new approaches in training. Youthful enthusiasm is balanced by experienced reaslism. Less experienced employees use the information about their home company provided by the more experienced employees to put the training material into proper perspective. If training is conducted at a company site, the trainee group can have a parallel organizational structure with the line organization responsible for the training. This will facilitate communications between trainers and trainees and provide role models for trainees at several levels, both organizationally and in the implicit norms and expectations of the company.

A Training Model

The training model analyzed here has been slowly developed over the past 6 years for use in intercompany transfers between the United States and the Far East and Middle East. It is intended to be used as a preliminary stage of international transfers where wide gaps are recognized between the sending and receiving cultures. Procter & Gamble wanted to reduce the time needed for employees from these diverse regions to develop adequate business skills in English, Procter & Gamble's corporate culture, and intercultural understanding between the U.S. company and the subsidiary abroad. The Intercultural Relations Institute, Inc., of Redwood City, California, provided the training expertise, initiated this model, and continues to refine it annually.

The training model consists of three components: (1) corporate business English, (2) corporate culture, and (3) intercultural communication skills.

Corporate Business English

Language skill is a major determinant in the length of a training program for international employees. Individuals selected for a training assignment abroad need to be critically evaluated for language competence prior to the transfer to give both trainers and line managers a clearer idea of the trainees' ability to meet the training objectives.

The language skill level needs evaluation both orally and in writing. The more comprehensive the evaluation, the more realistically the trainers can establish their materials. Once the language skill level is determined, the technical training can be properly phased and a rough timetable for completion established.

If the language level is low, initial training will need to be exclusively oriented toward language acquisition. The training materials used may be based on the technical subjects to be trained later and the specific vocabulary used may be unique to the subjects involved in the process, but the need being met at first is linguistic, and this fact must be understood by all parties involved in the training process.

Conversational English, typically the starting level for most transferees for training, is inadequate for most international training. In order to meet the need to understand and use the technical terminology of daily business, a specific vocabulary must be built into the training process.

To begin to develop an appropriate jargon and vocabulary, it is essential to collect actual operating materials to use as reference material for the language component of the training. If possible, videotapes of both formal and informal meetings can be developed for training. These videotapes will initially be used to assist in the integration of on-the-job idiom with the textbook language skills typically held by second or third language users. Later in training, these same tapes will be useful in the intercultural analysis of information flow.

Written procedures, administrative guides, training materials used for native speakers, and normal correspondence from one office to another are extremely useful in developing a core vocabulary for the foreign employee. These materials are best used with accomplished second language trainers to ensure that the subtleties and idioms are explained in such a way that the new information can be retained.

Once real language materials are obtained for use, the language training can be integrated into a preliminary phase of overall training to prepare the foreign employee for the core training to be conducted after adequate language skills are evidenced.

Language training is divided into two areas in this model: productive and receptive.

Productive language is related to speaking and writing. Speaking skills need to include meeting management and participation, interactive skills for formal and informal opportunities, clarification of ideas, basic grammar, pronunciation, and vocabulary building. Written skills taught need to include organization writing norms, complex grammar, vocabulary, clarity, simplicity, and speed.

Receptive language skills relate to listening and reading. Listening skills include understanding jargon, understanding meanings, and following one or two speakers to understand main ideas. Reading skills include skimming material to identify main ideas and important facts, understanding inferences, jargon use, and vocabulary development.

Language training is usually conducted in small groups of two to five participants supplemented with individual tutoring. Trainees are also given individual independent study exercises to complement the classroom work.

The design of the language training is to enable the trainee to gain understanding in the business language needed to succeed in the core training to follow. This requires attention to materials used, starting point of the trainee, and the knowledge of the organization held by the trainer. The careful integration of the language component to overall training objectives is essential to international training.

Corporate Culture

The second component of international training is corporate culture. Each company or organization has a distinctive character which is transmitted via unwritten means from level to level and generation to generation. For international training it is necessary to identify the company's dominant characteristics and to describe these as they fit into the overall national culture. This process enables the international trainee to understand the "why" of many of the business practices of the host location which may be otherwise confusing or seemingly arbitrary.

Since most of the material included in the generic term "culture" is implicit in the daily actions of the members of an organization, resources abound but do not seem readily apparent. For example, evaluation criteria are a direct reflection of corporate values and norms. Items like press releases, interoffice memoranda, approval levels, and procedures for expenditures or decisions, policy statements, speeches made by company officers, the physical layout of offices and manufacturing facilities, meeting management norms, and telephone manners each reflect the company's culture. If these are analyzed as part of the corporate culture, put into the appropriate context, and woven into the overall training program, the international employee will gain a broad appreciation for the home company's implicit view of itself.

The analysis of the alien culture is best begun with self-analysis. This step needs to be done by bicultural trainers who can assist the natives in identifying their home company's cultural characteristics. Once initiated, this process leads to comparison exercises, clear identification of points of convergence and divergence, and an awareness of the diversity of the ways common ends can be obtained.

It is important to emphasize the necessity of remaining objective at this early analytical state. Often the newcomer to this field becomes judgmental and trapped in comparisons between home and host countries which become win-lose or good-bad in nature. The trainer must be especially cautious not to lose sight of the established training objectives at this critical point.

Components of corporate culture training need to include managerial expectations, norms and values, and the identification of individual skills needed to succeed within the corporate culture. These subjects provide a rich source of business vocabulary at the same time that the transfer of values takes place.

The result of this training is an employee who understands the company from a unique perspective. The study of daily activities as a reflection of the overall whole of the organization gives the foreign employee the skills needed not only to survive but also to integrate skills acquired abroad and to adapt these to the established practices of the home organization. This potential for synergy is often overlooked in international training dynamics and results in the loss of organization potential. The international trainer must find ways to integrate the effectiveness of the international employee into the home organization by expanding established practices to include the more efficient or productive methods used by the overseas organization.

Intercultural Communication Skills

The third component of international training is the acquisition of appropriate behaviors to communicate effectively within the organization. These are termed intercultural communication skills. The successful development of these skills gives the international employee confidence to use the newly acquired language and corporate culture knowledge. These behaviors also give a needed feeling of confidence to the home country employee with whom the foreign employee must work to learn home company systems or technology.

Intercultural communication skills begin with an analysis of the communication process within the host country. During this analysis, the foreign employee will integrate the corporate culture and business language into the learning process. As this integration develops, the way the new organization evolved within its home culture will begin to be understood by the foreign employee.

Specific skills for behavior within the culture being analyzed need to be identified and taught. In general, interactive listening, maintaining discussions, and identifying and resolving miscommunications in both formal and informal settings need to be presented to and understood by the foreign employee. As these basic skill areas are mastered, additional topics can be identified and developed as appropriate for the duration of the training and the organization's objectives identified earlier. For example, formal presentations to peers and higher management levels, giving and receiving feedback, persuasion and initiating and participating in extemporaneous conversations are appropriate intercultural skills for presentation and analysis.

As the foreign employee gains a unique view of both host and home cultures, the concept of cultural informant is developed. The cultural informant is one who has a bicultural understanding of company operations and is able to help parties from both sides work more effectively together. For example, the trainer for this model must be a cultural informant.

At the beginning of the training, the trainer models this role for the trainee and establishes a way of using a cultural informant. During the training, the foreign employee needs to develop new ways to identify and use cultural informants other than the trainers. Sources of potential cultural informants include employees previously assigned to the foreign employee's home company, those previously assigned to a similar country, those who have studied abroad, and finally those who want to work abroad. Each source has varying degrees of expertise which can be used by the foreign employee to help integration into the host organization. After the conclusion of training, the foreign employee will be able to act as a cultural informant for the host location with regard to the foreign employee's home company and culture.

The training for intercultural skills is effective using videotaped meetings, role plays, and scenes which highlight normal communication and interactions between employees. The emphasis of this training is on miscommunication and misinterpretation of the videotapes on the part of the trainee and the consequences of such mistakes. The analysis of events in which the trainee will be expected to participate gives realism to the training. This training model clearly identifies the trainee's ineffective behavior and the negative consequences of continuing such action. This motivates employees to want to change their behavior to get positive feedback once they are committed to the fact they need help in learning to become effective in the host culture. The positive role play provides the model for effectiveness in communication, thereby giving confidence to the foreign employee as successes are established. This further develops an attitude predisposed to success through an analysis of miscommunication which is essential to the foreign employee once this preparatory phase of training has been completed.

Timing of the Three-Part Model

As previous stated, the language competence of the trainees will largely influence the duration of this training model. However, for general planning purposes, 3 to 5 months are needed to complete this model for most groups of nonnative employees.

For a basic program, with minimal language skill, about 60 percent of the time is devoted to corporate language training, 20 percent to corporate culture, and 20 percent to intercultural skills. This can be adjusted as the language level of those to be trained improves.

Location of Training

It is recommended that this preparatory training be accomplished in the host company's country, if not at the actual location. The necessity for constant reinforcement in the host language is best done in that country. Additionally, the experience of living abroad provides immediate incentive to the foreign employee to learn the skills presented by the trainers. The immediacy of the language and cultural training cannot be duplicated effectively in the foreign employee's home country. Finally, if at all possible, employees need to be separated from their families for as much of this initial training as possible. If this training is a preliminary step to a technology transfer, it should be done in advance of the family's arrival. This puts a total immersion effect on the training which gives reinforcement to all aspects of the program, 24 hours a day. This will not occur if families accompany the employee at the same time the training is initiated.

Conclusion

As organizations become more multicultural in their scope and influence, it is increasingly difficult to assume that individual employees from outside the main-stream organization's culture are prepared to adapt to training offered by the home organization. Differences in cultures need to be recognized and adapted to training techniques if desired results are to be met. The stronger the home organization's norms, the more difficult it will be to accommodate foreign expectations and values.

The foregoing model is intended to prepare employees for successful training in a foreign location. The counterpoint of this model is one which prepares home company employees to work effectively abroad. Similar preparation is needed to avoid costly errors and unsuccessful expatriate experiences as home organization resources prepare to work abroad.

Prior to any international training or assignment, the cost, selection process, and skills identification and development must be thoroughly managed to obtain the maximum benefit both organizationally and personally. Once this model has been adapted to the organization's needs, it can be used for virtually all functional areas and skills. Trainers need to be sensitized as well as trainees. Clear organizational expectations need to be developed and communicated. Realistic outcomes must be agreed to by both sending and receiving organizations. Finally, active management of the training process must occur throughout the duration of training. The size of the investment and need for the ongoing development of international resources justifies the unique training model and can result in significantly increased value to the multinational organization.

41

Literacy in the Workplace

Rosalyn E. Stoker

Linda Stoker is a member of The Polaroid Corporation's Human Resource Development Group. She manages the company's in-house education programs for nonexempt employees. An advocate of literacy and lifelong learning, Stoker has been a consultant to higher education and to other corporations in planning basic skills programs and has been active as an advocate at the local, state, and federal level in establishing education policy for undereducated populations. Stoker is a member of the editorial board of Life Long Learning. She has served as a member of the White House Conference on Productivity, as the chairman of The National Advisory Committee to the G.E.D. Testing Service, and as a senior policy advisor to the National Adult Literacy Project. She has testified before the House Sub-Committee on Post-Secondary Education on the Problem of Illiteracy in the Workforce.

Literacy and Jobs: What Are Job-Related Literacy Skills?

While the academic community is still coming to agreement on a common definition of literacy, most researchers agree that job-related literacy includes several sets of skills, each set arranged along a continuum from very simple cognitive tasks to very complex ones. Any job-related discussion of these skills may combine or overlap tasks from more than one set, but it is useful to describe them separately. Job-related literacy includes:*

---

* Some researchers also include skills associated with good work habits and/or skills and knowledge that orient a learner in the world of work, such as a general understanding of "how things work" in a technological environment.

- Skills in reading, writing, and speaking English
- Computation skills
- The solution of certain kinds of problems

Skills in Reading, Writing, and Speaking English

These skills are the most universally agreed-upon forms of literacy. While not all jobs require equal amounts of literacy in reading, writing, or speaking, as work and the working environment change, there is a clear tendency toward and an increased dependence on these skills.

Reading Skills and Writing Skills. The most basic level of job-related literacy includes an ability to sign one's name and to respond appropriately to safety signs in the work environment.

More advanced job-related reading and writing skills include the ability to find relevant facts on a work order and maintain a log requiring the writing of a limited set of frequently repeated words or phrases.

More difficult are tasks that require the worker to read material such as a simply written work change order and apply its conditions appropriately. An equivalent writing task might be to fill out a critical incident report which requires a short narrative of an accident or other unusual event.

Still more complex reading might include training manuals, work-related technical articles, and letters explaining changes in health benefits. Equivalent writing tasks involve the composition of simple letters and memos and the written organization of routine findings as in a lab report.

Skills in Speaking English. The most basic job-related *oral* English skills include understanding routine work instructions such as "Stop the belt" and "Please take your break at ten o'clock," as well as the ability to communicate simple, routine information clearly such as "More piece parts, please," or "Thank you for the raise."

More complex speaking and listening skills include the ability to sustain a conversation on a job-related subject with which both participants are highly familiar. Still more complex are the ability to organize and present information or recommendations to an unfamiliar audience and the ability to comprehend the job-related implications of an oral presentation of unfamiliar material.

Computation Skills

Computation skills underlie a new shape of work on the production floor. Workers who a few years ago were asked to read dials and punch a button if the needle crossed a line are now being introduced to the mysteries of dimensional control. The development or reacquisition of computation skills is increasingly important for the work force.

Very basic computational tasks include checking a digital readout and copying the numbers in the correct order in a log, accurately reading a readout at the beginning and at the end of a run and subtracting correctly to report the number of units made, or accepting cash in payment and counting out the correct change.

Examples of more sophisticated skills include the use of fractions or decimals to measure materials; computing of percentages; and the computation of means, modes, and medians. More complex computation skills might include the keeping and balancing of a petty cash account, reviewing routine data and projecting trends and inferences, or routinely using a set of simple formulas in tasks like computing airflow for an air-conditioning system or changing the yield of a recipe.

In addition to these job-related applications, fairly sophisticated computation skills are a prerequisite for mastery of subjects such as electronics instrumentation.

Skills in Solving Problems

One of the most significant shifts in job redesign is the increase in involvement of members of the production team in problem solving. In addition to requiring employees to work together differently, calling on communication skills and presentation skills to a new degree, new work designs require employees to develop new approaches to solving problems.

Workers may be asked to use analytic skills to troubleshoot a machine breakdown, to work in a team to brainstorm recommendations for a more efficient production layout, to make real-time choices among several options to avoid stoppages in a production run, or to collect data of operation and project their implications under variable conditions. All of these are problem-solving approaches production workers are being asked to do in a variety of settings. Workers who have not yet developed these skills can learn to do so while performing work operations ranging from the most concrete to the most abstract.

An inability to perform these literacy tasks is never in itself a sign of intellectual incompetence. Basic literacy skills are vital to the ongoing operations of even the most unsophisticated work environment. Yet these skills cannot be inferred either by an educational credential or from a previously satisfactory work record. Every day workers with poor literacy skills make valuable contributions in the workplace; the oral communication skills an illiterate adult may develop to compensate for lack of reading can be highly desired in some jobs. In fact, when a worker "comes out of the closet" and reveals his or her lack of skills both supervisors and colleagues are often surprised to learn of their colleague's disability.

Providing Services

Basic Skills

More and more human resource groups are deciding that employees' basic skills needs warrant in-house basic skills support. Basic skills classes in math, reading and study skills, writing, English as a second language, and/or problem solving are regularly offered at the worksite on and off and across shifts. Job-related basic skills programs can be successful when the employees learn skills they need to improve job performance or for job growth. They are most cost-effective when the students can demonstrate those skills in new performance behavior on the job.

Several kinds of direct and indirect services can be included in a comprehensive program. Critical to the success of any program are the base lines, establishing minimum competencies and conducting skills assessments. Other direct and indirect service program components can include advocacy, basic skills job studies, job-related literacy tutorial, literacy support groups, referral networks, basic skills classes, and course and program evaluation.

Whether a program is developed and run in-house or contracted from a vendor, several factors are critical in mounting job-related basic skills programs. While inadequate consideration of any one factor may render a program ineffective, it is the interaction of the combination of factors that assures program success. Factors to consider include needs assessment, organizational culture and environment, employee motivation and management support, resources in-house and in the community, delivery systems, course of study, evaluation and planning, and program management.

In many cases it will be in a company's interests to make basic skills education available to its employees. While all employee educational needs and aspirations cannot be the responsibility of employers, it is clear that there can be a convergence of the needs of individuals for improved literacy skills at any point along a skill continuum and of the needs of their employers for those skills to be enhanced in the workplace.

A basic skills program will include a variety of activities. Some classes may or may not be appropriate to any given work setting. Not every job-related literacy skill deficiency warrants a course offering. A number of factors need to be considered when deciding whether to offer a job-related basic skills course or design another type of intervention. First, the skills needed should be priority skills for the corporation, and the human resources professional should develop a specific rationale for the program that can be agreed to by line management.

Human resource groups can develop targeted programs of literacy training and basic skills education using in-house or community resources or a combination of the two. Components of a comprehensive basic skills program feature both direct services to employees and indirect services to work groups. Organizational and individual needs assessments, planning, and inventories of community resources will help determine which program components and content areas as well as which target groups of workers should have top priority in a corporate literacy program.

Culture and Environment

Another set of factors to consider when planning a basic skills program is the culture and environment of the corporation. Cultural considerations include the traditional relationship between workers and management. Stress between the two groups can sabotage the best-designed program. Production schedules are also critical. Courses should not be planned to start, for example, during a peak production period. No matter how committed management may be to the program supervisors will have trouble releasing people for classes that conflict with a production run. Other factors to consider are shift, age, and sex of the target employees, accessibility of the classrooms, and the reputation of the group offering the program.

Characteristics of the community in which the plant is located must be taken into consideration. Women with school-age children or workers who share transportation are less likely to be able to stay after work for a shared-time program. One basic skills program almost never got off the ground because the courses were inadvertently set up in competition with the company's share-a-ride campaign.

Employee Motivation and Management Support

Motivation and support are perhaps the two key factors in deciding how to develop a basic skills program. In the situation described above, supervisors incorrectly regarded the lack of employee response as evidence of lack of interest. Employees interpreted the conflicting messages of the two programs as proof of management's insincerity.

The visibility of management support is paramount to success. Much of this chapter is directed toward developing pragmatic rationales to present to management for offering site-appropriate programs. Many managers will be predisposed to view basic skills interventions as charitable efforts, benefits, or frills. Unless key management, from the plant manager who pays the bill to the first-line supervisor who releases the employee, is *convinced* that the program is relevant to short- or long-term production goals, the program will not succeed.

Equally important is employee motivation. Motivating the undereducated to return to schooling is a subtle process. They are predisposed by prior experience to expect difficulty in the classroom. A machinist who had trouble with math in the sixth grade has no reason based in experience to expect to be any more successful as an adult. However, some of the best research in adult education shows that when adults with limited expectations of schooling can be shown that they do benefit from adult education experiences, those experiences themselves become highly motivating. In other words, once they can experience education working for them, the undereducated participate. Basic skills programs work when they are focused on concrete, job-related content, when the content shows specific relationships to the tasks students need to perform to earn their livings, and when students can learn techniques that transfer learning to new settings.

Establishing Minimum Competencies.   A strong in-house basic skills program should be anchored in job-related basic skills criteria (minimum competencies). These can be established for all hourly positions. If a comprehensive minimum competency study is too complex to take on at once, at the very least, basic skills competencies should be established for target jobs or job groups. The target might be a specific job, a family of jobs such as machine operators, or clerical workers, or a cluster of jobs in a specific location. Samples at similar jobs or sites should be made in order to determine whether the minimum competency being required is unique or generic.

Comprehensive basic skills studies do not need to be expensive. They should be done in two parts, team inventories and technical studies. If necessary, well-executed team inventories can be used alone, but to be useful technical studies must always be backed up by team inventories.

Developing a Team Inventory.   This inventory is useful for three reasons. First, it gives human resource planners a definite frame of reference within which to develop programs. Second, it allows employees to reflect on the relationship between basic skills and work and schooling options within a pragmatic context. Finally, the process of developing this list is a useful one for engaging supervisors, compensation analysts, and others to think about how basic skills are used on the work floor.

An inventory of minimum competencies may be conducted throughout a corporation, at a work site, or for a group of targeted jobs. For literacy programming, the study should be reliable but does not need to be either highly formal or structured. In one corporate study the human resources group called together a group of line managers, supervisors, compensation analysts, personnel administrators, and labor representatives all of whom had direct experience with a family of jobs such as secretarial, hand assembly, or skilled trades. In another, divisional study of quality assurance operations, the training group included all the quality organization's major clients on the team.

Minimum competencies should be listed in terms of job tasks rather than years of schooling or course names. In each case, the study team was given examples of job-related basic skills statements and was asked to develop their own lists of minimum competencies for each hourly job in their group. When the team lists were completed, the training and education specialist reconvened the team and reviewed their combined work. In both cases the teams were told that they could establish the skills threshold at whatever level they wished, but a "must" competency should be the lowest level of skill that workers needed to perform a given job adequately. In other words, team members were asked what was the lowest level of reading, writing, English speaking, or computation skill that employees had to have in order to get the job done. In all cases there was surprising agreement across the several interest groups on each job team.

Developing a Technical Study. Technical studies may be conducted in-house by trained human resources professionals or they may be contracted from local educational institutions. An outside agency can be particularly useful in establishing baseline studies, but trainers with education backgrounds can conduct periodic updates themselves. If an educational institution is contracted, the human resources staff should work closely with them, orienting the contractor to the workplace.

One approach to basic skills technical studies is similar to job analysis for compensation. Examples of all the reading, writing, or computational materials or oral communications that workers are expected to use in a particular operation are collected and analyzed. Reading levels are computed if appropriate and the material compared and correlated to a hierarchy of basic skills to establish sequences for planning or instruction.

A number of skill lists have developed. One useful one was developed by the National Center for Research in Vocational Education at Ohio State University. This document was designed to assist vocational educators in identifying competency-based adult literacy skills. Since it was designed for adult education purposes, it avoids describing skills in grade levels which are not particularly useful in literacy program planning and often are counterproductive to literacy program implementation.

There will be discrepancies between a team inventory and a technical analysis of basic skills. The data from the two kinds of study can form the basis of discussion of performance expectations and basic skills needs in the workplace. The data provide the human resource group with a general skills-based context from which to begin, and periodically revisit, discussions of basic skills needs within the corporation, division, department, or work team.

Basic Skills Assessments

Reading, English as a second language, and basic math assessments should be selected or developed and correlated to job tasks. Many excellent testing instruments are available, but not all well-designed tests are equally appropriate for a job-related education program.

Tests selected for a job-related basic skills program should be easy to take, easy to administer, and criterion referenced. Criterion referencing ties test items to specific skills instead of group performance norms. This is important for basic skills programs because it allows the program planner to correlate the test items to specific job duties and gives employees immediate, specific, and useful information about steps to take to improve job performance or prepare for job growth.

Selecting Items or Tests. Whether assessments are developed in-house or purchased ready-made, the process of selection remains the same. Using the job-related basic skills competencies identified in the minimum competency inventory described above, the training team reviews possible test material and selects items that match the competencies required for the job or range of jobs for which the assessment is being developed.

The format of the material should be carefully considered. In the United States, tests are used to select and support the academically successful in furthering their schooling. At the same time tests reinforce the inability of poor academic performers to compete in schooling. Since most school leavers end up in the work force, trainers should expect, as a rule of thumb, that workers will have poor performance expectations and relatively high levels of anxiety when faced with formal tests.

Test anxiety can badly bias performance to the degree that the training team should consider whether there is a net advantage to using formal testing for basic skills assessment. Informal assessments, composed of demonstrably job-related items and administered in an informal although supervised environment, can deliver more reliable feedback to both the assessor and the employee about the employee's skills and skill deficiencies.

The ideal job-related assessment system is easy for employees to use. Employees should feel that they are getting as much useful job-related information as the tester gets. Employee feedback should be specific. In the best circumstances, employee participation is voluntary and the job-related assessment system is designed to protect the confidentiality of the employee's results. Technological advances in computer-assisted testing and computer-based interactive video are making it feasible to use these powerful tools for employee assessments.

Advocacy for Basic Skills

As part of an overall basic skills program a consulting and advocacy role can be developed for employees at risk of losing job classification or at risk of termination because of basic skills deficiencies.

As the workplace becomes more sophisticated there is a trend for work to become more complex. Employees are asked to be more flexible and to work on a variety of tasks. The need for increased flexibility means that some employees with formerly good performance records may be unable to adapt to new situations quickly enough to meet schedule demands. In this way a good worker can quickly become a problem employee.

Whatever a corporation's policies and procedures, the human resource development group will want to explore this problem with other personnel professionals and explore the possibility of establishing a review process for employees who cannot manage reassignments. One possibility to take into consideration is whether the employee's literacy skills are congruent with the requirements of the new assignment.

The Basic Skills Job Study

If a basic skills job study is called for, an educational consultant would be called in to conduct it. The consultant might be a member of the training team who has skills in job analysis, counseling, and basic skills education. Or an educational specialist may be contracted from outside the company to perform this service. If an outside person is brought in, care should be taken to select a consultant who has educational assessment competencies, understands job analysis, and can maintain a neutral role. If an outside consultant is used, it may be useful to find one or two people who can consult regularly. Over time these consultants will develop a rich knowledge of the basic skills required in a variety of tasks across the organization.

The consultant's first task is to meet with the supervisor and document the basic skills required for the assignment in question. Using specific job information and material from the basic competency studies and job-related assessments described above, the consultant then develops a specific assignment-related assessment for the employee. Next, the consultant meets with the employee and, after explaining the procedure and how the results will be used, conducts the assessment. Wherever possible, preliminary feedback should be given to the employee right away. Finally, the consultant reviews the results of the assessment and writes a confidential report for the training group.

The member of the training group who meets with the review board writes a report to the board summarizing the consultant's findings and making official recommendations. If there appears to be a mismatch between the employee and the assignment, reassignment to a more appropriate position or training to support the employee may be more appropriate than disciplinary action. For an employee who needs additional basic skills the training group may recommend intensive job-related literacy training, a referral to an outside program, or enrollment in a regular basic skills program.

Job-Related Literacy Tutorials

Occcasionally an employee may need an individualized job-related tutorial. This will be the case when no programs in the organization or nearby communities meet the employee's needs and the organization's objectives. The tutorial may be the outcome of a reassignment review, a performance evaluation, or in anticipation of new job skill demands.

Job-related tutorials are the most expensive form of job-related education. Tutors may need to spend as much time learning job material and designing exercises as they spend in instruction. Therefore, tutorials should be run only for people needing intensive, individual attention who would not benefit from group instruction. One explicit objective of any job-related literacy tutorial should be for the student to develop a skill level that would enable him or her to transfer to group instruction.

Selecting an Instructor. Tutorial instructors must have highly developed skills as adult educators in reading, writing, computation, or English as a second language as well as an ability to earn the confidence of both the employee and the supervisor. The tutor may be a training professional from the human resources organization or an outside consultant. The time required to make a job-related tutorial effective and the intensity of instruction suggest that literacy tutoring should not be done by the employee's peers or supervisor.

Contracting. Three elements are essential to a successful job-related tutorial: careful assessment of the job-related skill needs and the individual's skills, carefully designed and reasonable performance objectives, and commitment to the process by both the employee and the supervisor.

These elements can be managed through a contract or agreement signed by both the supervisor and the employee as well as training management. The contract should stipulate the specific, job-related objectives, the time frame, and the supervisor's participation in helping developing job-related material and conducting periodic reviews of the employee's progress.

At one large corporation which supports significant basic skills education out of a corporate budget, the cost of job-related tutorials is stipulated in the contract and cross-charged to the employee's home department on the premise that supervisors are more inclined to pay close attention to and participate in the tutorial process when they are paying for it.

Literacy Support Groups

Employees with low levels of literacy but without immediate, job-related reading needs may benefit from literacy support groups. These groups, usually run by a trained instructor and a counselor, assist members in coming to grips with their literacy problems and in testing their ability to learn new skills in a safe environment. They are most effective with participants who both know they need to improve their basic skills but are anxious about going back to school *and* have the time to explore their feelings and motivations. Literacy support groups have been run by community learning centers, corporations, and health care facilities. They can be particularly effective for men and women with learning disabilities.

An important feature of successful support groups is the dual leadership. The counselor and the instructor each bring a mixed set of skills. Groups led by an instructor alone tend to become instructional settings while counselors seldom have the specific adult educational experience necessary to understand the unique problems of the disabled reader. Since the prime objective of the group is motivation, literacy support groups should not be established unless a support network of courses and/or referrals is in place.

Referral and Linkage Networks

Even if the human resources group was prepared to offer all educational services to employees, in-house community resource networks for referrals would be critical to the program's success.

In-House Networks. In-house networks are necessary to communicate the aims of the literacy program. Overtime, the training group should become a resource to the company's medical department, assisting them in evaluating and referring employees with literacy-related or literacy-compounded disabilities.

Job analysts from the compensation group can provide cross training in conducting job studies and need to understand the relationships between the literacy skills embedded in tasks and the factors they measure to establish job values.

Personnel administrators, personal, career, and retirement counselors, union representatives, and other helping group members need to know about the literacy programs in order to represent the program and its interests to employees and to management.

First-line supervisors, industrial engineers, and process engineers are all members of corporate systems whose effectiveness can be limited by employee literacy problems. These groups should be acquainted with the literacy program, educated to how the program can increase productivity, and coached in ways to refer employees who may need assistance.

Community Networks. Human resources groups managing job-related literacy programs must be acquainted with the literacy resources in the community. Volunteer tutoring networks, hospital-based learning disorder units, community learning centers, community colleges, and libraries are all potential sources of information, staff, and consulting, as well as possible referrals for individual employees.

Every state and territory in the United States has an adult education office as part of the department of education. This body in turn supports high school equivalency programs, targeted community based education programs, and a network of local educational agencies funded to offer basic education through either local or county school systems or community colleges. Information about federally and state-funded adult basic education programs can be obtained by contacting the director of adult services in the state department of education. Some corporations have contracted with local adult education programs to tailor their services to company needs and provide programs at the workplace.

Libraries may be a source of tutoring or a resource for information about community education. In Massachusetts, for example, the state Board of Library Examiners funded the development of a comprehensive guide to publicly and privately funded literacy and basic skills programs available in the state.

The American Association for Adult and Continuing Education has a unit on Basic Skills in Business, Labor Organizations, and Industry. The unit publishes profiles of member private sector programs. In 1980, fewer than 10 programs were identified. By 1985, unit members reported private sector programming in 31 states. Copies of the unit's publications can be obtained by writing the unit chairperson in care of AAACE.

Other networks for developing programs and sharing information, such as Chamber of Commerce education committees, community college advisory boards, and ASTD chapters, are becoming increasingly important as awareness of the need for reeducation in the work force becomes more widespread.

Basic Skills Classes

When a sufficiently large portion of the work force needs skill development, it becomes worthwhile to develop and offer classes in-house. Not everyone will be able to take classes at the same time, so the pool of employees needing the skill must be big enough to support classes over two or more course cycles. If only a few people need a priority skill, tutorials or referrals to a community program plus additional support to facilitate job-related transfer might be more appropriate.

Finally, to warrant including in-house classes in a basic skills program, the skills need must be sufficiently long-term to allow time for employees to develop the skills. Employees with immediate, critical skills problems or who work in operations that are in the process of revision will not receive immediate benefit from basic skills classes, because classes require time for the employees to develop and apply skills. More appropriate program responses might be intensive tutoring or training or even redesign of the operation to accommodate the group's skill deficiencies. Of course these are short-term responses. But they can buy production time while the requisite skills are being developed by other means.

Direct, instructor-led group instruction remains the most cost-effective delivery system for many kinds of basic skills learning. A well-trained instructor, a competency-based, job-related curriculum, and individualized learning are the keys to effective adult basic skills classes.

Needs Assessment. The beginning of any successful basic skills class is in three broad forms of needs assessment. The identification of minimum competencies needed in a job or group of jobs provides a baseline to begin program planning— telling the planners what people *must be able* to do today. The planning group should then identify the optimal skill proficiencies the organization desires from the work force—what they *would like* workers to be able to do. These exercises provide program goals and establish a skills continuum within which a course of study can be developed.

Finally, summary information from individual and group basic skills assessments and from studying and cataloging operational errors in the target jobs will show clusters of skill deficiencies at various levels of sophistication along the continuum—telling the planners what workers *can* do. Since the purpose of the needs assessment exercise is to determine how well a group performs a skill, it is only necessary to have reliable measures of the overall performance of a statistically valid subset of members of the group. By comparing these data the planning team can identify clusters of skill needs that require program priority.

This approach to planning is useful for several reasons. It is relatively inexpensive. The results can be easily expressed in terms that make sense to line management and will generate employee motivation. Further, the data give the planners the most effective context for planning high transferability as each skill specified in the program can be documented by the data as both needed by the operation and lacking in the group.

The course of study will be developed from the needs assessment materials. Instructional materials may be a combination of commercial adult education materials and lessons and examples built by the staff from job-related work examples. To run efficiently, the course should be divided into sessions; 3 to 6 hours a week for 10 to 15 weeks per session appears to be normal. Whatever the content of the class, the pace at which the students move through the material should be individualized. Individuals will move through course content at very different paces, depending on their developmental level and the complexity of the material they are studying.

Staffing. Successful instructors in job-related basic skills programs must have special skills. They must know their field of study and be able to interpret it to adults. Successful instructors have a strong background—whether developed formally or informally—in learning theory and psychology of learning. They must know traditional instructional methodology to understand how it did not work with their students. And they must be able to apply developmental learning principles to their students' learning needs in order to teach the course content and clarify the learning process. This will enable students to apply course content back on the job.

Few companies can afford to employ math, reading, writing, and English as a second language instructors full time. Some basic skills programs use company employees to teach basic skills. While the employee population can be an excellent resource, the instructor or employee must always consider his or her principal assignment as the first priority, and changes in shift or primary assignment can mean a sudden loss of an instructor.

Another approach is to hire part-time instructors. This approach allows for more flexible scheduling. The human resources manager who uses part-time staff has the problem of integrating staff with disparate schedules into a team, but the payoff in program flexibility and quality is very high.

A third way of staffing basic skills classes is to contract with an outsider vendor. Many community colleges, adult learning centers, and independent adult education consultants can provide this service. The program manager should be very careful that the vendor understands the company's goals and objectives and is prepared to meet them. Instructors should also be interviewed before they are accepted to ensure they will be able to meet the company's goals as well as their own. Key attributes to consider in a vendor or instructor are an ability to focus on both the company's need *and* the employee's, a willingness to learn more about the job-related context of instruction, an understanding of a developmental approach to instruction, and high professional standards.

Alternatives to Formal Classes. In any setting there will be individuals who cannot arrange their work or personal time to make scheduled classes. For these individuals, print- or computer-based programmed and guided study materials, referrals to community programs, and computer-driven interactive video may be alternatives. The company's tuition assistance program can be tapped for tuition for community programs. As the cost of computer-based interactive video systems is driven down, publishing companies will produce more material in this medium.

In using any of these alternatives, the program manager must be sure to make additional support available to the student. Study skills might be necessary for students to understand how to arrange their time. Computer literacy skills might be a prerequisite. The program manager should be prepared to establish that outside programs are capable of delivering the skills and services the employee needs. One reason some companies end up investing in in-house classes is the difficulty in finding individualized, developmental approaches in community education. If the basic skills program has developed an individual employee assessment system, that component can be used to help employees who are using outside resources or informal learning experiences outside the classroom to document their progress.

Evaluation and Feedback. Since the purpose of a basic skills program is to support employees in developing skills for improving job performance or for job growth, good evaluation and feedback measures must be established that give unambiguous performance feedback to both the employees and their supervisors. Even if a class or program meets all the human resource group's performance criteria, both the students and line management must understand how the program worked to meet the students' needs—and how meeting those needs helped meet the line's performance objectives. The advantage of offering a competency-based program built on job-related performance objectives is that the instructor and the program manager can easily interpret classroom progress into measures understandable by the line.

Progress Reports. Individual progress reports are vital to program success. They are especially useful where the course content is individualized and each student is working at his or her own pace. This report can be in the form of a one-page memorandum on company letterhead. It can be printed in bulk. The memo is addressed to the employee with copies for the supervisor (if the student is attending class on company time or at company expense), and for the training office file.

The first section should be a brief, simply worded description of the course and its overall objectives. It can be part of the printed copy. The hardest part usually is writing this description simply but completely.

The second section should detail the student's class attendance. Lines should be included for the inclusive dates of the course and for a list of specific dates the student was absent from class. It is important that attendance be documented, both for the record and to provide a context for the student's rate of progress. Most programs also note perfect attendance. And some make note, in the case of absences, of the reason.

The third section is a narrative of the student's specific goals and his or her progress toward achieving them. This section may be brief but must be clearly and simply written. If there is little progress, this is the place for an explanation.

The final section should include a few lines about next steps for the student's education. There should always be recommendations for next steps in a world of lifelong learning.

The progress report should be discussed with the student before the course ends. He or she should understand that a copy will be forwarded to the supervisor. The supervisor might be encouraged to include the progress report in the employee's folder. A few days after the report has been sent the instructors or program manager should contact the supervisor to see if there are any questions about the employee's performance in the classroom. This is the instructor's or program manager's opportunity to engage the supervisor in reflecting on the relationship between what the student learned in the classroom and what the employee does on the job.

Course and Program Evaluation

Objective tests are only one way to measure course success—and in the job-related program they are often not the most effective. To determine if a program has been effective, the program manager will want to review student attendance records, look at progress reports and compare the results with earlier assessments, conduct ongoing discussions with supervisors and instructors about the progress of the students and the evolution of the course objectives, and observe in the classroom. As a program evolves and stabilizes, these activities might be sampled over a period of time, but in general, half of the program manager's time devoted to the program should be spent in evaluation and planning. The more of this groundwork that is done the more successful the program will be, especially if the program is largely staffed by part-time instructors or by a vendor. In that case the program manager becomes the key link back to the production line and his or her evaluation role becomes doubly significant.

It is important to include supervisors and line managers in the evaluation process. In a job-related program, success of the program is measured by behavior change back on the job. The degree and means of support of supervisors and line management for the students attending classes and practicing new skills in the job setting should be looked at as well as the performance of the students and instructors. The program manager can use the evaluation session as a teaching tool to educate management in how the program can be useful to them and about the role they need to play to make the program successful.

Summary

The workplace of the future will be inhabited largely by the workers of today. Assisting them to be ready to learn the skills they will be needing is one of the most important contributions the human resource professional can make. Sensitive management of job-related basic skills programs is one means for assisting marginal contributors to become more employable and enabling good workers to become better.

Resources

Newsletters

Basic Training
Lorrie Verplagtse & Associates
201 Maple Street
Attleboro, MA 02703

Business Council for Effective Literacy
1221 Avenue of the Americas—35th Floor
New York, NY 10020

Organizations

American Association for Adult &
Continuing Education
Business and Industry Unit
1201 Sixteenth St., N.W., Suite 1301
Washington, DC 20036

National Center for Research in Vocational
Education
Ohio State University
1960 Kenny Road
Columbus, OH 4321

San Mateo County Office of Education
Redwood City, CA 94063

Further Reading

Davies, W., *How To Teach Adults*, Learning Resources Network, Manhattan, KS, 1981.

DeLong, D., "A Look at Return on Investment: The Cost of Remediation," *Training News*, March 1982.

Duggan, P., *Literacy at Work*, Northeast-Midwest Institute: The Center for Regional Policy, Washington, DC, 1985.

Elsasser, N., and V. John-Steiner, "An Interactional Approach to Advancing Literacy," in *Thought and Language/Language and Reading*, edited by H. Wolf, M. McQuillan, and E. Radwin, *Harvard Educational Review*, Cambridge, MA, 1980.

Functional Literacy and the Workplace, American Council of Life Insurance, Washington, DC, 1986.

Hunter, C., and D. Harmon, *Adult Illiteracy in the United States*, McGraw-Hill, New York, 1979.

Jordan, D., *Dyslexia in the Classroom*, Charles E. Merrill, Columbus, OH, 1972.

Lean, E., "Learning Disabled Trainees: Finding and Helping the 'Hidden Handicapped,'" *Training and Development Journal*, September 1983.

Lerche, R., *Effective Adult Literacy Programs*, Cambridge Books, New York, 1985.

McCord, A., *The Impact of Basic Skills on Human Resource Management in the Retailing Industry*, National Retail Merchants Association, New York, 1983.

Martin, A., "Help Wanted: Only Skilled Labor Need Apply," *Training and Development Journal*, June 1983.

Mayer, S., *Guidelines for Effective Literacy Programs*, B. Dalton, Bookseller, Minneapolis, MN, 1984.

Patience, W., and D. Whitney, *What Competencies Are Measured by the Tests of General Educational Development (GED)*? The GED Testing Service of the American Council on Education, Washington, DC, 1982.

Resnick, D., and L. Resnick, "The Nature of Literacy: An Historical Exploration," in *Thought and Language/Language and Reading*, edited by H. Wolf, M. McQuillan, and E. Radwin, *Harvard Educational Review*, Cambridge, MA, 1980.

Sticht, T., and L. Mikulecky, *Job-Related Basic Skills: Cases and Conclusions*, The National Center for Research in Vocational Education, Columbus, OH, 1984.

Sticht, T., ed., *Reading for Working*, Human Resources Research Organization, Alexandria, VA, 1975.

Stoker, R., "Building Intellectual Capital: The Role of Education in Industry," in *The Yearbook of Adult and Continuing Education*, 1980–1981, edited by P. Cunningham, Marquis Academic Media, Chicago, IL, 1980.

Winterbauer, M., *Basic Skills Needs in Business and Industry*, Literacy 85, St. Paul, MN, 1985.

42
Communication Training*

Thomas E. Anastasi, Jr.

Thomas E. Anastasi, Jr., has been in private practice as a communication training consultant in Medfield, Massachusetts, since 1969. Since then, he has served over 200 clients throughout the United States and Canada with training and consulting services in all aspects of written and oral communication. Before starting his own firm, he served as director of the Communication Training Institute of the U.S. Civil Service Commission's Boston Regional Training Center, as a management development specialist for Bethlehem Steel, and as assistant professor of Adult Education at Northeastern University. Anastasi has published widely. His most recent books are Listen! and the Desk Guide to Communication. He is also active as a member of the faculty of the Center for Management Development at Bryant College.

Every organization, public or private, large or small, needs clear, effective communication to function well. So, who needs communication training? Just about anyone at any level is a possible candidate for it, and prime candidates are those people who aren't functioning effectively in meeting their communication responsibilities or taking best advantage of their opportunities to communicate. Of course, sometimes it's a good idea to reinforce the communication skills of good communicators, but that's best left until you've dealt with the deficiencies of the less skilled.

Good communication training should conform to two principal criteria: It should

---

* In part, this chapter is an update of "Manpower and Career Planning," by John E. McMahon and Joseph C. Yeager, which was Chapter 11 of the Second Edition of the *Training and Development Handbook*.

be simple, and it should be skill-oriented. Good communication training, like good communication, needs to be simple. It needs to be simply designed to meet the needs of our participants. It should not have a convoluted design intended to comfort the soul of the trainer. It should be skill-oriented. It should not aim to make the participants *aware*, or *sensitive*, or even *knowledgeable*, rather it should leave them with the ability to communicate better.

Training in the sending skills, speaking and writing, should not be directed to helping the participants to achieve some given level of glibness. Style is a fine thing, but when it's merely a mask for a lack of competent content, it's not good communication, and trainers do their clients a disservice by fostering it.

Training in the receiving skills, reading and listening, should help participants dig for meaning. It's not enough to teach people to read at the speed of light or to absorb words in an environment plagued with aural static.

A good program will do more than teach skills in the medium that is its subject. It will help the participants to see that medium and their skills in the context of the situations in which they must actually communicate. A writing course, for example, should show people when to write and when to choose some other medium. A program to train interviewers should not only give skill in that process but also show participants the limitations of the process as an information gathering tool.

Because any training experience is finite and shortlived, it should show the learners how to continue to build skill on their own, after the program is over. Communication, as a process or as a skill, must always be seen in the context of the situation and the people involved. Good skill training never overlooks that.

Communication Training as Part of Other Programs

Much skill training is offered on its own, for example, programs in technical writing, oral presentation, interviewing, and the like. But a communication skills section can also be an important adjunct to your other training. Executive, management, and supervisory development programs can benefit from a communication skills component, as can courses in appraisal interviewing, sales, customer relations, secretarial effectiveness, and others.

Communication is another word for dealing with people, and any other program that involves human relations, in any way, may offer an opportunity for increasing communication skills. I recently conducted a program for a large insurance company as part of its customer relations training. The participants had to deal with customers in many ways, including writing letters to them. The firm's management felt it was extremely important that the tone and content of its correspondence reflect the company's commitment to meet the needs of its policyholders; so I was retained to train their letter writers in the skills necessary to do that. A review of your own training objectives may disclose similar opportunities to use communication training to achieve your own goals.

Program Planning

In planning communication training, as an independent course or as a part of another program, consider your objectives. What are you trying to accomplish? What skills will prospective participants need to do their jobs better? What are the problems, if any, which prompted the training?

Are you, for instance, planning a management course to help reduce an unacceptable turnover rate? If so, why do you have such high turnover? If it's due to poor communication by management, communication skills training for those people may help. But if it's due to a poor wage or benefit package or dissatisfaction with working conditions, then communication training, while "nice," will do little to remedy the underlying causes of the turnover problem.

If you don't know the causes, you must explore them. Are your supervisors conducting exit interviews? Should they be? Do they have the skill to do so? Do they need training in how to do so? Would this provide management with better information, and would that help to alleviate the problem? If the answers to questions like these suggest an affirmative trend, maybe communication skills training should be part of your strategy for dealing with your turnover problem.

Performance Orientation

Are you getting the most productive performance from your secretaries? Are they using their abilities fully? Could they, for instance, contribute more by writing for their managers or by editing what comes to their managers for signature? Would this kind of job enrichment make the secretaries' work more satisfying? It probably would, and that probably means you should give them the skills to do it.

How about your sales force? Do your people need any skill work? What makes a successful sales rep in your organization? Is communication skill, in any form, critical to maximum performance? Should training in those skills be a part of your regular sales training? Is it? If not, why not?

Identifying Needs

Talk to potential participants in your training programs to see if they perceive any needs for increased communication skills. Talk, too, with the people with whom they work: customers, colleagues, suppliers, subordinates, superiors. These interviews may flag areas susceptible to improvement through increased communication skill. Several times, I've conducted programs in proposal writing for companies. Wherever possible, with the client's permission, I try to interview their customers before designing the program. These people know better than anyone what needs to be done and what will constitute the most effective program objectives.

A review of performance appraisals can yield information useful for planning independent training in communication or for including some communication work in your other programs.

Sometimes, your evaluation program for your own training may provide useful information. I do quite a bit of work with programs designed to review and reinforce basic language skills, grammar, and punctuation. I first became aware of the need for this when I reviewed evaluation sheets from writing courses. Many people felt they needed to brush up on the basics and that such a review would enhance both their skill and their confidence in writing—and they were right. It has proved to be very useful in many instances.

Performance Analysis.   Beyond all this, there is another way to determine communication skill needs: analysis of communication results. You can do it yourself, or you can hire someone else to do it for you. Essentially, it's a market research approach.

One company looked at its correspondence and found that it often took several letters and phone calls to resolve customer questions or complaints. The analysis showed this was happening because the letters that went to customers were unclear or unresponsive. This affected not only customer relations but also the cost of doing business; all those extra letters and calls were very expensive. Training the letter writers to produce better, clearer, more responsive letters had positive results. Customer relations improved, and so did its cost. There was another side benefit: the letter writers felt a lot better about themselves and their job performance. They were proud of their skill.

One caution with this kind of analysis. Make sure that you're identifying causes and not symptoms. The instance I've just cited would have turned out differently if the cause of the poor letters had been the style faults insisted upon by management as part of the perceived or actual policy. That is to say that the problem would not have been eliminated if management had not allowed the trainees to use the skills the training gave them.

A staff member or consultant can analyze your correspondence or reports or meetings or presentations to see whether there are factors which suggest training needs. This kind of quality control check can be done routinely if a staff member is competent to do the job. If a consultant must be retained for the work, you should be pretty sure a problem exists before you hire one of us for diagnosis—unless your budget has provisions for prophylaxis.

Program Design

Let your need statement read, "We need a training program which will. . . ." Then complete that statement with specific objectives. Don't be satisfied with "We need a listening course," or "We need a course in report writing," or anything that general. Those statements indicate an awareness of a problem. They should mark the beginning of your need determination, not its end. In other words, you should write the specifications before you design the product.

To help you specify your needs, think about the part of your organization and the type of skill or activity for which you're considering training. What level of performance are you getting now? Is it acceptable? If not, can training give you an acceptable level of performance? If so, what kind of training?

When you can answer those questions, you're ready for the next batch of questions:

- Who are the proposed trainees?
- What are their training needs?
- Do they have similar needs? If they do, you can develop and conduct one program of the entire population. If not, you should be thinking of more than one program, or, at least, of a branching program that will offer the same core curriculum to all, and elective modules to those who can benefit from them.
- What are the specific objectives? By *specific* objectives I mean statements like "skill in researching and writing replies to complaint letters sent to senior management" or "ability to edit the work of a technical proposal team" or "skill at planning and delivering elements of the sales training program for new hires." Those objectives are likely to be more useful than general objectives like "writing skill," "learn how to edit," or "develop presentation skill." Of course, there are times when people need to develop general writing, editing, or speaking skills because their work calls for them to make many applications of those skills. Fine. But if the skill need is specific, let the objectives be similarly specific.

- What, if any, are the other considerations? There may be elements like time, money, resources, and organizational constraints. You'll probably learn more about these as you go through the design phase, but it's good to begin considering them as early as you can so you'll have more time to think about alternatives.

If you have an internal capability to conduct your own program, you'll be concerned with design; if not, your concern will be selecting an outside resource or package. For either use, let's consider design criteria and the process through which we can develop or select a well-designed program. This involves extensive work with the potential participants and their managers. Communication skill training should lead to behavior change, to improved performance, and the forces that inhibit or enhance behavior come from the people and customs of the organization.

If you know what you're doing, you can, without undue effort, design a program to improve performance in some skill area. But it will come to naught if the participants refuse to change, or if their managers refuse to allow them to do so, or if the organizational climate—or, at least, what is perceived as the organizational climate—militates against change. To avoid running afoul of those resistances, involve the participants and their managers early in the design phase. Your program will accomplish little unless it matches the behavior the trainees are willing and able to emit and which their managers and the organizational culture will permit and reinforce. Discussion and negotiation of acceptable behavior change should take place before the training program starts, not during or after it.

That doesn't mean that the participants should design the program; it means that the trainer should be familiar with their perceptions of training needs and program objectives. The trainer may decide to go ahead with aspects of the program the participants will resist, but if the trainer has explored this ahead of time, the resistance will not come as a surprise, and the trainer will be prepared to deal with it. I don't mean to suggest that precourse discussions should center on resistance; there well may be none. What is more likely is that the participants, who know their own communication problems and opportunities well, will be able to offer valuable comments and suggestions.

Precourse meetings with the participants' managers are different. The managers can contribute because they see the participants' communication behavior—and from a different and wider perspective than the participants have. It is also they who must support and reinforce any lasting behavior change—and it is they who can advertently or inadvertently thwart anything that happens in the training experience. Behavior change happens back on the job, not in the training room, and the manager to a great extent determines what happens on the job. The manager and the trainer, then, are partners in designing and bringing about improved performance. A precourse meeting is an excellent time to clarify and harmonize that partnership and to plan for follow-up support. For communication skill training to be effective, you must have management support. Training from the top down can often be the best way to get this. Failing that, precourse conferences can be very helpful.

Build on Existing Skills

Your participants are experienced communicators. Take advantage of that experience. If, for instance, you'll be training people in oral presentation skills, realize that most of them have given many presentations and that most of those presentations have been acceptable. Your task is not to turn bad presenters into good presenters. Your task is to help each participant to improve, to take better advantage of his or her presentation opportunities. Take advantage of their experience. It will have made them aware of their problem areas and receptive to your suggestions for improvement. Many presentations, for instance, are poorly organized, not because the speakers want them that way but because they've never had the chance to learn how to organize their presentations. If you can give them skill in organizing, they'll be receptive, but make sure you give adequate, effective instruction. If your exposition of organizing techniques for presentations is cursory or unskilled, you'll encounter resistance—not because your participants don't want to organize their presentations, but because a cursory or inadequate treatment fails to teach them the skills they need to do the job.

Building Skill

Expository treatment alone is not adequate for good communication training. You don't want your learners merely *to know* about the subject, you want to give them skills they can use to communicate better; so design your program to develop skill and ability, not merely knowledge and awareness. Design your program to build skill.

There's another kind of experience you can build on. Good communication is other-centered. Good writing is reader-centered; good speaking, listener-centered; good reading, writer-centered. Your student writers have been readers, and you can use that experience to let them develop insights into what makes good writing. The same is certainly true of the other skills.

People are often insecure about their communication skills. They realize those skills are important to them and to their proper functioning, but they often don't feel competent. That is true of people at all levels in organizations; it is sometimes not obvious at the higher levels. This insecurity can make some participants defensive. Few people, regardless of the length of their educational experience, have had adequate training in communication. Unfortunately, that is becoming truer each year. What many people have learned about communication they have learned by repeating the wrong ways of doing it time after time. In school, people learn how to write term papers. When they leave school, they try to write business reports the same way, and that produces very bad writing. Yet they think it's supposed to be the right way to do it because that's what they were taught. As a communication trainer, you have to deal with these issues.

Can you overcome these previous experiences and the habits they have engendered? Sure. Fortunately, the practices of these folk are ungrounded in logic. The tie is emotional. They write (or speak, or read, or listen) as they do because they know no other way to do it. If you can show them another way, you well may effect the desired changes.

You won't do that by following the course that many trainers do. Their approach is to use horrible examples to show the participants how poor their communication skills are—and then they tell them to stop doing it that way. But they don't show them how to do it. If you are trying to extinguish undesirable communication habits and practices, you must be prepared to help your participants develop useful skill in the desired behaviors.

Of course, examples and cases of poor communication can be helpful, but they should not be the main focus. Make the main focus a positive approach to learning how it should be done. Don't let it become an exercise in avoiding poor communication. Your skill training program should be designed to give the trainees the maximum number of positive experiences with the skill being learned. Design your program so that it allows the participants to succeed often.

A Checklist for Program Design

As you design your own program or check the design of a vendor's program, compare it with this list:

- Are your program goals consistent with behavior change that is:
  - Likely to be acceptable to the trainees?
  - Likely to be reinforced by their managers?
- Are the skills to be learned likely to be useful back on the job?
- Do you have enough support from the top to assure that the organizational climate will be receptive to the new skills?
- Does your course announcement accurately communicate the course content and objectives?
- Does the design take advantage of the participants' precourse experiences?
- Is positive skill building the main thrust of the course?
- Will the course develop skill, or will it merely provide information?
- Does the course allow for the development of individual styles of communication?
- Is there adequate opportunity for application and reinforcement of the skilled behaviors? Is the proposed instructor broadly enough prepared to make the learning experience useful to the participants?

Identifying and Using Resources

People

A communication skills trainer should have sufficient background to see the skill in the context of the trainees' job responsibilities, and sufficient depth and skill to develop the participants' individual styles.

Experience is vital. Members of a training staff who will conduct communication training will benefit from an apprenticeship with an experienced trainer. This should begin with observation, followed by discussion with the experienced trainer, followed by team teaching with the lead trainer, followed by solo teaching. It is not enough to have the new instructor observe a program, note another instructor's materials and approach, and then attempt to teach the skill. The result of this approach will be shallow training that wastes time.

Academic preparation is a variable of undetermined value. Some course preparation in the skill area is helpful, but experience may substitute for it. The trainer should have a fluency in the principles of human behavior because communication is a social process and is best taught in that context, lest the training produce mere word arrangers who operate in the blissful ignorance of a vacuum. Experience in dealing with adults is essential. Someone whose experience has been solely with children will likely fare ill with a group of adults who have a background of experience in the skill being taught and a need for useful, immediately applicable skills. This does not mean that a high school English teacher cannot teach an industrial writing course, but it does mean that such a teacher's qualification must extend beyond those required by the local school board.

The instructor should be adept in the skill taught. It does not necessarily hold true that the best speaker in the house should be asked to teach an oral presentation seminar. Your experience has, no doubt, shown you the difference between being able to use a skill and being able to teach others to do so. An instructor's credibility and effectiveness both depend on his or her ability to use well the skill being taught. Your interviewing skills instructor should be a good interviewer, and your presentation skills instructor should be a good speaker whose own presentations to the class are well organized and competently delivered.

Experience should be as directly related as possible. If, for instance, you're going to offer a letter writing course, it should probably not be taught by someone whose experience has been exclusively in training report writers or advertising copywriters.

Consultants may prove to be a helpful resource, and are of two kinds: There are those of us who earn our livings in that field, the outside, fee-paid consultants; and your own colleagues from other departments within your organization who, though they do not work in training, may have valuable skills you can use in your training work.

A consultant may take care of your entire program from needs determination, through program design, to actual presentation of the training, or the consultant may work on only one or more of those processes.

A consultant may serve as a guest lecturer for part of a larger program. You may be able to handle the design and presentation in all but a few topical areas and may find it helpful to have a consultant augment your program in those areas. I've done that sort of thing for clients in their sales training programs, for instance. Their own training and sales staff have been quite capable of designing and presenting the bulk of the program, but have lacked expertness in training the salespeople in oral presentation skills or in proposal writing. Thus, I was able to work on only those parts of the overall training program.

You may choose to hire a consultant to design a program for you and your colleagues to teach. Consultants often get assignments like this when working for clients who have large populations to train and who cannot afford to hire the consultant to do all the training. In that type of relationship, we design the package and the supporting material, pilot or field test it, then train the client's instructors to do the rest of the work.

Commercial Packages

Some are good, others bad. Some are so bad that they're always bad. None is so good that it's always good. Before selecting any package, clarify your requirements. Know what you want the package to do before you check to see what's available. The package should fit your needs; you should not modify your needs to fit what's available in the market. Sure, you may sometimes have to trade a requirement against availability, but those trades should be made only for incidental requirements. Your basic goals should remain intact.

Commercial packages, by their nature, must be prepared to meet general needs, but your needs are specific. Of course, if your needs are common ones, there may be a package that will meet them. You may want to consider blending a commercial package with some material of your own design to produce a program that will do just what you want it to do.

Training packages, particularly programmed instruction and other self-paced mediums, may be quite well suited to tutorial or remedial situations.

Texts

As with commercial packages, plan your objectives first. Your objectives, not text availability, should determine the course content and method. The instructor who will have to work with the book and with the class should have the right to choose the text to be used.

The text shouldn't duplicate the course content, but it should amplify and expand the in-class coverage. It should also be chosen to serve as a postclass reference. A text may serve as an excellent reference and refresher. It is therefore usually unwise to try to cut costs by collecting the texts at the end of a course to use with subsequent classes.

Conducting Communication Training

1. *Keep class size small.* Groups of 12 to 18 usually prove to be best. They provide enough people for spirited discussion and allow each trainee to have ample opportunity for skill building practice and application.

2. *Emphasize workshop sessions.* The majority of sessions, particularly when the subject is any form of oral skill, should be practical sessions in which the students practice the skill under the guidance of a skilled instructor. The comments of the other participants are a valuable contribution and allow a greater sharing of experience. For oral programs, in particular, it is a good idea to confine lecture to the beginning of the program. The rest of the instructor's contribution can then be offered in comments and suggestions or through short impromptu lectures suggested by the development of the class.

For programs in writing and other skills, we have found it best to interweave exposition and practical application.

3. *Meet individual needs.* The skills of communication are those which many trainees associate with English classes in school, and for many of them, this was not one of life's high points; so deemphasize any similarities with those earlier experiences.

In any communication skills training group, you'll find people who, before the first session begins, already have more skill than some of their fellow trainees will have when the course is over. You must help both kinds of trainees to grow in skill. The better skilled can develop still greater skill, and the less skilled can develop within the limitations of their own potentials. An informal atmosphere will help to dispel the notion that the class is really the training ground for the National Indoor Communication Championships. Encourage each participant to compete only with him- or herself, not with colleagues.

If you're not careful, a communication skills class can be a dangerous place for marginal communicators. A poorly conducted class can reinforce their feelings of inadequacy and destroy any confidence they might have had.

This doesn't mean that you should withhold honest, helpful criticism, but it does mean that your sessions should be businesslike, though informal and spontaneous. Create an atmosphere which encourages growth in skill rather than progress toward some undefined, arbitrary, and probably impossible goal.

This is where the skill and depth of the instructor that I mentioned earlier comes in. It's not enough merely to identify the participants' weaknesses. They could do that on their own, and they are quite aware of those weaknesses even without a class in communication. You must be prepared to go beyond that—to tell them what they can do about those weaknesses, and how they can remedy them. And generalities won't do the job. If a participant's writing tends to be poorly organized, it's not enough to tell that person to "focus"; you must be prepared to tell how that can be done. If a trainee speaks in a monotone, you can't just tell him or her to stop doing so; you must be prepared to tell that particular person the specific things he or she can do to remedy the problem.

Training Programs in Communication Skills

This section outlines some typical programs in the various skill areas. These outlines aren't models, for every program should be prepared and conducted to meet the needs of the men and women being trained, but they will give an idea of scope and are intended to serve as foundations and, perhaps, as themes upon which individual trainers may compose variations.

Writing Skills

This sample seminar focuses on no particular written medium, though it can be adapted to many, and could be presented to people who must write in many different mediums. Letters and reports are treated as they are the most common mediums. Develop workshop and illustrative material from a sampling of the trainees' own writing, or at least from the files that are typical of the subject matter and forms of writing typical of the participants' work.

This program is arranged in six ½-day sessions. It can be scheduled in any convenient pattern from 3 full days at once to ½ day a week for 6 weeks.

Session 1: Foundations of effective writing:
Writing for the reader
How to save time: the three steps of effective writing:
  Think
  Write
  Edit
How to approach the writing task:
  Set purpose for reader response
  Control the scope
  Organize and outline the ideas
  Get approval of the concepts and approach
  Expand the outline
  Write the rough draft
  Edit the rough and write the final copy

Session 2: How to develop a readable style:
Why we write as we do—and what to do about it
How simplicity promotes readability
The natural approach to clarity
How to use verbs for a clearer, stronger style

Session 3: How to write effective sentences:

How to make modifiers work for you
How to combine relevant ideas
How to separate irrelevant ideas
Transition: linking ideas for clarity and understanding
Parallelism: form for clarity

Session 4: How to write paragraphs that communicate:
How good paragraphs make your writing easier to read
How to use the paragraph as the basic structural unit
How to build topic focus
How to develop ideas through paragraph structure
How to build structural emphasis

Session 5: The forms of writing:
Reports that communicate
Letters and memos that get the job done

Session 6: Writing clinic: An opportunity for each participant to bring actual samples of his or her writing for discussion and analysis by the group and the seminar leader.

Oral Presentation Skills

This seminar is also arranged in four ½-day sessions and can be scheduled in any convenient pattern from 2 full days to ½ day a week for 4 weeks.

Session 1: Lecture and discussion on:
What makes a presentation effective
    Audience expectations
    Audience centeredness
    How presentations differ from speeches
Can you give an effective presentation?
    The elements of effectiveness:
      The subject
      The audience
      You
Nervousness, apprehension, tension, and butterflies
    How planning can help
    How to keep them from affecting your effectiveness
How to plan a presentation
    How to develop a clear outline
    How to begin a presentation
    How to develop the body
    How to end with impact
    How to use organization for emphasis
    How to prepare for objections and questions
    How to turn features into audience benefits
    How to point the presentation to the audience's needs
    How to prepare for the audience of people with different needs for information
    How to prepare and use notes that work for you
Session 2: Lecture and discussion on:
Communication aids
    How and when to use them
    How to keep them from distracting the audience

How to handle quantitative data
Criteria for effective visuals
Discussion on and demonstration of the more frequently used mediums
Delivery
Script, memory, or notes?
Practice and dry runs
Contact with the audience
Eye contact
Voice contact
Gesture and movement
Techniques for the tense

Session 3: Workshop: In this and the following session, the participants give presentations. Allow them to choose their own topics, but suggest that they should be typical of actual, on-the-job presentation opportunities. Videotape the presentations; then play them back for discussion and analysis. Class comments are particularly helpful as the other participants are typical of the people in the actual audiences the participants will address in their own real presentations outside the class. The instructor should be ready to give specific, concrete help to correct any deficiencies and to recognize and reinforce skilled behavior.

Session 4: Essentially a repetition of the last session, only this one should build on the learning of the previous session. Conclude the workshop by showing the participants how to build on the learning experience of the seminar and continue their skill development on their own.

The seminar outlined above is suitable for six to eight participants. To double that number, keep sessions 1 and 2 as outlined, then divide the group into two subgroups (let's call them *A* and *B*), and follow this schedule:

Session 1: All attend
Session 2: All attend
Session 3: Subgroup *A* attends
Session 4: Subgroup *B* attends
Session 5: Subgroup *A* attends
Session 6: Subgroup *B* attends

If you use this schedule, don't let your seminar get too spread out. Conduct sessions 3 and 4 on the same day and do the same with sessions 5 and 6.

To develop greater levels of skill, add more practice sessions. The pattern suggested here is basic and can be adapted to other uses, for example, sales presentation skills training and public speaking training.

Listening Skills

Listening is a skill. It's neither a character trait nor an aspect of personality. It's a skill that can be developed, a skill that can make people more productive and help them to improve the quality of their work—particularly if that work involves dealing with people.

Listening is an emotional and intellectual process, a search for meaning. That differentiates it from hearing, a purely physical process, the apprehension of sound; thus, good listening training will not stress hearing. Many training programs have been developed with hearing as a focus. These programs have featured tapes of speakers with difficult accents and situations with extensive background noise or other distractions. They may have their place if your goal is to teach people to discriminate sound, but if listening is your goal, they probably won't do much good.

Participants in your listening training should be learning what promotes and what inhibits their own listening. You can tell them about some things that all listeners share as advantages and limitations, but you should also help them to learn their individual strengths and weaknesses. In any case, your training program will offer only a start to listening improvement. The real learning and skill development will come after the program ends as your participants learn to listen better by consciously applying and striving to better their skills. Skill development comes with application. That's true of javelin throwing, bricklaying, surgery, cooking, and all communication skill—but it's particularly true of listening skill.

There's not a great deal that most people need to know about listening. They've already had a lifetime's use of the skill. The purpose of the training should be to help them to reconceptualize much of what they already know and to focus their attention on a few other points. I've found that a one-day training program can do the job of getting people started on the lifelong road to better listening. Lecture on and extensive discussion of the following topics have worked best for me in this one-day format:

1. You *can* listen better
   What listening really means
   Why hearing is not enough
   How to focus on the benefits of better listening

2. Your barriers to better listening—and what you can do about them
   Internal distractions
   External distractions
   How to manage and control distractions
   The trap of listening politely
   The content-delivery equation
   The scripts you write to distract yourself
   How to listen when you're arguing
   How to use listening as a persuasive technique
   The speech and thought differential
   How your lack of confidence in your listening skills can work against you
   How echoes of your own ideas distort your listening

3. How to listen with greater skill
   Recognizing and dealing with the emotional component of meaning
   How to work with the speaker for better messages
   The value of nonevaluative listening
   The appearance of listening
   Patience and how to cultivate it
   How to check your listening performance
   How to show you're really listening
   How to use a personal listening log to improve listening quality

4. Meetings worth listening to
   Agenda for an effective meeting
   Do you need a meeting?
   The cost of meetings and how to reduce it
   How to plan and participate in meetings worth listening to

5. How to listen to presentations
   Prelistening techniques
   Defending against distraction
   Visual aids can be listening aids

Dealing with a distracting style of delivery
How to work with the speaker

6. The listener interviews
The skills of an effective interviewer
How to prepare for an interview
Interview settings that maximize listening
How to keep tension low
Questions that stimulate information
Tips for specific interviews
Selection interviews
Appraisal interviews
Exit interviews

7. Epilogue: How to continue your skill development

Reading Skills

Many years ago, reading programs abounded. They had titles like "Rapid Reading" and "Speed Reading" and promised that their participants would learn to read faster than a speeding locomotive and comprehend tall buildings at a single bound, and they were quite popular for quite a while. Many used machinery of various types—tachistoscopes and shutters and the like—and others had films and other devices to train eyeballs to flick along and fixate only on groups of words. There don't seem to be as many of them around these days.

Many alumni of these programs questioned their long-term value, and many trainers began to think that the whole idea was only a fad. Well, is there a place in a valid training plan for a reading skills program? There may be. Some people do have to plow through vast quantities of written material as part of their jobs, and they may need to learn how to handle that chore more efficiently. In the main, they don't need speed reading or much work on perceptual technique, but they well may use some help in managing their reading loads and processing the piles in their in baskets. A little work on speed and one or two perceptual tips might also be in order—mainly those that help participants to avoid bad habits like vocalization, lip reading, and regression.

Then, too, people might need to understand many of the same things that they need to know to develop listening skill. The receiving skills, listening and reading, have much in common; so a couple of hours on reading might well be a useful adjunct to a listening program. Of course, you could offer a brief reading program as an independent offering. However you decide to do it, consider the following topics as you build your program.

1. How to manage your reading
Purposeful reading
Prereading techniques
How to evaluate what you read
How to categorize your reading load
How to delegate your reading load
How to control the volume of paper that comes to you
How to train the people who write to you

2. Perception and reading
Lip reading
Tracing and panning

Regression and how to deal with it
The importance of varied reading rates

3. Specialized reading
How to read graphs and statistics (you should add to this section any special formats the participants regularly read, such as contracts, proposals, or specifications)

Multiple Skills Programs

As I've already noted, some programs combine naturally, such as listening and reading. The same happy blending can be true of the sending skills, speaking and writing. Participants in either of those programs must learn to organize ideas and how to link ideas for coherence. Both must learn to analyze their intended receivers and to construct receiver-centered messages. Both must know when to write and when to speak, and there are other common skills.

You can often take advantage of these commonalities, by designing one program to impart both skills to people who have need of both. This not only saves time and money, but it provides additional reinforcement as well.

The same blending can occur with contrasting skills. Speakers can learn much about their skill by considering the listening process and how their messages can take best advantage of it.

I have several times designed for clients programs which spanned the range of communication skills for their personnel who needed facility in all aspects of communication. These programs have dealt with a blending of skill training in speaking, writing, listening, interviewing, and meeting and conference leadership and participation. Because the skills have much in common, they reinforced each other and we were able to accomplish a great deal in a relatively short time—certainly in much less time than it would have taken for several courses, one on each of the skills. Your own training needs may suggest similar combinations to you. If so, don't hesitate to explore the possibilities.

Evaluating Communication Training

Communication training is skill training; thus, the best measure is the skills the participants show on the job after the training program is long over. Long-term evaluation yields the most reliable results. Sure, you may choose to conduct an end-of-course evaluation and this may give you some useful information, but it may also measure only the pleasingness of the program rather than its value.

Skill takes time and application to develop. Your participants need time to try the course principles and techniques back on the job, and to adapt them to their own styles and environments. Thus, a delayed evaluation conducted 2 to 6 months after the completion of the training program can be most helpful to trainers who want to keep their program responsive to their trainees' needs.

This delayed evaluation should be of two types: participant reaction and communication skill analysis. For the first type, ask the participants for their impressions of the program and its usefulness back on the job. For the second, the trainer should analyze the former participants' current skill as demonstrated by their job performance for comparison with precourse behavior and the program's goals.

More simply put, if the program was on report writing, read the participants' reports before and after the course. If the results are positive, you can be pretty sure the course did its job. If the results are negative or show no change, check into it. Perhaps the course was at fault, or perhaps the fault lies with what we have called organizational climate. People or policies which inhibit skill application may have kept the participants from applying the skills they learned. If that's the case, you'll have to change your course selection procedures or do something to neutralize the inhibiting people or processes.

However you choose to evaluate your programs, remember that skill in communication, not knowledge about it, should have been the goal of your communication training program. That skill, then, is not just the best measure of your program—it is its only real measure.

Bibliography

Anastasi, Thomas E., Jr., *Desk Guide to Communication*, 2d ed., Van Nostrand Reinhold, New York, 1981.

Anastasi, Thomas E., Jr., *Listen! Techniques for Improving Communication Skills*, Van Nostrand Reinhold, New York, 1982.

Ebbitt, Wilma R., and David R. Ebbitt, *Writer's Guide and Index to English*, 7th ed., Scott, Foresman and Company, Chicago, 1982.

Gallagher, William J., *Report Writing for Management*, Addison-Wesley Publishing Company, Reading, MA, 1969.

Gallagher, William J., *Writing the Business and Technical Report*, Van Nostrand Reinhold, New York, 1981.

Hall, E.C., *The Silent Language*, Doubleday & Company, Garden City, NY, 1973.

Haney, William V., *Communication and Interpersonal Behavior*, 4th ed., Richard D. Irwin, Inc., Homewood, IL, 1979.

Hayakawa, S.I., *Language in Thought and Action*, 4th ed., Harcourt Brace Jovanovich, New York, 1978.

Leedy, Paul D., *Read with Speed and Precision*, McGraw-Hill Book Company, New York, 1963.

Meuse, Leonard F., Jr., *Mastering the Business and Technical Presentation*, Van Nostrand Reinhold, New York, 1980.

Nichols, Ralph G., and Leonard A. Stevens, *Are You Listening?* McGraw-Hill Book Company, New York, 1957.

Santeuesanio, Richard P., *Developing Reading Skills for Business and Industry*, Van Nostrand Reinhold, New York, 1981.

Strunk, William, and E.B. White, *The Elements of Style*, 3d ed., The Macmillan Company, New York, 1973.

43
Career Development

John E. McMahon

Stephen K. Merman

John E. McMahon is Director of Worldwide Management Development at Johnson Wax in Racine, Wisconsin, where he directs executive succession planning and management development. He joined Johnson Wax in 1977 after 20 years with Union Carbide and 5 years with Smith Kline, in Human Resource Development. He graduated with a B.S. from St. Vincent College and added an M.S. from Canisius College. He also attended advanced courses in personnel administration and organization development. He has designed and conducted human resource planning, career planning, and management resource development programs at several colleges and universities, including the University of Michigan (Division of Management Education). He has also conducted life/career planning workshops and management development programs for many business organizations. He served as the 1985–1986 chairman of the Career Development Professional Practice Area for ASTD, and received the Society's Career Development Professional Award in 1983.

Stephen K. Merman is a principal of PMG, Inc., a Denver-based career development company. Merman has a national reputation for his extensive involvement, research, and publication in the areas of career development and career management programs for organizations and individuals. He is a proponent of change and growth, and is considered a catalyst and facilitator in helping individuals take responsibility for their personal and professional growth and development. He has held leadership positions in activities for ASTD at both the local and national levels and received the 1986 ASTD Torch Award. A graduate of the University of Colorado, he completed his master's and doctoral programs at the American University in Washington, D.C.

Some Definitions

Career development of employees is for many organizations the next logical phase in human resources planning. This chapter is offered as a tool for both studying and contributing to the state-of-the-art career development program. This tool can be used by the individual to describe career goals to be accomplished, assess career development actions, and choose appropriate action. For the organization, it can be used to promote systematic inquiry and communication on the organizational level and to encourage a professional interchange of ideas and experiences.

The question "How can we have a common understanding of what we are talking about?" constantly challenged our initial resistance to work on definitions. What terms are most important to understand? How do we define terms based on diverse views and expertise of academics, counselors, consultants, and industrially employed professionals?

The following commonly used terms evolved from a synthesis of concepts from the literature and the expertise of Dr. Walter Storey and the first ASTD Career Development Executive Committee, which included the authors. The twofold purpose is to provide a point of reference and to aid in the interchange among professionals in human resource development. It is hoped that these definitions will focus attention on describing the "state of planning processes" which bear on career development as defined here.

- *Life planning.* A self-analysis process for identifying relative emphasis in one's life among work, family, leisure, education, and spiritual development.

- *Career.* The sequence of a person's work-related activities and behaviors and associated attitudes, values, and aspirations over the span of one's life.

- *Career planning.* A deliberate process for becoming aware of self, opportunities, constraints, choices, and consequences; identifying career-related goals; and "career pathing" or programming work, education, and related developmental experiences to provide the direction, timing, and sequence of steps to attain a specific career goal.

- *Career management.* An ongoing process of preparing, implementing, and monitoring career plans undertaken by the individual alone or in concert with the organization.

- *Career development.* The outcomes of actions on career plans. The outcomes that are pursued may be based on the needs of the organization and/or the individual.[1]

Career Planning

Organizational Awareness

Organizations are becoming more aware of how the basic beliefs and values of the company affect the productivity of employees. Understanding this is a skill that must not only be applied by management but must be fully understood by employees seeking to manage their careers as well. Organizational reactions to changing economic and market conditions have resulted in some questionable management decisions in many companies. Uncertainty and fear, plus rapidly changing work values among employees, have caused confusion and frustrated efforts to make sound long-term business decisions.

Rapid changes have also affected how individuals perceive the organization. Employees affected by cutbacks or job loss are more apt to reassess their traditional beliefs and values about organizations and be less committed to organizational goals, products, or company missions. Many individuals no longer believe that the organization will take care of them for the rest of their working life.

In managing a career, the individual is confronted with having to reorder priorities, review the role of the organization in his or her life, and develop strategies to cope with the organization's response to rapid change. Many individuals select self-employment, while others adopt strategies to maintain options in their chosen careers, determine their value to other career fields, and work toward creating more visibility in their profession and among business associates.

John Naisbitt and Patricia Aburdene point out that: "We are shifting the ideal of the model employee from one who carries out orders correctly to one who takes responsibility and initiative, monitors his or her own work, and uses managers and supervisors in their new roles as facilitators, teachers and consultants."[2] The term used most commonly among the enlightened careerist is "self-management," which Naisbitt and Aburdene label "the new ideal" for the American worker.

Whatever the culture, an organization must consider its basic values and beliefs and then put into action career development systems and mechanisms that reflect that culture. Organizations who fund large career centers and allow employees to attend career management seminars are examples of companies who put positive beliefs into concrete action. Examples such as these are becoming more common and represent a growing concern for employee welfare and protection.

Career planning affects the relationship the individual has with the corporate culture and the way the systems of the organization fit with individual systems.

Integrating career and organizational needs is the "new strategy," and it is becoming increasingly critical to ensure organizational effectiveness. The futurist Naisbitt states: "Today, work must provide more than just a paycheck. We want it to express ourselves and our values, to make a difference in society, and to fit harmoniously with other priorities—family, health, spirituality."[3] Career planning and development help employees achieve this balance.

The Basic Unit

The basic unit of career planning is the individual. Two different viewpoints are involved: the organization's perspective and the individual's perspective. The relationship between the organization and the individual, while reciprocal and interdependent, is also quite distinct. Human resource planning is often viewed as the macroscopic system that provides guidance for the optimum use of the organization's human resources. The human resource planning system must, however, incorporate programs and subsystems which maximize the growth of the individuals who collectively make up its human resources, and it must determine ways in which these two will interact.

Career planning is used to identify those programs which deal with the issue of individual growth and productivity within the organizational environment. Career planning deals with the determinants which will improve the individual's ability to perform given tasks as needed and to smooth the interface between the individual and the system.

The I-O Relationship

As in most relationships, the one that exists between the individual (I) and the organization (O) may change over a period of years. Such changes can be clearly seen when one compares the role of organizations toward employees 20 years ago with the role of the organization today.

Business has always involved risks; however, in the past, the general stability of the organization was communicated and generally accepted by the employees. Employment was viewed as secure if performance was acceptable. As a result, there was more allegiance and loyalty to the organization on the part of the employee. The organization's role was that of a caretaker; high productivity, loyalty, and competence were the duties of the individual.

In addition, employees expected substantial support and benefits from organizations. It was not uncommon for companies to view employees as family and to care for their health and welfare through comprehensive benefit programs and services. The organization helped employees save money, invest money, stop smoking, lose weight, gain weight, buy products at low prices, create good health through innovative exercise programs, and even send their children to college. They provided for an employee's transportation needs, counseled their families on substance abuse, assisted them in times of crisis, and provided loans at reduced interest rates. In short, an employee could expect that virtually all of his or her daily living needs would be met through some type of organizational benefit program. All he or she had to do was to go to work, remain loyal and committed, and be productive.

All these benefits and more were common among organizations, and they still exist in many of the larger companies in the United States. However, when organizations started reacting to changed market conditions, the responsiveness that was once prevalent was no longer provided. Benefits previously lavished on employees were suddenly cut. Organizations not only expected employees to give up the company car or pay their own bus fare but asked them to cut their salaries as well. The work values that many middle-aged employees grew up with were suddenly being threatened. In short, the individual-organization (I-O) relationship began to change.

How that relationship is changing and what the new relationship means in terms of organizational effectiveness is largely the function of a sound career development program.

The I-O Relationship Today.   Today, employees and organizations are searching for ways they can redefine the I-O relationship and still meet the needs of both the individual and the organization.

Career development helps individuals reassess priorities and assists them in taking personal responsibility for their careers. There are no guarantees, no certainty that an organization will be in existence 10, 5, or even 3 years in the future. If the individual is to maintain a productive, financially rewarding lifestyle, he or she must assume responsibility for career development.

Individuals must take the new attitude that "I will go to work and be loyal, committed and productive; however, if I start getting cues that the company may not be in business next year, I will exercise my options and seek other employment." Clearly, there is a trend toward "self-management."

This attitude has also caused changes in management style and philosophy. Realizing that the individual may not be as committed to the company as in the past, and may leave, even in a tight job market, the manager is confronted with new challenges in maintaining the traditional I-O relationship.

In a recent study of 25 CEOs and general managers of small to medium-sized organizations, it was learned that they had become increasingly more sensitive to the needs of their employees. These senior executives were developing a more supportive and reinforcing management style that focused on the quality of their relationship with employees rather than on a hard-nosed results orientation.

They felt that the more supportive attitude would better maintain employee commitment, loyalty, and productivity. They acknowledged that this was a significant difference in their approach to their employees compared with 10 or 15 years before.[4]

As Bradford and Cohen describe in their management book, "the focus is on quality, on genuinely collaborative team effort, on confronting differences about work without petty infighting, and on continual attention to the development of members as integral to achieving the task."[5]

Rarely were line managers responsible for ensuring the personal and professional needs of employees. This was traditionally handled by employee relations or personnel. With downsizing and strong decentralization trends, line managers are increasingly being called upon to perform human resource responsibilities.

Bradford and Cohen state it best when they discuss the "manager as developer": "A manager must first believe in the concept (of developer) and then act in the creation of a team of key subordinates who are jointly responsible with the manager for the department's success. At the same time that the manager works to develop management responsibility in subordinates, he or she must help develop the subordinates' abilities to share management of the unit's performance."[6]

Now the manager and supervisor are being asked to conduct career discussions with employees to assure that skill and developmental needs are being met. Although many find they agree with this "facilitative approach," however, actions have been slow in coming.

Marlys Hanson, a leader in training managers to conduct career discussions, comments that managers often look for easy answers to complex problems. Training managers and supervisors to be "human" and conduct effective developmental or career discussions is a challenge. In the first place, there is general agreement that the manager must have his or her own career development in order before he or she can assist others. Second, there is often a danger in conducting career discussions with employees of professional concerns spilling over to personal issues.

However, as Hanson points out: "Many organizations are beginning to respond with creative approaches for meeting employees' needs for influence and interaction independent of management positions. Career management programs also prepare both (employees) and managers to better fulfill their responsibilities for effective use of human resources."[7]

Managerial Coaching.   When to put on the "manager's" hat and when to put on the "counselor" or "coach" hat is a key issue with most managers. It is often felt that if a manager counsels, it erodes the authority as a manager, because he or she may have to reveal something personal to the employee in order to gain the rapport necessary for a productive developmental discussion. Effective managers, however, know that losing control is a remote possibility and there are considerable benefits to performing this duty effectively.

Successfully integrating the individual into the organizational culture is a key function of the manager or supervisor. Accepting the role as a coach or counselor becomes easier when one considers *why* employees need help in the first place. In most cases employees have either

- Negative self-concept and need support

- Need to take some risks, but don't know how and need support

- Need to create some options for a career and need support

- Need to resolve a conflict and need support in doing it

The bottom line regarding an employee's need for help is *support*—support in managing the changes coming at him or her in the personal, social, and professional realms, support in dealing with organizations that appear directionless, and support in coping with the vast amount of change that confronts all aspects of our society.

In most situations, the manager will be dealing with an employee able to adjust to the stresses of organizational life. The manager should be aware of the possibility of coaching employees who may have psychological disfunctions. The manager should be ready to refer that employee to more skilled professionals if the need arises.

The I-O relationship, as it has for years, will continue to change and develop new dimensions and characteristics. Especially in the service economy, now being more fully realized in American business, human resources are the organization's newest weapon in the battle against competition. Self-management, as a strategy, is more popular and the computer is vastly influencing how line managers approach their jobs. Flexible work hours, contract workers, newer demands on leisure time, and the emergence of the American entrepreneur are all influencing this relationship. What it means in terms of business environments in the twenty-first century will depend largely on how well the organization and the individual collaborate in recreating this fascinating relationship.

Organizational Commitment

Since adults in our culture have a strong tendency to define themselves in terms of the work they do, facilitating the career planning process would seem to be of value as a means of maximizing the individual's contribution to the organization. Yet some organizations resist career planning efforts in the attempt to manipulate the decisions of the individuals under their control. Usually this is rationalized as an attempt to preserve organizational stability or to limit decisions by individuals which are inconvenient to the organization. But a contrasting attitude was observed during a career planning program conducted by McMahon at a career center in a midwestern university. As a result of a life planning exercise in that program, a staff member resigned to pursue a career in industry. The director of the center responded with the enlightened comment that 'I would rather have people here because they plan to be here than because of a sense of accident or apathy.''[8]

Individuals should be primarily responsible for their own career planning. Even in apparently hopeless organizational settings, the individual always has the option to leave. But it is certainly a desirable goal for career planning programs to facilitate the individual's achievement of personal objectives. Where there is choice, there may be more commitment from the individual, and a more productive relationship may result.

One other item is important to mention. Career planning is not always synonymous with upward mobility, for only a few make significant upward strides. Rather, career planning is more comparable with the notion of growth and development, which is for everybody.

The objective of career planning is simply the mutual I-O establishment of a course of action which seems reasonable in terms of what is known about the individual and the environment of the organization.

Five Career Planning Criteria

Five features or criteria important to the success of career planning are dialogue, guidance, the individual's involvement in the process, feedback to the individual, and the mechanisms by which the process operates.

- *I-O dialogue.* Dialogue represents the relationship between the individual and the organization. It might be between the individual and his or her immediate manager, the manager's manager, other interested parties, or a third party who can facilitate and help increase the objectivity and validity of the decisions. Through dialogue, openness and trust can be generated to the advantage of both the individual and the organization. Dialogue may be implemented in a number of ways, but the essential point is that without it, there is no career planning.

- *Guidance.* Guidance from management is, in essence, the provision of information about the career milieu in which the individual must function. An individual can plan intelligently with knowledge about options, opportunities, and goals available. The information can be provided by means of seminars or third-party counseling, or it can be given informally if no systematic program is developed.

- *The individual's involvement.* To ensure a high degree of involvement, means must be established to allow individuals to input their career objectives, timetables, values, and other personally meaningful issues. Provision must be made to use this information once it is solicited in order to optimize the relationship between what the individual wants and what is possible. It may be necessary to structure a sequence of events in order to obtain clear statements from individuals of what they, in fact, want. This is not easy, since experience shows that individuals' desires are often poorly defined and are sometimes in conflict with the organization's goals. Special career planning workshops can be developed that will help identify and resolve this problem. These are described later in this chapter.

- *Feedback.* Feedback to the individual is important in that it provides the basis for calibrating his or her behavior or for initiating appropriate changes in terms of what is learned. It may take the form of one-to-one discussions with superiors, or often it emerges from developmental experiences which point out areas requiring change.

- *Mechanisms of career planning.* The mechanisms of career planning, or the processes and the techniques, must interface with one another as subsystems. The potentially useful devices are rather numerous. Because they are the means by which the above four items are brought into being, considerable discussion will be devoted to several of them in the following sections.

Techniques and Methods of Career Planning

Career guidance discussions between managers, supervisors, and subordinates are those links in the organizational career management process that facilitate employee growth and development.

Career development programs take many forms, depending on the organization, the commitment, and a variety of other factors. One important link in the process of establishing career development opportunities is a formally structured discussion between a manager or supervisor and his or her subordinate where the focus is primarily developmental.[9]

Many other devices are available, and full descriptions appear in the literature in the field (see Gutteridge and Sekaran's annotated bibliography, commissioned by the Career Development Professional Practice Area of ASTD, as listed in the reference notes at the end of this chapter).[10]

Three methods will be described briefly: the life and career planning process, career paths, and job posting.

Life and Career Planning

The life and career planning process is instrumental for career planning activities in a growing number of organizations. It is a reasonably simple method to use and can be administered independently of any other program or system. Its costs are negligible, requiring only blank paper and a pencil for each participant for recording thoughts and reactions to stimulating career questions. An ordinary conference room can be used as long as chairs can be arranged in small circular groups of three or four people. There are many variations of this process, but common to most is the idea that the individual is primarily responsible for his or her own career and that the result of the process is to have a written career plan in the individual's hands at the completion of the workshop. This plan can be used to fit together the purposes of the individual and the organization.

Many people make the assumption that their future life or career is determined largely by their past or is controlled largely by people other than themselves. Career planning, dealing with a base of "here and now," often slips back into the past. It might be more effective if the process could slip more into the future.

The following sequence of exercises is a way of bringing the future of one's choice into being. Any of the exercises, or the entire sequence, could be done by individuals, pairs, or groups. The latter method permits more sharing of one's plans with others and may generate more self-growth goals than could be achieved through self-insight alone.

Career by Objectives—A Hands-On Approach. The following exercises should help participants to confront various issues in their own lives and work and to begin making choices that will lead to greater fulfillment of their potential. Career by Objectives helps the participants take stock of where they are now, what their plans are for the future, and how their career fits in with their situation. You might try this exercise by yourself now, or later, with a small group of peers.

Where I Am. This first step involves an examination of your current position in life and career and addresses the questions of where you are.

- For a few moments, think about your entire life, from beginning to end, birth to death, womb to tomb (or, as one student asked, "you mean sperm to worm?"). You might draw a line that represents your life from beginning to end (see Fig. 43-1). Your line may show peak experiences or events you remember vividly, important things that happened or may happen. Draw your line to include the past; present and draw it the way you think it will be or how you'd like it to be in the future. Draw the line out to the end of your life. Think about it! How would you like it to look?
- Now put an X on your line to indicate where you are now.

Figure 43-1. Career by Objectives—where I am.

Who I Am.   Think about who you are, the different roles you play.

- Ponder the question, "Who am I?" Think of as many answers as you can and write each one down on a separate slip of paper or 3 by 5 card. Use nouns (son, daughter, friend, sister, brother, names, woman, man) or adjectives (quiet, talkative, active, athletic) or mixtures (an active athlete, a loving son). You have many roles, responsibilities, and characteristics. Write statements if you want.
- Use a different card for each answer or statement.
- When you're finished, put them in order of importance to you. Think about which are temporary and which are permanent. Which would you like to take into the future with you? Which would you like to leave behind? Which would you like to amend? Are there others you'd like to add?

Where I Would Like to Be and What I Would Like to Happen.   We'll spend the rest of the process on the part of your line from the X into the future. Now that you know *where* you are and *who* you are, look out to the very end of your line and think about where you would like to be or what you would like to happen by then.

- Write your eulogy, epitaph, or autobiography to answer:
    - What do you want to have accomplished by then?
    - What do you want to be remembered for?
    Think about it; then take pen to paper and write. Don't worry about the grammar. Write an outline, a few paragraphs, or a few thoughts. In a sense, as concrete or as broad as your ideas may be, you are setting some life goals.

An Ideal Year in the Future.   Now come back in time and select a 12-month portion in the *future* that you can arrange for yourself (see Fig. 43-2).

- If you had unlimited resources—money or material, for example—what would you do?
- You have 12 months, 1 year in the future. Write down what you would do. Think, fantasize, dream a little!
- Is it in line with what you wrote as your life goals, or what you want to be remembered for, in the previous exercise? Or should you think a little more about what you want in life?

Unlimited resources is difficult to imagine. We have found that even in this "fantasy" people put limits on their resources. Even though parts of your ideal year

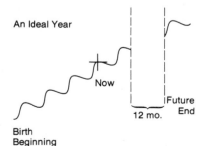

Figure 43-2. Career by Objectives—an ideal year in the future.

may seem farfetched, you may find many that are not so far from real, and could be accomplished at least in part.

An Ideal Job for You.   Returning to the present and immediate future, think of an ideal job for you with your resources as you know them.

- Don't think of titles or job labels or specific disciplines or individual organizations.
- Think of specific *things* you want in a job.
- What kind of training and schooling will you need?
- How can you apply your present training?

Career-by-Objectives Inventory.   Now let's take an inventory of how you view your current status using the following questions.

- In your career and life, what "turns you on?" When do you feel really alive?
- What do you do well?
- What do you not do so well?
- What do you feel you need—need to learn, need to expand your authority, need for additional experiences?
- What resources do you have?
- What should you stop doing that you are now doing?
- What should you start doing now?
- What is your long-term career objective? Can you write one for yourself?

Summary.   As illustrated in Fig. 43-3, this exercise is a suggested *continuous* sequence of simplistic, yet not so easily answered questions. Essentially the exercise deals with the questions where am I, who am I, where am I going, how can I

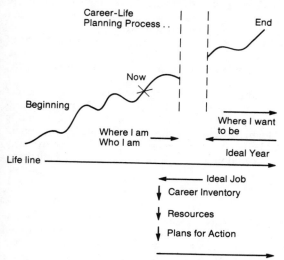

Figure 43-3. Career by Objectives—career life planning process.

influence getting there. The sequence requires periodic review. It is an educational process. Personal goals are desirable and worth working for.

In Management by Objectives, goals are set for certain time periods. Strategies, using available resources, flow from the objectives. Specific actions and subsequent results achieved help input the objectives for the next time period. Career by Objectives is analogous to the life and career planning approach, and can even prove to be fun.[11]

There are numerous variations and extensions of this process. Lippitt[12] illustrates another version, as do Bolles[13] and Hanson.[14] Experience has shown that a one-day workshop is very flexible and revealing. In between questions and group interaction on sharing responses, information is given to participants about the organizational career environment. When the first half of the workshop deals with life values and the second section focuses on career issues, there is a helpful integration of the goals the individual wants to actualize through the medium of the career. This process has been used by the authors at numerous organizations with very positive results.

The Small Group Model.   The small group model as a method for generating career planning information has been widely and successfully used by both business and academic institutions. It has a number of advantages. For instance, individuals participate at a personally comfortable rate and exchange useful information. Interaction among participants produces a controlled forum for the testing of individual thoughts and positions, and it can produce useful additions to the human resource planning database.

One component of the authors' programs has consisted of sets of instructions and projects to stimulate guided group interaction on shared concerns and to ground the interaction on a base of data which relates directly to participants' needs and to the organizational culture affecting career planning. A great deal of experience has also been gathered by other organizations and experts on the usefulness and cost-effectiveness of the small group model in career planning to generate action-oriented information.

A unique combination of corporate career information and personal experience delivered through small group techniques is seen as an advantageous feature of economical career planning programs. Group techniques are often selected for their relative efficiency, supplemented by one-to-one sessions as needed.

One program objective should be to produce comparative indices by means of which individuals could evaluate themselves in relation to peer achievement, salary, technical obsolescence, interpersonal and managerial effectiveness, lifestyle, and especially, personal goals and values.

From these baseline data, individuals can assess objective and subjective career progress, in terms that are personally meaningful and from which short-, medium- and long-range career plans may be plotted in a source document. The resulting plan must be worked out in dialogue with the cognizant individuals who represent the corporate point of view in order to harmonize the needs of the parties involved, and appropriate data should be entered in the human resource planning database.

Career Paths

A common device often confused with career planning is known as *career paths* or *career ladders*. In essence, career paths imply a structured series of predetermined on-the-job experiences which result in movement up a hierarchy.

Career paths can be a two-edged sword. While they do provide some closure for a career plan, they do not easily provide for the dynamics of either the organization or the individual in a changing environment. A major argument against "pathing" is that it assumes that an individual is being prepared for a job whose date of availability and content are known. It also assumes that the "when" and the "what" of the job are not likely to change prior to the individual's arrival. But there are intervening variables such as reorganizations and maturation of the individual which occur and the requirement to avoid preparing for tomorrow's job according to today's I-O needs emerges.

Where structured experience is a technical necessity, there may be a place for career paths. But in many situations where organizational environments have become volatile, it makes little sense to structure careers much more than 2 to 5 years into the future. Structuring careers only a short time into the future also avoids the embarrassing problem of having to explain to an individual why a career path must be abandoned after the individual has been sold on the long-range idea. New organizational structures such as the matrix concept (nonhierarchical work environments) and project management may eventually provide many optional ways of arranging developmental experiences which allow more flexibility in dealing with opportunities as they arise in a dynamic organization. They also point out the need for continuously assessing the individual's cognitive and personal growth in order to optimize opportunities for I-O as they occur.

Job Posting

Job posting is the intraorganizational equivalent of publicly announcing position vacancies in the classified section of a newspaper. Candidates apply according to their aspirations and career plans. Individuals, motivated to apply for vacancies on their own, produce a vastly superior organizational climate for I-O optimization than can be attained through any other single method of career planning. Systems combining job posting with other devices such as life and career planning, assessment centers, organizational development, and manager development are experiencing efficient and effective results. There is often a great deal of management resistance to the openness of announcing vacancies and their relative positions in the hierarchy, usually stated in terms meaning that individuals cannot be trusted to behave conveniently and rationally if they are given options. But in terms of the Johari window, described below, openness and honesty are assumed to be ends in themselves.

The Career Development Window

Underlying many emerging career planning systems is an assumption that the more the individual and the organization know about each other, the better. This issue, concerning how much reciprocal knowledge there is about the individual within the context of a career, can be represented by the Johari window. This device was named after its creators, Joseph Luft and Harry Ingham—hence the name "Johari." The assumption made about career planning is that the more open and honest the relationship between I-O, the better.

The career development version of the Johari window provides a way of conceptualizing the individual's relationships and the criteria for evaluating the effectiveness of his or her role in the building of these relationships in the career planning setting (see Fig. 43-4).

The upper left-hand square of the window represents the area that the individual knows and the area that the supervisor or manager knows. This is the common knowledge or OPEN/PUBLIC area in their relationship.

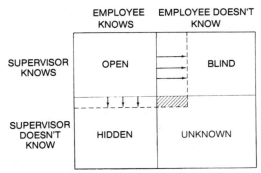

Figure 43-4. The career development window—an adaptation of the Johari window concept of disclosure and feedback process in personal growth in the employee-supervisor interview.

The area in the lower left-hand block indicates the things which the individual knows but which the supervisor does not know. This is referred to as the HIDDEN or DEFENSIVE area. These are things the individual does not tell his or her supervisor.

The upper right-hand block shows the area of knowledge that the supervisor has but does not tell the individual. Since the person does not know about the things in this area, it is referred to as the BLIND area. Without feedback from the career planning process, this can be a debilitating and sometimes dishonest area.

The bottom block on the right indicates an area about which neither the individual nor the supervisor knows. This is called the UNKNOWN area. In this area one may find undiscovered potential and creativity or other untapped capabilities or resources.

In line with the objective of the career planning process—to foster a clearer understanding, a sharper definition of purpose and commitment between an individual and his or her supervisor (or with a third party in many cases) through a frank, participative discussion of climate, needs, strengths, feelings, aspirations, performance, and compensation—the Johari process might be applied in the following way.

If the person tells the supervisor some of the things that the supervisor does not know, the HIDDEN area is reduced, and this may stimulate some response or feedback from the supervisor in the area about which the person does not know, thereby reducing the BLIND area. In both cases it increases the arena or OPEN area between them and may expose more of the UNKNOWN or potential areas.

This concept and the emphasis on future planning can be helpful in meeting the objectives of career planning.

Interdependency

One outgrowth of the I-O relationship is the growing use of interdependency as a career management and development tool by individuals. The concept is simply the act of creating a positive, win-win relationship with another person for purposes of creating value for each. The idea goes beyond the traditional ideas of networking, which is reserved for information gathering and sharing. Interdependency requires much heavier involvement, participation, energy, time, and money to successfully complete.

Interdependency requires that an individual be quite selective in choosing another individual with whom to create the relationship. The choice must assure a relationship of benefit to both parties and must involve a project or program in which both can share acknowledgment and recognition equally. It may be a joint article, a book, a task force, or a special committee within an organization.

In terms of career management and development for an employee, interdependency becomes a powerful strategy used to enhance one's value, not only to the organization, but to one's profession as well. It is a strategy which can effectively increase a person's versatility or the options available to him or her. Finally, if done correctly, interdependency serves to enhance an individual's visibility to the organization, as well as to the profession.

In terms of an organization's career and human resource planning systems, interdependent relationships among employees can produce significant benefits. Not only are they motivating and rewarding for the employees, the relationships often produce increased productivity, new products and services, ways to decrease costs and increase profits, and new ways to produce collaborative problem solving among departments.

Organizations can promote this valuable strategy among employees through innovative career management programs. Skills needed to create such relationships are often taught in career management seminars. These skills include the ability to build relationships, mentoring, and determining self-marketing strategies for seeking opportunities. Organizations can also support interdependency among employees by open and supportive management styles that encourage, reinforce, and credit employees for their contributions.

Summary

Human resource management as a function in its broadest sense is very much like a comprehensive list of personnel functions, old and new, ranging from wage and salary and recruiting to behavioral science. It is an operational concept in action.

Often, reading the list of functions carried out by a human resource planning function is very much like reading the table of contents in a comprehensive textbook on personnel. Policy, procedure, practices, legislation—all these things are subsumed under the concept of human resource planning and range from the traditional to the exotic. Often, the human resource management function will be circumscribed to human resource planning, but human resources are one-third of a corporation's resources (money and physical facilities being the others). Human resources is perhaps the most important because of the human element involved. These are the resources which "wear out" or "burn out" with disuse or improper use. Human resource management is synonymous with the scope of the personnel or human resource function and is not merely a narrow planning role within a corporate personnel operation. It is the total human resource concept or system.

Career planning, on the other hand, can often be translated into programs and procedures which are designed to give the individual leverage in carving out a personal career within the corporate environment in dialogue with the organization. It is hoped that career planning will open a facilitating dialogue between the individual and the organization in order to optimize their mutual needs as they are set in the context of human resource planning.

Some desirable features or criteria of career planning programs are the ideas that individuals should be able to articulate and specify their desires (consistent with the jobs available), that the corporation will endeavor to match those needs as much as possible and not be capricious or arbitrary, and that the corporation will follow through on commitments and expectations which are raised. In addition to the career planning techniques already discussed in this chapter, numerous others are available which can be used. See the reference list for suggested readings.

What most organizations lack, however, is a systematic means of allowing employees to participate fully in their own growth and development. The data which are elicited from the individual in career planning programs tend to age rapidly because people are dynamic, changing entities. The half-life of career planning data seems, as a rule of thumb, to be reached within 18 to 24 months in many cases; family circumstances change, career aspirations are modified, interests shift, and new goals emerge.

Of course, at appropriate points in the career planning dialogue, individuals have the obligation to achieve whatever developmental goals are required to prepare them for the career objectives which have been delineated. From a programmatic point of view, it is preferable to have career planning programs which are easily administered and maintained. If career planning can transcend being viewed as "just another personnel program" overlaid upon the busy line manager, the chances of success are increased.

With all its promise, career planning is a concept which relates to programs that most organizations already have in place. It is important to recognize that career planning is not independent of ongoing personnel activities. It is an emerging influence on human resource management that should add new dimensions to existing human resource practices.

References

1. Storey, Walter D., *A Guide for Career Development Inquiry*, ASTD, Madison, WI, 1979, pp. 4,5.

2. Naisbitt, John, and Patricia Aburdene, *Re-Inventing the Corporation*, Warner Books, 1985, p. 83.

3. Naisbitt, John, and Patricia Aburdene, op. cit., p. 87.

4. Merman, Stephen, *Study of Facilitative Management Techniques*, PMG Incorporated, Denver, CO, 1985.

5. Bradford, David L., and Allan R. Cohen, *Managing for Excellence*, John Wiley and Sons, New York, 1984, p. 6.

6. Bradford, David L., and Allan R. Cohen, op. cit. p. 7.

7. Hanson, Marlys, "Job Fit and Creativity," *IEEE Potentials*, July 30, 1985.

8. McMahon, John, *Life-Career Planning Seminar*, University of Cincinnati, November 1973.

9. Callahan, Ed, *INFO-LINE*, ASTD, August 1985, from the introduction.

10. Gutteridge, Thomas G., and Uma Sekaran, *Career Planning and Development: A Multi-Dimensional Perspective, An Annotated Bibliography*, Third Edition, ASTD, April 1986.

11. McMahon, John, "Career Choices: A Hands-On Approach" in *Engineering Horizons*, November 1985, pp. 11,12.

12. Lippitt, Gordon, "Developing Life Plans," *Training and Development Journal*, May 1970.

13. Bolles, Richard N., *What Color Is Your Parachute?*, Ten Speed Press, Berkeley, CA, 1972.

14. Hanson, Marlys, "Implementing a Career Development Program," *Training and Development Journal*, 35 (7), 1981, pp. 80–90.

44

Employee Participation and Involvement

Carl E. Boyer

Preston Pond

Carl E. Boyer is the Vice President of Human Resources for Clark Material Systems Technology Co., a business unit of Clark Equipment Co. Prior to assuming his current position in 1983, he spent 25 years with General Motors, the last 10 years as director of organization development for the Packard Electric Division. While with GM, he was involved in the development of self-autonomous work teams in new-plant start-ups, and union-management collaboration projects to increase the participation of factory employees in established plants.

Preston Pond is an independent management and organization development consultant based in Lexington, Kentucky. He is currently working with Ford Motor Company, IBM, and the James River Corporation on a variety of new start-up, employee involvement, and redesign activities. He holds a master's degree in Organization Behavior from Brigham Young University. Past experience includes several years with Procter and Gamble as an internal Organization Development Consultant on greenfield start-ups and redesign efforts in the United States, Japan, and Mexico. As director of organization development for Clark Equipment Company, he worked closely with employee involvement and collaborative redesign efforts.

Most documented experience with employee involvement has come from the shop floor of manufacturing operations. The principles and techniques involved, however, have been tried and are applicable to a variety of organizational settings. We believe that employee involvement groups can be established in any industry at any level of the organization. The intent of this chapter is to describe what is meant by "employee involvement and participation" and to outline some basic guidelines for initiating and maintaining such efforts with an ongoing organization.

Definitions

Participation and Involvement. Because of the similarity in meaning and usage of the words "participation" and "involvement," both words will be used interchangeably throughout the chapter.

Employee involvement is a **process** which accomplishes the following:

1. *Involves employees in organization decision making.* Successful involvement is most often accomplished by asking employees to discuss what goes wrong within their work areas and then acting on their suggestions. Through this process, members from various parts of the organization can have a voice in decisions to be made—especially cost, quality, quality of work life, and productivity decisions—that directly affect their own work area or job responsibilities.

2. *Gains management support and commitment.* Often management is not even aware of problems, roadblocks, or improvement opportunities surfaced by employee involvement groups. After thorough group problem identification and problem solving, new information, suggestions, alternatives, and action plans can be presented to management, putting it in a much better position to understand the actual needs and difficulties of the organization. With that input, management can and generally does find it easier to take a clear stand and make appropriate commitments to support suggestions and recommended plans.

3. *Builds a strong sense of employee ownership and commitment.* We are generally committed to those things we have worked hardest for. Individual involvement in the problem-identification, problem-solving, and decision-making process takes effort, an investment of personal time and mental energy. For most employees, this personal investment, and the desire for improvement that accompany it, lead to a strong sense of ownership and commitment to resulting activities. Further, to the extent that suggested plans, improvements, and programs are followed up and implemented, employee trust, satisfaction, and identification with the company seem to increase.

4. *Helps to focus organization resources on their best use.* Allocation of resources like time, money, equipment, and manpower can be difficult, political, and highly emotional. When many individuals are involved from several parts of the organization, their collective view of resource use and application is improved. Furthermore, the recommendations of many individuals carry more weight and credibility than the ideas of a few isolated individuals. Equipped with better facts, clearer problems, concrete recommendations, and backed by a committed group and a more committed management, employee involvement groups can have strong influence on the deployment of resources.

Employee Involvement Group. This is a selected group of employees working together to improve business results through enhanced information sharing and group cooperation, problem solving, and decision making.

A variety of involvement groups are currently in common use throughout industry, ranging from recreation and blood drive committees to full-scale organization redesign groups. Different kinds of groups may be used within the same organization, sequentially or concurrently, with some form of coordination to link their efforts. The important identifying characteristics are:

1. Members are deliberately selected from appropriate parts of the department or larger organization.

2. The individuals cooperate, using group problem-solving and decision-making techniques.

3. The clear task is to improve business results in concrete and measurable ways.

Examples of involvement groups include quality circles, cross-functional business teams, fair treatment committees, and special task forces.

Why Participation and Involvement Is Important

Organizations that genuinely respect their employees find ways of involving them—from the top to bottom—in decision-making activities that will later affect them. This esteem for the contributions of each employee is a basic organizational and cultural value. Employee involvement is often an expression of the importance the organization places on its individual members and can be effective in moving organizations to higher commitment and valuing of their employees.

More significantly, however, employee participation is beginning to make good business sense. Richard Walton, in a recent article on commitment in the workplace, observed:

> Only lately have they [managers] begun to see that workers respond best—and most creatively—not when they are tightly controlled by management, placed in narrowly defined jobs, and treated like an unwelcome necessity, but instead, when they are given broader responsibilities, encouraged to contribute and help to take satisfaction in their work. It should come as no surprise that eliciting worker commitment—and providing the environment in which it can flourish—pays tangible dividends for the individuals and for the companies.[1]

Many companies that involve their employees in problem identification and decision making are discovering that employees are happier, costs are down, and quality, productivity, and profits are up.

It is interesting and instructive to consider some of the circumstances which have led businesses to seek participation and involvement among their employees. During the 1960s, American industry in general experienced unprecedented growth and productivity. As that productivity waned during the recessions of the 1970s, companies began to look for ways to continue to maintain higher productivity and quality in the face of rising wage and raw material costs. Meanwhile, Japanese competition, in electronics, automobiles, heavy equipment, and many other industries, became a real contending force. Their participative decision making and group involvement in quality circles caught the attention of the world, heralded by lower costs and the increasingly superior product quality.

In addition to a more competitive business environment, there has been a gradual, yet general, recognition in management circles that the nineteenth century traditional autocratic management styles of the sixties no longer fit the values and expectations of a newer generation of workers who expect more from their work—

employees who want to feel ownership and who expect to be able to make a contribution to the organization.

With lagging productivity, aggressive competitors, and the threat of extinction looming on the horizon, many companies looked to employee involvement as a productivity improvement tool to meet pressing business needs. As a response to these demands, quality circles and employee involvement found their start in a variety of industrial settings, with the primary focus on quality. In many cases, that quality focus expanded to include cost productivity and quality of work life issues as well. It is significant that these efforts often improved the waning trust between employees and management.

Concurrent with the expansion of quality circles during the middle to late sixties, several companies such as Procter and Gamble, Kodak, Pet Foods, and General Motors began experimenting with and implementing more participative new plant start-ups. These as well as more recent efforts at a systemic redesigning of existing work locations have led to a variety of participation and involvement methods. Based on this variety and the success of many participative activities, there seems to be less question about whether they are legitimate productivity tools and more and more focus on how and when to use them.

Training, Facilitation, and Consulting Roles

As interest and experience with involvement groups have grown during the 1970s and in the 1980s, organizations have increasingly felt the need for skilled help in training and development. Three related though differing roles seem to have emerged to meet the needs to train participants in basic skills, develop group cohesiveness and direction, and coordinate activities within the framework of the larger organization: trainer, group facilitator, and internal change consultant. Since these roles are somewhat distinct, and since the terms "trainer," "facilitator," and "consultant" have different meanings in different organizations, it is important to clarify what is meant by each, and how they might be successfully combined.

The Trainer's Role

One of the most effective means of reducing resistance to participative efforts, and more importantly of building support for new projects, is training. Unfortunately, in many involvement activities, this crucial initial step is omitted, most often because of management's zeal to get the group formed and seek quick results. Initial training of involvement participants, properly done, normally takes the form of basic education on the philosophy and principles of participation and human motivation. This orientation training also identifies those who are interested and readily able to contribute to the participative process. Furthermore, the training itself provides a model of openness and information sharing that not only is necessary to successful involvement but signals the incipient change within the organization.

The trainer's role, as it has evolved, is twofold:

1. To identify the range of skills needed to help the involvement group(s) reach its objectives

2. To train inexperienced members in those skills needed to reach group and project objectives

Beyond basic education and orientation training, the range of skills needed for involvement groups to meet their objectives often includes the following:

- Core technical skills
- Statistical process control skills (in manufacturing)
- Giving and receiving feedback
- Conflict resolution skills
- Group decision-making skills
- Group problem-solving skills
- Planning and follow-up skills
- Leadership and motivation skills

Some organizations have separate trainers for technical training and human effectiveness training; others combine them into one role. In some organizations, quality control managers become trainers; in others, human resources group or line management has taken time to develop the training packages and present them in seminar-like settings.

The Facilitator's Role

Beyond the basic orientation and skills training, there is an additional need to develop group cohesiveness and direction throughout the participation process. This challenge is being met by group facilitators.

The two basic aspects of the facilitator's role are:

1. To manage the employee involvement group process during meetings. This includes ensuring group membership equity, encouraging group discussion, suggesting decision-making and problem-solving alternatives (keeping the group "unstuck"), pushing and pulling toward resolution, and promoting development of action and follow-up plans.

2. To provide and administer a variety of team-building exercises and sessions to involvement groups. These sessions help group members learn to be sensitive to fellow members, to seek input from even the most quiet and reserved, and to establish guidelines and group norms which help them function more effectively.

This role has tended to be filled by trained human resources professionals or by highly interested internal managers who have acquired group process skills.

The Change Consultant's Role

The third role extends into the framework of the larger organization. With the emergence of organizational development, the internal change agent, or consultant, has often filled this role. Two basic aspects of the consultant's role are:

1. To diagnose organizational problems and readiness for change
2. To manage and coordinate the involvement process within the larger organization

This person is the "glue" or, in other words, the one who holds management and other levels of employees together in the participative process. It is the change consultant, in short, who works with management to ensure their motives and behaviors are philosophically consistent with the principles of participation and involvement and who then seeks to prevent employees from being manipulated by the process. More specifically, the consultant's activities include establishing a clear mission for the group, seeing that an overall plan is developed, ensuring proper group representation to accomplish its task, choosing proper group size, planning initial meetings with sanction or steering groups, serving as a meeting leader during early stages, and coordinating communication between various groups and levels throughout the project.

The Combined Role

Some organizations have separate trainers, facilitators, and consultants, all three working together to accomplish participation objectives. Others successfully combine the training and facilitation roles into one, or the facilitation and consulting into one separate from the trainer. Still others successfully combine all three—the trainer, facilitator, and consultant roles.

It is easy to separate roles during the early stages, because in initial training and start-up meetings, the planning, coordination, and orientation are in these leaders' hands. However, as the groups mature and teams acquire more control and responsibility and as individuals take more leadership initiative for accomplishment of objectives, it becomes more difficult to differentiate the roles. At this point, the trainer-facilitator-consultant needs to interact spontaneously with the evolving training, group development, and larger organization coordination needs of the group(s). For these reasons, we recommend combining the skills into one role. This provides an overall continuity and allows participants in various parts of the organization to know where to go for help. The combined role further allows for a top-to-bottom look at things in order to hold the process together and keep it rolling. Keep in mind, however, that any combination of these roles will work, though care should be taken to fit the right mix of roles and people to the particular situation.

Throughout the remainder of this chapter we will use the word "trainer" to represent the participative group leader, whether it is in fact a trainer, facilitator, consultant, or any combination of these roles.

Beginning

Because of the nature of the involvement process, assessing the readiness of the members of the organization is essential. The obvious need for the individual to do more than just carry out a directive of the supervisor demands that the leaders of the organization know the feelings of its members about becoming involved in the participation process. Without their willingness, there is no involvement. But there are other aspects of this question of readiness, and we need to look at each of them.

1. *Is management truly willing to consider the input of the people below them?* This is essential in any involvement plan. It is sometimes answered too quickly "yes," and later turns out to be the reason projects fail. The answer to this question is deeply rooted in the values and beliefs of the individual leaders. Do managers believe their role is to make decisions for others to carry out? If they do not fulfill that role, are they failing as the leaders? On the other side of the question, do they believe that the motivation of workers below them comes primarily from making

money and other tangible rewards, and therefore being involved in organizational decision making is not important to the average worker anyway?

Trainers can find the answer to this question in several ways. First, a variety of readiness assessment instruments are available. Or trainers can simply make their own judgments about top management's attitudes toward employee involvement. Finally, there is the direct approach: the trainer can talk to upper management and discover their reaction to the concept of employee participation, stressing the importance of their support to success.

2. *Is the organization culture conducive to involvement?*   In spite of the importance of the organizational leaders' attitude, the history and culture of the rest of the organization is also an important readiness factor. A leader cannot decree participation and expect it to work. Not only is this a contradiction of terms, but participation cannot flourish in an environment of directives. Therefore, the same tests for readiness we used for management should be applied to the organization as a whole. A dilemma may occur at this juncture if the leader is ready to change management style long before the rest of the organization is ready. It is here that the strengths of trainers play a role in establishing support for involvement or overcoming resistance to it. They might begin by educating lower levels of management as to the reasons for increasing involvement and how they plan to implement the change. We will address this intervention a little later.

3. *Has the union been included in planning involvement?*   In organizations represented by a union, top management support and understanding is necessary but not sufficient. No meaningful change will happen where the union has not been involved in the assessment process and included in the planning and implementation. There are several good reasons for this. One is that an effort to involve employees in matters where they normally have no say is perceived by the union as an attempt by management to develop a relationship with its employees that will reduce or eliminate the role of the union. Sometimes that is exactly what is intended; but whether it is or not, the fear of such an outcome is sufficient to motivate a union to make certain that this new effort by management does not succeed. The degree of resistance is, of course, dependent on the relationship between the company and the union, and especially on the union's faith that management is not trying to undermine them. The irony of this situation is that carefully implemented participation and involvement has done more to improve union-management relationships than anything in the history of the labor movement. What is required is time, patience, honesty, and sincerity. With these elements, the participative process has the power to strip away the roles people play and let them interact with each other simply as human beings. No other management tool can accomplish this.

4. *Does the experiment have enough priority within the organization?*   "What does this participation stuff have to do with getting widgets out the back door?" When the answer to this question is, "Nothing. We can't afford for that group to meet this week," then little improvement will result from the experiment. In fact, it is likely that the disillusionment which will result if this priority persists will cause more harm to the organization than no attempt at participation at all. Therefore, another measurement of readiness is the willingness to commit the time required to produce results.

The question for the trainer is, "How much time and what resources are required?" The answer varies greatly with the size and scope of the project, but every effort requires time for orienting and training participants, for regular meeting schedules that allow for continuity, and for building cooperation and gathering information from staff departments.

5. *Can this project be successful in our organization?* The degree of sophistication of the project is an important consideration in the readiness assessment. Most organizations where trust between management and the other employees is low, and especially organizations with adversarial labor relations, need to begin in safe, noncontroversial areas. Some examples are blood drives, United Way campaigns, and Christmas projects for needy adults or children. Members of the organization can come together to work on these efforts with the assumption that the motives and objectives of each person are similar. This is a critical criterion for the success of any collaboration, but it is very difficult to accomplish in normal work settings. Work relationships in the United States between management and labor are adversarial by nature, and therefore distrust is more common within the group than trust. This level 1 type of project—United Way, Christmas projects, etc.—allows the individuals to experience the positive feelings that come from accomplishing a task as a group and working together with those people who they feel are normally in opposition to them. The members of the group can drop their negative labels and identify with their fellow participants.

As a trainer associated with a noncontroversial project, you have an opportunity to further the cause of participation by encouraging the development of a common bond among members of the group as they share in success. People need help in understanding why they feel a bond for a person with whom there is normally no sympathy. The best way to accomplish this is for the group to spend some time together discussing their feelings. The trainer can assist them in this learning process.

These are the five major criteria for ensuring that an organization is ready to begin the participation process. Having done the best assessment possible, the trainer is in a position to proceed or to recommend further preparation before implementation.

Other Levels of Participation

Level 2

This involvement centers around resolution of work-related issues, beginning with issues most important to employees. These issues may also be important to management but tend to seem less critical to them. Examples are:

1. Quality improvements that assist employees in their daily work.

2. Housekeeping improvements that make the workplace safer or more pleasant.

3. Input into cafeteria decorating, menus, or arrangements.

In level 2 projects, the trainer hopes to continue building trust that began in level 1 and to test it where there is a greater possibility of disagreement. This experience further develops joint problem-solving skills for work-related topics.

Level 3

This level of participation is characterized by the impact of the results on the organization. Level 3 projects encompass the highly visible, complex, and controversial issues that test the ability of the organization to keep communication open and test the patience of all involved. Examples of this type of project are:

1. Productivity improvements that require changes in work assignments, manpower levels, outsourcing of work, or other controversial areas.
2. Any form of pay changes, such as gainsharing plans, pay for knowledge systems, or changes in classification.
3. Any project in which there is a high degree of difference among the members as to the best course of action. Often this is the point where some employees begin to tell management that they are the ones being paid to make just that type of decision.

These are only rough definitions for determining whether a project falls in level 1, level 2, or level 3. The final judgment will be up to the trainer.

Sanctions

Sometimes for level 2 projects and almost always for level 3, there is a need for a steering group to provide sanction, advice, and support. This is a group of management (and union, where appropriate) members who can assist in the following ways:

1. *Act as a chartering body for the larger group.*   Most often the steering group's membership will cut across the various departments of the organization. This representation will then legitimize the participation in the general involvement group of other employees from those departments.
2. *Meet periodically with work groups to review their progress.*   A good review bolsters the confidence of a work group, giving them hope that their recommendations will eventually be accepted by management. Although members of the steering group cannot give final approval, they do serve as the sanctioning body for upper management.
3. *Assist groups preparing presentations of their findings and recommendations for top management.*   The presentation itself, however, will always have more impact if it is made by the people who developed it rather than by the steering committee.

Throughout this entire process, trainers are key players. They are the link between the involvement groups and the sanctioning group. Often they are facilitators of both groups and decide when it is important for the steering group to meet and what to discuss.

Getting Yourself Organized

If this is the first time you have led a particular group, there are some basic points to consider first:

1. *Is the group chosen representative of those involved?*   Involved individuals could either be those who have input and information needed by the group or those who have a stake in the outcome and/or have to implement the final recommendations. There is need for representation on both sides, even though everyone who fits these categories often cannot be included.
2. *Is the group size manageable?*   Theory says that a person can separate and monitor the input from seven other people. This number can vary plus or minus

two, so that a group of five to nine is ideal. Fewer may deprive the group of energy and ideas. More than nine and the group may be too large for all members to express their opinions and grasp the ideas and views of others. If the group must be larger, the trainer needs to be aware of the potential difficulties and work to minimize them.

3. *Do you have a well-developed orientation and training plan?* Never bring a new group together, whether it includes the top person in the organization or the bottom ones, without a clear plan of what the group will do during the first meeting. The best plan is one that is flexible enough to accommodate the unforeseen needs of the group—but flexibility does not mean being unprepared. Preparation for this first meeting includes:

   a. Introduction of members to each other. This is very important and includes more than just exchanging names. Talking together about why each chose to work in the group (in a participative environment, everyone is a volunteer) is a productive way to learn about the values and interests of the members. Developing a list of expectations for the task before them is another effective way to begin.

   b. Defining the purpose of the group. Each person brings a slightly different view, and spending time early to flush out agreement and disagreement is time well spent. It also allows the group to seek help or clarification from others outside the group if they are not able to resolve the differences.

   c. Setting norms for the group concerning meeting times and frequency, how absences are viewed, and whether substitutes are welcome when members cannot be present. Other norms, including how decisions will be made, how differences will be resolved, and who outside the group is to be informed about the actions and decisions made, are important issues which require some group training before consensus can be reached.

   d. Creating the proper climate. This is the responsibility of the trainer. Participative groups need a leadership style and climate within the group which communicate that members are equal within the confines of the group and that each member shares in the success or failure of accomplishing the purpose. A caring and open manner demonstrated by the trainer is the best way to establish such a climate.

What to Do Once the Groups Are Formed

Once an involvement project is fully underway, with general objectives, involvement groups or teams established, and management support formalized in some sort of sanctioning body, a new challenge surfaces—that of maintaining group energy, project credibility, and continued organization support. Based on our learning over the past 10 years, following are several recommendations for managing the ongoing process.

Group Development

Maintaining involvement, group energy, and commitment is not easy. As with all groups, involvement teams are subject to the emotional cycle that is typically a part of change efforts. Don Kelley and Daryl Conner describe a predictable group emotional cycle in their article "The Emotional Cycle of Change," in the 1979 *Annual Handbook for Group Facilitators*.[2] The stages of this cycle are uninformed optimism, informed pessimism, hopeful realism, informed optimism, and rewarding completion. Once the honeymoon effect of the initial kick-off wears off, most groups move firmly into the informed pessimism stage as they become increasingly aware of other parts of the organization, the complex systemic nature of problems, and the real existence of politics and other organizational barriers. This stage is perhaps the most difficult to manage. If groups are advised ahead of time of the group emotional cycle phenomenon, this sometimes avoids unnecessarily violated expectations when things get tough. Close group facilitation, conflict resolution, and team-building activities at this point can also help maintain group commitment.

To the extent that each team sets its own mission and scope of action, the members of the team will be more committed. After initial problem identification activities, they should be encouraged to set aggressive short-term and long-term objectives and secure management's agreement and support early. This is best done by taking each group through the goal-setting process where they clarify their mission, set objectives, and establish concrete goals and action plans to support each objective.

Setting Measurements

Measures to evaluate group and project results are often overlooked or simply not established. Group and project objectives, goals, and action plans form the basis for clear measurement of progress—a key involvement effort issue from beginning to end.

There are both hard and soft measures. Facilitators and trainers are often accused of depending too heavily on soft measures, while their evaluators tend to be looking for harder, more concrete measures.

Hard measures are best developed during early stages of the project and, when done properly, can define the project itself. These measures can be effectively developed by answering the question, "What will be changed as a result of this effort?" Concrete objectives, goals, and actions are needed to establish these hard measures. More specifically, they should be set in quantifiable terms, such as percent fewer rejects, percent more machines up per shift, percent of market increase, price gap reduction, product superiority, profit margin improvement, percent quality improvement, and customer services levels. Target dates for completion, cost reduction amounts, and specific technical changes should also be noted. By setting sights on these hard measures early, groups can gauge efforts along the way and increase chances of achieving superior results. Further, if goals and objectives are backed by specific action plans and the teams meet regularly, they can assess their progress against their own measures.

Soft measures deal with the relationships that are developed through association and cooperation while striving for common objectives. As we mentioned before, to the extent groups define their own group decision-making methods, resolve their own conflicts, define their own roles, and establish their own means of communicating with each other, they will take more responsibility and initiative on an ongoing basis to meet established objectives on their own. These accomplishments should not be minimized, because they are necessary to the success and continuation of cooperative involvement. Furthermore, they can have other measurable side results, such as dramatic reductions in the number of grievances or debilitating organization conflicts and critical incidents. Facilitators of involvement efforts should keep in mind, however, that these soft measures, though necessary and important, are not sufficient for continued sanctioning of the project and should not be depended on to sustain support for ongoing participative efforts.

Updating the Steering Committee

Some words are needed about managing the ongoing interface between the management sanctioning body, or steering committee, and the involvement group. Since the sanctioning body will tend not to be involved with day-to-day activities, they should be regularly updated. We recommend that representatives of involvement groups meet with them at least monthly to review goals and objectives, give an update on current progress, and discuss the next steps. Sharing critical incidents, concrete progress measures, and casual anecdotes helps all involved feel good about progress being made. It further arms them with facts and ideas to share with others in the organization at large. Sharing with the larger organization in informal ways is an effective means of managing the organization's expectation of the whole involvement process. We further recommend that the monthly sanctioning body meetings be summarized, including critical incidents, dates, and concrete progress results, and distributed appropriately up and down the organization. These brief summaries should not be confused with a more lengthy collection of meeting minutes.

Who is involved in progress updates and their formats may vary according to the circumstances. Of critical importance, however, is that some form of regular update pass between the key management support group and the participants in the involvement groups at the bottom of the chain, and that key events be recorded for future reference.

Principles of Participation

It may be helpful to the organizer of a participative group to have a set of guidelines or principles to assist in anticipating problems. Listed below are several that will help maintain the integrity and credibility not only of the process of participation but also of those trainers who are the managers of it:

1. Management must know why they want employee input, and these reasons need to be ethically congruent with the philosophy of participation and involvement.
2. Management must listen to and be willing to consider the input of employees.
3. Top management must support the process and have a visible role.
4. There must be a willingness to share information about the organization, its objectives, and its performance.
5. Time must be available to train people to work in a participative environment.

These principles can be incorporated into the involvement process in a variety of ways. For example, they can be used as part of the assessment for readiness by the trainer, or they can be emphasized during the early organizing meetings of the sanctioning group. In any case, it is better to make these principles explicit early in the process than to attempt to introduce them after problems arise.

Cautions

1. *Looking for the quick fix and wanting to initiate a participation and involvement process at the same time.* These two aspirations are totally incongruent, since

time is one of the investments required for a successful participative effort. Participation is often described as "beginning a journey, not a destination."

2. *Skipping over middle and first-line supervisors by beginning participation efforts with the factory line workers.* This happens frequently and is often caused by a desire to get quick action and see short-term results. Since supervisors are part of management, the false assumption is that they will automatically see the benefits and will support the "program." That, however, is usually not true, since the direct involvement of employees in the decision-making process is as much of a threat to the security of the supervisor as to the union steward.

3. *Unwillingness of a group to take a risk.* Sometimes a group is too timid to propose anything they feel management will not like. This prevents them from exploring their innovativeness and the full range of possible solutions to problems. The trainer needs to encourage them to brainstorm and take necessary risks.

Knowing When to Dissolve a Group or Project

There are three criteria for deciding when a participative group needs to be discontinued:

1. When the objectives of the group have been reached.
2. When the effort has outlived its usefulness.
3. When it's time to admit a failure and learn from it.

Some groups are created to accomplish a particular objective and, upon achieving it, are disbanded. They may be brought together again to tackle a new objective, with the same or different membership, but the accomplishment of the original purpose was their end.

The second possibility applies to groups which are formed for less specific objectives and which could continue indefinitely. When groups of this kind become institutionalized, they run the risk of becoming ineffective. They continue to meet because they have been meeting for a long time, and they believe that someone expects them to continue. At this point, the effectiveness of the group needs to be evaluated and a decision made as to its future.

We read a lot about successful participative activities but not much about the failures. This is understandable, but the fact remains there are unsuccessful participative ventures. There can obviously be a multitude of reasons for failures, but it is up to the trainer to recognize when the effort has failed and to dissolve the project. As in many things in life, an organization frequently learns more from a mistake than from a success.

Summary

Throughout this chapter we have stressed the importance of evaluating your motives for initiating employee involvement and your organization's readiness for implementing such a program. Once you have determined that both management and employees are committed to undertaking a participative effort, it is up to the trainer to implement necessary training, facilitate the group projects, and maintain an organizational and group climate which will nurture their progress. If the basic principles of successful participation are thoroughly understood by those involved and are used as guidelines in establishing involvement groups, then the process itself, and the resulting heightened cooperative spirit, should yield quality resolutions to all types of organizational problems.

References

1. Walton, Richard E., "From Control to Commitment in the Work Place," *Harvard Business Review*, March–April 1985, p. 77.

2. Conner, Daryl R., and Don Kelley, "Emotional Cycle of Change," in John E. Jones and J. William Pfeiffer, eds., *1979 Annual Handbook for Group Facilitators*, University Associates, LaJolla, CA, p. 117.

Further Reading

Ackoff, Russell L., and William B. Deane, "The Revitalization of ALCOA's Tennessee Operations," *National Productivity Review*, summer 1984, Vol. 3, No. 3, pp. 239–245.

Carlson, Howard C., and D. L. Landen, "Strategies for Defusing, Evolving, and Institutionalizing Quality of Work Life at General Motors," In R. Zager and M.P. Rosow, eds., *The Innovative Organization: Productivity Programs in Action*, Pergamon Press/Work in America Institute, New York, 1982, pp. 291–335.

Dewar, Donald L., "The Quality Circle Handbook," Quality Circles Institute, 1425 Vista Way, Red Bluff, CA 96080-1335.

Goodman, Paul S., "Why Productivity Programs Fail: Reasons and Solutions," *National Productivity Review*, autumn 1982, pp. 369–380.

Kanter, Rosebeth Moss, "Dilemmas of Managing Participation," *Organizational Dynamics*, summer 1982, pp. 5–27.

Klein, Janice A., "Why Supervisors Resist Employee Involvement," *Harvard Business Review*, September–October 1984, No. 5, pp. 87–95.

Lawler, Edward E. III, and David E. Nadler, "Quality of Work Life: Perspectives and Directions," *Organization Dynamics*, winter 1983, pp. 20–30.

Lawler, Edward E. III, "Increasing Worker Involvement to Enhance Organizational Effectiveness," in Paul S. Goodman and Associates, eds., *Change in Organizations*, Jossey-Bass Publishers, 1982, pp. 280–315.

Macy, Barry A., "Employee Involvement: A Summary Report," Presentation to Environmental Scanning Association, October 1984.

Oshry, Barry, and Leonard A. Schlesinger, "Quality of Work Life and the Manager: Muddle in the Middle," *Organizational Dynamics*, summer 1984, pp. 5–19.

Sashkin, Marshall, "Participative Management Is an Ethical Imperative," *Organizational Dynamics*, spring 1984, pp. 5–22.

Section 5

Resources

45

Information Resources

L. James Olivetti

L. James Olivetti is Information Center Manager at ASTD where he is responsible for development of information-based products and services. Prior to joining ASTD in 1984, Olivetti held positions of User Services Associate and Associate Editor for Acquisition & Selection with the American Psychological Association's PsycINFO database. His experience with PsycINFO included database administration and customer training. For 6 years, he served as Education/Psychology Librarian and Head of Reference at George Mason University Library, Fairfax, VA, where he initiated online information retrieval services for students and faculty. He received his M.S. in Library and Information Science from Simmons College and his M.A. in Industrial/Organizational Psychology from George Mason University.

Training professionals need to make efficient use of two kinds of knowledge about the training field. They need to be grounded in "academic" knowledge and keep abreast of new findings generated by academic research. They also need to be aware of, and make use of, "street" knowledge generated within the training practitioners day-to-day world of the workplace.[1]

The primary purpose of this chapter is to describe resources that trainers can use to tap into both academic and street knowledge about training. The subject matters trainers teach, safety, welding, customer relations, etc., will not be addressed here.

Sources of information and information access methods are always in flux. This change is fueled, in part, by the power of computers to store, manipulate, and disseminate information. The resources and strategies presented here have achieved some stability and longevity. However, new technological developments and new resources appear at an alarming rate. Trainers need to be alert to developments that will supersede information in this chapter.

Sources of Academic Knowledge

Several academic disciplines contribute to formal theory and research in training. This can be seen in the variety of university departments that offer coursework in training including behavioral sciences, communications, instructional media, education, adult education, vocational education, business, and counseling.[2] This diversity is important in that a resource for academic knowledge may be oriented toward only one discipline's viewpoint or approach.

Overview Sources

For trainers not well versed in the academic knowledge base of a particular topic, a good place to begin is a handbook such as this one. Handbooks provide an overview of major theoretical issues and point out key research studies. Examples of some other overview sources for training include *Handbook of Industrial and Organizational Psychology, Human Resources Management and Development Handbook, Handbook of Human Resource Development,* and *Annual Review of Psychology.*

Books

Books provide a source of detailed information on a topic and often serve to synthesize and interpret a large body of academic research. Two bibliographies that provide excellent listings of landmark books in training are the Ontario Society for Training and Development's *Weighted Bibliography: Learning Resources for T&D/ HRD Practitioners* and the University of Minnesota's *Human Resource Development Bibliography.* A monthly printed bibliography of books, as well as government documents and journal articles, that is both relevant and inexpensive is *Personnel Literature.*

Trainers who have an ongoing need for books but who do not have large budgets for book purchase should consider building a relationship with a nearby university library. University libraries, in some cases, offer corporate borrowing privileges, allowing trainers many services normally reserved for students and faculty.

Most university libraries use the Library of Congress subject headings to provide subject access to the library's book collection through a card catalog or computerized catalog. Trainers will find the bulk of the library's training collection listed under the following headings taken from the Library of Congress Subject Headings:

Employees, Training of

see also:

Apprentices

Assessment centers

Business education (Internship)

Employee induction

Employee training directors

Executives, Training of

International business enterprises—Employees, Training of

Occupational retraining

Sales personnel, Training of
Technical education
Training manuals

Academic Journals

Trainers seeking the most up-to-date academic knowledge in their field must look beyond overview sources and books and consult academic journals. The typical academic journal article focuses on a single research study or synthesizes a group of such studies on a discrete topic. Journal articles reporting the results of academic research often have a standardized format that includes:

- Brief literature review
- Research hypothesis
- Experimental design
- Results
- Summary and conclusions

This format allows for easy initial scanning of the articles.

A sample of the U.S. journals that regularly publish academic knowledge relevant to trainers is listed below. However, keep in mind that new journals are introduced and existing journals change their names or cease publication on a continuing basis. A thorough search of the literature necessitates use of computerized databases, or printed indexes and abstracts, described in a later section.

Adult Education Quarterly, American Association for Adult and Continuing Education

California Management Review, University of California, Graduate School of Business Administration

Education Communications & Technology Journal (ECTJ), Association for Educational Communications & Technology

Group and Organization Studies, American Society for Training and Development

Harvard Business Review, Harvard University, Graduate School of Business Administration

Human Resource Management, John Wiley & Sons, Inc.

Journal of Applied Psychology, American Psychological Association

Journal of Industrial Teacher Education, National Association of Industrial & Technical Teacher Educators

Performance & Instruction, National Society for Performance and Instruction

Personnel Psychology, Personnel Psychology, Inc.

Public Personnel Management, International Personnel Management Association

Sloan Management Review, Massachusetts Institute of Technology

Sources of Street Knowledge

Street knowledge is less defined and less controlled than academic knowledge. It is knowledge that is gathered by "word of mouth," informally on a trainer-to-trainer basis. Therefore, the trainer's entire work-related environment can be said to serve as a source of street knowledge.

Trainers can take certain steps to fine tune the channels by which they are receiving street knowledge. Resources and strategies for achieving this fine tuning are described below.

Professional Associations

Being an active member of at least one professional association is probably the single most important thing a trainer can do to tie into sources of street knowledge. Some examples of practitioner-oriented resources professional associations typically provide are demographic and salary surveys, newsletters on national issues, employment opportunity announcements, professional standards, specialized libraries or information centers, and professional development opportunities in the form of workshops and conferences.

Networking. A source of practitioner-based knowledge that professional associations uniquely offer is the availability of networking among members. Effective networks provide at least four kinds of benefits to participants:

- Insider information on latest developments

- Expert opinion and advice

- Morale support and alliance building

- Access to still other networks[3]

Such networks can be formally structured by the association for its members or self-generated by the members. An example of a formal network is ASTD's Member Information Exchange (MIX). Administered by ASTD's Information Center, this network is an in-house database of members' expertise profiles that can be tapped by other members seeking information on specific training topics. "Experts" in the database have volunteered to assist their peers by sharing their practical expertise and knowledge.

Informal networking can take place during national conferences, committee meetings, or simply through creative use of an association's membership directory.

Mailing Lists. A sometimes overlooked, and occasionally maligned, benefit of association membership is the opportunity to be included on professional mailing lists that are made available to vendors of training-related products and services. Some trainers may feel that unsolicited promotional material in their mail is burdensome. However, regular scanning of direct mail announcements can serve as a valuable current awareness resource for practitioners.

Major Associations. While ASTD is the major U.S. association for training professionals, a number of other organizations have special interest groups for trainers, or at least a substantial number of members who are in the training field. There are also a growing number of associations that focus on a single aspect of training. Finally, trade associations of many industries, such as health, construction, or transportation, are good resources for highly focused training information. Major U.S. training-related associations include:

American Association for Adult and
   Continuing Education
1201 16th Street, N.W., Suite 230
Washington, DC 20036
202/822-7866

American Society for Personnel
   Administration
606 N. Washington Street
Alexandria, VA 22314
703/548-3440

American Society for Training and
   Development
1630 Duke Street
Box 1443
Alexandria, VA 22313
703/683-8100

Association for the Development of
   Computer-Based Instructional Systems
Miller Hall 409
Western Washington University
Bellingham, WA 98225
206/676-2860

Association for Educational
   Communications and Technology
1126 16th Street, N.W.
Washington, DC 20036
202/466-4780

Human Resource Planning Society
P.O. Box 2553

Grand Central Station
New York, NY 10163
212/490-6387

International High Technology Training
   Association
P.O. Box 1565
Melbourne, FL 32901
305/676-3747

International Society for Intercultural
   Education, Training and Research
1414 22nd Street, N.W., Suite 102
Washington, DC 20037
202/296-4710

National Society for Performance and
   Instruction
1126 16th Street, N.W., Suite 214
Washington, DC 20036
202/861-0777

National Society of Sales Training
   Executives
1040 Woodcock Road
Orlando, FL 32803
305/894-8312

OD Network
P.O. Box 69329
Portland, OR 97201
503/246-0148

Seminars

Seminars can vary in content from the very theoretical to the very applied. Their overall goal is not to produce scholars but rather to bring attendees up to speed in a new field in a concentrated period of time. They may originate as offshoots of university curricula but are also sponsored by associations, businesses, government agencies, or private consultants. A side benefit of seminar attendance that should not be overlooked is the opportunity to share mutual experiences with like-minded participants.

The large number and diversity of seminars available presents a significant selection problem to the practitioners. Various print and computerized services exist to assist trainers in identifying seminars for themselves or employees in their firms. Among the best known are:

SIS Workbook.   An annual printed directory with supplements providing seminar descriptions listed by subject with sponsors and dates.

Seminars Directory.   A semiannual publication that lists seminars with descriptions under 150 subject areas.

Seminar Clearinghouse International. A telephone referral service that provides descriptions of seminars and evaluations provided by SCI subscribers. Seminar Clearinghouse International is located in St. Paul, MN.

EdVENT Database. A computerized database of 70,000 seminars that is accessible over personal computer or terminal. The database is produced by Timeplace, Inc., Waltham, MA.

Professional Conferences and Trade Shows

The professional associations listed above all hold annual conferences for their memberships with nonmembers welcomed. These conferences typically have concurrent sessions with papers delivered on a range of topics. One-day workshops are often held before or after the conference as well. Conference presentations are an excellent source of the most current knowledge—knowledge that may take a year or more to reach publication in a journal or book.

Beyond learning from these formal presentations, much practical knowledge can be gained from visiting product expositions, socializing with peers at conference receptions, and rubbing elbows with training "gurus" who are often keynote speakers or association officers.

Several training-related enterprises have evolved annual events similar to association conferences. Among the most widely publicized are:

- Training Annual Conference, Lakewood Publications, Inc.
- U.A. Annual Conference, University Associates, Inc.
- COMMTEX, International Communications Industries Association
- Computer-Based Training Conference, Weingarten Publications, Inc.

Practitioner Journals

A number of training-related journals are oriented toward publishing street knowledge rather than solely research reports. The typical article in such a journal is written by a practitioner and describes how a practical problem can be addressed in an actual training setting. Other articles provide "how-to" advice, checklists of steps to follow in conducting a training activity, or news of products and events in the field.

Aside from the articles, trainers can pick up additional useful street knowledge from advertisements, book and media reviews, letters and editorials, and events calendars.

Major U.S. practitioner journals are:

Bulletin on Training, Bureau of National Affairs, Inc.

OD Practitioner, OD Network

Personnel, American Management Association

Personnel Administrator, American Society for Personnel Administration

Training, Lakewood Publications, Inc.

Training and Development Journal, American Society for Training and Development

Training News, Weingarten Publications, Inc.

Performance Aids

A wide variety of printed performance aids are available that trainers can turn to for practical advice and assistance on the job. The following list of such aids is a sample of the kinds available; it is not comprehensive. Prices have been omitted, as they would soon be out of date.

ASTD Buyer's Guide and Consultant Directory published by ASTD and *Training Marketplace Directory* published by Lakewood Publications. These are two annual directories of products and services available to training practitioners. Both are organized by topic and contain full producer contact information.

Trainer's Resource published by HRD Press. A regularly updated guide to several hundred commercially produced learning programs deliverable at a company's site. Program prices and recent program users are provided.

Annual: Developing Human Resources published by University Associates. An annual handbook of practical materials: lectures, instrumentation, and structured experiences for use in training, career development, and organization development functions. The materials may be reproduced from the volumes for educational training events.

Info-Line published by ASTD. A monthly booklet series with each issue devoted to a single topic related to training delivery. The booklets contain job aids, checklists, guidelines, and extensive resource lists.

HRD Review published by G. F. Khoury. A monthly looseleaf publication providing reviews of new books, videocassettes, games and simulations, packaged programs, etc. Evaluative reviews are written by practicing trainers.

ASTD Training Video Directory published by ASTD. A two-volume directory of over 12,000 training-related video programs. Indexed by subject, each program entry includes information on date, producer-distributor, target audience, length, and a brief program description.

Media Profiles: The Career Development Edition published by Olympic Media Information. A bimonthly guide to training film and video programs. Training professionals prepare reviews that include target audience, content summary, and brief evaluation. Approximately 150 current programs are profiled each year.

Training and Development Organization Directory published by Gale Research. An irregularly revised directory of approximately 2000 firms, institutes, specialized university programs, and other agencies which offer training and development programs. The work is organized geographically with a detailed subject index.

Hope Reports U.S. Training Business published by Hope Reports, Inc., Rochester, NY. A market study report of the commercial training business with data about suppliers of off-the-shelf training programs, custom design services, and generic seminars. Includes commercial training revenues by year since 1977, region, subject matter, client industry, media, etc.

Computer Databases

The conscientious trainer who wants to use published academic and street knowledge available to improve the quality of his or her training programs is faced with the formidable task of harnessing the wealth of published material that is growing along with the general information explosion in our society. Fortunately, the 1970s and 1980s have witnessed successful application of computers to the control of this literature.

The Search Process

Computerized searching of databases for literature provides a number of advantages over precomputerized manual searching of printed abstracts and indexes. Among the major advantages are:

- Speed of machine, as opposed to human, searching of files containing several hundred thousand references

- Currency of information on-line, not requiring lag time for printing and mailing of a printed source

- Flexibility of combining several concepts in a single search

- Automated output of a sorted bibliography in print or machine readable format

In a typical computerized database search, a searcher at a terminal, or microcomputer with modem, types out a search query statement, for example, "locate articles on stress management training." The statements are transmitted via a telecommunications network to a vendor mainframe computer that has loaded a variety of databases. The search query is processed by the vendor and a response, "located 28 references on stress management training" is returned on-line to the searcher.

All 28 references can be viewed or printed on-line, or printed off-line by the vendor and mailed. Most vendors provide on-line ordering of full text of the referenced articles for an additional fee through a document delivery service. This interactive searching process is illustrated in Fig. 45-1.

Do-It-Yourself Searching

Trainers interested in performing their own on-line searches may wish to consult an introductory text such as *Online Searching: A Primer* by Fenichel and Hogan.[4] A glossary of basic on-line searching terms is included at the end of this chapter.

An on-line database search usually involves obtaining from a database vendor a password that serves as a billing mechanism for vendor charges. Searches can be performed either on a terminal with an acoustic coupler or modem, or on a microcomputer with modem and telecommunications software. Training in both

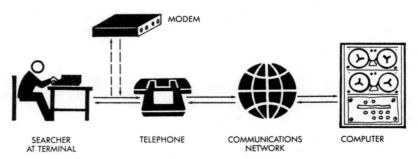

SEARCHER   TELEPHONE   COMMUNICATIONS   COMPUTER
AT TERMINAL   NETWORK

Figure 45-1. Interactive searching process.

the system commands of the on-line vendor and the special features of particular databases is essential to really efficient searching.

Two database vendors in the United States that provide computer access to the most important training-related databases are BRS and Dialog Information Retrieval Service. Their addresses are:

BRS
1200 Route 7
Latham, NY 12110

Dialog
3460 Hillview Avenue
Palo Alto, CA 94304

Brokered Searching

Trainers who are not in a position to perform their own database searching still can take advantage of the technology in one of two ways.

Many major database producers perform searches of their own files and provide printouts off-line, for example, PsycINFO through its PASAR service or ERIC through its Clearinghouses. An advantage to producer searches is the producer's familiarity with the database content, indexing, etc. The search result is, therefore, typically of high quality. However, these "custom searches" are usually fairly expensive and the trainer loses a great deal of control of the research process.

Alternatively, the trainer may contract with a search intermediary to perform on-line searches. The difference between this alternative and the first is that the intermediary is not a member of the database producer's staff. The typical intermediary is an information professional in an academic library, public library, or corporate setting. Private information consultants or brokers often offer searching as one of their client services.

The intermediary is not usually as familiar with a specific database as is the database producer. However, fees for intermediary searches are often low, particularly in public library or public supported universities. Often there is opportunity for face-to-face discussions prior to the search. By making inquiries, it is usually possible to identify an intermediary locally with knowledge of training-related databases who can provide searches at a reasonable cost.

Training-Related Databases

The databases described here are reference databases. They refer or "point" researchers to other sources, rather than contain the actual information referenced. Furthermore, these databases are all bibliographic; that is, they provide access to published information such as journal articles, conference reports, dissertations, or books.

In most cases, these computer databases are used to produce the printed indexes and abstracts that are found on the shelves of many university and public libraries. Printed versions of the databases are noted below where appropriate.

ERIC (Educational Resources Information Center)
Producer: National Institute of Education

U.S. Department of Education
1200 19th Street, N.W.
Washington, DC 20208

The ERIC database is a national information system providing access to education literature by and for educational practitioners and scholars. ERIC includes references to journal literature from 750 education-related publications and nonjournal literature such as curriculum materials, conference proceedings, program descriptions, and research reports.

The ERIC Clearinghouse on Adult, Career, and Vocational Education has primary responsibility for adding to the database information relevant to training, from "basic literacy training through professional skill upgrading."

Two monthly printed publications parallel the major divisions of the ERIC database: *Current Index to Journals in Education* covering the journal literature, and *Resources in Education* covering the nonjournal material.

ABI/Inform   620 South Fifth Street
Producer: Data Courier, Inc.   Louisville, KY 40202

ABI/Inform is a business database covering articles from 650 journals, including 200 journals published outside the United States. The full range of business topics is covered by ABI/Inform including human resources, general management, marketing, finance, accounting, etc. Each record includes a 200-word summary of the article content. There is no printed resource corresponding to the on-line database.

The database is segmented by management function codes to increase on-line searching precision. The human resource management functional area is subdivided into five narrow classifications: human resource planning, training and development, labor relations, employee benefits and compensation, and employee problems. As of fall 1985, approximately 10,500 articles in the database were classified with the code for training and development.

PsycINFO

Producer: American Psychological   1200 17th Street, N.W.
  Association   Washington, DC 20036

The PsycINFO database covers the world's journal literature in psychology and related behavioral sciences. Articles from over 1100 journals, half of which are published outside the United States, are indexed and abstracted for inclusion in PsycINFO. The print counterpart to the PsycINFO database is the monthly abstract journal *Psychological Abstracts*.

A significant segment of the PsycINFO database references publications in the field of applied psychology, and includes topics very relevant to training research. The major category "applied psychology" is broken down into eight subdivisions including occupational attitudes and interests, personnel selection and training, personnel evaluation and performance, management and management training, organizational behavior, and job satisfaction. As of fall 1985, about 21,500 articles in PsycINFO were classified as applied psychology.

NTIS   U.S. Department of Commerce
Producer: National Technical Information   5285 Port Royal Road
  Service   Springfield, VA 22161

NTIS is the central source for public dissemination and sale of U.S. government-sponsored research. The database includes technical reports and other analyses prepared by national and local government agencies, their contractors or grantees.

The NTIS database includes a substantial number of technical reports on training. These often are in the form of model curricula, training manuals, demonstration programs, case studies, and simulations. The database is particularly strong in computer-based training documents. Much of the material is sponsored by one of the branches of the armed forces for application to military personnel training. In fall 1985, over 7000 reports were classified in the section of the database designated as "job training and career development."

The NTIS computerized database is represented in print by the biweekly publication *Government Reports Announcements and Index*. Copies of NTIS-referenced reports are available for ordering from NTIS in paper or microfiche.

WILSONLINE—Business Periodicals Index   950 University Avenue
Producer: H.W. Wilson Company   Bronx, NY 10452

Business Periodicals Index (BPI), available for on-line searching through WILSONLINE, indexes 300 of the most important English-language journals in trade and business research. Key training-related journals are included in the coverage. BPI is unlike other databases described here in that the database producer, H.W. Wilson, serves as the database vendor through WILSONLINE. BPI is not available on Dialog or BRS. Therefore, to search the database, a unique system command language must be learned.

BPI is updated twice per week, which makes it a source of very current information. Because it covers the core business journals, most of the articles it references are available in local libraries. However, as of fall 1985, no abstracts were provided for articles referenced in the database. A unique feature provided by WILSONLINE is the ability to conduct a simultaneous search over BPI and Education Index, another H.W. Wilson database. This may be advantageous for researching some training topics that span the education and business disciplines. The print counterpart to BPI online is the printed source, *Business Periodicals Index*.

Glossary

Connect time: The amount of time a remote terminal is connected to a vendor's computer.

Database: A collection of numeric data and/or textual information that is processed by publishers in computer-readable form for electronic publishing of printed materials and/or for electronic distribution.

Database producer: An organization that compiles and/or publishes information in machine-readable form.

Database record: A collection of related items of data treated as a unit. In a bibliographic database, a record is typically all the information stored to represent a document (author, title, date, abstract, etc.).

Database vendor: An organization that provides standardized computer access to a large number of databases through a contract or fee arrangement.

Free-tax searching: Searching for concepts or words without relying solely on thesaurus vocabulary. Free-text searching usually includes searching titles and abstracts.

Modem: A device that converts digital signals from a terminal or personal computer into analog tones which phone lines are capable of transmitting and that reverses the process when the terminal or personal computer receives information from the vendor's computer.

Off-line: Computer processing that takes place after the searcher has disconnected and is no longer interacting with the computer.

On-line: Ongoing communication between searcher and vendor's computer involving immediate transmission of queries and results.

Telecommunications network: A system that links user terminals to vendor computers for purposes of long-distance transmission of data.

Thesaurus: List of subject headings used by indexers to assign headings to items in a database, usually cross-referenced and showing relationships among terms. Searchers employing thesaurus terms are likely to produce highly relevant results.

References

1. Mitroff, I. I., "Why Our Old Pictures of the World Do Not Work Anymore," Chapter 2 in Edward E. Lawler III, ed., *Doing Research That Is Useful for Theory and Practice*, Jossey-Bass, San Francisco, 1985, pp. 35–36.

2. Pace, R. W., B. D. Peterson, and W. M. Porter, "Competency-Based Curricula," *Training and Development Journal*, 40(3): 71–78 (1986).

3. Ferguson, J., "Networks: Beyond the Hoopla," *Issues & Observations*, 1(3): 1–3 (1981).

4. Fenichel, C. H., and T. H. Hogan, *Online Searching: A Primer*, 2d ed., Learned Information, Marlton, NJ, 1984.

Bibliography

Annual: Developing Human Resources, University Associates, Inc., San Diego, CA.

Annual Review of Psychology, Annual Reviews, Inc., Palo Alto, CA.

ASTD Buyer's Guide & Consultant Directory, ASTD, Alexandria, VA.

DeGideo, S., and R. A. Swanson, *Human Resource Development Bibliography*, University of Minnesota, Department of Vocational and Technical Education, St. Paul, MN, 1985.

Dunnette, M. D., ed., *Handbook of Industrial and Organizational Psychology*, John Wiley & Sons, Inc., New York, 1983.

HRD Review, George F. Khoury, Glen Rock, NJ.

Info-Line, ASTD, Alexandria, VA.

Media Profiles: The Career Development Edition, Olympic Media Information, Hoboken, NJ.

Nadler, L., ed., *Handbook of Human Resource Development*, John Wiley & Sons, Inc., New York, 1984.

Personnel Literature, U.S. Office of Personnel Management Library, Washington, DC.

Seminars Directory, Creative Communications, Inc., Madison, WI.

SIS Workbook, Seminar Information Service, Inc., New York.

Seussmuth, P. F., and W. H. Cumberland, *Weighted Bibliography: Learning Resources for the HRD Practitioner*, Ontario Society for Training and Development, Toronto, Ont., 1985.

Tracey, W. R., ed., *Human Resources Management and Development Handbook*, Amacom, New York, 1985.

Trainer's Resource, Human Resource Development Press, Amherst, MA.

Training Marketplace Directory, Lakewood Publications, Inc., Minneapolis, MN.

Wasserman, Paul, ed., *Training and Development Organizations Directory*, Gale Research, Detroit, MI.

46

Colleges and Universities

Theodore J. Settle

Theodore J. Settle is Director of the NCR Management College at NCR Corporation in Dayton, Ohio. He is responsible for the design, development, delivery, and evaluation of management education programs for NCR managers worldwide. Settle received his doctorate in education at the University of Michigan and his MBA from Harvard University. He had 9 years of experience in teaching, research, and administration in higher education and a Woodrow Wilson Foundation fellowship before joining NCR in 1980. He is a frequent speaker at national forums and has authored several articles on the benefits of partnerships between business and higher education. Settle is a member of the advisory committees at several universities and the Educational Opportunity Center in Dayton. He was a charter member of the Advisory Committee to the Program on Noncollegiate Sponsored Instruction of the American Council on Education, is on the board of directors of the Council on the Continuing Education Unit, and recently served as a member of the project review panel for the Standards Project that was responsible for the Principles of Good Practice. He is a Major in the United States Army Reserve.

Although most training and development professionals have at least one college degree and have spent many years in the academic world, institutions of higher education are not often considered as resources to address the training, development, and research needs of business. This chapter explores the concept of partnerships in education and training between business and higher education, cites some working examples, and lists some do's and don'ts in building these relationships.

The New Environment in
Higher Education

Colleges and universities did not just happen upon the scene. Likewise, using higher education as a resource to address employees' educational needs is not a new idea. The difference between the past and present is higher education's receptivity to the education and training of fully employed adults.the following hypothetical conversation between a training person and college representative highlights this difference:

> TRAINING PERSON: The training needs in my company are far greater than we can address. We need outside help. We can use some combination of vendors, consultants, and additional internal staff. But, since many of the consultants are college faculty, I wonder if the college would help us identify the kind of faculty support we need and possibly even deliver the program at our site.

> COLLEGE REPRESENTATIVE'S RESPONSE (circa 1960): Our faculty resources are really strained right now. We can't keep up with the demands for additional faculty caused by the steady enrollment increases. Furthermore, our primary purpose is to teach full-time 18- to 22-year-olds. Our faculty teach on-campus on Mondays, Wednesdays, and Fridays from 9 to 12 and 1 to 3. Even if we had the faculty, they certainly don't teach in the evenings and weekends. And to teach at the company's site? We've never done that.

> COLLEGE REPRESENTATIVE'S RESPONSE (circa 1986): The recent enrollment declines have reduced our class sizes to manageable, desirable, academically defensible levels. Our faculty don't teach fewer classes, but they now have opportunities to pursue other activities, like research, consulting, and public service. For example, ABC Company is opening a new development and manufacturing facility 30 miles away. We could meet with them, explain our capabilities and interests, identify their business needs, and explore mutual areas of interest. The success of that facility can have a major impact on the economic development in this area and, over the long term, possibly increase our enrollment.

The mock dialogue from the two time periods clearly does not represent all faculty and administrators from all colleges and universities, but it does accurately reflect a substantial shift in attitude that has occurred for a variety of reasons. The most widely accepted reason is the actual or pending decrease in enrollment. The campus, which once had an ever-increasing student population of full-time 18- to 22-year-olds, has lost some of its clientele. Replacing this lost clientele is a significant number of part-time students who are also full-time employees, but it takes about three part-time students to create the same demand for faculty resources as one full-time student. Consequently, with its traditional client base shrinking, higher education is considerably more receptive to overtures from business.

While the enrollment prognosis for higher education is stable, at best, employee participation in company-sponsored education and training programs has grown dramatically. It is difficult to document the actual number of students in employer training programs, but membership in ASTD has multiplied five times in the past 25 years. Since these professionals design, develop, deliver, and evaluate training programs for their companies, it is quite clear that corporations are investing heavily in developing their human resources.

The growth in employer-sponsored education and training over the past several years has been a well-kept secret from the halls of academe. Now, all of a sudden, faculty are beginning to see the magnitude of this "shadow system" of education. In fact, some experts judge that the current number of students and the amount of money spent on education and training in business approximates that in higher education. The systems are almost equal in size.

In addition to the enrollment decline in higher education and the growing recognition of enrollment growth in employer-sponsored education, continuing education throughout one's life is a much more widely accepted phenomenon. For example, adult education through neighborhood high schools, churches, museums, and libraries has reached new heights as individuals pursue multiple careers in a lifetime or seek enrichment in new areas. Changing technology in the health sciences and engineering requires continuous investments in education by professionals in these fields.

Finally, the importance of education as a necessary ingredient for local and national economic development is no longer debated. The location of Research Triangle Park near Duke University, the University of North Carolina, and North Carolina State University and the location of Microelectronics and Computer Technology Corporation near the University of Texas are not coincidental. Many other cities are attempting to replicate this environment to solicit new high-technology businesses. In fact, North Carolina and South Carolina promise to provide whatever training is necessary to guarantee a qualified labor force to potential industry. At the national level, there are periodic discussions on investment tax credits for employer-provided education and training like the existing tax credits for investments in equipment.

The reasons for the new environment in higher education are many and varied, but there now exists a substantially improved climate for higher education to assist business in satisfying its education and training needs. Peter Drucker assessed the situation as follows: "The fastest growing industry in America today is continuing education for professionals or highly skilled mid-career adults, and most of this is going on outside the education establishment." Higher education is finally beginning to understand that it may be missing a tremendous opportunity.

What's New in Employee Training?

The traditional role of training and development professionals typically involved the design, development, delivery, and evaluation of live instruction. In this environment, few companies, if any, offered so much training that employees said, "We get too much." Rather, most employees said, "I needed this ten years ago. What took so long? This is really helpful. When is the next dose? My boss needs this." Likewise, few training organizations had adequate staff and resources to satisfactorily address the company's education and training needs. And, despite major new commitments to education and training by our employers over the past few years, we have been operating, are operating, and will continue to operate in a shortfall position. Consequently, without significant increases in our staffs, we must take on a new role and perform our trade differently to increase the effectiveness of—as well as the number of persons affected by—education and training.

A global objective for training and development professionals is to deliver the right training to the right people at the right time at the least cost. This implies that these professionals give participants only what they need vs. an entire 1-week course, that specific individuals be targeted for training vs. all sales managers, that the training be provided when it is needed vs. when enough people can be assembled for a class, and that this be done with fewer resources. The only way to achieve or even progress toward this objective is for training and development professionals to evolve from the traditional delivery role to a managerial role involving multiple development and delivery channels.

These professionals should appeal to multiple learning styles, both to create greater choice and to enhance learning. Likewise, alternative delivery systems need to supplement and sometimes replace live instruction. But in their new role, these development and delivery channel managers should greatly increase the number of courses offered and the overall effectiveness of the education and training. As a channel manager, these training and development professionals will supplement traditional, live, in-house delivery with live delivery by external presenters, external course development, off-the-shelf vendor programs, consultants, self-instruction courses (print, computer-aided instruction, interactive videodisc), and credit and noncredit programs by colleges and universities. For example, a 1-day, live, in-house course on time management could be developed and/or delivered by a college or an outside consultant, or it could be purchased from a reputable vendor for live delivery. Alternatively, it could be converted to a self-instruction format using videotape, computer-assisted instruction, or videodisc. Under any of these live or self-instruction options, the prior time commitment of the training and development professional to deliver the live course is now available for other course development or delivery activities, thereby multiplying the results of the individual's talents.

Since the high-tech features of new delivery systems are covered elsewhere in this handbook, this chapter focuses on credit and noncredit programs by colleges and universities.

Win-Win Relationships

Business and higher education have operated relatively autonomously for many years. What opportunities do both sectors in our society envision that could nudge the relationship from curious observers to serious courting, to engagement, and finally to marriage? The driving force behind this relationship derives from the central importance of education in our knowledge-intensive society. The potential benefits to both business and higher education prod the sectors to consummate the relationship.

Higher education offers much to business. Most importantly, it has people— expert faculty in addition to graduates for our work force. The faculty can develop courses and create new windows on research that can result in new products. The students of today are the employees of tomorrow.

Colleges and universities offer, and their faculty deliver, an impressive array of academic courses, degree programs, and credit and noncredit continuing education opportunities at cost-effective rates. The tuition and miscellaneous charges are generally modest, and the study is frequently on the employee's own time. Colleges and universities also provide an opportunity through executive-in-residence programs to challenge senior managers on various issues. For example, many current managers lived through the Vietnam War, but few are equipped to discuss apartheid in South Africa and the threat of nuclear war, both major issues on today's campuses and increasingly in the international business environment. Finally, college faculty as adjunct faculty to corporate education and training organizations represent a way to add status, quality, and quantity to live delivery.

Higher education also has much to gain in this symbiotic relationship. Its students and faculty are major beneficiaries. Business offers significant numbers of students who want and need additional formal study. These students are generally serious, mature, highly motivated, and challenging. They bring experience to the classroom and a need for relevance to their lives. These qualities tend to create a more rich and rewarding learning experience for the other students and faculty. Not insignificantly, their full-time salaries and the companies' tuition-refund assistance programs minimize the need for financial aid.

Faculty development is another major benefit for colleges and universities. Working with business gives faculty the opportunity to road-test their theories, improve their curricula, develop consulting arrangements, and gain access to corporate data and funds for research projects. Executive-in-residence programs add a real-world flavor to the academic environment—an insight into "What's happening out there?" Business also offers job opportunities through part-time positions and internship experiences. Finally, business has resources for faculty time, support services, travel, consulting, new equipment, and technology. In sum, both sides bring much to this developing relationship.

Much is already occurring on a one-company–one-college basis. However, several major organizations representing associations of colleges and universities are quite active in extending the horizon of this relationship.

For one, the American Council on Education has three major initiatives. First, a recent annual conference focused on college-corporation cooperation. Second, the Business-Higher Education Forum,[1] an organization of presidents and chief executive officers from business and higher education, discusses issues of mutual concern. For example, a recent study[2] focused on the state of business education in the United States. And third is ACE's Program on Noncollegiate Sponsored Instruction.[3] In this program, companies invite college faculty to evaluate selected company courses against comparable courses in colleges and universities. If this visiting team recommends a course as being equivalent to a comparable course at the associate, baccalaureate, or graduate level, an employee who completes the course can take this recommendation to the local college or university. The institution can accept or reject the transfer credit, as it can with credit from another college or university. This program provides companies with a third-party assessment of the quality and level of their educational offerings, adds status to both the instructional staff and participants when credit recommendations are awarded, encourages course development personnel and delivery personnel to modify and upgrade their courses, and helps employees narrow the gap between the credits they have and the credits they need for degree completion.

The American Association for Higher Education[4] is another major organization that is working to expand the partnership between business and higher education. AAHE membership consists largely of college presidents, academic vice presidents, and department chairpersons. The theme for an annual conference was business–higher education partnerships. Subsequent annual conferences have further promoted discussion on this topic.

Another such organization, The College Board,[5] is best known for the SAT tests which it annually administers to thousands of high school students. Their Office of Adult Learning Services has sponsored a series of workshops across the country under the following titles: "Making Business and Industry Your New Clientele," "Beyond Alliances: Corporations as Colleges," and "Building Partnerships with Business and Industry."

A major organization working to expand the relationship between business and higher education is the Council on the Continuing Education Unit (CCEU).[6] The members of this organization are continuing education personnel from higher education and education and training personnel from the private and public sectors. It is most widely known for the continuing education unit (CEU), a unit of measurement where one CEU equals ten contact hours of instruction. CEUs are most important for continuing certification in certain professions, such as medicine and allied health, engineering, and quality assurance. The greatest contribution of

CCEU, with cosponsorship from the National University Continuing Education Association, was the development of "Standards of Good Practice in Continuing Education." The standards can assist education and training personnel in higher education and business in conducting a self-appraisal of the quality of their programs.

The National University Continuing Education Association[7] (NUCEA) includes members from accredited, degree-granting institutions of higher education and comparable organizations, like museums, dedicated to the concept of continuing education for adults. Its primary mission is to encourage the further expansion of and quality improvement in continuing education, particularly at the postsecondary level, through educational and related activities.

The involvement of these major national higher education organizations underscores the perceived significance by colleges and universities of establishing relationships between higher education and business. Both sides have much to offer and much to gain from each other.

Examples of Working Partnerships

As evidence that much is already occurring between colleges and companies on a one-to-one basis, this section highlights some past and present partnerships between NCR Corporation and colleges and universities. These examples are illustrative but not unique to NCR. Your partnerships will need to focus on your needs and circumstances. Once again, partnerships occur only when both parties have something to gain.

Curriculum Development

The Executive Development Program at NCR consisted of a series of seminars for the company's top executives. The University of Dayton designed and delivered, on-campus, one series on Law and Society and another on The International Economy. These programs stretched the participants, and the University of Dayton gained faculty development and financial support.

The NCR Management College recently developed a computer-assisted instruction course on Basic English Grammar for NCR employees. Before the course was released, it was pilot-tested with students from the Developmental Studies Program and the Department of English at Sinclair Community College. Sinclair students were exposed to another delivery system, and NCR gained a higher-quality product.

Improved Quality of New Employees

Wright State University's Department of Management invited senior managers from several Dayton-area employers to discuss their new, competency-based, undergraduate management curriculum. NCR gained an entree to the university and ultimately a higher-quality new employee. Wright State gained a better relationship with several consumers of their products and assurances that they were more effectively preparing their students for the world of work.

Visits

NCR educators and faculty from the College of Education at Ohio State University exchanged site visits. From these visits, NCR gained an entree to Ohio State

University, an exposure to their faculty and Ph.D. graduates, and an awareness of their research on computer-assisted instruction and videodisc technology. Ohio State gained a window into a major educational enterprise in a corporate setting, a research contract, and participation on a dean's advisory committee.

Internships

NCR and other corporations hire a substantial number of undergraduate and graduate interns for employment during the summer and throughout the academic year. The companies gain an opportunity to employ individuals on a short-term basis prior to offering full-time employment. In addition, the students bring considerable enthusiasm and the latest technology to the workplace—a refreshing combination that is also cost-effective. The students gain valuable work experience, a look at full-time employment with one employer, a paying job, and, if successful, an offer for full employment.

On-Site Degree and Continuing Education Programs

NCR is exploring the feasibility of offering on-site bachelor's degree coursework in Computer Science and Business and master's degree coursework in Business and Communications from Wright State University. NCR will gain geographic proximity, thus eliminating another barrier to employee participation in its Tuition Refund Plan. Wright State will better serve its urban clientele and potentially benefit from relationships that typically follow classroom instruction, such as consulting, research contracts, and corporate contacts.

NCR is one of many employers participating in the Association for Media-Based Continuing Education for Engineers[8] (AMCEE) and the National Technological University[9] (NTU). AMCEE is a nonprofit consortium of 33 engineering universities that was formed to increase the national effectiveness of continuing education for engineers, industrial scientists, and technical managers. Its activities include the development and distribution of media-based graduate and continuing education courses. Programs distributed through AMCEE vary from a seminar lasting an hour or two to regular college courses requiring 20 to 30 hours. Most programs are videotape-based. However, more are now being offered interactively through the NTU/AMCEE satellite delivery system.

NTU is a consortium of 21 colleges and universities which uses advanced educational and telecommunications technology to deliver instructional programs to graduate engineers and technical professionals at their place of employment. Technical master's degrees via satellite are available in five major fields, including computer engineering, computer science, electrical engineering, engineering management, and manufacturing systems engineering. NTU is covered more extensively elsewhere in the handbook.

Research

NCR and the University of Michigan have been involved in two research projects. One project, involving employee career progression within and between major job families, was fairly traditional and resembled contract work. NCR supplied money and corporate data; the university supplied the research talent. NCR gained some insight into the research question; the university received support and gained a better understanding of career progression in a large, private sector organization.

The second example is more in the partnership spirit. A major need was perceived at NCR, as in most other training organizations, to substantially improve the evaluation procedures of courses, students, and instructional staff. A doctoral student at the University of Michigan was interested in evaluation and in private sector education. Together an outline was designed for a mutually agreeable project. NCR provided modest resources and access to employees for interviews and survey purposes; the student provided the labor and the research talent. Everybody won. NCR learned more about evaluation methodologies for management education. The doctoral student gained considerable firsthand experience with corporate education and a completed dissertation. NCR is interested in replicating the process on other topics, and the academic department is willing to encourage other doctoral students to work with NCR.

National Forum

Cornell University's School of Industrial and Labor Relations hosted a one-week conference for NCR's personnel managers from around the world. The university exposed these NCR managers to some of the best minds at Cornell. NCR gained stimulating insights from the conference in a highly creative atmosphere. Cornell gained money and an opportunity to have a significant impact on the personnel function in a major corporation. Since NCR is a major employer in Ithaca, New York, this further bonded the NCR-Cornell relationship.

Dayton, Ohio, has a long history of innovative people, including the Wright brothers and Charles F. Kettering. The University of Dayton, several area companies, and a local nonprofit organization called Creativity 80's hosted a conference on innovation in organizations that featured Rosabeth Kantor and Gifford Pinchot III, authors of *The Change Masters*[10] and *Intrapreneuring*,[11] respectively. In this instance, the university and Creativity 80's are serving as a catalyst to bring a program to southwestern Ohio that no one organization could have hosted. NCR and the other area companies obtained access to speakers and presentations that otherwise would have been impossible. The University of Dayton earned considerable recognition as a community resource that addresses community needs.

Tuition Refund Plans

NCR's Tuition Refund Plan is similar to that of many other major corporations. NCR reimburses employees for the full tuition and fees upon successful completion of a course or degree program. The plans of some other companies reimburse on a sliding scale depending on the grade earned, while others pay at the beginning of the term. A small percentage of plans reimburse for combinations of books, supplies, travel, parking, and child care.

NCR is currently in the process of updating the plan by including alternative delivery systems (e.g., National Technological University) and returning adult programs (e.g., credit for life experience, portfolio development, proficiency testing, CLEP, and ACE-PONSI transfer credit), but the major theme remains: to encourage more employees to complete formal degree programs and selective courses through company support.

NCR gains a more educated work force that is also more receptive to change in the workplace. Colleges and universities gain serious, motivated, mature students who generally have no financial aid requirements. Unfortunately, despite a working partnership where the employee, employer, and college all win, the nagging question remains: Why is employee participation in tuition refund plans so low? It is generally accepted that less than 10 percent of all eligible employees are actually participating at any one time. (As one involved in management education, training efforts at NCR could focus on higher-order skills and yield greater results if all managers had at least a bachelor's degree.)

Colleges and universities represent a tremendous resource to help fulfill our training and development needs. As education and training professionals, we need to find additional ways to encourage employees to develop themselves on their own time. At present, tuition refund is a grossly underused resource to address corporate education and training needs.

Who Wins?

This section has focused on some examples of partnerships. Colleges gain and companies gain; however, let us not lose sight of the fact that a working partnership is a collection of individuals (students to the college and employees to the employer) who are learners. The learners drive this process for all parties.

What to Do and What Not to Do

If you are at least partially persuaded that colleges and universities are potential resources to address your company's education and training needs, please consider some personal lessons from the past several years.

The most important step is to know the players in nearby colleges and universities. Find out who they are, what they are like, and what values they share. Channel all your energies in this direction. Remember that the pump is primed: colleges want your business as much as you want their assistance, but they don't know how to take the first step and, like you, they don't know either the people or the correct access point into our organizations. You should lay the first plank in the bridge, instead of waiting for your counterpart to initiate the action. Have a high-ranking official from your company contact his counterpart at the target college. Ask them to discuss the relative interest of both parties in working together. If the college is interested, arrange a meeting at the company site between your vice president for personnel and their vice president for academic affairs for further exploratory discussions. The vice president for personnel can broadly describe his or her business needs, and the vice president for academic affairs can broadly describe university resources and their willingness to engage with a new partner. The next step involves actual discussions around a specific business need, such as on-site courses or degree programs. The college will provide the appropriate expert. The resulting product will largely be a function of the chemistry between the two representatives, especially since colleges tend to be far less hierarchical than companies. It is much more difficult for a vice president in a college to mandate an action. Both parties may need to compromise to yield mutually beneficial results.

The above process is a "by the book" method. You also need to use "street" methods. You need to maximize the number of contacts in your target college. What about your social network? Does your neighbor, golf team, church choir, kid's soccer team, Rotary Club, or other relationship include a faculty member from the target college? If yes, talk to that person about the role of developing employees through company and university sponsored education. If not, you have to spread the word. Networking is critical. Is the faculty member interested in talking to your company? Can he or she recommend someone else? The idea is to get several balls in the air simultaneously. Not all will be caught, but the greater the number the greater the chance for success. Much of your initial effort is to encourage the college representatives to think outside their traditional markets. You want them to color outside the lines!

The primary concerns in obtaining external assistance in either course development or delivery are quality, flexibility of instructional delivery, and evaluation. You want a high-quality product that will do what it is supposed to do and will be delivered at the stated time and place. However, you should be aware of two other issues on many campuses: (1) organization of the continuing education function and (2) price.

Organization is a difficult but important issue. A separate continuing education organization exists on many campuses today. It may be a one-person operation, or it may have a large staff. The crucial issue for you is whether continuing education on the campus is an integral part of the mission, and therefore of the academic program of the institution, or whether it is an appendage operation that is not directly tied to the academic program. (Size of organization is not a factor in determining this; some small and some large continuing education organizations are woven into the fabric of the college and others are separate.) Ideally, you want a college that has integrated continuing education into the mission and the daily life of the campus and its faculty because that college has made a commitment to continuing education. In this environment, continuing education has substantially greater status and ready access to the institution's faculty. These faculty typically participate in credit and noncredit continuing education activities as part of their routine faculty duties. Institutional commitment typically provides other attractive features, such as (1) evening registration, (2) a greater willingness to deliver courses on-site vs. on-campus, and (3) a faculty that is more experienced with adult learners. Frequently, one measure of institutional commitment is the involvment of an institution's own faculty in its continuing education programs. In general, the lower the percentage of its own faculty, the lower the institutional commitment. The continuing education organization in these instances more closely resembles a broker between consultants and students. This does not mean that the programs are of necessarily low quality; however, it does mean that there is little opportunity for other fallout benefits from the partnership. Because you are not working with resident faculty, this kind of relationship generally stops when you pay your money and the course ends.

The other issue is price. It is difficult to give any guidelines about what is a good deal and what is too much. The most important message to continually repeat is quality, quality, quality. Personal experience says that price is a secondary issue, although not unimportant. Some institutions will add a full overhead charge; others will not. At a minimum, consider this a negotiable item. It is far more negotiable than direct costs of faculty salaries, facilities charges, and materials.

Following these do's and don'ts and being sensitive to campus issues are necessary behaviors to consummate the relationship. These mechanics must be grounded on a foundation of faith, flexibility, and positive attitude toward the other party and the desired outcome.

Conclusion

Partnerships can happen only if the people in higher education and business get to know each other, develop relationships, and build personal trust and confidence. Training and development professionals can and should be more active in helping colleges and universities build and maintain relationships with business and the needs of the workplace.

Working with colleges and universities represents a new way for these professionals to address the education and training needs of today's work force. Colleges and universities represent a cost-effective method to augment our current system of meeting education and training needs. The time is ripe to capitalize on this interested third party. Take the first step . . . everybody wins.

References

1. For more information contact American Council of Education, One Dupont Circle, NW, Washington, DC 20036-1193.

2. *America's Business Schools: Priorities for Change*, American Council on Education, Business –Higher Education Forum, Washington, DC, 1985.

3. For more information contact American Council on Education, Office on Educational Credit and Credentials, One Dupont Circle, NW, Washington, DC 20036-1193.

4. For more information contact American Association for Higher Education, One Dupont Circle, NW, Suite 600, Washington, DC 20036.

5. For more information contact The College Board, Office of Adult Learning Services, 888 Seventh Avenue, New York, NY 10019.

6. For more information contact Council on the Continuing Education Unit, 1101 Connecticut Avenue, NW, Washington, D.C. 20036.

7. For more information contact National University Continuing Education Association, One Dupont Circle, NW, Suite 420, Washington, DC 20036-1168.

8. For more information contact Association for Media-Based Continuing Education for Engineers, Inc., 225 North Avenue, NW, Atlanta, GA 30332.

9. For more information contact National Technological University, P. O. Box 700, Fort Collins, CO 80522.

10. Kanter, Rosabeth Moss, *The Change Masters*, Simon and Schuster, New York, 1983.

11. Pinchot, Gifford III, *Intrapreneuring*, Harper & Row, New York, 1985.

Bibliography

Business-Higher Education Forum, *America's Business Schools: Priorities for Change*, Washington, DC, Business-Higher Education Forum in affiliation with the American Council on Education, 1985.

Eurich, Nell P., *Corporate Classrooms*, A Carnegie Foundation Special Report, The Carnegie Foundation for the Advancement of Teaching, Princeton, NJ, 1985.

Fenwick, Dorothy D., ed., *Directory of Campus-Business Linkages*, American Council on Education/Macmillan Series in Higher Education, Macmillan Publishing Company, New York, 1983.

Fenwick, Dorothy D., ed. *Campus-Business Linkage Programs: Education and Business Prospering Together*, 2d ed., American Council on Education/Macmillan Series in Higher Education, Macmillan Publishing Company, New York, 1986.

Gold, Gerald G., ed., *Business and Higher Education: toward New Alliances*, New Directions in Experiential Learning, Number 13, Jossey-Bass, San Francisco, 1981.

Johnson, Lynn G., *The High-Technology Connection: Academic/Industrial Cooperation for Economic Growth*, ASHE-ERIC Higher Education Research Reports. Report 6, Association for the Study of Higher Education, Washington, DC, 1984.

Lynton, Ernest A., *The Missing Connection between Business and the Universities*, American

Council on Education/Macmillan Series in Higher Education, Macmillan Publishing Company, New York, 1984.

Matthews, Jana B., and Rolf Norgaard, *Managing the Partnership between Higher Education & Industry*, National Center for Higher Education Management Systems, Boulder, CO, 1984.

Morse, Suzanne W., *Employee Educational Programs: Implications for Industry and Higher Education*, ASHE-ERIC Higher Education Research Reports, Report 7, Association for the Study of Higher Education, Washington, DC, 1984.

Yeager, Douglas M., and M. Daniel Henry, "Cooperative Planning between NCR and the University of Dayton," *Planning for Higher Education* 12:2 (winter 1984), pp. 6–13.

47

Consultants

Scott B. Parry

William M. Ouweneel

Scott B. Parry is president of Training House in Princeton, New Jersey, and consultant to more than 50 of the Fortune 500 organizations. Active in ASTD, he is a frequent speaker at national conferences and regional meetings. Prior to founding Training House in 1971, Parry was president of Training Development Center, a division of Sterling Institute, in New York. He worked with the ASTD Metropolitan chapter and New York University to set up an adult education program of 10 courses for training and development professionals, and served on the faculty of NYU as principal instructor of the program. Parry's speaking and consulting engagements have taken him to 6 continents and 21 countries. When not on the road, he retreats to his 14-acre farm in Princeton.

William M. Ouweneel is a program manager with the Corporate Education Department of International Business Machines in Armonk, New York. He has worked in both the United States and overseas, having been education manager for IBM Brazil. During a public service leave of absence he was director of the U.S. Peace Corps in Brazil. Subsequently, as Manager of Administration Education for the IBM World Trade Americas/Far East Corporation, he established a computer-based training project that developed and delivered courses from a central location to more than 30 countries via satellite. As an internal consultant with IBM, he has made frequent use of outside training consultants, including his coauthor Parry.

According to the membership list of ASTD, one out of every seven members is a training consultant. A growth in the number of books, articles, and workshops on the subject of HRD consulting is further evidence that more and more organizations have turned to outside resources for help in training and developing their employees. The hiring of consultants must be done on the same basis that any sound purchasing decision is made: through cost-benefit analysis. A client invests in training to help people perform in ways that benefit them and their enterprise. Consultants who cannot earn an organization more money than they cost should not be retained.

Consultant Defined

Let us start by agreeing on what a consultant is—and is not. Most trainers are familiar with one or two of the negative, tongue-in-cheek definitions that abound:

- A consultant is someone who borrows your watch, tells you the time, then keeps it.
- A consultant is someone who can help you go wrong with confidence.
- A consultant is an expert, which comes from the Latin *ex* meaning "has been" or "former," and *spurt*, meaning "a large drip or gush."
- Those who *can do* will do; those who *can't do* will consult.
- A consultant is anyone farther than 50 miles from home and carrying an attaché case costing more than $100.

Fortunately, similar derogatory comments are made about doctors, lawyers, and other professionals, and so we need not take them too seriously. They are, in fact, symptomatic of a universal problem that all of us face: knowing when we do and do not need outside help, be it the help of a consultant, doctor, lawyer, or TV repairman. Because we lack the knowledge and experience that professionals bring us, we are uncertain about how to utilize their services and how to evaluate their performance.

For our purposes, let's agree to define a training consultant as any outside individual or firm who is paid primarily to deliver professional training advice, instruction, or customized development of material. Notice that this definition excludes outside suppliers of films, public seminars, cassettes, audiovisual hardware or software, tests, and other training products or services that are purchased "off the shelf." Of course, our definition does not bar consultants from having a product line. Indeed, those who have been in the consulting business for at least several years are likely to have favorite activities and exercises that they bring to new clients. Experience in using these is one of the consultant's main assets provided they fit the client's needs. Many publishers of instructional systems have a capability and interest in customizing their products to meet their user's requirements. It is here that their publishing activity ends and consulting begins.

In short, a consultant may offer both products and services, but the primary focus must be on the client's needs and not on the sale of existing products. This requires an ability to carry out a needs analysis, to customize, and to provide the supportive service needed to enable a client to get the performance that was specified at the start.

Although our definition and discussion so far have been based on the assumption that the consultant is an outsider, an increasing number of organizations now have internal consultants—specialists in organizational development, human resource utilization, technical training, and so on. An increasing trend is to charge their services to the using department through a system of cross-budget credits and debits. These staff specialists often have more in common with the outside consultant than they do with a training director who is still functioning as the principal of an internal "little red schoolhouse."

When to Use a Consultant

Three major reasons, or needs, prompt companies to use training consultants:

- The need to expand capability on a "crash" basis—when time is short and stakes are high (e.g., using office temporaries to supplement your own staff on a crash project). Many organizations keep a lean training department whose staff members are problem solvers, internal consultants, or project managers who call on outsiders to create and/or deliver courses.

- The need for specialized *expertise* or *facilities* (e.g., calling in the doctor or TV repairman). The design or selection of needs-analysis instruments and/or specialized instructional techniques may require professional skills that can be purchased from an outsider as needed for much less than it would cost to recruit or develop and maintain this expertise internally.

- Need for the "intangibles" of *objectivity* or *corporate leverage* to get a job done. This is a political reason for using an outside consultant whose neutrality and/or credibility is an asset in terms of seeing the problem in a fresh perspective and getting top management to listen. Training directors know all too well that prophets are never heeded in their own country. Outsiders may command attention and be catalysts in getting things done, whereas insiders would have difficulty (either because their personal stakes in the outcome render them suspect or simply because they lack experience, credentials, or leverage).

Given these reasons for employing outside help, let us examine some of the major types of client engagements that consultants accept. Some training consultants are specialists, and others are generalists who have competence in a broad range of activities. Surveying the range of firms and individuals that identify themselves *primarily* as training consultants, we find their activities falling into one or more of the categories listed in Fig 47-1.

Note that we have avoided any reference to the consultant's area of expertise—sales management, bank teller training, etc. A company seeking outside help should look for a consultant with experience in the same industry or functional area (sales). Of course, it is often not possible to find a consultant who is both the subject matter expert (SME) and the behavorial technologist. In most engagements, the client provides the SME who works with the outside consultant. This kind of partnership usually produces a more satisfactory and more cost-effective end result than is possible when the client and consultant work separately on the assumption that the consultant possesses all the subject matter expertise needed to fill the engagement.

Defining the Job

From the client's viewpoint, our "inventory of activities" listed in Fig. 47-1 should help to identify the nature and scope of services you are looking for. Thereafter, it is much easier to *select* the type of consultant who can best meet your needs and to agree on the division of labor between your staff and the consultant's.

Let us illustrate this:

- If you are interested in carrying out a needs analysis and in receiving professional advice on systems design (items a, b, e, and f in Fig. 47-1), then you should seek a consultant who has problem-solving skills, research design experience, maturity, and a following of clients for whom these services have been performed satisfactorily.

a. ANALYSIS—analysis of human performance and assessment of organizational and individual needs. Includes task analysis, systems analysis, behavioral analysis, establishing behavioral objectives and performance criteria, and use of tests and survey research.

b. DESIGN—design of training programs. Includes research to determine course content and a design rationale for selecting methods and media, instructional strategies, criterion tests, and decisions on administering the instruction—when, where, how often, for whom, by whom, etc.

c. PRODUCTION—preparation of instructional materials. Writing of training manuals, programmed instruction, cases, role plays, instructor guidelines, games and simulations, assessments, script for tape, creation of slides, film, videotape or disc, computer-based training, etc.

d. INSTRUCTING—presenting in-company courses (either public, tailored, or homegrown) in such areas as sales training, management by objectives, problem solving, management development, transactional analysis, sensitivity training, "train-the-trainer" workshops, and dozens of other topics.

e. IMPLEMENTING—installing instructional systems, pilot testing, revising as needed, and training of client's instructors in how to administer the course(s) on a continuing basis.

f. EVALUATING—evaluation and/or design of performance development systems. Performance appraisal, job analysis, preparation of job descriptions, assessment labs, skills inventories, placement, career planning succession programs, and OD work.

Figure 47-1. Major types of activities of training consultants.

- If you are interested in finding outside help in putting together a course (items b and c), then you should find a consultant who has experience and creative skills in the various instructional methods and media, including both *presentation systems* (film, slides, overhead, etc.) and *practice and feedback systems* (role play, case method, games and simulations, etc.).

- If you are interested in finding a consultant to teach in-company courses for you (item d), then you will look for someone with a dynamic personality, subject matter expertise, and a catalytic teaching style that produces a high degree of learner interest and participation.

These three examples illustrate the same point: You must know what you want done before you seek out a consultant, and you should look for and be able to identify a consultant who has the skills to do the job. This sounds like a truism, and yet we could all point to examples of firms that have engaged consultants without first establishing the nature and scope of their involvement and the performance criteria against which they would be evaluated. Figure 47-2 might be useful to client and consultant alike in helping them to define what work is to be done and by whom.

Guidelines for Selecting Consultants

Unlike the purchase of tangible goods, the selection of a consultant carries with it a mystique that often finds buyers putting their trust in the seller's hands. To a

PLANNING AND DEFINING	1. Specify organizational objectives.
	2. Perform a needs analysis. (Identify the knowledge, attitudes, skills needed to perform.)
	3. Specify performance objectives for the workplace.
	4. Specify terminal behaviors (learning objectives).
	5. Specify entering behaviors of trainees.
	6. Develop a criterion test.
STRUCTURING AND ENLARGING	7. Determine course content: facts, skills, procedures, attitudes, concepts, principles, rules, techniques, etc.
	8. Organize material in a "teachable" way: a. Progression from simple to complex. b. Relate the new to the old; build a web of learning. c. Organize material in a "logical" way: chronological and psychological, in addition to the "logical" order in which it has always been done.
	9. Flesh out the content outline: draw examples from the real world of behavior, illustrations, anecdotes to bring things to life.
	10. Ask management to review materials developed to this point: make revisions, if necessary, and obtain go-ahead.
STRATEGY AND METHOD	11. Determine instructional strategies—concepts vs. rote, inductive vs. deductive, etc. Keep in mind, "We learn not by being told, but by experiencing the consequences of our actions."
	12. Decide on instructional methods—lecture, text, slides, photos. Both presentation and response methods must be built into the instructional system, so that the learner may respond in an audial mode (discussion, question and answer, cases) or a visual mode (draw diagram, make visual discrimination).
	13. Determine the media and packaging of the course.
DEVELOPMENT AND TESTING	14. Write the course (or supervise the writing of it).
	15. Review by management and SMEs of the material in as close to finished production form as possible. (This review is for content—not format.)
	16. Developmentally test the course with 1, 2, or 3 trainees at a time.
	17. Revise accordingly.
	18. Prepare a field tryout edition of the course.
	19. Select a sample of the population of trainees to try out the course.
	20. Train the administrators of the field test.
	21. Conduct the field test.
	22. Analyze the data from the field test.
	23. Revise accordingly (another tryout necessary?)
PRODUCTION AND INSTALLATION	24. Prepare final version of course, using professional narration, artwork, etc. Order in quantity (or schedule seminars, etc.).
	25. Distribute materials and train the trainers (provide instructor guidelines, test score key, data collection forms).

Figure 47-2. Steps in the design of an instructional system. (*Training House, Inc.*)

certain degree this is true—much as you trust your doctor, lawyer, or TV repairman. What we are discussing, of course, is *trust* and *confidence*. This is perhaps the first quality to look for.

Does your consultant inspire confidence, or do you think twice about giving out information and being completely candid? A professional consultant will protect the interest of your company; a nonprofessional may carry tales outside the company, steal key people from you, or work for your competitor immediately after completing your contract. (You may want to include a "noncompetitive work" clause in your contract.)

The client should examine the consultant's desire for a long-term relationship—many consultants develop a pattern of going from client to client rather than building longer relationships with a base group of clients.

A second quality you should look for in a training consultant is a solid *understanding* of your problem or need. Listen to the questions your consultant asks and the manner in which he or she goes about testing you and your assumptions relating to the need. Some consultants have one or two techniques, instruments, or methods which, they will assure you, are just what you need. Others may focus on the abilities or experience of key persons in their firm. Still others spend much of their time describing specific problems they solved for other clients relating an impressive array of success stories.

However useful it might be to have a consultant that can bring you proved methods, key people, and success stories, the real test of professional consultants is their ability to listen, probe, test, analyze, and thereby come to grips with *your* problem. Listen to see how much time the consultant spends discussing his or her satisfiers versus your needs. What is the ratio between the two? Which does the consultant want to talk about first? The answers to these two questions can be quite revealing, and they may help you to separate professionals from those who have solutions in search of problems.

The outstanding training consultants are those who have sold their services and proved their worth on the basis of their understanding of the client's problems, needs, resources, and constraints. In entering a new engagement, they bring with them experience, but they reserve judgment on what is called for until they have first listened to the client and done their own independent data gathering. Professionals know that their objectivity is a major part of their value.

A third quality to look for is the consultant's ability to *reduce uncertainty*. Uncertainty always accompanies change. Often the solving of one set of problems or needs may produce another set. We identified earlier the three most common reasons for engaging a consultant: shortage of *time*, shortage of *expertise*, and shortage of *objectivity* or *corporate leverage*. Behind each of these is the client's desire to reduce uncertainty. This is the fundamental service that the experienced, professional consultant can provide. The novice can bring specialized knowledge and skills to a client, but an inexperienced consultant is often unable to reduce risk for the client (and, in many cases, may actually increase the probability of failure).

In selecting a consultant, find out how he or she proposes to reduce risk or develop benefits. What controls and check points will be used to measure progress? What prior successes and failures (with reasons why) has the consultant had with other clients? Does the consultant talk about results and successes, or does the talk center on products and services to be provided? In selecting a consultant, you should check with two or three current clients to get the answers to these questions.

There are many other factors to look for in selecting consultants, of course. Here are a few:

- Is your consultant concerned with making you and your program a success, or is he or she on an ego trip, using your organization to meet personality needs?

(Many consultants have strong ego needs; the issue is whether these needs are satisfied as a by-product of meeting the needs of your organization.)

- How fast does the consultant grasp your operations, the opportunities and constraints, and the nature of the interpersonal relations (company politics, personal rivalries, etc.)? Are the consultant's people-handling skills equal to his or her task-handling skills?

- How will your fellow managers perceive the consultant? Will the consultant make friends for you in making contacts with other employees, or is there a danger that he or she will embarrass you or cause others to wonder why you brought in such a person?

- How much time will the principal or principals in the consulting firm be spending with you? Do you know who will be assigned to the contract? Are you getting the "first team" or "second stringers"?

- Are you seeking a "bargain" or a "value" in selecting a consultant? Can the consultant contribute ways that will build the success of your own organization while adding to his or her own business strength? Is the consultant a good businessperson?

- What successful projects has the consultant handled? What is the quality of the samples of work submitted? What references can the consultant give you, and what do they have to say?

- Does your consultant have back-up capability? Or are you putting all your eggs in one basket? Is the consultant an individual or an organization? If the latter, what depth?

- What interest does the consultant show in your business? How important is your project to the financial vitality of the consultant?

- How does the consultant go about managing projects? Deadlines and control of the "critical path"? What evidence do you have of the consultant's planning, scheduling, and controlling skills (PERT, CPM, Gantt charts, etc.)?

Once an organization has determined the qualities needed in a consultant, a decision matrix can be drawn up and numerical ratings assigned to each candidate. This is illustrated in Fig. 47-3. The qualities listed are not all of equal importance. Hence, each one has been assigned a "weight" from 1 to 10 to reflect its relative importance. Each option (in this case, three candidates) can then be rated on a scale of 1 to 5. By multiplying the *weight* of each quality by the *rating* assigned to each potential consultant, and adding the resulting products, we arrive at a "bottom line" evaluation that identifies the best-qualified consultant. . . in our example, William Smith and Associates.

The Needs Analysis

When we select a doctor, lawyer, accountant, architect, or other professional, their work for us usually begins with a needs analysis. Questions are asked and data are collected and analyzed. So it is with training consultants. Sometimes the organization will have already completed a needs analysis before locating a consultant, although experience suggests that the client-consultant relationship and the quality of the information obtained will be better if both parties work on the needs analysis as a team.

Since it is sometimes difficult to agree on a contract for services to be rendered

Qualities Desired and weight of each (on a 1-10 scale)		The Optima Group	Wm. Smith & Associates	Klein, Fraser, and Co.
1. Trust and confidence	10	4 \ 40	5 \ 50	5 \ 50
2. Fast learner quick to understand	8	4 \ 32	5 \ 40	2 \ 16
3. Experience in our industry	8	1 \ 8	3 \ 24	1 \ 8
4. Evaluation by references	9	5 \ 45	5 \ 45	5 \ 45
5. Back-up capability (depth of orgn.)	6	5 \ 30	4 \ 24	4 \ 24
6. Desire to have our business	5	5 \ 25	5 \ 25	5 \ 25
7. Prior work of a similar nature	7	3 \ 21	4 \ 28	2 \ 14
8. Writing and organizing skills	6	4 \ 24	3 \ 18	4 \ 24
9. Needs analysis skills	4	2 \ 8	4 \ 16	2 \ 8
10. Project management skills	8	3 \ 24	4 \ 32	1 \ 8
		257	302	222
		Second choice	First choice	Third choice

Options (consultants being considered)

Figure 47-3. Decision matrix for selecting a consultant.

until the needs analysis is complete, many consulting firms will undertake this phase of a project on a per diem basis, billing only for labor and out-of-pocket expenses until the nature and scope of the consultancy has been defined. The major kinds of methods and tools used in conducting a needs analysis are listed in Fig. 47-4. Typically, a needs analysis may last from several days to several months. It gives both client and consultant the opportunity to see one another at work, to decide how they can work together to best advantage, and to establish criteria for evaluating the success of the project. It is extremely important that this be a joint activity of both parties; the consultant should not be expected to go back to his or her office and write up a program or proposal until this dual investment is made.

The end product of the needs analysis is a blueprint—a plan of action that both

There are five major methods for collecting data in a needs analysis. Each is listed below, along with examples of the tools that can be used to generate new information (as in 1 and 2) or to capture existing information (as in 3). In a typical needs analysis, no more than two or three are employed. Organizational audits (3) are best when they yield *reliable, valid,* and *sufficient* data, since 3 does not take employees away from their work. However, these criteria are often not present in 3, and trainers must use survey research (1) and simulation assessments (2) to generate information that cannot be captured via organizational audits (3).

1. SURVEY RESEARCH
   - interviewing—present job holders, new trainees, supervisors, customers
   - questionnaire—mailed or filled out at work, alone, or in researcher's presence
   - "climate survey"—to measure morale, commitment, work environment, attitude
   - tests of proficiency—writing skill, knowledge of supervisory practices, circuitry
   - attitude survey—management style, communication style, etc.
   - "critical incident" research ("Recall a recent situation in which . . .")

2. SIMULATION ASSESSMENTS
   - assessment lab in managerial skills, via videotape or live experience
   - in-basket and managerial appraisals
   - role playing (e.g., selling skills, interviewing, supervisory skills)
   - case analysis (e.g., in problem-solving and decision-making skills)

3. ORGANIZATIONAL AUDITS
   A. TASK ANALYSIS AND SYSTEM ANALYSIS
   - flow charting of procedures and work flow
   - work distribution study and analysis of time sheets
   - methods improvement and work simplification
   - "present vs. proposed" analysis of work elements
   - operation analysis, person-machine analysis

   B. OBSERVATION ON THE JOB
   - participant observer (as "coworker")
   - nonparticipant observer: obtrusive and unobtrusive research
   - "shopping survey"—retail sales, banks, airlines, etc.
   - telephone shopping of employees at work

   C. RECORDS CHECK
   - reports on file: call reports, incidents reports, grievances, etc.
   - systems and procedures documentation (flowcharts, etc.)
   - methods and procedures manuals, training guides, etc.
   - complaints, error rates, "squeaky wheel" data
   - job descriptions, performance appraisals, etc.
   - library research—trade association data, competitor's data, studies by industry, use of experts, commercially available courses, etc.

Figure 47-4. Needs-analysis methods and tools. (*Training House, Inc.*)

parties feel is appropriate to pursue. This plan of action usually lists the behavioral objectives (terminal behaviors, performance criteria) that trainees will have reached upon completion of their training. In smaller engagements, the needs analysis may take only a few weeks to complete and may be paid for under a per diem arrangement. (Fees and billing will be discussed later.) When the consulting engagement and training project are more ambitious in nature, the needs analysis may make use of a combination of research techniques (see Fig. 47-4) and may require many months. In such cases, the client and consultant usually enter into contract to cover the needs-analysis phase of the work (with a subsequent contract to cover the materials development phase). Their preliminary per diem time is then spent together in determining what information they want and why and how they plan to get it during the needs analysis.

A word of caution regarding the needs analysis: Many training directors (or their top management) are action-oriented and do not enjoy seeing a lot of time and money spent on research to determine the need. "We *know* we need training," they are quick to tell the consultant. "So why spend a lot of time carrying out a needs analysis?" A little selling (educating, if you prefer) may be called for to make sure that client and consultant are agreed on the values obtained. A list of the major reasons for doing a needs analysis is shown in Fig. 47-5. But all these reasons can be summed up in Bob Mager's delightful parable of the seahorse who observed that "if you don't know where you are or where you want to be, you're not very likely to get there."[1]

Note our seventh reason in Fig. 47-5. This is the one that enables client and consultant to make decisions regarding the design and implementation of the instructional system: Who will be trained? Where, when, and in what sequence will they be trained? What criteria, standards, objectives, etc., will be used to measure performance? What course content, methods, media, and instructional strategies will be employed? How will the system be administered? Who will teach, who will collect performance data, who will promote the program and enroll the trainees, etc.? These are the questions that should be answered at the end of the needs-analysis phase. These answers mark the beginning of the materials development and systems design phase.

Those who have been in the field of training for some time have learned, often painfully, that not every problem is a training problem. We could point to courses we have put together which were very good training programs (from an instructional systems design standpoint) but which failed to produce the desired terminal behavior in the trainee. A consultant who has (1) experience working with many firms, (2) a behavioral scientist's outlook, and (3) an understanding of the many organizational factors affecting human performance can be especially helpful in counseling a client on the degree to which training per se will and will not be useful in producing behavior change. The research tools used to carry out a needs analysis are valuable in helping a firm to identify the factors that are at work in producing or hindering the desired performance (organizational climate, reinforcement and feedback systems, work-station design, work flow, design of forms and procedures, recruitment and placement policies, and so on).

Contracts and Agreements

Once the nature and scope of the work to be performed have been determined by client and consultant, a contract or letter of agreement can be drawn up. Some consultants write their proposal in such a way that it can be signed by both parties and serve as the agreement. However, a proposal is mainly written to sell, and it may lack protections that the client wants (e.g., noncompetitive assurances, nondisclosure warranty, terms of nonacceptability).

Organizations that make frequent or recurring use of consultants to deliver seminars, conduct interviews, handle needs analyses and assessments, etc., have found it convenient to use a standard consulting agreement (Fig. 47-6) that can be

1. To find out <u>what</u> the present level of performance is. By establishing a "bench level" of present behavior (performance), we can measure change over time. That is, a needs analysis will give us pretraining measures which we can compare with our posttraining measures (assuming we give training. . . there may be other ways besides training to improve performance).

2. To determine <u>why</u> present performance is what it is. Why are those whom we'll be training performing as they are? What reinforcers are maintaining their behavior? What contingencies and constraints are preventing better performance? What is the relative strength of each of the factors affecting human performance, both positively and negatively? What can be done to increase the positive and reduce the negative?

3. To find out <u>who</u> the trainees are. What entering behavior do they bring to the job? What strengths can we build on? What deficiencies do they possess? How universal are these? How homogeneous or heterogenous is our population of trainees? Should they be subgrouped for ease of administering different modules of training to deal with individual differences?

4. To assess the <u>organizational climate</u> or work environment within which the trainee operates. Will it support and nourish the behavior we will shape through training, or will it discourage and cause it to die? What can we do to improve climate? How can we prepare the trainee, his or her boss, customers, etc., to maintain a supportive climate?

5. To <u>examine the systems and procedures</u> employed with a view toward identifying ways of working smarter instead of harder. Can steps, tasks, forms, etc., possibly be eliminated, resequenced, combined, simplified to produce better behavior (increased output, reduced error, easier work, etc.)? Methods improvement and work simplification should always be examined as a possibility throughout your study of tasks performed, work stations, work flow, and who does what.

6. To <u>establish behavioral objectives</u>. . . measurable, observable, specific performance goals that each trainee must achieve as a result of training and/or whatever other changes (e.g., organizational, motivational) you identify as essential to producing and maintaining the desired behaviors. These objectives can be analyzed and sorted into subcategories for convenience in designing our subsequent behavior-shaping strategies. For example, behavior might be classified as cognitive, affective, and psychomotor (knowing, feeling, doing). . . or as knowledge, attitudes, skills (since not all skills are psychomotor—e.g., interviewing, proofreading). Skills might be further classified as task-handling and people-handling.

7. To <u>establish policy and make decisions</u> regarding the length, scope, format, location, cost, frequency, etc., of training. Examples of these decisions: initial vs. continuation (i.e., how much or how little to teach initially vs. subsequently); formal vs. OJT (i.e., "vestibule" and classroom vs. training by supervisor on the job); make vs. buy; head vs. book (must know "cold" vs. can look up or ask someone); centralized vs. decentralized training; individual vs. group (self-instruction vs. group-based); etc.

8. To <u>involve line managers</u> and others in your organization whose support and whose inputs are important to the success of your training efforts (e.g., the bosses of your trainees, the subject matter experts, the influentials. By getting them ego-involved at the start and forming a "partnership" with them you can rely on them to promote and sell training (or make changes in procedures, systems, reinforcement schedules, etc.).

Figure 47-5. Reasons for conducting a needs analysis. (*Training House, Inc.*)

kept on file as an "umbrella contract." Each new assignment is treated as an addendum and referred to in the agreement as an exhibit. This can be a one- or two-page description of the assignment, the time frame, and the costs and payment schedule.

A major advantage of the standard consulting agreement is that training managers do not have to wait for the legal department to draft or approve contracts for each new consulting engagement, which can be time-consuming. The training

THIS CONSULTING AGREEMENT (the "Agreement") made and entered into this —day of —, 19— by and between _____ ("Company") and _____ ("Consultant").

WITNESSETH:

WHEREAS, Consultant is in the business of preparing and conducting seminars and providing training services relating to the business of Company; and

WHEREAS, Company desires Consultant to present such seminars and/or perform related services for Company, on the terms and conditions hereinafter set forth;

NOW, THEREFORE, in consideration of the premises and the mutual promises and agreements contained herein, the parties hereto, intending to be legally bound, hereby agree as follows:

SECTION 1. *Consultant Undertakings.*

a. Consultant shall prepare for and carry out each Assignment (seminar, survey, assessment, etc.) according to the guidelines set forth in this agreement and the terms and conditions contained in a supplemental letter agreement ("Supplemental Agreement"), which, when signed by Consultant and Company, will become an exhibit to this agreement and will be incorporated herein. The Supplemental Agreement will set forth the specifics of each Assignment, including but not limited to, the description of work, dates, and fees to be paid to Consultant in connection with the services rendered.

SECTION 2. *Confidentiality.*

In conjunction with the rendering of services by Consultant, it is anticipated that Company has disclosed or may disclose to Consultant or Consultant may come in contact with or observe certain confidential information, including trade secrets, that is the property of the Company. Such information shall be held in strict confidence by Consultant and, from the date hereof through two years following the termination of this Agreement, shall not be disclosed to any third party without the prior written permission of Company.

SECTION 3. *Fees.*

a. The fees to be paid to Consultant ("Consulting Fee") for each Assignment conducted by Consultant during the term of this agreement will be specified in the Supplemental Agreement mentioned above. In the event of the cancellation of any scheduled Assignment, Company shall give Consultant thirty (30) days prior written notice of such cancellation. Subject to the Company's timely notification of cancellation, Company shall not be obligated to pay Consultant the Consulting Fee for the seminar cancelled. Company and Consultant may mutually agree upon a rescheduled date during the same calendar year for any Assignment cancelled without any liability to either party.

b. The Consulting Fee is payable within thirty (30) days of receipt by Company of Contractor's invoice and is subject to the provisions of Section 4 hereof.

c. Company shall reimburse Consultant for reasonable out-of-pocket expenses and traveling expenses (tourist class only) incurred at the direction of Company. Consultant shall submit invoices with documentation satisfactory to Company in order to receive reimbursement for such expenses.

SECTION 4. *Term of Agreement.*

a. This Agreement shall have an initial term of one (1) year, automatically extending for renewal terms of one (1) year unless either party gives written notice to the other of its intention not to renew the agreement at least thirty (30) days prior to the end of the initial term or any renewal term.

b. The Agreement may be terminated as follows:

   (i) At any time by the mutual consent of the parties;

   (ii) By Company, unilaterally by, and effective upon, the giving of written notice to Consultant, if Consultant breaches any warranty contained in the Agreement;

   (iii) By Company, unilaterally for any reason by, and effective upon, the giving of thirty (30) days' written notice to Consultant.

Figure 47-6. Standard consulting agreement.

c. If the Agreement is terminated at any time after the date hereof pursuant to subsection 4b(i) or 4b(ii) of this Section 4, Company's sole obligation shall be to pay Consultant any amount properly accrued to the account of Consultant under Section 3 hereof to the date of termination, and Consultant shall have no right to receive any other payment of any nature whatsoever.

SECTION 5. *Representations and Warranties.*

Consultant represents and warrants that it has the experience, ability and expertise to carry out the Assignment as described in the Agreement; that Consultant's services hereunder shall be performed in a good, professional and workmanlike manner; that the services furnished hereunder will be suitable to Company's purposes; that no part of the services furnished hereunder will in any way infringe upon or violate any rights whatsoever of any third persons; and that Consultant is authorized to enter into the Agreement and that the undersigned is authorized to sign the Agreement on behalf of Consultant.

SECTION 6. *Indemnification.*

Consultant agrees to indemnify and hold Company, its divisions and subsidiaries and agents, representatives and employees thereof, harmless from and defend same against every claim, damage, loss, liability and suit (including interest and attorneys' fees) caused or alleged to have been caused by any breach of warranty or by acts or omissions of Consultant in connection with performance under the Agreement or arising out of any contractual obligations of Consultant to third parties in connection with the services to be provided pursuant to the Agreement.

SECTION 7. *Miscellaneous.*

a. *Independent Contractor.* Consultant is and shall be an independent contractor, and it has no authority to bind Company in any way.

b. *Governing Law.* The Agreement shall be interpreted, construed and governed by and in accordance with the laws of the State of _____, where Company is located.

c. *Headings.* The section and paragraph headings contained in the Agreement are for reference purposes only and shall not affect in any way the meaning or interpretation of this Agreement.

d. *Waivers.* All waivers must be in writing, and the waiver by either party of a breach or violation of any provision of this Agreement shall not operate as or be construed to be a waiver or subsequent breach hereof.

e. *Assignment.* The Agreement shall not be assigned in whole or in part without the written consent of Company.

f. *Entire Agreement.* The Agreement embodies the full and complete understanding of the parties hereto and supersedes any previous agreement, written or oral, relating to the subject matter hereof. The Agreement may be modified only by written instrument signed by each of the parties hereto.

IN WITNESS WHEREOF, Company and Consultant have executed this Agreement under seal as of the date first above written.

COMPANY: _____
By: _____
Title: _____

CONSULTANT: _____
By: _____
Title: _____

manager can usually draft a letter for each new engagement (Exhibit A, B, C, etc.) without legal approval.

Many organizations have made use of consultants over the years without entering into contracts with them. Both parties may feel that a contract is unnecessary . . . perhaps even a statement of distrust, a step backward in their relationship. These are the same feelings that managers experience when an organization embarks on a management by objectives (MBO) program and now requires managers to put down on paper the things they plan to accomplish, with time frames and costs. "Haven't I been doing a good job?" is their natural reaction. "Don't you trust me?"

Although issues of trust are addressed in a contract or letter of agreement, their primary purpose is to make sure that both parties have given enough thought to the assignment that it will be performed to the satisfaction and benefit of both parties. Contracts are a form of self-discipline; they force clearer and deeper thinking than is usually present in face-to-face (oral) agreements. As such, they minimize the chance of a "win-lose" outcome in which one party benefited at the expense of the other. In short, a contract is the proverbial "ounce of prevention, worth a pound of cure."

Fees and Billing

As discussed earlier, consultants generally charge for their services on either a project basis (i.e., fixed-fee) or a time-plus-expenses basis (i.e., per diem). Either way, charges are based primarily on the consultant's time. When the nature and scope of the work to be done can be defined very specifically in advance, with agreement between consultant and client on the amount of time each will spend on the project, then it is appropriate to have a fixed fee for the project. However, many consulting engagements are subject to the "iceberg" phenomenon: Neither client nor consultant knows what lies beneath the surface—they can see only a small fraction of the mass. Projects of this nature should be priced on a per diem basis; otherwise, one party will inevitably end up being "short-changed."

For this reason, many consulting engagements are planned in two phases, with Phase 1 being the needs-analysis phase (the activities described in Fig. 47-4). Here it is appropriate for the consultant to bill on a per diem basis. One of the objectives of a needs analysis, of course, is to define in precise terms the kinds of activities (courses, materials, etc.) that are needed. Once client and consultant have defined these, a fixed-fee contract is usually desired by both parties: *Clients* must budget specific amounts and are glad to have the "open-ended" Phase 1 behind them, and *consultants* like the incentive of performing within the time estimates on which the fixed fee was based, thereby increasing the profit margin.

Both client and consultant have cash-flow needs, and it is important for both to agree on how and when fees are to be paid. Some contracts simply divide the total contract price into equal payments payable monthly (or at equal time intervals) throughout the contract. Others will make payments contingent on delivery of the specified products or services. Thus a contract covering the production of a course to be done in eight modules (lessons, cassettes, weeks, locations, etc.) might be billed in nine equal payments: the first is payable upon signing the agreement, the second is payable upon delivery of module 1, and so on. However, if the course is useless until all eight modules are delivered, the payment schedule might be weighted toward the back end of the contract. For example, there might be nine payments, as just noted, but the last one might constitute one-fourth of the cost of the contract. Such a schedule helps to protect the client from a consultant who may lose interest during the contract or be lured into a more profitable assignment elsewhere.

Epilogue

Nowhere in the preceding comments have we addressed one of the major benefits that client and consultant enjoy from working together. It is this: professionals want to continue their growth and development, and to stay on the cutting edge of their discipline. Many training departments are relatively small and lack the perspective that an outsider brings to the table. Similarly, consultants need the structure and framework of an organization as their "laboratory" in which new courses, techniques, instruments, etc., can be refined and brought to life. In short, each party needs the other, and the professional growth of both should be a major by-product of any consultancy.

Reference

1. Mager, Robert F., *Preparing Instructional Objectives*, Lear Siegler, Inc./Fearon Publishers, Inc., Belmont, CA, 1962, preface.

48

Packages and Seminars

Vincent W. Hope

Mary B. Hope

Thomas W. Hope

Vincent W. Hope *is vice president and a senior research analyst at Hope Reports, Inc. He is responsible for the market research and is editor of* Hope Reports U.S. Training Business. *His background includes scriptwriting, film production, and business consulting. Hope has served on ASTD's Research Advisory Committee and is a member of the Society of Motion Picture & Television Engineers and the Council of International Nontheatrical Events, among other organizations.*

Mary B. Hope *is Assistant Director of Graduate Programs, College of Business at the Rochester Institute of Technology. Her background is in anthropology, and she spent a decade as a teacher, program designer, and media producer at major U.S. museums. Most recently she chaired the Department of Education & Public Programs at the Rochester (N.Y.) Museum & Science Center. Hope is a member of the National Association of Women Deans, Administrators and Counselors.*

Thomas W. Hope *is president of Hope Reports, Inc., a market research and consulting firm focusing on visual and audio communications media. He is publisher of* Hope Reports U.S. Training Business *and author of numerous articles and books. Hope is fellow and former governor of the Society of Motion Picture & Television Engineers, listed in* Who's Who in Industry *and* Who's Who in the East, *a founding director of CINE, the Council on International Nontheatrical Events, on the advisory board of the University Film & Video Foundation, and member of numerous other boards and organizations. Previously he was film manager for General Mills and a market research analyst at Eastman Kodak Company. Hope founded Hope Reports in 1970 at Rochester, New York.*

Increasing demand for training services within corporations has given rise to greater use of prepared packages and seminars provided by outside "vendors." Unfortunately there is a dearth of information on when to produce inside versus buying a ready-made program. Likewise, there is little on evaluating and choosing titles. This chapter addresses both needs with examination of:

- The initial decision to "go outside" rather than develop a program "in-house"
- Locating sources of programs and seminars
- Choosing the most effective package
- Opting to rent, lease, or buy
- Tailoring your choice to specific needs
- Evaluating the results

Today's trainer must be a consummate manager of human, monetary, and material resources. This chapter supports that challenge. Over the past decade American business and industry has recognized training and development as a key factor in corporate productivity, with a growing commitment to human resource functions.

An Expanding Training Business

Commercially Available Training

Industry surveys and a variety of case studies document increased budgets and training activities in recent years.[1] The most conservative 1986 estimates of American investment in training are in the $25 billion to $40 billion range, without consideration of trainees' salaries, downtime, and other indirect costs associated with the process.[2]

The U.S. Training Business generated by commercial vendors has exploded in the past decade. As Fig. 48-1 indicates, well over half of all commercial training

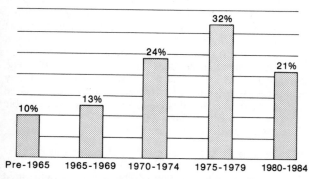

Figure 48-1. Growth of commercial training suppliers. New company formations—percentage of known vendors. The percentage for the years 1980 to 1984 is based on partial data only. Many new, local, or regional firms are not yet "visible" for national analysis. (*Source: Hope Reports U.S. Training Business, 1986.*)

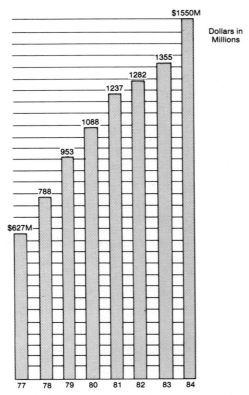

Figure 48-2. Training business trends—commercial revenues from seminars, off-the-shelf programs, and materials. (*Source: Hope Reports U.S. Training Business, 1986.*)

suppliers have begun service since 1975. Less than one quarter of today's training vendors were operating prior to 1970.

The number of major suppliers has jumped from less than 100 in the early 1970s to more than 1000 today. When the smallest training "houses" are added to the count, the 1986 list exceeds 3500 sources of programs and seminars. These are just the commercial suppliers and do not include colleges, universities, vocational, and other educational organizations which sponsor training programs for industry.[3]

Business spending with these commercial vendors has tripled since 1977 (Fig. 48-2), growing steadily through the dual recessions of the early 1980s.[4] The vitality of the commercial training business is good news for trainers. A wealth of prepared materials now exists to meet a variety of training needs. And the scope of available programs will continue to expand to meet growing demand.

Two assumptions underlie the following discussion:

1. The packaged program or seminar you purchase will perform as the "centerpiece" of your training event; that is, the program you buy, rent, or lease will carry most of the training burden. In this sense you will be purchasing a finished program rather than materials to integrate into a larger scheme.

2. Any program you buy will require some tailoring to meet your specific objectives.

As the training function grows, so too does reliance on effective packages available off the shelf. As the scope of sources and titles can reach overwhelming proportions, effective methods for evaluating the marketplace become critical to the efficiency and eventual growth of your internal operations. The need for buying wisely has never been greater. That need promises to be with us as the training function takes on even greater corporate prominence in years ahead.

In-House vs. Outside—When to Go Where

Homework

Before any decision can be made or program assessment begin, initial efforts should define:

- Specific performance problem(s)
- Specific training content (learning objectives)
- Specific desired outcomes (behavioral objectives)
- Impact of new behavior on the organization (goals)
- Any other information which serves to delineate the project

This basic approach to business planning will initially focus on the identified problem area to ensure that training is indeed the solution of choice.

Does the problem represent ultimate cause? Many programs which fail to achieve desired goals have been aimed at symptoms. This is the least expensive stage in which to identify potential mistakes. Be sure of your underlying problem.

From that goal will come concrete training objectives: knowledge and behaviors trainees will acquire. Where possible, clarify objectives in terms of measurable competency. They will become the final gauge of mastery for individuals in your program.

Defining Your Project

As you pinpoint various factors, evaluate them regarding your in-house capabilities. Keep a running scorecard on opportunities as well as constraints of cost, facilities, staff, and time. Some of the following may seem obvious. Other areas may be well researched from previous projects. Each of the following, however, deserves consideration:

- Estimate, as best you can, actual numbers of workers who presently need this training. Will this need recur in the future? How often and for how many?
- Is the subject conducive to tiered programs—elementary levels followed by intermediate and advanced segments?
- Where are the trainees based, both regionally and in terms of physical training space?
- What related skills do the trainees possess? Is your target audience homogeneous? Will prerequisite skills need to be standardized?
- With regard to homogeneity, are there physical or cultural characteristics specific to your trainees?

Factors Regarding Your In-House Option

- Identify the timetable for the entire process from design through implementation. Is follow-up evaluation built into the schedule?
- Locate in-house experts and pinpoint levels, availability, and timing of their support.
- Confirm numbers of trainers available for testing, adapting, supplementing, and implementing the program.
- Speak to in-house media personnel. Solicit their views of your firm's strengths and weaknesses with respect to potential media systems—and production capabilities, availability, maintenance, costs to you the user, costs to your media center.
- Inventory existing equipment with your target audience and learning facilities in mind. If new equipment is envisioned, how will your accountants depreciate it? Method may impact options.
- Does equipment rental meet your needs?
- Confirm your budget regarding:
  - Program development (or purchase)
  - Equipment and facilities (direct or charge back)
  - Personnel costs to implement and evaluate
  - Miscellaneous costs (pretesting, preview fees, travel, departmental overhead)
- Judge your budget regarding trainee demographics. Do you need multiple copies, duplicating rights, or format changes to "bicycle" the program to training sites? Will a trainer have to travel to multiple sites?

Any or all of your project and audience criteria can suggest particular methods, media, and program sources while eliminating others.

When Logic Points Outside

Any number of limitations regarding in-house design or production capabilities can send you searching outside. You may not find the proper content specialists, program designers, producers, or production facilities in-house. Even when they exist, they may be unavailable in your time frame. Or their combined costs may outweigh the value of your intended results (as measured by your budget).

Internal constraints may also stem from your immediate department. When time, money, or staff limits your options, off-the-shelf programs become a viable choice. They, of course, bring with them a set of unique concerns. But the sharp training buyer will mix purchases with customized programs to meet corporate needs for a variety of training with a modest staff and reasonable budget.

Here's where packaged programs typically fit best.

- When time is of the essence. Good, tested programs are available immediately.
- When budgets are tight. A program used by many companies will have a much lower break-even point than a single, custom package.
- When targeted skills or knowledge are general, functional topics. If the training does not require special adaptation to your firm's systems, language, or culture, generic programming will work.

- When your target audience is spread horizontally throughout the company. Generic programs can present broad topics for a variety of applications.

- When program needs are short-term. If technologies or the environment are changing and the training will have limited life, the lower costs of "off-the-shelf" programs will make sense. Rent or lease options can provide additional savings.

- Even where budget and time allow the "perfect fit" of a custom-designed program, the variety of available programs may include packages which meet your needs. There may be no need to "reinvent the wheel."

Defining your project, audience, objectives, and goals at the outset now allows you to evaluate your in-house capabilities and potential benefits of buying a program outside. Those parameters will serve as functional guidelines through each of the following stages as you make your program selection, decide among purchase options, tailor the program to your specific audience, and evaluate learning results.

There are bottom-line, cost-benefit reasons for the growth of off-the-shelf programs in corporate training. Sales have climbed steadily. On average, spending on purchased programs has increased 16 percent each year since 1977, through healthy times and recessions alike.[5]

Expenditures for public seminars, special in-house seminars provided by vendors, customized program design under private contract and the services of outside consultants tend to fluctuate widely, depending upon general economic and business conditions. During the 1980 and 1982 recessions, downturns for companies and organizations which provide these specialty services were well publicized in the trade press. Purchase of "off-the-shelf" programs, however, grew steadily throughout.[6] In relative proportions of budget, trainers placed greater reliance on the economies of purchased programs when recessions set in.[7]

As a result, "off-the-shelf" programs now account for over half of all commercial training purchases in America.[8] And that growth is not surprising since it is getting easier to find effective programs in packaged formats.

Locating Sources

Networking in Action

At first glance, searching out available programs and making your choice may appear a monumental task. It's easier than it seems.

You will eventually be examining materials from two kinds of vendors:

- Industry-specific (e.g., working with banks, petroleum firms, utilities), with programs for a particular industry.

- Topic-specific with programs for many industries, such as sales training, accounting, or productivity

Investigating vendors and selecting programs need not be a "blind" task. You already have informed, professional networks in place.

If you work in a large firm, a primary source of information can be peers in other divisions, departments, or subsidiaries. Their experience can save hours of search and analysis. If programs have been purchased by others in the company, you may be able to take advantage of "multiple-copy" discounts or piggyback on their investment by sharing costs via internal charge-backs.

You may also find that media producers in your firm's in-house audiovisual or video department are aware of recent programs worth your attention. Next, consult your peers outside the firm.

Professional Societies

American Association for Adult and Continuing Education (AAACE)

American Society for Personnel Administration (ASPA)

American Society for Training & Development (ASTD)

Association for Educational Communications and Technology (AECT)

Instructional Systems Association (ISA)

National Society for Performance and Instruction (NSPI)

Society for Applied Learning Technology (SALT)

Training Media Distributors Association (TMDA)

These societies and associations are comprised of either trainers and educators (ASTD, NSPI, SALT) or training vendors (ISA, TMDA). Each type of association can be helpful. See also Chapter 45, Information Resources.

Obviously vendor associations will provide answers with a particular "slant." They may provide enthusiastic recommendations on programs from their members. Aware of this bias, you will find them helpful in locating programs or vendors of a given speciality.

Clearly the most candid assessments will come from your closest professional associates in training societies.[9] ASTD has active regional chapters, for instance, as well as an informed national staff. Discreet questions of the right people may result in titles of "hot" programs or packages which have been found to work well.

Directories and Magazines

ASTD Buyer's Guide and Consultant Directory

Gale Research Company Training and Development Organizations Directory

Hope Reports Training Business Directory

Lakewood/Training Magazine Marketplace Directory

Olympia Media Information

Schrello direct marketing publications

Seminar Information Services

Local business magazines

Local chamber of commerce directories

Local yellow pages

Data Training

Training

Training and Development Journal

Training News

See Chapter 45 for a selected list of publishers.

Some training service directories may prove more valuable than others because of layout, cross referencing, or frequency. Try several.

You may want to contact your local chamber of commerce to inquire about training suppliers among its members. Querying staff of local business magazines or papers may prove fruitful, as most devote issues or major articles to human resource development.

The yellow pages of the phone book may be an overlooked source. A recent addition to many telephone directories is a "training programs and services" category. Since some companies are unaware of the new "training" category, also check other key words, such as alcoholism, associations, business, communications, computers, counselors, management, personnel, safety, sales, schools, or writing.

Magazines which specialize in training will be helpful. Advertising can be as informative as editorial coverage. Some magazines present reviews of individual programs. Others merely reprint press releases on new offerings. Both are valuable. In addition to general journals, periodicals specializing in applied areas (health, data processing, etc.) are available.

Industrial Trade Associations

American Arbitration Association

American Association of Industrial Management

American Bar Association

American Electronics Association

American Hospital Association

Trade groups specialize in either entire industries (banking, law, insurance) or job functions which cut across many industries (arbitration, data processing, sales training). There are also professional scientific, technical, and engineering societies which serve specific fields. Because of the targeted nature of individual associations, they can be helpful if you know what you are looking for.

All these industry groups offer "information services." Many are also direct providers or sponsors of training and continuing education programs for members. At the very least, trade groups will know of specialized training firms which serve their constituents.

If you need help getting started, public or business libraries can provide addresses and phone numbers. Your contacts within professional societies may also lead to specialty trade associations.

Educational Organizations

Universities and colleges

Two-year (community) colleges

Institutes affiliated with academia

Vocational schools

Private trade and technical schools

State educational cooperatives

High school continuing education departments

Academic organizations provide training services and programs. They range from sessions at national business colleges to local programs sponsored by private trade schools or the continuing education department of a public school district. Each has unique qualities which may fit corporate needs.

Universities, 4-year colleges, and affiliated research, consulting, and training "institutes" offer a full spectrum of services ranging from the hard realities of science and engineering to business management, planning, and human relations. Many university-based institutes have popped up in recent years.

Contact various offices on a campus, which may sponsor training programs or coordinate off-campus activities of professors: offices of continuing education, graduate studies, institutional liaison, deans or directors of particular academic programs as well as aforementioned institutes. A call to the registrar can also be helpful.

Shifting population demographics have created new priorities for many universities. With traditional undergraduate enrollments shrinking, many schools are working actively to promote new services for adult learners. Trainers can benefit as college planners expand their traditional academic roles to better serve the corporations which underwrite "adult learning."

Community colleges are undergoing the same strain from declining enrollments as their 4-year counterparts. Many 2-year schools, however, pursue training business more actively than the larger universities. Two-year schools tend to specialize in more applied levels of technical and vocational skills.

Private trade or technical schools are privately run learning centers which run the gamut from industrial skills, auto repair, and electronics servicing to driver education, modeling, and office skills. Contrary to enrollment trends in academia, many of these "schools" have been growing successfully in recent years. While there are a few large national "schools" (National Education Corp. or Bell & Howell's DeVry Institute), most trade schools are local or regional. There may be several in your area.

High school adult education and cooperative centers offer adult and continuing education programs. Many public school districts have been expanding their adult education offerings from traditional subjects such as foreign languages, checkbook balancing, crafts, and athletics to include wellness programs, time management, and other business topics.

Cooperative education centers are funded by states for several school districts. These co-op centers sponsor vocational youth programs and other skills training which require capital equipment (printing, media production, etc.)

All the preceding academic organizations consider industrial or training business secondary to their traditional "student" services. Most, however, may enter into contracts with individual corporations. Many companies work closely with educational organizations via tuition reimbursement programs for individual employees. And as the next section indicates, your community offers an even wider range of training services than you might imagine.

Community Organizations and Sources

Chamber of Commerce

Public library

Civic groups

Community agencies

Religious groups

Besides educational institutions, other local organizations can serve as sources of programs or information. Most obvious is your local Chamber of Commerce which may sponsor business and training seminars directly or, at minimum, publish listings of local vendors. Other sources in the community are often overlooked. Public libraries, museums, the local Red Cross, the YMCA or YWCA, religious groups, Lions or Rotary Clubs, local associations, and other civic groups may provide many types of expertise, often at modest cost. They can also serve as important links in a local "information" network. Depending upon your needs, nontraditional sources can be surprisingly productive.

Staying in Touch

Once you target promising vendors, call or write for brochures, catalogs, and price lists. Ask also to be placed on their mailing list. With smaller companies in particular your name may not be added to their routine mailing list unless you have purchased from them recently.

Some companies make a business of not letting you fall through the cracks—they sell mailing lists. An innocent inquiry to these firms can pyramid into a mountain of promotional mail. If you're willing to sort through junk mail, there will be valuable literature in your in-basket.

A few tips for the collector of catalogs and brochures:

- Include your local educational institutions when asking for catalogs.
- Create alphabetical file folders for vendors' literature. You can always reference a specific company via the topical index of a national directory.
- When new catalogs arrive, throw out the old ones. Date stamping materials will help.
- Finally, if you know beyond any doubt that you will never use a particular flyer, don't handle it twice. Toss it now. But be careful on this judgment.

Choosing the Package

Targeting Subject Areas and Techniques

Your program search should first key on your subject. You may concentrate on firms or sources which specialize in serving your industry, but your primary discrimination among programs will be based on topic. A second criterion will be program relevance to your objectives. Here is where your earlier delineation of problems, and objectives will provide guidelines for choosing programs with effective techniques.

By categorizing primary objectives, you can match technique to your needs. You should be able to identify a technique which:

1. Most closely approximates the conditions under which your trainees will be expected, ultimately, to perform on the job
2. Allows the trainee to perform the desired behavior (as closely as possible)
3. Provides the trainee the most opportunity to practice[10]
4. Utilizes in-house personnel, equipment, and facilities to best advantage.

Appropriate applications of popular off-the-shelf methods are summarized in Table 48-1. While most techniques can be used to achieve different performance objectives, Table 48-1 provides an outline of "best fit" applications.

Table 48-1. Techniques and Objectives – Best Fit Matching*

	Performance objectives				
Training techniques	Acquisition of body of knowledge	Managerial supervisory skills	Inter-personal skills	Association and discrimination	Psychomotor skills
Presentation:					
Lecture	√				
Demonstration		√		√	√
Both:					
Seminar discussion	√	√			
Programmed instruction	√			√	
Practice:					
Equipment simulation					√
Game simulation		√			
Role playing		√	√		
Case study		√	√		

* Other combinations work but these matches indicate optimal effect.
SOURCE: Based on and summarized from Vincent Miller, *The Guidebook for International Trainers in Business and Industry* ASTD, Madison, WI, 1979, pp. 110–111; and Hilton D. Goldman, "Instructional System Development in The United States Air Force" in *Instructional Development: The State of the Art II*, Ronald K. Bass and Charles R. Dills eds., Kendall/Hunt Publishing Co., Dubuque, IA, 1984, p. 487.

The first two techniques, stand-up lecture and demonstration, emphasize one-way presentation from the "front of the classroom." The bottom four techniques in Table 48-1 emphasize participation—practice and feedback. The two middle techniques, seminar discussion and programmed instruction, incorporate both phases of learning—presentation of new information and practice.

An effective program may mix several techniques. Thus lecture or demonstration methods are often used in combination with the six practice methods.

Lecture alone works best in nonskills knowledge transfer. It is less effective as the primary experience in skills training. As a result, care should be taken in evaluating vendors' seminars when they rely heavily on lecture. Other programs may be available which address a specific skills area with strong emphasis on practice, and thus greater potential for retention.

Targeting Media to Method and Budget

Once you have generated a list of potential programs which fit content and technique, the selection process will center on quality, cost, and availability.

You may discover that your list includes a cross section of different "instructional" media. In most cases a number of delivery systems are adaptable to your needs. Media constraints will usually arise directly from your organization—equipment in place, available facilities, or policies regarding use of specific systems.

Wallington has identified key features of training media in Chapter 29 of this handbook. Table 48-2 is a summary of critical media considerations. The table has been set up to evaluate appropriate systems for a specific project.

It omits videodisc. While the disc system is being used creatively by some large

Table 48-2. Project Worksheet – Media Consideration
Place checkmarks in gray columns indicating suitability of media to this project

Equipment[1] available this project	Audience size		Need for updating		Program shipping		Equipment portability		Darkened room needed	Overall system suitability for this project
	Best	This project	Capability	This project	Compact	This project	Compact	This project	System Available	
Audiocassette	Small[2]		Low cost		Yes		Yes		No	
Film, 16-mm	Large[3]		No		Easy[4]		Rent		Yes	
Videocassette: 3/4 inch, VHS, beta	Small[2]		No		Feasible[5]		Yes or rent[7]		Limited[8]	
Slides	All		Easy		Bulky[6]		Yes		Limited[9]	
Slide tape	All		Low cost		Bulky[6]		Bulky		Limited[9]	
Filmstrip	All		No		Yes		Yes		Yes	

[1] Do you own? If you must rent, consider these costs.
[2] Most effective with smaller audiences or individualized instruction.
[3] Most effective with larger groups.
[4] While not necessarily compact, virtually all motion pictures are packaged in mailing containers.
[5] More compact than film, but usually requires repackaging in shipping containers.
[6] Slides mounted in carousel trays are bulky. Compact shipping packages of slides require trays at the user location.
[7] Portable one-piece VCR/TVs are available for individual viewing. On-site equipment will be needed for larger audiences.
[8] Video projection needs a darkened room. Multiple monitors may require dimmed lighting.
[9] Most effective with dimmed lighting.

corporations, few vendors offer disc programs off-the-shelf at this time. Generic videodiscs should become more available as design and software costs decline. At some point critical criteria for using videodiscs could match those of videocassettes in Table 48-2.

Today, actual costs of materials—tape, film, slides, and print—are a small portion of total package price. (Add-on fees or additional copies can be minimal, for example.) Price variations among media formats may at first appear significant, but indirect implementation "costs" will be your true measure. These will include operational convenience and the effectiveness of the system with your target audience. Hidden costs associated with either of these factors can dwarf the price differential of a program available on filmstrip or videotape, for example.

If actual materials play a small role in total price, the cost of a vendor representative to teach the program usually accounts for a major share. The following section deals with this and other concerns for final decision making.

Determining Quality

When considering a 10-minute motivational film with Vince Lombardi, Zig Zigler, Eddie Murphy, or the Muppets, for just a $40 preview fee, your staff can enjoy an office break as a "pretest" audience. But how do you preview a full program that takes an entire day, or 3 days, or 5 and then compare it with six other "finalists" in your search?

The answer is that you don't sit through it. Instead request and look at the materials. Examine the structure of the program, underlying learning models, sequencing of information, classroom events, and testing or evaluation instruments.

Balance of new information with practice sessions for trainees is a key consideration. Is the program biased toward practice? All the better. Is there adequate feedback for participants during the practice sessions? Will practice actually lead to improved behavior? If the program is weak on any of these counts, keep looking elsewhere.

Evaluation devices should meet your standards for testing mastery of the targeted skills. Methods of evaluation will vary from vendor to vendor and even within one supplier's offerings. Be prepared to evaluate the evaluation method within the context of the program. And be prepared to tailor this part of the program to your final specifications. This should be only a modest task.

Beware of programs which do not include evaluation devices. Costs of designing reliable evaluations from scratch, which test with accuracy and which are based on the language, style, and models of a program can be costly—prohibitively so. Again, affordable programs with market-tested evaluations are available. If posttesting appears to be a problem, you may want to keep looking.

Program closure is another vital element. Does the program focus on a concluding case study, practice session, or exercise which brings all key ideas into perspective? If not, the program designers may have been too hasty or may not have properly understood the processes. In either case closure becomes critical. Without final focus, program effectiveness usually suffers. The cost of adding a wrap-up yourself, after the fact, may be prohibitive. There are few justifications for buying a program which fails on this key issue.

Tiered packages. If a program includes both elementary and advanced sessions, it is usually best to examine the segments as a single package. It may be tempting to buy the very best introductory session, but then shift vendors for the best advanced program. Very few packages, however, share language, models, and learning constructs. The result of mixing sessions will be confusion for trainees. It may be best to stick with one program, even if neither module would be your top individual choice.

Additionally, the best multiple-level package will usually include a strong introductory module. Unless your key project objectives are addressed only at the advanced level, basic learning models and the underlying constructs presented in the elementary level will be primary factors in overall package quality.

Further measure of a program combines both sequenced sessions and the closure concept. Are there adequate closure activities throughout the program so that employees can put skills to work before completing the entire program? The degree to which a program meets this standard can affect the timing and location of training. There may actually be advantage to interrupting the learning process with on-the-job applications, with trainees spending short times in the classroom once a day or once a week. This may also minimize the operational costs associated with pulling an employee off the job.

The reverse of this scenario is the program which is not sequenced with step-by-step learning "levels." The implementation of the "holistic" program, if you will, may require advance planning throughout the company so that business flows as normal while trainees are in your keeping.

Keep your eyes open for unexpected or unidentified materials or equipment costs which can result in add-on expenses. Besides money, are there unexpected time factors built into the program? What is a realistic timetable for implementation? What is the total timetable through final evaluation?

Finally ask the vendor for names of others who have used the program, not just company names, but people's names and phone numbers. Most suppliers will oblige. Call those previous users who can answer candidly, without conflict of interest. Ask direct questions. Probe to learn not just whether the program worked, but with what type of audience, in what time frame and why?

Special Considerations

International programs are examples of special circumstances which require additional research. Without multiple language versions, for example, tailoring costs can become exorbitant. It may seem modest to translate a sound track on video, but what of printed materials? And what of underlying "social" translation? Are there aspects to visuals that will cause repercussions in certain cultures? Will a concluding case study require reformatting to a different cultural business environment? Are you capable of judging the subtleties of such translations? There are companies which specialize in multicultural training and have packages available. Try them first when faced with overseas considerations.

Full-scale preview may be desirable. Questions may exist even after examination. It may be worth the expense of putting one of your own people through the program, as a "real-time" pretest. If the program is being run elsewhere by the vendor, if train-the-trainer sessions are underway, it may be to your advantage to enroll an experienced associate who can judge the program prior to final commitment. You might also want to send a trainer who will eventually implement the program and lead your in-house sessions. You may also be able to negotiate "tuition" waivers or rebates on condition of purchase.

Staff certification by the vendor is another reality of off-the-shelf purchasing. As mentioned earlier, the cost of a vendor's representative to teach a program is often the most expensive portion of an off-the-shelf package. Some vendors require that your in-house staff be certified prior to implementing training sessions on their own. In other cases it may be prudent to use a vendor's representative even when not required and "pepper" your audience of trainees with staff who will eventually conduct the program.

Inquire about a vendor's conditions of sale. Certification may be optional or required. In either case it will affect your budget.

Arriving at a Decision

The preceding suggestions are intended to bring you to a point decision, but are not all-inclusive. It is hoped that those which apply to your project will spark further ideas from your particular perspective.

There are probably only two real-life scenarios within which you will ultimately opt to buy most programs. If media constraints exist ("We have to use the video system installed last year") or if personnel constraints dictate a medium or format, then your choice will be the best program within that format. If on the other hand, the content of a specific program is so outstanding that additional costs or problems of using that program become insignificant or at least surmountable, then again you have your "buy."

Final Negotiations

And You Thought You Were Done

There may be several key factors to examine, even after you've found your program.

Copyright restrictions need to be clarified. Once you purchase the program, are you free to alter different segments? Indiscriminately? Are there restrictions regarding program use? Will the vendor assist with modifications? (The vendor may have experience with field-tested variations or tailoring by other purchasers.) Will the vendor actually provide a "tailored" version to your specifications? At what price above standard rates?

Regarding duplication, what copying rights do you acquire with purchase? For "protection" copies? For private internal use? What defines internal? Overseas divisions? Regional sales offices?

Over what "performance" and copying rights does the vendor retain control after selling the package? What discount multiple copy prices are available for consumable materials? Even with permission to copy, the vendor's pricing may be below your true internal cost of duplicating materials (people, equipment, overhead).

Questions which center on the vendor's copyright will be compounded further if you rent the program for the short term or lease the program (or series) over a longer period. In those circumstances, tailoring may not be a viable alternative, and legal duplication will be out of the question unless otherwise negotiated.

Rent or Lease Options

Some programs are not available for purchase by vendor design. Or, if purchase is feasible, cost of ownership may be prohibitive. The lease or long-term rental option may result in lower overall costs of materials for the buyer. Some materials may be expensive if new evolving technologies are used. Others may carry a high purchase price because of specialized, limited market potential.

Leasing brings lower up-front costs and the convenience of no materials to store or dispose of following program completion. The cost advantage of leasing will appeal if the training targets skills which will be changing over time (as technologies develop, for example). Also if there will be no recurring demand, the leasing option makes sense. Even a few years on the shelf can lessen the impact of a theoretically sound program. Outdated styles of clothing, hair, and cars may seem minor distractions, but they undermine timeliness and thus credibility of information.

Leasing will also make sense if the training applies to an experimental operation. With no certainty of future demand you might lease now and negotiate an option to buy later at a reduced rate.

Finally, leasing will be advantageous when a package of multiple modules (progressive topics in data processing, for example) can be bicycled around the country. The contract may cover 15 modules over a 2-year time, but each module will only be in your system for 4 months. Every 6 weeks you receive a new module. Costs of such arrangements can be half the purchase price.

Short-term rentals apply more to individual materials, such as films and videotapes, than to full packages. When you find programs which can be rented for a week, prices should be significantly lower than the leasing rates for use over several weeks or months.

Signing the Contract

Negotiation is above and beyond program concerns discussed to this point. Many options are open to negotiation. A vendor may state that there are set options only, beyond which the salesperson has no control. You are about to hand that person a commission, however. There are many ways representatives will work flexibly with you to ensure their income. So goes negotiation. You should not buy a package or aspects of a package you do not need. Negotiate around the many angles that have been discussed so that your purchase is close to what you would have designed yourself.

Budget can also create unique concerns. The larger your purchase, the larger the financial stakes and thus the more flashy salesmanship you will likely encounter. You may be prepared with your expertise to cut through a spiel, but if you do not have final sign-off authority on money, be prepared for potential problems at the sales and demonstration meeting.

A salesperson will often ask or require that the executive with sign-off authority be present at the demonstration. If your boss is not a trainer, the flash and sizzle may be effective beyond your control. Rather than chance a public "discussion" you may want to reach agreement prior to the sales meeting not to make a final decision on the spot.

Once you reach agreement with the vendor, ask that all details be put in writing. Time factors relating to your purchase should be included. Are there contingencies for rebate or replacement that should be in writing? Are there warranties which apply to the software or any related hardware? Get it in black and white.

Tailoring Your Package

In Theory

You have put your corporation's name on the bottom line and purchased a program. If it's typical, the generic package you own evolved from custom programs developed for previous clients. Common needs and similar patterns emerge as clients repeatedly ask for programs on a particular topic. Through recognition of these "common denominators" many vendors have evolved over the past decade from custom "houses" to distributors of off-the-shelf programming.[11]

Awareness of this process is important for the buyer. Ideally, what the vendor removed from custom programs, the uncommon denominators if you will, is what you will want to "tailor" back into the generic program. The underlying premise is that certain specifics, applications, and personalization have been omitted from off-the-shelf packages. Thus all generic programs require some degree of adaptation by the user.

Obviously if you overtailor a package to exact fit, your budget and efforts could begin to equal those of a custom program. Since you have purchased a package in part to avoid that expense, controlling the tailoring becomes a key factor.

Assumptions

Scope of your tailoring will depend on your objectives, audience, and success in searching out the best package. This discussion assumes that your purchased program:

- Has been acquired with no copyright restrictions on adaptation or duplication
- Includes a balance of trainee "listening and doing" behaviors
- Includes closure exercises which bring content into final focus
- Includes tests and assessment instruments for measuring acquired skills and knowledge
- Does not need massive adaptation for multicultural audiences

Avoid Costly Redesign

The conclusion of these assumptions is that you did, indeed, find a good program. Careful selection is the easiest way to reduce tailoring costs.

Adapting to Fit Your Audience

Internal modifications to fine-tune content may be required, even in the best of programs. For example, you may want to alter timing of segments, expand practice sessions, shorten or eliminate segments with which your audience is familiar. In addition, every company has its own procedures which need to be woven into a standard program.

This tailoring should be limited to improvements which optimize the learning for particular audiences. If a program is run for three types of managers, for example, each group may need slight variations based on their previous skills, need to know, and perspectives of their different jobs.

This level of tailoring may cost little aside from time devoted to modifying a syllabus or trainers' guide. Some packages are designed by the vendor for flexibility of presentation and include recommendations for various audiences and circumstances.

More extensive variation will probably require more staff time. Modifying the program into discrete segments for use once a week, for example, will require adequate closure for each session. This might be accomplished by expanding or creating additional practice sessions.

You may want to take the tailoring further by adding exercises or adapting practice techniques. Certain methods may work especially well in your company—because of facilities or because your audience is practiced with the format.

Evaluation instruments may also require adaptation to measure particular learning objectives. This may only involve deleting portions of tests, but may also create additional questions which test applied concepts or skills from your trainees' perspective.

Transfer of materials to other media formats is an alteration which may involve still greater expense. Your company may be standardized on a particular medium which differs from your purchased format. Certain field offices or training sites may not use standard corporate equipment, thus requiring reformatted versions.

Transfer services are available in most metropolitan areas. Often, lowest price may reflect lesser quality. Good image and audio quality is essential for audience acceptance. It can be worth your effort to shop around.

In-house media people will be most helpful. But without that resource, you may want to seek advice from local equipment dealers or other informed, yet "unbiased," media professionals.

Changing actual content within media programs will vary in difficulty with the format (see Table 48-2). Visual change in a slide program is the easiest adaptation. Changing visuals in videotapes, or audio tracks in motion pictures, are much more involved. With these adaptive processes, primary limitation will be budget—staff salaries, materials costs, and "postproduction" media fees.

Tailoring Audience Expectations

This is the simplest form of alteration and the least expensive when feasible. Via simple explanation let the audience adapt rather than change the program. This commonsense approach works well for one or two simple items, such as when words differ from your corporate usage.

But weigh the impact of learning when asking the audience to adapt. Some requests may be totally inconsequential. Others may subtly alter trainee perceptions and attitudes. Costs of modifying programs should be weighed carefully against subtle influences on learning.

Sources for Tailoring

There are several sources of content expertise on which to draw. Cost and perceived value trade-offs may influence your choice.

Staff experts within your own department should be able to handle most tailoring and program adaptation. Supervisors throughout your firm probably serve as final content authorities. You may already be in the practice of calling on their assistance.

Another case for going outside your department will be need for media production assistance. Your in-house media staff should be cost-effective. Your other options in media expertise are independent producers, contract media production companies, or postproduction facilities.

Outside content specialists may also be needed. You may know of a consultant with direct experience who can improve a program.

Your program vendor may offer assistance and may provide more for your dollar. The vendor knows the program and is likely to have experience adapting the package. The vendor may offer consulting assistance or may reconfigure the program to your specification.

Evaluating Results

Other chapters of this handbook discuss evaluation procedures. They deserve application here. As training becomes a more visible function in the competitive corporate environment, measures of effectiveness and of cost-effectiveness take on new political importance.

Literature on training evaluation historically targets four areas of feedback:[12]

1. Trainee attitudes—as measured by *reaction* surveys

2. Measures of learning objectives—trainee mastery of new *knowledge*

3. Application of that knowledge—measures of *behavioral* change

4. Measures of program goals—the *results*—change brought about by training

Each level of evaluation applies directly to your purchased program. From these measures you should be able to judge the quality of your problem and solution statement, the cost-effectiveness of your project, and the fit of your off-the-shelf selection.

Purchased Program Evaluation

Evaluation of your purchase should target two primary issues:

- Was outside purchase the right decision? Would added time and expense of customizing have improved results? Significantly? Justifiably?

- Did I buy the most effective program? Was learning optimized? Was this the best methodology? Would another have improved outcomes?

Assessment of your packaged program need not be a formal, structured test. Answers for these two primary issues can often be derived from "testing" carried out with trainees in the name of closure. Postprogram measures will add that much more to your specific program evaluation.

Trainee Attitude Surveys

This simplest form of feedback intrinsically provides the least quantifiable measure of training. Subjective answers reflect bias and can be difficult to measure statistically. But measured bias is a key to your program evaluation.

Where other measures address "what" has been achieved, the attitude survey reveals clues to "how" and "why" a program worked or failed. Trainees' reactions address the issue of whether the program was a best buy.

Invite candid comment. Ensure anonymity via a third party besides the trainer. With candid response, attitude surveys may prove as valuable as statistical measures.

Measuring Primary Objectives—
Mastery of Knowledge

Mastery of new knowledge is a critical training objective. Similarly, evaluation at this level will be a key measure of your chosen program. With your planning and previous efforts in tailoring, this testing should serve as smooth closure for trainees.

Measuring Applied Objectives—
Behavior and Performance

More challenging is measurement of performance objectives—behavorial change. Many training objectives do not translate well to behaviors, particularly in measurable terms. Key is a standard measure of behavior *prior* to training.

Ideal measurement requires careful design. Isolating training as a critical catalyst and avoiding bias, such as the Hawthorne effect,[13] are expensive considerations. As a result behavioral testing may be ignored in favor of less costly, indirect measures of behavior—impact on the corporation.

Measuring Goals—Corporate Results

Business measures are the most visible evidence of training's effectiveness in the organization. Whether viewed statistically or by seat-of-the-pants observation, this is where top executives often see and judge the training function.

It is often in a training department's interest to verify that a program, whether purchased or built from scratch, achieved ultimate corporate goals. Training's primary role as *the* agent of change may be difficult to prove. The presence of training as an influence, however, deserves documentation and recognition.

Measuring Cost-Effectiveness

Financial measures of business changes provide necessary grist for measures of training's cost-effectiveness. Comparison of full implementation cost with value of impact on the organization produces a net measure of training's worth. Business measures provide existing quantifiable data, where measures of behavior and learning objectives can be costly and elusive.

Several key points are worth noting.

- Placing value on either behavioral or business change requires statistically significant measures.

- Indirect program costs, such as trainees' salaries and increased operational costs incurred while trainees are off the job, need to be factored into the equation if "true" cost-effectiveness is being measured.

- Finally, standardize results via your firm's methods for capital budgeting. Use of payback period, rate of return, or net present values will put your department on equal business footing with manufacturing, marketing, and other operating units.

Obviously, since costs of off-the-shelf packages are considerably less than those of custom-made equivalents, final cost-effectiveness measures of your purchased program should produce convincing evidence.

Pragmatic Evaluation

Posttraining evaluation of your purchase is but one measure of training. Measures of effectiveness can serve as key tools for future budgets or result in a corporate priority, even bias, toward human resource development. Also it can serve your department by identifying productivity gains available to your own staff.

But there are many roadblocks to evaluation.

- Inherently, evaluation follows training, when priorities usually turn to new projects.
- Evaluation does not improve learning outcomes—this time around—so who pays?
- Benchmarks for judging a program may not exist, especially with the question "Could I have purchased a better program?"
- Political risk of an unexpected poor showing may be a very real consideration in some corporate environments.

These and other evaluation problems tend to be short-term. Long-term rejoinders center on true cost-effectiveness. Evaluation conducted to improve training department and corporate productivity plays well from a variety of angles.

One final thought should guide evaluation. Trainees become the true judges of a program's merit. They are the ones who put ideas and skills to work. And some of them may eventually become your corporate superiors.

Full Circle

The evaluation process ties together the training cycle. Information gleaned from evaluation becomes a building block for future projects and efficiencies. As a result the training process moves through its cycles toward higher levels of impact on the organization.

Purchasing off the shelf is in many ways a safety hatch or escape valve as the training cycle evolves. Faced with fixed resources, growing demand, and greater visibility in the corporate environment, the training department will realize greater flexibility as it utilizes this growing outside resource.

References

1. Reports are available from many sources—ASTD's *Training America's Bankers* study and publications by Anthony Carnevale or Robert Calvert, Lakewood Publications, American Vocational Assocation, Schrello Direct Marketing, *New York Times* biannual reports, Human Resources Research Organization, ITT Educational Services, federal and state government agencies, as well as Hope Reports, just to name several. A telephone call to ASTD can result in names, addresses, and telephone numbers.

2. Eurich, Nell P., *Corporate Classrooms—The Learning Business*, The Carnegie Foundation for the Advancement of Teaching, Princeton, NJ, 1985.

3. *Hope Reports U.S. Training Business*, Hope Reports, Inc., Rochester, NY, 1986.

4. Ibid.

5. Ibid.

6. *Training* Magazine's "Industry Report" which supersedes the Census & Trends Reports, Lakewood Publications, Minneapolis, MN, October issues, 1985, 1984, 1983, 1982.

7. *Hope Reports U.S. Training Business,* Hope Reports, Inc., Rochester, NY, 1986.

8. Ibid.

9. Wilson, Albro C., Jr., training consultant, personal communications. The authors acknowledge contributions of Mr. Wilson, who provided key insights for this and following sections on topics such as networking, materials assessment, balance of listening vs. doing, closure, multiple-level packages, indirect assessment sources, and certification.

10. Mager, Robert F., and Kenneth M. Beach, Jr., *Developing Vocational Instruction,* Lear Siegler, Inc./Fearon Publishing, Belmont, CA, 1967, pp. 55, 56.

11. *Hope Reports U.S. Training Business,* Hope Reports, Inc., Rochester, NY, 1986.

12. Kirkpatrick, Donald L., "Techniques for Evaluating Training Programs," *Journal of the ASTD,* November 1959, December 1959, January 1960, February 1960.

13. The Hawthorne effect is a form of testing bias—generally, the impact on behavior of environmental change, including the very presence of a tester. First documented in industrial experiments at Western Electric Co.'s Hawthorne plant in Illinois by a team led by Elton Mayo (1927–1932). Mayo, Elton, *The Human Problems of an Industrial Civilization,* copyright The Macmillan Co., New York, 1933, as republished by the Viking Press, New York, 1960; copyright assigned to The President and Fellows of Harvard College, 1946.

49

Professional Networking

James P. McHale

James P. McHale is a consultant in human resources and benefits with Sun Company, Inc., in Radnor, Pennsylvania. He is formerly the manager of executive and management training at Sun and has held management roles in financial systems, benefits, and computer systems consulting at Sun since 1967. McHale is a graduate of the Pennsylvania State University with a B.S. in Management and of the University of Maryland with an M.B.A. He is a former captain in the U.S. Army. He has taught at American University, Temple University, University of Pennsylvania, and elsewhere on topics including human resource management, employee benefits, training and development, supervision, leadership, management information systems, and systems analysis. He is active in community affairs as well as ASTD, Association for Systems Management, and the Professional Ski Instructors of America. He is now serving on the ASTD National Committee for Professional Development and the ASTD National Conference Design Committee.

What Is Networking?

"Networking" is a term for a set of activities now being recognized but not yet given a standard definition. Networking has many different meanings shown in the activity or work of a person which can include:

1. Finding the right track to multiple sources of information related to a project
2. Bridging the information flow between functions such as finance and marketing
3. Communicating by informal as well as formal means to accomplish projects
4. Getting things done and/or gathering information without overpowering others
5. Managing the give and take of information flow within an organization or between organizations often outside of formal organization lines

6. Facilitating the interchange among a collection of individuals who serve as resources to obtain a specific goal

How to Define a Network

Given the preceding definition, it is important to take another look and define the meaning of a network. A typical network can involve many general-purpose contacts in the form of people and informational resources. A network will involve peers, subordinates, and superiors in different configurations including:

1. A set of relationships without normal structures and without line authority
2. A set of relationships in the normal formal organization with line authority
3. A mixture of informal and formal relationships not shown on any organizational chart
4. The set of relationships involved in a specific project
5. The set of relationships commonly known as business contacts
6. A person's entire collection of social and personal contacts
7. A person's major network of all of the people who will recognize his or her name when called or visited

Networking Process Discussion

One of the dilemmas in networking is that it contradicts the old behavioral rules such as:

1. Rigid adherence to formal communication style
2. Compliance with traditional chain of command
3. Tight control over who gets what information
4. The tradition that written communication is better than verbal

These hierarchial rules of life came from the church, the school, or the first formal employment with the military or a strict employer. This creates a dilemma because networking is not well understood by some people, and they see it as threat to their comfortable way of life. In some cases, powerful entrenched leaders, or "up through the ranks" managers, resist the informality of networking. Networking violates their needs for typical hierarchy and control systems. Concerns may arise because networking works across functional lines and could spark conflict if not done properly. On the other hand, many organizations encourage networking and get their work done through multifunctional projects. That naturally involves good networking skills and challenges former approaches.

The networking process essentially involves establishing and using an interpersonal style which shares and gathers appropriate information to assist in accomplishing necessary tasks. Certain assumptions are necessary for networking to work effectively.

1. Individuals have rights, responsibilities, and freedom to do their work creatively.

2. Reasonable verbal and written communication is encouraged and supported through necessary equipment and allowance of time.
3. Organizations are becoming more flexible in their people and project management concepts and will relax former rules of interpersonal communication.
4. Individuals will use networking in a professional and responsible fashion to help the organization meet its goals.

Basic Skills in Networking

The basic skills in networking include addressing the issues of networking via:

1. Building effective networks in a multidiscipline function
2. Maintaining proper "politic" relationships
3. Managing the overlap of internal and external networks
4. Overcoming the barriers to networking
5. Balancing and coordinating the networking activities with other activities of your work
6. Recognizing the existence of a network contact in the formal or informal organization and nurturing such contacts for eventual use
7. Building a network
8. Improving a network

How to build effective networks in a multidiscipline function is a critical networking skill in training and development. Training activities take place to educate people in skills and content from the basic to the complex. The audience or client can vary from barely literate to extremely well educated and experienced. Trainers or training design specialists are often expert in the training process but not in the content or subject. An ability to build, maintain, and use networks thus becomes critical to success. Networking is not the solution to all management or training problems. In fact, a concern that should be addressed is the possibility that excessive networking is going on and people are just acting as "busy bodies." The manager may want to have an awareness of whether the right information is getting shared with the right people. A dilemma can exist when there is excessive networking and people are buried with information that serves no business need. A professional should understand networking and work to assure good networking in the organization.

A classic example of the effective use of networking skills in the multidiscipline function of training and development occurs whenever a new course is needed and a trainer or consultant is assigned to the task. Assuming that some form of course needs analysis has been well done, the consultant will probably sketch a rough outline of a potential course using creative skills, memory, and reference materials. The consultant will then begin active networking by calling other consultants, trainers, or former associates to outline the project and ask for leads or ideas. The networking assistance may come in the form of suggested books, recent journal articles, names of people doing related work, etc. Networking proceeds as the consultant calls or visits individuals, collects materials, and designs. The original design is tested by informal discussions with others in the organization or outside professionals in the field. When the design is ready for formal testing, a small group of people is assembled and a "dry run" of the course is conducted with the group as students and evaluators. The whole approach is based on expanding the use of skills and inputs by the use of a good design process and networking activity. It also utilizes the concept that a good result will naturally evolve if multiple disciplines are used early in a design effort and significant testing and review occurs prior to formal implementation.

An important aspect of networking is maintaining the proper "politic" relationship with various people. This is obviously a sensitive area. Two basic forms of relationships exist when networking in any business environment. The first is the form of networking involved with contacts internal to any private or corporate organization. The second is the form of networking dealing with the external contacts such as elected or appointed politicians or bureaucrats in relevant forms of government or individuals from other organizations. Depending upon the kind of work, individuals may deal extensively with such external networks or a mixture of internal and external networks. Such networks often overlap. The skill is in the management of the networks to be sure that the overlap is effective. Involvement with networking should be done with careful balance and coordination, given the limitations on time and resources.

Your networking skills should be applied with an awareness of the differences between formal and the informal organizations. The formal-informal arena is where a lot of the organizational stress and strain exists. Networking can be helpful in that arena where few traditional behaviors are clearly applicable. Until recently, there was minimal information published on professional networking. People didn't even really know what it meant. Literature searches on networking surfaced only a few miscellaneous articles and books and there was not much of any academic quality to serve as a theoretical base. Fortunately that is beginning to improve. An example is the *Megatrends* series of video tapes which are based on the book by the same title by John Naisbitt. Those tapes include a segment where Naisbitt talks about networking as a new major trend. He discusses the beginnings of the networking concept and his opinion that many networks spring into existence because the traditional hierarchies of organizations fail to meet people's needs. He emphasizes the lateral aspects of networking and how traditionally unrelated individuals make networking connections and achieve mutual objectives. A lot of people have been networking for years. People just didn't have as much of a handle on it or a name for it. Barriers to networking exist such as:

1. Lack of freedom to use informal communication procedures, to make personal visits to peers in related organizations, and to participate in professional society activities.

2. The networking process is not broadly understood and used in some organizations.

3. The existence of old behavior rules and practices as discussed earlier.

4. Lack of confidence in some people to use new approaches.

These and other barriers can be somewhat reduced by the implementation of the concepts in this chapter. How one manager reduced such barriers is best described by example. The organization involved consisted of a number of different functions under one general manager. These functions varied from legal to materials management to financial, and they involved people with various backgrounds. The lack of a common language or understanding was a problem within this organization, and an informal communications network to address the problems had to be continuously maintained. The manager's solution is an annual conference when all functions of his organization gather to review issues of mutual concern. The event itself is designed to model and encourage networking. This works even though the people involved represent several functions and removes many of the barriers.

What gets the definitions of networking and a network complicated is the fact that the concept of a network ranges from three people working on something informally to virtually thousands of people. The working network definition could be that the network is the set of all individuals who recognize and will help the networker use the process. From that definition a specific network can be identified around any issue or topic. Any particular network can always be expanded. Whenever an issue or problem arises, a person in a network with related experience can become the nucleus of a customized network. A call might go out: "I am working in this new area and I understand you have some friends who work in that field or have related expertise." This process is like a living organism; a network is activated and friends connect and that leads to an expanded network contact which builds on their preestablished relationship. An example of the potential reaction in this scenario is that the initial contact calls a friend and says "I have an associate who needs your expertise. Is it okay if he gives you a call tomorrow?" Instantly the network is going to expand. Even the formal organization itself can be a part of an expanded network because the members will recognize names and perhaps will do something for others just because they work for the same company. It is important to balance and coordinate your networking activities with full recognition that networking is one of many ways to accomplish work and is not an end in itself.

A point for consideration is that when a career evolves and individuals rise up in the organization, many people may recognize their names. Therefore, a potential exists for many network involvements. The broad definition includes such potential members because there is the power implication that these individuals would respond to a request especially if some prior relationship or even informal contact existed.

When an individual rises into any hierarchy his or her network literally includes thousands of people. One of the dilemmas of senior professionals or general managers is managing the give and take in that whole network of thousands of people. Realistically, that may not be a normal working network on a daily basis for most individuals; however, care must be taken to balance and coordinate networking activities with other work activity.

The subtlety here is not to confuse the formal organization and a true working network. However, do not underestimate the potential of a network forming where an unused but "okay" circuit exists because of a formal organization or functional requirement such as staff service. Obviously, there are differing degrees of utilization in any network. Just the mere fact that two individuals are in the same company provides a basis of a network contact. The formal organization initially opens up functional networking channels that aren't available otherwise.

A very interesting example of functional networking exists when the director of compensation and benefits for a major corporation sponsors a benefits breakfast meeting every month. He invites a wide variety of individuals from across the corporation from groups such as legal, tax, corporate insurance, and all of his key staff in the formal organization. Several different benefit-related functions or departments give a short update on issues at that breakfast and typically you'll have a guest speaker give a short presentation, like a government regulation update or a subsidiary issue review. It is a 2-hour meeting usually starting at 7:30 a.m. which works well to stimulate the network that this manager would like to see in his area. A natural networking spinoff of the breakfast meeting is a series of follow-up minimeetings on issues or topics that need attention.

A common question in the area of networking is: "Are committees networks?" Some are, but many are not. Words such as committee, network, or task force vary in meaning by organization. Current observations show that the networks are more fluid, informal ways of interacting and moving information and getting work done than the old formal committees and structures. The split between committees vs. networks is in the formal vs. informal nature of their structure. Networks can function and do the work that is sometimes done in committees or task forces, but networks are characterized by the process of being more fluid and informal in the way work is done.

Networking relationships tend to get complex as careers evolve and customized networks come into existence and multiple interactions take place. This will become more clear in our upcoming network exercise.

Networking Exercise

Given the preceding definitional material as background, networking may be best understood in the form of a personal exercise. Start with a blank sheet of paper. Across the top of the page write "professional and business network." Consider yourself as the center of your network. Using either initials or last names, put the names around the center which represents individuals in your network for some major activity of your job. Link the names that are connected to each other. As you continue with this exercise, you will sketch out what you consider as your daily personal network. Then begin to ask yourself the following: What does it look like? How does it work? What kinds of links does it have? Show your professional and business contacts that make up your network when you are working on a real business issue. That is not normally the same as a formal organization chart.

Analyze this diagram of your active professional business network. Does it have five names in it or does it have 100 names in it? Obviously, if it has 100 or more (not unusual) you will need significant time to put them all down. List all relevant types of people like lawyers, finance people, professors, engineering consultants, bankers, production planners, craftspeople, and audiovisual technicians. List everyone by name and/or by function.

The next step of this exercise is where it can really pay off. Place a check next to the individuals you have contacted in the last business month. For those not checked, ask yourself: What is the quality of the contact or relationship? The suggestion is that it may be valuable to document your network periodically and think about when you have activated or used portions of it. A network contact may occur when you helped someone, they helped you, whatever the case might be. Use this as the basis of analyzing the quality of your network. Ask yourself, do you want to proactively improve the quality of the network? A network is a collection of relationships, and stale relationships are not effective. So it is perfectly acceptable and appropriate to work at networking by continually making informal contacts. Some need only annual refreshing, some weekly. Most people find that their network is a lot bigger than they think and realize that it can and should be even bigger. This can only be done through proactive network maintenance.

A reference book, *The General Managers*, by Dr. John Kotter of the Harvard Business School, is one source of some additional ideas and reflections on networking. Kotter studied many of the successful managers in major corporations and other significant organizations. The section of the book that is very relevant includes those chapters about the general manager's working style in the use of networks. Exhibits A, B, and C are reprinted with permission. Figure 49-1 is a typical general manager (GM) network from Kotter's book.

Key points of Kotter's observations on the content and process of networks are best shown in Exhibit B—Networking Building as follows:

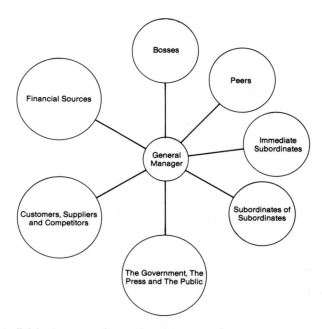

Figure 49-1. Exhibit A—a typical general manager network.

I. Content: The GMs created networks of cooperative relations that

- Included hundreds or thousands of people
- Included subordinates, subordinates of subordinates, bosses, peers, and outsiders such as customers, suppliers, the press, and bankers
- Were different from formal structure
- Included a variety of types and intensities of relationships to and among people
- Often included very strong ties to and among subordinates

II. Process: The GMs created networks by

- Focusing on people they felt dependent upon, or people they felt were needed to implement their emerging agendas
- Making others feel obliged to them
- Encouraging others to identify with them
- Establishing their reputation in the eyes of others
- Making others feel dependent on them
- Replacing or removing incompetent subordinates
- Changing suppliers or bankers or other outsiders
- Shaping the "environment," especially among their subordinates, to foster teamwork, minimize politics, etc., by using both formal management tools (e.g., planning processes, organization structure, control systems) and more informal methods

Exhibit B: Networking Building. Kotter describes the process of using the network which is summarized in Exhibit C—Executing: Getting networks to implement agendas as follows:
  I. Choosing what to act on. The GMs

- Selected items on agendas that were not being effectively attended to by networks
- Selected people in the networks who could help get action on those items
- Selected an approach to influencing others which accomplished multiple objectives at once
- Selected an approach which minimally disturbed important relationships in the networks

  II. Influencing those people. The GMs did so

- Directly, by approaching a network member who could help on some agenda items and using their relationships to influence the person by asking, demanding, cajoling, intimidating
- Indirectly, by shaping an event or a set of events by directly influencing a number of people, and by using time and space, meetings, architecture, language, and stories as symbols

Exhibit C: Executing: Getting Networks to Implement Agendas. Look at the sketch of your network from the exercise and compare it with Exhibit A. It is likely that your sketch is a lot less complete than what you see outlined in Exhibit A and discussed in Exhibits B and C.
  When analyzing a network using the above concepts, many observe that they have a network that is one or two jobs out of date. Most never have gone through an exercise of putting a network on paper. Some individuals move through the hierarchy from an individual contributor such as a professional to a consultant, to a supervisor, and then to a general manager. Often such individuals invest a fair amount of energy maintaining the old network and forget to build the network needed for the current role. How can a network be improved relevant to the present job? How should a person be improving his or her network now to get ready for the job they think they might have in the future? Many in the training and development field move laterally through several jobs or organizations. Do they adjust their network accordingly?

How to Build a Network

Some people say "Well, how do I build a network? I don't have one. I only have three or four people I really work with." The preceding exercise may remove that as an impression. The reality is that there are many ways to build or expand a network. Several are addressed throughout this chapter. A favorite way of expanding networks quickly is through joining organizations such as:

1. Professional societies
2. College alumni organizations
3. Study groups
4. Graduate schools
5. Community groups and not-for-profit organizations
6. Church activities

The challenge is: How can networks be established quickly and accurately and then used effectively to aid communication in the training and development function or any other key business function? A related issue is how to encourage participation in sharing of data within the network. These topics will be addressed in the following pages.

An answer to the challenge is that networks need to be developed and maintained continually. At the moment of need, the appropriate network is activated and the earlier investment is appreciated. Quite often the network is not fully effective if you have just built it when needed. A recent example of how a network was activated quickly involved the testing of a new employee benefit concept. The benefits consultant who was evaluating the new benefit concept called six people in his network and invited them to a meeting to preview it. He explained why their help is needed in an evaluation of this new benefit concept. The example could easily be the same in the training and development field when the selection of a consultant or course is required. The benefits consultant then arranged and conducted the "proposal meeting," provided lunch for the "network members," and expressed respect and gratitude for their assistance. In turn, the people gave a few hours of their time, knowing that the process works both ways. As the group listened to the proposal presentation, they provided objective analysis and feedback. The internal consultant's enthusiasm about the topic was balanced by the network members' reflections. The group feedback was that they could see why the consultant was excited about the new concept but, given the current corporate political and budget environment, it was best to move slowly with implementation of the concept. They caused the consultant to stop and think and recognize that his enthusiasm overwhelmed his analysis, and he revised his schedule and plans.

In some organizations the absence of effective networking would prevent the above process. What could happen when networks or informal relationships do not exist is that a similar need would arise and a "test" audience would react to the invitation more formally by comments such as "I've got to get permission from my manager," or "You know, I can't really do that, it's not part of my job." The result then could be that more time and money is required to obtain similar results. Networking can save money and bureaucratic delays.

How to Improve a Network

Internal networks can be improved through a variety of techniques such as:

1. Appropriate (and legal) use of gifts
2. Phone calls to those you do not see regularly
3. Lunches (often a thank you for networking support)
4. Recreation
5. Slide or videotape presentations
6. Effective use of travel time
7. Customer meetings
8. Functional conferences
9. Special projects
10. Professional associations
11. Conferences and seminars

12. Trade shows

13. Focus groups or user groups

14. Community groups

A favorite "gifts" story is about a training consultant in a large company who helped an individual in a significant way. The individual showed up one day with a rose for the consultant picked out of his yard. That personal touch meant a lot and certainly improved the networking spirit. Cautions are always in order when gifts are contemplated in networking behaviors. Be aware of legal and corporate culture limits, especially with gifts. Remembrance kind of gifts like meeting portfolios or pens with company logos can often be mutually acceptable.

The value of *recreation* and sports in networking is very high. When a common interest, recreation, sport, concert, etc., is shared with either a current or a potential member of a network, stronger connections are built. The formal contact might exist through the business, but real networking considers social realities and encourages the extra step. Some avoid that. It can be a dilemma for some in terms of how much social or sports time is shared with business contacts. Some have a "hurdle" between the personal life and business life. Part of any general management role is the more involved social and business networking with business associates often done in a recreational setting. If the position warrants it, flexibility in time management exists. For example, a general manager will never get critiqued for taking a long lunch if he is out with a supplier or a potential customer.

A fascinating example of how recreation led to a good opportunity for networking involved a fellow professional who recently took a bike trip and spent a lot of time with an individual who works for the United Nations. About a week later an issue came up requiring quick information from the United Nations. A quick phone call obtained the necessary information, totally bypassing the bureaucracy. No one could ever predict that such a need and connection would have ever happened. Good networking nurtures such happenings.

Some women see sports such as golf and the related men's locker room as one of the oldest forms of "good old boy" networking. Historically, they were left out of this exchange. Now that there are more women's locker rooms and shared athletic activities, they understand what goes on and take an active part. This is a healthy social change, and everyone can be effectively involved in this form of networking.

A form of networking to get people up to speed on an issue or project could be an introductory *slide presentation* or videotape prior to a working sessions. People will often volunteer their involvement if it is easy for them to get started and they are informed on why they should cooperate.

Another networking technique that is not always available but should be well managed is *travel time*. Those who spend 2 to 10 hours on a plane with a fellow professional, manager, or executive have a captive audience. Intelligent use of that time is potentially valuable to your network development and management.

Another technique used to improve a network is to have *customer meetings* that includes both business and recreational aspects. Some organizations invite customers and their spouses and develop the broad external network as well as the internal network at the same time.

Functional internal conferences of such groups as finance, marketing, production, human resources, and technology can be very valuable forums for networking. Such meetings can also communicate management philosophy that it is "okay" to network in addition to getting other agenda work done.

Individuals can expand their company network through *special project activities*. For example, a common training assignment involves recruiting internal or external speakers for training or general company events. That is an excellent opportunity to meet many people and develop relationships.

How do *professional associations* help with network building or maintenance?

1. Information and contact exchange

2. Newsletters

3. Educational events

4. Dinner meetings with guest speakers

Active involvement in attending and organizing professional society events obviously expands a network. Such professional contacts can stimulate creativity and expand the entire approach to networking and professional work.

An excellent example of networking through *conference and seminar attendance* is seen at the annual American Society for Training and Development (ASTD) conference. This author's experiences at ASTD conferences have been very rewarding in that they presented opportunities to personally meet many of the experts on all aspects of training and development. These meetings led to follow-up discussions and classic give and take networking. It is fascinating how competitors take off their competitive stance at conferences when they are delivering papers and sharing information. Obviously this sharing has been approved by their company and they share their current "state of the art." Things are seen as they emerge, long before they are published. At the related vendor or trade shows and equipment demonstrations, the technology being developed for tomorrow is on display. Demonstrations of physical equipment, computer systems, visual aids, electronic devices, etc., take place continuously. Break-throughs in pricing are available for consideration.

Trade shows in the training and development field are extremely valuable as they are an excellent form of continued professional education at little or no personal cost beyond the time. The related literature that is available to those attending trade shows is also excellent and an education in itself. A by-product is that the office mailbox will be filled with good material for months after these shows. Demonstration of computer equipment and software at these shows related to training and development is usually quite helpful in locating and implementing programs.

Another example of networking in the broader sense that exists in many functions are *focus groups, user groups,* or published data-sharing groups involving professionals from the same function from several companies. These are very common with computer hardware or software "user groups." Some of the functional "networks" have been going on for 20 years or more. One or two representatives from each of the companies come together for a working conference. Each representative has a summary of all the current functional data which is shared with all the other participants followed by a question and answer session. They talk about a recent change in laws and regulations and frankly try to collectively make sense of the world and their business function. Other company staff can give their representative questions to ask at the meeting which is conducted in the roundtable format; i.e., is anybody doing such and such, and answers are available either verbally or through a follow-up contact. Contact information and business cards are freely exchanged.

Community and civic groups are great eye-opening opportunities for improvement of external networks. This form of building network contacts is complex but it pays off. Think of the field of networking as a big energy pocket. Each participant puts energy into the pocket; occasionally a participant takes some out.

Use of Modern Communications in Networking

Advanced networking techniques involve the application of electronic mail that many companies are beginning to install—especially those with multiple locations. In addition to general memo-style mail, access can be made to information electronically from company, public, and private databases. It takes about an hour and a half to get comfortable in using electronic mail. Therefore, a person who can spare a long lunch has the time to learn this technique. Electronic mail can be especially relevant to networking in that it can help eliminate telephone tag or message trading. Most professionals may wish to get comfortable with electronic networking tools, as the day is approaching when most will have terminals on the desk. These tools allow a trainer to utilize a vast set of resources and individuals in a cost-effective manner. It is an ideal tool for locating appropriate speakers and making related arrangements.

General Contact Development Skills

It may be helpful to develop a reminder sheet for contact development skills and ideas. Consider the following:

1. Talk about other topics in addition to professional specialities in general business conversations.
2. Vary participation in conversations. Ask occasional serious questions in conversations and expand the range of discussion.
3. Monitor contact time around who, how, why.
4. Take on volunteer or special project opportunities.
5. Use versatility in influence tactics.
6. Break your routines and do something unusual once in a while.
7. Mix the mode of contact by changing patterns of your lunch, commute, etc.
8. Learn the technical terminology of the business.
9. Learn the business facts and figures of the organization.
10. Study the journal articles and review the professional literature periodically.
11. Visit other departments in the company or organization.
12. Use networks to implement agendas.
13. Prepare for important meetings by previsits to those involved.
14. Learn people's names and family information. Make a practice of keeping a current Rolodex file and periodically review it.
15. Establish and maintain a file of business cards with personal notes on the back. Loose-leaf "album" books are available for such files.
16. Maintain a cross-functional Rolodex file. List functions or services alphabetically with the associated individual's name. Such a file can also be maintained on a personal computer.

Networking Technique

Networking technique involves the use of all the preceding networking skills with a touch of grace and judgment based on good interpersonal relations. For example, instead of always aggressively pursuing your agenda and timetable with associates, suggest an informal arrangement to have lunch or a cup of coffee together. The process is to build a relationship and a network first and subsequently use it.

High-quality networking is like a loving relationship—it involves a lot of give and take. Once in a while everyone needs information or help. If the networks are properly built and maintained, a person can just call and say "I need help with . . .". People will usually respond and sometimes actually appreciate the opportunity to help.

Maintenance of the political contacts related to the network involves the use of good common sense and skills valuable in maintaining any kind of relationship. People who press their computer system hard and insist on printing a big report immediately pay heavily for it. If they can say they need it tomorrow, they can get that service at one-third the cost. Typically, the same things happen in personal relations. When pressed too hard, people may or may not give the answer and it will eventually cost more.

A fascinating aspect of sharing a professional courtesy such as networking is that it is never clear how it is going to be of direct personal value. Networking is spiritual in nature. It is similar to: "Do unto others as you would have them do unto you." That is the essence and basic principle of networking. If someone in a company has been very gracious in helping an individual in another company to understand an issue, another network contact begins to form. If a contact is necessary with that particular organization even a year or two later, a positive image exists. People remember someone being gracious, perhaps inviting them over and giving a tour or orientation on a training issue or course.

Use common sense in external contacts but generally never be hesitant about calling your professional counterparts in other companies and building a professional network. There are some cautions around situations where information should not be shared or contacts should not be made. Obviously, confidential information about what a company is doing is not shared. It is very inappropriate to press for information about what another company is doing on confidential topics. If a disclosure question exists, there is a potential problem, and it is appropriate to get legal advice.

Another aspect of networking is that it provides an opportunity to obtain answers to cultural questions that can often be helpful if training and development assignments involve meeting new people or going to new companies. For example, common questions are how should a consultant dress or what is the acceptable way of greeting people in an unfamiliar company. This can be a very subtle process, and understanding of organizational culture through good networking can be very valuable in training and development.

It may be informative to close by sharing a personal experience. It involved trying to arrange interviews with selected senior faculty at a major university in California as part of design and staffing of an executive education program. A basic problem in such a project is how to get started. When I remembered that my fraternity brother and former college roommate is now head of a department at that university, I was off and running. Our company also had an existing relationship on a research project and I located the names of the professors involved. I called the professors to check out the reputations of other faculty and related connections. When I went to California for the meetings, the premeeting contacts paid off and many good events and discussions evolved. One such event was a dinner with a professor developing some new concepts related to executive training. Several of the concepts learned were influential in our seminar designs. Again, the networking process paid off.

Bibliography

Kahn, Joseph P., "Networking a Little Help from Your Friends," *Inc.* Magazine, June 1985.

Kotter, John P., *The General Managers,* The Free Press of Macmillan Publishing Co., Inc., New York, 1982, pp. 68, 72, 75.

Limpert, John, Jr., "The Fine Art of Dealing with CEO's," *Business Horizons,* May–June 1985.

McInnis, Noel, "Networking: A way to Manage Our Changing World?" *The Futurist,* June 1984.

Naisbitt, John, *Megatrends,* Warner Books, Inc., New York, 1982.

Stark, Peter B., "Networking: The Brilliant Art of the 1980's," *Vital Speeches of the Day,* Vol. LI, No. 24, October 1, 1985.

Index

About the editor

Robert L. Craig has worked actively in the field of employee training since its early days in the 1950s. He has been especially prominent in building the literature of the field, as editor of the two earlier editions of this best-selling handbook and as editor of the *Training Directors Journal/ Training and Development Journal* for fifteen years. He also established the *National Report for Training and Development* as a key source of information about human resource development and national issues. Mr. Craig recently retired as vice president of the American Society for Training and Development. In 1985 he received ASTD's highest award, the Gordon M. Bliss Memorial Award.